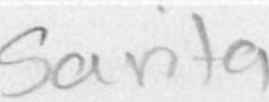

Age	Physical Developments	Neurological Developments	Cognitive Developments	Language Developments	Emotional Developments	Social Developments	Self/Gender/ Identity Developments	Moral Developments
18–24 months	Toddler can walk up steps.	Number of synapses increases.	Toddler uses mental representations and symbols. Object permanence is achieved. Toddler can form concepts and categories. Episodic memory emerges.	Naming explosion takes place. First sentences are often telegraphic.	Self-conscious emotions (embarrassment, envy, empathy) have emerged, as well as precursors of shame and guilt. Negativism begins.	Urge for autonomy is developing. Conflicts with older siblings increase.	Child recognizes self in a mirror. Use of first-person pronouns shows consciousness of self. Parental gender-typing peaks.	Child may show prosocial (helping) behavior.
24–30 months	Artwork consists of scribbles.	Number of synapses peaks; unneeded synapses are pruned. Myelination of frontal lobes occurs; this development may underlie self-awareness, self-conscious emotions, and capacity for self-regulation.	Preoperational stage begins.	Child uses many two-word phrases. Child begins to engage in conversations. Child overregularizes language rules.	Self-evaluative emotions (pride, shame, guilt) have emerged. Empathic responses are less egocentric, more appropriate.	Play with others is mostly parallel.	Child can describe and evaluate self. Gender awareness emerges. Preference for gender-appropriate toys and activities emerges.	Guilt, shame, and empathy promote moral development. Aggression occurs primarily in conflicts over toys and space.
30–36 months	Child has full set of primary teeth. Child can jump in place.	Neurons continue to undergo integration and differentiation.	Child can count. Child knows basic color words. Child understands analogies about familiar items. Child can explain familiar causal relations. Child becomes more accurate in gauging others' emotional states.	Child learns new words almost daily. Child combines three or more words. Child understands language well. Child says up to 1,000 words. Child uses past tense.	Child shows growing ability to "read" others' emotions, mental states, and intentions.	Child shows increasing interest in other people, especially children.	Child begins to be aware of a continuous self.	Aggression becomes less physical, more verbal.
3 years	Child draws shapes. Child can pour liquids and eat with silverware. Child can use toilet alone.	Brain is about 90 percent adult weight. Handedness is apparent. Hormonal changes in autonomic nervous system are associated with emergence of evaluative emotions.	Child understands symbolic nature of pictures, maps, and scale models. Autographical memory may begin. Child engages in pretend play. Child can do pictorial calculations involving whole numbers. IQ tests may predict later intelligence.	Vocabulary, grammar, and syntax are improving. Emergent literacy skills are developing.	Negativism peaks; temper tantrums are common.	Initiative is developing. Play with others becomes more coordinated. Child chooses friends and playmates on basis of proximity.	Children play with others of same sex. Peers reinforce gender-typed behavior.	Altruism and other prosocial behavior become more common; motive is to earn praise and avoid disapproval.

IMPORTANT

HERE IS YOUR REGISTRATION CODE TO ACCESS MCGRAW-HILL PREMIUM CONTENT AND MCGRAW-HILL ONLINE RESOURCES

For key premium online resources you need THIS CODE to gain access. Once the code is entered, you will be able to use the web resources for the length of your course.

Access is provided only if you have purchased a new book.

If the registration code is missing from this book, the registration screen on our website, and within your WebCT or Blackboard course will tell you how to obtain your new code. Your registration code can be used only once to establish access. It is not transferable.

To gain access to these online resources

1. **USE** your web browser to go to: **www.com/papaliaacw10**
2. **CLICK** on "First Time User"
3. **ENTER** the Registration Code printed on the tear-off bookmark on the right
4. After you have entered your registration code, click on "Register"
5. **FOLLOW** the instructions to setup your personal UserID and Password
6. **WRITE** your UserID and Password down for future reference. Keep it in a safe place.

If your course is using WebCT or Blackboard, you'll be able to use this code to access the McGraw-Hill content within your instructor's online course.
To gain access to the McGraw-Hill content in your instructor's WebCT or Blackboard course simply log into the course with the user ID and Password provided by your instructor. Enter the registration code exactly as it appears to the right when prompted by the system. You will only need to use this code the first time you click on McGraw-Hill content.

These instructions are specifically for student access. Instructors are not required to register via the above instructions.

Thank you, and welcome to your McGraw-Hill Online Resources.

0-07-312623-3
Paplia
A Child's World: Infancy through Adolescence, 10/e

6BWP-V8GB-GKHN-XDNM-ACH-3

REGISTRATION CODE

REGISTRATION CODE

The McGraw-Hill Companies
Mc Graw Hill Higher Education

A Child's World

Tenth Edition

A Child's World

Infancy Through Adolescence

Diane E. Papalia

Sally Wendkos Olds

Ruth Duskin Feldman

Boston Burr Ridge, IL Dubuque, IA Madison, WI New York San Francisco St. Louis
Bangkok Bogotá Caracas Kuala Lumpur Lisbon London Madrid Mexico City
Milan Montreal New Delhi Santiago Seoul Singapore Sydney Taipei Toronto

The McGraw·Hill Companies

Higher Education

A CHILD'S WORLD: INFANCY THROUGH ADOLESCENCE

Published by McGraw-Hill, a imprint of The McGraw-Hill Companies, Inc., 1221 Avenue of the Americas, New York, NY 10020.

This book is printed on acid-free paper.

2 3 4 5 6 7 8 9 0 CTP/CTP 0 9 8 7 6

ISBN-13: 978-0-07-296731-9
ISBN-10: 0-07-296731-5

Editor-in-chief: *Emily Barrosse*
Publisher: *Stephen D. Rutter*
Executive Editor: *Michael J. Sugarman*
Marketing Manager: *Melissa Caughlin*
Senior Developmental Editor: *Elsa Peterson*
Managing Editor: *Jean Dal Porto*
Project Manager: *Richard H. Hecker*
Manuscript Editor: *Sarah Lane*
Art Director: *Jeanne Schreiber*
Senior Designer: *Kim Menning*
Text Designer: *Ellen Pettengell/Glenda King*
Cover Designer: *Lisa Adamitis*
Art Editor: *Emma C. Ghiselli*
Photo Research Coordinator: *Nora Agbayani*
Cover Credit: © *Jack Deutsch Studio*
Senior Print Supplements Producer: *Louis Swaim*
Media Project Manager: *Alexander Rohrs*
Production Supervisor: *Janean A. Utley*
Senior Media Producer: *Stephanie George*
Permissions Editor: *Marty Granahan*
Composition: *10/12 Times Roman by Cenveo*

Credits: The credits section for this book begins on page A-1 and is considered an extension of the copyright page.

Library of Congress Cataloging-in Publication Data

A child's world : infancy through adolescence / Diane E. Papalia ... [et al.].-- 10th ed.
p. cm.
Rev. ed. of: A child's world / Diane E. Papalia, Sally Wendkos Olds, Ruth Duskin Feldman. Updated 9th ed. c2004.
Includes bibliographical references and index.
ISBN 0-07-296731-5 (hc. : alk. paper)
1. Child development. 2. Child psychology. 3. Adolescence. I. Papalia, Diane E. II. Papalia, Diane E. Child's world.
HQ767.9.P36 2006
305.231--dc22 2004061124

http://www.mhcollege.com

About the Authors

As a professor, **Diane E. Papalia** taught thousands of undergraduates at the University of Wisconsin-Madison. She received her bachelor's degree, majoring in psychology, from Vassar College and both her master's degree in child development and family relations and her doctorate in life-span developmental psychology from West Virginia University. She has published numerous articles in such professional journals as *Human Development, International Journal of Aging and Human Development, Sex Roles, Journal of Experimental Child Psychology*, and *Journal of Gerontology.* Most of these papers have dealt with her major research focus, cognitive development from childhood through old age. Dr. Papalia is especially interested in intellectual development and factors that contribute to the maintenance of intellectual functioning. She is a Fellow in the Gerontological Society of America. Dr. Papalia also is the coauthor, with Sally Wendkos Olds and Ruth Duskin Feldman, of *Human Development*, now in its ninth edition; of *Adult Development and Aging* with Harvey L. Sterns, Ruth Duskin Feldman, and Cameron J. Camp, now in its second edition; and of *Child Development: A Topical Approach* with Dana Gross and Ruth Duskin Feldman.

Sally Wendkos Olds is an award-winning professional writer who has written more than 200 articles in leading magazines and the author or coauthor of seven books addressed to general readers, in addition to the three textbooks she has coauthored with Dr. Papalia. Her newest book, *A Balcony in Nepal: Glimpses of a Himalayan Village,* describes her encounters with the people and way of life in a remote hill village in eastern Nepal. The updated and expanded third edition of her classic book *The Complete Book of Breastfeeding* was published in 1999. She is also the author of *The Working Parents' Survival Guide* and *The Eternal Garden: Seasons of Our Sexuality* and the coauthor of *Raising a Hyperactive Child* (winner of the Family Service Association of America National Media Award) and *Helping Your Child Find Values to Live By.* She has spoken widely on the topics of her books and articles to both professional and lay audiences, in person and on television and radio. She received her bachelor's degree from the University of Pennsylvania, where she majored in English literature and minored in psychology. She was elected to Phi Beta Kappa and was graduated summa cum laude.

Ruth Duskin Feldman is an award-winning writer and educator. With Diane E. Papalia and Sally Wendkos Olds, she coauthored the fourth, seventh, eighth, and ninth editions of *Human Development* and the eighth, ninth, and updated ninth editions of *A Child's World.* She also is coauthor of *Adult Development and Aging* and *Child Development: A Topical Approach.* A former teacher, she has developed educational materials for all levels, from elementary school through college, and has prepared ancillaries to accompany the Papalia-Olds books. She is author or coauthor of four books addressed to general readers, including *Whatever Happened to the Quiz Kids? Perils and Profits of Growing Up Gifted* (republished in 2000 as an Authors Guild Backinprint edition of iUniverse). She has written for numerous newspapers and magazines and has lectured extensively and made national and local media appearances throughout the United States on education and gifted children. She received her bachelor's degree from Northwestern University, where she was graduated with highest distinction and was elected to Phi Beta Kappa.

To our parents,
Madeline and Edward Papalia,
Leah and Samuel Wendkos,
and Boris and Rita Duskin,
for their unfailing love, nurturance, and
confidence in us and for their abiding conviction
that childhood is a wondrous time of life.

And to our children,
Anna Victoria,
Nancy, Jennifer, and Dorri,
Steven, Laurie, and Heidi,
and our grandchildren,
Stefan, Maika, Anna, Lisa, and Nina,
Daniel, Emmett, Rita, Carol, Eve, Isaac, and Delilah,
who have helped us revisit childhood
and see its wonders and challenges
with new eyes.

Dana Gross, chief consultant to this edition, is a professor of psychology at St. Olaf College. She received her bachelor's degree, majoring in psychology, from Smith College and her Ph.D. in child psychology from the Institute of Child Development at the University of Minnesota. Her broad teaching and research interests include perception, language, cognition, and social cognition, as well as cross-cultural child development. She has published articles in such professional journals as *Child Development, Cognitive Development, Educational Gerontology,* and the *International Journal of Behavioral Development* and has presented her work at numerous conferences. She has also published chapters in edited books, including *Developing Theories of Mind* and *Play & Culture Studies* (vol. 5). In addition to being a member of several national professional societies, Dr. Gross is a founding member of the Division of Academic Psychology of the Minnesota Psychological Association. Dr. Gross has authored supplements for several McGraw-Hill textbooks and served as chief consultant on the eighth and ninth editions of Papalia et al.'s *Human Development* and the eighth and ninth editions of *A Child's World*. She is coauthor, with Dr. Papalia and Ruth Duskin Feldman, of *Child Development: A Topical Approach*.

Brief Contents

Contents

Preface

The title *A Child's World* reflects our vision of the study of child development as an exciting journey of exploration into the special world of childhood. Through vibrant illustrations, real-life examples, and tightly integrated pedagogical features, we seek to make that world come alive. By studying this book, students will gain a perspective, not only on what earlier "explorers" have discovered about children's development, but also on how the world looks from the standpoint of a child.

In the three decades since the first publication of *A Child's World,* the field of child development has increasingly come into its own as a rigorous scientific enterprise. This book, too, has "grown up." Like a child reaching maturity, it has gained in depth, breadth, and objectivity while retaining its unique "personality": the engaging tone and accessible style that have contributed to its popularity over the years.

Our Aims for This Edition

In recent editions of *A Child's World,* our author team has revamped virtually the entire book—its design, content, and pedagogical features—and substantially streamlined the text. In this tenth edition our primary aim is to build on these foundations by revising and adding much new material. We have sifted through the plethora of literature published each year to select cutting-edge research that will add significantly to students' understanding. We have broadened the research base of each chapter and have updated throughout, using the most current statistics available. We have striven to make our coverage as concise and readable as possible while still doing justice to the vast scope and significance of current theoretical and research work. As always, we have sought to emphasize the continuity of development, highlight interrelationships among the physical, cognitive, and psychosocial domains, and integrate theoretical, research-related, and practical concerns.

The Tenth Edition at a Glance

Organization

This book takes a *chronological* approach, examining all aspects of development at each period of childhood. With this approach students gain a sense of the multifaceted sweep of child development. The 17 chapters fall into six parts:

- Part 1 summarizes the history, basic concepts, theories, and research tools of the field of child development.
- Part 2 explores the beginnings of life, including the influences of heredity and environment, pregnancy and prenatal development, birth, and the newborn baby.
- The remaining four parts are divided into three chapters each, covering physical, cognitive, and psychosocial development during infancy and toddlerhood, early childhood, middle childhood, and adolescence.

In this edition, we have carefully assessed and improved the organization of material within and among chapters. For example, material on basic memory processes and capacities, previously introduced in Part 5, Middle Childhood, is now in Part 4, Early Childhood, to reflect the growing research interest in memory development at that age.

Pedagogical Features

We are gratified by the overwhelmingly favorable response to our comprehensive Learning System, a unique, coordinated set of marginal features to guide and check students' learning. The pedagogical features (Guideposts, Checkpoints, and critical thinking questions entitled "What's Your View?") are designed to reinforce our central theme of exploration and discovery of a child's world. So are the four types of boxed material: The Research World, The Everyday World, The Social World, and Around the World. As before, each box refers the student to relevant links on the On-Line Learning Center to accompany *A Child's World,* tenth edition, at http://www.mhhe.com/papaliaacw10. Also well-received are the biographical Focus vignettes that introduce each chapter and the interpretive Refocus questions that conclude it. A Landmark Table in the front and back of the book (inside covers and endsheets) helps students "find" the whole child at each period of development. The Visual Walk-Through following this preface previews the book's features in detail.

New in the Tenth Edition

Each of the book's parts begins with a distinctive, illustrated two-page spread. This opener contains a Part Preview Table outlining each chapter, a Part Overview introducing important themes, and, for parts 2 through 6, a list of Linkups to Look For, examples of interaction among the physical, cognitive, and psychosocial domains of development. Also new are marginal links to the multimedia resources on our LifeMap CD, a learning tool that is packaged with each new copy of the book. The LifeMap CD includes video interviews with child development experts as well as video of children and teens discussing issues and engaged in behaviors discussed in the text. It also offers interactive quizzes.

Content Changes

An important theme of the chapter-by-chapter changes is our continually expanding coverage of *cultural* and *historical* influences on development. Reviewers have praised our emphasis on culture as a particular strength of this book. Cross-cultural research is fully integrated throughout the text as well as highlighted in Around the World boxes, reflecting the diversity of the population in the United States and in other nations. In this edition are new or enhanced discussions of such topics as ethnic gloss, acculturation, and how culture affects various aspects of development, from memory to self-definition. Our photo illustrations, too, show an ever greater commitment to depicting cultural diversity. Our strengthened attention to historical influences begins with Chapter 1, which introduces the concept of historical generations, expands our treatment of the history of the study of child development, and updates Elder's work on the life course. Discussions in other parts of the book place in a historical context subjects ranging from infant feeding to the comprehensive high school.

New in the Tenth Edition

Following is a chapter-by-chapter list of the most important new material in our 10th edition.

Chapter 1—Studying a Child's World

- Expanded discussions of early approaches to the study of child development, history of childhood, effects of socioeconomic status on poor and affluent families, culture, and race/ethnicity, including concepts of ethnic gloss and acculturation patterns
- Revised discussion of cohort, introducing the concept of historical generations
- Revised Social World box updating Elder's work

Chapter 2—A Child's World: How We Discover It

- New section on collaborative research
- New Research World box on adaptive value of immaturity
- Greatly expanded section on ethics of research
- Expanded treatment of cognitive neuroscience approach
- Revised discussion of qualitative research methods

Chapter 3—Forming a New Life: Conception, Heredity, and Environment

- Introduction to concept of incomplete dominance
- Updated information on multiple births, human genome, sex determination, Down syndrome, autistic spectrum disorders, infertility, and assisted reproduction techniques

Chapter 4—Pregnancy and Prenatal Development

- New section on maternal stress
- New information on maternal attachment to the fetus
- Updated sections on prenatal influences, including maternal nutrition, fetal alcohol effects, maternal nicotine ingestion, and environmental hazards
- Updated Social World box on fetal welfare and mothers' rights

Chapter 5—Birth and the Newborn Baby

- Updated information on childbirth safety, electronic fetal monitoring, cesarean births, medicated deliveries, neonatal screening, low birth weight, and stillbirth

Chapter 6—Physical Development and Health During the First Three Years

- New section on shaken baby syndrome
- New information on screening for hearing loss
- Updated information on infant feeding, outcomes for Romanian orphans, infant mortality (U.S. and world statistics), Sudden Infant Death Syndrome (SIDS), deaths from accidental injuries, and immunization

Chapter 7—Cognitive Development During the First Three Years

- New sections on locating objects in space and on symbolic development and spatial thinking, including some material moved from Chapter 10
- New Everyday World box on whether infants and toddlers watch too much television
- Revised section on cognitive neuroscience
- Updated information on infant imitation and violation-of-expectations research

Chapter 8—Psychosocial Development During the First Three Years

- New sections on emotional communication as a developmental process and impact of child care on disadvantaged children and minorities
- New Around the World box on struggles with toddlers
- Updated information on measuring temperament, goodness of fit, intergenerational transmission of attachment patterns, still-face paradigm, and effects of early child care

Chapter 9—Physical Development and Health in Early Childhood

- New Around the World box on surviving the first five years of life (international data)
- Updated information on nutrition, overweight, lead exposure, and child abuse

Chapter 10—Cognitive Development in Early Childhood

- New sections on children's ideas about prayer, the order in which theory-of-mind abilities develop, and how culture affects memory
- Updated information on theory-of-mind research, delayed language development, scaffolding, compensatory early childhood education, and the transition to kindergarten

Chapter 11—Psychosocial Development in Early Childhood

- New section on cultural differences in self-definition
- Updated information on biological influences on gender identity, gender development, significance of solitary play, parental psychological aggression, and cultural influences on parenting styles

Chapter 12—Physical Development and Health in Middle Childhood

- New section on recess-time play
- Updated sections on organized sports and maintaining health and fitness
- Updated information on nutrition, overweight, asthma, and influences of SES/ethnicity on health

Chapter 13—Cognitive Development in Middle Childhood

- New sections on school environment, educational innovations (such as charter schools), and computer and Internet use
- New discussion of ability to understand reciprocal obligations
- Updated information on math abilities, genetic influences on IQ, K-ABC-II, teaching of reading, school enrollment statistics, effects of parenting and maternal employment on school achievement, learning disabilities, and Attention Deficit/Hyperactivity Disorder (ADHD)

Chapter 14—Psychosocial Development in Middle Childhood

- New section on companion animals
- New information on relationship between self-esteem and volunteer work and on effortful (voluntary) control
- Updated information on poverty and parenting, adoption, effects of divorce, popularity, and bullies and victims

Chapter 15—Physical Development and Health in Adolescence

- New section on the adolescent brain
- Updated information on obesity and physical inactivity, drug use and abuse, adolescent depression, and death during adolescence

Chapter 16—Cognitive Development in Adolescence

- New sections on changes in information-processing abilities, stages of faith development, and gender differences in school achievement
- Expanded discussion of the secondary educational system, including historical background and current trends, such as Early College High Schools
- Updated information on high school dropouts

Chapter 17—Psychosocial Development in Adolescence

- New sections on romantic relationships and emerging adulthood
- New information on relationship between aggressiveness and popularity
- Updated information on homosexual identity and behavior, adolescent risk taking, sexual activities and attitudes, adolescent pregnancy and childbearing, antisocial behavior and violence, and cultural variations in time use

Supplementary Materials

A Child's World, tenth edition, is accompanied by a complete learning and teaching package keyed into the Learning System. Each component of this package has been thoroughly revised and expanded to include important new course material. Please contact your McGraw-Hill representative for more information.

For the Instructor

Instructor's Manual

Kathleen A. Bey, Palm Beach Community College
S. Peter Resta, University of Maryland–Baltimore County

Designed specifically for the tenth edition, this manual will be a valuable aid to new as well as experienced instructors. It is organized around the book's Guideposts for Study and offers a Total Teaching Package Outline that ties each Guidepost to lecture topics, classroom activities, and the like. In addition to an Expanded Outline there is a Transparency-Ready Topic Outline. Teaching and Learning Activities include topics for lecture and discussion, independent study assignments, a Ten-Minute Test, and more. The Choosing Sides feature provides a starter for class discussions and debates. Each chapter concludes with Resources for Instructors, citing publications and videos to enrich your teaching experience, as well as Linkups to help integrate each chapter with the others in the book.

Test Bank

Barbara Lane Radigan, Community College of Allegheny County

This comprehensive Test Bank includes more than 1,500 multiple-choice questions as well as more than 100 essay questions. The test questions are organized by chapter and are designed to test factual, applied, and conceptual understanding. New to the tenth edition is the inclusion of test questions pertaining to the video resources on the LifeMap student CD. The Test Bank is found on the Instructor Resource CD-ROM and can be ordered in print as well.

Dual Platform Computerized Test Bank on CD-ROM

The Computerized Test Bank is compatible with both Macintosh and Windows platforms. This CD-ROM provides a fully functioning editing feature that enables instructors to integrate their own questions, scramble items, and modify questions. The CD-ROM also offers an instructor the option of implanting the following unique features: On-Line Testing Program, Internet Testing, and Grade Management. Additional information regarding these features can be found in the accompanying CD-ROM documentation.

PowerPoint Slides

These presentations cover the key points of each chapter, serving as a springboard for your lectures. They can be used as is, or you may modify them to meet your specific needs.

Instructor's Resource CD-ROM

For instructors' convenience, the Instructor's Manual, Test Bank, and PowerPoints are offered on a single CD-ROM.

Online Learning Center: Instructor Center

http://www.mhhe.com/papaliaacw10

This extensive Web site, designed specifically to accompany *A Child's World,* tenth edition, offers an array of resources for both instructor and student. Among the features included on the Instructor's side of the Web site, which is password protected, are an online version of the Instructor's Manual, PowerPoint Slides, and links to professional resources. These resources and more can be found by logging onto the text site at http://www.mhhe.com/papaliaacw10. Contact your McGraw-Hill representative for your password.

PowerWeb

This unique online reader, which is fully integrated into the Online Learning Center, provides readings, *New York Times* news feeds, and weekly updates with refereed Web links. You will be excited by this powerful tool for helping keep your lectures up-to-date and timely.

PageOut

PageOut™ is the easiest way to create a Web site for your course. It requires no prior knowledge of HTML coding or graphic design and is free with every McGraw-Hill textbook. Visit www.pageout.net to learn more about PageOut™.

McGraw-Hill's Visual Asset Database (VAD) for Lifespan Development

Jasna Jovanovic, University of Illinois–Urbana-Champaign

McGraw-Hill's Visual Asset Database is a password-protected online database of hundreds of multimedia resources for use in classroom presentations. It includes original video clips, audio clips, photographs, and illustrations—all designed to bring to life concepts in developmental psychology. In addition to offering ready-made multimedia presentations for every stage of the lifespan, the VAD search engine and unique My Modules program allows instructors to select from the database's resources to create customized presentations, or modules. Instructors can save these customized presentations in specially marked module folders on the McGraw-Hill site and then run presentations directly from VAD to the Internet-equipped classroom. Contact your McGraw-Hill representative for a password to this valuable resource.

Multimedia Courseware for Child Development

Charlotte J. Patterson, University of Virginia

This video-based two-CD-ROM set covers classic and contemporary experiments in child development. Respected researcher Charlotte J. Patterson selected the video and wrote modules that can be assigned to students. The modules also include suggestions for additional projects as well as a testing component. Multimedia Courseware can be packaged with the text at a discount.

As a full service publisher of quality educational products, McGraw-Hill does much more than just sell textbooks to your students. We create and publish an extensive array of print, video, and digital supplements to support instruction on your campus. Orders of new (versus used) textbooks help us defray the cost of developing such supplements, which is substantial. We have a broad range of other supplements in psychology that you may wish to tap for your course. Ask your local McGraw-Hill representative about the availability of supplements that may help with your course design.

For the Student

Study Guide

Kathleen Bey, Palm Beach Community College

This comprehensive study guide is extensively revised for the tenth edition. Organized by chapter, it integrates the Guideposts for Study, which are found in the main text as well as in the Instructor's Manual. The Study Guide includes a chapter summary; multiple choice and true-false quizzes with answer keys; discussion topics; ideas for independent projects and papers; suggestions for further reading including journals, books, and Web sites; and an extensive outline that includes all important terms, people, theories, and concepts mentioned in the text.

LifeMap CD-ROM

Mary Lawrence Wathen

This CD-ROM, packaged free with each new copy of the book, gives students an opportunity to test their knowledge of course material. In addition to offering a multiple-choice quiz with feedback for each chapter, the LifeMap CD includes videos of children engaged in activities described in the text; interviews with children, teens, and expectant parents; and comments from experts on various child development topics. Each video is accompanied by an overview, study questions, and Web links to encourage further exploration of the topic.

Online Learning Center with PowerWeb

http://www.mhhe.com/papaliaacw10

This extensive Web site, designed specifically to accompany *A Child's World,* tenth edition, offers an array of resources for both instructor and student. The student side of the Online Learning Center provides a variety of learning tools, including a chapter outline, Guideposts for Study that match those in the text, a Key Terms matching exercise, multiple choice questions, true-false questions, short answer/essay questions, and Web links for each chapter. These resources and more can be found by logging on to the text site at http://www.mhhe.com/papaliaacw10.

PowerWeb

Bound into each new copy of the book is a password that students should save so that they can benefit from this unique online reader, which is fully integrated into the Online Learning Center. Here you will find readings, *New York Times* news feeds, and weekly updates with refereed Web links; tools for research, study, and assessment; and interactive exercises.

Acknowledgments

We would like to express our gratitude to the many friends and colleagues who, through their work and their interest, helped us clarify our thinking about child development. We are especially grateful for the valuable help given by those who reviewed the updated ninth edition of *A Child's World* and the manuscript drafts of this tenth edition, whose evaluations and suggestions helped greatly in the preparation of this new edition. These reviewers, who are affiliated with both two-year and four-year institutions, are as follows.

Donna Andersen, Bob Jones University
Kathy Baumwart, Rose State College
Kathleen A. Bey, Palm Beach Community College
Belinda Blevins-Knabe, University of Arkansas at Little Rock
Claire Etaugh, Bradley University
Kathleen E. Fite, Texas State University
Janet Fuller, Mansfield University
Gene Geist, Ohio University
Donna Gray, Irvine Valley College
Robyn M. Holmes, Monmouth University
Kathy E. Johnson, Indiana University–Purdue University at Indianapolis
Iris Lafferty, MiraCosta College

Deborah Laible, Southern Methodist University
Debbie Lewis, Miramar College
Miriam Linver, Montclair State University
Sonia Nieves, Broward Community College
Susan L. O'Donnell, George Fox University
Robert Pasnak, George Mason University
Elizabeth Pearce, Manchester Community College
Sandra Portko, Grand Valley State University
Lillian Range, University of Southern Mississippi
S. Peter Resta, Anne Arundel Community College, Prince Georges Community College, University of Maryland–Baltimore County
Lilliette J. Smith, Southwest Tennessee Community College
Julianne Stermer, Lane Community College

We appreciate the strong support we have had from our publisher. We would like to express our special thanks to publisher Steve Rutter, executive editor Mike Sugarman, senior developmental editor Elsa Peterson, project manager Rick Hecker, designer Kim Menning, photo research coordinator Nora Agbayani, and Malvine Litten, who coordinated the supplements. Freelance photo researcher Toni Michaels used her sensitivity and her good eye to find outstanding photographs.

As before, we wish to thank Dana Gross, Ph.D., who again has served admirably as chief consultant for this edition, helping us keep up with the latest findings in a rapidly expanding field. Her current classroom experience provides a valuable perspective on the needs of today's students. In addition, as a parent of two young children, Dana rounds out our author team, which consists of the parent of an adolescent and two grandparents of children of various ages.

As always, we welcome and appreciate comments from readers, which help us continue to improve *A Child's World.*

Diane E. Papalia
Sally Wendkos Olds
Ruth Duskin Feldman

Visual Walk-Through

Part Preview Tables

These tables, visually keyed to each chapter of the text, preview the main features of each chapter. The contents of the part preview tables for Parts 2 through 6 are coordinated with Table 1-1 in Chapter 1, which summarizes major developments of each period of the life span.

Part 3

Infancy and Toddlerhood: A Preview

Chapter 6
Physical Development and Health During the First Three Years

- All senses and body systems operate at birth to varying degrees.
- The brain grows in complexity and is highly sensitive to environmental influence.
- Physical growth and development of motor skills are rapid.

Chapter 7
Cognitive Development During the First Three Years

- Abilities to learn and remember are present, even in early weeks.
- Use of symbols and ability to solve problems de
- Comprehension and use of language develop r

Chapter 8
Psychosocial Development Duri
the First Three Years

- Attachments to parents and others form.
- Self-awareness develops.
- Shift from dependence to autonomy occurs.
- Interest in other children increases.

Beginnings

By the time babies are born, they already have an impressive history. Part of this early history, which began long before conception, is the hereditary endowment. Another part is environmental, for the new organism is affected by many events that occur during its nine months in the womb. As this organism grows from a single cell to a newborn baby, both inheritance and experience affect its development. At birth, babies are already individuals, distinguishable not just by sex, but by size, temperament, appearance, and history.

The changes that occur between conception and the first months after birth are broader and faster paced than any a person will ever experience again. Although these initial changes may seem to be mostly physical, they have repercussions on other aspects of development. For example, the *physical* growth of the brain before and immediately after birth makes possible a great burst of *cognitive* and *emotional* growth.

In Part II, we focus on this earliest period of development. Chapter 3 examines the two great forces—heredity and environment—that work together to make each child a unique person. Chapter 4 considers effects

Linkups to Look For

- A combination of biological, psychological, social, economic, and cultural factors may shape development beginning at conception.
- Fetuses seem to prefer their mother's voice to the voice of another woman.
- A family's socioeconomic status and other aspects of the social and cultural environment may affect the availability and utilization of prenatal care and, thus, the health of a newborn.
- Many prospective mothers are as concerned about emotional and social aspects of the setting in which their infants come into the world as they are about medical arrangements.
- Protective factors that

Part Overviews and *Linkups* to Look For

At the beginning of each part, an overview introduces the period of life discussed in the chapters that follow. The part overviews include *Linkups* to Look For: bulleted lists that point to examples of the interaction of physical, cognitive, and psychosocial aspects of development.

Chapter-Opening Outlines

At the beginning of each chapter, an outline previews the major topics included in the chapter.

Biographical "snapshots" from the lives of well-known people introduce and illustrate chapter themes.

Physical Development and Health in Middle Childhood

The healthy human child will keep
Away from home, except to sleep.
Were it not for the common cold,
Our young we never would behold.

—Ogden Nash, *You Can't Get There from Here*

Focus *Ann Bancroft, Polar Explorer*

Growth and Physiological Development
Height and Weight
Nutrition and Oral Health
Overweight and Body Image

Motor Development and Physical Play
Rough-and-Tumble Play
Organized Sports

Health, Fitness, and Safety
Maintaining Health and Fitness
Medical Conditions
Accidental Injuries
Factors in Health and Access to Health Care

BOXES
12-1 The Re... Childre... Health...
12-2 Around... Cultura... Health...

Focus *Ann Bancroft, Polar Explorer*

Ann Bancroft
AP/Wide World Photos

Ann Bancroft is the first woman in history to reach both the North and South Poles by nonmotorized means. In 1986, she dogsledded 1,000 miles from the Northwest Territories in Canada to the North Pole as the only female member of an international expedition. After surviving eight months of grueling training and enduring temperatures as low as −70°F for 56 days, Bancroft stood on top of the world. Seven years later she led three other women in a 67-day, 660-mile ski trek to the South Pole, reaching it on January 14, 1993. For these exploits, she was inducted into the National Women's Hall of Fame, was named Woman of the Year by *Ms.* magazine, and won numerous other awards and honors. Bancroft also was the first woman to ski across Greenland. In 2000, she and Liv Arneson of Norway became the first team of women to ski across the landmass of Antarctica; and in 2002 the two women reunited for a kayaking voyage from the north shore of Lake Superior to the St. Lawrence Seaway.

How did this 5-foot 3-inch, 125-pound woman achieve these remarkable feats? The answers go back to her childhood in then-rural Mendota Heights, Minnesota.

Born September 29, 1955, into what she calls a family of risk takers, Ann showed her climbing instincts as soon as she could walk. As a toddler, she would climb her grandmother's bookcase to reach things on top. Instead of trying to stop her from climbing, her

engineering, with questions. His uncle told him about the earth's north and south poles and about magnetic fields, but Albert still was not satisfied. He believed there must be some mysterious force in what appeared to be the empty space around the needle. He carried the compass around for weeks, trying to figure out its secret. Years later, at the age of 67, he wrote, ". . . this experience made a deep and lasting impression upon me. Something deeply hidden had to be behind things" (Schilpp, 1970, p. 9).

That sense of wonder was reawakened several years later, when Uncle Jacob, noticing that Albert showed an interest in arithmetic, introduced him to algebra and geometry. Albert solved every problem in the books his uncle brought him and then went searching for more. It was that same insatiable curiosity and persistence—what Einstein himself called "a furious impulse to understand" (Michelmore, 1962, p. 24)—that underlay his lifetime quest for scientific knowledge.

• • •

Albert Einstein's story touches on several themes of cognitive development in early childhood. One is the variation in normal language development. Another is that although Einstein's reaction to the compass may have been unusually intense, it was characteristic of young children's understanding of the physical world: their growing recognition that natural phenomena have causes, though those causes are not always apparent. Einstein's lifelong memory of that engrossing incident may shed light on why some kinds of early memories last while others do not. Finally, his parents' and teachers' underestimation of his cognitive abilities raises issues about how intelligence can be accurately assessed.

In this chapter, we examine these and other aspects of cognitive development in early childhood, as revealed by recent research as well as by such theorists as Piaget and Vygotsky. We see how children's thinking advances after toddlerhood and in what ways it remains immature. We look at children's increasing fluency with language and what impact this has on other aspects of development. We examine the beginnings of autobiographical memory, such as Einstein's memory of the compass; and we compare psychometric intelligence tests with assessments based on Vygotsky's theories. Finally, we look at the widening world of preschool and kindergarten.

After you have read and studied this chapter, you should be able to answer each of the Guidepost questions that follow. Look for them again in the margins, where they point to important concepts throughout the chapter. To check your understanding of these Guideposts, review the end-of-chapter Summary. Checkpoints located at periodic spots throughout the chapter will help you verify your understanding of what you have read.

Chapter Overviews

Near the beginning of each chapter, a brief overview of topics to be covered leads the reader smoothly from the opening vignette into the body of the chapter.

A comprehensive, unified **Learning System** helps students focus their reading and review and retain what they learn. It forms the conceptual framework for each chapter, is carried across all text supplements, and contains five parts:

Guideposts for Study

These topical questions, similar to learning objectives, are first posed near the beginning of each chapter to capture students' interest and motivate them to look for answers as they read. The questions are broad enough to form a coherent outline of each chapter's content but specific enough to invite careful study. Each Guidepost is repeated in the margin at the beginning of the section that deals with the topic in question and is repeated in the Chapter Summary to facilitate study.

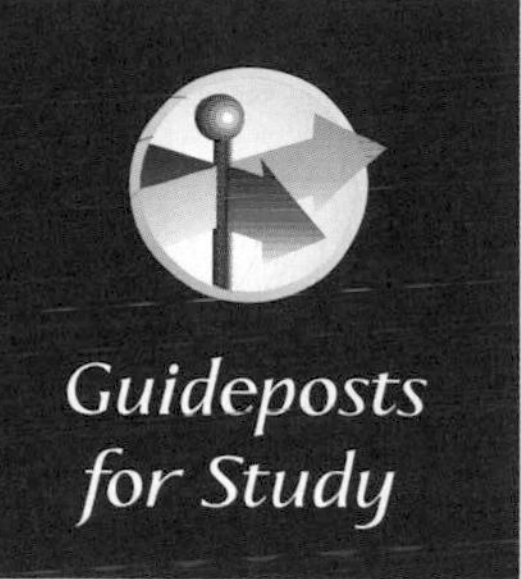

1. What is child development, and how has its study evolved?
2. What are six fundamental points about child development on which consensus has emerged?
3. What do developmental scientists study?
4. What are the three major domains and five periods of child development?
5. What kinds of influences make one child different from another?

Checkpoints

These detailed marginal questions, placed at the end of major sections of text, enable students to test their understanding of what they have read. Students should be encouraged to stop and review any section for which they cannot answer one or more Checkpoints.

Checkpoint 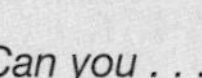

Can you . . .

✔ Trace highlights in the evolution of the study of child development?

✔ Name some pioneers in that study and summarize their most important contributions?

✔ Give examples of practical applications of research on child development?

What's your view 

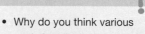

- Why do you think various societies divide the periods of development differently?

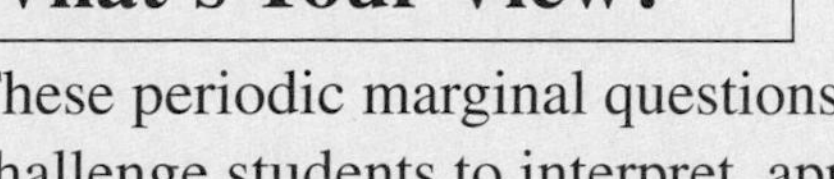

What's Your View?

These periodic marginal questions challenge students to interpret, apply, or critically evaluate information presented in the text.

Refocus

New in this update, this series of interpretive questions near the end of each chapter encourages students to think back over major chapter themes and their application to the famous person described in the opening vignette.

Refocus

How does the story of Victor, the Wild Boy of Aveyron, illustrate the following chapter themes?

- How the study of child development has become more scientific
- The interrelationship of domains of development
- The influences of heredity, environment, and maturation
- The importance of contextual and historical influences
- The roles of nonnormative influences and critical or sensitive periods

Now that you have had a brief introduction to the field of child development and its basic concepts, we can look more closely at the issues developmental scientists think about and how they do their work. In Chapter 2, we will discuss some influential theories of how development takes place and the methods investigators commonly use to study it.

Summary and Key Terms

The Study of Child Development: Then and Now

Guidepost 1 What is child development, and how has its study evolved?

- Child development is the scientific study of processes of change and stability.
- The scientific study of child development began toward the end of the 19th century. Adolescence was not considered a separate phase of development until the 20th century. The field of child development is now part of the study of the entire life span, or human development.
- The concept of periods of development is a social construction. In this book, child development is divided into five periods: the prenatal period, infancy and toddlerhood, early childhood, middle childhood, and adolescence. In each period, children have characteristic developmental needs and tasks.

social construction (11)

Influences on Development

Guidepost 5 What kinds of influences make one child different from another?

Summary and Key Terms

The Chapter Summaries are organized by the major topics in the chapter. The Guideposts for Study questions appear under the appropriate major topics. Each Guidepost is followed by a series of brief statements restating the most important points that fall under it, thus creating a self-testing question-answer format. Students should be encouraged to try to answer each Guidepost question before reading the summary material that follows. In this edition, key terms are listed for review under relevant topics, in the order in which they first appear, and are cross-referenced to pages where they are defined.

Boxed Series in This Edition

This edition includes four different types of boxed material. Each box contains a critical-thinking What's Your View question, as well as Check It Out Web site links, which direct students to further information located on the World Wide Web.

The Research World Boxes

These boxes report on exciting new developments or current controversies in the field of child development. These include new treatments of such contemporary topics as whether there is a critical period for language acquisition; whether early temperament can predict adult personality; the case against corporal punishment; and the homework debate.

The Research World

Box 1-2 *Is There a Critical Period for Language Acquisition?*

In 1970, a 13-year-old girl called Genie (not her real name) was discovered in a suburb of Los Angeles (Curtiss, 1977; Fromkin, Krashen, Curtiss, Rigler, & Rigler, 1974; Pines, 1981; Rymer, 1993). The victim of an abusive father, she had been confined for nearly 12 years to a small room in her parents' home, tied to a potty chair and cut off from normal human contact. She weighed only 59 pounds, could not straighten her arms or legs, could not chew, had no bladder or bowel control, and did not speak. She recognized only her own name and the word *sorry.*

Only three years before, Eric Lenneberg (1967, 1969) had proposed that there is a critical period for language acquisition, beginning in early infancy and ending around puberty. Lenneberg argued that it would be difficult, if not impossible, for a child who had not yet acquired language to do so after that age.

The discovery of Genie offered the opportunity for a test of Lenneberg's hypothesis. Could Genie be taught to speak, or was it too late? The National Institutes of Mental Health (NIMH) funded a study, and a series of researchers took over Genie's care and gave her intensive testing and language training.

Genie's progress during the next few years—before the NIMH withdrew funding and her mother regained custody and cut her off from contact with the professionals who had been teaching her—both challenges and supports the idea of a critical period for language acquisition. Genie did learn some simple words and could string them together into primitive, but rule-governed, sentences. She also learned the fundamentals of sign language. But she never used language normally, and "her speech remained, for the most part, like a somewhat garbled telegram" (Pines, 1981, p. 29). When her mother, unable to care for her, turned her over to a series of abusive foster homes, she regressed into total silence.

What explains Genie's initial progress and her inability to sustain it? The fact that she was just beginning to show signs of puberty at age 13 may indicate that she was still in the critical period, though near its end. The fact that she apparently had learned a few words before being locked up at the age of 20 months may mean that her language-learning mechanisms were triggered early in the critical period, allowing later learning to occur. On the other hand, her extreme abuse and neglect may have retarded her so much—emotionally, socially, and cognitively—that, like Victor, the wild boy of Aveyron, she could not be considered a true test of the critical period (Curtiss, 1977).

Case studies like those of Genie and Victor dramatize the *difficulty* of acquiring language after the early years of life, but, because there are too many complicating factors, they do not permit conclusive judgments about whether such acquisition is *possible.* Brain imaging research has found that even if the parts of the brain best suited to language processing are damaged early in childhood, nearly normal language development can continue as other parts of the brain take over (Boatman et al., 1999; Hertz-Pannier et al., 2002, M. H. Johnson, 1998). In fact, shifts in brain organization and utilization occur throughout the course of normal language learning (M. H. Johnson, 1998; Neville & Bavelier, 1998). Neuroscientists also have observed different patterns of brain activity during language processing between people who learned American Sign Language (ASL) as a native language and those who learned it as a second language, after puberty (Newman, Bavelier, Corina, Jezzard, & Neville, 2002). It is possible to learn a second language, signed or spoken, even in adulthood but typically not as easily or as well as in early childhood (Newport, 1991).

Because of the brain's plasticity, some researchers consider the prepubertal years a *sensitive* rather than *critical* period for learning language (Newport, Bavelier, & Neville, 2001; Schumann, 1997). But if either a critical or a sensitive period for language learning exists, what explains it? Do the brain's mechanisms for acquiring language decay as the brain matures? That would seem strange, since other cognitive abilities improve. An alternative hypothesis is that this very increase in cognitive sophistication interferes with an adolescent's or adult's ability to learn a language. Young children acquire language in small chunks that can be digested readily. Older learners, when they first begin learning a language, tend to absorb a great deal at once and then may have trouble analyzing and interpreting it (Newport, 1991).

What's your view ?

Do you see any ethical problems in the studies of Genie and Victor? Is the knowledge gained from such studies worth any possible damage to the individuals involved? (Keep this question, and your answer, in mind when you read the section on ethics of research in Chapter 2.)

Check it out

For more information on this topic, go to **http://www.facstaff.bucknell.edu/rbeard/acquisition.html.** This Web site was developed by Professor Robert Beard of the Linguistics Program at Bucknell University. The page at that URL gives a brief, accurate overview of the nature-nurture question as it concerns language acquisition. Links to other related sites of interest are also given.

Around the World

Box 8-2 *Are Struggles with Toddlers Necessary?*

Are the "terrible twos" a normal phase in child development? Many western parents and psychologists think so. Actually, though, this transition does not appear to be universal.

In Zinacantan, Mexico, toddlers do not typically become demanding and resistant to parental control. Instead of asserting independence from their mothers, toddlerhood in Zinacantan is a time when children move from mama's babies toward the new status of "mother's helpers," responsible children who tend a new baby and help with household tasks (Edwards, 1994). A similar developmental pattern seems to occur in Mazahua families in Mexico and among Mayan families in San Pedro, Guatemala. San Pedro parents "do not report a particular age when they expect children to become especially contrary or negative" (Mosier & Rogoff, 2003, p. 1058).

One arena in which issues of autonomy and control appear in western cultures is in sibling conflicts over toys and the way children respond to parental handling of these conflicts. To explore these issues, a cross-cultural study compared 16 San Pedro families with 16 middle-class European-American families in Salt Lake City. All of the families had toddlers 14 to 20 months old and older siblings 3 to 5 years old. The researchers interviewed each mother about her child-raising practices. They then handed the mother a series of attractive objects (such as nesting dolls and a jumping-jack puppet) and, in the presence of the older sibling, asked the mother to help the toddler operate them, with no instructions about the older child. Researchers who observed the ensuing interactions found striking differences in the way siblings interacted in the two cultures and in the way the mothers viewed and handled sibling conflict.

The older siblings in Salt Lake City often tried to take and play with the objects, but this did not generally happen in San Pedro. Instead, the older San Pedro children would offer to help their younger siblings work the objects, or the two children would play with them together. When there was a conflict over possession of the objects, the San Pedro mothers almost always favored the toddlers (94 percent of the time), even taking an object away from the older child if the younger child wanted it; and the older siblings tended to go along, willingly handing the objects to the toddlers or letting them have the objects from the start. By contrast, in more than one-third of the interactions in Salt Lake City, the mothers tried to treat both children equally, negotiating with them or suggesting that they take turns or share. These observations were consistent with reports of mothers in both cultures of how they handled such issues at home. San Pedro children are given a privileged position until age 3; then they are expected to willingly cooperate with social expectations.

What explains these cultural contrasts? A possible clue emerged when the mothers were asked at what age children can be held responsible for their actions. Most of the Salt Lake mothers maintained that their toddlers already understood the consequences of touching prohibited objects; several said this understanding arises as early as 7 months. Yet all but one of the San Pedro mothers placed the age of understanding social consequences of actions much later—between 2 and 3 years. Whereas the Salt Lake mothers regarded their toddlers as capable of intentionally misbehaving, most San Pedro mothers did not. More than half of the Salt Lake mothers reporting punishing toddlers for such infractions; none of the San Pedro mothers did. All of the Salt Lake preschoolers were under direct caregiver supervision, much like their toddler siblings, while 11 of the 16 San Pedro preschoolers were already on their own much of the time. The San Pedro preschoolers also had more mature household responsibilities.

The researchers suggest that the "terrible twos" may be a phase specific to societies that place individual freedom before the needs of the group. Ethnographic research suggests that, in societies that place higher value on group needs, freedom of choice does exist, but it goes hand in hand with interdependence, responsibility, and expectations of cooperation. Salt Lake parents seem to believe that responsible behavior develops gradually from engaging in fair competition and negotiations. San Pedro parents seem to believe that responsible behavior develops rapidly when children are old enough to understand the need to respect others' desires as well as their own.

What's your view ?

From your experience or observation of toddlers, which of the two ways of handling sibling conflict would you expect to be more effective?

Check it out !

For more information on this topic, go to **http://www.zerotothree.org/**. Here you will find links to a survey of 3,000 parents and other adults about commonly asked questions regarding the handling of young children and a downloadable article on "Cultural Models for Early Caregiving."

Around the World Boxes

This boxed feature offers windows on child development in societies other than our own (in addition to the cultural coverage in the main body of text). A new topic under this heading is Are Struggles with Toddlers Necessary?

The Everyday World Boxes

These boxes highlight practical applications of research findings. Among the new or greatly revised subjects are imaginary companions, the math wars, and whether parents should stay together for the sake of their children.

The Everyday World

Box 10-1 *Imaginary Companions*

At 3½, Anna had 23 "sisters" with such names as Och, Elmo, Zeni, Aggie, and Ankie. She often talked to them on the telephone, since they lived about 100 miles away, in the town where her family used to live. During the next year, most of the sisters disappeared, but Och continued to visit, especially for birthday parties. Och had a cat and a dog (which Anna had begged for in vain), and whenever Anna was denied something she saw advertised on television, she announced that she already had one at her sister's house. But when a live friend came over and Anna's mother happened to mention one of her imaginary companions, Anna quickly changed the subject.

All 23 sisters—and some "boys" and "girls" who have followed them—lived only in Anna's imagination, as she well knew. Like an estimated 25 to 65 percent of children between ages 3 and 10 (Woolley, 1997), Anna created imaginary companions with whom she talked and played. This normal phenomenon of childhood is seen most often in firstborn and only children who lack the close company of siblings. Like Anna, most children who create imaginary companions have many of them (Gleason, Sebanc, & Hartup, 2000). Girls are more likely than boys to have imaginary "friends" (or at least to acknowledge them). Girls' imaginary playmates are usually other children, whereas boys' are more often animals (D. G. Singer & Singer, 1990).

Children who have imaginary companions can distinguish fantasy from reality, but in free-play sessions they are more likely to engage in pretend play than are children without imaginary companions (M. Taylor, Cartwright, & Carlson, 1993). They play more happily and more imaginatively than other children and are more cooperative with other children and adults (D. G. Singer & Singer, 1990; J. L. Singer & Singer, 1981); and they do not lack for friends at preschool (Gleason et al., 2000). They are more fluent with language, watch less television, and show more curiosity, excitement, and persistence during play. In one study, 4-year-olds—regardless of verbal intelligence—who reported having imaginary companions did better on theory-of-mind tasks (such as differentiating appearance and reality and recognizing false beliefs) than children who did not create such companions (M. Taylor & Carlson, 1997).

Children's relationships with imaginary companions are like peer relationships; they are usually sociable and friendly, in contrast with the nurturing relationships children have with personified objects, such as stuffed animals and dolls (Gleason et al., 2000). Imaginary playmates are good company for an only child like Anna. They provide wish-fulfillment mechanisms ("There was a monster in my room, but Elmo scared it off with magic dust"), scapegoats ("I didn't eat those cookies—Och must have done it!"), displacement agents for the child's own fears ("Aggie is afraid she's going to be washed down the drain"), and support in difficult situations (one 6-year-old "took" her imaginary companion with her to see a scary movie).

What's your view ?

How should parents respond to children's talk about imaginary companions?

Check it out !

For more information on this topic, go to **http://harbaugh.uoregon.edu/mtaylor/**. This Web page by Marjorie Taylor is about children's imaginary companions.

The Social World Boxes

This box series includes new discussions or substantial updates or revisions of such topics as Elder's work on growing up in hard times; fetal welfare versus mothers' rights; and "pubilect," the dialect of adolescence.

The Social World

Box 1-1 *Studying the Life Course: Growing up in Hard Times*

Our awareness of the need to look at the life course in its social and historical context is indebted in part to Glen H. Elder, Jr. In 1962, Elder arrived on the campus of the University of California at Berkeley to work on the Oakland Growth Study, a longitudinal study of social and emotional development in 167 urban young people born around 1920, about half of them from middle-class homes. The study had begun at the outset of the Great Depression of the 1930s, when the participants, who had spent their childhoods in the boom years of the Roaring '20s, were entering adolescence. Elder observed how societal disruption can alter family processes and, through them, children's development (Elder, 1974).

As economic stress changed parents' lives, it changed children's lives, too. Deprived families reassigned economic roles. Fathers, preoccupied with job losses and irritable about their loss of status within the family, sometimes drank heavily. Mothers got outside jobs and took on more parental authority. Parents argued more. Adolescents tended to show developmental difficulties.

Still, for boys, particularly, the long-term effects of the ordeal were not entirely negative. Boys who got jobs to help out became more independent and were better able to escape the stressful family atmosphere than were girls, who helped at home. These boys grew up to be strongly work oriented but also valued family activities and cultivated dependability in their children.

Elder noted that effects of a major economic crisis depend on a child's stage of development. The children in the Oakland sample were already teenagers during the 1930s. They could draw on their own emotional, cognitive, and economic resources. A child born in 1929 would have been entirely dependent on the family. On the other hand, the parents of the Oakland children, being older, may have been less resilient in dealing with the loss of a job, and their emotional vulnerability may well have affected the tone of family life and their treatment of their children.

Fifty years after the Great Depression, in the early 1980s, a precipitous drop in the value of midwestern agricultural land pushed many farm families into debt or off the land. This farm crisis gave Elder the opportunity to replicate his earlier research, this time in a rural setting. In 1989, he and his colleagues (Conger & Elder, 1994; Conger et al., 1993) interviewed 451 Iowa farm and small-town two-parent families with a seventh grader and a sibling no more than four years younger. The researchers also videotaped family interactions. Because there were virtually no minorities living in Iowa at the time, all the participating families were white.

As in the Depression-era study, many of these rural parents, under pressure of economic hardship, developed emotional problems. Depressed parents were more likely to fight with each other and to mistreat or withdraw from their children. The children, in turn, tended to lose self-confidence, to be unpopular, and to do poorly in school. But whereas in the 1980s this pattern of parental behavior fit both mothers and fathers, in the 1930s it was less true of mothers, whose economic role before the collapse had been more marginal (Conger & Elder, 1994; Conger et al., 1993; Elder, 1998).

This study, now called the Family Transitions Project, continues. The family members have been reinterviewed yearly, with a focus on how a family crisis experienced in early adolescence affects the transition to adulthood. The adolescents who were in seventh grade when the study began were followed through high school. Each year they completed a list of stressful events they had experienced and were tested on measures of anxiety and depression and self-reported delinquent activities. For both boys and girls, a self-reinforcing cycle appeared. Such negative events as economic crisis, illness, and getting in trouble at school tended to intensify sadness, fear, and antisocial conduct, which, in turn, contributed to future adversities, such as the divorce of parents (Kim, Conger, Elder, & Lorenz, 2003).

Glen Elder's studies of children growing up during the Great Depression showed how a major sociohistorical event can affect children's current and future development.

Elder's work, like other studies of the life course, gives researchers a window into processes of development and their links with socioecoconomic change. Eventually it may enable us to see long-term effects of early hardship on the lives of people who experienced it at different ages and in varying family situations.

What's your view?

Can you think of a major cultural event within your lifetime that shaped the lives of families and children? How would you go about studying such effects?

Check it out!

For more information on this topic, go to **http://www.sos.state.mi.us/history/museum/techstuf/depressn/teacup.html.** This article, "Reminiscences of the Great Depression" was originally published in *Michigan History Magazine,* January–February, 1982 (Vol. 66, No. 1). Read one of the oral histories at this Web site and consider how the Great Depression seems to have affected the person whose story is told.

Source: Unless otherwise referenced, this discussion is based on Elder, 1998.

Other Teaching and Learning Aids

Key Terms

Whenever an important new term is introduced in the text, it is highlighted in **boldface** and defined, both in the text and, sometimes more formally, in the end-of-book glossary. Key terms and their definitions appear in the margins near the place where they are introduced in the text, and all key terms appear in **boldface** in the Chapter Summaries and subject index.

substance abuse Repeated, harmful use of a substance, usually alcohol or other drugs.

substance dependence Addiction (physical, psychological, or both) to a harmful substance.

an escape from overwhelming problems. They thereby endanger their present and future physical and psychological health.

Substance abuse is harmful use of alcohol or other drugs. It is a poorly adaptive behavior pattern lasting more than one month, in which a person continues to use a substance after knowingly being harmed by it or uses it repeatedly in a hazardous situation, such as while driving (APA, 1994). Abuse can lead to **substance dependence** (addiction), which may be physiological, psychological, or both and is likely to continue into adulthood.

Trends in Drug Use

Use of illicit drugs among U.S. adolescents declined 11 percent overall between 2001 and 2003 and is well below the peak during the late 1970s and early 1980s (see Figure 15-2). An upsurge during the early 1990s accompanied a decline in perception of the dangers of drug use and a softening of peer disapproval. That trend has now begun to reverse itself, including a drop in use of crack cocaine and a sharp decline in the use of ecstasy, a hallucinatory, amphetaminelike drug popular at night-long "raves" or "trances" (L. D. Johnston,

Tables

Periodic tables summarize or illustrate important concepts and developments.

Table 1-1 Typical Major Developments in Five Periods of Child Development

Age Period	Physical Developments	Cognitive Developments	Psychosocial Developments
Prenatal Period (conception to birth)	Conception occurs by normal fertilization or other means The genetic endowment interacts with environmental influences from the start. Basic body structures and organs form; brain growth spurt begins. Physical growth is most rapid in the life span. Vulnerability to environmental influences is great.	Abilities to learn and remember and to respond to sensory stimuli are developing.	Fetus responds to mother's voice and develops a preference for it.
Infancy and Toddlerhood (birth to age 3)	All senses and body systems operate at birth to varying degrees. The brain grows in complexity and	Abilities to learn and remember are present, even in early weeks. Use of symbols and ability to solve	Attachments to parents and others form. Self-awareness develops.

Today, research using operant conditioning with nonverbal, age-appropriate tasks suggests that infants' memory processes may not differ fundamentally from those of older children and adults except that infants' retention time is shorter. These studies have found that babies will repeat an action days or weeks later—*if* they are periodically reminded of the situation in which they learned it (Rovee-Collier, 1999).

In a series of experiments by Carolyn Rovee-Collier and her associates, infants were operantly conditioned to kick to activate a mobile attached to one ankle by a ribbon. Babies 2 to 6 months old, when again shown the mobiles days or weeks later, repeated the kicking, even though their legs were no longer attached to the mobiles. When the infants saw the mobiles, they kicked more than before the conditioning, showing that recognition of the mobiles triggered a memory of their initial experience with them (Rovee-Collier, 1996, 1999). In a similar task designed for older infants and toddlers, a child was conditioned to press a lever to make a miniature train go around a track. The length of time a conditioned response can be retained increases with age, from two days for 2-month-olds to 13 weeks for 18-month-olds (Hartshorn et al., 1998; Rovee-Collier, 1996, 1999; see Figure 7-2).

Young infants' memory of a behavior seems to be linked specifically to the original cue. Two- to 6-month-olds repeated the learned behavior only when they saw the original mobile or train. However, older infants, between 9 and 12 months, would "try out" the behavior on a different train if no more than two weeks had gone by since the training (Rovee-Collier, 1999).

Babies 2 to 6 months old can remember, after a hiatus of two days to two weeks, that they were able to activate a mobile by kicking; they show this by kicking as soon as they see the mobile.

Context can affect recollection when a memory has weakened. Three-, 9-, and 12-month-olds initially could recognize the mobile or train in a different setting from the one in which they were trained, but not after long delays. Periodic nonverbal reminders through brief exposure to the original stimulus can sustain a memory from early infancy through 1½ to 2 years of age (Rovee-Collier, 1999).

Since infants can remember, why don't their early memories last? It may be because the crucial match between the situation in which something is learned and the situation in which it can be recalled is lost after a long period of time—a period in which the child begins to rely more on verbal than on nonverbal cues (Rovee-Collier, 1999).

Checkpoint

Can you . . .

- ✔ Contrast the goals of the behaviorist, psychometric, and Piagetian approaches to the study of cognitive development?
- ✔ Give examples of classical and operant conditioning in infants?
- ✔ Summarize what studies of operant conditioning have shown about infant memory?

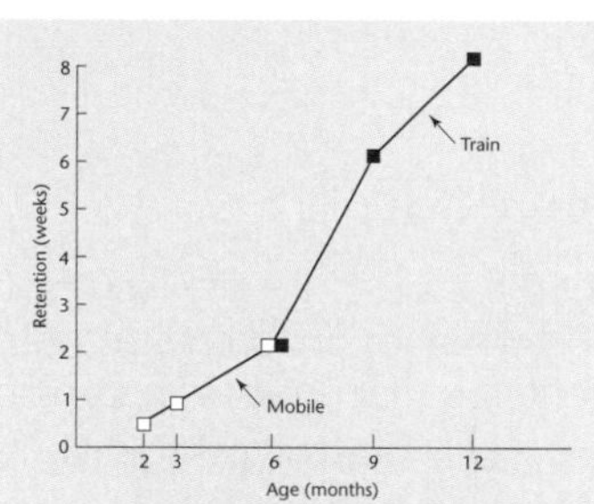

Figure 7-2

Maximum number of weeks that infants of varying ages show retention of how to operate either a mobile or a miniature train. Regardless of the task, retention improves with age.

Source: Rovee-Collier, 1999, Fig. 4, p. 83.

Chapter 7 Cognitive Development During the First Three Years 165

Art Program

Many points in the text are underscored pictorially through carefully selected drawings, graphs, and photographs. The illustration program includes new or revised figures and many full-color photographs.

Index

Separate indexes, by author name and by subject, appear at the end of the book.

Name Index

AAAS (American Association for the Advancement of Science), 364
Aalsma, M. C., 470
Allen, J. R., 179
Allen, K. R., 214, 387
Allen, N. B., 400

Subject Index

A, not-B error, 172, 183
AAI (Adult Attachment Interview), 219
Abecedarian Project, 168, 169
gender differe
high school c
homework, 3

End-of-Book Glossary

The extensive glossary at the back of the book gives definitions of key terms.

Glossary

A

A, not-B error Tendency for 8- to 12-month-old infants to search for a hidden object in a place where they previously found it rather than in the place where they most recently saw it being hidden.

acceleration Approach to educating the

Apgar scale Standard meas newborn's condition; it as appearance, pulse, grimac respiration.

art therapy Therapeutic ap a child to express troubled words, using a variety of a media.

Part 1

Entering a Child's World: A Preview

Chapter 1
Studying a Child's World

- The scientific study of child development began during the late 19th century and has evolved to become part of the study of the full life span.
- Developmental scientists study change and stability in the physical, cognitive, and psychosocial domain.
- Development is subject to internal and external influences.
- Important contextual influences on development include family, neighborhood, socioeconomic status, culture, ethnicity, and history.

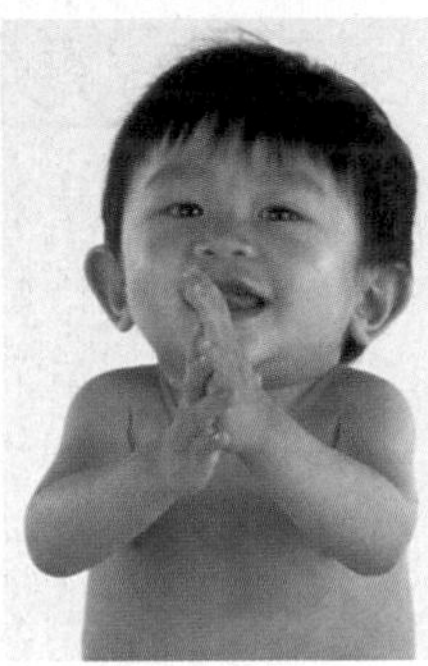

Chapter 2
A Child's World: How We Discover It

- Theoretical perspectives on child development differ on three key issues: (1) the relative importance of heredity and environment, (2) whether children contribute to their own development, and (3) whether development is continuous or occurs in stages.
- Major theoretical perspectives include psychoanalytic, learning, cognitive, evolutionary/biological, and contextual. Various theories of development are influenced by these perspectives.
- Basic methods of data collection include self-reports, tests, and observation. Basic research designs include case studies, ethnographic studies, correlational studies, and experiments.
- To study development, researchers may follow children over a period of time to see how they change, or may compare children of different ages to see how they differ.

Entering a Child's World

If you look at pictures of yourself as a child, it may seem as if you are stepping back onto a terrain that is familiar yet strange. Is that really you in those images frozen in time? When you study a photograph of yourself soon after birth, do you wonder how it felt to come into this world? How about that photo taken on your first day of school—were you nervous about meeting your teacher? Now flip ahead to your high school graduation picture. How did that helpless baby turn into the sturdy schoolchild and then into the cap-and-gowned young person about to step into the world of adulthood?

Snapshots tell us little about the processes of change that take place as a child grows up. Even a series of home videos, which can follow children from moment to moment as they get older, will not capture a progression of changes so subtle that we often cannot detect them until after they have occurred. The processes and influences that produce those developmental changes are the subject of this book.

Part I is a guide map to a child's world. It traces routes that investigators have followed in the quest for information about what makes children develop as they do and points out the main directions students of development follow today. In Chapter 1, we explore how the study of child development has evolved and examine its basic concepts. In Chapter 2, we consider how developmental scientists study children, what theories guide them, what research methods they use, and what ethical standards govern their work.

As you enter a child's world again, remember that real children are not abstractions on the printed page. They are living, laughing, crying, shouting, tantrum-throwing, question-asking human beings. Observe the children about you in grocery stores, parks, movie theaters, and on the street. Listen to them. Look at them. Pause to pay attention as they confront and experience the wonder of life. Look back at the child you once were, and ask yourself what made you the person you are. Jot down questions you hope this course will help you answer. With the insights you gain as you read this book, you will be able to look at yourself and at every child you see with new eyes.

chapter
1

Studying a Child's World

There is nothing permanent except change.

—Heraclitus, fragment (6th century B.C.)

Focus *Victor, the Wild Boy of Aveyron*

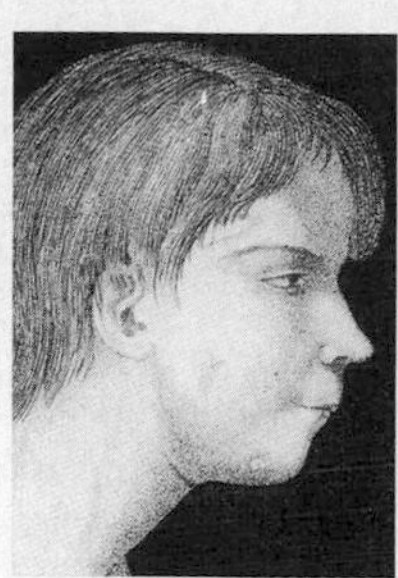

Victor

On January 8, 1800, a naked boy, his face and neck heavily scarred, appeared on the outskirts of the village of Saint-Sernin in the sparsely populated province of Aveyron in south central France. The boy, who was only four and a half feet tall but looked about 12 years old, had been spotted several times during the previous two and a half years, climbing trees, running on all fours, drinking from streams, and foraging for acorns and roots.

When the dark-eyed boy came to Saint-Sernin, he neither spoke nor responded to speech. Like an animal accustomed to living in the wild, he spurned prepared foods and tore off the clothing people tried to put on him. It seemed clear that he had either lost his parents or been abandoned by them, but how long ago this had occurred was impossible to tell.

The boy appeared during a time of intellectual and social ferment, when a new, scientific outlook was beginning to replace mystical speculation. Philosophers debated questions about the nature of human beings—questions that would become central to the study of child development. Are the qualities, behavior, and ideas that define what it means to be human inborn or acquired or both? How important is social contact during the formative years? Can its lack be overcome? A study of a child who had grown up in isolation might provide evidence of the relative impacts of "nature" (inborn characteristics) and "nurture" (upbringing, schooling, and other societal influences).

After initial observation, the boy, who came to be called Victor, was sent to a school for deaf-mutes in Paris. There, he was turned over to Jean-Marc-Gaspard Itard, an ambitious 26-year-old practitioner of the emerging science of "mental medicine," or psychiatry. Itard believed that Victor's development had been limited by isolation and that he simply needed to be taught the skills that children in civilized society normally acquire.

Itard took Victor into his home and, during the next five years, gradually "tamed" him. Itard first awakened his pupil's ability to discriminate sensory experience through hot baths and dry rubs. He then moved on to painstaking, step-by-step training of emotional responses and instruction in moral and social behavior, language, and thought. The methods Itard used—based on principles of imitation, conditioning, and behavioral modification, all of

Sources of information about the wild boy of Aveyron are Frith (1989) and Lane (1976).

which we discuss in Chapter 2—were far ahead of their time, and he invented many teaching devices used today.

But the education of Victor (which was dramatized in François Truffaut's film *The Wild Child*) was not an unqualified success. The boy did make remarkable progress; he learned the names of many objects and could read and write simple sentences. He could express desires, obey commands, and exchange ideas. He showed affection, especially for Itard's housekeeper, Madame Guérin, as well as such emotions as pride, shame, remorse, and the desire to please. However, aside from uttering some vowel and consonant sounds, he never learned to speak. Furthermore, he remained totally focused on his own wants and needs and never seemed to lose his yearning "for the freedom of the open country and his indifference to most of the pleasures of social life" (Lane, 1976, p. 160). When the study ended, Victor—no longer able to fend for himself, as he had done in the wild—went to live with Madame Guérin until his death in his early 40s in 1828.

• • •

Why did Victor fail to fulfill Itard's hopes for him? The boy may have been a victim of brain damage, autism (a brain disorder involving lack of social responsiveness), or severe early maltreatment. Itard's instructional methods, advanced as they were for his time, may have been inadequate. Itard himself came to believe that the effects of long isolation could not be fully overcome and that Victor may have been too old, especially for language learning.

Although Victor's story does not yield definitive answers to the questions Itard set out to explore, it is important because it was one of the first systematic attempts to study child development. Since Victor's time, we have learned much about how children develop, but developmental scientists are still investigating such fundamental questions as the relative importance of nature and nurture and how they work together. Victor's story dramatizes the challenges and complexities of the scientific study of child development—the study on which you are about to embark.

In this chapter, we examine how the field of child development has itself developed as scientists have learned more about infants, children, and adolescents. We review the goals and basic concepts of the field today. We consider aspects of development and how they interrelate. We survey major developments during each period of a child's life. We look at influences on development and the contexts in which it occurs.

After you have read and studied this chapter, you should be able to answer each of the Guidepost questions that follow. Look for them again in the margins, where they point to important concepts throughout the chapter. To check your understanding of these Guideposts, review the end-of-chapter Summary. Checkpoints located at periodic spots throughout the chapter will help you verify your understanding of what you have read.

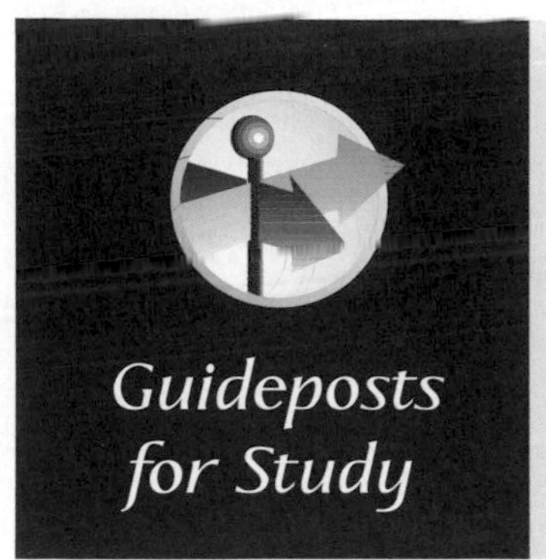

1. What is child development, and how has its study evolved?
2. What are six fundamental points about child development on which consensus has emerged?
3. What do developmental scientists study?
4. What are the three major domains and five periods of child development?
5. What kinds of influences make one child different from another?

The Study of Child Development: Then and Now

What is child development, and how has its study evolved?

child development Scientific study of processes of change and stability from conception through adolescence.

From the moment of conception, human beings undergo processes of development. The field of **child development** is the scientific study of those processes. Developmental scientists—people engaged in the professional study of child development—look at ways in which children change from conception through adolescence as well as at characteristics that remain fairly stable.

Child development has, of course, been going on as long as children have existed, but its formal scientific study is relatively new. Looking back, we can see dramatic changes in the ways of investigating the world of childhood.

Early Approaches

Forerunners of the scientific study of child development were *baby biographies,* journals kept to record the early development of a single child. One such journal, published in 1787 in Germany, contained Dietrich Tiedemann's (1897/1787) observations of his son's sensory, motor, language, and cognitive behavior during the first two and a half years. Typical of the speculative nature of such observations was Tiedemann's erroneous conclusion, after watching the infant suck more continuously on a cloth tied around something sweet than on a nurse's finger, that sucking appeared to be "not instinctive, but acquired" (Murchison & Langer, 1927, p. 206).

It was Charles Darwin, originator of the theory of evolution, who first emphasized the *developmental* nature of infant behavior as an orderly process of change. Darwin believed that human beings could better understand themselves by studying their origins—both as a species and as individuals. In 1877 he published an abstract of his notes on his son Doddy's sensory, cognitive, and emotional development during the first 12 months (Keegan & Gruber, 1985; see *Focus* at the beginning of Chapter 7). Darwin's journal gave baby biographies scientific respectability; about 30 more were published during the next three decades (Dennis, 1936).

By the end of the 19th century, several important trends in the western world were preparing the way for the scientific study of child development. Scientists had unlocked the mystery of conception and (as in the case of the wild boy of Aveyron) were arguing about the relative importance of "nature" and "nurture" (inborn characteristics and external influences). The discovery of germs and immunization made it possible for many more children to survive infancy. Because of an abundance of cheap labor, children were less needed as workers. Laws protecting them from long workdays let them spend more time in school, and parents and teachers became more concerned with identifying and meeting children's developmental needs. The new science of psychology taught that people could understand themselves by learning what had influenced them as children.

Still, this new discipline had far to go. Adolescence was not considered a separate period of development until the early 20th century, when G. Stanley Hall, a pioneer in child study, published a popular (though unscientific) book called *Adolescence* (1904/1916). The

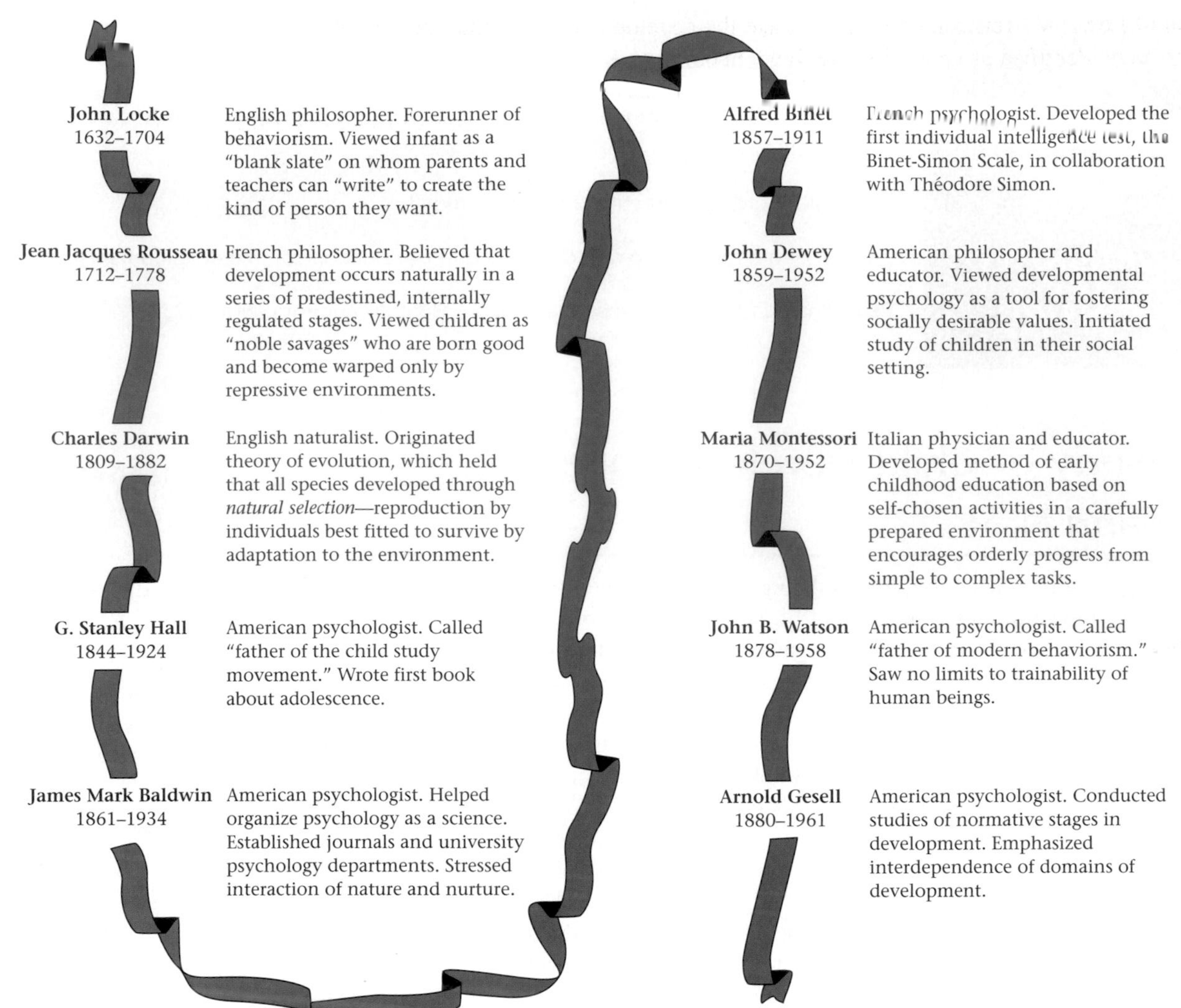

John Locke
1632–1704
English philosopher. Forerunner of behaviorism. Viewed infant as a "blank slate" on whom parents and teachers can "write" to create the kind of person they want.
Jean Jacques Rousseau
1712–1778
French philosopher. Believed that development occurs naturally in a series of predestined, internally regulated stages. Viewed children as "noble savages" who are born good and become warped only by repressive environments.
Charles Darwin
1809–1882
English naturalist. Originated theory of evolution, which held that all species developed through *natural selection*—reproduction by individuals best fitted to survive by adaptation to the environment.
G. Stanley Hall
1844–1924
American psychologist. Called "father of the child study movement." Wrote first book about adolescence.
James Mark Baldwin
1861–1934
American psychologist. Helped organize psychology as a science. Established journals and university psychology departments. Stressed interaction of nature and nurture.
Alfred Binet
1857–1911
French psychologist. Developed the first individual intelligence test, the Binet-Simon Scale, in collaboration with Théodore Simon.
John Dewey
1859–1952
American philosopher and educator. Viewed developmental psychology as a tool for fostering socially desirable values. Initiated study of children in their social setting.
Maria Montessori
1870–1952
Italian physician and educator. Developed method of early childhood education based on self-chosen activities in a carefully prepared environment that encourages orderly progress from simple to complex tasks.
John B. Watson
1878–1958
American psychologist. Called "father of modern behaviorism." Saw no limits to trainability of human beings.
Arnold Gesell
1880–1961
American psychologist. Conducted studies of normative stages in development. Emphasized interdependence of domains of development.

Figure 1-1

A timeline of developments in the study of a child's world.

establishment of research institutes in the 1930s and 1940s at universities such as Iowa, Minnesota, Columbia, Berkeley, and Yale marked the emergence of child psychology as a true science with professionally trained practitioners. Longitudinal studies, such as Arnold Gesell's (1929) studies of stages in motor development, provided research-based information about developments that normally occur at various ages. Other major studies that began around 1930—-the Fels Research Institute Study, the Berkeley Growth and Guidance Studies, and the Oakland (Adolescent) Growth Study—produced much information on long-term development. Figure 1-1 presents summaries, in historical order, of the ideas and contributions of some of the early pioneers in the study of child development.

With the work of Gesell and the classic theories of Sigmund Freud and Jean Piaget (introduced in Chapter 2), developmental science became interdisciplinary (Parke, 2004). Today students of child development draw collaboratively from a wide range of disciplines, including psychology, psychiatry, sociology, anthropology, biology, genetics (the study of inherited characteristics), family science (the interdisciplinary study of family relations), education, history, philosophy, and medicine. This book includes findings from research in all these fields.

Studying the Life Span

Life-span studies in the United States grew out of programs designed to follow children through adulthood. The Stanford Studies of Gifted Children, begun in 1921 under the direction of Lewis M. Terman, continue to trace the development of people (now in old age) who were identified as unusually intelligent in childhood.

Today the study of child development is part of the broader study of *human development,* which covers the entire life span from conception to death. Although growth and development are most obvious in childhood, they occur throughout life. Indeed, such varied aspects of adult development as the timing of parenthood, maternal employment, and marital satisfaction have an impact on the way children develop (Parke, 2004).

New Frontiers

Although children have been the focus of scientific study for more than 100 years, this exploration is an ever-evolving endeavor. The questions that developmental scientists seek to answer, the methods they use, and the explanations they propose are more sophisticated and more eclectic than they were even 25 years ago (Parke, 2004). These shifts reflect progress in understanding, as new investigations build on or challenge those that went before. They also reflect the changing cultural and technological context.

Sensitive instruments that measure eye movements are turning up intriguing connections between infant visual attentiveness and childhood intelligence. Cameras, videocassette recorders, and computers enable investigators to scan infants' facial expressions for early signs of emotions and to analyze how mothers and babies communicate. Advances in brain imaging make it possible to probe the mysteries of temperament and to pinpoint the sources of logical thought.

The classic distinction between *basic research,* the kind undertaken purely in a spirit of intellectual inquiry, and *applied research,* which addresses a practical problem, is becoming less meaningful. Increasingly, research findings have direct application to child rearing, education, health, and social policy (Parke, 2004). For example, research into preschool children's understanding of death can enable adults to help a child deal with bereavement; research on children's memory can help determine the weight to be given children's courtroom testimony; and research on factors that increase the risks of low birth weight, antisocial behavior, and teenage suicide can suggest ways to prevent these ills.

What's your view

- What reasons do you have for studying child development?

Checkpoint

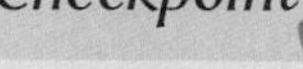

Can you . . .

✔ Trace highlights in the evolution of the study of child development?

✔ Name some pioneers in that study and summarize their most important contributions?

✔ Give examples of practical applications of research on child development?

An Emerging Consensus

Guidepost 2

What are six fundamental points about child development on which consensus has emerged?

As the study of children has matured, a broad consensus has emerged on several fundamental points:

1. *All domains of development are interrelated.* Although developmental scientists often look separately at various *domains,* or dimensions, of development, each affects the others. For example, increasing physical mobility helps a baby learn about the world. The hormonal and physical changes of puberty affect emotional development.
2. *Normal development includes a wide range of individual differences.* Each child, from the start, is unlike anyone else in the world. One child is outgoing, another shy. One is agile, another awkward. How do those differences and a multitude of others come about? Some of the influences on individual development are inborn; others come from experience. Most often, both types of influences work together. Family characteristics, gender, social class, ethnicity, and the presence or absence of physical, mental, or emotional disability all affect the way a child develops.
3. *Children help shape their own development and influence others' responses to them.* Right from the start, through the responses they evoke in others, infants mold their environment and then respond to the environment they have helped create. Influence is *bidirectional:* When babies babble and coo, adults tend to talk to them, which then makes babies "talk" more.
4. *Historical and cultural contexts strongly influence development.* Each child develops within a specific environment, bounded by time and place. A child born in the United States today is likely to have very different experiences from a child born in colonial America or from a child born in Greenland or Afghanistan.

5. *Early experience is important, but children can be remarkably resilient.* A traumatic incident or a severely deprived childhood may well have grave emotional consequences, but the life histories of countless people show that the effects of painful experience, such as growing up in poverty or the death of a parent, can often be overcome.
6. *Development in childhood is connected to development throughout the rest of the life span.* At one time, it was believed that growth and development end, as this book does, with adolescence. Today most developmental scientists agree that development goes on throughout life. As long as people live, they have the potential to change.

Checkpoint

Can you . . .

✔ Summarize six fundamental points of agreement that have emerged from the study of child development?

Guidepost 3

What do developmental scientists study?

The Study of Child Development: Basic Concepts

The processes of change and stability that developmental scientists study occur in all aspects of development and throughout all periods of the life span.

Developmental Processes: Change and Stability

quantitative change Change in number or amount, such as in height, weight, or size of vocabulary.

qualitative change Change in kind, structure, or organization, such as the change from nonverbal to verbal communication.

Developmental scientists study two kinds of change: *quantitative* and *qualitative.* **Quantitative change** is a change in number or amount, such as in height, weight, size of vocabulary, or frequency of communication. **Qualitative change** is a change in kind, structure, or organization. It is marked by the emergence of new phenomena that cannot be anticipated easily on the basis of earlier functioning, such as the change from a nonverbal child to one who understands words and can communicate verbally.

Despite these changes, most people show an underlying *stability,* or constancy, of personality and behavior. For example, about 10 to 15 percent of children are consistently shy, and another 10 to 15 percent are very bold. Although various influences can modify these traits somewhat, they persist to a moderate degree, especially in children at one extreme or the other (see Chapter 3).

Which of a child's characteristics are likely to endure? Which are likely to change, and why? These are among the questions that developmental scientists seek to answer.

Guidepost 4

What are three major domains and five periods of child development?

Domains of Development

Change and stability occur in various domains of the self. Developmental scientists talk separately about *physical development, cognitive development,* and *psychosocial development.* Actually, though, these domains are interrelated. Throughout life, each affects the others.

Growth of the body and brain, the development of sensory capacities and motor skills, and health are aspects of *physical development* and may influence other domains. For example, a child with frequent ear infections may develop language more slowly than a child without this problem. During puberty, dramatic physiological and hormonal changes affect the developing sense of self.

Change and stability in mental abilities, such as learning, memory, language, thinking, moral reasoning, and creativity constitute *cognitive development.* Cognitive advances are closely related to physical, social, and emotional growth. The ability to speak depends on the physical development of the mouth and brain. A child who has difficulty expressing herself in words may evoke negative reactions in others, influencing her popularity and sense of self-worth.

Change and stability in personality, emotional life, and social relationships are aspects of *psychosocial development,* and this can affect cognitive and physical functioning. Anxiety about taking a test can impair performance. Social support can help children cope with the potentially negative effects of stress on physical and mental health. Conversely, physical and cognitive capacities influence psychosocial development. They contribute greatly to self-esteem and can affect social acceptance.

Although we will be looking separately at physical, cognitive, and psychosocial development, a child is more than a bundle of isolated parts. Development is a unified process. Throughout the text, we will highlight links among the three major domains of development.

A Grecian vase painting (from about 460 B.C.) depicts a mother and toddler reaching out to one another. The toddler is seated in a tall stool with a removable potty chamber on top. Such stools, which seem to have been fairly common, were the only type of furniture known to have been made specifically for children.

Periods of Development

The concept of periods of development is a **social construction:** an idea about the nature of reality accepted by members of a particular society at a particular time on the basis of shared subjective perceptions or assumptions. There is no single, objectively definable moment when a child becomes an adolescent or an adolescent becomes an adult. Indeed, the concept of childhood itself can be viewed as a social construction. Some evidence indicates, though it has been disputed, that children in earlier times were regarded and treated much like small adults (Ariès, 1962; Elkind, 1986; Pollock, 1983). Even now, in some developing countries, children labor alongside their elders, doing the same kinds of work for equally long hours.

In industrial societies, as mentioned earlier, the concept of adolescence as a period of development is quite recent. Until the early 20th century, young people in the United States were considered children until they left school (often well before age 13), married or got a job, and entered the adult world. By the 1920s, with the establishment of comprehensive high schools to meet the needs of a growing industrial and commercial economy and with more families able to support extended formal education for their children, the teenage years came to be seen as a distinct period of development. Yet it was not until after the 1930s that teenagers adopted distinctive styles of dress different from those of their elders (Keller, 1999). In some preindustrial societies, the concept of adolescence still does not exist. The Chippewa Indians, for example, have only two periods of childhood: from birth until the child walks, and from walking to puberty. What we call *adolescence* is part of adulthood (Broude, 1995), as was true in western societies before industrialization.

social construction Concept about the nature of reality, based on societally shared perceptions or assumptions.

What's your view 

- Why do you think various societies divide the periods of development differently?

In this book, we follow a sequence of five periods generally accepted in western industrial societies. After examining the crucial changes that occur in the first period, before birth, we will trace all three domains of development through infancy and toddlerhood, early childhood, middle childhood, and adolescence (see Table 1-1). These age divisions are approximate and somewhat arbitrary. Individual differences exist in the way children deal with the characteristic events and issues of each period. One toddler may be toilet trained by 18 months and another not until 3 years.

Checkpoint 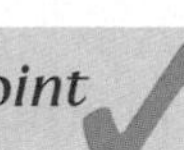

Can you . . .

✔ Distinguish between quantitative and qualitative development and give an example of each?

✔ Identify three domains of development and give examples of how they are interrelated?

✔ Name five periods of human development (as defined in this book) and list several key issues or events of each period?

Despite these differences, however, developmental scientists suggest that certain basic developmental needs must be met and certain developmental tasks must be mastered during each period for normal development to occur. Infants, for example, are dependent on adults to meet their basic needs for food, clothing, and shelter as well as for human contact and affection. They form attachments to parents or caregivers, who also become attached to them. With the development of speech and self-locomotion, toddlers become more self-reliant; they need to assert their autonomy but also need parents to help them keep their impulses in check. During early childhood, children develop more self-control and more interest in other children. During middle childhood, control over behavior gradually shifts from parent to child, and the peer group becomes increasingly important. A main task of adolescence is the search for identity—personal, sexual, and occupational. As adolescents become physically mature, they deal with sometimes conflicting needs and emotions as they prepare to separate from the parental nest.

Table 1-1 Typical Major Developments in Five Periods of Child Development

Age Period	Physical Developments	Cognitive Developments	Psychosocial Developments
Prenatal Period (conception to birth)	Conception occurs by normal fertilization or other means The genetic endowment interacts with environmental influences from the start. Basic body structures and organs form; brain growth spurt begins. Physical growth is most rapid in the life span. Vulnerability to environmental influences is great.	Abilities to learn and remember and to respond to sensory stimuli are developing.	Fetus responds to mother's voice and develops a preference for it.
Infancy and Toddlerhood (birth to age 3)	All senses and body systems operate at birth to varying degrees. The brain grows in complexity and is highly sensitive to environmental influence. Physical growth and development of motor skills are rapid.	Abilities to learn and remember are present, even in early weeks. Use of symbols and ability to solve problems develop by end of second year. Comprehension and use of language develop rapidly.	Attachments to parents and others form. Self-awareness develops. Shift from dependence to autonomy occurs. Interest in other children increases.
Early Childhood (3 to 6 years)	Growth is steady; appearance becomes more slender and proportions more adultlike. Appetite diminishes, and sleep problems are common. Handedness appears; fine and gross motor skills and strength improve.	Thinking is somewhat egocentric, but understanding of other people's perspectives grows. Cognitive immaturity results in some illogical ideas about the world. Memory and language improve. Intelligence becomes more predictable. Preschool experience is common, and kindergarten experience is more so.	Self-concept and understanding of emotions become more complex; self-esteem is global. Independence, initiative, and self-control increase. Gender identity develops. Play becomes more imaginative, more elaborate, and usually more social. Altruism, aggression, and fearfulness are common. Family is still the focus of social life, but other children become more important.
Middle Childhood (6 to 11 years)	Growth slows. Strength and athletic skills improve. Respiratory illnesses are common, but health is generally better than at any other time in the life span.	Egocentrism diminishes. Children begin to think logically but concretely. Memory and language skills increase. Cognitive gains permit children to benefit from formal schooling. Some children show special educational needs and strengths.	Self-concept becomes more complex, affecting self-esteem. Coregulation reflects gradual shift in control from parents to child. Peers assume central importance.
Adolescence (11 to about 20 years)	Physical growth and other changes are rapid and profound. Reproductive maturity occurs. Major health risks arise from behavioral issues, such as eating disorders and drug abuse.	Ability to think abstractly and use scientific reasoning develops. Immature thinking persists in some attitudes and behaviors. Education focuses on preparation for college or vocation.	Search for identity, including sexual identity, becomes central. Relationships with parents are generally good. Peer group may exert a positive or negative influence.

Influences on Development

Guidepost 5

What kinds of influences make one child different from another?

Students of development are interested in processes of development, but they also want to know about **individual differences**, both in influences on development and in its outcome. Children differ in sex, height, weight, and body build; in constitutional factors such as health and energy level; in intelligence; and in personality characteristics and emotional reactions. The contexts of their lives and lifestyles differ too: the homes, communities, and societies they live in, the relationships they have, the kinds of schools they go to (or whether they go to school at all), and how they spend their free time.

individual differences Differences among children in characteristics, influences, or developmental outcomes.

Why does one child turn out unlike any other? Because development is complex and the factors that affect it cannot always be measured precisely, scientists cannot answer that question fully. However, they have learned much about what children need to develop normally, how they react to the many influences upon and within them, and how they can best fulfill their potential.

Heredity, Environment, and Maturation

Some influences on development originate primarily with **heredity:** the genetic endowment inherited from the biological parents at conception. Other influences come largely from the **environment:** the world outside the self, beginning in the womb. Individual differences increase as children grow older. Many typical changes of infancy and early childhood seem to be tied to **maturation** of the body and brain—the unfolding of a natural sequence of physical changes and behavior patterns, including readiness to master new abilities such as walking and talking. As children grow into adolescents and then into adults, differences in innate (inborn) characteristics and life experience play a greater role as children adapt to, or deal with, their internal and external conditions.

heredity Inborn influences or traits inherited from biological parents.

environment Totality of nonhereditary, or experiential, influences on development.

maturation Unfolding of a natural sequence of physical and behavioral changes, including readiness to master new abilities.

Even in processes that all children go through, rates and timing of development vary. Throughout this book, we talk about average ages for the occurrence of certain behaviors: the first word, the first step, the first menstruation or "wet dream," the development of logical thought. But these ages are *merely* averages. Only when deviation from the average is extreme should we consider development exceptionally advanced or delayed.

In trying to understand the similarities and differences in development, we need to look at the *inherited* characteristics that give each person a special start in life. We also need to consider the many *environmental* factors that affect people, especially such major contexts as family, neighborhood, socioeconomic status, ethnicity, and culture. We need to see how heredity and environment interact. We need to look at influences that affect many or most children at a certain age or a certain time in history and also at those that affect only certain individuals. Finally, we need to look at how timing can affect the impact of certain influences.

LifeMap CD

To learn more about how psychologists study influences on development, watch the "Career in Developmental Psychology" video in Chapter 1 of your CD.

Major Contextual Influences

Human beings are social beings. Right from the start, they develop within a social and historical context. For an infant, the immediate context normally is the family; and the family in turn is subject to the wider and ever-changing influences of neighborhood, community, and society.

Family

Family may mean something different in different times and places. The **nuclear family** is a two-generational kinship, economic, and household unit consisting of one or two parents and their biological children, adopted children, or stepchildren. Historically, the two-parent nuclear family has been the dominant family unit in the United States and other western societies. Parents and children typically worked side by side on the family farm. Today most U.S. families are urban; they have fewer children, and both parents are likely to work outside the home. Children spend much of their time in school or child care. Children of

nuclear family Two-generational kinship, economic, and household unit consisting of one or two parents and their biological children, adopted children, or stepchildren.

Table 1-2 Poverty Hurts Children

Outcomes	Low-Income Children's Higher Risk
Health	
Death in infancy	1.6 times more likely
Premature birth (under 37 weeks)	1.8 times more likely
Low birth weight	1.9 times more likely
Inadequate prenatal care	2.8 times more likely
No regular source of health care	2.7 times more likely
Having too little food sometime in the last 4 months	8.0 times more likely
Education	
Lower math scores at ages 7 to 8	5 test points lower
Lower reading scores at ages 7 to 8	4 test points lower
Repeating a grade	2.0 times more likely
Being expelled from school	3.4 times more likely
Being a dropout at ages 16 to 24	3.5 times more likely
Finishing a four-year college	50 percent as likely

Source: Children's Defense Fund, 2004.

divorced parents may live with one or the other parent or may move back and forth between them. The household may include a stepparent and stepsiblings or a parent's live-in partner. There are increasing numbers of single and childless adults, unmarried parents, and gay and lesbian households (Hernandez, 1997, 2004; Teachman, Tedrow, & Crowder, 2000).

extended family Multigenerational kinship network of parents, children, and other relatives, sometimes living together in an extended-family household.

In many societies in Asia, Africa, and Latin America and among some U.S. families that trace their lineage to those countries, the **extended family**—a multigenerational kinship network of grandparents, aunts, uncles, cousins, and more distant relatives—is the traditional family form. Many or most people live in *extended-family households,* where they have daily contact with kin. Adults often share breadwinning and child raising responsibilities, and children are responsible for younger brothers and sisters. Often these households are headed by women (Aaron, Parker, Ortega, & Calhoun, 1999; Harrison, Wilson, Pine, Chan, & Buriel, 1990; Johnson et al., 2003; Levitt, Guacci-Franco, & Levitt, 1993; Perex, 1994; Smith, 1997). Today the extended-family household is becoming less typical in developing countries due to industrialization and migration to urban centers (Brown, 1990; Gorman, 1993), particularly among upwardly mobile groups (Peterson, 1993).

Socioeconomic Status and Neighborhood

socioeconomic status (SES) Combination of economic and social factors describing an individual or family, including income, education, and occupation.

Socioeconomic status (SES) includes income, education, and occupation. Throughout this book, we examine many studies that relate SES to developmental processes (such as mothers' verbal interactions with their children) and to developmental outcomes (such as health and cognitive performance; see Table 1-2). SES affects these outcomes indirectly, through such associated factors as the kinds of homes and neighborhoods children live in and the quality of nutrition, medical care, supervision, schooling, and other opportunities available to them.

Poverty, especially if it is chronic, is harmful to the physical, cognitive, and psychosocial well-being of children and families (Evans, 2004). Poor children are more likely than other children to have emotional or behavioral problems, and their cognitive potential and school performance suffer even more (Brooks-Gunn, Britto, & Brady, 1998; Brooks-Gunn & Duncan, 1997; Duncan & Brooks-Gunn, 1997; McLoyd, 1998). The harm done by poverty may be indirect, through its impact on where families can live, on parents' emotional state and parenting practices, and on the home environment they create (see

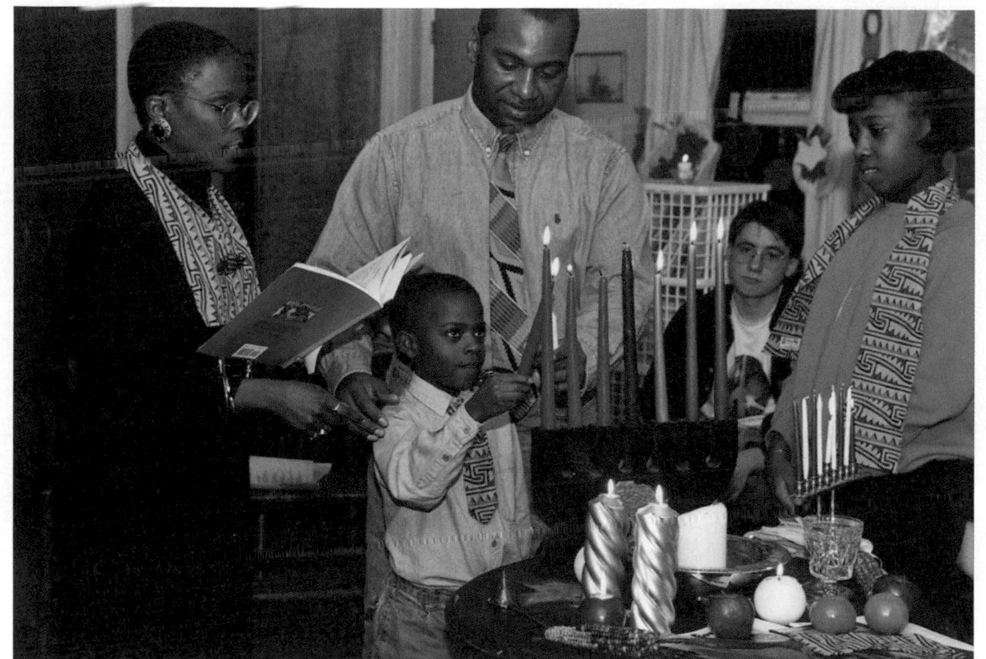

In Auburn, New York, a family lights the Kinara, a ceremony celebrating the first harvest, part of the African American celebration of Kwanzaa. The family joined others at a local Unitarian Universalist Church to celebrate the winter solstice, Hanukkah, and Kwanzaa. The gathering shared stories and songs from varied cultural traditions.

Chapter 14). Threats to well-being multiply if, as often happens, several **risk factors**—conditions that increase the likelihood of a negative outcome—coexist (Evans, 2004).

risk factors Conditions that increase the likelihood of a negative developmental outcome.

The composition of a neighborhood affects the way children turn out. The most powerful factors seem to be average neighborhood *income* and *human capital*—the presence of educated, employed adults who can build the community's economic base and provide models of what a child can hope to achieve (Brooks-Gunn et al., 1997; Leventhal & Brooks-Gunn, 2000). In a poor neighborhood with large numbers of residents unemployed and on welfare, effective social support is less likely to be available (Black & Krishnakumar, 1998).

Children in affluent families also may be at risk (Evans, 2004). Under pressure to achieve and often left on their own by busy parents, these children have high rates of substance abuse, anxiety, and depression (Luthar, 2003; Luthar & Becker, 2002).

Culture and Race/Ethnicity

Culture refers to a society's or group's total way of life, including customs, traditions, beliefs, values, language, and physical products, from tools to artworks—all of the learned behavior passed from parents to children. Culture is constantly changing, often through contact with other cultures. For example, when Europeans arrived on American shores, they learned from the native Indians how to grow corn. Today computers and telecommunications enhance cross-cultural contact, and American music is downloaded around the world.

culture A society's or group's total way of life, including customs, traditions, beliefs, values, language, and physical products—all learned behavior passed on from parents to children.

Some cultures have variant *subcultures* associated with ethnic groups. An **ethnic group** consists of people united by ancestry, religion, language, and/or national origin, all of which contribute to a sense of shared identity and shared attitudes, beliefs, and values. The term *race,* historically viewed as a biological category, is now considered a perceived social construct, not readily distinguishable from ethnicity. In fact, there is more genetic variation *within* races than among them (American Academy of Pediatrics Committee on Pediatric Research, 2000; Lin & Kelsey, 2000). Categories of culture, race, and ethnicity are "continuously shaped and redefined by social and political forces" (Fisher et al., 2002, p. 1026), and there is no clear consensus on the definitions of these terms.

ethnic group Group united by ancestry, religion, language, and/or national origins, all of which contribute to a sense of shared identity.

Most ethnic groups trace their roots to a country of origin, where they or their forebears shared a common culture that continues to influence their way of life. Ethnic and

What's your view?

- How might you be different if you had grown up in a culture other than your own?

cultural patterns may influence the composition of a household, its economic and social resources, the way its members act toward one another, the foods they eat, the games children play, the way they learn, how well they do in school—and even the way they think and perceive the world (Parke, 2004).

In 2003, 31 percent of the U.S. population belonged to a racial or ethnic minority—black, Hispanic, American Indian, or Asian and Pacific Islander—representing a threefold increase since the 1930s (U.S. Census Bureau, 1930, 2003). By 2050, the minority population is projected to rise to 50 percent (McKinney & Bennett, 1994). Actually, the United States always has been a nation of immigrants and ethnic groups. The European-descended "white majority" consists of many distinct ethnic groups—German, Belgian, Irish, French, Italian, and so on. Cuban Americans, Puerto Ricans, and Mexican Americans—all Hispanic Americans—have different histories and cultures and may be of African, European, Native American, or mixed descent (Johnson et al., 2003). African Americans from the rural South differ from those of Caribbean ancestry. Asian Americans hail from a variety of countries with distinct cultures, from modern, industrial Japan to communist China to the remote mountains of Nepal, where many people still practice their ancient way of life. American Indians consist of hundreds of recognized nations, tribes, bands, and villages (Lin & Kelsey, 2000).

Furthermore, although statistics often refer to distinct racial or ethnic classifications, a person (such as the golf champion Tiger Woods, who has a black father and an Asian-American mother) may fall into more than one such category and may identify more strongly with one or another at different times (Lin & Kelsey, 2000). Such a term as *black* or *Hispanic,* then, can be an **ethnic gloss**—an overgeneralization that obscures cultural differences within such a group (Parke, 2004; Trimble & Dickson, in press).

ethnic gloss Overgeneralization about an ethnic or cultural group that obscures differences within the group.

The dynamic nature of cultural change further confounds ethnic identity (Parke, 2004). In large, multiethnic societies such as the United States, immigrant or minority groups *acculturate,* or adapt, by learning the language, customs, and attitudes needed to get along in the dominant culture while trying to preserve some of their own cultural practices and values (Johnson et al., 2003). Individuals acculturate at different rates depending on such factors as how long they have lived in the majority culture, how old they were when they immigrated, their treatment by the dominant community, and how closely they want to maintain ties with their native culture (Chun, Organista, & Marin, 2002; Johnson et al., 2003).

Although researchers today are paying much more attention to ethnic and cultural differences than in the past, it is difficult, if not impossible, to present a truly comprehensive picture of these differences. Minorities are still underrepresented in developmental research, and minority samples are often unrepresentative, in part because of wariness about participating (Parke, 2004). Many studies reported in this book are limited to the dominant group within a culture, and others compare only two groups, such as white Americans and African Americans. When multiple groups *are* studied, often only one or two are noticeably different and therefore worth noting. Even cross-cultural studies cannot capture all of the variations within and among cultures.

Checkpoint

Can you . . .

✔ Explain why individual differences tend to increase with age?

✔ Give examples of the influences of family and neighborhood composition, socioeconomic status, culture, ethnicity, and historical context?

The Historical Context

At one time developmental scientists paid little attention to the historical context—the time in which people live and grow. Then, as the early longitudinal studies of childhood extended into the adult years, investigators began to focus on how certain experiences, tied to time and place, affect the course of children's lives. The Terman sample, for example, reached adulthood in the 1930s, during the Great Depression; the Oakland sample, during World War II (see Box 1-1); and the Berkeley sample, around 1950, the postwar boom period. What did it mean to be a child in each of these periods? To be an adolescent? To become an adult? The answers differ in specific and important ways.

Today, as we will discuss in the next section, the historical context is part and parcel of the study of development.

The Social World

Box 1-1 *Studying the Life Course: Growing up in Hard Times*

Our awareness of the need to look at the life course in its social and historical context is indebted in part to Glen H. Elder, Jr. In 1962, Elder arrived on the campus of the University of California at Berkeley to work on the Oakland Growth Study, a longitudinal study of social and emotional development in 167 urban young people born around 1920, about half of them from middle-class homes. The study had begun at the outset of the Great Depression of the 1930s, when the participants, who had spent their childhoods in the boom years of the Roaring '20s, were entering adolescence. Elder observed how societal disruption can alter family processes and, through them, children's development (Elder, 1974).

As economic stress changed parents' lives, it changed children's lives, too. Deprived families reassigned economic roles. Fathers, preoccupied with job losses and irritable about their loss of status within the family, sometimes drank heavily. Mothers got outside jobs and took on more parental authority. Parents argued more. Adolescents tended to show developmental difficulties.

Still, for boys, particularly, the long-term effects of the ordeal were not entirely negative. Boys who got jobs to help out became more independent and were better able to escape the stressful family atmosphere than were girls, who helped at home. These boys grew up to be strongly work oriented but also valued family activities and cultivated dependability in their children.

Elder noted that effects of a major economic crisis depend on a child's stage of development. The children in the Oakland sample were already teenagers during the 1930s. They could draw on their own emotional, cognitive, and economic resources. A child born in 1929 would have been entirely dependent on the family. On the other hand, the parents of the Oakland children, being older, may have been less resilient in dealing with the loss of a job, and their emotional vulnerability may well have affected the tone of family life and their treatment of their children.

Fifty years after the Great Depression, in the early 1980s, a precipitous drop in the value of midwestern agricultural land pushed many farm families into debt or off the land. This farm crisis gave Elder the opportunity to replicate his earlier research, this time in a rural setting. In 1989, he and his colleagues (Conger & Elder, 1994; Conger et al., 1993) interviewed 451 Iowa farm and small-town two-parent families with a seventh grader and a sibling no more than four years younger. The researchers also videotaped family interactions. Because there were virtually no minorities living in Iowa at the time, all the participating families were white.

As in the Depression-era study, many of these rural parents, under pressure of economic hardship, developed emotional problems. Depressed parents were more likely to fight with each other and to mistreat or withdraw from their children. The children, in turn, tended to lose self-confidence, to be unpopular, and to do poorly in school. But whereas in the 1980s this pattern of parental behavior fit both mothers and fathers, in the 1930s it was less true of mothers, whose economic role before the collapse had been more marginal (Conger & Elder, 1994; Conger et al., 1993; Elder, 1998).

This study, now called the Family Transitions Project, continues. The family members have been reinterviewed yearly, with a focus on how a family crisis experienced in early adolescence affects the transition to adulthood. The adolescents who were in seventh grade when the study began were followed through high school. Each year they completed a list of stressful events they had experienced and were tested on measures of anxiety and depression and self-reported delinquent activities. For both boys and girls, a self-reinforcing cycle appeared. Such negative events as economic crisis, illness, and getting in trouble at school tended to intensify sadness, fear, and antisocial conduct, which, in turn, contributed to future adversities, such as the divorce of parents (Kim, Conger, Elder, & Lorenz, 2003).

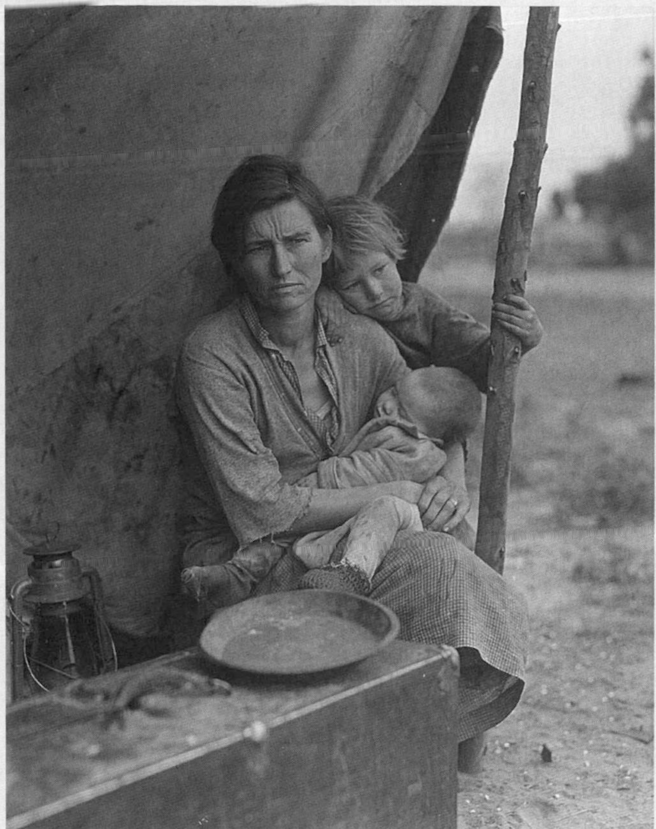

Glen Elder's studies of children growing up during the Great Depression showed how a major sociohistorical event can affect children's current and future development.

Elder's work, like other studies of the life course, gives researchers a window into processes of development and their links with socioecoconomic change. Eventually it may enable us to see long-term effects of early hardship on the lives of people who experienced it at different ages and in varying family situations.

What's your view?

Can you think of a major cultural event within your lifetime that shaped the lives of families and children? How would you go about studying such effects?

Check it out!

For more information on this topic, go to **http://www.sos.state.mi.us/history/museum/techstuf/depressn/teacup.html.** This article, "Reminiscences of the Great Depression" was originally published in *Michigan History Magazine,* January–February, 1982 (Vol. 66, No. 1). Read one of the oral histories at this Web site and consider how the Great Depression seems to have affected the person whose story is told.

Source: Unless otherwise referenced, this discussion is based on Elder, 1998.

Normative and Nonnormative Influences

To understand similarities and differences in development, we must look at influences, including those of time and place, that impinge on large numbers of people and at those that touch only certain individuals (Baltes, Reese, & Lipsitt, 1980).

normative Characteristic of an event that is experienced in a similar way by most people in a group.

A **normative** event is experienced in a similar way by most people in a group. *Normative age-graded influences* are highly similar for people in a particular age group. They include biological events (such as puberty) and social events (such as entry into formal education). The timing of biological events is fixed, within a normal range. (Children do not experience puberty at age 3.) The timing of social events is more flexible and varies in different times and places, within maturational limits. Children in western industrial societies generally begin formal education around age 5 or 6. In some developing countries, schooling begins much later, if at all.

Normative history-graded influences are significant events (such as the Great Depression or World War II) that shape the behavior and attitudes of a **historical generation:** a group of people who experience the event at a formative time in their lives. For example, the generations that came of age during the Depression and World War II tend to show a strong sense of social interdependence and trust that has declined among more recent generations (Rogler, 2002). Depending on when and where they live, entire generations may feel the impact of famines, nuclear explosions, or terrorist attacks. In western countries, medical advances as well as improvements in nutrition and sanitation have dramatically reduced infant and child mortality. Children today are influenced by computers, digital cameras, the Internet, and other technological developments. Social changes, such as the increase in employed mothers, have greatly altered family life.

historical generation Group of people strongly influenced by a major historical event during their formative period.

cohort Group of people born at about the same time.

nonnormative Characteristic of an unusual event that has an impact on a particular person or a typical event that happens at an unusual time of life.

A historical generation is not quite the same as an age **cohort:** a group of people born at about the same time. A historical generation may contain more than one cohort, but not all cohorts are part of historical generations unless they experience major, shaping historical events at a formative point in their lives (Rogler, 2002).

Nonnormative influences are unusual events that have a major impact on *individual* lives and may cause stress because they are unexpected. They are either typical events that happen at an atypical time of life (such as marriage in the early teens or the death of a parent when a child is young) or atypical events (such as having a birth defect or being in an airplane crash). They can also, of course, be happy events (such as winning the lottery). Young people may help create their own nonnormative life events—say, by driving after drinking or by applying for a scholarship—and thus participate actively in their own development.

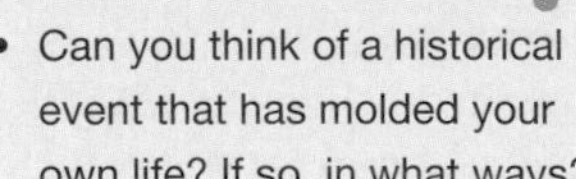

- Can you think of a historical event that has molded your own life? If so, in what ways?

Timing of Influences: Critical or Sensitive Periods

critical period Specific time when a given event, or its absence, has the greatest impact on development.

plasticity Modifiability of performance.

sensitive periods Times in development when a person is particularly open to certain kinds of experiences.

A **critical period** is a specific time when a given event, or its absence, has a specific impact on development. For example, if a woman receives X-rays, takes certain drugs, or contracts certain diseases at certain times during pregnancy, the fetus may show specific ill effects. The amount and kind of damage will vary, depending on the nature of the "shock" and on its timing.

A child deprived of certain kinds of experience during a critical period is likely to show permanent stunting of physical development. For example, if a muscle problem interfering with the ability to focus both eyes on the same object is not corrected early in life, the brain mechanisms necessary for binocular depth perception probably will not develop (Bushnell & Boudreau, 1993).

The concept of critical periods is controversial. Because many aspects of development, even in the biological/neurological domain, have been found to show **plasticity,** or modifiability of performance, it may be more useful to think about **sensitive periods,** when a developing person is especially responsive to certain kinds of experiences (Bruer, 2001). Further research is needed to discover "which aspects of behavior are likely to be altered by environmental events at specific points in development and which aspects remain more plastic and open to influence across wide spans of development" (Parke, 2004, p. 8). Box 1-2 discusses how the concepts of critical and sensitive periods apply to language development.

Checkpoint

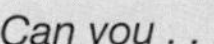

Can you . . .

✔ Give examples of normative age-graded, normative history-graded, and nonnormative influences?

✔ Explain the concept of "critical" periods and give examples?

The Research World

Box 1-2 *Is There a Critical Period for Language Acquisition?*

In 1970, a 13 year-old girl called Genie (not her real name) was discovered in a suburb of Los Angeles (Curtiss, 1977; Fromkin, Krashen, Curtiss, Rigler, & Rigler, 1974; Pines, 1981; Rymer, 1993). The victim of an abusive father, she had been confined for nearly 12 years to a small room in her parents' home, tied to a potty chair and cut off from normal human contact. She weighed only 59 pounds, could not straighten her arms or legs, could not chew, had no bladder or bowel control, and did not speak. She recognized only her own name and the word *sorry.*

Only three years before, Eric Lenneberg (1967, 1969) had proposed that there is a critical period for language acquisition, beginning in early infancy and ending around puberty. Lenneberg argued that it would be difficult, if not impossible, for a child who had not yet acquired language to do so after that age.

The discovery of Genie offered the opportunity for a test of Lenneberg's hypothesis. Could Genie be taught to speak, or was it too late? The National Institutes of Mental Health (NIMH) funded a study, and a series of researchers took over Genie's care and gave her intensive testing and language training.

Genie's progress during the next few years—before the NIMH withdrew funding and her mother regained custody and cut her off from contact with the professionals who had been teaching her—both challenges and supports the idea of a critical period for language acquisition. Genie did learn some simple words and could string them together into primitive, but rule-governed, sentences. She also learned the fundamentals of sign language. But she never used language normally, and "her speech remained, for the most part, like a somewhat garbled telegram" (Pines, 1981, p. 29). When her mother, unable to care for her, turned her over to a series of abusive foster homes, she regressed into total silence.

What explains Genie's initial progress and her inability to sustain it? The fact that she was just beginning to show signs of puberty at age 13 may indicate that she was still in the critical period, though near its end. The fact that she apparently had learned a few words before being locked up at the age of 20 months may mean that her language-learning mechanisms were triggered early in the critical period, allowing later learning to occur. On the other hand, her extreme abuse and neglect may have retarded her so much—emotionally, socially, and cognitively—that, like Victor, the wild boy of Aveyron, she could not be considered a true test of the critical period (Curtiss, 1977).

Case studies like those of Genie and Victor dramatize the *difficulty* of acquiring language after the early years of life, but, because there are too many complicating factors, they do not permit conclusive judgments about whether such acquisition is *possible.* Brain imaging research has found that even if the parts of the brain best suited to language processing are damaged early in childhood, nearly normal language development can continue as other parts of the brain take over (Boatman et al., 1999; Hertz-Pannier et al., 2002; M. H. Johnson, 1998). In fact, shifts in brain organization and utilization occur throughout the course of normal language learning (M. H. Johnson, 1998; Neville & Bavelier, 1998). Neuroscientists also have observed different patterns of brain activity during language processing between people who learned American Sign Language (ASL) as a native language and those who learned it as a second language, after puberty (Newman, Bavelier, Corina, Jezzard, & Neville, 2002). It is possible to learn a second language, signed or spoken, even in adulthood but typically not as easily or as well as in early childhood (Newport, 1991).

Because of the brain's plasticity, some researchers consider the prepubertal years a *sensitive* rather than *critical* period for learning language (Newport, Bavelier, & Neville, 2001; Schumann, 1997). But if either a critical or a sensitive period for language learning exists, what explains it? Do the brain's mechanisms for acquiring language decay as the brain matures? That would seem strange, since other cognitive abilities improve. An alternative hypothesis is that this very increase in cognitive sophistication interferes with an adolescent's or adult's ability to learn a language. Young children acquire language in small chunks that can be digested readily. Older learners, when they first begin learning a language, tend to absorb a great deal at once and then may have trouble analyzing and interpreting it (Newport, 1991).

What's your view?

Do you see any ethical problems in the studies of Genie and Victor? Is the knowledge gained from such studies worth any possible damage to the individuals involved? (Keep this question, and your answer, in mind when you read the section on ethics of research in Chapter 2.)

Check it out!

For more information on this topic, go to **http://www.facstaff.bucknell.edu/rbeard/acquisition.html.** This Web site was developed by Professor Robert Beard of the Linguistics Program at Bucknell University. The page at that URL gives a brief, accurate overview of the nature-nurture question as it concerns language acquisition. Links to other related sites of interest are also given.

Refocus

How does the story of Victor, the Wild Boy of Aveyron, illustrate the following chapter themes?

- How the study of child development has become more scientific
- The interrelationship of domains of development
- The influences of heredity, environment, and maturation
- The importance of contextual and historical influences
- The roles of nonnormative influences and critical or sensitive periods

Now that you have had a brief introduction to the field of child development and its basic concepts, we can look more closely at the issues developmental scientists think about and how they do their work. In Chapter 2, we will discuss some influential theories of how development takes place and the methods investigators commonly use to study it.

Summary and Key Terms

The Study of Child Development: Then and Now

Guidepost 1 What is child development, and how has its study evolved?

- Child development is the scientific study of processes of change and stability.
- The scientific study of child development began toward the end of the 19th century. Adolescence was not considered a separate phase of development until the 20th century. The field of child development is now part of the study of the entire life span, or human development.
- Ways of studying child development are still evolving, making use of advanced technologies.
- The distinction between basic and applied research has become less meaningful.

child development (7)

Guidepost 2 What are six fundamental points about child development on which consensus has emerged?

- Consensus has emerged on several important points. These include (1) the interrelationship of domains of development, (2) the existence of a wide range of individual differences, (3) the bidirectionality of influence, (4) the importance of history and culture, (5) children's potential for resilience, and (6) continuity of development throughout life.

The Study of Child Development: Basic Concepts

Guidepost 3 What do developmental scientists study?

- Developmental scientists study developmental change, both quantitative and qualitative, as well as stability of personality and behavior.

quantitative change (10) **qualitative change (10)**

Guidepost 4 What are three major domains and five periods of child development?

- The three major domains, or dimensions, of development are physical, cognitive, and psychosocial. Each affects the others.
- The concept of periods of development is a social construction. In this book, child development is divided into five periods: the prenatal period, infancy and toddlerhood, early childhood, middle childhood, and adolescence. In each period, children have characteristic developmental needs and tasks.

social construction (11)

Influences on Development

Guidepost 5 What kinds of influences make one child different from another?

- Influences on development come from both heredity and environment. Many typical changes during childhood are related to maturation. Individual differences increase with age.

individual differences (13) **heredity (13)** **environment (13)** **maturation (13)**

- In some societies, the nuclear family predominates; in others, the extended family.
- Socioeconomic status (SES) affects developmental processes and outcomes through the quality of home and neighborhood environments and of nutrition, medical care, supervision, and schooling. The most powerful neighborhood influences seem to be neighborhood income and human capital. Multiple risk factors increase the likelihood of poor outcomes.
- Important environmental influences stem from ethnicity, culture, and historical context. In large, multiethnic societies, immigrant groups often acculturate to the majority culture while preserving aspects of their own.

nuclear family (13) **extended family (14)** **socioeconomic status (SES) (14)** **risk factors (15)** **culture (15)** **ethnic group (15)** **ethnic gloss (16)**

- Influences may be normative (age graded or history graded) or nonnormative.
- There is strong evidence of critical periods for certain kinds of early development.

normative (18) **historical generation (18)** **cohort (18)** **nonnormative (18)** **critical period (18)** **plasticity (18)** **sensitive periods (18)**

chapter 2

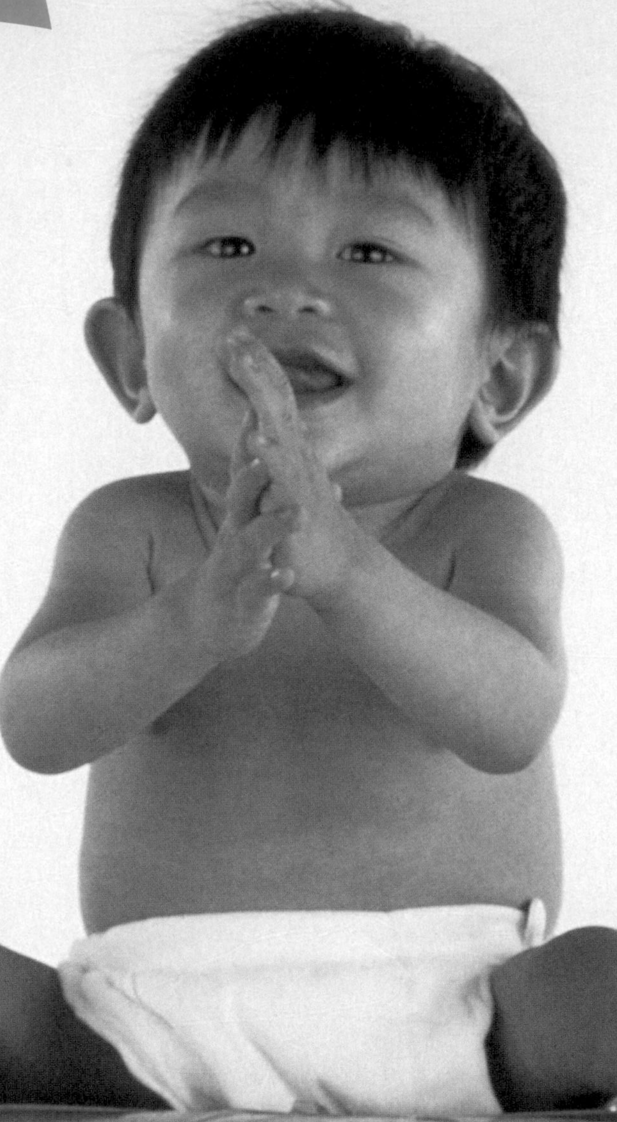

A Child's World: How We Discover It

There is one thing even more vital to science than intelligent methods; and that is, the sincere desire to find out the truth, whatever it may be.

—Charles Sanders Peirce, *Collected Papers*, vol. 5

Focus *Margaret Mead, Pioneer in Cross-Cultural Research*

Margaret Mead

Margaret Mead (1901–1978) was a world-famous American anthropologist. In the 1920s, at a time when it was rare for a woman to take on the rigors of field work with remote, preliterate peoples, Mead spent nine months on the South Pacific island of Samoa, studying girls' adjustment to the transition to adulthood. Her best-selling first book, *Coming of Age in Samoa* (1928), challenged accepted views about the inevitability of adolescent rebellion.

An itinerant childhood built around her parents' academic pursuits prepared Mead for a life of roving research. In New Jersey, her mother, who was working on her doctoral thesis in sociology, took Margaret along on interviews with recent Italian immigrants—the child's first exposure to fieldwork. Her father, a professor at the University of Pennsylvania's Wharton business school, taught her respect for facts and "the importance of thinking clearly" (Mead, 1972, p. 40). He stressed the link between theory and application—as Margaret did when, years later, she applied her theories of child rearing to her daughter. Margaret's grandmother, a former schoolteacher, sent her out in the woods to collect and analyze mint specimens. "I was not well drilled in geography or spelling," Mead wrote in her memoir *Blackberry Winter* (1972, p. 47). "But I learned to observe the world around me and to note what I saw."

Margaret took copious notes on the development of her younger brother and two younger sisters. Her curiosity about why one child in a family behaved so differently from another led to her later interest in temperamental variations within a culture.

How cultures define male and female roles was another research focus. Margaret saw her mother and her grandmother as educated women who had managed to have husbands, children, and professional careers; and she expected to do the same. She was dismayed when, at the outset of her career, the distinguished anthropologist Edward Sapir told her she "would do better to stay at home and have children than to go off to the South Seas to study adolescent girls" (Mead, 1972, p. 11).

Margaret's choice of anthropology as a career was consistent with her homebred respect for the value of all human beings and their cultures. Recalling her father's insistence that the only thing worth doing is to add to the store of knowledge, she saw an urgent need to document once-isolated cultures now "vanishing before the onslaught of modern civilization" (Mead, 1972, p. 137).

"I went to Samoa—as, later, I went to the other societies on which I have worked—to find out more about human beings, human beings like ourselves in everything except their culture," she wrote. "Through the accidents of history, these cultures had developed so differently from ours that knowledge of them could shed a kind of light upon us, upon our potentialities and our limitations" (Mead, 1972, p. 293). The ongoing quest to illuminate those "potentialities and limitations" is the business of theorists and researchers in human development.

• • •

Margaret Mead's life was all of a piece. The young girl who filled notebooks with observations about her siblings became the scientist who traveled to distant lands and studied cultures very different from her own.

Mead's story underlines several important points about the study of child development. First, the study of children is not dry, abstract, or esoteric. It deals with the substance of real life.

Second, a cross-cultural perspective can reveal which patterns of behavior, if any, are universal and which are not. Most studies of child development have been done in western, developed societies, using white, middle-class participants. Today developmental scientists are increasingly conscious of the need to expand the research base, as Mead and her colleagues sought to do.

Third, theory and research are two sides of the same coin. As Mead reflected on her own experiences and observed the behavior of others, she constantly formed tentative explanations to be tested by later research.

Fourth, although the goal of science is to obtain verifiable knowledge through open-minded, impartial investigation, observations about human behavior are products of very human individuals whose inquiries and interpretations may be influenced by their own background, values, and experiences. As Mead's daughter, Mary Catherine Bateson (1984), herself an anthropologist, noted in response to methodological criticism of Mead's early work in Samoa, a scientific observer is like a lens, which may introduce some distortion into what is observed. This is why scientists have others check their different results. In striving for greater objectivity, investigators must scrutinize how they and their colleagues conduct their work, the assumptions on which it is based, and how they arrive at their conclusions. And in studying the results of research, it is important to keep these potential biases in mind.

In the first part of this chapter, we examine major issues and theoretical perspectives that underlie much research in child development. In the remainder of the chapter, we look at how researchers gather and assess information, so that you will be better able to judge whether their conclusions rest on solid ground.

After you have read and studied this chapter, you should be able to answer each of the Guidepost questions that follow. Look for them again in the margins, where they point to important concepts throughout the chapter. To check your understanding of these Guideposts, review the end-of-chapter summary. Checkpoints located at periodic spots throughout the chapter will help you verify your understanding of what you have read.

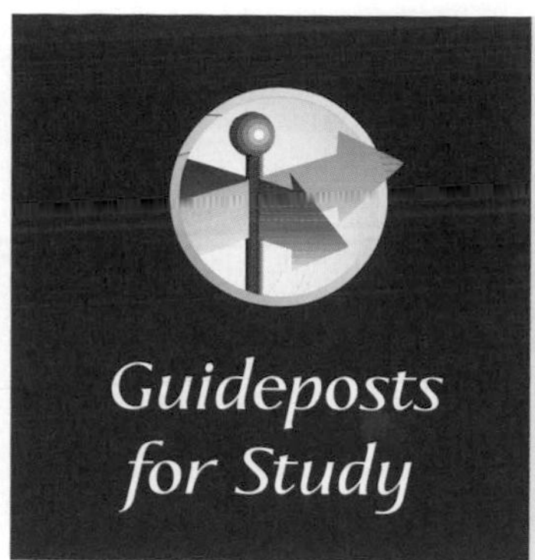

1. What purposes do theories serve?
2. What are three basic theoretical issues on which developmental scientists differ?
3. What are five theoretical perspectives on child development, and what are some theories representative of each?
4. How do developmental scientists study children, and what are the advantages and disadvantages of each research method?
5. What ethical problems may arise in research on children?

Basic Theoretical Issues

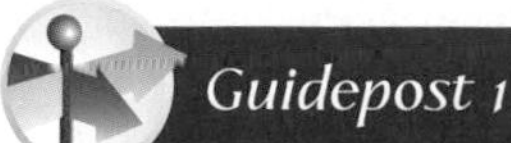

What purposes do theories serve?

Developmental scientists have come up with many theories about how children develop. A **theory** is a set of logically related concepts or statements that seeks to describe and explain development and to predict what kinds of behavior might occur under certain conditions. Theories organize data, the information gathered by research, and are a rich source of **hypotheses**—tentative explanations or predictions that can be tested by further research.

theory Coherent set of logically related concepts that seeks to organize, explain, and predict data.

hypotheses Possible explanations for phenomena, used to predict the outcome of research.

Theories change to incorporate new findings. Sometimes research supports a hypothesis and the theory on which it was based. At other times, as with Mead's findings challenging the inevitability of adolescent rebellion, scientists must modify their theories to account for unexpected data. Research findings often suggest additional questions and hypotheses to be examined and provide direction for dealing with practical issues.

The way theorists explain development depends in part on the way they view three basic issues: (1) the relative weight given to heredity and environment; (2) whether children are active or passive in their own development; and (3) whether development is continuous or occurs in stages.

Issue 1: How Do Heredity and Environment Affect Development?

Guidepost 2

What are three basic theoretical issues on which developmental scientists differ?

Which has more impact on development: heredity or environment? This issue once aroused intense debate. Theorists differed in the relative importance they gave to *nature* (the inborn traits and characteristics inherited from the biological parents) and *nurture* (environmental influences, both before and after birth, including influences of family, peers, schools, neighborhoods, society, and culture).

How much is inherited? How much is environmentally influenced? These questions matter. If parents believe that intelligence can be strongly influenced by experience, they may make special efforts to talk to and read to their children and offer them toys that help them learn. If parents believe that intelligence is inborn and unchangeable, they may be less likely to make such efforts.

Today, scientists have found ways to measure more precisely the roles of heredity and environment in the development of specific traits within a population. When we look at a particular child, however, research with regard to almost all characteristics points to a blend of inheritance and experience. Thus, even though intelligence has a strong hereditary component, parental stimulation, education, peer influence, and other variables make a difference. Although there still is considerable dispute about the relative importance of nature and nurture, many contemporary theorists and researchers are more interested in finding ways to explain how they work together.

Issue 2: Is Development Active or Passive?

Are children active or passive in their development? This controversy goes back to the 18th century. The English philosopher John Locke held that a young child is a *tabula rasa*—a "blank slate"—on which society "writes." In contrast, the French philosopher Jean Jacques Rousseau believed that children are born "noble savages" who develop according to their own positive natural tendencies unless corrupted by a repressive society. We now know that both views are too simplistic. Children have their own internal drives and needs as well as hereditary endowments that influence development; but children also are social animals, who cannot achieve optimal development in isolation.

mechanistic model Model that views development as a passive, predictable response to stimuli.

The debate over Locke's and Rousseau's philosophies led to two contrasting models, or images, of development: *mechanistic* and *organismic*. Locke's view was the forerunner of the **mechanistic model** of development. In this model, people are like machines that react to environmental input (Pepper, 1942, 1961). Fill a car with gas, turn the ignition key, press the accelerator, and the vehicle will move. In the mechanistic view, human behavior is much the same. If we know enough about how the human "machine" is put together and about the internal and external forces impinging on it, we can predict what a person will do. Mechanistic research seeks to identify and isolate the factors that make people behave—or react—as they do. For example, in seeking to explain why some adolescents drink too much alcohol, a mechanistic theorist might look for environmental influences such as advertising and whether the person's friends drink to excess.

organismic model Model that views development as internally initiated by an active organism and as occurring in a sequence of qualitatively different stages.

Rousseau's ideas were precursors of the **organismic model** of development. This model sees people as active, growing organisms that set their own development in motion (Pepper, 1942, 1961). They initiate events; they do not just react. The impetus for change is internal. Environmental influences do not cause development, though they can speed or slow it. Human behavior is an organic whole; it cannot be predicted by breaking it down into simple responses to environmental stimulation. An organismic theorist, in studying why some adolescents drink too much, would be likely to look at what kinds of situations they choose to participate in and with whom. Do they choose friends who like to party or who are more studious?

Issue 3: Is Development Continuous, or Does It Occur in Stages?

The mechanistic and organismic models also differ on the third issue: Is development continuous, or does it occur in stages?

Mechanistic theorists see development as continuous, like walking or crawling up a ramp (see Figure 2-1). These theorists describe development as always governed by the

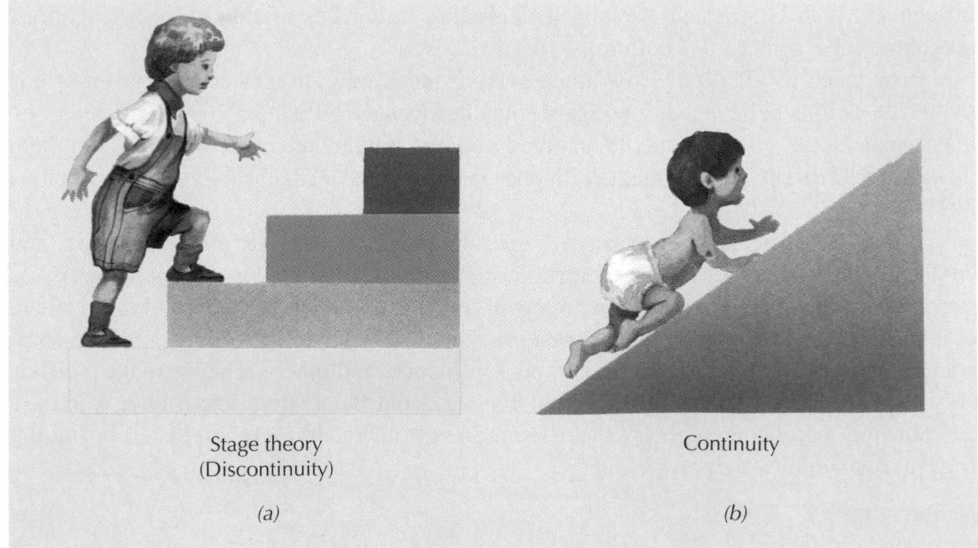

Figure 2-1
A major difference among developmental theories is (*a*) whether development occurs in distinct stages, as Piaget, Freud, and Erikson maintained, or (*b*) whether it proceeds continuously, as learning theorists and information-processing theorists propose.

same processes, enabling prediction of later behaviors from earlier ones. These theorists focus on *quantitative* change (refer back to Chapter 1): for example, changes in the frequency with which a response is made, rather than changes in the kind of response.

Organismic theorists emphasize *qualitative* change (refer back to Chapter 1). They see development as occurring in a series of distinct stages, like stair steps. At each stage, people cope with different kinds of problems and develop different kinds of abilities. Each stage builds on the previous one and prepares the way for the next.

An Emerging Consensus

As the study of child development has evolved, the relative influence of the mechanistic and organismic models has shifted (Parke, Ornstein, Rieser, & Zahn-Waxler, 1994). Most of the early pioneers in the field, such as G. Stanley Hall, Alfred Binet, and Arnold Gesell (refer back to Figure 1-2 in Chapter 1), favored organismic or stage approaches. So did Sigmund Freud, Erik Erikson, and Jean Piaget. However, the mechanistic view gained support during the 1960s with the popularity of learning theories derived from the work of John B Watson. (We discuss these last four theorists in the next section.)

Today the pendulum has swung back part way. Quasi-organismic approaches centered on the biological bases of behavior are on the rise; but instead of attempting to delineate broad stages, theorists seek to discover what specific kinds of behavior show continuity or lack of continuity and what processes are involved in each. There is wide agreement that influences on development are bidirectional: Children change their world even as it changes them. A baby born with a cheerful disposition is likely to get positive responses from adults, which strengthen her trust that her smiles will be rewarded and motivate her to smile more. As children grow older, their natural tendencies lead them to choose or initiate activities, such as studying a musical instrument, that further develop those tendencies.

Checkpoint

Can you . . .

- ✔ State three basic issues regarding the nature of child development?
- ✔ Contrast the mechanistic and organismic models of development?

Theoretical Perspectives

Guidepost 3

What are five theoretical perspectives on child development, and what are some theories representative of each?

Despite the growing consensus on the basic issues just discussed, many investigators still view development from differing theoretical perspectives. Theories generally fall within these broad perspectives, each of which emphasizes different kinds of developmental processes. These perspectives may influence the questions researchers ask, the methods they use, and the ways they interpret data. Therefore, to evaluate and interpret research, it may be important to recognize the theoretical perspective on which it is based.

Five major perspectives (summarized in Table 2-1) underlie much influential theory and research on child development: (1) *psychoanalytic* (which focuses on unconscious emotions and drives); (2) *learning* (which studies observable behavior); (3) *cognitive* (which analyzes thought processes); (4) *evolutionary/sociobiological* (which considers evolutionary and biological underpinnings of behavior); and (5) *contextual* (which emphasizes the impact of the historical, social, and cultural context).

psychoanalytic perspective View of development as shaped by unconscious forces.

Perspective 1: Psychoanalytic

The **psychoanalytic perspective** views development as shaped by unconscious forces that motivate human behavior. Sigmund Freud (1856–1939), a Viennese physician, developed *psychoanalysis,* a therapeutic approach aimed at giving patients insight into unconscious emotional conflicts. Other theorists and practitioners, including Erik H. Erikson, have expanded and modified the psychoanalytic perspective.

The Viennese physician Sigmund Freud developed an influential but controversial theory of childhood emotional development.

Sigmund Freud: Psychosexual Development

Freud (1953, 1964a, 1964b) believed that people are born with biological drives that must be redirected to make it possible to live in society. By asking his patients questions designed to summon up long-buried memories, Freud concluded that the sources of emotional disturbances lay in repressed traumatic experiences of early childhood. He proposed that personality is formed in childhood, as children deal with unconscious conflicts

Table 2-1 Five Perspectives on Human Development

Perspective	Important Theories	Basic Beliefs
Psychoanalytic	Freud's psychosexual theory	Behavior is controlled by powerful unconscious urges.
	Erikson's psychosocial theory	Personality is influenced by society and develops through a series of crises.
Learning	Behaviorism, or traditional learning theory (Pavlov, Skinner, Watson)	People are responders; the environment controls behavior.
	Social-learning (social-cognitive) theory (Bandura)	Children learn in a social context by observing and imitating models. Children are active contributors to learning.
Cognitive	Piaget's cognitive-stage theory	Qualitative changes in thought occur between infancy and adolescence. Children are active initiators of development.
	Information-processing theory	Human beings are processors of symbols.
Evolutionary/ sociobiological	Bowlby's attachment theory	Human beings have the adaptive mechanisms to survive; critical or sensitive periods are stressed; evolutionary and biological bases for behavior and predisposition toward learning are important.
Contextual	Bronfenbrenner's bioecological theory	Development occurs through interaction between a developing person and five surrounding, interlocking contextual systems of influences, from microsystem to chronosystem.
	Vygotsky's sociocultural theory	Sociocultural context is central to development.

psychosexual development In Freudian theory, unvarying sequence of stages of personality development during infancy, childhood, and adolescence, in which gratification shifts from the mouth to the anus and then to the genitals.

between these inborn urges and the requirements of civilized life. These conflicts occur in an unvarying sequence of five maturationally based stages of **psychosexual development** (see Table 2-2), in which pleasure shifts from one body zone to another—from the mouth to the anus and then to the genitals. At each stage, the behavior that is the chief source of gratification (or frustration) changes—from feeding to elimination and eventually to sexual activity.

Freud considered the first three stages—those of the first few years of life—crucial for personality development. He suggested that if children receive too little or too much gratification in any of these stages, they are at risk of *fixation*—an arrest in development that can show up in adult personality. Babies whose needs are not met during the *oral stage,* when feeding is the main source of pleasure, may become nail-biters or develop "bitingly" critical personalities. A person who, as a toddler, had too-strict toilet training may be fixated at the *anal stage.* Such a person may be obsessively clean, rigidly tied to schedules and routines, or defiantly messy.

According to Freud, a key event in psychosexual development occurs in the *phallic stage* of early childhood. Boys develop sexual attachment to their mothers, and girls to their fathers, and they have aggressive urges toward the same-sex parent, whom they regard as a rival. (Freud called these developments the *Oedipus* and *Electra complexes.*) Children eventually resolve their anxiety over these feelings by identifying with the same-sex parent and move into the *latency stage* of middle childhood. They become socialized, develop skills, and learn about themselves and society. The *genital stage,* the final one, lasts throughout adulthood. The sexual urges repressed during latency now resurface to flow in socially approved channels, which Freud defined as heterosexual relations with persons outside the family of origin.

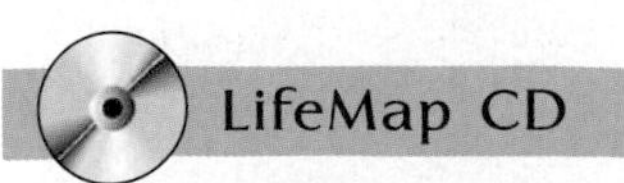

For more on the psychoanalytic perspective, watch the video on "Freud's Contribution to Psychology" in Chapter 2 of your CD.

In addition to the five stages, Freud proposed three hypothetical parts of the personality—the *id,* the *ego,* and the *superego*—that develop early in life. Newborns are governed by the *id,* which seeks immediate satisfaction under the *pleasure principle.* When gratification is delayed, as it is when infants have to wait to be fed, they begin to see themselves as separate from the outside world. The *ego,* which represents reason, develops gradually during the first year or so of life and operates under the *reality principle.* The ego's

(continued)

Technique Used	State-Oriented	Causal Emphasis	Active or Passive Individual
Clinical observation	Yes	Innate factors modified by experience	Passive
Clinical observation	Yes	Interaction of innate and experiential factors	Active
Rigorous scientific (experimental) procedures	No	Experience	Passive
Rigorous scientific (experimental) procedures	No	Experience modified by innate factors	Active and passive
Flexible interviews; meticulous observation	Yes	Interaction of innate and experiential factors	Active
Laboratory research; technological monitoring of physiologic responses	No	Interaction of innate and experiential factors	Active and passive
Naturalistic and laboratory observation	No	Interaction of innate and experiential factors	Active and passive (theorists vary)
Naturalistic observation and analysis	No	Interaction of innate and experiential factors	Active
Cross-cultural research; observation of child interacting with more competent person	No	Experience	Active

aim is to find realistic ways to gratify the id that are acceptable to the *superego,* which develops at about age 5 or 6. The *superego* includes the conscience and incorporates socially approved "shoulds" and "should nots" into the child's own value system. The superego is highly demanding; if its standards are not met, a child may feel guilty and anxious. The ego mediates between the id and superego.

Freud's theory made historic contributions, and several of his central themes have been validated by research, though others have not (Emde, 1992; Westen, 1998). Freud made us aware of the importance of unconscious thoughts, feelings, and motivations; the role of childhood experiences in forming personality; the ambivalence of emotional responses, especially responses to parents; and ways in which early relationships affect later ones. Freud also opened our eyes to the presence from birth of sexual urges. Although many psychoanalysts today reject his narrow emphasis on sexual and aggressive drives, his psychoanalytic method greatly influenced modern-day psychotherapy.

We need to remember that Freud's theory grew out of his place in history and in society. Freud based his theories about normal development, not on a population of average children, but on a clientele of upper-middle-class adults, mostly women, in therapy. His concentration on early emotional experience does not take into account other, and later, influences on personality—including the influences of society and culture, which many heirs to the Freudian tradition, notably Erikson, stress.

The psychoanalyst Erik H. Erikson departed from Freudian theory in emphasizing societal, rather than chiefly biological, influences on personality.

Erik Erikson: Psychosocial Development

Erik Erikson (1902–1994), a German-born psychoanalyst who originally was part of Freud's circle in Vienna, modified and extended Freudian theory by emphasizing the influence of society on the developing personality. Erikson was a pioneer in the life-span perspective. Whereas Freud maintained that early childhood experiences permanently shape personality, Erikson contended that development is lifelong.

Erikson's (1950, 1982; Erikson, Erikson, & Kivnick, 1986) theory of **psychosocial development** covers eight stages across the life span (refer to Table 2-2), which we will discuss in the appropriate chapters. Each stage involves what Erikson originally called a

psychosocial development In Erikson's eight-stage theory, socially and culturally influenced process of development of the ego, or self.

Table 2-2 Developmental Stages According to Various Theories

Psychosexual Stages (Freud)	Psychosocial Stages (Erikson)	Cognitive Stages (Piaget)
Oral (birth to 12–18 months). Baby's chief source of pleasure involves mouth-oriented activities (sucking and feeding).	*Basic trust versus mistrust (birth to 12–18 months).* Baby develops sense of whether world is a good and safe place. Virtue: hope.	*Sensorimotor (birth to 2 years).* Infant gradually becomes able to organize activities in relation to the environment through sensory and motor activity.
Anal (12–18 months to 3 years). Child derives sensual gratification from withholding and expelling feces. Zone of gratification is anal region, and toilet training is important activity.	*Autonomy versus shame and doubt (12–18 months to 3 years).* Child develops a balance of independence and self-sufficiency over shame and doubt. Virtue: will.	*Preoperational (2 to 7 years).* Child develops a representational system and uses symbols to represent people, places, and events. Language and imaginative play are important manifestations of this stage. Thinking is still not logical.
Phallic (3 to 6 years). Child becomes attached to parent of the other sex and later identifies with same-sex parent. Superego develops. Zone of gratification shifts to genital region.	*Initiative versus guilt (3 to 6 years).* Child develops initiative when trying out new activities and is not overwhelmed by guilt. Virtue: purpose.	
Latency (6 years to puberty). Time of relative calm between more turbulent stages.	*Industry versus inferiority (6 years to puberty).* Child must learn skills of the culture or face feelings of incompetence. Virtue: skill.	*Concrete operations (7 to 11 years).* Child can solve problems logically if they are focused on the here and now but cannot think abstractly.
Genital (puberty through adulthood). Reemergence of sexual impulses of phallic stage, channeled into mature adult sexuality.	*Identity versus identity confusion (puberty to young adulthood).* Adolescent must determine own sense of self ("Who am I?") or experience confusion about roles. Virtue: fidelity.	*Formal operations (11 years through adulthood).* Person can think abstractly, deal with hypothetical situations, and think about possibilities.
	Intimacy versus isolation (young adulthood). Person seeks to make commitments to others; if unsuccessful, may suffer from isolation and self-absorption. Virtue: love.	
	Generativity versus stagnation (middle adulthood). Mature adult is concerned with establishing and guiding the next generation or else feels personal impoverishment. Virtue: care.	
	Integrity versus despair (late adulthood). Elderly person achieves acceptance of own life, allowing acceptance of death, or else despairs over inability to relive life. Virtue: wisdom.	

Note: All ages are approximate.

Checkpoint

Can you . . .

✔ Identify the chief focus of the psychoanalytic perspective?

✔ Name Freud's five stages of development and three parts of the personality?

✔ Tell how Erikson's theory differs from Freud's and list its eight stages?

"crisis" in personality—a major psychosocial theme that is particularly important at that time and will remain an issue to some degree throughout the rest of life.* These issues, which emerge according to a maturational timetable, must be satisfactorily resolved for healthy ego development.

Each stage requires the balancing of a positive trait and a corresponding negative one. Although the positive quality should predominate, some degree of the negative is needed as well. The critical theme of infancy, for example, is *basic trust versus basic mistrust.* People need to trust the world and the people in it, but they also need to learn some mistrust to protect themselves from danger. The successful outcome of each stage is the development of a particular "virtue" or strength—in this first stage, the "virtue" of *hope.*

Erikson's theory has held up better than Freud's, especially in its emphasis on social and cultural influences and on development beyond adolescence. However, some of Erikson's concepts (like Freud's) do not lend themselves to rigorous testing.

*Erikson later dropped the term *crisis* and referred instead to *conflicting* or *competing tendencies.*

Perspective 2: Learning

The **learning perspective** maintains that development results from *learning,* a long-lasting change in behavior based on experience, or adaptation to the environment. Learning theorists are concerned with finding out the objective laws that govern changes in observable behavior. They see development as continuous (not in stages) and emphasize quantitative change.

learning perspective View of development that holds that changes in behavior result from experience, or adaptation to the environment.

Learning theorists have helped to make the study of human development more scientific. Their terms are defined precisely, and their theories can be tested in the laboratory. By stressing environmental influences, they help explain cultural differences in behavior.

Two important learning theories are *behaviorism* and *social learning theory.*

Learning Theory 1: Behaviorism

Behaviorism is a mechanistic theory, which describes observed behavior as a predictable response to experience. Although biology sets limits on what people do, behaviorists view the environment as much more influential. They hold that human beings at all ages learn about the world the same way other organisms do: by reacting to conditions, or aspects of their environment, that they find pleasing, painful, or threatening. Behaviorists look for events that determine whether a particular behavior will be repeated. Behavioral research focuses on *associative learning,* in which a mental link is formed between two events. Two kinds of associative learning are *classical conditioning* and *operant conditioning.*

behaviorism Learning theory that emphasizes the predictable role of environment in causing observable behavior.

Classical Conditioning The Russian physiologist Ivan Pavlov (1849–1936) devised experiments in which dogs learned to salivate at the sound of a bell that rang at feeding time. These experiments were the foundation for **classical conditioning**, in which a response (salivation) to a stimulus (the bell) is evoked after repeated association with a stimulus that normally elicits it (food).

classical conditioning Learning based on association of a stimulus that does not ordinarily elicit a response with another stimulus that does elicit the response.

The American behaviorist John B. Watson (1878–1958) applied stimulus-response theories to children, claiming that he could mold any infant in any way he chose. His writings influenced a generation of parents to apply principles of learning theory to child raising. In one of the earliest and most famous demonstrations of classical conditioning in human beings (Watson & Rayner, 1920), he taught an 11-month-old baby known as "Little Albert" to fear furry white objects.

In this study, Albert was exposed to a loud noise just as he was about to stroke a furry white rat. The noise frightened him, and he began to cry. After repeated pairings of the rat with the loud noise, Albert whimpered with fear whenever he saw the rat. Although such research would be considered unethical today, the study showed that a baby could be conditioned to fear things he or she had not been afraid of before.

What's your view 

- In an experiment with classical conditioning, what standards would you suggest to safeguard participants' rights?

Critics of such methods sometimes associate conditioning with thought control and manipulation. Actually, as we will discuss in Chapter 7, classical conditioning is a natural form of learning that occurs even without intervention. By learning what events go together, children can anticipate what is going to happen, and this knowledge makes their world a more orderly, predictable place.

Operant Conditioning Baby Terrell lies peacefully in his crib. When he happens to smile, his mother goes over to the crib and plays with him. Later his father does the same thing. As this sequence is repeated, Terrell learns that his behavior (smiling) can produce a desirable consequence (loving attention from a parent); and so he keeps smiling to attract his parents' attention. An originally accidental behavior (smiling) has become a conditioned response.

This kind of learning is called **operant conditioning** because the individual learns from the consequences of "operating" on the environment. Unlike classical conditioning, operant conditioning involves voluntary behavior, such as Terrell's smiling.

operant conditioning Learning based on association of behavior with its consequences.

The American psychologist B. F. Skinner (1904–1990), who formulated the principles of operant conditioning, worked primarily with rats and pigeons, but Skinner (1938) maintained that the same principles apply to human beings. He found that an organism will tend to repeat a response that has been reinforced and will suppress a response that has been

The American psychologist B. F. Skinner formulated the principles of operant conditioning.

punished. **Reinforcement** is a consequence of behavior that *increases* the likelihood that the behavior will be repeated; in Terrell's case, his parents' attention reinforces his smiling. **Punishment** is a consequence of behavior that *decreases* the likelihood of repetition. If Terrell's parents frowned when he smiled, he would be less likely to smile again. What is reinforcing for one person may be punishing for another. For example, for a child who likes being alone, being sent to his or her room could be reinforcing rather than punishing.

Reinforcement can be either positive or negative. *Positive reinforcement* consists of *giving* a reward, such as food, gold stars, money, praise, or focused attention. *Negative reinforcement* consists of *taking away* something the individual does not like (known as an *aversive event*), such as a loud noise. Negative reinforcement is sometimes confused with punishment. However, they are different. Punishment *suppresses* a behavior by *bringing on* an aversive event (such as spanking a child or giving an electric shock to an animal) or by *withdrawing* a positive event (such as watching television). Negative reinforcement *encourages* repetition of a behavior by *removing* an aversive event. When an older baby signals a wet diaper, the removal of the diaper may encourage the child to signal again the next time a diaper is wet.

Reinforcement is most effective when it immediately follows a behavior. If a response is no longer reinforced, it will eventually be *extinguished*; that is, it will return to its original (baseline) level. If, after a while, no one plays with Terrell when he smiles, he may not stop smiling but will smile far less than if his smiles still brought reinforcement.

reinforcement In operant conditioning, stimulus that encourages repetition of a desired behavior.

punishment In operant conditioning, stimulus that discourages repetition of a behavior.

Behavior modification, or behavior therapy, is a form of operant conditioning used to eliminate undesirable behavior or to instill positive behavior. Behavior modification is particularly effective among children with special needs, such as those with mental or emotional disabilities. However, Skinnerian psychology is limited in application because it does not adequately address individual differences and cultural and social influences (Parke, 2004).

Learning Theory 2: Social Learning (Social Cognitive) Theory

social learning theory Theory that behaviors are learned by observing and imitating models. Also called *social cognitive theory.*

observational learning Learning through watching the behavior of others.

The American psychologist Albert Bandura (b. 1925) developed many of the principles of **social learning theory.** Whereas behaviorists see the environment, acting upon the person, as the chief impetus for development, social learning theorists (Bandura, 1977, 1989; Bandura & Walters, 1963) suggest that the impetus for development comes from the person.

Classic social learning theory maintains that people learn appropriate social behavior chiefly by observing and imitating models—that is, by watching other people. This process is called *modeling* or **observational learning.** People initiate or advance their own learning by choosing models to imitate—say, a parent or a popular sports hero. Imitation of models is the most important element in how children learn a language, deal with aggression, develop a moral sense, and learn gender-appropriate behaviors. However, observational learning can occur even if the child does not imitate the observed behavior.

The specific behavior people imitate depends on what they perceive as valued in their culture. If all the teachers in Carlos's school are women, he probably will not copy their behavior, which he may consider "unmanly." However, if he meets a male teacher he likes, he may change his mind about the value of teachers as models.

Bandura's (1989) newest version of social learning theory is called *social cognitive theory.* The evolution from one name to the other reflects Bandura's increasing emphasis on cognitive processes as central to development. Cognitive processes are at work as people observe models, learn "chunks" of behavior, and mentally put the chunks together into complex new behavior patterns. Rita, for example, imitates the toes-out walk of her dance teacher but models her dance steps after those of Carmen, a slightly more advanced student. Even so, she develops her own style of dancing by putting her observations together into a new pattern.

Through feedback on their behavior, children gradually form standards for judging their own actions and become more selective in choosing models who exemplify those standards. They also begin to develop a sense of *self-efficacy,* or confidence that they have the characteristics they need to succeed.

Checkpoint

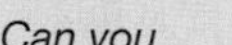

Can you . . .

- ✔ Identify the chief concerns, strengths, and weaknesses of the learning perspective?
- ✔ Tell how classical conditioning and operant conditioning differ?
- ✔ Distinguish among positive reinforcement, negative reinforcement, and punishment?
- ✔ Compare behaviorism and social learning (social cognitive) theory?

Perspective 3: Cognitive

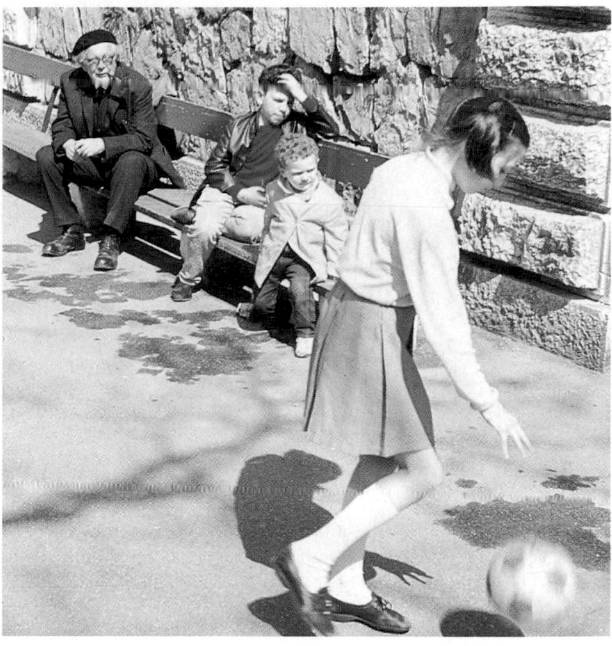

The Swiss psychologist Jean Piaget studied children's cognitive development by observing and talking with his own youngsters and others.

The **cognitive perspective** focuses on thought processes and the behavior that reflects those processes. This perspective encompasses both organismic and mechanistically influenced theories. It includes the cognitive-stage theory of Piaget, the newer information-processing approach, and neo-Piagetian theories, which combine elements of both. It also includes contemporary efforts to apply findings of brain research to the understanding of cognitive processes. (Vygotsky's theory, which deals largely with social contexts of cognition, is discussed under the contextual perspective.)

Jean Piaget's Cognitive-Stage Theory

Much of what we know about how children think comes from the work of the Swiss theoretician Jean Piaget (1896–1980). Piaget's theory was the forerunner of today's "cognitive revolution" with its emphasis on mental processes. Piaget took an organismic perspective, viewing cognitive development as the product of children's efforts to understand and act on their world.

As a young man studying in Paris, Piaget set out to standardize the tests Alfred Binet had developed to assess the intelligence of French schoolchildren (see Chapter 7). Piaget became intrigued by the children's wrong answers, finding in them clues to their thought processes. Piaget's *clinical method* combined observation with flexible questioning. To find out how children think, Piaget followed up their answers with more questions, and he designed tasks to test his tentative conclusions. In this way he discovered that a typical 4-year-old believes that pennies or flowers are more numerous when arranged in a line than when heaped or piled up. From his observations of his own and other children, Piaget created a comprehensive theory of cognitive development.

cognitive perspective View that thought processes are central to development.

Piaget suggested that cognitive development begins with an inborn ability to adapt to the environment. By rooting for a nipple, feeling a pebble, or exploring the boundaries of a room, young children develop a more accurate picture of their surroundings and greater competence in dealing with them.

Piaget described cognitive development as occurring in four qualitatively different stages (listed in Table 2-2 and discussed in detail in later chapters), which represent universal patterns of development. At each stage a child's mind develops a new way of operating. From infancy through adolescence, mental operations evolve from learning based on simple sensory and motor activity to logical, abstract thought. Cognitive growth occurs through three interrelated processes: *organization, adaptation,* and *equilibration.*

Organization is the tendency to create increasingly complex cognitive structures: systems of knowledge or ways of thinking that incorporate more and more accurate images of reality. These structures, called **schemes,** are organized patterns of behavior that a person uses to think about and act in a situation. As children acquire more information, their schemes become more and more complex. An infant has a simple scheme for sucking but soon develops varied schemes for how to suck at the breast, a bottle, or a thumb.

Adaptation is Piaget's term for how children handle new information in light of what they already know. Adaptation involves two steps: (1) **assimilation,** taking in new information and incorporating it into existing cognitive structures, and (2) **accommodation,** adjusting one's cognitive structures to fit the new information.

Equilibration—a constant striving for a stable balance, or equilibrium—dictates the shift from assimilation to accommodation. When children cannot handle new experiences within their existing cognitive structures and thus experience disequilibrium, they organize new mental patterns that integrate the new experience, restoring a more comfortable state of equilibrium. A breast- or bottle-fed baby who begins to suck on the spout of a "sippy" cup is showing assimilation—using an old scheme to deal with a new situation. When the infant discovers that sipping from a cup requires different tongue and mouth movements

organization Piaget's term for the creation of systems of knowledge.

schemes Piaget's term for organized patterns of behavior used in particular situations.

adaptation Piaget's term for adjustment to new information about the environment.

assimilation Piaget's term for incorporation of new information into an existing cognitive structure.

accommodation Piaget's term for adjustments in a cognitive structure to fit new information.

equilibration Piaget's term for the tendency to seek a stable balance among cognitive elements.

from those used to suck on a breast or bottle, she accommodates by modifying the old scheme. She has adapted her original suckling scheme to deal with a new experience: the cup. Thus, assimilation and accommodation work together to produce equilibrium. Throughout life, the quest for equilibrium is the driving force behind cognitive growth.

Piaget's observations have yielded much information and some surprising insights. Who, for example, would have thought that most children younger than 7 do not realize that a ball of clay that has been rolled into a "worm" before their eyes still contains the same amount of clay? Or that an infant might think that a person who has moved out of sight no longer exists? Piaget has shown us that children's minds are not miniature adult minds. Knowing how children think makes it easier for parents and teachers to understand them and teach them.

Yet Piaget seems to have seriously underestimated the abilities of infants and young children. Some contemporary psychologists question his distinct stages, pointing instead to evidence that cognitive development is more gradual and continuous (Flavell, 1992). Furthermore, as we will see, later research has challenged Piaget's idea that thinking develops in a single, universal progression leading to formal thought. Instead, children's cognitive processes seem closely tied to specific content (what they are thinking *about*) as well as to the context of a problem and the kinds of information and thought a culture considers important (Case & Okamoto, 1996).

Checkpoint

Can you . . .

- ✔ Contrast Piaget's assumptions and methods with those of classical learning theory?
- ✔ List three principles that bring about cognitive growth, according to Piaget, and give an example of each?

The Information-Processing Approach

information-processing approach Approach to the study of cognitive development by observing and analyzing the mental processes involved in perceiving and handling information.

The newer **information-processing approach** attempts to explain cognitive development by observing and analyzing the mental processes involved in perceiving and handling information. The information-processing approach is not a single theory but a framework, or set of assumptions, that underlies a wide range of theories and research.

The information-processing approach has practical applications. It enables researchers to estimate an infant's later intelligence from the efficiency of his or her sensory perception and processing. It enables parents and teachers to help children learn by making them more aware of their own mental processes and of strategies to enhance them. Psychologists use information-processing models to test, diagnose, and treat learning problems (R. M. Thomas, 1996; Williams, 2001).

Computer-Based Models Some information-processing theorists compare the brain to a computer. Sensory impressions go in; behavior comes out. But what happens in between? How does the brain take sensation and perception, say, of an unfamiliar face and use it to recognize that face again?

Information-processing researchers *infer* what goes on between a stimulus and a response. For example, they may ask a person to recall a list of words and then observe any difference in performance when the person repeats the list over and over before being asked to recall the words. Through such studies, some information-processing researchers have developed *computational models* or flow charts analyzing the specific steps children go through in gathering, storing, retrieving, and using information.

Despite the use of the "passive" computer model, information-processing theorists, like Piaget, see people as actively thinking about their world. Unlike Piaget, these theorists generally do *not* propose stages of development. They view development as continuous and note age-related increases in the speed, complexity, and efficiency of mental processing and in the amount and variety of material that can be stored in memory.

Neo-Piagetian Theories

During the 1980s, in response to criticisms of Piaget's theory, neo-Piagetian developmental psychologists began to integrate some elements of his theory with the information-processing approach. Instead of describing a single, general system of increasingly logical mental operations, neo-Piagetians focus on *specific* concepts, strategies, and skills. They suggest that children develop cognitively by becoming more efficient at processing information, thus freeing mental "space" for additional information and more complex problem solving.

Robbie Case (Case & Okamoto, 1996) tested a model that modifies Piaget's idea of cognitive structures. Unlike Piaget's *operational* structures, such as concrete and formal operations, which apply to any domain of thought, Case proposes *conceptual* structures within specific domains such as number, story understanding, and spatial relations. As children acquire knowledge, they go through stages in which their conceptual structures become more complex, better coordinated, and multidimensional. For example, a child's understanding of spatial concepts begins with the recognition of the shapes of objects, moves on to a sense of their relative size and location, and then progresses to an understanding of perspective.

Because of its emphasis on efficiency of processing, the neo-Piagetian approach helps account for individual differences in cognitive ability and for uneven development in various domains. Currently some French and Swiss researchers are exploring the multiple processes and individual pathways of development that Piaget, for the most part, treated merely as variations on a general pattern (Larivée, Normandeau, & Parent, 2000).

The Cognitive Neuroscience Approach

For most of the history of psychology, theorists and researchers have studied cognitive processes apart from the physical structures of the brain in which these processes occur. Now that sophisticated instruments make it possible to see the brain in action, adherents of the **cognitive neuroscience approach** argue that an accurate understanding of cognitive functioning must be linked to what happens in the brain (Gazzaniga, 2000; Humphreys, 2002; Posner & DiGirolamo, 2000). As we discuss in later chapters, brain research supports important aspects of information-processing models, such as the existence of separate physical structures to handle conscious and unconscious memory.

cognitive neuroscience approach Approach to the study of cognitive development that links brain processes with cognitive ones.

social cognitive neuroscience An emerging interdisciplinary field that draws on cognitive neuroscience, information process, and social psychology.

Developmental cognitive neuroscience focuses on how cognitive growth occurs as the brain interacts with the environment (Johnson, 1999, 2001) and why some children do not develop normally (Posner & DiGirolamo, 2000). It may be able to shed light on whether intelligence is general or specialized and what influences a young child's readiness for formal learning (Byrnes & Fox, 1998).

Social cognitive neuroscience is an emerging interdisciplinary field that bridges brain, mind, and behavior, bringing together data from cognitive neuroscience, social psychology, and the information-processing approach. Social cognitive neuroscientists use brain imaging and studies of people with brain injuries to figure out how neural pathways control such behavioral processes as memory and attention and how these processes influence attitudes and emotions (Azar, 2002; Ochsner & Lieberman, 2001).

Ultimately, by shedding light on what neural and cognitive processes best explain particular social behaviors, social cognitive neuroscience may help sift through competing theoretical explanations (Azar, 2002; Ochsner & Lieberman, 2001). On a practical level, researchers can use tests of memory, attention, and language performance to figure out what brain systems are involved in such disorders as schizophrenia, anxiety, phobias, and obsessive-compulsive disorder (Ochsner & Lieberman, 2001).

Checkpoint

Can you . . .

- ✔ Describe what information-processing researchers do?
- ✔ Tell how neo-Piagetian theory draws from the information-processing approach?
- ✔ Explain how brain research contributes to understanding of cognitive processes?

Perspective 4: Evolutionary/Sociobiological

The **evolutionary/sociobiological perspective** proposed by E. O. Wilson (1975) focuses on evolutionary and biological bases of social behavior. It looks beyond an individual's immediate behavior to its function in promoting the survival of the group or species. Influenced by Darwin's theory of evolution, it draws on findings of anthropology, ecology, genetics, ethology, and evolutionary psychology to explain the adaptive, or survival, value of behavior for an individual or species.

evolutionary/sociobiological perspective View of development that focuses on evolutionary and biological bases of behavior.

According to Darwin, all animal species have developed through the related processes of *survival of the fittest* and *natural selection.* Individuals with traits better adapted to their environments survive; those less adapted do not. Through reproduction, more adaptive characteristics are passed on to future generations, and less adaptive characteristics die out. As environments change, some characteristics become more or less adaptive than before; this accounts for the emergence and extinction of species such as dinosaurs.

ethology Study of distinctive adaptive behaviors of species of animals that have evolved to increase survival of the species.

evolutionary psychology Application of Darwinian principles of natural selection and survival of the fittest to individual behavior.

Checkpoint

Can you . . .

- ✔ Identify the chief focus of the evolutionary/sociobiological perspective, and explain how Darwin's theory of evolution underlies this perspective?
- ✔ Tell what kinds of topics ethologists and evolutionary psychologists study?

Ethology is the study of the distinctive behaviors of species of animals that have adaptive value. Ethologists suggest that, for each species, certain innate behaviors—such as squirrels' burying of nuts in the fall and spiders' spinning of webs—have evolved to increase the odds of survival. By observing animals, usually in their natural surroundings, ethologists seek to identify which behaviors are universal and which are specific to a particular species or are modified by culture. Konrad Lorenz, an Austrian zoologist, observed that infant animals become attached to the first animal they see, usually their mothers—a process he called *imprinting* (see Chapter 5). The British psychologist John Bowlby applied ethological principles to human development, such as infants' attachment to a caregiver.

Evolutionary psychology applies Darwinian principles to individual behavior. According to this theory, people unconsciously strive not only for personal survival, but also to perpetuate their genetic legacy. The result for the species is the development of mechanisms that solve problems. For example, sudden aversion to certain foods during pregnancy may be an evolved mechanism for protecting the vulnerable fetus from toxic substances (Bjorklund & Pellegrini, 2000, 2002). However, such "evolved mechanisms" are not as universal or automatic as the innate mechanisms found in animals.

Evolutionary *developmental* psychologists seek to identify behaviors that are adaptive at different ages (see Box 2-1). For example, an infant needs to stay close to the mother, but for an older child independent exploration is important.

Perspective 5: Contextual

contextual perspective View of development that sees the individual as inseparable from the social context.

According to the **contextual perspective,** development can be understood only in its social context. Contextualists see the individual, not as a separate entity interacting with the environment, but as an inseparable part of it.

Urie Bronfenbrenner's Bioecological Theory

bioecological theory Bronfenbrenner's approach to understanding processes and contexts of development.

American psychologist Urie Bronfenbrenner's (1979, 1986, 1994; Bronfenbrenner & Morris, 1998) influential **bioecological theory** describes the range of interacting influences that affect a developing child. Every biological organism develops within the context of ecological systems that support or stifle its growth. Just as we need to understand the ecology of the ocean or the forest if we wish to understand the development of a fish or a tree, we need to understand the ecology of the human environment if we wish to understand how children develop.

According to Bronfenbrenner, development occurs through increasingly complex processes of regular, active, two-way interaction between a developing child and the immediate, everyday environment—processes that are affected by more remote contexts of which the child may not even be aware. To understand these processes, we must study the multiple contexts in which they occur. These begin with the home, classroom, and neighborhood; connect outward to societal institutions, such as educational and transportation systems; and finally encompass cultural and historical patterns that affect the family, the school, and virtually everything else in a person's life. By highlighting the interrelated contexts of, and influences on, development, Bronfenbrenner's theory provides a key to understanding the processes that underlie such diverse phenomena as antisocial behavior and academic achievement.

Bronfenbrenner identifies five interlocking contextual systems, from the most intimate to the broadest: the *microsystem, mesosystem, exosystem, macrosystem,* and *chronosystem* (see Figure 2-2 on page 38). Although, for purposes of illustration, we will look at each of these levels of influence separately, they continually interact.

microsystem Bronfenbrenner's term for a setting in which a child interacts with others on an everyday, face-to-face basis.

A **microsystem** is a pattern of activities, roles, and relationships within a setting, such as the home, school, workplace, or neighborhood, in which a person functions on a firsthand, day-to-day basis. It is through the microsystem that more distant influences, such as social institutions and cultural values, reach the developing child.

A microsystem involves personal, face-to-face relationships, and bidirectional influences flow back and forth. How, for example, does a new baby affect the parents' lives? How do their feelings and attitudes affect the baby?

The Research World

Box 2-1 *The Adaptive Value of Immaturity*

In comparison with other animals, and even with other primates, human beings take a long time to grow up. Chimpanzees reach reproductive maturity in about eight years, rhesus monkeys in about four years, and lemurs in only two years or so. Human beings, by contrast, do not mature physically until the early teenage years and, at least in modern industrialized societies, typically reach cognitive and psychosocial maturity even later.

From the point of view of Darwinian evolutionary theory, this prolonged period of immaturity is essential to the survival and well-being of the species. Human beings, more than any other animal, live by their intelligence. Human communities and cultures are highly complex, and there is much to learn in order to "know the ropes." A long childhood serves as essential preparation for adulthood.

Some aspects of immaturity serve immediate adaptive purposes. For example, some primitive reflexes, such as rooting for the nipple, are protective for newborns and disappear when no longer needed. The development of the human brain, despite its rapid prenatal growth, is much less complete at birth than the development of brains of other primates; if the fetus's brain attained full human size before birth, its head would be too big to go through the birth canal. Instead, the human brain continues to grow throughout childhood, eventually far surpassing the brains of our simian cousins in the capacities for language and thought.

The human brain's slower development gives it greater flexibility, or *plasticity,* as not all connections are "hard wired" at an early age. One theorist has called this plasticity the "human species's greatest adaptive advantage" (Bjorklund, 1997, p. 157).

The extended period of immaturity and dependency during infancy and childhood allows children to spend much of their time in play; and, as Piaget maintained, it is largely through play that cognitive development occurs. Play also enables children to develop motor skills and experiment with social roles. It is a vehicle for creative imagination and intellectual curiosity, the hallmarks of the human spirit.

Research on animals suggests that the immaturity of early sensory and motor functioning may protect infants from overstimulation. By limiting the amount of information they have to deal with, it may help them make sense of their world and focus on experiences essential to survival, such as feeding and attachment to the mother. Later, infants' limited memory capacity may simplify the processing of linguistic sounds and thus facilitate early language learning.

Limitations on young children's thought also may have adaptive value. For example, Piaget observed that young children are *egocentric*; they tend to see things from their own point of view. This tendency toward egocentrism may actually help children learn. In one study (Ratner & Foley, 1997), 5-year-olds took turns with an adult in placing furniture in a doll house. In a control group, the adult had already placed half of the items, and the children were then asked to place the other half. When questioned afterward, the children who had taken turns with the adult remembered more about the task and were better able to repeat it. It may be that an "I did it!" bias helps young children's recall by avoiding the need to distinguish between their own actions and the actions of others. Young children also tend to be unrealistic in assessing their own abilities, believing they can do more than they actually can. This immature self-judgment can encourage children to try new things by reducing their fear of failure.

All in all, evolutionary theory and research suggest that immaturity is not necessarily equivalent to deficiency and that some attributes of infancy and childhood have persisted because they are appropriate to the tasks of a particular time of life.

What's your view?

Can you think of additional examples of the adaptive value of immaturity? Can you think of ways in which immaturity may *not* be adaptive?

Check it out!

For more information on this topic, go to **http://www.brazelton-institute.com/**. This is the Web site for the Brazelton Institute at Harvard Medical School. Follow the link *The Brazelton Scale: What Is It?* to learn about the scale. The scale shows how much such immature creatures as human newborns can do in responding to the world. This Web site also offers a preview of the discussion of the Brazelton scale in Chapter 5.

Source: Bjorklund, 1997; Bjorklund & Pellegrini, 2000, 2002.

A **mesosystem** is the interaction of two or more microsystems that contain the developing child. It may include linkages between home and school or between the family and the peer group. Attention to mesosystems can alert us to differences in the ways the same person acts in different settings. For example, a child who can satisfactorily complete a school assignment at home may become tongue-tied when asked a question about the assignment in class.

mesosystem Bronfenbrenner's term for linkages between two or more microsystems.

An **exosystem,** like a mesosystem, consists of linkages between two or more settings; but in an exosystem, unlike a mesosystem, at least one of these settings—such as parents' workplaces—does *not* contain the developing child and thus affects the child only indirectly. A woman whose employer encourages breast-feeding by providing pumping and milk storage facilities may be more likely to continue nursing her baby.

exosystem Bronfenbrenner's term for linkages between two or more settings, one of which does not contain the child.

The **macrosystem** consists of overall cultural patterns, like those Margaret Mead studied: dominant values, beliefs, customs, and economic and social systems of a culture or subculture, which filter down in countless ways to individuals' daily lives. For example,

macrosystem Bronfenbrenner's term for a society's overall cultural patterns.

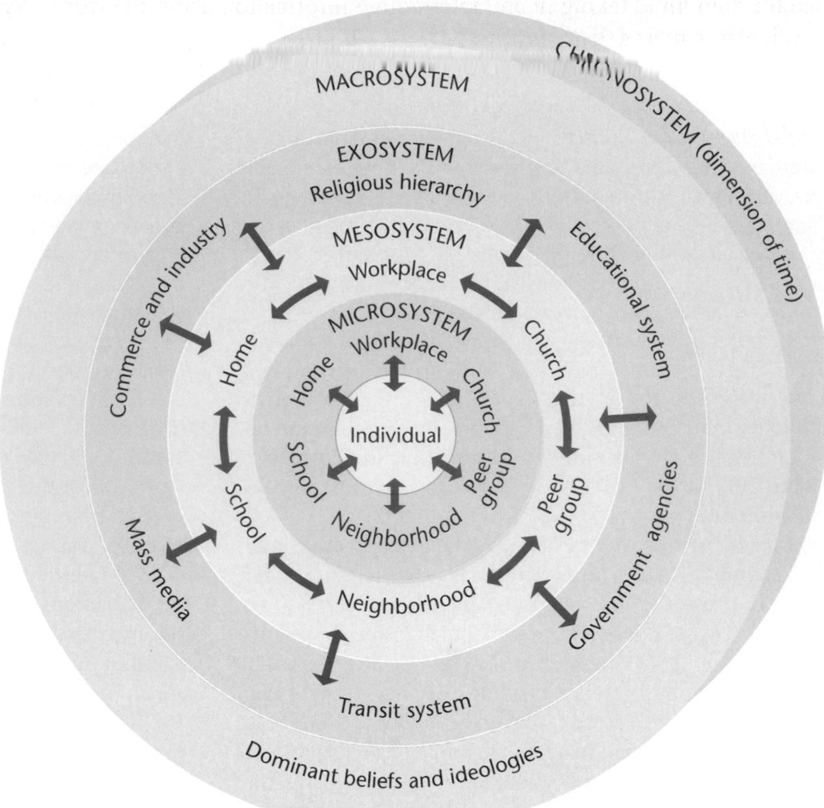

Figure 2-2

Bronfenbrenner's bioecological theory. Concentric circles show five levels of environmental influence, from the most intimate environment (innermost circle) to the broadest—all within the dimension of time. The circles form a set of nested influences, like egg-shaped boxes that fit inside one another, encasing the developing person. The figure shows what we would see if we sliced the nested "boxes" across the middle and looked inside. Keep in mind that the boundaries between the "boxes" are fluid, and the "boxes" are interconnected.

Source: Adapted from Cole & Cole, 1989.

chronosystem Bronfenbrenner's term for effects of time on other developmental systems.

According to the Russian psychologist Lev Semenovich Vygotsky, children learn through social interaction.

whether a child grows up in a nuclear or extended-family household is strongly influenced by a culture's macrosystem.

The **chronosystem** adds the dimension of time: the degree of stability or change in a child's world. This can include changes in family composition, place of residence, or parents' employment, as well as larger events such as wars, economic cycles, and waves of migration. Changes in family patterns (such as the increase in the number of working mothers in western industrial societies and the decline of the extended-family household in developing countries) are chronosystem factors.

According to Bronfenbrenner, a person is not merely an outcome of development, but also a shaper of it. People affect their own development through their biological and psychological characteristics, talents and skills, disabilities, and temperament.

Lev Vygotsky's Sociocultural Theory

The Russian psychologist Lev Semenovich Vygotsky (1896–1934) was a prominent proponent of the contextual perspective, particularly as it applies to children's cognitive development. In contrast with Bronfenbrenner, who sees contextual systems as centered around the individual person, Vygotsky's central focus was the social, cultural, and historical complex of which a child is a part. To understand cognitive development, he maintained, one must look to the social processes from which a child's thinking is derived.

Vygotsky's (1978) **sociocultural theory,** like Piaget's theory of cognitive development, stresses children's active engagement with their environment. But whereas Piaget described the solo mind taking in and interpreting information about the world, Vygotsky saw cognitive growth as a *collaborative* process. Children, said Vygotsky, learn through social interaction. They acquire cognitive skills as part of their induction into a way of life. Shared activities help children to internalize their society's ways of thinking and behaving and to make those ways their own.

sociocultural theory Vygotsky's theory of how contextual factors affect children's development.

According to Vygotsky, adults (or more advanced peers) must help direct and organize a child's learning before the child can master and internalize it. This guidance is most effective in helping children cross the **zone of proximal development (ZPD)**, the gap between what they are already able to do and what they are not quite ready to accomplish by themselves. (*Proximal* means "nearby.") Children in the ZPD for a particular task can almost, but not quite, perform the task on their own. With the right kind of guidance, however, they can do it successfully. Responsibility for directing and monitoring learning gradually shifts from the adult to the child.

zone of proximal development (ZPD) Vygotsky's term for the difference between what a child can do alone and what the child can do with help.

scaffolding Temporary support to help a child master a task.

When an adult teaches a child to float, the adult first supports the child in the water and then lets go gradually as the child's body relaxes into a horizontal position. When the child seems ready, the adult withdraws all but one finger and finally lets the child float freely. Some followers of Vygotsky (Wood, 1980; Wood, Bruner, & Ross, 1976) have applied the metaphor of scaffolds—the temporary platforms on which construction workers stand—to this way of teaching. **Scaffolding** is the temporary support that parents, teachers, or others give a child in doing a task until the child can do it alone.

Vygotsky's theory has important implications for education and for cognitive testing. Tests based on the ZPD, which focus on a child's potential, provide a valuable alternative to standard intelligence tests that assess what the child has already learned; and many children may benefit from the sort of expert guidance Vygotsky prescribed.

A major contribution of the contextual perspective has been its emphasis on the social component of development. Research attention has shifted from the individual to larger, interactional units—parent and child, sibling and sibling, the entire family, the neighborhood, and broader societal institutions. The contextual perspective also reminds us that the development of children in one culture or one group within a culture (such as white, middle-class Americans) may not be an appropriate norm for children in other societies or cultural groups.

Checkpoint

Can you . . .

- ✔ Identify the chief assumptions of the contextual perspective?
- ✔ Name Bronfenbrenner's five systems of contextual influence?
- ✔ Explain how Vygotsky's theory differs from Bronfenbrenner's and Piaget's?
- ✔ Tell how Vygotsky's theory applies to educational teaching and testing?

How Theory and Research Work Together

No one theory of human development is universally accepted, and no one theoretical perspective explains all facets of development. In the absence of a single, widely accepted "grand" theory (such as those of Freud and Piaget), the trend is toward smaller, more limited "minitheories" aimed at explaining specific phenomena, such as how poverty influences family relations (Parke, 2004). At the same time, as you will see throughout this book, there is increasing theoretical and research exploration of the interplay among developmental domains. There also is growing awareness of the importance of historical change and of the need to explore cultural diversity.

What's your view 

- Which theoretical perspective would be most useful for (a) a mother trying to get her child to say "please," (b) a teacher interested in stimulating critical thinking, and (c) a researcher studying siblings' imitation of one another?

Theories of child development often grow out of, and are tested by, research. Thus, research questions and methods tend to reflect the theoretical orientation of the researcher. For example, in trying to understand how a child develops a sense of right and wrong, a behaviorist would examine what kinds of behavior the parents have punished or praised; a social learning theorist would focus on imitation of moral examples; and an information-processing researcher might analyze the steps a child goes through in determining the range of moral options available and deciding which to pursue.

Research Methods

Guidepost 4

How do developmental scientists study children, and what are the advantages and disadvantages of each research method?

Two key issues at the outset of a scientific investigation are how the participants will be chosen and how the data will be collected. These decisions often depend on what questions the researcher wants to answer. All these issues play a part in a research design, or plan.

quantitative research Research that focuses on objectively measurable data.

qualitative research Research that focuses on nonnumerical data, such as subjective experiences, feelings, or beliefs.

scientific method System of established principles and processes of scientific inquiry.

Researchers in child development work within two methodological traditions: *quantitative* and *qualitative*. **Quantitative research** deals with objectively measurable data; for example, how much fear or anxiety children feel before surgery, as measured by standardized tests, physiological changes, or statistical analysis. **Qualitative research** involves the interpretation of nonnumerical data, such as the nature or quality of participants' subjective experiences, feelings, or beliefs—for instance, how children describe their emotions before surgery (Morse & Field, 1995) or, as with Margaret Mead's research, how girls in the South Sea islands describe their experience of puberty.

Quantitative research is based on the **scientific method,** which generally characterizes any scientific inquiry. Its usual steps are (1) *identifying a problem* to be studied, often on the basis of a theory or of previous research; (2) *formulating hypotheses* to be tested by research; (3) *collecting data*; (4) *analyzing the data* to determine whether they support the hypothesis; and (5) *disseminating findings* so that other observers can check, learn from, analyze, repeat, and build on the results.

Although most developmental scientists have been trained in quantitative methods, the need for qualitative research is increasingly recognized (Parke, 2004). Qualitative research is open-ended and exploratory. Instead of generating hypotheses from previous research, qualitative researchers gather and examine data to see what hypotheses or theories may emerge. Qualitative research can be a rich source of insights into attitudes and behavior.

The selection of quantitative or qualitative methods depends on a number of factors: the topic for study, how much is already known about it, the researcher's theoretical orientation, and the setting. Quantitative research is often done in controlled laboratory settings. Qualitative research is conducted in everyday settings. Each of these two distinct methodologies can provide rich information about child development. And the two methods can complement each other. For example, computerized statistical analysis can be applied to verbal reports generated by focus groups (Parke, 2004).

Checkpoint ✓

Can you . . .

✔ Compare quantitative and qualitative research, and give an example of each?

✔ Summarize the five steps in the scientific method and tell why each is important?

Sampling

sample Group of participants chosen to represent the entire population under study.

To be sure that the results of research are true generally, and not just for specific participants, quantitative researchers need to control who gets into the study. Because studying an entire *population* (a group to which we want to apply the findings) is usually too costly and time-consuming, investigators select a **sample,** a smaller group within the population. The sample should adequately represent the population under study—that is, it should show relevant characteristics in the same proportions as in the entire population. Otherwise the results cannot properly be *generalized,* or applied to the population as a whole. To judge how generalizable the findings are likely to be, researchers carefully compare the characteristics of the people in the sample with those of the population as a whole.

Often researchers seek to achieve representativeness through *random selection,* in which each person in a population has an equal and independent chance of being chosen. If we wanted to study the effects of a pilot educational program, one way to select a random sample would be to put all the names of participating children into a large bowl, stir it, and then draw out a certain number of names. A random sample, especially a large one, is likely to represent the population well. Unfortunately, a random sample of a large population is often difficult to obtain. Instead, many studies use samples selected for convenience or accessibility (for example, children born in a particular hospital or attending a particular day care center). The findings of such studies may not apply to the population as a whole.

In qualitative research, samples tend to be small and need not be random. Participants in this kind of research may be chosen for their ability to communicate the nature of their experience—say, what it feels like to go through surgery—or because they have undergone a particular type of surgery.

Forms of Data Collection

Common ways of gathering data (see Table 2-3) include self-reports (verbal reports by study participants), tests and other behavioral measures, and observation. Depending in

Table 2-3 Characteristics of Major Methods of Data Collection

Type	Main Characteristics	Advantages	Disadvantages
Self-report: diary, interview, or questionnaire	Participants are asked about some aspect of their lives; questioning may be highly structured or more flexible.	Can provide firsthand information about a person's life, attitudes, or opinions.	Participant may not remember information accurately or may distort responses in a socially desirable way; how question is asked or by whom may affect answer.
Behavioral measures	Participants are tested on abilities, skills, knowledge, competencies, or physical responses.	Provides objectively measurable information; avoids subjective distortions.	Cannot measure attitudes or other nonbehavioral phenomena; results may be affected by extraneous factors.
Naturalistic observation	People are observed in their normal setting, with no attempt to manipulate behavior.	Provides good description of behavior; does not subject people to unnatural settings that may distort behavior.	Lack of control; observer bias.
Laboratory observation	Participants are observed in the laboratory, with no attempt to manipulate behavior.	Provides good descriptions; offers greater control than naturalistic observation, since all participants are observed under same conditions.	Observer bias; controlled situation can be artificial.

part on time and financial constraints, researchers may use one or more of these data collection techniques in any research design. Currently there is a trend toward increased use of self-reports and observation in combination with more objective measures.

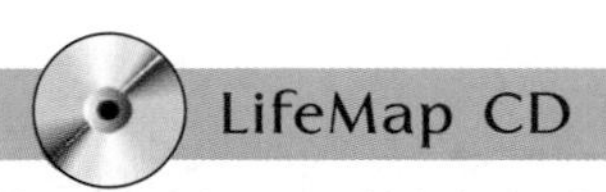

For an opinion on which form of data collection is most valuable, watch the video called "Judy Dunn on How to Develop a Study of Children" in Chapter 2 of your CD.

Self-Reports: Diaries, Interviews, Questionnaires

The simplest form of self-report is a *diary* or log. Adolescents may be asked, for example, to record what they eat each day or the times when they feel depressed. In studying young children, *parental self-reports*—diaries, journals, interviews, or questionnaires—are commonly used, often with other methods, such as videotaping or recording. Parents may be videotaped playing with their babies and then may be shown the tapes and asked to explain their responses to their infants.

In a face-to-face or telephone *interview,* researchers ask questions about attitudes, opinions, or behavior. Interviews may cover such topics as parent-child relationships, sexual activities, and occupational goals. In a *structured* interview, each participant is asked the same set of questions. An *open-ended* interview is more flexible; as in Piaget's clinical method, the interviewer can vary the topics and order of questions and can ask follow-up questions based on the responses. To reach more people and protect their privacy, researchers sometimes distribute a printed *questionnaire,* which participants fill out and return.

By questioning a large number of people, investigators get a broad picture—at least of what the respondents *say* they believe or do or did. However, people willing to participate in interviews or fill out questionnaires tend to be unrepresentative of the population. Furthermore, heavy reliance on self-reports may be unwise, since people may not have thought about what they feel and think, or they honestly may not know. Some people forget when and how events actually took place, and others consciously or unconsciously distort their replies to fit what is considered socially desirable.

How a question is asked, and by whom, can affect the answer. When researchers at the National Institute on Drug Abuse reworded a question about alcohol use to indicate that a "drink" meant "more than a few sips," the percentage of teenagers who reported drinking alcohol dropped significantly (National Institute on Drug Abuse, 1996). When questioned about risky or socially disapproved behavior, such as sexual habits and drug use, respondents may be more candid in responding to a computerized survey than to a paper-and-pencil one (Turner et al., 1998).

Behavioral and Performance Measures

For many kinds of research, investigators use more objective measures instead of, or in addition to, self-reports. A behavioral or performance measure *shows* something about a child rather than asking the child or someone else, such as a parent, to *tell* about it. Tests and other behavioral and neuropsychological measures, including mechanical and electronic devices, may be used to assess abilities, skills, knowledge, competencies, or physiological responses, such as heart rate and brain activity. Although these measures are less subjective than self-reports, results can be affected by such factors as fatigue and self-confidence.

Some tests, such as intelligence tests, compare performance with that of other test takers. Such tests can be meaningful and useful only if they are both *valid* (that is, they measure the abilities they claim to measure) and *reliable* (that is, the results are reasonably consistent from one time to another). To avoid bias, intelligence tests must be *standardized* (that is, given and scored by the same methods and criteria for all test takers).

operational definition Definition stated solely in terms of the operations or procedures used to produce or measure a phenomenon.

When measuring a characteristic such as intelligence, it is important to define exactly what is to be measured in a way that other researchers will understand so that they can comment on the results. For this purpose, research scientists use an **operational definition**—a definition stated solely in terms of the operations or procedures used to produce or measure a phenomenon. *Intelligence,* for example, can be defined as the ability to achieve a certain score on a test covering logical relationships, memory, and vocabulary recognition. Some people may not agree with this definition, but no one can reasonably claim that it is not clear.

Checkpoint

Can you . . .

- ✔ Compare quantitative and qualitative research and give examples?
- ✔ Summarize the five steps in the scientific method and tell why each is important?
- ✔ Explain the purpose of random selection and tell how it can be achieved?
- ✔ Compare the advantages and disadvantages of various forms of data collection?

Naturalistic and Laboratory Observation

naturalistic observation Research method in which behavior is studied in natural settings without intervention or manipulation.

laboratory observation Research method in which all participants are observed under the same controlled conditions.

Observation can take two forms: *naturalistic observation* and *laboratory observation.* In **naturalistic observation,** researchers look at children in real-life settings. The researchers do not try to alter behavior or the environment; they simply record what they see. In **laboratory observation,** researchers observe and record behavior in a controlled situation, such as a laboratory. By observing all participants under the same conditions, investigators can more clearly identify any differences in behavior not attributable to the environment.

Both kinds of observation can provide valuable descriptions of behavior, but they have limitations. For one, they do not explain *why* children behave as they do, though they may suggest interpretations. Then, too, an observer's presence can alter behavior. When children know they are being watched, they may act differently. Finally, there is a risk of *observer bias:* the researcher's tendency to interpret data to fit expectations or to emphasize some aspects and minimize others.

During the 1960s, laboratory observation was most commonly used so as to achieve more rigorous control. Today, naturalistic observation is supplemented by such technological devices as portable videotape recorders and computers, which increase objectivity and enable researchers to analyze moment-by-moment changes in facial expressions or other behavior.

Basic Research Designs

A research design is a plan for conducting a scientific investigation: what questions are to be answered, how participants are to be selected, how data are to be collected and interpreted, and how valid conclusions can be drawn. Four of the basic designs used in developmental research are case studies, ethnographic studies, correlational studies, and experiments. Each design has advantages and drawbacks, and each is appropriate for certain kinds of research problems (see Table 2-4).

Case Studies

case study Study covering a single case or life.

A **case study** is a study of a single case or individual, such as Victor, the wild boy of Aveyron (discussed in the Focus of Chapter 1). A number of theories, such as Freud's, have grown out of clinical case studies, which include careful observation and interpretation of what patients say and do. Case studies also may use behavioral or neuropsychological measures and biographical, autobiographical, or documentary materials.

Table 2-4 Basic Research Designs			
Type	**Main Characteristics**	**Advantages**	**Disadvantages**
Case study	Study of single individual in depth.	Flexibility; provides detailed picture of one person's behavior and development; can generate hypotheses.	May not generalize to others; conclusions not directly testable; cannot establish cause and effect.
Ethnographic study	In-depth study of a culture or subculture.	Can help overcome culturally based biases in theory and research; can test universality of developmental phenomena.	Subject to observer bias.
Correlational study	Attempt to find positive or negative relationship between variables.	Enables prediction of one variable on basis of another; can suggest hypotheses about causal relationships.	Cannot establish cause and effect.
Experiment	Controlled procedure in which an experimenter controls the independent variable to determine its effect on the dependent variable; may be conducted in the laboratory or field.	Establishes cause-and-effect relationships; is highly controlled and can be repeated by another investigator; degree of control greatest in the laboratory experiment.	Findings, especially when derived from laboratory experiments, may not generalize to situations outside the laboratory.

Case studies offer useful, in-depth information. They can explore sources of behavior and can test treatments. They also can suggest a need for other research. Another advantage is flexibility: The researcher is free to explore avenues of inquiry that arise during the course of the study. However, case studies have shortcomings. From studying Victor, for instance, we learn much about the development of a single child but not how the information applies to children in general. Furthermore, case studies cannot explain behavior with certainty, because there is no way to test their conclusions. Even though it seems reasonable that Victor's severely deprived environment caused or contributed to his language deficiency, it is impossible to know whether he would have developed normally with a normal upbringing.

Ethnographic Studies

An **ethnographic study** seeks to describe the patterns of relationships, customs, beliefs, technology, arts, and traditions that make up a society's way of life. Ethnographic research can be qualitative, quantitative, or both. It uses a combination of methods, including **participant observation.** Participant observation is a form of naturalistic observation in which researchers live or participate in the societies or groups they observe, as Margaret Mead (1928, 1930, 1935) did, often for long periods of time; thus, their findings are especially open to observer bias.

ethnographic study In-depth study of a culture using a combination of methods including participant observation.

participant observation Research method in which the observer lives with the people or participates in the activity being observed.

In response to later controversy over Mead's sampling methods and her findings on adolescence (D. Freeman, 1983; L. D. Holmes, 1987), the anthropologist Robert LeVine wrote, "Mead's basic message to the child development field remains as valid today as in 1930: To understand how children grow up under varied environmental conditions, one must be willing to go to where those conditions already exist, to examine them with respect and in detail, and to change one's assumptions in the face of new observations" (LeVine et al., 1994, p. 9).

Ethnographic research can help overcome cultural biases in theory and research (see Box 2-2). Ethnography demonstrates that principles developed from research in western cultures are not necessarily universally applicable. It also can reveal processes that may account for differences in outcomes within a single ethnic group (Parke, 2004).

Correlational Studies

correlational study Research design intended to discover whether a statistical relationship between variables exists.

A **correlational study** is an attempt to find a *correlation,* or statistical relationship, between *variables,* phenomena that change or vary among people or can be varied for

Around the World

Box 2-2 *Purposes of Cross-Cultural Research*

When David, an American child, was asked to identify the missing detail in a picture of a face with no mouth, he said, "The mouth." But Ari, an Asian immigrant child in Israel, said that the *body* was missing. Since art in his culture does not present a head as a complete picture, he thought the absence of a body was more important than the omission of "a mere detail like the mouth" (Anastasi, 1988, p. 360).

By looking at children from different cultural groups, researchers can learn in what ways development is universal (and thus intrinsic to the human condition) and in what ways it is culturally determined. For example, children everywhere learn to speak in the same sequence, advancing from cooing and babbling to single words and then to simple combinations of words. The words vary from culture to culture, but around the world toddlers put them together to form sentences similar in structure. Such findings suggest that the capacity for learning language is universal and inborn.

On the other hand, culture can exert a surprisingly large influence on early motor development. African babies, whose parents often prop them in a sitting position and bounce them on their feet, tend to sit and walk earlier than U.S. babies (Rogoff & Morelli, 1989). The society in which children grow up also influences the skills they learn. In the United States, children learn to read, write, and, increasingly, to operate computers. In rural Nepal, they learn how to drive water buffalo and find their way along mountain paths.

One important reason to conduct research among different cultural groups is to recognize biases in traditional western theories and research that often go unquestioned until they are shown to be a product of cultural influences. Since so much research in child development has focused on western industrialized societies, many people have defined typical development in these societies as the norm, or standard of behavior. Measuring against this "norm" leads to narrow—and often wrong—ideas about development. Pushed to its extreme, this belief can cause the development of children in other ethnic and cultural groups to be seen as deviant (Rogoff & Morelli, 1989).

Barriers exist to our understanding of cultural differences, particularly those involving minority subcultures. As with David and Ari in our opening example, a question or task may have different conceptual meanings for different cultural groups. Sometimes the barriers are linguistic. In a study of children's understanding of kinship relations among the Zinacanta people of Chiapas, Mexico (Greenfield & Childs, 1978), instead of asking "How many brothers do you have?" the researchers—knowing that the Zinacantas have separate terms for older and younger siblings—asked, "What is the name of your older brother?" Using the same question across cultures might have obscured, rather than revealed, cultural differences and similarities (Parke, 2004).

Results of observational studies of ethnic or cultural groups may be affected by the ethnicity of the researchers. For example, in one study European-American observers noted more conflict and restrictiveness in African-American mother-daughter relationships than African-American observers did (Gonzales, Cauce, & Mason, 1996).

In this book we discuss several influential theories developed from research in western societies that do not hold up when tested on people from other cultures—theories about gender roles, abstract thinking, moral reasoning, and a number of other aspects of human development. Throughout this book, we consistently look at children in cultures and subcultures other than the dominant one in the United States to show how closely development is tied to society and culture and to add to our understanding of normal development in many settings. In so doing, however, we need to keep in mind the pitfalls involved in cross-cultural comparisons.

What's your view?

Can you think of a situation in which you made an incorrect assumption about a person because you were unfamiliar with her or his cultural background?

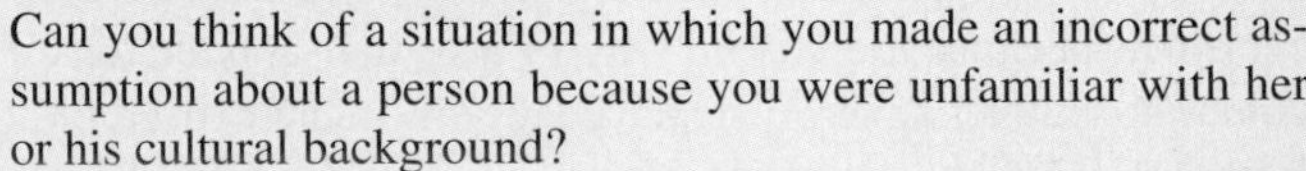

Check it out!

For more information on this topic, go to **http://zzyx.ucsc.edu/Psych/psych.html**. This is the Web site for the Department of Psychology at the University of Santa Cruz. Select the *Faculty* link and read about the work of faculty members who conduct cross-cultural research in human development: Barbara Rogoff, David Harrington, Ronald Tharp, and Stephen Wright.

purposes of research. Correlations are expressed in terms of direction (positive or negative) and magnitude (degree). Two variables that are related *positively* increase or decrease together. A positive, or direct, correlation between televised violence and aggressiveness would exist if children who watched more violent television hit, bit, or kicked more than children who watched less violent television. Two variables have a *negative,* or inverse, correlation if, as one increases, the other decreases. Studies show a negative correlation between amount of schooling and the risk of developing dementia (mental deterioration) due to Alzheimer's disease in old age. In other words, the less education a person has, the more dementia is likely (Katzman, 1993).

Correlations are reported as numbers ranging from -1.0 (a perfect negative relationship) to $+1.0$ (a perfect positive relationship). Perfect correlations are rare. The closer a correlation comes to $+1.0$ or -1.0, the stronger the relationship, either positive or negative. A correlation of 0.0 means that the variables have no relationship (see Figure 2-3).

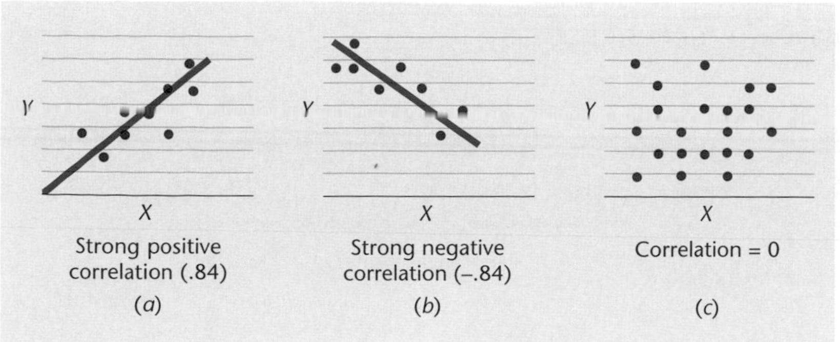

Figure 2-3

Correlational studies may find positive or negative correlations or no correlation. In a positive, or direct, correlation (*a*), data plotted on a graph cluster around a line showing that one variable (*X*) increases as the other variable (*Y*) increases. In a negative, or inverse, correlation (*b*), one variable (*X*) increases as the other variable (*Y*) decreases. No correlation, or a zero correlation (*c*), exists when increases and decreases in two variables show no consistent relationship (that is, data plotted on a graph show no pattern).

Correlations enable us to predict one variable on the basis of another. If, for example, we found a positive correlation between watching televised violence and fighting, we would predict that children who watch violent shows will be more likely to get into fights. The greater the magnitude of the correlation between two variables, the greater the ability to predict one from the other.

Although strong correlations may suggest possible causes, these possible cause-and-effect relations need to be examined very critically. We cannot be sure from a positive correlation between televised violence and aggressiveness that watching televised violence *causes* aggressive play; we can conclude only that the two variables are related. It is possible that the causation goes the other way: aggressive play may lead children to watch more violent programs. Or a third variable—perhaps an inborn predisposition toward aggressiveness or a violent environment—may cause a child both to watch violent programs and to act aggressively. Similarly, we cannot be sure that schooling protects against dementia; it may be that another related variable, such as socioeconomic status, can explain both lower levels of schooling and higher levels of dementia. The only way to show with certainty that one variable causes another is through a controlled experiment—something that, in studying human beings, is not always possible for practical or ethical reasons.

Experiments

An **experiment** is a controlled procedure in which the experimenter manipulates variables to learn how one affects another. Scientific experiments must be conducted and reported in such a way that another experimenter can *replicate* them; that is, repeat them in exactly the same way with different participants to verify the results and conclusions. Figure 2-4 shows how an experiment might be designed.

experiment Rigorously controlled, replicable procedure in which the researcher manipulates variables to assess the effect of one on the other.

Groups and Variables A common way to conduct an experiment is to divide the participants into two kinds of groups. An **experimental group** is composed of people who are to be exposed to the experimental manipulation or *treatment*—the phenomenon the researcher wants to study. Afterward, the effect of the treatment will be measured one or more times to find out what changes, if any, it caused. A **control group** is composed of people who are similar to the experimental group but do not receive the treatment or receive a different treatment. An experiment may include one or more of each type of group. Or, if the experimenter wants to compare the effects of different treatments (say, of two methods of teaching), the overall sample may be divided into *treatment groups,* each of which receives one of the treatments under study.

experimental group In an experiment, group receiving the treatment under study.

control group In an experiment, group of people, similar to those in the experimental group, who do not receive the treatment under study.

One team of researchers (Whitehurst et al., 1988) wanted to find out what effect *dialogic reading,* a special method of reading picture books to very young children might have

Checkpoint

Can you . . .

- ✔ Compare the uses and drawbacks of case studies, ethnographic studies, correlational studies, and experiments?
- ✔ Explain why only a controlled experiment can establish causal relationships?
- ✔ Distinguish among laboratory, field, and natural experiments, and tell what kinds of research seem most suitable to each?

When, for practical or ethical reasons, it is impossible to conduct a true experiment, a *natural experiment* may provide a way of studying certain events. A natural experiment compares people who have been accidentally "assigned" to separate groups by circumstances of life—one group of children who were exposed, say, to famine or HIV or superior educational opportunities and another group who were not. A natural experiment, despite its name, is actually a correlational study, since controlled manipulation of variables and random assignment to treatment groups are not possible.

One natural experiment dealt with what happened when a casino opened on an Indian reservation in North Carolina, raising the income of tribal members (Costello, Compton, Keeler, & Angold, 2003). The study found a decline in behavioral disorders among children in these families as compared with children in the same area whose families did not receive increased income. However, being correlational, the study could not prove that the increased income *caused* improvements in mental health.

Controlled experiments have important advantages over other research designs: the ability to establish cause-and-effect relationships and to permit replication. However, such experiments can be too artificial and too narrowly focused. In recent decades, therefore, many researchers have concentrated less on laboratory experimentation or have supplemented it with a wider array of methods.

Developmental Research Designs

The two most common research strategies used to study child development are *cross-sectional* and *longitudinal* studies (see Figure 2-5). Cross-sectional studies show similarities and differences among age groups; longitudinal studies reveal how children change or stay the same as they grow older. Because each of these designs has drawbacks, researchers also have devised *sequential* designs. To directly observe change, *microgenetic studies* can be used.

Cross-Sectional, Longitudinal, and Sequential Studies

cross-sectional study Study design in which people of different ages are assessed on one occasion.

In a **cross-sectional study,** children of different ages are assessed at one time. In one cross-sectional study, researchers asked 3-, 4-, 6-, and 7-year-olds about what a pensive-looking woman was doing or about the state of someone's mind. There was a striking increase with age in children's awareness of mental activity (J. H. Flavell, Green, & Flavell, 1995). These findings strongly suggest that, as children become older, their understanding of mental processes improves. However, we cannot draw such a conclusion with certainty. We don't know whether the 7-year-olds' awareness of mental activity when they were 3 years old was the same as that of the current 3-year-olds in the study. The only way to see whether change occurs with age is to conduct a longitudinal study of a particular person or group.

longitudinal study Study designed to assess changes in a sample over time.

In a **longitudinal study,** researchers study the same child or children more than once, sometimes years apart. They may measure a single characteristic, such as vocabulary size, height, or aggressiveness, or they may look at several aspects of development to find relationships among them. The Oakland (Adolescent) Growth Study (refer back to

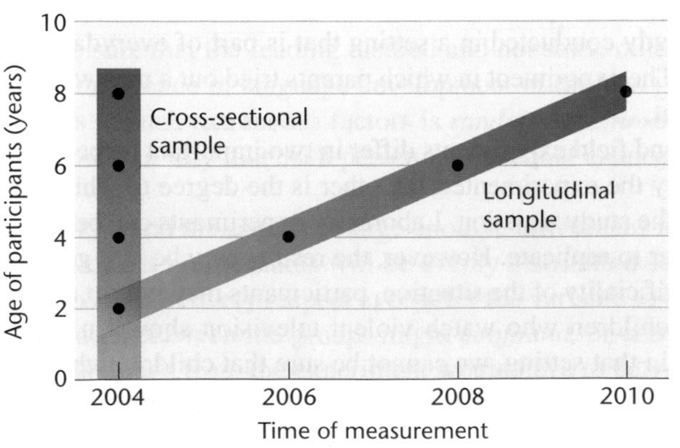

Figure 2-5

Developmental research designs. In the *cross-sectional* study, groups of 2-, 4-, 6-, and 8-year-olds were tested in 2004 to obtain data about age differences. In the *longitudinal* study, a sample of children were first measured in 2004, when they were 2 years old; follow-up testing is done when the children are 4, 6, and 8, to measure age-related changes in performance. Note: Dots indicate times of measurement.

Table 2-5	Longitudinal, Cross-Sectional, and Sequential Research: Pros and Cons		
Type of Study	**Procedure**	**Advantages**	**Disadvantages**
Longitudinal	Data are collected on same person or persons over a period of time.	Can show age-related change or continuity; avoids confounding age with cohort effects.	Is time-consuming, expensive; presents problems of attrition, bias in sample, and effects of repeated testing; results may be valid only for cohort tested or sample studied.
Cross-sectional	Data are collected on people of different ages at the same time.	Can show similarities and differences among age groups; speedy, economical; presents no problem of attrition or repeated testing.	Cannot establish age effects; masks individual differences; can be confounded by cohort effects.
Sequential	Data are collected on successive cross-sectional or longitudinal samples.	Can avoid drawbacks of both cross-sectional and longitudinal designs.	Requires large amount of time and effort and analysis of very complex data.

Chapter 1) initially was designed to assess social and emotional development from the preteen through the senior high school years; ultimately, many of the participants were followed into old age. The study found that participants who as teenagers showed self-confidence, intellectual commitment, and dependable effectiveness made good choices in adolescence and also in early adulthood, which often led to promising opportunities (scholarships, good jobs, and competent spouses). Less competent teenagers made poorer early decisions and tended to lead crisis-ridden lives (Clausen, 1993).

Both cross-sectional and longitudinal designs have strengths and weaknesses (see Table 2-5). Advantages of cross-sectional research include speed and economy; data can be gathered fairly quickly from large numbers of people. And, since participants are assessed only once, there is no problem of attrition or repeated testing. A drawback of cross-sectional studies is that they may overlook individual differences by focusing on group averages. Their major disadvantage, however, is that the results may be affected by cohort differences (the differing experiences of children born, for example, before and after the advent of the Internet). Cross-sectional studies are sometimes interpreted as yielding information about developmental changes in groups or individuals, but such information is often misleading. Thus, although cross-sectional studies still dominate the field—no doubt because they are so much easier to do—the proportion of research devoted to longitudinal studies, especially short-term ones, is increasing (Parke et al., 1994).

Longitudinal research, by repeatedly studying the same people, can track individual patterns of continuity and change. However, a longitudinal study done on one cohort may not apply to another. (The results of a study of children born in the 1920s may not apply to children born in the 1990s.) Furthermore, longitudinal studies generally are more time-consuming and expensive than cross-sectional studies; it is hard to keep track of a large group of participants over the years, to keep records, and to keep the study going despite possible turnover in research personnel. Then there is the problem of attrition; participants may die, move away, or drop out. Also, longitudinal studies tend to be biased; those who stay with the study tend to be above average in intelligence and socioeconomic status. Finally, results can be affected by repeated testing; participants may do better in later tests because of familiarity with test procedures.

The **sequential study**—a sequence of cross-sectional and/or longitudinal studies—is a complex strategy designed to overcome the drawbacks of longitudinal and cross-sectional research (again see Table 2-5). Researchers may assess a cross-sectional sample on two or more occasions (that is, in sequence) to find out how members of each age cohort have changed. This procedure permits researchers to separate age-related changes from cohort effects. Another sequential design consists of a sequence of longitudinal studies, running concurrently but starting one after another. This design enables researchers to compare individual differences in the course of developmental change. A combination of cross-sectional and longitudinal sequences (as shown in Figure 2-6) can provide a more complete picture of development than would be possible with longitudinal or cross-sectional

sequential study Study design that combines cross-sectional and longitudinal techniques.

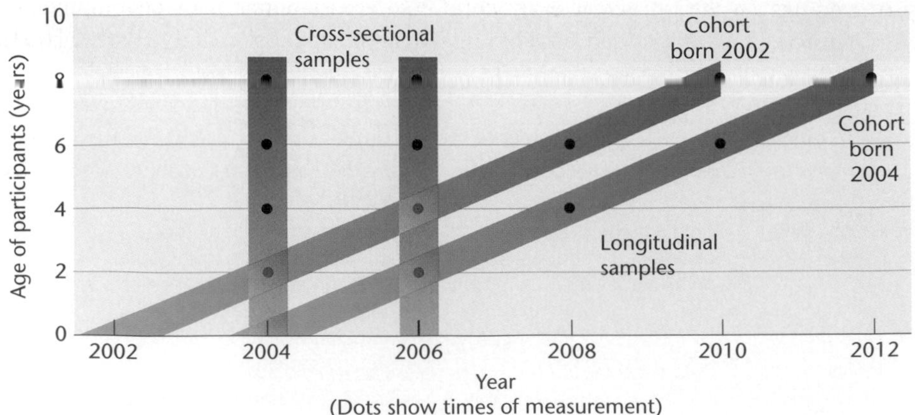

Figure 2-6

A sequential design. Two successive cross-sectional groups of 2-, 4-, 6-, and 8-year-olds are tested in 2004 and 2006. Also, a longitudinal study of a sample of children first measured in 2004, when they were 2 years old, is followed by a similar longitudinal study of another group of children who were 2 years old in 2006.

research alone. The major drawbacks of sequential studies involve time, effort, and complexity. Sequential designs require large numbers of participants and the collection and analysis of huge amounts of data over a period of years. Interpreting their findings and conclusions can demand a high degree of sophistication.

Microgenetic Studies

microgenetic study Study design that enables researchers to directly observe change by repeated testing over a short time.

Developmental scientists rarely can observe change directly in everyday life because it usually happens so slowly. But what if the process could be compressed into a very short time frame? A **microgenetic study** does just that, by repeatedly exposing participants to a stimulus for change, or opportunity for learning, over a short period of time, enabling researchers to see and analyze the processes by which change occurs. Vygotsky, for example, used what he called "microgenesis experiments" in which he manipulated conditions to see how much children's performance could be improved over a short period of time.

In one series of experiments using operant conditioning (Rovee-Collier & Boller, 1995; see Chapter 5), infants as young as 2 months old learned to kick to set in motion a brightly colored mobile to which one leg was attached—if the infants were exposed to a similar situation repeatedly within a few days or weeks. Building on this work, Esther Thelen (1994) tied 3-month-olds' left and right legs together with soft elastic fabric. Would they learn to kick with both legs at once to activate the mobile? The infants' movements were videotaped, and the frequency and speed of kicks, using one or both legs, were then analyzed with the help of a computer. The results showed that the infants gradually switched to kicking with both legs when it proved more effective, and observers were able to chart exactly how and when this change occurred.

Checkpoint

Can you . . .

- ✔ List advantages and disadvantages of longitudinal, cross-sectional, and sequential research?
- ✔ Explain how microgenetic studies are done and what kinds of data they can reveal?

Collaborative Research

Throughout much of the history of the field, investigators of child development have worked individually or in small groups at a single laboratory or site. Although many important advances have come from such research, the current trend is to broaden the research base.

Researchers use various means to share and pool data. One is the archiving of data sets for use by other researchers. Another is *meta-analysis,* a statistical analysis of the findings of multiple studies. A third and increasingly common approach is collaborative research by multiple researchers at multiple sites, sometimes with government or foundation funding. This collaborative model makes possible larger, more representative samples; makes it easier to carry out longitudinal studies that might otherwise be hampered by researcher attrition and burnout; and permits a blending of theoretical perspectives (Parke, 2004).

An example of collaborative research is the National Institute of Child Health and Human Development (NICHD) Study of Early Child Care (discussed in Chapter 8). This study, which began in 1990, has followed more than 1,300 children, of varied socioeconomic status and ethnicity, at 10 widely separated research sites. It has produced a complex array of findings on the impact of early child care across domains of development—findings that would not have been possible in a smaller, single-site study (Parke, 2004).

A difficulty with the collaborative model is the need for group consensus on all aspects of the research, from the initial design to the writing of the report. Achieving consensus can be cumbersome and may require difficult compromises. The more flexible single-investigator or single-site model may be better suited to experimental work and to the development of novel methods and approaches.

Ethics of Research

What ethical problems may arise in research on children?

Should research that might harm its participants ever be undertaken? How can we balance the possible benefits against the risk of mental, emotional, or physical injury to individuals?

Objections to the study of "Little Albert" (described earlier in this chapter) as well as to a number of other early studies gave rise to today's more stringent ethical standards. Institutional review boards at colleges, universities, and other institutions that receive federal funding must review proposed research from an ethical standpoint. Guidelines of the American Psychological Association (2002) and the Society for Research in Child Development (1996) cover such issues as informed consent, avoidance of deception, protection of participants from harm and loss of dignity, guarantees of privacy and confidentiality, the right to decline or withdraw from an experiment at any time, and the responsibility of investigators to correct any undesirable effects.

In resolving ethical dilemmas, researchers are supposed to be guided by three principles: (1) *beneficence,* the obligation to maximize potential benefits to participants and minimize possible harm; (2) *respect* for participants' autonomy and protection of those who are unable to exercise their own judgment; and (3) *justice,* the inclusion of diverse groups combined with sensitivity to any special impact the research situation may have on them. In evaluating risks and benefits, researchers should consider children's developmental needs (Thompson, 1990) and be sensitive to cultural issues and values (Fisher et al., 2002).

To learn more about developmental considerations in research ethics, watch the video on "Ethical Issues in Studying Infants" in Chapter 2 of your CD.

Let's look more closely at a few of the ethical considerations that can present problems.

Right to Informed Consent

Informed consent exists when participants voluntarily agree to be in a study, are competent to give consent, are fully aware of the risks as well as the potential benefits, and are not being exploited. The National Commission for the Protection of Human Subjects of Biomedical and Behavioral Research (1978) recommends that children age 7 or over be asked to give their own consent to take part in research and that children's objections should be overruled only if the research promises direct benefit to the child, as in the use of a new experimental drug.

However, some ethicists argue that young children cannot give meaningful, voluntary *consent,* since they cannot fully understand what is involved. They can merely *assent;* that is, agree to participate. The usual procedure, therefore, when children under 18 are involved, is to ask the parents or legal guardians and sometimes school personnel to give consent.

Avoidance of Deception

Can informed consent exist if participants are deceived about the nature or purpose of a study or about the procedures to which they will be subjected? Suppose that children are told they are trying out a new game when they are actually being tested on their reactions to success or failure? Experiments like these, which cannot be carried out without deception, have been done—and they have added significantly to our knowledge but at the cost of the participants' right to know what they were getting involved in.

Ethical guidelines call for withholding information *only* when it is essential to the study; and then investigators should avoid methods that could cause pain, anxiety, or harm. Participants should be debriefed afterward to let them know the true nature of the study and why deception was necessary and to make sure they have not suffered as a result.

Right to Self-Esteem

Should children be subjected to research that may damage their self-esteem? Some studies have a built-in "failure factor." For example, the researchers may keep giving harder and harder tasks until the participant is unable to do them. Might this inevitable failure affect a participant's self-confidence? Similarly, when researchers publish findings that middle-class children are academically superior to poor children, unintentional harm may be done to some participants' self-esteem. And, although such studies may lead to beneficial interventions for poor children, they also may affect teachers' expectations and students' performance.

Right to Privacy and Confidentiality

Is it ethical to use one-way mirrors and hidden cameras to observe children without their knowledge? How can we protect the confidentiality of personal information that participants may reveal in interviews or questionnaires?

What if, during the course of research, an investigator notices that a child seems to have a learning disability or some other treatable condition? Is the researcher obliged to share such information with parents or guardians or to recommend services that may help the child, when sharing the information might contaminate the research findings? Such a decision should not be made lightly, since sharing information of uncertain validity may create damaging misconceptions about a child. On the other hand, researchers need to know of their legal responsibility to report child abuse or neglect or any other illegal activity of which they become aware.

Checkpoint

Can you . . .

- ✔ Identify three principles that should govern inclusion of participants in research?
- ✔ Discuss four rights of research participants?

Refocus

- Based on the information given about Margaret Mead, what position do you think she might have taken on the issue of the relative influences of heredity and environment?
- Does Mead seem to fit within any of the five theoretical perspectives described in this chapter?
- What research methods described in the chapter did she use? What advantages and disadvantages existed because her research was done in the field rather than in a laboratory?
- What ethical issues might be relevant to cross-cultural research such as Mead's?

The final word in these introductory chapters is that this entire book is far from the final word. Although the authors have tried to incorporate the most important and up-to-date information about how children develop, developmental scientists are constantly learning more. As you read this book, you are certain to come up with your own questions. By thinking about them and perhaps eventually conducting research to find answers, it is possible that you, now just embarking on the study of child development, will someday add to our knowledge about the interesting species to which we all belong.

Summary and Key Terms

Basic Theoretical Issues

Guidepost 1 What purposes do theories serve?

- A theory is used to organize and explain data and generate hypotheses that can be tested by research.

theory (25) **hypotheses (25)**

Guidepost 2 What are three basic theoretical issues on which developmental scientists differ?

- Developmental theories differ on three basic issues: the relative importance of heredity and environment, the active or passive character of development, and the existence of stages of development.
- Some theorists subscribe to a mechanistic model of development; others to an organismic model.

mechanistic model (26) **organismic model (26)**

Theoretical Perspectives

Guidepost 3 What are five theoretical perspectives on human development, and what are some theories representative of each?

- The psychoanalytic perspective sees development as motivated by unconscious emotional drives or conflicts. Leading examples are Freud's and Erikson's theories.

  psychoanalytic perspective (27) psychosexual development (28) psychosocial development (29)

- The learning perspective views development as a result of learning based on experience. Leading examples are Watson's and Skinner's behaviorism and Bandura's social learning (social cognitive) theory.

  learning perspective (31) behaviorism (31) classical conditioning (31) operant conditioning (31) reinforcement (32) punishment (32) social learning theory (32) observational learning (32)

- The cognitive perspective is concerned with thought processes. Leading examples are Piaget's cognitive-stage theory, the information-processing approach, and the cognitive neuroscience approach.

  cognitive perspective (33) organization (33) schemes (33) adaptation (33) assimilation (33) accommodation (33) equilibration (33) information-processing approach (34) cognitive neuroscience approach (35) social cognitive neuroscience (35)

- The evolutionary/sociobiological perspective, represented by O. W. Wilson, describes adaptive behaviors that promote group survival.

  evolutionary/sociobiological perspective (35) ethology (36) evolutionary psychology (36)

- The contextual perspective focuses on interaction between the individual and the social context. Leading examples are Bronfenbrenner's and Vygotsky's theories.

  contextual perspective (36) bioecological theory (36) microsystem (36) mesosystem (37) exosystem (37) macrosystem (37) chronosystem (38) sociocultural theory (39) zone of proximal development (ZPD) (39) scaffolding (39)

Research Methods

Guidepost 4 How do developmental scientists study children, and what are the advantages and disadvantages of each research method?

- Research can be quantitative, qualitative, or both.
- To arrive at sound conclusions, quantitative researchers use the scientific method.
- Random selection of a research sample can ensure generalizability.

  quantitative research (40) qualitative research (40) scientific method (40) sample (40)

- Three forms of data collection are self-reports (diaries, interviews, and questionnaires); behavioral and performance measures; and observation.

  operational definition (42) naturalistic observation (42) laboratory observation (42)

- Two basic designs used in developmental research are the case study and ethnographic study. Two quantitative designs are the correlational study and the experiment. Only experiments can firmly establish causal relationships. Cross-cultural research can indicate whether certain aspects of development are universal or culturally influenced.

  case study (42) ethnographic study (43) participant observation (43) correlational study (43) experiment (45)

- Experiments must be rigorously controlled so as to be valid and replicable. Random assignment of participants can ensure validity.
- Laboratory experiments are easiest to control and replicate, but findings of field experiments may be more generalizable. Natural experiments may be useful in situations in which true experiments would be impractical or unethical.

  experimental group (45) control group (45) independent variable (46) dependent variable (46)

- The two most common designs used to study age-related development are longitudinal and cross-sectional. Cross-sectional studies compare age groups; longitudinal studies describe continuity or change in the same participants. The sequential study is intended to overcome the weaknesses of the other two designs. A microgenetic study enables direct observation of change over a short period of time.

  cross-sectional study (48) longitudinal study (48) sequential study (49) microgenetic study (50)

Guidepost 5 What ethical problems may arise in research on children?

- Researchers seek to resolve ethical issues on the basis of principles of beneficence, respect, and justice.
- Ethical issues in research on child development involve the rights of participants to informed consent, avoidance of deception, protection from harm and loss of dignity or self-esteem, and guarantees of privacy and confidentiality.

Part 2

Beginnings: A Preview

Chapter 3
Forming a New Life

- Conception occurs by normal fertilization or other means.
- The genetic endowment interacts with environmental influences from the start.

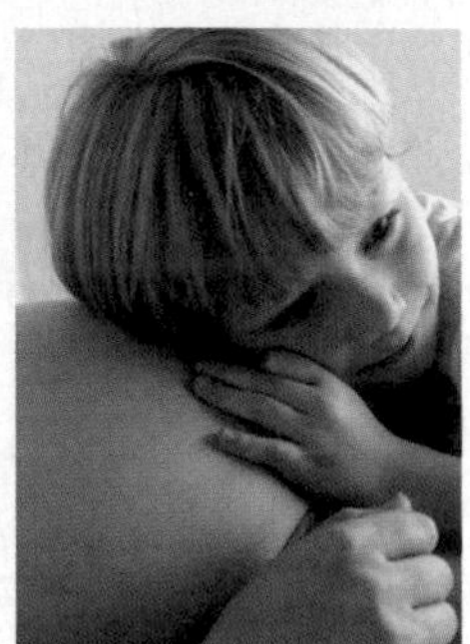

Chapter 4
Pregnancy and Prenatal Development

- Basic body structures and organs form; brain growth spurt begins.
- Physical growth is most rapid in the life span.
- Abilities to learn and remember and to respond to sensory stimuli are developing.
- Vulnerability to environmental influences is great.

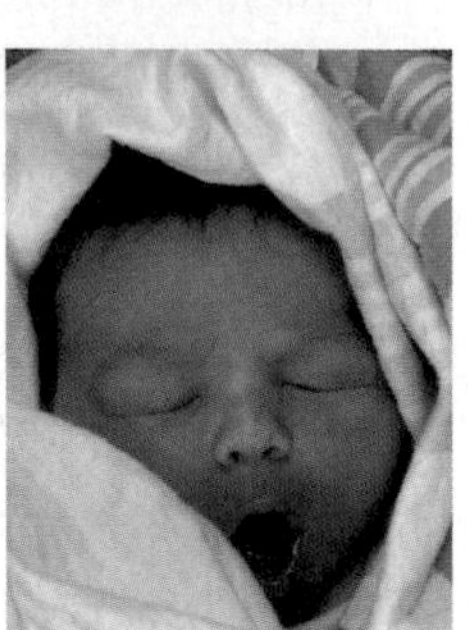

Chapter 5
Birth and the Newborn Baby

- A method and setting for childbirth are chosen, and the progress of the birth is monitored.
- The newborn emerges and is assessed for immediate health, developmental status, and any complications of childbirth.
- All body systems operate at birth to some extent.

Beginnings

By the time babies are born, they already have an impressive history. Part of this early history, which began long before conception, is the hereditary endowment. Another part is environmental, for the new organism is affected by many events that occur during its nine months in the womb. As this organism grows from a single cell to a newborn baby, both inheritance and experience affect its development. At birth, babies are already individuals, distinguishable not just by sex, but by size, temperament, appearance, and history.

The changes that occur between conception and the first months after birth are broader and faster paced than any a person will ever experience again. Although these initial changes may seem to be mostly physical, they have repercussions on other aspects of development. For example, the *physical* growth of the brain before and immediately after birth makes possible a great burst of *cognitive* and *emotional* growth.

In Part II, we focus on this earliest period of development. Chapter 3 examines the two great forces—heredity and environment—that work together to make each child a unique person. Chapter 4 considers effects of the prenatal environment. Chapter 5 describes the birth process and the tiny traveler who emerges into a child's world.

Linkups to Look For

- A combination of biological, psychological, social, economic, and cultural factors may shape development beginning at conception.
- Fetuses seem to prefer their mother's voice to the voice of another woman.
- A family's socioeconomic status and other aspects of the social and cultural environment may affect the availability and utilization of prenatal care and, thus, the health of a newborn.
- Many prospective mothers are as concerned about emotional and social aspects of the setting in which their infants come into the world as they are about medical arrangements.
- Protective factors that reduce the impact of complications of birth include an affectionate, supportive family and rewarding experiences in school, work, or place of worship.

chapter

3

Forming a New Life: Conception, Heredity, and Environment

Of the cell, the wondrous seed
Becoming plant and animal and mind
Unerringly forever after its kind . . .

—William Ellery Leonard, *Two Lives,* 1923

Focus *Louise Brown, the First "Test-Tube Baby"*

Louise Brown

The writer Aldous Huxley foresaw it in 1932: human life created in the laboratory. As Huxley described it in his novel *Brave New World,* the feat would be accomplished by immersing female *ova* (egg cells), which had been incubated in test tubes, in a dish of free-swimming male sperm. Huxley envisioned his "brave new world" as 600 years off; yet it took only 46 years for a birth through *in vitro fertilization,* or fertilization outside the mother's body, to become a reality.

Louise Brown, the world's first documented "test-tube baby," was born July 25, 1978, at a four-story red brick hospital in the old textile mill town of Oldham in northwest England. She had been conceived, not in a test tube, but by placing a ripe ovum from her 30-year-old mother, Lesley Brown, in a shallow glass dish with fluid containing sperm from her 38-year-old father, John Brown. After 2 days, during which the resulting single-celled organism multiplied to 8 cells, the embryo was implanted in Lesley's womb.

Until this event, Lesley and her husband, a truck driver for the British Railway Network, were—by their own description—an ordinary couple who lived in a low-rent row house in Bristol. Although they were raising John's 17-year-old daughter from a previous marriage, they desperately wanted to have a baby together. After seven years of failure to conceive, they turned to the then-experimental *in vitro* method. The fulfillment of the Browns' wish was the culmination of more than a decade of painstaking preparatory research by Patrick Steptoe, a gynecologist, and Robert Edwards, a physiologist at Cambridge University. The outcome was far more than a single baby. Steptoe's and Edwards's work gave birth to a new branch of medicine: *assisted reproductive technology.*

Questions were in the air as Lesley and John Brown awaited the birth of what was to be called, in banner headlines, the "Miracle Baby" and "Baby of the Century." Despite strenuous efforts by the couple and their doctors to keep the birth secret, the news leaked out. Hordes of newspaper and television reporters from around the world hovered outside the hospital and, later, camped on the Browns' front lawn.

The story launched a debate about the moral implications of tampering with nature—and, down the road, the possibility of mass baby farms and reproductive engineering, which

Sources of information about Louise Brown are Barthel (1982); Faltermayer et al. (1996); Lawson (1993); "Louise Brown" (1984); "Louise Brown" (1994); "Test-Tube Baby" (1978); "The First Test-Tube Baby" (1978); & Van Dyck (1995).

could alter or custom design the "products" of reproduction. People raised more immediate concerns about the risks to mother and baby. What if the baby was born grossly deformed? Could *any* baby conceived in a laboratory dish have a normal life?

Lesley was checked and monitored more frequently than most expectant mothers are, and, as a precaution, spent the last three months of her pregnancy in the hospital. The birth took place about two weeks before the due date, by cesarean delivery, because Lesley had developed toxemia (blood poisoning), and the fetus did not seem to be gaining weight. The delivery went smoothly without further complications.

The blond, blue-eyed, 5-pound 12-ounce baby was, from all accounts, a beautiful, normal infant, who emerged crying lustily. "There's no difference between her and any other little girl," her father maintained. "We just helped nature a bit" ("Louise Brown," 1984, p. 82).

By the time Louise celebrated her fourth birthday, she had a "test-tube" sister, Natalie, born June 14, 1982. Lesley and John used part of the nest egg obtained from interview, book, and film rights to buy a modest house; the rest remained in trust for the children.

On Louise Brown's 25th birthday, about 1,000 of the more than 1 million in vitro children estimated to have been born as a result of that procedure gathered to celebrate the occasion. Brown, who had recently become engaged to a 33-year-old bank security officer, said she had no immediate plans to start a family and just wanted to be treated as a "normal person." Her sister Natalie, at 20, had two children, both conceived normally (Daley, 2003).

• • •

What made Louise Brown the person she is? Like any other child, she began with a hereditary endowment from her mother and father. For example, she has her father's stocky build, wide forehead, and chubby cheeks and her mother's tilted nose and curved mouth—as well as her mother's sudden temper. Louise also has been affected by a host of environmental influences, from that famous laboratory dish to the tremendous public interest in her story. As a preschooler, she was mentally precocious, mischievous, and (by her parents' admission) spoiled. As a teenager, like many of her classmates, she liked to swim and ride horses, wore two gold studs in each ear, watched MTV, and had a crush on the actor Tom Cruise.

Most children do not become famous, especially at birth; but every child is the product of a unique combination of hereditary and environmental influences set in motion by the parents' decision to form a new life. We begin this chapter by examining how a life is conceived, either through normal reproduction or through alternative technologies, some of them developed since Louise Brown's birth. We consider the mechanisms and patterns of heredity—the inherited factors that affect development—and how genetic counseling can help couples make the decision to become parents. We look at how heredity and environment work together and how their effects on development can be studied.

After you have read and studied this chapter, you should be able to answer each of the Guidepost questions that follow. Look for them again in the margins, where they point to important concepts throughout the chapter. To check your understanding of these Guideposts, review the end-of-chapter summary. Checkpoints located at periodic spots throughout the chapter will help you verify your understanding of what you have read.

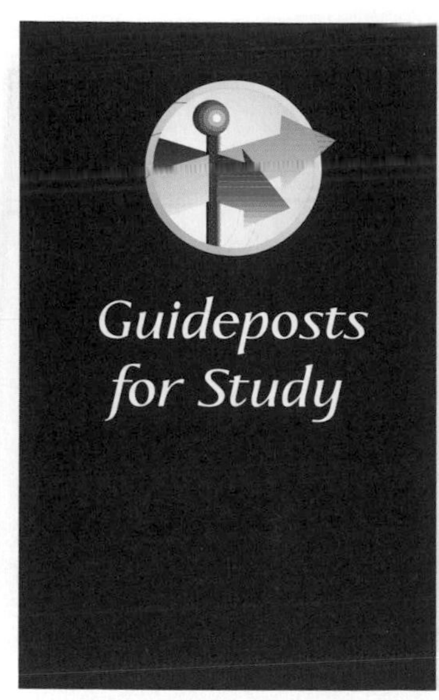

1. How does conception normally occur, and how have beliefs about conception changed?
2. What causes multiple births?
3. What causes infertility, and what are alternative ways of becoming parents?
4. What genetic mechanisms determine sex, physical appearance, and other characteristics?
5. How are birth defects and disorders transmitted?
6. How do scientists study the relative influences of heredity and environment, and how do heredity and environment work together?
7. What roles do heredity and environment play in physical health, intelligence, and personality?

Becoming Parents

The choice, timing, and circumstances of parenthood can have vast consequences for a child. Whether a birth is planned or accidental, whether the pregnancy is welcomed or unwanted, whether it comes about through normal or extraordinary means, whether the parents are married or unmarried, whether they are of the same sex or different sexes, and how old the parents are when a child is conceived or adopted all are factors in the *microsystem* identified in Bronfenbrenner's bioecological approach (refer to Chapter 2). Whether the culture encourages large or small families, whether it values one sex over the other, and how much it supports families with children are *macrosystem* issues likely to influence that child's development.

We'll explore such contextual issues throughout this book. For now, let us look at the act of conception and then at options for couples unable to conceive normally.

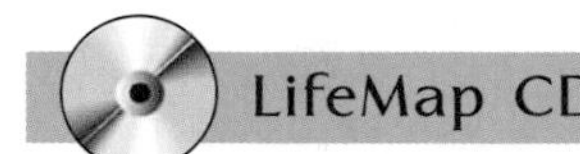

To learn more about what it's like to become a parent, watch the "Transition to Parenting" video in Chapter 3 of your CD.

Conception

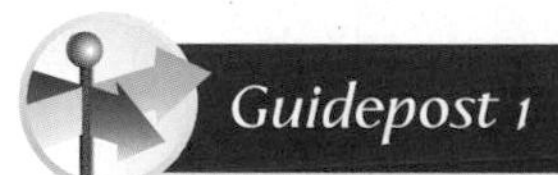

How does conception normally occur, and how have beliefs about conception changed?

Most adults, and even most children in developed countries, have a reasonably accurate idea of where babies come from. Yet only a generation or two ago, many parents told their children that a stork had brought them. The folk belief that children came from wells, springs, or rocks was common in north and central Europe as late as the beginning of the 20th century. Conception was believed to be influenced by cosmic forces. A baby conceived under a new moon would be a boy; during the moon's last quarter, a girl (Gélis, 1991).

*Changing Theories of Conception**

Theories about conception go back to ancient times. The Greek physician Hippocrates, known as the father of medicine, held that a fetus results from the joining of male and female seeds. The philosopher Aristotle had a contrary view that "the woman functions only as a receptacle, the child being formed exclusively by means of the sperm" (Fontanel & d'Harcourt, 1997, p. 10). According to Aristotle, the production of male babies was in the natural order of things; a female came about only if development was disturbed.

Between the 17th and 19th centuries, a debate raged between two schools of biological thought. Harking back to Aristotle, the *animalculists* (so named because the male sperm were then called *animalcules*) claimed that fully formed "little people" were contained in

*Unless otherwise referenced, this discussion is based on Eccles, 1982, and Fontanel & d'Harcourt, 1997.

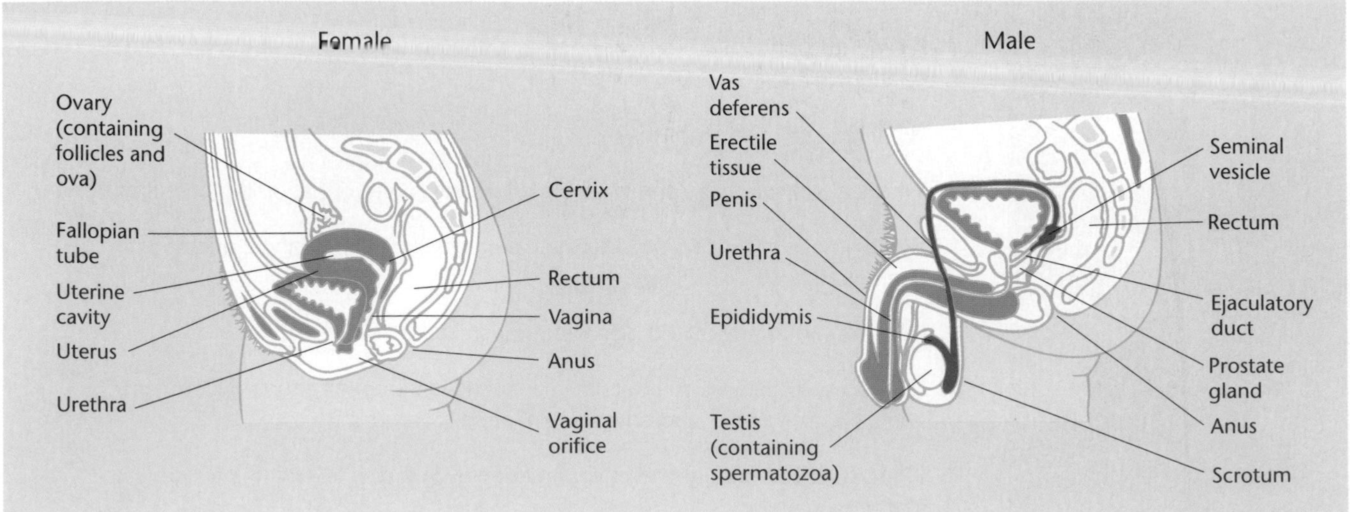

Figure 3-1
Human reproductive systems.

the heads of sperm, ready to grow when deposited in the nurturing environment of the womb. The *ovists,* inspired by the influential work of the English physician William Harvey, held an opposite but equally incorrect view: that a female's ovaries contained tiny, already formed humans whose growth was activated by the male's sperm. Finally, in the late 18th century, German-born anatomist Kaspar Friedrich Wolff demonstrated that embryos are not preformed in either parent and that both parents contribute equally to the formation of a new being.

How Fertilization Takes Place

clone *(verb)* To make a genetic copy of an individual; *(noun)* a genetic copy of an individual.

Although scientists have now found a way to **clone** (make a genetic copy of) a human being, and this has value for therapeutic research purposes (Cibelli, Lanza, & West, 2002), ethical and religious concerns about the dignity of individual human life make it unlikely—at least in the near future—that cloning will become a common means of reproduction. Until that happens, virtually every person's biological beginning will continue to be a split-second event when a single sperm from the biological father joins an ovum from the biological mother. As we will see, which sperm meets which ovum has tremendous implications for the new person.

fertilization Fusion of sperm and ovum to produce a zygote; also called *conception.*

zygote One-celled organism resulting from fertilization.

Fertilization, or conception, is the process by which sperm and ovum—the male and female *gametes,* or sex cells—combine to create a single cell called a **zygote**, which then duplicates itself again and again by cell division to become a baby. It has long been believed that at birth, a girl has about 2 million immature ova in her two ovaries (see Figure 3-1), each ovum in its own small sac, or *follicle.* However, new research in mice has found that new ova continue to develop during adulthood from stem cells in the ovary, and this may well be true of adult women as well (Johnson, Canning, Kaneko, Pru, & Tilly, 2004). In a sexually mature woman, *ovulation*—rupture of a mature follicle in either ovary and expulsion of its ovum—occurs about once every 28 days until menopause. The ovum is swept along through the fallopian tube by tiny hair cells, called *cilia,* toward the uterus, or womb. Fertilization normally occurs during the brief time the ovum is passing through the fallopian tube.

Sperm are produced in the testicles (testes), or reproductive glands, of a mature male (refer to Figure 3-1) at a rate of several hundred million a day and are ejaculated in the semen at sexual climax. They enter the vagina and try to swim through the *cervix* (the opening of the uterus) and into the fallopian tubes, but only a tiny fraction make it that far.

Fertilization is most likely if intercourse occurs on the day of ovulation or during the five days before (Wilcox, Weinberg, & Baird, 1995). If fertilization does not occur, the

These monozygotic twins look almost exactly alike but may differ in temperament or in other ways.

ovum and any sperm cells in the woman's body die. The sperm are absorbed by the woman's white blood cells, and the ovum passes through the uterus and exits through the vagina.

What Causes Multiple Births?

Guidepost 2

What causes multiple births?

The incidence of multiple births in the United States has grown rapidly. Between 1980 and 2002, the number of live twin births more than doubled, from 68,339 to 125,134, and the number of triplets and larger multiples nearly sextupled from 1,337 to 7,401 (Martin, Hamilton, Ventura, Menacker, & Park, 2002; Martin et al., 2003).

Multiple births may occur in two ways. Most commonly, the mother's body releases two ova within a short time (or sometimes, perhaps, a single unfertilized ovum splits), and then both are fertilized. The resulting babies are **dizygotic (two-egg) twins**, commonly called *fraternal twins*. The second way is for a single *fertilized* ovum to split into two. The babies that result from this cell division are **monozygotic (one-egg) twins**, commonly called *identical twins*. Triplets, quadruplets, and other multiple births can result from either of these processes or a combination of both.

dizygotic (two-egg) twins Twins conceived by the union of two different ova (or a single ovum that has split) with two different sperm cells; also called *fraternal twins*.

monozygotic (one-egg) twins Twins resulting from the division of a single zygote after fertilization; also called *identical twins*.

temperament Characteristic disposition, or style of approaching and reacting to situations.

Monozygotic twins have the same hereditary makeup and are the same sex, but—in part because of differences in prenatal as well as postnatal experience—they differ in some respects. They may not be identical in **temperament** (disposition, or style of approaching and reacting to situations). In some physical characteristics, such as hair whorls, dental patterns, and handedness, they may be mirror images of each other; for example, one may be left-handed and the other right-handed. Dizygotic twins, who are created from different sperm cells and usually from different ova, are no more alike in hereditary makeup than any other siblings and may be different sexes.

The main factor in the rise in multiple births is the increased use of fertility drugs, which spur ovulation, and of such techniques as in vitro fertilization. Their use varies among ethnic groups; twinning rates are approximately equal among non-Hispanic white and black mothers—about 35 per 1,000—but less than 21 per 1,000 among Hispanic mothers. Another factor in the rise in multiple births is a trend toward delayed childbearing. Multiple births are more common among older women (Martin et al., 2003).

The explosion of multiple births, especially triplets and higher-order multiples, is of concern, since such births are associated with increased risks: pregnancy complications, premature delivery, low-birth-weight infants, and disability or death of the infant. Perhaps because of such concerns, the proportion of artificial procedures involving three or more embryos declined between 1997 and 2001, and the birth rate for triplets and higher multiples has taken a slight downturn (Jain, Missmer, & Hornstein, 2004; Martin et al., 2003; Wright, Schieve, Reynolds, & Jeng, 2003).

Guidepost 3

What causes infertility, and what are alternative ways of becoming parents?

infertility Inability to conceive after 12 to 18 months of trying.

Infertility

At some point in their lives, an estimated 7 percent of U.S. couples experience **infertility**: inability to conceive a baby after 12 to 18 months of trying (Centers for Disease Control & Prevention, 2001a). Women's fertility begins to decline in the late 20s, with substantial decreases during the 30s. Men's fertility is less affected by age but declines significantly by the late 30s (Dunson, Colombo, & Baird, 2002).

Infertility is far from a new concern. To enhance fertility, ancient doctors advised men to eat fennel, and women to drink the saliva of lambs and wear necklaces of earthworms. It was recommended that, after intercourse, a woman lie flat with her legs crossed and "avoid becoming angry" (Fontanel & d'Harcourt, 1997, p. 10). By the Renaissance, the list of foods recommended to spur conception ranged from squabs and sparrows to cocks' combs and bull's genitals. In the early 17th century, Louise Bourgeois, midwife to Marie de Médicis, the queen of France, advocated bathing the vagina with chamomile, mallow, marjoram, and catmint boiled in white wine.

Today we know that the most common cause of infertility in men is production of too few sperm. Although only one sperm is needed to fertilize an ovum, a sperm count lower than 60 to 200 million per ejaculation makes conception unlikely. In some instances an ejaculatory duct may be blocked, preventing the exit of sperm, or sperm may be unable to "swim" well enough to reach the cervix. Some cases of male infertility seem to have a genetic basis (King, 1996; Reijo, Alagappan, Patrizio, & Page, 1996; Phillips, 1998).

In a woman, the cause of infertility may be the failure to produce ova or to produce normal ova; mucus in the cervix, which might prevent sperm from penetrating it; or a disease of the uterine lining, which might prevent implantation of the fertilized ovum. A major cause of declining fertility in women after age 30 is deterioration in the quality of ova (van Noord-Zaadstra et al., 1991). However, the most common cause is the problem Lesley Brown had: blockage of the fallopian tubes, preventing ova from reaching the uterus. In about half of these cases, the tubes are blocked by scar tissue from sexually transmitted diseases (King, 1996).

Infertility can burden a marriage emotionally. Partners may become frustrated and angry with themselves and each other and may feel empty, worthless, and depressed (Abbey, Andrews, & Halman, 1992; Jones & Toner, 1993). However, only when infertility leads to permanent, involuntary childlessness is it associated with long-term psychological distress (McQuillan, Greil, White, & Jacob, 2003).

Sometimes hormone treatment, drug therapy, or surgery may correct the problem. However, as we have mentioned, fertility drugs increase the likelihood of multiple, high-risk births. Also, men undergoing fertility treatment are at increased risk of producing sperm with chromosomal abnormalities (Levron et al., 1998). Daily supplements of coenzyme Q10, an antioxidant, may help increase sperm motility (Balercia et al., 2004).

Couples who have been unable to bear children after one year should not necessarily rush into fertility treatments. Unless there is a known cause for failure to conceive, the chances of success after 18 months to two years are high. Among 782 women in six European countries, 9 out of 10 even of those in their late 30s were able to conceive by the end of the second year of trying, unless the male partner was over 40 (Dunson, 2002). Pregnancies that occur after a year or more of trying—even if they occur without treatment—need to be monitored closely, as there is greater risk of preterm births, low birth-weight babies, and cesarean deliveries (Basso & Baird, 2003).

Since human beings seldom abandon their desires simply because they run into obstacles, it is no surprise that many infertile adults who want children, like Lesley and John Brown, eagerly embrace techniques that bypass ordinary biological processes (see Box 3-1). Others choose the more traditional route of adoption (see Chapter 14).

Checkpoint

Can you . . .

- ✔ Explain how and when fertilization normally takes place?
- ✔ Distinguish between monozygotic and dizygotic twins, and tell how each comes about?
- ✔ Identify several causes of male and female infertility?
- ✔ Describe four means of assisted reproduction, and mention several issues they raise?

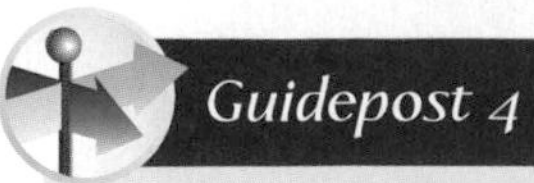

Guidepost 4

What genetic mechanisms determine sex, physical appearance, and other characteristics?

Mechanisms of Heredity

The science of genetics is the study of *heredity*—the inborn factors, inherited from the biological parents, that affect development. When ovum and sperm unite—whether by normal fertilization or by assisted reproduction, as with Louise Brown—they endow the

The Everyday World

Box 3-1 *Alternative Ways to Parenthood*

Since the birth of Louise Brown in 1978 as a result of *in vitro fertilization (IVF),* 1.4 million children worldwide have been conceived through assisted reproduction (Reaney, 2003). In 2000, more than 25,000 U.S. women delivered with technological help, giving birth to more than 35,000 babies (Wright, Schieve, Reynolds, & Jeng, 2003), nearly 1 percent of all babies born in the United States in that year (Martin, Hamilton et al., 2002).

In IVF, the most common assisted reproduction procedure, fertility drugs are given to increase production of ova. Then one or more mature ova are surgically removed, fertilized in a laboratory dish, and implanted in the woman's uterus. Usually 50,000 to 100,000 sperm are used to increase the chances of fertilization, and several embryos are transferred to the uterus to increase the chances of pregnancy. This also increases the likelihood of multiple, usually premature, births (Wennerholm & Bergh, 2000). A newer technique, *in vitro maturation (IVM)* is performed earlier in the monthly cycle, when as many as 30 to 50 egg follicles are developing. Normally, only one of these will mature. Harvesting a large number of follicles before ovulation is complete and then allowing them to mature in the laboratory can make hormone injections unnecessary and diminish the likelihood of multiple births (Duenwald, 2003).

Many women, like Louise Brown's mother, have turned to IVF because their fallopian tubes were blocked or scarred beyond surgical repair. IVF also can address severe male infertility, since a single sperm can be injected into the ovum—a technique called *intracytoplasmic sperm injection (ICSI).* However, there is a significant risk of transmission of a genetic defect that can cause infertility in the offspring.

Artificial insemination—injection of sperm into a woman's vagina, cervix, or uterus—can be used to facilitate conception if a man has a low sperm count. Sperm from several ejaculations can be combined for one injection. Thus, with help, a couple can produce their own biological offspring. If the man is infertile, a couple may choose *artificial insemination by a donor (AID).* If the woman has no explainable cause of infertility, the chances of success can be greatly increased by stimulating her ovaries to produce excess ova and injecting semen directly in the uterus (Guzick et al., 1999).

A woman who is producing poor-quality ova or who has had her ovaries removed may try *ovum transfer.* In this procedure, an ovum, or *donor egg*—provided, usually anonymously, by a fertile young woman—is fertilized in the laboratory and implanted in the prospective mother's uterus. In *blastocyst transfer,* the fertilized ovum is kept in the culture until it grows to the blastocyst stage; but this method has been linked to an increase in identical twin births (Duenwald, 2003). Alternatively, the ovum can be fertilized in the donor's body by artificial insemination. The donor's uterus is flushed out a few days later, and the embryo is retrieved and inserted into the recipient's uterus.

Although success rates have improved since 1978 (Duenwald, 2003), only 30.8 percent of the 99,629 U.S. women who attempted assisted reproduction in 2000 had live births, and 53 percent of these were multiple births. Chances of success are highest for women under age 35 (Wright et al., 2003). Whether a woman's own eggs or donor eggs are used does not seem to make a significant difference (Thum et al., 2003). Two relatively new techniques with higher success rates are *gamete intrafallopian transfer (GIFT)* and *zygote intrafallopian transfer (ZIFT),* in which either the egg and sperm or the fertilized egg are inserted in the fallopian tube (CDC, 2002b; Schieve et al., 2002; Society for Assisted Reproductive Technology, 1993, 2002).

How do children conceived by artificial means turn out? Results vary. In Western Australia between 1993 and 1997, babies conceived by IVF or ICSI were twice as likely to show major birth defects during the first year as infants conceived naturally (Hansen, Kurinczuk, Bower, & Webb, 2002). A survey of Danish mothers who gave birth in 1997 found the general health of IVF and ICSI twins to be comparable to that of other twins born the same year but poorer than that of IVF/ICSI singletons, who tended to have higher birth weight (Pinbrog, Loft, Schmidt, & Andersen, 2003). In a longitudinal study of 1,523 British, Belgian, Danish, Swedish, and Greek infants, there were no major differences in physical development, health, and other aspects of development at age 5 between those born through IVF or ICSI and those conceived normally. The groups also did not differ in behavioral problems or temperamental difficulties. However, children born through ICSI did have a higher rate of congenital urological and kidney abnormalities (Barnes et al., 2003; Sutcliffe, Loft, Wennerholm, Tarlatzis, & Bonduelle, 2003). Longitudinal studies of children conceived by IVF or by donor insemination found little or no difference in socioemotional development at age 12 between these children and naturally conceived or adopted children (Golombok, MacCallum, & Goodman, 2001; Golombok, MacCallum, Goodman, & Rutter, 2002).

In *surrogate motherhood,* a fertile woman is impregnated by the prospective father, usually by artificial insemination. She carries the baby to term and gives the child to the father and his mate. Surrogate motherhood is in legal limbo; courts in most states view surrogacy contracts as unenforceable, and some states have either banned the practice or placed strict conditions on it. The American Academy of Pediatrics (AAP) Committee on Bioethics (1992) recommends that surrogacy be considered a tentative, preconception adoption agreement. The committee also recommends a prebirth agreement on the period of time in which the surrogate may assert her parental rights.

Perhaps the most objectionable aspect of surrogacy, aside from the possibility of forcing the surrogate to relinquish the baby, is the payment of money. The creation of a "breeder class" of poor and disadvantaged women who carry the babies of the well-to-do strikes many people as wrong. Similar concerns have been raised about payment for donor eggs. Exploitation of the would-be parents is an issue, too (Gabriel, 1996). However, a study of 42 families with infants born through surrogacy found that these parents adjusted better to their first year of parenthood than parents in control groups who had conceived children naturally or through egg donation. The surrogacy parents reported lower stress, showed more warmth to their babies, and enjoyed parenthood more than the other two groups—perhaps because these were highly committed parents raising extremely wanted children (Golombok, Murray, Jadva, MacCallum, & Lycett, 2004).

One thing seems certain: As long as there are people who want children but are unable to conceive or bear them, human ingenuity and technology will come up with ways to satisfy their need.

What's your view?

If you or your partner were infertile, would you seriously consider or undertake one of the methods of assisted reproduction described here? Why or why not?

Check it out!

For more information on this topic, go to **http://www.nichd.nih.gov/publications/pubs/counrs/sub3.htm**. This Web site features research highlights about assisted reproduction technology.

baby-to-be with a genetic makeup that influences a wide range of characteristics from color of eyes and hair to health, intellect, and personality.

The Genetic Code

deoxyribonucleic acid (DNA) Chemical that carries inherited instructions for the formation and function of body cells.

The basis of heredity is a chemical called **deoxyribonucleic acid (DNA),** which contains all the inherited material passed from biological parents to children. DNA carries the biochemical instructions that direct the formation of each cell in the body and tell the cells how to make the proteins that enable them to carry out specific body functions.

The structure of DNA resembles a long, spiraling ladder made of four chemical units called *bases* (see Figure 3-2). The bases—adenine, thymine, cytosine, and guanine—are known by their initials: A, T, C, and G. They pair up in four combinations—AT, TA, CG, and GC—and coil around each other. The sequence of 3 billion base pairs constitutes the **genetic code,** which determines all inherited characteristics.

genetic code Sequence of base pairs within DNA, which determine inherited characteristics.

chromosomes Coils of DNA that carry genes.

genes Small segments of DNA located in definite positions on particular chromosomes.

human genome Complete sequence or mapping of genes in the human body and their locations.

Within each cell nucleus are **chromosomes,** coils of DNA that contain smaller segments called **genes,** the "molecules of life," which are the functional units of heredity. Each gene is a small unit of DNA, located in a definite position on its chromosome, and each gene contains the chemical blueprint for building a specific protein that affects a specific aspect of the body's functioning, such as eye color or physical build. A typical gene contains thousands of base pairs.

The complete sequence of genes in the human body constitutes the **human genome.** The genome specifies the order in which genes are expressed, or activated. In 2001, two teams of scientists completed the mapping of the human genome, which is estimated to contain between 30,000 and 40,000 genes, far fewer than the 80,000 to 100,000 previously estimated (McKusick, 2001). This project has greatly advanced our ability to identify which genes control specific traits or behaviors (Parke, 2004).

Most human genes seem to be similar to those of other animals; all but 300 human genes have counterparts in mice (Wade, 2001), and the genomes of humans and chimpanzees are nearly 99 percent alike (Clark et al., 2003). Indeed, chimps and humans of the same sex are no more different genetically than are men and women (Rozen et al., 2003).

Every cell in the normal human body except the sex cells has 23 pairs of chromosomes—46 in all. Through a type of cell division called *meiosis,* each sex cell, or gamete (sperm or ovum), ends up with only 23 chromosomes—one from each pair. Thus, when sperm and ovum fuse at conception, they produce a zygote with 46 chromosomes, half from the father and half from the mother.

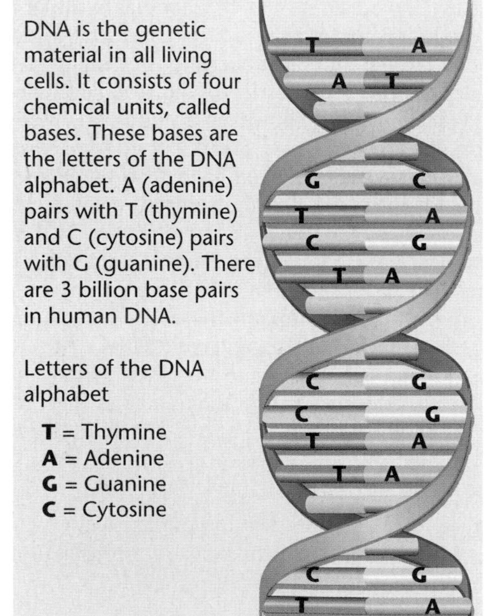

DNA is the genetic material in all living cells. It consists of four chemical units, called bases. These bases are the letters of the DNA alphabet. A (adenine) pairs with T (thymine) and C (cytosine) pairs with G (guanine). There are 3 billion base pairs in human DNA.
Letters of the DNA alphabet
T = Thymine
A = Adenine
G = Guanine
C = Cytosine
T A
A T
G C
T A
C G
T A
C G
C G
T A
T A
C G
T A

Figure 3-2

DNA: The genetic code.

Source: Ritter, 1999.

Three-quarters of the genes every child receives are identical to those received by every other child; they are called *monomorphic genes.* The other one-quarter of a child's genes are *polymorphic genes,* which define each person as an individual. Since many of these come in several variations, and since meiotic division is random, it is virtually impossible for any two children (other than monozygotic twins) to receive exactly the same combination of genes.

At conception, then, the single-celled zygote has all the biological information needed to guide its development into a human baby. This happens through *mitosis,* a process by which the cells divide over and over again. When a cell divides, the DNA spirals replicate themselves, so that each newly formed cell has the same DNA structure as all the others. Thus, each cell division creates a duplicate of the original cell, with the same hereditary information. When development is normal, each cell (except the gametes) continues to have 46 chromosomes identical to those in the original zygote. As the cells divide and the child grows and develops, the cells differentiate, specializing in a variety of complex bodily functions.

Genes control, not only specific traits, but also the developmental unfolding of these traits (Parke, 2004). Genes spring into action when conditions call for the information they can provide. Genetic action that triggers growth of body and brain is often regulated by hormonal levels, which are affected by such environmental conditions as nutrition and stress. Thus, from the start, heredity and environment are interrelated (Brown, 1999).

What Determines Sex?

In many villages in Nepal, it is common for a man whose wife has borne no male babies to take a second wife. In some societies, a woman's failure to produce sons is justification for divorce. The irony in these customs is that it is the father's sperm that normally determines a child's sex.

At the moment of conception, the 23 chromosomes from the sperm and the 23 from the ovum form 23 pairs. Twenty-two pairs are **autosomes,** chromosomes that are not related to sexual expression. The 23d pair are **sex chromosomes**—one from the father and one from the mother—which govern the baby's sex.

autosomes Twenty-two pairs of chromosomes not related to sexual expression.

sex chromosomes Pair of chromosomes that determines sex: XX in the normal female, XY in the normal male.

Sex chromosomes are either *X chromosomes* or *Y chromosomes.* The sex chromosome of every ovum is an X chromosome, but the sperm may contain either an X or a Y chromosome. The Y chromosome contains a gene for maleness, the *SRY gene.* When an ovum (X) is fertilized by an X-carrying sperm, the zygote formed is XX, a female. When an ovum (X) is fertilized by a Y-carrying sperm, the resulting zygote is XY, a male (see Figure 3-3).

Initially, the embryo's rudimentary reproductive system is no different in males than in females. About 6 to 8 weeks after conception, male embryos normally start producing the male hormone testosterone, and exposure of a genetically male embryo to steady, high levels of testosterone ordinarily results in the development of a male body with male sexual organs. However, the process is not automatic. Research with sex-reversed mice suggests that hormones in the insulin family must first signal the SRY gene, which then triggers cell differentiation and formation of the testes. Testis formation in mice also depends on the presence of another gene, *Dax1.* Without insulin family signaling and Dax1, a genetically male mouse will develop female genitals instead of male ones. It is possible that similar mechanisms occur in human males (Meeks, Weiss, & Jameson, 2003; Nef et al., 2003). Conversely, the development of female characteristics is controlled by a signaling molecule called *Wnt-4,* a mutation of which can "masculinize" a genetically female fetus (Vainio, Heikkiia, Kispert, Chin, & McMahon, 1999). Thus, sexual differentiation appears to be a more complex process than simple genetic determination.

Sometimes, after many generations, a gene may deteriorate. Because most chromosomes come in pairs (one from the mother and one from the father), they can repair damaged genes by trading parts with each other. But the Y chromosome does not have a counterpart from the mother. Instead, it carries backup copies of important genes and can use them to repair itself (Rozen et al., 2003; Skaletsky et al., 2003). In one in several thousand boys, a mistake in this process results in deletion of segments of DNA, and this is one cause of male infertility (Page, quoted in Wade, 2003).

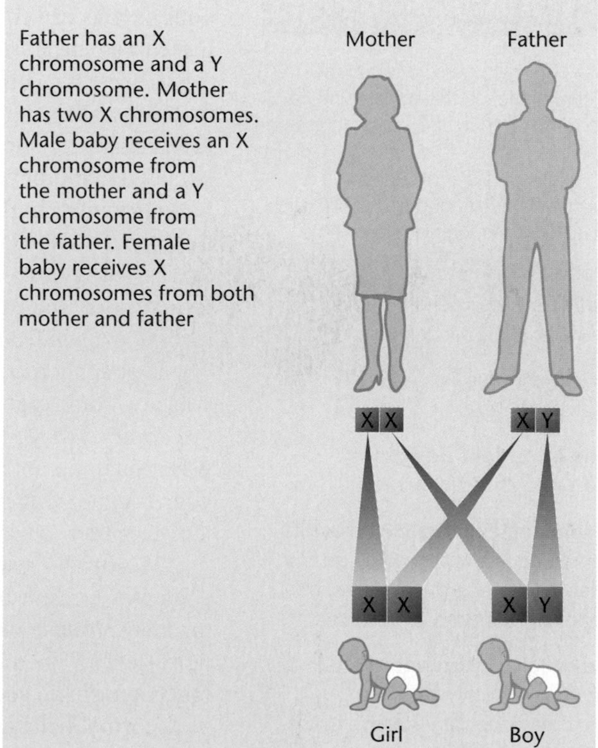

Father has an X chromosome and a Y chromosome. Mother has two X chromosomes. Male baby receives an X chromosome from the mother and a Y chromosome from the father. Female baby receives X chromosomes from both mother and father
Mother
Father
X X
X Y
X X
X Y
Girl
Boy

Figure 3-3

Determination of sex. Since all babies receive an X chromosome from the mother, sex is determined by whether an X or Y chromosome is received from the father.

Patterns of Genetic Transmission

During the 1860s, Gregor Mendel, an Austrian monk, laid the foundation for our understanding of patterns of inheritance. He crossbred pea plants that produced only yellow seeds with pea plants that produced only green seeds. The resulting hybrid plants produced only yellow seeds, meaning, he said, that yellow was *dominant* over green. Yet when he bred the yellow-seeded hybrids with each other, only 75 percent of their offspring had yellow seeds, and the other 25 percent had green seeds. This showed, Mendel said, that a hereditary characteristic (in this case, the color green) can be *recessive*; that is, carried by an organism that does not express, or show, it.

Mendel also tried breeding for two traits at once. Crossing pea plants that produced round yellow seeds with plants that produced wrinkled green seeds, he found that color and shape were independent of each other. Mendel thus showed that hereditary traits are transmitted separately.

Figure 3-4

Dominant and recessive inheritance. Because of dominant inheritance, the same observable phenotype (in this case, the ability to curl the tongue lengthwise) can result from two different genotypes (DD and Dd). A phenotype expressing a recessive characteristic (such as inability to curl the tongue) must have a homozygous genotype (dd).

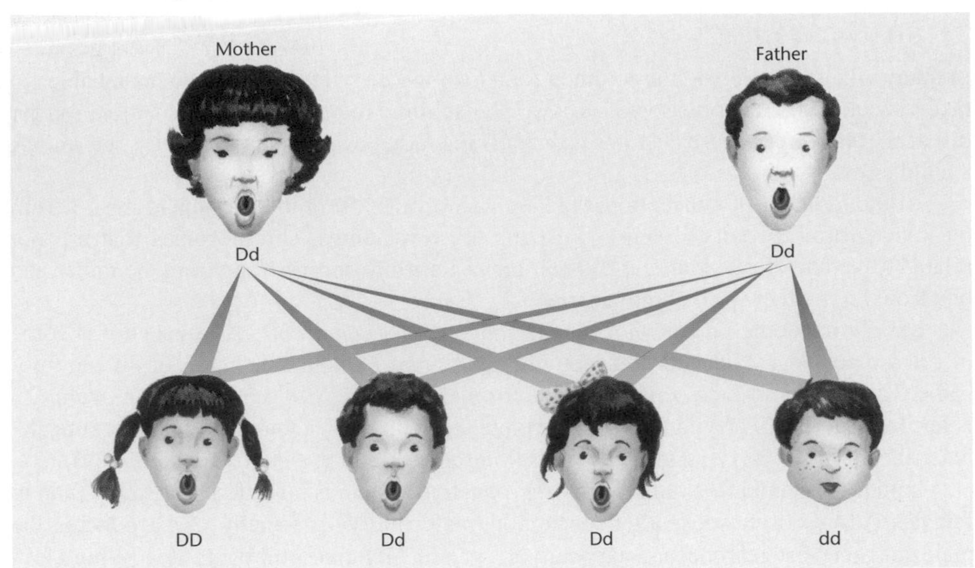

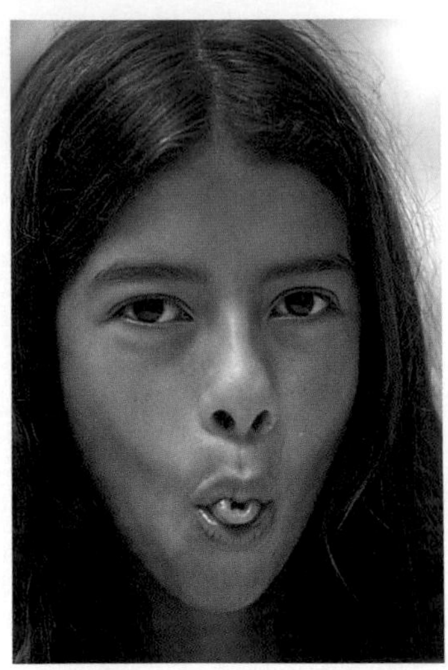

The ability to curl the tongue lengthwide, as this girl is doing, is unusual in that it is inherited through simple dominant transmission. Most normal traits are influenced by multiple genes, often in combination with environmental factors.

alleles Paired genes (alike or different) that affect a trait.

homozygous Possessing two identical alleles for a trait.

heterozygous Possessing differing alleles for a trait.

dominant inheritance Pattern of inheritance in which, when a child receives contradictory alleles, only the dominant one is expressed.

recessive inheritance Pattern of inheritance in which a child receives identical recessive alleles, resulting in expression of a nondominant trait.

polygenic inheritance Pattern of inheritance in which multiple genes affect a complex trait.

Today we know that the genetic picture in humans is far more complex than Mendel imagined. Most human traits fall along a continuous spectrum (for example, from light skin to dark). It is hard to find a single normal trait that people inherit through simple dominant transmission other than the ability to curl the tongue lengthwise.

Dominant and Recessive Inheritance

Can you curl your tongue? If so, you inherited this ability through *dominant inheritance.* If your parents can curl their tongues but you cannot, *recessive inheritance* occurred. How do these two types of inheritance work?

Genes that can produce alternative expressions of a characteristic (such as ability or inability to curl the tongue) are called **alleles.** Every person receives a pair of alleles for a given characteristic, one from each biological parent. When both alleles are the same, the person is **homozygous** for the characteristic; when they are different, the person is **heterozygous.** In **dominant inheritance**, when a person is heterozygous for a particular trait, the dominant allele governs. In other words, when an offspring receives contradictory alleles for a trait, only one of them, the dominant one, will be expressed. **Recessive inheritance**, the expression of a recessive trait, occurs only when a person receives the recessive allele from both parents.

If you inherited one allele for tongue-curling ability from each parent (see Figure 3-4), you are homozygous for tongue curling. If, say, your mother passed on an allele for the ability and your father passed on an allele lacking it, you are heterozygous. Either way, since the ability is dominant (D) and its lack is recessive (d), you, again, can curl your tongue. But if you received the recessive allele from both parents, you are not a tongue-curler.

Most traits result from **polygenic inheritance,** the interaction of several genes. Skin color is the result of three or more sets of genes on three different chromosomes, which together produce varying shades of brown pigment. Intelligence may be affected by 50 or more genes. Whereas more than a 1,000 rare genes individually determine abnormal traits, no known single gene by itself significantly accounts for individual differences in any complex normal behavior. Instead, such behaviors are likely to be influenced by many genes with small but sometimes identifiable effects. Furthermore, there may be an average of 12 different versions, or variants, of each gene, each with varying influences (Stephens et al., 2001).

Researchers in *molecular genetics* have begun to identify specific genes that contribute to particular behavioral traits, such as reading disabilities (Plomin, 2001). The locations and relative effect sizes of contributing genes, called **quantitative trait loci (QTL),** can be determined by comparing the frequency of a certain allele in large samples of unrelated people who do and do not show a trait or disorder. The larger the sample size, the smaller the effect size that can be detected (McGuffin, Riley, & Plomin, 2001; Plomin, 1995; Plomin & DeFries, 1999). In addition, **multifactorial transmission**, a combination of genetic and environmental factors, plays a role in the expression of most traits.

quantitative trait loci (QTL) Interaction of multiple genes, each with effects of varying sizes, to produce a complex trait.

multifactorial transmission Combination of genetic and environmental factors to produce certain complex traits.

Genotypes and Phenotypes: Multifactorial Transmission

If you can curl your tongue, that ability is part of your **phenotype**, the array of observable characteristics through which your **genotype**, or underlying genetic makeup, is expressed. Except for monozygotic twins, no two people have the same genotype. The phenotype is the product of the genotype and any relevant environmental influences. This is why even a clone can never be an exact duplicate of another human being.

phenotype Observable characteristics of a person.

genotype Genetic makeup of a person, containing both expressed and unexpressed characteristics.

As Figure 3-4 shows, the same phenotypical characteristic may arise from different genotypes: either a homozygous combination of two dominant alleles or a heterozygous combination of one dominant allele and one recessive allele. If you are heterozygous for tongue curling, and you and a mate who is also heterozygous for the trait have four children, the statistical probability is that one child will be homozygous for the ability, one will be homozygous lacking it, and the other two will be heterozygous. Thus, three of your children will likely have phenotypes that include tongue curling (they will be able to curl their tongues), but this ability will arise from two different genotypical patterns (homozygous and heterozygous).

Tongue curling has a strong genetic base; but for most traits, experience modifies the expression of the genotype. Imagine that Steven has inherited musical talent. If he takes music lessons and practices regularly, he may delight his family with his performances. If his family likes and encourages classical music, he may play Bach preludes; if the other children on his block influence him to prefer popular music, he may eventually form a rock group. However, if from early childhood he is not encouraged and not motivated to play music, and if he has no access to a musical instrument or to music lessons, his genotype for musical ability may not be expressed (or may be expressed to a lesser extent) in his phenotype. Some physical characteristics (including height and weight) and most psychological characteristics (such as intelligence and personality traits, as well as musical ability) are products of multifactorial transmission.

Checkpoint

Can you . . .

- ✔ Explain why no two people, other than monozygotic twins, have the same genetic heritage?
- ✔ Explain why it is the sperm that determines a baby's sex?
- ✔ Tell how dominant inheritance and recessive inheritance work, and why most normal traits are *not* the products of simple dominant or recessive transmission?

Genetic and Chromosomal Abnormalities

Guidepost 5

How are birth defects and disorders transmitted?

One of John and Lesley Brown's chief worries before Louise's birth—whether she would be a "normal" baby—is shared by every prospective biological parent. Babies born with serious birth defects are at high risk of dying at or shortly after birth or during infancy or childhood (Skjaerven, Wilcox, & Lie, 1999). Although most of these abnormalities are fairly rare, they were the leading cause of infant death in the United States in 2001, accounting for 20 percent of all deaths in the first year (Mathews, Menacker, & MacDorman, 2003). Most of the serious malformations involve the circulatory or central nervous systems (see Table 3-1).

Because many defects are hereditary, affected people risk passing them on to their children. This may be one reason that women with birth defects are less likely than other women to have children (Lie, Wilcox, & Skjaerven, 2001; Skjaerven et al., 1999).

It is in genetic defects and diseases that we see most clearly the operation of dominant and recessive transmission in humans and also of a variation, *sex-linked inheritance* (discussed in a subsequent section). Some defects are due to abnormalities in genes or chromosomes, which may result from **mutations:** permanent alterations in genetic material that may produce harmful characteristics. Mutations can occur spontaneously or can be induced by environmental hazards, such as radiation. It has been estimated that the human species undergoes at least 1.6 harmful mutations per person in each generation. Eventually, mutations may be eliminated from the human genome by **natural selection,** the failure of affected individuals to survive and reproduce (Crow, 1999; Eyre-Walker & Keightley, 1999; Keightley & Eyre-Walker, 2001).

mutations Permanent alterations in genes or chromosomes that may produce harmful characteristics.

natural selection According to Darwin's theory of evolution, process by which characteristics that promote survival of a species are reproduced in successive generations, and characteristics that do not promote survival die out.

Table 3-1 Some Birth Defects

Problem	Characteristics of Condition	Who Is at Risk	What Can Be Done
Alpha$_1$ antitrypsin deficiency	Enzyme deficiency that can lead to cirrhosis of the liver in early infancy and emphysema and degenerative lung disease in middle age.	1 in 1,000 white births	No treatment.
Alpha thalassemia	Severe anemia that reduces ability of the blood to carry oxygen; nearly all affected infants are stillborn or die soon after birth.	Primarily families of Malaysian, African, and Southeast Asian descent	Frequent blood transfusions.
Beta thalassemia (Cooley's anemia)	Severe anemia resulting in weakness, fatigue, and frequent illness; usually fatal in adolescence or young adulthood.	Primarily families of Mediterranean descent	Frequent blood transfusions.
Cystic fibrosis	Overproduction of mucus, which collects in the lung and digestive tract; children do not grow normally and usually do not live beyond age 30; the most common inherited *lethal* defect among white people.	1 in 2,000 white births	Daily physical therapy to loosen mucus; antibiotics for lung infections; enzymes to improve digestion; gene therapy (in experimental stage).
Duchenne muscular dystrophy	Fatal disease usually found in males, marked by muscle weakness; minor mental retardation is common; respiratory failure and death usually occur in young adulthood.	1 in 3,000 to 5,000 male births	No treatment.
Hemophilia	Excessive bleeding, usually affecting males rather than females; in its most severe form, can lead to crippling arthritis in adulthood.	1 in 10,000 families with a history of hemophilia	Frequent transfusions of blood with clotting factors.
Neural-tube defects:			
Anencephaly	Absence of brain tissues; infants are stillborn or die soon after birth.	1 in 1,000	No treatment.
Spina bifida	Incompletely closed spinal canal, resulting in muscle weakness or paralysis and loss of bladder and bowel control; often accompanied by hydrocephalus, an accumulation of spinal fluid in the brain, which can lead to mental retardation.	1 in 1,000	Surgery to close spinal canal prevents further injury; shunt placed in brain drains excess fluid and prevents mental retardation.
Phenylketonuria (PKU)	Metabolic disorder resulting in mental retardation.	1 in 15,000 births	Special diet begun in first few weeks of life can offset mental retardation.
Polycystic kidney disease	*Infantile form:* enlarged kidneys, leading to respiratory problems and congestive heart failure. *Adult form:* kidney pain, kidney stones, and hypertension resulting in chronic kidney failure.	1 in 1,000	Kidney transplants.
Sickle-cell anemia	Deformed, fragile red blood cells that can clog the blood vessels, depriving the body of oxygen; symptoms include severe pain, stunted growth, frequent infections, leg ulcers, gallstones, susceptibility to pneumonia, and stroke.	1 in 500 African Americans	Painkillers, transfusions for anemia and to prevent stroke, antibiotics for infections.
Tay-Sachs disease	Degenerative disease of the brain and nerve cells, resulting in death before age 5.	Historically found mainly in eastern European Jews	No treatment.

Source: Adapted from AAP Committee on Genetics, 1996; NIH Consensus Development Panel, 2001; Tisdale, 1988, pp 68–69.

Table 3-2 Chances of Genetic Disorders for Various Ethnic Groups

If You Are	The Chance Is About	That
African American	1 in 12	You are a carrier of sickle-cell anemia.
	7 in 10	You will have milk intolerance as an adult.
African American and male	1 in 10	You have a hereditary predisposition to develop hemolytic anemia after taking sulfa or other drugs.
African American and female	1 in 50	You have a hereditary predisposition to develop hemolytic anemia after taking sulfa or other drugs.
White	1 in 25	You are a carrier of cystic fibrosis.
	1 in 80	You are a carrier of phenylketonuria (PKU).
Jewish (Ashkenazic)	1 in 100	You are a carrier of familial dysautonomia.
Italian American or Greek American	1 in 10	You are a carrier of beta thalassemia.
Armenian or Jewish (Sephardic)	1 in 45	You are a carrier of familial Mediterranean fever.
Afrikaner (white South African)	1 in 330	You have porphyria.
Asian	almost 100%	You will have milk intolerance as an adult.

Source: Adapted from Milunsky, 1992, p. 122.

Many disorders arise when an inherited predisposition interacts with an environmental factor, either before or after birth. Attention deficit disorder with hyperactivity, discussed in Chapter 13, is one of a number of behavioral disorders thought to be transmitted multifactorially.

Not all genetic or chromosomal abnormalities show up at birth. Symptoms of Tay-Sachs disease (a fatal degenerative disease of the central nervous system that at one time occurred mostly among Jews of eastern European ancestry) and sickle-cell anemia (a blood disorder most common among African Americans) may not appear until at least 6 months of age; cystic fibrosis (a condition, especially common in children of northern European descent, in which excess mucus accumulates in the lungs and digestive tract), not until age 4; and glaucoma (a disease in which fluid pressure builds up in the eye) and Huntington's disease (a progressive degeneration of the nervous system), usually not until middle age.

Defects Transmitted by Dominant or Recessive Inheritance

As Mendel discovered, characteristics can be passed on from parent to child by dominant or recessive inheritance. Most of the time, normal genes are dominant over those carrying abnormal traits, but sometimes the gene for an abnormal trait is dominant. When one parent has a dominant abnormal gene and one recessive normal gene and the other parent has two recessive normal genes, each of their children has a 50-50 chance of inheriting the abnormal gene. Among the 1,800 disorders known to be transmitted by dominant inheritance are achondroplasia (a type of dwarfism) and Huntington's disease.

Recessive defects are expressed only if a child receives the same recessive gene from each biological parent. Some defects transmitted recessively, such as Tay-Sachs disease and sickle-cell anemia, are more common among certain ethnic groups, which, through inbreeding (marriage and reproduction within the group), have passed down recessive characteristics (see Table 3-2).

Defects transmitted by recessive inheritance are more likely to be lethal at an early age than those transmitted by dominant inheritance. If a dominantly transmitted defect killed before the age of reproduction, it could not be passed on to the next generation and therefore would soon disappear. A recessive defect can be transmitted by carriers who do not have the disorder and thus may live to reproduce.

incomplete dominance Partial expression of a trait.

Some traits are only partly dominant or partly recessive. In **incomplete dominance** a trait is not fully expressed. For example, people with only one sickle-cell allele and one normal allele do not have sickle-cell anemia but do show some manifestations of the condition, such as shortness of breath at high altitudes.

Defects Transmitted by Sex-Linked Inheritance

sex-linked inheritance Pattern of inheritance in which certain characteristics carried on the X chromosome inherited from the mother are transmitted differently to her male and female offspring.

In **sex-linked inheritance** (see Figure 3-5) certain recessive disorders linked to genes on the sex chromosomes show up differently in male and female children. Red-green color blindness is one of these sex-linked conditions. Another is hemophilia, a disorder in which blood does not clot when it should.

Sex-linked recessive traits are carried on one of the X chromosomes of an unaffected mother. The mother is a *carrier*; she does not have the disorder but can pass on the gene for it to her children. Sex-linked disorders almost always appear only in male children; in females, a normal dominant gene on the X chromosome from the father overrides the defective gene on the X chromosome from the mother. Boys are more vulnerable to these disorders because there is no opposite dominant gene on the shorter Y chromosome from the father to override a defect on the X chromosome from the mother. Occasionally, a female does inherit a sex-linked condition. For example, if her father is a hemophiliac and her mother happens to be a carrier for the disorder, the daughter has a 50 percent chance of receiving the abnormal X chromosome from each parent and having the disease.

Genome Imprinting

Genome, or *genetic, imprinting* is the differential expression of genetic traits, depending on whether the trait has been inherited from the mother or the father. In a few specific regions of the genome, genetic information is activated when inherited from the parent of one sex but not from the other. Since both maternal and paternal genetic material is necessary for normal development, genetic imprinting results in abnormal development.

Genome imprinting may explain why the child of a diabetic father but not of a diabetic mother is likely to develop diabetes and why the opposite is true for asthma (Day, 1993). Imprinting also may explain why children who inherit Huntington's disease from their fathers are far more likely to be affected at an early age than children who inherit the Huntington's gene from their mothers (Sapienza, 1990) and why children who receive a certain allele from their mothers are more likely to have autism than those who receive that allele from their fathers (Ingram et al., 2000).

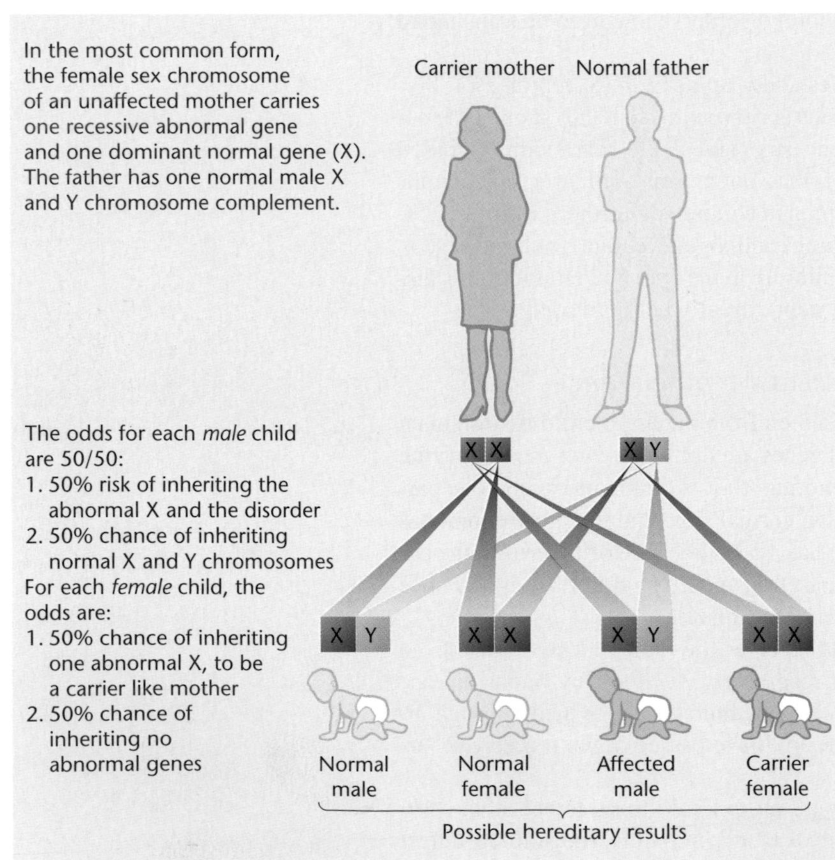

In the most common form, the female sex chromosome of an unaffected mother carries one recessive abnormal gene and one dominant normal gene (X). The father has one normal male X and Y chromosome complement.
Carrier mother
Normal father
X X
X Y
The odds for each *male* child are 50/50:
1. 50% risk of inheriting the abnormal X and the disorder
2. 50% chance of inheriting normal X and Y chromosomes
For each *female* child, the odds are:
1. 50% chance of inheriting one abnormal X, to be a carrier like mother
2. 50% chance of inheriting no abnormal genes
X Y
X X
X Y
X X
Normal male
Normal female
Affected male
Carrier female
Possible hereditary results

Figure 3-5
Sex-linked inheritance.

Chromosomal Abnormalities

About 1 in every 156 children born in western countries is estimated to have a chromosomal abnormality (Milunsky, 1992). Some of these abnormalities are inherited; others result from accidents during prenatal development and are not likely to recur in the same family.

Some chromosomal disorders, such as Klinefelter syndrome, are caused by an extra sex chromosome (shown by the pattern XXY). Others, such as Turner syndrome,

Table 3-3 Sex Chromosome Abnormalities

Pattern/Name	Characteristics*	Incidence	Treatment
XYY	Male; tall stature; tendency to low IQ, especially verbal.	1 in 1,000 male births	No special treatment
XXX (triple X)	Female; normal appearance, menstrual irregularities, learning disorders, mental retardation.	1 in 1,000 female births	Special education
XXY (Kleinfelter)	Male; sterility, underdeveloped secondary sex characteristics, small testes, learning disorders.	1 in 1,000 male births	Hormone therapy, special education
XO (Turner)	Female; short stature, webbed neck, impaired spatial abilities, no menstruation, infertility, underdeveloped sex organs, incomplete development of secondary sex characteristics.	1 in 1,500 to 2,500 female births	Hormone therapy, special education
Fragile X	Minor-to-severe mental retardation; symptoms, which are more severe in males, include delayed speech and motor development, speech impairments, and hyperactivity; the most common *inherited* form of mental retardation.	1 in 1,200 male births; 1 in 2,000 female births	Educational and behavioral therapies when needed

*Not every affected person has every characteristic.

result from a missing sex chromosome (XO). Characteristics of the most common sex chromosome disorders are shown in Table 3-3.

Other chromosomal abnormalities occur in the autosomes. **Down syndrome,** the most common of these, is responsible for about 40 percent of all cases of moderate-to-severe mental retardation (Pennington, Moon, Edgin, Stedron, & Nadel, 2003). The condition is also called *trisomy-21,* because it is usually caused by an extra 21st chromosome or the translocation of part of the 21st chromosome onto another chromosome. The most obvious physical characteristic associated with the disorder is a downward-sloping skin fold at the inner corners of the eyes.

Down syndrome Chromosomal disorder characterized by moderate-to-severe mental retardation and by such physical signs as a downward-sloping skin fold at the inner corners of the eyes.

Approximately 1 in every 600 babies born alive has Down syndrome. About 94 percent of these babies are born to normal parents (Pennington et al., 2003). The risk is greatest with older parents; when the mother is under age 35, the disorder is more likely to be hereditary. The extra chromosome seems to come from the mother's ovum in 95 percent of cases (Antonarakis & Down Syndrome Collaborative Group, 1991); the other 5 percent of cases seem to be related to the father.

The brains of these children appear normal at birth but shrink in volume by young adulthood, particularly in the hippocampal area, resulting in cognitive dysfunction (Pennington et al., 2003). The prognosis for children with Down syndrome is brighter than was once thought. As adults, many live in small group homes and support themselves; they tend to do well in structured job situations. More than 70 percent of people with Down syndrome live into their 60s, but they are at elevated risk of dying early from various causes, including leukemia, cancer, Alzheimer's disease, and cardiovascular disease (Hayes & Batshaw, 1993; Hill et al., 2003).

This boy shows the chief identifying characteristic of Down syndrome: a downward sloping skinfold at the inner corner of the eye. Although Down syndrome is a major cause of mental retardation, children with this chromosomal abnormality have a good chance of living productive lives.

Genetic Counseling and Testing

Genetic counseling can help prospective parents assess their risk of bearing children with genetic or chromosomal defects. People who have already had a child with a genetic defect, who have a family history of hereditary illness, who suffer from conditions known or suspected to be inherited, or who come from ethnic groups at higher-than-average risk of passing on genes for certain diseases can get information about their likelihood of producing affected children.

genetic counseling Clinical service that advises couples of their probable risk of having children with hereditary defects.

Figure 3-6

A karyotype is a photograph that shows the chromosomes when they are separated and aligned for cell division. We know that this is a karyotype of a person with Down syndrome, because there are three chromosomes instead of the usual two on chromosome 21.

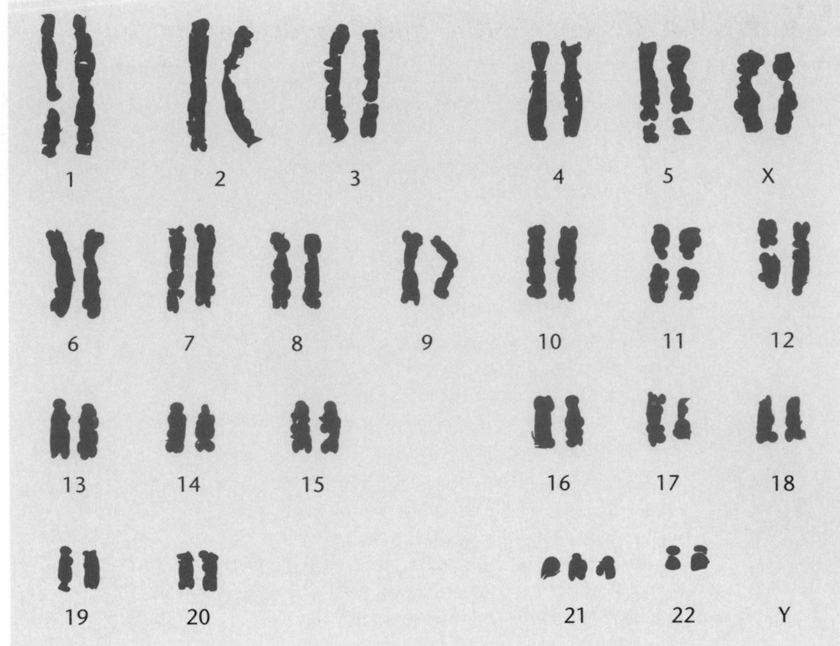

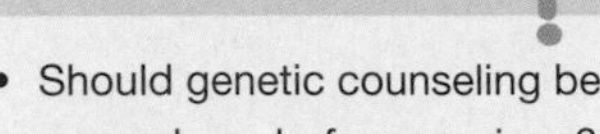

What's your view

- Should genetic counseling be compulsory before marriage?

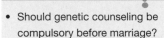

Checkpoint

Can you . . .

✔ Explain the operation of dominant inheritance, recessive inheritance, sex-linked inheritance, and genome imprinting in transmission of birth defects?

✔ Describe three ways chromosomal disorders occur?

✔ Explain the purposes of genetic counseling?

A genetic counselor may be a pediatrician, an obstetrician, a family doctor, a nurse, or a genetic specialist. She or he takes a family history and gives the prospective parents and any biological children physical examinations. Laboratory investigations of blood, skin, urine, or fingerprints may be performed. Chromosomes from body tissues may be analyzed and photographed, and the photographs enlarged and arranged according to size and structure on a chart called a *karyotype.* This chart can show chromosomal abnormalities and can indicate whether a person who appears normal might transmit genetic defects to a child (see Figure 3-6). The counselor tries to help clients understand the mathematical risk of a particular condition, explains its implications, and presents information about alternate courses of action.

Geneticists have made great contributions to avoidance of birth defects. For example, since so many Jewish couples have been tested for Tay-Sachs genes, far fewer Jewish babies have been born with the disease; in fact, it is now far more likely to affect non-Jewish babies (Kaback et al., 1993). Similarly, screening and counseling of women of childbearing age from Mediterranean countries, where beta thalassemia (refer back to Table 3-1) is common, have resulted in a decline in births of affected babies and greater knowledge of the risks of being a carrier (Cao, Saba, Galanello, & Rosatelli, 1997).

Today, researchers are rapidly identifying genes that contribute to many serious diseases and disorders as well as those that influence normal traits. Their work is likely to lead to widespread genetic testing to reveal genetic profiles—a prospect that involves dangers as well as benefits (see Box 3-2).

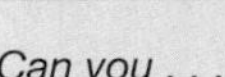

Guidepost 6

How do scientists study the relative influences of heredity and environment, and how do heredity and environment work together?

Nature and Nurture: Influences of Heredity and Environment

Which is more important, nature or nurture? That question was hotly debated by early psychologists and the general public (refer back to Chapters 1 and 2). Today it has become clear that, although certain rare physical disorders are virtually 100 percent inherited, phenotypes for most complex normal traits, such as those having to do with health, intelligence, and personality, are subject to a complex array of hereditary and environmental forces. Let us explore how scientists study and explain the influences of heredity and environment and how these two forces work together.

The Research World

Box 3-2 *Genetic Testing and Genetic Engineering*

The Human Genome Project, under the joint leadership of the National Institutes of Health and the U.S. Department of Energy in cooperation with Celera Genomics, a private firm in Rockville, Maryland, has mapped the order of DNA base pairs in all the genes in the human body. The mapping of the human genome has led to a new field of science: *genomics,* the study of the functions and interactions of the various genes in the genome. Genomics will have untold implications for *medical genetics,* the application of genetic information to therapeutic purposes (McKusick, 2001; Patenaude, Guttmacher, & Collins, 2002). As efforts shift from finding genes to understanding how they affect behavior (behavioral genomics), scientists will be able to identify genes that cause, trigger, or increase susceptibility to particular disorders (Plomin & Crabbe, 2000) so as to screen at-risk population groups (Khoury, McCabe, & McCabe, 2003).

The genetic information gained from such research could increase our ability to predict, prevent, control, treat, and cure disease—even to pinpoint specific drug treatments to specific individuals (McGuffin et al., 2001; McKusick, 2001; Patenaude et al., 2002; Rutter, 2002; Subramanian, Adams, Venter, & Broder, 2001). Already, genetic screening of newborns is saving lives and preventing mental retardation by permitting identification and treatment of infants with such disorders as sickle-cell anemia and phenylketonuria (PKU) (Holtzman, Murphy, Watson, & Barr, 1997; Khoury et al., 2003). Genetic screening for breast cancer probably would identify 88 percent of all high-risk persons, significantly more than are identified by currently used risk factors (Pharaoh et al., 2002). Genetic information can help people decide whether to have children and with whom, and it can help people with family histories of a disease to know the worst that is likely to happen (Post, 1994; Wiggins et al., 1992).

Gene therapy (repairing or replacing abnormal genes) is already an option for some genetic disorders and has been tried *in utero* (Flake et al., 1996). In 2000, French researchers reversed severe combined immunodeficiency, a serious immune disease, in three babies from 1 to 11 months old by taking bone marrow cells from the babies, genetically altering the cells, and then injecting them into the babies. The patients remained healthy as much as a year later (Cavazanna-Calvo et al., 2000).

However, human gene transfer experiments raise ethical concerns about safety, benefit to participants, and the difficulty of obtaining meaningful informed consent (Sugarman, 1999). Gene therapy carries serious risks. An 18-year-old died after being given an experimental infusion of gene-altered viruses intended to treat a liver disorder (Stolberg, 2000). A group of scientists, ethicists, lawyers, and theologians concluded that gene therapy can damage reproductive cells and that it cannot yet be safely performed on human beings (Chapman & Frankel, 2000).

Genetic testing itself involves such ethical and political issues as privacy and fair use of genetic information (Clayton, 2003; Jeffords & Daschle, 2001; Patenaude et al., 2002). Although medical data are supposed to be confidential, it is almost impossible to keep such information private. Some courts have ruled that blood relatives have a legitimate claim to information about a patient's genetic health risks that may affect them, even though such disclosures violate confidentiality (Clayton, 2003).

A major concern is *genetic determinism:* the misconception that a person with a gene for a disease is bound to get the disease. All genetic testing can tell us is the *likelihood* that a person will get a disease. Most diseases involve a complex combination of genes or depend in part on lifestyle or other environmental factors (Clayton, 2003; Plomin & Rutter, 1998; Rutter, 2002). Job and insurance discrimination on the basis of genetic information has occurred—even though tests may be imprecise and unreliable and people deemed at risk of a disease may never develop it (Clayton, 2003; Khoury et al., 2003; Lapham, Kozma, & Weiss, 1996). Federal and state antidiscrimination laws provide some protection, but it is not consistent or comprehensive (Clayton, 2003). Policies protecting confidentiality of research also are needed (Jeffords & Daschle, 2001).

The psychological impact of test results is another concern (Patenaude et al., 2002). Predictions are imperfect; a false positive result may cause needless anxiety, and a false negative result may lull a person into complacency. And what if a genetic condition is incurable? Is there any point in knowing you have the gene for a potentially debilitating condition if you cannot do anything about it? A panel of experts has recommended against genetic testing for diseases for which there is no known cure (Institute of Medicine [IOM], 1993).

Additional concerns involve the testing of children. Should a child be tested to benefit a sibling or someone else? How will a child be affected by learning that he or she is likely to develop a disease 20, 30, or 50 years later? The American Academy of Pediatrics Committee on Bioethics (2001) recommends against genetic testing of children for conditions that cannot be treated in childhood.

Particularly chilling is the prospect that genetic testing could be misused to justify sterilization of people with "undesirable" genes or abortion of a normal fetus with the "wrong" genetic makeup (Plomin & Rutter, 1998). Gene therapy has the potential for similar abuse. Should it be used to make a short child taller or a chubby child thinner? To improve an unborn baby's appearance or intelligence? The path from therapeutic correction of defects to genetic engineering for cosmetic or functional purposes may well be a slippery slope (Anderson, 1998), leading to a society in which some parents could afford to provide the "best" genes for their children and others could not (Rifkin, 1998).

Within the next 15 years, genetic testing and gene therapy "will almost certainly revolutionize the practice of medicine" (Anderson, 1998, p. 30). It is not yet clear whether the benefits of these new biotechnologies will outweigh the risks.

What's your view?

Would you want to know that you had a gene predisposing you to lung cancer? To Alzheimer's disease? Would you want your child to be tested for these genes?

Check it out!

For more information on this topic, go to **http://www.ornl.gov/hgmis/resource/medicine.html**. This is the Human Genome Project Web site. Information about disease diagnosis and prediction, disease intervention, genetic counseling, and ethical, legal, and social issues is presented.

Studying the Relative Influences of Heredity and Environment

behavioral genetics Quantitative study of relative hereditary and environmental influences.

One approach to the study of heredity and environment is quantitative: It seeks to measure *how much* heredity and environment influence particular traits. This is the traditional goal of the science of **behavioral genetics.**

Measuring Heritability

heritability Statistical estimate of the contribution of heredity to individual differences in a specific trait within a given population.

Heritability is a statistical estimate of how great a contribution heredity makes toward individual differences in a specific trait at a certain time *within a given population.* Heritability does *not* refer to the relative influence of heredity and environment in a particular individual; those influences may be virtually impossible to separate. Nor does heritability tell us how traits develop. It merely indicates the statistical extent to which genes contribute to a trait.

Heritability is expressed as a percentage ranging from 0.0 to 1.0; the greater the number, the greater the heritability of a trait, with 1.0 meaning that genes are 100 percent responsible for differences in the trait. Since heritability cannot be measured directly, researchers in behavioral genetics rely chiefly on three types of correlational research: family, adoption, and twin studies.

Such studies are based on the assumption that immediate family members are more genetically similar than more distant relatives, monozygotic twins are more genetically similar than dizygotic twins, and adopted children are genetically more like their biological families than their adoptive families. Thus, if heredity is an important influence on a particular trait, siblings should be more alike than cousins with regard to that trait, monozygotic twins should be more alike than dizygotic twins, and adopted children should be more like their biological parents than their adoptive parents. By the same token, if a shared environment exerts an important influence on a trait, persons who live together should be more similar than persons who do *not* live together.

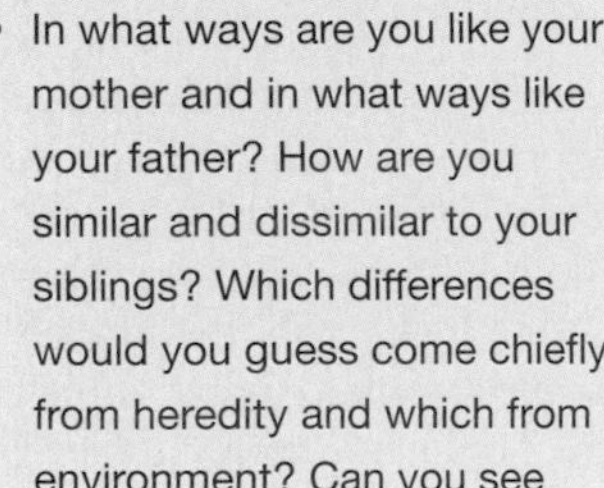

- In what ways are you like your mother and in what ways like your father? How are you similar and dissimilar to your siblings? Which differences would you guess come chiefly from heredity and which from environment? Can you see possible effects of both?

Family studies go beyond noting similarities in traits among family members, as we did for Louise Brown and her mother and father. Researchers measure the *degree* to which biological relatives share certain traits and whether the closeness of the familial relationship is associated with the degree of similarity. If the correlation is strong, the researchers infer a genetic influence. However, family studies cannot rule out environmental influences on a trait. A family study alone cannot tell us whether obese children of obese parents inherited the tendency or whether they are overweight because their diet is like that of their parents. For that reason, researchers do adoption studies, which can separate the effects of heredity from those of a shared environment.

Adoption studies look at similarities between adopted children and their adoptive families and also between adopted children and their biological families. When adopted children are more like their biological parents and siblings in a particular trait (say, obesity), we see the influence of heredity. When they resemble their adoptive families more, we see the influence of environment.

Studies of twins compare pairs of monozygotic twins and same-sex dizygotic twins. (Same-sex twins are used so as to avoid any confounding effects of gender.) Monozygotic twins are twice as genetically similar, on average, as dizygotic twins, who are no more genetically similar than other same-sex siblings. When monozygotic twins are more **concordant** (that is, have a statistically greater tendency to show the same trait) than dizygotic twins, we see the likely effects of heredity. Concordance rates, which may range from 0.0 to 1.0, estimate the probability that a pair of twins in a sample will be concordant for that trait.

concordant Term describing tendency of twins to share the same trait or disorder.

When monozygotic twins show higher concordance for a trait than do dizygotic twins, the likelihood of a genetic factor can be studied further through adoption studies. Studies of monozygotic twins separated in infancy and reared apart have found strong resemblances between the twins. Twin and adoption studies support a moderate to high hereditary basis for many normal and abnormal characteristics (McGuffin et al., 2001).

Critics of behavioral genetics claim that its assumptions and methods tend to maximize the importance of hereditary effects and minimize environmental ones. Furthermore,

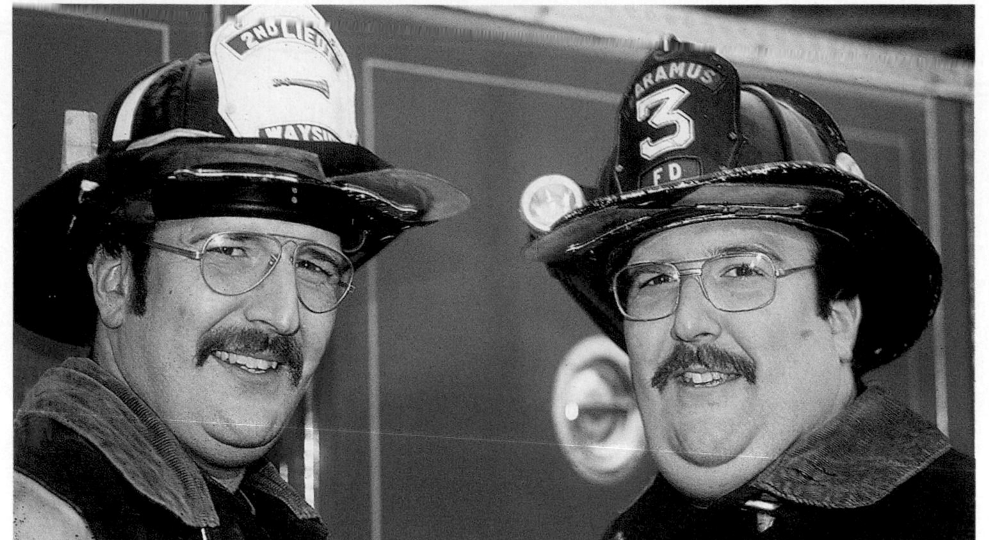

Monozygotic twins separated at birth are sought after by researchers who want to study the impact of genes on personality. These twins, adopted by different families and not reunited till age 31, both became firefighters. Was this a coincidence, or did it reflect the influence of heredity?

there are great variations in the findings, depending on the source of the data. For example, twin studies generally come up with higher heritability estimates than adoption studies do. This wide variability, critics say, "means that no firm conclusions can be drawn about the relative strength of these influences on development" (Collins, Maccoby, Steinberg, Hetherington, & Bornstein, 2000, p. 221).

Even behavioral geneticists recognize that the effects of genetic influences, especially on behavioral traits, are rarely inevitable. Even in a trait strongly influenced by heredity, the environment can have substantial impact (Rutter, 2002), as much as 50 percent. In fact, environmental interventions sometimes can overcome genetically "determined" conditions. A special diet begun soon after birth often can prevent mental retardation in children with the genetic disease phenylketonuria (PKU) (Plomin & DeFries, 1999; refer back to Table 3-1).

Effects of the Prenatal Environment

Two newer types of twin studies—*co-twin control* and *chorion control* studies—enable researchers to look at the nature and timing of nongenetic influences in the womb (Phelps, Davis, & Schartz, 1997). *Co-twin control studies* compare the prenatal (or postnatal) development and experiences of one monozygotic twin with those of the other, who serves as a one-person "control group." *Chorion control studies* focus on prenatal influences by comparing two types of monozygotic twins: (1) *monochorionic* twins, who developed within the same fluid-filled sac and thus had a similar prenatal environment, and (2) *dichorionic* twins, who grew within separate sacs, as about one-third of monozygotic twins, like all dizygotic twins, do.

Monochorionic twins normally share blood and have similar hormonal levels, which affect brain development. They also share exposure to any infectious agents that come from the mother's body. Because dichorionic twins are attached to different parts of the uterine wall, one twin may be better nourished than the other and better protected against infection. Twin studies that do not take account of these factors may either underestimate or overestimate genetic influences. Monochorionic twins tend to be more concordant than dichorionic twins in IQ, certain personality patterns, and cholesterol levels.

Checkpoint

Can you . . .

- ✔ State the basic assumption underlying studies of behavioral genetics and explain how it applies to family studies, adoption studies, and twin studies?
- ✔ Cite criticisms of the behavioral genetics approach?
- ✔ Identify two types of twin studies that focus on environmental influences in the womb?

How Heredity and Environment Work Together

Today, as research in cognitive neuroscience and molecular biology increasingly underlines the complexity of development, many developmental scientists have come to regard a solely quantitative approach to the study of heredity and environment as simplistic (Collins, Maccoby, Steinberg, Hetherington, & Bornstein, 2000). They see these two forces as fundamentally intertwined (Parke, 2004). Instead of looking at genes and experience as

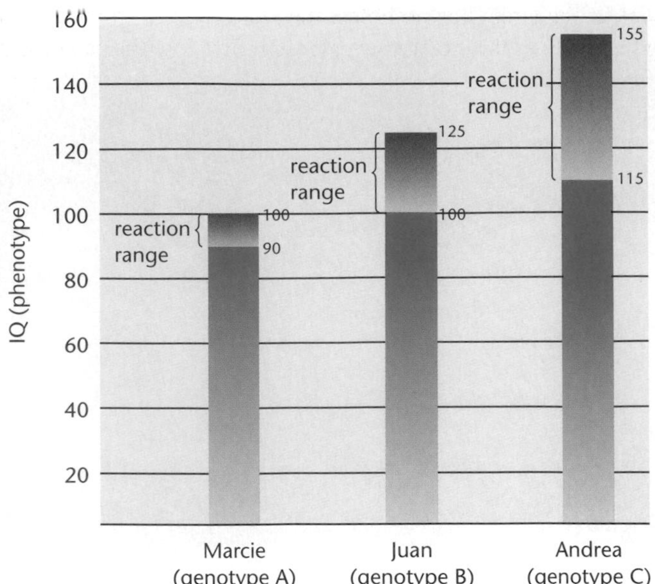

Figure 3-7

Intelligence and reaction range. Children with different genotypes for intelligence will show varying reaction ranges when exposed to a restricted (blue portion of bar) or enriched (entire bar) environment.

operating directly on an organism, they see both as part of a complex *developmental system* (Gottlieb, 1991). From conception on, throughout life, a combination of constitutional (biological and psychological), social, economic, and cultural factors help shape development. The more advantageous these circumstances and the experiences to which they give rise, the greater is the likelihood of optimum development (Horowitz, 2000).

Let us consider several ways in which inheritance and experience work together.

Reaction Range and Canalization

Many characteristics vary, within limits, under varying hereditary or environmental conditions. The concepts of *reaction range* and *canalization* can help us visualize how this happens.

reaction range Potential variability, depending on environmental conditions, in the expression of a hereditary trait.

Reaction range is the conventional term for a range of potential expressions of a hereditary trait. Body size, for example, depends largely on biological processes, which are genetically regulated. Even so, a range of sizes is possible, depending on environmental opportunities and constraints and a person's own behavior. In societies in which nutrition has dramatically improved, an entire generation has grown up to tower over the generation before. The better-fed children share their parents' genes but have responded to a healthier world. Once a society's average diet becomes adequate for more than one generation, however, children tend to grow to heights similar to their parents'. Ultimately, height has genetic limits; we do not see people who are only a foot tall or any who are 10 feet tall.

Heredity can influence whether a reaction range is wide or narrow. For example, a child born with a defect producing mild retardation is more able to respond to a favorable environment than a child born with more severe limitations. A child of normal native intelligence is likely to have a higher IQ if raised in an enriched home and school environment than if raised in a more restrictive environment; but a child with more native ability will probably have a much wider reaction range (see Figure 3-7).

Instead of envisioning a reaction range, advocates of a developmental system model prefer to think of a *norm of reaction.* Although they recognize that heredity does set some limits, they argue that, because development is so complex, these limits are unknowable and their effects unpredictable (Gottlieb, 1991).

canalization Limitation on variance of expression of certain inherited characteristics.

The metaphor of **canalization** illustrates how heredity restricts the range of development for some traits. After a heavy storm, the rainwater that has fallen on a pavement has to go somewhere. If the street has potholes, the water will fill them. If deep canals have been dug along the edges of the street, the water will flow into the canals instead. Some human characteristics, such as eye color, are so strongly programmed by genes that they are said to be highly canalized; there is little opportunity for variance in their expression.

Certain behaviors also develop along genetically "dug" channels; it takes an extreme change in environment to alter their course. Behaviors that depend largely on maturation seem to appear when a child is ready. Normal babies follow a typical sequence of motor development: crawling, walking, and running, in that order, at certain approximate ages. Still, this development is not completely canalized; experience can affect its pace and timing.

Cognition and personality are more subject to variations in experience: the kinds of families children grow up in, the schools they attend, and the people they encounter. Consider language. Before children can talk, they must reach a certain level of neurological and muscular maturation. No 6-month-old could speak this sentence, no matter how enriched the infant's home life might be. Yet environment does play a large part in language development. If parents encourage babies' first sounds by talking back to them, children are likely to start to speak earlier than if their early vocalizing is ignored.

Recently scientists have begun to recognize that a usual or typical *experience,* too, can dig canals, or channels for development (Gottlieb, 1991). For example, infants who hear only the sounds peculiar to their native language soon lose the ability to perceive sounds characteristic of other languages (see Chapter 7). Throughout this book you will find many examples of how socioeconomic status, neighborhood conditions, and educational opportunity can powerfully shape developmental outcomes, from the pace and complexity of language development to the likelihood of early sexual activity and antisocial behavior.

Genotype-Environment Interaction

Genotype-environment interaction usually refers to the effects of similar environmental conditions on genetically different individuals. To take a familiar example, many people are exposed to pollen and dust, but people with a genetic predisposition are more likely to develop allergic reactions. Some researchers point out that interactions can work the other way as well: Genetically similar children often develop differently depending on their home environment (Collins et al., 2000). As we will discuss in Chapter 8, a child born with a "difficult" temperament may develop adjustment problems in one family and thrive in another, depending largely on parental handling. Thus, it may take the interaction of hereditary and environmental factors, not just one or the other, to produce certain conditions.

genotype-environment interaction Portion of phenotypic variation that results from the reactions of genetically different individuals to similar environmental conditions.

Genotype-Environment Correlation

The environment often reflects or reinforces genetic differences. That is, certain genetic and environmental influences tend to act in the same direction. This is called **genotype-environment correlation**, or *genotype-environment covariance,* and it works in three ways to strengthen the phenotypic expression of a genotypic tendency (Bergeman & Plomin, 1989; Scarr, 1992; Scarr & McCartney, 1983):

genotype-environment correlation Tendency of certain genetic and environmental influences to reinforce each other; may be passive, reactive (evocative), or active. Also called *genotype-environment covariance.*

- *Passive correlations:* Generally parents, who provide the genes that predispose a child toward a trait, also provide an environment that encourages the development of that trait. For example, a musical parent is likely to create a home environment in which music is heard regularly, to give a child music lessons, and to take the child to musical events. If the child inherited the parent's musical talent, the child's musicality will reflect a combination of genetic and environmental influences. This type of correlation is called *passive* because the child does not control it. It is most applicable to young children, whose parents, the source of their genetic legacy, also have a great deal of control over their early experiences.
- *Reactive, or evocative, correlations:* Children with differing genetic makeups evoke different responses from adults. Parents who are *not* musically inclined may make a special effort to provide musical experiences to a child who shows interest and ability in music. This response, in turn, strengthens the child's genetic inclination toward music.

- *Active correlations:* As children get older and have more freedom to choose their own activities and environments, they actively select or create experiences consistent with their genetic tendencies. A child with a talent for music will probably seek out musical friends, take music classes, and go to concerts if such opportunities are available. A shy child is likely to spend more time in solitary pursuits than an outgoing youngster. This tendency to seek out environments compatible with one's genotype is called **niche-picking;** it helps explain why identical twins reared apart tend to be quite similar.

niche-picking Tendency of a person, especially after early childhood, to seek out environments compatible with his or her genotype.

What Makes Siblings So Different? The Nonshared Environment

LifeMap CD

To learn more about the interplay of heredity and environment, watch the video on "Nature and Nurture: The Study of Twins" in Chapter 3 of your CD.

Although two children in the same family may bear a striking physical resemblance, siblings can be very different in intellect and especially in personality. One reason may be genetic differences, which lead children to need different kinds of stimulation or to respond differently to a similar home environment. A child with a high IQ may be more stimulated by a roomful of books and puzzles than a child with a markedly lower IQ—an example of genotype-environment interaction. One child may be more affected by family discord than another (Rutter, 2002). In addition, studies in behavioral genetics suggest that many of the experiences that strongly affect development are different for different children in a family (McGuffin et al., 2001; Plomin & Daniels, 1987; Plomin & DeFries, 1999).

nonshared environmental effects Unique environment in which each child grows up, consisting of distinctive influences or influences that affect one child differently than another.

These **nonshared environmental effects** result from the unique environment in which each child in a family grows up. Children in a family have a shared environment—the home they live in, the people in it, and the activities a family jointly engage in—but they also, even if they are twins, have experiences that are not shared by their brothers and sisters. Parents and siblings may treat each child differently. Certain events, such as illnesses and accidents, and experiences outside the home (for example, with teachers and peers) affect one child and not another. Indeed, some behavioral geneticists have claimed that heredity accounts for most of the similarity between siblings, and the nonshared environment accounts for most of the difference (McClearn et al., 1997; Plomin, 1996; Plomin & Daniels, 1987; Plomin & DeFries, 1999; Plomin, Owen, & McGuffin, 1994). However, methodological challenges and additional empirical evidence point to the more moderate conclusion that nonshared environmental effects do not greatly outweigh shared ones; rather, there seems to be a balance between the two (Rutter, 2002).

Genotype-environment correlations may play an important role in the nonshared environment. Children's genetic differences may lead parents and siblings to react to them differently and treat them differently, and genes may influence how children perceive and respond to that treatment and what its outcome will be. Children also mold their own environments by the choices they make—what they do and with whom—and their genetic makeup influences these choices. A child who has inherited artistic talent may spend a great deal of time creating "masterpieces" in solitude, whereas a sibling who is athletically inclined may spend more time playing ball with others. Thus, not only will the children's abilities (in, say, painting or soccer) develop differently, but their social lives will be different as well. These differences tend to be accentuated as children grow older and have more experiences outside the family (Bergeman & Plomin, 1989; Bouchard, 1994; Plomin, 1990, 1996; Plomin et al., 1994; Scarr, 1992; Scarr & McCartney, 1983).

Critics of behavioral genetics research say that these studies give short shrift to the influence of parenting (Collins et al., 2000; Rutter, 2002). Some critics point to the narrow range of families sampled in some studies and to a lack of direct observation of family life. Instead, they look to longitudinal studies of effects of parenting practices and direct interventions that seem to foster effective parenting. Such studies offer evidence that parental influence contributes greatly to developmental outcomes, independent of hereditary effects or bidirectional processes. At the same time, this research points to "the interrelated effects of parenting, nonfamilial influences, and the role of the broader context in which families live" (Collins et al., 2000, p. 228).

The old nature-nurture puzzle is far from resolved; we know now that the problem is far more complex than previously thought. A variety of research designs can continue to augment and refine our understanding of the forces affecting development.

Checkpoint

Can you . . .

- ✔ Explain and give at least one example of reaction range, canalization, genotype-environment interaction, and genotype-environment correlation?
- ✔ List three types of influences that contribute to nonshared environmental effects?
- ✔ Cite criticisms of behavioral genetics research?

Some Characteristics Influenced by Heredity and Environment

What roles do heredity and environment play in physical health, intelligence, and personality?

Keeping in mind the complexity of unraveling the influences of heredity and environment, let us look at what is known about their roles in producing certain characteristics.

Physical and Physiological Traits

Not only do monozygotic twins generally look alike, but they are also more concordant than dizygotic twins in their risk for such medical disorders as hypertension (high blood pressure), heart disease, stroke, rheumatoid arthritis, peptic ulcers, and epilepsy (Brass, Isaacsohn, Merikangas, & Robinette, 1992; Plomin et al., 1994). Lifespan, too, seems to be influenced by genes (Sorensen, Nielsen, Andersen, & Teasdale, 1988).

Obesity—sometimes called simply *overweight* and defined in childhood as having a body mass index, or BMI (comparison of weight to height), at or above the 95th percentile for age and sex—is a multifactorial condition. Twin studies, adoption studies, and other research suggest that 40 to 70 percent of the risk is genetic (Chen et al., 2004). As many as 250 genes or chromosome regions are associated with obesity (Pérusse, Chagnon, Weisnagel, & Bouchard, 1999). A longitudinal study of risk factors for heart disease, begun in 1973 in the Bogalusa, Louisiana, area, has linked specific genes and their chromosomal locations to body mass measurements taken over several decades (Chen et al., 2004). One key gene, *GAD2* on chromosome 10, normally controls appetite; but an abnormal version of this gene can stimulate hunger and overeating (Boutin et al., 2003).

obesity Overweight in relation to age, sex, height, and body type; sometimes defined as having a body mass index (weight for height) at or above the 95th percentile of growth curves for children of the same age and sex.

The kind and amount of food eaten in a particular home or in a particular social or ethnic group and the amount of exercise that is encouraged can increase or decrease the likelihood that a person will become overweight. The rapid rise in the prevalence of obesity in western countries seems to result from the interaction of a genetic predisposition with inadequate exercise (Leibel, 1997; see Chapters 9, 12, and 15).

Intelligence and School Achievement

Heredity seems to exert a strong influence on general intelligence and also on specific abilities (McClearn et al., 1997; Plomin et al., 1994; Plomin & DeFries, 1999). Still, experience counts too; an enriched or impoverished environment can substantially affect the development and expression of innate ability (Neisser et al., 1996; see Chapter 13). This seems to be an example of QTL: Many genes, each with its own small effect, combine to establish a range of possible reactions to a range of possible experiences (Scarr, 1997a; Weinberg, 1989; refer to Figure 3-7).

Evidence of the role of heredity in intelligence has emerged from adoption and twin studies. Adopted children's IQs are consistently closer to the IQs of their biological mothers than to those of their adoptive parents and siblings, and monozygotic (identical) twins are more alike in intelligence than dizygotic (fraternal) twins. This is also true of performance on elementary school achievement tests and on National Merit Scholarship examinations given to high school students. The studies yield a consistent estimate of heritability: 50 to 60 percent for verbal abilities and 50 percent for spatial abilities, meaning that genetic differences explain at least half of the observed variation among members of a population. The close correlation between verbal and spatial abilities suggests a genetic link among the components of intelligence (Plomin & DeFries, 1999).

Furthermore, the measured genetic influence increases with age. The family environment seems to have more influence on younger children, whereas adolescents are more apt to find their own niche by actively selecting environments compatible with their hereditary abilities and related interests (McClearn et al., 1997; McGue, 1997; McGue, Bouchard, Iacono, & Lykken, 1993; Plomin & DeFries, 1999).

The main environmental influences on intelligence, then, seem to occur early in life (McGue, 1997). In fact, an analysis of 212 studies (Devlin, Daniels, & Roeder, 1997) points to the impact of the earliest environment: the womb. According to this analysis, the prenatal environment may account for 20 percent of the similarity in IQ between twins and 5 percent of the similarity in nontwin siblings (who occupy the same womb at different times), bringing heritability of IQ below 50 percent. Thus, the influence of genes on intelligence may be weaker and the influence of the prenatal environment stronger than was previously thought, underlining the importance of a healthy prenatal environment.

Personality

Certain aspects of personality appear to be inherited, at least in part. Analyses of five major groupings of traits—extraversion, neuroticism (a group of traits involving anxiety), conscientiousness, agreeableness, and openness to experience—suggest a heritability of about 40 percent. Setting aside variances attributable to measurement error brings heritability closer to 66 percent for these trait groupings, meaning that environment would have no more than a 34 percent influence (Bouchard, 1994).

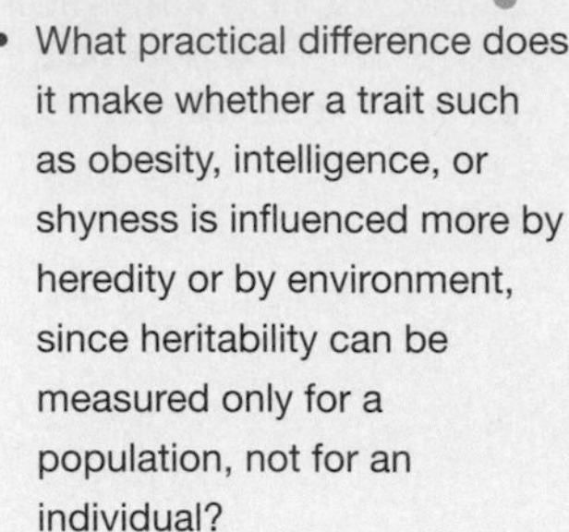

- What practical difference does it make whether a trait such as obesity, intelligence, or shyness is influenced more by heredity or by environment, since heritability can be measured only for a population, not for an individual?

Temperament (discussed in detail in Chapter 8) appears to be largely inborn and is often consistent over the years, though it may respond to special experiences or parental handling (A. Thomas & Chess, 1984; A. Thomas, Chess, & Birch, 1968). An observational study of 100 pairs of 7-year-old siblings (half of them adoptive siblings and half siblings by birth) found significant genetic influences on activity, sociability, and emotionality (Schmitz, Saudino, Plomin, Fulker, & DeFries, 1996). A large body of research (also discussed in Chapter 8) strongly suggests that shyness and its opposite, boldness, are largely inborn and tend to stay with a person throughout life.

Scientists have begun to identify genes directly linked with specific personality traits. One of these genes has been found to play a part in neuroticism, which may contribute to depression. An estimated 10 to 15 other genes also may be involved in anxiety (Lesch et al., 1996). Future work in molecular genetics and brain physiology is likely to further illuminate the sources of personality traits (Bouchard & Loehlin, 2001).

Psychopathology

There is evidence for a strong hereditary influence on schizophrenia, autism, and depression. All tend to run in families and to show greater concordance between monozygotic twins than between dizygotic twins. However, heredity alone does not produce such disorders; an inherited tendency can be triggered by environmental factors. For example, researchers have linked a gene or genes on chromosome 1 to vulnerability to depression (Nurnberger et al., 2001). (Depression is discussed later in this book.)

schizophrenia Mental disorder marked by loss of contact with reality; symptoms include hallucinations and delusions.

Schizophrenia, a disorder characterized by loss of contact with reality and by such symptoms as hallucinations and delusions, has a strong genetic component (Tuulio-Henriksson et al., 2002; Vaswani & Kapur, 2001). The risk of schizophrenia is 10 times greater among siblings and offspring of schizophrenics than among the general population; and twin and adoption studies suggest that this increased risk comes from shared genes, not shared environments. The estimated genetic contribution is between 63 and 85 percent (McGuffin, Owen, & Farmer, 1995). A postmortem study of brain tissue of schizophrenics identified a gene variant, which, through its role in regulating a neurotransmitter or chemical messenger called *glutamate,* results in slower processing in the prefrontal cortex and an increased risk of schizophrenia (Egan et al., 2004).

However, since not all monozygotic twins are concordant for the illness, its cause cannot be purely genetic. Co-twin studies suggest that a prenatal viral infection, carried in the blood shared by monochorionic twins, may play a part (Phelps et al., 1997). In a study of all births in Denmark between 1935 and 1978, people born in urban areas were more likely to be schizophrenic than those born in rural areas, perhaps because of greater likelihood of birth complications and of exposure to infections (Mortenson et al., 1999). Among 87,907 babies born in Jerusalem between 1964 and 1976, the risk of the disorder was four times higher when the father was 50 years old or more than when the father was younger than 25 (Malaspina et al., 2001). In addition, a study of 7,086 persons born in Helsinki, Finland, between 1924 and 1993 found indications that fetal undernutrition increases the risk of schizophrenia (Wahlbeck, Forsen, Osmond, Barker, & Eriksson, 2001).

Autism, a severe disorder of brain functioning, is characterized by lack of normal social interaction, impaired communication and imagination, and a highly restricted range of activities and interests. It usually appears within the first 3 years and continues to varying degrees throughout life (AAP Committee on Children with Disabilities, 2001; National Institute of Neurological Disorders and Stroke, 1999; Rapin, 1997; Rodier, 2000). Its onset appears to be preceded by abnormal brain growth: a small head size at birth followed by a sudden, excessive spurt in size during the first year (Courchesne, Carper, & Akshoomoff, 2003). Four out of five autistic children are boys (Yeargin-Allsopp et al., 2003), possibly because of girls' greater early sensitivity to social stimuli (Constantino, 2003), and about three out of four are mentally retarded (American Psychological Association, 1994).

autism Pervasive developmental disorder of the brain, characterized by lack of normal social interaction, impaired communication and imagination, and repetitive, obsessive behaviors.

An autistic baby may fail to notice the emotional signals of others and may refuse to cuddle or make eye contact. An autistic child may speak in a sing-song voice, paying little or no attention to the listener. Severely autistic children often show repetitive behaviors, such as spinning, rocking, hand flapping, and head banging, and are obsessed with certain subjects, rituals, or routines (National Institute of Neurological Disorders and Stroke, 1999).

Autism is one of a group of *autistic spectrum disorders (ASDs)* ranging from mild to severe, which may be more common than previously thought. Estimates are that as many as 6 children in 1,000 may have one of these disorders (Yeargin-Allsopp et al., 2003). The most common of these is *Asperger's disorder,* which affects about 1 in 500 children. Children with Asperger's disorder usually have normal or even high verbal intelligence, are curious, and do good schoolwork; but they have limited, fixed interests, repetitive speech and behavior, and difficulty understanding social and emotional cues ("Autism—Part I," 2001). Preschoolers with ASDs tend to focus on individual bits of information instead of on the total picture. They are weak in verbal ability and in *joint attention*—pointing to an object to call attention to it or looking at another person to see whether the two of them are paying attention to the same event. Lack of joint attention may underlie delayed development of *theory of mind* (see Chapter 10), awareness of the mental processes of oneself and others (Morgan, Mayberry, & Durkin, 2003).

Autistic disorders run in families and seem to have a strong genetic basis (Bailey, Le Couteur, Gottesman, & Bolton, 1995; Constantino, 2003; National Institute of Neurological Disorders and Stroke, 1999; Ramoz et al., 2004; Rodier, 2000; Szatmari, 1999; Trottier et al., 1999). Family members of an autistic child may show symptoms too mild to qualify for a diagnosis of ASD (Constantino, 2003). Monozygotic twins are more concordant for autism than dizygotic twins. Several genes may be involved in cases of varying symptoms and severity (Cook et al., 1997; Szatmari, 1999). One is a variant of HOXA1, involved in the development of the brain stem (Ingram et al., 2000; Rodier, 2000). Another is a gene involved in providing energy to brain cells (Ramoz et al., 2004).

Environmental factors, such as exposure to certain viruses or chemicals, may trigger an inherited tendency toward autism (National Institute of Neurological Disorders and Stroke, 1999; Rodier, 2000; Trottier, Srivastava, & Walker, 1999). Certain complications of pregnancy, such as uterine bleeding and vaginal infection, seem to be associated with a higher incidence of autism (Juul-Dam, Townsend, & Courchesne, 2001). Major stress during the 24th to 28th weeks of pregnancy may deform the developing brain (Beversdorf et al., 2001). The claim that autism is related to administration of the measles-mumps-rubella vaccine has not been substantiated (AAP Committee on Children with Disabilities, 2001; Fombonne, 2001, 2003; Madsen et al., 2003).

Autism has no known cure, but improvement, sometimes substantial, can occur. Some autistic children can be taught to speak, read, and write. Behavior therapy can help them learn such basic social skills as paying attention, sustaining eye contact, and feeding and dressing themselves. Physical and occupational therapy, highly structured social play, and extensive parent training may be part of the treatment. New, safer medications are effective in managing specific symptoms (AAP Committee on Children with Disabilities, 2001). However, only about 2 percent of autistic children grow up to live independently; most need some degree of care throughout life. Children with Asperger's syndrome generally fare better ("Autism—Part II," 2001).

Checkpoint

Can you . . .

- ✔ Assess the evidence for genetic and environmental influences on obesity, intelligence, and temperament?
- ✔ Name and describe two mental disorders that show a strong genetic influence?

Refocus

- Since Louise Brown's birth, how have alternate means of conception affected the likelihood of multiple births and the treatment of infertility?
- What hereditary and environmental influences may explain some of Louise Brown's characteristics?
- The "Focus" vignette gives very little information about Louise Brown's test-tube sister, Natalie, but what factors do you imagine might have affected any similarities and differences between them?

In this chapter we have looked at some ways in which heredity and environment act to make children what they are. A child's first environment is the world within the womb, which we discuss in Chapter 4.

Summary and Key Terms

Becoming Parents

Guidepost 1 How does conception normally occur, and how have beliefs about conception changed?

- Early beliefs about conception reflected incorrect beliefs about nature and about male and female anatomy.
- Fertilization, the union of an ovum and a sperm, results in the formation of a one-celled zygote, which then duplicates itself by cell division.

clone (60) **fertilization (60)** **zygote (60)**

Guidepost 2 What causes multiple births?

- Multiple births can occur either by the fertilization of two ova (or one ovum that has split) or by the splitting of one fertilized ovum. Larger multiple births result from either one of these processes or a combination of the two.
- Dizygotic (fraternal) twins have different genetic makeups and may be of different sexes; monozygotic (identical) twins have the same genetic makeup. Because of differences in prenatal and postnatal experience, "identical" twins may differ in temperament and other respects.

dizygotic (two-egg) twins (61) **monozygotic (one-egg) twins (61)** **temperament (61)**

Guidepost 3 What causes infertility, and what are alternative ways of becoming parents?

- The most common cause of infertility in men is a low sperm count; the most common cause in women is blockage of the fallopian tubes. Assisted reproduction by in vitro fertilization or other means may involve ethical and practical issues.

infertility (62)

Mechanisms of Heredity

Guidepost 4 What genetic mechanisms determine sex, physical appearance, and other characteristics?

- The basic functional units of heredity are the genes, which are made of deoxyribonucleic acid (DNA). DNA carries the biochemical instructions that govern the formation and functions of various body cells. The genetic code, the chemical structure of DNA, determines all inherited characteristics. Each gene seems to be located by function in a definite position on a particular chromosome. The complete sequence of genes in the human body is the human genome.

deoxyribonucleic acid (DNA) (64) **genetic code (64)** **chromosomes (64)** **genes (64)** **human genome (64)**

- At conception, each normal human being receives 23 chromosomes from the mother and 23 from the father. These form 23 pairs of chromosomes—-22 pairs of autosomes and 1 pair of sex chromosomes. A child who received an X chromosome from each parent is genetically female. A child who received a Y chromosome from the father is genetically male.
- The simplest patterns of genetic transmission are dominant and recessive inheritance. When a pair of alleles are the same, a person is homozygous for the trait; when they are different, the person is heterozygous.

autosomes (65) **sex chromosomes (65)** **alleles (66)** **homozygous (66)** **heterozygous (66)** **dominant inheritance (66)** **recessive inheritance (66)** **polygenic inheritance (66)**

- Most normal human characteristics are the result of quantitative trait loci (QTL) effects or multifactorial transmission. Except in the case of monozygotic twins, each child inherits a unique genotype, but the phenotype may not express the underlying genotype.

quantitative trait loci (QTL) (67) **multifactorial transmission (67)** **phenotype (67)** **genotype (67)**

Guidepost 5 How are birth defects and disorders transmitted?

- Birth defects and diseases may result from simple dominant, recessive, or sex-linked inheritance; from mutations; from genome imprinting; or from chromosomal abnormalities.
- Genetic counseling can provide information about the mathematical odds of bearing children with certain defects. Genetic testing involves risks as well as benefits.

mutations (67) **natural selection (67)** **incomplete dominance (70)** **sex-linked inheritance (70)** **Down syndrome (71)** **genetic counseling (71)**

Nature and Nurture: Influences of Heredity and Environment

Guidepost 6 How do scientists study the relative influences of heredity and environment, and how do heredity and environment work together?

- Research in behavioral genetics is based on the assumption that the relative influences of heredity and environment can be measured statistically. If heredity is an important influence on a trait, genetically closer persons will be more similar in that trait. Family studies, adoption studies, and studies of twins enable researchers to measure the heritability of traits.
- Critics claim that traditional behavioral genetics is too simplistic. Instead, they study complex developmental systems, reflecting a confluence of constitutional, economic, social, and biological influences.
- The concepts of reaction range, canalization, genotype-environment interaction, genotype-environment correlation (or covariance), and niche-picking describe ways in which heredity and environment work together.
- Siblings tend to be more different than alike in intelligence and personality. Many experiences that strongly affect development are different for each sibling.

behavioral genetics (74) heritability (74) concordant (74) reaction range (76) canalization (76) genotype-environment interaction (77) genotype-environment correlation (77) niche-picking (78) nonshared environmental effects (78)

Guidepost 7 What roles do heredity and environment play in physical health, intelligence, and personality?

- Health, obesity, longevity, intelligence, and temperament are influenced by both heredity and environment, and their relative influences may vary across the life span.
- Schizophrenia and autism are psychopathological disorders influenced by both heredity and environment.

obesity (79) schizophrenia (80) autism (81)

chapter

4

Pregnancy and Prenatal Development

If I could have watched you grow
as a magical mother might,
if I could have seen through my magical transparent
belly,
there would have been such ripening within . . .

—Anne Sexton, 1964

Focus *Abel Dorris and Fetal Alcohol Syndrome*

Abel Dorris

Fetal alcohol syndrome (FAS), a cluster of abnormalities shown by children whose mothers drank during pregnancy, is a leading cause of mental retardation. But in 1971, when the writer Michael Dorris adopted a 3-year-old Sioux boy whose mother had been a heavy drinker, the facts about FAS had not been widely publicized or scientifically investigated, though the syndrome had been observed for centuries. Not until 11 years later, as Dorris related in *The Broken Cord* (1989), did he discover the source of his adopted son's developmental problems.

The boy, named Abel ("Adam" in the book), had been born almost seven weeks premature, with low birthweight. He had shown signs of abuse and undernourishment before being removed to a foster home. His mother had died at 35 of alcohol poisoning. His father had been beaten to death in an alley after a string of arrests. The boy was small for his age, was not toilet trained, and could speak only about 20 words. Although Abel had been diagnosed as mildly retarded, Dorris was certain that with a positive environment he would catch up.

Abel did not catch up. When he turned 4, he was still in diapers and weighed only 27 pounds. He had trouble remembering names of playmates. His activity level was unusually high, and the circumference of his skull was unusually small. He suffered severe, unexplained seizures.

As the months went by, Abel had trouble learning to count, to identify primary colors, and to tie his shoes. Before entering school, he was labeled "learning disabled." His IQ was and remained in the mid-60s. Thanks to the efforts of a devoted first-grade teacher, Abel did learn to read and write, but his comprehension was low. When the boy finished elementary school in 1983, he "still could not add, subtract, count money, or consistently identify the town, state, country, or planet of his residence" (Dorris, 1989, pp. 127–128).

By then, Michael Dorris had solved the puzzle of what was wrong with his son. As an associate professor of Native American studies at Dartmouth College, he was acquainted with the cultural pressures that make drinking prevalent among American Indians. In 1982, the year before Abel's graduation, Michael visited a treatment center for chemically dependent teenagers at a Sioux reservation in South Dakota. There he was astonished to see three boys who "could have been [Abel's] twin brothers" (Dorris, 1989, p. 137). They not only looked like Abel but also acted like him.

Fetal alcohol syndrome had been identified as a medical condition during the 1970s, when Abel was growing up. Once alcohol enters a fetus's bloodstream, it remains there in high concentrations for long periods of time, causing brain damage and harming other body organs. There is no cure. As one medical expert wrote, "for the fetus the hangover may last a lifetime" (Enloe, 1980, p. 15).

For the family, too, the effects of FAS can be devastating. The years of constant attempts first to restore Abel to normality and then to come to terms with the damage irrevocably done in the womb may well have been a factor in later problems in Michael Dorris's marriage to the writer Louise Erdrich, which culminated in divorce proceedings, and in his suicide in 1997 at age 52. According to Erdrich, Dorris suffered from extreme depression, possibly exacerbated by the difficulties he faced as a father (L. Erdrich, personal communication, March 1, 2000).

As for Abel Dorris, by the age of 20 he had entered a vocational training program and had moved into a supervised home, taking along his collections of stuffed animals, paper dolls, newspaper cartoons, family photographs, and old birthday cards. At 23, five years before his father's death, he was hit by a car and killed (Lyman, 1997).

• • •

The story of Abel Dorris is a reminder of the responsibility prospective biological parents have for the crucial development that goes on before birth. The womb is the developing child's first environment, and its impact on the child is immense. In addition to what the mother does and what happens to her, there are other environmental influences, from those that affect the father's sperm to the technological, social, and cultural environment, which may affect the kind of prenatal care a woman gets.

In this chapter we begin by looking at the experience of pregnancy and how prospective parents prepare for a birth. We trace how the fertilized ovum becomes an embryo and then a fetus, already with a personality of its own. Then we discuss environmental factors that can affect the developing person-to-be, examine techniques for determining whether development is proceeding normally, and point out the importance of prenatal care.

After you have read and studied this chapter, you should be able to answer each of the Guidepost questions that follow. Look for them again in the margins, where they point to important concepts throughout the chapter. To check your understanding of these Guideposts, review the end-of-chapter summary. Checkpoints located at periodic spots throughout the chapter will help you verify your understanding of what you have read.

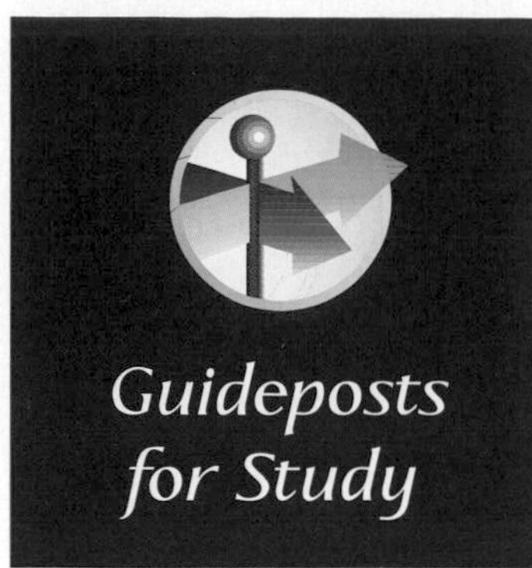

1. What are the three stages of prenatal development, and what happens during each stage?
2. What can fetuses do?
3. What environmental influences can affect prenatal development?
4. What techniques can assess a fetus's health and well-being, and what is the importance of prenatal care?

Prenatal Development: Three Stages

What are the three stages of prenatal development, and what happens during each stage?

If you had been born in China, you would probably celebrate your birthday on your estimated date of conception rather than your date of birth. This Chinese custom recognizes the importance of *gestation,* the approximately nine-month (or 266-day) period of development between conception and birth. Scientists, too, date *gestational age* from conception.

What turns a fertilized ovum, or *zygote,* into a creature with a specific shape and pattern? Research suggests that an identifiable group of genes is responsible for this transformation in vertebrates, presumably including human beings. These genes produce molecules called *morphogens,* which are switched on after fertilization and begin sculpting arms, hands, fingers, vertebrae, ribs, a brain, and other body parts (Echeland et al., 1993; Kraus, Concordet, & Ingham, 1993; Riddle, Johnson, Laufer, & Tabin, 1993).

Prenatal development takes place in three stages: *germinal, embryonic,* and *fetal.* (Table 4-1 gives a month-by-month description.) During these three stages of gestation, the original single-celled zygote grows into an *embryo* and then a *fetus.* Both before and after birth, development proceeds according to two fundamental principles. Growth and motor development occur from top down and from the center of the body outward.

The **cephalocaudal principle** (from Latin, meaning "head to tail") dictates that development proceeds from the head to the lower part of the trunk. An embryo's head, brain, and eyes develop earliest and are disproportionately large until the other parts catch up. At 2 months of gestation, the embryo's head is half the length of the body. By the time of birth, the head is only one-fourth the length of the body but is still disproportionately large. According to the **proximodistal principle** (from Latin, for "near to far"), development proceeds from parts near the center of the body to outer ones. The embryo's head and trunk develop before the limbs, and the arms and legs, before the fingers and toes.

cephalocaudal principle Principle that development proceeds in a head-to-tail direction; that is, that upper parts of the body develop before lower parts.

proximodistal principle Principle that development proceeds from within to without; that is, that parts of the body near the center develop before the extremities.

Germinal Stage (Fertilization to 2 Weeks)

During the **germinal stage,** from fertilization to about 2 weeks of gestational age, the zygote divides, becomes more complex, and is implanted in the wall of the uterus (see Figure 4-1).

germinal stage First 2 weeks of prenatal development, characterized by rapid cell division, increasing complexity and differentiation, and implantation in the wall of the uterus.

Within 36 hours of fertilization, the zygote enters a period of rapid cell division and duplication, or *mitosis.* Seventy-two hours after fertilization it has divided into 16 to 32 cells; a day later it has 64 cells. This division continues until the original single cell has developed into the 800 billion or more specialized cells that make up the human body.

While the fertilized ovum is dividing, it is also making its way down the fallopian tube to the uterus, a journey of three or four days. Its form changes into a fluid-filled sphere, a *blastocyst,* which floats freely in the uterus until the sixth day after fertilization, when it begins to implant itself in the uterine wall. The blastocyst actively participates in the implanting process through a complex system of hormonally regulated signaling (Norwitz, Schust, & Fisher, 2001).

Table 4-1 Prenatal Development

Month	Description
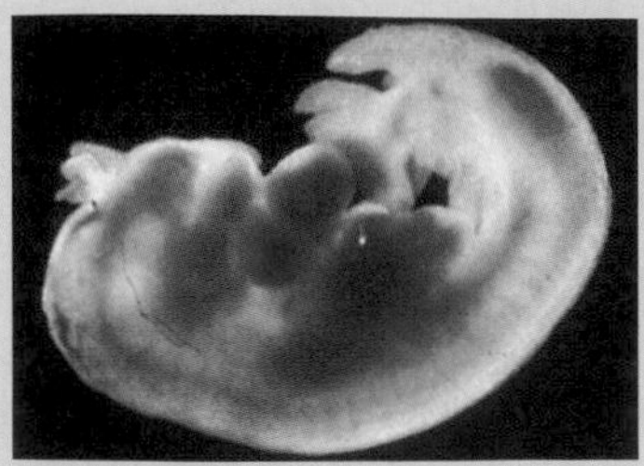 1 month	During the first month, growth is more rapid than at any other time during prenatal or postnatal life: The embryo reaches a size 10,000 times greater than the zygote. By the end of the first month, it measures about ½ inch in length. Blood flows through its veins and arteries, which are very small. It has a minuscule heart, beating 65 times a minute. It already has the beginnings of a brain, kidneys, liver, and digestive tract. The umbilical cord, its lifeline to the mother, is working. By looking very closely through a microscope, it is possible to see the swellings on the head that will eventually become eyes, ears, mouth, and nose. Its sex cannot yet be determined.
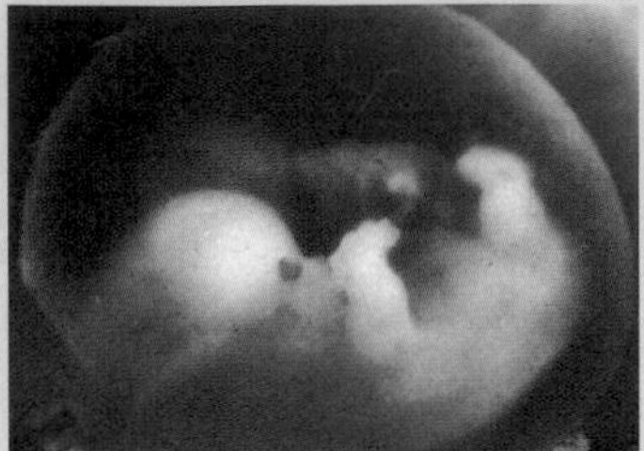 7 weeks	By the end of the second month, the fetus is less than 1 inch long and weighs only 1/13 ounce. Its head is half its total body length. Facial parts are clearly developed, with tongue and teeth buds. The arms have hands, fingers, and thumbs, and the legs have knees, ankles, and toes. The fetus has a thin covering of skin and can make handprints and footprints. Bone cells appear at about 8 weeks. Brain impulses coordinate the function of the organ system. Sex organs are developing; the heartbeat is steady. The stomach produces digestive juices; the liver, blood cells. The kidneys remove uric acid from the blood. The skin is now sensitive enough to react to tactile stimulation. If an aborted 8-week-old fetus is stroked, it reacts by flexing its trunk, extending its head, and moving back its arms.
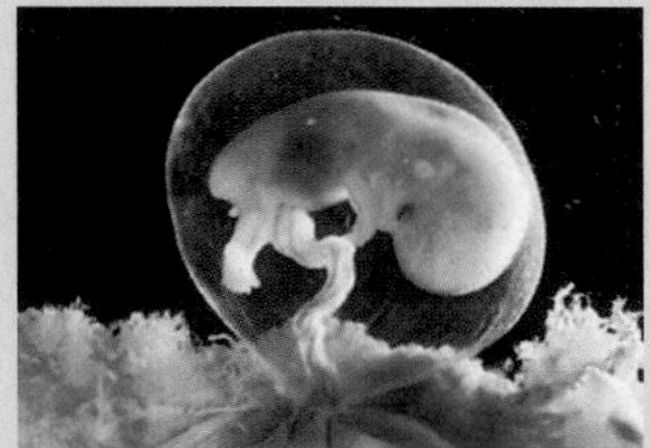 3 months	By the end of the third month, the fetus weighs about 1 ounce and measures about 3 inches in length. It has fingernails, toenails, eyelids (still closed), vocal cords, lips, and a prominent nose. Its head is still large—about one-third its total length—and its forehead is high. Sex can easily be determined. The organ systems are functioning, and so the fetus may now breathe, swallow amniotic fluid into the lungs and expel it, and occasionally urinate. Its ribs and vertebrae have turned into cartilage. The fetus can now make a variety of specialized responses: It can move its legs, feet, thumbs, and head; its mouth can open and close and swallow. If its eyelids are touched, it squints; if its palm is touched, it makes a partial fist; if its lip is touched, it will suck; and if the sole of the foot is stroked, the toes will fan out. These reflexes will be present at birth but will disappear during the first months of life.
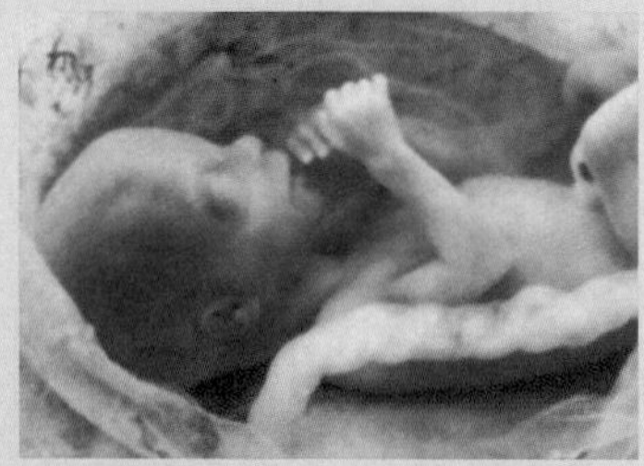 4 months	The body is catching up to the head, which is now only one-fourth the total body length, the same proportion it will be at birth. The fetus now measures 8 to 10 inches and weighs about 6 ounces. The umbilical cord is as long as the fetus and will continue to grow with it. The placenta is now fully developed. The mother may be able to feel the fetus kicking, a movement known as *quickening,* which some societies and religious groups consider the beginning of human life. The reflex activities that appeared in the third month are now brisker because of increased muscular development.
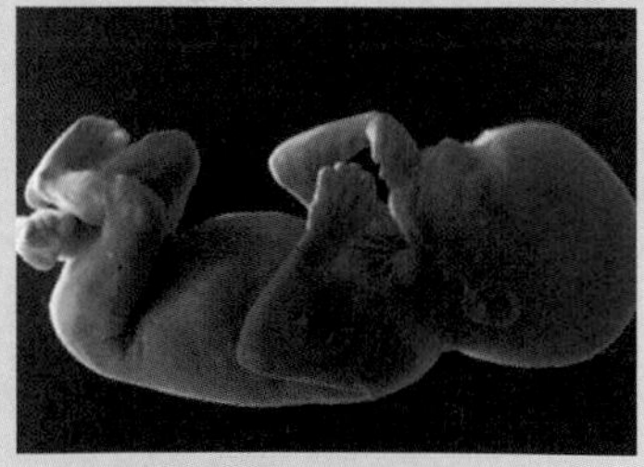 5 months	The fetus, now weighing about 12 ounces to 1 pound and measuring about 1 foot, begins to show signs of an individual personality. It has definite sleep-wake patterns, has a favorite position in the uterus (called its *lie*), and becomes more active—kicking, stretching, squirming, and even hiccuping. By putting an ear to the mother's abdomen, it is possible to hear the fetal heartbeat. The sweat and sebaceous glands are functioning. The respiratory system is not yet adequate to sustain life outside the womb; a baby born at this time does not usually survive. Coarse hair has begun to grow for eyebrows and eyelashes, fine hair is on the head, and a woolly hair called *lanugo* covers the body.

Table 4-1 Prenatal Development (*continued*)

Month	Description
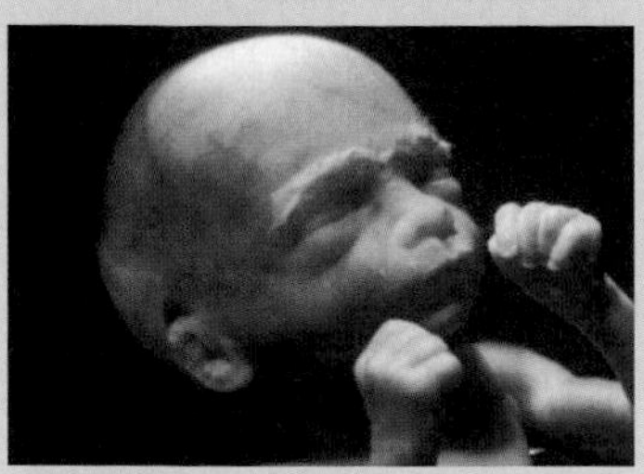 6 months	The rate of fetal growth has slowed down a little—by the end of the sixth month, the fetus is about 14 inches long and weighs 1¼ pounds. It has fat pads under the skin; the eyes are complete, opening, closing, and looking in all directions. It can hear, and it can make a fist with a strong grip. A fetus born during the sixth month still has only a slight chance of survival, because the breathing apparatus has not matured. However, some fetuses of this age do survive outside the womb.
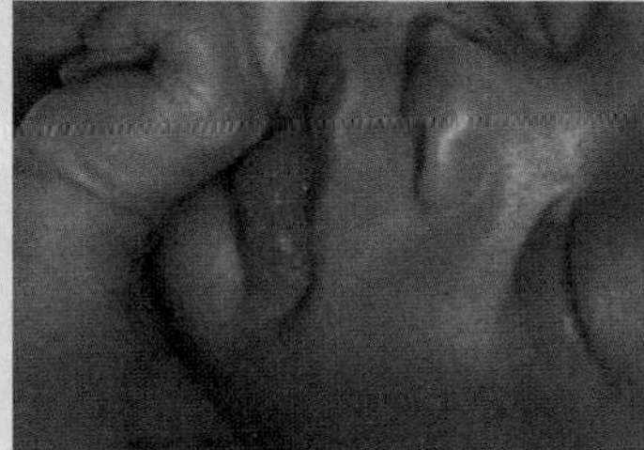 7 months	By the end of the seventh month, the fetus, about 16 inches long and weighing 3 to 5 pounds, now has fully developed reflex patterns. It cries, breathes, and swallows, and it may suck its thumb. The lanugo may disappear at about this time, or it may remain until shortly after birth. Head hair may continue to grow. The chances that a fetus weighing at least 3½ pounds will survive are fairly good, provided it receives intensive medical attention. It will probably need to be kept in an isolette until a weight of 5 pounds is attained.
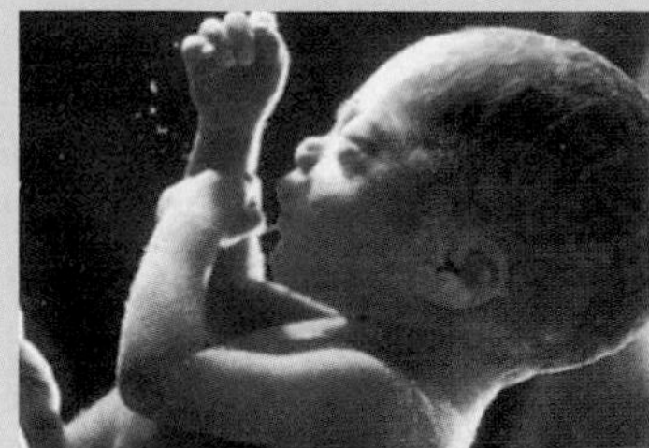 8 months	The 8-month-old fetus is 18 to 20 inches long and weighs between 5 and 7 pounds. Its living quarters are becoming cramped, and so its movements are curtailed. During this month and the next, a layer of fat develops over the fetus's entire body, which will enable it to adjust to varying temperatures outside the womb.
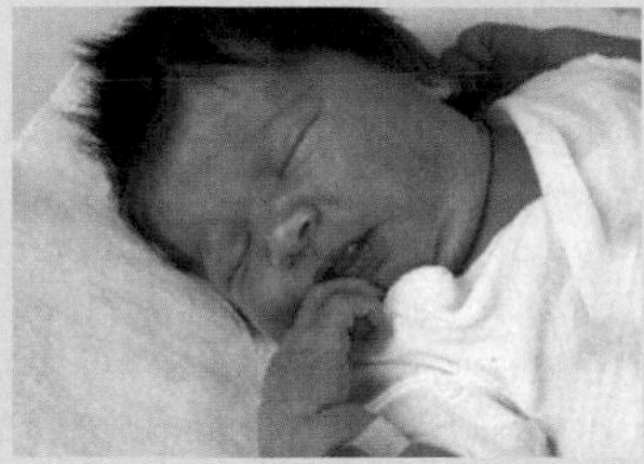 9 months—newborn	About a week before birth, the fetus stops growing, having reached an average weight of about 7½ pounds and a length of about 20 inches, with boys tending to be a little longer and heavier than girls. Fat pads continue to form, the organ systems are operating more efficiently, the heart rate increases, and more wastes are expelled through the umbilical cord. The reddish color of the skin is fading. At birth, the fetus will have been in the womb for about 266 days, although gestational age is usually estimated at 280 days, since most doctors date the pregnancy from the mother's last menstrual period.

Note: Even in these early stages, individuals differ. The figures and descriptions given here represent averages.

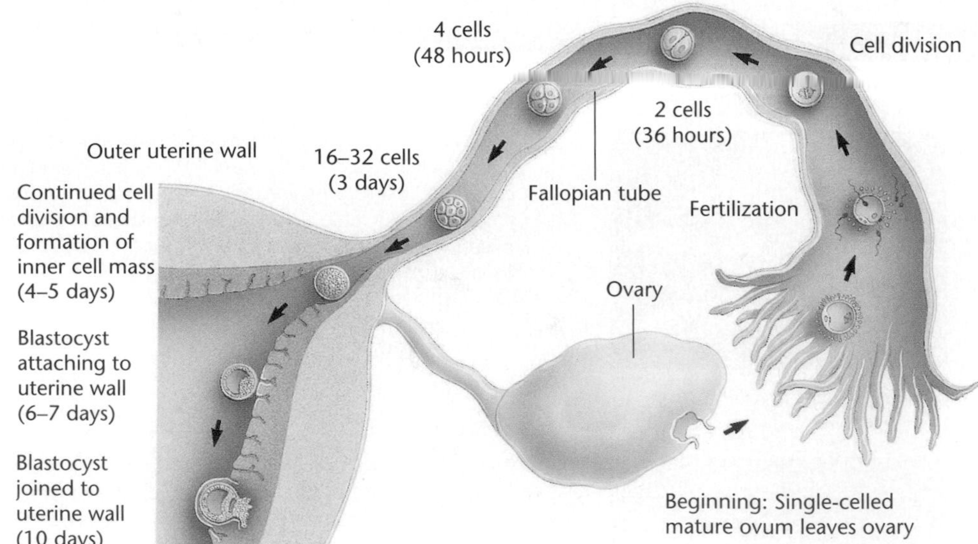

Figure 4-1
Early development of a human embryo. This simplified diagram shows the progress of the ovum as it leaves the ovary, is fertilized in the fallopian tube, and then divides while traveling to the lining of the uterus. Now a blastocyst, it is implanted in the uterus, where it will grow larger and more complex until it is ready to be born.

Meanwhile, as cell differentiation begins, some cells around the edge of the blastocyst cluster on one side to form the *embryonic disk,* a thickened cell mass from which the embryo begins to develop. This mass is already differentiating into two layers. The upper layer, the *ectoderm,* will become the outer layer of skin, the nails, hair, teeth, sensory organs, and the nervous system, including the brain and spinal cord. The lower layer, the *endoderm,* will become the digestive system, liver, pancreas, salivary glands, and respiratory system. Later a middle layer, the *mesoderm,* will develop and differentiate into the inner layer of skin, muscles, skeleton, and excretory and circulatory systems.

Other parts of the blastocyst begin to develop into organs that will nurture and protect the unborn child: the *placenta,* the *umbilical cord,* and the *amniotic sac* with its outermost membrane, the *chorion.* The *placenta,* which has several important functions, will be connected to the embryo by the *umbilical cord.* Through this cord the placenta delivers oxygen and nourishment to the developing baby and removes its body wastes. The placenta also helps to combat internal infection and gives the unborn child immunity to various diseases. It produces the hormones that support pregnancy, prepare the mother's breasts for lactation, and eventually stimulate the uterine contractions that will expel the baby from the mother's body. The *amniotic sac* is a fluid-filled membrane that encases the developing baby, protecting it and giving it room to move. The *trophoblast,* the outer cell layer of the blastocyst (which later becomes part of the placenta), produces tiny fingerlike extensions that will penetrate the lining of the uterine wall and will become the pipeline to the mother's blood supply.

Only about 10 to 20 percent of fertilized eggs complete the task of implantation and continue to develop. Researchers have identified a gene called *Hoxa10,* which appears to affect whether an embryo will be successfully implanted in the uterine wall (Taylor, Arici, Olive, & Igarashi, 1998). For implantation to be successful, a protein called *L-selectin,* which coats the trophoblast, must interlock with carbohydrate molecules on the surface of the uterus, stopping the blastocyst's free-floating motion. Since the uterus secretes these molecules for only a short time during a woman's monthly cycle, timing of the attempted implantation is crucial (Genbacev et al., 2003). Implantation more than 8 to 10 days after ovulation increases the risk of pregnancy loss (Wilcox, Baird, & Weinberg, 1999).

Embryonic Stage (2 to 8 Weeks)

embryonic stage Second stage of gestation (2 to 8 weeks), characterized by rapid growth and development of major body systems and organs.

spontaneous abortion Natural expulsion from the uterus of an embryo or fetus that cannot survive outside the womb; also called *miscarriage.*

During the **embryonic stage,** the second stage of gestation, from about 2 to 8 weeks, the organs and major body systems—respiratory, digestive, and nervous—develop rapidly. This is a critical period, when the embryo is most vulnerable to destructive influences in the prenatal environment (see Figure 4-2). An organ system or structure that is still developing at the time of exposure is most likely to be affected. Defects that occur later in pregnancy are likely to be less serious. (In Chapter 6, we discuss brain growth and development, which begins during the embryonic stage and continues after birth and beyond.)

The most severely defective embryos usually do not survive beyond the first *trimester,* or three-month period, of pregnancy. A **spontaneous abortion,** commonly called a *mis-*

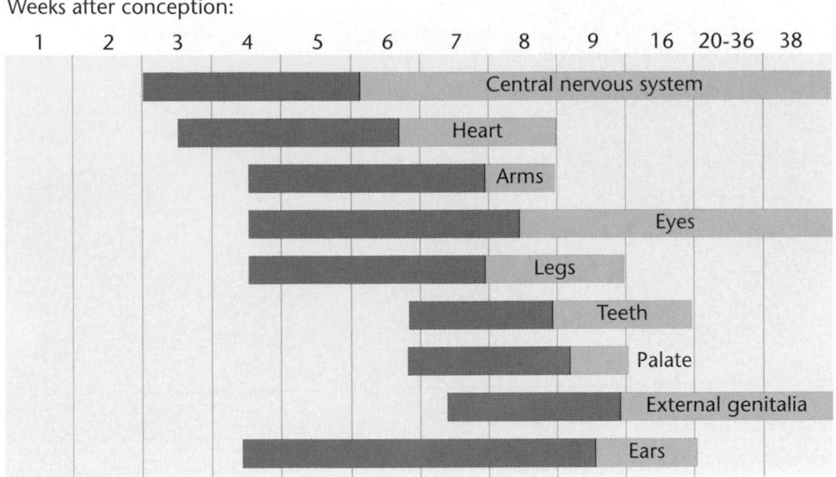

Figure 4-2

When birth defects occur. Body parts and systems are most vulnerable to damage when they are developing most rapidly (*blue shaded areas*), generally within the first trimester of pregnancy.

Note: Intervals of time are not all equal.

Source: J. E. Brody, 1995; data from March of Dimes.

carriage, is the expulsion from the uterus of an embryo or fetus that is unable to survive outside the womb. Most miscarriages result from abnormal pregnancies; about 50 to 70 percent involve chromosomal abnormalities.

Males are more likely than females to be spontaneously aborted or to be *stillborn* (dead at birth). Thus, although about 125 males are conceived for every 100 females—a fact that has been attributed to the greater mobility of sperm carrying the smaller Y chromosome—only 106 boys are born for every 100 girls. Males' greater vulnerability continues after birth. More of them die early in life, and at every age they are more susceptible to many disorders. Furthermore, the proportion of male births appears to be falling in the United States, Canada, and several European countries, while the incidence of birth defects among males is rising, perhaps reflecting effects of environmental pollutants (Davis, Gottlieb, & Stampnitzky, 1998).

Fetal Stage (8 Weeks to Birth)

What can fetuses do?

The appearance of the first bone cells at about 8 weeks signals the **fetal stage,** the final stage of gestation. During this period, the fetus grows rapidly to about 20 times its previous length, and organs and body systems become more complex. Right up to birth, "finishing touches" such as fingernails, toenails, and eyelids develop.

fetal stage Final stage of gestation (from 8 weeks to birth), characterized by increased detail of body parts and greatly enlarged body size.

ultrasound Prenatal medical procedure using high-frequency sound waves to detect the outline of a fetus and its movements so as to determine whether a pregnancy is progressing normally.

Fetuses are not passive passengers in their mothers' wombs. They breathe, kick, turn, flex their bodies, do somersaults, squint, swallow, make fists, hiccup, and suck their thumbs. The flexible membranes of the uterine walls and amniotic sac, which surround the protective buffer of amniotic fluid, permit and stimulate limited movement.

Scientists can observe fetal movement through **ultrasound,** using high-frequency sound waves to detect the outline of the fetus. Other instruments can monitor heart rate, changes in activity level, states of sleep and wakefulness, and cardiac reactivity. In one study, fetuses monitored from 20 weeks of gestation until term had increasingly slower but more variable heart rates, possibly in response to the increasing stress of the mother's pregnancy, and greater cardiac response to stimulation. They also showed less—but more vigorous—activity, perhaps a result of the increasing difficulty of movement for a growing fetus in a constricted environment, as well as of maturation of the nervous system (DiPietro, Hodgson, Costigan, Hilton, & Johnson, 1996b). A significant "jump" in all these aspects of fetal development seems to occur between 28 and 32 weeks; it may help explain why infants born prematurely at this time are more likely to survive and flourish than those born earlier (DiPietro et al., 1996). This "jump" occurred among fetuses observed in two contrasting cultures, Baltimore and Lima, Peru, suggesting that this aspect of fetal neurological development is universal. On the other hand, there were significant differences in the course of this development, with the Lima fetuses lagging behind the Baltimore fetuses. The explanation of these differences was unclear, though they may have been related to differences in maternal nutrition (DiPietro et al., 2004).

The movements and activity level of fetuses show marked individual differences, and their heart rates vary in regularity and speed. There also are differences between males and females. Male fetuses, regardless of size, are more active and tend to move more

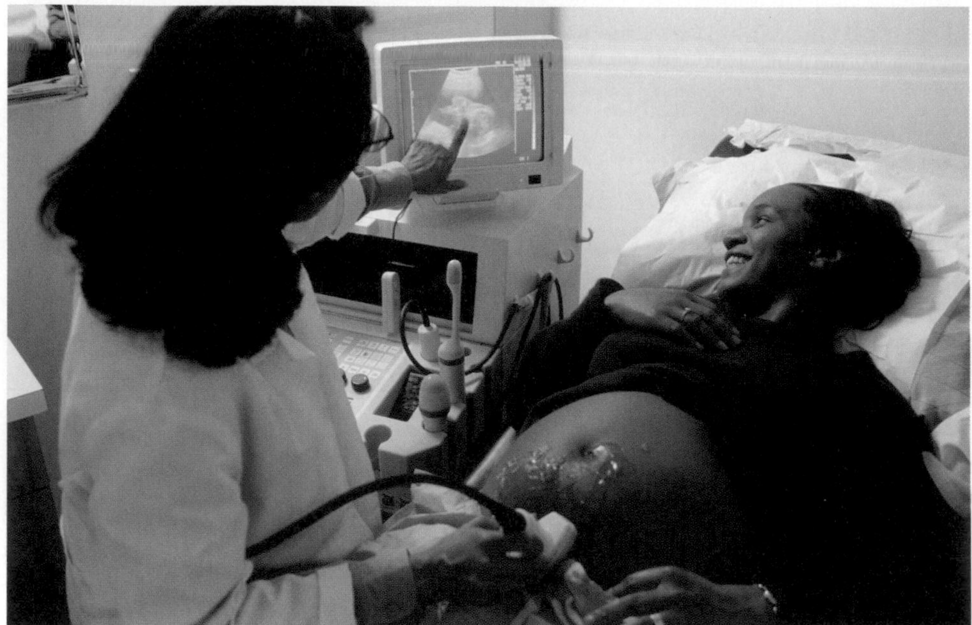

The most effective way to prevent birth complications is early prenatal care, which may include ultrasound checkups, such as this woman is having, to follow the fetus's development. Ultrasound is a diagnostic tool that presents an immediate image of the fetus in the womb.

vigorously than female fetuses throughout gestation. Thus, infant boys' tendency to be more active than girls may be at least partly inborn (DiPietro et al., 1996).

Beginning at about the 12th week of gestation, the fetus swallows and inhales some of the amniotic fluid in which it floats. The amniotic fluid contains substances that cross the placenta from the mother's bloodstream and enter the fetus's own bloodstream. Partaking of these substances may stimulate the budding senses of taste and smell and may contribute to the development of organs needed for breathing and digestion (Mennella & Beauchamp, 1996a; Ronca & Alberts, 1995; Smotherman & Robinson, 1995, 1996). Mature taste cells appear at about 14 weeks of gestation. The olfactory system, which controls the sense of smell, also is well developed before birth (Bartoshuk & Beauchamp, 1994; Mennella & Beauchamp, 1996a).

Fetuses respond to the mother's voice and heartbeat and the vibrations of her body, suggesting that they can hear and feel. Familiarity with the mother's voice may have a basic survival function: to help newborns locate the source of food. Hungry infants, no matter on which side they are held, turn toward the breast in the direction from which they hear the mother's voice (Noirot & Algeria, 1983, cited in Rovee-Collier, 1996). Responses to sound and vibration seem to begin at 26 weeks of gestation, rise, and then reach a plateau at about 32 weeks (Kisilevsky, Muir, & Low, 1992).

Fetuses seem to learn and remember. In one experiment, 3-day-old infants sucked more on a nipple that activated a recording of a story their mother had frequently read aloud during the last 6 weeks of pregnancy than they did on nipples that activated recordings of two other stories. Apparently, the infants recognized the pattern of sound they had heard in the womb. A control group, whose mothers had not recited a story before birth, responded equally to all three recordings (DeCasper & Spence, 1986). Similar experiments have found that newborns 2 to 4 days old prefer musical and speech sequences heard before birth. They also prefer their mother's voice to those of other women, female voices to male voices, and their mother's native language to another language (DeCasper & Fifer, 1980; DeCasper & Spence, 1986; Fifer & Moon, 1995; Lecanuet, Granier-Deferre, & Busnel, 1995; Moon, Cooper, & Fifer, 1993).

How do we know that these preferences develop before rather than after birth? When 60 fetuses heard a female voice reading, their heart rate increased if the voice was their mothers' and decreased if it belonged to a stranger (Kisilevsky et al., 2003). In another study, newborns were given the choice of sucking to turn on a recording of the mother's voice or a "filtered" version of her voice as it might sound in the womb. The newborns sucked more often to turn on the filtered version, suggesting that fetuses develop a preference for the kinds of sounds they hear before birth (Fifer & Moon, 1995; Moon & Fifer, 1990).

Checkpoint

Can you . . .

- ✔ Identify two principles that govern physical development and give examples of their application during the prenatal period?
- ✔ Describe how a zygote becomes an embryo?
- ✔ Explain why defects and miscarriages are most likely to occur during the embryonic stage?
- ✔ Describe findings about fetal activity, sensory development, and memory?

Prenatal Development: Environmental Influences

What environmental influences can affect prenatal development?

The pervasive influence of the prenatal environment underlines the importance of providing an unborn child with the best possible start in life. Only recently have scientists become aware of some of the myriad environmental influences that can affect the developing organism. The role of the father used to be virtually ignored; today we know that various environmental factors can affect a man's sperm and the children he conceives. Although the mother's role has been recognized far longer, researchers are still discovering environmental hazards that can affect her fetus. On the positive side, prospective mothers' feelings of attachment to their fetuses seem to have increased in the past three or four decades, as infant and maternal mortality have decreased. Technology that permits a woman to view images of her fetus early in her pregnancy may motivate her to engage in nurturing behaviors, such as eating properly and abstaining from alcohol and drugs (Salisbury, Law, LaGasse, & Lester, 2003).

Maternal Factors

Since the prenatal environment is the mother's body, virtually everything that impinges on her well-being, from her diet to her moods, may alter her unborn child's environment and affect its growth.

Not all environmental hazards are equally risky for all fetuses at all times during gestation. Some factors that are **teratogenic** (birth defect-producing) at one stage of pregnancy have little or no effect earlier or later. The timing of exposure to a teratogen, the size of the dose, and its interaction with other factors may be important (Brent, 2004; refer back to Figure 4-2). Vulnerability may depend on a gene in the fetus or in the mother. Fetuses with a particular variant of a growth gene, called *transforming growth factor alpha,* have six times more risk than other fetuses of developing a cleft palate if the mother smokes while pregnant (Hwang et al., 1995).

teratogenic Capable of causing birth defects.

Nutrition and Maternal Weight

Women need to eat more than usual when pregnant: typically, 300 to 500 more calories a day, including extra protein. The more a pregnant woman gains—up to 40 pounds—the less likely she is to have a baby whose weight at birth is dangerously low. However, excessive weight gain is linked with other risks, such as an infant so large that cesarean delivery is necessary. Desirable weight gain depends on individual factors, such as weight and height before pregnancy. For a woman of normal weight, recommended weight gain is 15 to 25 pounds (Martin, Hamilton, et al., 2003).

Undernourishment during fetal growth may have long-range effects. In rural Gambia, in western Africa, people born during the "hungry" season, when foods from the previous harvest are badly depleted, are 10 times more likely to die in early adulthood than people born during other parts of the year (Moore et al., 1997). In rural areas of northern England and Wales, rising stroke rates among middle-aged adults were associated with poverty and poor nutrition 50 years earlier, when those adults were born (Barker & Lackland, 2003). Psychiatric examinations of Dutch military recruits whose mothers had been exposed to wartime famine during pregnancy suggest that severe prenatal nutritional deficiencies in the first or second trimesters affect the developing brain, increasing the risk of antisocial personality disorders at age 18 (Neugebauer, Hoek, & Susser, 1999). And, as reported in Chapter 3, a Finnish study found a link between fetal undernutrition and schizophrenia (Wahlbeck et al., 2001).

Certain nutrients can positively affect cognitive development. In one study, babies whose mothers, at the time of delivery, had high blood levels of the omega-3 fatty acid docosahexaenoic acid (DHA), an ingredient of breast milk, showed better attentional abilities at 12 and 18 months (Colombo et al., 2004). DHA, which is found naturally in Atlantic salmon, Pacific cod fish, and tuna, also can be taken in the form of supplements derived from algae.

Undernourished women who take dietary supplements while pregnant tend to have bigger, healthier, more active, and more visually alert infants (J. L. Brown, 1987; Vuori et al., 1979); and women with low zinc levels who take daily zinc supplements are less likely to have babies with low birth weight and small head circumference (Goldenberg et al., 1995). However, certain vitamins (including A, B_6, C, D, and K) can be harmful in excessive amounts. Iodine deficiency, unless corrected before the third trimester of pregnancy, can cause cretinism, which may involve severe neurological abnormalities or thyroid problems (Cao et al., 1994; Hetzel, 1994).

Only in recent decades have we come to know the critical importance of folic acid, or folate (a B vitamin), in a pregnant woman's diet. China has the highest incidence in the world of babies born with the neural-tube defects anencephaly and spina bifida (refer back to Table 3-1), but it was not until the 1980s that researchers linked that fact with the timing of the babies' conception. Traditionally, Chinese couples marry in January or February and try to conceive as soon as possible. That means pregnancies often begin in the winter, when rural women have little access to fresh fruits and vegetables, important sources of folic acid.

Did your diet change while you were pregnant?
how about your physical activity?

After medical detective work established the lack of folic acid as a cause of neural-tube defects, China embarked on a massive program to give folic acid supplements to prospective mothers. The result was a large reduction in the prevalence of these defects (Berry et al., 1999). Addition of folic acid to enriched grain products has been mandatory in the United States since 1998, and the incidence of neural-tube defects has fallen by 19 percent (Honein, Paulozzi, Mathews, Erickson, & Wong, 2001). Women of childbearing age are urged to take folate supplements and to include this vitamin in their diets by eating plenty of fresh fruits and vegetables even before becoming pregnant, since damage from folic acid deficiency can occur during the early weeks of gestation (American Academy of Pediatrics [AAP] Committee on Genetics, 1999; Mills & England, 2001). If all women took 5 milligrams of folic acid each day before pregnancy and during the first trimester, an estimated 85 percent of neural-tube defects could be prevented (Wald, 2004).

Obese women (regardless of folate intake) risk having children with neural-tube defects, as well as heart defects and other birth defects (G. M. Shaw, Velie, & Schaffer, 1996; Werler, Louik, Shapiro, & Mitchell, 1996; Watkins, Rasmussen, Honein, Botto, & Moore, 2003). Obesity also increases the risk of other complications of pregnancy, including miscarriage, stillbirth, and *neonatal death* (death during the first month of life) (Cnattingius, Bergstrom, Lipworth, & Kramer, 1998; Goldenberg & Tamura, 1996). Either overweight or underweight before pregnancy can be risky. Among women having their first babies, those who were overweight before pregnancy had the most risk of stillbirth or of losing their babies during the first week of life. On the other hand, underweight women are more likely to have dangerously small babies (Cnattingius et al., 1998).

Physical Activity and Strenuous Work

Moderate exercise does not seem to endanger the fetuses of healthy women (Carpenter et al., 1988). Regular exercise prevents constipation and improves respiration, circulation, muscle tone, and skin elasticity, all of which contribute to a more comfortable pregnancy and an easier, safer delivery and may result in a bigger baby. Pregnant women should avoid activities that could cause abdominal trauma (Committee on Obstetric Practice, 2002).

The American College of Obstetrics and Gynecology (1994) recommends that women in low-risk pregnancies be guided by their own abilities and stamina. The safest course seems to be for pregnant women to exercise moderately, not pushing themselves and not raising their heart rate above 150, and, as with any exercise, to taper off at the end of each session rather than stop abruptly.

Employment during pregnancy generally entails no special hazards. However, strenuous working conditions, occupational fatigue, and long working hours may be associated with a greater risk of premature birth (Luke et al., 1995).

Checkpoint

Can you . . .

✔ Summarize recommendations concerning an expectant mother's diet and physical activity?

Drug Intake

Practically everything an expectant mother takes in makes its way to the uterus. Drugs may cross the placenta, just as oxygen, carbon dioxide, and water do. Vulnerability is greatest in the first few months of gestation, when development is most rapid. Some problems resulting from prenatal exposure to drugs can be treated if the presence of a drug can be detected early.

What are the effects of the use of specific drugs during pregnancy? Let's look first at medical drugs; then at alcohol, nicotine, and caffeine; and finally at some illegal drugs: marijuana, opiates, and cocaine.

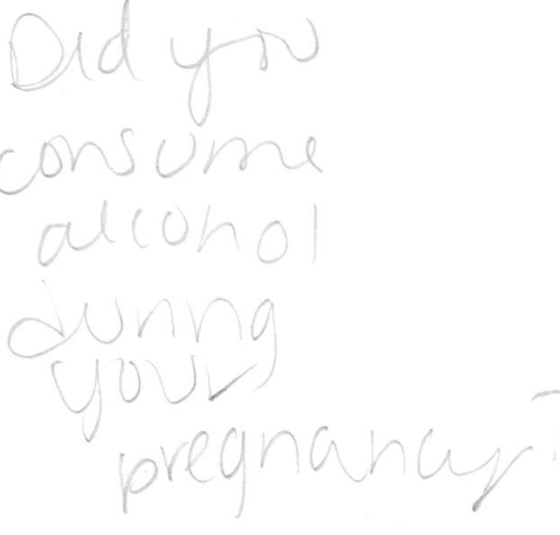
Did you consume alcohol during your pregnancy?

Medical Drugs In the early 1960s, the tranquilizer *thalidomide* was banned after it was found to have caused stunted or missing limbs, severe facial deformities, and defective organs in some 12,000 babies. The thalidomide disaster sensitized medical professionals and the public to the potential dangers of taking drugs while pregnant. Today, nearly 30 drugs have been found to be teratogenic in clinically recommended doses (Koren, Pastuszak, & Ito, 1998). Among them are the antibiotic tetracycline; certain barbiturates, opiates, and other central nervous system depressants; several hormones, including diethylstilbestrol (DES) and androgens; certain anticancer drugs, such as methotrexate; Accutane, a drug often prescribed for severe acne; and aspirin and other nonsteroidal anti-inflammatory drugs, which should be avoided during the third trimester.

The effects of taking a drug during pregnancy do not always show up immediately. In the late 1940s and early 1950s, the synthetic hormone diethylstilbestrol (DES) was widely prescribed (ineffectually, as it turned out) to prevent miscarriage. Not until years later, when the daughters of women who had taken DES during pregnancy reached puberty, did as many as 1 in 1,000 develop a rare form of vaginal or cervical cancer (Giusti, Iwamoto, & Hatch, 1995; Swan, 2000; Treffers, Hanselaar, Helmerhorst, Koster, & van Leeuwen, 2001). DES daughters may have abnormalities of the genital tract and may have trouble bearing children, with higher risks of miscarriage or premature delivery (Mittendorf, 1995; Swan, 2000; Treffers et al., 2001). DES sons also have had malformations in the genital tract, which do not seem to affect fertility (Treffers et al., 2001; Wilcox, Baird, Weinberg, Hornsby, & Herbst, 1995). Findings of an association between DES exposure and testicular cancer are controversial (Giusti, Iwamoto, & Hatch, 1995). However, in male mice early exposure to DES led to long-term adverse effects on testicular development and sperm function (Fielden et al., 2002), as well as an increase in genital tumors (Treffers et al., 2001). DES mothers may have a heightened risk of breast cancer (Mittendorf, 1995; Treffers et al., 2001).

Certain antipsychotic drugs used to manage severe psychiatric disorders may have serious potential effects on the fetus, including withdrawal symptoms at birth. It is advisable to taper off and then discontinue the use of such drugs as the delivery date approaches or, if necessary, to take the lowest dose possible (AAP Committee on Drugs, 2000). The American Academy of Pediatrics (AAP) Committee on Drugs (1994) recommends that *no* medication be prescribed for a pregnant or breast-feeding woman unless it is essential for her health or her child's. Pregnant women should not take over-the-counter drugs without consulting a doctor (Koren et al., 1998).

> *What's your view?*
>
> • Thousands of adults now alive suffer from gross abnormalities because, during the 1950s, their mothers took the tranquilizer thalidomide during pregnancy. As a result, the use of thalidomide was banned in the United States and some other countries. Now thalidomide has been found to be effective in treating or controlling many illnesses, from mouth ulcers to brain cancer. Should its use for these purposes be permitted even though there is a risk that pregnant women might take it? If so, what safeguards should be required?

Alcohol Like Abel Dorris, as many as 5 infants in 1,000 born in the United States suffers from **fetal alcohol syndrome (FAS),** a combination of retarded growth, face and body malformations, and disorders of the central nervous system—and its incidence seems to be increasing. Problems related to the central nervous system can include, in infancy, reduced responsiveness to stimuli and slow reaction time and, throughout childhood, short attention span, distractibility, restlessness, hyperactivity, learning disabilities, memory deficits, and mood disorders (Sokol, Delaney-Black, & Nordstrom, 2003). FAS and other, less severe alcohol-related conditions—all classified under the umbrella of *fetal alcohol spectrum disorder (FASD)*—are estimated to occur in nearly 1 in every 100 births. Prenatal alcohol exposure is the most common cause of mental retardation and the leading preventable cause of birth defects in the United States (Sokol et al., 2003).

fetal alcohol syndrome (FAS) Combination of mental, motor, and developmental abnormalities affecting the offspring of some women who drink heavily during pregnancy.

A woman who drinks and smokes while pregnant is taking grave risks with her future child's health.

Prebirth exposure to alcohol seems to affect a portion of the *corpus callosum,* which coordinates signals between the two hemispheres of the brain. In macaques (short-tailed monkeys) and, presumably, in humans as well, the affected portion, toward the front of the head, is involved in initiating voluntary movement and other higher-order processing (Miller, Astley, & Clarren, 1999).

As many as 50 percent of women of childbearing age consume alcohol, and 15 to 20 percent admit that they continue to drink during pregnancy. Even small amounts of social drinking may harm a fetus (Sokol et al., 2003), and the more the mother drinks, the greater the effect. Moderate or heavy drinking during pregnancy seems to disturb an infant's neurological and behavioral functioning, and this may affect early social interaction with the mother, which is vital to emotional development (Nugent, Lester, Greene, Wieczorek-Deering, & O'Mahony, 1996). In a longitudinal study of 501 women at an urban university's maternity clinic, women who consumed even small amounts of alcohol during pregnancy tended to have children who were unusually aggressive at ages 6 to 7, and prospective mothers who drank moderately to heavily tended to have problem or delinquent children (Sood et al., 2001). Unfortunately, underreporting of maternal alcohol use during pregnancy is common; physicians and researchers generally have to rely on women's self-reports, and diagnosis of FAS is often missed or delayed (Martin, Hamilton, et al., 2002; Sokol et al., 2003).

Some FAS problems recede after birth; others, such as retardation, behavioral and learning problems, and hyperactivity, tend to persist, as with Abel Dorris. Enriching these children's education or general environment does not seem to enhance their cognitive development (Kerns, Don, Mateer, & Streissguth, 1997; Spohr, Willms, & Steinhausen, 1993; Streissguth et al., 1991; Strömland & Hellström, 1996). However, interviews with caregivers of patients with either FAS or a related condition, fetal alcohol effects (FAE), ranging in age from 6 to 51, suggest that children are less likely to develop behavioral and mental health problems if they are diagnosed early and are reared in stable, nurturing environments (Streissguth et al., 2004). Nevertheless, since there is no known safe level of drinking during pregnancy, it is best to avoid alcohol from the time a woman begins *thinking* about becoming pregnant until she stops breast-feeding (AAP Committee on Substance Abuse and Committee on Children with Disabilities, 1993; Sokol et al., 2003).

To learn more about the effects of maternal drinking, watch the "Effects of Prenatal Exposure to Alcohol" video in Chapter 4 of your CD.

Nicotine Although smoking during pregnancy has declined by 42 percent since 1989, 11.4 percent of women who gave birth in the United States in 2002 reported that they had smoked while pregnant. Smoking is especially prevalent among pregnant 18- and 19-year-olds (Martin, Hamilton et al., 2003).

Women who smoke during pregnancy are more than one and a half times as likely as nonsmokers to bear low-birth-weight babies (weighing less than 5½ pounds at birth) (Martin, Hamilton, et al., 2003). Even light smoking (fewer than five cigarettes a day) is associated with a greater risk of low birth weight (Martin, Hamilton, et al. 2002; Ventura, Hamilton, Mathews, & Chandra, 2003). Tobacco use during pregnancy also brings increased risks of miscarriage, prenatal growth retardation, stillbirth, infant death, colic in early infancy, and long-term health, cognitive, and behavioral problems (American Academy of Pediatrics Committee on Substance Abuse, 2001; Martin, Hamilton, et al., 2002; Sondergaard, Henriksen, Obel, & Wisborg, 2001). In a controlled study, newborns whose mothers had smoked during pregnancy (but had not used drugs and had taken no more than three alcoholic drinks per month) showed more evidence of neurological toxicity (such as overexcitability and stress) than infants of nonsmoking mothers (Law et al., 2003). A mother's smoking during pregnancy also may increase her child's risk of cancer (Lackmann et al., 1999). The effects of prenatal exposure to secondhand smoke on cognitive development tend to be worse when the child also experiences socieconomic hardships, such as substandard housing, malnutrition, and inadequate clothing during the first two years of life (Rauh et al., 2004).

Women who smoke during pregnancy also tend to smoke after giving birth, so it is hard to separate the effects of prenatal and postnatal exposure. One study did this by examining 500 newborns about 48 hours after birth, while they were still in the hospital's nonsmoking maternity ward and thus had not been exposed to smoking outside the womb. Newborns whose mothers had smoked during pregnancy were shorter and lighter and had poorer respiratory functioning than babies of nonsmoking mothers (Stick, Burton, Gurrin, Sly, & LeSouëf, 1996).

Smoking during pregnancy seems to have some of the same effects on children when they reach school age as drinking during pregnancy: poor attention span, hyperactivity, anxiety, learning and behavior problems, perceptual-motor and linguistic problems, poor IQ scores, low grade placement, and neurological problems (Landesman-Dwyer & Emanuel, 1979; Milberger, Biederman, Faraone, Chen, & Jones, 1996; Naeye & Peters, 1984; Olds, Henderson, & Tatelbaum, 1994a, 1994b; Streissguth et al., 1984; Thapar et al., 2003; Wakschlag et al., 1997; Weitzman, Gortmaker, & Sobol, 1992; Wright et al., 1983). A 10-year longitudinal study of 6- to 23-year-old offspring of women who reported having smoked heavily during pregnancy found a fourfold increase in risk of conduct disorder in boys, beginning before puberty, and a fivefold increased risk of drug dependence in girls, beginning in adolescence, in comparison with young people whose mothers had not smoked during pregnancy (Weissman, Warner, Wickramaratne, & Kandel, 1999).

Caffeine Can the caffeine a pregnant woman swallows in coffee, tea, cola, or chocolate cause trouble for her fetus? The answer is not clear. It does seem clear that caffeine is *not* a teratogen for human babies (Christian & Brent, 2001; Hinds, West, Knight, & Harland, 1996). A controlled study of 1,205 new mothers and their babies showed no effect of reported caffeine use on low birth weight, premature birth, or retarded fetal growth (Santos, Victora, Huttly, & Carvalhal, 1998). On the other hand, four or more cups of coffee a day may dramatically increase the risk of sudden death in infancy (Ford et al., 1998). Studies of a possible link between caffeine consumption and spontaneous abortion have had mixed results (Cnattingius et al., 2000; Dlugosz et al., 1996; Infante-Rivard, Fernández, Gauthier, David, & Rivard, 1993; Klebanoff, Levine, DerSimonian, Clemens, & Wilkins, 1999; Mills et al., 1993; Signorello et al., 2001).

Marijuana, Opiates, and Cocaine Although findings about marijuana use by pregnant women are mixed, some evidence suggests that heavy use can lead to birth defects. A Canadian study found temporary neurological disturbances, such as tremors and startles, as well as higher rates of low birth weight in the infants of marijuana smokers (Fried, Watkinson, & Willan, 1984). An analysis of blood samples from the umbilical cords of 34 newborns found a greater prevalence of cancer-causing mutations in the infants of mothers who smoked marijuana. These women did not use tobacco, cocaine, or opiates, suggesting that marijuana use alone can increase cancer risk (Ammenheuser, Berenson, Babiak, Singleton, & Whorton, 1998).

Women addicted to morphine, heroin, or codeine are likely to bear premature, addicted babies who will be addicted to the same drugs and will suffer the effects until at least age 6. Prenatally exposed newborns are restless and irritable and often have tremors, convulsions, fever, vomiting, and breathing difficulties (Cobrinick, Hood, & Chused, 1959; Henly & Fitch, 1966; Ostrea & Chavez, 1979). Those who survive cry often and are less alert and less responsive than other babies (Strauss, Lessen-Firestone, Starr, & Ostrea, 1975). They tend to show acute withdrawal symptoms during the neonatal period, requiring prompt treatment (Wagner, Katikaneni, Cox, & Ryan, 1998).

At 1 year, these infants are likely to show somewhat slowed psychomotor development (Bunikowski et al., 1998). In early childhood they weigh less than average, are shorter, are less well adjusted, and score lower on tests of perceptual and learning abilities (G. Wilson, McCreary, Kean, & Baxter, 1979). These children tend not to do well in school, to be unusually anxious in social situations, and to have trouble making friends (Householder, Hatcher, Burns, & Chasnoff, 1982).

Cocaine use during pregnancy has been associated with a variety of risks, including spontaneous abortion, delayed growth, and impaired neurological development (Chiriboga, Brust, Bateman, & Hauser, 1999; Macmillan et al., 2001; Scher, Richardson, & Day, 2000). So great has been the concern about "crack babies" that some states have brought criminal charges against expectant mothers suspected of using cocaine. However, the U.S. Supreme Court in 2001 overturned one such policy as violating the mother's constitutional rights (see Box 4-1).

The Social World

Box 4-1 Fetal Welfare Versus Mothers' Rights

A Wisconsin woman persisted in using cocaine while pregnant. A juvenile court ordered her unborn child placed in protective custody by forcing the expectant mother into inpatient treatment. The Wisconsin Supreme Court later held that she was wrongfully detained (Lewin, 1997).

A South Carolina hospital routinely tested the urine of pregnant women suspected to be using illegal drugs and reported the evidence to police. Ten women were arrested, some of them in their hospital rooms almost immediately after childbirth. They sued, arguing that the urine tests constituted an unconstitutional search of their persons without their consent (Greenhouse, 2000a).

In both these cases, the issue was the conflict between protection of a fetus and a woman's right to privacy or to make her own decisions about her body. It is tempting to require a pregnant woman to adopt practices that will ensure her baby's health or to stop or punish her if she does not. But what about her personal freedom? Can civil rights be abrogated for the protection of the unborn?

The argument about the right to choose abortion, which rests on similar grounds, is far from settled. But the examples just given deal with a different aspect of the problem. What can or should society do about a woman who does *not* choose abortion but instead goes on carrying her baby while engaging in behavior destructive to it or refuses tests or treatment that medical providers consider essential to the baby's welfare?

Ingesting Harmful Substances

Does a woman have the right to knowingly ingest a substance, such as alcohol or another drug, which can permanently damage her unborn child? Some advocates for fetal rights think it should be against the law for pregnant women to smoke or use alcohol, even though these activities are legal for other adults. Other experts argue that incarceration for substance abuse is unworkable and self-defeating. They say that expectant mothers who have a drinking or drug problem need education and treatment, not prosecution (Marwick, 1997, 1998).

Since 1985, at least 240 women in 35 states have been prosecuted for using illegal drugs or alcohol during pregnancy, even though no state legislature has specifically criminalized such activity (Harris & Paltrow, 2003; Nelson & Marshall, 1998). Instead, these women have been charged with the broader crimes of child endangerment or abuse, illegal drug delivery to a minor, murder, or manslaughter. In all states except South Carolina, courts have refused to expand these existing laws to cover claims of fetal rights. Only in South Carolina has drug use during pregnancy been held to be a crime (Harris & Paltrow, 2003).

However, in March 2001 the Supreme Court did invalidate the South Carolina hospital's nonconsensual urine testing policy (Harris & Poltrow, 2003). Meanwhile, criticism of the policy, along with a decline in cocaine use, has led to a statewide policy stressing treatment, rather than punishment (Greenhouse, 2000b).

Intrusive Medical Procedures

In January 2004, Melissa Ann Rowland of Salt Lake City was charged with the murder of one of her newborn twins, who was born dead. Until it was too late, Rowland had refused doctors' urgent recommendation that she have a cesarean section. The second child, a girl, was born alive with cocaine and alcohol in her system and was subsequently adopted. Rowland, who had a history of mental health problems, pleaded guilty to a reduced charge of child endangerment, agreed to enter a drug treatment program, and was sentenced to 18 months of probation (Associated Press, 2004; Johnson, 2004).

Should a woman be forced to submit to intrusive procedures that pose a risk to her, such as a surgical delivery or intrauterine transfusions, when doctors say such procedures are essential to the delivery of a healthy baby? Should a woman from a fundamentalist sect that rejects modern medical care be taken into custody until she gives birth? Such measures have been defended as protecting the rights of the unborn. But women's rights advocates claim that they reflect a view of women as mere vehicles for carrying offspring and not as persons in their own right (Greenhouse, 2000b). Courts have held that "neither fetal rights nor state interests on behalf of the fetus supersede women's rights as ultimate medical decision maker" (Harris & Paltrow, 2003, p. 1698). However, the United States Congress in March 2004, in response to the notorious murder of a pregnant woman, which also took the life of her unborn son, made it a federal crime to harm or kill an unborn child (Reuters, 2004b). That law, if not overturned by the courts, for the first time establishes a fetal right to life separate from the mother's and could have repercussions in cases in which fetal welfare conflicts with women's rights.

Forcing intrusive measures on a pregnant woman may have important practical drawbacks, jeopardizing the doctor-patient relationship. If failure to follow medical advice could bring forced surgery, confinement, or criminal charges, some women might avoid doctors altogether and thus deprive their fetuses of needed prenatal care (Nelson & Marshall, 1998). Indeed, in South Carolina, fewer women are seeking such care (Jonsson, 2001).

What's your view?

- Does society's interest in protecting an unborn child justify coercive measures against pregnant women who ingest harmful substances or refuse medically indicated treatment?
- Should pregnant women who refuse to stop drinking or get treatment be incarcerated until they give birth?
- Should mothers who repeatedly give birth to children with FAS be sterilized?
- Should liquor companies be held liable if adequate warnings against use during pregnancy are not on their products?
- Would your answers be the same regarding smoking or use of cocaine or other potentially harmful substances?

Check it out!

For more information on this topic, go to **http://www.nofas.org/**. You will find information on behaviors of those affected by Fetal Alcohol Syndrome and Fetal Alcohol Effects, including national statistics and contacts. Resources include newsletters, support groups, audiovisual materials, and information packets.

Since then, a review of the literature found no specific effects of prenatal cocaine exposure on physical growth, cognition, language skills, motor skills, neurophysiology, behavior, attention, and emotional expressiveness in early childhood that could not also be attributed to other risk factors, such as exposure to tobacco, alcohol, marijuana, or a poor home environment (Frank, Augustyn, Knight, Pell, & Zuckerman, 2001). Even more recently, though, a longitudinal study of 376 newborns in a high-risk population did pinpoint some cognitive risks of cocaine exposure. Although cocaine-exposed children did not differ from a control group in average IQ (verbal, performance, or total) at age 4, the cocaine-exposed group tended to have lower scores on certain specific tasks (information, arithmetic, and object assembly) and were less likely to have above-normal IQs. Home environment made a difference; cocaine-exposed children who remained with their biological mothers or with other relatives had lower IQs than those placed in foster or adoptive care, who originally had had the most severe cocaine exposure. The foster and adopted children had more stimulating home environments, and their IQs were equivalent to those of the nonexposed controls (Singer et al., 2004).

Sexually Transmitted Diseases

Acquired immune deficiency syndrome (AIDS) is a disease caused by the human immunodeficiency virus (HIV), which undermines functioning of the immune system. If an expectant mother has the virus in her blood, it may cross over to the fetus's bloodstream through the placenta. After birth, the virus can be transmitted through breast milk. Infants born to HIV-infected mothers tend to have small heads and slowed neurological development (Macmillan et al., 2001).

acquired immune deficiency syndrome (AIDS) Viral disease that undermines effective functioning of the immune system.

Important advances have been made in the prevention, detection, and treatment of HIV infection in infants. These include prenatal administration of the drug zidovudine (formerly called *azidothymidine*), commonly called AZT, together with other antiretroviral drugs, to curtail transmission (Peters et al., 2003); the recommendation that women with HIV should not breast-feed; and the availability of new drugs to treat AIDS-related pneumonia. Between 1992 and 1997, when zidovudine therapy became widespread, the number of babies who got AIDS from their mothers dropped by about two-thirds, raising the hope that mother-to-child transmission of the virus can be virtually eliminated (Lindegren et al., 1999). The risk of transmission also can be reduced by choosing cesarean delivery (International Perinatal HIV Group, 1999).

Syphilis can cause problems in fetal development, and gonorrhea and genital herpes can have harmful effects on the baby at the time of delivery. The incidence of genital herpes simplex virus (HSV) has increased among newborns, who may acquire the disease from the mother or father either at or soon after birth (Sullivan-Bolyai, Hull, Wilson, & Corey, 1983), causing blindness, other abnormalities, or death. Again, cesarean delivery may help avoid infection.

Other Maternal Illnesses

All prospective parents should try to prevent any infections—common colds, flu, urinary tract and vaginal infections, as well as sexually transmitted diseases. If the mother does contract an infection, she should have it treated promptly. Pregnant women also should be screened for thyroid deficiency, which can affect their children's future cognitive performance (Haddow et al., 1999).

Rubella (German measles), if contracted by a woman before her 11th week of pregnancy, is almost certain to cause deafness and heart defects in her baby. Chances of catching rubella during pregnancy have been greatly reduced in Europe and the United States since the late 1960s, when a vaccine was developed that is now routinely administered to infants and children. However, rubella is still a serious problem in developing countries where inoculations are not routine (Plotkin, Katz, & Cordero, 1999).

A diabetic mother's metabolic regulation, especially during the second and third trimesters of pregnancy, unless carefully managed, may affect her child's long-range neurobehavioral development and cognitive performance (Rizzo, Metzger, Dooley, & Cho,

1997). These risks can be greatly reduced by screening pregnant women for diabetes, followed by careful monitoring and a controlled diet (Kjos & Buchanan, 1999). Use of multivitamin supplements during the three months before conception and the first three months of pregnancy can reduce the risk of birth defects in offspring of diabetic mothers (Correa, Botto, Lin, Mulinare, & Erickson, 2003).

An infection called *toxoplasmosis,* caused by a parasite harbored in the bodies of cattle, sheep, and pigs and in the intestinal tracts of cats, typically produces either no symptoms or symptoms like those of the common cold. In a pregnant woman, however, especially in the second and third trimesters of pregnancy, it can cause brain damage, severely impaired eyesight or blindness, seizures, miscarriage, stillbirth, or death of the baby. Although as many as 9 out of 10 of these babies may appear normal at birth, more than half of them have later problems, including eye infections, hearing loss, and learning disabilities. To avoid infection, expectant mothers should not eat raw or very rare meat, should wash hands and all work surfaces after touching raw meat, should peel or thoroughly wash raw fruits and vegetables, and should not dig in a garden where cat feces are buried. Women who have a cat should have it checked for the disease, should not feed it raw meat, and, if possible, should have someone else empty the litter box (March of Dimes Foundation, 2002) or should do it often, wearing gloves (Kravetz & Federman, 2002).

Maternal Stress

Maternal stress during pregnancy may affect the offspring. Prenatal stress in animals increases the risk of a wide variety of psychological disorders (Dingfelder, 2004; Huizink, Mulder, & Buitelaar, 2004). Some of the limited research on prenatal stress in humans suggests negative effects as well. Maternal anxiety in late pregnancy has been associated with reduced blood flow to the fetus (Sjostrom, Valentin, Thelin, & Marsal, 1997), and fetal levels of stress hormones rise and fall with those of the mother (Gitau, Cameron, Fisk, & Glover, 1998). In one study, women whose partners or children died or were hospitalized for cancer or heart attacks were at elevated risk of giving birth to children with cranial-neural-crest malformations, such as cleft lip, cleft palate, and heart malformations (Hansen, Lou, & Olsen, 2000). This finding fits with one reported in Chapter 3 that major stress during the 24th to 28th weeks of pregnancy may produce autism by deforming the developing brain (Beversdorf et al., 2001).

A mother's self-reported anxiety during pregnancy has been associated with 8-month-olds' inattentiveness during a developmental assessment (Huizink, Robles de Medina, Mulder, Visser, & Buitelaar, 2002) and preschoolers' negative emotionality or behavioral disorders in early childhood (Martin, Noyes, Wisenbaker, & Huttunen, 2000; O'Connor, Heron, Golding, Beveridge, & Glover, 2002). Other studies have found links between expectant mothers' perceptions of stress and their fetuses' activity levels (DiPietro, Hilton, Hawkins, Costigan, & Pressman, 2002) as well as between maternal stress and the synchrony of fetal movements and heart rates (DiPietro, Hodgson, Costigan, Hilton, & Johnson, 1996a). In a study that did *not* depend on maternal self-reports, expectant mothers were given a mildly stressful cognitive task (to read aloud, for example, the word *red* when printed in blue). While the women engaged in this task, their fetuses' motor activity tended to decline, though individual responses varied (DiPietro, 2004).

Moderate maternal stress is not necessarily bad for fetuses; in fact, some stress at certain times during gestation may spur organization of the formative brain. In a follow-up study of 100 two-year-olds who as fetuses had participated in studies of maternal stress, those whose mothers had shown greater anxiety midway through pregnancy scored higher on measures of motor and mental development (DiPietro, 2004).

Maternal Age

Women today typically start having children later in life than was true 15 or 20 years ago, often because they spend their early adult years getting advanced education and establishing careers (Mathews & Ventura, 1997; Ventura et al., 1999). Births to women in their late 30s and 40s and even in their 50s have steadily risen since the late 1970s (Martin, Hamilton et al., 2003; Ventura, Martin, Curtin, Menacker, & Hamilton, 2001)—an example of a history-graded influence.

How does delayed childbearing affect the risks to mother and baby? Pregnant women over 35 are more likely to suffer complications due to diabetes, high blood pressure, or severe bleeding. Although most risks to the infant's health are not much greater than for babies born to younger mothers, there is more chance of miscarriage or stillbirth. There is also more likelihood of premature delivery, retarded fetal growth, other birth-related complications, and birth defects, such as Down syndrome (refer back to Chapter 3). However, due to widespread screening for fetal defects among older expectant mothers, fewer malformed babies are born nowadays (Berkowitz, Skovron, Lapinski, & Berkowitz, 1990; P. Brown, 1993; Cunningham & Leveno, 1995).

Women age 40 and over are at increased risk of needing operative deliveries (cesarean or by forceps or vacuum extraction; see Chapter 5). Risks of all birth complications are increased in delayed pregnancies, and the infants are more likely to be born prematurely and underweight (Gilbert, Nesbitt, & Danielsen, 1999). Women who give birth after age 50 are two to three times more likely than younger women to have babies who are very small, born prematurely, or stillborn (Salihu, Shumpert, Slay, Kirby, & Alexander, 2003).

Although multiple births generally tend to be riskier than single births, twins and triplets born to older mothers do as well or better than those born to younger mothers—unless the mothers have low socioeconomic status. Many multiple births to older women with higher SES are conceived through assisted reproductive technology, and these pregnancies tend to be monitored closely (Zhang, Meikle, Grainger, & Trumble, 2002).

Adolescents also tend to have premature or underweight babies—perhaps because a young girl's still-growing body consumes vital nutrients the fetus needs (Fraser, Brockert, & Ward, 1995). These newborns are at heightened risk of death in the first month, disabilities, or health problems. Risks of teenage pregnancy are discussed further in Chapter 17.

Outside Environmental Hazards

Air pollution, chemicals, radiation, extremes of heat and humidity, and other hazards of modern life can affect prenatal development. Blood samples taken from 265 New York City mothers and their newborns showed as much DNA damage from combustion-related pollutants in the infants as in the mothers, even though the infants had received a tenfold lower dose in the womb due to the protection of the placenta (Perera et al., 2004).Women who work with chemicals used in manufacturing semiconductor chips have about twice the rate of miscarriage as other female workers (Markoff, 1992), and women exposed to DDT tend to have more preterm births (Longnecker, Klebanoff, Zhou, & Brock, 2001). Two common insecticides, chlorpyrifos and diazinon, apparently cause stunting of prenatal growth. Infants born in New York City after a U.S. ban on household use of these substances were heavier and longer and had substantially less insecticide in blood drawn from their umbilical cords than babies born before the ban (Whyatt et al., in press).

Children born to mothers who live near toxic landfills may be at elevated risk for various types of birth defects. Research in the United Kingdom reported a 33 percent increase in risk of nongenetic birth defects among families living within two miles of certain hazardous-waste sites (Vrijheld et al., 2002). Childhood cancers, including leukemia, have been linked to pregnant mothers' drinking chemically contaminated ground water (Boyles, 2002). Infants exposed prenatally to high levels of lead score lower on tests of cognitive abilities than those exposed to low or moderate levels (Bellinger, Leviton, Watermaux, Needleman, & Rabinowitz, 1987; Needleman & Gatsonis, 1990); children exposed prenatally to heavy metals are more prone to illness and have lower measured intelligence than children not exposed to these metals (Lewis, Worobey, Ramsay, & McCormack, 1992).

In Taiwan, children born between 1978 and 1985 to mothers who had used contaminated cooking oil showed skin defects, developmental delays, and disordered behavior, and some died. A controlled follow-up study of 118 school-aged survivors found long-lasting cognitive and behavioral damage (Lai et al., 2002).

Prenatal radiation exposure (for example, through X-rays of a mother's abdomen) can lead to stunted growth, birth defects, abnormal brain function, or cancer later in life. The impact depends on the dose and the timing; risks are greatest before the 15th week of gestation (CDC, undated). Women who have routine dental X-rays during pregnancy triple their risk of having full-term, low-birth-weight babies (Hujoel, Bollen, Noonan, & del Aguila, 2004).

Checkpoint

Can you . . .

- ✔ Describe the short-term and long-term effects on the developing fetus of a mother's use of medical and recreational drugs during pregnancy?
- ✔ Summarize the risks of maternal illnesses and stress, delayed childbearing, and exposure to chemicals and radiation?

Radiation can cause genetic mutations. In utero exposure to radiation has been linked to mental retardation, small head size, chromosomal malformations, Down syndrome, seizures, and poor performance on IQ tests and in school. The critical period seems to be 8 through 15 weeks after fertilization (Yamazaki & Schull, 1990).

Paternal Factors

A man's exposure to lead, marijuana or tobacco smoke, large amounts of alcohol or radiation, DES, or certain pesticides (Swan et al., 2003) may result in abnormal or poor quality sperm. Offspring of male workers at a British nuclear processing plant were at elevated risk of being born dead (Parker, Pearce, Dickinson, Aitkin, & Craft, 1999). Babies whose fathers had diagnostic X-rays within the year prior to conception or had high lead exposure at work tended to have low birth weight and slowed fetal growth (Lin, Hwang, Marshall, & Marion, 1998; Shea, Little, & the ALSPAC Study Team, 1997). And fathers whose diet is low in vitamin C are more likely to have children with birth defects and certain types of cancer (Fraga et al., 1991).

What's your view?

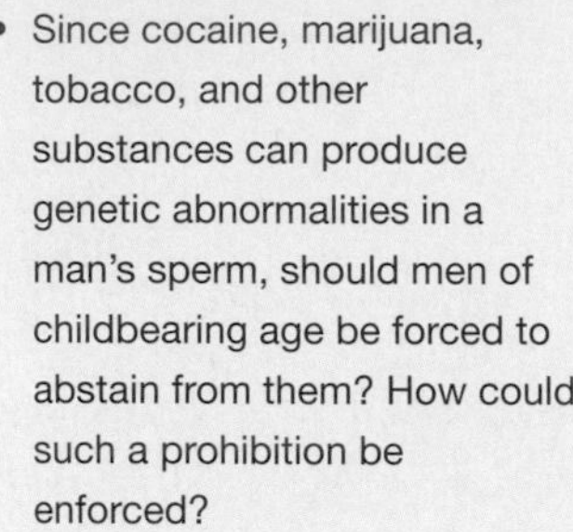

- Since cocaine, marijuana, tobacco, and other substances can produce genetic abnormalities in a man's sperm, should men of childbearing age be forced to abstain from them? How could such a prohibition be enforced?

A man's use of cocaine can cause birth defects in his children. The cocaine seems to attach itself to his sperm, and this cocaine-bearing sperm then enters the ovum at conception. Other toxins, such as lead and mercury, may "hitchhike" onto sperm in the same way (Yazigi, Odem, & Polakoski, 1991).

Men who smoke are at increased risk of impotence and of transmitting genetic abnormalities (AAP Committee on Substance Abuse, 2001). A pregnant woman's exposure to the father's secondhand smoke has been linked with low birth weight and cancer in childhood and adulthood (Ji et al., 1997; D. H. Rubin, Krasilnikoff, Leventhal, Weile, & Berget, 1986; Sandler, Everson, Wilcox, & Browder, 1985). In a study of 214 nonsmoking mothers in New York City, exposure to *both* paternal smoking and urban air pollution resulted in a 7 percent reduction in birth weight and a 3 percent reduction in head circumference (Perera et al., 2004). Paternal smoking brings increased risk of infant respiratory infections and sudden infant death, whether or not the mother also smokes (Wakefield, Reid, Roberts, Mullins, & Gillies, 1998).

Checkpoint

Can you . . .

✔ Identify at least three ways in which environmentally caused defects can be influenced by the father?

Older fathers may be a significant source of birth defects (Crow, 1993, 1995). A later paternal age (averaging in the late 30s) is associated with increases in the risk of several rare conditions, including Marfan's syndrome (deformities of the head and limbs) and dwarfism (G. Evans, 1976). Advanced age of the father may be a factor in about 5 percent of cases of Down syndrome (Antonarakis & Down Syndrome Collaborative Group, 1991) and in some cases of schizophrenia (Byrne, Agerbo, Ewald, Eaton, & Mortensen, 2003). More male cells than female ones undergo mutations, and mutations may increase with paternal age.

Guidepost 4

What techniques can assess a fetus's health and well-being, and what is the importance of prenatal care?

Monitoring Prenatal Development

Not long ago, almost the only decision parents had to make about their babies before birth was the decision to conceive; most of what happened in the intervening months was beyond their control. Now we have an array of tools to assess an unborn baby's progress and well-being (see Box 4-2), and even to intervene to correct some abnormal conditions. In line with these developments is a growing emphasis on the importance of early prenatal care.

Conditions detected by prenatal assessment can be corrected before birth in three ways: through administration of medicine, blood transfusion, and surgery. Fetuses can swallow and absorb medicines, nutrients, vitamins, and hormones that are injected into the amniotic fluid, and drugs that might not pass through the placenta can be injected through the umbilical cord. Blood can be transfused through the cord as early as the 18th week of gestation. In 1996, surgeons successfully performed a bone marrow transplant in the womb to prevent the development of a rare sex-linked genetic disorder, severe combined immunodeficiency, in a fetus identified by chorionic villus sampling as having the mutant gene for it. The baby was born healthy by cesarean delivery and showed no sign of the disorder throughout infancy (Flake et al., 1996). Eventually transplantation procedures, in the form of gene therapy, may be used to treat other congenital diseases in utero.

The Everyday World

Box 4-2 *Prenatal Assessment Techniques*

Techniques for monitoring fetal development, coupled with increased knowledge of ways to improve the child's prenatal world, make pregnancy much less a cause for concern than in earlier times. Access to prenatal diagnosis of birth defects, coupled with the legal availability of abortion and the possibility of fetal therapy, has encouraged many couples with troubling medical histories to take a chance on conception.

Ultrasound and Amniocentesis

Some parents see their baby for the first time in a *sonogram,* a picture of the uterus, fetus, and placenta created by *ultrasound* directed into the mother's abdomen. Ultrasound is used to measure fetal growth, to judge gestational age, to detect multiple pregnancies, to evaluate uterine abnormalities, to detect major structural abnormalities in the fetus, and to determine whether a fetus has died, as well as to guide other procedures, such as amniocentesis.

A newer technique called *sonoembriology,* which involves high-frequency transvaginal probes and digital image processing, has made possible earlier detection of unusual defects. Sonoembryology reportedly can detect 60 percent of all malformations during the first trimester of pregnancy and, in combination with ultrasound, more than 80 percent during the second trimester (Kurjak, Kupesic, Matijevic, Kos, & Marton, 1999).

In *amniocentesis,* a sample of the amniotic fluid, which contains fetal cells, is withdrawn and analyzed to detect the presence of certain genetic or multifactorial defects and all recognizable chromosomal disorders. Only 2 percent of mothers with live births used amniocentesis in 2002, as compared with 68 percent who had ultrasound (Martin et al., 2003). Amniocentesis is recommended for pregnant women ages 35 and over. It is also recommended if the woman and her partner are both known carriers of such diseases as Tay-Sachs and sickle-cell anemia or if they have a family history of such conditions as Down syndrome, spina bifida, and muscular dystrophy. However, a new ultrasound test that measures the nose bone of the fetus can improve early detection of Down syndrome and avoid the need for amniocentesis, which has a small risk of miscarriage (Cicero, Curcio, Papageorghiou, Sonek, & Nicolaides, 2001).

Both amniocentesis and ultrasound can reveal the sex of the fetus, which may help in diagnosing sex-linked disorders. In some Asian countries in which sons are preferred, both procedures have been used (in some places, illegally) for "sex-screening" of unborn babies, with the result that in these populations males now predominate (Burns, 1994; Kristof, 1993; WuDunn, 1997).

Other Assessment Methods

In *chorionic villus sampling (CVS),* tissue from the ends of *villi*—hairlike projections of the *chorion,* the membrane surrounding the fetus, that are made up of fetal cells—are tested for the presence of birth defects and disorders. This procedure can be performed between 8 and 13 weeks of pregnancy (earlier than amniocentesis) and yields results within about a week. However, there is almost a 5 percent greater chance of miscarriage or neonatal death after CVS than after amniocentesis (D'Alton & DeCherney, 1993).

Embryoscopy, insertion of a tiny viewing scope into a pregnant woman's abdomen, can provide a clear look at embryos as young as 6 weeks. The procedure is promising for early diagnosis and treatment of embryonic and fetal abnormalities (Quintero, Abuhamad, Hobbins, & Mahoney, 1993).

Preimplantation genetic diagnosis can identify some genetic defects in embryos of four to eight cells, which were conceived by in vitro fertilization and have not yet been implanted in the mother's uterus. Defective embryos are not implanted. This technique was used successfully on a woman with a genetic predisposition for early-onset Alzheimer's disease, to avoid the transmission of the mutant gene (Verlinsky et al., 2002).

By inserting a needle into tiny blood vessels of the umbilical cord under the guidance of ultrasound, doctors can take samples of a fetus's blood. This procedure, called *umbilical cord sampling* or *fetal blood sampling,* can test for infection, anemia, heart failure, and certain metabolic disorders and immunodeficiencies and seems to offer promise for identifying other conditions. However, the technique is associated with miscarriage, bleeding from the umbilical cord, early labor, and infection (Chervenak, Isaacson, & Mahoney, 1986; D'Alton & DeCherney, 1993; Kolata, 1988).

A blood sample taken from the mother between the 16th and 18th weeks of pregnancy can be tested for the amount of alpha fetoprotein (AFP) it contains. This *maternal blood test* is appropriate for women at risk of bearing children with defects in the formation of the brain or spinal cord, such as anencephaly or spina bifida, which may be detected by high AFP levels. To confirm or refute the presence of suspected conditions, ultrasound or amniocentesis or both may be performed. Blood tests of samples taken between the 15th and 20th weeks of gestation can predict about 60 percent of cases of Down syndrome. This blood test is particularly important for women under 35, who bear 80 percent of all Down syndrome babies but usually are not targeted to receive amniocentesis because their individual risk is lower (Haddow et al., 1992). In a 10-year study in England and Wales, screening programs based on blood tests or ultrasound were more effective in diagnosing Down syndrome than programs based on maternal age alone (Smith-Bindman et al., 2003).

The discovery that fetal cells that "leak" into the mother's blood early in pregnancy can be isolated and analyzed (Simpson & Elias, 1993) will make it possible to detect genetic as well as chromosomal disorders from a maternal blood test without using riskier procedures. Already researchers have succeeded in screening fetal blood cells for single genes for sickle-cell anemia and thalassemia (Cheung, Goldberg, & Kan, 1996).

What's your view?

In the United States, women who undergo ultrasound or amniocentesis can choose whether to be told their unborn babies' sex. Suppose substantial numbers of American women were aborting their fetuses for reasons of sex preference, as has happened in some East Asian countries. In that case, would you favor a law forbidding use of a prenatal diagnostic procedure to reveal the sex of a fetus?

Check it out!

For more information on this topic, go to **http://www.noah.cuny.edu/pregnancy/march_of_dimes/testing/amniocen.html** or **http://www.epregnancy.com/info/prenataltests/test-amnio.htm**. These are Web sites with facts about amniocentesis and links to fact sheets about other prenatal tests.

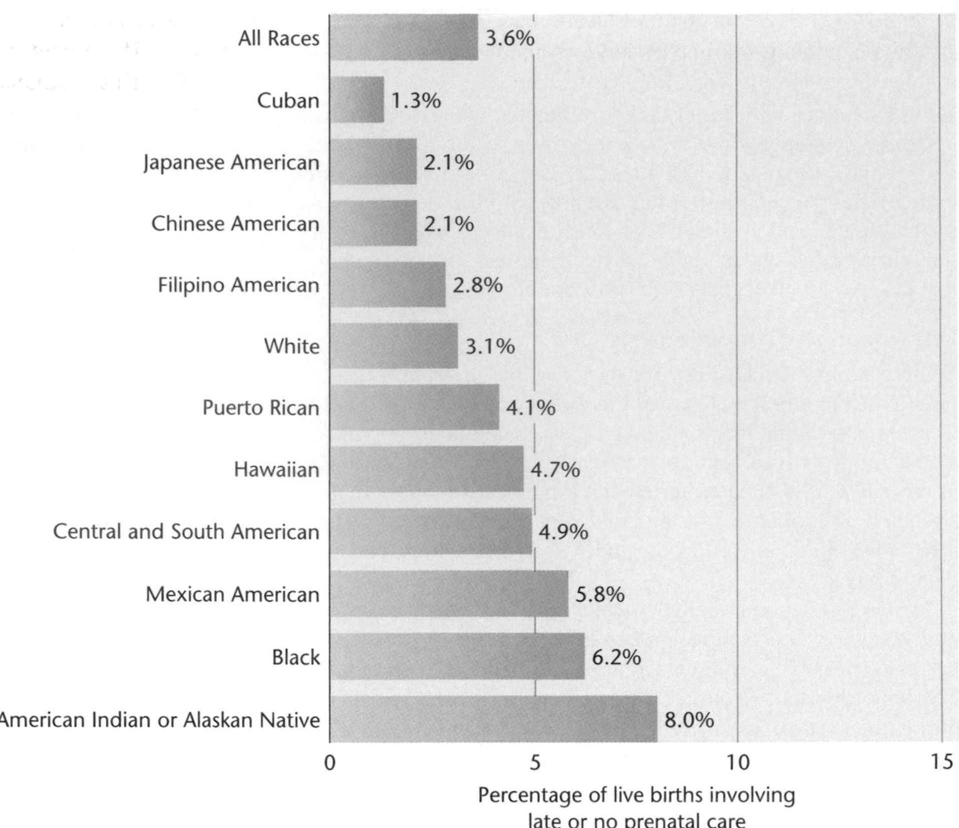

Figure 4-3

Proportion of U.S. mothers with late or no prenatal care, according to race or ethnicity, 2002. Late prenatal care begins in the last three months of pregnancy.

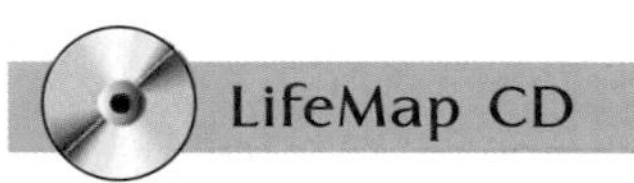

Every pregnant woman should see a health care professional as soon as she suspects she is pregnant. Watch the video on "Midwives" in Chapter 4 of your CD to learn more about prenatal care.

Screening for treatable defects and diseases is only one reason for the importance of prenatal care. Early, high-quality prenatal care, which includes educational, social, and nutritional services, can help prevent maternal and infant death and other complications of birth. It can provide first-time mothers with information about pregnancy, childbirth, and infant care. Poor women who get prenatal care benefit by being put in touch with other needed services, and they are more likely to get medical care for their infants after birth (Shiono & Behrman, 1995).

In the United States prenatal care is widespread but not universal as in many European countries, and it lacks uniform national standards and guaranteed financial coverage. Use of early prenatal care (during the first three months of pregnancy) has risen since 1990 from 75.8 percent to 83.7 percent of pregnant women. Still, in 2002, nearly 1 in 6 expectant mothers got no care until after the first trimester, and more than 1 in 25 received no care until the last trimester or no care at all (Martin et al., 2003).

Although prenatal care has increased, rates of low birth weight and premature birth have worsened (Kogan et al., 1998; Martin et al., 2001). Why? One answer is the increasing number of multiple births, which require especially close prenatal attention. Twin pregnancies often end, for precautionary reasons, in early births, either induced or by cesarean delivery. Intensive prenatal care may permit early detection of problems requiring immediate delivery, as, for example, when one or both fetuses are not thriving. This may explain why a U.S. government study of twin births between 1981 and 1997 found parallel upward trends in use of prenatal care and rates of preterm birth—along with a decline in mortality of those twin infants whose mothers obtained intensive prenatal care (Kogan et al., 2000).

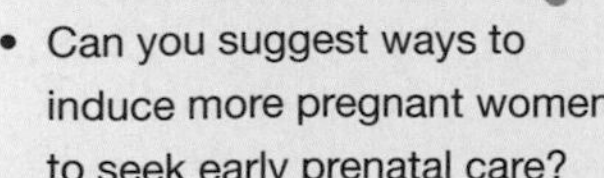

- Can you suggest ways to induce more pregnant women to seek early prenatal care?

A second answer is that the benefits of prenatal care are not evenly distributed. Although usage of prenatal care has grown, especially among ethnic groups that tend *not* to receive early care, the women most at risk of bearing low-birth-weight babies—teenage and unmarried women, those with little education, and some minority women—are still least likely to receive it (Martin et al., 2003; National Center for Health Statistics, 1994a,

1998, 2001; U.S. Department of Health and Human Services, 1996a). Although 85 percent of white expectant mothers receive prenatal care in the first trimester, only 75 percent of Hispanic Americans, 74 percent of African Americans, and 69 percent of American Indians and Alaska Natives do (American Public Health Association, 2004). Figure 4-3 shows percentages of various ethnic groups that receive late or no prenatal care.

Merely increasing the quantity of prenatal care does not address the *content* of care (Misra & Guyer, 1998). Most prenatal care programs in the United States focus on screening for major complications and are not designed to attack the causes of low birth weight. A national panel has recommended that prenatal care be restructured to provide more visits early in the pregnancy and fewer in the last trimester. In fact, care should begin *before* pregnancy. Prepregnancy counseling could make more women aware, for example, of the importance of getting enough folic acid in their diet and could make sure that they are immune to rubella. In addition, care needs to be made more accessible to poor and minority women (Shiono & Behrman, 1995).

Checkpoint

Can you . . .

- ✔ Describe seven techniques for identifying defects or disorders prenatally?
- ✔ Tell why early, high-quality prenatal care is important, and how it can be improved?

Refocus

- What light does Abel Dorris's case shed on the role of the prenatal environment in a child's development?
- Why did Michael Dorris's belief that Abel would "catch up," given a positive adoptive home environment, prove unfounded?
- Does Abel's story illustrate the concept of reaction range? Of canalization? Of critical periods? If so, how?
- What sorts of information might be helpful in counseling prospective parents on adoption of a child whose prenatal history is unknown?

Good prenatal care can give every child the best possible chance for entering the world in good condition to meet the challenges of life outside the womb—challenges we will discuss in the next three chapters.

Summary and Key Terms

Prenatal Development: Three Stages

Guidepost 1 What are the three stages of prenatal development, and what happens during each stage?

- Prenatal development occurs in three stages of gestation: the germinal, embryonic, and fetal stages.
- Growth and development both before and after birth follow the cephalocaudal principle (head to tail) and the proximodistal principle (center outward).
- About one-third of all conceptions end in spontaneous abortion, usually in the first trimester of pregnancy.

cephalocaudal principle (87) proximodistal principle (87) germinal stage (87) embryonic stage (90) spontaneous abortion (90)

Guidepost 2 What can fetuses do?

- As fetuses grow, they move less but move more vigorously. Swallowing amniotic fluid, which contains substances from the mother's body, stimulates taste and smell. Fetuses seem able to hear, exercise sensory discrimination, learn, and remember.

fetal stage (91) ultrasound (91)

Prenatal Development: Environmental Influences

Guidepost 3 What environmental influences can affect prenatal development?

- The developing organism can be affected greatly by its prenatal environment. The likelihood of a birth defect may depend on the timing and intensity of an environmental event and its interaction with genetic factors.
- Important environmental influences involving the mother include nutrition, physical activity, smoking, intake of alcohol or other drugs, maternal illnesses, maternal stress, maternal age, and external environmental hazards, such as chemicals and radiation. External influences and paternal age may affect the father's sperm.

teratogenic (93) fetal alcohol syndrome (FAS) (95) acquired immune deficiency syndrome (AIDS) (99)

Monitoring Prenatal Development

Guidepost 4 What techniques can assess a fetus's health and well-being, and what is the importance of prenatal care?

- Ultrasound, amniocentesis, chorionic villus sampling, embryoscopy, preimplantation genetic diagnosis, umbilical cord sampling, and maternal blood tests can be used to determine whether an unborn baby is developing or will develop normally. Some abnormal conditions can be corrected through fetal therapy.
- Early, high-quality prenatal care is essential for healthy development. It can lead to detection of defects and disorders and, especially if begun early and targeted to the needs of at-risk women, may help reduce maternal and infant death, low birth weight, and other birth complications.

chapter 5

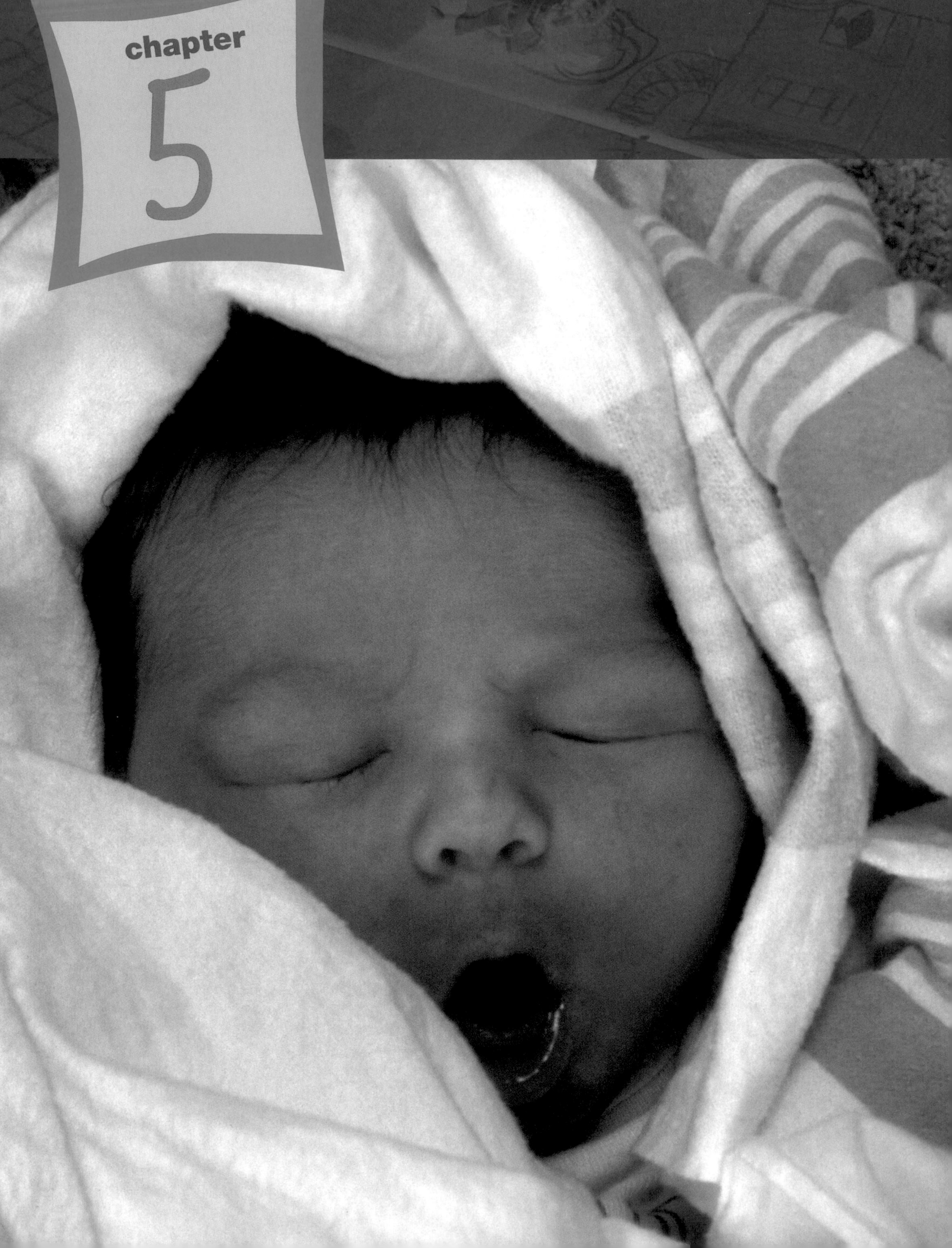

Birth and the Newborn Baby

A newborn baby is an extraordinary event; and I have never seen two babies who looked exactly alike. Here is the breathing miracle who could not live an instant without you, with a skull more fragile than an egg, a miracle of eyes, legs, toenails, and lungs.

—James Baldwin, *No Name in the Street*, 1972

Focus *The Birth of Elvis Presley*

Elvis Presley

Elvis Presley (1935–1977) was born in a 30- by 15-foot cottage in East Tupelo, Mississippi. Today, the modest birthplace of the now-legendary "king" of rock music is painted sparkling white, the walls are papered with primroses, and dainty curtains hang at the windows—among the many homey touches added for the benefit of tourists. But, like many of the popular myths about Elvis's early life, this "cute little doll house" (Goldman, 1981, p. 60) bears only slight resemblance to the reality: a bare board shack with no indoor plumbing or electricity, set in a dirt-poor hamlet that wasn't much more than "a wide spot in the road" (Clayton & Heard, 1994, p. 8).

During the Great Depression, Elvis's near-illiterate father, Vernon Presley, sometimes did odd jobs for a farmer named Orville Bean, who owned much of the town. Elvis's mother, Gladys, was vivacious and high-spirited, as talkative as Vernon was taciturn. She, like Vernon, came from a family of sharecroppers and migrant workers. She had moved to East Tupelo to be close to the garment factory where she worked.

Gladys first noticed handsome Vernon on the street and then, soon after, met him in church. They eloped on June 17, 1933. Vernon was 17 and Gladys, 21. They borrowed three dollars to pay for the marriage license.

At first the young couple lived with friends and family. When Gladys became pregnant, Vernon borrowed $180 from his employer, Bean, to buy lumber and nails and, with the help of his father and older brother, built a two-room cabin next to his parents' house on Old Saltillo Road. Bean, who owned the land, was to hold title to the house until the loan was paid off.

Vernon and Gladys moved into their new home in December 1934, about a month before Gladys gave birth. Her pregnancy was a difficult one; her legs swelled, and she finally quit her job at the garment factory, where she had to stand on her feet all day pushing a heavy steam iron.

When Vernon got up for work in the wee hours of January 8, a bitterly cold morning, Gladys was hemorrhaging. The midwife told Vernon to get the doctor, Will Hunt. (His $15 fee was paid by welfare.) At about 4 o'clock in the morning, Dr. Hunt delivered a stillborn

Sources of information about Elvis Presley's birth were Clayton & Heard (1994); Dundy (1985); Goldman (1981); Guralnick (1994); and Marling (1996).

baby boy, Jesse Garon. The second twin, Elvis Aron, was born about 35 minutes later. Gladys—extremely weak and losing blood—was taken to the hospital charity ward with baby Elvis. They stayed there for more than three weeks.

Baby Jesse remained an important part of the family's life. Gladys frequently talked to Elvis about his brother. "When one twin died, the one that lived got the strength of both," she would say (Guralnick, 1994, p. 13). Elvis took his mother's words to heart. Throughout his life, his twin's imagined voice and presence were constantly with him.

Elvis lived in his birthplace only until the age of 3, when his father went to prison for altering a $4 check. When the payment on the house loan came due, Bean evicted Gladys and her son, who had to move in with family members. In later years, Elvis would drive back to East Tupelo (now Tupelo's suburban Presley Heights). He would sit in his car in the dark, looking at the cottage on what is now called Elvis Presley Drive and "thinking about the course his life had taken" (Marling, 1996, p. 20).

• • •

Elvis Presley is just one of many well-known people—including almost all the presidents of the United States—who were born at home. At one time, medical care during pregnancy was rare even in the United States. Many infants, like Jesse Presley, were born dead, and many women died in childbirth. Today, medical advances and a rising standard of living in industrialized countries have reduced the risks of giving birth. The overwhelming majority of births in the United States (but a smaller proportion in some European countries) now occur in hospitals. However, as we will see, there is a small but growing movement back to home birth—still the norm in many developing countries.

In this chapter, we examine how babies come into the world. We describe how newborn infants look and how their body systems work. We discuss ways to assess their health and how birth complications can affect development. We also consider how the birth of a baby affects the people most vital to the infant's well-being: the parents.

After you have read and studied this chapter, you should be able to answer each of the Guidepost questions that follow. Look for them again in the margins, where they point to important concepts throughout the chapter. To check your understanding of these Guideposts, review the end-of-chapter summary. Checkpoints located at periodic spots throughout the chapter will help you verify your understanding of what you have read.

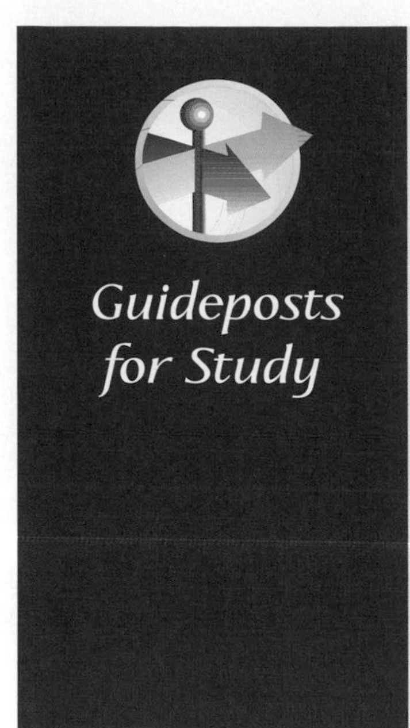

Guideposts for Study

1. How do customs surrounding birth reflect culture, and how has childbirth changed in developed countries?
2. How does labor begin, and what happens during each of the four stages of childbirth?
3. What alternative methods of delivery are available?
4. How do newborn infants adjust to life outside the womb?
5. How can we tell whether a new baby is healthy and is developing normally?
6. How do newborns' patterns of sleep, waking, and activity vary and change?
7. How do parents bond with their baby, and how does parenthood change their relationship with one another?
8. What complications of childbirth can endanger newborn babies, and what are the long-term prospects for infants with complicated births?

Childbirth and Culture: How Birthing Has Changed

Guidepost 1

How do customs surrounding birth reflect culture, and how has childbirth changed in developed countries?

Customs surrounding childbirth reflect the beliefs, values, and resources of a culture. A Mayan woman in Yucatan gives birth in the hammock in which she sleeps every night; the father-to-be is expected to be present, along with the midwife. To evade evil spirits, mother and child remain at home for a week (Jordan, 1993). By contrast, among the Ngoni in East Africa, men are excluded from the event. In rural Thailand, a new mother generally resumes normal activity within a few hours of giving birth (Broude, 1995; Gardiner & Kosmitzki, 2005).

Before the 20th century, childbirth in Europe and in the United States followed somewhat similar patterns. Birth was a female social ritual. The woman, surrounded by female relatives and neighbors, sat up in her own bed or perhaps in the stable, modestly draped in a sheet; if she wished, she might stand, walk around, or squat over a birth stool. Chinks in the walls, doors, and windows were stuffed with cloth to keep out chills and evil spirits. The prospective father was nowhere to be seen. Nor, until the 15th century, was a doctor present, and then only for wealthy women if complications arose.

The midwife who presided over the event had no formal training; she offered "advice, massages, potions, irrigations, and talismans." Salves made of fat of viper, gall of eel, powdered hoof of donkey, tongue of chameleon, or skin of snake or hare might be rubbed on the prospective mother's abdomen to ease her pain or hasten her labor; but "the cries of the mother during labor were considered to be as natural as those of the baby at birth" (Fontanel & d'Harcourt, 1997, p. 28).

Given the lack of accurate knowledge about female anatomy and the birth process, the midwives' ministrations sometimes did more harm than good. A 16th-century textbook instructed midwives to stretch and dilate the membranes of the genital parts and cut or break them with their fingernails, to urge the patient to go up and down stairs screaming at the top of her lungs, to help her bear down by pressing on her belly, and to pull out the placenta immediately after the birth (Fontanel & d'Harcourt, 1997).

After the baby emerged, the midwife cut and tied the umbilical cord and cleaned and examined the newborn, testing the reflexes and joints. The other women helped the new

Source: This discussion is based largely on Eccles (1982); Fontanel & d'Harcourt (1997); Gelis (1991); and Scholten (1985).

mother wash and dress, made her bed with clean sheets, and served her food to rebuild her strength. Within a few hours or days, a peasant mother would be back at work in the fields; a more affluent or noble woman could "lie in" and rest for several weeks.

What's your view ?

- If you or your partner were expecting a baby, and the pregnancy seemed to be going smoothly, would you prefer (a) hospital, birth center, or home birth, (b) attendance by a physician or midwife, and (c) medicated or nonmedicated delivery? Give reasons.
- If you are a man, would you choose to be present at the birth?
- If you are a woman, would you want your partner present?

Reducing the Risks of Childbirth

Childbirth in those times was "a struggle with death" (Fontanel & d'Harcourt, 1997, p. 34) for both mother and baby. In 17th- and 18th-century France, a woman had a 1 in 10 chance of dying while or shortly after giving birth. Thousands of babies were stillborn, and 1 out of 4 who were born alive died during their first year. At the end of the 19th century, in England and Wales, an expectant mother was almost 50 times more likely to die in childbirth than is a woman giving birth today (Saunders, 1997).

The development of the science of obstetrics early in the 19th century professionalized childbirth, especially in urban settings. Most deliveries still occurred at home and women were on hand to help and offer emotional support, but a (male) physician was usually in charge, with surgical instruments ready in case of trouble. Midwives were now given training, and obstetrics manuals were widely disseminated.

After the turn of the 20th century, maternity hospitals, where conditions were antiseptic and medical management was easier, became the birth setting of choice for those who could afford them (though not for many country women, like Gladys Presley). In 1900, only 5 percent of U.S. deliveries occurred in hospitals; by 1920, rates in various cities ranged from 30 to 65 percent (Scholten, 1985). A similar trend took place in Europe. In the United States today, about 99 percent of babies are born in hospitals, and more than 91 percent of births are attended by physicians. A small but growing proportion are attended by midwives (Martin et al., 2003).

LifeMap CD

To consider the pros and cons of having a baby with a midwife, watch the "Midwifery" video in Chapter 5 of your CD.

The dramatic reductions in risks surrounding pregnancy and childbirth, particularly during the past 50 years, are largely due to the availability of antibiotics, blood transfusions, safe anesthesia, improved hygiene, and drugs for inducing labor when necessary. In addition, improvements in prenatal assessment and care make it far more likely that a baby will be born healthy.

Still, childbirth is not risk free—for women or babies. Among the nearly 4 million U.S. women giving birth each year between 1993 and 1997, 31 percent experienced medical problems (Daniel, Berg, Johnson, & Atrash, 2003). Maternal mortality is at least four times as high for black women as for white women. Black women, obese women, those with difficult medical histories, those who have had previous cesarean deliveries, and those who have had several children are at elevated risk of hemorrhage and other dangerous complications (Chazotte, quoted in Bernstein, 2003).

Contemporary Settings for Childbirth

The medicalization of childbirth has had social and emotional costs. To many modern women, "a hospital birth has become a surgical act in which the woman is hooked up to a monitor and stretched out on a table under glaring lights and the stares of two or three strangers, her feet in stirrups" (Fontanel & d'Harcourt, 1997, p. 57). Today some women in developed countries are going back to the intimate, personal experience of home birth, which can involve the whole family. Home births usually are attended by a trained nurse-midwife, with the resources of medical science close at hand in case of need. Freestanding, homelike birth centers are another option. Studies suggest that both of these settings can be as safe and much less expensive than hospital births in low-risk deliveries attended by skilled practitioners (Anderson & Anderson, 1999; Durand, 1992; Guyer, Strobino, Ventura, & Singh, 1995; Korte & Scaer, 1984).

Checkpoint ✔

Can you . . .

✔ Identify at least three ways in which childbirth has changed in developed countries?

✔ Give reasons for the reduction in risks of pregnancy and childbirth?

✔ Weigh the comparative advantages of various settings and attendants for childbirth?

Hospitals, too, are finding ways to "humanize" childbirth. Labor and delivery may take place in a quiet, homelike birthing room, under soft lights, with the father present as a "coach" and older siblings invited to visit after the birth. The woman is given local anesthesia if she wants and needs it, but she can see and participate in the birth process and can hold her newborn on her belly immediately afterward. Rooming-in policies allow a baby to stay in the mother's room much or all of the time. By "demedicalizing the experience, some hospitals and birthing centers are seeking to establish—or reestablish—around childbirth an environment in which tenderness, security, and emotion carry as much weight as medical techniques" (Fontanel & d'Harcourt, 1997, p. 57).

The Birth Process

How does labor begin, and what happens during each of the four stages of childbirth ?

parturition Process of uterine, cervical, and other changes, usually lasting about two weeks, preceding childbirth.

Birth is both a beginning and an end: the climax of all that has happened from the moment of fertilization. *Labor* is an apt term for the process of giving birth. Birth is hard work for both mother and baby—but work that yields a rich reward.

What brings on labor, or normal vaginal childbirth, is a series of uterine, cervical, and other changes called **parturition.** Parturition typically begins about two weeks before delivery, when sharply rising estrogen levels stimulate the uterus to contract and the cervix to become more flexible. The timing of parturition seems to be determined by the rate at which the placenta produces a protein called *corticotropin-releasing hormone (CRH),* which also promotes maturation of the fetal lungs to ready them for life outside the womb. The rate of CRH production as early as the fifth month of pregnancy may predict whether a baby will be born early, "on time," or late (Smith, 1999).

The uterine contractions that expel the fetus begin—typically, 266 days after conception—as mild tightenings of the uterus. A woman may have felt similar "false" contractions at times during the final months of pregnancy, but she may recognize birth contractions as the "real thing" because of their greater regularity and intensity.

Stages of Childbirth

Labor takes place in four overlapping stages (see Figure 5-1). The *first stage,* the longest, typically lasts 12 hours or more for a woman having her first child. In subsequent births the first stage tends to be shorter. During this stage, regular and increasingly frequent uterine contractions cause the cervix to dilate, or widen.

The *second stage* typically lasts about 1½ hours or less. It begins when the baby's head begins to move through the cervix into the vaginal canal, and it ends when the baby emerges completely from the mother's body. If this stage lasts longer than 2 hours, signaling that the baby needs help, a doctor may grasp the baby's head with forceps or, more often, use vacuum extraction with a suction cup to pull it out of the mother's body (Curtin & Park, 1999). At the end of this stage, the baby is born; but it is still attached to the placenta in the mother's body by the umbilical cord, which must be cut and clamped.

During the *third stage,* which lasts about 5 to 30 minutes, the placenta and the remainder of the umbilical cord are expelled from the mother. The couple of hours after

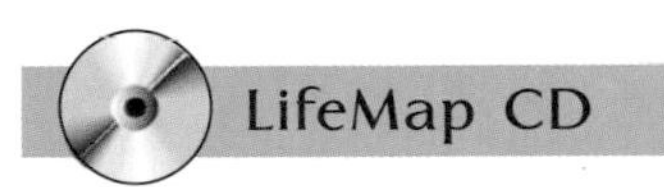

To learn more about the experience of having a baby, watch the "Childbirth" video in Chapter 5 of your CD.

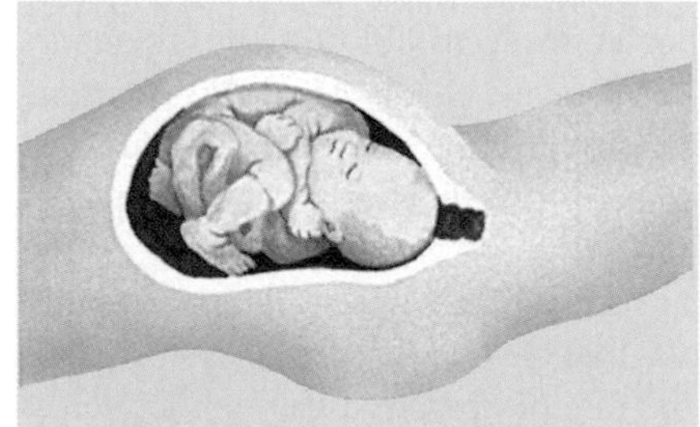
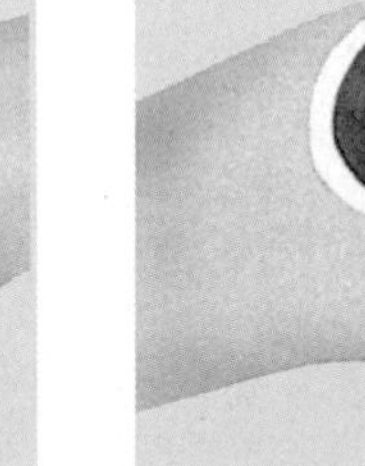

(*a*) First stage

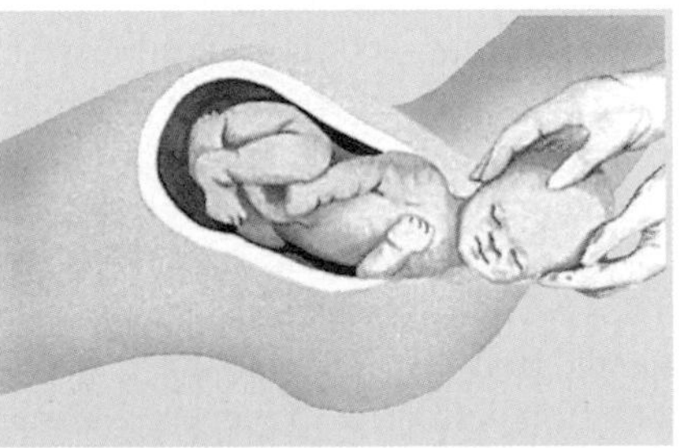

(*b*) Second stage

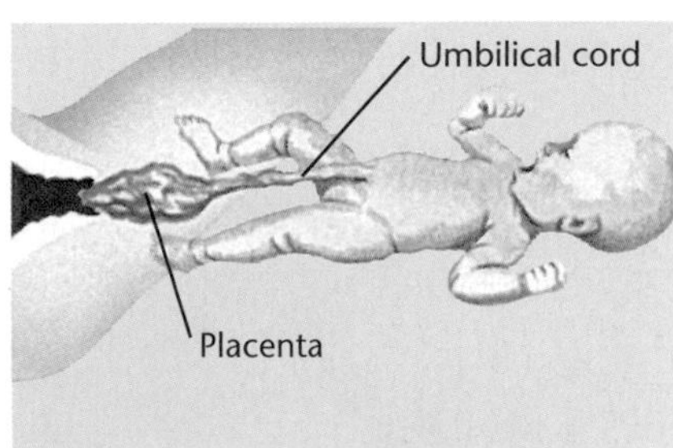

(*c*) Third stage

Figure 5-1

The first three stages of childbirth. (*a*) During the first stage of labor, a series of stronger and stronger contractions dilates the cervix, the opening to the mother's womb. (*b*) During the second stage, the baby's head moves down the birth canal and emerges from the vagina. (*c*) During the brief third stage, the placenta and umbilical cord are expelled from the womb. Then the cord is cut. During the fourth stage (not shown), recovery from delivery, the mother's uterus contracts.

Source: Adapted from Lagercrantz & Slotkin, 1986.

delivery constitute the *fourth stage,* when the mother rests in bed while her recovery is monitored.

Guidepost 3

What alternative methods of delivery are available?

cesarean delivery Delivery of a baby by surgical removal from the uterus.

Methods of Delivery

The primary concern in choosing a method for delivering a baby is the safety of both mother and baby. Also of concern is the mother's comfort.

Vaginal Versus Cesarean Delivery

The usual method of childbirth, just described, is vaginal delivery. **Cesarean delivery** is a surgical procedure to remove the baby from the uterus by cutting through the abdomen. In 2002, 26.1 percent of U.S. births occurred this way, as compared with only 5.5 percent in 1970 (Centers for Disease Control and Prevention, 1993; Martin et al., 2003). Cesarean birthrates in the United States are among the highest in the world, despite increased rates in European countries during the 1990s (International Cesarean Awareness Network, 2003; Notzon, 1990; Sachs et al., 1999).

The operation is commonly performed when labor progresses too slowly, when the fetus seems to be in trouble, or when the mother is bleeding vaginally. Often a cesarean is needed when the fetus is in the breech position (feet first) or in the transverse position (lying crosswise in the uterus) or when its head is too big to pass through the mother's pelvis. Surgical deliveries are more likely when the birth involves a first baby, a large baby, an older mother, or a mother who has had a previous cesarean. Thus, the increase in cesarean rates since 1970 is in part a reflection of a proportional increase in first births, a rise in average birth weight, and a trend toward later childbirth (Guyer et al., 1999; Martin et al., 2003; Parrish, Holt, Easterling, Connell, & LeGerfo, 1994). Other suggested explanations are the increased use of electronic fetal monitoring and induced labor, physicians' fear of malpractice litigation, and mothers' desire to avoid a difficult labor (Martin et al., 2003; Sachs, Kobelin, Castro, & Frigoletto, 1999).

During the early to mid-1990s the U.S. rate of cesarean births decreased by 9 percent, and the percentage of vaginal births after a previous cesarean increased by about 50 percent (from 18.9 in 1989 to 27.4 in 1997), reflecting a growing belief that cesarean delivery is unnecessary or harmful in many cases (Curtin & Park, 1999; Ventura, Martin, Curtin, Menacker, & Hamilton, 2001). About 4 percent of cesareans result in serious complications, such as bleeding and infections (Nelson et al., 1996).

Still, some physicians have argued that efforts to push for reduction in cesarean deliveries are misguided because such a reduction would result in greater reliance on operative vaginal deliveries (which use forceps or suction) and encouragement of vaginal delivery for women who have had previous cesarean deliveries. Although these procedures are fairly safe, they do carry risks, which must be weighed against the risks of cesarean delivery (Sachs et al., 1999). At greatest risk are women with previous cesarean births whose labor must be medically induced—who may suffer uterine rupture (Lydon-Rochelle, Holt, Easterling, & Martin, 2001)—and those whose labor is unsuccessful and who therefore must undergo a cesarean after all (McMahon, Luther, Bowes, & Olshan, 1996). Among 313,238 Scottish women giving birth after previous cesareans, the risk of the infant's dying during delivery was about 11 times higher in vaginal births than in planned repeat cesareans (Smith, Pell, Cameron, & Dobbie, 2002).

Perhaps because of such considerations, there has been a virtually complete reversal of earlier trends. Between 1996 and 2002, the rate of vaginal births after previous cesareans dropped to 12.6 percent, a 55 percent decline, and the rate of operative vaginal deliveries declined to 5.9 percent, a 61 percent decline since their high in 1994. Meanwhile, since 1996, the total cesarean rate for both first and repeat deliveries has increased by 26 percent to its present all-time high (Martin et al., 2003).

In many traditional cultures, childbearing women are attended by a *doula,* an experienced helper who can furnish emotional support and can stay at a woman's bedside throughout labor (see Box 5-1). In eleven randomized, controlled studies, women attended by doulas had shorter labor, less anesthesia, and fewer forceps and cesarean deliveries than mothers who had not had doulas (Klaus & Kennell, 1997).

Around the World

Box 5-1 *Having a Baby in the Himalayas*

Between 1993 and 1995, Sally Olds, one of the authors of this book, made four visits to Badel, a remote hill village in the small Asian country of Nepal, where she stayed with local families. The following account (Olds, 2002) describes a visit that she, the friend she traveled with, and their guide, Buddi, made to the village midwife.

Sabut Maya Mathani Rai has been helping childbearing mothers for almost 50 of her 75 years. Only three days ago she attended the birth of a baby girl.

When Sabut Maya attends a woman about to give birth, she says, "First I feel on the outside of the woman's belly. I look to see where is the head and the other organs. I help the mother push down when her time comes."

She does not use forceps. "I don't have any instruments," she says. "I just use my hands. If the baby is upside down, I turn it from the outside."

Nepali hill women usually give birth right after, or in the middle of, working in house or fields. The delivery may occur inside or outside of the house, depending on when the woman goes into labor. Women usually give birth on their knees. This kneeling position allows the mother to use her strong thigh and abdominal muscles to push the baby out. If the mother has other children, they usually watch, no matter how small they are. But the husbands don't want to watch, and the women don't want them there.

Most women are not attended by a midwife; they handle the delivery and dispose of the placenta and umbilical cord themselves. Buddi's mother once gave birth on the path as she was walking back from working in the fields, and then asked for her husband's knife to cut the cord.

"If the baby is not coming fast, I use special medicine," the midwife says. "I put grasses on the mother's body and I massage her with oil from a special plant. I don't give the mother any herbs or anything like that to eat or drink, only hot water or tea."

In a complicated birth—if, say, the baby is not emerging or the mother gets sick—the midwife calls the *shaman* (spiritual healer). Inevitably, some babies and some mothers die. In most cases, however, all goes well, and most deliveries are easy and quick.

How is the newborn cared for? "After the baby is born I wash the baby," says the midwife. "I leave this much of the cord on the baby [indicating about half an inch] and I tie it up with very good cotton. Then I wrap a piece of cotton cloth around the baby's tummy. This stays on for a few days until the cord falls off." Sometimes a small piece of the umbilical cord is saved and inserted into a metal bead that will be given to the child to wear on a string around the neck, to ward off evil spirits. A family member flings the placenta high up on a tree near the house to dry out; eventually it is thrown away.

No one but the mother—not even the father—is allowed to hold the baby at first. This may help to protect both mother and baby from infection and disease when they are most vulnerable. Then, at 3 days of age for a girl or 7 days for a boy (girls are thought to mature earlier), a purification rite and naming ceremony take place. My friend and I tell how in our culture women lie on their backs, a position unknown in most traditional societies, and how the doctor sometimes breaks the woman's water. We also describe how a doctor sometimes puts on surgical gloves and reaches inside the woman to turn a baby in a breech or other position. "We don't have gloves and we don't have instruments," the midwife repeats. "We don't do any of those things. I'm just a helper." What Sabut Maya really is is a combination of midwife and doula (described in this chapter)—a kind of helper now seen with growing frequency in western delivery rooms. It seems ironic that it has taken the western world so long to rediscover some of the wisdom that "primitive" societies have known for centuries.

A midwife in Kathmandu, Nepal, oils a newborn baby.

What's your view ?

- What aspects of traditional ways of delivering babies might enhance western childbearing practices without giving up medical techniques that save lives?
- Could advanced medical techniques be introduced into traditional societies without invalidating practices that seem to serve women in those societies well?

Check it out !

For more information on this topic, go to **http://www.dolna.com.** This is the Web site for Doulas of North America (DONA), an international association of doulas, founded in 1992 by Marshall Klaus, John Kennell, and others.

Medicated Versus Unmedicated Delivery

In the mid-19th century, England's Queen Victoria became the first woman in history to be put to sleep during delivery, that of her eighth child. Sedation with ether or chloroform became common practice as more births took place in hospitals (Fontanel & d'Harcourt, 1997).

Today, general anesthesia, which renders the woman completely unconscious, is rarely used, even in cesarean births. The woman is given local anesthesia if she wants and needs it, but she can see and participate in the birth process and can hold her newborn immediately afterward. Regional (local) anesthesia blocks the nerve pathways that would carry the sensation of pain to the brain, or the mother can receive a relaxing analgesic (painkiller). All these drugs pass through the placenta to enter the fetal blood supply and tissues, and thus may potentially pose dangers to the baby.

Alternative methods of childbirth were developed to minimize the use of drugs while maximizing both parents' active involvement. In 1914 a British physician, Dr. Grantly Dick-Read, suggested that pain in childbirth was caused mostly by fear. To eliminate fear, he advocated **natural childbirth**: educating women about the physiology of reproduction and training them in physical fitness and in breathing and relaxation during labor and delivery. By midcentury, Dr. Fernand Lamaze was using the **prepared childbirth** method to prepare expectant mothers for giving birth. This technique substitutes voluntary, or learned, physical responses to the sensations of uterine contractions for the old responses of fear and pain.

natural childbirth Method of childbirth that seeks to prevent pain by eliminating the mother's fear through education about the physiology of reproduction and training in breathing and relaxation for use during delivery.

prepared childbirth Method of childbirth that uses instruction, breathing exercises, and social support to induce controlled physical responses to uterine contractions and reduce fear and pain.

In the Lamaze method, a woman learns about the anatomy and physiology of childbirth. She is trained to pant or breathe rapidly "in sync" with the contractions and to concentrate on other sensations. She learns to relax her muscles as a conditioned response to the voice of her "coach" (usually the partner or a friend), who attends classes with her, takes part in the delivery, and helps with the exercises.

Advocates of natural methods argue that use of drugs poses risks for babies and deprives mothers of what can be an empowering and transforming experience. In some early studies, infants appeared to show immediate ill effects of obstetric medication in poorer motor and physiologic responses (A. D. Murray, Dolby, Nation, & Thomas, 1981) and, through the first year, in slower motor development (Brackbill & Broman, 1979). However, later research suggested that medicated delivery may *not* do measurable harm (Kraemer, Korner, Anders, Jacklin, & Dimiceli, 1985).

Improvements in medicated delivery have led many mothers to choose pain relief. Today approximately 60 percent of women in labor have regional (epidural or combined spinal-epidural) injections. The combined treatment provides almost immediate relief while enabling a woman to keep her balance, move around, and fully participate in the birth, with *no* increased risk of adverse outcomes for the fetus. However, there *is* evidence of greater use of instruments in vaginal deliveries when epidurals are given and a greater tendency for the woman to run a fever. Epidural techniques are increasingly used in both elective and emergency cesareans; a woman's risk of dying during a cesarean delivery is 17 times higher with general anesthesia, which can cause breathing problems (Eltzschig et al., 2003).

Pain relief should not be the only consideration in a decision about whether a woman should have anesthesia. More important to her satisfaction with the childbirth experience may be her involvement in decision making, her relationship with the professionals caring for her, and her expectations about labor. Social and cultural attitudes and customs also may play a part (Eltzschig et al., 2003).

Checkpoint

Can you . . .

- ✔ Describe the four stages of vaginal childbirth?
- ✔ Discuss the uses and disadvantages of cesarean births?
- ✔ Compare medicated delivery, natural childbirth, and prepared childbirth?

Guidepost 4

How do newborn infants adjust to life outside the womb ?

The Newborn Baby

A newborn baby, or **neonate,** is, in an extreme sense, an immigrant. After struggling through a difficult passage, the newcomer is faced with much more than learning a language and customs. A baby must start to breathe, eat, adapt to the climate, and respond to confusing surroundings—a mighty challenge for someone who weighs but a few pounds and whose organ systems are not fully mature. As we'll see, most infants arrive with systems ready to meet that challenge.

neonate Newborn baby, up to 4 weeks old.

neonatal period First four weeks of life, a time of transition from intrauterine dependency to independent existence.

The first four weeks of life, the **neonatal period,** is a time of transition from the uterus, where a fetus is supported entirely by the mother, to an independent existence. What are the physical characteristics of newborn babies, and how are they equipped for this crucial transition?

Size and Appearance

An average newborn in the United States is about 20 inches long and weighs about 7½ pounds. At birth, 95 percent of full-term babies weigh between 5½ and 10 pounds and are between 18 and 22 inches long. Boys tend to be slightly longer and heavier than girls, and a firstborn child is likely to weigh less at birth than laterborns.

In their first few days, neonates lose as much as 10 percent of their body weight, primarily because of a loss of fluids. They begin to gain weight again by about the fifth day and are generally back to birth weight by the 10th to the 14th day.

New babies have distinctive features, including a large head (one-fourth the body length) and a receding chin (which makes it easier to nurse). At first, a neonate's head may be long and misshapen because of the "molding" that eased its passage through the mother's pelvis. This temporary molding is possible because an infant's skull bones are not yet fused; they will not be completely joined for 18 months. The places on the head where the bones have not yet grown together—the soft spots, or **fontanels**—are covered by a tough membrane.

fontanels Soft spots on the head of a young infant.

Many newborns have a pinkish cast; their skin is so thin that it barely covers the capillaries through which blood flows. During the first few days, some neonates are very hairy because some of the **lanugo,** a fuzzy prenatal hair, has not yet fallen off. All new babies are covered with **vernix caseosa** ("cheesy varnish"), an oily protection against infection that dries within the first few days.

lanugo Fuzzy prenatal body hair, which drops off within a few days after birth.

vernix caseosa Oily substance on a neonate's skin that protects against infection.

Body Systems

Before birth, blood circulation, respiration, nourishment, elimination of waste, and temperature regulation are accomplished through the mother's body. After birth, all of the baby's systems and functions must operate on their own (see Table 5-1).

The fetus and mother have separate circulatory systems and separate heartbeats; the fetus's blood is cleansed through the umbilical cord, which carries "used" blood to the placenta and returns a fresh supply. A neonate's blood circulates wholly within the baby's own body; the heartbeat at first is fast and irregular, and blood pressure does not stabilize until about the 10th day of life.

The fetus gets oxygen through the umbilical cord, which also carries away carbon dioxide. A newborn needs much more oxygen than before and must now get it alone. Most babies start to breathe as soon as they are exposed to air. If breathing has not begun within about 5 minutes, the baby may suffer permanent brain injury caused by **anoxia**, lack of oxygen. Because infants' lungs have only one-tenth as many air sacs as adults' do, infants (especially those born prematurely) are susceptible to respiratory problems.

anoxia Lack of oxygen, which may cause brain damage.

In the uterus, the fetus relies on the umbilical cord to bring food from the mother and to carry fetal body wastes away. At birth, babies have a strong sucking reflex to take in milk and their own gastrointestinal secretions to digest it. During the first few days infants secrete **meconium**, a stringy, greenish-black waste matter formed in the fetal intestinal tract. When the bowels and bladder are full, the sphincter muscles open automatically; a baby will not be able to control these muscles for many months.

meconium Fetal waste matter, excreted during the first few days after birth.

neonatal jaundice Condition, in many newborn babies, caused by immaturity of the liver and evidenced by yellowish appearance; can cause brain damage if not treated promptly.

Three or four days after birth, about half of all babies (and a larger proportion of babies born prematurely) develop **neonatal jaundice**: Their skin and eyeballs look yellow. This kind of jaundice is caused by the immaturity of the liver. Usually it is not serious, does

Table 5-1 A Comparison of Prenatal and Postnatal Life

Characteristic	Prenatal Life	Postnatal Life
Environment	Amniotic fluid	Air
Temperature	Relatively constant	Fluctuates with atmosphere
Stimulation	Minimal	All senses stimulated by various stimuli
Nutrition	Dependent on mother's blood	Dependent on external food and functioning of digestive system
Oxygen supply	Passed from maternal bloodstream via placenta	Passed from neonate's lungs to pulmonary blood vessels
Metabolic elimination	Passed into maternal bloodstream via placenta	Discharged by skin, kidneys, lungs, and gastrointestinal tract

Source: Timiras, 1972, p. 174.

Checkpoint

Can you . . .

- ✔ Describe the normal size and appearance of a newborn, and name several changes that occur within the first few days?
- ✔ Compare four fetal and neonatal body systems?
- ✔ Identify two dangerous conditions that can appear soon after birth?

not need treatment, and has no long term effects. However, because healthy U.S. newborns usually go home from the hospital within 48 hours or less, jaundice may go unnoticed and may lead to complications (AAP Committee on Quality Improvement, 2002). Severe jaundice that is not monitored and treated promptly may result in brain damage.

The layers of fat that develop during the last two months of fetal life enable healthy full-term infants to keep their body temperature constant after birth despite changes in air temperature. Newborn babies also maintain body temperature by increasing their activity when air temperature drops. Exposure to cold around the time of birth can have far-reaching health effects, perhaps by inducing excess fat storage. In a study of 4,286 British women ages 60 to 79, those born during cold weather—especially those whose families were poor and may have lacked effective shelter—were more likely to develop coronary heart disease (Lawlor, Smith, Mitchell, & Ebrahim, 2004).

Guidepost 5

How can we tell whether a new baby is healthy and is developing normally ?

Medical and Behavioral Assessment

Although the great majority of births result in normal, healthy babies, some do not. The first few minutes, days, and weeks after birth are crucial for development. It is important to know as soon as possible whether a baby has any problem that needs special care.

The Apgar Scale

Apgar scale Standard measurement of a newborn's condition; it assesses appearance, pulse, grimace, activity, and respiration.

One minute after delivery and then again 5 minutes after birth, most babies are assessed using the **Apgar scale** (see Table 5-2). Its name, after its developer, Dr. Virginia Apgar (1953), helps us remember its five subtests: *a*ppearance (color), *p*ulse (heart rate), *g*rimace (reflex irritability), *a*ctivity (muscle tone), and *r*espiration (breathing). The newborn is rated 0, 1, or 2 on each measure, for a maximum score of 10. A 5-minute score of 7 to 10—achieved by 98.6 percent of babies born in the United States in 2000—indicates that the baby is in good to excellent condition (Martin et al., 2003). A score below 7 means the baby needs help to establish breathing; a score below 4 means the baby needs immediate lifesaving treatment. If resuscitation is successful, bringing the baby's score to 4 or more, no long-term damage is likely to result. Scores of 0 to 3 at 10, 15, and 20 minutes after birth are increasingly associated with cerebral palsy (muscular impairment due to brain damage before or during birth) or other neurological problems (AAP Committee on Fetus and Newborn and American College of Obstetricians and Gynecologists [ACOG] Committee on Obstetric Practice, 1996).

In general, Apgar scores reliably predict survival during the first month of life (Casey, McIntire, & Leveno, 2001). However, a low Apgar score alone does not necessarily indicate anoxia. Prematurity, medication given to the mother, and other conditions may affect

Table 5-2 Apgar Scale

Sign*	0	1	2
Appearance (color)	Blue, pale	Body pink, extremities blue	Entirely pink
Pulse (heart rate)	Absent	Slow (below 100)	Rapid (over 100)
Grimace (reflex irritability)	No response	Grimace	Coughing, sneezing, crying
Activity (muscle tone)	Limp	Weak, inactive	Strong, active
Respiration (breathing)	Absent	Irregular, slow	Good, crying

*Each sign is rated in terms of absence or presence from 0 to 2; highest overall score is 10.

Source: Adapted from V. Apgar, 1953.

the results (AAP Committee on Fetus and Newborn and ACOG Committee on Obstetric Practice, 1996).

Assessing Neurological Status: The Brazelton Scale

The **Brazelton Neonatal Behavioral Assessment Scale (NBAS)** is used in high-risk situations to assess neonates' responsiveness to their physical and social environment, to identify problems in neurological functioning, and to predict future development. The test is named for its designer, Dr. T. Berry Brazelton (1973, 1984; Brazelton & Nugent, 1995). It assesses *motor organization* as shown by such behaviors as activity level and the ability to bring a hand to the mouth; *reflexes*; *state changes,* such as irritability, excitability, and ability to quiet down after being upset; *attention and interactive capacities,* as shown by general alertness and response to visual and auditory stimuli; and indications of *central nervous system instability,* such as tremors and changes in skin color. The NBAS takes about 30 minutes, and scores are based on a baby's best performance.

Brazelton Neonatal Behavioral Assessment Scale (NBAS) Neurological and behavioral test to measure a neonate's responses to the environment.

Neonatal Screening for Medical Conditions

Children who inherit the enzyme disorder phenylketonuria, or PKU (refer back to Table 3-1 in Chapter 3), will become mentally retarded unless they are fed a special diet beginning in the first three to six weeks of life (National Institutes of Health [NIH] Consensus Development Panel, 2001). Screening tests that can be administered soon after birth often can discover such correctable defects.

Routine screening of all newborn babies for such rare genetic conditions as PKU (1 case in 15,000 births), congenital hypothyroidism (1 in 3,600 to 5,000), galactosemia (1 in 60,000 to 80,000), and other, even rarer biochemical disorders can be extremely expensive because of the need for separate tests for each disorder. Although all states require screening for PKU and hypothyroidism, states vary on requirements for other screening tests (AAP Newborn Screening Task Force, 2000; NIH Consensus Development Panel, 2001). Now, with tandem mass spectrometry, in which a single blood specimen can be screened for 20 or more disorders, about half of all states have expanded their mandatory screening programs. In a study of newborns in several New England states, infants identified by screening were less likely to be retarded or to need hospitalization than those identified by clinical diagnosis, and their parents reported less stress. However, the tests can generate false-positive results, suggesting that a problem exists when it does not, and may trigger anxiety and costly, unnecessary treatment (Waisbren et al., 2003).

Checkpoint

Can you . . .

✔ Discuss the uses of the Apgar test, the Brazelton Scale, and routine postbirth screening for rare disorders?

States of Arousal and Activity Levels

Guidepost 6

How do newborns' patterns of sleep, waking, and activity vary and change ?

Newborns show their individuality as well as their neurological maturation through their patterns of sleeping and waking and of activity when awake. Babies have an internal "clock" that regulates their daily cycles of eating, sleeping, and elimination and perhaps even their moods. These periodic cycles of wakefulness, sleep, and activity, which govern an infant's **state of arousal,** or degree of alertness (see Table 5-3), seem to be inborn and highly individual. Newborn babies average about 16 hours of sleep a day, but one may sleep only 11 hours while another sleeps 21 hours (Parmelee, Wenner, & Schulz, 1964). Changes in state are coordinated by multiple areas of the brain and are accompanied by changes in the functioning of virtually all body systems: heart rate and blood flow, breathing, temperature regulation, cerebral metabolism, and the workings of the kidneys, glands, and digestive system (Ingersoll & Thoman, 1999).

state of arousal Infant's physiological and behavioral status at a given moment in the periodic daily cycle of wakefulness, sleep, and activity.

Most new babies wake up every two to three hours, day and night. Short stretches of sleep alternate with shorter periods of consciousness, which are devoted mainly to feeding. Newborns have about six to eight sleep periods, which vary between quiet and active sleep. Active sleep is probably the equivalent of rapid eye movement (REM) sleep, which in adults is associated with dreaming. Active sleep appears rhythmically in cycles of about one hour and accounts for 50 to 80 percent of a newborn's total sleep time.

Table 5-0 States of Arousal in Infancy

State	Eyes	Breathing	Movements	Responsiveness
Regular sleep	Closed; no eye movement	Regular and slow	None, except for sudden, generalized startles	Cannot be aroused by mild stimuli.
Irregular sleep	Closed; occasional rapid eye movements	Irregular	Muscles twitch, but no major movements	Sounds or light bring smiles or grimaces in sleep.
Drowsiness	Open or closed	Irregular	Somewhat active	May smile, startle, suck, or have erections in response to stimuli.
Alert inactivity	Open	Even	Quiet; may move head, limbs, and trunk while looking around	An interesting environment (with people or things to watch) may initiate or maintain this state.
Waking activity and crying	Open	Irregular	Much activity	External stimuli (such as hunger, cold, pain, being restrained, or being put down) bring about more activity, perhaps starting with soft whimpering and gentle movements and turning into a rhythmic crescendo of crying or kicking or perhaps beginning and enduring as uncoordinated thrashing and spasmodic screeching.

Source: Adapted from information in Prechtl & Beintema, 1964; P. H. Wolff, 1966.

Premature infants tend to be uneven in their state development compared with full-term infants the same age. They are more alert and wakeful, have longer stretches of quiet sleep, and show more REMs in active sleep. On the other hand, their sleep is more fragmented, and they have more transitions between sleeping and waking (Ingersoll & Thoman, 1999).

Parents and caregivers spend a great deal of time and energy trying to change babies' states—mostly by soothing a fussy infant to sleep. Although crying is usually more distressing than serious, it is particularly important to quiet low-birth-weight babies, because quiet babies maintain their weight better. Steady stimulation is the time-proven way to soothe crying babies: by rocking or walking them, wrapping them snugly, or letting them hear rhythmic sounds (see Box 5-2).

At about 3 months, babies grow more wakeful in the late afternoon and early evening and start to sleep through the night. By 6 months, more than half their sleep occurs at night. By this time, active sleep accounts for only 30 percent of sleep time, and the length of the cycle becomes more consistent (Coons & Guilleminault, 1982). The amount of REM sleep continues to decrease steadily throughout life.

Babies' sleep rhythms vary across cultures. Among the Micronesian Truk and the Canadian Hare peoples, babies and children have no regular sleep schedules; they fall asleep whenever they feel tired. Nor do infants necessarily have special places to sleep. Gusii infants in Kenya fall asleep in someone's arms or on a caregiver's back. In many cultures an infant sleeps in the parents' or mother's bed, and this practice may continue into early childhood. Cultural variations in feeding practices may affect sleep patterns. Many U.S. parents time the evening feeding so as to encourage nighttime sleep. Mothers in rural Kenya allow their babies to nurse as they please, and their 4-month-olds continue to sleep only four hours at a stretch (Broude, 1995).

Some new babies are more active than others. These activity levels reflect temperamental differences that continue throughout childhood, and often throughout life. Neonates' unique behavior patterns elicit varying responses from their caregivers. Adults react very differently to a placid baby than to an excitable one; to an infant they can quiet easily than to one who is often inconsolable; to a baby who is often awake and alert than to one who seems uninterested in the surroundings. Babies, in turn, respond to the way their caregivers treat them. This bidirectional influence can have far-reaching effects on what kind of person a baby turns out to be. From the start, children affect their own lives by molding the environment in which they grow.

Checkpoint ✓

Can you . . .

✔ Describe patterns of sleep, arousal, and activity during the first few months?

The Everyday World

Box 5-2 *Comforting a Crying Baby*

All babies cry. It is their only way to let us know they are hungry, uncomfortable, lonely, or unhappy. And since few sounds are as distressing as a baby's cry, parents or other caregivers usually rush to feed or pick up a crying infant. As babies quiet down and fall asleep or gaze about in alert contentment, they may show that their problem has been solved. At other times, the caregiver cannot figure out what the baby wants. The baby keeps crying. It is worth trying to find ways to help. Babies whose cries bring relief seem to become more self-confident, seeing that they can affect their own lives.

In Chapter 7 we will discuss several kinds of crying and what the crying may mean. Unusual, persistent crying patterns may be early signs of trouble. For healthy babies who just seem unhappy, the following may help (Eiger & Olds, 1999):

- Hold the baby, perhaps laying the baby on his or her stomach on your chest, to feel your heartbeat and breathing. Or sit with the baby in a comfortable rocking chair.
- Put the baby in a carrier next to your chest and walk around.
- If you are upset, ask someone else to hold the baby; infants sometimes sense and respond to their caregivers' moods.
- Pat or rub the baby's back, in case a bubble of air is causing discomfort.
- Wrap the baby snugly in a small blanket; some infants feel more secure when firmly swaddled from neck to toes, with arms held close to the sides.
- Make the baby warmer or cooler; put on or take off clothing or change the room temperature.
- Give the baby a massage or a warm bath.
- Sing or talk to the baby. Or provide a continuous or rhythmic sound, such as music from the radio, a simulated heartbeat, or background noise from a whirring fan, vacuum cleaner, or other appliance.
- Take the baby out for a ride in a stroller or car seat—at any hour of the day or night. In bad weather, some parents walk around in an enclosed mall; the distraction helps them as well as the baby.
- If someone other than a parent is taking care of the baby, it sometimes helps if the caregiver puts on a robe or a sweater that the mother or father has recently worn so the baby can sense the familiar smell.
- Pick up on the baby's signals.

This crying baby may quiet when held stomach down on his father's chest.

What's your view ?

Have you ever tried to soothe a crying baby? What techniques seemed to work best?

Check it out !

For more information on this topic, go to **http://www.parenting-qa.com/cgi-bin/detail/behavior/crying/**. This is the Parenting Questions and Answers section of a Web site called Local Mom.com, which covers all the basic questions new parents might have. Or go to **http://www.zerotothree.org/brainworks/care_2-6cry.html**. This is an article from *Zero to Three,* which discusses various types of cries and offers advice about whether and how parents should respond.

Newborns and Their Parents

Guidepost 7

How do parents bond with their baby, and how does parenthood change their relationship with one another ?

The birth process is a major transition, not only for the baby, but for the parents as well. The mother's body systems have undergone massive physical change. For both mother and father, especially with a first birth, the newcomer in their lives brings insistent demands that challenge their ability to cope and force adjustments in their relationship. Meanwhile, parents (and, perhaps, siblings) are getting acquainted with this newcomer—developing emotional bonds and becoming familiar with the infant's patterns of behavior.

Childbirth and Bonding

How and when does the **mother-infant bond**—the close, caring connection between mother and newborn—develop? Some researchers studying this topic have followed the ethological approach (introduced in Chapter 2), which considers behavior in human beings, as in animals, to be biologically determined and emphasizes critical or sensitive periods for development of certain behaviors.

mother-infant bond Mother's feeling of close, caring connection with her newborn.

Newly hatched ducklings will follow and become attached to the first moving object they see, as the ethologist Konrad Lorenz showed. He called this behavior *imprinting.*

In one well-known study, Konrad Lorenz (1957) waddled, honked, and flapped his arms—and got newborn ducklings to follow him as they would the mother duck. Lorenz showed that newly hatched ducklings will follow the first moving object they see, whether or not it is a member of their own species. This phenomenon is called **imprinting**, and Lorenz believed that it is automatic and irreversible. Usually, this first attachment is to the mother; but if the natural course of events is disturbed, other attachments (like the one to Lorenz)—or none at all—can form. Imprinting, said Lorenz, is the result of a *predisposition toward learning:* the readiness of an organism's nervous system to acquire certain information during a brief critical period in early life.

imprinting Instinctive form of learning in which, during a critical period in early development, a young animal forms an attachment to the first moving object it sees, usually the mother.

Does something similar to imprinting happen between human newborns and their mothers? Apparently not. Research has concluded that, unlike the animals Lorenz studied, a critical period for bonding does *not* exist for human beings (Chess & Thomas, 1982; Klaus & Kennell, 1982; M. E. Lamb, 1983). This finding has relieved the worry and guilt sometimes felt by adoptive parents and parents who had to be separated from their infants after birth.

Fathers, like mothers, form close bonds with their babies soon after birth. The babies contribute simply by doing the things normal babies do: opening their eyes, grasping their fathers' fingers, or moving in their fathers' arms. Fathers who are present at the birth of a child often see the event as a "peak emotional experience" (May & Perrin, 1985), but a man can become emotionally committed to his newborn whether or not he attended the birth (Palkovitz, 1985).

How Parenthood Affects a Marriage

Along with feeling excitement, wonder, and awe, most new parents experience some anxiety about the responsibility of caring for a child, the commitment of time and energy it entails, and the feeling of permanence that parenthood imposes on a marriage. Pregnancy and the recovery from childbirth can affect a couple's future sexual relationship, sometimes making it more intimate and sometimes creating barriers.

Marital satisfaction typically declines during the child-raising years. In a 10-year longitudinal study of predominantly white couples who married in their late 20s, both husbands and wives reported a sharp decline in satisfaction during the first four years of marriage, followed by a plateau and then another decline (Kurdek, 1999).

Of course, this statistical pattern is an average; it is not necessarily true of all couples. One research team followed 128 middle- and working-class couples in their late 20s from the first pregnancy until the child's third birthday. Some marriages got stronger, and others deteriorated, especially in the eyes of the wives. In the marriages that deteriorated, the partners tended to be younger and less well educated, to earn less money, to have been married a shorter time, and to have lower self-esteem. The mothers who had the hardest time were those whose babies had difficult temperaments. Surprisingly, women who had planned their pregnancies were unhappier, possibly because they had expected life with a baby to be better than it turned out to be (Belsky & Rovine, 1990).

Checkpoint

Can you . . .

- ✔ Summarize findings on bonding between parents and infants?
- ✔ Cite at least three factors that can influence a new baby's effect on the parents' marriage?

One problem involves the division of household tasks. If a couple share these tasks fairly equally before becoming parents, and then, after the birth, the burden shifts to the wife, marital happiness tends to decline, especially for nontraditional wives (Belsky, Lang, & Huston, 1986). Among young Israeli first-time parents, fathers who saw themselves as caring, nurturing, and protecting experienced less decline in marital satisfaction than other fathers and felt better about parenthood. Men who were less involved with their babies and whose wives were more involved tended to be more dissatisfied. The mothers who became most dissatisfied with their marriages were those who saw themselves as disorganized and unable to cope with the demands of motherhood (Levy-Shiff, 1994).

Are adoptive parents' experiences different from those of biological parents? Researchers in Israel looked at 104 couples before they became parents and then again when their babies—half of whom were adopted and half biological offspring—were 4 months old (Levy-Shiff, Goldschmidt, & Har-Even, 1991). The adoptive parents reported more positive expectations and more satisfying parenting experiences than did the others. The adoptive parents, who tended to be older and married longer, may have been more mature and resourceful, or they may have appreciated parenthood more when it finally came. Or they may have felt the need to speak positively about parenthood, since they had gone to special lengths to achieve it.

Complications of Childbirth—and Their Aftermath

What complications of childbirth can endanger newborn babies, and what are the long-term prospects for babies with complicated births ?

"It must be a boy," say some mothers whose labor and delivery prove long and difficult. This old adage seems to bear some truth: boys' deliveries are somewhat more likely to involve complications than girls', in part because boy babies tend to be larger. In two large Irish and Dutch studies, male babies took longer to emerge and were more likely to suffer fetal distress, to require forceps or caesarean delivery, and to have low Apgar scores five minutes after birth (Bekedam, Engelsbel, Mol, Buitendijk, & van der Pal-de Bruin, 2002; Eogan, Geary, O'Connell, & Keane, 2003).

Although most babies are born healthy, some are injured in the birth process, and some are born dead or die soon after birth. Some remain in the womb too long or too briefly or are born very small—complications that can impair their chances of survival and well-being. Let's look at these potential complications of birth and how they can be avoided or treated so as to maximize the chances of favorable outcomes.

Birth Trauma

For a small minority of babies, the passage through the birth canal is a particularly harrowing journey. About 2 newborns in 1,000 are injured in the process (Wegman, 1994). **Birth trauma** (injury sustained at the time of birth) may be caused by anoxia (oxygen deprivation), diseases or infections, or physical injury. Sometimes the trauma leaves permanent brain damage, causing mental retardation, behavior problems, or even death.

birth trauma Injury sustained at the time of birth.

Electronic fetal monitoring can be used to track the fetus's heartbeat during labor and delivery so as to detect any lack of oxygen that could cause brain damage. The procedure was used in 85.2 percent of live births in the United States in 2002 (Martin et al., 2003). Electronic fetal monitoring can provide valuable information in high-risk deliveries, including those in which the fetus is very small or seems to be in distress. Yet monitoring has drawbacks when used routinely in low-risk pregnancies. It is costly; it restricts the mother's movements during labor; and, most important, it has an extremely high "false positive" rate, suggesting that fetuses are in trouble when they are not. Such warnings may prompt doctors to deliver by the riskier cesarean method rather than vaginally (Nelson, Dambrosia, Ting, & Grether, 1996).

electronic fetal monitoring Mechanical monitoring of fetal heartbeat during labor and delivery.

Postmaturity

Close to 7 percent of pregnant women have not gone into labor after 42 or more weeks' gestation (Martin et al., 2003). At that point, a baby is considered **postmature**. Postmature babies tend to be long and thin, because they have kept growing in the womb but have had an insufficient blood supply toward the end of gestation. Possibly because the placenta has aged and become less efficient, it may provide less oxygen. The baby's greater size also complicates labor; the mother has to deliver a baby the size of a normal 1-month-old.

postmature Referring to a fetus not yet born as of 42 weeks' gestation.

Because postmature fetuses are at risk of brain damage or even death, doctors sometimes induce labor with drugs or perform cesarean deliveries. However, if the due date has been miscalculated, a baby who is actually premature may be delivered. To help make the decision, doctors monitor the baby's status with ultrasound to see whether the heart rate speeds up when the fetus moves; if not, the baby may be short of oxygen. Another test involves examining the volume of amniotic fluid; a low level may mean the baby is not getting enough food.

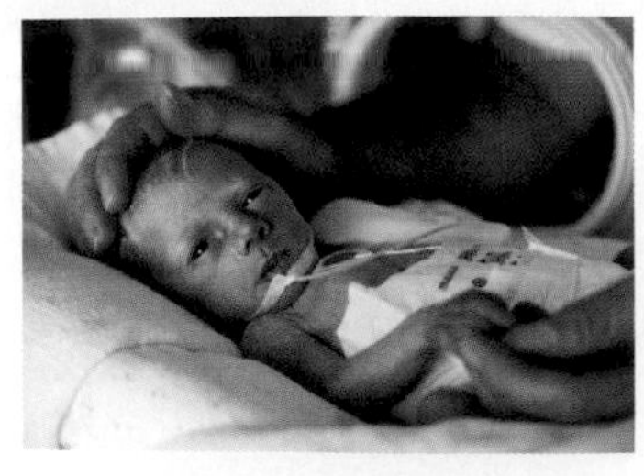

The antiseptic, temperature-controlled crib, or isolette, in which this premature baby lies has holes through which the infant can be examined, touched, and massaged. Frequent human contact helps low-birthweight infants thrive.

low birth weight Weight of less than 5½ pounds (2,500 grams) at birth because of prematurity or being small-for-date.

preterm (premature) infants Infants born before completing the 37th week of gestation.

small-for-date (small-for-gestational-age) infants Infants whose birth weight is less than that of 90 percent of babies of the same gestational age, as a result of slow fetal growth.

Low Birth Weight

In 2002, 7.8 percent of babies born in the United States had **low birth weight,** weighing less than 2,500 grams (5½ pounds) at birth, the highest rate of low birth weight in three decades. Very low-birth-weight babies, who weigh less than 1,500 grams (3⅓ pounds), accounted for less than 1.5 percent of births (Martin et al., 2003). Low birth weight is the second leading cause of death in infancy, after birth defects (Mathews, Menacker, & MacDorman, 2003), so preventing and treating low birth weight can greatly increase the number of babies who survive the first year of life.

Although the United States is more successful than any other country in the world in *saving* low-birth-weight babies, the rate of such births to U.S. women is higher than in 21 European, Asian, and Middle Eastern nations (UNICEF, 2002). Much of the increased prevalence of low birth weight in the United States since the mid-1980s is attributed to the rise in multiple births (Lockwood, 2002; Martin et al., 2003).

Low-birth-weight babies may be *preterm* or *small-for-date.* Babies born before completing the 37th week of gestation are called **preterm (premature) infants**; they may or may not be the appropriate size for their gestational age. In 2002, 12.1 percent of infants were born preterm, 29 percent more than in 1981. In addition to multiple births (Martin et al., 2003), this increase may reflect the rise in cesarean deliveries and induced labor and in births to women ages 35 and up (Kramer et al., 1998). **Small-for-date (small-for-gestational-age) infants**, who may or may not be preterm, weigh less than 90 percent of all babies of the same gestational age. Their small size is generally the result of inadequate prenatal nutrition, which slows fetal growth.

As many as 50 percent of preterm births are associated with uterine infection, which does not seem to respond to antibiotics once labor has begun. Other causes are maternal or fetal stress, placental hemorrhaging, and overstretching of the uterus, usually in multiple gestations. Such measures as enhanced prenatal care, nutritional interventions, home monitoring of uterine activity, and administration of drugs, bed rest, and hydration for women who go into early labor have proved unable to stem the tide of premature births (Goldenberg & Rouse, 1998; Lockwood, 2002). One promising treatment is a form of the hormone progesterone, called *hydroxyprogesterone caproate,* or *17P.* In a two-and-a-half-year trial at 13 major medical research centers, giving 17P to women who had previously borne premature babies reduced repeat preterm births by as much as one-third. The newborns whose mothers had received 17P were in better condition immediately after birth (Meis et al., 2003).

Who Is Likely to Have a Low-Birth-Weight Baby?

Factors increasing the likelihood that a woman will have an underweight baby include (1) *demographic and socioeconomic factors,* such as being African American, under age 17 or over 40, poor, unmarried, or undereducated; (2) *medical factors predating the pregnancy,* such as having no children or more than four, being short or thin, having had previous low-birth-weight infants or multiple miscarriages, having had low birth weight oneself, or having genital or urinary abnormalities or chronic hypertension; (3) *prenatal behavioral and environmental factors,* such as poor nutrition, inadequate prenatal care, smoking, use of alcohol or other drugs, or exposure to stress, high altitude, or toxic substances; and (4) *medical conditions associated with the pregnancy,* such as vaginal bleeding, infections, high or low blood pressure, anemia, too little weight gain, and having last given birth fewer than 6 months or more than 9 years before (Arias, MacDorman, Strobino, & Guyer, 2003; S. S. Brown, 1985; Chomitz, Cheung, & Lieberman, 1995; Nathanielsz, 1995; Shiono & Behrman, 1995; Wegman, 1992; Zhu, Rolfs, Nangle, & Horan, 1999). The safest interval between pregnancies is 18 to 23 months (Zhu et al., 1999). Depression during pregnancy is another risk factor; screening for depression is a critical part of prenatal care (Yonkers, quoted in Bernstein, 2003).

The high proportion (13.3 percent) of low-birth-weight babies in the African-American population—more than twice as high as among white and Hispanic babies—is the major factor in the high mortality rates of black babies (Martin et al., 2003; see Table 6-3 in Chapter 6). The higher risks of low birth weight and of preterm births among African-American babies seem to be independent of socioeconomic status and may reflect higher levels of stress and of vaginal infections in that population. Babies of African- or Caribbean-born black women are not at such high risk (David & Collins, 1997).

Immediate Treatment and Outcomes

The most pressing fear for very small babies is that they will die in infancy. Because their immune systems are not fully developed, they are especially vulnerable to infection; feeding them mothers' milk can help prevent this (Furman, Taylor, Minich, & Hack, 2003). Their nervous systems may not be mature enough for them to perform functions basic to survival, such as sucking, and they may need to be fed intravenously (through the veins). Because they do not have enough fat to insulate them and to generate heat, it is hard for them to stay warm. Respiratory distress syndrome, also called *hyaline membrane disease,* is common. Low Apgar scores in preterm newborns are a strong indication of heightened risk and of the need for intensive care (Weinberger et al., 2000).

In a study of 122,754 live births at a Dallas hospital, full-term newborns who were severely undergrown—at or below the third percentile of weight for their gestational age—were at high risk of endangered health and neonatal death. Among preterm infants, the less they weighed, the higher their risk (McIntire, Bloom, Casey, & Leveno, 1999).

Many very small preterm babies lack surfactant, an essential lung-coating substance that keeps air sacs from collapsing; they may breathe irregularly or stop breathing altogether. Administering surfactant to high-risk preterm newborns, along with other medical interventions, has dramatically increased the survival rate of infants who weigh as little as 500 grams (about 1 pound 2 ounces), enabling 4 out of 5 in this lowest-weight group to survive (Corbet et al., 1995; Goldenberg & Rouse, 1998; Horbar et al., 1993). However, these infants are likely to be in poor health and to have neurological deficits—at 20 months, a 20 percent rate of mental retardation and 10 percent likelihood of cerebral palsy (Hack, Friedman, & Fanaroff, 1996). In a randomized, controlled study, administering magnesium sulfate to women who were about to give birth before 30 weeks of gestation reduced infants' risks of cerebral palsy or death (Crowther, Hiller, Doyle, & Haslam for the Australasian Collaborative Trial of Magnesium Sulfate [ACTOMgSO4] Collaborative Group, 2003).

A low-birth-weight baby is placed in an *isolette* (an antiseptic, temperature-controlled crib) and fed through tubes. To counteract the sensory impoverishment of life in an isolette, hospital workers and parents are encouraged to give these small babies special handling. Gentle massage seems to foster growth, weight gain, motor activity, alertness, and behavioral organization, as assessed by the Brazelton NBAS (T. M. Field, 1986, 1998b; T. Field, Hernandez-Reif, & Freedman, 2004; Schanberg & Field, 1987), and can shorten the hospital stay (T. Field, Hernandez-Reif, & Freedman, 2004; Standley, 1998).

Long-Term Outcomes

Even if low-birth-weight babies survive the dangerous early days, as more and more are doing, there is concern about their development. Small-for-gestational age infants are more likely to be neurologically and cognitively impaired than equally premature infants whose weight was appropriate for their gestational age (McCarton, Wallace, Divon, & Vaughan, 1996), and preterm infants who are neurologically impaired often remain so as they grow older (McGrath, Sullivan, Lester, & Oh, 2000).

A longitudinal study of 1,064 full-term British infants who were small-for-gestational-age found small but significant deficits in academic achievement at ages 5, 10, and 16 as compared with children born during the same week with normal birth weight. At age 26, this group had lower incomes and professional attainments than the control group and were physically shorter. Still, they were just as likely to have completed their education and to be employed, married, and satisfied with life (Strauss, 2000).

Very low-birth-weight babies may have a less promising prognosis. Cognitive deficits, especially in memory and processing speed, are apparent by 5 or 6 months of age and may continue through childhood (Rose & Feldman, 2000; Rose, Feldman, & Jankowski, 2002). At school age, those who weighed the least at birth have the most behavioral, social, attentional, and language problems (Klebanov, Brooks-Gunn, & McCormick, 1994). As teenagers, the less they weighed at birth, the lower their IQs and achievement test scores and the more likely they are to require special education or to have repeated a grade (Saigal, Hoult, Streiner, Stoskopf, & Rosenbaum, 2000). By age 20, very low-birth-weight girls are more likely than very low-birth-weight boys to catch up with their peers in growth, but this abnormal growth may increase risk of obesity, heart disease, and diabetes later in life (Hack et al., 2003). Adults who had very low birth weight tend to have more neurosensory deficits and illnesses, higher systolic blood pressure, lower IQs, and poorer educational achievement than adults who had normal birth weight. Still, in one longitudinal study of 242 adult survivors of very low birth weight, 51 percent had IQs in normal range, 74 percent had finished high school, and 41 percent had gone on to higher learning (Greene, 2002; Hack et al., 2002; Hardy, Kuh, Langenberg, & Wadsworth, 2003).

Among 179 Canadian infants of *extremely* low birth weight (501 to 1,000 grams, or about 1 to 2 pounds) those who survived to adolescence tended to be smaller than a control group of full-term children and were far more likely to have neurological impairments and other problems (Saigal, Stoskopf, Streiner, & Burrows, 2001). Despite advances in treatment of low-birth-weight babies in the 1990s, school-aged children in Victoria, Australia, who had been born during that period with extremely low birth weight showed continuing cognitive, educational, and behavioral impairments (Anderson, Doyle, and the Victorian Infant Collaborative Study Group, 2003).

What's your view?

- In view of the long-term outlook for very low-birth-weight babies and the expense involved in helping them survive, how much of society's resources should be put into rescuing these babies?

On the other hand, in a longitudinal study of 296 infants who weighed, on average, just over 2 pounds at birth and were considered borderline retarded, most showed cognitive improvement in early childhood and intelligence in the normal range by age 8. Children in two-parent families, those whose mothers were highly educated, those who had not suffered significant brain damage, and those who did not need special help, did best (Ment et al., 2003). Birth weight alone, then, does not necessarily determine the outcome. Environmental factors make a difference, as we will discuss further in a subsequent section.

Stillbirth

A stillbirth is a tragic union of opposites—birth and death. Sometimes fetal death is diagnosed prenatally; in other cases, as with Elvis Presley's twin brother, the baby's death is discovered during labor or delivery.

Stillbirth accounts for more than half of perinatal deaths (deaths that occur during or within 24 hours after childbirth) in developing countries; 3 to 4 babies per 1,000 are born dead in Sweden and in the United States (Surkan, Stephansson, Dickman, & Cnattingius, 2004). Boys are more likely to be stillborn than girls (Bekedam, Engelsbel, Mol, Buitendijk, & van der Pal-de Bruin, 2002; Eogan, Geary, O'Connell, & Keane, 2003). Although the cause of stillbirth is not clearly understood, fetal growth restriction seems to be a major factor. Many stillborn infants are small for their gestational age, indicating malnourishment in the womb. A woman whose first baby was small for gestational age is at elevated risk of a stillbirth in a second pregnancy, especially if the first baby was preterm (Surkan et al., 2004).

Checkpoint

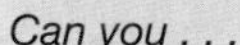

Can you . . .

- ✔ Explain the risks attending birth trauma and postmaturity, and discuss the use and value of fetal monitoring techniques?
- ✔ Discuss the risk factors, treatment, and outcomes for low-birth-weight babies?
- ✔ Describe coping responses of parents who have experienced stillbirth?

The number of third-trimester stillbirths in the United States has been substantially reduced during the past two decades. This improvement may be due to electronic fetal monitoring, ultrasound, and other measures to identify fetuses at risk for preeclampsia (a toxic condition) or restricted growth. Fetuses believed to have these problems can then be delivered prematurely (Goldenberg & Rouse, 1998).

How do parents cope with the loss of a child they never, or barely, got to know? Fathers and mothers tend to react somewhat differently. Men tend to worry, ignore the situation, or seek social support, whereas women are more likely to engage in wishful thinking, turn to spiritual support, or seek out others who have had a similar loss (McGreal, Evans, & Burrows, 1997). For 15 months, researchers followed 127 young adults who had lost an infant through stillbirth, neonatal death, or sudden infant death syndrome. Those whose adjustment was most positive tended to be better educated, and the women tended to have more friends in whom they could confide (Murray & Terry, 1999).

Can a Supportive Environment Overcome Effects of Birth Complications?

Prospects for overcoming the early disadvantage of low birth weight depend on two interrelated factors: the family's socioeconomic circumstances and the quality of the early environment (Aylward, Pfeiffer, Wright, & Verhulst, 1989; McGauhey, Starfield, Alexander, & Ensminget, 1991; Ross, Lipper, & Auld, 1991). Two major studies, the Infant Health and Development Program, and the Kauai Study, show that resilience can occur under favorable conditions.

The Infant Health and Development Program

The Infant Health and Development Program (IHDP) (1990) has successfully enhanced cognitive development for low-birth-weight children in a variety of family situations, especially those in which the family was poor and the mother had no more than a high school education (Brooks-Gunn, 2003). The study followed 985 preterm, low-birth-weight babies, most of them from disadvantaged families, in eight parts of the United States from birth to age 3. One-third of the heavier (but still low-birth-weight) babies and one-third of the lighter ones were randomly assigned to "intervention" groups. Their parents received home visits, counseling, information about children's health and development, and instruction in children's games and activities; at 1 year, these babies entered an educational day care program.

When the program stopped, the 3-year-olds in both the lower and higher birth weight intervention groups were doing better on cognitive and social measures, were much less likely to show mental retardation, and had fewer behavioral problems than control groups of similar birth weight who had received only pediatric follow-up (Brooks-Gunn, Klebanov, Liaw, & Spiker, 1993). However, by age 5, the lower birth weight intervention group lost their cognitive edge (Brooks-Gunn et al., 1994). By age 8, the higher birth weight intervention group averaged only 4 IQ points more than the controls. All groups had substantially below-average IQs and vocabulary scores (McCarton et al., 1997; McCormick, McCarton, Brooks-Gunn, Belt, & Gross, 1998). Perhaps for such an intervention to have lasting effects, it needs to continue beyond age 3. It may be that difficulties in controlling negative emotions—a particular risk for low-birth-weight babies that has been linked to lower IQ—resurfaced once the intervention stopped (Blair, 2002).

Additional studies of the full IHDP sample underline the importance of what goes on in the home. Children whose mothers reported having experienced stressful events—illnesses, deaths of friends or family members, moves, or changes in schooling or work—during the last six months of the child's first year showed less cognitive benefit from the intervention at age 3 (Klebanov, Brooks-Gunn, & McCormick, 2001). Children who got little parental attention and care were more likely to be undersized and to do poorly on cognitive tests than children from more favorable home environments (Kelleher et al., 1993; McCormick et al., 1998). Those whose cognitive performance stayed high had mothers who scored high themselves on cognitive tests and who were responsive and stimulating. Babies who had more than one risk factor (such as poor neonatal health combined with having a mother who did not receive counseling or was less well educated or less responsive) fared the worst (Liaw & Brooks-Gunn, 1993).

Thanks to positive environments and their own resilience, fully a third of the at-risk children studied by Emmy Werner and her colleagues developed into self-confident, successful adults.

The Kauai Study

As the IHDP research suggests, given a supportive environment many infants can overcome a poor start in life. That is also the conclusion of a longitudinal study of 698 children born in 1955 on the Hawaiian island of Kauai.

For nearly five decades, Emmy E. Werner (1987, 1995; Werner & Smith, 2001) and a team of pediatricians, psychologists, public health workers, and social workers have followed these children from gestation to middle adulthood. The researchers interviewed the mothers-to-be, monitored their pregnancies, and interviewed them again when the children were 1, 2, and 10 years old. They observed the children at home, gave them aptitude, achievement, and personality tests in elementary and high school, and obtained progress reports from their teachers. The young people themselves were interviewed periodically as adults.

The physical and psychological development of children who had suffered low birth weight or other complications at or before birth were seriously impaired *only* when the children grew up in persistently poor environmental circumstances. Unless the early damage was so serious as to require institutionalization, those children who had a stable and enriching environment did well (E. E. Werner, 1985, 1987). They had fewer language, perceptual, emotional, and school problems than children who had *not* experienced unusual stress at birth but who had received little intellectual stimulation or emotional support at home (E. E. Werner, 1989; E. E. Werner et al., 1968). The children who had been exposed to *both* birth-related problems and later stressful experiences had the worst health and the most retarded development (E. E. Werner, 1987).

Most remarkable is the resilience of children who escaped damage despite *multiple* sources of stress. Even when birth complications were combined with chronic poverty, family discord, divorce, or parents who were mentally ill, many children came through relatively unscathed. Of the 276 children who at age 2 had been identified as having four or more risk factors, two-thirds developed serious learning or behavior problems by the age of 10 or, by age 18, had become pregnant, gotten in trouble with the law, or become emotionally disturbed. Yet by age 30, one-third of these highly at-risk children had managed to become "competent, confident, and caring adults (E. E. Werner, 1995, p. 82). Of the full sample, about half of those on whom the researchers were able to obtain follow-up data successfully weathered the age-30 and age-40 transitions. Women tended to be better adapted than men (E. Werner & Smith, 2001).

protective factors Influences that reduce the impact of early stress and tend to predict positive outcomes.

Checkpoint

Can you . . .

✔ Discuss the effectiveness of the home environment and of intervention programs in overcoming effects of low birthweight and other birth complications?

✔ Name three protective factors identified by the Kauai study?

Protective factors, which tended to reduce the impact of early stress, fell into three categories: (1) individual attributes that may be largely genetic, such as energy, sociability, and intelligence; (2) affectionate ties with at least one supportive family member; and (3) rewards at school, work, or place of worship that provide a sense of meaning and control over one's life (E. E. Werner, 1987). Although the home environment seemed to have the most marked effect in childhood, in adulthood the individuals' own qualities made a greater difference (E. E. Werner, 1995).

These studies underline the need to look at child development in context. They show how biological and environmental influences interact, making resiliency possible even in babies born with serious complications. (Characteristics of resilient children are further discussed in Chapter 14.)

Refocus

- What changes in the customs and risks surrounding childbirth have occurred since Elvis Presley's birth?
- What resources available today might have changed the course of Gladys Presley's pregnancy and delivery?

Although most births are uneventful and most children turn out well, risk factors, protective factors, and resiliency are concerns that will come up again and again throughout this book as we report on what developmental scientists have learned about ways to promote the most desirable outcomes for children. In Part 3, we will examine our rapidly growing understanding of the physical, cognitive, and psychosocial developments of infancy and toddlerhood.

Summary and Key Terms

Childbirth and Culture: How Birthing Has Changed

Guidepost 1 How do customs surrounding birth reflect culture, and how has childbirth changed in developed countries?

- In Europe and the United States, childbirth before the 20th century was similar to childbirth in some developing countries today. Birth was a female ritual that occurred at home and was attended by a midwife. Pain relief was minimal, and risks for mother and baby were high.
- The development of the science of obstetrics professionalized childbirth. Births took places in hospitals, attended by physicians. Medical advances dramatically improved safety.
- Today delivery at home or in birth centers attended by midwives can be a relatively safe alternative to physician-attended hospital delivery for women with normal, low-risk pregnancies.

The Birth Process

Guidepost 2 How does labor begin, and what happens during each of the four stages of childbirth?

- Birth normally occurs after a preparatory period of parturition.
- The birth process consists of four stages: (1) dilation of the cervix; (2) descent and emergence of the baby; (3) expulsion of the umbilical cord and the placenta; and (4) contraction of the uterus and recovery of the mother.

parturition (111)

Guidepost 3 What alternative methods of delivery are available?

- About 26 percent of births in the United States are by cesarean delivery—an unnecessarily high rate, according to critics.
- Natural or prepared childbirth can minimize the need for pain-killing drugs and maximize parents' active involvement. Modern epidurals can give effective pain relief with smaller doses of medication than in the past.
- The presence of a doula can provide physical benefits as well as emotional support.

cesarean delivery (112) **natural childbirth (114)** **prepared childbirth (114)**

The Newborn Baby

Guidepost 4 How do newborn infants adjust to life outside the womb?

- The neonatal period is a time of transition from intrauterine to extrauterine life. During the first few days, the neonate loses weight and then regains it; the lanugo (prenatal hair) falls off, and the protective coating of vernix caseosa dries up. The fontanels (soft spots) in the skull close within the first 18 months.
- At birth, the circulatory, respiratory, gastrointestinal, and temperature regulation systems become independent of the mother's. If a newborn cannot start breathing within about 5 minutes, brain injury may occur.
- Newborns have a strong sucking reflex and secrete meconium from the intestinal tract. They are commonly subject to neonatal jaundice, due to immaturity of the liver.

neonate (114) **neonatal period (114)** **fontanels (115)** **lanugo (115)** **vernix caseosa (115)** **anoxia (115)** **meconium (115)** **neonatal jaundice (115)**

Guidepost 5 How can we tell whether a new baby is healthy and is developing normally?

- At 1 minute and 5 minutes after birth, a neonate's Apgar score can indicate how well he or she is adjusting to extrauterine life. The Brazelton Neonatal Behavioral Assessment Scale can assess an infant's responses to the environment and predict future development.
- Neonatal screening is done for certain rare conditions, such as PKU and congenital hypothyroidism.

Apgar scale (116) **Brazelton Neonatal Behavioral Assessment Scale (NBAS) (117)**

Guidepost 6 How do newborns' patterns of sleep, waking, and activity vary and change?

- A newborn's state of arousal is governed by periodic cycles of wakefulness, sleep, and activity, which seem to be inborn.
- Sleep takes up the major but a diminishing amount of a neonate's time.
- Individual differences in newborns' activity levels show stability and may be early indicators of temperament.
- Parents' responsiveness to babies' states and self-initiated activity levels is an important bidirectional influence on development.

state of arousal (117)

Newborns and Their Parents

Guidepost 7 How do parents bond with their baby, and how does parenthood change their relationship with one another?

- Researchers following the ethological approach have suggested that there is a critical period for the formation of the mother-infant bond. However, research has not confirmed this hypothesis. Fathers may bond with their babies whether or not they are present at the birth.
- Marital satisfaction typically declines during the child-raising years. Expectations and sharing of tasks can contribute to a marriage's deterioration or improvement.

mother-infant bond (119) **imprinting (120)**

Complications of Childbirth—and Their Aftermath

Guidepost 8 What complications of childbirth can endanger newborn babies, and what are the long-term prospects for babies with complicated births?

- A small minority of infants suffer lasting effects of birth trauma. Other complications include postmature birth, low birth weight, and stillbirth.
- Electronic fetal monitoring is widely used (and may be overused) during labor and delivery. It is intended to detect signs of fetal distress, especially in high-risk births.
- Low-birth-weight babies may be either preterm (premature) or small-for-date (small-for-gestational-age). Low birth weight is a major factor in infant mortality and can cause long-term physical and cognitive problems. Very low-birth-weight babies have a less promising prognosis than those who weigh more.
- A supportive postnatal environment and other protective factors often can improve the outcome for babies suffering from birth complications.

birth trauma (121) **electronic fetal monitoring (121)** **postmature (121)** **low birth weight (122)** **preterm (premature) infants (122)** **small-for-date (small-for-gestational-age) infants (122)** **protective factors (126)**

Part 3

Infancy and Toddlerhood: A Preview

Chapter 6
Physical Development and Health During the First Three Years

- All senses and body systems operate at birth to varying degrees.
- The brain grows in complexity and is highly sensitive to environmental influence.
- Physical growth and development of motor skills are rapid.

Chapter 7
Cognitive Development During the First Three Years

- Abilities to learn and remember are present, even in early weeks.
- Use of symbols and ability to solve problems develop by end of second year.
- Comprehension and use of language develop rapidly.

Chapter 8
Psychosocial Development During the First Three Years

- Attachments to parents and others form.
- Self-awareness develops.
- Shift from dependence to autonomy occurs.
- Interest in other children increases.

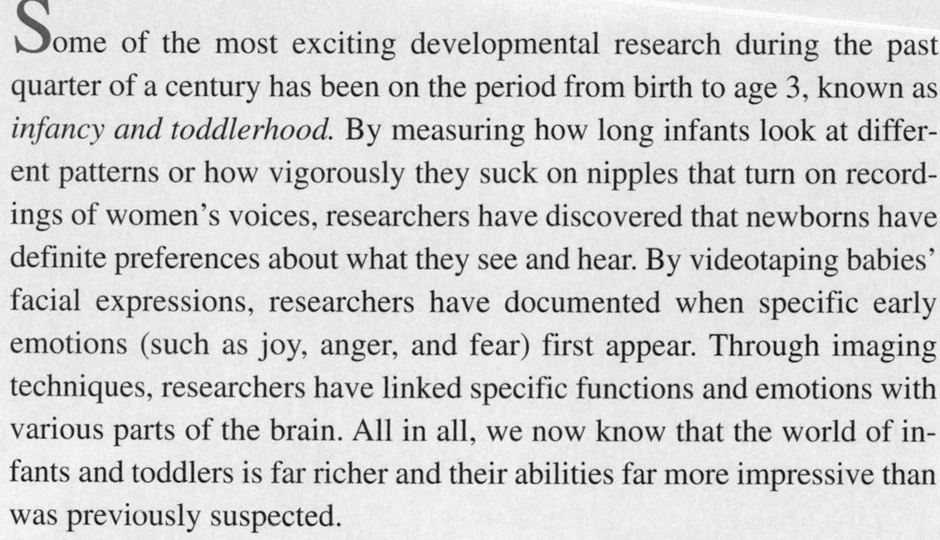

Infancy and Toddlerhood

Some of the most exciting developmental research during the past quarter of a century has been on the period from birth to age 3, known as *infancy and toddlerhood.* By measuring how long infants look at different patterns or how vigorously they suck on nipples that turn on recordings of women's voices, researchers have discovered that newborns have definite preferences about what they see and hear. By videotaping babies' facial expressions, researchers have documented when specific early emotions (such as joy, anger, and fear) first appear. Through imaging techniques, researchers have linked specific functions and emotions with various parts of the brain. All in all, we now know that the world of infants and toddlers is far richer and their abilities far more impressive than was previously suspected.

Infancy begins at birth and ends when a child begins walking and stringing words together—two events that typically take place between 12 and 18 months of age. Toddlerhood lasts from about 18 to 36 months, a period when children become more verbal, independent, and able to move about. As we study how newborns become infants and toddlers (and, later, grow into older children and adolescents), we see how each of the three aspects of development is bound up with the others. Thus, although we focus on the *physical* development of infants and toddlers in Chapter 6, on their *cognitive* development in Chapter 7, and on their *psychosocial* development in Chapter 8, we will see many examples of how these aspects of development intertwine.

Linkups to Look For

- The physical growth of the brain before and after birth makes possible a great burst of cognitive and emotional development. Fetuses whose ears and brains have developed enough to hear sounds from the outside world seem to retain a memory of these sounds after birth.
- An infant's earliest smiles arise from central nervous system activity and may reflect nothing more than a pleasant physiological state, such as drowsiness and a full stomach. As the infant becomes cognitively aware of the warm responses of caregivers and as his or her vision becomes sharp enough to recognize a familiar face, the infant's smiles become more emotionally expressive and more socially directed.
- Infants learn through their physical movements where their bodies end and everything else begins. As they drop toys, splash water, and hurl sand, their minds grasp how their bodies can change their world, and their sense of self begins to flourish.
- Without the vocal structures and motor coordination to form sounds, babies would not be able to speak. Physical gestures precede and often accompany early attempts to form words. The acquisition of language dramatically advances cognitive understanding and social communication.

chapter

6

Physical Development and Health During the First Three Years

There he lay upon his back
The yearling creature, warm and moist with life
To the bottom of his dimples,—to the ends
Of the lovely tumbled curls about his face.

—Elizabeth Barrett Browning, *Aurora Leigh*, 1857

Focus *Helen Keller and the World of the Senses*

Hellen Keller

"What we have once enjoyed we can never lose," the author Helen Keller (1880–1968) once wrote. "A sunset, a mountain bathed in moonlight, the ocean in calm and in storm—we see these, love their beauty, hold the vision to our hearts. All that we love deeply becomes a part of us" (Keller, 1929, p. 2).

This quotation is especially remarkable—and especially poignant—in view of the fact that Helen Keller never saw a sunset, or a mountain, or moonlight, or an ocean, or anything else after the age of 19 months. It was then that she contracted a mysterious fever, which left her deaf and with inexorably ebbing sight.

Before her illness, Helen had been a normal, healthy baby—lively, affectionate, and precocious, with excellent vision. After her illness, she became expressionless and unresponsive. At 1 year, she had begun to walk; after her illness, she clung to her mother's skirts or sat in her lap, endlessly rubbing her face. She had also begun to talk; one of her first words was *water.* After her illness, she continued to say, "wah-wah," but not much else.

Her distraught parents first took her to a mineral spa and then to medical specialists, but there was no hope for a cure. At a time when physical and cognitive development normally enter a major growth spurt, the sensory gateways to the exploration of Helen's world had slammed shut—but not entirely. Deprived of two senses, she leaned more heavily on the other three, especially smell and touch. She later explained that she could tell a doctor from a carpenter by the odors of ether or wood that came from them. She used her ever-active fingertips to trace the "delicate tremble of a butterfly's wings . . . , the soft petals of violets . . . , the clear, firm outline of face and limb, the smooth arch of a horse's neck and the velvety touch of his nose" (Keller, 1920, pp. 6–7). Memories of the daylight world she had once inhabited helped her make sense of the unrelieved night in which she now found herself.

Helen realized that she was not like other people, but at first she had no clear sense of who or what she was. She later wrote, "I lived in a world that was a no-world. . . . I did not know that I knew [anything], or that I lived or acted or desired" (1920, p. 113). Sometimes, when family members were talking to each other, she would stand between them and touch

Sources of information about Helen Keller include Keller (1903/1905, 1920, 1929, 2003), Herrmann (1999), Lash (1980), and Ozick (2003).

their lips and then frantically move her own—but nothing happened. Her frustration found its outlet in violent, inconsolable tantrums; she would kick and scream until she was exhausted.

Out of pity, her parents indulged her whims. Finally, more in desperation than in hope, they engaged a teacher for her: a young woman named Anne Sullivan, who herself had limited vision and who had been trained in a school for the blind. Arriving at the Keller home, Sullivan found 6-year-old Helen to be "wild, wilful, and destructive" (Lash, 1980, p. 348). Upon meeting her new teacher, the child knocked out one of Sullivan's front teeth. Once, after figuring out how to use a key, she locked her mother in the pantry. Another time, she overturned her baby sister's cradle. Frustrated by her teacher's attempts to spell the word *doll* into her palm, Helen hurled her new doll to the floor, smashing it to bits.

Yet, that same day, the little girl made her first linguistic breakthrough. As she and her teacher walked in the garden, they stopped to get a drink at the pump. Sullivan placed Helen's hand under the spout, at the same time spelling "w-a-t-e-r" over and over into her other hand. "I stood still," Keller later wrote, "my whole attention fixed upon the motions of her fingers. Suddenly I felt a misty consciousness as of something forgotten—a thrill of returning thought; and somehow the mystery of language was revealed to me. I knew then that 'w-a-t-e-r' meant the wonderful cool something that was flowing over my hand. That living word awakened my soul, gave it light, hope, joy, set it free!" (Keller, 1905, p. 35).

• • •

The story of how Anne Sullivan tamed this unruly child and brought her into the light of language and thought is a familiar and inspiring one. One lesson we can draw from the story of Helen Keller's early development is the central importance of the senses—the windows to a baby's world—and their connection with all other aspects of development. Had Helen Keller not lost her vision and hearing or had she been born without one or the other, or both, her physical, cognitive, and psychosocial development undoubtedly would have been quite different.

In this chapter, we explore how sensory perception goes hand in hand with an infant's growing motor skills and shapes the astoundingly rapid development of the brain. We examine typical growth patterns of body and brain, and we see how a nourishing environment can stimulate both. We study how infants, who spend most of their time sleeping and eating, become busy, active toddlers and how parents and other caregivers can foster healthy growth and development. We discuss threats to infants' life and health and how to ward them off.

After you have read and studied this chapter, you should be able to answer each of the Guidepost questions that follow. Look for them again in the margins, where they point to important concepts throughout the chapter. To check your understanding of these Guideposts, review the end-of-chapter summary. Checkpoints located at periodic spots throughout the chapter will help you verify your understanding of what you have read.

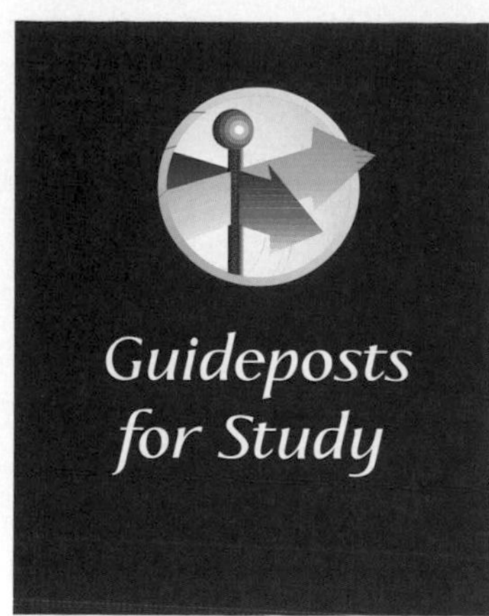

Guideposts for Study

1. How do babies grow, and what influences their growth?
2. How and what should babies be fed?
3. How does the brain develop, and how do environmental factors affect its early growth?
4. How do the senses develop during infancy?
5. What are the early milestones in motor development, and what are some influences on it?
6. How can we enhance babies' chances of survival and health?

Growth and Nutrition

Guidepost 1

How do babies grow, and what influences their growth?

Patterns of Growth

Children grow faster during the first three years, especially during the first few months, than they ever will again (see Figure 6-1). By 5 months, the average baby boy's birth weight has doubled to 16 pounds and, by 1 year, has nearly tripled to 23 pounds. This rapid growth rate tapers off during the second and third years; a boy typically gains about 5 pounds by his second birthday and 3½ pounds by his third, when he tips the scales at 31½ pounds. A boy's height typically increases by 10 inches during the first year (making the typical 1-year-old boy nearly 30 inches tall), by almost 5 inches during the second year (so that the average 2-year-old boy is approaching 3 feet tall), and by a little more than 3 inches during the third year to top 37 inches. Girls follow a parallel pattern but are slightly smaller; at 3, the average girl weighs a pound less and is half an inch shorter than the average boy (Kuczmarski et al., 2000).

Teething usually begins around 3 or 4 months, when infants begin grabbing almost everything in sight to put into their mouths; but the first tooth may not actually arrive until sometime between 5 and 9 months of age, or even later. By the first birthday, babies generally have six to eight teeth; by age 2½, they have a mouthful of 20.

As a baby grows, body shape and proportions change too; a 3-year-old typically is slender compared with a chubby, potbellied 1-year-old. Physical growth and development follow the maturational principles introduced in Chapter 3: the *cephalocaudal principle* and *proximodistal principle.* According to the cephalocaudal principle, growth occurs from top down. Because the brain grows so rapidly before birth, a newborn baby's head is

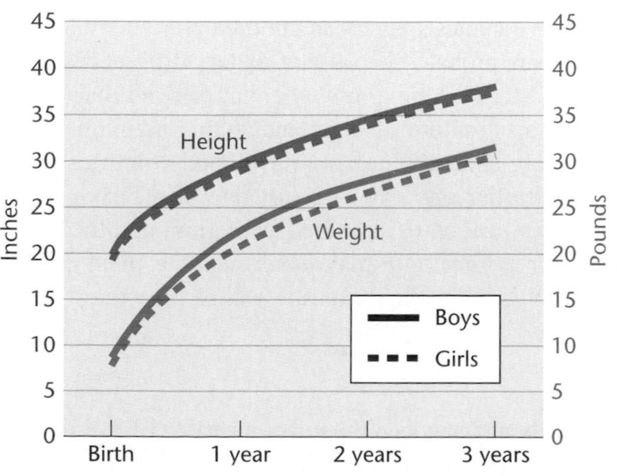

Figure 6-1

Growth in height and weight during infancy and toddlerhood. Babies grow most rapidly in both height and weight during the first few months of life and then taper off somewhat by age 3. Baby boys are slightly larger, on average, than baby girls.

Note: Curves shown are for the 50th percentiles for each sex.

Source: Kuczmarski et al., 2000.

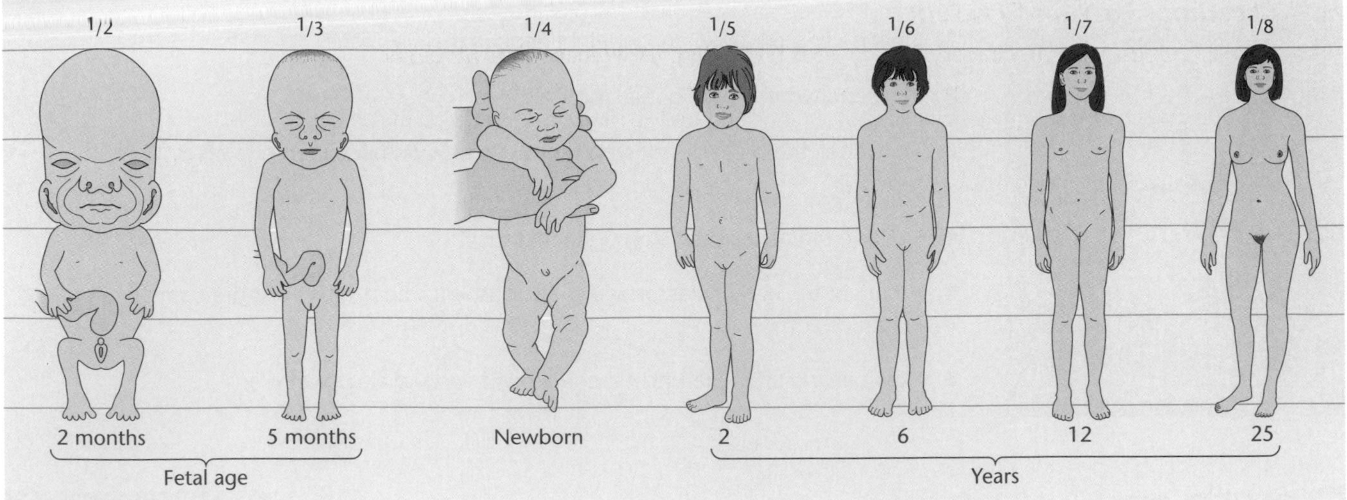

Figure 6-2

Changes in proportions of the human body during growth. The most striking change is that the head becomes smaller relative to the rest of the body. The fractions indicate head size as a proportion of total body length at several ages. More subtle is the stability of the trunk proportion (from neck to crotch). The increasing leg proportion is almost exactly the reverse of the decreasing head proportion.

disproportionately large. By 1 year, the brain is 70 percent of its adult weight, but the rest of the body is only about 10 to 20 percent of adult weight. The head becomes proportionately smaller as the child grows in height and the lower parts of the body develop (see Figure 6-2). As we'll see later in this chapter, sensory and motor development proceed according to the same principle; infants learn to use the upper parts of the body before the lower parts. They see objects before they can control their trunk, and they learn to do many things with their hands long before they can crawl or walk. According to the proximodistal principle (inner to outer), growth and motor development proceed from the center of the body outward. In the womb, the head and trunk develop before the arms and legs, then the hands and feet, and then the fingers and toes. During infancy and early childhood, the limbs continue to grow faster than the hands and feet. Similarly, babies first develop the ability to use their upper arms and upper legs (which are closest to the center of the body), then the forearms and forelegs, then hands and feet, and finally fingers and toes.

Influences on Growth

The genes an infant inherits have a strong influence on whether the child will be tall or short, thin or stocky, or somewhere in between. This genetic influence interacts with such environmental influences as nutrition and living conditions, which also affect general health and well-being. For example, Japanese American children are taller and weigh more than children the same age in Japan, probably because of dietary differences (Broude, 1995).

Well-fed, well-cared-for children grow taller and heavier than less well nourished and nurtured children. They also mature sexually and attain maximum height earlier, and their teeth erupt sooner. Today, children in many developed countries are growing taller and maturing sexually at an earlier age than a century ago (see Chapter 15), probably because of better nutrition and medical care, improved sanitation, and the decrease in child labor. Children who are ill for a long time may never achieve their genetically programmed stature because they may never make up for the loss of growth time during their sickness.

Checkpoint

Can you . . .

✔ Summarize typical patterns of growth during the first three years?

✔ Mention several factors that affect growth?

Guidepost 2

How and what should babies be fed?

Nourishment

Babies can grow normally and stay healthy under a variety of feeding regimens. Still, some feeding practices are more beneficial than others.

Early Feeding: Past and Present

From the beginnings of human history, babies were breast-fed.* A woman who was either unable or unwilling to nurse her baby usually found another woman, a wet nurse, to do it. At first a prerogative of upper-class women too busy with social rounds to breast-feed, the custom of wet-nursing spread by the Middle Ages to the working class in cities and villages, and it persisted in some places until the early 20th century.

Ironically, the babies of peasant women, who could not afford wet nurses, often thrived better than the children of the rich. The greater mortality rates among high-born, wet-nursed infants may have been due in part to the stress of separation as well as to the lack of built-in immunity from the mother's *colostrum,* an antibody-rich fluid produced in the first few days after childbirth.

Between the 16th and 18th centuries, in an effort to bring down the high rate of infant deaths, doctors and clergy in Europe and the American colonies urged mothers to nurse their own babies. Wet-nursing, it was said, was "against nature" and could cause great harm, not only to the baby but also to the mother, whose unconsumed milk could back up into her system and make her ill (Fontanel & d'Harcourt, 1997, p. 99). Babies fed nonhuman milk were even more likely to fall ill and die, and by the 19th century doctors were warning mothers to avoid the "poisonous bottle" at all costs (Fontanel & d'Harcourt, 1997, p. 121). Not until the first decade of the 20th century, some 20 years after the discovery of germs in 1878, did the medical establishment agree on the need to boil animal milk fed to infants.

By this time, maternal breast-feeding had come back in vogue. Diarrhea was the main cause of infant deaths, and artificially fed infants died of it at much higher rates than breast-fed babies (Brosco, 1999). Then, with the advent of dependable refrigeration, pasteurization, and sterilization, manufacturers began to develop formulas to modify and enrich cow's milk for infant consumption. With improvements in the design of bottles, bottle-feeding became safe, nutritious, and popular.

During the next half-century, formula feeding became the norm in the United States and some other industrialized countries. By 1971, only 25 percent of U.S. mothers even tried to nurse. Since then, recognition of the benefits of breast milk has brought about a reversal of this trend, so that in 2001, 69.5 percent of new mothers in the United States (the highest proportion ever recorded) breast-fed. However, only about 32.5 percent still breast-feed infants at 6 months, and many of these supplement breast milk with formula (AAP Work Group on Breastfeeding, 1997; Ryan, Wenjun, & Acosta, 2002; USDHHS, 2000a). Worldwide, only about one-half of all infants are ever breast-fed (UNICEF, 2002).

Breast milk can be called the "ultimate health food" because it offers so many benefits to babies—physical, cognitive, and emotional.

Increases in breast-feeding in the United States are most notable in socioeconomic groups that historically have been less likely to breast-feed: black women, teenage women, poor women, working women, and those with no more than high school education (Ryan et al., 2002). Lower-income and less-educated mothers and those who return to work or school are less likely to continue breast-feeding. Flexible scheduling and privacy for nursing mothers at work and at school, as well as education about the benefits of breast-feeding, may increase its prevalence in these groups (Ryan et al., 2002; Taveras et al., 2003).

Breast or Bottle?

Breast milk is almost always the best food for infants. The only acceptable alternative is an iron-fortified formula based on either cow's milk or soy protein and containing supplemental vitamins and minerals. Breast milk is more digestible and more nutritious than formula

* Unless otherwise referenced, the historical material in this section is based on Eccles (1982) and Fontanel & d'Harcourt (1997).

and is less likely to produce allergic reactions (AAP, 1989a, 1996; AAP Work Group on Breastfeeding, 1997; Eiger & Olds, 1999). Human milk is a complete source of nutrients for at least the first six months; during this time breast-fed babies normally do not need any other food. Neither they nor formula-fed infants need additional water (AAP Work Group on Breastfeeding, 1997).

The health advantages of breast-feeding are striking during the first two years and even later in life (A. S. Cunningham, Jelliffe, & Jelliffe, 1991; J. Newman, 1995; A. L. Wright, Holberg, Taussig, & Martinez, 1995). Among the illnesses prevented or minimized by breast-feeding are diarrhea, respiratory infections (such as pneumonia and bronchitis), otitis media (an infection of the middle ear), and staphylococcal, bacterial, and urinary tract infections (AAP Work Group on Breastfeeding, 1997; Black, Morris, & Bryce, 2003; A. S. Cunningham et al., 1991; Dewey, Heinig, & Nommsen-Rivers, 1995; J. Newman, 1995; Scariati, Grummer-Strawn, & Fein, 1997). Breast-feeding may reduce the risk of sudden infant death syndrome (discussed later in this chapter) (National Institute of Child Health and Human Development [NICHD], 1997, updated 2000) and of postneonatal deaths, which occur between 28 days and one year (Chen & Rogan, 2004). Resistance to some illnesses (influenza, diphtheria, and diarrhea) can be enhanced in bottle-fed babies by fortifying their formula with nucleotides, components of human milk that stimulate the immune system; but babies breast-fed more than six months do better overall (Pickering et al., 1998). Unfortunately, in developing countries where bottle-feeding has been promoted as the more modern method, some poor mothers dilute formula or use unclean water to make it, unwittingly endangering their babies' health and lives. Even in highly developed countries, breast-fed babies are healthier than formula-fed infants (AAP Work Group on Breastfeeding, 1997).

Breast-feeding seems to have benefits for visual acuity (Makrides, Neumann, Simmer, Pater, & Gibson, 1995), neurological development (Lanting, Fidler, Huisman, Touwen, & Boersma, 1994), and long-term cardiovascular health (Owen, Whincup, Odoki, Gilg, & Cook, 2002), including cholesterol levels (Singhal, Cole, Fewtrell, & Lucas, 2004). It may help prevent obesity (AAP Committee on Nutrition, 2003; Dietz, 2001; Gillman et al., 2001; Hediger, Overpeck, Kuczmarski, & Ruan, 2001; von Kries et al., 1999).

Most studies also show benefits for cognitive development (AAP Work Group on Breastfeeding, 1997; Angelsen, Vik, Jacobsen, & Bakketeig, 2001; Horwood & Fergusson, 1998; Jacobson, Chiodo, & Jacobson, 1999), even into young adulthood (Mortensen, Michaelson, Sanders, & Reinisch, 2002). However, a literature review found that many of these studies had methodological flaws (Jain, Concato, & Leventhal, 2002). Nevertheless, in a randomized clinical trial, when two fatty acids present in breast milk were added to infant formula, infants fed the fortified formula had better cognitive scores at 18 months than infants who had been fed unfortified formula (Birch, Garfield, Hoffman, Uauy, & Birch, 2000).

Since 1991, 16,000 hospitals and birthing centers worldwide have been designated as "Baby-Friendly" under a United Nations initiative for encouraging institutional support of breast-feeding. At Boston Medical Center, breast-feeding increased substantially after the program went into effect (Philipp et al., 2001). In a randomized controlled study of 17,046 new mothers in Belarus, in Eastern Europe, mothers trained to promote successful breast-feeding were more likely than a control group to breast-feed exclusively for the first three to six months and, to some degree, throughout the first year; and their infants were less likely to contract gastrointestinal infections and eczema (Kramer et al., 2001).

Nursing mothers need to be as careful as pregnant women about what they take into their bodies. Breast-feeding is inadvisable if a mother is infected with the AIDS virus or any other infectious illness, if she has untreated active tuberculosis, or if she is taking any drug that would not be safe for the baby (AAP Work Group on Breastfeeding, 1997; Eiger & Olds, 1999; Miotti et al., 1999; Nduati et al., 2000; Read and Committee on Pediatric AIDS, 2003). The risk of transmitting HIV infection to an infant continues as long as an infected mother breast-feeds (The Breastfeeding and HIV International Transmission Study Group, 2004).

Feeding a baby is an emotional as well as a physical act. Warm contact with the mother's body fosters emotional linkage between mother and baby. Such bonding can take place through either breast- or bottle-feeding and through many other caregiving activities,

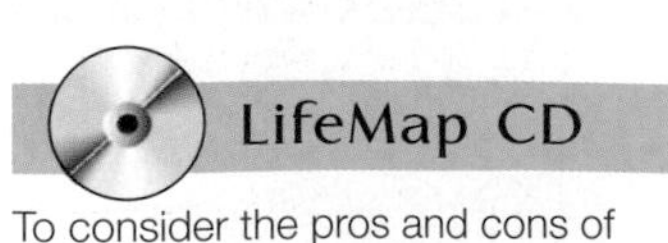

To consider the pros and cons of breast and bottle feeding, watch the "Breast vs. Bottle Feeding" video in Chapter 6 of your CD.

most of which can be performed by fathers as well as mothers. The quality of the relationship between parent and child and the provision of abundant affection and cuddling may be more important than the feeding method.

What's your view

- "Every mother who is physically able should breastfeed." Do you agree or disagree? Give reasons.

Cow's Milk, Solid Foods, and Juice

Iron-deficiency anemia is the world's most common nutritional disorder, affecting as many as one-fourth of all 6- to 24-month-old babies in the United States. Infants with iron-deficiency anemia do more poorly on cognitive tests than other infants. They also tend to be less independent, joyful, attentive, and playful and more wary, hesitant, and easily tired (Lozoff et al., 1998). Because infants fed plain cow's milk in the early months of life may suffer from iron deficiency, the American Academy of Pediatrics (AAP, 1989b, 1996; AAP Committee on Nutrition, 1992b) recommends that babies receive breast milk or, alternatively, iron-fortified formula for at least the first year.

Iron-enriched solid foods—usually beginning with cereal—should be gradually introduced during the second half of the first year (AAP Work Group on Breastfeeding, 1997). At this time, too, fruit juice may be introduced (Skinner, Carruth, Moran, Houck, & Coletta, 1999).

At 1 year, babies can switch from breast (or bottle) to cow's milk if they are getting a balanced diet of supplementary solid foods that provide one-third of their caloric intake (AAP, 1989b). To promote proper growth, the milk should be homogenized whole milk fortified with vitamin D, not skim milk or reduced-fat (1 or 2 percent) milk (AAP, 1996).

Nutritional Concerns

Unfortunately, many parents do not follow the guidelines just stated. According to random telephone interviews with parents and caregivers of more than 3,000 U.S. infants and toddlers, 29 percent of infants are given solid food before 4 months, 17 percent drink juice before 6 months, and 20 percent drink cow's milk before 12 months. Furthermore, like older children and adults, these very young children eat too much, especially of the wrong kinds of food. From 7 to 24 months, the median food intake is 20 to 30 percent over normal daily requirements. Up to one-third of the children eat no fruits and vegetables; but large percentages regularly consume hot dogs, sausage, bacon, dessert or candy, salty snacks, French fries, sugary fruit drinks, and soda (Fox, Pac, Devaney, & Jankowski, 2004).

In many low-income communities around the world, malnutrition in early life is widespread—and often fatal. Undernourished children who survive their first five years are at high risk for stunted growth and poor health and functioning throughout life. In a longitudinal study of a large-scale government-sponsored nutritional program in 347 poor rural communities of Mexico, infants who received fortified nutrition supplements—along with nutrition education, health care, and financial assistance for the family—showed better growth and lower rates of anemia than infants not yet assigned to the program (Rivera, Sotres-Alvarez, Habicht, Shamah, & Villalpando, 2004).

Although overweight is not usually a problem in infancy, food patterns developed early in life may be hard to break. Two factors seem to influence most strongly the chances that an overweight child will become an obese adult: whether the child has an obese parent and the age of the child. Before 3 years of age, parental obesity is a stronger predictor of a child's obesity as an adult than the child's own weight (AAP Committee on Nutrition, 2003). Having one obese parent increases the odds of obesity in adulthood by 3 to 1, and if both parents are obese, the odds increase to more than 10 to 1 (AAP Committee on Nutrition, 2003). Thus an overweight 1- or 2-year-old who has an obese parent—or especially two obese parents—may be a candidate for prevention efforts if it can be determined what factors, such as a too-rich diet or too little exercise, are contributing to the problem.

Checkpoint

Can you . . .

- ✔ Summarize pediatric recommendations regarding early feeding and the introduction of cow's milk, solid foods, and fruit juices?
- ✔ Cite factors that contribute to obesity and cardiac problems in later life?

Another concern is a potential buildup of *cholesterol,* a waxy substance found in human and animal tissue. High levels of one type of cholesterol (LDL, or "bad" cholesterol) can dangerously narrow blood vessels, leading to heart disease. This condition is called *atherosclerosis.* Although intake of breast milk, with its high fat content, is linked to high cholesterol levels during the first year of life, it tends to lead to lower LDL cholesterol in adolescence and adulthood. This suggests that formula prepared for bottle-fed infants should match the fat content of breast milk as closely as possible (Owen et al., 2002; Singhal et al., 2004).

All in all, the best ways parents can avoid obesity and cardiac problems in themselves and in their children is to adopt a more active lifestyle for the entire family—and to breastfeed their babies.

Guidepost 3

How does the brain develop, and how do environmental factors affect its early growth?

The Brain and Reflex Behavior

central nervous system Brain and spinal cord.

What makes newborns respond to a nipple? What tells them to start the sucking movements that allow them to control their intake of fluids? These are functions of the **central nervous system**—the brain and *spinal cord* (a bundle of nerves running through the backbone)—and of a growing peripheral network of nerves extending to every part of the body. Through this network, sensory messages travel to the brain, and motor commands travel back.

Building the Brain

The growth of the brain both before birth and during the childhood years is fundamental to future physical, cognitive, and emotional development. Throughout this period, the brain's growth and development depend on proper nutrition, including such nutrients as proteins, iron, iodine, zinc, vitamin A, vitamin B6, and folic acid (Rao & Georgieff, 2000). Through various brain-imaging tools, researchers are gaining a clearer picture of how brain growth occurs (Behrman, 1992; Casaer, 1993; Gabbard, 1996).* For example, from brain imaging studies we have learned that the brain's maturation takes much longer than was previously thought (Chugani, 1998)—well into the adolescent years (see Chapter 15).

brain growth spurts Periods of rapid brain growth and development.

The brain at birth weighs only about 25 percent of its eventual adult weight of 3½ pounds. It reaches nearly 90 percent of that weight by age 3. By age 6, it is almost adult size; but growth and functional development of specific parts of the brain continue into adulthood. The brain's growth occurs in fits and starts. **Brain growth spurts,** periods of rapid growth and development, coincide with changes in cognitive behavior (Fischer & Rose, 1994, 1995). Different parts of the brain grow more rapidly at different times.

Major Parts of the Brain

Beginning about two weeks after conception, the brain gradually develops from a long hollow tube into a spherical mass of cells (see Figure 6-3). By birth, the growth spurt of the spinal cord and *brain stem* (the part of the brain responsible for such basic bodily functions as breathing, heart rate, body temperature, and the sleep-wake cycle) has almost run its course. The *cerebellum* (the part of the brain that maintains balance and motor coordination) grows fastest during the first year of life (Casaer, 1993).

lateralization Tendency of each of the brain's hemispheres to have specialized functions.

The *cerebrum,* the largest part of the brain, is divided into right and left halves, or hemispheres, each with specialized functions. This specialization of the hemispheres is called **lateralization.** The left hemisphere is mainly concerned with language and logical thinking, the right hemisphere with visual and spatial functions such as map reading and drawing. Language lateralization increases with age in childhood and young adulthood, peaking between ages 25 and 35, and enables growth in language skills (Szaflarski, Holland, Schmithorst, & Weber-Byars, 2004). The two hemispheres are joined by a tough band of tissue called the *corpus callosum,* which allows them to share information and coordinate commands. The corpus callosum grows dramatically during childhood, reaching adult size by about age 10.

Each cerebral hemisphere has four lobes, or sections: the *occipital, parietal, temporal,* and *frontal* lobes, which control different functions (see Figure 6-4) and develop at different rates. The regions of the *cerebral cortex* (the outer surface of the cerebrum) that govern vision and hearing are mature by 6 months of age, but the areas of the frontal lobe responsible

* Unless otherwise referenced, the discussion in this section is largely based on Gabbard (1996).

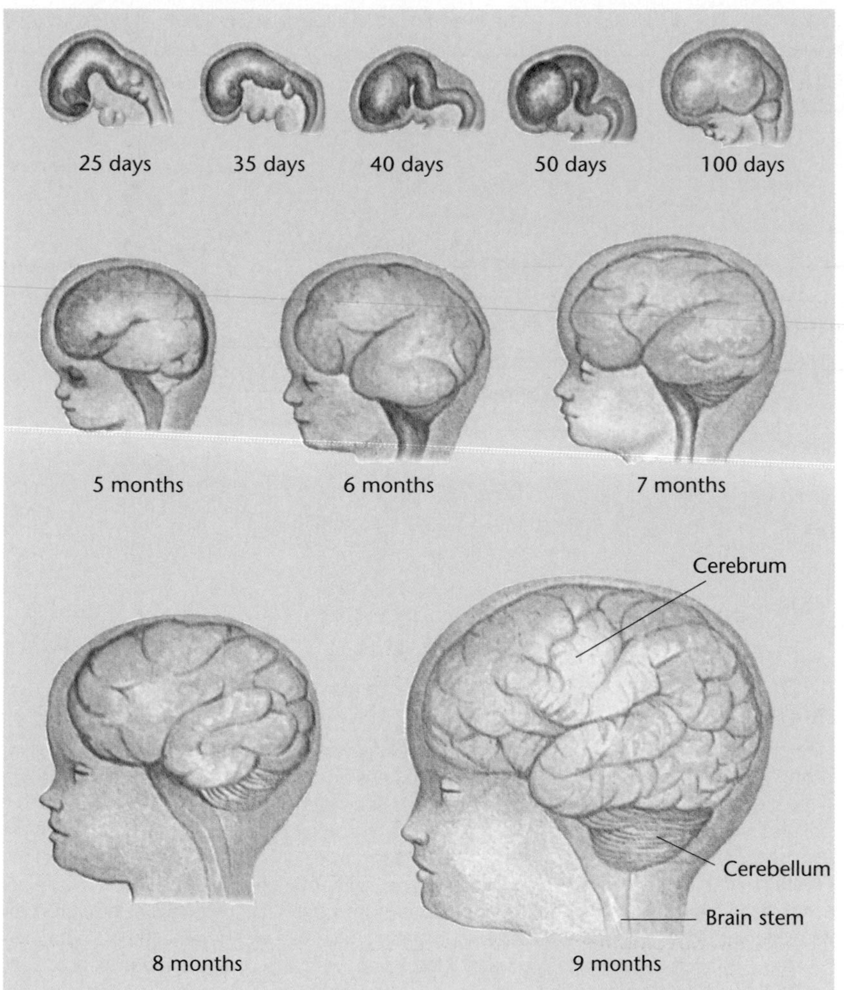

Figure 6-3

Fetal brain development from 25 days of gestation through birth. The brain stem, which controls basic biological functions such as breathing, develops first. As the brain grows, the front part expands greatly to form the cerebrum (the large, convoluted upper mass). Specific areas of the cerebral cortex (the gray outer covering of the brain) have specific functions, such as sensory and motor activity; but large areas are "uncommitted" and thus are free for higher cognitive activity, such as thinking, remembering, and problem solving. The brain stem and other structures below the cortical layer handle reflex behavior and other lower-level functions. The cerebellum, which maintains balance and motor coordination, grows most rapidly during the first year of life.

Source: Casaer, 1993; Restak, 1984.

for making mental associations, remembering, and producing deliberate motor responses remain immature for several years.

Brain Cells

The brain is composed of *neurons* and *glial cells.* **Neurons**, or nerve cells, send and receive information. *Glial cells* support and protect the neurons.

neurons Nerve cells.

Beginning in the second month of gestation, an estimated 250,000 immature neurons are produced every minute through cell division (mitosis). At birth, most of the more than 100 billion neurons in a mature brain are already formed but are not yet fully developed. The number of neurons increases most rapidly between the 25th week of gestation and the first few months after birth. This cell proliferation is accompanied by a dramatic growth in cell size.

Originally the neurons are simply cell bodies with a nucleus, or center, composed of deoxyribonucleic acid (DNA), which contains the cell's genetic programming. As the brain grows, these rudimentary cells migrate to various parts of it. There they sprout *axons* and *dendrites*—narrow, branching extensions. Axons send signals to other neurons, and dendrites receive incoming messages from them, through *synapses,* the nervous system's communication links. The synapses are tiny gaps, which are bridged with the help of chemicals called *neurotransmitters.* Eventually a particular neuron may have anywhere from 5,000 to 100,000 synaptic connections to and from the body's sensory receptors, its muscles, and other neurons within the central nervous system.

The multiplication of dendrites and synaptic connections, especially during the last two and one-half months of gestation and the first six months to two years of life (see

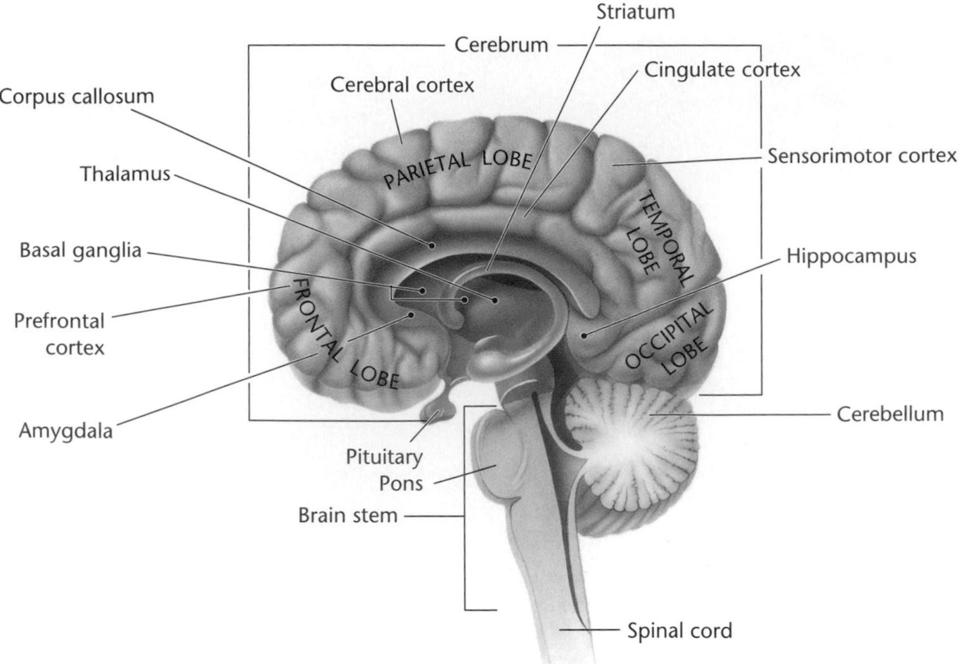

Figure 6-4

Parts of the brain, side view. The brain consists of three main parts: the brain stem, the cerebellum, and, above those, the large cerebrum. The brain stem, an extension of the spinal cord, is one of the regions of the brain most completely developed at birth. It controls such basic bodily functions as breathing, circulation, and reflexes. The cerebellum, at birth, begins to control balance and muscle tone; later it coordinates sensory and motor activity. The cerebrum constitutes almost 70 percent of the weight of the nervous system and handles thought, memory, language, and emotion. It is divided into two halves, or hemispheres, each of which has four sections, or lobes (right to left): (a) The occipital lobe processes visual information. (b) The temporal lobe helps with hearing and language. (c) The parietal lobe enables an infant to receive touch sensations and spatial information, which facilitates eye-hand coordination. (d) The frontal lobe develops gradually during the first year, permitting such higher-level functions as speech and reasoning. The cerebral cortex, the outer surface of the cerebrum, consists of gray matter; it is the seat of thought processes and mental activity. Parts of the cerebral cortex—the sensorimotor cortex and cingulate cortex—as well as several structures deep within the cerebrum, the thalamus, hippocampus, and basal ganglia, all of which control basic movements and functions, are largely developed at birth.

Figure 6-5), accounts for much of the brain's growth in weight and permits the emergence of new perceptual, cognitive, and motor abilities. Most of the neurons in the cortex, which is responsible for complex, high-level functioning, are in place by 20 weeks of gestation, and its structure becomes fairly well-defined during the next 12 weeks. Only after birth, however, do the cells begin to form connections that allow communication to take place.

As the neurons multiply, migrate to their assigned locations, and develop connections, they undergo the complementary processes of *integration* and *differentiation.* Through **integration,** the neurons that control various groups of muscles coordinate their activities. Through **differentiation,** each neuron takes on a specific, specialized structure and function.

integration Process by which neurons coordinate the activities of muscle groups.

differentiation Process by which neurons acquire specialized structure and function.

cell death Elimination of excess brain cells to achieve more efficient functioning.

At first the brain produces more neurons and synapses than it needs. Those that are not used or do not function well die out. This process of **cell death,** or pruning of excess cells, begins during the prenatal period and continues after birth (see Figure 6-6), helping to create an efficient nervous system. The number of synapses seems to peak at about age 2, and their elimination continues well into adolescence. Even as some neurons die out, new research suggests, others may continue to form during adult life (Eriksson et al., 1998; Gould, Reeves, Graziano, & Gross, 1999). Connections among cortical cells continue to improve into adulthood, enabling more flexible and more advanced motor and cognitive functioning.

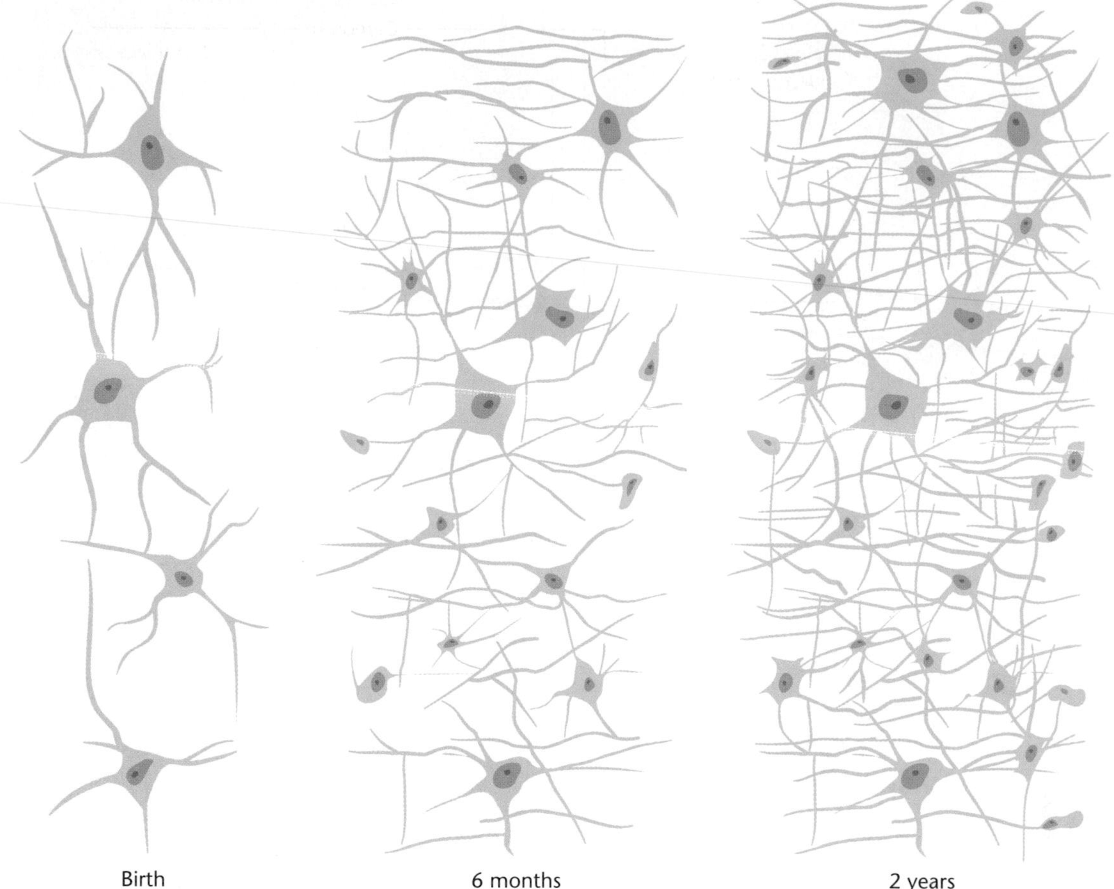

Figure 6-5

Growth of neural connections during the first two years of life. The rapid increase in the brain's density and weight is due largely to the formation of dendrites, extensions of nerve cell bodies, and the synapses that link them. This mushrooming communications network sprouts in response to environmental stimulation and makes possible impressive growth in every domain of development.

Source: Conel, 1959.

Myelination

Much of the credit for improvement in efficiency of communication goes to the glial cells, which coat the neural pathways with a fatty substance called *myelin.* This process of **myelination** enables signals to travel faster and more smoothly, permitting the achievement of mature functioning. Myelination begins about halfway through gestation in some parts of the brain and continues into adulthood in others. The pathways related to the sense of touch—the first sense to develop—are myelinated by birth. Myelination of visual pathways, which are slower to mature, begins at birth and continues during the first five months of life. Pathways related to hearing may begin to be myelinated as early as the fifth month of gestation, but the process is not complete until about age 4. The parts of the cortex that control attention and memory, which are slower to develop, are not fully myelinated until young adulthood. Myelination in an information-relay zone of the *hippocampus,* a structure deep in the temporal lobe that plays a key role in memory, and related formations continues to increase until at least age 70 (Benes, Turtle, Khan, & Farol, 1994).

Myelination of sensory and motor pathways, first in the fetus's spinal cord and later, after birth, in the cerebral cortex, may account for the appearance and disappearance of early reflexes.

myelination Process of coating neural pathways with a fatty substance (myelin) that enables faster communication between cells.

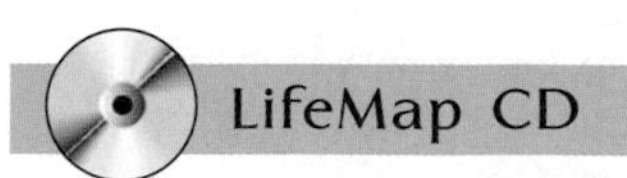

To learn more about early brain development, watch the video on "The Baby's Brain" in Chapter 6 of your CD.

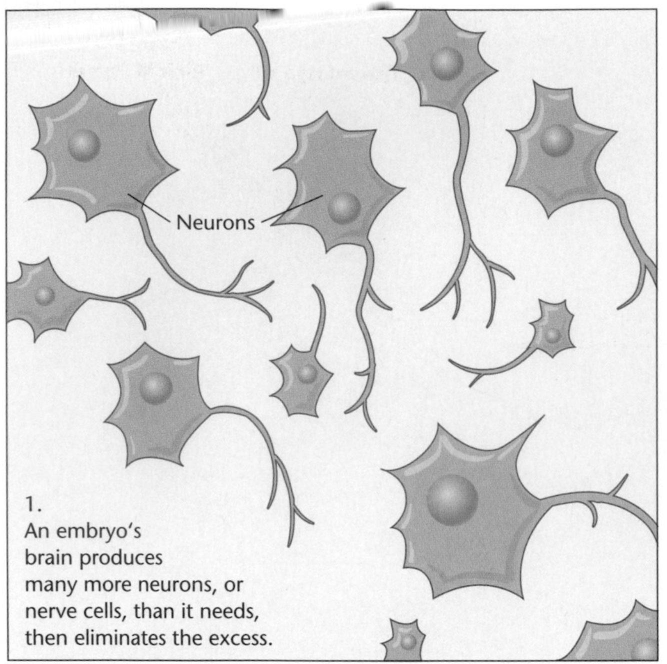

Neurons
1.
An embryo's
brain produces
many more neurons, or
nerve cells, than it needs,
then eliminates the excess.

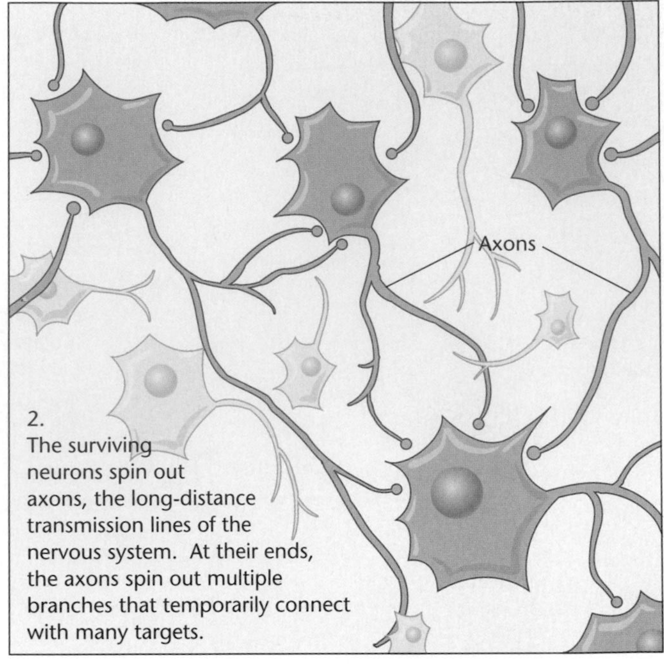

Axons
2.
The surviving
neurons spin out
axons, the long-distance
transmission lines of the
nervous system. At their ends,
the axons spin out multiple
branches that temporarily connect
with many targets.

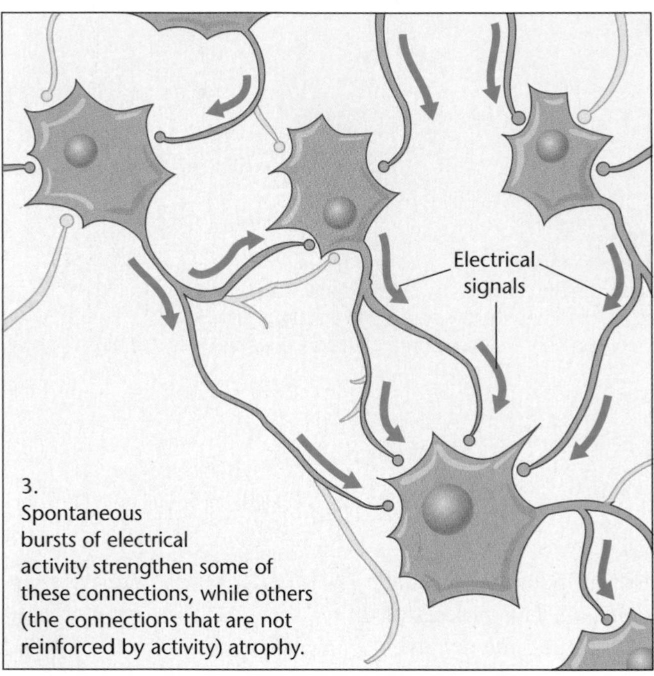

Electrical
signals
3.
Spontaneous
bursts of electrical
activity strengthen some of
these connections, while others
(the connections that are not
reinforced by activity) atrophy.

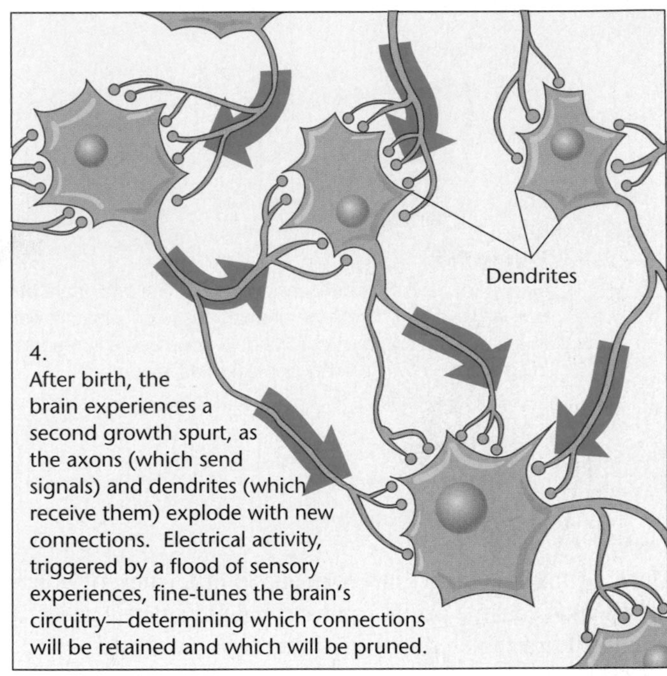

Dendrites
4.
After birth, the
brain experiences a
second growth spurt, as
the axons (which send
signals) and dendrites (which
receive them) explode with new
connections. Electrical activity,
triggered by a flood of sensory
experiences, fine-tunes the brain's
circuitry—determining which connections
will be retained and which will be pruned.

Figure 6-6

Wiring the brain: development of neural connections before and after birth.

Source: Nash, 1997, p. 51.

Early Reflexes

reflex behavior Automatic, involuntary, innate response to stimulation.

When you blink at a bright light, your eyelids are acting involuntarily. Such an automatic, innate response to stimulation is called a **reflex behavior.** Reflex behaviors are controlled by the lower brain centers that govern other involuntary processes, such as breathing and heart rate. These are the parts of the brain most fully myelinated at birth. Reflex behaviors play an important part in stimulating the early development of the central nervous system and muscles.

Human infants have an estimated 27 major reflexes, many of which are present at birth or soon after (Gabbard, 1996; see Table 6-1 for examples). *Primitive reflexes,* such as

Table 6-1	Early Human Reflexes			
Reflex	**Stimulation**	**Baby's Behavior**	**Typical Age of Appearance**	**Typical Age of Disappearance**
Moro	Baby is dropped or hears loud noise.	Extends legs, arms, and fingers, arches back, draws back head.	7th month of gestation	3 months
Darwinian (grasping)	Palm of baby's hand is stroked.	Makes strong fist; can be raised to standing position if both fists are closed around a stick.	7th month of gestation	4 months
Tonic neck	Baby is laid down on back.	Turns head to one side, assumes "fencer" position, extends arms and legs on preferred side, flexes opposite limbs.	7th month of gestation	5 months
Babkin	Both of baby's palms are stroked at once.	Mouth opens, eyes close, neck flexes, head tilts forward.	Birth	3 months
Babinski	Sole of baby's foot is stroked.	Toes fan out; foot twists in.	Birth	4 months
Rooting	Baby's cheek or lower lip is stroked with finger or nipple.	Head turns; mouth opens; sucking movements begin.	Birth	9 months
Walking	Baby is held under arms, with bare feet touching flat surface.	Makes steplike motions that look like well-coordinated walking.	1 month	4 months
Swimming	Baby is put into water face down.	Makes well-coordinated swimming movements.	1 month	4 months

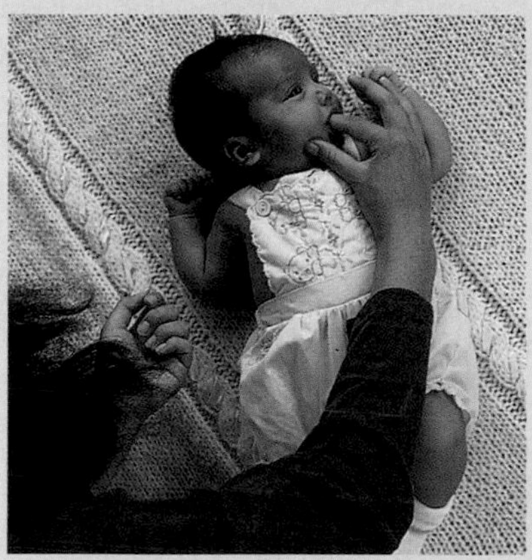

Rooting reflex

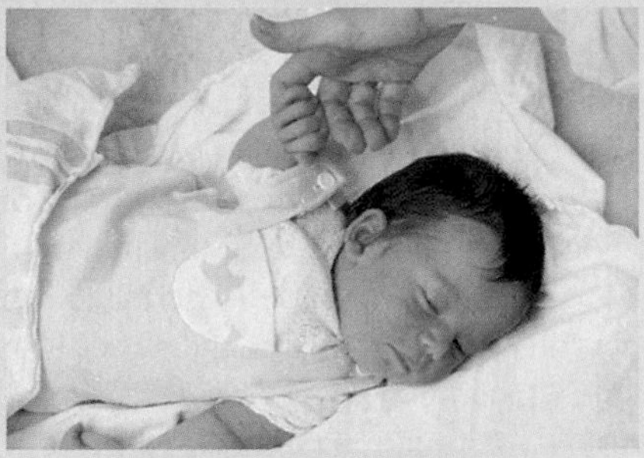

Darwinian reflex

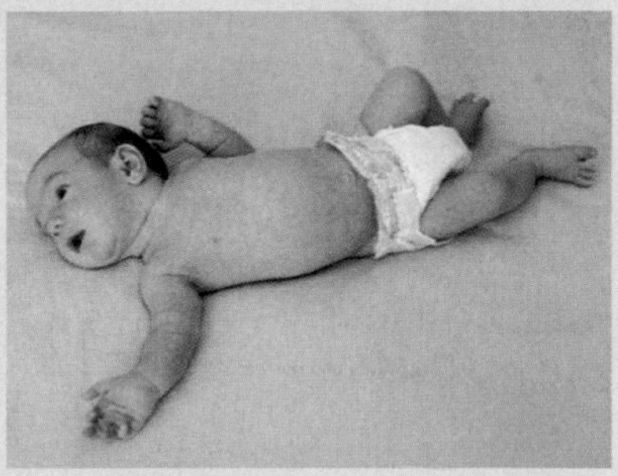

Tonic neck reflex

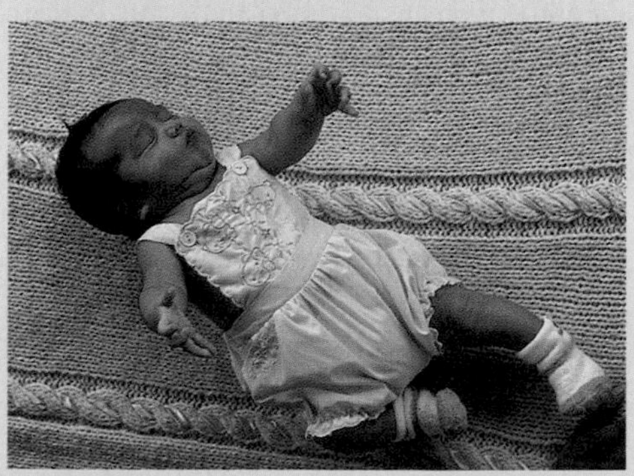

Moro reflex

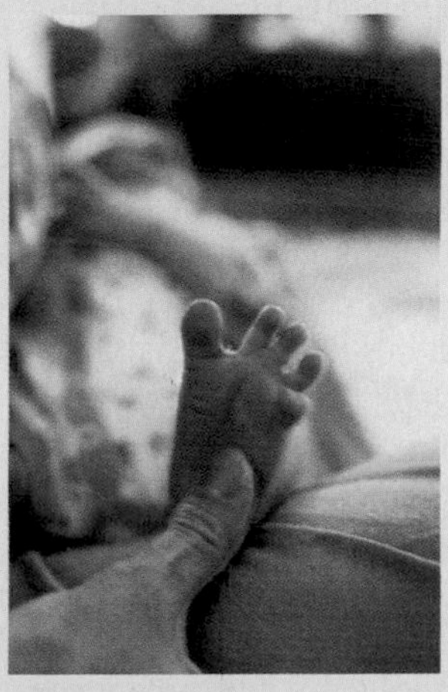

Babinski reflex

Walking reflex

sucking, rooting for the nipple, and the Moro reflex (a response to being startled or beginning to fall), are related to instinctive needs for survival and protection. Some primitive reflexes may be part of humanity's evolutionary legacy. One example is the grasping reflex, by which infant monkeys hold on to the hair of their mothers' bodies. As the higher brain centers become active during the first two to four months, infants begin to show *postural reflexes:* reactions to changes in position or balance. For example, infants who are tilted downward extend their arms in the parachute reflex, an instinctive attempt to break a fall.

Locomotor reflexes, such as the walking and swimming reflexes, resemble voluntary movements that do not appear until months after the reflexes have disappeared. As we'll see, there is debate about whether locomotor reflexes prepare the way for their later, voluntary counterparts.

Most of the early reflexes disappear during the first six months to one year. Reflexes that continue to serve protective functions, such as blinking, yawning, coughing, gagging, sneezing, shivering, and the pupillary reflex (dilation of the pupils in the dark), remain. Disappearance of unneeded reflexes on schedule is a sign that motor pathways in the cortex have been partially myelinated, enabling a shift to voluntary behavior. Thus, we can evaluate a baby's neurological development by seeing whether certain reflexes are present or absent.

Molding the Brain: The Role of Experience

The brain growth spurt that begins at about the third trimester of gestation and continues until at least the fourth year of life is important to the development of neurological functioning. Smiling, babbling, crawling, walking, and talking—all the major sensory, motor, and cognitive milestones of infancy and toddlerhood—are made possible by this rapid development of the brain, particularly the cerebral cortex.

Until the middle of the 20th century, scientists believed that the brain grew in an unchangeable, genetically determined pattern. This does seem to be largely true before birth. But it is now widely believed, largely on the basis of animal studies, that the postnatal brain is "molded" by experience. This is so especially during the early months of life, when the cortex is still growing rapidly and organizing itself (J. E. Black, 1998). The technical term for this malleability, or modifiability, of the brain is **plasticity.** Early synaptic connections, some of which depend on sensory stimulation, refine and stabilize the brain's genetically designed "wiring." Thus, early experience can have lasting effects on the capacity of the central nervous system to learn and store information (J. E. Black, 1998; Chugani, 1998; Greenough, Black, & Wallace, 1987; Pally, 1997; Wittrock, 1980).

plasticity Modifiability of the brain through experience.

We know that malnutrition can interfere with cognitive growth (Rose, 1994). So, too, early abuse or sensory impoverishment may leave an imprint on the brain (J. E. Black, 1998). In one experiment, kittens fitted with goggles that allowed them to see only vertical lines grew up unable to see horizontal lines and bumped into horizontal boards in front of them. Other kittens, whose goggles allowed them to see only horizontal lines, grew up blind to vertical columns (Hirsch & Spinelli, 1970). This did not happen when the same procedure was carried out with adult cats. Apparently, neurons in the visual cortex became programmed to respond only to lines running in the direction the kittens were permitted to see. Thus, if certain cortical connections are not made early in life and if no further intervention occurs (Bruer, 2001), these circuits may "shut down" forever. This is why the sensory and cognitive stimulation Anne Sullivan provided was so important to Helen Keller's development.

Early emotional development, too, may depend on experience. Infants whose mothers are severely depressed show less activity in the left frontal lobe, the part of the brain that is involved in positive emotions such as happiness and joy, and more activity in the right frontal lobe, which is associated with negative emotions (Dawson, Klinger, Panagiotides, Hill, & Spieker, 1992; Dawson, Frey, Panagiotides, Osterling, & Hessl, 1997).

Sometimes corrective experience can make up for past deprivation (J. E. Black, 1998). Plasticity continues throughout life as neurons change in size and shape in response to environmental experience (M. C. Diamond, 1988; Pally, 1997; Rutter, 2002). Brain-damaged rats, when raised in an enriched setting, grow more dendritic connections (M. C. Diamond, 1988). Such findings have sparked successful efforts to stimulate the physical and mental development of children with Down syndrome and to help victims of brain damage recover function.

Ethical constraints prevent controlled experiments on the effects of environmental deprivation on human infants. However, the discovery of thousands of infants and young chil-

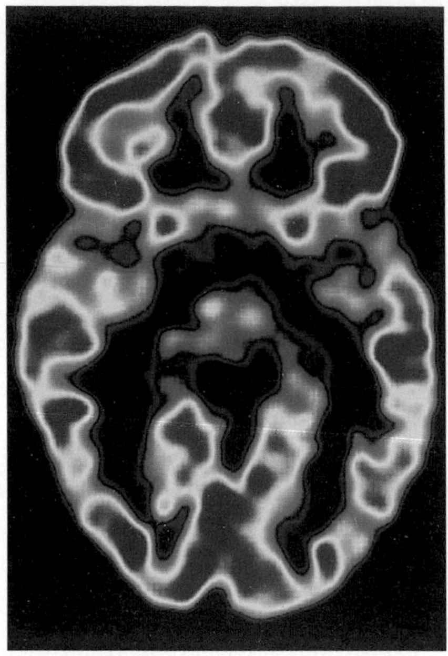

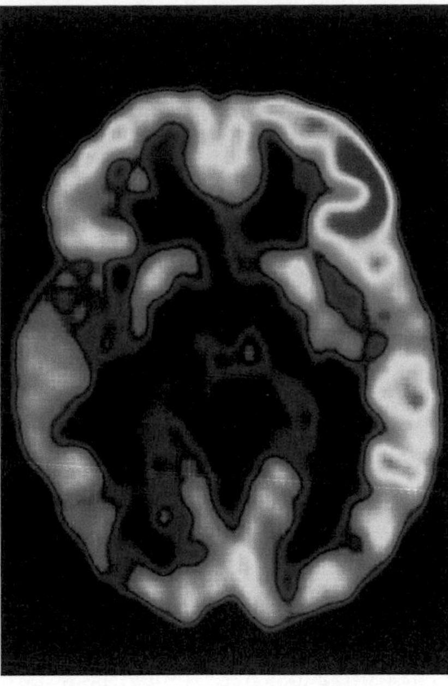

Extreme environmental deprivation in infancy can affect the structure of the brain, resulting in cognitive and emotional problems. A PET scan of a normal child's brain (*left*) shows regions of high (*red*) and low (*blue* and *black*) activity. A PET scan of the brain of a Romanian orphan institutionalized after birth (*right*) shows little activity.

dren who had spent virtually their entire lives in overcrowded Romanian orphanages offered an opportunity for a natural experiment (Ames, 1997). Discovered after the fall of the dictator Nicolae Ceauşescu in December 1989, these abandoned children appeared to be starving, passive, and emotionless. They had spent much of their time lying quietly in their cribs or beds, with nothing to look at. They had had little contact with one another or with their caregivers and had heard little conversation or even noise. Most of the 2- and 3-year-olds did not walk or talk, and the older children played aimlessly. PET scans of their brains showed extreme inactivity in the temporal lobes, which regulate emotion and receive sensory input.

Many of these children were adopted by Canadian families. At the time of adoption, all the children showed delayed motor, language, or psychosocial development, and nearly 8 out of 10 were behind in all these areas. Three years later, when compared with children left behind in the Romanian institutions, many of the adoptees showed remarkable progress. About one-third had no serious problems and were doing well—in a few cases, better than the average home-raised child. Another one-third—generally those who had been in institutions the longest—still had serious developmental problems. The rest were moving toward average performance and behavior (Ames, 1997; Morison, Ames, & Chisholm, 1995).

Age of adoption made a difference. At 4½, those who had spent eight months or more in the orphanages and had been adopted into Canada by age 2 had average IQs and verbal comprehension. But the orphanage group as a whole had not caught up with Canadian-born nonadopted children nor with a control group of Romanian children adopted by 4 months of age, who had not been in orphanages (Morison & Ellwood, 2000). In preschool, the previously institutionalized children showed poorer social skills and social interaction than Canadian-born children or Romanian early adoptees (Thompson, 2001); and at age 8½, PET scans found persistent underactivity in portions of their brains (Chugani et al., 2001).

Similarly, among 111 Romanian children adopted in England before age 2, those adopted before 6 months of age had largely caught up physically and had made a complete cognitive recovery by age 4, as compared with a control group of English adopted children. However, 85 percent of the English adoptees were more cognitively advanced than the average Romanian child adopted *after* 6 months of age (Rutter & the English and Romanian Adoptees [ERA] Study Team, 1998). By age 6, although the Romanian adoptees as a group showed a remarkable degree of recovery, many continued to exhibit substantial cognitive and social deficits (Rutter, O'Connor, and the English and Romanian Adoptees [ERA] Study Team, 2004). Apparently, then, it may take very early environmental stimulation to fully overcome the effects of extreme deprivation.

What's your view

- In view of what is now known about the plasticity of the infant brain, should society make sure that every baby has access to an appropriately stimulating environment?
- If so, how can this be done?

Checkpoint

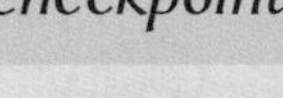

Can you . . .

✔ Describe important features of early brain development?

✔ Explain the functions of reflex behaviors and why some drop out during the early months?

✔ Discuss how early experience affects brain growth and development?

How do the senses develop during infancy?

Early Sensory Capacities

"The baby, assailed by eyes, ears, nose, skin, and entrails at once, feels that all is one great blooming, buzzing confusion," wrote the psychologist William James in 1890. We now know that this is far from true. The developing brain enables newborn infants to make fairly good sense of what they touch, see, smell, taste, and hear; and their senses develop rapidly in the early months of life.

Touch and Pain

Touch seems to be the first sense to develop, and for the first several months it is the most mature sensory system. When a newborn's cheek is stroked near the mouth, the baby responds by trying to find a nipple. Early signs of this rooting reflex (refer back to Table 6-1) show up in the womb, two months after conception. By 32 weeks of gestation, all body parts are sensitive to touch, and this sensitivity increases during the first five days of life (Haith, 1986).

In the past, physicians performing surgery on newborn babies often used no anesthesia because of a mistaken belief that neonates cannot feel pain or feel it only briefly. Actually, even on the first day of life, babies can and do feel pain; and they become more sensitive to it during the next few days. Furthermore, pain experienced during the neonatal period may sensitize an infant to later pain, perhaps by affecting the neural pathways that process painful stimuli. In one study, circumcised 4- and 6-month-olds had stronger reactions to the pain of vaccination than uncircumcised infants. The reaction was muted among infants who had been treated with a painkilling cream before being circumcised (Taddio, Katz, Ilersich, & Koren, 1997). The American Academy of Pediatrics and Canadian Paediatric Society (2000) now maintain that prolonged or severe pain can do long-term harm to newborns and that pain relief is essential.

Smell and Taste

The senses of smell and taste also begin to develop in the womb. The flavors and odors of foods an expectant mother consumes may be transmitted to the fetus through the amniotic fluid. After birth, a similar transmission occurs through breast milk (Mennella & Beauchamp, 1996b).

A preference for pleasant odors seems to be learned in utero and during the first few days after birth, and the odors transmitted through the mother's breast milk may further contribute to this learning (Bartoshuk & Beauchamp, 1994). Six-day-old breast-fed infants prefer the odor of their mother's breast pad over that of another nursing mother, but 2-day-olds do not, suggesting that babies need a few days' experience to learn how their mothers smell (Macfarlane, 1975). Bottle-fed babies do not make such a distinction (Cernoch & Porter, 1985). This preference for the fragrance of the mother's breast may be a survival mechanism.

Certain taste preferences seem to be largely innate (Bartoshuk & Beauchamp, 1994). Newborns prefer sweet tastes to sour, bitter, or salty ones. The sweeter the fluid, the harder they suck and the more they drink (Haith, 1986; Harris, 1997). Sweetened water calms crying newborns, whether full term or two to three weeks premature—evidence that not only the taste buds themselves (which seem to be fairly well developed by 20 weeks of gestation), but also the mechanisms that produce this calming effect are functional before normal term (B. A. Smith & Blass, 1996). An inborn "sweet tooth" may help a baby adapt to life outside the womb, since breast milk is quite sweet (Harris, 1997). Newborns' rejection of bitter tastes is probably another survival mechanism, since many bitter substances are toxic (Bartoshuk & Beauchamp, 1994). Newborns generally are not interested in tastes not associated with sources of available nutrition; their reactions range from indifference to rejection, depending in part on the concentration of the flavor (Harris, 1997). Taste preferences developed in infancy may last into early childhood. Four- and five-year-olds who, as infants, had been fed different types of formula had differing food preferences: As compared with those who had been fed milk-based formulas, those fed on protein hydrolysate formulas were more likely to prefer sour-flavored juice, whereas those fed on soy formulas were more likely to prefer bitter-flavored juice (Mennella & Beauchamp, 2002).

Hearing

Hearing, too, is functional before birth; fetuses respond to sounds and seem to learn to recognize them. As we discussed in Chapter 4, babies less than 3 days old respond differently to a story heard while in the womb than to other stories; can tell their mother's voice from a stranger's; and prefer their native language to a foreign tongue (DeCasper & Fifer, 1980; DeCasper & Spence, 1986; C. Moon, Cooper, & Fifer, 1993). Early recognition of voices and language heard in the womb may lay the foundation for the relationship between parents and child.

Auditory discrimination develops rapidly after birth. Three-day-old infants can tell new speech sounds from those they have heard before (L. R. Brody, Zelazo, & Chaika, 1984). At 1 month, babies can distinguish sounds as close as ba and pa (Eimas, Siqueland, Jusczyk, & Vigorito, 1971).

Because hearing is a key to language development, hearing impairments should be identified as early as possible. Hearing loss occurs in 1 to 3 of 1,000 live births and, if left undetected, can lead to developmental delays. In 2001, 24 states identified 1,306 infants with hearing loss; nearly 2 of 3 of those infants were placed in early intervention programs, most of them by 6 months (Gaffney et al., 2003). Among 10,372 infants born in Honolulu during a 5-year period, hearing screening within the first three days, followed by hearing aids and aural therapy before age 6 months for those found to have hearing problems, enabled them to achieve normal speech and language development (Mason & Herrmann, 1998).

Sight

Vision is the least developed sense at birth. The eyes of newborns are smaller than those of adults, the retinal structures are incomplete, and the optic nerve is underdeveloped. A neonate's eyes focus best from about 1 foot away—just about the typical distance from the face of a person holding a newborn. This may be an adaptive measure to promote mother-infant bonding.

Newborns blink at bright lights. Their peripheral vision is very narrow; it more than doubles between 2 and 10 weeks of age (E. Tronick, 1972). The ability to follow a moving target also develops rapidly in the first months, as does color perception. By about 2 months, babies can tell red from green; by about 3 months, they can distinguish blue (Haith, 1986). Four-month-old babies can discriminate among red, green, blue, and yellow. Like most adults, they prefer red and blue (M. Bornstein, Kessen, & Weiskopf, 1976; Teller & Bornstein, 1987).

Visual acuity at birth is approximately 20/400 but improves rapidly, reaching the 20/20 level by about 8 months (Kellman & Arterberry, 1998; Kellman & Banks, 1998). (This measure of vision means that a person can read letters on a specified line on a standard eye chart from 20 feet away.) *Binocular vision*—the use of both eyes to focus, enabling perception of depth and distance—usually does not develop until 4 or 5 months (Bushnell & Boudreau, 1993).

Early screening is essential to detect any problems that interfere with vision, such as retinal abnormalities, congenital cataracts, muscle imbalances, and amblyopia (failure of coordination between the images produced by the two eyes). Infants with known medical or genetic risks should be examined soon after birth. All infants should be examined by 6 months for visual fixation preference, ocular alignment, and any signs of eye disease. Formal vision screening should begin by 3 years and continue at regular intervals throughout childhood (AAP Committee on Practice and Ambulatory Medicine and Section on Opthalmology, 1996, 2002).

Checkpoint

Can you . . .

- ✔ Give evidence for early development of the senses?
- ✔ Tell how breast-feeding plays a part in the development of smell and taste?
- ✔ Tell how auditory discrimination in newborns is related to fetal hearing?
- ✔ List three ways in which newborns' vision is underdeveloped?

Motor Development

Guidepost 5

What are the early milestones in motor development, and what are some influences on it?

Babies do not have to be taught such basic motor skills as grasping, crawling, and walking. They just need room to move and freedom to see what they can do. When the central nervous system, muscles, and bones are ready and the environment offers the right opportunities for exploration and practice, babies keep surprising the adults around them with their new abilities.

Milestones of Motor Development

systems of action Increasingly complex combinations of skills that permit a wider or more precise range of movement and more control of the environment.

Denver Developmental Screening Test Screening test given to children 1 month to 6 years old to determine whether they are developing normally.

gross motor skills Physical skills that involve the large muscles.

fine motor skills Physical skills that involve the small muscles and eye-hand coordination.

Motor development is marked by a series of "milestones": achievements that develop systematically, each newly mastered ability preparing a baby to tackle the next. Babies first learn simple skills and then combine them into increasingly complex **systems of action**, which permit a wider or more precise range of movement and more effective control of the environment. In developing the precision grip, for example, an infant first tries to pick things up with the whole hand, fingers closing against the palm. Later the baby masters the *pincer grasp,* in which thumb and index finger meet at the tips to form a circle, making it possible to pick up tiny objects. In learning to walk, an infant first gains control of separate movements of the arms, legs, and feet before putting these movements together to take that momentous first step.

The **Denver Developmental Screening Test** (Frankenburg, Dodds, Fandal, Kazuk, & Cohrs, 1975) is used to chart normal progress between the ages of 1 month and 6 years and to identify children who are not developing normally. The test measures **gross motor skills** (those using large muscles), such as rolling over and catching a ball, and **fine motor skills** (using small muscles), such as grasping a rattle and copying a circle. It also assesses language development (for example, knowing the definitions of words) and personality and social development (such as smiling spontaneously and dressing without help). The newest edition, the Denver II Scale (Frankenburg et al., 1992), includes revised norms (see Table 6-2 for examples).

When we talk about what the "average" baby can do, we refer to the 50 percent Denver norms. Actually, normality covers a wide range; about half of all babies master these skills before the ages given, and about half do so afterward. Also, the Denver norms were developed with reference to a western population and are not necessarily valid in assessing children from other cultures. For example, Southeast Asian children who were given the Denver test did not play pat-a-cake, did not pick up raisins, and did not dress themselves at the expected ages (V. Miller, Onotera, & Deinard, 1984). Yet that did not indicate slow development. In their culture, children do not play pat-a-cake; raisins look like a medicine they are taught to avoid; and their parents continue to help them dress much longer than western parents do.

As we trace typical progress in head control, hand control, and locomotion, notice how these developments follow the *cephalocaudal* (head to tail) and *proximodistal* (inner to outer) principles outlined earlier. Note, too, that although boy babies tend to be a little bigger and more active than girl babies, there are no gender differences in infants' motor development (Mondschein, Adolph, & Tamis-Lemonda, 2000).

Table 6-2 Milestones of Motor Development

Skill	50 percent	90 percent
Rolling over	3.2 months	5.4 months
Grasping rattle	3.3 months	3.9 months
Sitting without support	5.9 months	6.8 months
Standing while holding on	7.2 months	8.5 months
Grasping with thumb and finger	8.2 months	10.2 months
Standing alone well	11.5 months	13.7 months
Walking well	12.3 months	14.9 months
Building tower of two cubes	14.8 months	20.6 months
Walking up steps	16.6 months	21.6 months
Jumping in place	23.8 months	2.4 years
Copying circle	3.4 years	4.0 years

Note: This table shows the approximate ages when 50 percent and 90 percent of children can perform each skill, according to the Denver Training Manual II.

Source: Adapted from Frankenburg et al., 1992.

Head Control

At 4 months, Delilah can raise her head high from a prone position.

At birth, most infants can turn their heads from side to side while lying on their backs. While lying chest down, many can lift their heads enough to turn them. Within the first two to three months, they lift their heads higher and higher—sometimes to a point at which they lose their balance and roll over on their backs. By 4 months of age, almost all infants can keep their heads erect while being held or supported in a sitting position.

Hand Control

Babies are born with a grasping reflex. If the palm of an infant's hand is stroked, the hand closes tightly. At about 3½ months, most infants can grasp an object of moderate size, such as a rattle, but have trouble holding a small object. Next they begin to grasp objects with one hand and transfer them to the other and then to hold (but not pick up) small objects. Some time between 7 and 11 months, their hands become coordinated enough to pick up a tiny object, such as a pea, using the pincer grasp. After that, hand control becomes increasingly precise. By 15 months, the average baby can build a tower of two cubes. A few months after the third birthday, the average toddler can copy a circle fairly well.

Locomotion

After 3 months, the average infant begins to roll over deliberately (rather than accidentally, as before)—first from front to back and then from back to front. The average baby can sit without support by 6 months and can assume a sitting position without help about two and one-half months later.

Between 6 and 10 months, most babies begin to get around under their own power by means of various forms of creeping or crawling. This achievement of self-locomotion has striking cognitive and psychosocial ramifications (see Box 6-1). There is no universal progression in crawling; some infants slither on their bellies before crawling on hands and knees, and some do not. But, as with most skills, practice is the key to success, and experience in one position (such as belly crawling) increases initial proficiency in another position (hands and knees) (Adolph, Vereijken, & Denny, 1998).

By holding onto a helping hand or a piece of furniture, the average baby can stand at a little past 7 months of age. A little more than four months later, most babies let go and stand alone. The average baby can stand well about two weeks or so before the first birthday.

All these developments are milestones along the way to the major motor achievement of infancy: walking. Humans begin to walk later than other species, possibly because babies' heavy heads, short legs, and relatively weak muscles make balance difficult. Again, practice is the most important factor in overcoming these difficulties (Adolph, Vereijken, & Shrout, 2003). For some months before they can stand without support, babies practice "cruising" while holding onto furniture. Soon after they can stand alone well, at about 11½ months, most infants take their first unaided steps—usually into their mothers' waiting arms. At this stage a baby typically practices standing and walking more than six hours a day, on and off, and may take enough steps (9,000) to cover the length of 29 football fields! Within a few weeks, soon after the first birthday, the child is walking fairly well, as Helen Keller did, and thus achieves the status of toddler.

During the second year, children begin to climb stairs one at a time, putting one foot after another on each step; later, they will alternate feet. Walking down stairs comes later. In their second year, toddlers run and jump. By age 3½, most children can balance briefly on one foot and begin to hop.

How Motor Development Occurs: Maturation in Context

The sequence just described was traditionally thought to be genetically programmed—a largely automatic, preordained series of steps directed by the maturing brain. Today, many

The Research World

Box 6-1 *The Far-Reaching Implications of Crawling*

Between 7 and 9 months, babies change greatly in many ways. They show an understanding of such concepts as *near* and *far.* They imitate more complex behaviors, and they show new fears; but they also show a new sense of security around their parents and other caregivers. Since these changes involve so many different psychological functions and processes and occur during such a short time span, some observers tie them all in with a reorganization of brain function. This neurological development may be set in motion by a skill that emerges in most babies at this time: the ability to crawl, which makes it possible to get around independently. Crawling has been called a "setting event" because it sets the stage for other changes in the infant and his or her relationships with the environment and the people in it (Bertenthal & Campos, 1987; Bertenthal, Campos, & Barrett, 1984; Bertenthal, Campos, & Kermoian, 1994).

Crawling exerts a powerful influence on babies' cognitive development by giving them a new view of the world. Infants become more sensitive to where objects are, how big they are, whether they can be moved, and how they look. Crawling helps babies learn to judge distances and perceive depth. As they move about, they see that people and objects look different close up than far away. Crawling babies can differentiate similar forms that are unlike in color, size, or location (J. Campos, Bertenthal, & Benson, 1980). Babies are more successful in finding a toy hidden in a box when they crawl around the box than when they are carried around it (Benson & Uzgiris, 1985).

The ability to crawl gets babies into new situations. As they become more mobile, they begin to hear such warnings as "Come back!" and "Don't touch!" They receive loving help as adult hands pick them up and turn them in a safer direction. They learn to look to caregivers for clues as to whether a situation is secure or frightening—a skill known as social referencing (see Chapter 8). Crawling babies do more social referencing than babies who have not yet begun to crawl (J. B. Garland, 1982). Crawling babies also may develop fear of heights; they learn to be afraid of places from which they might fall.

The ability to move from one place to another has other emotional and social implications. Crawling babies are no longer "prisoners" of place. If Ashley wants to be close to her mother and far away from a strange dog, she can move toward the one and away from the other. This is an important step in developing a sense of mastery, enhancing self-confidence and self-esteem.

Thus, the physical milestone of crawling has far-reaching effects in helping babies see and respond to their world in new ways.

What's your view?

Which do you think has more important overall effects on development: crawling or walking? Why? Would you consider walking to be a setting event? Can you think of any other milestones that might be considered setting events?

Check it out!

For more information on this topic, go to **http://www.zerotothree.org/hop.htm**. This is an article by Lois Barclay Murphy from *Zero to Three,* "Hopping, Jumping, Leaping, Skipping, and Loping: Savoring the Possibilities of Locomotion." Or go to **http://www.zerotothree.org/toddler.htm**. This is an article by Lois Barclay Murphy and Colleen Small from *Zero to Three,* "Parent Information: Toddlers: Themes and Variation." The article takes "a close look at very young children as they develop locomotion."

developmental scientists consider this view too simplistic. Instead, according to Esther Thelen (1995), motor development is a continuous process of interaction between baby and environment.

Thelen points to the *walking reflex:* stepping movements a neonate makes when held upright with the feet touching a surface. This behavior usually disappears by the fourth month. Not until the latter part of the first year, when a baby is getting ready to walk, do such movements appear again. The usual explanation is a shift to cortical control: thus, an older baby's deliberate walking is a new skill masterminded by the developing brain. But, Thelen observes, a newborn's stepping involves the same kinds of movements the neonate makes while lying down and kicking. Why would stepping stop, only to reappear months later, whereas kicking continues? The answer, she suggests, may be that babies' legs become thicker and heavier during the early months but not yet strong enough to carry the increased weight (Thelen & Fisher, 1982, 1983). In fact, when young infants are held in warm water, which helps support their legs, stepping reappears. Their ability to produce the movement has not changed—only the physical and environmental conditions that inhibit or promote it.

Maturation alone cannot explain such observations, says Thelen. Infant and environment form an interconnected system, and development has interacting causes. One is the infant's motivation to do something (say, pick up a toy or get to the other side of the room). The infant's physical characteristics and his or her position in a particular setting (for example, lying in a crib or being held upright in a pool) offer opportunities and constraints that affect whether and how the baby can achieve the goal. Ultimately, a solution emerges as the baby tries out behaviors and retains those that most efficiently contribute to that achievement. Rather than being solely in charge of this process, the maturing brain is only one part of it.

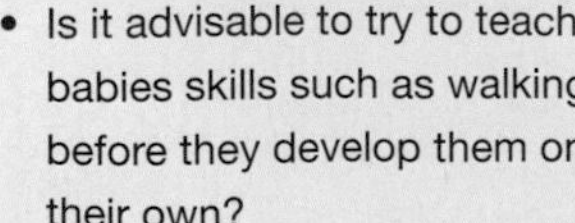

- Is it advisable to try to teach babies skills such as walking before they develop them on their own?

According to Thelen, normal babies develop the same skills in the same order because they are built approximately the same way and have similar physical challenges and needs. Thus, they eventually discover that walking is more efficient than crawling in most situations. That this discovery arises from each particular baby's experience in a particular context may help explain why some babies learn to walk earlier than others.

Motor Development and Perception

Early motor development is an excellent example of the interrelationship among the physical and cognitive domains. Sensory perception enables infants to learn about themselves and their environment so they can make better judgments about how to navigate in it. Motor experience, together with awareness of their changing bodies, sharpens and modifies their perceptual understanding of what is likely to happen if they move in a certain way. This bidirectional connection between perception and action, mediated by the developing brain, gives infants much useful information about themselves and their world (Adolph & Eppler, 2002).

Sensory and motor activity seem to be fairly well coordinated from birth (Bertenthal & Clifton, 1998). Infants begin reaching for and grasping objects at about 4 to 5 months; by 5½ months, they can adapt their reach to moving or spinning objects (Wentworth, Benson, & Haith, 2000). Piaget and other researchers long believed that reaching depended on **visual guidance:** the use of the eyes to guide the movement of the hands (or other parts of the body). Now, research has found that infants in that age group can use other sensory cues to reach for an object. They can locate an unseen rattle by its sound, and they can reach for a glowing object in the dark, even though they cannot see their hands (Clifton, Muir, Ashmead, & Clarkson, 1993). They even can reach for an object based only on their memory of its location (McCarty, Clifton, Ashmead, Lee, & Goubet, 2001). Slightly older infants, 5 to 7½ months old, can grasp a moving, fluorescent object in the dark—a feat that requires awareness, not only of how their own hands move, but also of the object's path and speed, so as to anticipate the likely point of contact (Robin, Berthier, & Clifton, 1996).

visual guidance The use of the eyes to guide the movement of the hands (or other parts of the body).

Depth perception, the ability to perceive objects and surfaces in three dimensions, depends on several kinds of cues that affect the image of an object on the retina of the eye. These cues involve not only binocular coordination, but also motor control (Bushnell & Boudreau, 1993). Kinetic cues come from movements of either the object or the observer. To find out which is moving, a baby might hold his or her head still for a moment, an ability that is well established by about 3 months.

depth perception Ability to perceive objects and surfaces in three dimensions.

Sometime between 5 and 7 months, babies respond to such cues as relative size and differences in texture and shading. These cues depend on **haptic perception,** the ability to acquire information by handling objects rather than just looking at them. Haptic perception comes only after babies develop enough eye-hand coordination to reach for objects and grasp them (Bushnell & Boudreau, 1993).

haptic perception Ability to acquire information about properties of objects, such as size, weight, and texture, by handling them.

In a classic experiment by Richard Walk and Eleanor Gibson (1961), 6-month-old babies were placed on a plexiglass tabletop, over a checkerboard pattern that created the illusion of a vertical drop in the center of the table—a **visual cliff** (see photo on p. 152). Would the infants perceive the illusion of depth? The babies did see a difference between the "ledge" and the "drop." They crawled freely on the "ledge" but avoided the "drop," even when they saw their mothers beckoning on the far side of the table.

visual cliff Apparatus designed to give an illusion of depth and used to assess depth perception in infants.

Eleanor and James Gibson's Ecological Theory

How do babies decide whether to move across a "ledge" or down a hill? According to Eleanor Gibson's and James J. Gibson's **ecological theory of perception** (E. J. Gibson, 1969; J. J. Gibson, 1979; Gibson & Pick, 2000), infants size up the "fit," or **affordance,** between their own changing physical attributes or capabilities (such as arm and leg length, endurance, balance, and strength) and the changing characteristics of their environment. Knowledge of affordances enables babies to make moment-to-moment decisions about what they can and cannot do in a given situation (Adolph, 2000; Adolph & Eppler, 2002). (Is the ground too rough to walk on? Can I keep my balance if I try?) According to the Gibsons, perceptual learning occurs through a growing ability to detect and differentiate the many

ecological theory of perception Theory developed by Eleanor and James Gibson, which describes developing motor and perceptual abilities as interdependent parts of a functional system that guides behavior in varying contexts.

affordance In the Gibsons' ecological theory of perception, the fit between a person's physical attributes and capabilities and characteristics of the environment.

No matter how enticing a mother's arms are, this baby is staying away from them. As young as he is, she can perceive depth and wants to avoid falling off what looks like a cliff.

features of a rich sensory environment. It is this ability that permits infants and toddlers to recognize affordances and thus to successfully negotiate a terrain.

Locomotor development depends on increasing sensitivity to affordances and is an outcome of both perception and action (Adolph & Eppler, 2002). With experience, babies become better able to gauge the environment in which they move and to adapt their movements accordingly (Adolph, 2000; Adolph et al., 2003; Adolph & Eppler, 2002). In visual cliff experiments, infants who have been crawling for some time are more likely than novices to avoid the "cliff." Similarly, when faced with actual downward slopes of increasing steepness, infants' judgments become more accurate and their explorations more efficient as they gain practice in crawling. They do not seem to learn from fear of heights or of falling or from trial and error. What they apparently learn from experience is how far they can push their limits without losing their balance (Adolph & Eppler, 2002).

This learning is flexible but posture-specific. Babies who learn how far they can reach for a toy across a gap while in a sitting position must acquire this knowledge anew when they begin to crawl (Adolph, 2000; Adolph & Eppler, 2002). Likewise, when crawling babies who have mastered slopes begin to walk, they have to learn to cope with slopes all over again (Adolph, 1997; Adolph & Eppler, 2002).

Many parents put their babies in mobile walkers in the belief that the babies will learn to walk earlier. Actually, by restricting babies' motor exploration and their view of their own movements, walkers may *delay* motor skill development. In one study, infants who used walkers sat, crawled, and walked later than babies who did not use walkers, and they also scored lower on tests of cognitive development (Siegel & Burton, 1999). Furthermore, walkers can be dangerous. In research on the visual cliff, crawling babies avoided the "edge," but the same babies, when supported in mechanical walkers, crossed over to the "deep" side (Rader, Bausano, & Richards, 1980). The American Academy of Pediatrics (AAP Committee on Injury and Poison Prevention, 2001b) has called for a ban on the manufacture and sale of baby walkers. In 2004, Canada became the first country in the world to ban their sale, advertising, or import (Reuters, 2004a).

Cultural Influences on Motor Development

Although motor development follows a virtually universal sequence, its pace does seem to respond to certain contextual factors. When children are well fed and well cared for and have physical freedom and the chance to explore their surroundings, their motor development is likely to be normal. However, what is normal in one culture may not be in another.

African babies tend to be more advanced than U.S. and European infants in sitting, walking, and running. In Uganda, for example, babies typically walk at 10 months, as compared with 12 months in the United States and 15 months in France (Gardiner & Komitzki, 2005). Asian babies tend to develop these skills more slowly. Such differences may in part be related to ethnic differences in temperament (H. Kaplan & Dove, 1987; see Chapter 8) or may reflect a culture's child-rearing practices (Gardiner & Komitzki, 2005).

Some cultures actively encourage early development of motor skills. In many African and West Indian cultures with advanced infant motor development, adults use special "handling routines," such as bouncing and stepping exercises, to strengthen babies' muscles (Hopkins & Westra, 1988). In one study, Jamaican infants, whose mothers used such handling routines daily, sat, crawled, and walked earlier than English infants, whose mothers gave them no such special handling (Hopkins & Westra, 1990).

On the other hand, some cultures discourage early motor development. Children of the Ache in eastern Paraguay do not begin to walk until 18 to 20 months of age—about nine months later than U.S. babies (H. Kaplan & Dove, 1987). Ache mothers pull their babies back to their laps when the infants begin to crawl away. The Ache mothers closely super-

Checkpoint

Can you . . .

- ✔ Trace a typical infant's progress in head control, hand control, and locomotion, according to the Denver norms?
- ✔ Discuss how maturation, perception, and cultural influences relate to early motor development.

vise their babies to protect them from the hazards of nomadic life and also because the women's primary responsibility is child raising rather than subsistence labor. Yet, as 8- to 10-year-olds, Ache children climb tall trees, chop branches, and play in ways that enhance their motor skills (H. Kaplan & Dove, 1987). Normal development, then, need not follow the same timetable to reach the same destination.

Health

Guidepost 6

How can we enhance babies' chances of survival and health?

Infancy and toddlerhood are risky times of life, though far less so than they were when Helen Keller contracted her mysterious illness. How many babies die during the first year, and why? What can be done to prevent dangerous or debilitating childhood diseases? How can we ensure that infants and toddlers live, grow, and develop as they should?

Reducing Infant Mortality

One of the most tragic losses is the death of an infant. Great strides have been made in protecting the lives of new babies, but these improvements are not evenly distributed throughout the population. Too many babies still die—some of them without warning and for no apparent reason.

Trends in Infant Mortality

Worldwide, in 2000 more than 1 infant of each 20 born alive died before the first birthday (UNICEF, 2002), 3.9 million of these during the neonatal period (Black, Morris, & Bryce, 2003). Infant deaths are much more frequent in many developing countries; as many as 193.8 Angolan infants die for every 1,000 born alive, and life expectancy at birth is only 37 years (U.S. Census Bureau, 2003). Furthermore, figures on infant deaths may be understated due to lack of uniformity in reporting. Most infant deaths are preventable, resulting from a combination of poverty, poor maternal health and nutrition, infection, and poor medical care (UNICEF, 2003).

In the United States, the **infant mortality rate**—the proportion of babies who die within the first year—rose slightly in 2002, according to preliminary data, from 6.8 to 7.0 deaths for every 1,000 live births, after falling steadily since 1958. The upturn may reflect the mounting complications from fertility treatments and multiple births. More than half of all infant deaths take place in the first week of life, and two-thirds occur during the neonatal period (Kochanek & Smith, 2004). Most likely to die in infancy are boy babies, those who were born preterm or of low birth weight, and those whose mothers are teenagers or in their 40s, did not finish high school, are unmarried, smoked during pregnancy, had late or no prenatal care, or had multiple births (Arias, MacDorman, Strobino, & Guyer, 2003; Mathews, Menacker, & MacDorman, 2003).

infant mortality rate Proportion of babies born alive who die within the first year.

Birth defects (congenital abnormalities) are the leading cause of infant deaths in the United States, followed by disorders related to prematurity or low birth weight (the leading cause of death in the first month), sudden infant death syndrome (SIDS), and maternal complications of pregnancy. These four causes together account for about half of all infant deaths (American Public Health Association, 2004; Arias et al., 2003; Kochanek & Smith, 2004).

The virtually continual improvement in U.S. infant mortality rates since 1990, even at a time when more babies were born perilously small, is attributable largely to prevention of SIDS (discussed in the next section) as well as to effective treatment of respiratory distress and medical advances in keeping very small babies alive (Arias et al., 2003). Another factor is a striking reduction in air pollution in some cities due to permanent losses of manufacturing after the 1980–1982 recession (Greenstone & Chay, 2003). Still, mainly because of the prevalence of low birth weight, U.S. babies have a poorer chance of reaching their first birthday than babies in many other developed countries (Arias et al., 2003; U.S. Census Bureau, 2003; see Figure 6-7).

Racial/Ethnic Disparities in Infant Mortality

Although infant mortality has declined overall for all races and ethnic groups since 1980, large disparities remain (Mathews et al., 2003; see Figure 6-8). Most strikingly, non-Hispanic black babies are more than twice as likely to die in their first year as white and

Figure 6-7

Infant mortality rates in industrialized countries, 2003. The United States has a higher infant mortality rate than 19 other industrialized nations, largely because of its very high mortality rate for African-American babies. In recent years most nations, including the United States, have shown dramatic improvement.

Source: U.S. Census Bureau, 2003.

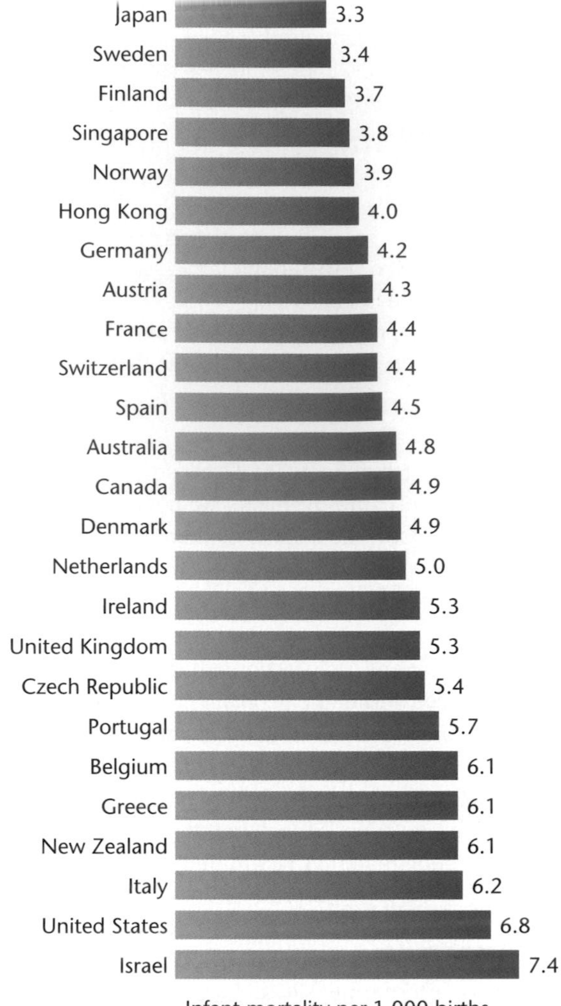

Hispanic babies (Kochanek & Smith, 2004; Mathews et al., 2003; see Table 6-3), largely reflecting the greater prevalence of low birth weight and SIDS among African Americans. African-American infants are nearly 4 times as likely as white infants to die of disorders related to premature birth or low birth weight (Kochanek & Smith, 2004) and twice as likely to die of SIDS. Infant mortality among American Indians and Alaska Natives is almost twice that among white babies, mainly due to SIDS and fetal alcohol syndrome (American Public Health Association, 2004).

Intragroup variations are often overlooked. Although Hispanic infants, as a group, die at a slightly lower rate than non-Hispanic white babies, the rate is higher for Puerto Rican infants. Although Asian Americans, overall, are least likely to die in infancy, Pacific Islander infants are 31 percent more likely to die than white babies (American Public Health Association, 2004; Mathews et al., 2003).

Certain behavioral factors help account for racial or ethnic disparities. For example, obesity, smoking, and alcohol consumption are factors in poor outcomes of pregnancy. Asians and Pacific Islanders have the lowest obesity rates and the lowest rates of smoking and drinking. African Americans have the highest obesity rates, and American Indians and Alaska Natives tend to be heavy smokers and drinkers. Another factor is unintended pregnancy; in one study, African-American women reported that 29 percent of their pregnancies as opposed to 9.2 percent for white women were unintended. Finally, rates of prenatal care vary from 85 percent of white expectant mothers down to 69 percent of American Indians and Alaska Natives (American Public Health Association, 2004; refer back to Chapter 4).

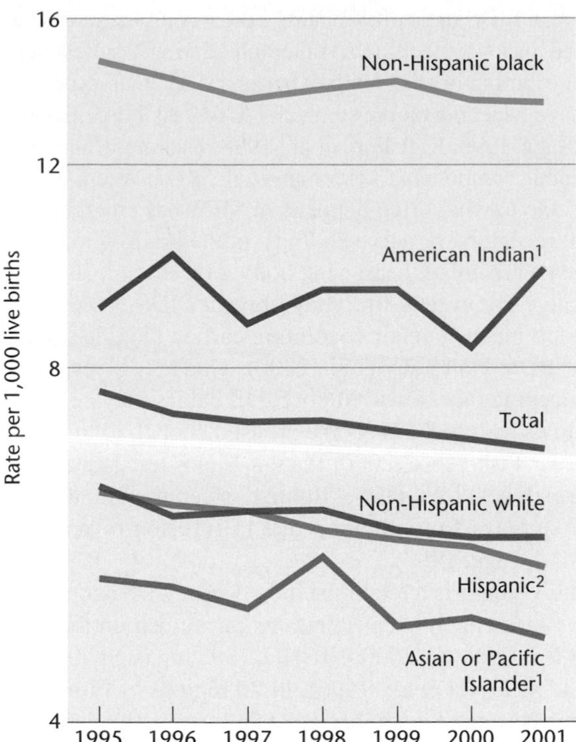

Figure 6-8

Trends in infant mortality rates by race and ethnicity of mother, 1995–2001. Infant mortality has dropped in recent years in most racial/ethnic groups but not among American Indians. Despite some decline, non-Hispanic blacks continue to have the highest infant mortality rates.

Source: Mathews et al., 2003, Fig. 1.

Table 6-3 Birth Weight, Mortality, and Race, 2002*

	Low Birth Weight (less than 5.5 pounds, or 2,500 grams), % of births	Very Low Birth Weight (less than 3.3 pounds, or 1,500 grams), % of births	Infant Mortality Rate** per 1,000	Neonatal Mortality Rate*** per 1,000	Postneonatal Mortality Rate**** per 1,000
Black infants	13.4	3.1	14.3	9.4	4.9
White (non-Hispanic) infants	6.9	1.2	5.9	3.9	1.9
Hispanic infants	6.5	1.2	5.6	3.8	1.8

Note: Black infants are more likely than white or Hispanic infants to die in the first year from birth defects or disorders, sudden infant death syndrome, respiratory distress syndrome, and disorders related to short gestation and low birth weight and as a result of maternal complications of pregnancy.

* Mortality rates from 2002 are preliminary.
** Deaths during the first year of life
*** Deaths during first 4 weeks
**** Deaths between 4 weeks and 11 months

Source: Kochanek & Smith, 2004; Martin et al., 2003.

Sudden Infant Death Syndrome (SIDS)

Sudden infant death syndrome (SIDS), sometimes called *crib death,* is the sudden death of an infant under 1 year of age in which the cause of death remains unexplained after a thorough investigation that includes an autopsy. In 2001, a total of 2,236 U.S. babies were victims of SIDS, representing an 11 percent decline in one year. The decline was even greater (21 percent) among Hispanic babies (Mathews et al., 2003). SIDS is the leading cause of postneonatal infant death (NCHS, 2003) and is most common among American Indian and black mothers (Mathews et al., 2003).

sudden infant death syndrome (SIDS) Sudden and unexplained death of an apparently healthy infant.

It seems likely that SIDS most often results from a combination of factors. An underlying biological defect may make some infants vulnerable, during a critical period in their development, to certain contributing or triggering experiences, such as exposure to smoke, prenatal exposure to caffeine, or sleeping on the stomach (AAP Task Force, 2000; Cutz, Perrin, Hackman, & Czegledy-Nagy, 1996; R. P. Ford et al., 1998; Kadhim, Kahn, & Sebire, 2003). SIDS also may have a genetic component (Ackerman et al., 2001; Weese-Mayer et al., 2003).

An important clue to what often happens in SIDS has emerged from the discovery of defects in chemical receptors, or nerve endings, in the brain stem, which receive and send messages that regulate breathing, heart beat, body temperature, and arousal. These defects, which may originate early in fetal life, may prevent SIDS babies from awakening when they are breathing too much stale air containing carbon dioxide trapped under their blankets (Kinney et al., 1995; Panigrahy et al., 2000). This may be especially likely to happen when the baby is sleeping face down. Many SIDS babies may be deficient in a protective mechanism that allows an infant to become aroused enough to turn the head when breathing is restricted (AAP Task Force, 2000; Waters, Gonzalez, Jean, Morielli, & Brouillette, 1996). Even in normal, healthy infants, "tummy" sleeping inhibits the swallowing reflex, which protects the airways from choking due to infusion of nasal and digestive fluids (Jeffery, Megevand, & Page, 1999).

Research strongly supports a relationship between SIDS and sleeping on the stomach. Side sleeping is not safe either, because infants put to bed on their sides often turn onto their stomachs (AAP Task Force, 2000; NICHD, 1997, updated 2000; Skadberg, Morild, & Markestad, 1998; J. A. Taylor et al., 1996). In 20 regions of Europe, nearly half (48 percent) of SIDS deaths between September 1992 and April 1996 were attributed to sleeping on the stomach or side (Carpenter et al., 2004). The decline in SIDS rates in the United States and in other countries (some by as much as 70 percent) followed recommendations that healthy babies be put to sleep on their backs (Dwyer, Ponsonby, Blizzard, Newman, & Cochrane, 1995; C. E. Hunt, 1996; Skadberg et al., 1998; Willinger, Hoffman, & Hartford, 1994).

Infants should not sleep on soft surfaces, such as pillows, quilts, or sheepskin, or under loose covers, which, especially when the infant is face down, may increase the risk of overheating or rebreathing (breathing the infant's own waste products) (AAP Task Force, 2000; Hauck et al., 2003). The risk of SIDS is increased 20-fold when infants sleep in adult beds, sofas, or chairs or on other surfaces not designed for infants (Scheers, Rutherford, & Kemp, 2003). Breast-feeding and use of pacifiers are associated with lower risk of SIDS (Hauck et al., 2003).

Unfortunately, about 20 percent of U.S. infants still sleep face down (AAP Task Force, 2000). As many as 20 percent of SIDS deaths occur in a child-care setting, where infants often sleep on their stomachs (Moon, Patel, & Shaefer, 2000).

In addition to being better protected against SIDS, infants who sleep on their backs tend to have fewer fevers, stuffy noses, ear infections, and other health problems than infants who sleep face down (Hunt et al., 2003). Sleeping on the back does tend to result in a slight temporary delay in the development of motor skills requiring upper-body strength, such as rolling over, sitting, crawling, and standing. However, these milestones are still attained within the normal age range (Davis, Moon, Sachs, & Ottolini, 1998), and no difference is detectable by 18 months. It is important for infants to have plenty of "tummy time" while awake and supervised, for development of shoulder strength (AAP Task Force, 2000).

Sharing a bed with the mother is a common practice in some cultures; its possible role in preventing or promoting SIDS has been controversial (see Box 6-2).

Death from Injuries

Unintentional injuries are the seventh leading cause of death in infancy in the United States and the third leading cause of death after the first four weeks of life, following SIDS and birth defects (Kochanek & Smith, 2004; Anderson, 2002). Between 1988 and 1998, injury deaths during the postneonatal period declined from 29.6 to 25.7 per 100,000 live births, but the decline was smaller among black infants, who were more than two and a half times as likely to die of injuries as white infants. Black infants are also more than three times as likely to be victims of homicide (Tomashek, Hsia, & Iyasu, 2003).

Around the World

Box 6-2 *Sleep Customs*

Newborns' sleeping arrangements vary considerably across cultures. In many societies, infants sleep in the same room with their mothers for the first few years of life and frequently in the same bed, making it easier to nurse at night (Broude, 1995). In the United States, it is customary to have a separate bed or a separate room for the infant, but bed sharing is common in low-income inner-city families (Brenner et al., 2003).

In interviews, middle-class U.S. parents and Mayan mothers in rural Guatemala revealed their societies' child-rearing values and goals in their explanations about sleeping arrangements (Morelli, Rogoff, Oppenheim, & Goldsmith, 1992). The U.S. parents, many of whom kept their infants in the same room but not in the same bed for the first 3 to 6 months, said they moved the babies to separate rooms because they wanted to make them self-reliant and independent. The Mayan mothers kept infants and toddlers in the maternal bed until the birth of a new baby, when the older child would sleep with another family member or in a bed in the mother's room. The Mayan mothers valued close parent-child relationships and expressed shock at the idea that anyone would put a baby to sleep in a room all alone.

Some investigators find health benefits in the shared sleeping pattern. One research team monitoring sleep patterns of mothers and their 3-month-old infants found that those who sleep together tend to wake each other up during the night. The researchers suggested that this may prevent the baby from sleeping too long and too deeply and having long breathing pauses that might be fatal (McKenna & Mosko, 1993).

Bed sharing also promotes breast-feeding. Infants who sleep with their mothers breast-feed about three times longer during the night than infants who sleep in separate beds (McKenna, Mosko, & Richard, 1997). By snuggling up together, mother and baby stay oriented toward each other's subtle bodily signals. Mothers can respond more quickly and easily to an infant's first whimpers of hunger, rather than having to wait until the baby's cries are loud enough to be heard from the next room.

However, under certain conditions, such as the use of soft bedding or maternal smoking or drug use, bed sharing can increase the risk of sudden infant death syndrome (American Academy of Pediatrics Task Force on Infant Positioning and SIDS, 1997; Hauck et al., 2003). There is also the possibility that a parent may roll over onto the baby while asleep. In a review of medical examiners' investigations of SIDS deaths in the St. Louis area between 1994 and 1997, a shared sleep surface was the site of death in nearly half (47.1 percent) of the cases investigated (Kemp et al., 2000). And, in an investigation of 84 SIDS cases in Cleveland, Ohio, bed sharing was associated with a younger age at death, especially when the mother was large (Carroll-Pankhurst & Mortimer, 2001).

Adult beds are not designed to meet safety standards for infants, as cribs are (NICHD, 1997, updated 2000; Scheers et al., 2003). Japan, where mothers and infants commonly sleep in the same bed, has one of the lowest SIDS rates in the world (Hoffman & Hillman, 1992), but this may be because Japanese families—as in many developing countries where bed sharing is practiced—generally sleep on thin mats on the floor.

Societal values influence parents' attitudes and behaviors. Throughout this book we will see many ways in which such culturally determined attitudes and behaviors affect children.

What's your view

Given the evidence about pros and cons of bed sharing between mother and infant, would you encourage this practice in cultures in which it is not customary?

Check it out!

For more information on this topic, go to **http://www.zerotothree.org/0-3_1198.htm**. This is an article from *Zero to Three* that explores "the complex developmental and relational issues surrounding infant sleep."

Many accidental injuries occur at home. In a study of 990 infants brought to emergency rooms in Kingston, Ontario, by far the most injuries were caused by falls (61.1 percent), followed by ingesting harmful substances (6.6 percent), and burns (5.7 percent) (Pickett, Streight, Simpson, & Brison, 2003).

Shaken Baby Syndrome

The scenario is all too common. A baby, usually 6 weeks to 4 months old, is brought to the emergency room by a parent or caregiver. The infant may show symptoms ranging from lethargy, tremors, or vomiting to seizures, convulsions, stupor, or coma and may be unable to suck or swallow, make sounds, or follow an object with his or her eyes. However, there is no visible sign of injury, and the parent or caregiver denies knowledge of what caused the condition or claims that the child fell. Closer examination may or may not reveal bruises indicative of abuse, but radiological studies (a CT scan, possibly followed by an MRI) find hemorraghing of the brain or retina—a result of the infant's having been violently shaken (AAP Committee on Child Abuse and Neglect, 2001; National Center on Shaken Baby Syndrome, 2000).

Shaken baby syndrome (SBS) is a form of maltreatment (see Chapter 9), found mainly in children under 2 years and especially in infants, that usually results in serious, irreversible brain trauma. Because it is frequently misdiagnosed and underreported, its true incidence is unknown (AAP Committee on Child Abuse and Neglect, 2001; King, MacKay,

shaken baby syndrome (SBS) Form of maltreatment found mainly in children under 2 years but as old as 5, usually resulting in serious, irreversible brain trauma.

Sirnick, & The Canadian Shaken Baby Study Group, 2003), but estimates range from 600 to 1,400 cases each year in the United States alone. Often these children have suffered previous abuse. About 20 percent die within a few days of being shaken. Survivors may be left with a range of disabilities, from learning and behavioral disorders to neurological injuries, retardation, paralysis, or blindness, or in a permanent vegetative state (King et al., 2003; National Center on Shaken Baby Syndrome, 2000).

Why would an adult bring such harm upon a helpless baby? A caregiver who is unable to handle stress or has unrealistic expectations for infant behavior may lose control and shake a crying baby in a desperate attempt to quiet the child. If the injured infant becomes drowsy or loses consciousness, the caregiver may think the shaking "worked" and may do it again when the crying resumes. Or the caregiver may put an unconscious baby to bed, hoping the infant will recover, thus missing the opportunity for early treatment (AAP Committee on Child Abuse and Neglect, 2001; National Center on Shaken Baby Syndrome, 2000).

Adults need to know that a baby's crying is normal and is not a reflection on their caregiving skills, that shaking is *never* "okay," and that help is available. (One resource is the National Center on Shaken Baby Syndrome, 888-273-0071.) Parents also need to know that age-appropriate physical play with a baby is *not* injurious (National Center on Shaken Baby Syndrome, 2000).

Immunization for Better Health

Such once-familiar and sometimes fatal childhood illnesses as measles, pertussis (whooping cough), and infantile paralysis (polio) are now largely preventable, thanks to the development of vaccines that mobilize the body's natural defenses. Unfortunately, many children still are not adequately protected.

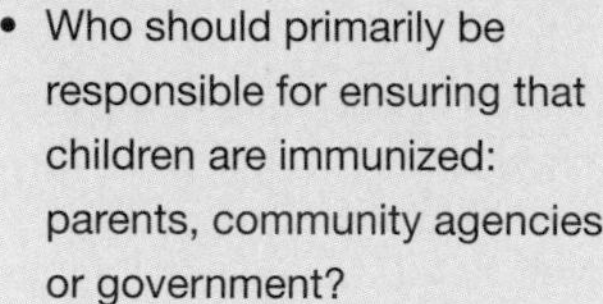

- Who should primarily be responsible for ensuring that children are immunized: parents, community agencies, or government?

In the developing world, 18 percent of deaths of children under age 5 are from vaccine-preventable diseases (Wegman, 1999). A five-year global Measles Initiative, currently focused on Africa, seeks to save lives by immunizing 200 million children. Between 1990 and 2000, such mass campaigns reached approximately 80 percent of the world's infants under 1 year old, and deaths from measles dropped to zero in Latin America. However, in 18 countries, 14 of them in Africa, less than 50 percent of eligible children are immunized (UNICEF Press Centre, 2002).

Checkpoint

Can you . . .

- ✔ Summarize trends in infant mortality, and explain why black infants are less likely to survive than white infants?
- ✔ Discuss risk factors for, causes of, and prevention of sudden infant death syndrome and shaken baby syndrome?
- ✔ Explain why full immunization of all infants and preschoolers is important?

In the United States, thanks to a nationwide immunization initiative, vaccine-preventable infectious diseases have dropped more than 95 percent since 1993 (AAP Committee on Infectious Diseases, 2000). In 2003, 79.4 percent of 19- to 35-month-olds completed a series of childhood vaccinations (NCHS, 2003). Still, many children lack one or more of the required shots, and there is substantial regional variation in coverage with lower immunization rates in urban areas (Centers for Disease Control and Prevention [CDC], 2004).

One reason some parents hesitate to immunize their children is fear that vaccines (especially pertussis vaccine) may cause brain damage. However, the association between pertussis vaccine and neurologic illness appears very small (Gale et al., 1994). The potential damage from the diseases that this vaccine prevents is far greater than the risks of the vaccine. Some parents worry that infants receive too many vaccines for their immune system to handle safely. (Today's children routinely receive 11 vaccines and as many as 20 shots by age 2.) Actually, the opposite is true. Multiple vaccines fortify the immune system against a variety of bacteria and viruses and reduce related infections (Offit et al., 2002).

New and improved vaccines are being devised. A vaccine for chicken pox is recommended for all children over 1 year of age and for adolescents and adults who have not had the disease (Centers for Disease Control and Prevention, 1999; Jefferson, 1999).

Refocus

- What connections does Helen Keller's story show among physical health, sensory capabilities, cognition, and pyschosocial development?
- How would a cognitive neuroscientist explain why Keller's senses of smell and touch became unusually sharp when she lost her hearing and sight?
- What hypotheses might explain why Keller's language development regressed and how she regained it? How might such hypotheses have been tested?
- Would the "mysterious fever" that Helen contracted likely be as damaging today? Why or why not?

Fortunately, most babies survive and grow up healthy. Their physical development forms the underpinning for cognitive and psychosocial developments that enable infants and toddlers to become more at home in their world, as we will see in Chapters 7 and 8.

Summary and Key Terms

Growth and Nutrition

Guidepost 1 How do babies grow, and what influences their growth?

- Normal physical growth and sensory and motor development proceed according to the cephalocaudal and proximodistal principles.
- A child's body grows most dramatically during the first year of life; growth proceeds at a rapid but diminishing rate throughout the first three years.

Guidepost 2 How and what should babies be fed?

- Historic shifts in feeding practices reflected efforts to improve infant survival and health.
- Breast-feeding offers many health advantages and sensory and cognitive benefits. However, the quality of the relationship between parents and infant may be more important than the feeding method.
- Babies should not start solid foods and fruit juices until 6 months of age and should not get cow's milk until 1 year.
- Obese babies are *not* at special risk of becoming obese adults, unless they have obese parents.

The Brain and Reflex Behavior

Guidepost 3 How does the brain develop, and how do environmental factors affect its early growth?

- The central nervous system controls sensorimotor functioning. Brain growth spurts coincide with changes in cognitive behavior. Lateralization enables each hemisphere of the brain to specialize in different functions.
- The brain grows most rapidly during the months before and immediately after birth as neurons migrate to their assigned locations, form synaptic connections, and undergo integration and differentiation. Cell death and myelination improve the efficiency of the nervous system.
- Reflex behaviors—primitive, locomotor, and postural—are indicators of neurological status. Most early reflexes drop out during the first year as voluntary, cortical control develops.
- Especially during the early period of rapid growth, environmental experience can influence brain development positively or negatively.

central nervous system (138) brain growth spurts (138) lateralization (138) neurons (139) integration (140) differentiation (140) cell death (140) myelination (141) reflex behavior (142) plasticity (144)

Early Sensory Capacities

Guidepost 4 How do the senses develop during infancy?

- Sensory capacities, present from birth and even in the womb, develop rapidly in the first months of life. Very young infants can discriminate among stimuli.
- Touch seems to be the first sense to develop and mature. Newborns are sensitive to pain. Smell, taste, and hearing also begin to develop in the womb.
- Vision is the least well-developed sense at birth but sharpens within the first six months.

Motor Development

Guidepost 5 What are the early milestones in motor development, and what are some influences on it?

- Motor skills develop in a certain sequence, which may depend largely on maturation but also on context, experience, and motivation. Simple skills combine into increasingly complex systems. The Denver Developmental Screening Test assesses gross and fine motor skills as well as linguistic, personality, and social development.
- Self-locomotion seems to be a "setting event," bringing about changes in all domains of development.
- Depth perception is present at a very early age and is related to motor development.
- Environmental factors, including cultural practices, may affect the pace of early motor development.

systems of action (148) Denver Developmental Screening Test (148) gross motor skills (148) fine motor skills (148) visual guidance (151) depth perception (151) haptic perception (151) visual cliff (151) eulogical theory of perception (151) affordance (151)

Health

Guidepost 6 How can we enhance babies' chances of survival and health?

- Although infant mortality has diminished in the United States, it is still disturbingly high for African-American babies. Birth defects are the leading cause of death in the first year; for black infants, low birth weight is the leading cause.
- Sudden infant death syndrome (SIDS) is the third leading cause of death in infants in the United States. Major risk factors are exposure to smoke and, prenatally, to caffeine, and sleeping in the prone position. SIDS rates have dropped dramatically since doctors have advised parents to put infants to sleep on their backs.
- Injuries are the third leading cause of death of U.S. infants after the first month.
- Shaken baby syndrome (SBS) is an underdiagnosed and underreported form of abuse, mainly of children under 2. It can cause severe, irreversible brain injury or death.
- Vaccine-preventable diseases have declined as rates of immunization have improved, but many preschoolers are not fully protected.

infant mortality rate (153) sudden infant death syndrome (SIDS) (155) shaken baby syndrome (SBS) (157)

chapter 7

Cognitive Development During the First Three Years

So runs my dream: but what am I?
An infant crying in the night:
An infant crying for the light,
And with no language but a cry.

—Alfred, Lord Tennyson, *In Memoriam*, Canto 54

Focus *William Erasmus Darwin, Naturalist's Son*

Charles and "Doddy" Darwin

On December 27, 1839, when the naturalist Charles Darwin was 30 years old, his first baby, William Erasmus Darwin, affectionately known as Doddy, was born. That day—20 years before his publication of *Origin of Species,* which outlined his theory of evolution based on natural selection—the proud father began keeping a diary of observations of his newborn son. It was these notes, published in 1877, that first called scientific attention to the developmental nature of infant behavior.

What abilities are babies born with? How do they learn about their world? How do they communicate, first nonverbally and then through language? These were among the questions Darwin sought to answer—questions still central to the study of cognitive development.

Darwin's keen eye illuminates how coordination of physical and mental activity helps an infant adapt to the world—as in this entry written when Doddy was 4 months old:

> Took my finger to his mouth & as usual could not get it in, on account of his own hand being in the way; then he slipped his own back & so got my finger in.—This was not chance & therefore a kind of reasoning. (diary, p. 12; quoted in Keegan & Gruber, 1985, p. 135)

In Darwin's notes, we can see Doddy developing new cognitive skills through interaction, not only with his father's finger, but with other objects as well. The diary depicts a series of encounters with reflected images. In these episodes Doddy gains knowledge, not in sudden bursts or jumps, but through gradual integration of new experience with existing patterns of behavior. In Darwin's view—as, later, in Piaget's—this was not merely a matter of piling new knowledge upon old; it involved an actual transformation of the way the mind is organized.

When Doddy, at 4½ months, saw his likeness and his father's in a mirror, Darwin noted that the baby "seemed surprised at my voice coming from behind him, my image being in front" (diary, p. 18; quoted in Keegan & Gruber, 1985, p. 135). Two months later, Doddy apparently had solved the mystery: Now, when his father, standing behind him, made a funny face in the mirror, the infant "was aware that the image . . . was not real & therefore . . . turned round to look" (diary, pp. 21–22; quoted in Keegan & Gruber, 1985, pp. 135–136).

The source for analysis of Darwin's diary is Keegan and Gruber (1985).

At first, this newfound understanding did not generalize to other reflective materials. Two weeks later, Doddy seemed puzzled to see his father's reflection in a window. By 9 months, however, the boy realized that "the shadow of a hand, made by a candle, was to be looked for behind, in [the] same manner as in [a] looking glass" (diary, p. 23; quoted in Keegan & Gruber, 1985, p. 136). His recognition that reflections could emanate from objects behind him now extended to shadows, another kind of two-dimensional image.

Darwin was particularly interested in documenting his son's progress in communication. He believed that language acquisition is a natural process, akin to earlier physical expressions of feelings. Through smiling, crying, laughing, facial expressions, and sounds of pleasure or pain, Doddy managed to communicate quite well with his parents even before uttering his first word. One of his first meaningful verbal expressions was "Ah!"—uttered when he recognized an image in a glass.

• • •

Darwin made these observations more than 160 years ago, at a time when infants' cognitive abilities were widely underestimated. We now know—as Darwin inferred from his observations of Doddy—that normal, healthy infants are born with the ability to learn and remember and with a capacity for acquiring and using speech. They use their growing sensory and cognitive capacities to exert control over their behavior and their world.

In this chapter we look at infants' and toddlers' cognitive abilities from three classic perspectives—behaviorist, psychometric, and Piagetian—and then from three newer perspectives: information processing, cognitive neuroscientific, and social-contextual. We trace the early development of language and discuss how it comes about.

After you have read and studied this chapter, you should be able to answer each of the Guidepost questions that follow. Look for them again in the margins, where they point to important concepts throughout the chapter. To check your understanding of these Guideposts, review the end-of-chapter summary. Checkpoints located at periodic spots throughout the chapter will help you verify your understanding of what you have read.

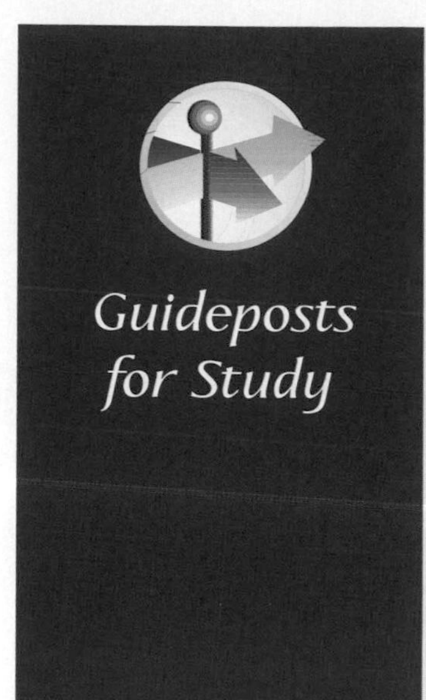

1. How do infants learn, and how long can they remember?
2. Can infants' and toddlers' intelligence be measured, and how can it be improved?
3. How did Piaget explain early cognitive development, and how have his claims stood up?
4. How can we measure infants' ability to process information, and how does this ability relate to future intelligence?
5. When do babies begin to think about characteristics of the physical world?
6. What can brain research reveal about the development of cognitive skills?
7. How does social interaction with adults advance cognitive competence?
8. How do babies develop language?
9. What influences contribute to linguistic progress?

Studying Cognitive Development: Classic Approaches

How and when do babies learn to solve problems? How and when does memory develop? What accounts for individual differences in cognitive abilities? Can we measure a baby's intelligence? Can we predict how smart that baby will be in the future? Many investigators have taken one of three classic approaches to the study of such questions:

- The **behaviorist approach** studies the basic *mechanics* of learning. It is concerned with how behavior changes in response to experience.
- The **psychometric approach** seeks to *measure quantitative differences* in cognitive abilities by using tests that indicate or predict these abilities.
- The **Piagetian approach** looks at changes, or stages, in the *quality* of cognitive functioning. It is concerned with how the mind structures its activities and adapts to the environment.

All three of these classic approaches, as well as the three newer ones we will discuss in the following section—the information-processing, cognitive neuroscience, and social-contextual approaches—help us understand the cognitive development of infants and toddlers.

behaviorist approach Approach to the study of cognitive development that is concerned with basic mechanics of learning.

psychometric approach Approach to the study of cognitive development that seeks to measure the quantity of intelligence a person possesses.

Piagetian approach Approach to the study of cognitive development that describes qualitative stages in cognitive functioning.

Behaviorist Approach: Basic Mechanics of Learning

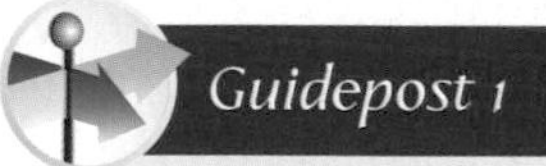

How do infants learn, and how long can they remember?

Babies are born with the ability to learn from what they see, hear, smell, taste, and touch, and they have at least some ability to remember what they learn. Of course, maturation is essential to this process, as learning theorists recognize; but the main interest of these theorists is in mechanisms of learning.

Let's look first at two simple learning processes, introduced in Chapter 2, that behaviorists study: *classical conditioning* and *operant conditioning.* Later we will consider *habituation,* form of learning that information-processing researchers study.

Classical and Operant Conditioning

Eager to capture Anna's memorable moments on film, her father took pictures of the infant smiling, crawling, and showing off her other achievements. Whenever the flash went off, Anna blinked. One evening when Anna was 11 months old, she saw her father hold the camera up to his eye—and she blinked *before* the flash. She had learned to associate the camera with the bright light, so that the sight of the camera alone activated her blinking reflex.

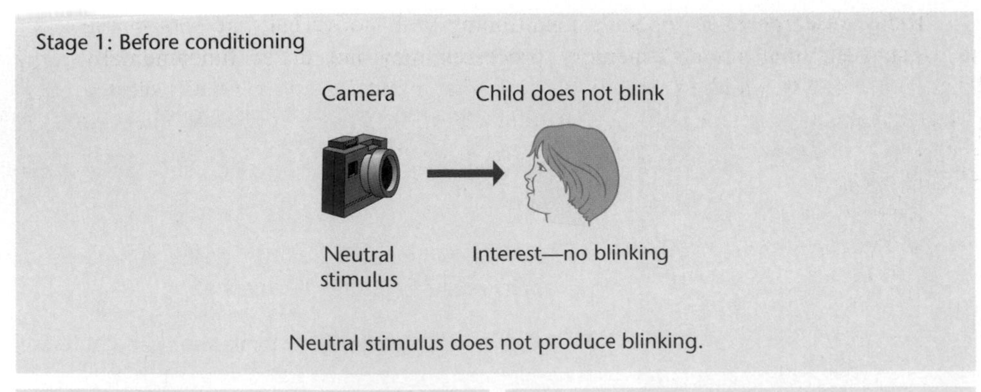
Stage 1: Before conditioning
Camera
Child does not blink
Neutral stimulus
Interest—no blinking
Neutral stimulus does not produce blinking.

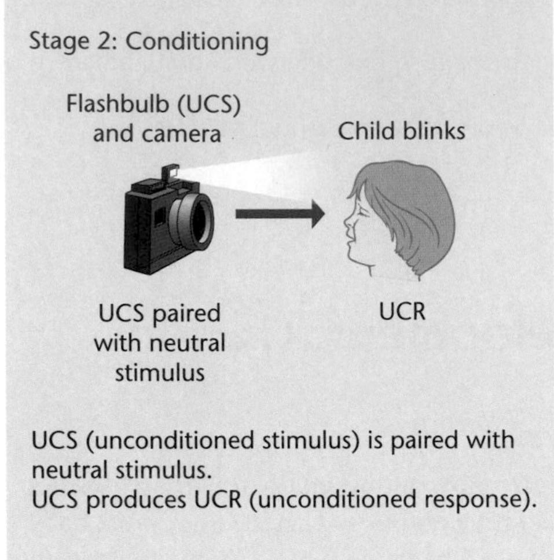
Stage 2: Conditioning
Flashbulb (UCS) and camera
Child blinks
UCS paired with neutral stimulus
UCR
UCS (unconditioned stimulus) is paired with neutral stimulus.
UCS produces UCR (unconditioned response).

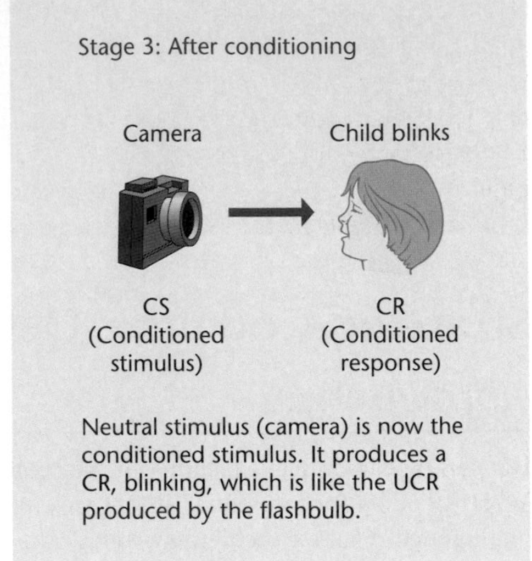
Stage 3: After conditioning
Camera
Child blinks
CS (Conditioned stimulus)
CR (Conditioned response)
Neutral stimulus (camera) is now the conditioned stimulus. It produces a CR, blinking, which is like the UCR produced by the flashbulb.

Figure 7-1
Three steps in classical conditioning.

classical conditioning Learning based on associating a stimulus that does not ordinarily elicit a response with another stimulus that does elicit the response.

operant conditioning Learning based on reinforcement or punishment.

Anna's blinking (see Figure 7-1) is an example of **classical conditioning,** in which a person or animal learns to make a reflex (involuntary) response (in this case, blinking) to a stimulus (the camera) that originally did not provoke the response. Classical conditioning enables infants to anticipate an event before it happens by forming associations between stimuli (such as the camera and the flash) that regularly occur together. Classically conditioned learning will fade, or become *extinct,* if it is not reinforced. Thus, if Anna frequently saw the camera without the flash, she eventually would stop blinking.

In classical conditioning, the learner is passive, absorbing and automatically reacting to stimuli. By contrast, in **operant conditioning**—as when a baby learns that smiling brings loving attention—the learner acts, or operates, on the environment. The infant learns to make a certain response to an environmental stimulus (smiling at the sight of her or his parents) in order to produce a particular effect (parental attention).

Infant Memory

Can you remember anything that happened to you before you were 3 years old? Chances are you can't. This inability to remember early events is called *infantile amnesia.* One explanation, held by Piaget (1969) and others, is that early events are not stored in memory because the brain is not yet developed enough. Freud, in contrast, believed that early memories are stored but are repressed because they are emotionally troubling. Other researchers suggest that children cannot store events in memory until they can talk about them (Nelson, 1992).

Today, research using operant conditioning with nonverbal, age-appropriate tasks suggests that infants' memory processes may not differ fundamentally from those of older children and adults except that infants' retention time is shorter. These studies have found that babies will repeat an action days or weeks later—*if* they are periodically reminded of the situation in which they learned it (Rovee-Collier, 1999).

In a series of experiments by Carolyn Rovee-Collier and her associates, infants were operantly conditioned to kick to activate a mobile attached to one ankle by a ribbon. Babies 2 to 6 months old, when again shown the mobiles days or weeks later, repeated the kicking, even though their legs were no longer attached to the mobiles. When the infants saw the mobiles, they kicked more than before the conditioning, showing that recognition of the mobiles triggered a memory of their initial experience with them (Rovee-Collier, 1996, 1999). In a similar task designed for older infants and toddlers, a child was conditioned to press a lever to make a miniature train go around a track. The length of time a conditioned response can be retained increases with age, from two days for 2-month-olds to 13 weeks for 18-month-olds (Hartshorn et al., 1998; Rovee-Collier, 1996, 1999; see Figure 7-2).

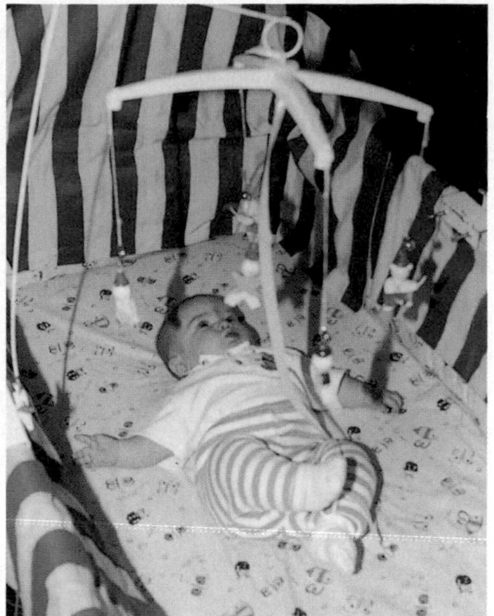

Babies 2 to 6 months old can remember, after a hiatus of two days to two weeks, that they were able to activate a mobile by kicking; they show this by kicking as soon as they see the mobile.

Young infants' memory of a behavior seems to be linked specifically to the original cue. Two- to 6-month-olds repeated the learned behavior only when they saw the original mobile or train. However, older infants, between 9 and 12 months, would "try out" the behavior on a different train if no more than two weeks had gone by since the training (Rovee-Collier, 1999).

Context can affect recollection when a memory has weakened. Three-, 9-, and 12-month-olds initially could recognize the mobile or train in a different setting from the one in which they were trained, but not after long delays. Periodic nonverbal reminders through brief exposure to the original stimulus can sustain a memory from early infancy through 1½ to 2 years of age (Rovee-Collier, 1999).

Since infants can remember, why don't their early memories last? It may be because the crucial match between the situation in which something is learned and the situation in which it can be recalled is lost after a long period of time—a period in which the child begins to rely more on verbal than on nonverbal cues (Rovee-Collier, 1999).

Checkpoint

Can you . . .

- ✔ Contrast the goals of the behaviorist, psychometric, and Piagetian approaches to the study of cognitive development?
- ✔ Give examples of classical and operant conditioning in infants?
- ✔ Summarize what studies of operant conditioning have shown about infant memory?

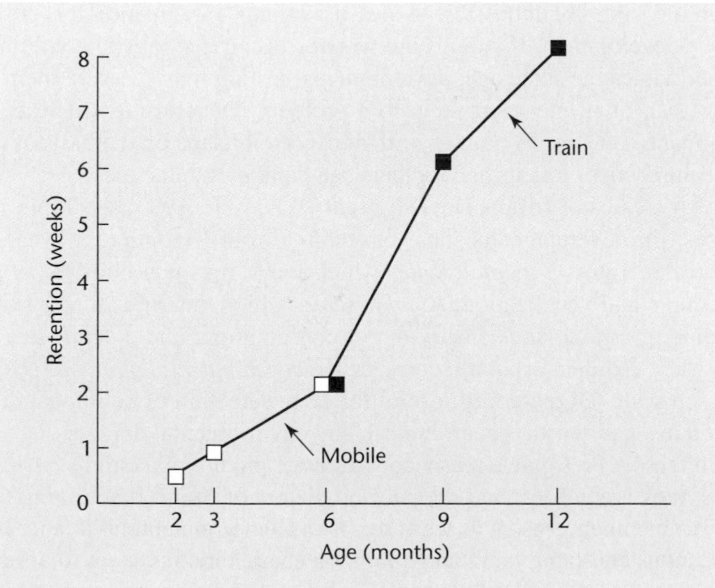

Figure 7-2

Maximum number of weeks that infants of varying ages show retention of how to operate either a mobile or a miniature train. Regardless of the task, retention improves with age.

Source: Rovee-Collier, 1999, Fig. 4, p. 83.

Can infants' and toddlers' intelligence be measured, and how can it be improved?

Psychometric Approach: Developmental and Intelligence Testing

When Doddy Darwin, at 4 months, figured out how to get his father's finger into his mouth by moving his own hand out of the way, he showed **intelligent behavior.** Intelligent behavior is *goal oriented* and *adaptive:* directed at adjusting to the circumstances and conditions of life. Intelligence enables people to acquire, remember, and use knowledge; to understand concepts and relationships; and to solve problems.

intelligent behavior Behavior that is goal oriented and adaptive to circumstances and conditions of life.

The precise nature of intelligence has been debated for many years, as has the best way to measure it. Beginning in the 19th century, there were attempts to measure intelligence by such characteristics as head size and reaction time and then by tests that scored strength of hand squeeze, pain sensitivity, weight discrimination, judgment of time, and rote recall. As we might expect, these tests had little predictive value.

Then, at the beginning of the 20th century, school administrators in Paris asked the psychologist Alfred Binet to devise a way to identify children who could not handle academic work and who should be removed from regular classes and given special training. The test that Binet and his colleague Theodore Simon developed was the forerunner of psychometric tests that score intelligence by numbers. One is the Stanford-Binet Intelligence Scale, described in Chapter 10.

The goals of psychometric testing are to measure quantitatively the factors that are thought to make up intelligence (such as comprehension and reasoning) and, from the results of that measurement, to predict future performance (such as school achievement). **IQ (intelligence quotient) tests** consist of questions or tasks that are supposed to show how much of the measured abilities a person has, by comparing that person's performance with that of other test takers.

IQ (intelligence quotient) tests Psychometric tests that seek to measure intelligence by comparing a test taker's performance with standardized norms.

Testing Infants and Toddlers

For school-age children, intelligence test scores can predict academic performance fairly accurately and reliably. Testing infants and toddlers is another matter. Since babies cannot tell us what they know and how they think, the most obvious way to gauge their intelligence is by assessing what they can do. But if they do not grasp a rattle, it is hard to tell whether they do not know how, do not feel like doing it, do not realize what is expected of them, or have simply lost interest.

Although it is virtually impossible to measure infants' intelligence, it *is* possible to test their cognitive development. If parents are worried because a baby is not doing the same things as other babies the same age, developmental testing may reassure them that development is normal, or it may alert them to a problem. **Developmental tests** compare a baby's performance on a series of tasks with norms established on the basis of observation of what large numbers of infants and toddlers can do at particular ages.

developmental tests Psychometric tests that compare a baby's performance on a series of nonverbal tasks with standardized norms for particular ages.

Bayley Scales of Infant Development Standardized test of infants' mental and motor development.

The **Bayley Scales of Infant Development** (Bayley II, 1993; see Table 7-1) are designed to assess the developmental status of children from 1 month to 3½ years. The Bayley II has three sections: a *mental scale,* which measures such abilities as perception, memory, learning, and vocalization; a *motor scale,* which measures motor skills, such as sitting, standing, grasping, and sensory-motor coordination; and a *behavior rating scale* completed by the examiner. Separate scores, called *developmental quotients (DQs),* are calculated for each scale. DQs are most useful for early detection of emotional disturbances, learning problems, and sensory, neurological, and environmental deficits.

Although these scores give a reasonably accurate picture of a child's *current* developmental status, they are not IQs and are poor predictors of future functioning (Anastasi & Urbina, 1997). One likely reason, as we'll see, is that environmental influences such as socioeconomic status and family and neighborhood characteristics seem to affect cognitive development more strongly as children approach age 3 (Klebanov, Brooks-Gunn, McCarton, & McCormick, 1998). Another reason is that the developmental tests traditionally used for babies measure mostly sensory and motor abilities, whereas intelligence tests for older children place more emphasis on verbal abilities (Bornstein & Sigman, 1986; Colombo, 1993; McCall & Carriger, 1993). Not until at least the third year of life, when children may

Table 7-1	Sample Tasks in the Bayley Scales of Infant Development	
Age (in months)	**Mental Scale***	**Motor Scale***
1	Eyes follow moving person	Lifts head when held at shoulder
3	Reaches for suspended ring	Turns from back to side
6	Manipulates bell, showing interest in detail	Turns from back to stomach
9	Jabbers expressively	Raises self to standing position
12	Pats toy in imitation	Walks alone
14–16	Uses two different words appropriately	Walks up stairs with help
20–22	Names three objects	Jumps off floor with both feet
26–28	Matches four colors	Imitates hand movements
32–34	Uses past tense	Walks up stairs, alternating feet
38–42	Counts	Walks down stairs, alternating feet

*Task most children this age can do

Source: Bayley, 1993.

be tested with the Stanford-Binet, do a child's IQ scores, along with such factors as the parents' IQ and educational level, usually help to predict later test scores (Kopp & Kaler, 1989; Kopp & McCall, 1982; McCall & Carriger, 1993). As children approach their fifth birthday, the relationship between current scores and those in later childhood becomes stronger (Bornstein & Sigman, 1986). IQ tests given near the end of kindergarten are among the best predictors of future school success (Tramontana, Hooper, & Selzer, 1988).

Assessing the Impact of the Home Environment

Intelligence was once thought to be fixed at birth; we now know that it is influenced by both inheritance and experience. What characteristics of the early home environment may influence intelligence? Using the **Home Observation for Measurement of the Environment (HOME)** (R. H. Bradley, 1989; Caldwell & Bradley, 1984), trained observers rate on a checklist the resources and atmosphere in a child's home.

Home Observation for Measurement of the Environment (HOME) Instrument to measure the influence of the home environment on children's cognitive growth.

One important factor that HOME assesses is parental responsiveness. HOME gives credit to the parent of an infant or toddler for caressing or kissing the child during an examiner's visit, to the parent of a preschooler for spontaneously praising the child, and to the parent of an older child for answering the child's questions. A longitudinal study found positive correlations between parents' responsiveness to their 6-month-olds and the children's IQ, achievement test scores, and teacher-rated classroom behavior through age 13 (Bradley, Corwyn, Burchinal, McAdoo, & Coll, 2001).

HOME also assesses the number of books in the home, the presence of playthings that encourage the development of concepts, and parents' involvement in children's play. In an analysis of HOME assessments of 29,264 European-American, African-American, and Hispanic-American children in the National Longitudinal Study of Youth (NLSY), learning stimulation was consistently associated with kindergarten achievement tests, as well as with language competence and motor and social development (Bradley et al., 2001).

However, because studies using HOME are correlational, we cannot be certain that parental responsiveness or an enriched home environment actually *causes* a child's intelligence to increase. All we can say is that these factors are associated with higher intelligence. Intelligent, well-educated parents may be more likely to provide a positive, stimulating home environment; and since they also pass their genes on to their children, there may be a genetic influence as well. (This is an example of a *passive genotype-environment correlation,* described in Chapter 3.)

Checkpoint

Can you . . .

- ✔ Tell why developmental tests are sometimes given to infants and toddlers, and describe one such widely used test?
- ✔ Explain why tests of infants and toddlers are unreliable in predicting later IQ?
- ✔ Identify aspects of the home environment that may influence intelligence, and tell why such influence is hard to show?
- ✔ Discuss the relationship between SES and cognitive development?

Socioeconomic Status and IQ

The correlation between socioeconomic status and IQ is well documented (Neisser et al., 1996). Family income is associated with cognitive development, achievement, and behavior in the preschool years and beyond. Poverty limits parents' ability to provide educational resources and may exert a negative psychological effect on the parents and their parenting practices (Brooks-Gunn, 2003; Evans, 2004; McLoyd, 1990, 1998; see Chapter 14).

A combination of genetic and environmental factors influences children's vulnerability to economic deprivation and their ability to surmount it cognitively and behaviorally. That was the conclusion of a study of 1,116 twin pairs born in England and Wales in 1994 and 1995 and assessed at age 5 (Kim-Cohen, Moffitt, Caspi, & Taylor, 2004). As in other studies, children in deprived families tended to have lower IQs and were more likely to engage in antisocial behavior. However, a child's outgoing temperament together with maternal warmth and stimulating activities in the home (which, again, may be influenced by parental IQ) served as intertwined protective factors. For example, children who inherit a pleasing temperament may elicit more attention, warmth, and stimulation from their parents—again, a gene-environment correlation—and end up with more sociable behavior and higher IQs.

Early Intervention

early intervention Systematic process of providing services to help families meet young children's developmental needs.

If an impoverished home environment can lower intelligence scores, can early intervention raise them? Research suggests that it can to some extent. **Early intervention,** as defined under the Individuals with Disabilities Education Act, is a systematic process of planning and providing therapeutic and educational services for families that need help in meeting infants', toddlers', and preschool children's developmental needs.

Some researchers have identified six aspects of the home environment that pave the way for normal cognitive and psychosocial development and help prepare children for school. These six conditions are (1) encouragement to explore the environment; (2) mentoring in basic cognitive and social skills, such as labeling, sequencing, sorting, and comparing; (3) celebration of accomplishments; (4) guidance in practicing and expanding skills; (5) protection from inappropriate punishment, teasing, or disapproval for mistakes or unintended consequences of exploring and trying out skills; and (6) stimulation of language and other symbolic communication. The consistent presence of all six of these conditions early in life may be essential to normal brain development (C. T. Ramey & S. L. Ramey, 1998a, 1998b; S. L. Ramey & C. T. Ramey, 1992). (Table 7-2 lists specific suggestions for helping babies develop cognitive competence.)

What's your view

- On the basis of the six essential aspects of the home environment listed in the text, can you suggest specific ways to help infants and toddlers get ready for schooling?

The goal of early intervention is to help children who may not be getting such developmental support. Two randomly assigned, controlled studies, among others, have tested the effectiveness of early intervention (C. T. Ramey & S. L. Ramey, 1998b).

Project CARE (Wasik, Ramey, Bryant, & Sparling, 1990) and the Abecedarian Project (C. T. Ramey & Campbell, 1991) involved a total of 174 North Carolina babies from at-risk homes. In each project, from 6 weeks of age until kindergarten, an experimental group was enrolled in Partners for Learning, a full-day, year-round early childhood education program at a university child development center. The program had a low child-teacher ratio and used learning games to foster specific cognitive, linguistic, perceptual-motor, and social skills. Control groups received pediatric and social work services, formula, and home visits, as the experimental groups did, but were not enrolled in Partners for Learning.

In both projects, the children who received the early intervention showed a widening advantage over the control groups in developmental test scores during the first 18 months. By age 3, the average IQ of the Abecedarian children was 101 and of CARE children, 105—equal to or better than average for the general population—as compared with only 84 and 93 for the control groups (C. T. Ramey & S. L. Ramey, 1998b).

As often happens with early intervention programs, these early gains were not fully maintained. IQs dropped between ages 3 and 8, especially among children from the most disadvantaged homes. Still, scores tended to be higher and more stable among children who had been in Partners for Learning than in the control groups (Burchinal et al., 1997).

Table 7-2 Fostering Competence

Findings from the Harvard Preschool Project, from studies using the HOME scales, and from neurological studies and other research suggest the following guidelines for fostering infants' and toddlers' cognitive development:

1. In the early months, *provide sensory stimulation* but avoid overstimulation and distracting noises.
2. As babies grow older, *create an environment that fosters learning*—one that includes books, interesting objects (which do not have to be expensive toys), and a place to play.
3. *Respond to babies' signals.* This establishes a sense of trust that the world is a friendly place and gives babies a sense of control over their lives.
4. *Give babies the power to effect changes,* through toys that can be shaken, molded, or moved. Help a baby discover that turning a doorknob opens a door, flicking a light switch turns on a light, and opening a faucet produces running water for a bath.
5. *Give babies freedom to explore.* Do not confine them regularly during the day in a crib, jump seat, or small room and only for short periods in a playpen. Baby-proof the environment and let them go!
6. *Talk to babies.* They will not pick up language from listening to the radio or television; they need interaction with adults.
7. In talking to or playing with babies, *enter into whatever they are interested in* at the moment instead of trying to redirect their attention to something else.
8. *Arrange opportunities to learn basic skills,* such as labeling, comparing, and sorting objects (say, by size or color), putting items in sequence, and observing the consequences of actions.
9. *Applaud new skills and help babies practice and expand them.* Stay nearby and do not hover.
10. *Read to babies in a warm, caring atmosphere from an early age.* Reading aloud and talking about the stories develop preliteracy skills.
11. *Use punishment sparingly.* Do not punish or ridicule results of normal trial-and-error exploration.

Sources: R. R. Bradley & Caldwell, 1982; R. R. Bradley, Caldwell, & Rock, 1988; R. H. Bradley et al., 1989; C. T. Ramey & Ramey, 1998a, 1998b; S. L. Ramey & Ramey, 1992; Staso, quoted in Blakeslee, 1997; J. H. Stevens & Bakeman, 1985; B. L. White, 1971; B. L. White, Kaban, & Attanucci, 1979.

From then on into adulthood, both the experimental and control groups' IQs and math scores increasingly fell below national norms while reading scores held steady but below average. However, the children in the Abecedarian Project who had been enrolled in Partners for Learning continued to outdo the control group by all measures and were less likely to repeat a grade in school (Campbell, Pungello, Miller-Johnson, Burchinal, & Ramey, 2001; C. T. Ramey et al., 2000).

These findings and others like them show that early educational intervention can help moderate the effects of environmental risks (Brooks-Gunn, 2003). The most effective early interventions are those that (1) start early and continue throughout the preschool years; (2) are highly time-intensive (i.e., occupy more hours in a day or more days in a week, month, or year); (3) are center-based, providing direct educational experiences, not just parental training; (4) take a comprehensive approach, including health, family counseling, and social services; and (5) are tailored to individual differences and needs. As in the two North Carolina projects, initial gains tend to diminish unless there is enough ongoing environmental support for further progress (Brooks-Gunn, 2003; C. T. Ramey & S. L. Ramey, 1996, 1998a).

Checkpoint

Can you . . .

- ✔ Identify six aspects of the home environment considered essential to normal cognitive development?
- ✔ Summarize findings about the value of early intervention?

Guidepost 3

How did Piaget explain early cognitive development, and how have his claims stood up?

Piagetian Approach: The Sensorimotor Stage

The first of Piaget's four stages of cognitive development is the **sensorimotor stage.** During this stage, from birth to approximately age 2, infants learn about themselves and their world through their developing sensory and motor activity. Babies change from creatures who respond primarily through reflexes and random behavior into goal-oriented toddlers. In Darwin's diary, for example, we saw Doddy progress from simple exploration of his father's finger to purposeful attempts to solve the mysteries of mirrors and shadows.

sensorimotor stage Piaget's first stage in cognitive development, during which infants learn through senses and motor activity.

Table 7-3 Six Substages of Piaget's Sensorimotor Stage of Cognitive Development*

Substage	Ages	Description	Behavior
Use of reflexes	Birth to 1 month	Infants exercise their inborn reflexes and gain some control over them. They do not coordinate information from their senses. They do not grasp an object they are looking at.	Dorri begins sucking when her mother's breast is in her mouth.
Primary circular reactions	1 to 4 months	Infants repeat pleasurable behaviors that first occur by chance (such as thumb sucking). Activities focus on the infant's body rather than the effects of the behavior on the environment. Infants make first acquired adaptations; that is, they suck different objects differently. They begin to coordinate sensory information and grasp objects.	When given a bottle, Dylan, who is usually breast-fed, is able to adjust his sucking to the rubber nipple.
Secondary circular reactions	4 to 8 months	Infants become more interested in the environment; they repeat actions that bring interesting results (such as shaking a rattle) and prolong interesting experiences. Actions are intentional but not initially goal directed.	Alejandro pushes pieces of dry cereal over the edge of his high chair tray one at a time and watches each piece as it falls to the floor.
Coordination of secondary schemes	8 to 12 months	Behavior is more deliberate and purposeful (intentional) as infants coordinate previously learned schemes (such as looking at and grasping a rattle) and use previously learned behaviors to attain their goals (such as crawling across the room to get a desired toy). They can anticipate events.	Anica pushes the button on her musical nursery rhyme book, and "Twinkle, Twinkle, Little Star" plays. She pushes this button over and over again, choosing it instead of the buttons for the other songs.
Tertiary circular reactions	12 to 18 months	Toddlers show curiosity and experimentation; they purposefully vary their actions to see results (for example, by shaking different rattles to hear their sounds). They actively explore their world to determine what is novel about an object, event, or situation. They try out new activities and use trial and error in solving problems.	When Bjorn's big sister holds his favorite board book up to his crib bars, he reaches for it. His first efforts to bring the book into his crib fail because the book is too wide. Soon, Bjorn turns the book sideways and hugs it, delighted with his success.
Mental combinations	18 to 24 months	Since toddlers can mentally represent events, they are no longer confined to trial and error to solve problems. Symbolic thought enables toddlers to begin to think about events and anticipate their consequences without always resorting to action. Toddlers begin to demonstrate insight. They can use symbols, such as gestures and words, and can pretend.	Jenny plays with her shape box, searching carefully for the right hole for each shape before trying—and succeeding.

*Note: Infants show enormous cognitive growth during Piaget's sensorimotor stage, as they learn about the world through their senses and their motor activities. Note their progress in problem solving and the coordination of sensory information. All ages are approximate.

Substages of the Sensorimotor Stage

schemes Piaget's term for organized patterns of behavior used in particular situations.

The sensorimotor stage consists of six substages (see Table 7-3), that flow from one to another as a baby's **schemes,** organized patterns of behavior, become more elaborate. During the first five substages, babies learn to coordinate input from their senses and organize their activities in relation to their environment. They do this by the processes of ***organization, adaptation,*** and ***equilibration,*** which we discussed in Chapter 2. During the sixth and last substage, they progress from trial-and-error learning to the use of symbols and concepts to solve simple problems.

circular reactions Piaget's term for processes by which an infant learns to reproduce desired occurrences originally discovered by chance.

Much of this early cognitive growth comes about through **circular reactions,** in which an infant learns to reproduce pleasurable or interesting events originally discovered by chance. Initially, an activity produces a sensation so enjoyable that the baby wants to repeat it. The repetition then feeds on itself in a continuous cycle in which cause and effect keep reversing (see Figure 7-3). The original chance behavior has been consolidated into a new scheme.

In the *first substage* (birth to about 1 month), neonates begin to exercise some control over their inborn reflexes, engaging in a behavior even when its normal stimulus is not present. For example, newborns suck reflexively when their lips are touched. But they soon learn to find the nipple even when they are not touched, and they suck at times when they are not hungry. These newer behaviors illustrate how infants modify and extend the scheme for sucking.

In the *second substage* (about 1 to 4 months), babies learn to repeat a pleasant bodily sensation first achieved by chance (say, sucking their thumbs, as in the first part of Figure 7-3). Piaget called this a *primary circular reaction.* Also, they begin to turn toward sounds, showing the ability to coordinate different kinds of sensory information (vision and hearing).

The *third substage* (about 4 to 8 months) coincides with a new interest in manipulating objects and learning about their properties. Babies engage in *secondary circular reactions:* intentional actions repeated not merely for their own sake, as in the second substage, but to get results *beyond the infant's own body.* For example, a baby this age will repeatedly shake a rattle to hear its noise or (as in the second part of Figure 7-3) coo when a friendly face appears, so as to make the face stay longer.

By the time infants reach the *fourth substage, coordination of secondary schemes* (about 8 to 12 months), they have built on the few schemes they were born with. They have learned to generalize from past experience to solve new problems, and they can distinguish means from ends. They will crawl to get something they want, grab it, or push away a barrier to it (such as someone else's hand). They try out, modify, and coordinate previous schemes to find one that works. This substage marks the development of complex, goal-directed behavior.

In the *fifth substage* (about 12 to 18 months), babies begin to experiment with new behavior to see what will happen. Once they begin to walk, they can more easily explore their environment. They now engage in *tertiary circular reactions,* varying an action to get a similar result, rather than merely repeating pleasing behavior they have accidentally discovered. For example, a toddler may squeeze a rubber duck that squeaked when stepped on, to see whether it will squeak again (as in the third part of Figure 7-3). For the first time, children show originality in problem solving. By trial and error, they try out behaviors until they find the best way to attain a goal.

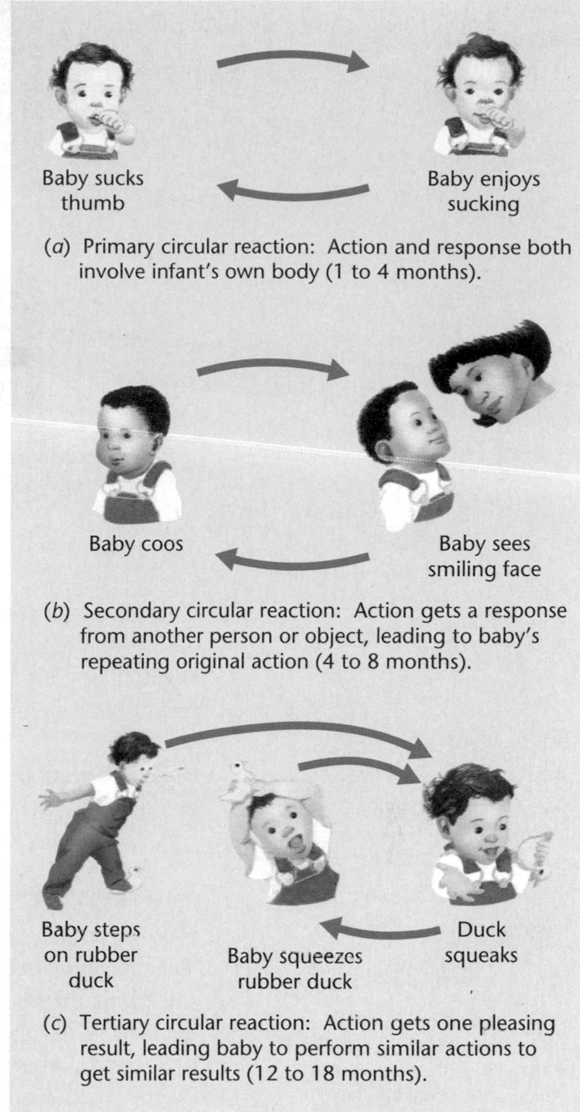
Baby sucks thumb
Baby enjoys sucking
(a) Primary circular reaction: Action and response both involve infant's own body (1 to 4 months).
Baby coos
Baby sees smiling face
(b) Secondary circular reaction: Action gets a response from another person or object, leading to baby's repeating original action (4 to 8 months).
Baby steps on rubber duck
Baby squeezes rubber duck
Duck squeaks
(c) Tertiary circular reaction: Action gets one pleasing result, leading baby to perform similar actions to get similar results (12 to 18 months).

Figure 7-3
Primary, secondary, and tertiary circular reactions.

The *sixth substage, mental combinations* (about 18 months to 2 years) is a transition into the preoperational stage of early childhood. **Representational ability**—the ability to mentally represent objects and events in memory, largely through symbols such as words, numbers, and mental pictures—blossoms. The ability to manipulate symbols frees children from immediate experience. They can now engage in **deferred imitation,** imitating actions they no longer see in front of them. They can engage in **pretend play**—also called *fantasy play, dramatic play,* or *imaginative play*—and their representational ability affects the sophistication of their pretending (Bornstein, Haynes, O'Reilly, & Painter, 1996). They can think about actions before taking them. They no longer have to go through laborious trial and error to solve problems. Piaget's daughter Lucienne seemed to show representational ability when, in figuring out how to pry open a partially closed matchbox to remove a watch chain, she opened her mouth wider to represent her idea of widening the opening in the box (Piaget, 1936/1952).

representational ability Piaget's term for capacity to store mental images or symbols of objects and events.

deferred imitation Piaget's term for reproduction of an observed behavior after the passage of time by calling up a stored symbol of it.

pretend play Play involving imaginary people or situations; also called *fantasy play, dramatic play,* or *imaginative play.*

During these six substages, infants develop specific knowledge about certain aspects of the physical world; notably, about objects and spatial relationships.

Development of Knowledge About Objects and Space

The *object concept*—the idea that objects have their own independent existence, characteristics, and locations in space—is fundamental to an orderly view of physical reality. The

This 8-month-old baby crawling after a ball is in the fourth substage of Piaget's sensorimotor stage, coordination of secondary schemes.

object concept is the basis for children's awareness that they themselves exist apart from objects and other people. It is essential to understanding a world full of objects and events. Doddy Darwin's struggle to understand the existence and location of reflective images was part of his development of an object concept.

object permanence Piaget's term for the understanding that a person or object still exists when out of sight.

LifeMap CD

How can you tell whether an infant grasps the concept of object permanence? To find out, watch the video on "Lacking Object Permanence at Four Months" in Chapter 7 of your CD.

A, not-B error Tendency for 8- to 12-month-old infants to search for a hidden object in a place where they previously found it rather than in the place where they most recently saw it being hidden.

egocentric In Piaget's terminology, unable to consider any point of view other than one's own; a characteristic of young children's thought.

Object Permanence One aspect of the object concept is **object permanence,** the realization that an object or person continues to exist when out of sight. The development of this concept in many cultures can be seen in the game of peekaboo (see Box 7-1).

Piaget believed that infants develop knowledge about objects by watching the results of their own actions; in other words, by coordinating visual and motor information. In this way, object permanence develops gradually during the sensorimotor stage. At first, infants have no such concept. By the third substage, from about 4 to 8 months, they will look for something they have dropped, but if they cannot see it, they act as if it no longer exists. In the fourth substage, about 8 to 12 months, they will look for an object in a place where they first found it after seeing it hidden, even if they later saw it being moved to another place. Piaget called this the **A, not-B error.** In the fifth substage, 12 to 18 months, they no longer make this error; they will search for an object in the *last* place they saw it hidden. However, they will *not* search for it in a place where they did *not* see it hidden. By the sixth substage, 18 to 24 months, object permanence is fully achieved; toddlers will look for an object even if they did not see it hidden.

Piaget (1954/1971) observed the A, not-B error when his son Laurent was 9½ months old. Piaget placed Laurent on a sofa, with a small blanket (A) on his right and a wool garment (B) on his left. As the baby watched, Piaget hid his watch under the blanket. Laurent lifted the blanket and retrieved the watch. After repeating this game several times, Piaget placed the watch under the garment instead of under the blanket. Laurent watched intently and then again lifted the blanket and searched for the watch there. Two analyses of research on the A, not-B error have verified its prevalence (Marcovitch & Zelazo, 1999; Wellman, Cross, & Bartsch, 1986).

Piaget saw the A, not-B error as a sign of incomplete understanding of the object concept, together with an **egocentric** (self-centered) view of spatial relations. He reasoned that the infant must believe that the object's existence is linked to a particular location (the one where it was first found) and to the infant's own action in retrieving it from that location. A more recent explanation is that infants—and even toddlers and preschoolers—may simply find it hard to restrain the impulse to repeat an earlier behavior that was previously reinforced by success (Diamond, Cruttenden, & Neiderman, 1994; Zelazo, Reznick, & Spinazzola, 1998). This interpretation may explain why even 2-year-olds and older preschoolers sometimes make the A, not-B error. If, on an earlier trial, they merely *observed* the object being found rather than finding it themselves, they are much less likely to

Around the World

Box 7-1 *Playing Peekaboo*

In rural South Africa, a Bantu mother smiles at her 9-month-old son, covers her eyes with her hands, and asks, "Uphi?" (Where?). After three seconds, the mother says, "Here!" and uncovers her eyes to the baby's delight. In Tokyo, a Japanese mother plays the same game with her 12-month-old daughter, who shows the same joyous response. In suburban Connecticut, a 15-month-old boy who sees his grandfather for the first time in two months raises his shirt to cover his eyes—as Grandpa did on his previous visit.

Peekaboo is played across diverse cultures, using similar routines (Fernald & O'Neill, 1993). In all cultures in which the game is played,* the moment when the mother or other caregiver reappears is exhilarating. It is marked by exaggerated gestures and voice tones. Infants' pleasure from the immediate sensory stimulation of the game is heightened by their fascination with faces and voices, especially the high-pitched tones an adult usually uses.

The game serves several important purposes. Psychoanalysts say that it helps babies master anxiety when their mother disappears. Cognitive psychologists see it as a way babies play with developing ideas about object permanence. It may also be a social routine that helps babies learn rules that govern conversation, such as taking turns. It may provide practice in paying attention, a prerequisite for learning.

"Peekaboo!" This game, played the world over, helps babies to overcome anxiety about a parent's disappearance and to develop cognitive concepts, such as anticipation of future events.

As babies develop the cognitive competency to predict future events, the game takes on new dimensions. Between 3 and 5 months, the baby's smiles and laughter as the adult's face moves in and out of view signal the infant's developing expectation of what will happen next. At 5 to 8 months, the baby shows anticipation by looking and smiling as the adult's voice alerts the infant to the adult's imminent reappearance. By 1 year, babies are no longer merely observers but usually initiate the game, actively engaging adults in play. Now it is the adult who generally responds to the baby's physical or vocal cues, which can become quite insistent if the adult doesn't feel like playing.

To help infants who are in the process of learning peekaboo or other games, parents often use *scaffolding* (see Chapter 2). In an 18-month longitudinal study at the University of Montreal, 25 mothers were videotaped playing peekaboo with their babies, using a doll as a prop (Rome-Flanders, Cronk, & Gourde, 1995). The amount and type of scaffolding varied with the infant's age and skill. Mothers frequently tried to attract a 6-month-old's attention to begin the game; this became less and less necessary as time went on. Modeling (performing the peekaboo sequence to encourage a baby to imitate it) also was most frequent at 6 months and decreased significantly by 12 months, when there was an increase in direct verbal instruction ("Cover the doll") as babies became more able to understand spoken language. Indirect verbal instruction ("Where is the doll?"), used to focus attention on the next step in the game, remained constant throughout the entire age range. Reinforcement (showing satisfaction with the infant's performance, for example, by saying, "Peekaboo!" when the infant uncovered the doll) was fairly constant from 9 months on. The overall amount of scaffolding dropped substantially at 24 months, by which time most babies have fully mastered the game.

What's your view ?

Have you ever played peekaboo periodically with the same infant? If so, did you notice changes with age in the child's participation, as described in this box?

Check it out !

For more information on this topic, go to **http://www.zerotothree.org/dynamic.html.** This is an article by Steve Harvey, Ph.D., from *Zero to Three,* "Dynamic Play Therapy: Integrated Expressive Arts Approach to the Family Treatment of Infants and Toddlers."

*The cultures included in this report are found in Malaysia, Greece, India, Iran, Russia, Brazil, Indonesia, Korea, and South Africa.

make this error (Zelazo et al., 1998). In one study, 2-year-olds' tendency to make the A, not-B error diminished the more times the hidden object was subsequently found in the B location (Spencer, Smith, & Thelen, 2001).

Locating Objects in Space According to Piaget (1954/1971), egocentrism also helps explain young infants' limited ability to locate objects in space. They can see things only from their own point of view, which, given their immobility, is very limited. They have no idea that objects exist in space independent of themselves. Not until the sixth substage, said Piaget, as egocentrism declines and mental representations develop, do babies develop an **allocentric** (objective) view of the world. They can consider relationships among all objects in a given space, including themselves.

allocentric In Piaget's terminology, able to objectively consider relationships among objects or people.

Research generally supports Piaget's timetable of spatial development (Haith & Benson, 1998). In a classic longitudinal study (Acredolo, 1978), infants were conditioned, at the sound of a buzzer, to turn their heads to one side to see a woman in a window playing with toys. Then the infants were turned around so that the window in which the woman appeared was now on their other side. At 6 months, the infants still turned their heads the same way as before, even though they could no longer see the woman in the window (an apparently egocentric response); but by 16 months, they turned their heads to the side where the woman now appeared, even though that was not the direction in which they had been conditioned to look (an apparently allocentric response).

However, it is not clear whether the increasing accuracy of spatial judgments stems from a decline in egocentrism, as Piaget maintained, or merely from a growing ability to coordinate information about the infant's own position with information about the environment. Some researchers suggest that improvements in spatial understanding near the end of the first year are related to the development of self-locomotion (Bremner, 1989; refer to Box 6-1 in Chapter 6). Crawling and walking may help babies learn that certain features of the environment are fixed and can be used as landmarks.

In the longitudinal study just described (Acredolo, 1978), 11-month-olds, after their position had been reversed, were more likely to turn toward the window in which the woman appeared if they had a direct landmark to guide them—a large yellow star framing the window. But if the landmark was indirect—that is, located on a wall near the window—the infants were less able to use it to guide their response. Most other studies support this finding: without a landmark directly marking the target location, infants younger than 9 to 11 months tend to repeat an earlier response, even if their position has changed (Acredolo, 1990; Bushnell, McKenzie, Lawrence, & Connell, 1995).

Symbolic Development and Spatial Thinking As Piaget suggested, the growth of representational thinking enables children to make more accurate judgments about objects and spatial relationships. In both the United States and Africa's Ivory Coast, infants were observed using their hands to explore pictures as if they were objects—feeling, rubbing, patting, or grasping them or attempting to lift a depicted object off the page. Not until about 19 months—according to Piaget, the dawn of representational thought—did they show, by pointing at a picture of a bear or telephone while saying its name ("beh" or "teltone"), an understanding that a picture is a representation of something else (DeLoache, Pierroutsakos, Uttal, Rosengren, & Gottlieb, 1998).

Two-year-olds can use this understanding to guide them to the actual location of something shown in a photograph (Suddendorf, 2003). But although U.S. children this age generally spend a good deal of time watching television, they may not at first realize that what they are seeing is a representation of reality. In one experiment, 2- and 2½-year-olds watched on a video monitor as an adult hid an object in an adjoining room. When taken to the room, the 2½-year-olds found the hidden object easily, but 2-year-olds could not. Yet the younger children did find the object if they had watched through a window as it was being hidden (Troseth & DeLoache, 1998). Apparently, what the 2-year-olds lacked was representational understanding of screen images. In a follow-up experiment, 2-year-olds watched themselves "live" on home videos while their parents pointed out that what they saw was actually happening. After two weeks of this training, the children were able to find an object after seeing it hidden on video (Troseth, 2003).

Young children also have difficulty using scale models, apparently because they tend to think of the model as an object in itself rather than a representation of something else (DeLoache, 2000). In one experiment, 2½-year-olds who were told that a "shrinking machine" had shrunk a room to the size of a miniature model were more successful in finding a toy hidden in the room on the basis of its position in the model than were children the same age who were told that the "little room" was just like the "big room." According to the **dual representation hypothesis,** what makes the second task harder is that it requires a child to mentally represent both the symbol (the "little room") and its relationship to the thing it stands for (the "big room") at the same time. With the "shrinking machine," children do not have to perform this dual operation, because they are told that the room and the model are one and the same. Three-year-olds do not seem to have this problem with models (DeLoache, Miller, & Rosengren, 1997).

dual representation hypothesis Proposal that children under the age of 3 have difficulty grasping spatial relationships because of the need to keep more than one mental representation in mind at the same time.

The dual representation hypothesis has practical implications. It means that preschool teachers should not assume that children will understand when they use concrete objects, such as blocks of varying sizes, to stand for abstract concepts, such as numerical relationships.

Estimation of Scale When 2-year-old Samantha tried to climb into her doll's buggy, her father laughed. But research has found that *scale errors*—momentary misperceptions of the relative sizes of objects—are common among toddlers. In one study, 25 out of 54 eighteen- to thirty-month-olds were videotaped trying to slide down tiny slides, sit in dollhouse chairs, and squeeze into miniature toy cars after similar, child-sized objects were removed from their playroom. Such scale errors were clearly distinguishable from pretend play with the objects (DeLoache, Uttal, & Rosengren, 2004).

The researchers suggested that two different brain systems normally work together during interactions with familiar objects. One system enables the child to recognize and categorize an object ("That's a buggy") and plan what to do with it ("I'm going to lie in it"). A separate system may be involved in perceiving the size of the object and using this information to control actions pertaining to it. A breakdown of the "teamwork" between these immature brain systems may explain young children's frequent scale errors. Another possible explanation is a lack of impulse control due to immaturity of the prefrontal cortex (DeLoache et al., 2004).

What Abilities May Develop Earlier Than Piaget Thought?

According to Piaget, the journey from reflex behavior to the beginnings of thought is a long, slow one. For a year and a half or so, babies learn only from their senses and movements; not until the last half of the second year do they make the breakthrough to conceptual thought. Although research has supported some of Piaget's findings, there is growing evidence that certain limitations Piaget saw in infants' early cognitive abilities may instead have reflected immature linguistic and motor skills. Researchers using simplified tasks and modern research tools have built an impressive case for babies' cognitive strengths. Their findings, some of them controversial, suggest that even very young infants may form mental representations—images or memories of objects not physically present—an ability Piaget said does not emerge before 18 months. Two of the abilities on which such research has focused are imitation and object permanence.

Imitation Piaget maintained that **invisible imitation**—imitation using parts of the body that a baby cannot see, such as the mouth—develops at about 9 months, after **visible imitation,** the use of hands or feet, for example, which babies can see. Yet in a series of studies by Andrew Meltzoff and M. Keith Moore (1983, 1989), babies less than 72 hours old appeared to imitate adults by opening their mouths and sticking out their tongues as well as by duplicating adults' head movements.

invisible imitation Imitation with parts of one's body that one cannot see.

visible imitation Imitation with parts of one's body that one can see.

However, a review of Meltzoff's and Moore's work and of attempts to replicate it found clear, consistent evidence of only one apparently imitative movement—sticking out the tongue (Anisfeld, 1996)—and that response disappears by about 2 months of age. Since it seems unlikely that an early and short-lived imitative capacity would be limited to one gesture, some researchers have instead suggested that the tongue thrust may serve other purposes, perhaps as an early attempt to interact with the mother or simply as exploratory behavior aroused by the intriguing sight of an adult tongue (Bjorklund, 1997; S. S. Jones, 1996). Pending further research, then, the age when invisible imitation begins will remain in doubt.

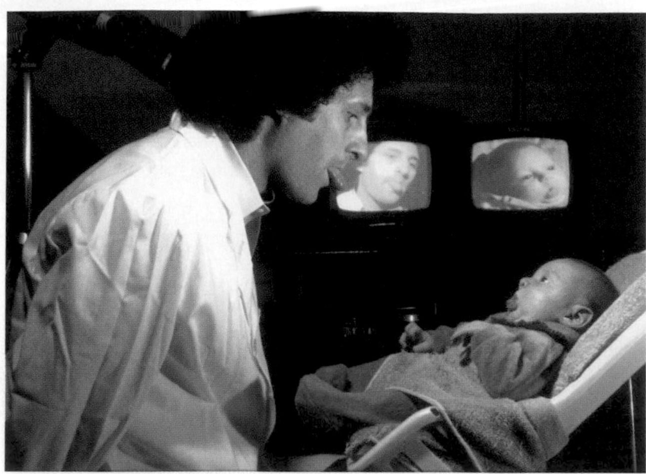

Is this infant imitating the researcher's stuck-out tongue? Studies by Andrew N. Meltzoff suggest that infants as young as 2 weeks are capable of invisible imitation. But other researchers found that only the youngest babies make this response, suggesting that the tongue movement may merely be exploratory behavior.

Piaget also held that children under 18 months lack the cognitive memory structures to engage in *deferred imitation* of an act they saw some time before. But Piaget may have underestimated infants' and toddlers' memory because of their limited ability to talk about what they remember. Babies as young as 6 *weeks* have imitated an adult's facial movements after a 24-hour delay, in the presence of the same adult, who this time was expressionless. This suggests that very young babies can retain a mental representation of an event (Meltzoff & Moore, 1994, 1998). Deferred imitation of novel or complex events seems to begin by 6 to 9 months (Meltzoff & Moore, 1998; Bauer, 2002). Thus, the findings on deferred imitation agree with those on operant conditioning (Rovee-Collier, 1999); infants do seem capable of remembering after a delay.

In **elicited imitation,** researchers induce infants and toddlers to imitate a specific series of actions they have seen but not necessarily done before. The initial demonstration may be accompanied by a simple verbal explanation (Bauer, 1996, 2002; Bauer, Wenner, Dropik, & Wewerka, 2000; Bauer, Wiebe, Carver, Waters, & Nelson, 2003). After a one-month delay, with no further demonstration or explanation, 42 to 45 percent of 9-month-olds can reproduce a simple two-step procedure, such as dropping a toy car down a vertical chute and then pushing the car with a rod to make it roll to the end of a track and turn on a light (Bauer, 2002; Bauer et al., 2003). One study reliably predicted individual differences in performance of this task from scans of the infants' brains as they looked at photos of the same procedure a week after first seeing it. The memory traces of infants who could not repeat the procedure in the right order were less robust, indicating that they had failed to consolidate the memory for long-term storage (Bauer et al., 2003).

elicited imitation Research method in which infants or toddlers are induced to imitate a specific series of actions they have seen but not necessarily done before.

Elicited imitation is much more reliable during the second year of life; nearly 8 out of 10 toddlers 13 to 20 months old can repeat an unfamiliar, multistep sequence (such as putting together a metal gong and causing it to ring) as much as a year later (Bauer, 1996; Bauer et al., 2000). Prior practice helps to reactivate children's memories, especially if some new items have been substituted for the original ones (Hayne, Barr, & Herbert, 2003). Four factors seem to determine young children's long-term recall: (1) the number of times a sequence of events has been experienced, (2) whether the child actively participates or merely observes, (3) whether the child is given verbal reminders of the experience, and (4) whether the sequence of events occurs in a logical, causal order (Bauer et al., 2000).

Apparently, then, the ability to talk about an event is not necessary for a child to remember it. However, as we will discuss in Chapter 10, verbal skills may affect whether memories can be carried forward into later life.

Object Permanence Piaget may have underestimated young infants' grasp of object permanence because of his testing methods. Babies may fail to search for hidden objects because they cannot yet carry out a two-step or two-handed sequence of actions, such as moving a cushion or lifting the cover of a box before grasping the object. But when given repeated opportunities, over a period of one to three months, to explore, manipulate, and learn about such a task, infants in the last half of their first year can do so (Bojczyk & Corbetta, 2004).

When object permanence is tested with a more age-appropriate procedure, in which the object is hidden only by darkness and thus can be retrieved in one motion, infants in the third substage (4 to 8 months) perform surprisingly well. In one study, 6½-month-olds saw a ball drop down a chute and land in one of two spots, each identifiable by a distinctive sound. When the light was turned off and the procedure was repeated, the babies reached for the ball in the appropriate location, guided only by the sound (Goubet & Clifton, 1998). This showed that they knew the ball continued to exist and could tell where it had gone.

What's your view?

- What comments might Piaget have made about Darwin's diary entries on his son's early cognitive development?
- On the basis of observations by Piaget and the research they inspired, what factors would you consider in designing or purchasing a toy for an infant or toddler?

Table 7-4 Key Developments of the Sensorimotor Stage

Concept or Skill	Piaget's View	More Recent Findings
Object permanence	Develops gradually between the third and sixth substage. Infants in the fourth substage (8–12 months) make the A, not-B error.	Infants as young as 3½ months (second substage) seem to show object knowledge, though interpretation of findings is in dispute. The A, not-B error may persist into the second year or longer.
Spatial knowledge	Development of object concept and spatial knowledge is linked to self-locomotion and coordination of visual and motor information.	Research supports Piaget's timetable and the relationship of spatial judgments to the decline of egocentrism. Link to motor development is less clear.
Causality	Develops slowly between 4–6 months and 1 year, based on an infant's discovery, first of effects of own actions and then of effects of outside forces.	Some evidence suggests early awareness of specific causal events in the physical world, but general understanding of causality may be slower to develop.
Number	Depends on use of symbols which begins in the sixth substage (18–24 months).	Infants as young as 5 months may recognize and mentally manipulate small numbers, but interpretation of findings is in dispute.
Categorization	Depends on representational thinking, which develops during the sixth substage (18–24 months).	Infants as young as 3 months seem to recognize perceptual categories, and 7-month-olds categorize by function.
Imitation	Invisible imitation develops around 9 months; deterred imitation begins after development of mental representations in the sixth substage (18–24 months).	Controversial studies have found invisible imitation of facial expressions in newborns and deferred imitation as early as 6 weeks. Deferred imitation of complex activities seems to exist as early as 6 months.

Methods based only on infants' looking behavior eliminate the need for *any* motor activity and thus can be used at even earlier ages. As we will discuss in the next major section of this chapter, controversial research since the late 1970s, using information-processing methodology, suggests that infants as young as 3 or 4 months old seem not only to have a sense of object permanence, but also to understand causality and categorization, to have a rudimentary concept of number, and to know other principles governing the physical world. (Table 7-4 compares these findings with Piaget's views; refer back to this table as you read on.)

In some ways, then, infants and toddlers seem to be more cognitively competent than Piaget imagined and to show earlier signs of conceptual thought. This does not mean that infants come into the world with minds fully formed. As Piaget observed, immature forms of cognition seem to give way to more mature forms. We can see this, for example, in the errors young infants make in searching for hidden objects. But Piaget may have been wrong in his emphasis on motor experience as the primary "engine" of cognitive growth. Infants' perceptions are far ahead of their motor abilities, and today's methods enable researchers to make observations and inferences about those perceptions. How perception relates to cognition is a major area of investigation, as we will see in the next section.

Checkpoint

Can you . . .

- ✔ Summarize major developments during the six substages of the sensorimotor stage?
- ✔ Explain how primary, secondary, and tertiary circular reactions work?
- ✔ Tell why the development of representational ability is important?
- ✔ Summarize Piaget's views on object permanence and spatial knowledge?
- ✔ Explain why Piaget may have underestimated some of infants' cognitive abilities, and discuss the implications of more recent research?

Studying Cognitive Development: Newer Approaches

information-processing approach Approach to the study of cognitive development by analyzing processes involved in perceiving and handling information.

cognitive neuroscience approach Approach to the study of cognitive development that links brain processes with cognitive ones.

social-contextual approach Approach to the study of cognitive development by focusing on environmental influences, particularly parents and other caregivers.

During the past few decades, researchers have turned to three new approaches to add to our knowledge about infants' and toddlers' cognitive development:

- The **information-processing approach** focuses on the processes involved in perception, learning, memory, and problem solving. It seeks to discover what children do with information from the time they encounter it until they use it.
- The **cognitive neuroscience approach** examines the "hardware" of the central nervous system. It seeks to identify what brain structures are involved in specific aspects of cognition.
- The **social-contextual approach** examines environmental aspects of the learning process, particularly the role of parents and other caregivers.

Guidepost 4

How can we measure infants' ability to process information, and how does this ability relate to future intelligence?

Information-Processing Approach: Perceptions and Representations

Like the psychometric approach, information-processing theory is concerned with individual differences in intelligent behavior. Unlike the psychometric approach, it aims to describe the mental processes involved in acquiring and remembering information or solving problems rather than merely inferring differences in mental functioning from answers given or problems solved.

Information-processing research uses new methods to test ideas about cognitive development that sprang from the psychometric and Piagetian approaches. For example, information-processing researchers analyze the separate parts of a complex task, such as Piaget's object search tasks, to figure out what abilities are necessary for each part of the task and at what age these abilities develop. Information-processing researchers also measure and draw inferences from what infants pay attention to and for how long.

Habituation

At about 6 weeks, Stefan lies peacefully in his crib near a window, sucking a pacifier. It is a cloudy day, but suddenly the sun breaks through, and an angular shaft of light appears on the end of the crib. Stefan stops sucking for a few moments, staring at the pattern of light and shade. Then he looks away and starts sucking again.

We don't know what was going on in Stefan's mind when he saw the shaft of light, but we can tell by his sucking and looking behavior at what point he began paying attention and when he stopped. These simple behaviors can be indicators of sensory perception and discrimination and even of future intelligence.

habituation Type of learning in which familiarity with a stimulus reduces, slows, or stops a response.

Much information-processing research with infants is based on **habituation,** a type of learning in which repeated or continuous exposure to a stimulus (such as the shaft of light) reduces attention to that stimulus. In other words, familiarity breeds loss of interest. As infants habituate, they transform the novel into the familiar, the unknown into the known (Rheingold, 1985).

Researchers study habituation in newborns by repeatedly presenting a stimulus (usually a sound or visual pattern) and then monitoring such responses as heart rate, sucking, eye movements, and brain activity. A baby who has been sucking typically stops when the stimulus is first presented and does not start again until after it has ended. After the same sound or sight has been presented again and again, it loses its novelty and no longer causes the baby to stop sucking. Resumption of uninterrupted sucking shows that the infant has habituated to the stimulus. A new sight or sound, however, will capture the baby's attention, and the baby will again stop sucking. This increased response to a new stimulus is called **dishabituation.**

dishabituation Increase in responsiveness after presentation of a new stimulus.

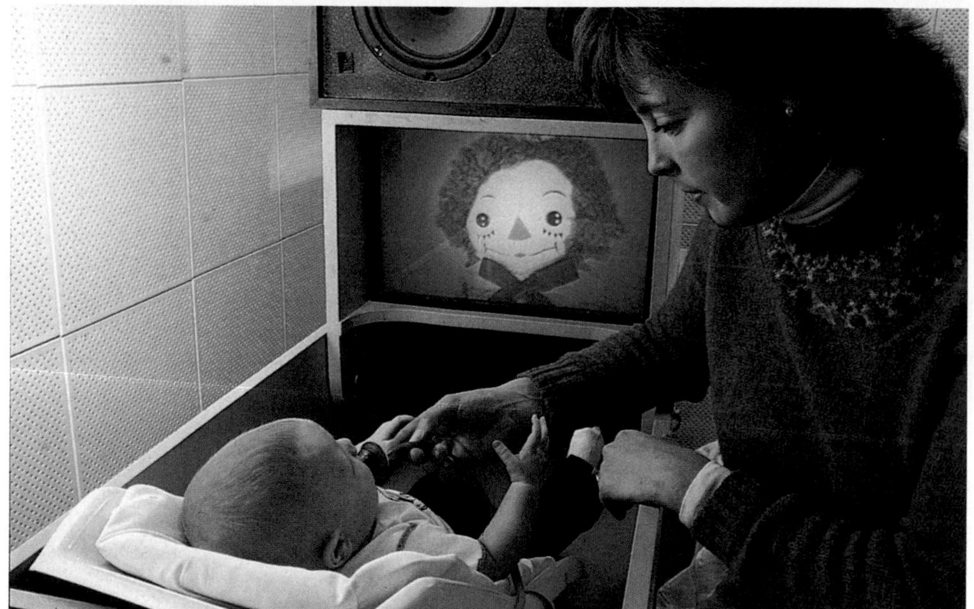

Can this baby tell the difference between Raggedy Ann and Raggedy Andy? This researcher may find out by seeing whether the baby has habituated—gotten used—to one face (as shown by sucking on a nipple) and then stops sucking on the nipple when a new face appears, showing recognition of the difference.

Researchers gauge the efficiency of infants' information processing by measuring how quickly babies habituate to familiar stimuli, how fast their attention recovers when they are exposed to new stimuli, and how much time they spend looking at the new and the old. Efficiency of habituation correlates with later signs of cognitive development, such as a preference for complexity, rapid exploration of the environment, sophisticated play, quick problem solving, and the ability to match pictures. In fact, as we will see, speed of habituation and other information-processing abilities show promise as predictors of intelligence (Bornstein & Sigman, 1986; Colombo, 1993; McCall & Carriger, 1993).

Visual and Auditory Processing Abilities

The amount of time a baby spends looking at different kinds of sights is considered a measure of **visual preference,** which is based on the ability to make visual distinctions. Babies less than 2 days old seem to prefer curved lines to straight lines, complex patterns to simple patterns, three-dimensional objects to two-dimensional objects, pictures of faces (or facelike configurations) to pictures of other things, and new sights to familiar ones (Fantz, 1963, 1964, 1965; Fantz, Fagen, & Miranda, 1975; Fantz & Nevis, 1967; Turati, Simion, Milani, & Umilta, 2002). The latter tendency is called *novelty preference.*

visual preference Tendency of infants to spend more time looking at one sight than another.

Visual recognition memory can be measured by showing an infant two stimuli side by side, one familiar and one novel. A longer gaze at the new stimulus indicates that the infant recognizes the other stimulus as something seen before. Visual recognition memory depends on comparing incoming information with information the infant already has—in other words, on the ability to form and refer to mental representations of previous visual experience (P. R. Zelazo, Kearsley, & Stack, 1995).

visual-recognition memory Ability to distinguish a familiar visual stimulus from an unfamiliar one when shown both at the same time.

Contrary to Piaget's view, habituation and novelty preference studies suggest that at least a rudimentary representational ability exists at birth or very soon after and quickly becomes more efficient. Individual differences in efficiency of information processing reflect the speed with which infants form and refer to such mental images. When shown two sights at the same time, infants who quickly shift attention from one to another tend to have better recognition memory and stronger novelty preference than infants who take longer looks at a single sight (Jankowski, Rose, & Feldman, 2001; Rose, Feldman, & Jankowski, 2001; Stoecker, Colombo, Frick, & Allen, 1998).

Researchers also study how attention itself develops (Colombo, 2001). From birth to 8 or 10 weeks, the amount of time infants typically gaze at a new sight increases. Between 3 and about 6 months, looking time becomes shorter as infants learn to scan objects more efficiently and shift attention. After 7 months, when sustaining attention becomes more voluntary and task oriented, looking time plateaus or slightly increases (Colombo, 2002). Five-month-olds have been trained to distribute attention more efficiently and thus to improve processing (Jankowski et al., 2001). The capacity for *joint attention,* or *joint perceptual exploration*—which may contribute to social interaction, language acquisition, and the understanding of others' mental states—develops by 12 months, when babies respond to adults' gaze by looking or pointing in the same direction (Brooks & Meltzoff, 2002).

Watching television in infancy and toddlerhood may impede attentional development (see Box 7-2). In a nationally representative longitudinal study, the more hours children spent watching television at ages 1 and 3, the more likely they were to have attentional problems at age 7 (Christakis, Zimmerman, DiGiuseppe, & McCarty, 2004).

Auditory discrimination studies also are based on attentional preference. Such studies have found that newborns can tell sounds they have already heard from those they have not. In one study, infants who heard a certain speech sound one day after birth appeared to remember that sound 24 hours later, as shown by a reduced tendency to turn their heads toward the sound and even a tendency to turn away (Swain, Zelazo, & Clifton, 1993). Indeed, as discussed in Chapter 4, newborns even seem to remember sounds they heard in the womb.

Piaget believed that the senses are unconnected at birth and are only gradually integrated through experience. If so, this integration begins almost immediately. The fact that neonates will look at a source of sound shows that they associate hearing and sight. A more sophisticated ability is **cross-modal transfer,** the ability to use information gained from one sense to guide another—as when a person negotiates a dark room by feeling for the location of familiar objects or identifies objects by sight after feeling them with eyes closed. In one study, 1-month-olds showed that they could transfer information gained from sucking (touch) to vision. When the infants saw a rigid object (a hard plastic cylinder) and a flexible one (a wet sponge) being manipulated by a pair of hands, the infants looked longer at the object they had just sucked (Gibson & Walker, 1984). The use of cross-modal transfer to judge some other properties of objects, such as shape, seems to develop a few months later (Maurer, Stager, & Mondloch, 1999). By 5 to 7 months, infants can link the feeling of their legs kicking to a visual image of that motion (Schmuckler & Fairhall, 2001).

cross-modal transfer Ability to use information gained by one sense to guide another.

Speed of processing increases rapidly during the first year of life. It continues to increase during the second and third years, as toddlers become better able to separate new information from information they have already processed (P. R. Zelazo et al., 1995). Children who were born preterm or with very low birth weight tend to process information more slowly than those born full term (Rose & Feldman, 2000; Rose, Feldman, & Jankowski, 2002).

A young child who watches television several hours a day may develop attentional problems and be late in learning to read.

Information Processing as a Predictor of Intelligence

Because of the weak correlation between infants' scores on developmental tests and their later IQ, many psychologists believed that the cognitive functioning of infants had little in common with that of older children and adults—in other words, that there was a discontinuity in cognitive development (Kopp & McCall, 1982). Piaget believed this too. However, when researchers assess how infants and toddlers process information, some aspects of mental development seem to be fairly continuous from birth (McCall & Carriger, 1993). Children who, from the start, are efficient at taking in and interpreting sensory information later score well on intelligence tests.

In many longitudinal studies, habituation and attention-recovery abilities during the first 6 months to 1 year of life were moderately useful in predicting childhood IQ. So was visual recognition memory (Bornstein & Sigman, 1986; Colombo, 1993; McCall & Carriger, 1993). In one study, a combination of visual recognition memory at 7 months and cross-modal transfer at 1 year predicted IQ at age 11 and also showed a modest (but nonetheless remarkable after 10 years!) relationship to processing speed and memory at that age (Rose & Feldman, 1995, 1997).

Visual reaction time and *visual anticipation* can be measured by the *visual expectation paradigm.* In this research design, a series of computer-generated pictures briefly appears,

The Everyday World

Box 7-2 *Do Infants and Toddlers Watch Too Much Television?*

Six-month-old Jenny reclines in her bouncy seat, watching a Baby Einstein DVD. She bounces up and down, claps, and laughs out loud as bright images flash across the screen. Jenny has been watching Baby Einstein videos since she was 5 weeks old.

Jenny is neither precocious nor unusual, according to a nationally representative random-dialed survey of 1,000 parents of preschoolers, sponsored by the Henry J. Kaiser Family Foundation. On a typical day, 59 percent of children under 2 watch television, 42 percent watch a video or DVD, 5 percent use a computer, and 3 percent play video games. These children spend an average of two hours and five minutes a day in front of a screen, more than twice as much time as they spend being read to (see figure).

An avalanche of media geared to infants and toddlers has occurred since the late 1990s: the first television show targeting children as young as 12 months, computer games with special keyboard toppers for infants as young as 9 months, and educational videotapes and DVDs (with accompanying books, flashcards, and puppets) aimed at infants from 1 to 18 months old.

According to the Kaiser survey, 74 percent of children under 2 watch television, and 26 percent have TV sets in their bedrooms. Two-thirds (66 percent) of children 3 and younger turn on the TV by themselves, 52 percent change channels with a remote device, and 30 percent put in a video or DVD by themselves.

Babies in whose households television is frequently on are more likely to start watching before their first birthday than babies not exposed to such heavy doses of TV. The "heavy watchers" are more likely to watch every day, watch for a longer time, and spend less time being read to. They also are less likely to learn to read by age 6.

All of this flies in the face of recommendations by the American Academy of Pediatrics Committee on Public Education (2001) that children under 2 be discouraged from watching television and instead be engaged in interactive activities that promote brain development, such as talking, playing, singing, and reading with parents. Most parents in the survey expressed faith in the educational value of the media and said their children were more likely to imitate positive behaviors, such as sharing and helping, than aggressive behaviors. Parents who value and exhibit positive behavior tend to steer children toward stories, films, and television programs that depict such behavior (Singer & Singer, 1998).

Further study is needed to find out whether this is so. Researchers also need to investigate such questions as whether the presence of background media interferes with infants' and toddlers' concentration on physical coordination and language development; whether time spent with media takes away time from playing outdoors, reading, or interacting with parents; whether it contributes to a sedentary lifestyle; whether video and computer game playing helps visual and spatial skills or risks eyestrain or ergonomic problems; how various types of media impact cognitive development and attention span; and what is the extent and effect of young children's exposure to noneducational content.

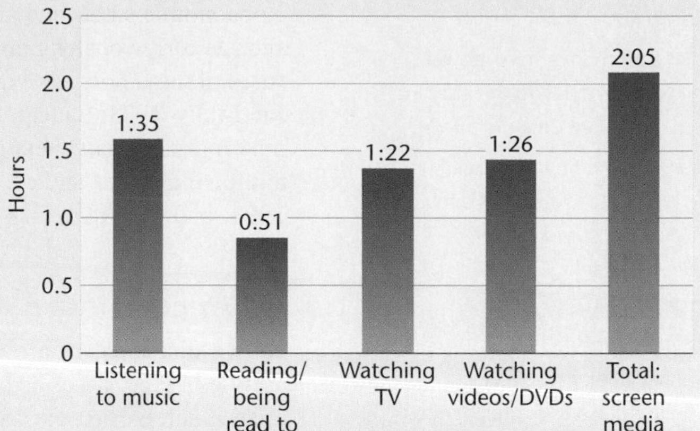

Average amount of time children under 2 spend on media and other activities in a typical day, according to mothers' reports. These data include only children who participate in these activities. The number of children this age who use a computer or play video games on a typical day is too small for reliable data on time spent with those media.

Source: Rideout et al., 2003.

What's your view ?

At what age would you let a baby watch television or a videotape or play a computer game, and what restrictions, if any, would you place on such activities?

Check it out !

For more information on this topic, go to **http://www.kff.org/entmedia102803nr.cfm.** This is the URL of the Kaiser Foundation report discussed in this box.

Source: Unless otherwise referenced, this box is based on Rideout, Vandewater, & Wartella, 2003.

some on the right and some on the left sides of an infant's peripheral visual field. The same sequence of pictures is repeated several times. The infant's eye movements are measured to see how quickly his or her gaze shifts to a picture that has just appeared (reaction time) or to the place where the infant expects the next picture to appear (anticipation). These measurements are thought to indicate attentiveness and processing speed, as well as the tendency to form expectations on the basis of experience. In a longitudinal study, visual reaction time and visual anticipation at 3½ months correlated with IQ at age 4 (Dougherty & Haith, 1997). Reaction time and anticipation seem to improve up to 8 or 9 months of age (Reznick, Chawarska, & Betts, 2000).

All in all, there is much evidence that the abilities infants use to process sensory information are related to the cognitive abilities intelligence tests measure. Still, we need to be cautious in interpreting these findings. Most of the studies used small samples. Also, the predictability of childhood IQ from measures of habituation and recognition memory is only modest. It is no higher than the predictability from parental educational level and socioeconomic status and not as high as the predictability from some other infant behaviors, such as early vocalization. Furthermore, predictions based on information-processing measures alone do not take into account the influence of environmental factors (Colombo & Janowsky, 1998; Laucht, Esser, & Schmidt, 1994; McCall & Carriger, 1993). For example, maternal responsiveness in early infancy seems to play a part in the link between early attentional abilities and cognitive abilities later in childhood (Bornstein & Tamis-LeMonda, 1994) and even at age 18 (Sigman, Cohen, & Beckwith, 1997).

Checkpoint

Can you . . .

- ✔ Summarize three newer approaches to the study of cognitive development?
- ✔ Explain how habituation measures the efficiency of infants' information processing?
- ✔ Identify several early perceptual and processing abilities that serve as predictors of intelligence?

Information Processing and the Development of Thought

As we discussed in a previous section, evidence suggests that several of the cognitive abilities Piaget described as developing toward the end of the sensorimotor stage actually arise much earlier. Research based on infants' visual processing—independent of motor abilities—has given developmental scientists a new window into the timing of such cognitive developments as causality, categorization, object permanence, and number, all of which depend on formation of mental representations (refer back to Table 7-3).

Guidepost 5

When do babies begin to think about characteristics of the physical world?

Causality An understanding of *causality,* the principle that one event causes another, is important because it "allows people to predict and control their world" (L. B. Cohen, Rundell, Spellman, & Cashon, 1999). Piaget believed that this understanding develops slowly during the first year of life. At about 4 to 6 months, as infants become able to grasp objects, they begin to recognize that they can act on their environment. Thus, said Piaget, the concept of causality is rooted in a dawning awareness of the power of one's own intentions. However, according to Piaget, infants do not yet know that causes must come before effects; and not until close to 1 year do they realize that forces outside of themselves can make things happen.

Some information-processing research suggests that a mechanism for recognizing causality may exist much earlier (Mandler, 1998). Infants 6½ months old have shown by habituation and dishabituation that they seem to see a difference between events that are the immediate cause of other events (such as a brick striking a second brick, which is then pushed out of position) and events that occur with no apparent cause (such as a brick moving away from another brick without having been struck by it). The researcher who conducted these experiments proposed that babies have an innate "brain module" for detecting causal motion or may develop it at an early age (Leslie, 1982, 1984).

Other researchers replicated these findings with 6½-month-olds, but not with younger infants, casting doubt on the brain module hypothesis (L. B. Cohen & Amsel, 1998). On the basis of additional experiments with infants of different ages looking at a variety of objects moving at varying trajectories, these investigators attribute the growth of causal understanding to a gradual improvement in information-processing skills. By 7 months, infants may make causal interpretations of a particular set of objects and simple events, but not until 10 to 15 months do they perceive causality in more complex circumstances involving a chain of several events. As infants accumulate more information about how objects behave, they are better able to see causality as a general principle operating in a variety of situations (L. B. Cohen & Amsel, 1998; L. B. Cohen & Oakes, 1993; L. B. Cohen et al., 1999; Oakes, 1994).

Categorization Dividing the world into meaningful categories is vital to thinking about objects or concepts and their relationships. According to Piaget, the ability to classify, or group things into categories, does not appear until the sixth substage, around 18 months. Yet, by looking longer at items in a new category, even 3-month-olds seem to know, for example, that a dog is not a cat (Quinn, Eimas, & Rosenkrantz, 1993).

At first infants seem to categorize on the basis of perceptual features (such as shape, color, and pattern); but toward the end of the first year their categories become more conceptual, based on real-world knowledge (Oakes, Coppage, & Dingel, 1997), particularly of function (Mandler, 1998; Mandler & McDonough, 1993, 1996, 1998). Seven- to 11-month-olds seem to realize that a bird with wide wings is not in the same category as an airplane,

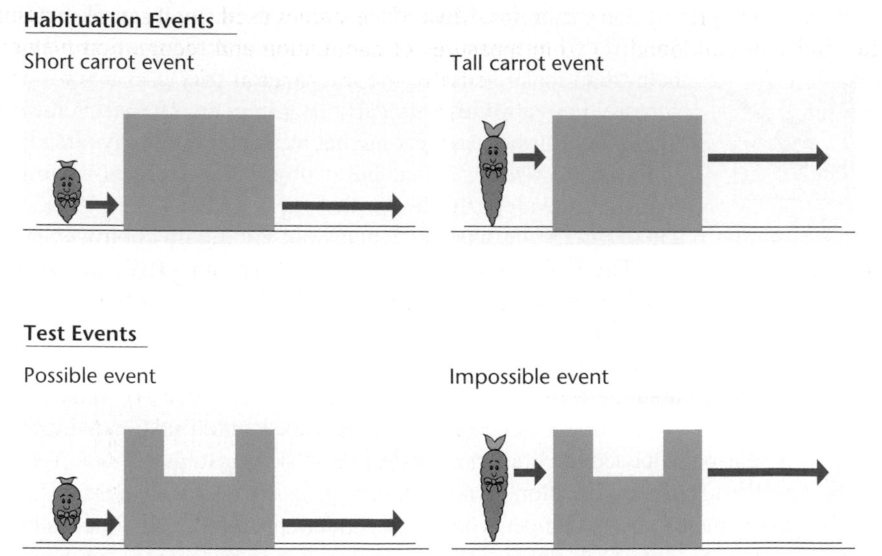

Figure 7-4
How early do infants show object permanence? In this violation-of-expectations experiment, 3½-month-olds watched a short carrot and then a tall carrot slide along a track, disappear behind a screen, and then reappear. After they became accustomed to seeing these events, the opaque screen was replaced by a screen with a large notch at the top. The short carrot did not appear in the notch when passing behind the screen; the tall carrot, which should have appeared in the notch, also did not. The babies looked longer at the tall than at the short carrot event, suggesting that they were surprised that the tall carrot did not reappear.
Source: Baillargeon & DeVos, 1991.

even though they may look somewhat similar and both can fly (Mandler & McDonough, 1993). In one series of experiments, 10- and 11-month-olds recognized that chairs with zebra-striped upholstery belong in the category of furniture, not animals (Pauen, 2002).

Results vary depending on the methodology of the study, the perceptual similarity of the items shown to the infant, and the context in which they are presented (Oakes, Coppage, & Dingel, 1997; Oakes & Madole, 2000). Infants who are allowed to touch and manipulate objects rather than just look at them are more likely to form functional categories (Madole, Oakes, & Cohen, 1993).

In the second year, language becomes a factor. Hearing an experimenter name an object and/or point out its function can help 14- to 18-month-olds with category formation (Booth & Waxman, 2002). Language learning also may desensitize infants to categorical distinctions not recognized by their own language. In one study based on novelty preference, 5-month-old infants from native English-speaking homes seemed to distinguish between tight fit (for example, a cap on a pen) and loose fit (a pen on a table), a distinction recognized in Korean language but not in English and one that English-speaking adults did not make. This suggests, the experimenters concluded, that babies have formed concepts about categories in the physical world before learning the words to express them (Hespos & Spelke, 2004).

Object Permanence **Violation-of-expectations** research begins with a familiarization phase, in which infants see an event or series of events happen normally. After the infant is habituated to this procedure, the event is changed in a way that conflicts with (violates) normal expectations. An infant's tendency to look longer at the changed event is interpreted as evidence that the infant recognizes it as surprising. Research using the violation-of-expectations method suggests that infants begin to think and reason about the physical world much earlier than Piaget proposed.

violation-of-expectations
Research method in which dishabituation to a stimulus that conflicts with experience is taken as evidence that an infant recognizes the new stimulus as surprising.

Using the violation-of-expectations method, Renée Baillargeon and her colleagues claim to have found evidence of object permanence in infants as young as 3½ months. The babies appeared surprised by the failure of a tall carrot that slid behind a screen of the same height to show up in a large notch in the upper part of the screen before appearing again on the other side (Baillargeon & DeVos, 1991; see Figure 7-4).

In other research, the ability to visually follow the path of a ball that briefly passed behind a box was present at 4 months and more firmly established at 6 months (Johnson et al., 2003). Of course, the perception that an object that disappears on one side of a visual barrier looks the same as the object that reappears on the other side need not imply cognitive knowledge that the object continues to exist behind the barrier (Meltzoff & Moore, 1998). Still, such research raises the possibility that at least a rudimentary form of object permanence may be present in the early months of life.

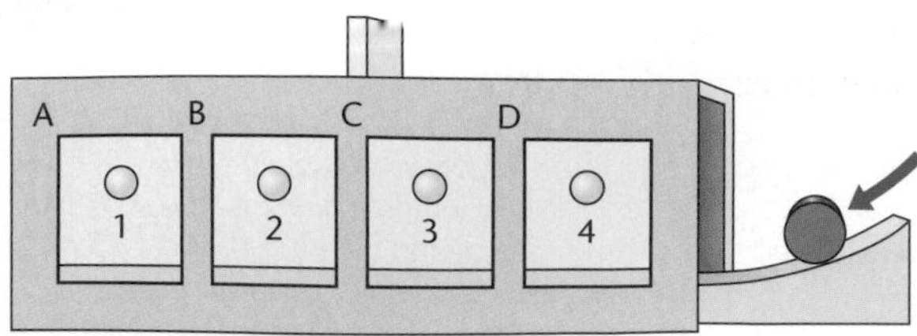

Figure 7-5

Apparatus for testing young children's object search abilities. When a barrier is placed behind the wall and the cylinder is set rolling, most 3-year-olds will open the right door to find where the cylinder stops. Most 2½-year-olds will open a different door.

Source: Hood, Cole-Davies, & Dias, 2003, Fig. 1.

On the basis of such research, it has been proposed that infants are born with reasoning abilities—*innate learning mechanisms* that help them make sense of the information they encounter—or may acquire these abilities very early (Baillargeon, 1994a). Some investigators go further, suggesting that infants at birth may already have intuitive *knowledge* about basic physical principles—knowledge that then develops further with experience (Spelke, 1994, 1998). These interpretations and conclusions are highly controversial.

The violation-of-expectations method also has been used with toddlers in object search tests, with puzzling results. In one study, children watched a cylinder roll down a ramp and disappear behind a wall containing a row of four doors. A barrier jutting up from behind the wall could be placed so that the cylinder would have to stop behind one of the doors (see Figure 7-5). When asked to find the cylinder, most 3-year-olds opened the correct door, but most 2½-year-olds did not. Yet, when watching an experimenter open the doors, the 2½-year-olds, like infants in such experiments, looked longer when the cylinder appeared in an "impossible" location. As with the A, not-B error reported earlier in this chapter, failure seemed to stem from the younger children's tendency to open the door where the cylinder had been found on previous trials (Hood, Cole-Davies, & Dias, 2003).

Additional studies were designed to narrow possible sources of young children's search errors. In one such study, the apparatus was translucent so that the children could visually follow a ball's path until it came to rest. At that point the wall containing the doors was lowered to conceal the ramp and the resting ball, and the children were asked to find the ball. The performance of 2½-year-olds improved in this situation, but 2-year-olds did little better than chance would predict—in part, it seems, because they did not keep their eyes on the point where the ball had landed. Also, it may be that the younger children could not translate their knowledge of what is physically possible into appropriate action (Keen, 2003).

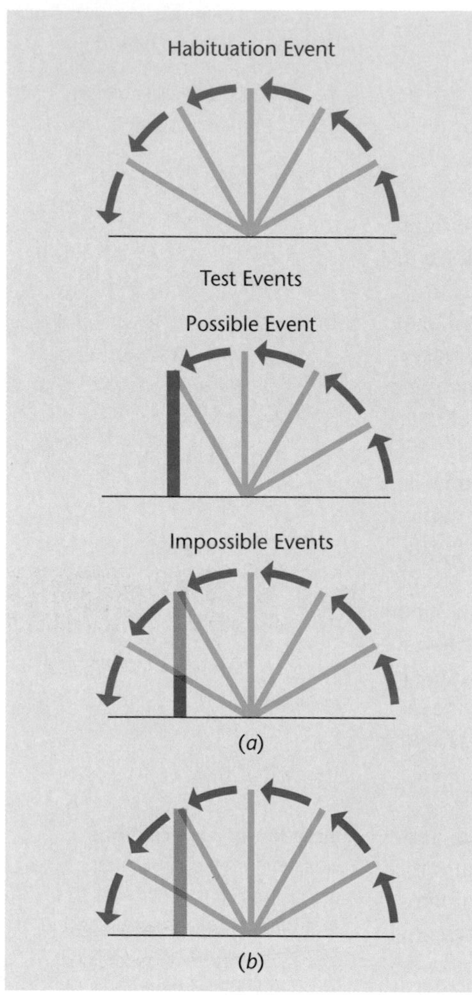

Figure 7-6

Test for infants' understanding of how a barrier works. Infants first become accustomed to seeing a "drawbridge" rotate 180 degrees on one edge. Then a box is placed beside the drawbridge. In the possible event, the drawbridge stops when it reaches the edge of the box. In the impossible events, the drawbridge rotates through part or all of the space occupied by the box. On the basis of how long they stare at each event, 4½-month-old infants seem to know that the drawbridge cannot pass through the entire box (*b*); but not until 6½ months do infants recognize that the drawbridge cannot pass through 80 percent of the box (*a*).

Source: Adapted from Baillargeon, 1994a.

Number Violation-of-expectations research suggests that an understanding of number may begin long before Piaget's sixth substage, when he claimed children first begin to use symbols. Karen Wynn (1992) tested whether 5-month-old babies can add and subtract small numbers of objects. The infants watched as Mickey Mouse dolls were placed behind a screen, and a doll was either added or taken away. The screen then was lifted to reveal either the expected number or a different number of dolls. In a series of experiments, the babies looked longer at surprising "wrong" answers than at expected "right" ones, suggesting (according to Wynn) that they had mentally "computed" the right answers. Other researchers who replicated these experiments got similar results (Baillargeon, 1994b; Koechlin, Dehaene, & Mehler, 1997; Simon, Hespos, & Rochat, 1995; Uller, Carey, Huntley-Fenner, & Klatt, 1999). Wynn (1996) also found that 6-month-olds seemed to know the difference between a puppet jumping twice in a row and three times in a row—numerical comparisons that could not be taken in at a glance.

According to Wynn, this research raises the possibility that numerical concepts are inborn—that when parents teach their babies numbers, they may only be teaching them the names ("one, two, three") for concepts the babies already know. However, this is mere speculation, since the infants in these studies were already 5 and 6 months old. Furthermore, infants may simply be responding perceptually to the puzzling presence of a doll they saw removed from behind the screen or the absence of a doll they saw placed there (Haith, 1998; Haith & Benson, 1998). Other studies suggest that, although infants do seem to discriminate visually between sets of, say, two and three objects, they merely notice differences in the overall contours, area, or collective mass of the sets of objects rather than compare the *number* of objects in the sets (Clearfield &

Mix, 1999; Mix, Huttenlocher, & Levine, 2002). Finally, a recent study—which Wynn (2000) disputes on procedural grounds—failed to replicate Wynn's findings consistently (Wakeley, Rivera, & Langer, 2000a).

Evaluating Violation-of-Expectations Research The interpretation of violation-of-expectations studies, like that of the causality studies, is controversial. Does an infant's visual interest in an "impossible" condition reveal a *conceptual* understanding of the way things work or merely a *perceptual* awareness that something unusual has happened? The fact that an infant looks longer at one scene than at another may show only that the infant can see a difference between the two. It does not show what the infant knows about the difference or that the infant is actually surprised. The "mental representation" the infant refers to may be no more than a brief sensory memory of something just seen. It's also possible that an infant, in becoming accustomed to the habituation event, develops the expectations that are then violated by the "surprising" event and did not have such knowledge or expectations before (Goubet & Clifton, 1998; Haith, 1998; Haith & Benson, 1998; Mandler, 1998; Munakata, 2001; Munakata, McClelland, Johnson, & Siegler, 1997).

Defenders of this research insist that a conceptual interpretation best accounts for the findings (Baillargeon, 1999; Spelke, 1998), but a recent variation on one of Baillargeon's experiments suggests otherwise. In her original research, Baillargeon (1994a) showed infants of various ages a "drawbridge" rotating 180 degrees. When the infants became habituated to the rotation, a barrier was introduced in the form of a box. At 4½ months, infants seemed to show (by longer looking) that they understood that the drawbridge could not move through the entire box (see Figure 7-6). Later investigators replicated the experiment but eliminated the box. Five-month-olds still looked longer at the 180-degree rotation than at a lesser degree of rotation, even though no barrier was present—suggesting that they simply were demonstrating a preference for greater movement (Rivera, Wakeley, & Langer, 1999). Until further research clarifies these issues, we must be cautious about inferring the existence of adultlike cognitive abilities from data that may have simpler explanations or may represent only partial achievement of mature abilities (Haith, 1998).

Checkpoint

Can you . . .

- ✔ Describe the violation-of-expectations research method, tell how and why it is used, and list some criticisms of it?
- ✔ Discuss four areas in which information-processing research seems to contradict Piaget's account of development?

Cognitive Neuroscience Approach: The Brain's Cognitive Structures

Guidepost 6

What can brain research reveal about the development of cognitive skills?

Piaget's belief that neurological maturation is a major factor in cognitive development is borne out by current brain research. Brain growth spurts (periods of rapid growth and development) coincide with changes in cognitive behavior similar to those Piaget described (Fischer & Rose, 1994, 1995).

Some researchers have recorded shifts in brain activity to determine which brain structures affect which cognitive functions and to chart developmental changes (Nelson & Monk, 2001). Studies of normal and brain-damaged adults point to two separate long-term memory systems—*explicit* and *implicit*—that acquire and store different kinds of information. **Explicit memory** is conscious or intentional recollection, usually of facts, names, events, or other things that people can state, or declare. **Implicit memory** refers to remembering that occurs without effort or even conscious awareness; it generally pertains to habits and skills, such as knowing how to throw a ball or ride a bicycle. Brain scans provide direct physical evidence of the location of these systems (Squire, 1992; Vargha-Khadem et al., 1997).

explicit memory Intentional and conscious memory, generally of facts, names, and events.

implicit memory Unconscious recall, generally of habits and skills; sometimes called *procedural memory.*

Integration and consolidation of brain structures produce developmental change. In early infancy, when the hippocampal structures largely responsible for memory storage are not fully formed, memories are relatively fleeting (Serres, 2001). The maturing of the hippocampus as well as the development of cortical structures coordinated by the hippocampal formation make longer-lasting memories possible (Bauer, 2002; Bauer et al., 2000, 2003). The hippocampal system continues to develop at least through the fifth year (Seress, 2001).

The *prefrontal cortex* (the large portion of the frontal lobe directly behind the forehead) is believed to control many aspects of cognition. This part of the brain develops more slowly than any other (M. H. Johnson, 1998). During the second half of the first year, the

LifeMap CD

Why is it important to study brain development? To find out, watch the "Brain Development and Cognition" video in Chapter 7 of your CD.

working memory Short term storage of information being actively processed

prefrontal cortex and associated circuitry develop the capacity for **working memory**—storage of information the brain is actively processing, or working on. It is in
emory that mental representations are prepared for, or recalled from, storage.
atively late appearance of working memory may be largely responsible for the
pment of object permanence, which seems to be seated in a rearward area of
l cortex (Nelson, 1995). By 12 months, this region may be developed enough
infant to avoid the A, not-B error by controlling the impulse to search in a
he object previously was found (Bell & Fox, 1992; Diamond, 1991).

explicit memory and working memory continue to develop beyond infancy,
rgence of the brain's memory structures underlines the importance of envi-
nulation during the first months of life. Social-contextual theorists and re-
particular attention to the impact of environmental influences.

textual Approach: Learning from Interactions ivers

enced by Vygotsky's sociocultural theory study how the cultural context
al interactions that may promote cognitive competence.

guided participation Participation of an adult in a child's activity in a manner that helps to structure the activity and to bring the child's understanding of it closer to that of the adult.

Guided participation refers to mutual interactions with adults that help structure children's activities and bridge the gap between a child's understanding and an adult's. This concept was inspired by Vygotsky's zone of proximal development (refer to Chapter 2) and his view of learning as a collaborative process. Guided participation often occurs in shared play and in everyday activities in which children learn informally the skills, knowledge, and values important in their culture.

In one cross-cultural study (Rogoff, Mistry, Göncü, & Mosier, 1993), researchers visited the homes of 14 one- to two-year-olds in each of four places: a Mayan town in Guatemala, a tribal village in India, and middle-class urban neighborhoods in Salt Lake City and Turkey. The investigators interviewed caregivers about their child-rearing practices and watched them help the toddlers learn to dress themselves and to play with unfamiliar toys.

Cultural differences affected the types of guided participation the researchers observed. In the Guatemalan town, where toddlers normally saw their mothers sewing and weaving at home to help support the family, and in the Indian village, where they accompanied their mothers at work in the fields, the children customarily played alone or with older siblings while the mother worked nearby. After initial demonstration and instruction, mostly nonverbal, in, for example, how to tie shoes, the children took over, while the parent or other caregiver remained available to help. The U.S. toddlers, who had full-time homemaker mothers or were in day care, interacted with their parents in the context of child's play rather than in the parents' work or social worlds. Caregivers spoke with the children as peers and managed and motivated their learning with praise and excitement. Turkish families, who were in transition from a rural to an urban way of life, showed a pattern somewhere between the other two.

The cultural context, then, influences the way caregivers contribute to cognitive development. Direct adult involvement in children's play and learning may be better adapted to a middle-class urban community, in which parents or caregivers have more time, greater verbal skills, and possibly more interest in children's play and learning, than in a rural community in a developing country, in which children frequently observe and participate in adults' work activities (Rogoff et al., 1993).

In a cross-cultural observational study of middle-class families in Washington, D.C., and Buenos Aires, 20-month-olds playing at home with their mothers engaged in similar activities in both cultures. However, the U.S. children and mothers tended to engage in more exploratory play with toys (such as dialing a telephone); Argentine children and mothers engaged in more symbolic and social play (such as feeding a doll or putting it to bed), and the mothers praised their children more. These differences seem to reflect cultural variations in goals of child raising; U.S. society is highly individualistic and stresses autonomy and assertiveness, whereas Argentine society places greater emphasis on social interdependence and connectedness (Bornstein, Haynes, Pascual, Painter, & Galperin, 1999).

Checkpoint

Can you . . .

- ✔ Identify the brain structures apparently involved in explicit, implicit, and working memory, and mention a task made possible by each?
- ✔ Tell how brain research helps explain Piagetian developments and memory operations?
- ✔ Tell how cultural patterns can affect guided participation in toddlers' learning?

Language Development

Guidepost 8

How do babies develop language?

Doddy Darwin's exclamation "Ah!" to express his recognition of an image in a glass is a striking example of the connection between **language,** a communication system based on words and grammar, and cognitive development. Once children know words, they can use them to represent objects and actions. They can reflect on people, places, and things; and they can communicate their needs, feelings, and ideas in order to exert control over their lives.

language Communication system based on words and grammar.

The growth of language illustrates the interaction of all aspects of development. As the physical structures needed to produce sounds mature and the neuronal connections necessary to associate sound and meaning become activated, social interaction with adults introduces babies to the communicative nature of speech. Let's look at the typical sequence of language development (see Table 7-5), at some characteristics of early speech, at how babies acquire language and make progress in using it, and at how parents and other caregivers help toddlers prepare for **literacy,** the ability to read and write.

lliteracy Ability to read and write.

Sequence of Early Language Development

Before babies can use words, they make their needs and feelings known—as Doddy Darwin did—through sounds that progress from crying to cooing and babbling, then to accidental imitation, and then to deliberate imitation. These sounds are known as **prelinguistic speech.** Infants also grow in the ability to recognize and understand speech sounds and to use meaningful gestures. Babies typically say their first word around the end of the first year, and toddlers begin speaking in sentences about eight months to a year later.

prelinguistic speech Forerunner of linguistic speech; utterance of sounds that are not words. Includes crying, cooing, babbling, and accidental and deliberate imitation of sounds without understanding their meaning.

Early Vocalization

Crying is a newborn's only means of communication. Different pitches, patterns, and intensities signal hunger, sleepiness, or anger (Lester & Boukydis, 1985).

Between 6 weeks and 3 months, babies start *cooing* when they are happy—squealing, gurgling, and making vowel sounds like "ahhh." At about 3 to 6 months, babies begin to play with speech sounds, matching the sounds they hear from people around them.

Babbling—repeating consonant-vowel strings, such as "ma-ma-ma-ma"—occurs between 6 and 10 months of age and is often mistaken for a baby's first word. Babbling is not real language, since it does not hold meaning for the baby, but it becomes more wordlike.

Language development continues with accidental *imitation of language sounds* babies hear and then imitation of themselves making these sounds. At about 9 to 10 months, infants deliberately imitate sounds without understanding them. Once they have a repertoire of sounds, they string them together in patterns that sound like language but seem to have no meaning.

Recognizing Language Sounds

The ability to perceive differences between sounds is essential to language development. As we have seen, this ability is present from or even before birth, and it becomes more refined during the first year of life. In getting ready to understand and use speech, infants first become familiar with the sounds of words and phrases and later attach meanings to them (Jusczyk & Hohne, 1997).

The process apparently begins in the womb. In one experiment, two groups of Parisian women in their 35th week of pregnancy each recited a different nursery rhyme, saying it three times a day for four weeks. At the end of that time, researchers played recordings of both rhymes close to the women's abdomens. The fetuses' heart rates slowed when the rhyme the mother had spoken was played but not for the other rhyme. Since the voice on the tape was not that of the mother, the fetuses apparently were responding to the linguistic sounds they had heard the mother use. This suggests that hearing the "mother tongue" before birth may "pretune" an infant's ears to pick up its sounds (DeCasper, Lecanuet, Busnel, Granier-Deferre, & Maugeais, 1994).

Before infants can connect sounds to meanings, they seem to recognize sound patterns they hear frequently, such as their own names. Infants 4½ months old listen longer to their

Table 7-5 Language Milestones from Birth to 3 Years

Age in Months	Development
Birth	Can perceive speech, cry, make some response to sound.
1½ to 3	Coos and laughs.
3	Plays with speech sounds
5 to 6	Makes consonant sounds, trying to match what she or he hears.
6 to 10	Babbles in strings of consonants and vowels.
9	Uses gestures to communicate and plays gesture games.
9 to 10	Begins to understand words (usually "no" and baby's own name); imitates sounds.
9 to 12	Uses a few social gestures.
10 to 12	No longer can discriminate sounds not in own language.
10 to 14	Says first word (usually a label for something).
10 to 18	Says single words.
13	Understands symbolic function of naming.
13	Uses more elaborate gestures.
14	Uses symbolic gesturing.
16 to 24	Learns many new words, expanding vocabulary rapidly, going from about 50 words to as many as 400; uses verbs and adjectives.
18 to 24	Says first sentence (2 words).
20	Uses fewer gestures; names more things.
20 to 22	Has comprehension spurt.
24	Uses many two-word phrases; no longer babbles; wants to talk.
30	Learns new words almost every day; speaks in combinations of three or more words; understands very well; makes grammatical mistakes.
36	Says up to 1,000 words, 80 percent intelligible; makes some mistakes in syntax.

Source: Bates, O'Connell, & Shore, 1987; Capute, Shapiro, & Palmer, 1987; Lalonde & Werker, 1995; Lenneberg, 1969.

own names than to other names, even names with stress patterns similar to theirs (Mandel, Jusczyk, & Pisoni, 1995). Six-month-olds look longer at a video of their mothers when they hear the word *mommy* and of their fathers when they hear *daddy,* suggesting that they are beginning to associate sound with meaning—at least with regard to special people (Tincoff & Jusczyk, 1999).

By 6 months of age, babies have learned to recognize the basic sounds, or *phonemes,* of their native language, and to adjust to slight differences in the way different speakers form those sounds. In one study, 6-month-old Swedish and U.S. babies routinely ignored variations in sounds common in their own language but noticed variations in an unfamiliar language (Kuhl, Williams, Lacerda, Stevens, & Lindblom, 1992).

By about 10 months, babies lose their earlier sensitivity to sounds that are not part of the language or languages they hear spoken. For example, Japanese infants no longer make a distinction between "ra" and "la," a distinction that does not exist in the Japanese language. Although the ability to perceive nonnative sounds is not entirely lost—it can be revived, with effort, in adulthood—the brain no longer routinely discriminates them (Bates, O'Connell, & Shore, 1987; Lalonde & Werker, 1995; Werker, 1989).

During the second half of the first year, as babies become increasingly familiar with the sounds of their language, they begin to become aware of its phonological rules—how sounds are arranged in speech. In one series of experiments (Marcus, Vijayan, Rao, & Vishton, 1999), 7-month-olds listened longer to "sentences" containing a different order of nonsense sounds (such as "wo fe wo," or ABA) from the order to which the infants had been habituated (such as "ga ti ti," or ABB). The sounds used in the test were different from those used in the habituation phase, so the infants' discrimination must have been based on the patterns of repetition alone. This finding suggests that infants may have a mechanism for discerning abstract rules of sentence structure.

Gestures

At 9 months, Maika *pointed* to an object, sometimes making a noise to show that she wanted it. Between 9 and 12 months, she learned some *conventional social gestures:* waving bye-bye, nodding her head to mean *yes,* and shaking her head to signify *no.* By about 13 months, she used more elaborate *representational gestures;* for example, she would hold an empty cup to her mouth to show that she wanted a drink or hold up her arms to show that she wanted to be picked up.

Symbolic gestures, such as blowing to mean *hot* or sniffing to mean *flower,* often emerge around the same time as babies say their first words, and they function much like words. By using them, children show an understanding that symbols can refer to specific objects, events, desires, and conditions. Gestures usually appear before children have a vocabulary of 25 words and drop out when children learn the word for the idea they were gesturing and can say it instead (Lock, Young, Service, & Chandler, 1990).

Gesturing seems to come naturally. In an observational study, blind children and adolescents used gestures while speaking as much as sighted children did and even while speaking to a blind listener. Thus, the use of gestures does not depend on having either a model or an observer but seems to be an inherent part of the speaking process (Iverson & Goldin-Meadow, 1998).

Learning gestures seems to help babies learn to talk. In one experiment (Goodwyn & Acredolo, 1998), 11-month-olds learned gestures by watching their parents perform them and say the corresponding words. Between 15 and 36 months, when tested on vocal language development, these children outperformed two other groups—one whose parents had only said words and another who had received neither vocal nor gestural training. Gestures, then, can be a valuable alternative or supplement to words, especially during the period of early vocabulary formation.

First Words

Doddy Darwin, at 11 months, said his first word—"ouchy"—which he attached to a number of objects. Doddy's development was typical in this respect. The average baby says a first word sometime between 10 and 14 months, initiating **linguistic speech**—verbal expression that conveys meaning. At first an infant's total verbal repertoire is likely to be "mama" or "dada." Or it may be a simple syllable that has more than one meaning depending on the context in which the child utters it. "Da" may mean "I want that," "I want to go out," or "Where's Daddy?" A word like this, which expresses a complete thought, is called a **holophrase.**

linguistic speech Verbal expression designed to convey meaning.

holophrase Single word that conveys a complete thought.

Babies understand many words before they can use them. The first words most babies understand are the ones they are likely to hear most often: their own names and the word *no.* By 13 months, most children understand that a word stands for a specific thing or event, and they can quickly learn the meaning of a new word (Woodward, Markman, & Fitzsimmons, 1994). Addition of new words to their *expressive* (spoken) vocabulary is slower at first. As children come to rely more on words than on gestures to express themselves, the sounds and rhythms of speech grow more elaborate.

Passive (understood) vocabulary continues to grow throughout the single-word stage, which generally lasts until about 18 months. At this age toddlers—especially those with larger vocabularies and faster reaction times—can recognize spoken words from just the first part of the word. For example, upon hearing "daw" or "ki," they will point to a picture of a dog or kitten (Fernald, Swingley, & Pinto, 2001). Sometime between 16 and 24 months, a "naming explosion" occurs. Within a few weeks, a toddler may go from saying about 50 words to saying about 400 (Bates, Bretherton, & Snyder, 1988). These rapid gains in spoken vocabulary reflect the increase in speed and accuracy of word recognition during the second year of life (Fernald, Pinto, Swingley, Weinberg, & McRoberts, 1998). Two-year-olds learn nouns more easily than verbs, and they retain new words best if they hear a word several times on more than one day (Childers & Tomasello, 2002).

First Sentences

The next important linguistic breakthrough comes when a toddler puts two words together to express one idea ("Dolly fall"). Generally, children do this between 18 and 24 months, about 8 to 12 months after they say their first word. However, this age range varies greatly. Although prelinguistic speech is fairly closely tied to chronological age, linguistic speech is not. Most children who begin talking fairly late catch up eventually—and many make up for lost time by talking nonstop to anyone who will listen! (True delayed language development is discussed in Chapter 10.)

A child's first sentences typically deal with everyday events, things, people, or activities (Braine, 1976; Rice, 1989; Slobin, 1973). Darwin noted instances in which Doddy expressed his developing moral sense in words. At 27 months the boy gave his sister the last bit of his gingerbread, exclaiming, "Oh, kind Doddy, kind Doddy!"

telegraphic speech Early form of sentence use consisting of only a few essential words.

At first children typically use **telegraphic speech,** consisting of only a few essential words. When Rita says, "Damma deep," she seems to mean "Grandma is sweeping the floor." Children's use of telegraphic speech and the form it takes vary, depending on the language being learned (Braine, 1976; Slobin, 1983). Word order generally conforms to what a child hears; Rita does not say "Deep Damma" when she sees her grandmother pushing a broom.

Does the omission of functional words such as *is* and *the* mean that a child does not know these words? Not necessarily; the child may merely find them hard to reproduce. Even during the first year, infants are sensitive to the presence of functional words; at 10½ months, they can tell a normal passage from one in which the functional words have been replaced by similar-sounding nonsense words (Jusczyk, 2003).

syntax Rules for forming sentences in a particular language.

Sometime between 20 and 30 months, children show increasing competence in **syntax,** the rules for putting sentences together in their language. They become somewhat more comfortable with articles (*a, the*), prepositions (*in, on*), conjunctions (*and, but*), plurals, verb endings, past tense, and forms of the verb *to be* (*am, are, is*). They also become increasingly aware of the communicative purpose of speech and of whether their words are being understood (Shwe & Markman, 1997)—a sign of growing sensitivity to the mental lives of others. By age 3, speech is fluent, longer, and more complex; although children often omit parts of speech, they get their meaning across well.

Characteristics of Early Speech

Early speech has a character all its own—no matter what language a child is speaking (Slobin, 1971).

As we have seen, children *simplify.* They use telegraphic speech to say just enough to get their meaning across ("No drink milk!").

Children *understand grammatical relationships they cannot yet express.* At first, Nina may understand that a dog is chasing a cat, but she cannot string together enough words to express the complete action. Her sentence comes out as "Puppy chase" rather than "Puppy chase kitty."

Children *underextend word meanings.* Lisa's uncle gave her a toy car, which the 13-month-old called her "koo-ka." Then her father came home with a gift, saying, "Look, Lisa, here's a little car for you." Lisa shook her head. "Koo-ka," she said and ran and got the one from her uncle. To her, *that* car—and *only* that car—was a little car, and it took some time before she called any other toy cars by the same name. Lisa was underextending the word *car* by restricting it to a single object.

Children also *overextend word meanings.* At 14 months, Eddie jumped in excitement at the sight of a gray-haired man on the television screen and shouted, "Gampa!" Eddie was overgeneralizing, or *overextending,* a word; he thought that because his grandfather had gray hair, all gray-haired men could be called "Grandpa." As children develop a larger vocabulary and get feedback from adults on the appropriateness of what they say, they overextend less. ("No, honey, that man looks a little like Grandpa, but he's somebody else's grandpa, not yours.")

Children *overregularize rules.* They apply them rigidly, not knowing that some rules have exceptions. When John says "mouses" instead of "mice" or Megan says "I thinked" rather than "I thought," this represents progress. Both children initially used the correct forms of these irregular words but merely in imitation of what they heard. Once children learn the rules for plurals and past tense (a crucial step in learning language), they apply them universally. The next step is to learn the exceptions to the rules, which they generally do by early school age.

Checkpoint

Can you . . .

- ✔ Trace the typical sequence of milestones in early language development, pointing out the influence of the language babies hear around them?
- ✔ Describe five ways in which early speech differs from adult speech?

Classic Theories of Language Acquisition: The Nature-Nurture Debate

How do children gain access to the secrets of verbal communication? Is linguistic ability learned or inborn? In the 1950s, a debate raged between two schools of thought: one led by B. F. Skinner, the foremost proponent of learning theory, and the other by the linguist Noam Chomsky.

Skinner (1957) maintained that language learning, like other learning, is based on experience. According to classic learning theory, children learn language through operant conditioning. At first, babies utter sounds at random. Caregivers reinforce the sounds that happen to resemble adult speech with smiles, attention, and praise. Infants then repeat these reinforced sounds. Sounds that are not part of the native language are not reinforced, and the child gradually stops making them. According to social-learning theory, babies imitate the sounds they hear adults make and, again, are reinforced for doing so. Word learning depends on selective reinforcement; the word *kitty* is reinforced only when the family cat appears. As this process continues, children are reinforced for speech that is more and more adultlike. Sentence formation is a more complex process. The child learns a basic word order (subject-verb-object—"I want ice cream") and then learns that other words can be substituted in each category ("Daddy eats meat").

Observation, imitation, and reinforcement probably do contribute to language development, but, as Chomsky (1957) persuasively argued, they cannot fully explain it (Flavell, Miller, & Miller, 1993; Owens, 1996). For one thing, word combinations and nuances are so many and so complex that they cannot all be acquired by specific imitation and reinforcement. Then, caregivers often reinforce utterances that are not strictly grammatical, as long as they make sense ("Gampa go bye-bye"). Adult speech itself is an unreliable model to imitate, as it is often ungrammatical, containing false starts, unfinished sentences, and slips of the tongue. Also, learning theory does not account for children's imaginative ways of saying things they have never heard—as when 2-year-old Anna described a sprained ankle as a "sprangle" and said she didn't want to go to sleep yet because she wasn't "yawny."

Chomsky's own view is called **nativism.** Unlike Skinner's learning theory, nativism emphasizes the active role of the learner. Since language is universal among human beings, Chomsky (1957, 1972) proposed that the human brain has an innate capacity for acquiring language; babies learn to talk as naturally as they learn to walk. He suggested that an inborn **language acquisition device (LAD)** programs children's brains to analyze the language they hear and to figure out its rules. More recently, Chomsky (1995) has sought to identify a simple set of universal principles that underlie all languages and a single multipurpose mechanism for connecting sound to meaning.

nativism Theory that human beings have an inborn capacity for language acquisition.

language acquisition device (LAD) In Chomsky's terminology, inborn mechanism that enables children to infer linguistic rules from the language they hear.

Support for the nativist position comes from newborns' ability to differentiate similar sounds, suggesting that they are "born with perceptual mechanisms that are tuned to the properties of speech" (Eimas, 1985, p. 49). Nativists point out that almost all children master their native language in the same age-related sequence without formal teaching. Furthermore, the brains of human beings, the only animals with fully developed language, contain a structure that is larger on one side than on the other, suggesting that an inborn mechanism for sound and language processing may be localized in the larger hemisphere—the left for most people (Gannon, Holloway, Broadfield, & Braun, 1998). Still, the nativist approach does not explain precisely how such a mechanism operates. It does not tell us why some children acquire language more rapidly and efficiently than others, why children differ in linguistic skill and fluency, or why (as we'll see) speech development appears to depend on having someone to talk with, not merely on hearing spoken language.

Figure 7-7

Example of manual babbling by a nonhearing baby who had been exposed to sign language. The baby repeated this series of hand movements over and over again in sequence. Each motion is comparable to a syllable in a sequence of vocal babbling.

Source: Petitto & Marentette, 1991.

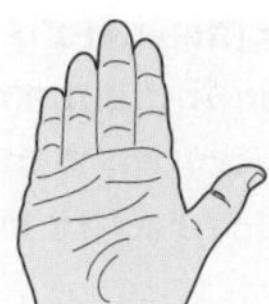

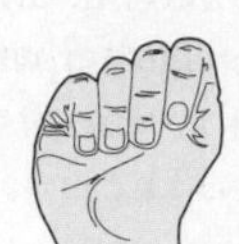
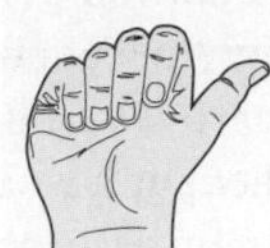

Aspects of both learning theory and nativism have been used to explain how deaf babies learn sign language, which is structured much like spoken language and is acquired in the same sequence. Just as hearing babies of hearing parents copy vocal utterances, deaf babies of deaf parents seem to copy the sign language they see their parents using, first stringing together meaningless motions and then repeating them over and over in what has been called *hand-babbling*. As parents reinforce these gestures, the babies attach meaning to them. Hand-babbling motions are slower, more systematic, and more deliberate than nonlinguistic hand movements and are restricted to the space in front of the body where signing normally takes place (Petitto & Marentette, 1991; Petitto, Holowka, Sergio, & Ostry, 2001; see Figure 7-7). Hearing babies of deaf parents also hand-babble (Petitto, Holowka, et al., 2001).

However, some deaf children make up their own sign language when they do not have models to follow—evidence that environmental influences alone cannot explain the emergence of linguistic expression (Goldin-Meadow & Mylander, 1998). That is how Nicaraguan Sign Language emerged in the 1970s among children who were being taught only lipreading in Spanish (Senghas & Coppola, 2001).

Furthermore, learning theory does not explain the correspondence between the ages at which linguistic advances in both hearing and nonhearing babies typically occur (Padden, 1996; Petitto, Katerelos, et al., 2001; Petitto & Kovelman, 2003). Deaf babies begin hand-babbling between 7 and 10 months of age, about the age when hearing infants begin voice-babbling (Petitto, Holowka, et al., 2001; Petitto & Marentette, 1991). Deaf babies also begin to use sentences in sign language at about the same time that hearing babies begin to speak in sentences (Meier, 1991; Newport & Meier, 1985). This suggests that an inborn language capacity may underlie the acquisition of both spoken and signed language and that advances in both kinds of language are tied to brain maturation.

Most developmental scientists today believe that language acquisition, like most other aspects of development, depends on an intertwining of nature and nurture. Children, whether hearing or deaf, probably have an inborn capacity to acquire language, which may be activated or constrained by experience.

Checkpoint

Can you . . .

✔ Summarize how learning theory and nativism seek to explain language acquisition, and point out strengths and weaknesses of each?

Influences on Language Development

Guidepost 9

What influences contribute to linguistic progress?

What determines how quickly and how well children learn to understand and use language? Research has focused on influences both within and outside the child.

Genetic and Neurological Factors

By studying a family whose members have passed on a severe speech and language disorder for three generations, researchers have discovered a gene that seems to underlie speech and language development. This gene may "turn on" other genes involved in various aspects of language in the brain of the developing fetus (Lai, Fisher, Hurst, Vargha-Khadem, & Monaco, 2001).

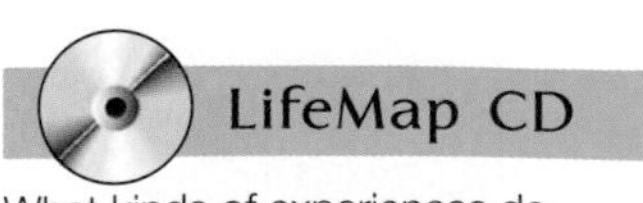

What kinds of experiences do babies need to develop to their full potential? For an expert's opinion on this question, watch the "Influences on Infant Brain Development" video in Chapter 7 of your CD.

The tremendous brain growth and reorganization during the early months and years is closely linked with language development. A newborn's cries are controlled by the *brain stem* and *pons,* the most primitive parts of the brain and the earliest to develop (refer back to Figure 6-4). Repetitive babbling may emerge with the maturation of parts of the *motor cortex,* which control movements of the face and larynx. Not until early in the second year, when most children begin to talk, do the pathways that link auditory and motor activity mature (Owens, 1996). Cortical regions associated with language continue to develop until at least the late preschool years or beyond—some, not even until adulthood.

In about 98 percent of people, the left hemisphere is dominant for language, though the right hemisphere participates as well (Nobre & Plunkett, 1997; Owens, 1996). Videotapes of babbling babies show that, as in adult speech, the mouth opens more on the right side than on the left. Since the left hemisphere of the brain controls activity on the right side of the body, lateralization of linguistic functions apparently takes place very early in life (Holowka & Petitto, 2002; refer back to Chapter 6).

Lateralization may be genetically determined, but it also seems to be environmentally influenced. Studies of brain-damaged children suggest that a sensitive period exists before lateralization of language is firmly fixed. The plasticity of the infant brain seems to allow functions to be transferred from damaged areas to other regions. Thus, whereas an adult whose left hemisphere is removed or injured will be severely language impaired, a young child who undergoes this procedure may eventually have nearly normal speech and comprehension (Nobre & Plunkett, 1997; Owens, 1996).

Brains of *normal* infants also show plasticity. In one study, researchers measured brain activity at various places on the scalp as babies listened to a series of words, some of which they did not understand. Between ages 13 and 20 months, a period of marked vocabulary growth, the infants showed increasing lateralization and localization of comprehension (Mills, Cofley-Corina, & Neville, 1997). Other evidence of neural plasticity comes from findings that the upper regions of the temporal lobe, which are involved in hearing and understanding speech, can be activated by a born-deaf person's use of sign language (Nishimura et al., 1999). Such findings suggest that the assignment of language functions to brain structures may be a gradual process linked to verbal experience and cognitive development (Nobre & Plunkett, 1997).

Checkpoint

Can you . . .

✔ Name areas of the brain involved in early language development, and tell the function of each?

✔ Give evidence for plasticity in the brain's linguistic areas?

Social Interaction: The Role of Parents and Caregivers

Language is a social act. Parents or other caregivers play an important role at each stage of language development.

Prelinguistic Period At the babbling stage, adults help an infant advance toward true speech by repeating the sounds the baby makes. The baby soon joins in the game and repeats the sounds back. Parents' imitation of babies' sounds affects the pace of language learning (Hardy-Brown & Plomin, 1985; Hardy-Brown, Plomin, & DeFries, 1981). It also helps babies experience the social aspect of speech, the sense that a conversation consists of taking turns, an idea most babies seem to grasp at about 7½ to 8 months of age. Even as early as 4 months, babies in a game of peekaboo show sensitivity to the structure of social exchange with an adult (Rochat, Querido, & Striano, 1999; refer back to Box 7-1).

Caregivers may help babies understand spoken words by, for example, pointing to a doll and saying, "Please give me Kermit." If the baby doesn't respond, the adult may pick up the doll and say, "Kermit." In one longitudinal study, mothers' responsiveness to 9-month-olds' and, even more so, to 13-month-olds' vocalization and play predicted the timing of language milestones, such as first spoken words and sentences. By 13 months, when children become better able to communicate, responses to their verbal initiatives become especially important (Tamis-LeMonda, Bornstein, & Baumwell, 2001).

Vocabulary Development When babies begin to talk, parents or caregivers often help them by repeating their first words and pronouncing them correctly. Vocabulary gets a boost when an adult seizes an appropriate opportunity to teach a child a new word. If Jordan's mother says, "This is a ball," when Jordan is looking at the ball, he is more likely to remember the word than if he were playing with something else and she tried to divert his attention to the ball (Dunham, Dunham, & Curwin, 1993). Adults help a toddler who has begun to put words together by expanding on what the child says. If Christina says, "Mommy sock," her mother may reply, "Yes, that is Mommy's sock."

Babies learn by listening to what adults say. A strong relationship has appeared between the frequency of various words in mothers' speech and the order in which children learn these words (Huttenlocher, Haight, Bryk, Seltzer, & Lyons, 1991) as well as between mothers' talkativeness and the size of toddlers' vocabularies (Huttenlocher, 1998). Mothers with higher socioeconomic status tend to use richer vocabularies and longer utterances, and their 2-year-olds tend to have larger spoken vocabularies (Hoff, 2003).

However, sensitivity and responsiveness to a child's level of development count more than the number of words a mother uses. In one longitudinal study, in which toddlers were observed interacting with their mothers at 13 and 20 months, the mothers increased their vocabulary use to match their children's growing language abilities; and the children with the biggest vocabularies had mothers who were most responsive (Bornstein, Tamis-LeMonda, & Haynes, 1999).

code mixing Use of elements of two languages, sometimes in the same utterance, by young children in households where both languages are spoken.

code switching Changing one's speech to match the situation, as in people who are bilingual.

In households where more than one language is spoken, babies achieve similar milestones in each language on the same schedule as children who hear only one language (Petitto, Katerelos, et al., 2001; Petitto & Kovelman, 2003). Bilingual children often use elements of both languages, sometimes in the same utterance—a phenomenon called **code mixing.** But this does not mean that they confuse the two languages (Petitto, Katerelos, et al., 2001; Petitto & Kovelman, 2003). A naturalistic observation in Montreal (Genesee, Nicoladis, & Paradis, 1995) suggests that children as young as 2 in dual-language households differentiate between the two languages, using French, for example, with a predominantly French-speaking father and English with a predominantly English-speaking mother. This ability to shift from one language to another is called **code switching.** (Chapter 13 discusses second-language learning.)

Child-Directed Speech

child-directed speech (CDS) Form of speech often used in talking to babies or toddlers; includes slow, simplified speech, a high-pitched tone, exaggerated vowel sounds, short words and sentences, and much repetition. Also called *parentese.*

You do not have to be a parent to speak "parentese." If, when you talk to an infant or toddler, you speak slowly in a high-pitched voice with exaggerated ups and downs, simplify your speech, exaggerate vowel sounds, and use short words and sentences and much repetition, you are using **child-directed speech (CDS)** (sometimes called *parentese* or *motherese*). Most adults and even children do it naturally. Such "baby talk" has been documented in many languages and cultures (Kuhl et al., 1997).

Many researchers believe that CDS helps infants learn their native language or at least pick it up faster by helping them hear the distinguishing features of speech sounds. In one cross-cultural observational study, mothers in the United States, Russia, and Sweden were audiotaped speaking to their 2- to 5-month-old infants. Whether the mothers were speaking English, Russian, or Swedish, they produced more exaggerated vowel sounds when talking to the infants than when talking to other adults. At 20 weeks, the babies' babbling contained distinct vowels that reflected the phonetic differences to which their mothers' speech had alerted them (Kuhl et al., 1997).

Other investigators challenge the value of CDS. They contend that babies speak sooner and better if they hear and can respond to more complex adult speech. In fact, some researchers say, children discover the rules of language faster when they hear complex sentences that use these rules more often and in more ways (Gleitman, Newport, & Gleitman, 1984; Oshima-Takane, Goodz, & Derevensky, 1996). Nonetheless, infants themselves prefer simplified speech. This preference is clear before 1 month of age, and it does not seem to depend on any specific experience (Cooper & Aslin, 1990; Kuhl et al., 1997; Werker, Pegg, & McLeod, 1994).

The preference for CDS is not limited to spoken language. In an observational study in Japan, deaf mothers were videotaped reciting everyday sentences in sign language, first to their deaf 6-month-old infants and then to deaf adult friends. The mothers signed more slowly and with more repetition and exaggerated movements when directing the sentences to the infants, and other infants the same age paid more attention and appeared more responsive when shown these tapes (Masataka, 1996). What's more, 6-month-old *hearing* infants who had never been exposed to sign language also showed a preference for infant-directed sign (Masataka, 1998). This is powerful evidence that infants, whether hearing or deaf, are universally attracted to child-directed communication.

Preparing for Literacy: The Benefits of Reading Aloud

Most babies love to be read to, and the frequency with which parents or caregivers read to them, as well as the way they do it, can influence how well children speak and eventually

Despite controversy over the value of child-directed speech, or "parentese," this simplified way of speaking does appeal to babies.

how well and how soon they read. Children who learn to read early are generally those whose parents read to them very frequently when they were very young. Reading to an infant or toddler offers opportunities for emotional intimacy and fosters parent-child communication.

Adults tend to have one of three styles of reading to children: the *describer style, comprehender style,* and *performance-oriented style.* A *describer* focuses on describing what is going on in the pictures and inviting the child to do so ("What are the Mom and Dad having for breakfast?"). A *comprehender* encourages the child to look more deeply at the meaning of a story and to make inferences and predictions ("What do you think the lion will do now?"). A *performance-oriented* reader reads the story straight through, introducing the main themes beforehand and asking questions afterward.

An adult's read-aloud style is best tailored to the needs and skills of the child. In an experimental study of 50 four-year-olds in Dunedin, New Zealand, the describer style resulted in the greatest overall benefits for vocabulary and print skills, but the performance-oriented style was more beneficial for children who started out with large vocabularies (Reese & Cox, 1999).

A promising technique, similar to the describer style, is *dialogic,* or *shared, reading.* In this method (mentioned in Chapter 2), "the child learns to become the storyteller" while the adult acts as an active listener (Whitehurst & Lonigan, 1998, p. 859). Parents ask challenging, open-ended questions rather than those calling for a simple yes or no ("What is the cat doing?" instead of "Is the cat asleep?"). They follow up the child's answers with more questions, repeat and expand on what the child says, correct wrong answers and give alternative possibilities, help the child as needed, and give praise and encouragement. They encourage the child to relate a story to the child's own experience ("Have you ever seen a duck swimming? What did it look like?").

Children who are read to often, especially in this way, when they are 1 to 3 years old show better language skills at ages 2½, 4½, and 5 and better reading comprehension at age 7 (Crain-Thoreson & Dale, 1992; Wells, 1985). In one study, 21- to 35-month-olds whose parents used this method scored six months higher in vocabulary and expressive language skills than a control group. The experimental group also got a boost in *prereading skills,* the competencies helpful in learning to read, such as learning how letters look and sound (Arnold & Whitehurst, 1994; Whitehurst et al., 1988).

Checkpoint

Can you . . .

- ✔ Explain the importance of social interaction, and give at least three examples of how parents or caregivers help babies learn to talk?
- ✔ Assess the arguments for and against the value of child-directed speech (CDS)?
- ✔ Tell why reading aloud to children at an early age is beneficial?
- ✔ Describe an effective way of reading aloud to infants and toddlers?

Refocus

- Which approach to cognitive development seems closest to the one Darwin took in observing and describing his son's development? Why?
- How might a behaviorist, a Piagetian, a psychometrician, an information-processing researcher, a cognitive neuroscientist, and a social-contextual theorist attempt to study and explain the developments Darwin described?
- Did Doddy's early linguistic development seem more consistent with Skinner's or Chomsky's theory of language development? How does it illustrate the role of social interaction?

Social interaction in reading aloud, play, and other daily activities is a key to much of childhood development. Children call forth responses from the people around them and, in turn, react to those responses. In Chapter 8, we will look more closely at these bidirectional influences as we explore early psychosocial development.

Summary and Key Terms

Studying Cognitive Development: Classic Approaches

behaviorist approach (163) **psychometric approach (163)** **Piagetian approach (163)**

Guidepost 1 How do infants learn, and how long can they remember?

- Two simple types of learning that behaviorists study are classical conditioning and operant conditioning.
- Rovee-Collier's research suggests that infants' memory processes are much like those of adults, and their memories can be jogged by periodic reminders.

classical conditioning (164) **operant conditioning (164)**

Guidepost 2 Can infants' and toddlers' intelligence be measured, and how can it be improved?

- Psychometric tests measure factors presumed to make up intelligence.

intelligent behavior (166) **IQ (intelligence quotient) tests (166)**

- Developmental tests, such as the Bayley Scales of Infant Development, can indicate current functioning but are generally poor predictors of later intelligence.

developmental tests (166) **Bayley Scales of Infant Development (166)**

- Socioeconomic status, temperament, parenting practices, and the home environment may affect measured intelligence.

Home Observation for Measurement of the Environment (167)

- If the home environment does not provide the necessary conditions that pave the way for cognitive competence, early intervention may be needed.

early intervention (168)

Guidepost 3 How did Piaget explain early cognitive development, and how have his claims stood up?

- During Piaget's sensorimotor stage, infants' schemes become more elaborate. They progress from primary to secondary to tertiary circular reactions and finally to the development of representational ability, which makes possible deferred imitation, pretending, and problem solving.

sensorimotor stage (169) **schemes (170)** **circular reactions (170)** **representational ability (171)** **deferred imitation (171)** **pretend play (171)**

- Object permanence develops gradually. Piaget saw the A, not-B error as a sign of incomplete object knowledge and the persistence of egocentric thought.

object permanence (172) **A, not-B error (172)** **egocentric (172)** **allocentric (174)** **dual representation hypothesis (175)**

- Research suggests that some abilities develop earlier than Piaget described. He may have underestimated young infants' imitative abilities and their grasp of object permanence.

invisible imitation (175) **visible imitation (175)** **elicited imitation (176)**

Studying Cognitive Development: Newer Approaches

information-processing approach (178) **cognitive neuroscience approach (178)** **social-contextual approach (178)**

Guidepost 4 How can we measure infants' ability to process information, and how does this ability relate to future intelligence?

- Information-processing researchers measure mental processes through habituation and other signs of visual and perceptual abilities. Contrary to Piaget's ideas, such research suggests that representational ability is present virtually from birth.
- Indicators of the efficiency of infants' information processing, such as speed of habituation, tend to predict later intelligence.

habituation (178) **dishabituation (178)** **visual preference (179)** **visual recognition memory (179)** **cross-modal transfer (180)**

Guidepost 5 When do babies begin to think about characteristics of the physical world?

- Such information-processing research techniques as habituation, novelty preference, and the violation-of-expectations method have yielded evidence that infants as young as 3½ to 5 months may have a rudimentary grasp of such Piagetian abilities as causality, categorization, object permanence, a sense of number, and an ability to reason about characteristics of the physical world. Some researchers suggest that infants may have innate learning mechanisms for acquiring such knowledge. However, the meaning of these findings is in dispute.

violation-of-expectations (183)

Guidepost 6 What can brain research reveal about the development of cognitive skills?

- Explicit memory and implicit memory are located in different brain structures. Working memory emerges between 6 and 12 months of age. Neurological developments help explain the emergence of Piagetian skills and memory abilities.

explicit memory (185) implicit memory (185) working memory (185)

Guidepost 7 How does social interaction with adults advance cognitive competence?

- Social interactions with adults contribute to cognitive competence through shared activities that help children learn skills, knowledge, and values important in their culture.

guided participation (186)

Language Development

Guidepost 8 How do babies develop language?

- The acquisition of language is an important aspect of cognitive development.

language (187) literacy (187)

- Prelinguistic speech includes crying, cooing, babbling, and imitating language sounds. By 6 months, babies have learned the basic sounds of their language and have begun to link sound with meaning.

prelinguistic speech (187)

- Before they say their first word, babies use gestures.
- The first word typically comes sometime between 10 and 14 months, initiating linguistic speech. A "naming explosion" typically occurs sometime between 16 and 24 months of age.

linguistic speech (189) holophrase (189)

- The first brief sentences generally come between 18 and 24 months. By age 3, syntax and communicative abilities are fairly well developed.

telegraphic speech (190) syntax (190)

- Early speech is characterized by simplification, underextending and overextending word meanings, and overregularizing rules.
- Two classic theoretical views about how children acquire language are learning theory and nativism. Today, most developmentalists hold that an inborn capacity to learn language may be activated or constrained by experience.

nativism (191) language acquisition device (LAD) (191)

Guidepost 9 What influences contribute to linguistic progress?

- Influences on language development include brain maturation and social interaction.
- Family characteristics, such as socioeconomic status, adult language use, and maternal responsiveness, affect a child's vocabulary development.
- Children who hear two languages at home generally learn both at the same rate as children who hear only one language, and they can use each language in appropriate circumstances.

code mixing (194) code switching (194)

- Child-directed speech (CDS) seems to have cognitive, emotional, and social benefits, and infants show a preference for it. However, some researchers dispute its value.

child-directed speech (CDS) (194)

- Reading aloud to a child from an early age helps pave the way for literacy.

chapter 8

Psychosocial Development During the First Three Years

I'm like a child
trying to do everything
say everything
and be everything
all at once

—John Hartford, "Life Prayer," 1971

Focus *Mary Catherine Bateson, Anthropologist*

Mary Catherine Bateson

Mary Catherine Bateson (b. 1939) is an anthropologist, the daughter of two famous anthropologists: Margaret Mead (refer back to Chapter 2 Focus) and Gregory Bateson, Mead's third husband and research partner. Hers was probably one of the most documented infancies on record—her mother taking notes, her father behind the camera. Margaret Mead's memoir, *Blackberry Winter* (1972), and Mary Catherine Bateson's *With a Daughter's Eye* (1984) together provide a rare and fascinating dual perspective on a child's first three years of life.

Cathy—Mead's only child—was born when her mother was 38 years old. Her parents divorced when she was 11. Their work during World War II often necessitated long absences and separations. But during her infancy and toddlerhood, when they were still together, Cathy was the focus of their love and wholehearted attention. Her early recollections include sitting with her parents on a blanket outdoors, being read to on her mother's lap, and watching the two of them hold up their breakfast spoons to reflect the morning light, making a pair of "birds" flash across the walls for her amusement.

To avoid subjecting her to frustration, her parents tried to respond quickly to her needs. Mead arranged her professional commitments around breast-feeding and nursed "on demand," like the mothers in the island cultures she had studied.

Like their friend Erik Erikson, Mead and Bateson placed great importance on the development of trust. They never left Cathy in a strange place with a strange person; she always met a new caregiver in a familiar place. "Her warm responsiveness, her trustingness, and her outgoing interest in people and things . . . set the stage for her expectation that the world was a friendly place" (Mead, 1972, p. 266). As an adult, Catherine observed that, during difficult periods in her life, she often found "resources of faith and strength, a foundation that must have been built in those [first] two years" (Bateson, 1984, p. 35). Yet, as Mead wrote, "How much was temperament? How much was felicitous accident? How much could be attributed to upbringing? We may never know" (1972, p. 268).

Mead tried to avoid overprotectiveness and to let Cathy be herself. Catherine remembers her father pushing her swing so high that he could run under it. Later he taught her to climb tall pine trees, testing every branch for firmness and making sure that she could find her way back down, while her mother, watching, tried not to show her fear.

Sources of biographical information about Mary Catherine Bateson are Bateson (1984) and Mead (1972).

When Cathy was 2 and her parents' wartime travel increased, they merged their household with that of a friend and colleague, Lawrence Frank. The decision fit in with Mead's belief, gleaned from her studies, that children benefit from having multiple caregivers and learning to adapt to different situations.

The menage in Frank's brownstone in Greenwich Village included his infant son and five older children. "Thus," Catherine writes, "I did not grow up in a nuclear family or as an only child, but as a member of a flexible and welcoming extended family . . . , in which five or six pairs of hands could be mobilized to shell peas or dry dishes." Her summertime memories are of a lakeside retreat in New Hampshire, where "each child was cared for by enough adults so that there need be no jealousy, where the garden bloomed and the evenings ended in song. . . . I was rich beyond other children . . . and yet there were all those partings. There were all those beloved people, yet often the people I wanted most were absent" (Bateson, 1984, pp. 38–39).

• • •

In Margaret Mead's and Mary Catherine Bateson's complementary memoirs, we can see how Mead put into practice the beliefs she had developed about child rearing, in part from memories of her own childhood and in part from observations of distant cultures. We see her seeking solutions to a problem that has become increasingly common: child care for children of working parents. And we see a bidirectionality of influence: how early experiences with parents help shape a child's development and how a child's needs can shape parents' lives.

This chapter is about the shift from the dependence of infancy to the independence of childhood. We first examine foundations of psychosocial development: emotions, temperament, and early experiences with parents and grandparents. We consider Erikson's views about the development of trust and autonomy. We look at relationships with caregivers, at the emerging sense of self, and at the foundations of conscience. We explore relationships with siblings and other children. Finally, we consider the increasingly widespread impact of early day care.

After you have read and studied this chapter, you should be able to answer each of the Guidepost questions that follow. Look for them again in the margins, where they point to important concepts throughout the chapter. To check your understanding of these Guideposts, review the end-of-chapter summary. Checkpoints located at periodic spots throughout the chapter will help you verify your understanding of what you have read.

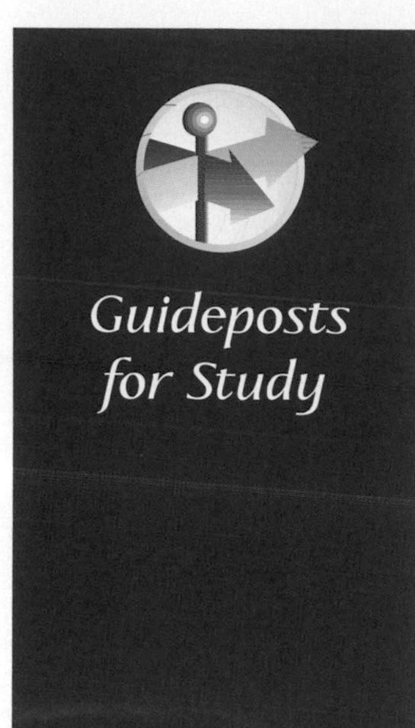

Guideposts for Study

1. When and how do emotions develop, and how do babies show them?
2. How do infants show temperamental differences, and how enduring are those differences?
3. What roles do parents and grandparents play in early personality development?
4. How do infants gain trust in their world and form attachments?
5. How do infants and caregivers “read” each other’s nonverbal signals?
6. When and how does the sense of self arise?
7. How do toddlers develop autonomy and standards for socially acceptable behavior?
8. How do infants and toddlers interact with siblings and other children?
9. How do parental employment and early child care affect infants’ and toddlers’ development?

Foundations of Psychosocial Development

Although babies share common patterns of development, they also—from the start—show distinct personalities, which reflect both inborn and environmental influences. From infancy on, personality development is intertwined with social relationships (see Table 8-1).

Emotions

Guidepost 1

When and how do emotions develop, and how do babies show them?

emotions Subjective reactions to experience that are associated with physiological and behavioral changes.

Emotions, such as sadness, joy, and fear, are subjective reactions to experience that are associated with physiological and behavioral changes (Sroufe, 1997). Fear, for example, is accompanied by a faster heartbeat and, often, by self-protective action. All normal human beings have the capacity to feel emotions, but people differ in how often they experience a particular emotion, in the kinds of events that may produce it, in their physical manifestations of it (such as heart rate changes), and in how they act as a result. Researchers disagree about how many emotions there are, when they arise, how they should be defined and measured, and even about what is or is not an emotion.

Emotions serve several protective functions. One is to communicate needs, intentions, or desires and to call forth a response. This communicative function is central to the development of social relationships and is especially important for infants, who must depend on adults to meet their basic needs. A second protective function, served by such emotions as fear and surprise, is to mobilize action in emergencies. A third function, that of such emotions as interest and excitement, is to promote exploration of the environment, which leads to learning that can protect or sustain life.

Emotional development is an orderly process; complex emotions unfold from simpler ones. A person’s characteristic pattern of emotional reactions begins to develop during infancy and is a basic element of personality. Indeed, an infant’s earliest awareness of self is intimately tied in with emotional development. However, as children grow older, some emotional responses may change. A baby who, at 3 months of age, smiled at a stranger’s face may, at 8 months, show wariness, or *stranger anxiety.* Also, different events may call forth similar emotions at different ages. An infant may smile or laugh when he sits on a plastic duck and hears a squeak; a toddler is likely to smile when she finds she can push a switch to turn on a light.

Table 8-1 Highlights of Infants' and Toddlers' Psychosocial Development, Birth to 36 Months

Approximate Age, Months	Characteristics
0–3	Infants are open to stimulation. They begin to show interest and curiosity, and they smile readily at people.
3–6	Infants can anticipate what is about to happen and experience disappointment when it does not. They show this by becoming angry or acting warily. They smile, coo, and laugh often. This is a time of social awakening and early reciprocal exchanges between the baby and the caregiver.
6–9	Infants play "social games" and try to get responses from people. They "talk" to, touch, and cajole other babies to get them to respond. They express more differentiated emotions, showing joy, fear, anger, and surprise.
9–12	Infants are intensely preoccupied with their principal caregiver, may become afraid of strangers, and act subdued in new situations. By 1 year, they communicate emotions more clearly, showing moods, ambivalence, and gradations of feeling.
12–18	Toddlers explore their environment, using the people they are most attached to as a secure base. As they master the environment, they become more confident and more eager to assert themselves.
18–36	Toddlers sometimes become anxious because they now realize how much they are separating from their caregiver. They work out their awareness of their limitations in fantasy and in play and by identifying with adults.

Source: Adapted from Sroufe, 1979.

Emotion is closely tied to other aspects of development. For example, a newborn baby who is emotionally neglected—not hugged, caressed, or talked to—may show *nonorganic failure to thrive;* that is, failure to grow and gain weight despite adequate nutrition. The baby often will improve when moved to a hospital and given emotional support. Among both children and adults, anxiety has been linked to asthma, irritable bowel syndrome, ulcers, inflammatory bowel disease, coronary heart disease, and shortened life (Twenge, 2000). Such emotions as anger and fear and especially shame, guilt, and sympathy may motivate moral behavior (Ben-Ze'ev, 1997; Eisenberg, 2000; Eisenberg, Guthrie, et al., 1999; Kochanska, 1997a).

Culture influences the way people feel about certain situations and the way they show their emotions (Parke, 2004). For example, some Asian cultures, which stress social harmony, discourage expression of anger but place much importance on shame. The opposite is often true in American culture, which stresses self-expression, self-assertion, and self-esteem (Cole, Bruschi, & Tamang, 2002).

Early Signs of Emotion

Newborns plainly show when they are unhappy. They let out piercing cries, flail their arms and legs, and stiffen their bodies. It is harder to tell when they are happy. During the first month, they become quiet at the sound of a human voice or when they are picked up, and they may smile when their hands are moved together to play pat-a-cake. As time goes by, infants respond more to people—smiling, cooing, reaching out, and eventually going to them.

These early signals or clues to babies' feelings are important steps in development. When babies want or need something, they cry; when they feel sociable, they smile or laugh. When their messages bring a response, their sense of connection with other people grows. Their sense of control over their world grows, too, as they see that their cries bring help and comfort and that their smiles and laughter elicit smiles and laughter in return. They become more able to participate actively in regulating their states of arousal and their emotional life.

The discussion in this section is largely indebted to Sroufe (1997).

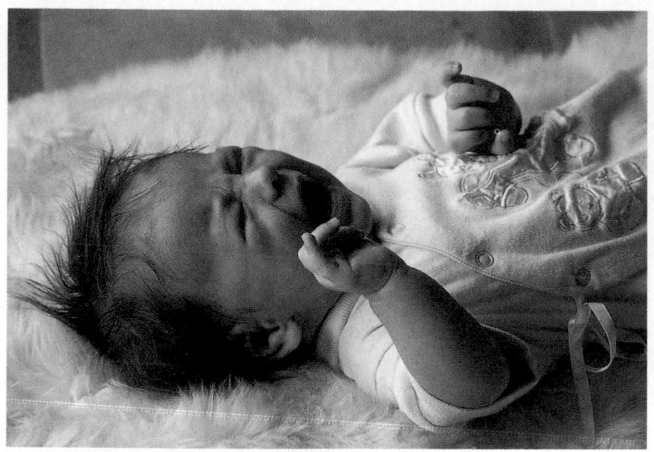

Crying enables this 7-week-old baby to communicate his needs. Parents generally learn to recognize whether their baby is crying because of hunger, anger, frustration, or pain.

An infant's earliest smiles are involuntary, but beginning at 1 month of age, smiles generally become more frequent and more social. This baby may be smiling at the sight of a parent or caregiver.

The meaning of babies' emotional signals changes. An early smile comes spontaneously as an expression of well-being; but by about 3 weeks, a smile may indicate pleasure in social contact. As babies get older, smiles and laughter at novel or incongruous situations reflect increasing cognitive awareness and growing ability to handle excitation (Sroufe, 1997).

Crying Crying is the most powerful way—and sometimes the only way—infants can communicate their needs. Almost all adults around the world respond quickly to a crying infant (Broude, 1995).

Some research has distinguished four patterns of crying (Wolff, 1969): the basic *hunger cry* (a rhythmic cry that is not always associated with hunger); the *angry cry* (a variation of the rhythmic cry, in which excess air is forced through the vocal cords); the *pain cry* (a sudden onset of loud crying without preliminary moaning, sometimes followed by holding the breath); and the *frustration cry* (two or three drawn-out cries, with no prolonged breath holding).

Some parents worry that they will spoil a child by picking up a crying baby. In one study, delays in responding did seem to reduce fussing during the first six months, perhaps because the babies learned to deal with minor irritations on their own (Hubbard & van IJzendoorn, 1991). But if parents wait until cries of distress escalate to shrieks of rage, it may become more difficult to soothe the baby; and such a pattern, if experienced repeatedly, may interfere with an infant's developing ability to regulate, or manage, his or her own emotional state (R. A. Thompson, 1991). Ideally, the most developmentally sound approach may be the one Cathy Bateson's parents followed: to *prevent* distress, making soothing unnecessary.

Smiling and Laughing The earliest faint smiles occur spontaneously soon after birth, apparently as a result of subcortical nervous system activity. These involuntary smiles frequently appear during periods of REM sleep, which is associated with dreaming. They become less frequent during the first three months as the cortex matures (Sroufe, 1997).

The earliest *waking* smiles may be elicited by mild sensations, such as gentle jiggling or blowing on the infant's skin. In the second week, a baby may smile drowsily after a feeding. By the third week, most infants begin to smile when they are alert and paying attention to a caregiver's nodding head and voice. At about 1 month, smiles generally become more frequent and more social. During the second month, as visual recognition develops, babies smile more at visual stimuli, such as faces they know (Sroufe, 1997; Wolff, 1963).

At about the fourth month, infants start to laugh out loud when kissed on the stomach or tickled. As babies grow older, they become more actively engaged in mirthful exchanges. A 6-month-old may giggle in response to the mother making unusual sounds or

Figure 8-1

Differentiation of emotions during the first 3 years. The primary, or basic, emotions emerge during the first 6 months or so; the self-conscious emotions develop beginning in the second half of the second year, as a result of the emergence of self-awareness (consciousness of self) together with accumulation of knowledge about societal standards and rules.

Note: There are two types of embarrassment. The earlier form does not involve evaluation of behavior and may simply be a response to being singled out as the object of attention. The second form, evaluative embarrassment, which emerges during the third year, is a mild form of shame.

Source: Adapted from Lewis, 1997, Fig. 1, p. 120.

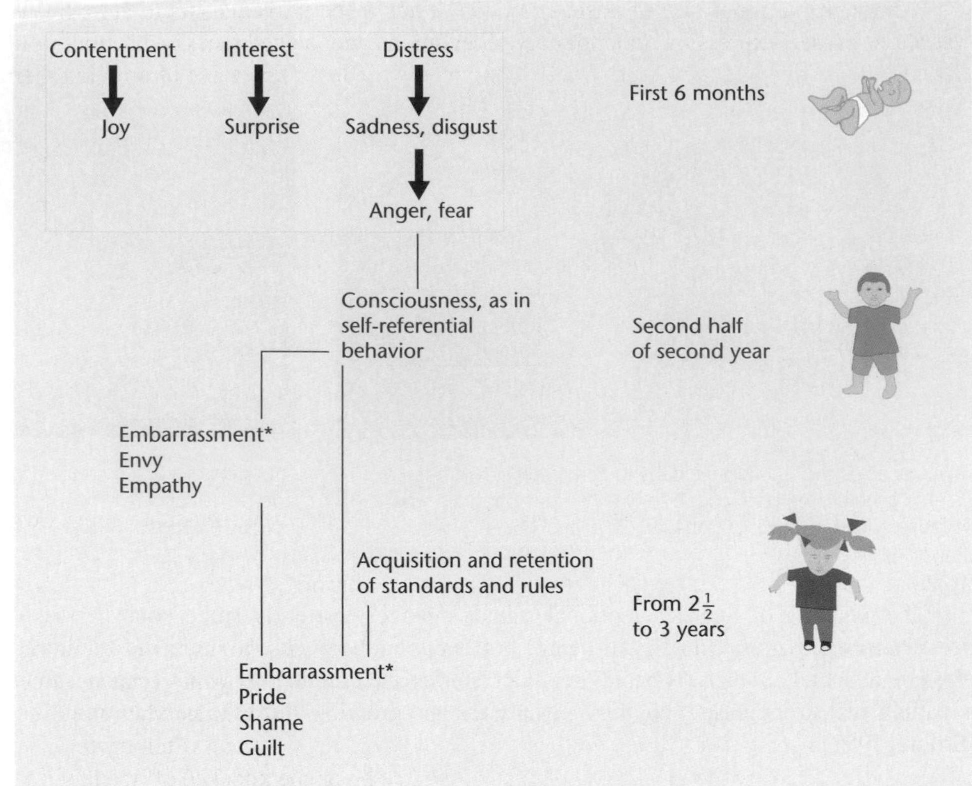

appearing with a towel over her face; a 10-month-old may laughingly try to put the towel back on her face. This change reflects cognitive development: by laughing at the unexpected, babies show that they know what to expect. By turning the tables, they show a dawning awareness that they can cause things to happen. Laughter also helps babies discharge tension, such as fear of a threatening object (Sroufe, 1997).

When Do Various Emotions Develop?

Identifying infants' emotions is a challenge because babies cannot tell us what they feel. Still, parents, caregivers, and researchers learn to recognize clues. Carroll Izard and his colleagues have videotaped infants' facial expressions and have interpreted them as showing joy, sadness, interest, and fear and, to a lesser degree, anger, surprise, and disgust (Izard, Huebner, Resser, McGinness, & Dougherty, 1980). Of course, we do not know that these babies actually *had* the feelings they were credited with showing, but their facial expressions were remarkably similar to adults' expressions when experiencing these emotions.

Facial expressions are not the only, or necessarily the best, index of infants' emotions; motor activity, body language, and physiological changes also are important indicators. For example, an infant can be fearful without showing a "fear face." Instead, a baby may show fear by turning away or averting the gaze or with a faster heartbeat. Different criteria may point to different conclusions about the timing of emergence of specific emotions. In addition, this timetable shows a good deal of individual variation (Sroufe, 1997).

Basic Emotions According to one model of emotional development (Lewis, 1997; see Figure 8-1), soon after birth babies show signs of contentment, interest, and distress. These are diffuse, reflexive, mostly physiological responses to sensory stimulation or internal processes. During the next six months or so, these early emotional states differentiate into true emotions: joy, surprise, sadness, disgust, and, later, anger and fear—reactions to events that have meaning for the infant. As we'll discuss in a subsequent section, the emergence of these basic, or primary, emotions is related to the biological "clock" of neurological maturation.

Although the repertoire of basic emotions seems to be universal, there are cultural variations in their expression. In laboratory observations, videotaped faces of 11-month-old Chinese infants whose arms were briefly restrained were less expressive of emotion than those of American and Japanese infants whose arm movements were similarly restricted (Camras et al., 1998). Whether these findings reflect cultural attitudes or innate differences in emotional reactivity is unclear.

Emotions Involving the Self **Self-conscious emotions,** such as embarrassment, empathy, and envy, can arise only after children have developed **self-awareness:** the cognitive understanding that they have a recognizable identity, separate and different from the rest of their world. This consciousness of self seems to emerge between 15 and 24 months, when, according to Piaget, infants become able to make mental representations—of themselves as well as of other people and things. Self-awareness is necessary before children can be aware of being the focus of attention, identify with what other "selves" are feeling, or wish they had what someone else has.

self-conscious emotions Emotions, such as embarrassment, empathy, and envy, that depend on self-awareness.

self-awareness Realization that one's existence and functioning are separate from those of other people and things.

By about age 3, having acquired self-awareness plus a good deal of knowledge about their society's accepted standards, rules, and goals, children can evaluate their own thoughts, plans, desires, and behavior against what is considered socially appropriate. Only then can they demonstrate the **self-evaluative emotions** of pride, shame, and guilt (Lewis, 1995, 1997, 1998).

self-evaluative emotions Emotions, such as pride, shame, and guilt, that depend on both self-awareness and knowledge of socially accepted standards of behavior.

Guilt and shame are distinct emotions, even though both may be responses to wrongdoing. Children who fail to live up to behavioral standards may feel guilty (that is, regret their behavior), but they do not necessarily feel a lack of self-worth, as when they feel ashamed. Their focus is on a bad *act,* not a bad *self.* A guilty child will often try to make amends, say, by trying to put together a broken dish that he or she knocked off the table; an ashamed child is more likely to try to hide the results of a misdeed (Eisenberg, 2000).

Empathy: Feeling What Others Feel **Empathy**—the ability to put oneself in another person's place and feel what that person feels or would be expected to feel in a particular situation—is thought to arise during approximately the second year and, like guilt, increases with age (Eisenberg, 2000; Eisenberg & Fabes, 1998). As toddlers become increasingly able to differentiate their own mental state from that of another person, they can respond to another child's distress as if it were their own (Hoffman, 1998). Empathy differs from *sympathy,* which merely involves sorrow or concern for another person's plight. Both empathy and sympathy tend to be accompanied by *prosocial behavior,* such as giving back a toy (see Chapter 11).

empathy Ability to put oneself in another person's place and feel what the other person feels.

Empathy depends on **social cognition,** the ability to understand that others have mental states, to gauge their feelings and intentions, and to be aware of how things look from their perspective. Piaget believed that egocentrism (a focus on a child's own viewpoint) delays the development of this ability until the concrete operational stage of middle childhood. But other research suggests that social cognition begins so early that it may be "an innate potential, like the ability to learn language" (Lillard & Curenton, 1999, p. 52).

social cognition Ability to understand that other people have mental states and to gauge their feelings and intentions.

Brain Growth and Emotional Development

The development of the brain after birth (refer back to Chapter 6) is closely connected with changes in emotional life. A newborn has only a diffuse sense of consciousness and is easily overstimulated and upset by sounds, lights, and other sources of sensory arousal. As the structures of the central nervous system develop and sensory pathways become myelinated, the baby's reactions become more focused and tempered, or modulated. Sensory processing becomes less reflexive as the cortex begins to function. This is a bidirectional process. Emotional experiences not only are affected by brain development but also can have long-lasting effects on the structure of the brain (Mlot, 1998; Sroufe, 1997).

There appear to be four major shifts in brain organization, which roughly correspond to changes in emotional processing (Schore, 1994; Sroufe, 1997; refer back to Figure 6-4). During the first three months, differentiation of basic emotions begins as the *cerebral cortex* becomes functional, bringing cognitive perceptions into play. REM sleep and reflexive behavior, including the spontaneous neonatal smile, diminish. The social smile reflects a growing desire to seek and maintain contact with outside stimuli.

The second shift occurs around 9 or 10 months, when the *frontal lobes* begin to interact with the *limbic system,* a seat of emotional reactions. At the same time, limbic structures such as the *hippocampus* become larger and more adultlike. Connections between the frontal cortex and the *hypothalamus* and limbic system, which process sensory information, may facilitate the relationship between the cognitive and emotional spheres. As these connections become denser and more elaborate, an infant can experience and interpret emotions at the same time. The development of recognition and recall, object permanence, and other cognitive advances makes it possible to coordinate past and present events and future expectations. A baby this age may become upset when a ball rolls under a couch and may smile or laugh when it is retrieved. Fear of strangers often develops at this time.

The third shift takes place during the second year, when infants develop self-awareness, self-conscious emotions, and a greater capacity for regulating their own emotions and activities. These changes, which coincide with greater physical mobility and exploratory behavior, may be related to myelination of the frontal lobes.

The fourth shift occurs around age 3, when hormonal changes in the autonomic nervous system coincide with the emergence of evaluative emotions. Underlying the development of such emotions as shame may be a shift away from dominance by the *sympathetic system,* which prepares the body for action, and the maturation of the *parasympathetic system,* which is involved in excretion and sexual excitation. The experience of shame may, in turn, activate the inhibitory circuits of the limbic system and deactivate the excitatory circuits, eventually bringing the two circuits into balance.

Neurological factors also may play a part in temperamental differences (Mlot, 1998), the topic we turn to next.

Checkpoint

Can you . . .

- ✔ Cite two important functions of emotions?
- ✔ Explain the significance of patterns of crying, smiling, and laughing?
- ✔ Trace a typical sequence of emergence of the basic, self-conscious, and evaluative emotions, and explain its connection with cognitive and neurological development?

Guidepost 2

How do infants show temperamental differences, and how enduring are those differences?

Temperament

temperament Characteristic disposition, or style of approaching and reacting to situations.

Temperament—sometimes defined as a person's characteristic, biologically based way of approaching and reacting to people and situations—has been described as the *how* of behavior: not *what* people do, but how they go about doing it (Thomas & Chess, 1977). Two toddlers, for example, may be equally able to dress themselves and may be equally motivated, but one may do it more quickly than the other, be more willing to put on a new outfit, and be less distracted if the cat jumps on the bed. Of course, a child may not act the same way in all situations. Temperament may affect not only the way children approach and react to the outside world, but also the way they regulate their own mental, emotional, and behavioral functioning (Rothbart et al., 2000).

Temperament has an emotional basis; but although emotions such as fear, excitement, and boredom come and go, temperament is relatively consistent and enduring. Individual differences in temperament, which are thought to derive from a person's basic biological makeup, form the core of a developing personality (Eisenberg, Fabes, Guthrie, & Reiser, 2000).

Aspects and Patterns of Temperament: New York Longitudinal Study

In the New York Longitudinal Study (NYLS), a pioneering study on temperament, researchers followed 133 infants into adulthood, interviewing, testing, and observing them and interviewing their parents and teachers. The researchers looked at how active the children were; how regular they were in hunger, sleep, and bowel habits; how readily they accepted new people and situations; how they adapted to changes in routine; how sensitive they were to noise, bright lights, and other sensory stimuli; how intensely they responded; whether their mood tended to be pleasant, joyful, and friendly or unpleasant, unhappy, and unfriendly; and whether they persisted at tasks or were easily distracted (A. Thomas, Chess, & Birch, 1968). The children differed in all these characteristics, almost from birth, and the differences tended to continue.

easy children Children with a generally happy temperament, regular biological rhythms, and a readiness to accept new experiences.

Almost two-thirds of the children in the NYLS fell into one of three categories (see Table 8-2). Forty percent were **easy children:** generally happy, rhythmic in biological

Table 8-2 Three Temperamental Patterns (according to the New York Longitudinal Study)

"Easy" Child	"Difficult" Child	"Slow-to-Warm-Up" Child
Has moods of mild to moderate intensity, usually positive.	Displays intense and frequently negative moods; cries often and loudly; also laughs loudly.	Has mildly intense reactions, both positive and negative.
Responds well to novelty and change.	Responds poorly to novelty and change.	Responds slowly to novelty and change.
Quickly develops regular sleep and feeding schedules.	Sleeps and eats irregularly.	Sleeps and eats more regularly than the difficult child, less regularly than the easy child.
Takes to new foods easily.	Accepts new foods slowly.	Shows mildly negative initial response to new stimuli (a first encounter with a new person, place, or situation).
Smiles at strangers.	Is suspicious of strangers.	
Adapts easily to new situations.	Adapts slowly to new situations.	
Accepts most frustrations with little fuss.	Reacts to frustration with tantrums.	
Adapts quickly to new routines and rules of new games.	Adjusts slowly to new routines.	Gradually develops liking for new stimuli after repeated, unpressured exposures.

Source: Adapted from A. Thomas & Chess, 1984.

functioning, and accepting of new experiences. This is how Margaret Mead described the infant Cathy. Ten percent were what the researchers called **difficult children:** more irritable and harder to please, irregular in biological rhythms, and more intense in expressing emotion. Fifteen percent were **slow-to-warm-up children:** mild but slow to adapt to new people and situations (A. Thomas & Chess, 1977, 1984).

difficult children Children with irritable temperament, irregular biological rhythms, and intense emotional responses.

slow-to-warm-up children Children whose temperament is generally mild but who are hesitant about accepting new experiences.

Many children (including 35 percent of the NYLS sample) do not fit neatly into any of these three groups. A baby may eat and sleep regularly but be afraid of strangers. A child may be easy most of the time but not always. Another child may warm up slowly to new foods but adapt quickly to new babysitters (A. Thomas & Chess, 1984). A child may laugh intensely but not show intense frustration, and a child with rhythmic toilet habits may show irregular sleeping patterns (Rothbart et al., 2000). All these variations are normal.

How Is Temperament Measured?

Many researchers have found the complex interviewing and scoring procedures used in the NYLS too cumbersome and have resorted to short-form questionnaires. A parental self-report instrument—the Rothbart Infant Behavior Questionnaire (IBQ), introduced in 1981 and revised in 2002—has been validated in part by home and laboratory observations (Gartstein & Rothbart, 2003; Rothbart et al., 2000). The original IBQ focused on several dimensions of infant temperament similar to those in the NYLS: activity level, positive emotion (smiling and laughing), fear, frustration, soothability, and duration of orienting (a combination of distractibility and attention span). Parents rate their infants on a scale, rather than compare them with other infants. The ratings focus on recent concrete events and behaviors rather than on overall judgments of infant behavior. ("How often during the past week did the baby smile or laugh when given a toy" rather than "Does the baby respond positively to new events?")

These researchers also developed a Children's Behavior Questionnaire (CBQ) for 3- to 7-year-olds that covers three clusters of personality characteristics: (1) *extraversion* (impulsiveness, intense pleasure, high activity level, boldness, risk taking, comfort in new social situations), (2) *negative affect* (sadness, discomfort, anger, frustration, fear, high reactivity), and (3) *effortful control* (inhibitory control of impulses, low-intensity pleasure, ability to focus attention, perceptual sensitivity). Some of these aspects of temperament, such as intensity of pleasure, perceptual sensitivity, and attentional shifting, have been added to the revised IBQ (Gartstein & Rothbart, 2003; Rothbart et al., 2000).

Today, parental ratings are the most commonly used measures of children's temperament. However, the reliability of parental ratings is in question. Studies of twins have found that parents tend to rate a child's temperament by comparison with other children in the family—for example, labeling one child inactive in contrast to a more active sibling (Saudino, 2003a). Still, not all types of parent-report instruments show this tendency (Hwang & Rothbart, 2003); and observations by researchers may reflect biases as well (Seifer, 2003). Parents see their children in a variety of day-to-day situations, whereas a laboratory observer sees only how the child reacts to particular standardized situations. Thus, a combination of methods may provide a more accurate picture of how temperament affects child development (Rothbart & Hwang, 2002; Saudino, 2003a, 2003b).

Effects of Temperament on Adjustment: "Goodness of Fit"

goodness of fit Appropriateness of environmental demands and constraints to a child's temperament.

According to the NYLS, the key to healthy adjustment is **goodness of fit**—the match between a child's temperament and the environmental demands and constraints the child must deal with. If a very active child is expected to sit still for long periods, if a slow-to-warm-up child is constantly pushed into new situations, or if a persistent child is constantly taken away from absorbing projects, trouble may occur.

Parents' responses to their children may reflect the amount of control the parents think they have over a child's behavior. In a home observation, parents who saw themselves as having little control over their 12-month-olds were more likely than other parents to play directively with their babies—urging, reminding, restraining, questioning, and correcting them; and mothers who felt and acted this way were more likely to consider their infants "difficult." Similar patterns have been found among parents of older children (Guzell & Vernon-Feagans, 2004).

When parents recognize that a child acts in a certain way, not out of willfulness, laziness, or stupidity or to spite the parents, but largely because of inborn temperament, they may be less likely to feel guilty, anxious, or hostile, to feel a loss of control, or to be rigid or impatient. They can anticipate the child's reactions and help the child adapt—for example, by giving early warnings of the need to stop an activity or, as Mead and Bateson did, by gradually introducing a child to new situations.

How Stable Is Temperament?

Temperament appears to be largely inborn, probably hereditary (Braungart, Plomin, DeFries, & Fulker, 1992; Emde et al., 1992; Schmitz et al., 1996; A. Thomas & Chess, 1977, 1984), and fairly stable. Newborn babies show different patterns of sleeping, fussing, and activity, and these differences tend to persist to some degree (Korner, 1996; Korner et al., 1985). That does not mean temperament is fully formed at birth. Temperament develops as various emotions and self-regulatory capacities appear (Rothbart et al., 2000) and can change in response to parental attitudes and treatment (Belsky, Fish, & Isabella, 1991; Lerner & Galambos, 1985).

Still, studies using the IBQ during infancy and the CBQ at age 7 found strong links between infant temperament and childhood personality (Rothbart et al., 2000, 2001). Other researchers, using temperamental types similar to those of the NYLS, have found that temperament at age 3 closely predicts personality at ages 18 and 21 (Caspi, 2000; Caspi & Silva, 1995; Newman, Caspi, Moffitt, & Silva, 1997; see Box 8-1).

Biological Bases of Temperament

Temperament, like emotion, seems to have a biological basis. In longitudinal research with about 400 children starting in infancy, Jerome Kagan and his colleagues have studied an aspect of temperament called *inhibition to the unfamiliar,* or shyness, which has to do with how sociable a child is with unfamiliar children and how boldly or cautiously the child approaches unfamiliar objects and situations. This characteristic is associated with differences in physical features and brain functioning, which are reflected in physiological signs such as heart rate, blood pressure, and pupil dilation. When asked to solve problems or learn new information, the shyest children (about 15 percent of the sample) showed higher and less variable heart rates than bolder children, and the pupils of their eyes dilated more. The boldest children (about 10 to 15 percent) tended to be energetic and spontaneous and to have very low heart rates (Arcus & Kagan, 1995).

The Research World

Box 8-1 *Does Early Temperament Predict Adult Personality?*

Do temperamental differences persist into adult life? The answer is yes, according to longitudinal studies in New Zealand and Finland.

In a study of 3-year-olds born in a single year in Dunedin, New Zealand (Caspi, 2000; Caspi & Silva, 1995; Newman, Caspi, Moffitt, & Silva, 1997), examiners tested 1,037 children on cognitive and motor skills and then rated them on a checklist of behavioral characteristics. Five personality types emerged, three of them much like the temperamental types identified by Thomas and Chess in the New York Longitudinal Study.

Well-adjusted children (about 40 percent of the sample, as in the NYLS) were similar to the "easy" type. They were reasonably self-confident, capable of self-control, and comfortable with new people and situations. *Undercontrolled* children (10 percent of the sample) resembled the "difficult" type. They were impulsive, restless, negative, distractible, and volatile. *Inhibited* children (again, about 10 percent) were somewhat like the "slow-to-warm-up" type. They were shy, fearful, and socially ill at ease. These three types have been validated using a variety of methods in a number of countries, including Iceland, Netherlands, Germany, and the United States. The researchers also identified two additional types—*confident* and *reserved*—which may be variations on the other categories.

When the participants were restudied at ages 18 (through self-report personality questionnaires) and 21 (through descriptions of people who knew them well), their early temperamental patterns proved remarkably predictive. Those who had been well adjusted as children remained so. By contrast, those who had been undercontrolled at age 3 were likely to be aggressive, socially alienated, reckless, careless, and thrill seeking. They tended to have problems at school and at work and to have conflicted personal and romantic relationships. They were prone to risky or antisocial behavior: dangerous driving, unsafe sex, alcohol dependence, violent crime, and suicide attempts. Friends described them as unreliable and untrustworthy.

Inhibited children showed a different pattern. They often grew up to be cautious, overcontrolled, unassertive, and subject to depression. They had few friends and companions, and those who knew them described them as low in affection, confidence, and vitality. They were less likely to get involved in antisocial behavior than the undercontrolled group, perhaps because they were more likely to be afraid of getting caught; but they too were prone to suicidal behavior.

In the Finnish study, the results were less striking, possibly because it measured different components of temperament. Researchers followed a population-based sample of 1,319 healthy children, ages 3 to 12, for more than 17 years. Initially, the children's mothers rated them on emotionality, activity, and sociability and on difficulty of temperament. As young adults, the participants rated themselves. Comparisons of the mothers' and adult children's ratings showed significant, though weak, continuity for activity, moderate continuity for difficult temperament, and an association between low sociability in childhood and anger in adulthood (Pesonen, Räikkönen, Keskivaara, & Keltikangas-Järvinen, 2003).

What accounts for stability of temperament? A proposed explanation points to the frequent similarity in temperament between parents and children (Caspi, 2000; Caspi & Silva, 1995; Newman, Caspi, Moffitt, & Silva, 1997). Warm, accepting parents tend to have easygoing children; parents who discipline harshly or inconsistently tend to have difficult children. This is an example of genotype-environment correlation (refer back to Chapter 3), in which the environment that parents create reinforces the genetic tendencies they have passed on to their children. It is also an example of bidirectional influence, since difficult children tend to elicit harsh or inconsistent discipline from their parents. As children grow up, they continue to seek out environments that strengthen their natural tendencies. It is not surprising, then, that temperamental patterns, both healthy and unhealthy, tend to persist.

This does not mean that nothing can be done about a "difficult" temperament. Although continuity is more likely than change, it is not inevitable. As the New York Longitudinal Study found, temperament can change, especially during infancy. Goodness of fit between parent and child is a key to healthy adjustment.

Seven-month-old Daniel's ready smile and willingness to try a new food are signs of an easy temperament.

What's your view?

- Ask your parents what you were like as an infant and as a toddler. What do they remember about you at ages 1, 2, and 3?
- How similar or different are the temperamental qualities you showed at those ages as compared with the way you are today?

Check it out!

For more information on this topic, go to **http://www.zerotothree.org/Archive/TEMPERAM.HTM**. This is an article from *Zero to Three,* "Temperamental Traits," which provides theoretical and empirical information about temperamental traits from birth to 3 years. It offers practical tips about how to apply this information when interacting with young children.

Four-month-olds who are highly reactive—that is, who show much motor activity and distress or who fret or cry readily in response to new stimuli—are likely to show the inhibited pattern at 14 and 21 months. Babies who are highly inhibited or uninhibited seem to maintain these patterns to some degree during childhood and adolescence (Kagan, 1997; Kagan & Snidman, 1991a, 1991b). However, behavioral distinctions between these two types of children tend to "smooth out" by preadolescence, even though the physiological distinctions remain (Woodward et al., 2001).

Again, experience can moderate or accentuate early tendencies. Male toddlers who were inclined to be fearful and shy were more likely to remain so at age 3 if their parents were highly accepting of the child's reactions. But if parents encouraged their sons to venture into new situations, the boys tended to become less inhibited (Park, Belsky, Putnam, & Crnic, 1997). In a separate four-year longitudinal study of 153 infants, those whose behavior patterns changed from inhibited to uninhibited showed different patterns of brain activity from those who remained inhibited. The infants who changed in temperament also were more likely to have had nonparental caregiving during the first two years (Fox, Henderson, Rubin, Calkins, & Schmidt, 2001).

What's your view?

- In the United States, many people consider shyness undesirable. How should a parent handle a shy child? Do you think it is best to accept the child's temperament or try to change it?

Checkpoint

Can you . . .

✔ List and describe nine aspects and three patterns of temperament identified by the New York Longitudinal Study?

✔ Assess evidence for the stability of temperament?

✔ Discuss how temperament can affect social adjustment, and explain the importance of "goodness of fit"?

✔ Give evidence of cultural differences in temperament, and discuss ways of interpreting it?

Cross-Cultural Differences

As Margaret Mead observed, temperament may be affected by culturally influenced child-raising practices. Infants in Malaysia, an island group in Southeast Asia, tend to be less adaptable, more wary of new experiences, and more readily responsive to stimuli than U.S. babies. This may be because Malay parents do not often expose young children to situations that require adaptability, and they encourage children to be acutely aware of sensations, especially uncomfortable ones such as the need for a diaper change (Banks, 1989).

A cross-cultural study of Chinese and Canadian 2-year-olds casts further light on the concept of goodness of fit. Canadian mothers of inhibited children tended to be punitive or overprotective, whereas Chinese mothers of shy children were warm and accepting and encouraged them to achieve. The Chinese toddlers were significantly more inhibited than the Canadian ones. In western countries such as Canada, shy, inhibited children tend to be seen as incompetent, immature, and unlikely to accomplish much; their mothers may emotionally reject them or give them special guidance and protection. In China, shyness and inhibition are socially approved. Thus, a naturally inhibited Chinese child may be less motivated to come out of his or her shell. However, because this was a correlational study, we don't know whether the children's temperament was a consequence or a cause of their mothers' treatment or perhaps a bidirectional effect (Chen et al., 1998).

Guidepost 3

What roles do parents and grandparents play in early personality development?

Earliest Social Experiences: The Infant in the Family

Infant care practices and patterns of interaction with infants vary greatly around the world, depending on environmental conditions and the culture's view of infants' nature and needs. In Bali, infants are believed to be ancestors or gods brought to life in human form and thus must be treated with utmost dignity and respect. The Beng of West Africa think that young babies can understand all languages, whereas people in the Micronesian atoll of Ifaluk believe that babies cannot understand language at all, and therefore adults do not speak to them (DeLoache & Gottlieb, 2000).

In some societies, as Margaret Mead found in the South Seas, infants have multiple caregivers. Among the Efe people of central Africa, for example, infants typically receive care from five or more people in a given hour and are routinely breast-fed by other women besides the mother (Tronick, Morelli, & Ivey, 1992). Among the Gusii in western Kenya, where infant mortality is high, parents are more likely than those in industrial societies to keep their infants close to them, respond quickly when they cry, and feed them on demand (LeVine, 1974, 1989, 1994). The same is true of Aka foragers in central Africa, who move around frequently in small, tightly knit groups marked by extensive sharing, cooperation, and concern about danger. However, Ngandu farmers in the same region, who tend to live farther apart and to stay in one place for long periods of time, are more likely to leave their infants alone and to let them fuss or cry, smile, vocalize, or play (Hewlett, Lamb, Shannon, Leyendecker, & Schölmerich, 1998).

We need to remember, then, that patterns of adult-infant interaction we take for granted may be culture based. With that caution in mind, let's look first at the roles of mother and father—how they care for and play with their babies and how their influence begins to shape personality differences between boys and girls. We'll also consider grandparents' roles. Later in this chapter, we will look more deeply at relationships with parents and, finally, at interactions with siblings. In Chapter 14, we will examine such nontraditional families as those headed by single parents and those formed by gay and lesbian couples.

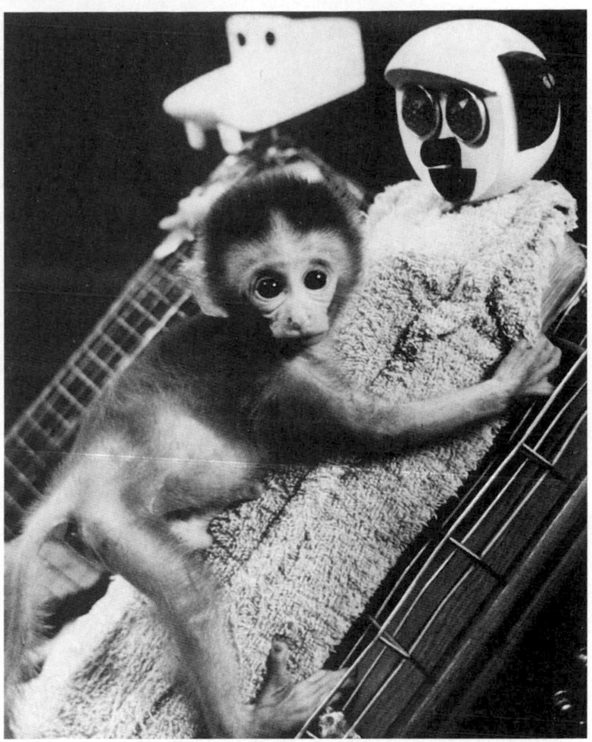

In a series of classic experiments, Harry Harlow and Margaret Harlow showed that food is not the most important way to a baby's heart. When infant rhesus monkeys could choose whether to go to a wire surrogate "mother" or a warm, soft terry-cloth "mother," they spent more time clinging to the cloth mother, even if they were being fed by bottles connected to the wire mother.

The Mother's Role

In a series of pioneering experiments by Harry Harlow and his colleagues, rhesus monkeys were separated from their mothers 6 to 12 hours after birth and raised in a laboratory. The infant monkeys were put into cages with one of two kinds of surrogate "mothers": a plain cylindrical wire-mesh form or a form covered with terry cloth. Some monkeys were fed from bottles connected to the wire "mothers"; others were "nursed" by the warm, cuddly cloth ones. When the monkeys were allowed to spend time with either kind of "mother," they all spent more time clinging to the cloth surrogates, even if they were being fed only by the wire ones. In an unfamiliar room, the babies "raised" by cloth surrogates showed more natural interest in exploring than those "raised" by wire surrogates, even when the appropriate "mothers" were there.

Apparently, the monkeys also remembered the cloth surrogates better. After a year's separation, the "cloth-raised" monkeys eagerly ran to embrace the terry-cloth forms, whereas the "wire-raised" monkeys showed no interest in the wire forms (Harlow & Zimmerman, 1959). None of the monkeys in either group grew up normally, however (Harlow & Harlow, 1962), and none were able to nurture their own offspring (Suomi & Harlow, 1972).

In another study, baby rats whose mothers licked them frequently turned out to be less anxious and fearful and produced lower levels of stress hormones than rats who had been licked less. The researchers found that maternal licking activated a gene that relieves stress (Caldji, Diorio, & Meaney, 2003).

It is hardly surprising that a dummy mother would not provide the same kinds of stimulation and opportunities for positive development as a live mother and that a mother's physical demonstrativeness would soothe her baby's stress. These experiments show that feeding is not the most important thing babies get from their mothers. Mothering includes the comfort of close bodily contact and, at least in monkeys, the satisfaction of an innate need to cling.

Human infants also have needs that must be satisfied if they are to grow up normally. A major task of developmental research is to find out what those needs are. In Chapter 5 we discussed the mother-infant bond, the close, caring connection that motivates mothers to care for their newborns. Later in this chapter we discuss the mutual attachment that develops during infancy, with far-reaching effects on psychosocial and cognitive development. We also examine the emotional signals that enable nonverbal communication between mothers and babies.

The Father's Role

The fathering role is essentially a social construction (Doherty, Kouneski, & Erickson, 1998), having different meanings in different cultures. The role may be taken or shared by someone other than the biological father: the mother's brother, as in Botswana (where young mothers remain with their own childhood family until their partners are in their 40s), or a grandfather, as in Vietnam (Engle & Breaux, 1998; Richardson, 1995; Townsend, 1997). In some societies, fathers are more involved in their young children's lives—economically, emotionally, and in time spent—than in other cultures. In many parts of the world, what it means to be a father has changed and is changing (Engle & Breaux, 1998).

Among the Huhot of Inner Mongolia, a province of China, fathers traditionally are responsible for economic support and discipline and mothers for nurturing (Jankowiak, 1992). Fathers are stern and aloof, and their children respect and fear them. Men almost never hold infants. Fathers interact more with toddlers but perform child care duties reluctantly and only if the mother is absent. However, urbanization and maternal employment are changing these attitudes. Fathers—especially college-educated ones—now seek more intimate relationships with children, especially sons. China's official one-child policy has accentuated this change, leading both parents to be more deeply involved with their only child (Engle & Breaux, 1998).

The Aka are hunter-gatherers in the tropical forests of central Africa who move frequently from camp to camp in small, tightly knit groups and are highly protective of young children. In contrast with the Huhot fathers, Aka fathers are as nurturant and emotionally supportive as Aka mothers. In fact, "Aka fathers provide more direct infant care than fathers in any other known society" (Hewlett, 1992, p. 169). This behavior is consistent with Aka cultural practices. In Aka families, husbands and wives frequently cooperate in subsistence tasks and other activities (Hewlett, 1992). Thus, the father's involvement in child care is part and parcel of his overall role in the family.

Fathers around the world differ in the way they play with their infants. A highly physical style of play, characteristic of many fathers in the United States, is not typical of fathers in all cultures. Swedish and German fathers usually do not play with their babies this way (Lamb, Frodi, Frodi, & Hwang, 1982; Parke, Grossman, & Tinsley, 1981). African Aka fathers (Hewlett, 1987) and those in New Delhi, India, also tend to play gently with small children (Roopnarine, Hooper, Ahmeduzzaman, & Pollack, 1993; Roopnarine, Talokder, Jain, Josh, & Srivastav, 1992). Such cross-cultural variations suggest that rough play is *not* a function of male biology, but instead is culturally influenced.

In the United States, fathers' involvement in caregiving and play has greatly increased since 1970 as more mothers have begun to work outside the home and concepts of fathering have changed (Cabrera et al., 2000; Casper, 1997; Pleck, 1997). A father's frequent and positive involvement with his child, from infancy on, is directly related to the child's well-being and physical, cognitive, and social development (Cabrera et al., 2000; Kelley, Smith, Green, Berndt, & Rogers, 1998; Shannon, Tamis-LeMonda, London, & Cabrera, 2002).

How Parents Shape Gender Differences

Being male or female affects how people look, how they move their bodies, and how they work, play, and dress. It influences what they think about themselves and what others think of them. All these characteristics—and more—are included in the word **gender:** what it means to be male or female.

gender Significance of being male or female.

Measurable gender differences in infancy are few, at least in U.S. samples. Baby boys are a bit longer and heavier than baby girls and may be slightly stronger, but they are physically more vulnerable from conception on. Newborn boys and girls react differently to stress, possibly suggesting genetic, hormonal, or temperamental differences (Davis & Emory, 1995). An analysis of a large number of studies found baby boys more active than baby girls, though this difference has not been consistently documented (Eaton & Enns, 1986).

The two sexes are equally sensitive to touch and tend to teethe, sit up, and walk at about the same ages (Maccoby, 1980). They also achieve the other motor milestones of infancy at about the same times. However, U.S. parents tend to *think* baby boys and girls are more different than they actually are. In a study of 11-month-old infants who recently had begun crawling, mothers consistently had higher expectations for their sons' success in crawling down steep and narrow slopes than for their daughters. Yet, when tested on the

In Japan, grandmothers like this one traditionally wear red as a sign of their noble status. Grandparenthood is an important milestone in western societies as well.

slopes, the baby girls and boys showed identical levels of performance (Mondschein, Adolph, & Tamis-LeMonda, 2000).

Parental shaping of boys' and girls' personalities appears to begin very early. Fathers, especially, promote **gender-typing,** the process by which children learn behavior that their culture considers appropriate for each sex (Bronstein, 1988). Fathers treat boys and girls more differently than mothers do, even during the first year (M. E. Snow, Jacklin, & Maccoby, 1983). During the second year, fathers talk more and spend more time with sons than with daughters (Lamb, 1981). Mothers talk more, and more supportively, to daughters than to sons. Overall, fathers are less talkative and supportive—but also less negative—in their speech than mothers are (Leaper, Anderson, & Sanders, 1998). Fathers of toddlers play more roughly with sons and show more sensitivity to daughters (Kelley et al., 1998). Home observations of 12-month-old, 18-month-old, and 5-year-old children found the biggest gender differences at 18 months, when both mothers and fathers tended to foster gender-typed play (Fagot & Hagan, 1991).

gender-typing Socialization process by which children, at an early age, learn appropriate gender roles.

We will discuss gender-typing and gender differences in more depth in Chapter 11.

Grandparents' Roles

In many developing societies and in some minority communities in the United States, extended-family households predominate, and grandparents play an integral role in child raising and family decisions. In Thailand and Taiwan, about 40 percent of the population aged 50 and over live with a minor grandchild, and half of those with grandchildren ages 10 or younger—usually grandmothers—provide care for the child (Kinsella & Velkoff, 2001).

Most U.S. children grow up in *nuclear families* limited to parents and siblings, and many grandparents live far away. However, distance does not necessarily affect the quality of relationships with grandchildren (Kivett, 1991, 1993, 1996). A major study of a nationally representative three-generation sample found that "grandparents play a limited but important role in family dynamics," and many have strong emotional ties to their grandchildren (Cherlin & Furstenberg, 1986a, p. 26).

What's your view

- How do you think your relationship with your father might have been different if you had grown up among the Huhot of Inner Mongolia? among the Aka people?
- Should parents try to treat male and female infants and toddlers alike?
- What was your grandparents' impact on your development?

Diane's sensitivity to Anna's needs contributes to the development of Anna's sense of basic trust—her ability to rely on the people and things in her world. Trust is necessary, according to Erikson, for children to form intimate relationships.

Checkpoint

Can you . . .

- ✔ Discuss the implications of research on monkeys "raised" by inanimate mothers?
- ✔ Compare the roles of fathers in various cultures?
- ✔ Discuss how parents influence gender-typing?
- ✔ Describe the changing roles of grandparents?

Many grandparents are their grandchildren's sole or primary caregivers. One reason, in developing countries, is the migration of rural parents to urban areas to find work. These "skip-generation" families exist in all regions of the world, particularly in Afro-Caribbean countries. In sub-Saharan Africa, the AIDS epidemic has left many orphans whose grandparents step into the parents' place (Kinsella & Velkoff, 2001).

In the United States, an increasing number of grandparents are serving as "parents by default" for children whose parents are unable to care for them—often as a result of teenage pregnancy, substance abuse, illness, divorce, or death (Allen et al., 2000). In 2002, 3.7 million children lived in grandparent-headed households, and 1.3 million of these children had no parent present. (Fields, 2003).

Guidepost 4

How do infants gain trust in their world and form attachments?

Developmental Issues in Infancy

How does a dependent newborn, with a limited emotional repertoire and pressing physical needs, become a child with complex feelings and the abilities to understand and control them? Much of this development revolves around issues regarding relationships with caregivers.

Developing Trust

For a far longer period than the young of other mammals, human babies are dependent on other people for food, for protection, and for their very lives. How do they come to trust that their needs will be met? According to Erikson (1950), early experiences are the key.

basic trust versus basic mistrust Erikson's first crisis in psychosocial development, in which infants develop a sense of the reliability of people and objects.

The first of the stages in psychosocial development that Erikson identified (refer back to Table 2-2 in Chapter 2) is **basic trust versus basic mistrust.** This stage begins in infancy and continues until about 18 months. In these early months, babies develop a sense of the reliability of the people and objects in their world. They need to develop a balance between trust (which lets them form intimate relationships) and mistrust (which enables them to protect themselves). If trust predominates, as it should, children develop the "virtue" of *hope:* the belief that they can fulfill their needs and obtain their desires (Erikson, 1982). If mistrust predominates, children will view the world as unfriendly and unpredictable and will have trouble forming relationships.

The critical element in developing trust is sensitive, responsive, consistent caregiving. Erikson saw the feeding situation as the setting for establishing the right mix of trust and mistrust. Can the baby count on being fed when hungry, and can the baby therefore trust the mother as a representative of the world? Trust enables an infant to let the mother out of sight "because she has become an inner certainty as well as an outer predictability" (Erikson, 1950, p. 247). This inner trust, in Cathy Bateson, may have formed a solid foundation for more difficult periods ahead.

Checkpoint

Can you . . .

✔ Explain the importance of basic trust, and identify the critical element in its development?

Developing Attachments

Attachment is a reciprocal, enduring emotional tie between an infant and a caregiver, each of whom contributes to the quality of the relationship. Attachments have adaptive value for babies, ensuring that their psychosocial as well as physical needs will be met. According to ethological theory (see Chapter 2), infants and parents are biologically predisposed to become attached to each other, and attachment promotes a baby's survival.

attachment Reciprocal, enduring tie between infant and caregiver, each of whom contributes to the quality of the relationship.

Studying Patterns of Attachment

The study of attachment owes much to the ethologist John Bowlby (1951), a pioneer in the study of bonding in animals. From his animal studies and from observations of disturbed children in a London psychoanalytic clinic, Bowlby became convinced of the importance of the mother-baby bond and warned against separating mother and baby without providing good substitute care. Mary Ainsworth, a student of Bowlby's in the early 1950s, went on to study attachment in African babies in Uganda through naturalistic observation in their homes (Ainsworth, 1967). Ainsworth later devised the **Strange Situation,** a now-classic laboratory-based technique designed to assess attachment patterns between an infant and an adult. Typically, the adult is the mother (though other adults have taken part as well), and the infant is 10 to 24 months old.

Strange Situation Laboratory technique used to study attachment.

The Strange Situation consists of a sequence of eight episodes, which takes less than half an hour. During that time, the mother twice leaves the baby in an unfamiliar room, the first time with a stranger. The second time she leaves the baby alone, and the stranger comes back before the mother does. The mother then encourages the baby to explore and play again and gives comfort if the baby seems to need it (Ainsworth, Blehar, Waters, & Wall, 1978). Of particular concern is the baby's response each time the mother returns.

When Ainsworth and her colleagues observed 1-year-olds in the Strange Situation and at home, they found three main patterns of attachment. These are *secure* (the most common category, into which about 60 to 75 percent of low-risk North American babies fall) and two forms of anxious, or insecure, attachment: *avoidant* (15 to 25 percent) and *ambivalent, or resistant* (10 to 15 percent) (Vondra & Barnett, 1999).

Babies with **secure attachment** cry or protest when the mother leaves and greet her happily when she returns. They use her as secure base, leaving her to go off and explore but returning occasionally for reassurance. They are usually cooperative and relatively free of anger. Babies with **avoidant attachment** rarely cry when the mother leaves, and they avoid her on her return. They tend to be angry and do not reach out in time of need. They dislike being held but dislike being put down even more. Babies with **ambivalent (resistant) attachment** become anxious even before the mother leaves and are very upset when she goes out. When she returns, they show their ambivalence by seeking contact with her while at the same time resisting it by kicking or squirming. Resistant babies do little exploration and are hard to comfort. These three attachment patterns are universal in all cultures in which they have been studied—cultures as different as those in Africa, China, and Israel—though the percentage of infants in each category varies (van IJzendoorn & Kroonenberg, 1988; van IJzendoorn & Sagi, 1999).

secure attachment Pattern in which an infant cries or protests when the primary caregiver leaves and actively seeks out the caregiver upon his or her return.

avoidant attachment Pattern in which an infant rarely cries when separated from the primary caregiver and avoids contact upon his or her return.

ambivalent (resistant) attachment Pattern in which an infant becomes anxious before the primary caregiver leaves, is extremely upset during his or her absence, and both seeks and resists contact on his or her return.

Later research (Main & Solomon, 1986) identified a fourth pattern, **disorganized-disoriented attachment.** This pattern is often subtle and difficult to observe, but it has been validated by more than 80 studies (Van IJzendoorn, Schuengel, & Bakermans-Kranenburg, 1999). Babies with the disorganized pattern seem to lack an organized strategy to deal with the stress of the Strange Situation. Instead, they show contradictory,

disorganized-disoriented attachment Pattern in which an infant, after separation from the primary caregiver, shows contradictory behaviors upon his or her return.

Table 8-3 Atatchment Behaviors in Strange Situation

Attachment Classification	Behavior
Secure	Gloria plays and explores freely when her mother is nearby. She responds enthusiastically when her mother returns.
Avoidant	When Sam's mother returns, Sam does not make eye contact or greet her. It is almost as if he has not noticed her return.
Ambivalent (Resistant)	James hovers close to his mother during much of the Strange Situation, but he does not greet her positively or enthusiastically during the reunion episode. Instead, he is angry and upset.
Disorganized/Disoriented	Erica responds to the Strange Situation with inconsistent, contradictory behavior. She seems to fall apart, overwhelmed by the stress.

Source: Based on Thompson, 1998, pp. 37–39.

repetitive, or misdirected behaviors (seeking closeness to the stranger instead of the mother). They may greet the mother brightly when she returns but then turn away or approach without looking at her. They seem confused and afraid. This may be the least secure pattern. It is most likely to occur in babies whose mothers are insensitive, intrusive, or abusive or have suffered unresolved loss. The child's temperament does not seem to be a factor (Carlson, 1998; Van IJzendoorn et al., 1999). Disorganized attachment tends to remain fairly stable and seems to be a risk factor for later behavioral problems, especially aggressive conduct (Van IJzendoorn et al., 1999). Disorganized attachment is thought to occur in at least 10 percent of low-risk infants but in much higher proportions in certain at-risk populations, such as premature children, those with autism or Down syndrome, and those whose mothers abuse alcohol or drugs (Vondra & Barnett, 1999). (Table 8-3 describes how babies with each of the four patterns of attachment react to the Strange Situation.)

Although much research on attachment has been based on the Strange Situation, some investigators have questioned its validity. The Strange Situation *is* strange; it is also artificial. It asks mothers not to initiate interaction, exposes babies to repeated comings and goings of adults, and expects the infants to pay attention to them. Since attachment influences a wider range of behaviors than are seen in the Strange Situation, some researchers have called for a more comprehensive, sensitive method to measure it, one that would show how mother and infant interact during natural, nonstressful situations (T. M. Field, 1987). Also, the Strange Situation may be less valid in some nonwestern cultures, which have different expectations for babies' interaction with their mothers and in which mothers may encourage different kinds of attachment-related behavior. Research on Japanese infants, who are less commonly separated from their mothers than U.S. babies, showed high rates of resistant attachment, which may reflect the extreme stressfulness of the Strange Situation for these babies (Miyake, Chen, & Campos, 1985).

Some researchers have begun to supplement the Strange Situation with methods that enable them to study children in natural settings. Using a Q-sort technique, observers sort a set of descriptive words or phrases ("cries a lot"; "tends to cling") into categories ranging from most to least characteristic of the child. The Waters and Deane (1985) Attachment Q-set (AQS) has mothers or other observers compare descriptions of children's everyday behavior with expert descriptions of the "hypothetical most secure child." The Preschool Assessment of Attachment (PAA) (Crittenden, 1993), an instrument for measuring attachment after 20 months of age, takes into account older preschoolers' more complex relationships and language abilities.

In a cross-cultural study using the AQS, mothers in China, Colombia, Germany, Israel, Japan, Norway, and the United States decribed their children as behaving more like than unlike the "most secure child." Furthermore, the mothers' descriptions of "secure-base" behavior were about as similar across cultures as within a culture. These findings suggest that the tendency to use the mother as a secure base is universal, though it may take somewhat varied forms (Posada et al., 1995).

How Attachment Is Established

This baby, like most infants, is developing a strong attachment to his mother. Both mother and baby contribute to the security of attachment by their personalities and behavior and their responsiveness to each other.

On the basis of a baby's interactions with the mother, proposed Ainsworth and Bowlby, the baby builds a "working model" of what can be expected from her. The various patterns of emotional attachment represent different cognitive representations that result in different expectations. As long as the mother continues to act the same way, the model holds up. If her behavior changes—not just once or twice but consistently—the baby may revise the model, and security of attachment may change.

A baby's working model of attachment is related to Erikson's concept of basic trust. Secure attachment evolves from trust; insecure attachment reflects mistrust. Securely attached babies have learned to trust not only their caregivers but their own ability to get what they need. Thus, babies who cry a lot and whose mothers respond by soothing them tend to be securely attached (Del Carmen, Pedersen, Huffman, & Bryan, 1993). Mothers of securely attached infants and toddlers tend to be sensitive and responsive (Ainsworth et al., 1978; Braungart-Rieker et al., 2001; De Wolff & van IJzendoorn, 1997; Isabella, 1993; NICHD Early Child Care Research Network, 1997a). Equally important are mutual interaction, stimulation, a positive attitude, warmth and acceptance, and emotional support (De Wolff & van IJzendoorn, 1997; Lundy, 2003).

The Role of Temperament

How much influence does temperament exert on attachment and in what ways? Findings vary (Susman-Stillman, Kalkoske, Egeland, & Waldman, 1996; Vaughn et al., 1992). In a study of 6- to 12-month-olds and their families, both a mother's sensitivity and her baby's temperament influenced attachment patterns (Seifer, Schiller, Sameroff, Resnick, & Riordan, 1996). Neurological or physiological conditions may underlie temperamental differences in attachment. For example, variability in heart rate is associated with irritability, and heart rate seems to vary more in insecurely attached infants (Izard, Porges, et al., 1991).

A baby's temperament may have not only a direct impact on attachment but also an indirect impact through its effect on the parents. In a series of studies in the Netherlands (van den Boom, 1989, 1994), 15-day-old infants classified as irritable were much more likely than nonirritable infants to be insecurely (usually avoidantly) attached at 1 year. However, irritable infants whose mothers received home visits, with instruction on how to soothe their babies, were as likely to be rated securely attached as the nonirritable infants. Thus, irritability on an infant's part may prevent the development of secure attachment but not if the mother has the skills to cope with the baby's temperament (Rothbart et al., 2000). "Goodness of fit" between parent and child may well be a key to understanding security of attachment.

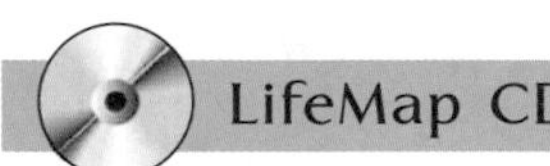

To learn more about the interplay between attachment and infant temperament, watch the "Attachment in Early Childhood" video in Chapter 8 of your CD.

Stranger Anxiety and Separation Anxiety

Sophie used to be a friendly baby, smiling at strangers and going to them, continuing to coo happily as long as someone—anyone—was around. Now, at 8 months, she turns away when a new person approaches and howls when her parents try to leave her with a babysitter. Sophie is experiencing both **stranger anxiety,** wariness of a person she does not know, and **separation anxiety,** distress when a familiar caregiver leaves her.

stranger anxiety Wariness of strange people and places, shown by some infants during the second half of the first year.

separation anxiety Distress shown by an infant when a familiar caregiver leaves.

Separation anxiety and stranger anxiety used to be considered emotional and cognitive milestones of the second half of infancy, reflecting attachment to the mother. However, newer research suggests that although stranger anxiety and separation anxiety are fairly typical, they are not universal. Whether a baby cries when a parent leaves or when someone new approaches may say more about the baby's temperament or life circumstances than about security of attachment (R. J. Davidson & Fox, 1989).

Babies rarely react negatively to strangers before 6 months of age, commonly do so by 8 or 9 months, and do so more and more throughout the rest of the first year (Sroufe, 1997). This change may reflect cognitive development. Sophie's stranger anxiety involves memory for faces, the ability to compare the stranger's appearance with her mother's, and perhaps the recollection of situations in which she has been left with a stranger. If Sophie is allowed to get used to the stranger gradually in a familiar setting, she may react more positively (Lewis, 1997; Sroufe, 1997). (As we've mentioned, Margaret Mead and Gregory Bateson made sure that Cathy always met a new caregiver in a familiar place.)

Separation anxiety may be due not so much to the separation itself as to the quality of substitute care. When substitute caregivers are warm and responsive and play with 9-month-olds *before* they cry, the babies cry less than when they are with less responsive caregivers (Gunnar, Larson, Hertsgaard, Harris, & Brodersen, 1992).

Stability of care is important. Pioneering work by René Spitz (1945, 1946) on institutionalized children emphasizes the need for substitute care to be as close as possible to good mothering. Research has underlined the value of continuity and consistency in caregiving, so children can form early emotional bonds with their caregivers. As Mead observed in southeast island cultures, bonds can be formed with multiple caregivers, as long as the caregiving situation is stable.

Today, neither intense fear of strangers nor intense protest when the mother leaves is considered to be a sign of secure attachment. Researchers measure attachment more by what happens when the mother returns than by how many tears the baby sheds at her departure.

Long-Term Effects of Attachment

As attachment theory proposes, security of attachment seems to affect emotional, social, and cognitive competence (van IJzendoorn & Sagi, 1997). The more secure a child's attachment to a nurturing adult, the easier it seems to be for the child eventually to become independent of that adult and to develop good relationships with others. The link between attachment in infancy and characteristics observed years later underscores the continuity of development and the interrelationships of its various aspects.

If, on the basis of early experience, children have positive expectations about their ability to get along with others and to engage in social give and take and if they think well of themselves, they may set up social situations that tend to reinforce these beliefs (Elicker et al., 1992; Sroufe et al., 1993). And if children, as infants, had a secure base and could count on parents' or caregivers' responsiveness, they are likely to feel confident enough to be actively engaged in their world (Jacobsen & Hofmann, 1997).

An analysis of seven studies found a substantial association between the quality of infant attachment and language development, as well as a smaller association with cognitive development (Van IJzendoorn, Dijkstra, & Bus, 1995). Securely attached toddlers tend to have larger, more varied vocabularies than those who are insecurely attached (Meins, 1998). They also tend to be more sociable (Elicker, Englund, & Sroufe, 1992; Main, 1983). They have more positive interactions with peers, and their friendly overtures are more likely to be accepted (Fagot, 1997). Insecurely attached toddlers tend to show more negative emotions (fear, distress, and anger), while securely attached children are more joyful (Kochanska, 2001).

From ages 3 to 5, securely attached children are likely to be more curious, competent, empathic, resilient, and self-confident, to get along better with other children, and to form closer friendships than children who were insecurely attached as infants (Arend, Gove, & Sroufe, 1979; Elicker et al., 1992; J. L. Jacobson & Wille, 1986; Waters, Wippman, & Sroufe, 1979; Youngblade & Belsky, 1992). They interact more positively with parents, preschool teachers, and peers and are better able to resolve conflicts (Elicker et al., 1992). They tend to have a more positive self-image (Elicker et al., 1992; Verschueren, Marcoen, & Schoefs, 1996).

Their advantages continue. In a French-Canadian laboratory observation, attachment patterns and the emotional quality of 6-year-olds' interactions with their mothers predicted the strength of the children's communicative skills, cognitive engagement, and mastery motivation at age 8 (Moss & St-Laurent, 2001).

Secure attachment seems to prepare children for the intimacy of friendship (Carlson, Sroufe, & Egeland, 2004). In middle childhood and adolescence, securely attached children (at least in western cultures, where most studies have been done) tend to have the closest, most stable friendships (Schneider, Atkinson, & Tardif, 2001; Sroufe et al., 1993). They also tend to be more self-reliant, self-assured, adaptable, resilient, and emotionally healthy (Sroufe et al., 1993).

Insecurely attached infants, by contrast, often have inhibitions and negative emotions in toddlerhood, hostility toward other children at age 5, and dependency during the school years (Calkins & Fox, 1992; Kochanska, 2001; Lyons-Ruth, Alpern, & Repacholi, 1993; Sroufe et al., 1993). Those with disorganized attachment tend to have behavior problems at all levels of schooling and psychiatric disorders at age 17 (Carlson, 1998).

It may be that correlations between attachment in infancy and later development stem, not from attachment itself, but from underlying personality characteristics that affect both attachment and parent-child interactions *after* infancy (Lamb, 1987). However, studies with rhesus monkeys suggest that secure attachment may counteract certain genetic risks. Monkeys with a variant of a gene linked to low levels of the brain chemical serotonin tend to be extremely impulsive and aggressive—but only if they experienced insecure early attachments. Securely attached monkeys do not show this behavior pattern, and their serotonin levels are normal (Suomi, 2003).

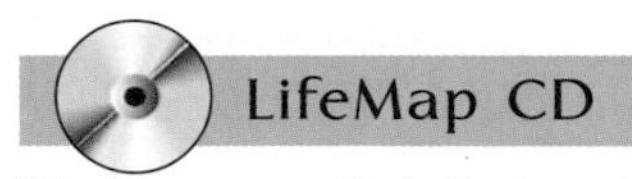

Would you agree that attachment theory led to a revolution in developmental psychology? See if the "Attachment Theory" video in Chapter 8 of your CD changes your opinion.

Intergenerational Transmission of Attachment Patterns

The way a mother remembers her attachment to her parents seems to predict the way her children will be attached to *her.* The *Adult Attachment Interview (AAI)* (George, Kaplan, & Main, 1985; Main, 1995; Main, Kaplan, & Cassidy, 1985) is a semistructured interview that asks adults to recall and interpret feelings and experiences related to their childhood attachments. An analysis of 18 studies using the AAI found that the clarity, coherence, and consistency of the responses reliably predict the security with which the respondent's own child will be attached to him or her (van IJzendoorn, 1995).

The way adults recall early experiences with parents or caregivers affects their emotional well-being and may also influence the way they respond to and deal with their own children (Adam, Gunnar, & Tanaka, 2004; Dozier, Stovall, Albus, & Bates, 2001; Pesonen, Räikkönen, Keltikangas-Järvinen, Strandberg, & Järvenpäa, 2003; Slade, Belsky, Aber, & Phelps, 1999). A mother who was securely attached to *her* mother or who understands why she was insecurely attached can accurately recognize the baby's attachment behaviors, respond encouragingly, and help the baby form a secure attachment to her (Bretherton, 1990). Mothers who are preoccupied with their past attachment relationships tend to show anger and intrusiveness in interactions with their children. Depressed mothers who dismiss memories of their past attachments tend to be cold and unresponsive to their children (Adam et al., 2003). Parents' attachment history also influences their perceptions of their baby's temperament, and those perceptions (as we have seen) often affect the parent-child relationship (Pesonen et al., 2003).

Checkpoint

Can you . . .

- ✔ Describe four patterns of attachment?
- ✔ Discuss how attachment is established, including the role of temperament?
- ✔ Discuss factors affecting stranger anxiety and separation anxiety?
- ✔ Describe long-term behavioral differences influenced by attachment patterns?

Emotional Communication with Caregivers: Mutual Regulation

Guidepost 5

How do infants and caregivers "read" each other's nonverbal signals?

Interactions that influence the security of attachment depend on the ability of both infant and caregiver to respond appropriately and sensitively to each other's mental and emotional states. Parents may contribute to these reciprocal, mutually rewarding interactions by making comments that show recognition of what is on an infant's mind (Lundy, 2003). Infants take an active part in the process by sending behavioral signals that influence the way caregivers behave toward them.

In this process of **mutual regulation,** healthy interaction occurs when a caregiver "reads" a baby's signals accurately and responds appropriately. When a baby's goals are met, the baby is joyful or at least interested (E. Z. Tronick, 1989). If a caregiver ignores an invitation to play or insists on playing when the baby has signaled "I don't feel like it," the baby may feel frustrated or sad. When babies do not achieve desired results, they keep on

mutual regulation Process by which infant and caregiver communicate emotional states to each other and respond appropriately.

sending signals to repair the interaction. Normally, interaction moves back and forth between well-regulated and poorly regulated states, and babies learn from these shifts how to send signals and what to do when their initial signals do not result in a comfortable emotional balance. Mutual regulation helps babies learn to "read" others' behavior and to develop expectations about it. Even very young infants can perceive emotions expressed by others and can adjust their own behavior accordingly (Legerstee & Varghese, 2001; Montague & Walker-Andrews, 2001; Termine & Izard, 1988).

Measuring Mutual Regulation: The "Still-Face" Paradigm

"still-face" paradigm Research procedure used to measure mutual regulation in infants 2 to 9 months old.

The **still-face paradigm** is a research procedure used to measure mutual regulation in 2- to 9-month-old infants. In the *still-face* episode, which follows a normal face-to-face interaction, the mother suddenly becomes stony-faced, silent, and unresponsive. Then, a few minutes later, she resumes normal interaction (the *reunion* episode). During the still-face episode, infants tend to stop smiling and looking at the mother. They may make faces, sounds, or gestures or may touch themselves, their clothing, or a chair, apparently to comfort themselves or to relieve the emotional stress created by the mother's unexpected behavior (Cohn & Tronick, 1983; E. Z. Tronick, 1980, 1989; Weinberg & Tronick, 1996).

How do infants react during the reunion episode? One study combined a microanalysis of 6-month-olds' facial expressions during this episode with measures of heart rate and nervous system reactivity. On the one hand, the infants showed even more positive behavior—joyous expressions and utterances and gazes and gestures directed toward the mother—than before the still-face episode. On the other hand, the persistence of sad or angry facial expressions, "pick-me-up" gestures, distancing, and indications of stress as well as an increased tendency to fuss and cry suggested that the negative feelings stirred by a breakdown in mutual regulation were not readily eased (Weinberg & Tronick, 1996).

The still-face reaction seems to be similar in eastern and western cultures and in interactions with both fathers and mothers (Braungart-Rieker, Garwood, Powers, & Notaro, 1998; Kisilevsky et al., 1998). However, gender differences have been found. In one laboratory observation, 6-month-old sons seemed to have a harder time than daughters in regulating their emotions during the still-face episode (Weinberg, Tronick, Cohn, & Olson, 1999).

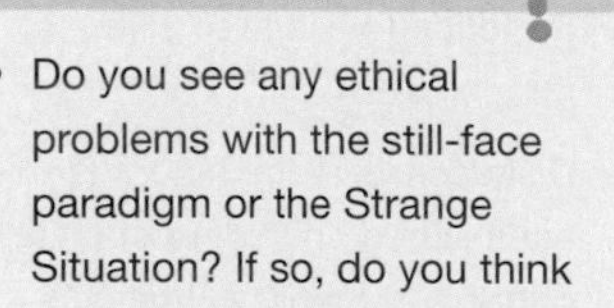

What's your view?

- Do you see any ethical problems with the still-face paradigm or the Strange Situation? If so, do you think the benefits of these kinds of research are worth any potential risks?

The way a mother sees and responds to her infant affects the infants' reactions to the still-face procedure (Rosenblum, McDonough, Muzik, Miller, & Sameroff, 2002; Tarabulsy et al., 2003). Infants whose parents are normally sensitive and responsive to their emotional needs seem better able to comfort themselves and show less negative emotion during the still-face episode and recover more readily during the reunion episode (Braungart-Rieker et al., 2001; Tarabulsy et al., 2003).

Emotional Communication as a Developmental Process

The ability to synchronize emotional interactions with a caregiver may be a crucial developmental achievement that facilitates social, emotional, and cognitive growth (Harrist & Waugh, 2002). In early infancy, synchrony depends largely on caregivers' *attunement,* or sensitivity, to the infant's signals. Infants may benefit from such interactions in four ways:

1. Synchronous interactions may enhance the infant's ability to coordinate sensory inputs: for example, awareness of the caregiver's gaze and vocalization with the sense of being held and touched.
2. Synchronous interactions may help an infant achieve emotional and physiological self-regulation, a balance between stimulation and arousal.
3. Synchronous interactions give an infant a sense that an interaction "feels right."
4. The frequency of synchronous interactions in early infancy predicts security of attachment.

Infants' ability to regulate emotions during the still-face procedure at 4 months has been shown to predict security of attachment at 12 months (Braungart-Rieker et al., 2001).

In toddlerhood, the child becomes a more active, intentional partner in interactions and sometimes initiates them. Caregivers can now more clearly "read" the child's signals.

Synchronous interactions may help toddlers gain communicative skills and social competence and may promote voluntary compliance with a parent's wishes (Harrist & Waugh, 2002).

How a Mother's Depression Affects Mutual Regulation

Reading emotional signals lets mothers assess and meet babies' needs; and it lets babies influence or respond to the mother's behavior toward them. What happens, then, if that communication system seriously breaks down, and what can be done about it?

Postpartum depression affects about 13 percent of new mothers—including the actress Brooke Shields, who has written a book about it. Unless treated promptly, it may have a negative impact on the way a mother interacts with her baby and on the child's future cognitive and emotional development (Gjerdingen, 2003).

Depressed mothers are less sensitive and less engaged with their infants than nondepressed mothers, and their interactions with their babies are generally less positive (NICHD Early Child Care Research Network, 1999b). Depressed mothers are less able to interpret and respond to an infant's cries (Donovan, Leavitt, & Walsh, 1998) and are less likely to comment on an infant's mental state (Lundy, 2003).

Babies of depressed mothers may give up on sending emotional signals and try to comfort themselves by sucking or rocking. If this defensive reaction becomes habitual, babies learn that they have no power to draw responses from other people, that their mothers are unreliable, and that the world is untrustworthy. They also may become depressed themselves (Ashman & Dawson, 2002; Gelfand & Teti, 1995; Teti et al., 1995).

We cannot be sure, however, that such infants become depressed through a failure of mutual regulation. They may inherit a predisposition to depression or acquire it prenatally through exposure to hormonal or other biochemical influences. Newborns of mothers with depressive symptoms are less expressive, less active and robust, more excitable, and less oriented to sensory stimuli than other newborns, suggesting an inborn tendency toward depression (Lundy, Field, & Pickens, 1996).

Infants of depressed mothers tend to show unusual patterns of brain activity, similar to the mothers' own patterns. Within 24 hours of birth, they show relatively less activity in the left frontal region of the brain, which seems to be specialized for "approach" emotions such as joy and anger, and more activity in the right frontal region, which controls "withdrawal" emotions, such as distress and disgust (G. Dawson et al., 1992, 1999; T. Field, 1998a, 1998c; T. Field, Fox, Pickens, Nawrocki, & Soutollo, 1995; N. A. Jones, Field, Fox, Lundy, & Davalos, 1997). Newborns of depressed mothers also tend to have higher levels of stress hormones (Lundy et al., 1999), lower scores on the Brazelton Neonatal Behavior Assessment Scale, and lower vagal tone, which is associated with attention and learning (T. Field, 1998a, 1998c; N. A. Jones et al., 1998). These findings suggest that a woman's depression during pregnancy may contribute to her newborn's neurological and behavioral functioning.

It may be that a combination of genetic, prenatal, and environmental factors puts infants of depressed mothers at risk. A bidirectional influence may be at work; an infant who does not respond normally may further depress the mother, and her unresponsiveness may in turn increase the infant's depression (T. Field, 1995, 1998a, 1998c; Lundy et al., 1999). Some depressed mothers do maintain good interactions with their infants, and these infants tend to have better emotional regulation than other infants of depressed mothers. These infants' characteristics may evoke more positive responses from their mothers (Field, Diego, Hernandez-Reif, Schanberg, & Kuhn, 2003). Interactions with a nondepressed adult—the father or a child care worker or nursery school teacher—can help infants compensate for the effects of depressed mothering (T. Field, 1995, 1998a, 1998c).

Both as infants and as preschoolers, children with depressed mothers tend to be insecurely attached to them (Gelfand & Teti, 1995; Teti et al., 1995). They are less motivated to explore and more apt to prefer relatively unchallenging tasks (Hart, Field, del Valle, & Pelaez-Nogueras, 1998; Redding, Harmon, & Morgan, 1990). They are likely to grow poorly, to perform poorly on cognitive and linguistic measures, and to have behavior problems (T. Field, 1998a, 1998c; T. M. Field et al., 1985; Gelfand & Teti, 1995; NICHD Early

Child Care Research Network, 1999b; B. S. Zuckerman & Beardslee, 1987). As toddlers these children tend to have trouble suppressing frustration and tension (Cole, Barrett, & Zahn-Waxler, 1992; Seiner & Gelfand, 1995), and in early adolescence they are at risk for violent behavior (Hay, 2003).

Techniques that may help improve a depressed mother's mood include listening to music, visual imagery, aerobics, yoga, relaxation, and massage therapy (T. Field, 1995, 1998a, 1998c). Massage also can help depressed babies (T. Field, 1998a, 1998b; T. Field et al., 1996), possibly through effects on neurological activity (N. A. Jones et al., 1997). In one study, such mood-brightening measures—plus social, educational, and vocational rehabilitation for the mother and day care for the infant—improved their interaction behavior. The infants showed faster growth and had fewer pediatric problems, more normal biochemical values, and better developmental test scores than a control group (T. Field, 1998a, 1998b).

Social Referencing

social referencing
Understanding an ambiguous situation by seeking out another person's perception of it.

If, at a formal dinner party, you have ever cast a sidelong glance to see which fork the person next to you was using, you have read another person's nonverbal signals to get information on how to act. Through **social referencing,** one person forms an understanding of how to act in an ambiguous, confusing, or unfamiliar situation by seeking out and interpreting another person's perception of it. Babies seem to use social referencing when they look at their caregivers upon encountering a new person or toy. This pattern of behavior may emerge some time after 6 months of age, when infants begin to judge the possible consequences of events, imitate complex behaviors, and distinguish among and react to various emotional expressions.

In a study using the visual cliff (a measure of depth perception described in Chapter 6), when the drop looked very shallow or very deep, 1-year-olds did not look to their mothers; they were able to judge for themselves whether to cross over. When they were uncertain about the depth of the "cliff," however, they paused at the "edge," looked down, and then looked up at their mothers. Most of the babies whose mothers showed joy or interest crossed the "drop," but very few whose mothers looked angry or afraid crossed it (Sorce, Emde, Campos, & Klinnert, 1985).

The idea that infants engage in social referencing has been challenged. When infants spontaneously look at caregivers in ambiguous situations, it is not clear that they are looking for information; they may be seeking comfort, attention, sharing of feelings, or simply reassurance of the caregiver's presence—typical attachment behaviors (Baldwin & Moses, 1996). However, newer research provides experimental evidence of social referencing at 1 year (Moses, Baldwin, Rosicky, & Tidball, 2001). When exposed to jiggling or vibrating toys fastened to the floor or ceiling, both 12- and 18-month-olds moved closer to or farther from the toys depending on the experimenters' expressed emotional reactions ("Yecch!" or "Nice!"). In a pair of studies, 12-month-olds (but not 10-month-olds) adjusted their behavior toward certain unfamiliar objects according to nonvocal emotional signals given by an actress on a television screen (Mumme & Fernald, 2003).

Checkpoint

Can you . . .

- ✔ Describe how mutual regulation works?
- ✔ Discuss how a mother's depression can affect her baby?
- ✔ Tell what social referencing is, and give examples of how infants seem to use it?

Developmental Issues in Toddlerhood

About halfway between their first and second birthdays, babies become toddlers. This transformation can be seen not only in such physical and cognitive skills as walking and talking, but also in the ways children express their personalities and interact with others. Let's look at three psychological issues that toddlers—and their caregivers—have to deal with: the emerging *sense of self;* the growth of *autonomy,* or self-determination; and the *internalization of behavioral standards.*

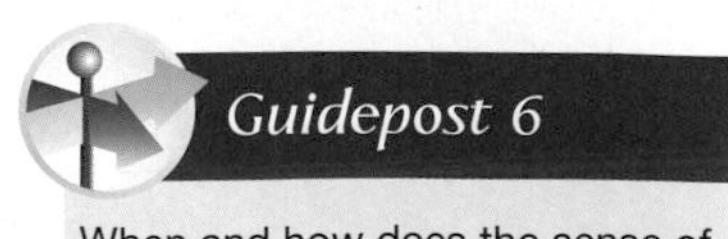

When and how does the sense of self arise?

The Emerging Sense of Self

William James, in the late 19th century, described two selves: the *I-self* and the *Me-self,* the knower and the known (James, 1950). The I-self is a subjective entity that constructs and seeks to know the Me-self. The Me-self, or **self-concept,** is what can be known about the self. It is what the I-self believes about the Me-self—our total picture of our abilities and traits.

self-concept Sense of self; descriptive and evaluative mental picture of one's abilities and traits.

The I-self is believed to emerge in the context of the infant-caregiver relationship, as an infant begins to form a rudimentary sense of self and others. Between 4 and 10 months, when infants learn to reach, grasp, and make things happen, they may begin to experience a sense of personal *agency,* a feature of the I-self. The sense of agency—the realization that one can control external events—is a forerunner of what Bandura (1994) calls **self-efficacy,** a sense of being able to master challenges and achieve goals. At about this time infants develop *self-coherence,* the sense of being a physical whole with boundaries, within which agency resides (Harter, 1998).

self-efficacy Sense of capability to master challenges and achieve goals.

The emergence of *self-awareness*—conscious knowledge of the self—may build on perceptual discrimination between self and others. In an experiment with 96 four- and nine-month-olds, the infants showed more interest in images of others than of themselves (Rochat & Striano, 2002). This early *perceptual* discrimination may be the foundation of the Me-self, the *conceptual* self-awareness that develops between 15 and 18 months. In a classic line of research, investigators dabbed rouge on the noses of 6- to 24-month-olds and sat them in front of a mirror. Three-fourths of 18-month-olds and all 24-month-olds touched their red noses more often than before, whereas babies younger than 15 months never did. This behavior suggests that the older babies knew they did not normally have red noses and recognized the image in the mirror as their own (Lewis, 1997; Lewis & Brooks, 1974).

Once infants can recognize themselves, they show interest in their own features. Periodically, between 9 and 24 months of age, babies saw video images of themselves and another infant the same age. In one of the images of themselves, a spot of red lipstick had surreptiously been placed on each cheek. In addition, from 12 months on, the infants were given a mirror recognition test like the one just described, except that a colored sticker was placed on their faces instead of rouge. At the same age when the infants showed self-recognition in the mirror (18 months), they also began to show a preference for looking at their own video image, both with and without the lipstick mark (Nielsen, Dissanayake, & Kashima, 2003).

What's your view 

- How would you expect each of the early stages in self-concept development to affect the parent-child relationship?

By 20 to 24 months, toddlers begin to use first-person pronouns, another sign of self-awareness (Lewis, 1997). Between 19 and 30 months, they begin to apply descriptive terms ("big" or "little"; "straight hair" or "curly hair") and evaluative ones ("good," "pretty," or "strong") to themselves. The rapid development of language enables children to think and talk about the self and to incorporate parents' verbal descriptions ("You're so smart!" "What a big boy!") into their own emerging self-image (Stipek, Gralinski, & Kopp, 1990). Self-evaluation and evaluation by others are steps toward the development of conscience.

Checkpoint 

Can you . . .

✔ Trace the early development of the sense of self?

Developing Autonomy

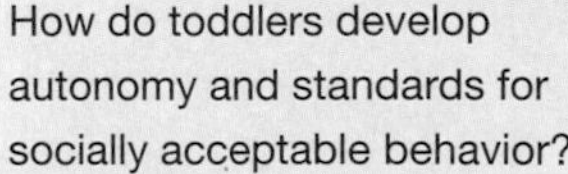

How do toddlers develop autonomy and standards for socially acceptable behavior?

Erikson (1950) identified the period from about 18 months to 3 years as the second stage in personality development, **autonomy versus shame and doubt,** which is marked by a shift from external control to self-control. Having come through infancy with a sense of basic trust in the world and an awakening self-awareness, toddlers begin to substitute their own judgment for their caregivers'. The "virtue" that emerges during this stage is *will.* Toilet training, which in most children is completed most rapidly if begun after 27 months (Blum, Taubman, & Nemeth, 2003), is an important step toward autonomy and self-control. So is language; as children are better able to make their wishes understood, they become more powerful and independent. Since unlimited freedom is neither safe nor healthy, said Erikson, shame and doubt have a necessary place. Toddlers need adults to set appropriate limits, and shame and doubt help them recognize the need for those limits.

autonomy versus shame and doubt Erikson's second crisis in psychosocial development, in which children achieve a balance between self-determination and control by others.

In the United States, the "terrible twos" are a normal manifestation of the drive for autonomy. Toddlers have to test the notions that they are individuals, that they have some control over their world, and that they have new, exciting powers. They are driven to try out their own ideas, exercise their own preferences, and make their own decisions. This drive

Table 8-4 Dealing with the "Terrible Twos"

The following research-based guidelines can help parents of toddlers discourage negativism and encourage socially acceptable behavior.

- *Be flexible.* Learn the child's natural rhythms and special likes and dislikes.
- *Think of yourself as a safe harbor,* with safe limits, from which a child can set out and discover the world and to which the child can keep coming back for support.
- *Make your home "child friendly."* Fill it with unbreakable objects that are safe to explore.
- *Avoid physical punishment.* It is often ineffective and may even lead a toddler to do more damage.
- *Offer a choice*—even a limited one—to give the child some control. ("Would you like to have your bath now or after we read a book?")
- *Be consistent* in enforcing necessary requests.
- *Don't interrupt an activity unless absolutely necessary.* Try to wait until the child's attention has shifted.
- *If you must interrupt, give warning.* ("We have to leave the playground soon.")
- *Suggest alternative activities* when behavior becomes objectionable. (When Ashley is throwing sand in Keiko's face, say, "Oh, look! Nobody's on the swings now. Let's go over and I'll give you a good push!")
- *Suggest; don't* command. Accompany requests with smiles or hugs, not criticism, threats, or physical restraint.
- *Link requests with pleasurable activities.* ("It's time to stop playing so that you can go to the store with me.")
- *Remind the child of what you expect:* "When we go to this playground, we *never* go outside the gate."
- *Wait a few moments before repeating a request* when a child doesn't comply immediately.
- Use *"time out"* to end conflicts. In a nonpunitive way, remove either yourself or the child from a situation.
- *Expect less self-control during times of stress* (illness, divorce, the birth of a sibling, or a move to a new home).
- *Expect it to be harder for toddlers to comply with "dos" than with "don'ts".* "Clean up your room" takes more effort than "Don't write on the furniture."
- *Keep the atmosphere as positive* as possible. Make your child *want* to cooperate.

Sources: Hasweli, Hock, & Wenar, 1981: Kochanska & Aksan, 1995; Kopp, 1982; Kuczynski & Kochanska 1995; Power & Chapieski, 1986.

socialization Development of habits, skills, values, and motives shared by responsible, productive members of a society.

internalization Process fundamental to socialization by which children accept societal standards of conduct as their own.

typically shows itself in the form of *negativism,* the tendency to shout, "No!" just for the sake of resisting authority. Almost all U.S. children show negativism to some degree; it usually begins before 2 years of age, tends to peak at about 3½ to 4, and declines by age 6. Caregivers who view children's expressions of self-will as a normal, healthy striving for independence, not as stubbornness, can help them learn self-control, contribute to their sense of competence, and avoid excessive conflict. (Table 8-4 gives specific, research-based suggestions for dealing with the "terrible twos.")

This toddler is showing autonomy—the drive to exert her own power over her environment.

Many U.S. parents might be surprised to hear that the "terrible twos" are not universal. In some developing countries, the transition from infancy to early childhood is relatively smooth and harmonious (Mosier & Rogoff, 2003; see Box 8-2).

Socialization and Internalization: Developing a Conscience

Socialization is the process by which children develop habits, skills, values, and motives that make them responsible, productive members of society. Compliance with parental expectations can be seen as a first step toward compliance with societal standards. Socialization rests on **internalization** of these standards. Children who are successfully socialized no longer merely obey

Around the World

Box 8-2 *Are Struggles with Toddlers Necessary?*

Are the "terrible twos" a normal phase in child development? Many western parents and psychologists think so. Actually, though, this transition does not appear to be universal.

In Zinacantan, Mexico, toddlers do not typically become demanding and resistant to parental control. Instead of asserting independence from their mothers, toddlerhood in Zinacantan is a time when children move from mama's babies toward the new status of "mother's helpers," responsible children who tend a new baby and help with household tasks (Edwards, 1994). A similar developmental pattern seems to occur in Mazahua families in Mexico and among Mayan families in San Pedro, Guatemala. San Pedro parents "do not report a particular age when they expect children to become especially contrary or negative" (Mosier & Rogoff, 2003, p. 1058).

One arena in which issues of autonomy and control appear in western cultures is in sibling conflicts over toys and the way children respond to parental handling of these conflicts. To explore these issues, a cross-cultural study compared 16 San Pedro families with 16 middle-class European-American families in Salt Lake City. All of the families had toddlers 14 to 20 months old and older siblings 3 to 5 years old. The researchers interviewed each mother about her child-raising practices. They then handed the mother a series of attractive objects (such as nesting dolls and a jumping-jack puppet) and, in the presence of the older sibling, asked the mother to help the toddler operate them, with no instructions about the older child. Researchers who observed the ensuing interactions found striking differences in the way siblings interacted in the two cultures and in the way the mothers viewed and handled sibling conflict.

The older siblings in Salt Lake City often tried to take and play with the objects, but this did not generally happen in San Pedro. Instead, the older San Pedro children would offer to help their younger siblings work the objects, or the two children would play with them together. When there was a conflict over possession of the objects, the San Pedro mothers almost always favored the toddlers (94 percent of the time), even taking an object away from the older child if the younger child wanted it; and the older siblings tended to go along, willingly handing the objects to the toddlers or letting them have the objects from the start. By contrast, in more than one-third of the interactions in Salt Lake City, the mothers tried to treat both children equally, negotiating with them or suggesting that they take turns or share. These observations were consistent with reports of mothers in both cultures of how they handled such issues at home. San Pedro children are given a privileged position until age 3; then they are expected to willingly cooperate with social expectations.

What explains these cultural contrasts? A possible clue emerged when the mothers were asked at what age children can be held responsible for their actions. Most of the Salt Lake mothers maintained that their toddlers already understood the consequences of touching prohibited objects; several said this understanding arises as early as 7 months. Yet all but one of the San Pedro mothers placed the age of understanding social consequences of actions much later—between 2 and 3 years. Whereas the Salt Lake mothers regarded their toddlers as capable of intentionally misbehaving, most San Pedro mothers did not. More than half of the Salt Lake mothers reporting punishing toddlers for such infractions; none of the San Pedro mothers did. All of the Salt Lake preschoolers were under direct caregiver supervision, much like their toddler siblings, while 11 of the 16 San Pedro preschoolers were already on their own much of the time. The San Pedro preschoolers also had more mature household responsibilities.

The researchers suggest that the "terrible twos" may be a phase specific to societies that place individual freedom before the needs of the group. Ethnographic research suggests that, in societies that place higher value on group needs, freedom of choice does exist, but it goes hand in hand with interdependence, responsibility, and expectations of cooperation. Salt Lake parents seem to believe that responsible behavior develops gradually from engaging in fair competition and negotiations. San Pedro parents seem to believe that responsible behavior develops rapidly when children are old enough to understand the need to respect others' desires as well as their own.

What's your view?

From your experience or observation of toddlers, which of the two ways of handling sibling conflict would you expect to be more effective?

Check it out!

For more information on this topic, go to **http://www.zerotothree.org/**. Here you will find links to a survey of 3,000 parents and other adults about commonly asked questions regarding the handling of young children and a downloadable article on "Cultural Models for Early Caregiving."

rules or commands to get rewards or avoid punishment; they have made society's standards their own (Grusec & Goodnow, 1994; Kochanska & Aksan, 1995; Kochanska, Tjebkes, & Forman, 1998).

Developing Self-Regulation

Katy, age 2, is about to poke her finger into an electric outlet. In her "child-proofed" apartment, the sockets are covered, but not here in her grandmother's home. When Katy hears her father shout, "No!" the toddler pulls her arm back. The next time she goes near an outlet, she starts to point her finger, hesitates, and then says, "No." She has stopped herself from doing something she remembers she is not supposed to do. She is beginning to show

self-regulation Child's independent control of behavior to conform to understood social expectations.

self-regulation: control of her own behavior to conform to a caregiver's demands or expectations, even when the caregiver is not present.

Self-regulation is the foundation of socialization, and it links all domains of development—physical, cognitive, social, and emotional. Until Katy was physically able to get around on her own, electric outlets posed no hazard. To stop herself from poking her finger into an outlet requires that she consciously understand and remember what her father told her. Cognitive awareness, however, is not enough; restraining herself also requires emotional control. By "reading" their parents' emotional responses to their behavior, children continually absorb information about what conduct their parents approve of. As children process, store, and act upon this information, their strong desire to please their parents leads them to do as they know their parents want them to, whether or not the parents are there to see.

Checkpoint ✓

Can you . . .

- ✔ Describe the conflict of autonomy versus shame and doubt?
- ✔ Explain why the "terrible twos" is considered a normal phenomenon, and suggest reasons this transition may not exist in some cultures?
- ✔ Tell when and how self-regulation develops and how it contributes to socialization?

Mutual regulation of emotional states during infancy contributes to the development of self-control, especially in temperamentally "difficult" children, who may need extra help in achieving it (R. Feldman, Greenbaum, & Yirmiya, 1999). Before they can control their own behavior, children may need to be able to regulate, or control, their *attentional processes* and to modulate negative emotions (Eisenberg, 2000). Attentional regulation enables children to develop willpower and cope with frustration (Sethi, Mischel, Aber, Shoda, & Rodriguez, 2000).

The growth of self-regulation parallels the development of the self-conscious and evaluative emotions, such as empathy, shame, and guilt (Lewis, 1995, 1997, 1998). It requires the ability to wait for gratification. It is correlated with measures of conscience development, such as resisting temptation and making amends for wrongdoing (Eisenberg, 2000). In most children, the full development of self-regulation takes at least three years (Kopp, 1982).

Origins of Conscience: Committed Compliance

conscience Internal standards of behavior, which usually control one's conduct and produce emotional discomfort when violated.

Conscience includes both emotional discomfort about doing something wrong and the ability to refrain from doing it. Before children can develop a conscience, they need to have internalized moral standards. Conscience depends on willingness to do the right thing because a child believes it is right, not (as in self-regulation) just because someone else said so. *Inhibitory control*—conscious, or effortful, holding back of impulses, a mechanism of self-regulation that emerges during toddlerhood—may contribute to the development of conscience by first enabling the child to comply voluntarily with parental dos and don'ts (Kochanska, Murray, & Coy, 1997).

Grazyna Kochanska (1993, 1995, 1997a, 1997b) and her colleagues have looked for the origins of conscience in a longitudinal study of a group of toddlers and mothers in Iowa. Researchers videotaped 103 children ages 26 to 41 months and their mothers playing together with toys for two to three hours, both at home and in a homelike laboratory setting (Kochanska & Aksan, 1995). After a free-play period, a mother would give her child 15 minutes to put the toys away. The laboratory had a special shelf with other, unusually attractive toys, such as a bubble gum machine, a walkie-talkie, and a music box. The child was told not to touch anything on the shelf. After about an hour, the experimenter asked the mother to go into an adjoining room, leaving the child alone with the toys. A few minutes later, a woman entered, played with several of the forbidden toys, and then left the child alone again for eight minutes.

committed compliance Kochanska's term for wholehearted obedience of a parent's orders without reminders or lapses.

situational compliance Kochanska's term for obedience of a parent's orders only in the presence of signs of ongoing parental control.

Children were judged to show **committed compliance** if they willingly followed the orders to clean up and not touch the special toys, without reminders or lapses. Children showed **situational compliance** if they needed prompting; their compliance depended on ongoing parental control. Committed compliance is related to internalization of parental values and rules (Kochanska, Coy, & Murray, 2001). Children whose mothers rated them as having internalized household rules refrained from touching the forbidden toys even when left alone with them, whereas children whose compliance was only situational tended to yield to temptation when their mothers were out of sight (Kochanska & Aksan, 1995).

Committed compliance and situational compliance can be distinguished in children as young as 13 months, but their roots go back to infancy. Committed compliers, who are more likely to be girls than boys, tend to be those who, at 8 to 10 months, could refrain from touching when told, "No!" Committed compliance tends to increase with age, while situational compliance decreases (Kochanska, Tjebkes, & Forman, 1998).

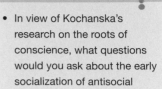

What's your view ?

- In view of Kochanska's research on the roots of conscience, what questions would you ask about the early socialization of antisocial adolescents and adults?

Factors in the Success of Socialization

Some children internalize societal standards more readily than others. The way parents go about the job of socializing a child together with a child's temperament and the quality of the parent-child relationship may help predict how hard or easy socialization will be (Kochanska, 1993, 1995, 1997a, 1997b, 2002). Factors in the success of socialization may include security of attachment, observational learning of parents' behavior, and the mutual responsiveness of parent and child (Maccoby, 1992). All these, as well as socioeconomic and cultural factors (Harwood, Schoelmerich, Ventura-Cook, Schulze, & Wilson, 1996), may play a part in motivation to comply.

Observational studies of more than 200 mothers and children highlight the importance to conscience development of a close, mutually binding and cooperative relationship between mother and child, in which both share positive emotions and are responsive to each other's emotional signals. Starting in the child's second year and extending until early school age, researchers observed mothers and children in lengthy, naturalistic interactions: caregiving routines, preparing and eating meals, playing, relaxing, and doing household chores. Mothers and children who were judged to have mutually responsive relationships tended to maintain them over time. These children tended to show *moral emotions* such as guilt and empathy; *moral conduct* in the face of strong temptation to break rules or violate standards of behavior; and *moral cognition,* as judged by their response to hypothetical, age-appropriate moral dilemmas (Kochanska, 2002).

Secure attachment and a warm, mutually responsive parent-child relationship seem to foster committed compliance and ultimately conscience development. Mothers of committed compliers, as contrasted with mothers of situational compliers, tend to rely on gentle guidance rather than force, threats, or other forms of negative control (Eisenberg, 2000; Kochanska & Aksan, 1995; Kochanska, Aksan, Knaack, & Rhines, 2004). Children may more readily comply with parental demands when the parent has repeatedly affirmed the child's autonomy—for example, by following the child's lead during play. Mothers who can readily see a child's point of view seem to be most successful in doing this (Kochanska, 1997b). In one observational study, 2½-year-olds whose mothers gave reasons for their requests, compromised, or bargained with the child showed greater conscience development at age 3 than children whose mothers had threatened, teased, insisted, or given in (Laible & Thompson, 2002).

Checkpoint ✓

Can you . . .

- ✔ Distinguish between committed and situational compliance?
- ✔ Discuss how temperament and parenting practices affect socialization?

Contact with Other Children

Guidepost 8

How do infants and toddlers interact with siblings and other children?

Although parents exert a major influence on children's lives, relationships with other children—both in the home and out of it—are important too, from infancy on.

Siblings

If you have brothers or sisters, your relationships with them are likely to be the longest lasting you will ever have. They share your roots; they "knew you when," they accepted or rejected the same parental values, and they probably deal with you more candidly than almost anyone else you know.

The Arrival of a New Baby

Children react in various ways to the arrival of a sibling. To bid for the mother's attention, some suck their thumbs, wet their pants, or use baby talk. Others withdraw. Some suggest taking the baby back to the hospital or flushing it down the toilet. Some take pride in being the "big ones," who can dress themselves, use the potty, and help care for the baby.

Much of the variation in children's adjustment to a new baby may have to do with such factors as the older child's age, the quality of his or her relationship with the mother, and the family atmosphere. Not surprisingly, attachment to the mother often becomes temporarily less secure (Teti, Sakin, Kucera, Corns, & Eiden, 1996).

The birth of a younger sibling may change the way a mother acts toward an older child, at least until the newcomer "settles in." The mother is likely to play less with the older child, to be less sensitive to her or his interests, to give more orders, to have more confrontations, to use physical punishment, and to initiate fewer conversations and games that help develop skills. An older boy, especially, may show temporary behavior problems (Baydar, Greek, & Brooks-Gunn, 1997; Baydar, Hyle, & Brooks-Gunn, 1997; Dunn, 1985; Dunn & Kendrick, 1982).

If the mother has been working outside the home and does not return to work, the arrival of a new baby may mean that the mother can spend more rather than less time with the older child. However, with less family income and another mouth to feed, fewer resources for learning (such as play materials and outings) may be available to the older child. Also, financial worries may affect the mother's emotional well-being, contributing to negative maternal interactions with the older sibling. On the positive side, the arrival of a baby tends to enhance the older child's language development, perhaps because the child talks more than before with the father and other family members (Baydar, Greek, & Brooks-Gunn, 1997; Baydar, Hyle, & Brooks-Gunn, 1997).

How Siblings Interact

Sibling relationships play a distinct role in socialization, different from the role of relationships with parents or peers (Vandell, 2000). Sibling conflicts can become a vehicle for understanding social relationships (Dunn & Munn, 1985; Ram & Ross, 2001). Lessons and skills learned from interactions with siblings carry over to relationships outside the home (Brody, 1998).

Young children usually become attached to their older brothers and sisters. Although rivalry may be present, so is affection. The more securely attached siblings are to their parents, the better they get along with each other (Teti & Ablard, 1989).

Nevertheless, as babies begin to move around and become more assertive, they inevitably come into conflict with siblings—at least in U.S. culture (refer back to Box 8-2). Sibling conflict increases dramatically after the younger child reaches 18 months of age (Vandell & Bailey, 1992). During the next few months, younger siblings begin to participate more fully in family interactions and become more involved in family disputes. As they do, they become more aware of others' intentions and feelings. They begin to recognize what kind of behavior will upset or annoy an older brother or sister and what behavior is considered "naughty" or "good" (Dunn & Munn, 1985).

As this cognitive and social understanding grows, sibling conflict tends to become more constructive, and the younger sibling participates in attempts to reconcile. Constructive conflict helps children recognize each other's needs, wishes, and point of view, and it helps them learn how to fight, disagree, and compromise within the context of a safe, stable relationship (Vandell & Bailey, 1992).

Checkpoint ✓

Can you . . .

- ✔ Discuss factors affecting a child's adjustment to a new baby sister or brother?
- ✔ Describe changes in sibling interaction and sibling conflict during toddlerhood?

Sociability with Nonsiblings

Infants and—even more so—toddlers show interest in people outside the home, particularly people their own size. During the first few months, they show interest in other babies by looking, smiling, and cooing (T. M. Field, 1978). During the last half of the first year, they increasingly smile at, touch, and babble to another baby (Hay, Pedersen, & Nash, 1982). At about 1 year, when the biggest items on their agenda are learning to walk and to manipulate objects, babies pay more attention to toys and less to other people (T. M. Field & Roopnarine, 1982). This stage does not last long, though; from about 1½ years of age to almost 3, children show more interest in what other children do and increasing understanding of how to deal with them (Eckerman, Davis, & Didow, 1989; Eckerman & Stein, 1982).

Toddlers learn by imitating one another. Games such as follow-the-leader help toddlers connect with other children and pave the way for more complex games during the preschool years (Eckerman et al., 1989). Imitation of each other's actions leads to more frequent verbal communication (such as "You go in playhouse," "Don't do it!" or "Look at me") which helps peers coordinate joint activity (Eckerman & Didow, 1996). As with siblings, conflict too can have a purpose: helping children learn how to negotiate and resolve disputes (Caplan, Vespo, Pedersen, & Hay, 1991).

Some children, of course, are more sociable than others, reflecting such temperamental traits as their usual mood, readiness to accept new people, and ability to adapt to change. Sociability is also influenced by experience; babies who spend time with other babies, as in child care, become sociable earlier than those who spend all their time at home alone.

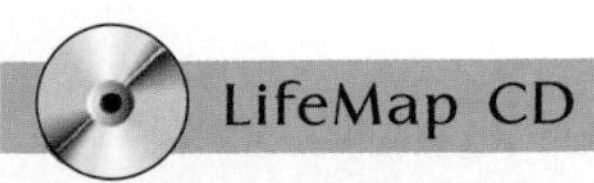

How does a two-year-old describe a social relationship? Find out by watching the video on "Describing a Best Friend at Age 2" in Chaper 8 of your CD.

Checkpoint

Can you . . .

✔ Trace changes in sociability during the first three years, and state two influences on it?

Children of Working Parents

How do parental employment and early child care affect infants' and toddlers' development?

A significant influence on the atmosphere in the home is the work one or both parents do for pay. Parents' work determines more than the family's financial resources. Much of adults' time, effort, and emotional involvement goes into their occupations. How do their work and their child care arrangements affect young children? Most research on this subject pertains to mothers' work. (We'll discuss the impact of parents' work on older children in later chapters.)

Effects of Parental Employment

More than half (50.6 percent) of mothers of infants in their first year of life and 56 percent of women with children under 3 were in the labor force in 2001 (Bureau of Labor Statistics, 2002). What effects does early maternal employment have on an infant or young child beyond the effects of child care?

The National Longitudinal Survey of Youth (NLSY) is an annual survey of some 12,600 women, accompanied by assessments of their children. An analysis of 1994 NLSY data (Harvey, 1999) found little or no effect of early maternal employment on children's compliance, behavior problems, self-esteem, cognitive development, or academic achievement. Three- and 4-year-olds whose mothers had returned to work later were slightly more compliant than children the same age whose mothers had returned to work sooner, and children whose mothers had worked long hours during the first 3 years scored slightly lower on tests of vocabulary and achievement during the early school years; but these differences were small and faded over time. As in a number of other studies, early maternal employment did seem to benefit children in low-income families by increasing the family's resources. The study found no significant effects of fathers' working hours.

On the other hand, longitudinal data on 900 European American children from the National Institute of Child Health and Human Development (NICHD) Study of Early Child Care, discussed in the next section, showed negative effects on cognitive development at 15 months to 3 years when mothers worked 30 or more hours a week by a child's ninth month. Maternal sensitivity, the quality of the home environment, and quality of child care made a difference but did not fully account for the findings (Brooks-Gunn, Han, & Waldfogel, 2002).

These findings suggest a need for generous family-leave policies to help mothers—and fathers—combine parenting and work. In the United States, however, legally required parental leave is unpaid and limited to three months, as compared with an average *paid* leave of nine months in European nations. Thus, many U.S. infants are in child care by the time they are 3 months old (Kamerman, 2000). How does early child care affect children?

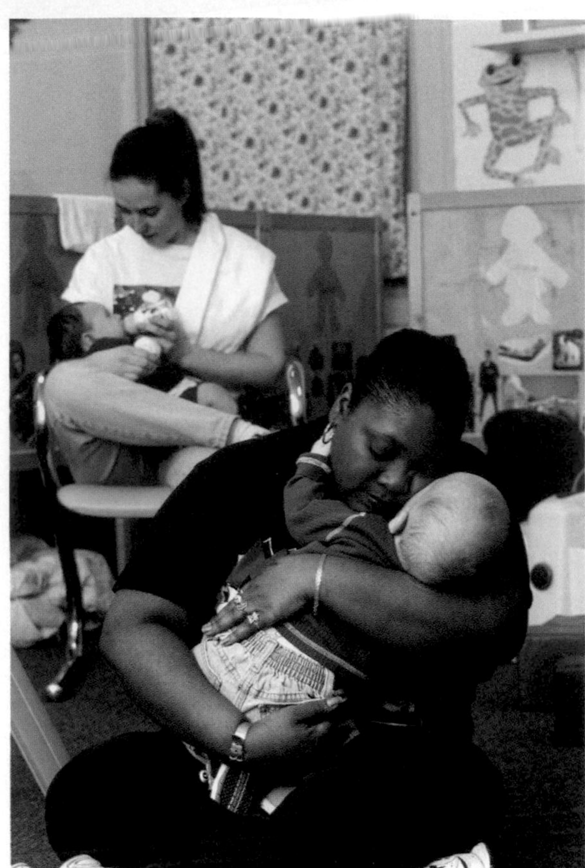

Caregivers' responsiveness to infants' needs is the most important factor in high-quality childcare.

Early Child Care

More than 2 out of 5 children under age 5 receive regular nonparental child care. Those with employed mothers average 30 hours a week in child care. But with an average cost of $4,000 to $6,000 a year, affordability of care is becoming a pressing issue for many families (Gardner, 2002). Parents of children with disabilities find it especially hard to find appropriate, affordable care (Shonkoff & Phillips, 2000).

Factors in Impact of Child Care

The impact of early child care may depend on a number of factors, including the type, amount, quality, and stability of care as well as the family's income and the age at which children start receiving nonmaternal care. Temperament and gender may make a difference (Crockenberg, 2003). In one study, 35 percent of infants and 71 percent of toddlers in a child care center experienced growing stress throughout the day, as measured by their secretion of cortisol, a stress hormone. The opposite occurred on days spent at home. Shy children in child care showed especially high cortisol levels, while sociable children did not. Stress levels tend to diminish during early childhood (Watamura, Donzella, Alwin, & Gunnar, 2003). Boys are more vulnerable to stress, in child care and elsewhere, than are girls (Crockenberg, 2003).

Quality of care contributes to cognitive and psychosocial development (Peisner-Feinberg et al., 2001). In home-based child care settings, typically used for infants, quality of care increases with the child's family income. This is less true in child care centers, more commonly used for preschoolers; poor families who receive federal child care subsidies may be able to afford higher quality care (NICHD Early Child Care Research Network, 1997b). However, the vast majority of children eligible for subsidies do not receive them (USDHHS, 2000b). Furthermore, most child care centers do not meet all recommended guidelines for child-staff ratios, group sizes, and teacher education (Bergen, Reid, & Torelli, 2000; NICHD Early Child Care Research Network, 1998c, 1999a). Table 8-5 lists guidelines for judging quality of care.

The most important element in quality of care is the caregiver; stimulating interactions with responsive adults are crucial to early cognitive, linguistic, and psychosocial development. Low staff turnover is important; infants need consistent caregiving in order to develop trust and secure attachments (Burchinal, Roberts, Nabors, & Bryant, 1996; Shonkoff & Phillips, 2000). Stability of care facilitates coordination between parents and child care providers, which may help protect against any negative effects of long hours of care (Ahnert & Lamb, 2003).

The NICHD Study: Isolating Child Care Effects

To assess the impact of child care on developmental outcomes, we need to separate it from other factors, such as the influences of family characteristics, the child's characteristics, and the care the child receives at home. The most comprehensive attempt to do so is an ongoing study sponsored by the National Institute of Child Health and Human Development (NICHD).

This longitudinal study of 1,364 children and their families began in 1991 in 10 university centers across the United States, shortly after the children's birth. The sample was diverse socioeconomically, educationally, and ethnically; nearly 35 percent of the families were poor or near poor. Most infants entered nonmaternal care before 4 months of age and received, on average, 33 hours of care each week. Child care arrangements varied widely in type and quality. Through observation, interviews, questionnaires, and tests, researchers measured the children's social, emotional, cognitive, and physical development at frequent

Table 8-5 Checklist for Choosing a Good Child Care Facility

- Is the facility licensed'? Does it meet minimum state standards for health, fire, and safety? (Many centers and home care facilities are not licensed or regulated.)
- Is the facility clean and safe? Does it have adequate indoor and outdoor space?
- Does the facility have small groups, a high adult-to-child ratio, and a stable, competent, highly involved staff?
- Are caregivers trained in child development?
- Are caregivers warm, affectionate, accepting, responsive, and sensitive? Are they authoritative but not too restrictive and neither too controlling nor merely custodial?
- Does the program promote good health habits?
- Does it provide a balance between structured activities and free play? Are activities age appropriate?
- Do the children have access to educational toys and materials, which stimulate mastery of cognitive and communicative skills at a child's own pace?
- Does the program nurture self-confidence, curiosity, creativity, and self-discipline?
- Does it encourage children to ask questions, solve problems express feelings and opinions, and make decisions?
- Does it foster self-esteem, respect for others, and social skills?
- Does it help parents improve their child-rearing skills?
- Does it promote cooperation with public and private schools and the community?

Sources: American Academy of Pediatrics [AAP], 1986; Belsky, 1984; K. A. Clarke-Stewart, 1987; NICHD Early Child Care Research Network, 1996; S. W. Olds, 1989: Scarr, 1998.

intervals from 1 month of age through the first seven years of life (Peth-Pierce, 1998). What do the findings show?

The amount and quality of care children received as well as the type and stability of care influenced specific aspects of development (Peth-Pierce, 1998; see Table 8-6). The more time a child spent in child care up to age 4½, the more likely that child was to be seen by adults as aggressive, disobedient, and hard to get along with, then and in kindergarten—though this effect was limited in size. As mentioned earlier, long days in child care have been associated with stress for 3- and 4-year-olds; and some children that age in the NICHD sample spent up to 92 hours a week in center care (NICHD Early Childhood Research Network, 2003).

High-quality child care had a positive influence on cognitive development. Children in child care centers with low child-staff ratios, small group sizes, and trained, sensitive, responsive caregivers who provided positive interactions and language stimulation scored higher on tests of language comprehension, cognition, and readiness for school. Their mothers also reported fewer behavior problems (NICHD Early Child Care Research Network, 1999a, 2000, 2002). In an analysis of NICHD data, quality of care predicted cognitive performance in early childhood (NICHD Early Child Care Research Network & Duncan, 2003).

However, factors related to child care seem less influential than family characteristics, such as income, the home environment, the amount of mental stimulation the mother provides, and the mother's sensitivity to her child. These characteristics strongly predict developmental outcomes, regardless of how much time children spend in outside care (NICHD Early Child Care Research Network, 1998b, 2000, 2003).

Although a caregiver's sensitivity and responsiveness influence a toddler's socialization, the mother's sensitivity has a greater influence, according to the NICHD research (NICHD Early Child Care Research Network, 1998a). Maternal sensitivity also is the strongest predictor of attachment. The researchers found that child care had no direct effect on attachment, no matter how early infants entered care or how many hours they spent in it. Nor did the stability and quality of care affect attachment in and of themselves. However, when unstable, poor quality, or more-than-minimal amounts of child care (10 or more hours a week) were combined with insensitive, unresponsive mothering, insecure

Table [illegible] Aspects of Development Affected by Characteristics of Early Child Care*

	Attachment	Parent-Child Relationships	Cooperation	Problem Behaviors	Cognitive Development and School Readiness	Language Development
Quality	•	•		+	+	+
Amount	•	•		•		
Type			•	•	+	+
Stability	•		•			

*Results after taking into account all family and child variables.

Source: Peth-Pierce, 1998, summary table of findings, p. 15.

+ Consistent effects

• Effects under some conditions

attachment was more likely. On the other hand, high-quality care seemed to help offset insensitive mothering (NICHD Early Child Care Research Network, 1997a, 2001b).

It should not be surprising that what look like effects of child care often may be related to family characteristics. After all, stable families with favorable home environments are more able, and therefore more likely, to place their children in high-quality care.

One area in which the NICHD study did find direct effects of child care, independent of characteristics of the family and child, is in interactions with peers. Between ages 2 and 3, children whose caregivers were sensitive and responsive tended to become more positive and competent in play with other children (NICHD Early Child Care Research Network, 2001a).

To sum up, the NICHD findings so far give high-quality child care good marks overall, especially for its impact on cognitive development and interaction with peers. Some observers say that the areas of concern the study pinpointed—stress levels in infants and toddlers and possible behavior problems related to amounts of care—might be counteracted by improving child care through activities that enhance children's attachment to caregivers and peers, emphasize child-initiated learning and internalized motivation, and focus on group social development (Maccoby & Lewis, 2003).

Impact on Disadvantaged Children

The NICHD sample is socioeconomically mixed, but other studies have focused on disadvantaged children. Children from low-income families or stressful homes especially benefit from care that supplies cognitive stimulation and emotional support, which may otherwise be lacking in their lives (Scarr, 1997b; Spieker, Nelson, Petras, Jolley, & Barnard, 2003). In one study at Early Head Start centers, low-income toddlers in center-based care who were insecurely attached to their mothers showed greater cognitive and language development at ages 2 and 3 than those cared for at home (Spieker et al., 2003). In a five-year longitudinal study of 451 poor, urban families in California and Florida with single mothers who were moving from welfare to work, children demonstrated stronger cognitive growth in center care than in home-based care (Loeb, Fuller, Kagan, & Carrol, 2004). Disadvantaged children in good child care programs tend not to show the declines in IQ often seen when such children reach school age, and they may be more motivated to learn (AAP, 1986; Belsky, 1984; Bronfenbrenner, Belsky, & Steinberg, 1977).

As we have mentioned, the NICHD study found that the more time a young child spends in nonmaternal care, the greater the risk of problem behavior (NICHD Early Childhood Research Network, 2003). But data from a study of 2,400 randomly selected low-income children in Boston, Chicago, and San Antonio suggest that extensive child care does *not* harm *poor* children's development unless it is of low quality. Low-income boys (but not girls) are more likely to develop behavior problems in low-quality care (Votruba-Drzal, Coley, & Chase-Lansdale, 2004).

Child Care for Ethnic Minorities

Studies of ethnically and socioeconomically mixed samples also may fail to reveal specific factors in minority experience with child care (Johnson et al., 2003).* Among these factors are workforce participation, socioeconomic status, family processes, and effects of racism. Studies that focus on low-income children, such as those discussed in the preceding section, often do not distinguish adequately between ethnicity and SES.

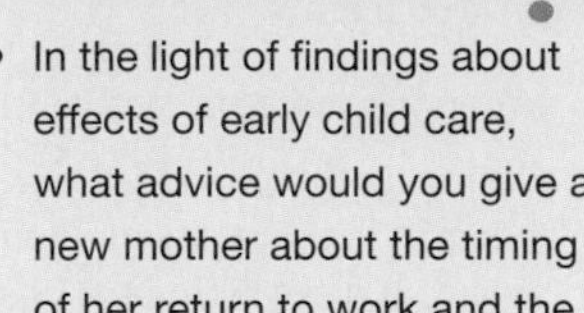

- In the light of findings about effects of early child care, what advice would you give a new mother about the timing of her return to work and the selection of child care?

Child care use among minority families reflects distinct patterns of maternal work, as well as differing historical and contextual factors, family structures, socialization practices, and parenting goals. Many minority families live in extended-family households. When child care centers began proliferating in the 1960s in response to the influx of middle-class women into the workplace, this new form of care was not widely available to families of color, who continued to turn to relatives or friends. Today, African-American and Latina women increasingly choose center care, which they see as promoting educational goals; but they are more likely to use family-based care or to rely on grandmothers.

Minority women tend to have different employment patterns than white women. Minority women are more likely to work night shifts or long hours, to hold seasonal, nonoffice jobs, and to be laid off periodically. Thus, child care settings designed for regular daytime employment may not meet their needs. In addition, residential segregation affects access to care.

Checkpoint

Can you . . .

✔ Evaluate the impact of a mother's employment on her baby's well-being?

✔ List at least five criteria for good child care?

✔ Compare the impact of child care and of family characteristics on emotional, social, and cognitive development?

✔ Point out special considerations regarding child care for low-income and minority children?

Concern about ethnic identity and continuity may influence a family's selection of child care. A Latino family intent on reinforcing traditional cultural values may choose one type of child care setting; an immigrant family interested in helping children adapt to the dominant culture may select a different type of setting.

Conventional standards of child care quality may not apply in evaluating child care for minority families. For example, caregiver turnover may not be a critical problem for children accustomed to the fluidity of an extended-family household. Indeed, some minority families may believe that children become more independent and adaptable through exposure to a variety of caregivers. More important to some families is whether the child care setting supports the values and parenting practices of the home. Strictness of discipline, the relative emphasis on autonomy versus obedience, attitudes toward the role of women and girls, and skills for coping with prejudice and discrimination are some of the issues that may have special implications for minority families. A caregiver of the same race or ethnicity as the family may be best able to collaborate with parents to foster consistent upbringing and competence in a child.

Refocus

- Which of the four types of temperament did Cathy Bateson show? Was there goodness of fit in her relationship with her parents?
- Did Cathy appear to be securely or insecurely attached?
- How did the child-raising practices Cathy's parents followed seem to contribute to her psychosocial development?
- Did Cathy's tree-climbing technique suggest that she had internalized her parents' safety rules?
- How did her mother's professional life affect Cathy as an infant? As a toddler? On balance, as an only child, did she seem to benefit from her family's unusual child care arrangement with the Frank family?

However infants and toddlers are cared for, the experiences of the first 3 years lay the foundation for future development. In Part 4, we'll see how young children build on that foundation.

*Unless otherwise referenced, this section is based on Johnson et al. (2003).

Summary and Key Terms

Foundations of Psychosocial Development

Guidepost 1 When and how do emotions develop, and how do babies show them?

- Emotions serve protective functions.
- Crying, smiling, and laughing are early signs of emotion. Other indices are facial expressions, motor activity, body language, and physiological changes.
- The repertoire of basic emotions seems to be universal, but there are cultural variations in their expression.
- Complex emotions seem to develop from earlier, simpler ones. Self-conscious and evaluative emotions arise after the development of self-awareness.
- Separate but interacting regions of the brain may be responsible for various emotional states.

emotions (201) **self-conscious emotions (205)** **self-awareness (205)** **self-evaluative emotions (205)** **empathy (205)** **social cognition (205)**

Guidepost 2 How do infants show temperamental differences, and how enduring are those differences?

- Many children seem to fall into one of three categories of temperament: "easy," "difficult," and "slow-to-warm-up." Temperamental patterns appear to be largely inborn and to have a biological basis. They are generally stable but can be modified by experience.
- Goodness of fit between a child's temperament and environmental demands aids adjustment.
- Cross-cultural differences in temperament may reflect child-raising practices.

temperament (206) **easy children (206)** **difficult children (207)** **slow-to-warm-up children (207)** **goodness of fit (208)**

Guidepost 3 What roles do parents and grandparents play in early personality development?

- Child-raising practices and caregiving roles vary around the world.
- Infants have strong needs for maternal closeness and warmth as well as physical care.
- Fatherhood is a social construction; fathering roles differ in various cultures.
- Although significant gender differences typically do not appear until after infancy, U.S. parents begin gender-typing boys and girls almost from birth.
- Distance or divorce may diminish the connection with grandparents, but many grandparents are heavily involved in grandchildren's lives.

gender (212) **gender-typing (213)**

Developmental Issues in Infancy

Guidepost 4 How do infants gain trust in their world and form attachments?

- According to Erikson, infants in the first 18 months are in the first stage of personality development, basic trust versus basic mistrust. Sensitive, responsive, consistent caregiving is the key to successful resolution of this conflict.
- Research based on the Strange Situation has found four patterns of attachment: secure, avoidant, ambivalent (resistant), and disorganized-disoriented.
- Newer instruments measure attachment in natural settings and in cross-cultural research.
- Attachment patterns may depend on a baby's temperament as well as on the quality of parenting and may have long-term implications for development. A parent's memories of childhood attachment can influence his or her own child's attachment.
- Separation anxiety and stranger anxiety may arise during the second half of the first year and appear to be related to temperament and circumstances.

basic trust versus basic mistrust (214) **attachment (215)** **Strange Situation (215)** **secure attachment (215)** **avoidant attachment (215)** **ambivalent (resistant) attachment (215)** **disorganized-disoriented attachment (215)** **stranger anxiety (217)** **separation anxiety (217)**

Guidepost 5 How do infants and caregivers "read" each other's nonverbal signals?

- Mutual regulation enables babies to play an active part in regulating their emotional states.
- A mother's depression, especially if severe or chronic, may have serious consequences for her infant's development.
- The belief that babies, after about 6 months of age, display social referencing is in dispute.

mutual regulation (219) **"still-face" paradigm (220)** **social referencing (222)**

Developmental Issues in Toddlerhood

Guidepost 6 When and how does the sense of self arise?

- According to William James, the self has two aspects: the I-self and the Me-self, or self-concept.
- The I-self emerges between 4 and 10 months, as infants experience a sense of agency and self-coherence.
- The Me-self, or self-concept, develops between 15 and 18 months and depends on self-awareness.

self-concept (223) **self-efficacy (223)**

Guidepost 7 How do toddlers develop autonomy and standards for socially acceptable behavior?

- Erikson's second stage concerns autonomy versus shame and doubt. Negativism is a normal manifestation of the shift from external control to self-control.
- Socialization, which rests on internalization of societally approved standards, begins with the development of self-regulation.

- A precursor of conscience is committed compliance to a caregiver's demands; toddlers who show committed compliance tend to internalize adult rules more readily than those who show situational compliance.
- Parenting practices, a child's temperament, the quality of the parent-child relationship, and cultural and socioeconomic factors may affect the ease and success of socialization.

autonomy versus shame and doubt (223) socialization (224) internalization (224) self-regulation (226) conscience (226) committed compliance (226) situational compliance (226)

Contact with Other Children

Guidepost 8 How do infants and toddlers interact with siblings and other children?

- A child's adjustment to a new baby may depend on the child's age, the quality of her or his relationship with the mother, and the family atmosphere.
- Sibling relationships play a distinct role in socialization; what children learn from relations with siblings carries over to relationships outside the home.
- Between 1½ and 3 years of age, children tend to show more interest in other children and increasing understanding of how to deal with them.

Children of Working Parents

Guidepost 9 How do parental employment and early child care affect infants' and toddlers' development?

- In general, mothers' workforce participation during a child's first three years seems to have little impact on development, but cognitive development may suffer when a mother works 30 or more hours a week by her child's ninth month.
- Substitute child care varies widely in type and quality. The most important element in quality of care is the caregiver.
- Although quality, quantity, stability, and type of care have some influence on psychosocial and cognitive development, the influence of family characteristics seems greater overall.
- Low-income children, especially, benefit from good child care. Minority children may need child care that meets their special needs and is consistent with their family upbringing.

Part 4

Early Childhood: A Preview

Chapter 9
Physical Development and Health in Early Childhood

- Growth is steady; appearance becomes more slender and proportions more adultlike.
- Appetite diminishes, and sleep problems are common.
- Handedness appears; fine and gross motor skills and strength improve.

Chapter 10
Cognitive Development in Early Childhood

- Thinking is somewhat egocentric, but understanding of other people's perspectives grows.
- Cognitive immaturity results in some illogical ideas about the world.
- Memory and language improve.
- Intelligence becomes more predictable.
- Preschool experience is common, and kindergarten experience is more so.

Chapter 11
Psychosocial Development in Early Childhood

- Self-concept and understanding of emotions become more complex; self-esteem is global.
- Independence, initiative, and self-control increase.
- Gender identity develops.
- Play becomes more imaginative, more elaborate, and usually more social.
- Altruism, aggression, and fearfulness are common.
- Family is still the focus of social life, but other children become more important.

Early Childhood

During the years from 3 to 6, often called the *preschool years,* children make the transition from toddlerhood to childhood. Their bodies become slimmer, their motor and mental abilities sharper, and their personalities and relationships more complex.

The 3-year-old is no longer a baby but a sturdy adventurer, at home in the world and eager to explore its possibilities as well as the developing capabilities of his or her own body and mind. A child of this age has come through a relatively dangerous time of life—the years of infancy and toddlerhood—to enter a healthier, less threatening phase.

Growth and change are less rapid in early childhood than in infancy and toddlerhood, but, as we will see in Chapters 9, 10, and 11, all domains of development—physical, cognitive, emotional, and social—continue to intertwine.

Linkups to Look For

- As muscles come under more conscious control, children can tend to more of their own personal needs, such as dressing and toileting, and thus gain a greater sense of competence and independence.
- Eating and sleep patterns are influenced by cultural attitudes.
- Even the common cold can have emotional and cognitive implications. Occasional minor illnesses not only build immunity; they also help children learn to cope with physical distress and understand its causes.
- Social interaction plays a major role in the development of preliteracy skills, memory, and measured intelligence.
- Cognitive awareness of gender has far-reaching psychosocial implications, affecting children's sense of self and their attitudes toward the roles males and females play in their society.

chapter
9

Physical Development and Health in Early Childhood

Children's playings are not sports and should be deemed as their most serious actions.

—Montaigne, *Essays*

Focus *Wang Yani, Self-Taught Artist*

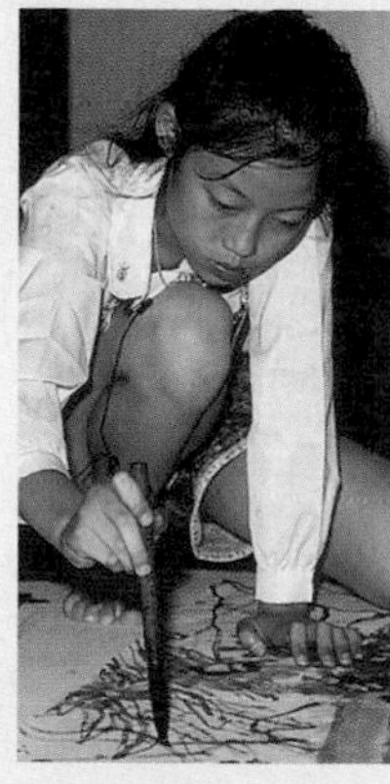

Wang Yani

Wang Yani (b. 1975) is a gifted young Chinese artist. She had her first exhibit in Shanghai at the age of 4 and had produced 4,000 paintings by the age of 6. Since she turned 10, her work has been shown throughout Asia and in Europe and the United States.

Yani (her given name)* began painting at 2½. Her father, Wang Shiqiang, was a professional artist and educator. He gave her big brushes and large sheets of paper to permit bold strokes. Rather than teach her, he let her learn in her own way and always praised her work. In contrast with traditional Chinese art education, which emphasizes conformity and imitation, he allowed his daughter's imagination free rein.

Yani went through the usual stages in preschoolers' drawing but far more quickly than usual. Her early paintings were made up of dots, circles, and lines, which represented people, birds, or fruit. By the age of 3, she could paint recognizable but highly original forms.

Yani's father encouraged her to paint what she saw outdoors near their home in the scenic riverside town of Gongcheng. Like traditional Chinese artists, she did not paint from life but constructed her brightly colored compositions from mental images of what she had seen. Her visual memory has been called astounding. When she was only 4, her father taught her Chinese characters (letters) of as many as 25 strokes by "writing" them in the air with his finger. Without hesitation, Yani would put them down on paper from memory.

Her father helped her develop powers of observation and imagery by carrying her on his shoulders as he hiked in the fields and mountains or lying with her in the grass and telling stories about the passing clouds. The pebbles along the riverbank reminded her of the monkeys at the zoo, which she painted over and over between the ages of 3 and 6. Yani made up stories about the monkeys she portrayed. They often represented Yani herself—eating a snack, refereeing an argument among friends, or trying to conquer her fear of her first shot at the doctor's office. Painting, to Yani, was not an objective representation of reality; it was a mirror of her mind, a way to transform her sensory impressions into simple but powerful semiabstract images onto which she projected her thoughts, feelings, and dreams.

Sources of biographical information about Wang Yani are Bond (1989), Costello (1990), Ho (1989), Stuart (1991), and Zhensun & Low (1991).

*In Chinese custom, the given name follows the family name.

Because of her short arms, Yani's brush strokes at first were short. Her father trained her to hold her brush tightly by trying to grab it from behind when she was not looking. She learned to paint with her whole arm, twisting her wrist to produce the effect she wanted. As her physical dexterity and experience grew, her strokes became more forceful, varied, and precise: broad, wet strokes to define an animal's shape; fuzzy, nearly dry ones to suggest feathers, fur, or tree bark. The materials she used—bamboo brushes, ink sticks, and rice paper—were traditional, but her style, popularly called *xieyi* or "idea writing," was not. It was and remains playful, free, and spontaneous.

With quick reflexes, a fertile imagination, remarkable visual abilities, strong motivation, and her father's sensitive guidance, Yani's artistic progress has been swift. As a young adult, she is considered an artist of great promise. Yet she herself finds painting very simple: "You just paint what you think about. You don't have to follow any instruction. Everybody can paint" (Zhensun & Low, 1991, p. 9).

• • •

Although Wang Yani's artistic growth has been unusual, it rests on typical developments of early childhood: rapid improvements in muscular control and eye-hand coordination. Children in this age group grow more slowly than before but still at a fast pace, and they make so much progress in muscle development and coordination that they can do much more than before. As is true for other children, Yani's gain in fine motor skills was accompanied by a growing cognitive understanding of the world around her—an understanding guided by her powers of observation and memory and her interactions with her father. Together these physical, cognitive, and social influences helped her express her thoughts and emotions through art.

In this chapter, as we look at physical development during the years from 3 to 6, we will see other examples of its interconnection with cognitive and psychosocial development. Nutrition and handedness are influenced by cultural attitudes, and sleep patterns by emotional experiences. Environmental influences, including the parents' life circumstances, affect health and safety. The links among developmental domains are especially evident in the tragic results of child abuse and neglect. Although the most obvious effects may be physical, these experiences can stunt cognitive growth and can leave lasting emotional scars.

After you have read and studied this chapter, you should be able to answer each of the Guidepost questions that follow. Look for them again in the margins, where they point to important concepts throughout the chapter. To check your understanding of these Guideposts, review the end-of-chapter summary. Checkpoints located at periodic spots throughout the chapter will help you verify your understanding of what you have read.

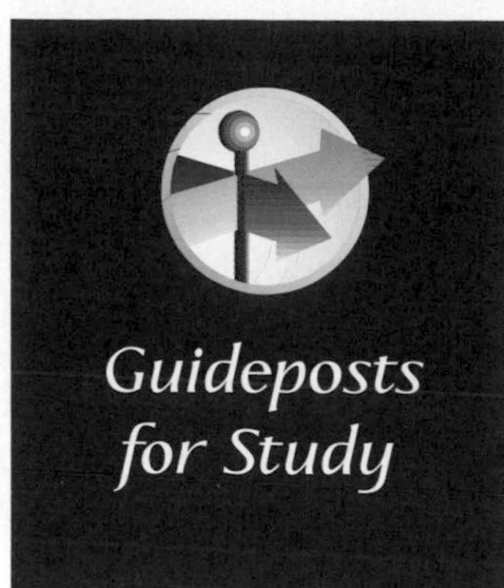

Guideposts for Study

1. How do children's bodies change between ages 3 and 6, and what are their nutritional and dental needs?
2. What sleep patterns and problems tend to develop during early childhood?
3. What are the main motor achievements of early childhood, and how does children's artwork show their physical and cognitive maturation?
4. What are the major health and safety risks for young children?
5. What are the causes and consequences of child abuse and neglect, and what can be done about it?

Aspects of Physiological Development

How do children's bodies change between ages 3 and 6, and what are their nutritional and dental needs?

In early childhood, children slim down and shoot up. They need less sleep than before and are more likely to develop sleep problems. They improve in running, hopping, skipping, jumping, and throwing balls. They also become better at tying shoelaces (in bows instead of knots), drawing with crayons (on paper rather than on walls), and pouring cereal (into the bowl, not onto the floor); and they begin to show a preference for either the right or left hand.

Bodily Growth and Change

Children grow rapidly between ages 3 and 6 but less quickly than in infancy and toddlerhood. At about age 3, children begin to take on the slender, athletic appearance of childhood. As abdominal muscles develop, the toddler potbelly tightens. The trunk, arms, and legs grow longer. The head is still relatively large, but the other parts of the body continue to catch up as proportions steadily become more adultlike.

The pencil mark on the wall that shows Eve's height at 3 years is 37½ inches from the floor, and she weighs about 30 pounds. Her twin brother Isaac, like most boys this age, is a little taller and heavier and has more muscle per pound of body weight, whereas Eve, like most girls, has more fatty tissue. Both boys and girls typically grow 2 to 3 inches a year during early childhood and gain 4 to 6 pounds annually (see Table 9-1). Boys' slight edge in height and weight continues until the growth spurt of puberty.

Muscular and skeletal growth progresses, making children stronger. Cartilage turns to bone at a faster rate than before, and bones become harder, giving the child a firmer shape

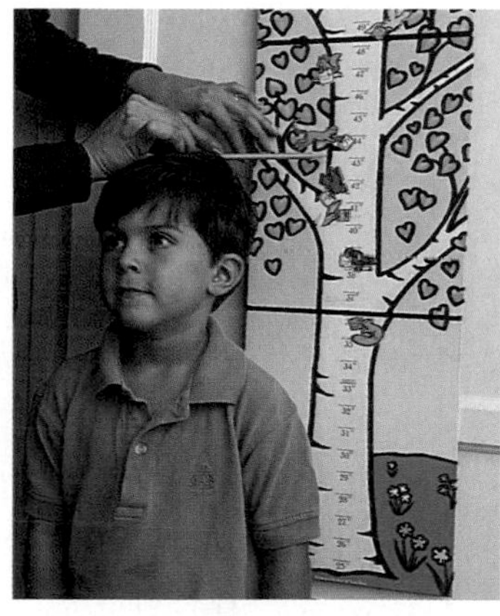

At age 4½, this boy's 43-inch height is 1½ inches above average but within normal range.

Table 9-1 Physical Growth, Ages 3 to 6 (50th percentile)*

Age	Height, Inches Boys	Height, Inches Girls	Weight, Pounds Boys	Weight, Pounds Girls
3	37½	37	32	30
3½	39	38½	34	32½
4	40½	39½	36	35
4½	41½	41	38	37
5	43	42½	40	40
5½	44½	44	43	42
6	45½	45½	46	45

*Fifty percent of children in each category are above this height or weight level, and 50 percent are below it.

Source: Kuczmarski et al., 2000.

The Everyday World

Box 9-1 *Helping Children Eat and Sleep Well*

One child refuses to eat anything but peanut butter and jelly sandwiches. Another seems to live on bananas. Mealtimes seem more like art class, as preschoolers make snowmen out of mashed potatoes or lakes out of applesauce, and food remains uneaten on the plate.

Although a diminished appetite in early childhood is normal, many parents make the mistake of insisting that children eat more than they want, setting in motion a contest of wills. Bedtime, too, often becomes an issue ("Daddy, leave the light on! . . . I want a drink of water. . . . What's that noise by the window? . . . I'm cold"). When a child delays or has trouble going to sleep or wakes often during the night, parents tend to become irritated, and the entire family feels the strain.

The following research-based suggestions can help make mealtimes and bedtimes pleasanter and children healthier (American Academy of Child and Adolescent Psychiatry [ACAP], 1997; American Academy of Pediatrics [AAP], 1992; L. A. Adams & Rickert, 1989; Graziano & Mooney, 1982; Rolls, Engell, & Birch, 2000; Williams & Caliendo, 1984):

Encouraging Healthy Eating Habits

- Keep a record of what a child eats. The child may in fact be eating enough.
- Serve simple, easily identifiable foods. Preschoolers often balk at mixed dishes, such as casseroles.
- Serve finger foods as often as possible.
- Introduce only one new food at a time, along with a familiar one the child likes.
- Offer small servings, especially of new or disliked foods; give second helpings if wanted.
- Don't pressure the child to clean the plate.
- After a reasonable time, remove the food and do not serve more until the next meal. A healthy child will not suffer from missing a meal, and children need to learn that certain times are appropriate for eating.
- Give the child a choice of foods containing similar nutrients: rye or whole wheat bread, a peach or an apple, yogurt or milk.
- Encourage a child to help prepare food; a child can help make sandwiches or mix and spoon out cookie dough.
- Have nutritious snack foods handy and allow the child to select favorites.
- Turn childish delights to advantage. Serve food in appealing dishes; dress it up with garnishes or little toys; make a "party" out of a meal.
- Don't fight "rituals," in which a child eats foods one at a time, in a certain order.
- Make mealtimes pleasant with conversation on interesting topics, keeping talk about eating itself to a minimum.

Helping Children Go to Sleep

- Establish a regular, unrushed bedtime routine—about 20 minutes of quiet activities, such as reading a story, singing lullabies, or having quiet conversation.
- Allow no scary or loud television shows.
- Avoid highly stimulating, active play before bedtime.
- Keep a small night-light on if it makes the child feel more comfortable.
- Don't feed or rock a child at bedtime.
- Stay calm but don't yield to requests for "just one more" story, one more drink of water, or one more bathroom trip.
- If you're trying to break a child's habit, offer rewards for good bedtime behavior, such as stickers on a chart or simple praise.
- Try putting your child to sleep a little later. Sending a child to bed too early is a common reason for sleep problems.
- If a child's fears about the dark or going to sleep have persisted for a long time, look for a program to help the child learn how to relax, how to substitute pleasant thoughts for frightening ones, and how to cope with stressful situations.

Helping Children Go Back to Sleep

- If a child gets up during the night, take him or her back to bed. Speak calmly and pat the child gently on the back, but be pleasantly firm and consistent.
- After a nightmare, reassure a frightened child and occasionally check in on the child. If frightening dreams persist for more than six weeks, consult your doctor.
- After night terrors, do not wake the child. If the child wakes, don't ask any questions. Just let the child go back to sleep.
- Help your child get enough sleep on a regular schedule; overtired or stressed children are more prone to night terrors.
- Walk or carry a sleepwalking child back to bed. Childproof your home with gates at the top of stairs and at windows and with bells on the child's bedroom door, so you'll know when she or he is out of bed.

What's your view?

Have you ever tried to get a young child to eat properly or go to sleep at bedtime? If so, did you find any of the tactics suggested in this box helpful?

Check it out!

For more information on this topic, go to **http://www.ParenthoodWeb.com/newsletter.htm**. This is a parent resource with many useful articles by experts in pediatric sleep disorders and nutrition. Select a topic from the list, search for articles using keywords, or choose one of the experts listed at the Web site.

and protecting the internal organs. These changes, coordinated by the still-maturing brain and nervous system (refer back to Chapter 6), promote the development of a wide range of motor skills. The increased capacities of the respiratory and circulatory systems build physical stamina and, along with the developing immune system, keep children healthier.

As in infancy and toddlerhood, proper growth and health depend on good nutrition and adequate sleep (see Box 9-1). However, preschoolers' dietary and sleep needs are quite different from those of infants or toddlers. Preschoolers are more likely to become overweight, especially if they are not active enough, and many develop sleep-related problems.

Nutrition: Preventing Overweight

Overweight has become a problem among U.S. preschoolers. More than 10 percent of 2- to 5-year-olds have a body mass index, or BMI, at or above the 95th percentile for their age and sex, compared with 7 percent in 1994 (Hedley et al., 2004; Ogden, Flegal, Carroll, & Johnson, 2002). About 12 percent more are at *risk* for overweight (with a BMI between the 85th and 95th percentiles). The increase is greatest among children in low-income families (Ritchie et al., 2001) and cuts across all ethnic groups (AAP Committee on Nutrition, 2003), but Mexican-American boys are especially prone to overweight (Hedley et al., 2004).

Worldwide, an International Obesity Task Force (Belizzi, 2002) estimates that 22 million children under age 5 are overweight. As "junk food" spreads through the developing world, as many as 20 to 25 percent of 4-year-olds in some countries, such as Egypt, Morocco, and Zambia, are overweight—a larger proportion than are malnourished.

A tendency toward overweight is partly hereditary, as discussed in Chapter 3, but it also depends on caloric intake and lack of exercise (Krebs, Jacobson, & AAP Committee on Nutrition, 2003; Jackson et al., 1997; Klesges, Klesges, Eck, & Shelton, 1995; Leibel, 1997; Ogden et al., 1997) As growth slows, preschoolers need fewer calories in proportion to their weight than they did before; and, according to a representative sampling in Glasgow, Scotland, many 3- to 5-year-olds have mostly sedentary lifestyles (Reilly et al., 2004).

As children move through the preschool period, their eating patterns become more environmentally influenced, like those of adults. Whereas 3-year-olds will eat only until they are full, 5-year-olds tend to eat more when a larger portion is put in front of them. Thus, a key to preventing overweight may be to make sure older preschoolers are served appropriate portions—and not to admonish them to clean their plates (Rolls et al., 2000). Preschoolers who are allowed to eat when they are hungry and are not pressured to eat everything given to them are more likely to regulate their own caloric intake than are children fed on a schedule (S. L. Johnson & Birch, 1994). However, children vary in their ability to recognize their internal cues of hunger and fullness and may be influenced by what their parents eat. In a study of 40 families in two child care facilities, a six-week program designed to teach children to recognize their own cues improved their ability to self-regulate, independent of what they saw their mothers do (Johnson, 2000).

What children eat is as important as how much they eat. To avoid overweight and prevent cardiac problems, young children should get only about 30 percent of their total calories from fat and less than 10 percent of the total from saturated fat. Lean meat and dairy foods should remain in the diet to provide protein, iron, and calcium. Milk and other dairy products can now be skim or low fat (AAP Committee on Nutrition, 1992a). Studies have found no negative effects on height, weight, body mass, or neurological development from a moderately low-fat diet (Rask-Nissilä et al., 2000; Shea et al., 1993).

Prevention of overweight is critical because the long-term success of treatment for obesity is limited (AAP Committee on Nutrition, 2003). Overweight children, especially those who have overweight parents, tend to become overweight adults (AAP Committee on Nutrition, 2003; Whitaker et al., 1997), and excess body mass can be a threat to health. Early to middle childhood is a good time to treat overweight, when a child's diet is still subject to parental influence or control (Whitaker et al., 1997). Overweight is discussed further in Chapters 12 and 15.

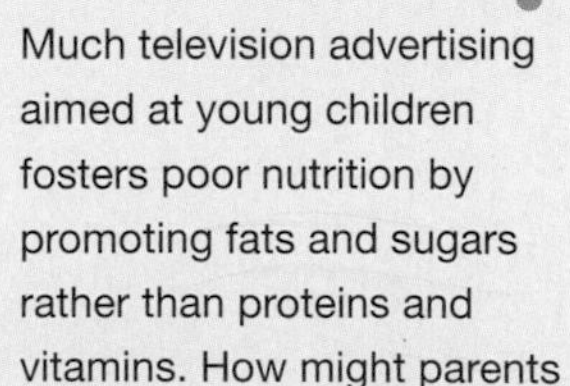

What's your view?

- Much television advertising aimed at young children fosters poor nutrition by promoting fats and sugars rather than proteins and vitamins. How might parents counteract these pressures?

Oral Health

By age 3, all the primary, or deciduous, teeth are in place, and the permanent teeth, which will begin to appear at about age 6, are developing. Thus, parents usually can safely ignore the common habit of thumb sucking in children under 4. If children stop sucking thumbs or fingers by that age, their permanent teeth are not likely to be affected (Herrmann & Roberts, 1987; Umberger & Van Reenen, 1995).

Checkpoint

Can you . . .

- ✔ Describe typical physiological changes between ages 3 and 6?
- ✔ Summarize preschoolers' dietary needs and explain why overweight and tooth decay can become concerns at this age?

Guidepost 2

What sleep patterns and problems tend to develop during early childhood?

Use of fluoride and improved dental care have dramatically reduced the incidence of tooth decay since the 1970s, but disadvantaged children still have more untreated cavities than other children (Bloom, Cohen, Vickerie, & Wondimu, 2003; Brown, Wall, & Lazar, 2000). Tooth decay in early childhood often stems from overconsumption of sweetened milk and juices in infancy together with a lack of regular dental care. In a longitudinal study of 642 Iowa children followed from ages 1 through 5, consumption of regular (nondiet) soda pop, powdered beverages, and, to a lesser extent, 100 percent juice increased the risk of tooth decay (Marshall et al., 2003).

The pain resulting from oral infection may contribute to slowed growth by interfering with normal eating and sleep. In one study of 300 three-year-olds, nearly 14 percent of those with serious tooth decay weighed less than 80 percent of their ideal weight. After a year and a half of dental rehabilitation, these children caught up in weight with a comparison group who had had relatively healthy teeth and normal weight (Acs, Shulman, Ng, & Chussid, 1999).

Sleep Patterns and Problems

Sleep patterns change throughout the growing-up years (Iglowstein, Jenni, Molinari, & Largo, 2003; see Figure 9-1), and early childhood has its own distinct rhythms. Young children usually sleep more deeply at night than they will later in life, but most U.S. children still need a daytime nap or quiet rest until about age 5. Children in other cultures may get the same amount of sleep each day, but its timing may vary. In many traditional cultures, such as the Gusii of Kenya, the Javanese in Indonesia, and the Zuni in New Mexico, young children have no regular bedtime and are allowed to stay up watching adult activities until they are sleepy. Among the Canadian Hare people, 3-year-olds do not take naps but are put to sleep right after dinner and are allowed to sleep as long as they wish in the morning (Broude, 1995).

Young children may develop elaborate routines to put off retiring, and it may take them longer than before to fall asleep. Bedtime may bring on a form of separation anxiety, and the child may do all she or he can to avoid it. Regular, consistent sleep routines can help minimize this common problem. Children past infancy should not be put to sleep by feeding or rocking, as this may make it hard for them to fall asleep on their own (American Academy of Child and Adolescent Psychiatry [AACAP], 1997).

Children are likely to want a light left on and to sleep with a favorite toy or blanket. Such *transitional objects,* used repeatedly as bedtime companions, help a child shift from the dependence of infancy to the independence of later childhood. Parents sometimes worry if their child cannot fall asleep without a tattered blanket or stuffed animal, but such worry seems unfounded. In one longitudinal study, children who at age 4 insisted on taking cuddly objects to bed were just as well adjusted at ages 11 and 16 as children who had not used transitional objects (Newson, Newson, & Mahalski, 1982).

Sleep Disturbances and Disorders

Walking and talking during sleep are fairly common in early childhood. Although sleepwalking itself is harmless, sleepwalkers may be in danger of hurting themselves (AACAP, 1997; Vgontzas & Kales, 1999). This and other sleep disturbances and disorders are caused by accidental activation of the brain's motor control system (Hobson & Silvestri, 1999). They are mostly occasional and usually outgrown. However, persistent sleep problems may indicate an emotional condition that needs to be examined.

A *nightmare* is a frightening dream. Nightmares are often brought on by staying up too late, eating a heavy meal close to bedtime, watching an overstimulating television program, seeing a terrifying movie, or hearing a frightening bedtime story (Vgontzas & Kales, 1999). Nightmares usually come toward morning and are often vividly recalled. They are quite common, especially among girls (AACAP, 1997); 50 percent of 3- to 6-year-olds experience them (Hobson & Silvestri, 1999). An occasional bad dream is no cause for alarm, but frequent or persistent nightmares, especially those that make a child fearful or anxious during waking hours, may signal excessive stress. A repeated theme may point to a specific problem the child cannot solve while awake.

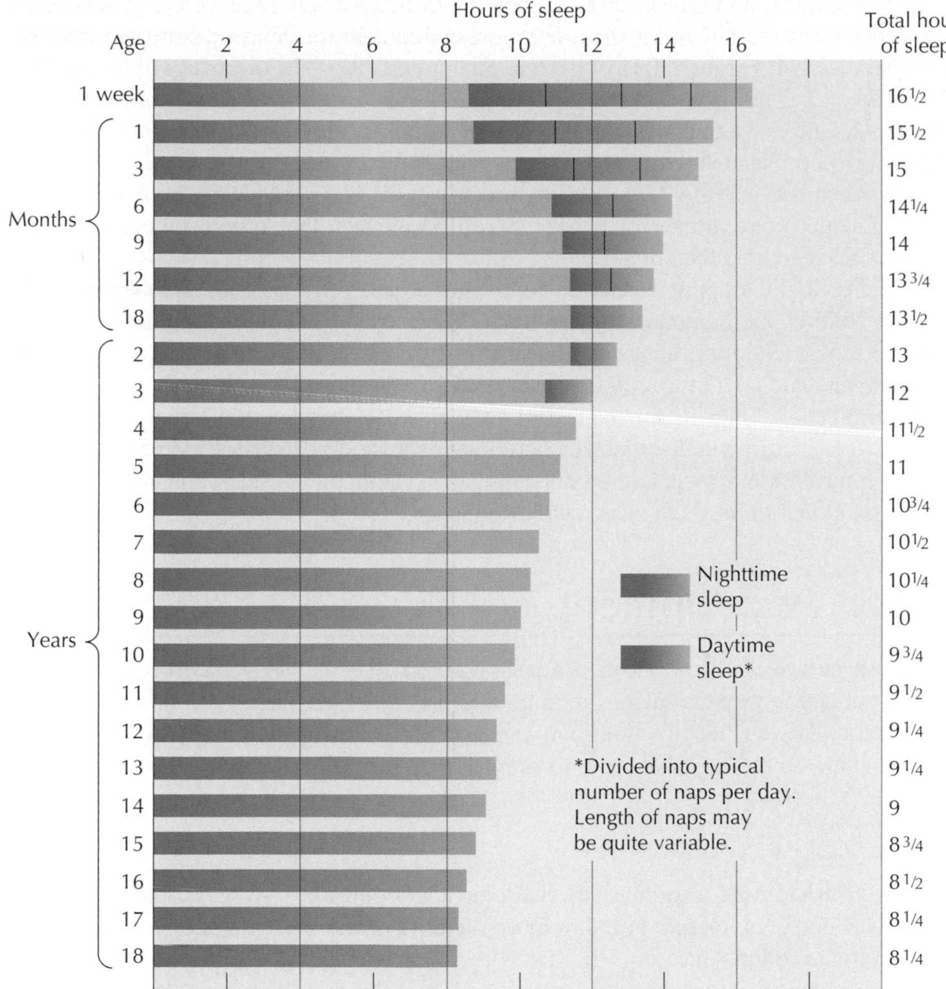

Figure 9-1

Typical sleep requirements in childhood. Unlike infants, who sleep about as long day and night, preschoolers get all or almost all their sleep in one long nighttime period. The number of hours of sleep steadily decreases throughout childhood, but individual children may need more or fewer hours than shown here.

Source: Ferber, 1985; similar data in Iglowstein et al., 2003.

A child who experiences a *sleep* (or *night*) *terror* appears to awaken abruptly from a deep sleep in a state of panic. The child may scream and sit up in bed, breathing rapidly and staring. Yet the child is not really awake, quiets down quickly, and the next morning remembers nothing about the episode. Unlike nightmares, night terrors tend to occur within an hour of falling asleep and affect boys more often than girls. They typically begin between ages 4 and 12. Like sleepwalking, they run in families (AACAP, 1997; Hobson & Silvestri, 1999). Night terrors alarm parents more than they do children and may simply be an effect of very deep sleep; they rarely signify a serious emotional problem and usually go away by age 6. Although the first concern is to protect the child from injury, it is best not to interrupt sleepwalking or night terrors; interruptions may confuse and further frighten the child (Vgontzas & Kales, 1999).

Bed-Wetting

Most children stay dry, day and night, by 3 to 5 years of age; but **enuresis,** repeated urination in clothing or in bed, is common, especially at night. About 7 percent of 5-year-old boys and 3 percent of girls wet the bed regularly. Most outgrow the condition without special help (American Psychiatric Association [APA], 1994; Schmitt, 1997).

enuresis Repeated urination in clothing or in bed.

Children this age normally recognize the sensation of a full bladder while asleep and awaken to empty it in the toilet. Children who wet the bed do not have this awareness. Fewer than 1 percent of bed wetters have a physical disorder, though they may have a small bladder capacity. Nor is persistent enuresis primarily an emotional, mental, or behavioral problem—though such problems can develop because of the way bed wetters are treated by playmates and family (National Enuresis Society, 1995; Schmitt, 1997).

Enuresis runs in families. About 75 percent of bed wetters have a close relative who also wets the bed, and identical twins are more concordant for the condition than fraternal twins (APA, 1994; Fergusson, Horwood, & Shannon, 1986). The discovery of the approximate site of a gene linked to enuresis (Eiberg, 1995; Eiberg, Berendt, & Mohr, 1995) points to heredity as a major factor, possibly in combination with slow motor maturation, allergies, or poor behavioral control (Goleman, 1995). The gene does not appear to account for occasional bed-wetting. Many children who wet the bed are lacking in an antidiuretic hormone, which concentrates urine during sleep. As a result, they produce more urine than their bladders can hold (National Enuresis Society, 1995).

Checkpoint

Can you . . .

✔ Identify four common sleep problems and give recommendations for handling them?

Children and their parents need to be reassured that enuresis is common and not serious. The child is not to blame and should not be punished. Generally parents need not do anything unless children themselves see bed-wetting as a problem. The most effective treatments include rewarding children for staying dry; waking them periodically throughout the night and taking them to the bathroom; waking them when they begin to urinate by using devices that ring bells or buzzers; cutting down on fluids before bedtime; hypnosis; and teaching children to practice controlling the sphincter muscles and to stretch the bladder (National Enuresis Society, 1995; Rappaport, 1993).

Guidepost 3

What are the main motor achievements of early childhood, and how does children's artwork show their physical and cognitive maturation?

Motor Development

Children ages 3 to 6 make great advances in motor skills—both **gross motor skills,** which involve the large muscles, such as running and jumping (see Table 9-2), and **fine motor skills,** manipulative skills involving eye-hand and small-muscle coordination, such as buttoning and drawing. They also begin to show a preference for either the right or left hand.

gross motor skills Physical skills that involve the large muscles.

fine motor skills Physical skills that involve the small muscles and eye-hand coordination.

Gross Motor Skills

At 3, David could walk a straight line and jump a short distance. At 4, he could hop a few steps on one foot. On his fifth birthday, he could jump nearly 3 feet and hop for 16 feet and was learning to roller-skate.

Motor skills do not develop in isolation. The skills that emerge in early childhood build on the achievements of infancy and toddlerhood. Development of the sensory and motor areas of the cerebral cortex permits better coordination between what children want to do and what they can do. Their bones and muscles are stronger, and their lung capacity is greater, making it possible to run, jump, and climb farther, faster, and better. As children's bodies change, permitting them to do more, they integrate their new and previously acquired skills into **systems of action,** producing ever more complex capabilities.

systems of action Increasingly complex combinations of skills that permit a wider or more precise range of movement and more control of the environment.

At about 2½, children begin to jump with both feet, a skill they have not been able to master before this time, probably because their leg muscles were not yet strong enough to propel their body weight upward. Hopping is hard to master until about 4 years of age. Going upstairs is easier than going down; by 3½, most children comfortably alternate feet going up, but not until about 5 do they easily descend that way. Children begin to gallop at

Table 9-2 Gross Motor Skills in Early Childhood

3-Year-Olds	4-Year-Olds	5-Year-Olds
Cannot turn or stop suddenly or quickly	Have more effective control of stopping, starting, and turning	Can start, turn, and stop effectively in games
Can jump a distance of 15 to 24 inches	Can jump a distance of 24 to 33 inches	Can make a running jump of 28 to 36 inches
Can ascend a stairway unaided, alternating feet	Can descend a long stairway alternating feet, if supported	Can descend a long stairway unaided, alternating feet
Can hop, using largely an irregular series of jumps with some variations added	Can hop four to six steps on one foot	Can easily hop a distance of 16 feet

Source: Corbin, 1973.

about 4, do fairly well by 5, and are quite skillful by 6½. Skipping is harder; although some 4-year-olds can skip, most children cannot do it until age 6 (Corbin, 1973). Of course, children vary in adeptness, depending on their genetic endowment and their opportunities to learn and practice motor skills.

The gross motor skills developed during early childhood are the basis for sports, dancing, and other activities that begin during middle childhood and may continue for a lifetime. However, children under 6 are rarely ready to take part in any organized sport. Only 20 percent of 4-year-olds can throw a ball well, and only 30 percent can catch well (AAP Committee on Sports Medicine and Fitness, 1992).

Young children develop best physically when they can be active at an appropriate maturational level in unstructured free play. Parents and teachers can help by offering young children the opportunity to climb and jump on safe, properly sized equipment, by providing balls and other toys small enough to be grasped easily and soft enough not to be harmful, and by offering gentle coaching when a child seems to need help.

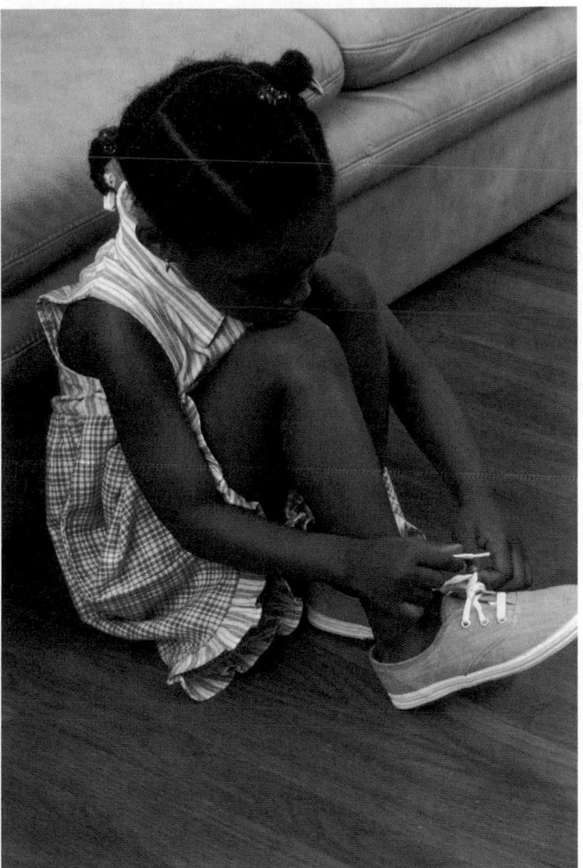
The ability to tie her own shoelaces enables this 5-year-old girl to be more self-reliant.

Fine Motor Skills and Artistic Development

Gains in *fine motor skills,* such as tying shoelaces and cutting with scissors, allow young children to take more responsibility for their personal care. At 3, Madison can pour milk into her cereal bowl, eat with silverware, and use the toilet alone. She can also draw a circle and a rudimentary person—without arms. At 4, Jordan can dress himself with help. He can cut along a line, draw a fairly complete person, make designs and crude letters, and fold paper into a double triangle. At 5, Juan can dress himself without much help, copy a square or triangle, and draw a more elaborate person than before.

Most 3- to 5-year-olds may not be as accomplished artists as Wang Yani, but with progress in fine motor coordination, they too can use their growing cognitive powers and express themselves emotionally through art. In pioneering research, Rhoda Kellogg (1970) examined more than one million drawings by children, half of them under age 6. Since she found drawings by young children similar in different cultures, she concluded that stages in early drawing (see Figure 9-2) reflect maturation of the brain as well as of the muscles.

Two-year-olds *scribble,* and their scribbles are not random. Kellogg identified 20 basic scribbles, such as vertical and zigzag lines, and 17 patterns of placement of scribbles on paper that appear by age 2. By age 3, the *shape* stage appears. Now a child draws in six basic shapes: circles, squares or rectangles, triangles, crosses, Xs, and odd forms. Children quickly move on to the *design* stage, in which they combine two basic shapes into a more complex abstract pattern. Most children enter the *pictorial* stage between ages 4 and 5, though Yani reached it at 3.

Kellogg views the switch from abstraction to representation during the late pictorial stage as a fundamental change in the purpose of children's drawing. Often, under the "guidance" of adults, children begin to aim for realistic portrayal and lose their concern with form and design, the primary elements of art (Kellogg, 1970).

Kellogg quotes artist Pablo Picasso: "Adults should not teach children to draw but should learn from them" (1970, p. 36). Like Wang Yani's father, adults can sustain children's early creativity by letting them draw what they like without imposing suggestions or standards.

LifeMap CD

Have you ever watched a 3-year-old draw? For more experience in observing motor development, watch the video on "Copying Shapes at Age 3" in Chaper 9 of your CD.

How does a 5-year-old's drawing ability differ from that of the 3-year-old in the previous video? To find out, watch the video on "Fine Motor Skills at Age 5" in Chapter 9 of your CD.

Handedness

Handedness, the preference for using one hand over the other, is usually evident by 3 years of age. Since the left hemisphere of the brain, which controls the right side of the body, is usually dominant, most people favor their right side. In people whose brains are less

handedness Preference for using a particular hand.

Figure 9-2

Artistic development in early childhood. There is a great difference between the very simple shapes shown in (*a*) and the detailed pictorial drawings in (*e*). The challenge for adults is to encourage children's creativity while acknowledging their growing facility in drawing.

Source: Kellogg, 1970.

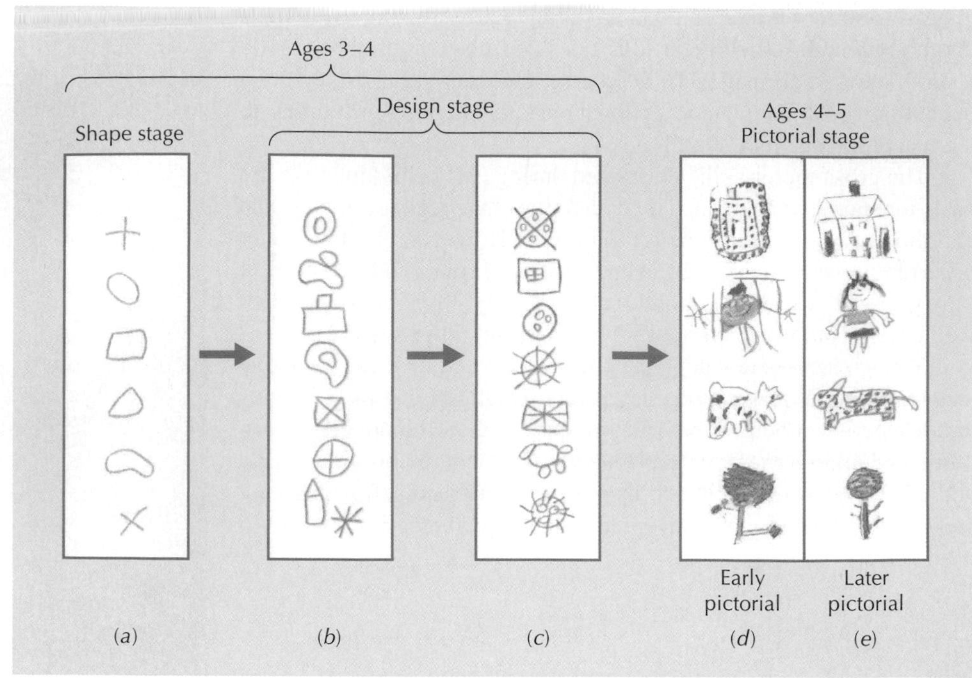

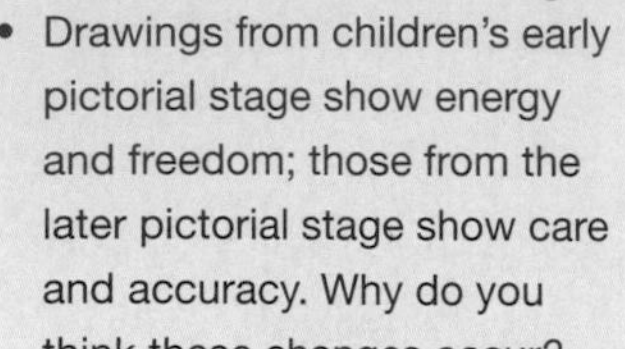

What's your view?

- Drawings from children's early pictorial stage show energy and freedom; those from the later pictorial stage show care and accuracy. Why do you think these changes occur?

asymmetrical, the right hemisphere tends to dominate, making them left-handed. Handedness is not always clear-cut; not everybody prefers one hand for every task. Boys are more likely to be left-handed than girls.

The incidence of left-handedness in a population depends in part on cultural attitudes. Many cultures discourage left-handedness, sometimes by forcing left-handed children to use the right hand or even by binding the left hand with tape. In the most restrictive societies, only 1.8 percent of the population is left-handed, as compared with 10.4 percent in more permissive societies (Hardyck & Petrinovich, 1977).

Is handedness genetic or learned? That question has been controversial. A new theory proposes the existence of a single gene for right-handedness. According to this theory, people who inherit this gene from either or both parents—about 82 percent of the population—are right-handed. Those who do *not* inherit the gene still have a 50-50 chance of being right-handed; otherwise they will be left-handed or ambidextrous. Random determination of handedness among those who do not receive the gene could explain why some monozygotic twins have differing hand preferences as well as why 8 percent of the offspring of two right-handed parents are left-handed. The theory closely predicted the proportion of left-handed offspring in a three-generational sample of families recruited through advertisements (Klar, 1996).

Since scientific evidence provides no reason for favoring "righties," prejudice against the left-handed has largely disappeared in western industrial countries. However, in other parts of the world superstitions surrounding left-handedness continue. If handedness is primarily genetic, such beliefs may eventually die out, and environments and tools designed to make life easier for the left-handed minority may become more common (Klar, 1996).

Checkpoint

Can you . . .

- ✔ List at least three gross motor skills and three fine motor skills, and tell when they typically develop?
- ✔ Identify four stages in young children's drawing?
- ✔ Tell how brain functioning is related to physical skills and handedness?

Guidepost 4

What are the major health and safety risks for young children?

Health and Safety

What used to be a very vulnerable time of life is now safer. Because of widespread immunization, many of the major diseases of childhood are now fairly rare in western industrialized countries. In the developing world, however, such vaccine-preventable diseases as measles, pertussis (whooping cough), and tuberculosis still take a large toll. About 74 percent of early deaths occur in poor, rural regions of sub-Saharan Africa and south Asia, where nutrition is inadequate, water is unsafe, and sanitary facilities are lacking (Black et al., 2003; see Box 9-2).

Around the World

Box 9-2 *Surviving the First Five Years of Life*

The chances of a child's living to his or her fifth birthday are substantially better than 35 years ago, but the prospects for survival depend to a great extent on where the child lives. Worldwide, more than 17 million children under 5 died in 1970. Today the number of deaths in this age group has dropped to 10.5 million each year—still far too many. And, although child mortality has lessened in most parts of the world, these gains have not benefited all children equally.

Fully 98 percent of child deaths occur in developing countries, almost 50 percent of them in Africa (see Figure 9-3). A baby born in Sierra Leone is three and a half times more likely to die before age 5 than a child born in India and more than 100 times more likely to die than a child born in Iceland, which has the world's lowest child mortality rate.

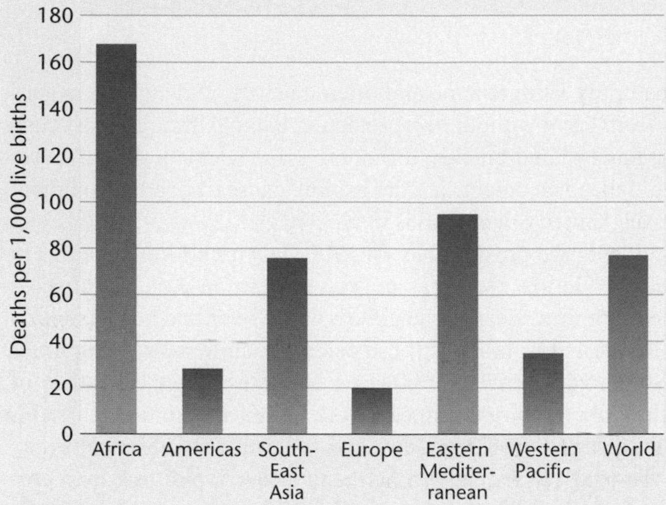

Figure 9-3

Comparative child mortality in six regions of the world, 2002.

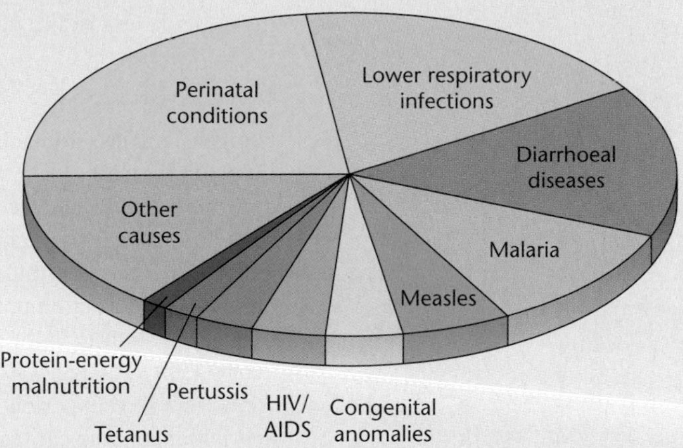

Figure 9-4

Leading causes of death for children in developing countries, 2002. Communicable diseases represent 7 of the 10 leading causes, and all 10 together represent 86 percent of all deaths.

The major causes of death in the developing world, accounting for about 60 percent of child deaths, are infectious and parasitic diseases, including HIV/AIDS (see Figure 9-4). Malnutrition, malaria, lower respiratory tract infections, and diarrheal diseases account for 45 percent of all deaths in sub-Saharan Africa, the site of 42 percent of all child deaths. In some African countries, HIV/AIDS is responsible for as many as 6 out of 10 child deaths, often in children who lose their mothers to the disease. More advanced developing countries of the Eastern Mediterranean region, Latin America, and Asia are experiencing a shift toward the pattern in more developed countries, where child deaths are most likely to be caused by complications of birth.

International efforts to improve child health focus on the first five years because nearly 9 out of 10 deaths of children under age 15 occur during those years. At least 169 countries have shown declines in child mortality in the past three decades. The most striking reduction was in Oman, on the southern end of the Arabian peninsula, from 242 child deaths per 1,000 live births in 1970 to only 15 per 1,000 in 2002. India and China also have achieved impressive declines.

In general, however, the strongest improvement has occurred in rich industrialized nations and in those developing countries where child mortality was already relatively low. Thus, although the mortality gap between the developed and developing world has narrowed, disparities among developing regions have widened.

In Africa, some promising gains have been wiped out, largely because of HIV/AIDS. Fourteen African countries, after achieving significant reductions in child mortality during the 1970s and 1980s, saw *more* young children die in 2002 than in 1990. On the other hand, eight countries in the region, among them Gabon, Gambia, and Ghana, have reduced child mortality by more than 50 percent since 1970.

In Latin America, the most dramatic reductions in child mortality have taken place in Chile, Costa Rica, and Cuba, where child deaths have dropped more than 80 percent since 1970. In contrast, Haitian children still die at a rate of 133 per 1,000, almost double the rate in Bolivia, which has the next worst mortality record in the Americas.

In most countries, with the exception of China, India, Pakistan, and Nepal, boys are more likely to die than girls. In China, where families traditionally prefer boys, young girls have a 33 percent greater risk of dying—often, it has been reported, through abandonment or infanticide (Carmichael, 2004; Hudson & den Boer, 2004; Lee, 2004; Rosenthal, 2003; see Box 11-2 in Chapter 11). Children in poor countries and children of the poor in rich countries are most likely to die young. Survival gains have been slower in rural than in urban areas and, in some countries, such as the United States, have disproportionately benefited those with higher incomes. But even poor U.S. children are less likely to die young than better-off children in Africa.

What's your view?

What can be done to produce more rapid and more evenly distributed improvements in child mortality throughout the world?

Check it out!

For more information on this topic, go to **http://www.who.int/whr/2003/chapter1/en/index2.html**. This is the Web site for the WHO report discussed in this box.

Source: World Health Organization (WHO), 2003.

In the United States, children's death rates from all causes have declined in recent years. Deaths in childhood are relatively few compared with deaths in adulthood, and most are caused by injury rather than illness (Arias et al., 2003). Still, environmental influences make this a less healthy time for some children than for others.

Minor Illnesses

Coughs, sniffles, stomachaches, and runny noses are a part of early childhood. These minor illnesses typically last a few days and are seldom serious enough to require a doctor's attention. Because children's lungs are not fully developed, respiratory problems are common, though less so than in infancy. Three- to 5-year-olds catch an average of seven to eight colds and other respiratory illnesses a year. It's a good thing they do, since these illnesses help build natural immunity (resistance to disease). During middle childhood, when the respiratory system is more fully developed, children average fewer than six such illnesses a year (Denny & Clyde, 1983). Minor illnesses may have emotional and cognitive benefits as well. Repeated experience with illness helps children learn to cope with physical distress and understand its causes, increasing their sense of competence (Parmelee, 1986).

Accidental Injuries

Because young children are naturally venturesome and often unaware of danger, it is hard for caregivers to protect them from harm without *over*protecting them. Although most cuts, bumps, and scrapes are "kissed away" and quickly forgotten, some accidental injuries result in lasting damage or death. Indeed, accidents are the leading cause of death throughout childhood and adolescence in the United States (Arias et al., 2003).

Many deaths from car accidents are preventable. In 1996, 1 in 5 children's deaths in automobile crashes—whether the victims were passengers, pedestrians, or bicyclists—were alcohol related. In 2 out of 3 of these deaths, the child's own driver had been drinking (Margolis, Foss, & Tolbert, 2000), and in most of these cases the child was riding unrestrained (Quinlan, Brewer, Sleet, & Dellinger, 2000). All 50 states and the District of Columbia require young children in cars to ride in specially designed seats or to wear standard seat belts. Four-year-olds who "graduate" from car seats to lap and shoulder belts may need booster seats until they grow bigger. Airbags designed to inflate rapidly so as to protect adults riding in the front seat of a car in high-impact collisions *increase* the risk of fatal injury to children under age 13 who are riding in the front seat by as much as 34 percent (Rivara, 1999). It is safer, therefore, for young children always to ride in the back seat.

More than one million cases of ingestion of toxic substances by children under 6 were reported to poison control centers in 1998, and the true figure may be more than four million. Medications are responsible for more than half (52 percent) of deaths from poisoning. Safe storage could prevent many of these deaths (Litovitz et al., 1999; Shannon, 2000).

U.S. laws requiring "childproof" caps on medicine bottles and other dangerous household products, regulation of product safety, mandatory helmets for bicycle riders, and safe storage of firearms have improved child safety. Making playgrounds safer would be another valuable measure. An estimated 3 percent of children in day care are hurt badly enough each year to need medical attention, and about half of accidents at child care centers occur on playgrounds. Nearly 1 in 5 are from falls, often resulting in skull injury and brain damage (Briss, Sacks, Addiss, Kresnow, & O'Neil, 1994). (Table 9-3 summarizes suggestions for reducing accident risks in various settings.)

Checkpoint

Can you . . .

- ✔ Identify two benefits of minor illnesses?
- ✔ Tell where and how young children are most likely to be injured, and list ways in which injuries can be avoided?

Health in Context: Bioecological Influences

Why do some children have more illnesses or injuries than others? As Bronfenbrenner's bioecological theory would predict, the child's characteristics interact with influences of the home, the child care facility, the neighborhood, and the larger society.

Temperament

Temperament may make some children injury prone. In a longitudinal study of 59 children, those who were more extraverted and had less inhibitory control as toddlers and preschool-

Table 9-3 Reducing Accident Risks for Children

Activity	Precautions
Bicycling	Helmets reduce risk of head injury by 85 percent and brain injury by 88 percent.
Skateboarding and Rollerblading	Children should wear helmets and protective padding on knees, elbows, and wrists.
Using fireworks	Families should not purchase fireworks for home use.
Lawn mowing	Children under 12 should not operate walk-behind mowers; those under 14 should not operate ride-on mowers; small children should not be close to a moving mower.
Swimming	Swimming pools should not be installed in backyards of homes with children under 5; pools already in place need a high fence around all four sides, with gates having high, out-of-reach, self-closing latches. Adults need to watch children very closely near pools, lakes, and other bodies of water.
Playing on a playground	A safe surface under swings, slides, and other equipment can be 10-inch-deep sand, 12-inch-deep wood chips, or rubber outdoor mats; separate areas should be maintained for active play and quiet play, for older and younger children.
Using firearms	Guns should be kept unloaded and locked up, with bullets locked in a separate place; children should not have access to keys; adults should talk with children about the risks of gun injury.
Eating	To prevent choking, young children should not eat hard candies, nuts, grapes, and hot dogs (unless sliced lengthwise, then across); food should be cut into small pieces; children should not eat while talking, running, jumping, or lying down.
Ingesting toxic substances	Only drugs and toxic household products with safety caps should be used; toxic products should be stored out of children's reach. Suspected poisoning should be reported immediately to the nearest poison control center.
Riding in motor vehicles	Young children should sit in approved car seats, in the back seat. Adults should observe traffic laws and avoid aggressive drivers.

Source: Adapted in part from American Academy of Pediatrics (AAP) Committee on Injury and Poison Prevention, 1995; AAP and Center to Prevent Handgun Violence, 1994; Rivara, 1999; Shannon, 2000.

ers tended to overestimate their physical abilities at age 6, and they also had had considerably more injuries requiring medical treatment. It is particularly important to ensure that injury-prone children be taught safety precautions. Still, protective measures, such as gates at railroad crossings, are imperative (Schwebel & Plumert, 1999).

Caregivers' Characteristics

Also at special risk are children whose primary caregivers are young, uneducated, and overburdened. In a study of all children born in Tennessee between 1985 and 1994, children born to mothers under 20 years old, with less than a high school education and three or more other children, were 15 times more likely to die of injuries before the age of 5 as children whose mothers were college educated, were more than 30 years old, and had fewer than three other children. If the mortality rate for all children could be reduced to that of this lowest-risk group, injury-related deaths might be reduced by more than 75 percent (Scholer, Mitchel, & Ray, 1997).

Exposure to Illness

Preschoolers in day care centers are 2 to 4 times more likely to pick up mild infectious diseases (such as colds, flu, and diarrhea) than are children raised at home. They also have a higher risk of contracting otitis media (middle ear infection), gastrointestinal diseases, and hepatitis A (Nafstad, Hagen, Oie, Magnus, & Jaakkola, 1999; Thacker et al., 1992). However, early mild infections may protect against more serious respiratory illness. In a longitudinal study of 1,035 Tucson children followed from birth, those who were exposed to older siblings at home or who were in day care during the first 6 months of life were less likely to develop asthma or frequent wheezing later in childhood (Ball et al., 2000).

Exposure to Smoking

Parental smoking is an important preventable cause of childhood illness and death. In the United States, 43 percent of children 2 months to 11 years old live with smokers and are exposed daily to secondhand smoke (AAP Committee on Substance Abuse, 2001; Pirkle et al., 1996). This passive exposure increases the risk of contracting a number of medical problems, including bronchitis, serious infectious illnesses, otitis media, burns, and asthma, and it increases the severity of asthma and decreased lung function in children who already have the disease. It also may lead to cancer in adulthood (Aligne & Stoddard, 1997; AAP Committee on Environmental Health, 1997; Bollinger, 2003; Mannino, Homa, & Redd, 2002; U.S. Environmental Protection Agency, 1994). The AAP Committee on Environmental Health (1997) recommends that children be raised in a smoke-free environment.

SES and Poverty

There is a striking relationship between socioeconomic status and health: the lower a family's SES, the greater a child's risks of illness, injury, and death (Chen, Matthews, & Boyce, 2002). Low income is the *chief* factor associated with poor health of children and adolescents, over and above race and family structure (Montgomery, Kiely, & Pappas, 1996; refer back to Table 1-2 in Chapter 1).

Nearly 1 in 5 U.S. children under 6—18.5 percent—were poor in 2002 (Proctor & Dalaker, 2003). Although poverty strikes all parts of the population, it besets young families—including working families—and minorities disproportionately. About 31 percent of black children and 28 percent of Hispanic children are poor, as compared with 13 percent of white children and 14.5 percent of Asian and Pacific Islander children. Three out of 4 poor children live with family members who work at least part-time. Furthermore, the safety net for needy families in a sluggish economy has weakened with the end of national welfare assistance (Children's Defense Fund [CDF], 2004). Only 4 out of 10 children in poor families are in excellent health, as compared with 6 out of 10 children in nonpoor families (Bloom, Cohen, Vickerie, & Wondimu, 2003).

The health problems of poor children often begin before birth. Many poor mothers do not eat well and do not receive adequate prenatal care; their babies are more likely than babies of nonpoor mothers to be of low birth weight or to die in infancy. Poor children who do not eat properly do not grow properly and thus are weak and susceptible to disease. Many poor families live in crowded, unsanitary housing in run-down, noisy, polluted, or dangerous neighborhoods. The children may lack adequate supervision, especially when the parents are at work. They are more likely than other children to suffer lead poisoning, hearing and vision loss, and iron-deficiency anemia, as well as such stress-related conditions as asthma, headaches, insomnia, and irritable bowel. They also tend to have more behavior problems, psychological disturbances, and learning disabilities (J. L. Brown, 1987; Chen et al., 2002; Egbuono & Starfield, 1982; Santer & Stocking, 1991; Starfield, 1991).

Many poor children do not get the medical care they need (Bloom et al., 2003; Chen et al., 2002). Medicaid has been an important "safety net" for poor children since 1965. However, it has not reached millions of children whose families earn too much to qualify but too little to afford private insurance. The federal government in 1997 authorized the Children's Health Insurance Program (CHIP) to help states extend health care coverage to uninsured children. By 2003, 5.8 million children had been enrolled. Still, 1 in 8 U.S. children (9.3 million) remain uninsured (CDF, 2004). Children with family incomes below $35,000 are almost nine times more likely to be uninsured than children in affluent families with incomes of $75,000 or more (Bloom et al., 2003). Latino children, now the nation's largest racial/ethnic minority, are more likely to lack regular, quality care and insurance than white or black children. Language and cultural barriers and the need for more Latino care providers may help explain these disparities (Flores et al., 2002). Among

What's your view?

- Who should be responsible for children's well-being when parents cannot provide adequate food, clothing, shelter, and health care: government, religious and community institutions, the private sector, or a combination of these?

Hispanic or Latino children, Mexican-American children are most likely to lack insurance and access to regular health care (Scott & Ni, 2004).

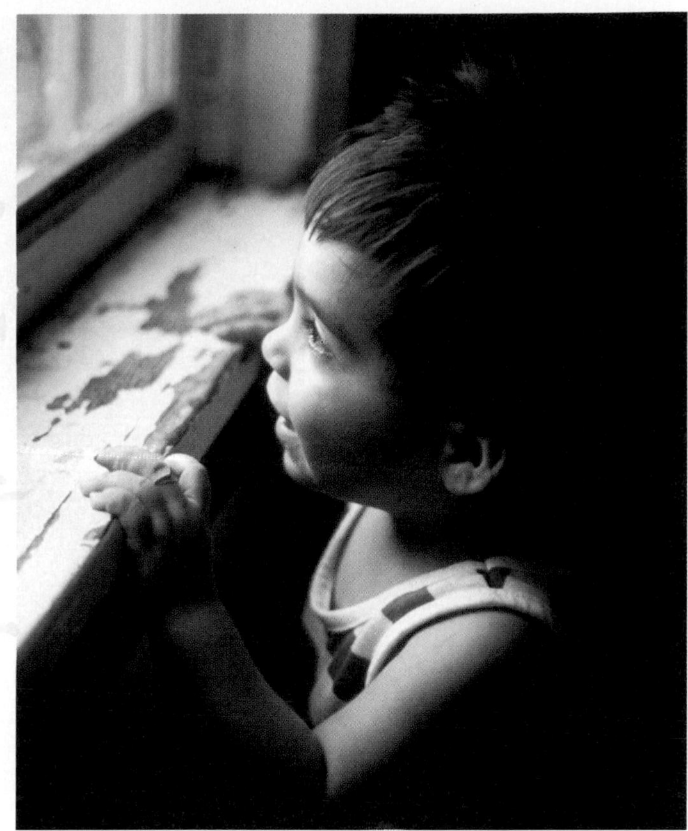

Young children who live in old, dilapidated buildings with peeling lead paint are at risk for lead poisoning, which can adversely affect the developing brain.

Exposure to Lead

Children can get lead in the bloodstream from lead-contaminated food or water, from putting contaminated fingers in their mouths, and from inhaling dust in homes or schools where there is lead-based paint. Lead poisoning can seriously interfere with cognitive development and can bring on a variety of neurological and behavioral problems (AAP Committee on Environmental Health, 1998; Canfield et al., 2003; Needleman, Riess, Tobin, Biesecker, & Greenhouse, 1996; Tesman & Hills, 1994). Yet it can be completely prevented by removing sources of lead from children's environment (Tesman & Hills, 1994).

Although children' blood lead levels have dropped by more than 80 percent in the past three decades, an estimated 8 percent of children in the United States, most of them poor and on Medicaid, still have dangerously elevated levels (Rogan et al., 2001). This includes about 1 child in 50 between the ages of 1 and 5. Furthermore, 1 in every 10 children in that age group has lead levels currently considered officially acceptable but high enough to lead to significant intellectual impairment (Canfield et al., 2003).

There is no safe level of exposure to lead. The degree of toxicity depends on the dose, how long a child is exposed, and the child's developmental and nutritional vulnerability (AAP Committee on Environmental Health, 1998). Even low levels of exposure may have detrimental effects in young preschoolers, particularly those who have other risk factors, such as poverty and maternal depression (Canfield et al., 2003).

In a five-year longitudinal study, treatment of lead-exposed children proved ineffective in improving psychological, behavioral, and cognitive functioning. Thus, prevention is critical (Rogan et al., 2001). Laws mandating removal of lead from gasoline, paints, and soldered food cans have helped prevention efforts, but dust and soil in many places are still contaminated (Pirkle et al., 1994; Tesman & Hills, 1994). The Centers for Disease Control and Prevention (1997) calls for universal screening of residential areas with at least 27 percent of housing built before 1950 and in populations in which the percentage of 1- and 2-year-olds with elevated blood lead levels is 12 percent or more.

Parents need to learn how to reduce lead exposure (AAP Committee on Environmental Health, 1998). Washing hands before meals and before bed, keeping fingernails clipped, and eating a well-balanced diet can help. Chipping or peeling paint should be removed carefully, and barriers can be put up to keep children away from areas that contain lead (Kimbrough, LeVois, & Webb, 1994).

Homelessness

Since the 1980s, as affordable rental housing has become scarce and poverty has spread, homelessness has increased dramatically in the United States (National Coalition for the Homeless, 2004). An estimated 1.35 million children experience homelessness each year (National Coalition for the Homeless, 2002, 2004; Urban Institute, 2000). In a survey of 25 cities, 49 percent of the homeless population were African American, 35 percent Caucasian, 13 percent Hispanic, 2 percent Native American, and 1 percent Asian American (U.S. Conference of Mayors, 2003).

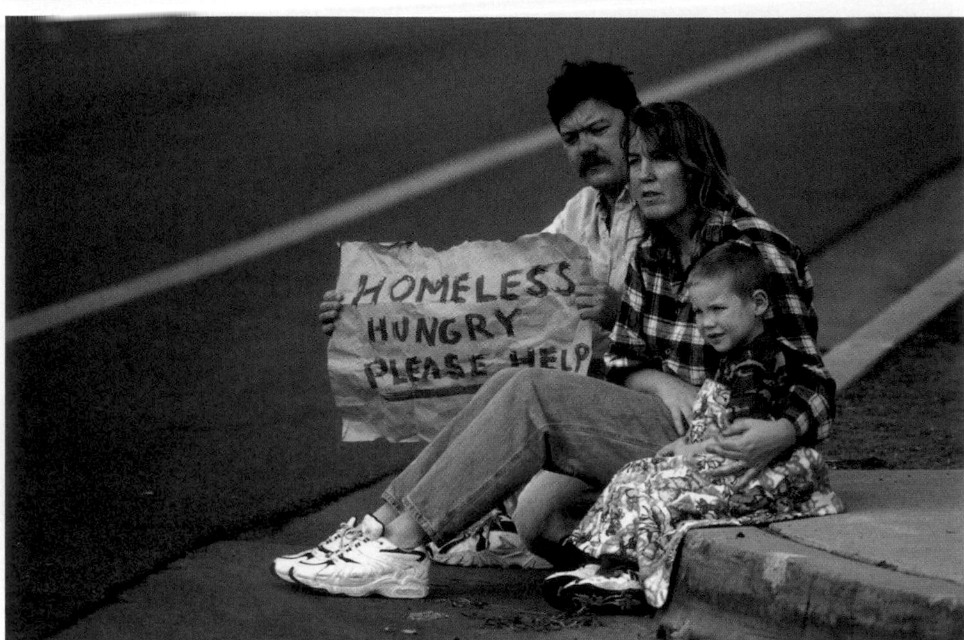

Families with children are the fastest growing part of the homeless population. Homeless children tend to have more health problems than children with homes.

Families now comprise 40 percent of the homeless population, and the proportion is probably higher in rural areas (National Coalition for the Homeless, 2004; U.S. Conference of Mayors, 2003). Many homeless families are headed by single mothers in their 20s (Buckner, Bassuk, Weinreb, & Brooks, 1999). Often these families are fleeing domestic violence (National Coalition for the Homeless, 2004). In New York City alone, the number of families living in shelters has almost doubled since 1998, and a family is likely to stay nearly a year before finding permanent housing (National Coalition for the Homeless, 2004; Santos & Ingrassia, 2002).

Many homeless children spend their crucial early years in unstable, insecure, and often unsanitary environments. They and their parents may be cut off from a supportive community, family ties, and institutional resources and from ready access to medical care and schooling.

These children suffer more health problems than poor children who have homes, and they are more likely to die in infancy. They are three times more likely than other children to lack immunizations and two to three times more likely to have iron deficiency anemia. They experience high rates of diarrhea; severe hunger, and malnourishment; obesity (from eating excessive carbohydrates and fats); tooth decay; asthma and other chronic diseases; respiratory, skin, and eye and ear infections; scabies and lice; trauma-related injuries; and elevated levels of lead. Homeless children also tend to suffer severe depression and anxiety and to have neurological and visual deficits, developmental delays, behavior problems, and learning difficulties. Uprooted from their neighborhoods, as many as half do not go to school; if they do, they tend to have problems, partly because they miss a lot of it and have no place to do homework. They tend to do poorly on standardized reading and math tests, even when their cognitive functioning is normal, and they are more likely to repeat a grade or be placed in special classes than are children with homes (AAP Committee on Community Health Services, 1996; Bassuk, 1991; CDF, 2004; Rafferty & Shinn, 1991; Rubin et al., 1996; Weinreb et al., 2002).

Checkpoint ✓

Can you . . .

✓ Discuss several environmental influences that endanger children's health and development?

Maltreatment: Abuse and Neglect

Guidepost 5

What are the causes and consequences of child abuse and neglect, and what can be done about it?

Although most parents are loving and nurturing, some cannot or will not take proper care of their children, and some deliberately hurt or kill them. *Maltreatment,* whether perpetrated by parents or others, is deliberate or avoidable endangerment of a child. It may consist of *abuse,* action that inflicts harm, or *neglect,* inaction that causes harm (U.S. Department of Health and Human Services [USDHHS], 1999a).

Maltreatment takes several specific forms, and any one form is likely to be accompanied by one or more of the others (Belsky, 1993). **Physical abuse** involves injury to the body through punching, beating, kicking, or burning. **Neglect** is failure to meet a child's basic needs, such as for food, clothing, medical care, protection, and supervision. **Sexual abuse** is sexual activity involving a child and an older person. **Emotional maltreatment** refers to acts of abuse or neglect that may cause behavioral, cognitive, emotional, or mental disorders. It may include rejection, terrorization, isolation, exploitation, degradation, ridicule, or failure to provide emotional support, love, and affection. Emotional maltreatment is hard to identify; its effects may not surface immediately and may be difficult to distinguish from signs of emotional disturbance and other developmental problems (USDHHS, 1999a).

physical abuse Action taken to endanger a child, involving potential bodily injury.

neglect Failure to meet a child's basic needs.

sexual abuse Sexual activity involving a child and an older person.

emotional maltreatment Action or inaction that may cause behavioral, cognitive, emotional, or mental disorders.

Maltreatment: Facts and Figures

Since its peak in 1993, the rate of child abuse and neglect in the United States has declined by 20 percent. Still, state and local child protective services agencies investigated and confirmed some 896,000 cases in 2002, and the actual number may have been considerably higher. An estimated 1,400 children died of abuse or neglect in that year (USDHHS, 2004).

The steep rise in reported cases and serious injuries since 1976, when the first national statistics were compiled, may reflect an increase in maltreatment, an increase in reporting, or (more likely) both. Still, the actual incidence of maltreatment is believed to be even higher. Many, if not most, cases are never reported, and many of those reported are not investigated (USDHHS, 1999a). On the other hand, some reported claims filed in the context of divorce proceedings, for example, turn out to be false.

Abused and neglected children are of all ages, but the highest rates are for ages 3 and younger. (Refer back to the discussion of shaken baby syndrome in Chapter 6.) American-Indian, Alaska-Native, and African-American children have the highest rates of victimization, about twice as high as those of white children (USDHHS, 2004). More than 60 percent of maltreated children are neglected, and almost 20 percent are physically abused. About 10 percent are sexually abused and 7 percent emotionally maltreated (USDHHS, 2004). Girls are four times more likely than boys to be sexually abused (NCANDS, 2001).

Psychological aggression, such as yelling and screaming (the most frequent form), swearing, calling names, threatening to spank, or threatening to kick a child out of the house, occurs at least once or twice a year in nearly 9 out of 10 households—especially among parents who are poor or less educated—and is often considered a form of discipline. However, some psychologists consider it emotional abuse. According to self-reports, about 10 to 20 percent of parents of toddlers engage in *severe* psychological aggression, and the prevalence rises to about 50 percent among parents of teenagers. Psychological aggression generally backfires, resulting in *more* behavior problems, not less, and may even lead to mental illness (Straus & Field, 2003).

Contributing Factors: An Ecological View

Abuse and neglect reflect the interplay of multiple layers of contributing factors involving the family, the community, and the larger society (USDHHS, 1999a). In more than 8 out of 10 cases of maltreatment, the perpetrators are the child's parents, usually the mother (USDHHS, 2004). Maltreatment by parents is a symptom of extreme disturbance in child rearing, usually aggravated by other family problems, such as poverty, alcoholism, or antisocial behavior. A disproportionate number of abused and neglected children are in large, poor, or single-parent families, which tend to be under stress and to have trouble meeting children's needs (Sedlak & Broadhurst, 1996). Yet what pushes one parent over the edge, another may take in stride. Although most neglect cases occur in very poor families, most low-income parents do not neglect their children.

Characteristics of Abusive Parents and Families

Abuse may begin when a parent who is already anxious, depressed, or hostile tries to control a child physically but loses self-control and ends up shaking or beating the child

(USDHHS, 1999a). When parents who had troubled childhoods, think poorly of themselves, and find negative emotions hard to handle have children who are particularly needy or demanding, who cry a lot, or who are unresponsive, the likelihood of maltreatment increases (NRC, 1993b; Reid, Patterson, & Loeber, 1982; USDHHS, 1999a).

Abusive parents tend to have marital problems and to fight physically. Their households tend to be disorganized, and they experience more stressful events than other families (Reid et al., 1982; Sedlak & Broadhurst, 1996). Many abusive parents cut themselves off from others, leaving them with no one to turn to in times of stress and no one to see what is happening.

Characteristics of Neglectful Parents and Families

Neglectful parents tend to be apathetic, incompetent, irresponsible, or emotionally withdrawn (Wolfe, 1985). The family atmosphere tends to be chaotic, with people moving in and out.

Neglectful parents tend to distance themselves from their children. They may be critical or uncommunicative. Often the mothers were neglected themselves as children and are depressed or feel hopeless. They may be mentally retarded or have limited knowledge about children's needs. Many are substance abusers. The fathers are not involved in their children's lives; many have deserted or do not give enough financial or emotional support. The child may be unresponsive or may have a "difficult" temperament and thus may be hard to care for. Often the children are of low birth weight. This may be related to SES and to lack of adequate prenatal care (Dubowitz, 1999).

Abuse and neglect often happen in the same households. Like abusive families, neglectful families tend to be socially isolated. Lack of social support makes it harder for these families to cope with difficult circumstances (Dubowitz, 1999). Substance abuse is a factor in at least one-third of cases of abuse and neglect (USDHHS, 1999a).

Neighborhood and Social Support

The outside world can create a climate for family violence. Poverty, unemployment, job dissatisfaction, social isolation, and lack of assistance for the primary caregiver are closely correlated with child and spouse abuse. None of these, however, is a determining factor.

What makes one low-income neighborhood a place where children are highly likely to be maltreated and another, matched for ethnic population and income levels, safer? In one inner-city Chicago neighborhood, the proportion of children who died from maltreatment (1 death for every 2,541 children) was about twice the proportion in another inner-city neighborhood. Researchers who interviewed community leaders found a depressed atmosphere in the high-abuse community. Criminal activity was rampant, and facilities for community programs were dark and dreary. This was an environment with "an ecological conspiracy against children" (Garbarino & Kostelny, 1993, p. 213). In the low-abuse neighborhood, people described their community as a poor but decent place to live. They painted a picture of a neighborhood with robust social support networks, well-known community services, and strong political leadership. In a community like this, maltreatment is less likely to occur.

Cultural Values and Patterns

Two cultural factors associated with child abuse are societal violence and physical punishment of children. In countries where violent crime is infrequent and children are rarely spanked, such as Japan, China, and Tahiti, child abuse is rare (Celis, 1990).

By comparison, the United States is a violent place. Homicide, domestic violence, and rape are common. A 1977 Supreme Court ruling that school personnel may strike disobedient children is still in effect, with some qualifications, and many states still permit corporal punishment in schools. According to one representative sampling, more than 9 out of 10 parents of preschoolers and about half of parents of school-age children report using physical punishment at home (Straus & Stewart, 1999; see Box 11-1 in Chapter 11).

Table 9-4	Developmentally Related Reactions to Sexual Abuse
Age	**Most Common Symptoms**
Preschoolers	Anxiety
	Nightmares
	Inappropriate sexual behavior
School-age children	Fear
	Mental illness
	Aggression
	Nightmares
	School problems
	Hyperactivity
	Regressive behavior
Adolescents	Depression
	Withdrawn, suicidal, or self-injurious behaviors
	Physical complaints
	Illegal acts
	Running away
	Substance abuse

Source: Adapted from Kendall-Tackett, Williams, & Finkelhor, 1993.

Effects of Maltreatment

Maltreatment can produce grave consequences—not only physical, but also emotional, cognitive, and social.

Maltreated children often show delayed speech (Coster, Gersten, Beeghly, & Cicchetti, 1989). They are more likely to repeat a grade, do poorly on cognitive tests, and have behavior problems in school (Eckenrode, Laird, & Doris, 1993). They often have disorganized-disoriented attachments to their parents (refer back to Chapter 8) and negative, distorted self-concepts. Deprived of early positive social interactions, they do not develop social skills and have difficulty making friends (Price, 1996). They may become either overly aggressive or withdrawn (USDHHS, 1999a).

Physically abused youngsters tend to be fearful, uncooperative, less able to respond appropriately to friendly overtures, and, consequently, less well liked than other children (Coie & Dodge, 1998; Haskett & Kistner, 1991; Salzinger, Feldman, Hammer, & Rosario, 1993). As adolescents, they tend to skip school and to show psychological and behavioral problems, and they are less likely to expect to go to college than teens who did not suffer abuse early in life (Lansford et al., 2002). Although most abused children do not become delinquent, criminal, or mentally ill, abuse makes it likelier that they will (Dodge, Bates, & Pettit, 1990; NRC, 1993b; Widom, 1989). They also are at increased risk of early initiation into illicit drug use (Dube et al., 2003) and of attempted suicide (Dube et al., 2001).

Chronic neglect during early childhood negatively affects later school performance, social relationships, adaptability, and problem solving (NRC, 1993b). Although effects of emotional maltreatment are harder to pin down, it has been linked to lying, stealing, low self-esteem, emotional maladjustment, dependency, underachievement, depression, aggression, learning disorders, homicide, and suicide, as well as psychological distress later in life (S. N. Hart & Brassard, 1987).

Consequences of sexual abuse vary with age (see Table 9-4). In a study that followed 68 sexually abused children for five years, these children showed more disturbed behavior, had lower self-esteem, and were more depressed, anxious, or unhappy than a control group (Swanston, Tebbutt, O'Toole, & Oates, 1997). Sexually abused children may become sexually active at an early age (Fiscella, Kitzman, Cole, Sidora, & Olds, 1998). Fearfulness and low self-esteem often continue into adulthood. Adults who were sexually abused as children tend to be anxious, depressed, angry, or hostile; to mistrust people; to feel isolated and stigmatized, to be sexually maladjusted (Browne & Finkelhor, 1986); and to abuse alcohol or drugs (NRC, 1993b; USDHHS, 1999a).

Still, many maltreated children show remarkable resilience. Above average intelligence, advanced cognitive abilities, and high self-esteem seem to help. Also important is the child's interpretation of the abuse or neglect. Children who see it as coming from a parent's weaknesses or frustrations seem to cope better than those who take it as parental rejection (Garmezy, Masten, & Tellegen, 1984; Zimrin, 1986).

Helping Families in Trouble or at Risk

Because maltreatment is a multifactorial problem, it needs many-pronged solutions. Effective community prevention and intervention strategies should be comprehensive, neighborhood based, centered on protecting children, and aimed at strengthening families if possible and removing children if necessary (USDHHS, 1999a).

Some abuse-prevention programs teach basic parenting skills (USDHHS, 1999a; Wolfe, Edwards, Manion, & Koverola, 1988). Other programs offer subsidized day care, volunteer homemakers, home visitors, and temporary "respite homes" or "relief parents" to take over occasionally. In a semirural New York community, nurses visited unmarried teenage first-time expectant mothers once a month during pregnancy and then during the child's first two years. At the end of that period, there were 80 percent fewer verified cases of abuse and neglect among the nurse-visited children than in a control group; and 15 years later, their mothers were only about half as likely to have been reported as abusers or neglecters (D. L. Olds, Eckenrode, et al., 1997; D. L. Olds, Henderson, et al., 1999).

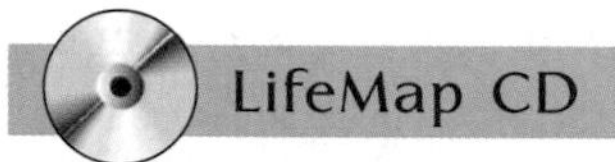

To learn how a social worker approaches the issue of maltreatment, watch the video on "Working with Children Who Are Abused and Neglected" in Chapter 9 of your CD.

Reports of child maltreatment go to state and local child protective services agencies for investigation. These agencies determine what steps, if any, need to be taken and marshal community resources to help. This may involve helping the family resolve their problems or arranging for alternative care for children who cannot safely remain at home (Larner, Stevenson, & Behrman, 1998).

Services for abused children and their parents include shelters, education in parenting skills, and therapy. Parents Anonymous and other organizations offer free, confidential support groups. Abused children may receive play or art therapy and day care in a therapeutic environment. In communities where abuse or neglect is widespread, school-based programs can be effective. However, availability of services is often limited. In a nationally representative survey, nearly half (47.9 percent) of 2- to 14-year-olds investigated by child welfare agencies after reported maltreatment had clinically significant emotional or behavioral problems, but only one-fourth of those with such problems received mental health care (Burns et al., 2004).

When authorities remove children from their homes, the usual alternative is foster care, which has grown substantially since the 1980s. More than 500,000 children were in foster care in 2001, more than one-fourth of them under age 5 (Chipungu & Bent-Goodley, 2004). Foster care removes a child from immediate danger, but it is often unstable, further alienates the child from the family, and may turn out to be another abusive situation. Often a child's basic health and educational needs are not met (David and Lucile Packard Foundation, 2004; NRC, 1993b). Due in part to a scarcity of traditional foster homes and an increasing caseload, a growing proportion of placements (31 percent), especially of African-American children, are in kinship foster care (Berrick, 1998; Geen, 2004). Although most foster children who leave the system are reunited with their families, about 28 percent reenter foster care within the next 10 years (Wulczyn, 2004). Children who have been in foster care are more likely than other children to become homeless, to become involved in criminal activity, and to become teenage mothers (David and Lucile Packard Foundation, 2004).

The plight of abused and neglected children is one for which society needs more effective remedies. Without help, maltreated children often grow up with serious problems, at great cost to themselves and to society, and many continue the cycle of maltreatment when they have children of their own (USDHHS, 1999a). Those who break the cycle of abuse are likely to have had a loving, supportive relationship with a nonabusive parent or someone else to whom they could turn for help; to have received therapy; and to have good marital or love relationships (Egeland, Jacobvitz, & Sroufe, 1988; Egeland & Sroufe, 1981; Kaufman & Zigler, 1987; NRC, 1993b).

Checkpoint ✓

Can you . . .

- ✔ Define four types of child abuse and neglect?
- ✔ Discuss the incidence of maltreatment and explain why it is hard to measure?
- ✔ Identify contributing factors having to do with the child, the family, the neighborhood, and the wider society?
- ✔ Give examples of effects of child abuse and neglect?
- ✔ Describe ways to prevent or stop maltreatment and help its victims?

Refocus

- What aspects of Wang Yani's physical development in early childhood seem to have been fairly typical? In what ways was her development advanced?
- Can you give examples of how Yani's physical, cognitive, and psychosocial development interacted?
- What more would you like to know about Yani's early development if you had the chance to interview her or her parents?

Fortunately, most children are not maltreated. Preschool children who are in good health and whose basic physical needs are met are able to make major advances in cognitive development, as we'll see in Chapter 10.

Summary and Key Terms

Aspects of Physiological Development

Guidepost 1 How do children's bodies change between ages 3 and 6, and what are their nutritional and dental needs?

- Physical growth increases during the years from 3 to 6 but more slowly than during infancy and toddlerhood. Boys are on average slightly taller, heavier, and more muscular than girls. Internal body systems are maturing, and all primary teeth are present.
- Preschool children generally eat less for their weight than before—and need less—but the prevalence of obesity has increased.
- Tooth decay has decreased since the 1970s but remains a problem among disadvantaged children.
- Thumb sucking can safely be ignored unless it continues beyond age 4, when permanent teeth begin to develop.

Guidepost 2 What sleep patterns and problems tend to develop during early childhood?

- Sleep patterns change during early childhood, as throughout life, and are affected by cultural expectations.
- It is normal for preschool children to develop bedtime rituals that delay going to sleep. Prolonged bedtime struggles or persistent sleep terrors or nightmares may indicate emotional disturbances that need attention.
- Bed-wetting is common and is usually outgrown without special help.

enuresis (245)

Motor Development

Guidepost 3 What are the main motor achievements of early childhood, and how does children's artwork show their physical and cognitive maturation?

- Children progress rapidly in gross and fine motor skills and eye-hand coordination, developing more complex systems of action.
- Stages of art production, which appear to reflect brain development and fine motor coordination, are the scribbling stage, shape stage, design stage, and pictorial stage.
- Handedness is usually evident by age 3, reflecting dominance by one hemisphere of the brain.

gross motor skills (246) **fine motor skills (246)**
systems of action (246) **handedness (247)**

Health and Safety

Guidepost 4 What are the major health and safety risks for young children?

- Although major contagious illnesses are rare today in industrialized countries due to widespread immunization, preventable disease continues to be a major problem in the developing world.
- Minor illnesses, such as colds and other respiratory illnesses, are common during early childhood and help build immunity to disease.
- Accidents, most commonly motor vehicle injuries, are the leading cause of death in childhood in the United States. Most fatal nonvehicular accidents occur at home.
- Environmental factors such as exposure to illness, smoking, poverty, and homelessness increase the risks of illness or injury. Lead poisoning can have serious physical, cognitive, and behavioral effects.

Maltreatment: Abuse and Neglect

Guidepost 5 What are the causes and consequences of child abuse and neglect, and what can be done about it?

- The incidence of reported maltreatment of children has increased greatly.
- Forms of maltreatment are physical abuse, neglect, sexual abuse, and emotional maltreatment.
- Characteristics of the abuser or neglecter, the victim, the family, the community, and the larger culture all contribute to child abuse and neglect.
- Maltreatment can interfere with physical, cognitive, emotional, and social development, and its effects can continue into adulthood. Still, many maltreated children show remarkable resilience.
- Preventing or stopping maltreatment may require multifaceted, coordinated community efforts.

physical abuse (255) **neglect (255)** **sexual abuse (255)** **emotional maltreatment (255)**

chapter
10

Cognitive Development in Early Childhood

Childhood is a world of miracle and wonder: as if creation rose, bathed in light, out of darkness, utterly new and fresh and astonishing. The end of childhood is when things cease to astonish us. When the world seems familiar, when one has got used to existence, one has become an adult.

—Eugene Ionesco, ***Fragments of a Journal***, 1976

Focus *Albert Einstein, Nuclear Physicist*

Albert Einstein

In the public mind, the name Albert Einstein (1879–1955) is synonymous with *genius*. His general theory of relativity ("the greatest revolution in thought since Newton"), his discovery of the fundamental principle of quantum physics, and his other contributions to the reshaping of our knowledge of the universe cause him to be considered "one of the greatest physicists of all time" (Whitrow, 1967, p. 1).

Yet the young Einstein, who was born in the German town of Ulm, hardly seemed destined for intellectual stardom. He was slow in learning to walk and did not begin talking until at least his third year. His parents feared he might be mentally retarded. Einstein himself always insisted that he did not *try* to speak until after the age of 3, skipping babbling and going directly into sentences. Actually, his sentences may have come a bit earlier. When his sister, Maja, was born four months before Albert's third birthday, Albert (who had been promised a new baby to play with and apparently thought it would be a toy) reportedly asked in disappointment, "Where are the wheels?"

Regardless of the exact timing, "Albert was certainly a late and reluctant talker" (Brian, 1996, p. 1). The reasons may have had more to do with personality than with cognitive development; he was a shy, taciturn child, whom adults thought backward and other children considered dull. He would not play marbles or soldiers or other games with his peers, but he would crouch for hours, observing an ant colony.

When he started school, he did poorly in most subjects; the headmaster predicted he would never amount to anything. Albert hated the regimentation and rote learning stressed in German schools; he did not have a retentive memory and could not give clear answers to his teachers' questions. He was a daydreamer, his questioning mind occupied with its own speculations. He would not even try to learn anything unless he was interested in it—and then his concentration was intense.

His wonder about the workings of the universe was awakened at the age of 4 or 5, when he was sick in bed and his father gave him a magnetic pocket compass to keep him amused. The boy was astonished: no matter which way he turned the compass, the needle pointed to *N* (for "north"). What controlled its motion? He pestered his Uncle Jacob, who had studied

Sources of biographical information about Albert Einstein are Bernstein (1973); Brian (1996); French (1979); Goldsmith, Mackay, & Woudhuysen (1980); Michelmore (1962); Quasha (1980); Schilpp (1970); and Whitrow (1967).

engineering, with questions. His uncle told him about the earth's north and south poles and about magnetic fields, but Albert still was not satisfied. He believed there must be some mysterious force in what appeared to be the empty space around the needle. He carried the compass around for weeks, trying to figure out its secret. Years later, at the age of 67, he wrote, ". . . this experience made a deep and lasting impression upon me. Something deeply hidden had to be behind things" (Schilpp, 1970, p. 9).

That sense of wonder was reawakened several years later, when Uncle Jacob, noticing that Albert showed an interest in arithmetic, introduced him to algebra and geometry. Albert solved every problem in the books his uncle brought him and then went searching for more. It was that same insatiable curiosity and persistence—what Einstein himself called "a furious impulse to understand" (Michelmore, 1962, p. 24)—that underlay his lifetime quest for scientific knowledge.

• • •

Albert Einstein's story touches on several themes of cognitive development in early childhood. One is the variation in normal language development. Another is that although Einstein's reaction to the compass may have been unusually intense, it was characteristic of young children's understanding of the physical world: their growing recognition that natural phenomena have causes, though those causes are not always apparent. Einstein's lifelong memory of that engrossing incident may shed light on why some kinds of early memories last while others do not. Finally, his parents' and teachers' underestimation of his cognitive abilities raises issues about how intelligence can be accurately assessed.

In this chapter, we examine these and other aspects of cognitive development in early childhood, as revealed by recent research as well as by such theorists as Piaget and Vygotsky. We see how children's thinking advances after toddlerhood and in what ways it remains immature. We look at children's increasing fluency with language and what impact this has on other aspects of development. We examine the beginnings of autobiographical memory, such as Einstein's memory of the compass; and we compare psychometric intelligence tests with assessments based on Vygotsky's theories. Finally, we look at the widening world of preschool and kindergarten.

After you have read and studied this chapter, you should be able to answer each of the Guidepost questions that follow. Look for them again in the margins, where they point to important concepts throughout the chapter. To check your understanding of these Guideposts, review the end-of-chapter summary. Checkpoints located at periodic spots throughout the chapter will help you verify your understanding of what you have read.

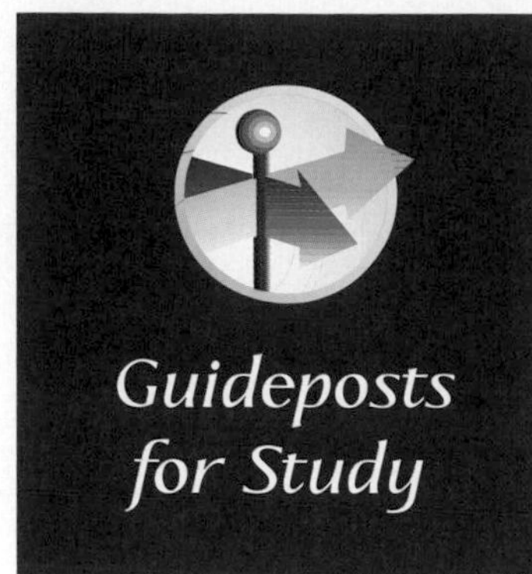

1. What are typical cognitive advances and immature aspects of preschool children's thinking?
2. What memory abilities expand in early childhood?
3. How is preschoolers' intelligence measured, and what factors influence it?
4. How does language improve, and what happens when its development is delayed?
5. What purposes does early childhood education serve, and how do children make the transition to kindergarten?

Piagetian Approach: The Preoperational Child

What are typical cognitive advances and immature aspects of preschool children's thinking?

Jean Piaget named early childhood the **preoperational stage.** The characteristic development in this second major stage of cognitive development, which lasts from approximately ages 2 to 7, is a great expansion in the use of symbolic thought, or representational ability, which first emerges at the end of the sensorimotor stage (refer back to Chapter 7). However, according to Piaget, children cannot think logically until the stage of concrete operations in middle childhood (Chapter 13). Let's look at some advances and immature aspects of preoperational thought (see Tables 10-1 and 10-2) and at recent research, some of which challenges Piaget's conclusions.

preoperational stage In Piaget's theory, second major stage of cognitive development, in which children become more sophisticated in their use of symbolic thought but are not yet able to use logic.

Advances of Preoperational Thought

Advances in symbolic thought are accompanied by a growing understanding of causality, identities, categorization, and number. Some of these understandings have roots in infancy and toddlerhood; others begin to develop in early childhood but are not fully achieved until middle childhood.

The Symbolic Function

"I want ice cream!" announces Kerstin, age 4, trudging indoors from the hot, dusty backyard. She has not seen anything that triggered this desire—no open freezer door, no television commercial. She no longer needs this kind of sensory cue to think about something. She remembers ice cream and its coldness and taste, and she purposefully seeks it out. This absence of sensory or motor cues characterizes the **symbolic function:** the ability to use symbols, or mental representations—words, numbers, or images to which a person has attached meaning. The use of symbols is a universal mark of human culture. Without symbols, people could not communicate verbally, make change, read maps, or treasure photos of distant loved ones. Having symbols for things helps children remember and think about them without having them physically present.

symbolic function Piaget's term for ability to use mental representations (words, numbers, or images) to which a child has attached meaning.

Preschool children show the symbolic function through deferred imitation, pretend play, and language. *Deferred imitation* (refer back to Chapter 7), which becomes more robust after 18 months, is based on having kept a mental representation of an observed action—as when 3-year-old Bart scolds his little sister, using the same words he heard his father say to the delivery boy who was late in bringing the pizza. In *pretend play,* also introduced in Chapter 7, children may make an object, such as a doll, stand for (symbolize) something else, such as a person. *Language,* discussed later in this chapter, uses a system of symbols (words or signs) to communicate.

As reported in Chapter 7, until at least age 3, most children do not reliably grasp the relationships between pictures, maps, or scale models and the objects or spaces they represent. Older preschoolers can use simple maps, and they can transfer the spatial understanding gained from working with models to maps and vice versa (DeLoache, Miller, & Pierroutsakos, 1998). In one experiment, 4-year-olds and most 3-year-olds were able to use

Table 10-1 Cognitive Advances During Early Childhood

Advance	Significance	Example
Use of symbols	Children do not need to be in sensorimotor contact with an object, person, or event in order to think about it.	Simon asks his mother about the elephants they saw on their trip to the circus several months earlier.
	Children can imagine that objects or people have properties other than those they actually have.	Rolf pretends that a slice of apple is a vacuum cleaner "vrooming" across the kitchen table.
Understanding of identities	Children are aware that superficial alterations do not change the nature of things.	Antonio knows that his teacher is dressed up as a pirate but is still his teacher underneath the costume.
Understanding of cause and effect	Children realize that events have causes.	Seeing a ball roll from behind a wall, Aneko looks behind the wall for the person who kicked the ball.
Ability to classify	Children organize objects, people, and events into meaningful categories.	Rosa sorts the pine cones she collected on a nature walk into two piles according to their size: "big" and "little."
Understanding of number	Children can count and deal with quantities.	Lindsay shares some candy with her friends, counting to make sure that each girl gets the same amount.
Empathy	Children become more able to imagine how others might feel.	Emilio tries to comfort his friend when he sees that his friend is upset.
Theory of mind	Children become more aware of mental activity and the functioning of the mind.	Blanca wants to save some cookies for herself, so she hides them from her brother in a pasta box. She knows her cookies will be safe there because her brother will not look in a place where he doesn't expect to find cookies.

Table 10-2 Immature Aspects of Preoperational Thought (According to Piaget)

Limitation	Description	Example
Centration: inability to decenter	Children focus on one aspect of a situation and neglect others.	Timothy teases his younger sister that he has more juice than she does because his juice box has been poured into a tall, skinny glass, but hers has been poured into a short, wide glass.
Irreversibility	Children fail to understand that some operations or actions can be reversed, restoring the original situation.	Timothy does not realize that the juice in each glass can be poured back into the juice box from which it came, contradicting his claim that he has more than his sister.
Focus on states rather than transformations	Children fail to understand the significance of the transformation between states.	In the conservation task, Timothy does not understand that transforming the shape of a liquid (pouring it from one container into another) does not change the amount.
Transductive reasoning	Children do not use deductive or inductive reasoning; instead they jump from one particular to another and see cause where none exists.	Sarah was mean to her brother. Then her brother got sick. Sarah concludes that she made her brother sick.
Egocentrism	Children assume everyone else thinks, perceives, and feels as they do.	Kara doesn't realize that she needs to turn a book around so that her father can see the picture she is asking him to explain to her. Instead, she holds the book directly in front of her, where only she can see it.
Animism	Children attribute life to objects not alive.	Amanda says that spring is trying to come but winter is saying, "I won't go! I won't go!"
Inability to distinguish appearance from reality	Children confuse what is real with outward appearance.	Courtney is confused by a sponge made to look like a rock. She states that it looks like a rock and it really is a rock.

a rectangle with a dot inside to find the corresponding location of a small black disk in a similarly shaped (but much larger) sandbox (Huttenlocher, Newcombe, & Vasilyeva, 1999).

Causality

Although Piaget recognized that toddlers have some understanding of a connection between actions and reactions, he believed that preoperational children cannot yet reason logically about cause and effect. Instead, he said, they reason by **transduction.** They mentally link two events, especially events close in time, whether or not there is logically a causal relationship. For example, they may think that their "bad" thoughts or behavior caused their own or another child's illness or their parents' divorce.

Yet when tested on situations they can understand, young children do seem to grasp cause and effect. One research team set up a series of microgenetic experiments using a device called a "blicket detector," rigged to light up and play music only when certain objects (called "blickets") were placed on it. Even 2-year-olds were able to decide, by observing the device in operation, which objects were blickets (because they activated the blicket detector) and which were not (Gopnik, Sobel, Schulz, & Glymour, 2001). Apparently, then, young children's understanding of familiar events in the physical world enables them to think logically about causation (Wellman & Gelman, 1998).

In naturalistic observations of 2½- to 5-year-olds' everyday conversations with their parents, children showed flexible causal reasoning, appropriate to the subject (Hickling & Wellman, 2001). However, preschoolers seem to view all causal relationships as equally and absolutely predictable. In one series of experiments, 3- to 5-year-olds, unlike adults, were just as sure that a person who does not wash his or her hands before eating will get sick as they were that a person who jumps up will come down (Kalish, 1998).

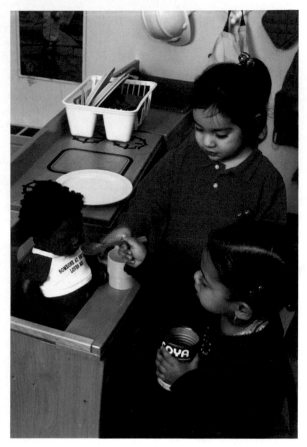

These girls "feeding" a doll are engaged in pretend play, which depends on the symbolic function.

transduction In Piaget's terminology, preoperational child's tendency to mentally link particular experiences, whether or not there is logically a causal relationship.

Understanding of Identities and Categorization

The world becomes more orderly and predictable as preschool children develop a better understanding of *identities:* the concept that people and many things are basically the same even if they change in form, size, or appearance. This understanding underlies the emerging self-concept (see Chapter 11).

Categorization, or classification, requires a child to identify similarities and differences. By age 4, many children can classify by two criteria, such as color and shape. Children use this ability to order many aspects of their lives, categorizing people as "good," "bad," "friend," "nonfriend," and so forth. Thus, categorization is a cognitive ability with psychosocial implications.

Can preschoolers distinguish living from nonliving things? When Piaget asked young children whether the wind and the clouds were alive, their answers led him to think they were confused about what is alive and what is not. (The tendency to attribute life to objects that are not alive is called **animism.**) But when later researchers questioned 3- and 4-year-olds about something more familiar to them—differences between a rock, a person, and a doll—the children showed they understood that people are alive and rocks and dolls are not. They did not attribute thoughts or emotions to rocks, and they cited the fact that dolls cannot move on their own as evidence that dolls are not alive (Gelman, Spelke, & Meck, 1983). Of course, plants do not move on their own either, nor do they utter sounds, as most animals do. Yet preschoolers know that both plants and animals can grow and decay and, when injured, can heal themselves (Rosengren, Gelman, Kalish, & McCormick, 1991; Wellman & Gelman, 1998).

animism Tendency to attribute life to objects that are not alive.

Number

In early childhood, children come to recognize five principles of counting (Gelman & Gallistel, 1978; Sophian, 1988):

1. The *1-to-1 principle:* Say only one number-name for each item being counted ("One . . . two . . . three . . .").
2. The *stable-order principle:* Say number-names in a set order ("One, two, three . . ." rather than "Three, one, two . . .").
3. The *order-irrelevance principle:* Start counting with any item, and the total count will be the same.
4. The *cardinality principle:* The last number-name used is the total number of items being counted. (If there are five items, the last number-name will be "5.")
5. The *abstraction principle:* The previous principles apply to any kind of object.

Contrary to an earlier belief that an understanding of these principles enables children to count (Gelman and Gallistel, 1978), recent findings suggest the reverse: that children extract the principles from their experience with counting (Ho & Fuson, 1998; Siegler, 1998). When asked to count six items, children younger than 3½ tend to recite the number-names (one through six) but not to say how many items there are altogether (six). In other words, children that age do not yet seem to understand the cardinality principle (Wynn, 1990), or they may have trouble applying or interpreting it.

By age 5, most children can count to 20 or more and know the relative sizes of the numbers 1 through 10, and some can do single-digit addition and subtraction (Siegler, 1998). Children intuitively devise strategies for adding by counting on their fingers or by using other objects.

How quickly children learn to count depends in part on the number system of their culture and in part on schooling (Naito & Miura, 2001). Through age 3, when most number learning is focused on counting from 1 through 10, U.S. and Chinese children perform about equally well. At ages 4 and 5, when U.S. children are learning separate names for the numbers between 11 and 20, Chinese youngsters learn their language's more efficient system based on 10s and 1s (10 + 1, 10 + 2, and so forth). It's not surprising, then, that U.S. children's performance begins to lag (Miller, Smith, Zhu, & Zhang, 1995).

Ordinality—the concept of *more* or *less*, *bigger* or *smaller*—seems to begin around 12 to 18 months and at first is limited to comparisons of very few objects (Siegler, 1998). By age 3 or 4, children have words for comparing quantities. They can say that one tree is *bigger* than another or one cup holds *more* juice than another. They know that if they have one cookie and then get another cookie, they have more cookies than they had before and that if they give one cookie to another child, they have fewer cookies. By age 4 or 5, children can solve ordinality problems ("Megan picked six apples, and Joshua picked four apples; which child picked more?") with up to nine objects (Byrnes & Fox, 1998). Ordinal knowledge appears to be universal, though it develops at different rates, depending on how important counting is in a particular family or culture (Resnick, 1989; Saxe, Guberman, & Gearhart, 1987; Siegler, 1998).

Immature Aspects of Preoperational Thought

According to Piaget, one of the main characteristics of preoperational thought is **centration:** the tendency to focus on one aspect of a situation and neglect others. He said preschoolers come to illogical conclusions because they cannot **decenter**—think about several aspects of a situation at one time. Centration can limit young children's thinking about both physical and social relationships.

centration In Piaget's theory, tendency of preoperational children to focus on one aspect of a situation and neglect others.

decenter In Piaget's terminology, to think simultaneously about several aspects of a situation.

conservation Piaget's term for awareness that two objects that are equal according to a certain measure remain equal in the face of perceptual alteration so long as nothing has been added to or taken away from either object.

horizontal décalage Piaget's term for inability to transfer learning about one type of conservation to other types, which causes a child to master different types of conservation tasks at different ages.

Conservation

A classic example is the failure to understand **conservation,** the fact that two things that are equal remain so if their appearance is altered, so long as nothing is added or taken away. Piaget found that children do not fully grasp this principle until the stage of concrete operations and that they develop different kinds of conservation at different ages—a phenomenon called **horizontal décalage.** (Table 10-3 shows how various dimensions of con-

Table 10-3 Tests of Various Kinds of Conservation

Conservation Task	What Child Is Shown*	Transformation	Question for Child	Preoperational Child's Usual Answers
Number	Two equal, parallel rows of candies	Space the candies in one row farther apart.	"Are there the same number of candies in each row or does one row have more?"	"The longer one has more."
Length	Two parallel sticks of the same length	Move one stick to the right.	"Are both sticks the same size or is one longer?"	"The one on the right (or left) is longer."
Liquid	Two identical glasses holding equal amounts of liquid	Pour liquid from one glass into a taller, narrower glass.	"Do both glasses have the same amount of liquid or does one have more?"	"The taller one has more."
Matter (mass)	Two balls of clay of the same size	Roll one ball into a sausage shape.	"Do both pieces have the same amount of clay or does one have more?"	"The sausage has more."
Weight	Two balls of clay of the same weight	Roll one ball into a sausage shape.	"Do both weigh the same or does one weigh more?"	"The sausage weighs more."
Area	Two toy rabbits, two pieces of cardboard (representing grassy fields), with blocks or toys (representing barns on the fields); same number of "barns" on each board	Rearrange the blocks on one piece of board.	"Does each rabbit have the same amount of grass to eat or does one have more?"	"The one with the blocks close together has more to eat."
Volume	Two glasses of water with two equal-sized balls of clay in them	Roll one ball into a sausage shape.	"If we put the sausage back in the glass, will the water be the same height in each glass, or will one be higher?"	"The water in the glass with the sausage will be higher."

*Child then acknowledges that both items are equal.

servation have been tested. The ages at which some forms of conservation develop are given in Chapter 13.)

In one type of conservation task, conservation of liquid, a 5-year-old we'll call Jeffrey is shown two identical clear glasses, each one short and wide and each holding the same amount of water. Jeffrey is asked, "Is the amount of water in the two glasses equal?" When he agrees, the researcher pours the water in one glass into a third glass, a tall, thin one. Jeffrey is now asked, "Do both glasses contain the same amount of water? Or does one contain more? Why?" In early childhood—even after watching the water being poured out of one of the short, fat glasses into a tall, thin glass or even after pouring it himself—Jeffrey will say that either the taller glass or the wider one contains more water. When asked why, he says, "This one is bigger this way," stretching his arms to show the height or width. Preoperational children cannot consider height *and* width at the same time. Since they center on one aspect, they cannot think logically, said Piaget.

To observe Piagetian tasks, watch the videos on "Lacking Concept of Conservation (Liquid) at Age 4" and "Understanding Conservation (Number) at Age 4" in Chapter 10 of your CD.

The ability to conserve is also limited by **irreversibility:** failure to understand that an operation or action can go in two or more directions. Once Jeffrey can imagine restoring the original state of the water by pouring it back into the other glass, he will realize that the amount of water in both glasses must be the same.

irreversibility Piaget's term for a preoperational child's failure to understand that an operation can go in two or more directions.

Preoperational children commonly think as if they were watching a slide show with a series of static frames: they *focus on successive states,* said Piaget, and do not recognize the transformation from one state to another. In the conservation experiment, they focus on the water as it stands in each glass rather than on the water being poured from one glass to another, and so they fail to realize that the amount of water is the same.

Egocentrism

Egocentrism is a form of centration. According to Piaget, young children center so much on their own point of view that they cannot take in another's. Three-year-olds are not as egocentric as newborn babies; but, said Piaget, they still think the universe centers on them.

egocentrism Piaget's term for inability to consider another person's point of view.

Figure 10-1
Piaget's three-mountain task. A preoperational child is unable to describe the "mountains" from the doll's point of view—an indication of egocentrism, according to Piaget.

Egocentrism may help explain why young children sometimes have trouble separating reality from what goes on inside their own heads and why they may show confusion about what causes what. When Emily believes that her "bad thoughts" have made her brother sick or that she caused her parents' marital troubles, she is thinking egocentrically.

To study egocentrism, Piaget designed the *three-mountain task* (see Figure 10-1). A child sits facing a table that holds three large mounds. A doll is placed on a chair at the opposite side of the table. The investigator asks the child how the "mountains" would look to the doll. Piaget found that young children usually could not answer the question correctly; instead, they described the "mountains" from their own perspective. Piaget saw this as evidence that preoperational children cannot imagine a point of view different from their own (Piaget & Inhelder, 1967).

However, another experimenter who posed a similar problem in a different way got different results (Hughes, 1975). A child sat in front of a square board divided by "walls" into four sections. A toy police officer stood at the edge of the board; a doll was moved from one section to another. After each move the child was asked, "Can the police officer see the doll?" Then another toy police officer was brought into the action, and the child was told to hide the doll from both officers. Thirty children between ages 3½ and 5 were correct 9 out of 10 times.

Why were these children able to take another person's point of view (the police officer's) when those doing the mountain task were not? It may be because the "police officer" task calls for thinking in more familiar, less abstract ways. Most children do not look at mountains and do not think about what other people might see when looking at one, but most preschoolers know something about dolls and police officers and hiding. Thus young children may show egocentrism primarily in situations beyond their immediate experience.

Checkpoint

Can you . . .

- ✔ Summarize findings about preschool children's understanding of symbols, causality, identities, categories, and number?
- ✔ Tell how centration limits preoperational thought?
- ✔ Give several reasons preoperational children have difficulty with conservation?
- ✔ Discuss research that challenges Piaget's views on egocentrism in early childhood?

Do Young Children Have Theories of Mind?

theory of mind Awareness and understanding of mental processes.

Piaget (1929) was the first scholar to investigate children's **theory of mind,** their emerging awareness of their own mental processes and those of other people. He asked children such questions as "Where do dreams come from?" and "What do you think with?" On the basis of their answers, he concluded that children younger than 6 cannot distinguish between thoughts or dreams and real physical entities and have no theory of mind. However, more recent research indicates that between ages 2 and 5 and especially around age 4, children's knowledge about mental processes—their own and others'—grows dramatically (Astington, 1993; Bower, 1993; Flavell et al., 1995; Wellman, Cross, & Watson, 2001).

Again, methodology seems to have made the difference. Piaget's questions were abstract, and he expected children to be able to put their understanding into words. Contemporary researchers use vocabulary and objects children are familiar with. Instead of talking in generalities, they observe children in everyday activities or give them concrete examples. In this way, we have learned, for example, that 3-year-olds can tell the difference between a boy who has a cookie and a boy who is thinking about a cookie; they know which boy can touch, share, and eat it (Astington, 1993).

Let's look at several aspects of theory of mind.

Knowledge About Thinking and Mental States

The young girl on the right is old enough to know that her cousin needs consoling. Empathy, the ability to understand another person's feelings, begins at an early age.

Between ages 3 and 5, children come to understand that thinking goes on inside the mind; that it can deal with either real or imaginary things; that someone can be thinking of one thing while doing or looking at something else; that a person whose eyes and ears are covered can think about objects; that someone who looks pensive is probably thinking; and that thinking is different from seeing, talking, touching, and knowing (Flavell et al., 1995).

However, preschoolers generally believe that mental activity starts and stops. Not until middle childhood do children know that the mind is continuously active (Flavell, 1993; Flavell et al., 1995). Preschoolers also have little or no awareness that they or other people think in words, or "talk to themselves in their heads," or that they think while they are looking, listening, reading, or talking (Flavell, Green, Flavell, & Grossman, 1997). Not until age 7 or 8 do most children realize that people who are asleep do *not* engage in conscious mental activity—that they do not know they are asleep (Flavell, Green, Flavell, & Lin, 1999).

Preschoolers tend to equate dreams with imagining; they believe they can dream about anything they wish. Five-year-olds show a more adultlike understanding, recognizing that physical experiences, emotions, knowledge, and thoughts can affect the content of dreams. Not until age 11, however, do children fully realize that they cannot control their dreams (Woolley & Boerger, 2002).

Social cognition, the recognition that others have mental states (refer back to Chapter 8), is a distinctly human capacity (Povinelli & Giambrone, 2001) that accompanies the decline of egocentrism and the development of empathy. At 14 to 18 months, children may be able to infer the intentions of another person from vocal expressions, by whether that person expresses, say, satisfaction ("There!") or surprise ("Woops!") (Carpenter, Akhtar, & Tomasello, 1998). By age 3, children realize that if someone gets what he wants he will be happy, and if not, he will be sad (Wellman & Woolley, 1990). Four-year-olds begin to understand that people have differing beliefs about the world—true or mistaken—and that these beliefs affect their actions.

False Beliefs and Deception

A researcher shows 3-year-old Mariella a candy box and asks what is in it. "Candy," she says. But when Mariella opens the box, she finds crayons, not candy. "What will a child who hasn't opened the box think is in it?" the researcher asks. "Crayons," says Mariella, not understanding that another child would be fooled by the box as she was. And then she says that she herself originally thought crayons would be in the box (Flavell, 1993; Flavell et al., 1995).

The understanding that people can hold false beliefs flows from the realization that people hold mental representations of reality, which can sometimes be wrong. Three-year-olds like Mariella appear to lack such an understanding (Flavell et al., 1995). An analysis of 178 studies in various countries, using a number of variations on false belief tasks, found this consistent developmental pattern (Wellman & Cross, 2001; Wellman, Cross, & Watson, 2001). However, some researchers claim that 3-year-olds do have a rudimentary understanding of false beliefs but may not show it when presented with complicated situations (Hala & Chandler, 1996).

Three-year-olds' failure to recognize false beliefs may stem from egocentric thinking. At that age, children tend to believe that everyone else knows what they know and believes what they do, and, like Mariella, they have trouble understanding that their own beliefs can be false (Lillard & Curenton, 1999). Older preschoolers' more advanced understanding of mental representations seems to be related to a decline in egocentrism. Four-year-olds understand that people who see or hear different versions of the same event may come away with different beliefs. Not until about age 6, however, do children realize that two people who see or hear the *same* thing may interpret it differently (Pillow & Henrichon, 1996).

Deception is an effort to plant a false belief in someone else's mind, and it requires a child to suppress the impulse to be truthful. Some studies have found that children become capable of deception as early as age 2 or 3, and others, at 4 or 5. The difference may have to do with the means of deception children are expected to use. In a series of experiments, 3-year-olds were asked whether they would like to play a trick on an experimenter by giving a false clue about which of two boxes a ball was hidden in. The children were better able to carry out the deception when asked to put a picture of the ball on the wrong box or to point to that box with an arrow than when they pointed with their fingers, which children this age are accustomed to doing truthfully (Carlson, Moses, & Hix, 1998).

Piaget maintained that young children regard all falsehoods—intentional or not—as lies. However, when 3- to 6-year-olds were told a story about a subject close to their experience—the danger of eating contaminated food—and were asked whether a character's incorrect statement about the food was a lie or a mistake, about three-fourths of the children of all ages characterized it accurately (Siegal & Peterson, 1998). Apparently, then, even 3-year-olds have some understanding of the role of intent in deception.

Distinguishing Between Appearance and Reality

Related to awareness of false beliefs is the ability to distinguish between appearance and reality; both require a child to refer to two conflicting mental representations at the same time. According to Piaget, not until about age 5 or 6 do children understand the distinction between what *seems* to be and what *is.* Much research bears him out, though some studies have found this ability beginning to emerge before age 4 (Friend & Davis, 1993; C. Rice, Koinis, Sullivan, Tager-Flusberg, & Winner, 1997).

In one series of experiments, 3-year-olds apparently confused appearance and reality in a variety of tests. For example, when the children put on special sunglasses that made milk look green, they said the milk *was* green, even though they had just seen white milk (Flavell, Green, & Flavell, 1986). However, when 3-year-olds were shown a sponge that looked like a rock and were asked to help trick someone else into thinking it was a rock, the children were able to make the distinction between the way the sponge looked (like a rock) and what it actually was (a sponge). Apparently, putting the task in the context of a deception helped the children realize that an object can be perceived as other than what it actually is (Rice et al., 1997).

Three-year-olds' difficulty distinguishing appearance from reality may itself be more apparent than real. When children were asked questions about the uses of such objects as a candle wrapped like a crayon, only 3 out of 10 answered correctly. But when asked to respond with actions rather than words ("I want a candle to put on a birthday cake"), 9 out of 10 handed the experimenter the crayonlike candle (Sapp, Lee, & Muir, 2000).

Distinguishing Between Fantasy and Reality

Sometime between 18 months and 3 years, children learn to distinguish between real and imagined events. Three-year-olds know the difference between a real dog and a dog in a dream and between something invisible (such as air) and something imaginary. They can pretend and can tell when someone else is pretending (Flavell et al., 1995).

Still, the line between fantasy and reality seems to blur at times; it may be difficult to tell, when questioning children about imaginary objects, whether the children are giving serious answers or are simply pretending (M. Taylor, 1997). In one study (Harris, Brown, Marriott, Whittall, & Harmer, 1991), the experimenter showed 40 four- to six-year-olds two cardboard boxes and asked them to pretend that there was a monster in one box and a bunny in the other. Each box had a small hole in it, and the experimenter asked the children whether they wanted to put a finger or a stick in the holes. The experimenter then left the room, and some of the children did touch the boxes. Even though most of the children claimed they were just pretending about the bunny and the monster, most preferred to touch the box holding the imaginary bunny, and more put their fingers in that box and put the stick in the monster box—suggesting that even though preschoolers seem to understand the distinction between fantasy and reality, they may be confused about whether the creatures of their imagination exist.

An alternative explanation is that the children may have been carrying on the unfinished pretend game in the experimenter's absence. In a partial replication of the study, the

The Everyday World

Box 10-1 *Imaginary Companions*

At 3½, Anna had 23 "sisters" with such names as Och, Elmo, Zeni, Aggie, and Ankie. She often talked to them on the telephone, since they lived about 100 miles away, in the town where her family used to live. During the next year, most of the sisters disappeared, but Och continued to visit, especially for birthday parties. Och had a cat and a dog (which Anna had begged for in vain), and whenever Anna was denied something she saw advertised on television, she announced that she already had one at her sister's house. But when a live friend came over and Anna's mother happened to mention one of her imaginary companions, Anna quickly changed the subject.

All 23 sisters—and some "boys" and "girls" who have followed them—lived only in Anna's imagination, as she well knew. Like an estimated 25 to 65 percent of children between ages 3 and 10 (Woolley, 1997), Anna created imaginary companions with whom she talked and played. This normal phenomenon of childhood is seen most often in firstborn and only children who lack the close company of siblings. Like Anna, most children who create imaginary companions have many of them (Gleason, Sebanc, & Hartup, 2000). Girls are more likely than boys to have imaginary "friends" (or at least to acknowledge them). Girls' imaginary playmates are usually other children, whereas boys' are more often animals (D. G. Singer & Singer, 1990).

Children who have imaginary companions can distinguish fantasy from reality, but in free-play sessions they are more likely to engage in pretend play than are children without imaginary companions (M. Taylor, Cartwright, & Carlson, 1993). They play more happily and more imaginatively than other children and are more cooperative with other children and adults (D. G. Singer & Singer, 1990; J. L. Singer & Singer, 1981); and they do not lack for friends at preschool (Gleason et al., 2000). They are more fluent with language, watch less television, and show more curiosity, excitement, and persistence during play. In one study, 4-year-olds—regardless of verbal intelligence—who reported having imaginary companions did better on theory-of-mind tasks (such as differentiating appearance and reality and recognizing false beliefs) than children who did not create such companions (M. Taylor & Carlson, 1997).

Children's relationships with imaginary companions are like peer relationships; they are usually sociable and friendly, in contrast with the nurturing relationships children have with personified objects, such as stuffed animals and dolls (Gleason et al., 2000). Imaginary playmates are good company for an only child like Anna. They provide wish-fulfillment mechanisms ("There was a monster in my room, but Elmo scared it off with magic dust"), scapegoats ("I didn't eat those cookies—Och must have done it!"), displacement agents for the child's own fears ("Aggie is afraid she's going to be washed down the drain"), and support in difficult situations (one 6-year-old "took" her imaginary companion with her to see a scary movie).

What's your view?

How should parents respond to children's talk about imaginary companions?

Check it out!

For more information on this topic, go to **http://harbaugh.uoregon.edu/mtaylor/**. This Web page by Marjorie Taylor is about children's imaginary companions.

experimenter remained in the room and clearly ended the pretense. Only about 10 percent of the children touched or looked in the boxes, and when questioned, almost all showed a clear understanding that the creatures were imaginary (Golomb & Galasso, 1995). If the experimenter had left the room after ending the pretense, the children might have felt more free to act on their fantasies, as in the earlier study (Woolley, 1997).

A review of the literature suggests that magical thinking in children age 3 and older does *not* stem from confusion between fantasy and reality. Often magical thinking is a way to explain events that do not seem to have obvious realistic explanations (usually because children lack knowledge about them, as young Einstein did about the workings of the compass). Or children may simply enjoy indulging in the pleasure of pretending—as with the belief in imaginary companions (see Box 10-1). Children, like adults, generally are aware of the magical nature of such fantasy figures but are more willing to entertain the possibility that they may be real (Woolley, 1997). Magical thinking tends to decline near the end of the preschool period (Woolley, Phelps, Davis, & Mandell, 1999).

All in all, then, the research on various theory-of-mind topics suggests that young children may have a clearer picture of reality than Piaget believed.

Young Children's Ideas about Prayer

What do young children understand about prayer? In one study, researchers asked 99 three- to eight-year-old Christian children whether adults, babies, cars, dogs, flowers, and tables could pray. They also asked the children to teach a puppet whose dog was sick how to pray.

Consistent with other theory-of-mind research, the study found that children first realize between ages 4 and 5 that prayer is a mental activity, that it involves "saying something 'in your head' " (Woolley, 2000, p. 121). They also understand that prayer involves knowing about God, and they believe that communicating their thoughts to God can make a prayer come true. Thus, children seem to regard prayer as a process apart from and even contrary to the natural causal relations of which they are becoming aware. By age 5 to 6, children associate prayer with morality, believing, for example, that a prayer for someone else to get hurt would be unacceptable.

In this study most of the families were active churchgoers, and, according to parents' reports, more than two-thirds of the children prayed at home and attended Sunday school. We cannot be sure that a child who grows up in a less religious family or community, or in a nonwestern culture, would develop similar concepts of prayer at the same ages.

In What Order Do Theory-of-Mind Abilities Develop?

Clearly, children's theory-of-mind skills become more sophisticated during the preschool years. But do some of these skills develop earlier than others? One research team (Wellman & Liu, 2004), on the basis of a review of the literature, constructed a *developmental scale* showing the order in which various theory-of-mind understandings develop. They then tested it on 75 three- to five-year-olds from three preschools serving a largely European-American but 25 percent minority population (see Table 10-4). The researchers found that understanding of desires precedes understanding of beliefs: children become aware that two people can have differing desires for the same object before they understand that two people can have different beliefs about the same object. Only after they show an understanding of diverse beliefs can they judge that someone can have a false belief. Even later comes the ability to differentiate between real and apparent emotion. What this means is that no single type of task, such as a false-belief test, can capture the course of children's theory-of-mind development. A scale such as this can make it easier to identify influences on that development and individual differences in it (Wellman & Liu, 2004).

What determines the order and timing of theory-of-mind development? Some investigators (de Villiers & de Villiers, 2000) suggest a sort of *linguistic determinism*—that grammatical development enables children to formulate concepts about certain states of mind. In this view, understanding of desire comes before understanding of belief because desires require less complex language to express them ("She wants to . . ." rather than "She believes that . . .). However, studies of young Chinese and German children, whose languages do *not* have different constructions for expressions about others' desires and beliefs, fail to support this view. Both Chinese and German children talk about desires earlier than beliefs, just as English-speaking children do (Perner, Sprung, Zauner, & Haider, 2003; Tardiff & Wellman, 2000). One way to interpret these findings is that the advance from desire-talk to belief-talk represents progress in conceptual or representational ability, independent of linguistic progress. Another is an *ecological explanation*: children may learn to gauge people's desires earlier than their beliefs because knowledge about desires has more immediate practical application (Perner et al., 2003).

Linguistic advances do appear to make a difference with regard to *false* beliefs. To express an understanding of a false belief, a child must be able to form a complex sentence with an embedded independent clause ("She thinks that *the doll is in the little room,* but it's really in the big room"). In one study, 4-year-olds but not 3-year-olds were able to handle such sentences, and success in doing so correlated with successful performance of false belief tasks (Smith, Apperly, & White, 2003).

Some researchers maintain that theory-of-mind skills are not a separate cognitive category but an extension of children's general cognitive development. In this view, children succeed in theory-of-mind tasks as they gain control over their own cognitive functioning, particularly the ability to avoid misleading distractions. This is called *inhibitory control* of attention (Bialystok & Senman, 2004). This ability may accompany and interact with growing conceptual and memory capacities (Blair, 2002; Carlson & Moses, 2001). The resulting ability to plan and carry out goal-directed mental activity is called *executive function* (Zelazo et al., 2003).

Table 10-4	Tasks in the Wellman-Liu Theory-of-Mind Scale in Typical Order of Development
Task	**Description**
1. Diverse Desires	Child judges that two persons (the child vs. someone else) have different desires about the same objects.
2. Diverse Beliefs	Child judges that two persons (the child vs. someone else) have different beliefs about the same object, when the child does not know which belief is true or false.
3. Knowledge Access	Child sees what is in a box and judges (yes–no) the knowledge of another person who does not see what is in a box.
4. Contents False Belief	Child judges another person's false belief about what is in a distinctive container when the child knows what it is in the container.
5. Explicit False Belief	Child judges how someone will search, given that person's mistaken belief.
6. Belief Emotion	Child judges how a person will feel, given a belief that is mistaken.
7. Real-Apparent Emotion	Child judges that a person can feel one thing but display a different emotion.

Source: Adapted from Wellman & Liu, 2004, Table 3, p. 531.

Influences on Individual Differences in Theory-of-Mind Development

Some children develop theory-of-mind abilities earlier than others. In part this development reflects brain maturation and general improvements in cognition. What other influences explain these individual differences?

Social competence and language development contribute to an understanding of thoughts and emotions (Cassidy, Werner, Rourke, Zubernis, & Balaraman, 2003). Children whose teachers and peers rate them high on social skills are better able to recognize false beliefs, to distinguish between real and feigned emotion, and to take another person's point of view; and these children also tend to have strong language skills (Cassidy et al., 2003; Watson, Nixon, Wilson, & Capage, 1999). Children with advanced language development and those with several siblings or older siblings to talk to are better able to take part in family discussions and tend to understand false beliefs earlier than other children (Astington & Jenkins, 1999; Cutting & Dunn, 1999; Hughes & Cutting, 1999; Lillard & Curenton, 1999).)

The *kind* of talk a young child hears at home may affect the child's understanding of mental states (Jenkins, Turrell, Kogushi, Lollis, & Ross, 2003). Three-year-olds whose mothers talk with them about others' mental states tend to show better theory-of-mind skills (Ruffman, Slade, & Crowe, 2002). In a two-year observational study of 40 Canadian families with 2- and 4-year-olds, children's *cognitive talk* (talk about beliefs and thoughts) increased with age, whereas talk about desires and feelings diminished. Parents addressed more cognitive talk to 4- and 6-year-olds than to 2-year-olds, and a 4-year-old with an older sibling tended to hear more cognitive talk (both from the sibling and the parents) than a 4-year-old with a younger sibling. Children with more educated mothers also heard more cognitive talk (Jenkins et al., 2003).

Families that encourage pretend play stimulate the development of theory-of-mind skills. As children play roles, they try to assume others' perspectives. When children pretend together, they must deal with other children's views of their imaginary world. Talking with children about how the characters in a story feel helps them develop social understanding (Lillard & Curenton, 1999). Empathy usually arises earlier in children whose families talk a lot about feelings and causality (Dunn, Brown, Slomkowski, Tesla, & Youngblade, 1991; Dunn, 1991).

Bilingual children, who speak and hear more than one language at home, do somewhat better than children with only one language on certain theory-of-mind tasks (Bialystok & Senman, 2004; Goetz, 2003). Bilingual children know that an object or idea can be represented linguistically in more than one way, and this knowledge may help them see that different people may have different perspectives. Bilingual children also recognize the need to match their language to that of their partner, and this may make them more aware of others' mental states. Finally, bilingual children tend to have better attentional control, and this may enable them to focus on what is true or real rather than on what only seems to be so (Bialystok & Senman, 2004; Goetz, 2003).

Heredity may play a part in theory-of-mind development. A study of 119 same-sex 3-year-old twins found a heritability of 67 percent in understanding of false beliefs and deception (Hughes & Cutting, 1999).

Different cultures have different ways of looking at the mind, and these cultural attitudes influence children (Lillard, 1998). For example, middle-class northern Europeans and Americans pay a lot of attention to how mental states affect behavior, whereas Asians focus on situations that call for certain behaviors. Japanese parents and teachers frequently talk to children about how their behavior affects other people's feelings (Azuma, 1994). A Japanese child who refuses to finish a meal may be told that the farmer who worked hard to grow the food will be hurt if the child doesn't eat it.

Checkpoint

Can you . . .

- ✔ Give examples of research that challenges Piaget's views on young children's cognitive limitations?
- ✔ Describe changes between the ages of 3 and 6 in children's knowledge about the way their minds work?

What memory abilities expand in early childhood?

Information-Processing Approach: Memory Development

During early childhood, children improve in attention and in the speed and efficiency with which they process information; and they begin to form long-lasting memories. Still, young children do not remember as well as older ones. For one thing, young children tend to focus on exact details of an event, which are easily forgotten, whereas older children and adults generally concentrate on the gist of what happened. Also, young children, because of their lesser knowledge of the world, may fail to notice important aspects of a situation, such as when and where it occurred, which could help jog their memory.

Basic Processes and Capacities

Information-processing theorists think of memory as a filing system that has three steps, or processes: *encoding, storage,* and *retrieval.* **Encoding** is like putting information in a folder to be filed in memory; it attaches a "code" or "label" to the information so that it will be easier to find when needed. Events are encoded along with information about the context in which they are encountered. **Storage** is putting the folder away in the filing cabinet. **Retrieval** occurs when the information is needed; the child then searches for the file and takes it out. Difficulties in any of these processes can interfere with efficiency.

encoding Process by which information is prepared for long-term storage and later retrieval.

storage Retention of memories for future use.

retrieval Process by which information is accessed or recalled from memory storage.

sensory memory Initial, brief, temporary storage of sensory information.

working memory Short-term storage of information being actively processed.

The way the brain stores information is believed to be universal, though the efficiency of the system varies (Siegler, 1998). Information-processing models depict the brain as containing three "storehouses": *sensory memory, working memory,* and *long-term memory.*

Sensory memory is a temporary "holding tank" for incoming sensory information. Sensory memory shows little change from infancy on (Siegler, 1998). However, without processing (encoding), sensory memories fade quickly.

Information being encoded or retrieved is kept in **working memory,** a short-term "storehouse" for information a person is actively working on: trying to understand, remember, or think about. Brain imaging studies have found that working memory is located partly in the *prefrontal cortex,* the large portion of the frontal lobe directly behind the forehead (Nelson et al., 2000). This region of the brain develops more slowly than any other (M. H. Johnson, 1998); not until the second half of the first year do the prefrontal cortex and associated circuitry develop the capacity for working memory (Nelson, 1995).

The efficiency of working memory is limited by its capacity. Researchers may assess the capacity of working memory by asking children to recall a series of scrambled digits (for example, 2-8-3-7-5-1 if they heard 1-5-7-3-8-2). The capacity of working memory—the number of digits a child can recall—increases rapidly (Cowan, Nugent, Elliott, Ponomarev, & Saults, 1999). At age 4, children usually remember only two digits; at 12 they typically remember six (Zelazo, Müller, Frye, & Marcovitch, 2003).

The growth of working memory may permit the development of *executive function,* the planning and carrying out of goal-directed mental activity (Zelazo et al., 2003). The development of executive function in early childhood can be seen in the complexity of the rules children formulate and use in solving problems (Zelazo et al., 2003).

According to a widely used model, a **central executive** controls processing operations in working memory (Baddeley, 1981, 1986, 1992, 1996, 1998). The central executive, which seems to mature between ages 8 and 10 (Cowan et al., 1999), orders information encoded for transfer to **long-term memory,** a "storehouse" of virtually unlimited capacity that holds information for long periods of time. The central executive also retrieves information from long-term memory for further processing. The central executive can temporarily expand the capacity of working memory by moving information into two separate subsidiary systems while the central executive is occupied with other tasks. One of these subsidiary systems holds verbal information (as in the digit task) and the other, visual/spatial images.

central executive In Baddeley's model, element of working memory that controls the processing of information.

long-term memory Storage of virtually unlimited capacity that holds information for very long periods.

Recognition and Recall

Recognition and *recall* are types of retrieval. **Recognition** is the ability to identify something encountered before (for example, to pick out a missing mitten from a lost-and-found box). **Recall** is the ability to reproduce knowledge from memory (for example, to describe the mitten to someone). Preschool children, like all age groups, do better on recognition than on recall, but both abilities improve with age. The more familiar children are with an item, the better they can recall it. Recall also depends on motivation and on the strategies a child uses to enhance it (Lange, MacKinnon, & Nida, 1989).

recognition Ability to identify a previously encountered stimulus.

recall Ability to reproduce material from memory.

How well do preschoolers recognize a familiar face? Not as well as older children and adults do, according to an Australian study—perhaps because young children have not yet had enough experience with faces. However, 4- and 5-year-olds do seem to process face-recognition information holistically, as adults do. Both young children and adults can more easily tell which of two noses belongs to a familiar face when the noses are depicted on the face than when the noses alone are shown (Pellicano & Rhodes, 2003).

Young children often fail to use strategies for remembering—even strategies they already know—unless reminded (Flavell, 1970). This tendency not to generate efficient strategies may reflect lack of awareness of how a strategy would be useful (Sophian, Wood, & Vong, 1995). Older children tend to become more efficient in the spontaneous use of memory strategies (see Chapter 13).

Checkpoint

Can you . . .

- ✔ Identify the three basic processes and three storehouses of memory and discuss their development?
- ✔ Compare preschoolers' recognition and recall ability?

Forming Childhood Memories

Memory of experiences in early childhood is rarely deliberate: young children simply remember events that made a strong impression, and most of these early conscious memories seem to be short-lived. One investigator has distinguished three types of childhood memory that serve different functions: *generic, episodic,* and *autobiographical* (Nelson, 1993b).

Generic memory, which begins at about age 2, produces a **script,** or general outline of a familiar, repeated event without details of time or place. The script contains routines for situations that come up again and again; it helps a child know what to expect and how to act. For example, a child may have scripts for riding the bus to preschool or having lunch at Grandma's house.

generic memory Memory that produces scripts of familiar routines to guide behavior.

script General remembered outline of a familiar, repeated event, used to guide behavior.

Episodic memory refers to awareness of having experienced a particular incident that occurred at a specific time and place. Young children remember more clearly events that are new to them. Three-year-olds may recall details about a trip to the circus for a year or longer (Fivush, Hudson, & Nelson, 1983), whereas generic memories of frequent events (such as going to the park) tend to blur together.

episodic memory Long-term memory of specific experiences or events, linked to time and place.

Given a young child's limited memory capacity, episodic memories are temporary. Unless they recur several times (in which case they are transferred to generic memory), they last for a few weeks or months and then fade. The reliability of children's episodic memory has become an important issue in lawsuits involving charges of child abuse (see Box 10-2).

Autobiographical memory refers to memories that form a person's life history. These memories are specific and long lasting. Although autobiographical memory is a type of

autobiographical memory Memory of specific events in one's own life.

The Social World

Box 10-2 *How Reliable Is Children's Eyewitness Testimony?*

Child abuse is a crime that often can be proved only by the testimony of a preschool child. If a child's testimony is inaccurate, an innocent adult may be unfairly punished. On the other hand, if a child's testimony is *not* believed, a dangerous adult may be set free.

Young children may not know whether they actually experienced an event or merely imagined it or were told or asked about it (Woolley & Bruell, 1996). Thus, children responding to adults' suggestions have been known to "remember" events that never occurred. In one experiment, researchers had a man called "Sam Stone" drop in at a child care center for a few minutes (Leichtman & Ceci, 1995). The visitor commented on a story that was being read, strolled around the room, and then waved good-bye and left. Some of the children who witnessed the event had repeatedly been told stories about "Sam Stone" before his visit, depicting him as a well-meaning bumbler, and/or were given false suggestions afterward that he had ripped a book and dirtied a teddy bear.

After four weekly interviews, nearly half of the 3- and 4-year-olds and 30 percent of 5- and 6-year-olds who had heard the stories about Sam Stone's bumbling and had been given the false suggestions spontaneously reported the book-ripping and teddy-bear-dirtying to a new interviewer; and when asked probing questions, nearly three-fourths of the younger children said the visitor had done one or both. By contrast, *none* of the children in a control group, who had *not* been given prejudicial information or false suggestions, made false reports. Thus, young children's testimony *can* be accurate when elicited neutrally.

As the Sam Stone study indicates, preschoolers tend to be more suggestible than older children. This difference may be due to younger children's weaker memory for specific events and their greater vulnerability to bribes, threats, and adult expectations (Bruck, Ceci, & Hembrooke, 1998; Ceci & Bruck, 1993; Leichtman & Ceci, 1995). Suggestibility seems to diminish after age 4½ (Portwood & Repucci, 1996). However, in one study, 5-year-olds were more likely to "remember" a false event than were 7- or 9-year-olds or adults (Ghetti & Alexander, 2004). And some children, regardless of age, are more suggestible than others (Bruck & Ceci, 1997).

Reports are likely to be more reliable if children are interviewed only once, soon after the event, by people who do not have an opinion about what took place; if the interviewers do not ask leading questions, ask open-ended rather than yes/no questions, and do not repeatedly ask the same questions; if interviewers are patient and nonjudgmental; and if they do not selectively reward or reinforce responses or convey veiled threats or accusations (Bruck & Ceci, 1997; Bruck, Ceci, & Hembrooke, 1998; Leichtman & Ceci, 1995; Steward & Steward, 1996).

Young children are apt to err in recalling precise details of a frequently repeated event (Powell & Thomson, 1996). They tend to confuse what happened during a particular episode with what happened during other, similar episodes. Thus, a child may have trouble answering questions about a *specific instance* of abuse, even though the child accurately remembers a *pattern* of abuse.

Often young children's testimony is excluded because they cannot demonstrate a clear understanding of the difference between truth and falsehood and of the morality and consequences of telling a lie. Often they do not understand such questions the way they are asked or cannot explain the concepts involved. Furthermore, abused children often have seriously delayed language skills. The Lyon-Saywitz Oath-Taking Competency Picture Task avoids these problems by simply asking a prospective young witness whether a child in a story is telling the truth about a pictured event and what would happen if the child told a lie. Among 192 maltreated 4- to 7-year-olds awaiting court appearances, a majority of 5-year-olds successfully performed this task, and even 4-year-olds did better than chance would predict (Lyon & Saywitz, 1999).

Issues concerning the reliability of young children's testimony are still being sorted out, but it appears that children *can* give reliable testimony if care is taken to avoid biased interviewing techniques. Researchers are trying to develop and validate "model" interview techniques that will expose adults who harm children while protecting those who may be falsely accused (Bruck et al., 1998).

What's your view ?

What information would you seek and what factors would you consider in deciding whether to believe a preschooler's testimony in a child abuse case?

Check it out !

For more information on this topic, go to **http://www.ojp.usdoj.gov/ovc/factshts/monograph.htm**. This is a June 1999 monograph from the U.S. Department of Justice Office for Victims of Crime, "Breaking the Cycle of Violence: Recommendations to Improve the Criminal Justice Response to Child Victims and Witnesses." Or go to **http://www.aap.org/policy/re9923.html**. This is a policy statement from the American Academy of Pediatrics, "The Child in Court: A Subject Review" (RE9923).

episodic memory, not everything in episodic memory becomes part of it—only those memories that have a special, personal meaning to the child. Autobiographical memory begins for most people around age 4 and rarely before age 3. It increases slowly between ages 5 and 8; from then on memories may be recalled for 20, 40, or more years. Individuals differ in the onset of autobiographical memory; some people have vivid memories from the age of 3, while others do not remember much before age 8 (Nelson, 1992).

A suggested explanation for the relatively late arrival of autobiographical memory is that children cannot store in memory events pertaining to their own lives until they develop a concept of self around which to organize those memories (Howe & Courage, 1993, 1997). The emergence of autobiographical memory also may be linked with the development of language. The ability to talk about an event, as Einstein and his uncle did, may affect whether and how the memory is carried into later life. Not until children can put memories into words can they hold them in their minds, reflect on them, and compare them with the memories of others (Fivush & Schwarzmueller, 1998).

Why do some early memories, like Einstein's memory of the compass, last longer than others? One factor is the uniqueness of the event. A second factor is children's active participation, either in the event itself or in its retelling or reenactment. Preschoolers tend to remember things they *did* better than things they merely *saw* (Murachver, Pipe, Gordon, Owens, & Fivush, 1996). A third factor is talk with parents about past events. In one study, 2½- to 3-year-olds engaged in pretend play with their mothers about a camping trip, a bird-watching adventure, and the opening of an ice cream shop. Children who jointly handled *and* jointly discussed with their mothers various items connected with these events recalled them better one to three days later than children who had only handled or only discussed the items (Haden, Ornstein, Eckerman, & Didow, 2001).

The *way* adults talk with a child about a shared experience can influence how well the child will remember it (Haden & Fivush, 1996; Reese & Fivush, 1993). When a child gets stuck, adults with a *repetitive* conversational style tend to repeat their own previous statements or questions. A repetitive-style parent might ask, "Do you remember how we traveled to Florida?" and then, receiving no answer, ask, "How did we get there? We went in the ______." Adults with an *elaborative* style would move on to a different aspect of the event or add more information: "Did we go by car or by plane?" Elaborative parents seem focused on having a mutually rewarding conversation and affirming the child's responses, whereas repetitive parents seem focused on checking the child's memory performance. Children of elaborative-style parents take part in longer, more detailed conversations about events at age 3 and tend to remember the events better at 5 and 6 (Reese, Haden, & Fivush, 1993). Even as early as 19 to 32 months, a mother's elaborative reminiscing predicts children's ability to repeat and elaborate on shared memories (Harley & Reese, 1999).

What's your view

- Since an elaborative conversational style seems most effective in jogging young children's memory, would you favor training mothers to use it? Why or why not?
- What difficulties or objections would you anticipate?

Memory and Culture

Social interaction not only helps children remember; it may also be the key to memory formation. Investigators influenced by Vygotsky's sociocultural theory support a **social interaction model,** which holds that children collaboratively construct autobiographical memories with parents or other adults as they talk about shared events (Nelson, 1993a). Adults initiate and guide these conversations, which show children how memories are organized in narrative form in their culture (Welch-Ross, 1997). When parents prompt 2- and 3-year-olds with frequent questions about context ("When did you find the pine cone?" "Where did you find it?" "Who was with you?"), children soon learn to include this information (Peterson & McCabe, 1994). When parents of 3-year-olds comment on subjective reactions ("You *wanted* to go on the slide," "It was a *huge* bowl," "Mommy was *wrong*"), the children at 5½ are more likely to weave such comments into their reminiscences (Haden, Haine, & Fivush, 1997).

social interaction model Model, based on Vygotsky's sociocultural theory, which proposes that children construct autobiographical memories through conversation with adults about shared events.

Checkpoint

Can you . . .

- ✔ Identify three types of memories in early childhood?
- ✔ Explain how language development may contribute to the onset of autobiographical memory?
- ✔ Identify factors that affect how well a preschool child will remember an event?
- ✔ Compare two types of parental styles of discussing shared memories with a child?
- ✔ Give examples of how culture influences autobiographical memory?

Culture affects what children remember about an experience and the way parents talk with them about it. In one study (Wang, 2004), 180 European-American and Chinese preschoolers, kindergartners, and second graders were asked such questions as "How did you spend your last birthday?" and "Tell me about a time when your mom or dad scolded you about something." The U.S. children told about particular events; their narratives were longer and more detailed and contained more opinion and emotion than those of the Chinese children. The Chinese children's accounts were shorter and more succinct and centered more on daily routines, group activities, and social interactions and roles. The U.S. children were the chief characters of their stories, whereas the Chinese children shared the "stage" with others. In discussions of shared memories with 3-year-olds, U.S. mothers used elaboration to encourage the child's active participation ("Do you remember when you went swimming at Nana's? What did you do that was really neat?"). Chinese mothers asked leading questions containing most of the content of the memory, and the child added little ("What did you play at the place of skiing? Sat on the ice ship, right?").

How is preschoolers' intelligence measured, and what factors influence it?

Intelligence: Psychometric and Vygotskian Approaches

One factor that may affect the strength of early cognitive skills is intelligence. Let's look at two ways intelligence is measured—through traditional psychometric tests and through newer tests of cognitive potential—and at influences on children's performance.

Traditional Psychometric Measures

Because 3-, 4-, and 5-year-olds are more proficient with language than younger children, intelligence tests can now include more verbal items; and these tests produce more reliable results than the largely nonverbal tests used in infancy. As children approach age 5, there is a higher correlation between their scores on intelligence tests and the scores they will achieve later (Bornstein & Sigman, 1986). IQ tests given near the end of kindergarten are among the best predictors of future school success (Tramontana et al., 1988).

Although preschool children are easier to test than infants and toddlers, they still need to be tested individually. The two most commonly used individual tests for preschoolers are the Stanford-Binet Intelligence Scale and the Wechsler Preschool and Primary Scale of Intelligence.

Stanford-Binet Intelligence Scales Individual intelligence test used to measure memory, spatial orientation, and practical judgment.

The **Stanford-Binet Intelligence Scales,** used for ages 2 and up, takes 45 to 60 minutes. The child is asked to define words, string beads, build with blocks, identify the missing parts of a picture, trace mazes, and show an understanding of numbers. The child's score is supposed to measure fluid reasoning (the ability to solve abstract or novel problems), knowledge, quantitative reasoning, visual-spatial processing, and working memory. The fifth edition, revised in 2003, includes nonverbal methods of testing all five of these dimensions of cognition and permits comparisons of verbal and nonverbal performance. The range of the scales has been extended to assess more accurately higher and lower levels of functioning. In addition to providing a full-scale IQ, the Stanford-Binet yields separate measures of verbal and nonverbal IQ plus composite scores spanning the five cognitive dimensions.

Wechsler Preschool and Primary Scale of Intelligence, Revised (WPPSI-III) Individual intelligence test for children ages 3 to 7 that yields verbal and performance scores as well as a combined score.

The **Wechsler Preschool and Primary Scale of Intelligence, Revised (WPPSI-III),** an individual test taking 30 to 60 minutes, has separate levels for ages 2½ to 4 and 4 to 7. It yields separate verbal and performance scores as well as a combined score. Its separate scales are similar to those in the Wechsler Intelligence Scale for Children (WISC-III), discussed in Chapter 13. The 2002 revision includes new subtests designed to measure both verbal and nonverbal fluid reasoning, receptive versus expressive vocabulary, and processing speed. Both the Stanford-Binet and the WPPSI-III have been restandardized on samples of children representing the population of preschool-age children in the United States. The WPPSI-III also has been validated for special populations, such as children with intellectual disabilities, developmental delays, language disorders, and autistic disorders.

Influences on Measured Intelligence

A common misconception is that IQ scores represent a fixed quantity of inborn intelligence. In reality, an IQ score is simply a measure of how well a child can do certain tasks at a certain time in comparison with others of the same age. Test scores of children in industrialized countries have risen steadily since testing began, forcing test developers to raise standardized norms. This is called the *Flynn effect* after the psychometrician James Flynn (1984, 1987), who first described it. The reasons for this upward trend are in dispute; it may in part reflect exposure to educational television, preschools, better-educated parents, and a wider variety of experiences, as well as changes in the tests themselves.

To consider some of the factors that contribute to intelligence, watch the "Parental Influence on Children's IQ" video in Chapter 10 of your CD.

How well a particular child does on intelligence tests may be influenced by several factors. These include temperament, the match between cognitive style and the tasks posed, social and emotional maturity, ease in the testing situation, preliteracy or literacy skills, socioeconomic status, and ethnicity or culture. (We will examine several of these factors in Chapter 13.)

At one time developmental scientists believed that the family environment played a major role in cognitive development. Now the extent of that influence is in question. We don't know how much of parents' influence on intelligence comes from their genetic contribution and how much from the fact that they provide a child's earliest environment for learning.

Twin and adoption studies suggest that family life has its strongest influence in early childhood, and this influence diminishes greatly by adolescence (McGue, 1997; Neisser et al., 1996). However, these studies have been done largely with white, middle-class samples; their results may not apply to low-income and nonwhite families (Neisser et al., 1996).

In two longitudinal studies of low-income African-American children, although the influence of the home environment did decline between infancy and middle childhood, it remained substantial—at least as strong as the influence of the mother's IQ (Burchinal et al., 1997). Among 175 African-American 3-year-olds, a father's satisfaction with his parenting role was associated with his child's IQ, and paternal involvement and nurturance were associated with language skills and other aspects of well-being (Black et al., 1999).

Family economic circumstances can exert a powerful influence, not so much in themselves as in the way they affect parenting practices and the atmosphere in the home. But socioeconomic status is only one of several social and family risk factors. Assessments of 152 children at ages 4 and 13 revealed no single pattern of risk. Instead, a child's IQ was affected by *the total number* of such risk factors as the mother's behavior, mental health, anxiety level, education, and beliefs about children's development; family size and social support; stressful life events; parental occupations; and disadvantaged status. The more risk factors there were, the lower the child's IQ score (Sameroff, Seifer, Baldwin, & Baldwin, 1993).

Giving suggestions and strategies for solving a puzzle or problem—without showing approval or disapproval—can foster cognitive growth. Parental influence on cognitive development may be strongest in early childhood.

Testing and Teaching Based on Vygotsky's Theory

According to Vygotsky, children learn by internalizing the results of interactions with adults. As mentioned in Chapter 2, this interactive learning is most effective in the *zone of proximal development (ZPD);* that is, with regard to tasks children are almost ready to accomplish on their own. The ZPD can be assessed by *dynamic tests* (see Chapter 13), which, according to Vygotsky's theory, provide a better measure of children's intellectual potential than do traditional psychometric tests that measure what children have already mastered.

The ZPD, in combination with the related concept of *scaffolding* (refer back to Chapter 2), also can help parents and teachers efficiently guide children's cognitive progress. The less able a child is to do a task, the more direction an adult must give. As the child can do more and more, the adult helps less and less. When the child can do the job alone, the adult takes away the "scaffold" that is no longer needed.

With scaffolding, parents can help their children acquire tools for learning, such as the motivation to learn, the ability to manage their own learning, and an understanding of their role in the learning process. By enabling children to become aware of and monitor their own cognitive processes and to recognize when they need help, parents can help children take responsibility for learning. Prekindergarten children who receive this kind of scaffolding are better able to regulate their own learning in kindergarten (Neitzel & Stright, 2003).

In a longitudinal study of 289 urban and rural low-SES, largely African-American families with infants, researchers observed the children at home and evaluated their development at ages 2, 3½, and 4½. The skills children developed during interactions with their mothers at 2 and 3½ enabled them, at 4½, to regulate their own goal-directed problem solving and to initiate social interactions. Two-year-olds whose mothers helped maintain the child's interest in an activity—for example, by asking questions, making suggestions or comments, or offering choices—tended, at 3½ and 4½, to show independence in cognitive and social skills, such as solving a problem and initiating social interaction (Landry, Smith, Swank, & Miller-Loncar, 2000).

What's your view?

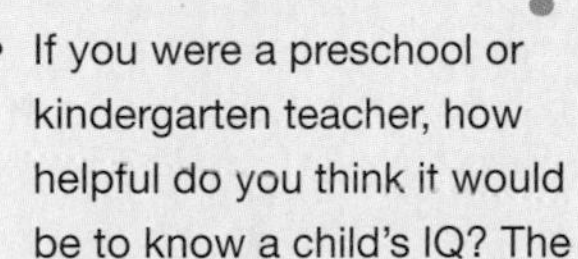

- If you were a preschool or kindergarten teacher, how helpful do you think it would be to know a child's IQ? The child's ZPD?

Checkpoint

Can you . . .

- ✔ Describe two commonly used individual intelligence tests for preschoolers?
- ✔ Discuss several influences on measured intelligence?
- ✔ Explain why an intelligence test score using the ZPD might be significantly different from a traditional psychometric test score?

In another study, 3- and 4-year-olds were asked to give their parents directions for finding a hidden mouse in a dollhouse. The parents gave the children feedback when their directions needed clarifying. The parents proved to be highly sensitive to the children's scaffolding needs; they gave more directive prompts to 3-year-olds, whose directions tended to be less clear than those of 4-year-olds, and used fewer directive prompts as the children gained experience in giving clear directions (Plumert & Nichols-Whitehead, 1996).

Guidepost 4

How does language improve, and what happens when its development is delayed?

Language Development

Preschoolers are full of questions: "How many sleeps until tomorrow?" "Who filled the river with water?" "Do babies have muscles?" "Do smells come from inside my nose?" Young children's growing facility with language helps them express their unique view of the world. Between ages 3 and 6, children make rapid advances in vocabulary, grammar, and syntax. The child who, at 3, describes how Daddy "hatches" wood (chops with a hatchet) or asks Mommy to "piece" her food (cut it into little pieces) may, by the age of 5, tell her mother, "Don't be ridiculous!" or proudly point to her toys and say, "See how I organized everything?"

Vocabulary

At 3 the average child knows and can use 900 to 1,000 words. By age 6, a child typically has an expressive (speaking) vocabulary of 2,600 words and understands more than 20,000 (Owens, 1996). With the help of formal schooling, a child's passive, or receptive, vocabulary (words she can understand) will quadruple to 80,000 words by the time she enters high school (Owens, 1996).

fast mapping Process by which a child absorbs the meaning of a new word after hearing it once or twice in conversation.

This rapid expansion of vocabulary may occur through **fast mapping,** which allows a child to pick up the approximate meaning of a new word after hearing it only once or twice in conversation. From the context, children seem to form a quick hypothesis about the meaning of the word, which then is refined with further exposure and usage (Owens, 1996). Linguists are not sure how fast mapping works, but it seems likely that children draw on what they know about the rules for forming words, about similar words, about the immediate context, and about the subject under discussion. Names of objects (nouns) seem to be easier to fast map than names of actions (verbs), which are less concrete. Yet one experiment showed that children just under 3 years old can fast map a new verb and apply it to another situation in which the same action is being performed (Golinkoff, Jacquet, Hirsh-Pasek, & Nandakumar, 1996).

Theory-of-mind development—the increasing ability to infer another's mental state—seems to play a role in vocabulary learning. In one study, preschoolers learned "nonsense" words better from a speaker who seemed certain what the word meant than from one who seemed unsure (Sabbagh & Baldwin, 2001).

Many 3- and 4-year-olds seem able to tell when two words refer to the same object or action (Savage & Au, 1996). They know that a single object cannot have two proper names (a dog cannot be both Spot and Fido). They also know that more than one adjective can apply to the same noun ("Fido is spotted and furry") and that an adjective can be combined with a proper name ("smart Fido!") (Hall & Graham, 1999).

The use of *metaphor,* a figure of speech in which a word or phrase that usually designates one thing is applied to another, becomes increasingly common during these years (Vosniadou, 1987). Once Vidya, upset by her parents' quarreling, exclaimed, "Why are you two being such grumpy old bears?" Vidya's spontaneous metaphor reflected her growing ability to see similarities between (in this case) parents and bears and thus was related to her ability to categorize. The use of metaphor shows an ability to draw on knowledge about one type of thing to better understand another, an ability needed for acquiring many kinds of knowledge.

Grammar and Syntax

The ways children combine syllables into words, and words into sentences, grow increasingly sophisticated during early childhood (Owens, 1996). At 3, children typically begin to use plurals, possessives, and past tense and know the difference between *I*, *you*, and *we*. Their sentences are generally short and simple, often omitting articles, such as *a* and *the*, but including some pronouns, adjectives, and prepositions. Although they most often use declarative sentences ("Kitty wants milk"), they can ask—and answer—*what* and *where* questions. (*Why* and *how* are harder to grasp.) However, they still overregularize because they have not yet learned or absorbed exceptions to rules (refer back to Chapter 7). Saying "holded" instead of "held" or "eated" instead of "ate" is a normal sign of linguistic progress. When young children discover a rule, such as adding *-ed* to a verb for past tense, they tend to overgeneralize—to use it even with words that do not conform to the rule. Eventually, they notice that *-ed* is not always used to form the past tense of a verb. Children are more likely to overgeneralize the use of transitive or intransitive verbs in constructions that call for the other type of verb ("He disappeared it" or "He's hitting") if the verb they are using is not very familiar to them (Brooks, Tomasello, Dodson, & Lewis, 1999).

Between ages 4 and 5, sentences average four to five words and may be declarative, negative ("I'm not hungry"), interrogative ("Why can't I go outside?"), or imperative ("Catch the ball!"). Four-year-olds use complex, multiclause sentences ("I'm eating because I'm hungry") more frequently if their parents often use such sentences (Huttenlocher, Vasilyeva, Cymerman, & Levine, 2002). Children this age tend to string sentences together in long run-on stories (". . . And then . . . And then . . ."). In some respects, comprehension may be immature. For example, 4-year-old Noah can carry out a command that includes more than one step ("Pick up your toys and put them in the cupboard"). However, if his mother tells him "You may watch TV after you pick up your toys," he may process the words in the order in which he hears them and think he can first watch television and then pick up his toys.

By ages 5 to 7, children's speech has become quite adultlike. They speak in longer and more complicated sentences. They use more conjunctions, prepositions, and articles. They use compound and complex sentences and can handle all parts of speech.

Still, although children this age speak fluently, comprehensibly, and fairly grammatically, they have yet to master many fine points of language. They rarely use the passive voice ("I was dressed by Grandpa"), conditional sentences ("If I were big, I could drive the bus"), or the auxiliary verb *have* ("I have seen that lady before") (C. S. Chomsky, 1969).

This preschool boy can use his growing vocabulary and knowledge of grammar and syntax to communicate more effectively. He has learned how to ask his father for things, to carry on a conversation, and to tell a story, perhaps about what happened at preschool.

Pragmatics and Social Speech

As children learn vocabulary, grammar, and syntax, they become more competent in **pragmatics**—the practical knowledge of how to use language to communicate. This includes knowing how to ask for things, how to tell a story or joke, how to begin and continue a conversation, and how to adjust comments to the listener's perspective (M. L. Rice, 1982). These are all aspects of **social speech:** speech intended to be understood by a listener.

pragmatics Practical knowledge needed to use language for communicative purposes.

social speech Speech intended to be understood by a listener.

Children use both gestures and speech communicatively from an early age. By age 2, they engage in conversation, trying to make their own speech relevant to what someone else has said. However, children this age have trouble keeping a conversation going without changing the subject (Owens, 1996).

With improved pronunciation and grammar, it becomes easier for others to understand what children say. Most 3-year-olds are quite talkative, and they pay attention to the effect of their speech on others. If people cannot understand them, they try to explain themselves more clearly. Four-year-olds, especially girls, use "parentese" when speaking to 2-year-olds (Owens, 1996; Shatz & Gelman, 1973; refer back to Chapter 7).

Most 5-year-olds can adapt what they say to what the listener knows. They can use words to resolve disputes, and they use more polite language and fewer direct commands in talking to adults than to other children. Almost half of all 5-year-olds can stick to a conversational topic for about a dozen turns—if they are comfortable with their partner and if the topic is one they know and care about (Owens, 1996).

Table 10-5 Types of Private Speech

Type	Child's Activity	Examples
Wordplay, repetition	Repeating words and sounds, often in playful, rhythmic recitation	José wanders around the room, repeating in a singsong manner, "Put the mushroom on your head, put the mushroom in your pocket, put the mushroom on your nose."
Solitary fantasy play and speech addressed to nonhuman objects	Talking to objects; playing roles; producing sound effects for objects	Darryl says, "Ka-powee ka-powee," aiming his finger like a gun. Ashley says in a high-pitched voice while playing in the doll corner, "I'll be better after the doctor gives me a shot." As she pokes herself with her finger (a pretend needle), she says, "Ow!"
Emotional release and expression	Expressing emotions or feelings directed inward rather than to a listener	Keiko is given a new box of crayons and says to no one in particular, "Wow! Neat!" Rachel is sitting at her desk with an anxious expression on her face, repeating to herself, "My mom's sick, my mom's sick."
Egocentric communication	Communicating with another person but expressing the information so incompletely or peculiarly that it can't be understood	David and Mark are seated next to one another on the rug. David says to Mark, "It broke," without explaining what or when. Susan says to Ann at the art table, "Where are the paste-ons?" Ann says, "What paste-ons?" Susan shrugs and walks off.
Describing or guiding one's own activity	Narrating one's actions; thinking out loud	Omar sits down at the art table and says to himself, "I want to draw something. Let's see, I need a big piece of paper. I want to draw my cat." Working in her arithmetic workbook, Cathy says to no one in particular, "Six." Then, counting on her fingers, she continues, "Seven, eight, nine, ten. It's ten, it's ten. The answer's ten."
Reading aloud, sounding out words	Reading aloud or sounding out words while reading	While reading a book, Tom begins to sound out a difficult word. "Sher-lock Holm-lock, he says slowly and quietly. Then he tries again. "Sher-lock-Holm-lock, Sherlock Holme," he says leaving off the final *s* in his most successful attempt.
Inaudible muttering	Speaking so quietly that the words cannot be understood by an observer	Tony's lips move as he works a math problem.

Source: Berk, L. and R. Garvin. (1984) Adapted from "Development of private speech among low income Appalachian children," *Developmental Psychology, 202*(2), 1984, 271–284. Copyright © 1984 by the American Psychological Association. Adapted with permission.

Private Speech: Piaget Versus Vygotsky

Anna, age 4, was alone in her room painting. When she finished, she was overheard saying aloud, "Now I have to put the pictures somewhere to dry. I'll put them by the window. They need to get dry now. I'll paint some more dinosaurs."

private speech Talking aloud to oneself with no intent to communicate.

Private speech—talking aloud to oneself with no intent to communicate with others—is normal and common in childhood, accounting for 20 to 50 percent of what 4- to 10-year-old children say (Berk, 1986a). Two- to 3-year-olds engage in "crib talk," playing with sounds and words. Four- and 5-year-olds use private speech as a way to express fantasies and emotions (Berk, 1992; Small, 1990). Older children "think out loud" or mutter in barely audible tones (see Table 10-5).

Piaget (1962/1923) saw private speech as a sign of cognitive immaturity. According to Piaget, because young children are egocentric, they are unable to recognize others' viewpoints and therefore are unable to communicate meaningfully. Instead, they simply vocalize whatever is on their own minds. Another reason young children talk while they do things, said Piaget, is that they do not yet distinguish between words and the actions the words stand for, or symbolize. By the end of the preoperational stage, he said, with cognitive maturation and social experience, children become less egocentric and more capable of symbolic thought and so discard private speech.

Like Piaget, Vygotsky (1962/1934) believed that private speech helps young children integrate language with thought. However, Vygotsky did not look upon private speech as egocentric. He saw it as a special form of communication: conversation with the self. As such, he said, it serves a very important function in the transition between early social speech (often experienced in the form of adult commands) and inner speech (thinking in words)—a transition toward the internalization of socially derived control of behavior ("Now I have to put the pictures somewhere to dry"). Vygotsky suggested that private speech follows an inverted U-shaped curve: it increases during the preschool years and then fades away during the early part of middle childhood as children become more able to guide and master their actions.

Research generally supports Vygotsky as to the functions of private speech. In an observational study of 93 low- to middle-income 3- to 5-year-olds, 86 percent of the children's remarks were *not* egocentric (Berk, 1986a). The most sociable children and those who engage in the most social speech tend to use the most private speech as well, apparently supporting Vygotsky's view that private speech is stimulated by social experience (Berk, 1986a, 1986b, 1992; Berk & Garvin, 1984; Kohlberg, Yaeger, & Hjertholm, 1968). There also is evidence for the role of private speech in self-regulation (Berk & Garvin, 1984; Furrow, 1984). Private speech tends to increase when children are trying to do difficult tasks, especially without adult supervision (Berk, 1992; Berk & Garvin, 1984).

According to one ranking (Bivens & Berk, 1988), children progress through at least three levels of private speech: (1) speech that is purely self-expressive (word play, repetition of syllables, expression of feelings, or talking to dolls or imaginary playmates); (2) vocal statements relevant to a task at hand (commenting on what one is doing or needs to do or has done, asking and then answering one's own questions, or sounding out words); and (3) external signs of task-directed inner speech (inaudible muttering or lip and tongue movements). Preschool girls, who tend to be more verbally advanced than preschool boys, use more mature forms of private speech; and middle-income children use more mature forms than low-income children (Berk, 1986a).

How much do children engage in private speech? The pattern now appears more complex than Vygotsky's U-shaped curve. Some studies have reported no age changes in overall use of private speech; others have found variations in the timing of its decline. The brightest children tend to use it earliest. Whereas Vygotsky considered the need for private speech a universal stage of cognitive development, studies have found a wide range of individual differences, with some children using it very little or not at all (Berk, 1992).

Understanding the significance of private speech has practical implications, especially in school (Berk, 1986a). Talking to oneself or muttering should not be considered misbehavior; a child may be struggling with a problem and may need to think out loud.

Checkpoint

Can you . . .

- ✔ Trace normal progress in 3- to 6-year-olds' vocabulary, grammar, syntax, and conversational abilities?
- ✔ Give reasons children of various ages use private speech?

Delayed Language Development

The fact that Albert Einstein did not start to speak until he was close to 3 years old may encourage parents of other children whose speech develops later than usual. About 3 percent of preschool-age children show language delays, though their intelligence is usually average or better (M. L. Rice, 1989). Boys are more likely than girls to be late talkers (Dale et al., 1998).

It is unclear why some children speak late. They do not necessarily lack linguistic input at home. These children may have a cognitive limitation that makes it hard for them to learn the rules of language (Scarborough, 1990). Children with delayed language may have problems in fast mapping; they may need to hear a new word more often than other children do before they can incorporate it into their vocabularies (M. L. Rice, 1989; M. Rice, Oetting, Marquis, Bode, & Pae, 1994).

Like Albert Einstein, many children who speak late—especially those whose comprehension is normal—eventually catch up (Dale, Price, Bishop, & Plomin, 2003; Thal, Tobias, & Morrison, 1991). Some late speakers have a history of otitis media (an inflammation of the middle ear) between 12 and 18 months of age; these children improve dramatically in language ability when the infection, with its related hearing loss, clears up (Lonigan, Fischel, Whitehurst, Arnold, & Valdez-Menchaca, 1992). But for some children, severe early language delays, if left untreated, may signal a persistent language impairment that can have far-reaching cognitive, social, and emotional consequences. In a longitudinal study, 31 children identified at age 2 as late talkers had less sophisticated narrative skills at ages 8 and 9 than a control group who had not been late talkers (Manhardt & Rescorla, 2002). Children who do not speak or understand as well as their peers tend to be judged negatively by adults and other children (M. L. Rice, Hadley, & Alexander, 1993) and to have trouble finding playmates or friends (Gertner, Rice, & Hadley, 1994).

It is not always easy to predict whether a late talker will need help. In longitudinal, community-based studies of 8,386 two-year-old twins born in England and Wales in 1994 and 1995, more than 40 percent of those reported to have early language delays showed language problems at ages 3 and 4. On the other hand, many 3- and 4-year-olds who developed language difficulties had not shown them earlier (Dale et al., 2003).

Heredity seems to play a major role, especially in the most severe and persistent cases of language delay, which may signal problems in early brain development and future language impairment (Dale et al., 1998). Thus, family history needs to be considered in recommending a child for treatment (Bishop, Price, Dale, & Plomin, 2003). In a Finnish study, late talkers with a family history of dyslexia had persistent language difficulties, but those without such a history had normal speech by age 3½ (Lyytinen, Poikkeus, Laakso, Eklund, & Lyytinen, 2001).

Among 3,039 pairs of 2-year-old twins in the English and Welsh sample, if one monozygotic twin fell in the bottom 5 percent in vocabulary knowledge, the other twin had an 80 percent chance of being equally delayed. Among dizygotic twins, the chances of equivalent delays were only 42 percent (Dale et al., 1998). In follow-up measurements at ages 3 and 4, heritability for this lower extreme of language disability was calculated at 49 percent (Spinath, Price, Dale, & Plomin, 2004). A study of 436 of these twins at age 4 found a genetically influenced association between language impairment and poor nonverbal cognitive skills (Viding et al., 2003).

Speech and language therapy may include strategies focusing on specific language forms, a specialized preschool program targeting language skills, and follow-up programs either in or out of school during the elementary school years (M. L. Rice, 1989). In a promising technique called *dialogic reading* (mentioned in Chapter 2), reading picture books becomes a vehicle for parent-child dialogue about the story. Three- to 6-year-olds with mild-to-moderate language delays whose mothers were trained in dialogic reading improved more than a comparison group whose mothers had been trained to use similar principles in talking with their children but not about books (Dale, Crain-Thoreson, Notari-Syverson, & Cole, 1996).

Why is shared reading more effective than just talking with a child? Shared reading affords a natural opportunity for giving information and increasing vocabulary. It provides a focus for attention and for asking and responding to questions. In addition, it is enjoyable for both children and adults; it fosters emotional bonding while enhancing cognitive development.

Social Interaction and Preparation for Literacy

emergent literacy Preschoolers' development of skills, knowledge, and attitudes that underlie reading and writing.

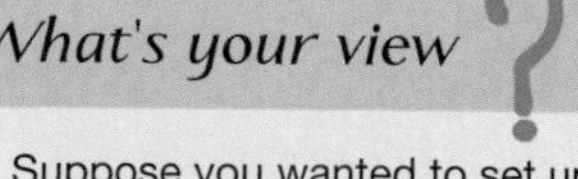

- Suppose you wanted to set up a program to encourage preliteracy development in high-risk children. What elements would you include in your program?
- How would you judge its success?

To understand what is on the printed page, children first need to master certain prereading skills (Lonigan, Burgess, & Anthony, 2000). **Emergent literacy** refers to the development of these skills, along with the knowledge and attitudes that underlie reading and writing. Prereading skills include (1) general linguistic skills, such as vocabulary, syntax, narrative structure, and the understanding that language is used to communicate; and (2) specific skills, such as *phonemic awareness,* the realization that words are composed of distinct sounds or *phonemes,* and *phoneme-grapheme correspondence,* the ability to link sounds with the corresponding letters or combinations of letters (Whitehurst & Lonigan, 1998; Lonigan et al., 2000). Children who have been taught the alphabet and other prereading skills before entering school tend to become better readers (Siegler, 1998; Lonigan et al., 2000; Whitehurst & Lonigan, 1998).

Social interaction can promote emergent literacy. Children are more likely to become good readers and writers if, during the preschool years, parents provide conversational challenges the children are ready for—if they use a rich vocabulary and center dinner-table talk on the day's activities or on questions about why people do things and how things work, as in young Einstein's discussions with his uncle Jacob (Snow, 1990, 1993). In a longitudinal study of 24 white, middle-class two-parent families (Reese, 1995), the quality of mother-child conversation at ages 3 and 4—particularly about past events—was a strong predictor of literacy skills prior to entering first grade. Most influential was the mothers' use of questions and comments that helped children elaborate on events or link them with other incidents.

As children learn the skills they will need to translate the written word into speech, they also learn that writing can express ideas, thoughts, and feelings. Preschool children pretend to write by scribbling, lining up their marks from left to right (Brenneman, Massey, Machado, & Gelman, 1996). Later they begin using letters, numbers, and letterlike shapes to represent words, syllables, or phonemes. Often their spelling is so inventive that they cannot read it themselves (Whitehust & Lonigan, 1998)!

Reading to children is one of the most effective paths to literacy. Children who are read to from an early age learn that reading and writing in English move from left to right and from top to bottom and that words are separated by spaces (Siegler, 1998; Whitehurst & Lonigan, 1998). They also are motivated to learn to read. A dialogic reading program combined with a phonetic awareness curriculum for 280 low-income preschoolers produced gains in emergent literacy that were maintained through the end of kindergarten (Whitehurst et al., 1999).

Moderate exposure to educational television can help prepare children for literacy, especially if parents talk with children about what they see. In one study, the more time 3- to 5-year-olds spent watching *Sesame Street,* the more their vocabulary improved (M. L. Rice, Huston, Truglio, & Wright, 1990). In a longitudinal study, the content of television programs viewed at ages 2 and 4 predicted academic skills three years later (Wright et al., 2001).

Checkpoint

Can you . . .

✔ Discuss possible causes, consequences, and treatment of delayed language development?

✔ Explain how social interaction can promote preparation for literacy?

Early Childhood Education

Guidepost 5

What purposes does early childhood education serve, and how do children make the transition to kindergarten?

Going to preschool is an important step, widening a child's physical, cognitive, and social environment. Today more 4-year-olds than ever and even many 3-year-olds are enrolled in early childhood education. The transition to kindergarten, the beginning of "real school," is another momentous step.

Goals and Types of Preschools

In some countries, such as China, preschools are expected to provide academic preparation for schooling. In contrast, most preschools in the United States and many other western countries have followed a "child-centered" philosophy stressing social and emotional growth in line with young children's developmental needs—though some, such as those based on the theories of Piaget or the Italian educator Maria Montessori (refer back to Chapter 1), have a stronger cognitive emphasis.

As part of a debate over how to improve education, pressures have built to offer instruction in basic academic skills in U.S. preschools. Defenders of the traditional developmental approach maintain that academically oriented programs neglect young children's need for exploration and free play and that, although children in such programs may learn more at first, too much teacher-centered instruction may stifle their interest and interfere with self-initiated learning (Elkind, 1986; Zigler, 1987).

What type of preschool is best for children? Studies in the United States support a child-centered, developmental approach. One field study (Marcon, 1999) compared 721 randomly selected, predominantly low-income and African-American 4- and 5-year-olds from three types of preschool classrooms in Washington, D.C.: *child-initiated, academically directed,* and *middle-of-the-road* (a blend of the other two approaches). Children from child-initiated programs, in which they actively directed their own learning experiences, excelled in basic academic skills in all subject areas. They also had more advanced motor skills than the other two groups and scored higher than the middle-of-the-road group in behavioral and communicative skills. These findings suggest that a single, coherent philosophy of education may work better than an attempt to blend diverse approaches and that a child-centered approach seems more effective than an academically oriented one.

These children in a Head Start program are getting a "head start" toward readiness for school. The most successful compensatory education programs start early and have well-trained staff, parental participation, and low staff-to-child ratios.

Compensatory Preschool Programs

Children from deprived socioeconomic backgrounds often enter school at a considerable disadvantage. They may make as much progress as more advantaged classmates, but because they start out behind, they remain behind (Stipek & Ryan, 1997). It has been estimated that more than two-thirds of children in poor urban areas enter school poorly prepared to learn (Zigler, 1998). Since the 1960s, large-scale programs have been developed to help such children compensate for what they have missed and to prepare them for school.

The best-known compensatory preschool program for children of low-income families in the United States is Project Head Start, a federally funded program launched in 1965. Consistent with its "whole child" approach, its goals are not only to enhance cognitive skills, but also to improve physical health and to foster self-confidence, relationships with others, social responsibility, and a sense of dignity and self-worth for the child and the family. The program provides medical, dental, and mental health care, social services, and at least one hot meal a day. Due to inadequate funding, Head Start serves only about 3 out of 5 eligible preschoolers (Children's Defense Fund, 2002b). However, virtually all states now offer their own prekindergarten programs (USDHHS, 2003a).

Has Head Start lived up to its name? Data support its effectiveness in improving school readiness (Ripple et al., 1999; USDHHS, 2003b). Similarly, children who attend the newer state programs tend to show better cognitive and language skills and do better in school than children who do not attend (USDHHS, 2003a). Yet, even though Head Start children make gains in vocabulary, letter recognition, early writing, and early mathematics, their readiness skills remain far below average (USDHHS, 2003b). And, although they do better on intelligence tests than other children from comparable backgrounds, this advantage disappears after they start school (Ripple et al., 1999; Zigler & Styfco, 1993, 1994).

Still, children from Head Start and other compensatory programs are less likely to be placed in special education or to repeat a grade and are more likely to finish high school than low-income children who did not attend such programs (Neisser et al., 1996). "Graduates" of one such program, the Perry Preschool Project, were also much less likely to become juvenile delinquents or to become pregnant in their teens (Berrueta-Clement, Schweinhart, Barnett, Epstein, & Weikart, 1985; Schweinhart, Barnes, & Weikart, 1993; see Chapter 17).

Outcomes are best with earlier and longer-lasting intervention through high quality, center-based programs (Brooks-Gunn, 2003; Reynolds & Temple, 1998; Zigler & Styfco,

1993, 1994, 2001). The most successful Head Start programs have been those with the most parental participation, the best-trained teachers, the lowest staff-to-child ratios, the longest school days and weeks, and the most extensive services (Ramey, 1999).

In 1995, an Early Head Start program began offering child and family development services to pregnant women and to infants and toddlers from birth to age 3. In a preliminary evaluation, 2-year-old participants scored higher on standardized developmental and vocabulary tests, spoke in more complex sentences, and were at less risk of slowed developmental learning than children not in the program. The Early Head Start parents read more to their children, played with them in more structured ways, set more regular bedtimes, and used less physical punishment (Commissioner's Office of Research and Evaluation and Head Start Bureau, 2001).

The Chicago Child Parent Centers, a large-scale, federally funded compensatory program, extends from preschool through third grade. The added years of academic enrichment significantly increased participants' reading achievement and decreased grade retention and special education placement through seventh grade, as compared with children who participated for only two or three years (Reynolds, 1994; Reynolds & Temple, 1998). At age 20, among 989 poverty-level children who had begun the program by age 4, nearly half (49.7 percent) had graduated from high school, as compared with 38.5 percent of a control group who had attended less intensive preschools or no preschool; and 16.9 percent had been arrested for juvenile crimes as compared with 25.1 percent of the control group (Reynolds, Temple, Robertson, & Mann, 2001).

Checkpoint

Can you . . .

✔ Compare goals and effectiveness of varying types of preschool programs?

✔ Assess the benefits of compensatory preschool education?

The Transition to Kindergarten

Originally a year of transition between the relative freedom of home or preschool and the structure of "real school," kindergarten in the United States has become more like first grade. Children spend less time on self-chosen activities and more time on worksheets and preparing to read.

Although some states do not require kindergarten programs or kindergarten attendance (Vecchiotti, 2003), most 5-year-olds attend either a public or private kindergarten. Since the late 1970s, an increasing number of kindergarteners (60 percent in 2001) spend a full day in school, rather than the traditional half day (National Center for Education Statistics, 2004). A practical impetus for this trend is the growing number of single-parent and dual-earner households. In addition, large numbers of children already have experienced preschool or full-time child care and are ready for a more rigorous, time-intensive kindergarten curriculum (Walston & West, 2004).

Full-day kindergarten is especially prevalent in Catholic schools. Among public schools, full-day kindergarten is most common in the south and in urban, small-town, or rural communities, whereas half-day kindergarten remains more prevalent in suburbs and large towns. Poor and minority children, especially black children, are disproportionately likely to spend a full day in kindergarten (National Center for Education Statistics, 2004; Walston & West, 2004).

Do children learn more in full-day kindergarten? According to ongoing longitudinal research sponsored by the U.S. Department of Education on a nationally representative sample of children who started kindergarten in the fall of 1998, public school children in full-day kindergarten are more likely to receive daily instruction in prereading skills, math skills, social studies, and science (Walston & West, 2004) and tend to do better by the end of kindergarten and in the early school years (Vecchiotti, 2003; Walston & West, 2004). However, when private school students are included, no differences between achievement of full-day and half-day students are detectable (West, Denton, & Reaney, 2001); and, by the end of third grade, both groups are substantially equal in reading, math, and science achievement (Rathburn, West, & Germino-Hausken, 2004).

Findings also highlight the importance of the preparation a child receives *before* kindergarten. The resources with which children come to kindergarten—early literacy skills and the richness of the home literacy environment—predict reading achievement in first grade, and these individual differences tend to persist or increase throughout the first two years of school (Denton, West, & Walston, 2003).

Because cutoff birth dates for kindergarten entrance vary among the states, children enter kindergarten at ages ranging from 4 to 6. In addition, as academic and emotional pressures mount, many parents are holding children back for a year, and some states are moving up their cutoff dates in the belief that children whose birthdays are close to the cutoff will be more ready for kindergarten if they wait a year. However, research gives limited support to that idea. Children who are older at kindergarten entry do have a modest initial academic advantage; but, by third grade, that advantage typically disappears (Stipek, 2002; Stipek & Byler, 2001).

Emotional and social adjustment are important factors in readiness for kindergarten and strongly predict school success. More important than knowing the alphabet or being able to count to 20, kindergarten teachers say, are the abilities to sit still, follow directions, wait one's turn, and regulate one's own learning (Blair, 2002; Brooks-Gunn, 2003; Raver, 2002). How well a child adjusts to kindergarten may depend on the child's age, gender, temperament, cognitive and social competencies, and coping skills as well as the support or stress generated by the home, school, and neighborhood environments (Blair, 2002; Ladd, 1996; Ladd, Birch, & Buhs, 1999). Children with extensive preschool experience tend to adjust to kindergarten more easily than those who spent little or no time in preschool (Ladd, 1996).

Proposals have been made to lengthen the school year. When an elementary school in a midsized southeastern city added 30 days to its school year, children who completed kindergarten outperformed their counterparts in a traditional 180-day program on tests of math, reading, general knowledge, and cognitive competence (Frazier & Morrison, 1998).

Checkpoint

Can you . . .

✔ Discuss factors that affect adjustment to kindergarten?

Refocus

- What aspects of preoperational thought are illustrated by Einstein's ideas about the compass?
- What does Einstein's story suggest about the relationship between delayed language development and intelligence? Between memory and intelligence?
- What information in this chapter would explain why Einstein's memory of the gift of a compass stayed with him throughout his life?
- Which do you think would have been more useful in testing Einstein's cognitive abilities: a traditional IQ test or a test based on Vygotsky's concept of the ZPD?
- Which type of preschool described in this chapter do you think would have been best for young Einstein?

The burgeoning physical and cognitive skills of early childhood have psychosocial implications, as we'll see in Chapter 11.

Summary and Key Terms

Piagetian Approach: The Preoperational Child

Guidepost 1 What are typical cognitive advances and immature aspects of preschool children's thinking?

- Children in the preoperational stage show several important advances, as well as some immature aspects of thought.
- The symbolic function enables children to reflect upon people, objects, and events that are not physically present. It is shown in deferred imitation, pretend play, and language.
- Early symbolic development helps preoperational children make more accurate judgments of spatial relationships. They can understand the concept of identity, link cause and effect, categorize living and nonliving things, and understand principles of counting.
- Centration keeps preoperational children from understanding principles of conservation, which develop gradually in middle childhood. Preoperational logic also is limited by irreversibility and a focus on states rather than transformations.
- Preoperational children appear to be less egocentric than Piaget thought; they (and even younger children) are capable of empathy.
- The theory of mind, which develops markedly between the ages of 3 and 5, includes awareness of one's own thought processes, social cognition, understanding that people can hold false beliefs, ability to deceive, ability to distinguish appearance from reality, and ability to distinguish fantasy from reality. Hereditary and environmental influences affect individual differences in theory-of-mind development.

preoperational stage (265) symbolic function (265) transduction (267) animism (267) centration (268) decenter (268) conservation (268) horizontal décalage (268) irreversibility (269) egocentrism (269) theory of mind (270)

Information-Processing Approach: Memory Development

Guidepost 2 What memory abilities expand in early childhood?

- Information-processing models describe three steps in memory: encoding, storage, and retrieval.
- Although sensory memory shows little change with age, the capacity of working memory increases greatly. The central executive controls the flow of information to and from long-term memory.
- At all ages, recognition is better than recall, but both increase during early childhood.
- Early episodic memory is only temporary; it fades or is transferred to generic memory. Autobiographical memory begins at about age 3 or 4 and may be related to early self-recognition ability and language development. According to the social interaction model, children and adults co-construct autobiographical memories by talking about shared experiences.
- Children are more likely to remember unusual activities that they actively participate in. The way adults talk with children about events influences memory formation.

encoding (276) storage (276) retrieval (276) sensory memory (276) working memory (276) central executive (277) long-term memory (277) recognition (277) recall (277) generic memory (277) script (277) episodic memory (277) autobiographical memory (277) social interaction model (279)

Intelligence: Psychometric and Vygotskian Approaches

Guidepost 3 How is preschoolers' intelligence measured, and what factors influence it?

- The two most commonly used psychometric intelligence tests for young children are the Stanford-Binet Intelligence Scale and the Wechsler Preschool and Primary Scale of Intelligence, Revised (WPPSI-III).
- Intelligence test scores may be influenced by social and emotional functioning as well as by parent-child interaction and socioeconomic factors.
- Newer tests based on Vygotsky's concept of the zone of proximal development (ZPD) indicate immediate potential for achievement. Such tests, when combined with scaffolding, can help parents and teachers guide children's progress.

Stanford-Binet Intelligence Scales (280) Wechsler Preschool and Primary Scale of Intelligence, Revised (WPPSI-III) (280)

Language Development

Guidepost 4 How does language improve, and what happens when its development is delayed?

- During early childhood, vocabulary increases greatly, and grammar and syntax become fairly sophisticated. Children become more competent in pragmatics.
- Private speech is normal and common; it may aid in the shift to self-regulation and usually disappears by age 10.
- Causes of delayed language development are unclear. If untreated, language delays may have serious cognitive, social, and emotional consequences.
- Interaction with adults can promote emergent literacy.

fast mapping (282) pragmatics (283) social speech (283) private speech (284) emergent literacy (286)

Early Childhood Education

Guidepost 5 What purposes does early childhood education serve, and how do children make the transition to kindergarten?

- Goals of preschool education vary across cultures. The academic content of early childhood education programs in the United States has increased, but studies support a child-centered approach.
- Compensatory preschool programs have had positive outcomes, but participants generally have not equaled the performance of middle-class children. Compensatory programs that start early and extend into the primary grades have better long-term results.
- Many children today attend full-day kindergarten. Success in kindergarten depends largely on emotional and social adjustment and prekindergarten preparation.

chapter
11

Psychosocial Development in Early Childhood

"I love you,"
said a great mother.
"I love you for what you are
knowing so well what you are.
And I love you more yet, child,
deeper yet than ever, child,
for what you are going to be,
knowing so well you are going far,
knowing your great works are ahead,
ahead and beyond,
yonder and far over yet."

—Carl Sandburg, *The People, Yes,* 1936

Focus *Isabel Allende, Militant Writer*

Isabel Allende

Isabel Allende has been called Latin America's foremost woman writer. Her best-selling novels and short stories, which evoke her imaginative inner world, have been translated into 30 languages and have sold an estimated 11 million copies worldwide. Perhaps her most moving work is *Paula* (1995), the memoir she began scribbling on yellow pads as she sat at the bedside of her 27-year-old daughter, Paula Frías, in a Madrid hospital, waiting for her to awaken from a coma that never lifted. The words Allende poured out were as much a reminiscence of her own tempestuous life as a tribute to her dying daughter.

Isabel Allende was born August 2, 1942, in Lima, Peru. Her father was a Chilean diplomat, a cousin of the Chilean revolutionary hero Salvador Allende, who was assassinated in a military coup in 1973. Her emotional connection with the cause of her oppressed people became the backdrop for much of her later writing. Her major theme is the role of women in a highly patriarchal society.

When Isabel was about 3, her father abandoned her mother, Doña Panchita, in childbirth; Isabel never saw him alive again. Left with no means of support and humiliated by the failure of her marriage, Doña Panchita returned in disgrace with her three young children to her parents' household in Santiago. She found a low-paying job in a bank and supplemented her salary by making hats. There was no divorce in Chile, so the marriage was annulled. "Those were difficult years for my mother," Allende (1995, p. 32) wrote; "she had to contend with poverty, gossip, and the snubs of people who had been her friends." For Isabel, the middle child and only daughter of "an attractive, abandoned woman who had many suitors and no money" (Ojito, 2003, p. E1), her mother's status was an embarrassment; because of it, Isabel once was expelled from a Roman Catholic school.

A second blow to young Isabel was the death of her beloved grandmother. Suddenly her home became dim and cheerless. A small, fearful, isolated child, often left in the care of a harsh, threatening maid, Isabel found refuge in silent games and in the fanciful stories her

Sources of information on Isabel Allende are Agosin (1999), Allende (1995), Ojito (2003), Perera (1995), Piña (1999), Rodden (1999), and Allende's Web site at http://www.isabelallende.com.

mother told at night in the dark. She felt "different," "like an outcast" (Allende, 1995, p. 50), and she had a rebellious streak. Although she loved her mother deeply and wanted to protect her, she did not want to be like her. She wanted to be strong and independent like her grandfather. "I think Tata was always sorry I wasn't a boy," she wrote in *Paula* (p. 37); "had I been, he could have taught me to play jai alai, and use his tools, and hunt." He tacitly condoned the "character-building" tactics of the two bachelor uncles who lived in the household and played rough "games" with the children that today would be considered physically or emotionally abusive. It was during these pivotal early years that Allende's fervent feminism was born. "When I was a little girl," she says, "I felt anger towards my grandfather, my stepfather, and all the men in the family, who had all the advantages while my mother was the victim. . . . She had to please everyone and everyone told her what to do" (Piña, 1999, pp. 174–175).

When Isabel was about 5, Ramón Huidobro, the Chilean consul who had helped the family return to Chile, moved in with Doña Panchita, displacing Isabel and her brothers from their mother's bedroom. It took Isabel years to accept her stepfather. "He raised us with a firm hand and unfailing good humor; he set limits and sent clear messages, without sentimental demonstrations, and without compromise. . . . he put up with my contrariness without trying to buy my esteem or ceding an inch of his authority, until he won me over totally," she writes (Allende, 1995, pp. 48–49).

Through her books, Allende has come to a greater understanding and acceptance of herself and her gender. Many of her characters are extraordinary women who break with tradition despite their place in society. Being a woman, she says, "was like being handicapped in many ways. In that macho culture where I was brought up . . . I would have liked to be a man." Not until she was 40 did she "finally accept that I was always going to . . . be the person I am" (Foster, 1999, p. 107).

• • •

The years from ages 3 to 6 are pivotal ones in children's psychosocial development, as they were for Isabel Allende. A child's emotional development and sense of self are rooted in the experiences of those years. Yet the story of the self is not completed in early childhood; like Allende, we continue to write it even as adults. Allende's story also highlights the importance of the cultural context. As a girl growing up in a male-dominated culture, she faced attitudes very different from what she might have experienced in a less tightly gender-based society.

In this chapter we discuss preschool children's understanding of themselves and their feelings. We see how their sense of male or female identity arises and how it affects their behavior. We describe the activity on which children, at least in industrialized cultures, typically spend most of their time: play. We consider the influence, for good or ill, of what parents do. Finally, we discuss relationships with siblings and other children.

After you have read and studied this chapter, you should be able to answer each of the Guidepost questions that follow. Look for them again in the margins, where they point to important concepts throughout the chapter. To check your understanding of these Guideposts, review the end-of-chapter summary. Checkpoints located at periodic spots throughout the chapter will help you verify your understanding of what you have read.

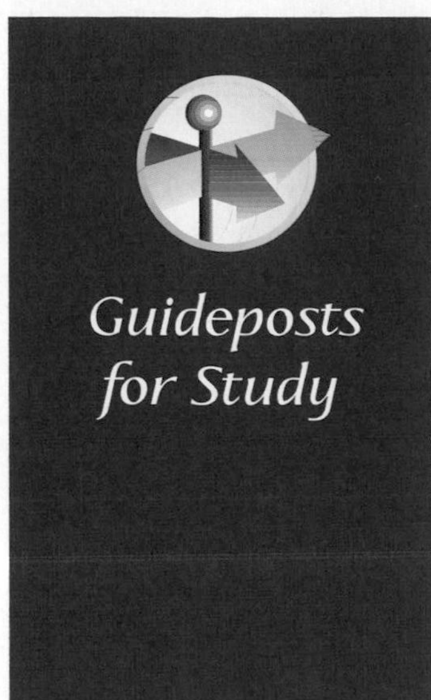

Guideposts for Study

1. How does the self-concept develop during early childhood, and how do children advance in understanding and regulating their emotions?
2. How do young children develop initiative and self-esteem?
3. How do boys and girls become aware of the meaning of gender, and what explains differences in behavior between the sexes?
4. How do preschoolers play, and how does play contribute to and reflect development?
5. How do parenting practices influence development?
6. Why do young children help or hurt others, and why do they develop fears?
7. How do young children get along with (or without) siblings?
8. How do young children choose playmates and friends, and why are some children more popular than others?

The Developing Self

Guidepost 1

How does the self-concept develop during early childhood, and how do children advance in understanding and regulating their emotions?

"Who in the world am I? Ah, *that's* the great puzzle," said Alice in Wonderland, after her size had abruptly changed—again. Solving Alice's "puzzle" is a lifelong process of getting to know one's self.

The Self-Concept and Cognitive Development

The **self-concept** is our image of ourselves. It is what we believe about who we are—our total picture of our abilities and traits. It is "a *cognitive construction,* . . . a system of descriptive and evaluative representations about the self," that determines how we feel about ourselves and guides our actions (Harter, 1996, p. 207). The sense of self also has a social aspect: children incorporate into their self-image their growing understanding of how others see them.

self-concept Sense of self; descriptive and evaluative mental picture of one's abilities and traits.

The picture of the self comes into focus in toddlerhood, as children develop self-awareness (refer back to Chapter 8). The self-concept becomes clearer and more compelling as a person gains in cognitive abilities and deals with the developmental tasks of childhood, of adolescence, and then of adulthood.

Early Self-Concept Development: The Continuous Self

How does the self-concept change in early childhood? A shift in self-awareness may occur near the age of 4, as autobiographical memory and a more sophisticated theory of mind develop. When 3½- and 4-year-olds were shown a videotape or photograph, taken a few minutes earlier, of a researcher placing a large sticker on their heads—an act of which they had been unaware—the children instantly reached up to feel and remove the sticker. Two-year-olds and younger 3-year-olds did not do that. Yet when shown the same thing happening in a mirror, the younger children did seem aware that a sticker was on their heads.

Does this mean that these children recognized themselves in a mirror but not in a photograph or videotape? That does not seem likely. Nor does it seem likely that they did not remember participating in a photograph session a few minutes earlier. A likelier explanation is that because younger children's memories are generic rather than autobiographical (refer back to Chapter 10), they may not have thought of the events in the videotape or photograph as having happened to *them* (Povinelli, Landau, & Perilloux, 1996).

Self-Definition: A Neo-Piagetian View

self-definition Cluster of characteristics used to describe oneself.

By age 4, Jason's attempts at **self-definition** are becoming more comprehensive as he begins to identify a cluster of characteristics to describe himself:

> My name is Jason and I live in a big house with my mother and father and sister, Lisa. I have a kitty that's orange and a television set in my own room. . . . I like pizza and I have a nice teacher. I can count up to 100, want to hear me? I love my dog, Skipper. I can climb to the top of the jungle gym, I'm not scared! Just happy. You can't be happy *and* scared—no way! I have brown hair, and I go to preschool. I'm really strong. I can lift this chair, watch me! (Harter, 1996, p. 208)

The way Jason describes himself is typical of U.S. children his age. He talks mostly about concrete, observable behaviors; external characteristics, such as physical features; preferences; possessions; and members of his household. He mentions particular skills (running and climbing) rather than general abilities (being athletic). His self-descriptions are unrealistically positive, and they frequently spill over into demonstrations; what he *thinks* about himself is almost inseparable from what he *does.* Not until middle childhood (around age 7) will he describe himself in terms of generalized traits, such as *popular, smart,* or *dumb;* recognize that he can have conflicting emotions; and be self-critical while holding a positive overall self-concept.

During the past 25 years, researchers have become interested in pinpointing the intermediate changes that make up this "age 5 to 7 shift." An analysis based on neo-Piagetian theory (Case, 1985, 1992; Fischer, 1980) describes the 5 to 7 shift as occurring in three steps, which actually form a continuous progression.* At 4, Jason is at the first step: his statements about himself are **single representations**—isolated, one-dimensional items. His thinking jumps from particular to particular, without logical connections. At this stage he cannot imagine having two emotions at once ("You can't be happy *and* scared"). He cannot decenter, in part because of his limited short-term memory capacity (see Chapter 13), and so he cannot consider different aspects of himself at the same time. His thinking is all-or-nothing. He cannot acknowledge that his **real self**, the person he actually is, is not the same as his **ideal self**, the person he would like to be. So he describes himself as a paragon of virtue and ability.

single representations In neo-Piagetian terminology, first stage in development of self-definition, in which children describe themselves in terms of individual, unconnected characteristics and in all-or-nothing terms.

real self Self one actually is.

ideal self Self one would like to be.

At about age 5 or 6, Jason moves up to the second step, as he begins to link one aspect of himself to another: "I can run fast, and I can climb high. I'm also strong. I can throw a ball real far, I'm going to be on a team some day!" (Harter, 1996, p. 215). However, these **representational mappings**—logical connections among parts of his image of himself—are still expressed in completely positive, all-or-nothing terms. Since good and bad are opposites, he cannot see how he might be good at some things and not at others.

representational mappings In neo-Piagetian terminology, second stage in development of self-definition, in which a child makes logical connections between aspects of the self but still sees these characteristics in all-or-nothing terms.

The third step, *representational systems,* takes place in middle childhood (see Chapter 14), when children begin to integrate specific features of the self into a general, multidimensional concept. As all-or-nothing thinking declines, Jason's self-descriptions will become more balanced ("I'm good at hockey but bad at arithmetic").

Cultural Differences in Self-Description

Does culture affect young children's self-concept? Research suggests that it does. Much as parents help children construct culturally defined autobiographical memories (refer back to Chapter 10), they subtly transmit, through everyday conversations, cultural ideas and beliefs about how to define the self. For example, Chinese parents tend to encourage *interdependent* aspects of the self: compliance with authority, appropriate conduct, humility, and a sense of belonging to the community. European-American parents encourage *independent* aspects of the self: individuality, self-expression, and self-esteem. These differing cultural values influence the way children in each culture perceive themselves (Wang, 2004).

*This discussion of children's developing understanding of themselves from age 4 on, including their understanding of their emotions, is indebted to Susan Harter (1990, 1993, 1996, 1998).

A comparative study of 180 European-American and Chinese preschoolers, kindergartners, and second graders (Wang, 2004) found that children absorb differing cultural styles of self-definition as early as age 3 or 4, and these differences increase with age. European-American children, like European-American adults, tend to describe themselves in terms of personal attributes and beliefs ("I am big"), whereas Chinese children, like Chinese adults, talk more about social categories and relationships ("I have a sister"). European-American children and adults more often describe themselves in terms of personality traits and tendencies ("I'm good at sports"), whereas Chinese children and adults describe specific, overt behaviors ("I play Snowmoon with my neighbor"). Finally, European-American children and adults tend to put themselves in an unqualifiedly positive light ("I am smart"), whereas Chinese children and adults describe themselves more neutrally ("I sometimes forget my manners").

Understanding and Regulating Emotions

"I hate you!" Maya, age 5, shouts to her mother. "You're a mean mommy!" Angry because her mother sent her to her room for pinching her baby brother, Maya cannot imagine ever loving her mother again. "Aren't you ashamed of yourself for making the baby cry?" her father asks Maya a little later. Maya nods, but only because she knows what response he wants. In truth, she feels a jumble of emotions—not the least of which is feeling sorry for herself.

Understanding and regulating their own emotions contributes to children's social competence, their ability to get along with others (Denham et al., 2003). It helps them guide their behavior and talk about feelings (Laible & Thompson, 1998). Understanding their emotions enables them to control the way they show their feelings and to be sensitive to how others feel (Garner & Power, 1996). As we will discuss in a later section, it even affects the types of play they engage in (Spinrad et al., 2004). Much of this development occurs during the preschool years (Denham et al., 2003).

Preschoolers can talk about their feelings and often can discern the feelings of others, and they understand that emotions are connected with experiences and desires (Saarni, Mumme, & Campos, 1998). By age 3, children know that if someone gets what he wants, he will be happy, and if not, he will be sad (Wellman & Woolley, 1990). However, they still lack a full understanding of such self-directed emotions as guilt, shame, and pride, and they have trouble reconciling conflicting emotions, such as being happy about getting a new bicycle but being disappointed because it's the wrong color (Kestenbaum & Gelman, 1995).

Emotions Directed Toward the Self

As we discussed in Chapter 8, emotions directed toward the self typically develop by the end of the third year, after children gain self-awareness and accept the standards of behavior their parents have set. Violating accepted standards can bring shame or guilt or both; living up to, or surpassing, standards can bring pride. But even children a few years older often lack the cognitive sophistication to *recognize* these emotions and what brings them on—a necessary step toward emotional control.

In one study (Harter, 1993), 4- to 8-year-olds were told two stories. In the first story, a child takes a few coins from a jar after being told not to do so; in the second story, a child performs a difficult gymnastic feat—a flip on the bars. Each story was presented in two versions: one in which a parent sees the child doing the act and another in which no one sees the child. The children were asked how they and the parent would feel in each circumstance.

The answers revealed a gradual progression in understanding of feelings about the self (Harter, 1996). At ages 4 to 5, children did not say that either they or their parents would feel pride or shame. Instead they used such terms as "worried" or "scared" (for the money jar incident) and "excited" or "happy" (about the gymnastic accomplishment). At 5 to 6, children said their parents would be ashamed or proud of them but did not acknowledge feeling these emotions themselves. At 6 to 7, children said they would feel proud or ashamed, but only if they were observed. Not until ages 7 to 8 (see Chapter 14) did children say that they would feel ashamed or proud of themselves even if no one saw them.

Checkpoint

Can you . . .

- ✔ Trace self-concept development between ages 3 and 6 and discuss cultural influences on self-definition?
- ✔ Describe the typical progression in understanding of (1) emotions directed toward the self and (2) simultaneous emotions?

Simultaneous Emotions

Part of the confusion in younger children's understanding of their feelings is difficulty recognizing that they can experience contrary emotional reactions at the same time, as Isabel Allende did toward her grandfather, both resenting and admiring him. Most children acquire a more sophisticated understanding of simultaneous emotions during middle childhood (Harter, 1996; see Chapter 14).

Individual differences in understanding conflicting emotions are evident by age 3. In one study, 3-year-olds who could identify whether a face looked happy or sad and who could tell how a puppet felt when enacting a situation involving happiness, sadness, anger, or fear were better able at the end of kindergarten to explain a story character's conflicting emotions. These children tended to come from families that often discussed why people behave as they do (J. R. Brown & Dunn, 1996).

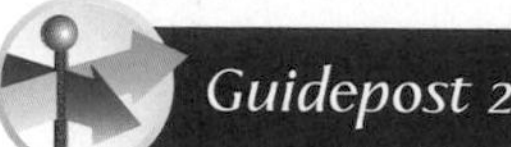

Guidepost 2

How do young children develop initiative and self-esteem?

Erikson: Initiative Versus Guilt

initiative versus guilt Erikson's third stage in psychosocial development, in which children balance the urge to pursue goals with moral reservations that may prevent carrying them out.

The need to deal with conflicting feelings about the self is at the heart of Erikson's (1950) third stage of personality development: **initiative versus guilt.** The conflict arises from the growing sense of purpose, which spurs a child to plan and carry out activities, and the growing pangs of conscience the child may have about such plans.

Preschool children can do—and want to do—more and more. At the same time, they are learning that some of the things they want to do meet social approval while others do not. How do they reconcile their desire to *do* with their desire for approval?

This conflict marks a split between two parts of the personality: the part that remains a child, full of an exuberant desire to try new things and test new powers, and the part that is becoming an adult, constantly examining the propriety of motives and actions. Children who learn how to regulate these opposing drives develop the "virtue" of *purpose,* the courage to envision and pursue goals without being unduly inhibited by guilt or fear of punishment (Erikson, 1982).

If this conflict is not resolved adequately, said Erikson, a child may turn into an adult who is constantly striving for success or showing off; is inhibited and unspontaneous or self-righteous and intolerant; or suffers from impotence or psychosomatic illness. With ample opportunities to do things on their own—but under guidance and consistent limits—children can attain a healthy balance between the tendency to overdo competition and achievement and the tendency to be repressed and guilt ridden.

Self-Esteem

self-esteem Judgment a person makes about his or her self-worth.

Self-esteem is the self-evaluative part of the self-concept, the judgment children make about their overall worth. From a neo-Piagetian perspective, self-esteem is based on children's growing cognitive ability to describe and define themselves.

Developmental Changes in Self-Esteem

Children do not generally articulate a concept of self-worth until about age 8, but younger children show by their behavior that they have one. Thus, attempts to measure young children's self-esteem often incorporate teacher and parent reports (Davis-Kean & Sandler, 2001) or puppets and doll play (Measelle, Ablow, Cowan, & Cowan, 1998) in addition to self-reports. In a study in Belgium (Verschueren, Buyck, & Marcoen, 2001), researchers measured 5-year-olds' self-representations using two measures: (1) the Harter (1985b) Self-Perception Profile for Children (SPPC), which covers overall (global) self-worth as well as specific perceptions about physical appearance, scholastic and athletic competence, social acceptance, and behavioral conduct; and (2) the Puppet Interview (Cassidy, 1988; Verschueren, Marcoen, & Schoefs, 1996), in which puppets are used to reveal a child's perception of what another person thinks of him or her. Children's positive or negative self-perceptions at age 5 tended to predict their self-perceptions and socioemotional functioning (as reported by teachers) at age 8.

But although young children can make judgments about their competence at various activities, they are not yet able to rank them in importance. Also, they tend to accept the judgments of adults, who often give positive, uncritical feedback, and thus may overrate their abilities. Self-esteem in early childhood tends to be all-or-none: "I am good" or "I am bad" (Harter, 1990, 1993, 1996, 1998). Not until middle childhood do personal evaluations of competence (based on internalization of parental and societal standards) normally become critical in shaping and maintaining a realistic sense of self-worth (Harter, 1990, 1996, 1998; see Chapter 14).

Contingent Self-Esteem: The "Helpless" Pattern

When self-esteem is high, a child is motivated to achieve. However, if self-esteem is *contingent* on success, children may view failure or criticism as an indictment of their worth and may feel helpless to do better. About one-third to one-half of preschoolers, kindergartners, and first-graders show elements of this "helpless" pattern: self-denigration or self-blame, negative emotion, lack of persistence, and lowered expectations of themselves (Burhans & Dweck, 1995; Ruble & Dweck, 1995). Instead of trying a different way to complete a puzzle, as a child with unconditional self-esteem might do, "helpless" children feel ashamed and give up or go back to an easier puzzle they have already done. They do not expect to succeed, and so they do not try. Whereas older children who fail may conclude that they are "dumb," preschoolers interpret poor performance as a sign of being "bad," and they believe that "badness" is permanent. This sense of being a bad person may persist into adulthood.

Individual differences in self-esteem, then, may hinge on whether children think their attributes are fixed or can be changed (Harter, 1998). Children with high self-esteem tend to attribute failure or disappointment to factors outside themselves or to the need to try harder. Children with contingent self-esteem become demoralized, believing there is nothing they can do to improve (Erdley, Cain, Loomis, Dumas-Hines, & Dweck, 1997; Pomerantz & Saxon, 2001). To avoid fostering the contingent, or "helpless," pattern, parents and teachers can give a child specific, focused feedback rather than criticize a child as a person (Burhans & Dweck, 1995).

What's your view ?

- Can you think of ways in which your parents or other adults helped you develop self-esteem?

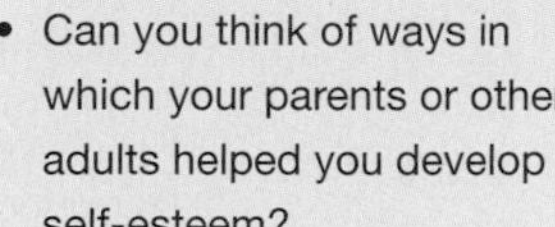

Checkpoint

Can you . . .

✔ Explain the significance of Erikson's third crisis of personality development?

✔ Tell how young children's self-esteem differs from that of school-age children?

Gender

Gender identity, awareness of one's femaleness or maleness and all it implies in a particular society, is an important aspect of the developing self-concept. Isabel Allende's awareness of what it meant to be a female in a "man's world" went back to her early years.

How different are young boys and girls? What causes those differences? How do children develop gender identity, and how does it affect their attitudes and behavior?

Guidepost 3

How do boys and girls become aware of the meaning of gender, and what explains differences in behavior between the sexes?

gender identity Awareness, developed in early childhood, that one is male or female.

Gender Differences

Gender differences are psychological or behavioral differences between males and females. How pronounced are these differences?

Measurable differences between baby boys and girls are few. Girls are less vulnerable than boys: they are less reactive to stress and more likely to survive infancy (Keenan & Shaw, 1997). On the other hand, baby boys, being a bit longer and heavier, may be slightly stronger. One of the earliest *behavioral* differences, appearing between 1 and 2 years of age, is in preferences for toys and play activities and for playmates of the same sex (Campbell, Shirley, Heywood, & Crook, 2000; Serbin et al., 2001; Turner & Gervai, 1995).

Although some gender differences become more pronounced after age 3, boys and girls on average remain more alike than different. The main difference is in boys' more aggressive behavior, discussed later in this chapter. Also, most studies find that girls are more empathic and helpful (Keenan & Shaw, 1997), and some find that girls are more compliant and cooperative with parents and seek adult approval more than boys do (N. Eisenberg,

Fabes, Schaller, & Miller, 1989; M. L. Hoffman, 1977; Maccoby, 1980; Turner & Gervai, 1995).

Overall, intelligence test scores show no gender differences (Keenan & Shaw, 1997); the most widely used tests are designed to eliminate gender bias (Neisser et al., 1996). However, there are differences in specific abilities. Females tend to do better at verbal tasks (but not analogies), at mathematical computation, and at tasks requiring fine motor and perceptual skills. Males excel in most spatial abilities and in abstract mathematical and scientific reasoning (Halpern, 1997). Some of these cognitive differences, which seem to exist across cultures, begin early in life. Girls' superiority in perceptual speed and verbal fluency appears during infancy and toddlerhood, and boys' greater ability to mentally manipulate figures and shapes and solve mazes becomes evident early in the preschool years. Other differences do not become apparent until preadolescence or beyond (Halpern, 1997; Levine, Huttenlocher, Taylor, & Langrock, 1999).

As toddlers, boys and girls are equally likely to hit, bite, and throw temper tantrums, and they are just as likely to show "difficult" temperament. Around age 4, however, problem behavior diminishes in girls, whereas boys tend to get in trouble or "act up." This difference persists into adolescence, when girls become more prone to anxiety and depression (see Chapter 15). Possible reasons for this divergence may lie in the biological and cognitive differences just discussed. Lower reactivity to stress may help girls control frustration or anger, and their greater facility with language may enable them to communicate their feelings in healthier ways. Another reason may be a difference in the way boys and girls are socialized. Girls, more than boys, are taught to control themselves, to share toys, and to think about how their actions affect others; and their greater empathic ability may help them internalize social standards (Keenan & Shaw, 1997).

Checkpoint ✓

Can you . . .

✔ Summarize the main behavioral and cognitive differences between boys and girls?

We need to remember, of course, that gender differences are valid for large groups of boys and girls but not necessarily for individuals. By knowing a child's sex, we cannot predict whether that *particular* boy or girl will be faster, stronger, smarter, more obedient, or more assertive than another child.

Perspectives on Gender Development: Nature and Nurture

What accounts for gender differences, and why do some of them emerge with age? The most influential explanations, until recently, centered on the differing experiences and social expectations that boys and girls meet almost from birth (Halpern, 1997; Neisser et al., 1996). These experiences and expectations concern three related aspects of gender identity: *gender roles, gender-typing,* and *gender stereotypes.*

gender roles Behaviors, interests, attitudes, skills, and traits that a culture considers appropriate for males or for females.

Gender roles are the behaviors, interests, attitudes, skills, and personality traits that a culture considers appropriate for males or females. All societies have gender roles. Historically, in most cultures, as in Isabel Allende's Chile, women have been expected to devote most of their time to caring for the household and children, and men have been providers and protectors. Women have been expected to be compliant and nurturant; men, to be active, aggressive, and competitive. It is these culturally defined roles that Allende rebelled against. Today, gender roles in western cultures have become more diverse and more flexible.

gender-typing Socialization process whereby children, at an early age, learn appropriate gender roles.

gender stereotypes Preconceived generalizations about male or female role behavior.

Gender-typing (refer back to Chapter 8), the acquisition of a gender role, takes place early in childhood; but children vary in the degree to which they become gender-typed. **Gender stereotypes** are preconceived generalizations about male or female behavior ("All females are passive and dependent; all males are aggressive and independent"). Gender stereotypes pervade many cultures. They appear to some degree in children as young as 2 or 3, increase during the preschool years, and reach a peak at age 5 (Campbell, Shirley, & Candy, 2004; Ruble & Martin, 1998). Preschoolers—and even older children—often attribute positive qualities to their own sex and negative qualities to the other sex. Still, among preschoolers, *both* boys and girls call boys strong, fast, and cruel and girls fearful and helpless (Ruble & Martin, 1998).

How do children acquire gender roles, and why do they adopt gender stereotypes? Are these purely social constructs, or do they reflect underlying biological differences between males and females? Do social and cultural influences create gender differences or merely

Table 11-1 Four Perspectives on Gender Development

Theories	Major Theorists	Key Processes	Basic Beliefs
Biological Approach		Genetic, neurological, and hormonal activity	Many or most behavioral differences between the sexes can be traced to biological differences.
Psychoanalytic Approach			
Psychosexual theory	Sigmund Freud	Resolution of unconscious emotional conflict	Gender identity occurs when child identifies with same-sex parent.
Cognitive Approach			
Cognitive-developmental theory	Lawrence Kohlberg	Self-categorization	Once a child learns she is a girl or he is a boy, child sorts information about behavior by gender and acts accordingly.
Gender-schema theory	Sandra Bem, Carol Lynn Martin, & Charles F. Halverson	Self-categorization based on processing of cultural information	Child organizes information about what is considered appropriate for a boy or a girl on the basis of what a particular culture dictates and behaves accordingly. Child sorts by gender because the culture dictates that gender is an important schema.
Socialization Approach			
Social cognitive theory	Albert Bandura	Modeling, reinforcement, and teaching	Gender-typing is a result of interpretation, evaluation, and internalization of socially transmitted standards.

accentuate them? Today investigators are uncovering evidence of biological explanations for gender differences: genetic, hormonal, and neurological. However, biological and sociocultural explanations are not necessarily either-or. Both nature and nurture probably play important parts in what it means to be male or female. Biological influences are not necessarily universal, inevitable, or unchangeable; nor are social and cultural influences easily overcome.

Let's look at four perspectives on gender development (summarized in Table 11-1): *biological, psychoanalytic, cognitive,* and *socialization-based* approaches. Each of these perspectives can contribute to our understanding; none fully explains why boys and girls turn out differently in some respects and not in others.

Biological Approach

The existence of similar gender roles in many cultures suggests that some gender differences, at least, may be biologically based. Hormones in the bloodstream before or about the time of birth may affect the developing brain and influence these differences. The male hormone testosterone, along with low levels of the neurotransmitter serotonin, may be related to aggressiveness, competitiveness, and dominance, perhaps through action on such brain structures as the hypothalamus and amygdala—though evidence of such a relationship is mixed (Bernhardt, 1997; Book, Starzyk, & Quinsey, 2001; Ramirez, 2003). In addition, scientists have identified 54 genes that may explain differences in anatomy and function between the brains of male and female mice. If similar genetic differences exist in humans, then sexual identity may be hardwired into the brain even before sexual organs form and hormonal activity begins (Dewing, Shi, Horvath, & Vilain, 2003).

By age 5, when the brain reaches approximate adult size, boys' brains are about 10 percent larger than girls' brains, mostly because boys have more gray matter in the cerebral cortex, whereas girls have greater neuronal density. What these findings may tell us about brain organization and functioning is unknown (Reiss, Abrams, Singer, Ross, & Denckla, 1996). We do have evidence that size differences in the *corpus callosum*, the band of tissue joining the right and left hemispheres, are correlated with verbal fluency (Hines, Chiu, McAdams, Bentler, & Lipcamon, 1992). Since girls have a larger corpus callosum, better coordination between the two hemispheres may help explain girls' superior verbal abilities (Halpern, 1997).

Other research focuses on children with unusual hormonal histories. Girls with a disorder called *congenital adrenal hyperplasia (CAH)* have high prenatal levels of *androgens* (male sex hormones). Although raised as girls, they tend to develop into "tomboys," showing preferences for "boys' toys," rough play, and male playmates, as well as strong spatial skills. *Estrogens* (female hormones), on the other hand, seem to have less influence on boys' gender-typed behavior. Since these studies are natural experiments, they cannot establish cause and effect; other factors besides hormonal differences, such as early interactions with parents, may play a role (Ruble & Martin, 1998).

Perhaps the most dramatic examples of biologically based research have to do with infant boys who have been medically assigned to female sex because of missing or ambiguous sexual organs (part male and part female). In the case of a 7-month-old boy whose penis was accidentally cut off during circumcision, the decision was made at 17 months to rear the child as a girl, and four months later doctors performed surgical reconstruction (Money & Ehrhardt, 1972). However, the child later rejected female identity and, at puberty, switched to living as a male (Diamond & Sigmundson, 1997).

Similarly, in a study of 27 genetically male children born without penises, although 25 of them were raised as girls, in childhood they considered themselves boys and engaged in rough-and-tumble play, suggesting that hormones do play a powerful role in gender identity (Reiner, 2000). A related study underlines the difficulty of predicting whether sex assignment at birth will "take." Fourteen genetically male children born without normal penises but with testes were legally and surgically assigned to female sex during the first month of life and were raised as girls. Between ages 5 and 16, however, eight of them declared themselves male (though two were living ambiguously). Five declared unwavering female identity but expressed difficulty fitting in with other girls; and one, after learning that she had been born male, refused to discuss the subject with anyone. Meanwhile, two boys whose parents had refused the initial sexual assignment remained male (Reiner & Gearhart, 2004). The implicit lesson of all these studies is that gender identity may be rooted in chromosomal structure or prenatal development and cannot easily be changed.

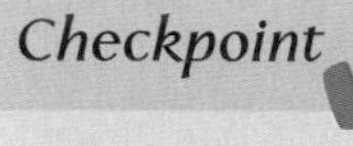

Checkpoint

Can you . . .

✔ Assess evidence for biological explanations of gender differences?

Psychoanalytic Approach

"Dad, where will you live when I grow up and marry Mommy?" asks Timmy, age 4. From the psychoanalytic perspective, Timmy's question is part of his acquisition of gender identity. That process, according to Freud, is one of **identification,** the adoption of characteristics, beliefs, attitudes, values, and behaviors of the parent of the same sex. Freud and other classical psychoanalytic theorists considered identification an important personality development of early childhood; some social learning theorists also have used the term.

identification In Freudian theory, process by which a young child adopts characteristics, beliefs, attitudes, values, and behaviors of the parent of the same sex.

According to Freud, identification will occur for Timmy when he represses or gives up the wish to possess the parent of the other sex (his mother) and identifies with the parent of the same sex (his father). But although this explanation for gender development has been influential, it has been difficult to test and has little research support (Maccoby, 1992). Despite some evidence that preschoolers tend to act more affectionately toward the other-sex parent and more aggressively toward the same-sex parent (Westen, 1998), most developmental psychologists today favor other explanations.

Cognitive Approach

Sarah figures out she is a girl because people call her a girl. As she continues to observe and think about her world, she concludes that she will always be female. She comes to understand gender the same way she comes to understand everything else: by actively thinking about and constructing her own gender-typing. This is the heart of Lawrence Kohlberg's (1966) cognitive-developmental theory.

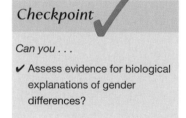

According to Kohlberg and other cognitive theorists, children actively search for cues about gender in their social world—who does what, and who can play with whom. As children come to realize which gender they belong to, they adopt behaviors they perceive as consistent with being male or female. Thus, 3-year-old Sarah prefers dolls to trucks because she sees girls playing with dolls and therefore views playing with dolls as consistent with her idea of herself as a girl. And she plays mostly with other girls, whom she assumes will share her interests (Ruble & Martin, 1998; Martin & Ruble, 2004).

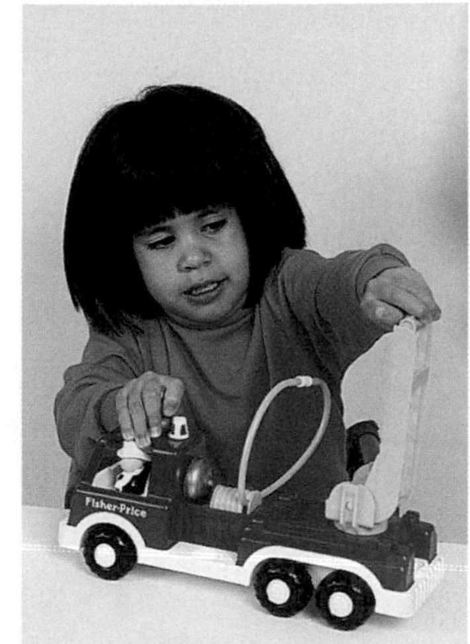

Anna's enjoyment of her truck shows that she is not restricted in her play by gender stereotypes. According to Bem's gender-schema theory, parents can help their children avoid such stereotypes by encouraging them to pursue their own interests, even when these interests are unconventional for their sex.

The acquisition of gender roles, said Kohlberg, hinges on **gender constancy,** more recently called *sex-category constancy*—a child's realization that his or her sex will always be the same. Once children realize they are permanently male or female, they adopt what they see as behaviors appropriate to their sex. Gender constancy seems to develop in three stages: *gender identity, gender stability,* and *gender consistency* (Ruble & Martin, 1998; Szkrybalo & Ruble, 1999). *Gender identity* (awareness of one's own gender and that of others) typically arrives between ages 2 and 3. *Gender stability* comes when a girl realizes that she will grow up to be a woman, and a boy that he will grow up to be a man—in other words, that gender remains the same across time. Children at this stage may base judgments about gender on superficial external appearances and stereotyped behaviors. Finally—sometime between ages 3 and 7 or even later—comes *gender consistency:* the realization that a girl remains a girl even if she has a short haircut and wears pants, and a boy remains a boy even if he has long hair and earrings.

Much research challenges Kohlberg's view that gender-typing depends on gender constancy. Long before children attain the final stage of gender constancy, they show gender-typed preferences (Bussey & Bandura, 1992; Ruble & Martin, 1998). They categorize activities and objects by gender, know a lot about what males and females do, and often acquire gender-appropriate behaviors (G. D. Levy & Carter, 1989; Luecke-Aleksa, Anderson, Collins, & Schmitt, 1995). As we have mentioned, gender preferences in toys and playmates appear as early as 12 to 24 months. However, gender-typing may be heightened by the more sophisticated understanding that gender constancy brings (Martin & Ruble, 2004).

gender constancy Awareness that one will always be male or female. Also called *sex-category constancy.*

gender-schema theory Theory, proposed by Bem, that children socialize themselves in their gender roles by developing a mentally organized network of information about what it means to be male or female in a particular culture.

Gender-schema theory, which combines elements of cognitive-developmental and social learning theory, seeks to describe a cognitive mechanism by which gender learning and gender-typing occur. Among its leading proponents is Sandra Bem (1983, 1985, 1993); others are Carol Lynn Martin and Charles F. Halverson (1981). A *schema* (much like Piaget's *schemes*) is a mentally organized network of information that influences a wide variety of behaviors. According to gender-schema theory, children begin (very likely in infancy) to categorize events and people, organizing their observations around the schema, or category, of gender. They organize information on this basis because they see that their society classifies people that way: males and females wear different clothes, play with different toys, and use separate bathrooms. Once children know what sex they are, they take on gender roles by developing a concept of what it means to be male or female in their culture. Children then match their own behavior to their culture's gender schema—what boys and girls are "supposed" to be and do.

According to this theory, gender schemas promote gender stereotypes by influencing judgments about behavior. When a new boy his age moves in next door, 4-year-old Brandon knocks on his door, carrying a toy truck. He assumes that the new boy will like the same toys he likes. However, there is little evidence that gender schemas are at the root of this assumption. Another problem with both gender-schema theory and Kohlberg's theory is that gender-stereotyping does not always become stronger with increased gender knowledge; in fact, the opposite is often true (Bussey & Bandura, 1999).

A current view, which has research support, is that gender-stereotyping rises and then falls in a developmental pattern (Ruble & Martin, 1998; Welch-Ross & Schmidt, 1996). Around ages 4 to 6, when, according to gender-schema theory, children are constructing and then consolidating their gender schemas, they notice and remember only information consistent with these schemas and even exaggerate it. In fact, they tend to *mis*remember information that challenges gender stereotypes, such as photos of a girl sawing wood or a boy cooking, and to insist that the genders in the photos were the other way around. Young children are quick to accept gender labels; when told that an unfamiliar toy is for the other sex, they will drop it like a hot potato, and they expect others to do the same (C. L. Martin, Eisenbud, & Rose, 1995; Martin & Ruble, 2004; Ruble & Martin, 1998).

To observe two preschoolers and the toys and play activities they prefer, watch the "Sex-Typed Play" video in Chapter 11 of your CD.

By ages 5 and 6, children develop a repertoire of rigid stereotypes about gender that they apply to themselves and others. A boy will pay more attention to what he considers "boys' toys" and a girl to "girls' toys." A boy will expect to do better at "boy things" than at "girl things," and if he does try, say, to dress a doll, he will be all thumbs. Then, around age 7 or 8, schemas become more complex as children begin to take in and integrate contradictory information, such as the fact that many girls wear pants. Children develop more complex beliefs about gender and become more flexible in their views about gender roles (Martin & Ruble, 2004; Ruble & Martin, 1998; M. G. Taylor, 1996; Trautner et al., 2003).

Cognitive approaches to gender development have made an important contribution by exploring how children think about gender and what they know about it at various ages. However, these approaches may not fully explain the link between knowledge and conduct. There is disagreement about precisely what mechanism prompts children to act out gender roles and why some children become more strongly gender-typed than others (Bussey & Bandura, 1992, 1999; Martin & Ruble, 2004; Ruble & Martin, 1998). Some investigators point to socialization.

Socialization-Based Approach

social cognitive theory Albert Bandura's expansion of social learning theory; holds that children learn gender roles through socialization.

Albert Bandura's (1986; Bussey & Bandura, 1999) **social cognitive theory,** an expanded version of social learning theory, sees gender identity as the outcome of a complex array of interacting influences, personal and social. Socialization—the way a child interprets and internalizes experiences with parents, teachers, peers, and cultural institutions—plays a central part.

As in traditional social learning theory, children initially acquire gender roles by observing models. Children generally choose models they see as powerful or nurturing. Typically, one model is a parent, often of the same sex, but children also pattern their behavior after other adults or after peers. (Isabel Allende, uncomfortable with the subordinate roles of the women she saw, sought to model herself after her grandfather.) Behavioral feedback, together with direct teaching by parents and other adults, reinforces gender-typing. A boy who models his behavior after his father or male peers is commended for acting "like a boy." A girl gets compliments on a pretty dress or hairstyle.

As we discussed in Chapter 8, socialization begins in infancy, long before a conscious understanding of gender begins to form. Gradually, as children begin to regulate their own activities, standards of behavior become internalized. A child no longer needs praise, rebukes, or a model's presence to act in socially appropriate ways. Children feel good about themselves when they live up to their internal standards and feel bad if they do not. A substantial part of the shift from socially guided control to self-regulation of gender-related behavior may take place between ages 3 and 4 (Bussey & Bandura, 1992). Let's look more closely at how parents, peers, and the media influence this development.

What's your view?

- Where would you place your own views on the continuum between the following extremes? Explain.
  1. Family A thinks girls should wear only ruffly dresses and boys should never wash dishes or cry.
  2. Family Z treats sons and daughters exactly alike, without making any references to the children's sex.

Family Influences Boys tend to be more strongly gender-socialized concerning play preferences than girls. Parents, especially fathers, generally show more discomfort if a boy plays with a doll than if a girl plays with a truck (Lytton & Romney, 1991; Ruble & Martin, 1998; Sandnabba & Ahlberg, 1999). Girls have more freedom than boys in their clothes, games, and choice of playmates (Miedzian, 1991).

In egalitarian households, the father's role in gender socialization seems especially important (Fagot & Leinbach, 1995). In an observational study of 4-year-olds in British and Hungarian cities, boys and girls whose fathers did more housework and child care were less aware of gender stereotypes and engaged in less gender-typed play (Turner & Gervai, 1995). Gender-role socialization also tends to be untraditional in single-parent families, in which a mother or father must play both the customary masculine and feminine roles (Leve & Fagot, 1997).

Peer Influences Anna, at age 5, insisted on dressing in a new way. She wanted to wear leggings with a skirt over them and boots—indoors and out. When her mother asked her why, Anna replied, "Because Katie dresses like this—and Katie's the king of the girls!"

Even in early childhood, the peer group is a major influence on gender-typing (Turner & Gervai, 1995). Peers begin to reinforce gender-typed behavior by age 3, and their influence increases with age (Ruble & Martin, 1998). Although both 3- and 4-year-olds know what behaviors peers consider gender-appropriate, 4-year-olds more consistently apply these judgments to themselves (Bussey & Bandura, 1992). Children show more disapproval of boys who act "like girls" than of girls who are tomboys (Ruble & Martin, 1998).

Indeed, play choices at this age may be more strongly influenced by peers and the media than by the models children see at home (Turner & Gervai, 1995). Generally, however, peer and parental attitudes reinforce each other. Social cognitive theory sees peers, not as an independent influence for socialization, but as part of a complex cultural system that encompasses parents and other socializing agents as well (Bussey & Bandura, 1999).

Cultural Influences When a Hindu girl in a village in Nepal touched the plow that her brother was using, she was severely rebuked. In this way she learned that as a female she was restricted from acts her brother was expected to perform (D. Skinner, 1989). Isabel Allende, at 5, received similar instruction when told that she must sit and knit with her legs together when her brothers were out climbing trees.

In the United States, television is a major channel for the transmission of cultural attitudes toward gender. Although women in television programs and commercials are now more likely to be working outside the home, and men are sometimes shown caring for children or doing the marketing, for the most part life as portrayed on television continues to be more stereotyped than life in the real world (Coltrane & Adams, 1997; Ruble & Martin, 1998).

Social cognitive theory predicts that children who watch a lot of television will become more gender-typed by imitating the models they see on the screen. Dramatic supporting evidence emerged from a natural experiment in several Canadian towns that obtained access to television transmission for the first time. Children who had had relatively unstereotyped attitudes showed marked increases in traditional views two years later (Kimball, 1986). In another study, children who watched a series of nontraditional episodes, such as a father and son cooking together, had less stereotyped views than children who had not seen the series (J. Johnston & Ettema, 1982).

Children's books have long been a source of gender stereotypes. Today, friendship between boys and girls is portrayed more often, and girls are depicted as braver and more resourceful. Still, male characters predominate, females are more likely to need help, and males are more likely to give it (Beal, 1994; Evans, 1998).

Major strengths of the socialization approach include the breadth and multiplicity of processes it examines and the scope for individual differences it reveals. But this very complexity makes it difficult to establish clear causal connections between the way children are raised and the way they think and act. Just what aspects of the home environment and the peer culture promote gender-typing? Do parents and peers treat boys and girls differently because they *are* different or because the culture says they *should be* different? Does differential treatment *produce* or *reflect* gender differences? Or, as social cognitive theory suggests, is there a bidirectional relationship? Further research may help show how socializing agents mesh with children's own biological tendencies and cognitive understandings with regard to gender-related attitudes and behavior.

Checkpoint

Can you . . .

✔ Distinguish among four basic approaches to the study of gender development?

✔ Compare how various theories explain the acquisition of gender roles, and assess the support for each theory?

Play: The Business of Early Childhood

Guidepost 4

How do preschoolers play, and how does play contribute to and reflect development?

Carmen, age 3, pretends that the pieces of cereal floating in her bowl are "fishies" swimming in the milk, and she "fishes," spoonful by spoonful. After breakfast, she puts on her mother's hat, picks up a briefcase, and is a "mommy" going to work. She rides her tricycle through the puddles, comes in for an imaginary telephone conversation, turns a wooden block into a truck and says, "Vroom, vroom!" Carmen's day is one round of play after another.

It would be a mistake to dismiss Carmen's activities as just "having fun." Play is the work of the young, and it contributes to all domains of development. Through play, children stimulate the senses, learn how to use their muscles, coordinate sight with movement, gain mastery over their bodies, and acquire new skills. As they sort blocks of different shapes, count how many they can pile on each other, or announce that "my tower is bigger than yours," they lay the foundation for mathematical concepts (Jarrell, 1998). As they play with computers, they learn new ways of thinking (Silvern, 1998).

Preschoolers engage in different types of play at different ages. Children have different styles of play, and they play at different things. Researchers categorize children's play by its *content* (what children do when they play) and its *social dimension* (whether they play alone or with others). What can we learn about children by seeing how they play?

Types of Play

Carol, at 3, "talked for" a doll, using a deeper voice than her own. Miguel, at 4, wore a kitchen towel as a cape and "flew" around as Batman. These children were engaged in pretend play involving make-believe people or situations.

Pretend play is one of four categories of play identified by Piaget and others as showing increasing levels of cognitive complexity (Piaget, 1951; Smilansky, 1968). The simplest form, which begins during infancy, is active **functional play** involving repetitive muscular movements (such as rolling or bouncing a ball). As gross motor skills improve, preschoolers run, jump, skip, hop, throw, and aim. Toward the end of this period and into middle childhood, *rough-and-tumble play* involving wrestling, kicking, and sometimes chasing becomes more common (Pellegrini, 1998; see Chapter 12).

functional play In Piaget's and Smilansky's terminology, lowest cognitive level of play, involving repetitive muscular movements.

constructive play In Piaget's and Smilansky's terminology, second cognitive level of play, involving use of objects or materials to make something.

pretend play In Piaget's and Smilansky's terminology, third cognitive level of play, involving imaginary people or situations; also called *fantasy play, dramatic play,* or *imaginative play.*

The second level of cognitive complexity is **constructive play**—using objects or materials to make something, such as a house of blocks or a crayon drawing. Four-year-olds in preschools or day care centers may spend more than half their time in this kind of play, and it becomes more elaborate by ages 5 and 6 (J. E. Johnson, 1998).

The third level, **pretend play,** also called *fantasy play, dramatic play,* or *imaginative play,* rests on the symbolic function, which emerges near the end of the sensorimotor stage (Piaget, 1962). It is easy to picture young Isabel Allende acting out the fanciful stories her mother told her. Pretend play typically begins during the last part of the second year, increases during the preschool years, and then declines as school-age children become more involved in the fourth cognitive level of play, *formal games with rules*—organized games with known procedures and penalties, such as hopscotch and marbles.

An estimated 10 to 17 percent of preschoolers' play and 33 percent of kindergartners' is pretend play, often using dolls and real or imaginary props (Bretherton, 1984; Garner, 1998; J. E. Johnson, 1998; K. H. Rubin, Fein, & Vandenberg, 1983). Through pretending, children try out roles, cope with uncomfortable emotions, gain understanding of other people's viewpoints, and construct an image of the social world. They develop problem-solving skills, experience the joy of creativity, and become more proficient with language (Bodrova & Leong, 1998; J. I. F. Davidson, 1998; Furth & Kane, 1992; J. E. Johnson, 1998; Nourot, 1998; Singer & Singer, 1990). By making "tickets" for an imaginary train trip or "reading" eye charts in a "doctor's office," they build emergent literacy (Christie, 1991, 1998).

Children who often play imaginatively tend to cooperate more with other children and to be more popular and more joyful than those who do not (Singer & Singer, 1990). Children who watch a great deal of television tend to play less imaginatively, perhaps because they are accustomed to passively absorbing images rather than generating their own (Howes & Matheson, 1992).

The Social Dimension of Play

In a classic study done in the 1920s, Mildred B. Parten (1932) identified six types of early play, ranging from the least to the most social (see Table 11-2). She found that as children get older, their play tends to become more social—that is, more interactive and more cooperative. At first children play alone, then alongside other children, and finally together. Today, however, many researchers view Parten's characterization of children's play development as too simplistic. Children of all ages engage in all of Parten's categories of play (K. H. Rubin et al., 1998).

Table 11-2 Parten's Categories of Social and Nonsocial Play

Category	Description
Unoccupied behavior	The child does not seem to be playing but watches anything of momentary interest.
Onlooker behavior	The child spends most of the time watching other children play. The onlooker talks to them, asking questions or making suggestions, but does not enter into the play. The onlooker is definitely observing particular groups of children rather than anything that happens to be exciting.
Solitary independent play	The child plays alone with toys that are different from those used by nearby children and makes no effort to get close to them.
Parallel play	The child plays independently but among the other children, playing with toys like those used by the other children but not necessarily playing with them in the same way. Playing *beside* rather than *with* the others, the parallel player does not try to influence the other children's play.
Associative play	The child plays with other children. They talk about their play, borrow and lend toys, follow one another, and try to control who may play in the group. All the children play similarly if not identically; there is no division of labor and no organization around any goal. Each child acts as she or he wishes and is interested more in being with the other children than in the activity itself.
Cooperative or organized supplementary play	The child plays in a group organized for some goal—to make something, play a formal game, or dramatize a situation. One or two children control who belongs to the group and direct activities. By a division of labor, children take on different roles and supplement each other's efforts.

Source: Adapted from Parten, 1932, pp. 249–251.

Is nonsocial play less mature than social play? Parten apparently thought so. She and some other observers suggested that young children who play alone may be at risk of developing social, psychological, and educational problems. However, certain types of nonsocial play, particularly parallel play and solitary independent play, may consist of activities that foster cognitive, physical, and social development. In one study of 4-year-olds, *parallel constructive play* (for example, working on puzzles near another child who is also doing so) was most common among children who were good problem solvers, were popular with other children, and were seen by teachers as socially skilled (K. Rubin, 1982).

LifeMap CD

To observe how young children play together without interacting, watch the "Parallel Play in the Sandbox" video in Chapter 11 of your CD.

Researchers now are beginning to look not only at *whether* a child plays alone but at *why.* Solitary or parallel play may show independence and maturity, not poor social adjustment (Harrist, Zain, Bates, Dodge, & Pettit, 1997; K. H. Rubin et al., 1998). Among 567 kindergartners, teachers, observers, and classmates rated almost 2 out of 3 children who played alone as socially and cognitively competent; they simply preferred to play that way (Harrist, Zain, Bates, Dodge, & Pettit, 1997). Children who prefer such play may be more object or task oriented than people oriented. They tend to have long attention spans and relatively placid dispositions (Coplan et al., 2004).

On the other hand, solitary play in some children is a sign of shyness, anxiety, fearfulness, or social rejection (Coplan et al., 2004; Henderson, Marshall, Fox, & Rubin, 2004; Spinrad et al., 2004). In two Canadian studies of preschoolers and kindergartners, boys who engaged in solitary passive play, drawing pictures or building with blocks while peers played nearby, tended to be shy or maladjusted (Coplan, Gavinski-Molina, Lagacé-Séguin, & Wichman, 2001; Coplan, Prakash, O'Neil, & Armer, 2004).

What's your view

- How do you think the growing use of computers for both games and educational activities might affect preschool children's cognitive and social development?

Reticent play, a combination of Parten's onlooker and unoccupied categories, is often a manifestation of shyness (Coplan et al., 2004). However, such reticent behaviors as playing near other children, watching what they do, or wandering aimlessly may sometimes be a prelude to joining in others' play (K. H. Rubin, Bukowski, & Parker, 1998; Spinrad et al., 2004). In a short-term longitudinal study, children were observed briefly in daily free play

Checkpoint

Can you . . .

- ✔ Describe four cognitive levels of play, according to Piaget and others, and six categories of social and nonsocial play, according to Parten?
- ✔ Explain the connection between the cognitive and social dimensions of play?

at two suburban university preschools. Reticent children, though hesitant to join in other children's play, were well-liked and showed few problem behaviors (Spinrad et al., 2004). Nonsocial play, then, seems to be far more complex than Parten imagined and bears further study.

One kind of play that typically becomes more social during the preschool years is imaginative play, which often shifts from solitary pretending to dramatic play involving other children (K. H. Rubin et al., 1998; Singer & Singer, 1990). Dramatic play offers rich opportunities to practice interpersonal and language skills and to explore social roles and conventions (Bodrova & Leong, 1998; Christie, 1991; J. E. Johnson, 1998; Nourot, 1998). Young children follow unspoken rules in organizing dramatic play, staking out territory ("I'm the daddy; you're the mommy"), negotiating ("Okay, I'll be the daddy tomorrow"), or setting the scene ("Watch out—there's a train coming!"). As imaginative play becomes more collaborative, story lines become more complex and innovative.

How Gender Influences Play

The tendency toward sex segregation in play seems to be universal across cultures. From an evolutionary viewpoint, gender differences in children's play provide practice for adult behaviors important for reproduction and survival. Boys' rough-and-tumble play mirrors adult males' competition for dominance and status and for fertile mates. Girls' play parenting prepares them to care for the young (Geary, 1999). Socialization reinforces those tendencies.

As we have mentioned, sex segregation is common among preschoolers, and it becomes even more prevalent in middle childhood (Fabes, Martin, & Hanish, 2003; Maccoby, 1988, 1990, 1994; Ramsey & Lasquade, 1996; Snyder, West, Stockemer, Gibbons, & Almquist-Parks, 1996). Even when boys and girls play with the same toys, they play more socially with others of the same sex (Neppl & Murray, 1997). Most of the time, though, boys and girls play differently. Most boys like active, forceful play in fairly large groups; girls are inclined to quieter, more harmonious play with one playmate. Boys play more boisterously; girls play more cooperatively. Boys play spontaneously on sidewalks, streets, or empty lots; girls tend to choose more structured, adult-supervised activities. All these tendencies are more exaggerated when children play in groups (Benenson, 1993; Fabes et al., 2003; Maccoby, 1980; Serbin, Moller, Gulko, Powlishta, & Colburne, 1994). In mixed-sex groups, however, play tends to revolve around traditionally masculine activities, perhaps because boys' play preferences are more stereotyped than girls' (Fabes et al., 2003).

Children's developing gender concepts influence dramatic play. Whereas boys' play often involves danger and discord, such as mock battles, girls' pretend stories generally focus on orderly social relationships, such as when playing house (Fagot & Leve, 1998; Nourot, 1998).

Preschool boys and girls prefer different types of play. Boys engage in rough-and-tumble play; girls play more quietly and cooperatively.

How Culture Influences Play

The frequency of specific forms of play differs across cultures and is influenced by the play environments adults set up for children, which in turn reflect cultural values (Bodrova & Leong, 1998). One observational study compared 48 middle-class Korean-American and 48 middle-class Anglo-American children in separate preschools (Farver, Kim, & Lee, 1995). The three Anglo-American preschools, in keeping with normative U.S. values, encouraged independent thinking and active involvement in learning by letting children select from a wide range of activities. The Korean-American preschool, in keeping with traditional Korean values, emphasized developing academic skills and completing tasks. The Anglo-American preschools encouraged social interchange among children and collaborative activities with teachers. In the Korean-American preschool, children were allowed to talk and play only during outdoor recess.

Not surprisingly, the Anglo-American children engaged in more social play, whereas the Korean Americans engaged in more unoccupied or parallel play. Korean-American children played more cooperatively, often offering toys to other children—very likely a reflection of their culture's emphasis on group harmony. Anglo-American children were more aggressive and often responded negatively to other children's suggestions, reflecting the competitiveness of American culture.

An ethnographic study compared pretend play among 2½- to 4-year-olds in five Irish-American families in the United States and nine Chinese families in Taiwan. Play was primarily social in both cultures. Irish-American children were more likely to pretend with other children, and Chinese children with caregivers, who often used the play as a vehicle to teach proper conduct. Children in both cultures used objects, such as toy soldiers, in play; but this was more typical of Irish-American children, whose play tended to center on fantasy or movie themes (Haight, Wang, Fung, Williams, & Mintz, 1999).

Checkpoint

Can you . . .

✔ Tell how gender and culture influence the way children play, and give examples?

Parenting

Guidepost 5

How do parenting practices influence development?

As children increasingly become their own persons, their upbringing can be a complex challenge. Parents must deal with small people who have minds and wills of their own but who still have a lot to learn about what kinds of behavior work well in society. How do parents handle discipline? Are some ways of parenting more effective than others?

Forms of Discipline

The word *discipline* means "instruction" or "training." In the field of child development, **discipline** refers to methods of molding character and of teaching self-control and acceptable behavior. It can be a powerful tool for socialization with the goal of developing self-discipline. What forms of discipline work best? Researchers have looked at a wide range of techniques.

discipline Methods of molding children's character and of teaching them to exercise self-control and engage in acceptable behavior.

Reinforcement and Punishment

"What are we going to do with that child?" Noel's mother says. "The more we punish him, the more he misbehaves!"

Parents sometimes punish children to stop undesirable behavior, but children usually learn more from being reinforced for good behavior. *External* reinforcements may be tangible (candy, money, toys, or gold stars) or intangible (a smile, a word of praise, a hug, extra attention, or a special privilege). Whatever the reinforcement, the child must see it as rewarding and must receive it fairly consistently after showing the desired behavior. Eventually, the behavior should provide its own *internal* reward: a sense of pleasure or accomplishment. In Noel's case, his parents often ignore him when he behaves well but scold or spank him when he acts up. In other words, they unwittingly reinforce his *mis*behavior by giving him attention when he does what they do *not* want him to do.

Harsh punishment can be especially counterproductive. Young children who have been punished harshly may act aggressively even though the punishment is intended to stop aggressive behavior (Dodge, Pettit, & Bates, 1997; Nix et al., 1999). Children who are punished harshly and frequently may have trouble interpreting other people's actions and words; they may perceive hostile intentions where none exist (B. Weiss, Dodge, Bates, & Pettit, 1992; see Chapter 14). Or such children may become passive because they feel helpless. Children may become frightened if parents lose control and may eventually try to avoid a punitive parent, undermining the parent's ability to influence behavior (Grusec & Goodnow, 1994).

corporal punishment Use of physical force with the intention of causing pain but not injury so as to correct or control behavior.

Corporal punishment has been defined as "the use of physical force with the intention of causing a child to experience pain, but not injury, for the purpose of correction or control of the child's behavior" (Straus, 1994a, p. 4). It can include spanking, hitting, slapping, pinching, shaking (which can be fatal to infants), and other physical acts. Its use is extremely common in the United States—it is a pervasive part of the socialization of many children. Corporal punishment is popularly believed to be more effective than other remedies and to be harmless if done in moderation by loving parents. However, a growing body of evidence suggests that these beliefs are untrue, that corporal punishment can have serious negative consequences, and that it should not be used (Straus, 1999; Straus & Stewart, 1999; see Box 11-1).

At times, of course, punishment is necessary. Children may have to be prevented from running out into traffic or hitting others. Sometimes a child is willfully defiant; parents who back down when confronted with a preschooler's coercive demands may reinforce repetition of the undesirable behavior (G. R. Patterson, 1995). Punishment, when necessary, should be consistent, immediate, and clearly tied to the offense. It should be administered calmly, in private, and aimed at eliciting compliance, not guilt. It is most effective when accompanied by a short, simple explanation (AAP Committee on Psychosocial Aspects of Child and Family Health, 1998; Baumrind, 1996a, 1996b).

Power Assertion, Induction, and Withdrawal of Love

Looking at reinforcement and punishment alone may be an oversimplification of how parents influence behavior. Contemporary research has focused on three broader categories of discipline: *power assertion, induction,* and *temporary withdrawal of love.*

power assertion Disciplinary strategy designed to discourage undesirable behavior through physical or verbal enforcement of parental control.

inductive techniques Disciplinary techniques designed to induce desirable behavior by appealing to a child's sense of reason and fairness.

withdrawal of love Disciplinary strategy that may involve ignoring, isolating, or showing dislike for a child.

Power assertion is intended to stop or discourage undesirable behavior through physical or verbal enforcement of parental control; it includes demands, threats, withdrawal of privileges, spanking, and other punishments. These kinds of techniques, used by the feared maid who took care of the Allende children, left psychological scars on Isabel. **Inductive techniques** are designed to encourage desirable behavior (or discourage undesirable behavior) by reasoning with a child; they include setting limits, demonstrating logical consequences of an action, explaining, discussing, negotiating, and getting ideas from the child about what is fair. **Withdrawal of love** may include ignoring, isolating, or showing dislike for a child. The choice and effectiveness of a disciplinary strategy may depend on the parent's personality, the child's personality and age, and the quality of the parent-child relationship, as well as on culturally based customs and expectations (Grusec & Goodnow, 1994).

Most parents call upon more than one strategy, depending on the situation. Parents tend to use reasoning to get a child to show concern for others. They use power assertion to stop play that gets too rough, and they use both power assertion and reasoning to deal with lying and stealing (Grusec & Goodnow, 1994). The strategy parents choose may depend not only on their belief in its effectiveness, but also on their confidence that they can carry it out (Perozynski & Kramer, 1999).

What's your view 

- As a parent, what forms of discipline would you favor in what situations? Give specific examples and tell why.

Induction is usually the most effective method and power assertion the least effective method of getting children to accept parental standards (M. L. Hoffman, 1970a, 1970b; Jagers, Bingham, & Hans, 1996; McCord, 1996). Inductive reasoning tends to arouse empathy for the victim of wrongdoing as well as guilt on the part of the wrongdoer (Krevans & Gibbs, 1996). Kindergartners whose mothers reported using reasoning were more likely to see the moral wrongness of behavior that hurts other people (as opposed to merely breaking rules) than children whose mothers took away privileges (Jagers et al., 1996).

The Research World

Box 11-1 *The Case Against Corporal Punishment*

"Spare the rod and spoil the child" may sound old-fashioned, but corporal punishment has become a live issue today. Although some professionals view corporal punishment as verging on child abuse (Straus, 1994b), others defend it as necessary or desirable in moderation when prudently administered by loving parents (Baumrind, 1996a, 1996b).

Corporal punishment has diminished in many European countries since the passage of laws against it in Sweden in 1979. Austria, Cyprus, Denmark, Finland, Italy, Norway, Croatia, and Latvia followed suit, and a number of other countries are considering such laws. Yet in the United States some professionals—and politicians—strongly advocate corporal punishment. In 1999 the Arizona and Arkansas legislatures adopted resolutions urging parents and teachers to use it. All states make it an exception to the crime of assault.

Some form of corporal, or bodily, punishment is widely used on infants, and it is almost universal among parents of toddlers. In interviews with a nationally representative sample of 991 parents, 35 percent reported using corporal punishment—usually hand slapping—on infants during the previous year, and fully 94 percent on 3- and 4-year-olds. About half of the parents were still hitting children by age 12, one-third were doing so at age 14, and 13 percent were still doing so at age 17 (Straus & Stewart, 1999).

Opponents of corporal punishment are not against disciplining children, but they maintain that there are more effective, less risky, or less harmful ways to do it. A large body of research has consistently found negative outcomes from its use. Apart from the risk of injury to the child, these outcomes include increased physical aggression in childhood and anxiety disorders, depression, alcohol problems, antisocial behavior, or partner abuse later in life (MacMillan et al., 1999; Strassberg, Dodge, Pettit, & Bates, 1994).

Most of this research was cross-sectional or retrospective, and the few longitudinal studies did not consider that the spanked children may have been aggressive in the first place and that their aggressive behavior might have led their parents to spank them. Since 1997 several large, nationally representative studies (Brezina, 1999; Gunnoe & Mariner, 1997; Simons, Lin, & Gordon, 1998; Strauss & Paschall, 1999; and Straus, Sugarman, & Giles-Sims, 1997) have overcome this defect by taking account of the child's own behavior at the time of first measurement.

These studies, which included children from age 3 through adolescence, found that corporal punishment is counterproductive; the more a child receives, the more aggressive the child's behavior tends to become and the more likely that child is to show antisocial or other maladaptive behavior, not only in childhood but also as an adult (Straus & Stewart, 1999). However, results of a more recent study of children spanked before age 2 were mixed. Frequently spanked non-Hispanic white children, but not black or Hispanic children, were more likely to have behavior problems after entering school (Shade & Wissow, 2004).

Why might corporal punishment lead to problem behavior? One answer comes from social learning theory. Children who are spanked not only suffer frustration, pain, and humiliation (which can be spurs to aggression), but also see aggressive behavior in an adult model and may learn to see infliction of pain as an acceptable response to problems (Dodge, Pettit, & Bates, 1997). Another explanation is that corporal punishment arouses anger and resentment, causing children to focus on their own hurts rather than on the wrong they have done to others and making them less receptive to parental teachings. Reliance on physical punishment may weaken parents' authority; as with any punishment, the effectiveness of spanking diminishes with repeated use (AAP Committee on Psychosocial Aspects of Child and Family Health, 1998; McCord, 1996).

Spanking may even inhibit cognitive development, according to data on 2- to 4-year-olds and 5- to 9-year-olds from the National Longitudinal Study of Youth. Children whose mothers used little or no corporal punishment during a two-week period showed greater cognitive gains than children who received such punishment (Straus & Paschall, 1999).

The American Academy of Pediatrics Committee on Psychosocial Aspects of Child and Family Health (1998) urges parents to avoid spanking. Instead, the committee suggests such inductive methods as helping children learn to use words to express feelings, giving children choices and helping them evaluate the consequences, and modeling orderly behavior and collaborative conflict resolution. The committee recommends positive reinforcement to encourage desired behaviors as well as verbal reprimands, "time-outs," or removal of privileges to discourage undesired behaviors—all within the context of a positive, supportive, loving parent-child relationship.

What's your view?

- Did your parents ever spank you? If so, how often and in what kinds of situations?
- Would you spank or have you ever spanked your own child? Why or why not?

Check it out!

For more information on this topic, go to **http://www.aap.org/policy/re9740.html**. This is the policy statement of the American Academy of Pediatrics, "Guidance for Effective Discipline" (RE9740).

The line between some forms of discipline and physical or emotional abuse (refer back to Chapter 9) is not always easy to draw, but "discipline" clearly becomes abusive when it results in injury to a child. **Psychological aggression** refers to verbal attacks that may result in psychological harm, such as (1) yelling or screaming, (2) threatening to spank or hit the child, (3) swearing or cursing at the child, (4) threatening to send the child away or kick the child out of the house, and (5) calling the child dumb or lazy. Some psychologists equate

psychological aggression Verbal attack by a parent that may result in psychological harm to a child.

the last three categories with emotional abuse. Psychological aggression, like physical aggression (spanking), is almost universal among U.S. parents. In a nationally representative sampling of 991 parents, 98 percent reported using some form of psychological aggression by the time a child was 5, and about 90 percent thereafter (Straus & Field, 2003).

The effectiveness of parental discipline may hinge on how well the child understands and accepts the parent's message, both cognitively and emotionally (Grusec & Goodnow, 1994). For the child to accept the message, the child has to recognize it as appropriate; so parents need to be fair and accurate as well as clear and consistent about their expectations. They need to fit the discipline to the misdeed and to the child's temperament and cognitive and emotional level. A child may be more motivated to accept the message if the parents are normally warm and responsive and if they arouse the child's empathy for someone the child has harmed (Grusec & Goodnow, 1994).

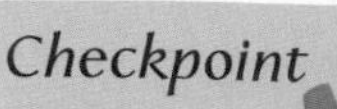

Can you . . .

✔ Compare various forms of discipline, and identify factors that influence their effectiveness?

One point on which experts agree is that a child interprets and responds to discipline in the context of an ongoing relationship with a parent. Some researchers therefore look beyond specific parental practices to overall styles, or patterns, of parenting.

Parenting Styles

Why does Stacy hit and bite the nearest person when she cannot finish a jigsaw puzzle? What makes David sit and sulk when he cannot finish the puzzle, even though his teacher offers to help him? Why does Consuelo work on the puzzle for 20 minutes and then shrug and try another? Why are children so different in their responses to the same situation? Temperament is a major factor, of course; but some research suggests that styles of parenting may affect children's competence in dealing with their world.

Baumrind's Model

Are some ways of socializing children more effective than others? In pioneering research, Diana Baumrind (1971, 1996b; Baumrind & Black, 1967) studied 103 preschool children from 95 families. Through interviews, testing, and home studies, she measured how children were functioning, identified three parenting styles, and described typical behavior patterns of children raised according to each. Baumrind's work and the large body of research it inspired have established strong associations between each parenting style and a particular set of child behaviors (Baumrind, 1989; Darling & Steinberg, 1993; Pettit, Bates, & Dodge, 1997).

authoritarian In Baumrind's terminology, parenting style emphasizing control and obedience.

Authoritarian parents, according to Baumrind, value control and unquestioning obedience. They try to make children conform rigidly to a set standard of conduct and punish them for violating it, often using power-assertive techniques. They are more detached and less warm than other parents. Their children tend to be more discontented, withdrawn, and distrustful.

permissive In Baumrind's terminology, parenting style emphasizing self-expression and self-regulation.

Permissive parents value self-expression and self-regulation. They make few demands and allow children to monitor their own activities as much as possible. They consult with children about policy decisions and rarely punish. They are warm, noncontrolling, and undemanding or even indulgent. Their preschool children tend to be immature—the least self-controlled and the least exploratory.

authoritative In Baumrind's terminology, parenting style blending respect for a child's individuality with an effort to instill social values.

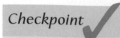

Authoritative parents value a child's individuality but also stress social constraints. They have confidence in their ability to guide children, but they also respect children's independent decisions, interests, opinions, and personalities. They are loving and accepting but also demand good behavior, are firm in maintaining standards, and are willing to impose limited, judicious punishment when necessary, within the context of a warm, supportive relationship. They favor inductive discipline, explaining the reasoning behind their stands and encouraging verbal negotiation and give-and-take. Their children apparently feel secure in knowing both that they are loved and what is expected of them. These preschoolers tend to be the most self-reliant, self-controlled, self-assertive, exploratory, and content. (Isabel Allende's description of how her stepfather, Tió Ramón, took charge and raised her and her brothers fits this description perfectly; his parenting style was more effective than those of their authoritarian grandfather and permissive mother.)

Eleanor Maccoby and John Martin (1983) added a fourth parenting style—*neglectful*, or *uninvolved*—to describe parents who, sometimes because of stress or depression, focus on their own needs rather than on those of the child. Neglectful parenting has been linked with a variety of behavioral disorders in childhood and adolescence (Baumrind, 1991; Parke & Buriel, 1998; R. A. Thompson, 1998).

Why does authoritative parenting seem to enhance children's social competence? It may be because authoritative parents like Ramón set sensible expectations and realistic standards. By making clear, consistent rules, they let children know what is expected of them. In authoritarian homes, children are so strictly controlled that often they cannot make independent choices about their own behavior; in permissive homes, children receive so little guidance that they may become uncertain and anxious about whether they are doing the right thing. In authoritative homes, children know when they are meeting expectations and can decide whether it is worth risking parental displeasure to pursue a goal. These children are expected to perform well, fulfill commitments, and participate actively in family duties as well as family fun. They know the satisfaction of accepting responsibilities and achieving success. Parents who make reasonable demands show that they believe their children can meet them—and that they care enough to insist that their children do.

What's your view 

- To what extent would you like your children to adopt your values and behavioral standards? Give examples.

When conflict arises, an authoritative parent can teach the child positive ways to communicate his or her own point of view and negotiate acceptable alternatives ("If you don't want to throw away those rocks you found, where do you think we should keep them?"). Internalization of this broader set of skills, not just of specific behavioral demands, may well be a key to the success of authoritative parenting (Grusec & Goodnow, 1994).

Support and Criticisms of Baumrind's Model

In research based on Baumrind's work, the superiority of authoritative parenting (or similar conceptions of parenting style) has repeatedly been supported (Baumrind, 1989; Darling & Steinberg, 1993). For example, a longitudinal study of 585 ethnically and socioeconomically diverse families in Tennessee and Indiana with children from prekindergarten through grade 6 found that four aspects of early supportive parenting—warmth, use of inductive discipline, interest and involvement in children's contacts with peers, and proactive teaching of social skills—predicted children's later behavioral, social, and academic outcomes (Pettit, Bates, & Dodge, 1997).

Still, because Baumrind's model seems to suggest that there is one "right" way to raise children well, it has provoked controversy. Because Baumrind's findings are correlational, they merely establish associations between each parenting style and a particular set of child behaviors. They do not show that different styles of child rearing *cause* children to be more or less competent. It is also impossible to know whether the children Baumrind studied were, in fact, raised in a particular style. It may be that some of the better-adjusted children were raised inconsistently, but by the time of the study their parents had adopted the authoritative pattern (Holden & Miller, 1999). In addition, Baumrind did not consider innate factors, such as temperament, that might have affected children's competence and exerted an influence on the parents.

Cultural Differences in Parenting Styles

Another concern is that Baumrind's categories reflect the dominant North American view of child development and may be misleading when applied to some cultures or socioeconomic groups. Among Asian Americans, obedience and strictness, rather than being associated with harshness and domination, have more to do with caring, concern, and involvement and with maintaining family harmony. Traditional Chinese culture, with its emphasis on respect for elders, stresses adults' responsibility to maintain the social order by teaching children socially proper behavior. This obligation is carried out through firm and just control and governance of the child and even by physical punishment if necessary

Checkpoint

Can you . . .

- ✔ Describe and evaluate Baumrind's model of parenting styles?
- ✔ Discuss how parents' way of resolving conflicts with young children can contribute to the success of authoritative child rearing?
- ✔ Discuss criticisms of Baumrind's model and cultural variations in parenting styles?

(Zhao, 2002). Although Asian-American parenting is frequently described as authoritarian, the warmth and supportiveness that characterize Chinese-American family relationships may more closely resemble Baumrind's authoritative parenting but without the emphasis on the American values of individuality, choice, and freedom (Chao, 1994) and with stricter parental control (Chao, 2001).

Still, the idea of a dichotomy between the individualistic values of western parenting and the collectivist values of Asian parenting may be overly simplistic. In interviews with 64 Japanese mothers of 3- to 6-year-olds (Yamada, 2004), the mothers' descriptions of their parenting practices reflected the search for a balance between granting appropriate autonomy and exercising disciplinary control. The mothers let children make their own decisions within what they saw as the child's personal domain, such as play activities, playmates, and clothing, and this domain enlarged with the child's age; but the mothers also encouraged their children to take responsibility for their decisions and not change their minds. When health or safety, moral issues, or conventional social rules were involved, the mothers set limits or exercised control. When conflicts arose, the mothers used reasoning rather than power-assertive methods or sometimes gave in to the child, apparently on the theory that the issue wasn't worth struggling over—or that the child might be right after all.

Why do young children help or hurt others, and why do they develop fears?

Promoting Altruism and Dealing with Aggression and Fearfulness

Three specific issues of special concern to parents, caregivers, and teachers of preschool children are how to promote altruism, curb aggression, and deal with fears that often arise at this age.

Prosocial Behavior

altruism Behavior intended to help others that comes from inner concern and without expectation of external reward; may involve self-denial or self-sacrifice.

prosocial behavior Any voluntary behavior intended to help others.

Alex, at 3½, responded to two preschool classmates' complaints that they did not have enough modeling clay, his favorite plaything, by giving them half of his. Alex was showing **altruism:** acting out of concern for another person with no expectation of reward. Altruistic acts like Alex's often entail cost, self-sacrifice, or risk. Altruism is the heart of **prosocial behavior,** voluntary activity intended to benefit another.

Even before the second birthday, children often help others, share belongings and food, and offer comfort. Such behaviors may reflect a growing ability to imagine how another person might feel (Zahn-Waxler, Radke-Yarrow, Wagner, & Chapman, 1992). An analysis of 179 studies found increasing evidence of concern for others from infancy throughout childhood and adolescence (Fabes & Eisenberg, 1996). Although girls tend to be more prosocial than boys, the differences are small (Eisenberg & Fabes, 1998).

Is there a prosocial personality or disposition? A longitudinal study that followed 32 four- and 5-year-olds into early adulthood suggests that there is and that it emerges early and remains somewhat consistent throughout life. Preschoolers who were sympathetic and spontaneously shared with classmates tended to show prosocial understanding and empathic behavior as much as 17 years later. A prosocial disposition may be partly temperamental or genetic, as it involves *inhibitory control* (self-control or self-denial). Preschoolers who are shy or withdrawn tend to be less prosocial, perhaps because they hesitate to reach out to others (Coplan et al., 2004).

The family is important as a model and as a source and reinforcer of explicit standards of behavior (Eisenberg & Fabes, 1998; Eisenberg, Guthrie, et al., 1999). Parents of prosocial children typically are prosocial themselves. They point out models of prosocial behavior and steer children toward stories, films, and television programs that depict cooperation, sharing, and empathy and encourage sympathy, generosity, and helpfulness (Singer & Singer, 1998). Parents encourage prosocial behavior when they use inductive disciplinary methods (Eisenberg & Fabes, 1998). When Sara took candy from a store, her father did not lecture her on honesty, spank her, or tell her what a bad girl she had been. Instead, he explained how the owner of the store would be harmed by her failure to pay for the candy, asked her how she thought the store owner might feel, and then took her back to the store to return the candy. Relationships with siblings (discussed later in this chapter) provide an important "laboratory" for trying out caring behavior and learning to see another person's point of view. Peers and teachers also can model and reinforce prosocial behavior (Eisenberg, 1992; Eisenberg & Fabes, 1998).

Motives for prosocial behavior may change as children grow older and develop more mature moral reasoning (see Chapters 13 and 16). Preschoolers tend to have egocentric motives; they want to earn praise and avoid disapproval. They weigh costs and benefits and consider how they would like others to act toward them. As children grow older, their motives become less self-centered. They adopt societal standards of "being good," which eventually become internalized as principles and values (Eisenberg & Fabes, 1998). Individual differences in prosocial behavior may reflect individual differences in moral reasoning (Eisenberg, Guthrie, et al., 1999).

Cultures vary in the degree to which they foster prosocial behavior. Traditional cultures in which people live in extended family groups and share work seem to foster prosocial values more than cultures that stress individual achievement (Eisenberg & Fabes, 1998).

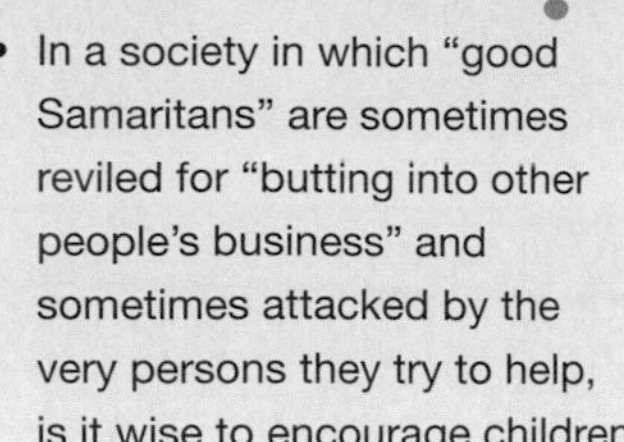

- In a society in which "good Samaritans" are sometimes reviled for "butting into other people's business" and sometimes attacked by the very persons they try to help, is it wise to encourage children to offer help to strangers?

Aggression

When Peter roughly snatches a ball away from Tommy, he is interested only in getting the ball, not in hurting or dominating Tommy. This is **instrumental aggression,** or aggression used as an instrument to reach a goal—the most common type in early childhood. Between ages 2½ and 5, children commonly struggle over toys and control of space. Aggression surfaces mostly during social play; children who fight the most also tend to be the most sociable and competent. In fact, the ability to show some instrumental aggression may be a necessary step in social development.

instrumental aggression Aggressive behavior used as a means of achieving a goal.

Between ages 2 and 4, as children develop more self-control and become better able to express themselves verbally, they typically shift from showing aggression with blows to doing it with words (Coie & Dodge, 1998). However, individual differences remain; children who more frequently hit or grab toys from other children at age 2 are likely to be more physically aggressive at age 5 (Cummings, Iannotti, & Zahn-Waxler, 1989); and children who, as preschoolers, often engaged in violent fantasy play may, at age 6, be prone to displays of anger (Dunn & Hughes, 2001). After age 6 or 7, most children become less aggressive as they grow more cooperative, less egocentric, more empathic, and better able to communicate. They can now put themselves in someone else's place, can understand why the other person may be acting in a certain way, and can develop more positive ways of asserting themselves. However, as aggression declines overall, **hostile aggression**—action intended to hurt another person—proportionately increases (Coie & Dodge, 1998; see Chapter 14).

hostile aggression Aggressive behavior intended to hurt another person.

Are boys more aggressive than girls? Much research says yes. Indeed, as we have mentioned, some studies suggest that the male hormone testosterone may underlie aggressive behavior. From infancy, boys are more likely to grab things from others. As children learn to talk, girls are more likely to rely on words to protest and to work out conflicts (Coie & Dodge, 1998).

However, girls may be more aggressive than they seem; they just show aggressiveness differently (McNeilly-Choque, Hart, Robinson, Nelson, & Olsen, 1996; Putallaz & Bierman, 2004). Boys engage in more **overt aggression,** either instrumental or hostile. Overt aggression, either physical or verbal, is openly directed against its target. Girls tend to practice **relational aggression** (also called *covert* or *social aggression*). This more subtle kind of aggression consists of damaging or interfering with relationships, reputation, or psychological well-being, often through teasing, manipulation, or bids for control. It may take such forms as spreading rumors, name-calling, put-downs, or excluding someone from a group or a team. Among preschoolers, it tends to be direct and face-to-face ("You can't come to my party if you don't give me that toy"). In middle childhood and adolescence, relational aggression becomes more sophisticated and indirect (Crick, Casas, & Nelson, 2002). Relational aggression may be no more frequent among girls than among boys, but its consequences may be more serious for girls, who tend to be more preoccupied with relationships than boys are (Cillessen & Mayeux, 2004; Crick et al., 2002).

overt aggression Aggression that is openly directed at its target.

relational aggression Aggression aimed at damaging or interfering with another person's relationships, reputation, or psychological well-being; also called *covert* or *indirect aggression.*

In a classic experiment by Albert Bandura, children who had seen a film of an adult hitting and kicking an inflated clown were more likely to imitate the aggressive behavior if they had seen the adult being rewarded or experiencing no consequences than if they had seen the adult punished.

Sources of Aggression Why are some children more aggressive than others? Biology may play a part. So may temperament: children who are intensely emotional and low in self-control tend to express anger aggressively (Eisenberg, Fabes, Nyman, Bernzweig, & Pinuelas, 1994). Aggressive behavior also tends to be bred from early childhood by a combination of a stressful and unstimulating home atmosphere, harsh discipline, lack of maternal warmth and social support, exposure to aggressive adults and neighborhood violence, and transient peer groups, which prevent stable friendships. Through such negative socializing experiences, children growing up in high-risk surroundings may absorb antisocial attitudes despite their parents' best efforts (Dodge, Pettit, & Bates, 1994; Grusec & Goodnow, 1994).

In longitudinal studies, insecure attachment and lack of maternal warmth and affection in infancy predicted aggressiveness in early childhood (Coie & Dodge, 1998; MacKinnon-Lewis, Starnes, Volling, & Johnson, 1997). Negative parent-child relationships may set the stage for prolonged, destructive sibling conflicts, in which children imitate their parents' hostile behavior. These coercive family processes may foster aggressive tendencies that are carried over to peer relations (MacKinnon-Lewis et al., 1997) and to conduct at home and at school (Garcia, Shaw, Winslow, & Yaggi, 2000).

Triggers of Aggression Exposure to violence can trigger aggression. In a classic social learning experiment (Bandura, Ross, & Ross, 1961), 3- to 6-year-olds individually watched adult models play with toys. Children in one experimental group saw the adult play quietly. The model for a second experimental group began to assemble Tinker Toys but then spent the rest of the 10-minute session punching, throwing, and kicking a life-size inflated doll. A control group did not see any model. After the sessions, the children, who were mildly frustrated by seeing toys they were not allowed to play with, went into another playroom. The children who had seen the aggressive model acted much more aggressively than those in the other groups, imitating many of the same things they had seen the model say and do. The children who had been with the quiet model were less aggressive than the control group. This finding suggests that parents may be able to moderate the effects of frustration by modeling nonaggressive behavior.

Television has enormous power for modeling either prosocial behavior or aggression. In Chapter 14 we will discuss the influence of televised violence on aggressive behavior.

Influence of Culture How much influence does culture have on aggressive behavior? One research team asked closely matched samples of 30 Japanese and 30 U.S. middle- to upper-middle-class preschoolers to choose pictured solutions to hypothetical conflicts or stressful situations (such as having one's block tower knocked down, having to stop playing and go to bed, being hit, hearing parents argue, or fighting on a jungle gym). The children also were asked to act out such situations using dolls and props. The U.S. children showed more anger, more aggressive behavior and language, and less emotional control than the Japanese children (Zahn-Waxler, Friedman, Cole, Mizuta, & Hiruma, 1996).

These results are consistent with child-rearing values in the two cultures. In Japan, anger and aggression contradict the cultural emphasis on harmony. Japanese mothers are more likely than U.S. mothers to use inductive discipline, pointing out how aggressive behavior hurts others. Japanese mothers show strong disappointment when children fail to meet behavioral standards. However, the cross-cultural difference in children's anger and aggressiveness was significant even apart from mothers' behavior, suggesting that temperamental differences also may have been at work (Zahn-Waxler et al., 1996).

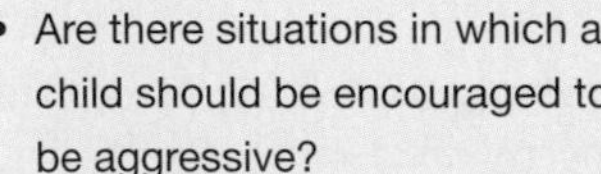

- Are there situations in which a child should be encouraged to be aggressive?

Fearfulness

"My childhood was a time of unvoiced fears," writes Isabel Allende (1995, p. 50): fear of her family's tyrannical maid; fear that her mother would die and her father would come back to claim her; fear of the devil; fear of her sadistic uncles; fear of gypsies; and fear of what "bad men can do to little girls."

Passing fears are common in early childhood. Many 2- to 4-year-olds are afraid of animals, especially dogs. By 6 years, children are more likely to be afraid of the dark. Other

Table 11-3 Childhood Fears

Age	Fears
0–6 months	Loss of support; loud noises
7–12 months	Strangers; heights; sudden, unexpected, and looming objects
1 year	Separation from parent; toilet; injury; strangers
2 years	Many stimuli, including loud noises (vacuum cleaners, sirens and alarms, trucks, and thunder), animals, dark rooms, separation from parent, large objects or machines, changes in personal environment, unfamiliar peers
3 years	Masks; dark; animals; separation from parent
4 years	Separation from parent; animals; dark; noises (including noises at night)
5 years	Animals; "bad" people; dark; separation from parent; bodily harm
6 years	Supernatural beings (e.g., ghosts, witches); bodily injury; thunder and lightning; dark; sleeping or staying alone; separation from parent
7–8 years	Supernatural beings; dark; media events (e.g., news reports on the threat of nuclear war or child kidnapping); staying alone; bodily injury
9–12 years	Tests and examinations in school; school performances; bodily injury; physical appearance; thunder and lightning; death; dark

Source: Adapted from Morris & Kratochwill, 1983; Stevenson-Hinde & Shouldice, 1996.

common fears are of thunderstorms, doctors, and imaginary creatures (DuPont, 1983; Stevenson-Hinde & Shouldice, 1996). Most of these disappear as children grow older and lose their sense of powerlessness.

Young children's fears stem largely from their intense fantasy life and their tendency to confuse appearance with reality. Sometimes their imaginations get carried away, and they worry about being attacked by a lion or being abandoned. Also, they are more likely to be frightened by something that looks scary, such as a cartoon monster, than by something capable of doing great harm, such as a nuclear explosion (Cantor, 1994). For the most part, older children's fears are more realistic and self-evaluative (for example, fear of failing a test) (Stevenson-Hinde & Shouldice, 1996; see Table 11-3).

Fears may come from personal experience or from hearing about other people's experiences (Muris, Merckelbach, & Collaris, 1997). A preschooler whose mother is sick in bed may become upset by a story about a mother's death, even the death of an animal mother. Often fears come from appraisals of danger, such as the likelihood of being bitten by a dog, or are triggered by events, as when a child who was hit by a car becomes afraid to cross the street. Children who have lived through an earthquake, a kidnapping, or some other frightening event may fear that it will happen again (Kolbert, 1994).

Parents can allay children's fears by instilling a sense of trust and normal caution without being too protective—and also by overcoming their own unrealistic fears. They can reassure a fearful child and encourage open expression of feelings. Ridicule ("Don't be such a baby!"), coercion ("Pat the nice doggie—it won't hurt you"), and logical persuasion ("The closest bear is 20 miles away, locked in a zoo!") are not helpful. Not until elementary school can children tell themselves that what they fear is not real (Cantor, 1994).

Children can be helped to overcome fears by *systematic desensitization,* a therapeutic technique in which a child is exposed in gradually increasing "doses" to a feared object or situation. This technique has been used successfully to help children overcome fears ranging from snakes to elevators (Murphy & Bootzin, 1973; Sturges & Sturges, 1998).

Checkpoint

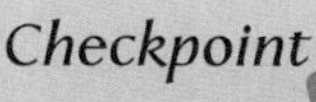

Can you . . .

✔ Discuss influences that contribute to altruism, aggression, and fearfulness?

Relationships with Other Children

Although the most important people in young children's world are the adults who take care of them, relationships with siblings and playmates become more important in early childhood. Virtually every characteristic activity and personality issue of this age, from gender development to prosocial or aggressive behavior, involves other children. Sibling and peer relationships in early childhood strengthen social cognition, or "mind reading"—the ability to understand others' intentions, desires, and feelings (Dunn, 1999). These relationships also provide a measuring stick for **self-efficacy,** children's growing sense of their ability to master challenges and achieve goals. By competing with and comparing themselves with other children, they can gauge their physical, social, cognitive, and linguistic competencies and gain a more realistic sense of self (Bandura, 1994).

self-efficacy Sense of capability to master challenges and achieve goals.

Guidepost 7

How do young children get along with (or without) siblings?

Siblings—or Their Absence

Ties between brothers and sisters often set the stage for later relationships. Let's look at sibling relationships and then at children who grow up with no siblings.

Brothers and Sisters

"It's mine!"
"No, it's mine!"
"Well, I was playing with it first!"

The earliest, most frequent, and most intense disputes among siblings are over property rights—who owns a toy or who is entitled to play with it. Although exasperated adults may not always see it that way, sibling disputes and their settlement can be viewed as socialization opportunities, in which children learn to stand up for moral principles (Ross, 1996).

Despite the frequency of conflict, sibling rivalry is *not* the main pattern between brothers and sisters early in life. Although some rivalry exists, so do affection, interest, companionship, and influence. Observations spanning three and a half years that began when younger siblings were about 1½ years old and the older ones ranged from 3 to 4½ found prosocial and play-oriented behaviors to be more common than rivalry, hostility, and competition (Abramovitch, Corter, & Lando, 1979; Abramovitch, Corter, Pepler, & Stanhope, 1986; Abramovitch, Pepler, & Corter, 1982). Older siblings initiated more behavior, both friendly and unfriendly; younger siblings tended to imitate the older ones. As the younger children reached their fifth birthday, the siblings became less physical and more verbal, both in showing aggression and in showing care and affection. At least one finding of this research has been replicated in many studies: same-sex siblings, particularly girls, are closer and play together more peaceably than boy-girl pairs (Kier & Lewis, 1998).

The quality of relationships with brothers and sisters often carries over to relationships with other children. A child who is aggressive with siblings is likely to be aggressive with friends as well (Abramovitch et al., 1986). Children with siblings get along better with kindergarten classmates than do only children (Downey & Condron, 2004).

Checkpoint

Can you . . .

- ✔ Explain how the resolution of sibling disputes contributes to socialization?
- ✔ Tell how birth order and gender affect typical patterns of sibling interaction?
- ✔ Compare development of only children with that of children with siblings?

The Only Child

Are only children spoiled, selfish, lonely, or maladjusted? Research does not bear out this stereotype. According to an analysis of 115 studies, "onlies" do comparatively well. In occupational and educational achievement and intelligence, they surpass children with siblings. Only children also tend to be more mature and motivated to achieve and to have higher self-esteem. They do not differ, however, in overall adjustment or sociability. Perhaps these children do better because their parents spend more time and focus more attention on them, talk to them more, do more with them, and expect more of them (Falbo & Polit, 1986; Polit & Falbo, 1987). On the other hand, more recent research found that children with siblings get along better with kindergarten classmates than do only children (Downey & Condron, 2004).

Research in China, which mandates one-child families, has produced largely encouraging findings about only children (see Box 11-2).

Around the World

Box 11-2 *A Nation of Only Children*

In 1979, to control an exploding population, the People's Republic of China established an official policy of limiting families to one child each. In addition to propaganda campaigns and incentives to induce voluntary compliance—money, child care, health care, housing, and preference in school placement—millions of involuntary abortions and sterilizations have taken place. People who have had children without first getting a permit have faced fines and loss of jobs. By 1985, at least 8 out of 10 young urban couples and half of those in rural areas had only one child (Yang, Ollendick, Dong, Xia, & Lin, 1995), and by 1997, the country's estimated population growth was holding steady at a little more than 1 percent.

Today the one-child policy is no longer rigorously or uniformly enforced. Economic growth is exerting a natural check on family size and also making it easier for families who want a second child to pay a fine (Faison, 1997). The State Family Planning Commission has prohibited forced sterilizations and abortions and instead has begun to stress education and contraceptive choice, while imposing extra taxes on families with more than one child. In a small but growing number of counties, fixed quotas and permit requirements have even been eliminated (Rosenthal, 1998).

Still, in many Chinese cities, kindergartens and primary classrooms are almost completely filled with children who have no brothers or sisters. This situation marks a great change in Chinese society, where newlyweds were traditionally congratulated with the wish, "May you have a hundred sons and a thousand grandsons." It offers researchers a natural experiment: an opportunity to study the adjustment of large numbers of only children.

Since 1979 the People's Republic of China has officially limited families to one child each. The implications of this policy are hotly debated by educators, researchers, and politicians.

Among 4,000 third and sixth graders, personality differences between only children and those with siblings—as rated by parents, teachers, peers, and the children themselves—were few. Only children's academic achievement and physical growth were about the same as, or better than, those with siblings (Falbo & Poston, 1993). In a randomized study in Beijing first-grade classrooms (Jiao, Ji, & Jing, 1996), only children outperformed classmates with siblings in memory, language, and mathematics skills. This finding may reflect the greater attention, stimulation, hopes, and expectations that parents shower on a baby they know will be their first and last. Fifth-grade only children, who were born before the one-child policy was strongly enforced—and whose parents may have originally planned on a larger family—did not show a pronounced cognitive edge.

A review of the literature found no significant differences in behavioral problems. The small number of severe problems that did appear in only children could be attributed to parental overindulgence and overprotection (Tao, 1998). Indeed, only children seem to be at a distinct psychological advantage in a society that favors and rewards such a child. Among 731 urban children and adolescents, those with siblings reported higher levels of fear, anxiety, and depression than only children, regardless of sex or age (Yang et al., 1995).

Both of these studies used urban samples. Further research may reveal whether the findings hold up in rural areas and small towns, where children with siblings are more numerous, and whether only children maintain their cognitive superiority as they move through school.

China's population policy has wider implications. If it succeeds, most Chinese will eventually lack aunts, uncles, nephews, nieces, and cousins, as well as siblings. How this will affect individuals, families, and the social fabric is incalculable.

A more sinister question is this: What happened to the girls? A 1990 census suggested that 5 percent of all infant girls born in China (some half a million each year) are unaccounted for. Since the adoption of the one-child policy, many parents have reportedly abandoned or killed baby girls so as to try to bear more culturally valued sons. A more benign explanation is that these girls were hidden and raised secretly to evade the one-child policy (Carmichael, 2004; Kristof, 1991, 1993). An increasing number are being sold or given up for adoption by foreigners; in 2000, the U.S. government issued 5,053 visas for orphans from China, as compared with only 61 visas in 1991 (Kreider, 2003; Rosenthal, 2003). These trends—together with prenatal sex selection through selective abortion of female fetuses—are producing a growing surplus of young men who cannot find mates and may threaten social stability (Hudson & den Boer, 2004; Lee, 2004). Concern about these unforeseen effects of China's one-child policy may be one factor in the recent relaxation of enforcement.

What's your view?

Governmental control of reproduction may seem like the ultimate in totalitarianism, but what course of action would you propose for a country that cannot support an exploding population?

Check it out!

For more information on this topic, go to **http://www.pbs.org/sixbillion/china/ch-repro.html**. This is the Web site of the Public Broadcasting Corporation, featuring a story on China and reproductive issues.

How do young children choose playmates and friends, and why are some children more popular than others?

What does friendship mean to a 5-year-old? Watch the video on "Describing Friends at Age 5" in Chapter 11 of your CD.

Playmates and Friends

Friendships develop as people develop. Toddlers play alongside or near each other, but not until about age 3 do children begin to have friends. Through friendships and interactions with casual playmates, young children learn how to get along with others. They learn that being a friend is the way to have a friend. They learn how to solve problems in relationships, they learn how to put themselves in another person's place, and they see models of various kinds of behavior. They learn moral values and gender-role norms, and they practice adult roles.

Choosing Playmates and Friends

Preschoolers usually like to play with children of their own age and sex. In preschool, they tend to spend most of their time with a few other children with whom they have had positive experiences and whose behavior is like their own. Children who have frequent positive experiences with each other are most likely to become friends (Rubin et al., 1998; Snyder et al., 1996). About 3 out of 4 preschoolers have such mutual friendships (Hartup & Stevens, 1999).

The traits that young children look for in a playmate are similar to the traits they look for in a friend (C. H. Hart, DeWolf, Wozniak, & Burts, 1992). In one study, 4- to 7-year-olds rated the most important features of friendships as doing things together, liking and caring for each other, sharing and helping one another, and to a lesser degree, living nearby or going to the same school. Younger children rated physical traits, such as appearance and size, higher than did older ones and rated affection and support lower (Furman & Bierman, 1983).

Preschool children prefer prosocial playmates (C. H. Hart et al., 1992). They reject disruptive, demanding, intrusive, or aggressive children and tend to ignore those who are shy, withdrawn, or tentative (Ramsey & Lasquade, 1996; Roopnarine & Honig, 1985). Shy boys, especially, may be excluded by peers (Coplan et al., 2004).

Well-liked preschoolers and kindergartners and those who are rated by parents and teachers as socially competent generally cope well with anger. They respond directly, in ways that minimize further conflict and keep relationships going. They avoid insults and threats. Unpopular children tend to hit back or tattle (Fabes & Eisenberg, 1992).

Characteristics and Effects of Friendships

Preschoolers act differently with their friends than with other children. They have more positive, prosocial interactions but also more quarrels and fights (Rubin et al., 1998). Children may get just as angry with a friend as with someone they dislike, but they are more likely to control their anger and express it constructively with a friend (Fabes, Eisenberg, Smith, & Murphy, 1996).

Friendships are more satisfying—and more likely to last—when children see them as relatively harmonious and as validating their self-worth. Being able to confide in friends and get help from them is less important at this age than when children get older (Ladd, Kochenderfer, & Coleman, 1996).

Children with friends enjoy school more. Among 125 kindergartners, those who had friends in their class when they entered in August liked school better two months later, and those who kept up these friendships continued to like school better the following May. Children whose friendships are a source of help and self-validation are happier, have more positive attitudes toward school, and feel they can look to classmates for support (Ladd et al., 1996).

Parenting and Popularity

Parenting styles and practices can influence peer relationships. Popular children generally have warm, positive relationships with both mother and father. The parents are likely to be authoritative and the children to be both assertive and cooperative (Coplan et al., 2004;

Isley, O'Neil, & Parke, 1996; Kochanska, 1992; Roopnarine & Honig, 1985). Children whose parents are authoritarian may become shy or withdrawn (Coplan et al., 2004). Children who are insecurely attached or whose parents are harsh, neglectful, or depressed or have troubled marriages are at risk of developing unattractive social and emotional patterns and of being rejected by peers (Rubin et al., 1998). Children, especially boys, with overprotective parents tend to be wary of associating with peers. Parents who place importance on their children's peer relationships tend to have more sociable children than parents who do not show such concern (Coplan et al., 2004).

Children whose parents rely on power-assertive discipline tend to use coercive tactics in peer relations; children whose parents engage in give-and-take reasoning are more likely to resolve conflicts with peers that way (Crockenberg & Lourie, 1996). Children whose parents clearly communicate disapproval rather than anger—as well as strong positive feelings—are more prosocial, less aggressive, and better liked (Boyum & Parke, 1995).

Checkpoint

Can you . . .

- ✔ Explain how preschoolers choose playmates and friends, how they behave with friends, and how they benefit from friendships?
- ✔ Discuss how relationships at home can influence relationships with peers?

Refocus

- From what you have read, would you guess that Isabel Allende had high or low self-esteem as a young child? Why?
- Which of the theories of gender formation seems to best describe Allende's development? Which do you think she would agree with most?
- Isabel Allende describes herself as a solitary child, who lived and played largely in the world of her own imagination. Would Parten have considered her immature? Would you?
- Allende and her mother shared an unconditional love, yet she seemed to have greater respect for her stepfather. Why?
- Allende says little about relationships with other children besides her younger brothers. Thinking about her personality, would you expect her to have been popular or unpopular with peers?

Peer relationships become even more important during middle childhood, which we will examine in Chapters 12, 13, and 14.

Summary and Key Terms

The Developing Self

Guidepost 1 How does the self-concept develop during early childhood, and how do children advance in understanding and regulating their emotions?

- The self-concept undergoes major change in early childhood. According to neo-Piagetians, self-definition shifts from single representations to representational mappings. Young children do not see the difference between the real self and the ideal self.
- Culture affects the self-definition.
- Understanding of emotions directed toward the self and of simultaneous emotions develops gradually.

self-concept (295) **self-definition (296)** **single representations (296)** **real self (296)** **ideal self (296)** **representational mappings (296)**

Guidepost 2 How do young children develop initiative and self-esteem?

- According to Erikson, the developmental conflict of early childhood is initiative versus guilt. Successful resolution of this conflict results in the "virtue" of *purpose.*
- Self-esteem in early childhood tends to be global and unrealistic, reflecting adult approval.

initiative versus guilt (298) **self-esteem (298)**

Gender

Guidepost 3 How do boys and girls become aware of the meaning of gender, and what explains differences in behavior between the sexes?

- Gender identity is an aspect of the developing self-concept.
- The main gender difference in early childhood is boys' greater aggressiveness. Girls tend to be more empathic and prosocial and less prone to problem behavior. Some cognitive differences appear early and others not until preadolescence or later.
- Children learn gender roles at an early age through gender-typing. Gender stereotypes peak during the preschool years.
- Four major perspectives on gender development are biological, psychoanalytic, cognitive, and socialization-based approaches.
- Evidence suggests that some gender differences may be biologically based.
- In Freudian theory, a child identifies with the same-sex parent after giving up the wish to possess the other parent.
- Cognitive-developmental theory maintains that gender identity develops from thinking about one's gender. According to Kohlberg, gender constancy leads to acquisition of gender roles. Gender-schema theory holds that children categorize gender-related information by observing what males and females do in their culture.

- According to social cognitive theory, children learn gender roles through socialization. Parents, peers, the media, and culture influence gender-typing.

  gender identity (299) **gender roles (300)** **gender-typing (300)** **gender stereotypes (300)** **identification (302)** **gender constancy (303)** **gender-schema theory (303)** **social cognitive theory (304)**

Play: The Business of Early Childhood

Guidepost 4 How do preschoolers play, and how does play contribute to and reflect development?

- Play has physical, cognitive, and psychosocial benefits. Changes in the types of play children engage in reflect cognitive and social development.
- According to Piaget and Smilansky, children progress cognitively from functional play to constructive play, pretend play, and then formal games with rules. Pretend play becomes increasingly common during early childhood and helps children develop social and cognitive skills. Rough-and-tumble play also begins during early childhood.
- According to Parten, play becomes more social during early childhood. However, later research has found that nonsocial play is not necessarily immature.
- Children prefer to play with (and play more socially with) others of their sex.
- Cognitive and social aspects of play are influenced by the culturally approved environments adults create for children.

  functional play (306) **constructive play (306)** **pretend play (306)**

Parenting

Guidepost 5 How do parenting practices influence development?

- Discipline can be a powerful tool for socialization.
- Both positive reinforcement and prudently administered punishment can be appropriate tools of discipline within the context of a positive parent-child relationship.
- Power assertion, inductive techniques, and withdrawal of love each can be effective in certain situations. Reasoning is generally the most effective and power assertion the least effective in promoting internalization of parental standards. Spanking and other forms of corporal punishment can have negative consequences.
- Baumrind identified three child-rearing styles: authoritarian, permissive, and authoritative. A fourth style, neglectful or uninvolved, was identified later. Authoritative parents tend to raise more competent children. However, Baumrind's findings may be misleading when applied to some cultures or socioeconomic groups.

  discipline (309) **corporal punishment (310)** **power assertion (310)** **inductive techniques (310)** **withdrawal of love (310)** **psychological aggression (311)** **authoritarian (312)** **permissive (312)** **authoritative (312)**

Guidepost 6 Why do young children help or hurt others, and why do they develop fears?

- The roots of altruism and prosocial behavior appear early. This may be an inborn disposition that can be cultivated by parental modeling and encouragement.
- Instrumental aggression—first physical, then verbal—is most common in early childhood.
- Most children become less aggressive after age 6 or 7, but the proportion of hostile aggression increases. Boys tend to practice overt aggression, whereas girls engage in relational aggression.
- Preschool children show temporary fears of real and imaginary objects and events; older children's fears tend to be more realistic.

  altruism (314) **prosocial behavior (314)** **instrumental aggression (315)** **hostile aggression (315)** **overt aggression (315)** **relational aggression (315)**

Relationships with Other Children

- Sibling and peer relationships contribute to self-efficacy.

  self-efficacy (318)

Guidepost 7 How do young children get along with (or without) siblings?

- Most sibling interactions are positive. Older siblings tend to initiate activities and younger ones to imitate. Same-sex siblings, especially girls, get along best.
- Siblings tend to resolve disputes on the basis of moral principles.
- The kind of relationship children have with siblings often carries over into other peer relationships.
- Only children seem to develop at least as well as children with siblings in most respects.

Guidepost 8 How do young children choose playmates and friends, and why are some children more popular than others?

- Preschoolers choose playmates and friends who are like them and with whom they have positive experiences. Aggressive children are less popular than prosocial children.
- Friends have more positive and negative interactions than other playmates.
- Parenting can affect children's social competence with peers.

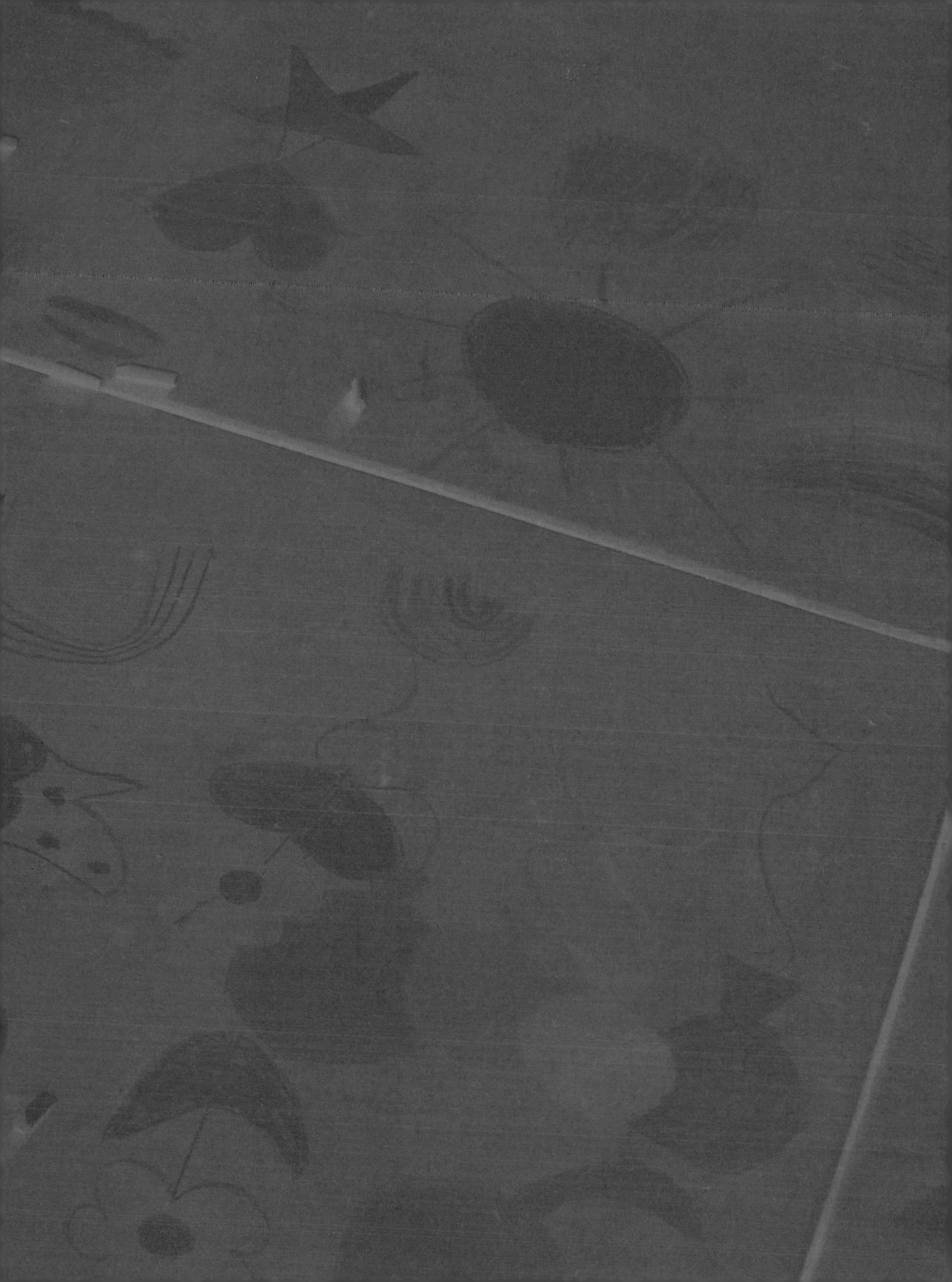

Part 5

Middle Childhood: A Preview

Chapter 12
Physical Development and Health in Middle Childhood

- Growth slows.
- Strength and athletic skills improve.
- Respiratory illnesses are common, but health is generally better than at any other time in the life span.

Chapter 13
Cognitive Development in Middle Childhood

- Egocentrism diminishes. Children begin to think logically but concretely.
- Memory and language skills increase.
- Cognitive gains permit children to benefit from formal schooling.
- Some children show special educational needs and strengths.

Chapter 14
Psychosocial Development in Middle Childhood

- Self-concept becomes more complex, affecting self-esteem.
- Coregulation reflects gradual shift in control from parents to child.
- Peers assume central importance.

Middle Childhood

The middle years of childhood, from about ages 6 to 11, are also called the *school years.* School is the central experience during this time—a focal point for physical, cognitive, and psychosocial development. As we will see in Chapter 12, children grow taller, heavier, and stronger and acquire the motor skills needed to participate in organized games and sports. As we will see in Chapter 13, they make major advances in thinking, in moral judgment, in memory, and in literacy. Individual differences become more evident and special needs more important as competencies affect success in school.

Competencies also affect self-esteem and popularity, as we will see in Chapter 14. Although parents continue to be important, the peer group is more influential than before. Children develop physically, cognitively, and emotionally as well as socially through contacts with other children.

Linkups to Look For

- Undernourishment can have cognitive and psychosocial as well as physical effects.
- Obese children often suffer social rejection.
- Moral development may be linked to cognitive growth.
- IQ can be affected by nutrition, socioeconomic status, culture, rapport with the examiner, and familiarity with the surroundings.
- Parenting styles can affect school achievement.
- Physical appearance plays a large part in self-esteem.
- A decline in egocentric thinking permits deeper, more intimate friendships.
- Children who are good learners and problem solvers tend to be resilient in coping with stress.

chapter 12

Physical Development and Health in Middle Childhood

The healthy human child will keep
Away from home, except to sleep.
Were it not for the common cold,
Our young we never would behold.

—Ogden Nash, *You Can't Get There from Here*

Focus *Ann Bancroft, Polar Explorer*

Ann Bancroft

Ann Bancroft is the first woman in history to reach both the North and South Poles by nonmotorized means. In 1986, she dogsledded 1,000 miles from the Northwest Territories in Canada to the North Pole as the only female member of an international expedition. After surviving eight months of grueling training and enduring temperatures as low as -70°F for 56 days, Bancroft stood on top of the world. Seven years later she led three other women in a 67-day, 660-mile ski trek to the South Pole, reaching it on January 14, 1993. For these exploits, she was inducted into the National Women's Hall of Fame, was named Woman of the Year by *Ms.* magazine, and won numerous other awards and honors. Bancroft also was the first woman to ski across Greenland. In 2000, she and Liv Arneson of Norway became the first team of women to ski across the landmass of Antarctica; and in 2002 the two women reunited for a kayaking voyage from the north shore of Lake Superior to the St. Lawrence Seaway.

How did this 5-foot 3-inch, 125-pound woman achieve these remarkable feats? The answers go back to her childhood in then-rural Mendota Heights, Minnesota.

Born September 29, 1955, into what she calls a family of risk takers, Ann showed her climbing instincts as soon as she could walk. As a toddler, she would climb her grandmother's bookcase to reach things on top. Instead of trying to stop her from climbing, her parents said, "Go ahead and try; you might just get what you want."

Ann was an outdoor girl. She and her two brothers and two sisters spent hours roaming the fields surrounding their farmhouse. Ann would "pretend she was a pirate building rafts to float down the creek, or an adventurer canoeing in the far north. During the winter she would build snow forts, sleeping shacks, and tunnels" (Wenzel, 1990, p. 15).

Her father often took the family on camping and canoe trips in the wilds of northern Minnesota. When she was 8, Ann started camping out in her backyard in winter with her cousins and the family dog. When she was 10, her parents went to Africa as missionaries. Ann's two years in Kenya kindled her thirst to see other parts of the world.

Biographical information about Ann Bancroft came primarily from Noone (2000), Wenzel (1990), and Bancroft's Web site, http://www.yourexpedition.com. Other sources were "Ann Bancroft, 1955–" (1998), "Ann Bancroft, 1955–" (1999), "Ann Bancroft, Explorer" (undated), "First Woman to Both Poles" (1997), and "Minnesota Explorer Ann Bancroft" (2002).

In school Ann was a poor student. A natural athlete, she liked gym class the best. Not until seventh grade did she learn that she had dyslexia, a reading disability. Around that time Ann came across a book about Sir Ernest Shackleton's unsuccessful effort to reach the South Pole in 1914. She was drawn to the photographs. "I was so fascinated by the images that I no longer was intimidated by the words and thickness of the book," Ann recalls. "I wanted to know about this adventure at the bottom of the world. This began my curiosity with Antarctica and the dream of one day crossing it."

Ann became a physical education teacher and athletic director in St. Paul. In 1983, she and a friend climbed Alaska's Mount McKinley, the highest peak in North America—an expedition that could have ended in disaster for her partner, who developed hypothermia, had it not been for Ann's training in first aid and emergency medicine. Two years later, Ann was invited to join the Steger International Polar Expedition to the North Pole as a medic and trip photographer.

"The goal was not so much reaching the pole itself," Bancroft recalls. "It was . . . more universal. Why do we all take on struggles? Why run a marathon? I think we're all striving to push ourselves. And in the process of overcoming struggle and challenges, we get to know ourselves better."

Today Bancroft is an instructor for Wilderness Inquiry, a program for both able-bodied people and those with disabilities. During her first South Pole expedition, she lugged a 30-pound radio set across the ice so she could send progress reports to students around the world. On her last expedition to Antarctica with Arneson, children in more than 40 countries followed the journey by e-mail, with the help of an interactive Web site and curriculum. She has coauthored a book about her adventures (Loewen & Bancroft, 2001).

Her goal is to "inspire children around the globe to pursue their dreams" as she has (Noone, 2000, p. 1). "It is totally energizing," she says, "to step out each day living a dream."

● ● ●

As a schoolgirl, Ann Bancroft may not have seemed extraordinary except that her dyslexia marked her as a child with special needs. Yet her achievements, based on her indomitable energy and will, are impressive. Her story illustrates how a dream formed in childhood can inspire later accomplishments. She is a living example of the power of attitudes and desires to shape development.

Although motor abilities improve less dramatically in middle childhood than before, these years are important for development of the strength, stamina, endurance, and motor proficiency needed for sports and outdoor activities. In this chapter we look at these and other physical developments, beginning with normal growth, which depends on proper nutrition and good health. As we explore health concerns, we examine children's understanding of health and illness, which links physical, cognitive, and emotional issues. As children do more, their risk of accidents increases; we examine some ways to lower the risks.

After you have read and studied this chapter, you should be able to answer each of the Guidepost questions that follow. Look for them again in the margins, where they point to important concepts throughout the chapter. To check your understanding of these Guideposts, review the end-of-chapter summary. Checkpoints located at periodic spots throughout the chapter will help you verify your understanding of what you have read.

1. What are normal growth patterns during middle childhood, and how can abnormal growth be treated?
2. What factors affect nutritional and oral health, and how can undernourishment and obesity be prevented and treated?
3. What gains in motor skills typically occur at this age, and what kinds of play do boys and girls engage in?
4. What are the principal health and fitness concerns in middle childhood, and what can adults do to make the school years healthier and safer?

Growth and Physiological Development

What are normal growth patterns during middle childhood, and how can abnormal growth be treated?

If we were to walk by a typical elementary school just after the three o'clock bell, we would see a virtual explosion of children of all shapes and sizes. Tall ones, short ones, husky ones, and skinny ones would be bursting out of the school doors into the open air. We would see that school-age children look very different from children a few years younger. They are taller, and most are fairly wiry; but more are likely to be overweight than in past decades, and some may be malnourished.

Height and Weight

Compared with its rapid pace in early childhood, growth in height and weight during middle childhood slows considerably. Still, although day-by-day changes may not be obvious, they add up to a startling difference between 6-year-olds, who are still small children, and 11-year-olds, many of whom are now beginning to resemble adults.

School-age children grow about 1 to 3 inches each year and gain about 5 to 8 pounds or more, doubling their average body weight (see Table 12-1). Girls retain somewhat more fatty tissue than boys, a characteristic that will persist through adulthood. Of course, these figures are just averages. Individual children vary widely—so widely that a child of average height at age 7 who did not grow at all for two years would still be within the normal limits of height at age 9.

African-American boys and girls tend to grow faster than white children. By about age 6, African-American girls have more muscle and bone mass than European-American or Mexican-American girls. Mexican-American girls have a higher percentage of body fat than white girls the same size (Ellis, Abrams, & Wong, 1997). (Racial comparisons in height and weight are not included in Table 12-1 because such data do not appear in the current charts published by the Centers for Disease Control.)

Table 12-1 Physical Growth, Age 6 to Age 11 (50th percentile)*

	Height, Inches		Weight, Pounds	
Age	**Boys**	**Girls**	**Boys**	**Girls**
6	45½	45½	46	45
7	48	48	51	50
8	50½	50½	57	57
9	52½	52½	63	64
10	54½	54½	70	73
11	56½	56½	79	82

*Fifty percent of children in each category are above this height or weight level, and 50 percent are below it.

Source: Data are from Kuczmarski at al., 2000.

Although most children grow normally, some do not. One type of growth disorder arises from the body's failure to produce enough growth hormone. Administration of synthetic growth hormone in such cases can produce rapid growth in height, especially during the first two years (Albanese & Stanhope, 1993; Vance & Mauras, 1999). However, synthetic growth hormone also is being used for children who are much shorter than other children their age but whose bodies *are* producing normal quantities of the hormone. Its use for this purpose is highly controversial (Macklin, 2000; Vance & Mauras, 1999). The procedure has been used for a relatively short time, and we do not know what the long-term effects may be. The treatment is costly and lengthy, and although it often brings short-term gains, there is mixed evidence as to whether it makes children who are normally short any taller as adults (Hintz, Attie, Baptista, & Roche for the Genentech Collaborative Group, 1999; Vance & Mauras, 1999). If unsuccessful, the therapy may do psychological harm by creating unfulfilled expectations or by giving short children the feeling that something is wrong with them. The American Academy of Pediatrics Committee on Drugs and Committee on Bioethics (1997) and other medical experts recommend extreme caution in prescribing growth hormone except as a replacement for natural hormone.

Checkpoint

Can you . . .

- ✔ Summarize typical growth patterns of boys and girls in middle childhood and give reasons for variations?
- ✔ Discuss the advisability of administering synthetic growth hormone to short children?

Guidepost 2

What factors affect nutritional and oral health, and how can undernourishment and obesity be prevented and treated?

Nutrition and Oral Health

Most schoolchildren have good appetites and eat far more than younger children. To support their steady growth and constant exertion, children need, on average, 2,400 calories every day—more for older children and less for younger ones. Breakfast should supply about one-fourth of total calories. Nutritionists recommend a varied diet including plenty of grains, fruits, and vegetables, which are high in natural nutrients.

Tooth Development and Dental Care

Most of the adult teeth arrive early in middle childhood. The primary teeth begin to fall out at about age 6 and are replaced by permanent teeth at a rate of about four teeth per year for the next five years.

Between 1971–1974 and 1988–1994, the number of U.S. children ages 6 to 18 with untreated cavities dropped nearly 80 percent. Improvements cut across ethnic and socioeconomic lines (Brown, Wall, & Lazar, 1999). Much of the improvement in children's dental health is attributed to use of adhesive sealants on the rough, chewing surfaces (L. J. Brown, Kaste, Selwitz, & Furman, 1996).

Undernourishment

Nearly half (46 percent) of young children in south Asia, 30 percent in sub-Saharan Africa, 8 percent in Latin America and the Caribbean, and 27 percent worldwide are moderately or severely underweight (UNICEF, 2002). In the United States, in 1998, 1 child in 5 did not get enough to eat (U.S. Department of Agriculture, 1999).

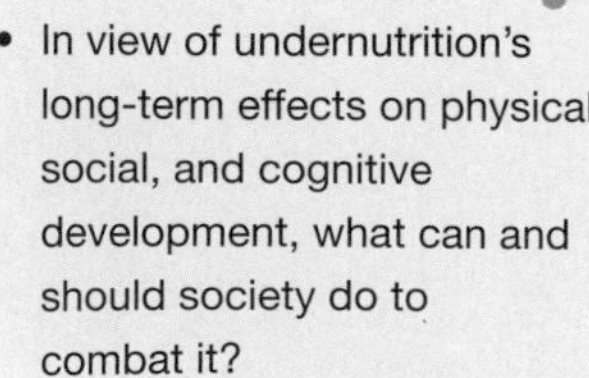

- In view of undernutrition's long-term effects on physical, social, and cognitive development, what can and should society do to combat it?

Because undernourished children usually live in extremely deprived circumstances, the specific effects of undernutrition may be hard to isolate. However, taken together, these deprivations may negatively affect not only growth and physical well-being but cognitive and psychosocial development as well. In an analysis of data on a nationally representative sample of 3,286 six- to 11-year-olds, those whose families had insufficient food were more likely to do poorly on arithmetic tests, to have repeated a grade, to have seen a psychologist, and to have had difficulty getting along with other children (Alaimo, Olson, & Frongillo, 2001). Moreover, cognitive effects of undernutrition may be long lasting. Among 1,559 Mauritian children born in a single year, those who were undernourished at age 3 had poorer verbal and spatial abilities, reading skills, scholastic ability, and neuropsychological performance than their peers at age 11 (Liu, Raine, Venables, Dalais, & Mednick, 2003).

Effects of undernutrition can be largely reversed with improved diet (Lewit & Kerrebrock, 1997), but because undernourishment affects all aspects of development, the most effective treatments may go beyond physical care. A longitudinal study (Grantham-McGregor, Powell, Walker, Chang, & Fletcher, 1994) followed two groups of Jamaican children with low developmental levels who had been hospitalized for severe undernour-

These girls proudly show off a childhood milestone—the normal loss of baby teeth, which will be replaced by permanent ones. U.S. children today have fewer dental cavities than in the early 1970s, probably owing to better nutrition, widespread use of fluoride, and better dental care.

ishment in infancy or toddlerhood. The children came from extremely poor and often unstable homes. Health care paraprofessionals played with an experimental group in the hospital and, after discharge, visited them at home every week for three years, showing the mothers how to make toys and encouraging them to interact with their children. Three years after the program stopped, the experimental group's IQs were well above those of a control group who received only standard medical care (though not as high as those of a third, well-nourished group). Furthermore, the IQs of the experimental group remained significantly higher 7, 8, 9, and 14 years after leaving the hospital.

Early education may help counter the effects of undernourishment. In the Jamaican study, the mothers in the experimental group enrolled their children in preschools at earlier ages than did the mothers in the control group. In another Mauritian study, 100 three- to 5-year-olds received nutritional supplements and medical inspections and were placed in special preschools with small classes. At age 17, these children had lower rates of antisocial behavior and mental health problems than a control group. The effects were greatest among those who had been undernourished to begin with (Raine et al., 2003).

Checkpoint

Can you . . .

- ✔ Identify nutritional needs of school-age children?
- ✔ Tell why health of permanent teeth has improved?
- ✔ Discuss effects of undernourishment and identify factors that may influence the long-term outcome?

Overweight and Body Image

Overweight in children has become a major health issue in the United States. About 16 percent of 6- to 11-year-olds are overweight, and an additional 15 percent are near-overweight. Boys are more likely to be overweight than girls (Hedley et al., 2004). Although overweight has increased in all ethnic groups (Center for Weight and Health, 2001), it is most prevalent among Mexican-American children (almost 22 percent) and non-Hispanic black children (nearly 20 percent) as compared with 13.5 percent of non-Hispanic white children (Ogden, Flegal, Carroll, & Johnson, 2002).

Unfortunately, children who try to lose weight are not always the ones who need to do so. Concern with **body image**—how one believes one looks—begins to be important toward the end of middle childhood, especially for girls, and may develop into eating disorders that become more common in adolescence (see Chapter 15).

body image Descriptive and evaluative beliefs about one's appearance.

Causes of Overweight

People become overweight when they consume more calories than they expend. But when two people eat the same amount of calories, why does only one get fat? And what makes some people eat more than they need?

Children who spend many hours watching television tend to be overweight. They are likely to get too little exercise and eat too many fattening snacks.

As we reported in Chapter 3, overweight, or obesity, often results from an *inherited tendency* aggravated by too little exercise and too much or the wrong kinds of food (AAP Committee on Nutrition, 2003). Researchers have identified several genes that seem to be involved in obesity (Chen et al., 2004; Clément et al., 1998; Jackson et al., 1997; Montague et al., 1997; Ristow, Muller-Wieland, Pfeiffer, Kroner, & Kahn, 1998). One of these genes governs production of a brain protein called *leptin,* which seems to help regulate body fat. A defect in this gene, originally found in mice, can disrupt appetite control (Campfield, Smith, Guisez, Devos, & Burn, 1995; Friedman & Halaas, 1998; Halaas et al., 1995; Kristensen et al., 1998; Pelleymounter et al., 1995; Zhang et al., 1994). Such research may lead to identification and treatment of children predisposed to overweight.

Environment is also influential. Children tend to eat the same kinds of foods and develop the same kinds of habits as the people around them (AAP Committee on Nutrition, 2003). U.S. children of all ages eat too much fat and sugar and artificially fortified or low-nutrient food (Muñoz et al., 1997; Subar, Krebs-Smith, Cook, & Kahle, 1998). On a typical day, more than 30 percent of a nationally representative sample of 6,212 children and adolescents reported eating fast foods. These children consumed more fat, carbohydrates, and sugar additives and less fiber, milk, fruits, and nonstarchy vegetables than other children (Bowman, Gortmaker, Ebbeling, Pereira, & Ludwig, 2004). Diets of poor and minority children are especially unbalanced, and they may lack access to safe places to work off what they eat (AAP Committee on Nutrition, 2003; Muñoz et al., 1997).

What's your view ?

- If overweight runs in families, either because of heredity or lifestyle, how can parents who have not been able to control their own weight help their children?

Inactivity may be a major factor in the sharp rise in childhood overweight. Children today are less likely than in previous generations to walk to school and to do household chores. In some communities, physical education has been cut back (AAP Committee on Nutrition, 2003). About 20 percent of 8- to 16-year-olds report engaging in vigorous physical activity no more than twice a week, and more than 25 percent watch at least 4 hours of television each day. Children who watch that much television tend to have more body fat and a higher body mass index (BMI) than those who watch less than two hours a day (Andersen, Crespo, Bartlett, Cheskin, & Pratt, 1998).

Why Is Childhood Overweight a Serious Concern?

When 106 severely obese children and adolescents were asked to rate their health-related quality of life (for example, their ability to walk more than one block, to sleep well, to get along with others, and to keep up in school), they reported significant impairment as compared with healthy peers. They also were more likely to miss school. In fact, the obese young people rated their quality of life as low as did children with cancer (Schwimmer, Burwinkle, & Varni, 2003).

For a discussion of a common childhood health problem, watch the video on "Obesity" in Chapter 12 of your CD.

Overweight children often suffer emotionally and may compensate by indulging themselves with treats, making their physical and social problems even worse. Chronically obese children are at risk for behavior problems, depression, and low self-esteem (AAP Committee on Nutrition, 2003; Mustillo et al., 2003). They commonly have medical problems, including high cholesterol and blood pressure and high insulin levels (AAP Committee on Nutrition, 2003; Freedman, Dietz, Srinivasan, & Berenson, 1999). Among nationally representative samples of U.S. children and adolescents ages 8 to 17, average blood pressure rose between 1988 and 2000, in part due to the increased prevalence of overweight (Muntner, He, Cutler, Wildman, & Whelton, 2004). Overweight children tend to become obese adults, at risk for heart disease, orthopedic problems, and diabetes. Indeed, childhood overweight may be a stronger predictor of some diseases than adult overweight (AAP Committee on Nutrition, 2003; Center for Weight and Health, 2001; Must, Jacques, Dallal, Bajema, & Dietz, 1992). Body mass index (BMI) and blood pressure, both risk factors for heart disease, tend to be higher in African-American and Mexican-American children than in white children (Winkleby, Robinson, Sundquist, & Kraemer, 1999).

Prevention and Treatment of Overweight

Prevention of weight gain is easier, less costly, and more effective than treating overweight once it develops (Center for Weight and Health, 2001). Parents should watch children's eating and activity patterns and address excessive weight gain *before* a child becomes severely overweight (AAP Committee on Nutrition, 2003).

Children with a BMI in the 95th percentile or higher are candidates for treatment. Treatment should begin early, involve the family, and promote permanent changes in lifestyle, not weight loss alone (Barlow & Dietz, 1998; Miller-Kovach, 2003). Parents need to find constructive, blame-free ways to encourage physical activity and build the child's self-esteem while providing a wide variety of healthful, low-fat foods (Committee for Weight and Health, 2001; Davison & Birch, 2001). During a 12-week experiment with 10 obese 8- to 12-year-olds, those whose television viewing was limited to the amount of time they spent pedaling an exercise bicycle watched much less television and showed significantly greater reductions in body fat than a control group (Faith et al., 2001).

Checkpoint

Can you . . .

✔ Discuss why childhood overweight has increased and how it can affect health?

Motor Development and Physical Play

Guidepost 3

What gains in motor skills typically occur at this age, and what kinds of play do boys and girls engage in?

During the middle years, children's motor abilities continue to improve (see Table 12-2). Children keep getting stronger, faster, and better coordinated, and they derive great pleasure from testing their bodies and learning new skills.

In nonliterate societies, children spend less time playing and more time on household chores than in industrial societies. By middle childhood, children in most nonliterate and transitional societies go to work, and girls, especially, do more household labor, leaving them little time and freedom to play (Larson & Verma, 1999). Even in the United States, children's lives today are more tightly scheduled than they were when Ann Bancroft was camping out in her backyard. Many children, as they grow older, spend less time in free, unstructured activities, such as rough-and-tumble play and informal games, and more time in organized sports (Hofferth & Sandberg, 1998). And a substantial minority—more than 1 in 5, according to one survey—engage in little or no free-time physical activity (Duke, Huhman, & Heitzler, 2003).

LifeMap CD

To observe fine motor skills in a school-age child, watch the video on "Copying Shapes at Age 7" in Chapter 12 of your CD.

Free Play

Should you come across a couple of schoolboys tumbling over each other, you might hardly be able to tell whether they were fighting or playing except by the expressions on their faces. About 10 percent of schoolchildren's free play at recess in the early grades consists of **rough-and-tumble play,** vigorous play that involves wrestling, kicking, tumbling, grappling, and sometimes chasing, often accompanied by laughing and screaming. This kind of play peaks in middle childhood; the proportion typically drops to about 5 percent at age 11, about the same as in early childhood (Pellegrini, 1998; Pellegrini & Smith, 1998).

rough-and-tumble play Vigorous play involving wrestling, hitting, and chasing, often accompanied by laughing and screaming.

Rough-and-tumble play seems to be universal; it takes place in such diverse places as India, Mexico, Okinawa, the Kalahari in Africa, the Philippines, Great Britain, and the United States (Humphreys & Smith, 1984). Rough-and-tumble play helps children jockey for dominance in the peer group by assessing their own and each other's strength. Boys

Table 12-2 Motor Development in Middle Childhood

Age	Selected Behaviors
6	Girls are superior in movement accuracy; boys are superior in forceful, less complex acts.
	Skipping is possible.
	Children can throw with proper weight shift and step.
7	One-footed balancing without looking becomes possible.
	Children can walk 2-inch-wide balance beams.
	Children can hop and jump accurately into small squares.
	Children can execute accurate jumping-jack exercise.
8	Children have 12-pound pressure on grip strength.
	The number of games participated in by both sexes is greatest at this age.
	Children can engage in alternate rhythmic hopping in a 2-2, 2-3, or 3-3 pattern.
	Girls can throw a small ball 40 feet.
9	Boys can run 16½ feet per second.
	Boys can throw a small ball 70 feet.
10	Children can judge and intercept pathways of small balls thrown from a distance.
	Girls can run 17 feet per second.
11	A standing broad jump of 5 feet is possible for boys and of 6 inches less for girls.

Source: Adapted from Cratty, 1986.

around the world participate in rough-and-tumble play more than girls do, a fact generally attributed to a combination of hormonal differences and socialization (Pellegrini, 1998; Pellegrini, Kato, Blatchford, & Baines, 2002; Pellegrini & Smith, 1998).

The games children play at recess tend to be informal and spontaneously organized. One child may play alone while nearby a group of classmates are chasing each other around the schoolyard. The games played at recess are not just fun; they affect children's growth in physical agility and social competence and their adjustment to school. For boys, playground games are a way to develop competitive skills important in male peer groups (Pellegrini et al., 2002).

In a longitudinal study, researchers observed the playground games of boys and girls in two primary schools in a large midwestern U.S. city across the first-grade year. Boys played more physically active games, whereas girls favored games that involve verbal expression or counting aloud, such as hopscotch and jumprope. Boys played a wider variety of games, even more so as the school year went on. Chasing games, which serve for boys as opening gambits for interaction with unfamiliar peers, gradually gave way to games with more complex rules, such as ball games. Boys who were leaders in games tended to become more socially competent and adjust better to school (Pellegrini et al., 2002).

Checkpoint

Can you . . .

- ✔ Explain the significance of rough-and-tumble play?
- ✔ Discuss differences in boys' and girls' free play?
- ✔ Tell what types of physical play children engage in as they grow older?

Organized Sports

After children outgrow rough-and-tumble play and begin playing games with rules, some join organized, adult-led sports. In a nationally representative survey of U.S. 9- to 13-year-olds and their parents, 38.5 percent reported participation in organized athletics outside of school hours during the previous week—most often in baseball, softball, soccer, and basketball. About twice as many children (77.4 percent) participated in unorganized physical activity, such as bicycling and shooting baskets. Black and Hispanic children and those in low-SES families were less likely than non-Hispanic white children to be involved in organized sports (Duke, Huhman, & Heitzler, 2003). Boys spend twice as much time on team sports as girls do, and the disparity widens as children grow older. Still, participation has risen 50 percent among both sexes since 1981 (Hofferth & Sandberg, 1998).

Health, Fitness, and Safety

What are the principal health and fitness concerns in middle childhood, and what can adults do to make the school years healthier and safer?

The development of vaccines for major childhood illnesses has made middle childhood a relatively safe time of life. The death rate in these years is the lowest in the life span. Still, many children get too little exercise, and some suffer from chronic medical conditions or accidental injuries or from lack of access to health care.

Maintaining Health and Fitness

Regular physical activity has immediate and long-term health benefits: weight control, lower blood pressure, improved cardiorespiratory functioning, and enhanced well-being. Furthermore, active children tend to become active adults. But although most U.S. schoolchildren get enough exercise to meet national goals, many children are not as active as they should be. In the national survey mentioned in the previous section, 22.6 percent of 9- to 13-year-olds engaged in *no* free-time physical activity (Duke, Huhman, & Heitzler, 2003).

Furthermore, many children, in and out of school, participate mainly in team and other competitive sports and games. After leaving school, most children will drop these activities, which typically are aimed at the fittest and most athletic children, like Ann Bancroft. A sound physical education program for *all* children should emphasize skill mastery based on realistic goals, rather than winning or losing. It should include a variety of competitive and recreational sports that can be part of a lifetime fitness regimen, such as tennis, bowling, running, swimming, golf, and skating (American Academy of Pediatrics [AAP] Committee on Sports Medicine and Committee on School Health, 1989; AAP Committee on Sports Medicine and Fitness, 1997).

Just changing everyday behavior can bring about improvement. Parents can make exercise a family activity by hiking or playing ball together, building strength on playground equipment, walking whenever possible, using stairs instead of elevators, and limiting television.

In addition to encouraging inactivity, too much television can deprive children of needed sleep. A questionnaire survey of parents of 495 kindergarten through fourth-grade children found that the more time children spent watching TV, especially at bedtime, the more likely they were to resist going to bed, to be slow in falling asleep, to be anxious around bedtime, and to wake up early (Owens et al., 1999). Indeed, according to the National Sleep Foundation (2004), U.S. children of all ages get less sleep than they need. First through fifth graders average 9½ hours a day, short of the recommended 10 to 11 hours.

Checkpoint

Can you . . .

✔ Explain the importance of adequate exercise and sleep, and give recommendations for parents?

Medical Conditions

Illness in middle childhood tends to be brief. **Acute medical conditions**—occasional, short-term conditions, such as infections and warts—are common. Six or seven bouts a year with colds, flu, or viruses are typical as germs pass among children at school or at play (Behrman, 1992). As children's experience with illness increases, so does their cognitive understanding of the causes of health and illness and of how people can promote their own health (see Box 12-1).

acute medical conditions Occasional illnesses that last a short time.

According to a nationwide survey of 30,032 families, an estimated 18 percent of children under age 18 have **chronic medical conditions:** physical, developmental, behavioral, and/or emotional conditions requiring special health services. Children with special health needs spend three times as many days sick in bed and miss school three times as often as other children (Newacheck et al., 1998). Let's look at some chronic conditions that affect everyday living.

chronic medical conditions Physical, developmental, behavioral, and/or emotional conditions that require special health services.

Vision and Hearing Problems

Most children have keener vision in middle childhood than when they were younger. Children under 6 years old tend to be farsighted. By age 6, vision typically is more acute; and because the two eyes are better coordinated, they can focus better.

The Research World

Box 12-1 *Children's Understanding of Health and Illness*

When Angela was sick, she overheard her doctor refer to *edema* (an accumulation of fluid, which causes swelling), and she thought her problem was "a demon." Being sick is frightening at any age. For young children, who do not understand what is happening, it can be especially distressing and confusing.

From a Piagetian perspective, children's understanding of health and illness is tied to cognitive development. As they mature, their explanations for disease change. Before middle childhood, children are egocentric; they believe that illness is magically produced by human actions, often their own ("I was a bad boy, so now I feel bad"). Later they explain all diseases—only a little less magically—as the doing of all-powerful germs. As children approach adolescence, they see that there can be multiple causes of disease, that contact with germs does not automatically lead to illness, and that people can do much to keep healthy.

Children's understanding of AIDS increases with age, like their understanding of colds, but they understand the cause of colds earlier, probably because they are more familiar with colds (Kistner et al., 1997; Schonfeld, Johnson, Perrin, O'Hare, & Cicchetti, 1993). Although most 6- and 7-year-olds have heard of HIV/AIDS, misconceptions about its causes and symptoms persist. Among 231 African-American children, ages 6 through 11, those whose mothers were infected showed fewer misconceptions than their peers (Armistead et al., 1999). Misconceptions about the disease can be harmful because children who harbor them are likely to unnecessarily avoid contact with classmates with AIDS (Kistner et al., 1997).

Interviews with 361 children in kindergarten through sixth grade (Schonfeld et al., 1993) found that children who give superficially correct explanations often lack real understanding of the processes involved in AIDS. For example, although 96 children mentioned drug use as a cause, most did not seem to realize that the disease is spread through blood adhering to a needle shared by drug users. One second grader gave this version of how someone gets AIDS: "Well, by doing drugs and something like that . . . by going by a drug dealer who has AIDS. . . . Well, you go by a person who's a drug dealer and you might catch the AIDS from 'em by standing near 'em" (Schonfeld et al., 1993, p. 393). From a young child's point of view, such a statement may be a logical extension of the belief that germs cause disease. The child may wrongly assume that AIDS can be caught, as colds are, from sharing cups and utensils, from being near someone who is coughing or sneezing, or from hugging and kissing.

To test Piaget's idea of an age-based progression in understanding of illness, an AIDS education program (Sigelman et al., 1996) sought to replace such intuitive "theories" with scientifically grounded ones. The developers of the program hypothesized that what young children lack is knowledge about the disease, not the ability to understand it. A total of 306 third, fifth, and seventh graders, mostly low-income Mexican Americans, in Catholic schools in Tucson participated in the carefully scripted program. Trained health instructors conducted two 50-minute sessions consisting of lectures, video clips, drawings, and discussion and using vocabulary appropriate for third graders. Content included an introduction to contagious and noncontagious diseases, specific information about HIV, an overview of the immune system, the meaning of the letters in *AIDS,* differences between transmission of colds and of AIDS, misconceptions about how the AIDS virus is transmitted, risk factors for AIDS, how the disease develops, and how it can be prevented. The instructors emphasized that there are only a few ways to get AIDS and that normal contact with infected people is *not* one of them. Flip charts summarized key points.

Experimental and control groups were tested before the program began and again about two weeks afterward. Students who had received instruction knew more about AIDS and its causes than those who had not, were no more (and no less) worried about it than before, and were more willing to be with people with AIDS. Almost a year later, they generally retained these gains. Third graders gained about as much from the program as seventh graders. It was somewhat less effective with fifth graders, perhaps because children that age already know more about AIDS than younger children but find it less relevant to their own lives than older ones do. The success of this program shows that, contrary to Piaget, even relatively young children can grasp complex scientific concepts about disease if teaching is geared to their level of understanding.

What's your view?

How old do you think children should be before being taught about AIDS?

Check it out!

For more information on this topic, go to **http://uhwww.unm.edu/childrens/child_life.shtml**. This is the Web site for the Children's Hospital at the University of New Mexico. It includes a link to a Family Resource Library. Or go to **http://www.pedinfo.org/**. This Web site is called "PEDINFO: An Index of the Pediatric Internet" and is dedicated to the dissemination of on-line information for those interested in child health.

Almost 13 percent of children under 18 are estimated to be blind or to have impaired vision. Vision problems are reported more often for white and Latino children than for African Americans (Newacheck, Stoddard, & McManus, 1993).

About 15 percent of 6- to 19-year-olds, preponderantly boys, have some hearing loss. Current screening guidelines may miss many children with very high frequency impairments. This is of concern, since even slight hearing loss can affect communication, behavior, and social relationships (Niskar et al., 1998).

Stuttering

Stuttering is involuntary, frequent repetition or prolongation of sounds or syllables. Its cause is unclear. Various theories point to faulty training in articulation and breathing, problems with brain functioning, parental pressure to speak properly, and deep-seated emotional conflicts. The condition runs in families, suggesting a genetic component. It is three times more common in boys than in girls. In 98 percent of cases, it begins before age 10. About 10 percent of prepubertal children stutter. Of these, 80 percent recover, usually before age 16—60 percent spontaneously and the other 20 percent in response to treatment (American Psychiatric Association [APA], 1994).

stuttering Involuntary, frequent repetition or prolongation of sounds or syllables.

Stuttering can interfere with social functioning. If stutterers become frustrated or anxious about ordinary conversation, their self-esteem may plummet. Yet a number of famous people, from the celebrated movie actress Marilyn Monroe to the World War II British prime minister Winston Churchill, have succeeded despite this disability.

Asthma

Asthma, a chronic respiratory disease, is the number one cause of childhood disability (Newacheck & Halfon, 2000). About 13 percent of U.S. children and adolescents have been diagnosed with asthma at some time. It is more common in boys than in girls (Bloom et al., 2003). Apparently allergy based, asthma is characterized by sudden attacks of coughing, wheezing, and difficulty in breathing. Its prevalence nearly doubled between 1980 and 1995 but seems to have leveled off (Akinbami & Schoendorf, 2002; Moss, 2003).

asthma Chronic respiratory disease characterized by sudden attacks of coughing, wheezing, and difficulty in breathing.

The cause of the asthma explosion is uncertain, but genetic factors may play a part. Researchers in the United States, Canada, and Australia have discovered a cluster of 291 genes, linked to asthma in mice, which also occur in human asthma patients. Most significant—and most promising for eventual treatment—seems to be a gene for the enzyme *arginase,* which regulates the way the body breaks down an amino acid in foods (Zimmerman et al., 2003). In addition, some experts point to tightly insulated houses that intensify exposure to indoor environmental toxins and allergens (Nugent, 1999; Sly, 2000; Stapleton, 1998), such as tobacco smoke, dust mites, molds, and cockroach droppings. Use of a gas stove for heat and allergies to household pets also may be risk factors (Bollinger, 2003; Etzel, 2003; Lanphear, Aligne, Auinger, Weitzman, & Byrd, 2001). Poor and minority children and those in single-parent families are most likely to be affected (Bloom et al., 2003; Newacheck & Halfon, 2000; Stapleton, 1998). Black children are three times more likely than white children to be hospitalized with asthma and four times more likely to die from it (Akinbami & Schoendorf, 2002).

Children with asthma miss an average of 10 days of school each year and experience 20 days of limited activity—almost twice the amount for children with other chronic ailments (Newacheck & Halfon, 2000). Most children with moderate to severe asthma, especially those from poor or Spanish-speaking families, do not get adequate treatment (Halterman, Aligne, Auinger, McBride, & Szilagyi, 2000). In a randomized, controlled study of 134 asthmatic inner-city children ages 8 to 16, a computerized, interactive device that used the Internet to educate patients and their families in symptom monitoring and medication use led to improved compliance and reduced symptoms (Dorsey & Schneider, 2003).

HIV and AIDS

Children infected with the human immunodeficiency virus (HIV) are at high risk of developing AIDS (acquired immune deficiency syndrome). Ninety percent of these children acquired the AIDS virus from their mothers, almost all of them in the womb (AAP Committee on Pediatric AIDS and Committee on Infectious Diseases, 1999; refer back to Chapter 4).

Prospects for children born with HIV infection have improved. Although some develop full-blown AIDS by their first or second birthday, others live for years without apparently being affected much, if at all (European Collaborative Study, 1994; Grubman et al., 1995; Nielsen et al., 1997; Nozyce et al., 1994). Genetic factors may affect the

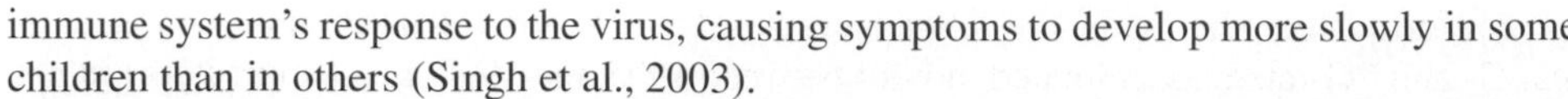

immune system's response to the virus, causing symptoms to develop more slowly in some children than in others (Singh et al., 2003).

Most children infected with HIV who reach school age function normally. Those with symptoms of AIDS may develop central nervous system dysfunction that can interfere with their ability to learn, but antiretroviral therapy can improve their functioning (AAP Committee on Pediatric AIDS, 2000). A combination therapy including protease inhibitors has markedly reduced mortality among HIV-infected children and adolescents (Gortmaker et al., 2001).

Since there is virtually no risk of infecting classmates (refer back to Box 12-1), children who carry the AIDS virus do not need to be isolated. They should be encouraged to participate in all school activities, including athletics, to the extent they are able (AAP Committee on Sports Medicine and Fitness, 1999; AAP Committee on Pediatric AIDS, 2000).

What's your view?

- There is virtually no medical evidence that children with HIV infection who are symptom free can transmit the virus to others except through bodily fluids. Yet many parents are afraid to have their children go to school with a child who is HIV-positive. What ways can you suggest to deal with this problem?

Accidental Injuries

Injuries increase between ages 5 and 14, as children take part in more physical activities and are supervised less. As in early childhood, accidental injuries are the leading cause of death (Anderson & Smith, 2003; Kochanek et al., 2004).

Parents tend to overestimate the safety skills of young children. Many kindergartners and first graders walk alone to school, often crossing busy streets without traffic lights, although they do not know how to do this safely. Many accidents could be prevented by providing school buses or more crossing guards (Dunne, Asher, & Rivara, 1992; Rivara, Bergman, & Drake, 1989; Zeedyk, Wallace, & Spry, 2002). Children, too, often overestimate their physical abilities. In one study, 6-year-olds who most overrated their abilities were most vulnerable to accidental injury. Eight-year-olds, with the benefit of more experience, were better judges of what they could safely do (Plumert, 1995).

Injuries tend to be repetitive, suggesting that some children are prone to take risks. In one study, 5- and 6-year-olds who tended to take risks in a gambling game were more likely than their peers to say it was safe to cross a busy street between cars without a traffic light or crosswalk (Hoffrage, Weber, Hertwig, & Chase, 2003). Risk taking may "run in families," perhaps due to risk factors or stress in the home and neighborhood. In a study of poor, urban children up to age 15 enrolled in Medicaid in King County, Washington, those who required emergency treatment for injuries were at elevated risk of repeat injuries during the next 90 days, and so were their siblings (Johnston, Grossman, Connell, & Koepsell, 2000). Children with behavioral disorders are particularly injury-prone (Brehaut, Miller, Raina, & McGrail, 2003).

Approximately 275 children die each year and about 430,000 go to emergency rooms for treatment of injuries from bicycle accidents. An estimated 23,000 of these are serious brain injuries. As many as 88 percent of these injuries could be prevented by using helmets (AAP Committee on Injury and Poison Prevention, 2001a). Protective headgear also is vital for baseball and softball, football, roller skating, rollerblading, skateboarding, scooter riding, horseback riding, hockey, speed sledding, and tobogganing. For soccer, protective goggles and mouth guards may help reduce head and facial injuries. "Heading" the ball should be minimized because of the danger of brain injury (AAP Committee on Sports Medicine and Fitness, 2000, 2001).

Many accidental injuries occur on school playgrounds. By wearing protective helmets when bicycling or roller skating, these children are dramatically reducing their risk of head injury.

Children under 14 suffered more than 1,260 snowmobile-related injuries, many of them severe and some fatal, in 1997 alone (Rice, Alvanos, & Kenney, 2000). The AAP Committee on Accident and Poison Prevention (1988) recommends that children under 16 *not* use snowmobiles, and that older riders be required by law to be licensed and to wear helmets at all times.

For a growing number of children, an important source of danger is the trampoline in the backyard (Furnival, Street, & Schunk, 1999; Smith & Shields, 1998). Because of the need for stringent safety precautions and constant supervision for trampoline use, the American Academy of Pediatrics (AAP Committee on Injury and Poison Prevention and Committee on Sports Medicine and Fitness, 1999) recommends that parents never buy trampolines and that children not use them on playgrounds or at school.

Unfortunately, the media do not encourage safety consciousness. In the 25 most popular G- and PG-rated nonanimated movies between 1995 and 1997, most characters did not wear automobile safety belts, look both ways when crossing streets, use crosswalks, wear helmets when bicycling, or wear flotation devices while boating (Pelletier et al., 2000).

Factors in Health and Access to Health Care

As we discussed in Chapter 9, socioeconomic status and race/ethnicity play an important part in children's health. Poor children—who are disproportionately minority children—and those living with a single parent are more likely than other children to be in fair or poor health, to have chronic conditions or health-related limitations on activities, to miss school due to illness or injury, to be hospitalized, to have unmet medical and dental needs, and to experience delayed medical care (Bloom et al., 2003; Collins & LeClere, 1997; Flores et al., 2002; Newacheck et al., 1998).

Why is this so? Parents with higher socioeconomic status tend to know more about good health habits and have better access to insurance and health care. Two-parent families tend to have higher incomes and more wholesome diets than single-parent families (Collins & LeClere, 1997), and their children are more likely to have health insurance (Fields, 2003). Children in low-income and minority families are more likely than other children to be uninsured, to have no usual place of health care, or to go to clinics or hospital emergency rooms rather than doctors' offices. In 2001, almost 18 percent of children in poor or near-poor households had no health insurance, and 15 percent of uninsured children had had no contact with a doctor or other health professional in more than two years (Bloom et al., 2003).

Access to health care is a particularly severe problem among Latino children, especially those who are poor or near poor and who have foreign-born parents with less than a high school education. More than 25 percent of Hispanic-American children, especially Mexican-American children, lack health insurance coverage, 14 percent have no usual place to go for health care, and nearly 18 percent have unmet health care needs due to cost (Scott & Ni, 2004). Even Asian-American children, who tend to be in better health than non-Hispanic white children (as measured, for example, by fewer school absences), are less likely to access and use health care, perhaps because of cultural and linguistic barriers (Yu, Huang, & Singh, 2004). Indeed, one factor in variations in health care is differing beliefs and attitudes about health and healing among cultural and ethnic groups (see Box 12-2 on page 340).

Checkpoint ✓

Can you . . .

- ✔ Distinguish between acute and chronic medical conditions, and discuss how chronic conditions can affect everyday life?
- ✔ Identify factors that increase the risks of accidental injury?
- ✔ Discuss how socioeconomic status and race/ethnicity influence health and access to health care?

Refocus

- How much impact do you think psychosocial factors such as motivation, determination, and self-confidence had in Ann Bancroft's physical development?
- How did Bancroft's childhood experiences with her parents and siblings influence her later achievements?
- What can we learn from Bancroft's experience about the kinds of activities that can lead to lifetime fitness?

One reason for some accidents is children's immaturity, both cognitive (preventing them from being aware of some dangers) and emotional (leading them to take dangerous risks). We will discuss cognitive development in middle childhood in Chapter 13 and emotional and social development in Chapter 14.

Box 12-2 *How Cultural Attitudes Affect Health Care*

One morning Buddi Kumar Rai, a university-educated resident of Badel, a remote hill village in Nepal, carried his 2½-year-old daughter, Kusum, to the shaman, the local "medicine man." Kusum's little face was sober, her usually golden complexion pale, and her almond-shaped eyes droopy from the upper-respiratory infection she had been suffering with the past week, complete with fever and a hacking cough.

Two days before, Kusum had been in her father's arms when he had slipped and fallen backwards off a veranda to the ground about 3 feet below, still tightly holding his little daughter. Neither was hurt, but little Kusum had screamed in fright.

Now the shaman told Buddi that Kusum's illness was due to that fright. He prescribed incantations and put a mark, a charcoal smudge the size of a silver dollar, on the child's forehead to drive away the evil spirit that had entered her body when she had her scare.

Adherence to ancient beliefs about illness is common in many parts of the industrialized world, where many people cling to beliefs that are at odds with mainstream scientific and medical thinking. To provide better medical care to members of ethnic minorities, policymakers need to understand the cultural beliefs and attitudes that influence what people do and the decisions they make and how they interact with the broader society.

Many cultures see illness and disability as a form of punishment inflicted upon someone who has transgressed in this or a previous life or is paying for an ancestor's sin. Another belief, common in Latin America and Southeast Asia, is that an imbalance of elements in the body causes illness, and the patient has to reestablish equilibrium. Arab Americans tend to attribute disease to such causes as the evil eye, grief and loss, exposure to drafts, and eating the wrong combinations of foods.

In many societies people believe that a severely disabled child will not survive. Since there is no hope, they do not expend time, effort, or money on the child—who then, of course, may *not* survive. In some religious households, parents hold out hope for a miracle and refuse surgery or other treatment.

Of course, standard medical practice in the United States is also governed by a cultural belief system. Often parents must make decisions about their child quickly, without consulting members of the extended family as would be done in many cultures. To foster independence and self-sufficiency, parents are discouraged from "babying" a disabled child. People from other cultures may not agree with these American values; parents may feel a need to consult their own parents about medical decisions and may not consider it important for a disabled child to become self-sufficient.

Professionals need to explain clearly, in the family's language whenever possible, what course of treatment they recommend, why they favor it, and what they expect to happen. Such concern can help prevent incidents like one that occurred when an Asian mother became hysterical as an American nurse took her baby to get a urine sample. The mother had had three children taken from her in Cambodia. None had returned.

This Peruvian healer treats a child with traditional methods, such as herbs and incantations. In many Latin American cultures, such practices are believed to cure illness by restoring the natural balance of elements in the body.

What's your view?

- How would Piaget interpret the belief in some cultures that illness and disabilities are punishments for human actions?
- Does such a belief suggest that Piaget's theory is limited in its applicability to nonwestern cultures?

Check it out!

For more information on this topic, go to **http://www.who.int/whr/**. This is the "World Health Report 2000, Health Systems: Improving Performance," published by the World Health Organization.

Sources: Al-Oballi Kridli (2002); S. W. Olds (2002); Groce & Zola (1993).

Summary and Key Terms

Growth and Physiological Development

Guidepost 1 What are normal growth patterns during middle childhood, and how can abnormal growth be treated?

- Physical development is less rapid in middle childhood than in earlier years. Wide differences in height and weight exist.
- Children with retarded growth due to growth hormone deficiency may be given synthetic growth hormone. The hormone is sometimes prescribed for short children who do *not* have hormone deficiency; extreme caution is advised in such cases.

Guidepost 2 What factors affect nutritional and oral health, and how can undernourishment and obesity be prevented and treated?

- Proper nutrition is essential for normal growth and health.
- The permanent teeth arrive in middle childhood. Dental health has improved, in part because of the use of sealants on chewing surfaces.
- Undernutrition can affect all aspects of development.
- Overweight, which is increasingly common among U.S. children, entails health risks. It is influenced by genetic and environmental factors and can often be treated.
- Concern with body image, especially among girls, may lead to eating disorders.

body image (331)

Motor Development and Physical Play

Guidepost 3 What gains in motor skills typically occur at this age, and what kinds of play do boys and girls engage in?

- Because of improved motor development, boys and girls in middle childhood can engage in a wide range of motor activities.
- About 10 percent of schoolchildren's recess-time play, especially among boys, is rough-and-tumble play.
- Informal, spontaneous play helps develop physical and social skills. Boys' games are more physical and girls' games more verbal.
- Many children, mostly boys, engage in organized, competitive sports, which are geared to the most athletic children. A sound physical education program should aim at skill development for all children.

rough-and-tumble play (333)

Health, Fitness, and Safety

Guidepost 4 What are the principal health and fitness concerns in middle childhood, and what can adults do to make the school years healthier and safer?

- Middle childhood is a relatively healthy period; the death rate is the lowest in the life span. However, many children do not meet fitness standards.
- Respiratory infections and other acute medical conditions are common. Chronic conditions such as asthma are most prevalent among poor and minority children, who are least likely to be insured and to have regular health care.
- Vision becomes keener during middle childhood, but a minority of children have defective vision or hearing. Stuttering is fairly common.
- Most children who are HIV-positive function normally in school and should not be excluded from any activities of which they are physically capable.
- Accidents are the leading cause of death in middle childhood. Use of helmets and other protective devices and avoidance of trampolines, snowmobiling, and other dangerous sports can greatly reduce injuries.
- Children's understanding of health and illness is related to their cognitive level. Cultural beliefs affect expectations regarding health care.

acute medical conditions (335) **chronic medical conditions (335)** **stuttering (337)** **asthma (337)**

chapter 13

Cognitive Development in Middle Childhood

What we must remember above all in the education of our children is that their love of life should never weaken.

—Natalia Ginzburg, *The Little Virtues*, 1985

Focus *Akira Kurosawa, Master Filmmaker*

Akira Kurosawa

The Japanese filmmaker Akira Kurosawa (1910–1998), who wrote and directed such classics as the Academy Award–winning *Rashomon* (1951) and *Seven Samurai* (1954), has been called a cinematographic genius. Kurosawa used the screen as if it were a canvas. Artistic intelligence—an unerring sense of composition, form, color, and texture—pervades his scenes.

In his mid-20s, as an apprentice to the great film director Kajiro Yamamoto, he was a quick study. Assigned to write scenarios, the talented novice came up with idea after idea. "He is completely creative," Yamamoto said of him (Richie, 1984, p. 12).

Yet, as a child, during his first two years at a westernized school in Tokyo, Kurosawa was a slow learner. Because he had trouble following the lessons, he just sat quietly, trying to amuse himself. His teacher eventually moved Akira's desk and chair away from the other students and frequently aroused snickers with such comments as "Akira probably won't understand this, but . . ." (Kurosawa, 1983, p. 8).

That initial school experience left an indelible mark on Kirosawa. He felt isolated and miserable. Then, toward the end of his second year of school, his family moved to another part of the city, and he was transferred to a traditional Japanese school. His new classmates, with their close-shaved heads, duck-cloth trousers, and wooden clogs, made fun of Akira's long hair and European-style clothing. The youngest of seven children, Akira had been a crybaby; now he became a laughingstock.

It was in third grade that he came out of his intellectual and emotional fog. The strongest catalyst for this change was his teacher, Mr. Tachikawa. In art class, instead of having all the students copy a picture and giving the top grade to the closest imitation, as was the custom, he let the children draw whatever they liked. Akira became so carried away that he pressed on his colored pencils until they broke, and then he licked his fingertips and smeared the colors all over the paper. When Mr. Tachikawa held up Akira's drawing, the class laughed boisterously. But the teacher lavished it with praise and gave it the highest grade.

"From that time on," Kurosawa later wrote, ". . . I somehow found myself hurrying to school in anticipation on the days when we had art classes . . . I became really good at drawing. At the same time my marks in other subjects suddenly began to improve. By the time

Sources of biographical information about Akira Kurosawa are Goodwin (1994), Kurosawa (1983), and Richie (1984).

Mr. Tachikawa left . . . , I was the president of my class, wearing a little gold badge with a purple ribbon on my chest" (1983, p. 13).

Academically, his performance was uneven: the best in his class in the subjects he liked, he did barely passable work in science and math. Still, he graduated as valedictorian. According to former classmate Uekusa Keinosuke, who became a scriptwriting colleague, "He certainly was not the little-genius type who merely gets good grades" but a "commanding" figure who became popular seemingly without effort (Richie, 1984, p. 10).

It was Mr. Tachikawa who introduced Akira to the fine arts and to film. Akira's father and his older brother Heigo discussed great literature with him and took him to Japanese vaudeville and western movies.

Even after Mr. Tachikawa left the school, Akira and his friend Uekusa would go to the teacher's home and sit around talking for hours. So strong was Akira's spirit by this time that when Mr. Tachikawa's conservative successor lambasted one of his paintings, the boy simply made up his mind to "work so hard that this teacher would never be able to criticize me again" (Kurosawa, 1983, p. 25).

• • •

We can learn several lessons from Akira Kurosawa's school experience. First, children—even highly gifted ones—develop at different rates. Second, Kurosawa's story illustrates the strong impact a teacher can have and how the influences of home and school interact. Finally, we see once again the tie-in between cognitive and psychosocial development. The flowering of Kurosawa's cognitive and social competence followed closely upon Mr. Tachikawa's move to boost his self-esteem. As Kurosawa later wrote, "When someone is told over and over again that he's no good at something, he loses more and more confidence and eventually does become poor at it. Conversely, if he's told he's good at something, his confidence builds and he actually becomes better at it" (1983, p. 40).

School is a major formative experience in middle childhood, impinging on every aspect of development. Children typically gain in self-confidence as they read, think, talk, play, and imagine in ways that were well beyond them only a few years before.

In this chapter we examine cognitive advances during the first five or six years of formal schooling, from about ages 6 to 11. Entry into Piaget's stage of concrete operations enables children to think logically and to make more mature moral judgments. As children improve in memory and problem solving, intelligence tests become more accurate in predicting school performance. The abilities to read and write open the door to a wider world. We discuss all these changes, and we look at controversies over IQ testing, bilingual education, homework, and mathematics instruction. Finally, we examine influences on school achievement and how schools try to meet special educational needs.

After you have read and studied this chapter, you should be able to answer each of the Guidepost questions that follow. Look for them again in the margins, where they point to important concepts throughout the chapter. To check your understanding of these Guideposts, review the end-of-chapter summary. Checkpoints located at periodic spots throughout the chapter will help you verify your understanding of what you have read.

1. How do school-age children's thinking and moral reasoning differ from those of younger children?
2. What advances in memory and other information-processing skills occur during middle childhood?
3. How accurately can schoolchildren's intelligence be measured?
4. How do communicative abilities expand during middle childhood?
5. What are some important influences on school achievement?
6. How do schools meet the needs of non-English-speaking children and those with learning problems?
7. How is giftedness assessed and nurtured?

Piagetian Approach: The Concrete Operational Child

Guidepost 1

How do school-age children's thinking and moral reasoning differ from those of younger children?

At about age 7, according to Piaget, children enter the stage of **concrete operations** when they can use mental operations to solve concrete (actual) problems. Children now can think logically because they can take multiple aspects of a situation into account. However, their thinking is still limited to real situations in the here and now.

concrete operations Third stage of Piagetian cognitive development (approximately from ages 7 to 12), during which children develop logical but not abstract thinking.

Cognitive Advances

In the stage of concrete operations, children can perform many tasks at a much higher level than they could in the preoperational stage (see Table 13-1). They have a better understanding of spatial concepts, causality, categorization, conservation, and number.

Space and Causality

Why can many 6- or 7-year-olds find their way to and from school, whereas most younger children cannot? One reason is that children in the stage of concrete operations can better understand spatial relationships. They have a clearer idea of how far it is from one place to another and how long it will take to get there, and they can more easily remember the route and the landmarks along the way. Experience plays a role in this development: a child who walks to school becomes more familiar with the neighborhood outside the home.

Both the ability to use maps and models and the ability to communicate spatial information improve with age (Gauvain, 1993). Although 6-year-olds can search for and find hidden objects, they usually do not give well-organized directions for finding the same objects—perhaps because they lack the appropriate vocabulary or do not realize what information the other person needs (Plumert, Pick, Marks, Kintsch, & Wegesin, 1994).

Judgments about cause and effect also improve during middle childhood. When 5- to 12-year-olds were asked to predict how levers and balance scales would perform under varying conditions, the older children gave more correct answers. Children understood the influence of physical attributes (the number of objects on each side of a scale) earlier than they recognized the influence of spatial factors (the distance of objects from the center of the scale) (Amsel, Goodman, Savoie, & Clark, 1996).

Categorization

The ability to categorize helps children think logically. Categorization includes such relatively sophisticated abilities as *seriation, transitive inference,* and *class inclusion,* which

Table 13-1 Advances in Selected Cognitive Abilities During Middle Childhood

Ability	Example
Spatial thinking	Danielle can use a map or model to help her search for a hidden object and can give someone else directions for finding the object. She can find her way to and from school, can estimate distances, and can judge how long it will take her to go from one place to another.
Cause and effect	Douglas knows which physical attributes of objects on each side of a balance scale will affect the result (i.e., number of objects matters but color does not). He does not yet know which spatial factors, such as position and placement of the objects, make a difference.
Classification	Elena can sort objects into categories, such as shape, color or both. She knows that a subclass (roses) has fewer members than the class of which it is a part (flowers).
Seriation and transitive inference	Catherine can arrange a group of sticks in order, from the shortest to the longest, and can insert an intermediate-size stick into the proper place. She knows that if one stick is longer than a second stick, and the second stick is longer than a third, then the first stick is longer than the third.
Inductive and deductive reasoning	Dara can solve both inductive and deductive problems and knows that inductive conclusions (based on particular premises) are less certain than deductive ones (based on general premises).
Conservation	Stacy, at age 7, knows that if a clay ball is rolled into a sausage, it still contains the same amount of clay (conservation of substance). At age 9, she knows that the ball and the sausage weigh the same. Not until early adolescence will she understand that they displace the same amount of liquid if dropped in a glass of water.
Number and mathematics	Kevin can count in his head, can add by counting up from the smaller number, and can do simple story problems.

improve gradually between early and middle childhood. Children show that they understand **seriation** when they can arrange objects in a series according to one or more dimensions, such as weight (lightest to heaviest) or color (lightest to darkest). By 7 or 8, children can grasp the relationships among a group of sticks on sight and arrange them in order of size (Piaget, 1952).

seriation Ability to order items along a dimension.

Transitive inference is the ability to infer a relationship between two objects from the relationship between each of them and a third object. Catherine is shown three sticks: a yellow one, a green one, and a blue one. She is shown that the yellow stick is longer than the green one, and the green one is longer than the blue. Without physically comparing the yellow and blue sticks, she immediately says that the yellow one is longer than the blue one (Chapman & Lindenberger, 1988; Piaget & Inhelder, 1967). However, we do not know whether Catherine arrives at this conclusion through conceptual reasoning, as Piaget suggested, or through perceptual comparison (Flavell, Miller, & Miller, 2002).

transitive inference Understanding of the relationship between two objects by knowing the relationship of each to a third object.

Class inclusion is the ability to see the relationship between a whole and its parts. Piaget (1964) found that when preoperational children are shown a bunch of 10 flowers—7 roses and 3 carnations—and are asked whether there are more roses or more flowers, they are likely to say there are more roses, because they are comparing the roses with the carnations rather than with the whole bunch. Not until age 7 or 8, and sometimes not even then, do children consistently reason that roses are a subclass of flowers and that, therefore, there cannot be more roses than flowers (Flavell, 1963; Flavell et al., 2002). However, even 3-year-olds show a rudimentary awareness of inclusion, depending on the type of task, the practical cues they receive, and their familiarity with the categories of objects they are tested on (Johnson, Scott, & Mervis, 1997).

class inclusion Understanding of the relationship between a whole and its parts.

Understanding of class inclusion is closely related to *inductive* and *deductive reasoning.* According to Piaget, children in the stage of concrete operations use only **inductive reasoning.** Starting with observations about particular members of a class of people, animals, objects, or events, they then draw general conclusions about the class as a whole.

inductive reasoning Type of logical reasoning that moves from particular observations about members of a class to a general conclusion about that class.

("My dog barks. So does Terry's dog and Melissa's dog. So it looks as if all dogs bark.") Inductive conclusions must be tentative because it is always possible to come across new information (a dog that does not bark) that does not support the conclusion.

Deductive reasoning, which Piaget believed does not develop until adolescence, starts with a general statement (premise) about a class and applies it to particular members of the class. If the premise is true of the whole class and the reasoning is sound, then the conclusion must be true: "All dogs bark. Spot is a dog. Spot barks."

deductive reasoning Type of logical reasoning that moves from a general premise about a class to a conclusion about a particular member or members of the class.

Researchers gave 16 inductive and deductive problems to 16 kindergartners, 17 second graders, 16 fourth graders, and 17 sixth graders. The problems were designed so as *not* to call upon knowledge of the real world. For example, one deductive problem was "All poggops wear blue boots. Tombor is a poggop. Does Tombor wear blue boots?" The corresponding inductive problem was "Tombor is a poggop. Tombor wears blue boots. Do all poggops wear blue boots?" Contrary to Piagetian theory, second graders (but not kindergartners) were able to answer both kinds of problems correctly, to see the difference between them, and to explain their responses, and they (appropriately) expressed more confidence in their deductive answers than in their inductive ones (Galotti, Komatsu, & Voelz, 1997).

What's your view 

- How can parents and teachers help children improve their reasoning ability?

Conservation

In solving various types of conservation problems, children in the stage of concrete operations can work out the answers in their heads; they do not have to measure or weigh objects.

If one of two identical clay balls is rolled or kneaded into a different shape—say, a long, thin "sausage"—Felipe, who is in the stage of concrete operations, will say that the ball and the "sausage" still contain the same amount of clay. Stacy, who is in the preoperational stage, is deceived by appearances. She says the long, thin roll contains more clay because it looks longer.

Felipe, unlike Stacy, understands the principle of *identity:* he knows the clay is still the same clay even though it has a different shape. He also understands the principle of *reversibility:* he knows he can change the sausage back into a ball. And he can *decenter:* he can focus on both length and width. He recognizes that although the ball is shorter than the "sausage," it is also thicker. Stacy centers on one dimension (length) while excluding the other (thickness).

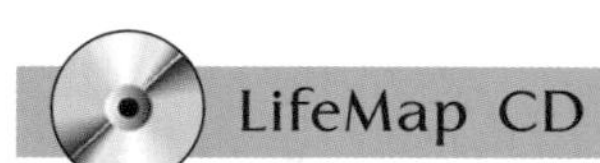

To observe a child in the concrete operational stage performing a Piagetian task, watch the "Development of Concept of Conservation" video in Chapter 13 of your CD.

Typically, children can solve problems involving conservation of substance, like this one, by about age 7 or 8. However, in tasks involving conservation of weight—in which they are asked, for example, whether the ball and the "sausage" weigh the same—children typically do not give correct answers until about age 9 or 10. In tasks involving conservation of volume—in which children must judge whether the "sausage" and the ball displace an equal amount of liquid when placed in a glass of water—correct answers are rare before age 12. Piaget's term for this inconsistency in the development of different types of conservation, as discussed in Chapter 10, is *horizontal décalage.* Children's thinking at this stage is so concrete, so closely tied to a particular situation, that they cannot readily transfer what they have learned about one type of conservation to another type, even though the underlying principles are the same.

Are there more red checkers or black checkers? This girl counting the checkers is solving a Piagetian conservation task. Because the red checkers are more spread out, a preoperational child would say there are more of them. A child in the stage of concrete operations will count, as this girl is doing, and say there are equal numbers of each color.

Number and Mathematics

By age 6 or 7, many children can count in their heads. They also learn to *count on:* to add 5 and 3, they start counting at 5 and then go on to 6, 7, and 8 to add the 3. It may take two or three more years for them to perform a comparable operation for subtraction, but by age 9 most children can either count up from the smaller number or down from the larger number to get the answer (Resnick, 1989).

Children also become more adept at solving simple story problems, such as "Pedro went to the store with $5 and spent $2 on candy. How much did he have left?" When the original amount is unknown ("Pedro went to the store, spent $2 and had $3 left. How much did he start out with?"), the problem is harder because the operation needed to solve it (addition) is not as clearly indicated. Few children can solve this kind of problem before age 8 or 9 (Resnick, 1989).

Research with minimally schooled people in developing countries suggests that the ability to add develops nearly universally and often intuitively, through concrete experience in a cultural context (Guberman, 1996; Resnick, 1989). These intuitive procedures are different from those taught in school. In a study of Brazilian street vendors ages 9 to 15, a researcher acting as a customer said, "I'll take two coconuts." Each one cost 40 cruzeiros; she paid with a 500-cruzeiros bill and asked, "What do I get back?" The child counted up from 80: "Eighty, 90, 100 . . ." and gave the customer 420 cruzeiros. However, when this same child was given a similar problem in the classroom ("What is 500 − 80?"), he arrived at the wrong answer by incorrectly using a series of steps learned in school (Carraher, Schliemann, & Carraher, 1988). This suggests that teaching math through concrete applications, not only through abstract rules, may be more effective.

Some intuitive understanding of fractions seems to exist by age 4 (Mix, Levine, & Huttenlocher, 1999), as children show when they deal a deck of cards or distribute portions of pizza (Frydman & Bryant, 1988; Sophian, Garyantes, & Chang, 1997). However, children tend not to think about the quantity a fraction represents; instead, they focus on the numerals that make it up. Thus, they may say that ½ plus ⅓ equals ⅖. Also difficult for many children to grasp at first is the fact that ½ is bigger than ¼—that the smaller fraction (¼) has the larger denominator (Siegler, 1998; Sophian & Wood, 1997).

The ability to estimate is important in many areas of daily life. How much time will I need to walk to school? How long will tonight's homework take? A study of 85 middle- and low-income schoolchildren found that estimating abilities progress with age (Siegler & Booth, 2004). When asked to place 24 numbers along a line from 0 to 100, almost all kindergartners exaggerated the differences between low numbers and minimized the distances between high numbers. Most second graders produced number lines that were more evenly spaced.

This developmental progression may result in part from the experience children gain in dealing with larger numbers in the latter part of first grade and throughout second grade, as well as with board games in which they move a token in accordance with a number shown on a spinner or on dice. A study in which second, fourth, and sixth graders placed numbers on a line from 0 to 1,000 found a similar progression, indicating again that experience with this larger range of numbers increases accuracy of estimation (Siegler & Opfer, 2003).

Checkpoint

Can you . . .

- ✔ Identify five kinds of cognitive abilities that emerge or strengthen during middle childhood, and explain how?
- ✔ Name three principles that help school-aged children understand conservation, and explain why children master different kinds of conservation at different ages?
- ✔ Weigh the evidence for influences of neurological development and cultural experience on Piagetian tasks?

Influences of Neurological Development and Culture

Piaget maintained that the shift from the rigid, illogical thinking of younger children to the flexible, logical thinking of older ones depends on both neurological development and experience in adapting to the environment. Support for a neurological influence comes from scalp measurements of brain activity during a conservation task. Children who had achieved conservation of volume had different brain wave patterns from those who had not yet achieved it, suggesting that they may have been using different brain regions for the task (Stauder, Molenaar, & Van der Molen, 1993).

Cross-cultural studies support the progression from preoperational to operational thought (Broude, 1995; Gardiner & Kosmitzki, 2005). However, abilities such as conservation may depend in part on familiarity with the materials being manipulated; children can think more logically about things they know something about. Mexican children who make pottery understand that a clay ball that has been rolled into a coil still has the same amount of clay sooner than they understand other types of conservation (Broude, 1995); and these children show signs of conservation of substance earlier than children who do not make pottery (Price-Williams, Gordon, & Ramirez, 1969). Thus, understanding of conservation may come not only from new patterns of mental organization, but also from culturally defined experience with the physical world.

Moral Reasoning

To draw out children's moral thinking, Piaget (1932) would tell them a story about two little boys: "One day Augustus noticed that his father's inkpot was empty and decided to help his father by filling it. While he was opening the bottle, he spilled a lot of ink on the tablecloth. The other boy, Julian, played with his father's inkpot and spilled a little ink on the cloth." Then Piaget would ask, "Which boy was naughtier, and why?" Children younger than 7 usually considered Augustus naughtier, since he made the bigger stain. Older children recognized that Augustus meant well and made the large stain by accident, whereas Julian made a small stain while doing something he should not have been doing. Immature moral judgments, Piaget concluded, center only on the degree of offense; more mature judgments consider intent.

Piaget (1932; Piaget & Inhelder, 1969) proposed that moral reasoning develops in three stages. Children move gradually from one stage to another, at varying ages.

The first stage (approximately ages 2–7, corresponding with the preoperational stage) is based on rigid obedience to authority. Because young children are egocentric, they cannot imagine more than one way of looking at a moral issue. They believe that rules cannot be bent or changed, that behavior is either right or wrong, and that any offense (like Augustus's) deserves punishment, regardless of intent.

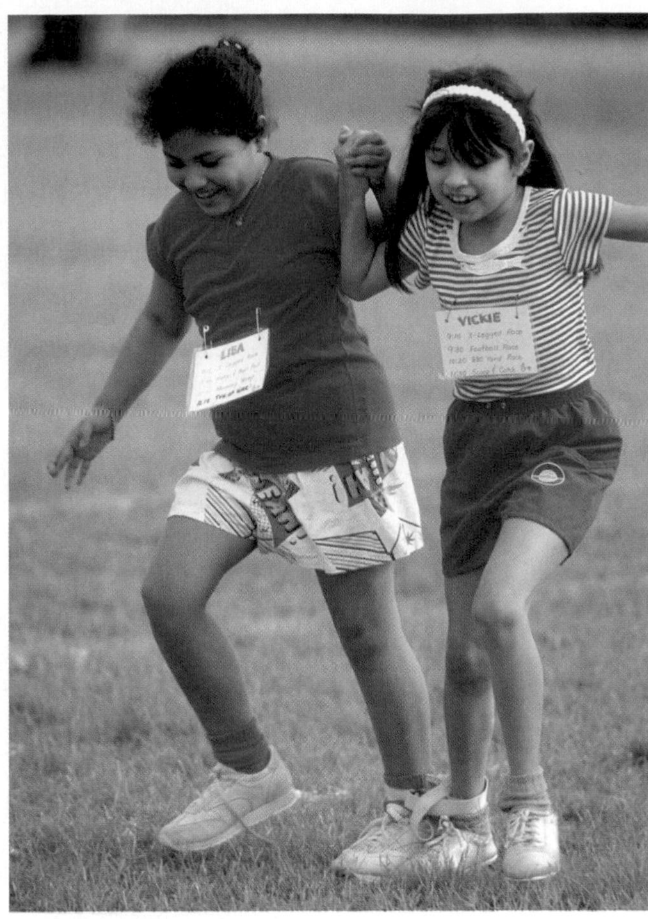

According to Piaget, children develop concepts of fairness through interaction with peers, often in games with rules, such as this three-legged race. As children grow older, they realize that rules need not be externally imposed but can be changed by mutual agreement.

The second stage (ages 7 or 8 to 10 or 11, corresponding with the stage of concrete operations) is characterized by increasing flexibility and some degree of autonomy based on mutual respect and cooperation. As children interact with more people and come into contact with a wider range of viewpoints, they begin to discard the idea that there is a single, absolute standard of right and wrong and to develop their own sense of justice based on fairness or equal treatment for all. Because they can consider more than one aspect of a situation, they can make more subtle moral judgments, such as taking into consideration the intent behind Augustus's and Julian's behavior.

What's your view 

- Do you agree that intent is an important factor in morality?
- How does the criminal justice system reflect this view?

Around age 11 or 12, when children may become capable of formal reasoning, the third stage of moral development arrives. Now "equality" takes on a different meaning for the child. The belief that everyone should be treated alike gradually gives way to the idea of *equity,* of taking specific circumstances into account. Thus, a child of this age might say that a 2-year-old who spilled ink on the tablecloth should be held to a less demanding moral standard than a 10-year-old who did the same thing.

One aspect of moral reasoning is the ability to understand reciprocal obligations and to anticipate how a person might feel when a promise has been violated. In a pair of studies, 122 three- to 10-year-old Berliners responded to stories involving hypothetical violations of agreements ("If Maxi keeps his room tidy for two weeks, his mother will give him a bike for Christmas"). Children of all age levels understood that the victim of a broken promise would feel bad, but preschoolers and kindergartners were less likely than older children to recognize that the person breaking the promise might feel bad as well (Keller, Gummerum, Wang, & Lindsey, 2004).

We'll discuss Lawrence Kohlberg's theory of moral reasoning, which builds on Piaget's, in Chapter 16.

Checkpoint 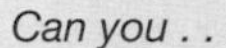

Can you . . .

✔ Describe Piaget's three stages of moral development and explain their links to cognitive maturation?

Guidepost 2

What advances in memory and other information-processing skills occur during middle childhood?

Information-Processing Approach: Memory and Other Processing Skills

As children move through the school years, they make steady progress in their abilities to process and retain information. Reaction time improves, and processing speed for such tasks as matching pictures, adding numbers in one's head, and recalling spatial information increases rapidly as unneeded synapses in the brain are pruned away (Hale et al., 1997; Janowsky & Carper, 1996; Kail, 1991, 1997; Kail & Park, 1994; refer back to Chapter 6). Faster, more efficient processing increases the amount of information a child can keep in working memory, making possible better recall and more complex, higher-level thinking (Flavell et al., 2002). School-age children also understand more about how memory works, and this knowledge enables them to use strategies, or deliberate techniques, to help them remember. As their knowledge expands, they become more aware of what kinds of information are important to pay attention to and remember.

LifeMap CD

Consider the information-processing abilities of a school-age child as you watch the video on "Memory ability at age 7" in Chapter 13 of your CD.

Metamemory: Understanding Memory

metamemory Understanding of processes of memory.

metacognition Awareness of one's own mental processes.

Between ages 5 and 7, the brain's frontal lobes may undergo significant development and reorganization. These changes may make improved recall and **metamemory,** knowledge about the processes of memory, possible (Janowsky & Carper, 1996). A related ability is **metacognition,** awareness of one's own thinking processes.

From kindergarten through fifth grade, children advance steadily in understanding memory (Flavell et al., 2002; Kreutzer, Leonard, & Flavell, 1975). Kindergartners and first graders know that people remember better if they study longer, that people forget things with time, and that relearning something is easier than learning it for the first time. By third grade, children know that some people remember better than others and that some things are easier to remember than others.

One pair of experiments looked at preschoolers', first graders', and third graders' beliefs about what influences remembering and forgetting. Most children in all three age groups believed that important events in a story about a birthday party (such as a guest falling into the cake) were more likely to be retained than minor details (such as a guest bringing a ball as a present). Most first and third graders but not most preschoolers believed that a later experience (playing with a friend who was not at the party) might color a child's recollection of who was at the party. Not until third grade did most children recognize that memory can be distorted by suggestions from others—say, a parent who suggests that the friend was at the party (O'Sullivan, Howe, & Marche, 1996).

Mnemonics: Strategies for Remembering

mnemonic strategies Techniques to aid memory.

external memory aids Mnemonic strategies using something outside the person.

rehearsal Mnemonic strategy to keep an item in working memory through conscious repetition.

organization Mnemonic strategy of categorizing material to be remembered.

elaboration Mnemonic strategy of making mental associations involving items to be remembered.

Devices to aid memory are called **mnemonic strategies.** The most common mnemonic strategy among both children and adults is use of *external memory aids.* Other common mnemonic strategies are *rehearsal, organization,* and *elaboration.*

Writing down a telephone number, making a list, setting a timer, and putting a library book by the front door are examples of **external memory aids:** prompts by something outside the person. Saying a telephone number over and over after looking it up, so as not to forget it before dialing, is a form of **rehearsal,** or conscious repetition. **Organization** is mentally placing information into categories (such as animals, furniture, vehicles, and clothing) to make it easier to recall. In **elaboration,** children associate items with something else, such as an imagined scene or story. To remember to buy lemons, ketchup, and napkins, for example, a child might imagine a ketchup bottle balanced on a lemon, with a pile of napkins handy to wipe up spilled ketchup.

As children get older, they develop better strategies, use them more effectively, and tailor them to meet specific needs (Bjorklund, 1997; see Table 13-2). When taught to use a strategy, older children are more likely to apply it to other situations (Flavell et al.,

Table 13-2 Four Common Memory Strategies

Strategy	Definition	Development in Middle Childhood	Example
External memory aids	Prompting by something outside the person	5- and 6-year-olds can do this, but 8-year-olds are more likely to think of it.	Dana makes a list of the things she has to do today.
Rehearsal	Conscious repetition	6-year-olds can be taught to do this; 7-year-olds do it spontaneously.	Tim says the letters in his spelling words over and over until he knows them.
Organization	Grouping by categories	Most children do not do this until at least age 10, but younger children can be taught to do it.	Luis recalls the animals he saw in the zoo by thinking first of the mammals, then the reptiles, then the amphibians, then the fish, and then the birds.
Elaboration	Associating items to be remembered with something else, such as a phrase, scene, or story	Older children are more likely to do this spontaneously and remember better if they make up their own elaboration; younger children remember better if someone else makes it up.	Yolanda remembers the lines of the musical staff (E, G, B, D, F) by associating them with the phrase "*Every good boy does fine.*"

2002). Children often use more than one strategy for a task and choose different kinds of strategies for different problems (Coyle & Bjorklund, 1997).

Selective Attention

School-age children can concentrate longer than younger children and can focus on the information they need and want while screening out irrelevant information. For example, they can summon up the appropriate meaning of a word they read and suppress other meanings that do not fit the context. Fifth graders are better able than first graders to keep discarded information from reentering working memory and vying with other material for attention (Harnishfeger & Pope, 1996).

This growing capacity for selective attention is believed to be due to neurological maturation and is one of the reasons memory improves during middle childhood (Bjorklund & Harnishfeger, 1990; Harnishfeger & Bjorklund, 1993). Older children may make fewer mistakes in recall than younger ones because they are better able to select what they want to remember and what they can forget (Lorsbach & Reimer, 1997).

Checkpoint

Can you . . .

- ✔ Identify at least three ways in which information processing improves during middle childhood?
- ✔ Name four common mnemonic aids and discuss developmental differences in their use?
- ✔ Explain the importance of metamemory and selective attention?

Information Processing and Piagetian Tasks

Improvements in information processing may help explain the advances Piaget described. For example, 9-year-olds may be better able than 5-year-olds to find their way to and from school because they can scan a scene, take in its important features, and remember objects in context in the order in which they were encountered (Allen & Ondracek, 1995).

Improvements in memory may contribute to the mastery of conservation tasks. Young children's working memory is so limited that they may not be able to remember all the

Checkpoint

Can you . . .

✔ Give examples of how improved information processing may help explain cognitive advances Piaget described?

relevant information (Siegler & Richards, 1982). They may forget, for example, that two differently shaped pieces of clay were originally identical. Gains in working memory may enable older children to solve such problems.

Robbie Case (1985, 1992), a neo-Piagetian theorist (refer back to Chapter 2), suggested that as a child's application of a concept or scheme becomes more automatic, it frees space in working memory to deal with new information. This may help explain horizontal décalage: children may need to be able to use one type of conservation without conscious thought before they can extend that scheme to other types of conservation.

Guidepost 3

How accurately can schoolchildren's intelligence be measured?

Psychometric Approach: Assessment of Intelligence

Intelligence tests (or IQ tests) are intended to measure the capacity to learn, as contrasted with *achievement tests,* which assess how much children have already learned. However, as we'll see, it is virtually impossible to design a test that requires no prior knowledge. In addition, intelligence tests are validated against measures of achievement, such as school performance, and these measures are affected by factors beyond innate intelligence. For this and other reasons, there is strong disagreement over how accurately IQ tests assess children's intelligence.

Traditional Group and Individual Tests

The original IQ tests, such as those of Alfred Binet and Theodore Simon (refer back to Chapter 7), were designed to be given to individuals, and their modern versions still are used that way. The first group tests, developed during World War I to screen army recruits for appropriate assignments, became models for the group tests now given in schools. As both individual and group tests have been refined, their developers have turned from the original emphasis on general intelligence to more sophisticated distinctions among various kinds of abilities and have sought to adapt the tests to special needs (Anastasi & Urbina, 1997; Daniel, 1997).

Wechsler Intelligence Scale for Children (WISC-III) Individual intelligence test for schoolchildren that yields verbal and performance scores as well as a combined score.

The most widely used individual test is the **Wechsler Intelligence Scale for Children (WISC-III).** This test for ages 6 through 16 measures verbal and performance abilities, yielding separate scores for each, as well as a total score. With separate subtest scores, it is

An individual intelligence test can help determine whether a child needs special help.

easier to pinpoint a child's strengths and to diagnose specific problems. For example, if a child does well on verbal tests (such as general information and basic arithmetic operations) but poorly on performance tests (such as doing a puzzle or drawing the missing part of a picture), the child may be slow in perceptual or motor development. A child who does well on performance tests but poorly on verbal tests may have a language problem. Another commonly used individual test is the Stanford-Binet Intelligence Scale (refer back to Chapter 10).

A popular group test, the **Otis-Lennon School Ability Test (OLSAT8),** has levels for kindergarten through twelfth grade. Children are asked to classify items, show an understanding of verbal and numerical concepts, display general information, and follow directions. Separate scores for verbal comprehension, verbal reasoning, pictorial reasoning, figural reasoning, and quantitative reasoning can identify strengths and weaknesses.

Otis-Lennon School Ability Test (OLSAT8) Group intelligence test for kindergarten through twelfth grade.

The IQ Controversy

The use of psychometric intelligence tests is controversial. On the positive side, because IQ tests have been standardized and widely used, there is extensive information about their norms, validity, and reliability (refer back to Chapters 2 and 7). IQ scores taken during middle childhood are fairly good predictors of school achievement, especially for highly verbal children, and scores are more reliable than during the preschool years. IQ at age 11 even has been found to predict length of life, functional independence late in life, and the presence or absence of dementia (Starr, Deary, Lemmon, & Whalley, 2000; Whalley & Deary, 2001; Whalley et al., 2000).

But are IQ tests fair? Critics claim that the tests underestimate the intelligence of children who, for one reason or another, do not do well on tests (Anastasi, 1988; Ceci, 1991). Because the tests are timed, they equate intelligence with speed and penalize a child who works slowly and deliberately. Their appropriateness for diagnosing learning disabilities has been questioned (Benson, 2003). A more fundamental criticism is that IQ tests infer intelligence from what children already know, but much of this knowledge is derived from schooling or culture and thus cannot measure native ability.

Influence of Schooling

Schooling does seem to increase tested intelligence (Ceci & Williams, 1997; Neisser et al., 1996). Children whose school entrance was significantly delayed (as happened, for example, in South Africa due to a teacher shortage and in the Netherlands during the Nazi occupation) lost as many as 5 IQ points each year, and some of these losses were never recovered (Ceci & Williams, 1997). IQ scores also drop during summer vacation (Ceci & Williams, 1997). Among a national sample of 1,500 children, language, spatial, and conceptual scores improved much more between October and April, the bulk of the school year, than between April and October, which includes summer vacation and the beginning and end of the school year (Huttenlocher, Levine, & Vevea, 1998).

Influences of Race/Ethnicity and Culture

Average test scores vary among racial or ethnic groups, inspiring claims that the tests are unfair to minorities. Although some African Americans score higher than most whites, black children, on average, score about 15 points lower than white children and show a comparable lag on school achievement tests. Average IQ scores of Hispanic children fall between those of black and white children, and their scores, too, tend to predict school achievement. Yet Asian Americans, whose scholastic achievements consistently outstrip those of other ethnic groups, do not seem to have a significant edge in IQ—a reminder of the limited predictive power of intelligence testing (Neisser et al., 1996). Instead, as we'll see later in this chapter, Asian-American children's strong scholastic achievement seems to be best explained by cultural factors.

What accounts for ethnic differences in IQ? Some writers have argued that part of the cause is genetic (Herrnstein & Murray, 1994; Jensen, 1969). However, while there is strong evidence of a genetic influence on *individual* differences in intelligence, there is *no* direct

cultural bias Tendency of intelligence tests to include items calling for knowledge or skills more familiar or meaningful to some cultural groups than to others.

culture-free Describing an intelligence test that, if it were possible to design, would have no culturally linked content.

culture-fair Describing an intelligence test that deals with experiences common to various cultures, in an attempt to avoid cultural bias.

evidence that differences among ethnic, cultural, or racial groups are hereditary (Neisser et al., 1996). Instead, the strength of genetic influence appears to vary with socioeconomic status. In a longitudinal study of 319 pairs of twins followed from birth, the genetic influence on IQ scores at age 7 among children from impoverished families was close to zero and the influence of environment was strong, whereas among children in affluent families the opposite was true. In other words, the genetic influence was accentuated in more favorable environments (Turkheimer, Haley, Waldron, D'Onofrio, & Gottesman, 2003).

Many scholars, therefore, attribute ethnic differences in IQ to inequalities in environment—in income, nutrition, living conditions, intellectual stimulation, schooling, culture, or other circumstances such as the effects of oppression and discrimination that can affect self-esteem, motivation, and academic performance. The IQ and achievement test gaps between white and black Americans appear to be narrowing as the life circumstances and educational opportunities of many African-American children improve. However, although socioeconomic status and IQ are strongly correlated, SES does not seem to explain the entire intergroup variance in IQ (Neisser et al., 1996; Suzuki & Valencia, 1997).

Some critics attribute ethnic differences in IQ to **cultural bias:** a tendency to include questions that use vocabulary or call for information or skills more familiar or meaningful to some cultural groups than to others (Sternberg, 1985a, 1987). These critics argue that intelligence tests are built around the dominant thinking style and language of white people of European ancestry, putting minority children at a disadvantage (Heath, 1989; Helms, 1992). Cultural bias also may affect the testing situation. For example, a child from a culture that stresses sociability and cooperation may be handicapped taking a test alone (Kottak, 1994). Still, although cultural bias may play a part in some children's performance, controlled studies have failed to show that it contributes substantially to overall group differences in IQ (Neisser et al., 1996).

Test developers have tried to design **culture-free** tests—tests with no culture-linked content—by posing tasks that do not require language, such as tracing mazes, putting the right shapes in the right holes, and completing pictures; but they have been unable to eliminate all cultural influences. Test designers also have found it virtually impossible to produce **culture-fair** tests consisting only of experiences common to people in various cultures.

Checkpoint ✓

Can you . . .

- ✔ Name and describe two traditional intelligence tests for schoolchildren?
- ✔ Give arguments for and against IQ tests?
- ✔ Assess explanations that have been given for differences in the performance of children of various ethnic and cultural groups on intelligence tests?

Is There More Than One Intelligence?

Another serious criticism of IQ tests is that they focus almost entirely on abilities used in school. They do *not* cover other important aspects of intelligent behavior, such as common sense, social skills, creative insight, and self-knowledge (Benson, 2003). Yet these abilities, in which some children with modest academic skills excel, may become equally or more important in later life and may even be considered separate forms of intelligence. Two of the chief advocates of this position are Howard Gardner and Robert Sternberg.

Gardner's Theory of Multiple Intelligences

theory of multiple intelligences Gardner's theory that each person has several distinct forms of intelligence.

Is a child who is good at analyzing paragraphs and making analogies more intelligent than one who can play a challenging violin solo or organize a closet or pitch a curve ball at the right time? The answer is no, according to Gardner's (1993) **theory of multiple intelligences.**

Gardner, a neuropsychologist and educational researcher at Harvard University, originally identified seven distinct kinds of intelligence. According to Gardner, conventional intelligence tests tap only three "intelligences": linguistic, logical-mathematical, and, to some extent, spatial. The other four, which are not reflected in IQ scores, are musical, bodily-kinesthetic, interpersonal, and intrapersonal. Gardner (1998) recently added an eighth intelligence, naturalist, to his original list. (Table 13-3 gives definitions of each intelligence and examples of fields in which it is most useful.)

High intelligence in one area does not necessarily accompany high intelligence in any of the others. A person may be extremely gifted in art (a spatial ability), precision of movement (bodily-kinesthetic), social relations (interpersonal), or self-understanding (intraper-

Table 13-3 Eight Intelligences, According to Gardner

Intelligence	Definition	Fields or Occupations Where Used
Linguistic	Ability to use and understand words and nuances of meaning	Writing, editing, translating
Logical-mathematical	Ability to manipulate numbers and solve logical problems	Science, business, medicine
Spatial	Ability to find one's way around in an environment and judge relationships between objects in space	Architecture, carpentry, city planning
Musical	Ability to perceive and create patterns of pitch and rhythm	Musical composition, conducting
Bodily-kinesthetic	Ability to move with precision	Dancing, athletics, surgery
Interpersonal	Ability to understand and communicate with others	Teaching, acting, politics
Intrapersonal	Ability to understand the self	Counseling, psychiatry, spiritual leadership
Naturalist	Ability to distinguish species	Hunting, fishing, farming, gardening, cooking

Source: Based on Gardner, 1993, 1998.

sonal) but not have a high IQ. Thus, Albert Einstein, the poet Gwendolyn Brooks and the cellist Pablo Casals may have been equally intelligent, each in a different area.

Gardner (1995) would assess each intelligence directly by observing its products—how well a child can tell a story, remember a melody, or get around in a strange area—and not by standardized tests. To monitor spatial ability, for example, the examiner might hide an object from a 1-year-old, ask a 6-year-old to do a jigsaw puzzle, and give a Rubik's cube to a preadolescent. The purpose would be, not to compare individuals, but to reveal strengths and weaknesses so as to help children realize their potential. Of course, such assessments would be far more time-consuming and more open to observer bias than paper-and-pencil tests.

What's your view

- Which of Gardner's types of intelligence are you strongest in?
- Did your education include a focus on any of these aspects?

Sternberg's Triarchic Theory of Intelligence

Robert Sternberg (1997) has defined *intelligence* as a group of mental abilities necessary for children or adults to adapt to any environmental context and to select and shape the contexts in which they live and act. By limiting his definition to universally necessary mental abilities, Sternberg excluded some of Gardner's "intelligences," such as musical and bodily-kinesthetic abilities.

Sternberg's (1985) **triarchic theory of intelligence** embraces three elements, or aspects, of intelligence: *componential, experiential,* and *contextual.*

- The **componential element** is the *analytic* aspect of intelligence; it determines how efficiently people process information. It tells people how to solve problems, how to monitor solutions, and how to evaluate the results.
- The **experiential element** is *insightful* or *creative;* it determines how people approach novel or familiar tasks. It allows people to compare new information with what they already know and to come up with new ways of putting facts together—in other words, to think originally.
- The **contextual element** is *practical;* it determines how people deal with their environment. It is the ability to size up a situation and decide what to do: adapt to it, change it, or get out of it.

According to Sternberg, everyone has these three kinds of abilities to a greater or lesser extent. A person may be strong in one, two, or all three.

triarchic theory of intelligence Sternberg's theory describing three types of intelligence: componential (analytical ability), experiential (insight and originality), and contextual (practical thinking).

componential element Sternberg's term for the analytic aspect of intelligence.

experiential element Sternberg's term for the insightful aspect of intelligence.

contextual element Sternberg's term for the practical aspect of intelligence.

Pragmatics: Knowledge About Communication

pragmatics Set of linguistic rules that govern the use of language for communication.

School-age children's major area of linguistic growth is in **pragmatics:** the practical use of language to communicate.* This includes both conversational and narrative skills.

Good conversationalists probe by asking questions before introducing a topic with which the other person may not be familiar. They quickly recognize a breakdown in communication and do something to repair it. There are wide individual differences in such conversational skills; some 7-year-olds are better conversationalists than some adults (Anderson, Clark, & Mullin, 1994). First graders respond to adults' questions with simpler, shorter answers than they give their peers. They also speak differently to parents than to other adults, issuing more demands and engaging in less extended conversation.

When children this age tell stories, they are usually not "made up" but based on personal experience. Most 6-year-olds can retell the plot of a short book, movie, or television show. By second grade, children's stories become longer and more complex. Fictional tales often have conventional beginnings and endings ("Once upon a time . . ." and "They lived happily ever after," or simply "The end"). Word use is more varied than before, but characters do not show growth or change, and plots are not fully developed.

Older children usually "set the stage" with introductory information about the setting and characters, and they clearly indicate changes of time and place. They construct more complex episodes than younger children do but with less unnecessary detail. They focus more on the characters' motives and thoughts, and they think through how to resolve problems in the plot.

Literacy

Learning to read and write frees children from the constraints of face-to-face communication. Now they have access to the ideas and imagination of people in faraway lands and long-ago times. Once children can translate the marks on a page into patterns of sound and meaning, they can develop increasingly sophisticated strategies to understand what they read. They also learn that they can use written words to express ideas, thoughts, and feelings.

Reading

decoding Process of phonetic analysis by which a printed word is converted to spoken form before retrieval from long-term memory.

visually-based retrieval Process of retrieving the sound of a printed word upon seeing the word as a whole.

phonetic, or code-emphasis, approach Approach to teaching reading that emphasizes decoding of unfamiliar words.

whole-language approach Approach to teaching reading that emphasizes visual retrieval and use of contextual clues.

Children can identify a printed word in two ways. One is called **decoding:** the child "sounds out" the word, translating it from print to speech before retrieving it from long-term memory. To do this, the child must master the phonetic code that matches the printed alphabet to spoken sounds. The second method is **visually-based retrieval:** the child simply looks at the word and then retrieves it. These two methods form the core of two contrasting approaches to reading instruction. The traditional approach, which emphasizes decoding, is called the **phonetic,** or **code-emphasis, approach.** The more recent **whole-language approach** emphasizes visual retrieval and the use of contextual cues.

The whole-language approach is based on the belief that children can learn to read and write naturally, much as they learn to understand and use speech. Whole-language proponents assert that children learn to read with better comprehension (understanding) and more enjoyment if they experience written language from the outset as a way to gain information and express ideas and feelings, not as a system of isolated sounds and syllables to be learned by memorization and drill. In contrast with the rigorous, teacher-directed tasks involved in phonics instruction, whole-language programs feature real literature and open-ended, student-initiated activities.

Despite the popularity of the whole-language approach, research has found little support for its claims. Critics say that whole-language teaching encourages children to skim through a text, guessing at words and their meaning, without trying to correct reading or spelling errors. A long line of research supports the view that phonemic awareness and early phonics training are keys to reading proficiency for most children (Booth, Perfetti, & MacWhinney, 1999; Hatcher, Hulme, & Ellis, 1994; Jeynes & Littell, 2000; Liberman & Liberman, 1990; National Reading Panel, 2000; Stahl, McKenna, & Pagnucco, 1994).

*This section is largely indebted to Owens (1996).

Many experts now recommend a blend of the best of both approaches (National Reading Panel, 2000). Children can learn phonetic skills along with strategies to help them understand what they read. Because reading skills are the joint product of many functions in different parts of the brain, instruction solely in specific subskills—phonetics or comprehension—is less likely to succeed (Byrnes & Fox, 1998). Children who can summon both visually-based and phonetic strategies, using visual retrieval for familiar words and phonetic decoding for unfamiliar words, become better, more versatile readers (Siegler, 1998).

The developmental processes that improve comprehension are similar to those that improve memory. As word identification becomes more automatic and the capacity of working memory increases, children can focus on the meaning of what they read and can adjust their speed and attentiveness to the importance and difficulty of the material. And, as children's store of knowledge increases, they can more readily check new information against what they already know (Siegler, 1998). Metacognition helps children monitor their understanding of what they read and enables them to develop strategies to clear up any problems—such strategies as reading slowly, rereading difficult passages, trying to visualize information, and thinking of examples. Having students recall, summarize, and ask questions about what they read can enhance comprehension (National Reading Panel, 2000).

Writing

The acquisition of writing skill goes hand in hand with the development of reading. Older preschoolers begin using letters, numbers, and letterlike shapes as symbols to represent words or parts of words—syllables or phonemes. Often their spelling is quite inventive—so much so that they may not be able to read it themselves (Whitehust & Lonigan, 1998).

Writing is difficult for young children, and early compositions usually are quite short. Unlike conversation, which offers constant feedback, writing requires the child to judge independently whether the goal has been met. The child also must keep in mind a variety of other constraints: spelling, punctuation, grammar, and capitalization, as well as the basic physical task of forming letters (Siegler, 1998).

In the typical classroom, children are discouraged from discussing their work with other children in the belief that they will distract one another. Research based on Vygotsky's social interaction model of language development suggests that this is not so. In one study, fourth graders working in pairs wrote stories with more solutions to problems, more explanations and goals, and fewer errors in syntax and word use than did children working alone (Daiute, Hartup, Sholl, & Zajac, 1993).

Efforts to improve the teaching of reading and writing seem to be paying off. The National Assessment of Educational Progress in 2002 and 2003 found significant improvements in the proportions of fourth and eighth graders who read and write proficiently. Still, fewer than one-third of students in both grades read and write at that level (NCES, 2004b, 2004c).

Checkpoint

Can you . . .

- ✔ Summarize improvements in language skills during middle childhood?
- ✔ Compare the phonetic and whole-language methods of teaching reading?
- ✔ Discuss how reading comprehension can be improved?
- ✔ Explain why writing is harder for younger children than for older ones?

The Child in School

Guidepost 5

What are some important influences on school achievement?

School is a major formative experience, as it was for Akira Kurosawa, affecting every aspect of development. In school, children gain knowledge, skills, and social competence, stretch their bodies and minds, and prepare for adult life. Unfortunately, despite efforts to achieve educational parity, 104 million primary-age children worldwide—57 percent of them girls—are *not* in school (UNESCO, 2003). In the United States, minorities constitute an increasing proportion of public school students—39 percent in 2000, a 17 percent increase since 1972 (Llagas & Snyder, 2003).

The earliest school experiences are especially critical in setting the stage for future success or failure. Let's look at the first-grade experience and at influences on school achievement. Then we'll consider how schools educate children with learning problems.

The Everyday World

Box 13-2 *The Math Wars*

Should children learn math by rules and formulas or by manipulating colored blocks or pie-shaped segments to illustrate mathematical concepts? By memorizing and drilling with the multiplication tables or by using computer simulations and relating math problems to real life?

These questions have spurred heated argument between proponents of traditional "skill-and-drill" math teaching and advocates of the newer *constructivist math* (or *whole math*), in which children actively construct their own mathematical concepts. This approach came into nationwide use after 1989, when the National Council of Teachers of Mathematics (NCTM) issued new standards of instruction based on constructivist principles.

The new standards deemphasized basic skills. Instead, they stressed understanding how mathematics works. Rather than passively absorb rules from a teacher or textbook, children were to discover mathematical concepts for themselves, often on the basis of intuitive learning gleaned from telling time, playing board games, dealing with money, and other everyday experiences. Instead of arriving at precise answers by multiplying, say, 19×6, children were encouraged to make estimates from more obvious relationships, such as 20×5.

Much like older arguments about reading instruction, the math wars split educators into opposing camps. Many parents complained that their children could not add, subtract, multiply, divide, or do simple algebra (Jackson, 1997a, 1997b). The reforms were widely pronounced a failure, but the first scientific studies on their effectiveness were generally favorable. Among 2,369 big-city middle-school students, the NCTM guidelines actually improved algebra performance (Mayer, 1998). Contrary to claims that the constructivist approach was inappropriate for diverse populations, a randomized study of 104 low-achieving, mostly poor and minority third and fourth graders' performance on computation and word problems found otherwise. Students taught by problem solving and/or peer collaboration outperformed students taught by more traditional methods (Ginsburg-Block & Fantuzzo, 1998).

Nevertheless, in the Third International Mathematics and Science Study (TIMSS) in 1998, U.S. twelfth graders scored lower than all but 2 of 21 competing nations on math literacy. Even students of advanced math lagged behind their counterparts in most nations (Smith, 1998). Furthermore, whereas in 1995 U.S. fourth graders had scored above average in math, by eighth grade their scores dipped below average (Holden, 2000).

The TIMSS intensified the math wars. Some educators blamed constructivist teaching, while others insisted the real problem was the persistence of traditional methods in many schools (Murray, 1998). Some argued that the reforms did not go far enough in rooting out the worst features of old curricula (Jackson, 1997a, 1997b). Superficial teaching and textbooks were among the reformers' complaints. In 1999, Project 2061, a group of classroom teachers and university faculty under auspices of the American Association for the Advancement of Science, rated math textbooks used in 3 out of 4 U.S. middle-school classrooms unsatisfactory in motivating mathematical thinking.

As in the reading wars, the best approach may be a combination of old and new methods. That is what the NCTM (2000) now advocates. Its latest revised standards strive for a balance between conceptual understanding and computational skills. In 2003, scores on the National Assessment of Educational Progress rose sharply to their highest levels since the test began in 1990; 77 percent of fourth graders and 68 percent of eighth graders scored at or above the basic level of achievement, and 32 percent of fourth graders and 68 percent of eighth graders were judged proficient (NCES, 2004a).

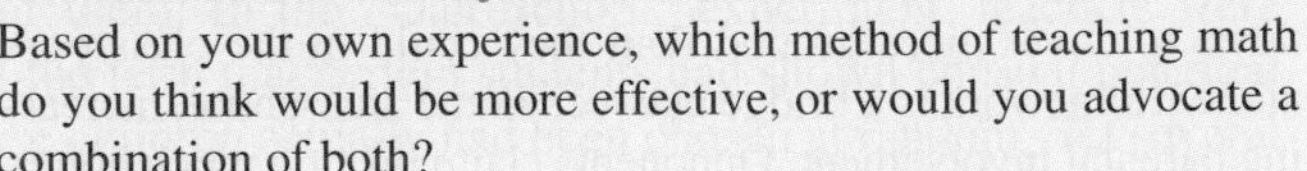

Based on your own experience, which method of teaching math do you think would be more effective, or would you advocate a combination of both?

Check it out !

For more information on this topic, go to **http://www.nctm.org**. This is the site of the National Council of Teachers of Mathematics. Also visit **http://www.ams.org**, the site of the American Mathematical Society. At **http://nces.ed.gov/timss/** you will find data from the TIMSS.

students were placed in regular-size classes. The students who had been in small classes did better than the comparison groups on standardized tests through eighth grade. They also were more likely to take college entrance exams and performed better on them. Strikingly, being assigned to a small class narrowed the black-white gap in college test taking by 54 percent (Krueger, 2003; Krueger & Whitmore, 2000).

social promotion Policy of automatically promoting children even if they do not meet academic standards.

Current Educational Innovations When the Chicago public schools in 1996 ended **social promotion,** the practice of promoting children who do not meet academic standards, many observers hailed the change. However, some educators argued that the alternative—forcing failing students to go to summer school before they could graduate, or to repeat a grade—was shortsighted (Bronner, 1999). Although retention in some cases can be a "wake-up call," more often it is the first step on a remedial track that leads to lowered expectations, poor performance, and dropping out of school (J. M. Fields & Smith, 1998; McCoy & Reynolds, 1999; McLeskey, Lancaster, & Grizzle, 1995; Temple, Reynolds, & Miedel, 2000). Indeed, studies by University of Chicago researchers found that Chicago's retention policy (which has since been modified) did not improve third graders' test scores, hurt sixth

An Internet search can put information needed for a school assignment at a student's fingertips. However, students need to learn to evaluate critically what they find using this tool.

graders' scores, and greatly increased eighth grade and high school dropout rates for retained students, though students who were *not* retained became less likely to drop out (Nagaoka & Roderick, 2004; Roderick et al., 2003).

Many educators say the only real solution to a high failure rate is to identify at-risk students early and intervene *before* they fail (Bronner, 1999). In 2000–2001, 39 percent of U.S. public school districts provided alternative schools or programs for at-risk students, offering smaller classes, remedial instruction, counseling, and crisis intervention (NCES, 2003). Summer school may be effective as an early intervention. A projected three-year study is following about 450 low-income Baltimore elementary school students randomly assigned to summer instruction in reading and writing. In the first year of the study, first graders who attended at least 75 percent of the time outscored 64 percent of their peers who did not participate (Borman, Boulay, Kaplan, Rachuba, & Hewes, 1999).

Some parents, disillusioned by the performance of their public schools or seeking a more innovative style of education, are choosing charter schools or homeschooling. More than 3,000 charter schools in 38 states serve more than 600,000 students, a disproportionate number of them low-income and minority (Center for Education Reform, 2004). Charter schools are relatively autonomous, publicly funded schools with voluntary enrollment that operate under a contract with a school district or other public body. In order to renew their contract, usually after five years, the schools must prove that they have achieved their stated goals. Charter schools tend to be smaller than regular public schools and have a unique philosophy, curriculum, structure, or organizational style. Although parents are generally satisfied with their charter schools, their effect on student outcomes is in dispute (Bulkley & Fisler, 2002; Center for Education Reform, 2004; Detrich, Phillips, & Durett, 2002; Nelson, Rosenberg, & Van Meter, 2004; Schemo, 2004).

Homeschooling is legal in all 50 states. In 2003 some 1.1 million U.S. students representing 2.2 percent of the school-age population were homeschooled, 4 out of 5 of them full time–a 29 percent increase from 1999. In a nationally representative government survey, the main reasons parents gave for choosing to school their children were concern about a poor learning environment in the schools and the desire to provide religious or moral instruction (Princiotta, Bielick, & Chapman, 2004). The success of homeschooling is yet to be assessed (Bielick, Chandler, & Broughman, 2001).

Computer and Internet Use Children's computer and Internet use has greatly increased in the past decade; 90.5 percent of 8- to 10-year-olds use computers, and 53.5 percent use the Internet for school assignments, e-mail, or computer games. However, a "digital divide" exists: fewer black and Hispanic children than white children and fewer poor children than nonpoor children use these technologies. Although about 90 percent of both girls and boys now use computers and 58 percent of both sexes use the Internet, girls tend to use the Internet primarily for e-mail, while boys are more likely to use it for games and information (DeBell & Chapman, 2003).

Computer literacy and the ability to navigate the World Wide Web are opening new possibilities for individualized instruction, global communication, and early training in independent research skills. However, this tool poses dangers. First is the risk of exposure to harmful or inappropriate material. Second, students need to learn to evaluate critically information they find in cyberspace and to separate facts from opinion and advertising (J. Lee, 1998). Finally, a focus on "visual literacy" could divert financial resources from other areas of the curriculum.

The Culture

Why do so many students of East Asian extraction do so well in school? Cultural influences in their countries of origin may hold the key.

East Asian cultures share values that foster educational success, such as obedience, responsibility, and respect for elders (Chao, 1994). Chinese and Japanese mothers view academic achievement as a child's most important pursuit (H. W. Stevenson, 1995; H. W. Stevenson, Chen, & Lee, 1993; H. W. Stevenson, Lee, Chen, & Lummis, 1990; H. W. Stevenson, Lee, Chen, Stigler, et al., 1990). Whereas U.S. students socialize after school and engage in sports and other activities, Asian students devote themselves almost entirely to study (Fuligni & Stevenson, 1995; H. W. Stevenson, 1995; H. W. Stevenson et al., 1993).

Checkpoint

Can you . . .

- ✔ Evaluate the effects of teachers' perceptions and expectations on children's achievement?
- ✔ Describe changes and innovations in educational philosophy and practice, and discuss views about social promotion, homework, and the teaching of math?
- ✔ Give reasons that children of East Asian extraction tend to do well in school?
- ✔ Identify some ways of addressing cultural differences in the classroom?

East Asians carry over these values and practices to their new land. Many Asian-American families see education as the best route to upward mobility (Chao, 1996; Sue & Okazaki, 1990). The child's school success is a prime goal of parenting (Chao, 1994, 1996; Huntsinger & Jose, 1995). Of course, as Asian-American children grow up in U.S. culture and absorb its values, their attitudes toward learning may change (C. Chen & Stevenson, 1995; Huntsinger et al., 1998).

Unlike Asian Americans, some minority children whose cultural values differ markedly from those of the dominant culture are at a disadvantage in school (Helms, 1992; Tharp, 1989). The Kamehameha Early Education Program (KEEP) has produced dramatic improvements in primary-grade Hawaiian children's cognitive performance by designing educational programs to fit cultural patterns—for example, having children work in small, collaborative groups and training teachers to adjust to cultural speaking and learning styles. A KEEP program also was established on the Navajo reservation in northern Arizona. Whereas children in non-KEEP classes score very low on standard achievement tests, children in KEEP classes approach national norms (Tharp, 1989).

Guidepost 6

How do schools meet the needs of non-English-speaking children and those with learning problems?

Second-Language Education

In two decades, between 1979 and 1999, the proportion of U.S. 5- to 24-year-olds who spoke a language other than English at home rose from 8 to 17 percent (NCES, 2003; see Figure 13-1). Increasingly, that primary language is Spanish. Largely due to recent increases in immigration, Hispanic students now represent 17 percent of public school enrollment. Although more than half of Hispanic students speak mostly English at home (LLagas & Snyder, 2003), many of the others need help learning English. According to one estimate, more than 3 million U.S. students have limited English proficiency (ProEnglish, 2002).

English-immersion Approach to teaching English as a second language in which instruction is presented only in English.

Some schools use an **English-immersion** approach (sometimes called ESL, or English as a Second Language), in which minority children are immersed in English from the beginning, in special classes. Other schools have adopted programs of **bilingual education,** in which children are taught in two languages, first learning in their native language with others who also speak it and then switching to regular classes in English when they become more proficient in it. These programs can encourage children to become **bilingual** (fluent in two languages) and to feel pride in their cultural identity.

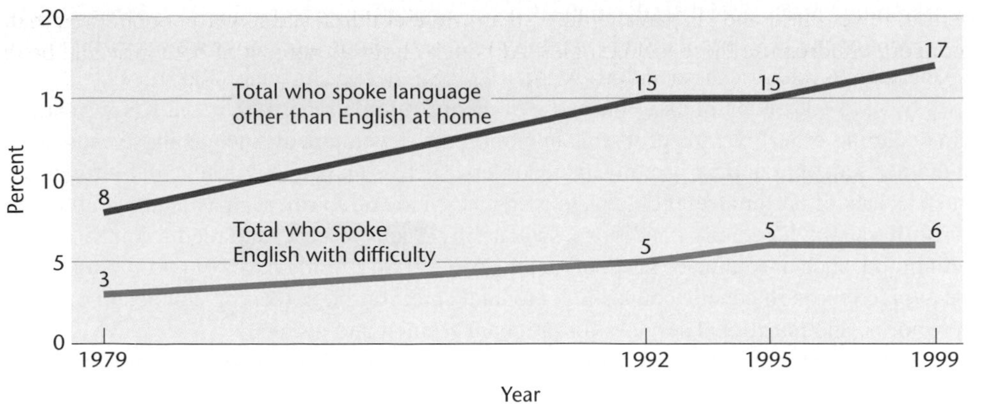

Figure 13-1

Language minority students. Percentage of U.S. 5- to 24-year-olds who spoke a language other than English at home and who spoke English with difficulty, selected years, 1979–1999.

Source: NCES, 2003.

Advocates of early *English immersion* claim that the sooner children are exposed to English and the more time they spend speaking it, the better they learn it. Support for this view comes from findings that the effectiveness of second-language learning declines from early childhood through late adolescence (Newport, 1991). Proponents of *bilingual* programs claim that children progress faster academically in their native language and later make a smoother transition to all-English classrooms (Padilla et al., 1991). Some educators maintain that the English-only approach stunts children's cognitive growth; because foreign-speaking children can understand only simple English at first, the curriculum must be watered down, and children are less prepared to handle complex material later (Collier, 1995).

bilingual education System of teaching non-English-speaking children in their native language while they learn English and later switching to all-English instruction.

bilingual Fluent in two languages.

A study of 70,000 non-English-speaking students in high-quality second-language programs in five districts across the United States offers strong support for a bilingual approach (Collier, 1995; W. P. Thomas & Collier, 1997). The study compared not only English proficiency but also long-term academic achievement. In the primary grades, the type of language teaching made little difference; but from seventh grade on, children who had remained in bilingual programs at least through sixth grade caught up with or even surpassed their native English-speaking peers. At the same time, the relative performance of children who had been in traditional immersion programs began to decline. By the end of high school, those in part-time ESL (immersion) programs trailed 80 percent of native English speakers their age.

Most successful was a third, less common approach: **two-way,** or **dual-language learning,** in which English-speaking and foreign-speaking children learn together in their own and each other's languages. This approach avoids any need to place minority children in separate classes. By valuing both languages equally, it helps build self-esteem and thus improves school performance. An added advantage is that English speakers learn a foreign language at an early age, when they can acquire it most easily (Collier, 1995; W. P. Thomas & Collier, 1997, 1998).

two-way (dual-language) learning Approach to second-language education in which English speakers and non-English speakers learn together in their own and each other's languages.

Despite such findings, many critics claim that bilingual education has produced millions of children who do not know enough English to hold a job. California, Arizona, and Massachusetts, which together account for one-half of students who speak languages other than English at home, have outlawed bilingual education by referendum and required English immersion. Initial results in California, the first state to ban bilingual education in 1998, were positive. In 2002, Colorado became the first state to vote down such an initiative (ProEnglish, 2002).

Checkpoint

Can you . . .

✔ Describe and evaluate various types of second-language education?

Children with Learning Problems

Some children, like Akira Kurosawa, are late bloomers when it comes to schoolwork, but an unfortunate minority have serious learning problems.

Mental Retardation

Mental retardation is significantly subnormal cognitive functioning. It is indicated by an IQ of about 70 or less, coupled with a deficiency in age-appropriate adaptive behavior such

mental retardation Significantly subnormal cognitive functioning.

as communication, social skills, and self-care, appearing before age 18. Approximately 1 percent of the U.S. population is mentally retarded, about three boys for every two girls (American Psychiatric Association [APA], 1994; Snyder & Hoffman, 2003).

In 30 to 40 percent of cases the cause of mental retardation is unknown. Known causes (in declining order) include problems in embryonic development, such as those caused by a mother's alcohol or drug use; mental disorders, such as autism; environmental influences, such as lack of nurturance; problems in pregnancy and childbirth, such as fetal malnutrition or birth trauma; hereditary conditions, such as Tay-Sachs disease; and medical problems in childhood, such as trauma or lead poisoning (APA, 1994). Many cases of retardation could be avoided through genetic counseling, prenatal care, routine screening and health care for newborns, and nutritional services for pregnant women and infants.

With a supportive and stimulating early environment and continued help and guidance, many mentally retarded children can expect a reasonably good outcome. Most retarded children can benefit from schooling. Intervention programs have helped many mildly or moderately retarded adults and those considered "borderline" (with IQs ranging from 70 up to about 85) to hold jobs, live in the community, and function fairly well in society. The profoundly retarded need constant care and supervision, usually in institutions. For some, day care centers, hostels for retarded adults, and homemaking services for caregivers can be less costly and more humane alternatives.

Learning Disabilities

dyslexia Developmental disorder in which reading achievement is substantially lower than predicted by IQ or age.

learning disabilities (LDs) Disorders that interfere with specific aspects of learning and school achievement.

Nelson Rockefeller, former vice president of the United States, had so much trouble reading that he ad-libbed speeches instead of using a script. Rockefeller is one of many eminent persons who have suffered from **dyslexia,** a language processing disorder in which reading is substantially below the level predicted by IQ or age. Other famous persons reportedly afflicted by dyslexia include the singer Harry Belafonte; the actors Tom Cruise, Whoopi Goldberg, and Cher; the fairy tale author Hans Christian Anderson; baseball Hall-of-Famer Nolan Ryan; television host Jay Leno; Alexander Graham Bell, inventor of the telephone; Albert Einstein, father of nuclear energy; and the novelist John Irving.

Dyslexia is the most commonly diagnosed of a large number of **learning disabilities (LDs).** These are disorders that interfere with specific aspects of school achievement, such as listening, speaking, reading, writing, or mathematics, resulting in performance substantially lower than would be expected given a child's age, intelligence, and amount of schooling (APA, 1994). Mathematical disabilities, as an example, include difficulty in counting, comparing numbers, calculating, and remembering basic arithmetic facts. Each of these may involve distinct disabilities. A growing number of children are served by federally supported programs for the learning disabled—almost 2.9 million, or 5 percent of the U.S. school population (National Center for Learning Disabilities, 2004b). Many others may be unserved.

Children with learning disabilities often have near-average to higher-than-average intelligence and normal vision and hearing, but they seem to have trouble processing sensory information. Although causes are uncertain, they may include genetic factors, complications of pregnancy or birth, or injuries after birth, such as head trauma, nutritional deprivation, and exposure to lead (National Center for Learning Disabilities, 2004b). Children in low-income families and children in fair or poor health are more likely than other children to have learning disabilities (Bloom, Cohen, Vickerie, & Wondimu, 2003).

Children with LDs tend to be less task oriented and more easily distracted than other children; they are less well organized as learners and less likely to use memory strategies. Learning disabilities can have devastating effects on self-esteem as well as on the report card. Of course, not all children who have trouble with reading, arithmetic, or other specific school subjects are learning disabled. Some haven't been taught properly, are anxious, have trouble reading or hearing directions, lack motivation or interest in the subject, or have a developmental delay, which may eventually disappear (Geary, 1993; Ginsburg, 1997; Roush, 1995).

About 4 out of 5 children with LDs have been identified as dyslexic. Dyslexia is generally considered to be a chronic, persistent medical condition and tends to run in families (S. E. Shaywitz, 1998, 2003). It hinders the development of oral as well as written language skills and may cause problems with writing, spelling, grammar, and understanding speech as well as with reading (National Center for Learning Disabilities, 2004a). Studies in the

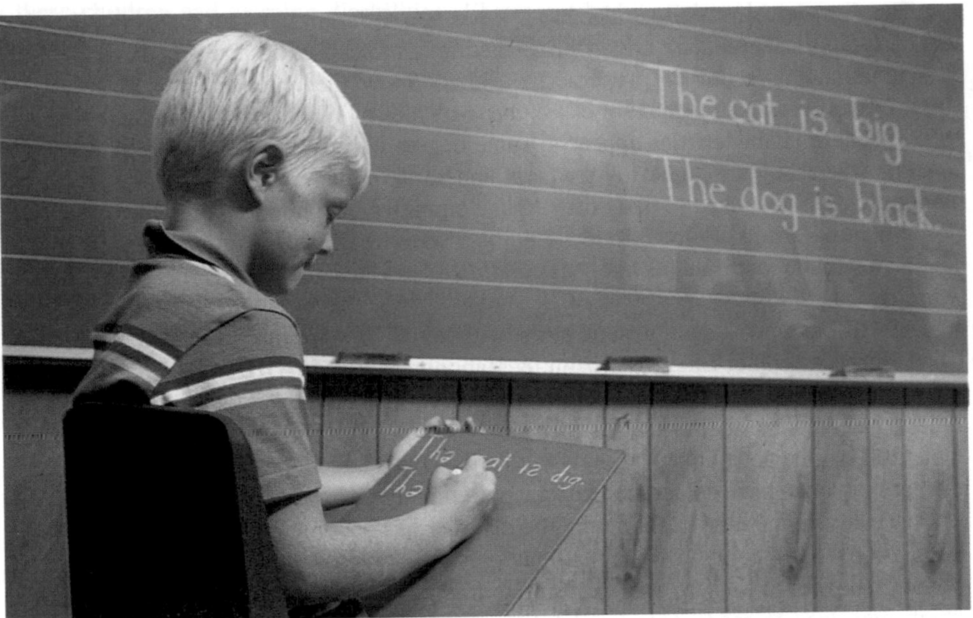

Children with dyslexia have trouble reading and writing and often doing arithmetic, because they may confuse up and down and left and right. Dyslexia may be part of a more general language impairment.

United States, United Kingdom, and New Zealand have found that reading disability affects children of all socioeconomic and ethnic backgrounds (National Center for Learning Disabilities, 2004a; Rutter et al., 2004).

Most often, dyslexia is believed to result from a neurological defect in processing speech sounds: an inability to recognize that words consist of smaller units of sound, which are represented by printed letters. This defect in phonological processing makes it harder to decode words (Morris et al., 1998; S. E. Shaywitz, 1998, 2003). Brain imaging has revealed differences in the regions of the brain activated during the processing of spoken language in dyslexic as compared with normal readers (Breier et al., 2003; Horwitz, Rumsey, & Donohue, 1998; T. L. Richards et al., 1999; Shaywitz, 2003; Shaywitz et al., 1998). Many of these children can be taught to read through early, systematic phonological training, but the process does not become automatic, as it does with most readers (S. E. Shaywitz, 1998, 2003). Other children identified as dyslexic remain poor readers. What makes the difference?

A study of 43 young adults identified in childhood as reading disabled suggests that there may be *two* types of dyslexia with differing outcomes. When asked to read real and made-up words on a screen, the better readers used different parts of the brain than normal readers do, apparently compensating for missing brain circuitry. The participants with the most serious reading problems had normal neural systems for reading but relied primarily on another part of the brain that is used primarily for memory. The better readers decoded the words, though slowly, while the poorer readers apparently used visually-activated retrieval (Shaywitz et al., 2003).

Hyperactivity and Attention Deficits

Attention-deficit/hyperactivity disorder (ADHD) affects an estimated 2 to 11 percent or more of school-age children worldwide (Zametkin & Ernst, 1999) and 6 percent in the United States (Bloom & Tonthat, 2002; Bloom et al., 2003), though some research suggests that its prevalence there may be underestimated (Rowland et al., 2002). Among the well-known people who reportedly have had the disorder are the singer and composer John Lennon, U.S. Senator Robert Kennedy, and the actors Robin Williams and Sylvester Stallone. It is a chronic condition usually marked by persistent inattention, distractibility, impulsivity, low tolerance for frustration, and a great deal of activity at the wrong time and the wrong place, such as the classroom (APA, 1994). Boys are more than twice as likely to be diagnosed as girls (Bloom et al., 2003).

attention-deficit/hyperactivity disorder (ADHD) Syndrome characterized by persistent inattention and distractibility, impulsivity, low tolerance for frustration, and inappropriate overactivity.

The Lives of Gifted Children

A classic longitudinal study of gifted children began in 1921, when Lewis M. Terman (who brought the Binet intelligence test to the United States) identified more than 1,500 California children with IQs of 135 or higher. The study demolished the widespread stereotype of the bright child as a puny, pasty-faced bookworm. These children were taller, healthier, better coordinated, better adjusted, and more popular than the average child, and, as a group, their cognitive, scholastic, and vocational superiority has held up in adulthood and old age (Shurkin, 1992; Terman & Oden, 1959). On the other hand, none of Terman's sample grew up to be Einsteins or Kurosawas, and those with the highest IQs became no more illustrious than those who were only moderately gifted. This lack of a close correlation between childhood giftedness and adult eminence has been supported by later research (Winner, 1997).

Defining and Measuring Creativity

In Kurosawa's directorial debut in *Sanshiro Saguto* in 1943, he surprised audiences and critics by combining traditional Japanese samurai themes with tension-building techniques from western action movies. Throughout his career, innovation was his hallmark.

One definition of *creativity* is the ability to see things in a new light—to produce something never seen before or to discern problems others fail to recognize and find new and unusual solutions. High creativity and high academic intelligence (or IQ) do not necessarily go hand in hand. Classic research found only modest correlations (Anastasi & Schaefer, 1971; Getzels, 1964, 1984; Getzels & Jackson, 1962, 1963).

J. P. Guilford (1956, 1959, 1960, 1967, 1986) distinguished two kinds of thinking: *convergent* and *divergent.* **Convergent thinking**—the kind IQ tests measure—seeks a single correct answer; **divergent thinking** comes up with a wide array of fresh possibilities. Tests of creativity call for divergent thinking. The Torrance Tests of Creative Thinking (Torrance, 1966, 1974; Torrance & Ball, 1984), among the most widely known tests of creativity, include such tasks as listing unusual uses for a paper clip, completing a figure, and writing down what a sound brings to mind.

One problem with many of these tests is that the score depends partly on speed, which is not a hallmark of creativity. Moreover, although the tests yield fairly reliable results, there is dispute over whether they are valid—whether they identify children who are creative in everyday life (Simonton, 1990). As Guilford recognized, divergent thinking may not be the only, or even the most important, factor in creative performance.

convergent thinking Thinking aimed at finding the one right answer to a problem.

divergent thinking Thinking that produces a variety of fresh, diverse possibilities.

enrichment Approach to educating the gifted that broadens and deepens knowledge and skills through extra activities, projects, field trips, or mentoring.

acceleration Approach to educating the gifted that moves them through the curriculum at an unusually rapid pace.

Educating Gifted, Creative, and Talented Children

About 68 percent of public elementary and secondary schools have special programs for the gifted (Snyder & Hoffman, 2003). These programs generally follow one of two approaches: *enrichment* or *acceleration.* **Enrichment** broadens and deepens knowledge and skills through extra classroom activities, research projects, field trips, or coaching by experts. **Acceleration,** often recommended for highly gifted children, speeds up their education through early school entrance, grade skipping, placement in fast-paced classes, or advanced courses in specific subjects. Moderate acceleration does not seem to harm social adjustment, at least in the long run (Winner, 1997).

Children in gifted programs not only make academic gains, but also tend to improve in self-concept and social adjustment (Ford & Harris, 1996). However, competition for funding and opposition to "elitism" threatens the continuation of these programs (Purcell, 1995; Winner, 1997). Some educators advocate moving away from an all-or-nothing definition of *giftedness* to including a wider range of students in more flexible programs (J. Cox, Daniel, & Boston, 1985; Feldhusen, 1992). Some say that if the level of education were significantly improved for all children, only the most exceptional would need special classes (Winner, 1997).

Checkpoint

Can you . . .

- ✔ Tell how gifted children are identified?
- ✔ Discuss the relationships between giftedness and life achievements, and between IQ and creativity?
- ✔ Describe two approaches to the education of gifted children?

Refocus

- How might a Piagetian or information-processing theorist explain Akira Kurosawa's cognitive advances in third grade?
- What kind of intelligence test would have been most likely to show accurately Kurosawa's abilities?
- What influences on school achievement mentioned in this chapter seemed most applicable to Kurosawa?
- What evidence of creativity did Kurosawa show as a child, and how does this tie in with his adult achievements?
- What does Kurosawa's story suggest about the difficulty of identifying gifted children, especially in the early years?

There is no firm dividing line between being gifted and not being gifted, creative and not creative. All children benefit from being encouraged in their areas of interest and ability. What we learn about fostering intelligence, creativity, and talent in the most able children may help all children make the most of their potential. The degree to which they do this will affect their self-concept and other aspects of personality, as we discuss in Chapter 14.

Summary and Key Terms

Piagetian Approach: The Concrete Operational Child

Guidepost 1 How do school-age children's thinking and moral reasoning differ from those of younger children?

- A child from about age 7 to age 12 is in the stage of concrete operations. Children are less egocentric than before and are more proficient at tasks requiring logical reasoning, such as spatial thinking, understanding of causality, categorization, inductive and deductive reasoning, conservation, and working with numbers. However, their reasoning is largely limited to the here and now.
- Cultural experience, as well as neurological development, seems to contribute to the rate of development of conservation and other Piagetian skills.
- According to Piaget, moral development is linked with cognitive maturation and occurs in three stages in which children move from strict obedience to authority toward more autonomous judgments based first on fairness and later on equity.

concrete operations (345) seriation (346) transitive inference (346) class inclusion (346) inductive reasoning (346) deductive reasoning (347)

Information-Processing Approach: Memory and Other Processing Skills

Guidepost 2 What advances in memory and other information-processing skills occur during middle childhood?

- Reaction time, processing speed, metamemory, metacognition, selective attention, and use of mnemonic strategies improve during the school years. These gains in information-processing abilities may help explain the advances Piaget described.

metamemory (350) metacognition (350) mnemonic strategies (350) external memory aids (350) rehearsal (350) organization (350) elaboration (350)

Psychometric Approach: Assessment of Intelligence

Guidepost 3 How accurately can schoolchildren's intelligence be measured?

- The intelligence of school-age children is assessed by group or individual tests. Although intended as aptitude tests, they are validated against measures of achievement.
- IQ tests are fairly good predictors of school success but may be unfair to some children.
- Differences in IQ among ethnic groups appear to result to a considerable degree from socioeconomic and other environmental differences. Schooling seems to increase measured intelligence.
- Attempts to devise culture-free or culture-fair tests have been unsuccessful.
- IQ tests tap only three of the "intelligences" in Howard Gardner's theory of multiple intelligences. According to Robert Sternberg's triarchic theory, IQ tests measure mainly the componential element of intelligence, not the experiential and contextual elements.
- New directions in intelligence testing include the Sternberg Triarchic Abilities Test (STAD), Kaufman Assessment Battery for Children (K-ABC-II), and dynamic tests based on Vygotskyan theory.

Wechsler Intelligence Scale for Children (WISC-III) (352) Otis-Lennon School Ability Test (OLSAT8) (353) cultural bias (354) culture-free (354) culture-fair (354) theory of multiple intelligences (354) triarchic theory of intelligence (355) componential element (355) experiential element (355) contextual element (355) Sternberg Triarchic Abilities Test (STAT) (356) Kaufman Assessment Battery for Children (K-ABC-II) (356)

Language and Literacy

Guidepost 4 How do communicative abilities expand during middle childhood?

- Use of vocabulary, grammar, and syntax become increasingly sophisticated, but the major area of linguistic growth is in pragmatics.
- Metacognition contributes to progress in reading.
- Despite the popularity of whole-language programs, early phonics training is a key to reading proficiency.
- Interaction with peers fosters development of writing skills.

pragmatics (358) decoding (358) visually based retrieval (358) phonetic, or code-emphasis, approach (358) whole-language approach (358)

The Child in School

Guidepost 5 What are some important influences on school achievement?

- Because schooling is cumulative, the foundation laid in first grade is very important.
- Children's and parents' self-efficacy beliefs affect school achievement.
- Parents influence children's learning by becoming involved in their schooling, motivating them to achieve, and transmitting attitudes about learning.
- Socioeconomic status can influence parental beliefs and practices that, in turn, influence achievement. Poor families whose children do well in school tend to have more social capital than poor families whose children do not do well. The neighborhood also is a factor.
- Although the power of the self-fulfilling prophecy may not be as great as was once thought, teachers' perceptions and expectations may have some influence.
- The school environment and class size affect learning.
- Current educational issues and innovations include the amount of homework assigned, methods of teaching math, social promotion, charter schools, homeschooling, and computer literacy.
- The superior achievement of children of East Asian extraction seems to stem from cultural factors. Some minority children may benefit from educational programs adapted to their cultural styles.

social capital (362) self-fulfilling prophecy (362) social promotion (364)

Guidepost 6 How do schools meet the needs of non-English-speaking children and those with learning problems?

- Methods of second-language education are controversial. Issues include speed and facility with English, long-term achievement in academic subjects, and pride in cultural identity.
- Three frequent sources of learning problems are mental retardation, learning disabilities (LDs), and attention-deficit/hyperactivity disorder (ADHD). Dyslexia is the most common learning disability.
- In the United States, all children with disabilities are entitled to a free, appropriate education. Children must be educated in the least restrictive environment possible, often in the regular classroom.

English-immersion (366) bilingual education (367) bilingual (367) two-way (dual-language) learning (367) mental retardation (367) dyslexia (368) learning disabilities (LDs) (368) attention-deficit/hyperactivity disorder (ADHD) (369)

Guidepost 7 How is giftedness assessed and nurtured?

- An IQ of 130 or higher is a common standard for identifying gifted children. Broader definitions include creativity, artistic talent, and other attributes and rely on multiple criteria for identification. Minorities are underrepresented in programs for the gifted.
- In Terman's classic longitudinal study of gifted children, most turned out to be well adjusted and successful but not outstandingly so.
- Creativity and IQ are *not* closely linked. Tests of creativity seek to measure divergent thinking, but their validity has been questioned.
- Special educational programs for gifted, creative, and talented children stress enrichment or acceleration.

convergent thinking (372) divergent thinking (372) enrichment (372) acceleration (372)

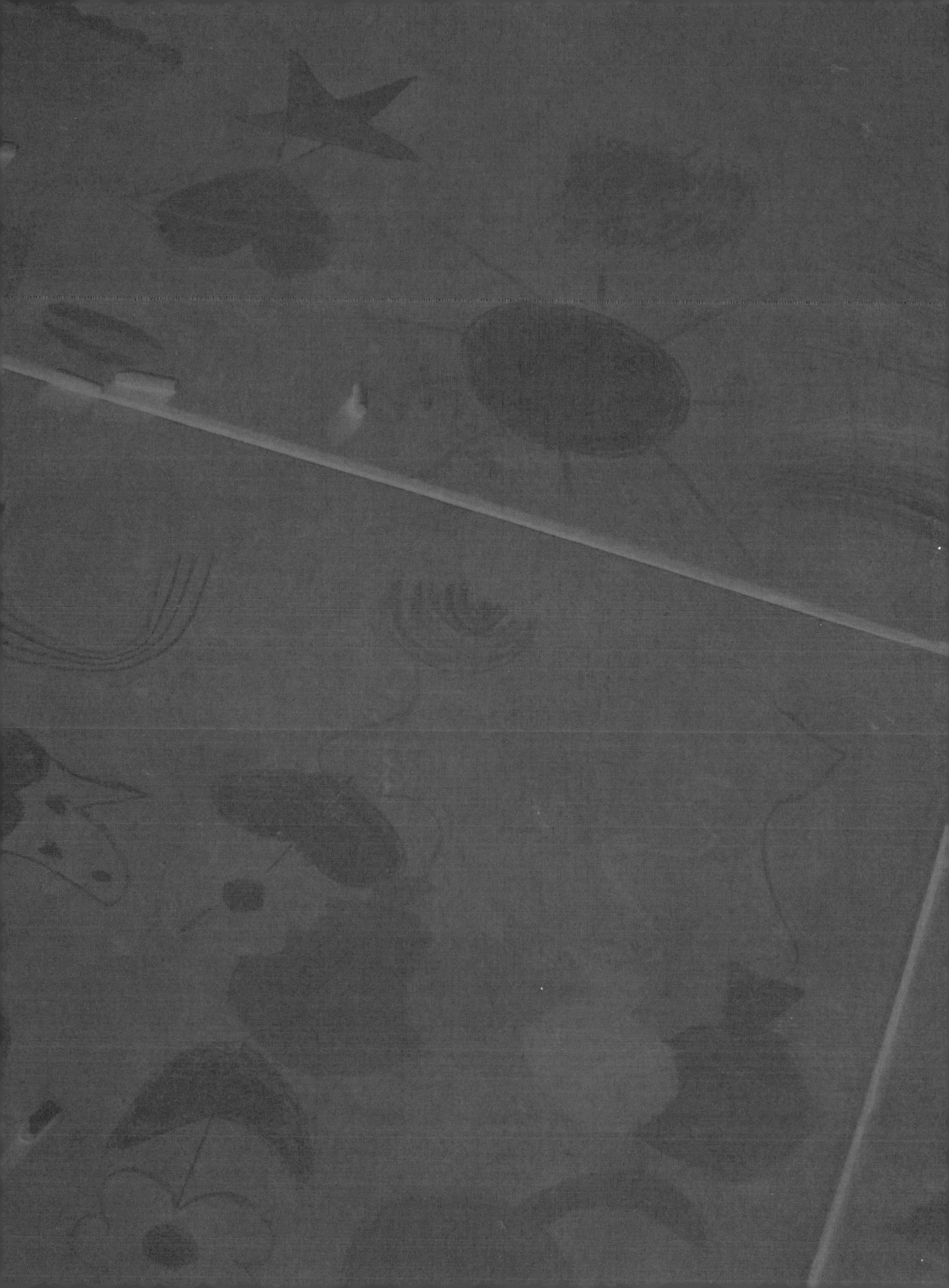

chapter
14
Sunday
Monday
Tuesday
Wednesday
Thursday
Friday

Psychosocial Development in Middle Childhood

Have you ever felt like nobody?
Just a tiny speck of air.
When everyone's around you,
And you are just not there.

—Karen Crawford, age 9

Focus *Marian Anderson, Operatic Trailblazer*

Marian Anderson

The African-American contralto Marian Anderson (1897*–1993) had—in the words of the great Italian conductor Arturo Toscanini—a voice heard "once in a hundred years." She was also a pioneer in breaking racial barriers. Turned away by a music school in her hometown of Philadelphia, she studied voice privately and in 1925 won a national competition to sing with the New York Philharmonic. When she was refused the use of a concert hall in Washington, D.C., First Lady Eleanor Roosevelt arranged for her to sing on the steps of the Lincoln Memorial. The unprecedented performance on Easter Sunday, 1939, drew 75,000 people and was broadcast to millions. Several weeks later, Marian Anderson became the first black singer to perform at the White House. But not until 1955 did Anderson, at age 57, become the first person of her race to sing with New York's Metropolitan Opera.

A remarkable story lies behind this woman's "journey from a single rented room in South Philadelphia" (McKay, 1992, p. xxx). It is a story of nurturing family ties—bonds of mutual support, care, and concern that extended from generation to generation.

Marian Anderson was the eldest of three children of John and Annie Anderson. Two years after her birth, the family left their one-room apartment to move in with her father's parents and then into a small rented house nearby. At the age of 6, Marian joined the junior choir at church. There she made a friend, Viola Johnson, who lived across the street from the Andersons. Within a year or two, they sang a duet together—Marian's first public performance.

When Marian was in eighth grade, her beloved father died, and the family again moved in with his parents, his sister, and her two daughters. Marian's grandfather had a steady job. Her grandmother took care of all the children, her aunt ran the house, and her mother contributed by cooking dinners, working as a cleaning woman, and taking in laundry, which Marian and her sister Alyce delivered.

The most important influence in Marian Anderson's life was the counsel, example, and spiritual guidance of her hardworking, unfailingly supportive mother. Annie Anderson

The chief source of biographical material about Marian Anderson and her family is Anderson (1992). Some details come from Freedman (2004), Jones (2004), Kernan (1993), Women in History (2004), and from obituaries published in *Time* (April 19, 1993), *People Weekly, The New Yorker,* and *Jet* (April 26, 1993).

*Although Anderson always gave her birthdate as 1902, her birth certificate, released after her death, showed it as 1897.

placed great importance on her children's schooling and saw to it that they didn't skimp on homework. Even when she was working full-time, she cooked their dinner every night, and she taught Marian to sew her own clothes. "Not once can I recall . . . hearing Mother lift her voice to us in anger . . . ," Marian wrote. "She could be firm, and we learned to respect her wishes" (Anderson, 1992, p. 92).

After Marian Anderson had become a world-renowned concert artist, she often returned to her old neighborhood in Philadelphia. Her mother and sister Alyce shared a modest house, and her other sister, Ethel, lived next door with her son.

"It is the pleasantest thing in the world to go into that home and feel its happiness, . . ." the singer wrote. "They are all comfortable, and they cherish and protect one another. . . . I know that it warms [Mother] to have her grandson near her as he grows up, just as I think that when he gets to be a man, making his own life, he will have pleasant memories of his home and family" (1992, p. 93). Anderson herself married but had no children. In 1992, widowed and frail at age 95, she went to live with her nephew, James DePriest, then music director of the Oregon Symphony. She died of a stroke at his home the following year.

• • •

Marian Anderson "lived through momentous changes in America and the world" and in African American life (McKay, 1992, p. xxiv), but one thing that never changed in her life was the strong, supportive network of relationships that sustained her and her family. The kind of household a child lives in and the relationships within the household can have profound effects on psychosocial development in middle childhood, when children are developing a stronger sense of what it means to be responsible, contributing members, first of a family and then of society. The family is part of a web of contextual influences, including the peer group, the school, and the neighborhood in which the family lives. Marian Anderson's first friend, her church choir, and the neighbors for whom she did odd jobs to earn the price of a violin all played parts in her development. Above and beyond these influences were the overarching cultural patterns of time and place, which presented special challenges to African-American families and communities and called forth mutually supportive responses.

In this chapter, we trace the rich and varied emotional and social lives of school-age children. We see how children develop a more realistic concept of themselves and achieve more competence, self-reliance, and emotional control. Through being with peers they make discoveries about their own attitudes, values, and skills. Still, as Anderson's story shows, the family remains a vital influence. Children's lives are affected, not only by the way parents approach the task of child raising, but also by whether and how they are employed, by the family's economic circumstances, and by its structure or composition—whether the child lives with one parent or two; whether the child has siblings and if so, how many; and whether the household includes other relatives, such as grandparents, aunt, and cousins. Although most children are emotionally healthy, some have mental health problems; we examine several of these. We also consider resilient children, who emerge from the stresses of childhood healthier and stronger.

After you have read and studied this chapter, you should be able to answer each of the Guidepost questions that follow. Look for them again in the margins, where they point to important concepts throughout the chapter. To check your understanding of these Guideposts, review the end-of-chapter summary. Checkpoints located at periodic spots throughout the chapter will help you verify your understanding of what you have read.

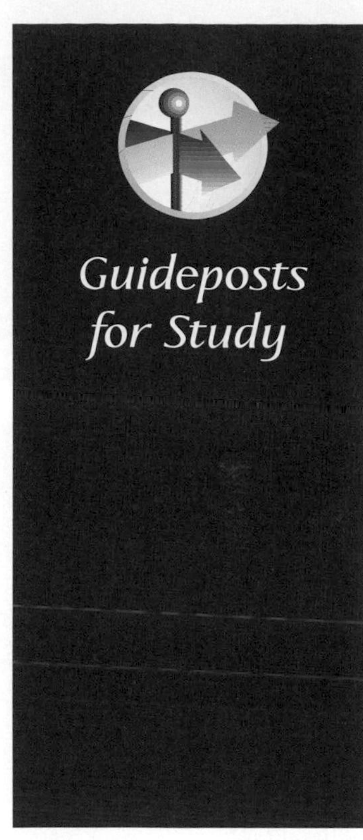

Guideposts for Study

1. How do school-age children develop a realistic self-concept, and what contributes to self-esteem?
2. How do school-age children show emotional growth?
3. How do parent-child relationships change in middle childhood?
4. What are the effects of parents' work and of poverty on family atmosphere?
5. What impact does family structure have on children's development?
6. How do siblings influence and get along with one another?
7. What part do pets play in children's development?
8. How do relationships with peers change in middle childhood, and what influences popularity and choice of friends?
9. What are the most common forms of aggressive behavior in middle childhood, and what influences contribute to such behavior?
10. What are some common emotional disturbances, and how are they treated?
11. How do the stresses of modern life affect children, and what enables "resilient" children to withstand them?

The Developing Self

The cognitive growth that takes place during middle childhood enables children to develop more complex concepts of themselves and to grow in emotional understanding and control.

Guidepost 1

How do school-age children develop a realistic self-concept, and what contributes to self-esteem?

Representational Systems: A Neo-Piagetian View

Around age 7 or 8, children reach the third of the neo-Piagetian stages of self-concept development described in Chapter 11. Judgments about the self become more conscious, realistic, balanced, and comprehensive as children form **representational systems:** broad, inclusive self-concepts that integrate various aspects of the self (Harter, 1993, 1996, 1998). "At school I'm feeling pretty smart in certain subjects, Language Arts and Social Studies," says 8-year-old Lisa. "I got As in these subjects on my last report card and was really proud of myself. But I'm feeling really dumb in Arithmetic and Science, particularly when I see how well the other kids are doing. . . . I still like myself as a person, because Arithmetic and Science just aren't that important to me. How I look and how popular I am are more important" (Harter, 1996, p. 208).

representational systems In neo-Piagetian terminology, third stage in development of self-definition, characterized by breadth, balance, and the integration and assessment of various aspects of the self.

Lisa's self-description shows that she can focus on more than one dimension of herself. She has outgrown an all-or-nothing, black-or-white self-definition; she recognizes that she can be "smart" in certain subjects and "dumb" in others. Her self-descriptions are more balanced; she can verbalize her self-concept better, and she can weigh different aspects of it ("How I look and how popular I am are more important."). She can compare her *real self* with her *ideal self* and can judge how well she measures up to social standards in comparison with others. All of these changes contribute to the development of self-esteem, her assessment of her *global self-worth* ("I like myself as a person").

Self-Esteem

According to Erikson (1982), a major determinant of self-esteem is children's view of their capacity for productive work. The issue to be resolved in middle childhood is

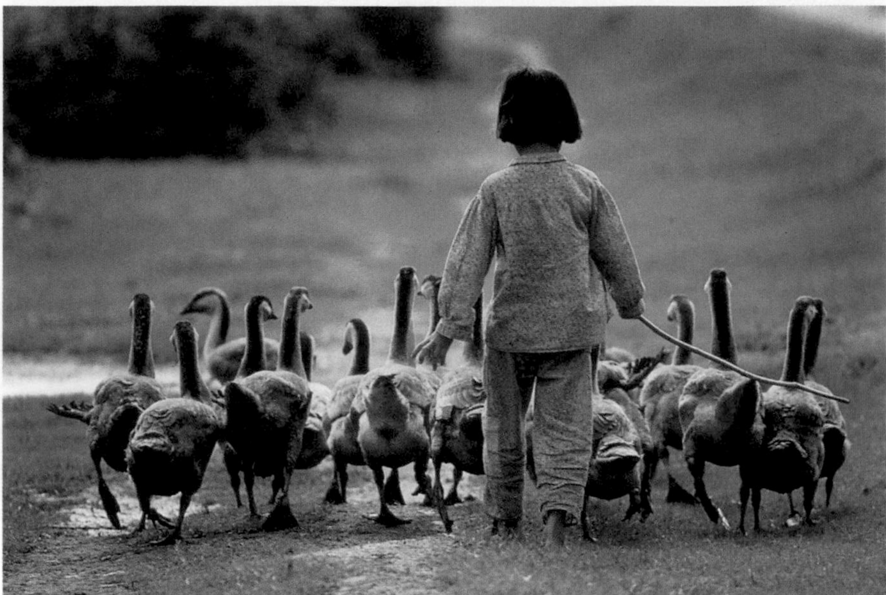

Middle childhood, according to Erikson, is a time for learning the skills one's culture considers important. In driving geese to market, this Vietnamese girl is developing a sense of competence and gaining self-esteem.

industry versus inferiority Erikson's fourth critical alternative of psychosocial development, in which children must learn the productive skills their culture requires or else face feelings of inferiority.

industry versus inferiority. Children need to learn skills valued in their society. Arapesh boys in New Guinea learn to make bows and arrows and to lay traps for rats; Arapesh girls learn to plant, weed, and harvest. Inuit children of Alaska learn to hunt and fish. Children in industrialized countries learn to read, write, count, and use computers. Like Marian Anderson, many children learn household skills and help out with odd jobs.

The "virtue" that develops with successful resolution of this stage of psychosocial development is *competence,* a view of the self as able to master skills and complete tasks. Children compare their abilities with those of their peers; if they feel inadequate, they may retreat to the protective embrace of the family. If, on the other hand, they become too industrious, they may neglect social relationships and turn into "workaholics."

A longitudinal study of 514 middle-class suburban U.S. children found an overall decline in their beliefs about their competence in math and sports throughout elementary and high school, presumably reflecting more realistic self-descriptions in comparison with peers. Boys tended to have a higher opinion of their abilities than girls did, but this gender gap narrowed with time, especially with regard to math. Parents' beliefs about their children's competence were strongly associated with their children's beliefs, especially with regard to fathers' beliefs about sports (Fredricks & Eccles, 2002).

A different perspective on self-worth comes from Susan Harter (1985a, 1990, 1993). In contrast to the importance Erikson placed on mastery of skills, Harter (1985a) found that 8- to 12-year-olds, at least in North America, judge themselves more by good looks and popularity. A major contributor to self-esteem, according to Harter, is social support from parents, peers, and teachers; but this generally will not compensate for a low self-evaluation. If Juanita thinks good looks are important but that she is not pretty, she will lose self-esteem no matter how much praise she gets from others.

Children who are withdrawn or isolated may be overly concerned about their performance in social situations. They may attribute rejection to their own personality deficiencies, which they believe they are helpless to change. Rather than trying new ways to gain approval, they repeat unsuccessful strategies or just give up. (This is similar to the "helpless pattern" in younger children, described in Chapter 11.) Children with high self-esteem, by contrast, tend to attribute failure to factors outside themselves or to the need to try harder. If initially unsuccessful, they persevere, trying new strategies until they find one that works (Erdley, Cain, Loomis, Dumas-Hines, & Dweck, 1997).

Children with high self-esteem tend to be more willing to volunteer to help those who are less fortunate than they are, and volunteering, in turn, helps build self-esteem. The reason may have to do with a belief that others, like oneself, can change and improve. In studies of fifth and sixth graders in Long Island, New York (Karafantis & Levy, 2004), children who expressed belief in people's potential for change were more likely to have positive

Checkpoint

Can you . . .

- ✔ From a neo-Piagetian perspective, tell how the self-concept develops in middle childhood as compared with early childhood?
- ✔ Compare Erikson's and Harter's views about sources of self-esteem?
- ✔ Describe how the "helpless pattern" can affect children's reactions to social rejection?
- ✔ Explain the relationship between volunteer activity and self-esteem?

attitudes toward disadvantaged groups and to see them as "like us." Such children were more willing to collect money for needy children abroad and to express interest in volunteering again and recommending the activity to peers.

Emotional Growth and Prosocial Behavior

How do school-age children show emotional growth?

As children grow older, they are more aware of their own and other people's feelings. They can better regulate their emotions and can respond to others' emotional distress (Saarni et al., 1998).

By age 7 or 8, children typically are aware of feeling shame and pride, and they have a clearer idea of the difference between guilt and shame (Harris, Olthof, Meerum Terwogt, & Hardman, 1987; Olthof, Schouten, Kuiper, Stegge, & Jennekens-Schinkel, 2000; refer back to Chapters 8 and 11). These emotions, now fully internalized, affect their opinions of themselves (Harter, 1993, 1996). Children also can verbalize conflicting emotions. As Lisa says, "Most of the boys at school are pretty yukky. I don't feel that way about my little brother Jason, although he does get on my nerves. I love him but at the same time, he also does things that make me mad. But I control my temper; I'd be ashamed of myself if I didn't" (Harter, 1996, p. 208).

By middle childhood, children are aware of their culture's "rules" for emotional expression (Cole, Bruschi, & Tamang, 2002), which parents communicate through reactions to children's displays of feelings (Eisenberg et al., 1996). Children learn the difference between having an emotion and expressing it. They learn what makes them angry, fearful, or sad and how other people react to a display of these emotions, and they learn to adapt their behavior accordingly. Kindergartners believe that a parent can make a child less sad by telling the child to stop crying or can make a child less afraid of a dog by telling the child there is nothing to be afraid of. Sixth graders know that an emotion may be suppressed, but it still exists (Rotenberg & Eisenberg, 1997).

Emotional self-regulation involves effortful (voluntary) control of emotions, attention, and behavior (Eisenberg et al., 2004). Children low in effortful control tend to become visibly angry or frustrated when interrupted or prevented from doing something they want to do. Children with high effortful control can stifle the impulse to show negative emotion at inappropriate times. Effortful control may be temperamentally based but generally increases with age; low effortful control may predict later behavior problems (Eisenberg et al., 2004).

Effortful control affects children's adjustment to school. Among 4½- to 8-year-olds in a southwestern U.S. city and 7- to 10-year-olds in Beijing, China, children with high effortful control tended to be well adjusted (Eisenberg et al., 2004; Zhou, Eisenberg, Wang, & Reiser, 2004). In the Chinese children, authoritarian parenting tended to predict low effortful control and high levels of anger and frustration (Zhou et al., 2004).

Children tend to become more empathic and more inclined to prosocial behavior in middle childhood, and such behavior is a sign of positive emotional adjustment. Prosocial children tend to act appropriately in social situations, to be relatively free from negative emotion, and to cope with problems constructively (Eisenberg, Fabes, & Murphy, 1996). Parents who acknowledge children's feelings of distress and help them focus on solving the root problem foster empathy, prosocial development, and social skills (Bryant, 1987; Eisenberg et al., 1996). When parents respond with disapproval or punishment, emotions such as anger and fear may become more intense and may impair children's social adjustment (Fabes, Leonard, Kupanoff, & Martin, 2001). Or the children may become secretive and anxious about negative feelings. As children approach early adolescence, parental intolerance of negative emotion may heighten parent-child conflict (Eisenberg, Fabes, et al., 1999).

Checkpoint

Can you . . .

✔ Identify some aspects of emotional growth in middle childhood, and tell how parental treatment may affect children's handling of negative emotions?

The Child in the Family

How do parent-child relationships change in middle childhood?

School-age children spend more time away from home than when they were younger and become less close to their parents (Hofferth, 1998). With the upsurge in dual-earner and single-parent families and the tighter pace of family life, children spend more time at

One of the most important influences on a child's development is the atmosphere in the home. Loving, supportive parents who enjoy being with their children, like this mother, are likely to raise children who feel good about themselves—and about their parents.

school and in other organized activities than a generation ago. They have less free time for unstructured play and leisurely family dinners. Much of the time parents and children spend together is task centered: shopping, preparing meals, cleaning house, and doing homework (Hofferth & Sandberg, 1998). Still, home and the people who live there remain an important part of a child's life.

To understand the child in the family we need to look at the family environment—its atmosphere and structure. These in turn are affected by what goes on beyond the walls of the home. As Bronfenbrenner's theory predicts, additional layers of influence—including parents' work and socioeconomic status and societal trends such as urbanization, changes in family size, divorce, and remarriage—help shape the family environment and, thus, children's development. Cultural experiences and values define rhythms of family life and roles of family members. African-American families like Marian Anderson's, for example, carry on extended-family traditions that include living near or with kin, a strong sense of family obligation, ethnic pride, and mutual aid (Parke & Buriel, 1998). As we look at the child in the family, then, we need to be aware of outside influences that impinge upon the family.

Family Atmosphere

The most important influences of the family environment on children's development come from the atmosphere within the home. Is it supportive and loving or conflict ridden? Does the family have enough money to provide for basic needs? Often these two facets of family atmosphere are interrelated.

Parenting Issues: Coregulation and Discipline

coregulation Transitional stage in the control of behavior in which parents exercise general supervision and children exercise moment-to-moment self-regulation.

During the course of childhood, control of behavior gradually shifts from parents to child. Middle childhood brings a transitional stage of **coregulation,** in which parent and child share power. Parents exercise oversight, but children enjoy moment-to-moment self-regulation (Maccoby, 1984). With regard to problems among peers, for example, parents now rely less on direct management and more on discussion with their own child (Parke & Buriel, 1998). Children are more apt to follow their parents' wishes when they recognize that the parents are fair and are concerned about the child's welfare and that they may "know better" because of experience. It also helps if parents try to defer to children's maturing judgment and take strong stands only on important issues (Maccoby, 1984).

The shift to coregulation affects the way parents handle discipline (Maccoby, 1984; Roberts, Block, & Block, 1984). Parents of school-age children are more likely to use inductive techniques. For example, 8-year-old Jared's father points out how his actions affect others: "Hitting Jermaine hurts him and makes him feel bad." In other situations, Jared's parents may appeal to his self-esteem ("What happened to the helpful boy who was here yesterday?"), sense of humor ("If you go one more day without a bath, we'll know when you're coming without looking!"), moral values ("A big, strong boy like you shouldn't sit on the train and let an old person stand"), or appreciation ("Aren't you glad that your father cares enough to remind you to wear boots so that you won't catch a cold?"). Above all, Jared's parents let him know that he must bear the consequences of his behavior ("No wonder you missed the school bus today—you stayed up too late last night! Now you'll have to walk to school").

Checkpoint

Can you . . .

✔ Describe how coregulation works and how discipline and the handling of family conflict change during middle childhood?

The way parents and children resolve conflicts may be more important than the specific outcomes. If family conflict is constructive, it can help children see the need for rules and standards. They also learn what kinds of issues are worth arguing about and what strategies can be effective (A. R. Eisenberg, 1996). However, as children become preadolescents and their striving for autonomy becomes more insistent, the quality of family problem solving often deteriorates (Vuchinich, Angelelli, & Gatherum, 1996).

Effects of Parents' Work

What are the effects of parents' work and of poverty on family atmosphere?

In 2002, nearly 4 out of 5 U.S. mothers with children ages 6 to 17 were in the workforce (Bureau of Labor Statistics, 2002a). With more than half of all new mothers in the United States going to work within a year of giving birth (Bureau of Labor Statistics, 2002b), many children have never known a time when their mothers were *not* working for pay.

Most studies of the impact of parents' work on children's well-being have focused on employed mothers. In general, the more satisfied a mother is with her employment status, the more effective she is likely to be as a parent (Parke & Buriel, 1998). However, the impact of a mother's work depends on many other factors, including the child's age, sex, temperament, and personality; whether the mother works full- or part-time; why she is working; whether she has a supportive or unsupportive partner, or none; the family's socioeconomic status; and the kind of care the child receives before and/or after school (Parke & Buriel, 1998). Often a single mother like Marian Anderson's must work to stave off economic disaster. How her working affects her children may hinge on how much time and energy she has left over to spend with them and what sort of role model she is (B. L. Barber & Eccles, 1992)—clearly, a positive one in Annie Anderson's case.

"Latch-key" children, who care for themselves after school while parents work, like this brother and sister, need to be mature, responsible, and resourceful and should know how to get help in an emergency.

How well parents keep track of their children may be more important than whether the mother works for pay (Crouter, MacDermid, McHale, & Perry-Jenkins, 1990). Some children of employed mothers are supervised before and after school by their fathers, other relatives, or babysitters. Some, especially if their mothers are single or employed full-time, go to structured child care programs or enrichment activities. Many children experience several types of out-of-school care (NICHD Early Child Care Research Network, 2004).

Like good child care for preschoolers, good after-school programs have relatively low enrollment, low child-staff ratios, and well-educated staff (Rosenthal & Vandell, 1996). Children, especially boys, in organized after-school programs with flexible programming and a positive emotional climate tend to adjust better and do better in school (Pierce, Hamm, & Vandell, 1999; Posner & Vandell, 1999).

About 9 percent of school-aged children and 23 percent of early adolescents are reported to be in *self-care,* regularly caring for themselves at home without adult supervision (Hofferth & Jankuniene, 2000; NICHD Early Childhood Research Network, 2004). This arrangement is advisable only for older children who are mature, responsible, and resourceful and know how to get help in an emergency–and, even then, only if a parent stays in touch by telephone.

What's your view 

- If finances permit, should one parent stay home to take care of the children?

Poverty and Parenting

Poverty can inspire people like Marian Anderson's mother to work hard and make a better life for their children—or it can crush their spirits. Close to 17 percent of all U.S. children under 18—about 12.1 million in all—lived in poverty in 2002. One-half (3.6 million) of the 7.2 million families in poverty were headed by single women (Proctor & Dalaker, 2003).

Poverty can harm children's development through its impact on parents' emotional state and parenting practices and on the home environment they create (Brooks-Gunn & Duncan, 1997; Brooks-Gunn et al., 1998). Vonnie McLoyd's (1990, 1998; Mistry, Vandewater, Huston, & McLoyd, 2002) ecological analysis of the effects of poverty traces a route that leads to adult psychological distress, to effects on child rearing, and finally to emotional, behavioral, and academic problems in children. Parents who live in poor housing (or none), who have lost their jobs, who are worried about their next meal, and who feel a lack of control over their lives are likely to become anxious, depressed, and irritable. They may become less affectionate with and less responsive to their children. They may discipline inconsistently, harshly, and arbitrarily. They may ignore good behavior and pay attention only to misbehavior. The children, in turn, tend to become depressed themselves, to have trouble getting along with peers, to lack self-confidence, to develop behavioral problems, and to engage in antisocial acts (Brooks-Gunn et al., 1998; Evans & English, 2002; McLoyd,

1990, 1998; Mistry et al., 2002). They also tend to do poorly in school. In a nationally representative study of 11,760 children ages 6 to 17, one-third of those with family incomes below poverty level were behind the normal grade level for their age (T. M. Fields & Smith, 1998).

Poverty can sap parents' confidence in their ability to affect their children's development. A father's involvement with his children tends to be related to his economic success; when he feels like a failure as a breadwinner, his demoralization is likely to affect negatively his relationships with his children (Doherty et al., 1998). Lack of financial resources also makes it harder for mothers and fathers to support each other in parenting (Brody et al., 1994). Families under economic stress are less likely to monitor their children's activities, and lack of monitoring is associated with poorer school performance and social adjustment (Bolger, Patterson, Thompson, & Kupersmidt, 1995).

Persistent poverty may be particularly damaging. Among 534 schoolchildren in Charlottesville, Virginia, those from persistently deprived families had lower self-esteem, got along less well with peers, and were more likely to have behavior problems than children whose families experienced intermittent hardship or none at all (Bolger et al., 1995). However, the effects of persistent poverty can be complex. In a six-year longitudinal study of children who had been in Head Start, those who had been continuously poor since age 5 showed no worse academic and behavioral outcomes in fifth grade than children who had been poor for only the last four of those six years or children who had been poor only intermittently. What seemed to be more damaging to children were family characteristics that may accompany poverty—unstable adult relationships, psychiatric problems, and violent or criminal behavior (Ackerman, Brown, & Izard, 2004).

Checkpoint

Can you . . .

- ✔ Identify ways in which parents' work can affect children?
- ✔ Discuss effects of poverty on child raising?

Parents who can turn to relatives (as Annie Anderson did) or to community representatives for emotional support, help with child care, and child-rearing information often can parent their children more effectively. A four-year longitudinal study of 152 single mother–headed African-American families in four economically depressed counties of Georgia found an ecological pattern opposite to the one McLoyd described. Mothers who, despite economic stress, were emotionally healthy and had relatively high self-esteem tended to have academically and socially competent children who reinforced the mothers' positive parenting; and this, in turn, supported the children's continued academic success and socially desirable behavior (Brody, Kim, Murry, & Brown, 2004).

Guidepost 5

What impact does family structure have on children's development?

Family Structure

Family structure in the United States has changed dramatically. In earlier generations, the vast majority of children grew up in traditional families with two married biological or adoptive parents. Today, although 7 in 10 children under 18 live with two parents (not necessarily married), the proportion has declined drastically (Fields, 2003; see Figure 14-1). In addition, many two-parent families are stepfamilies resulting from divorce and remarriage. Other increasingly common family types include single-parent families, gay and lesbian families, and grandparent-headed families (discussed in Chapter 8). How do these various family structures affect children?

Other things being equal, children tend to do better in traditional two-parent families than in divorced, single-parent, or stepfamilies (Bramlett & Mosher, 2001; Bray & Hetherington, 1993; Bronstein, Clauson, Stoll, & Abrams, 1993; D. A. Dawson, 1991; Hetherington, Bridges, & Insabella, 1998). However, structure in itself is not the key; the parents' relationship with each other and their ability to create a favorable atmosphere affect children's adjustment more than does marital status (Bray & Hetherington, 1993; Bronstein et al., 1993; D.A. Dawson, 1991).

Adoptive Families

Adoption is found in all cultures throughout history. It is not only for infertile people; single people, older people, gay and lesbian couples, and people who already have biological children have become adoptive parents. In 2000, about 1.6 million U.S. children under

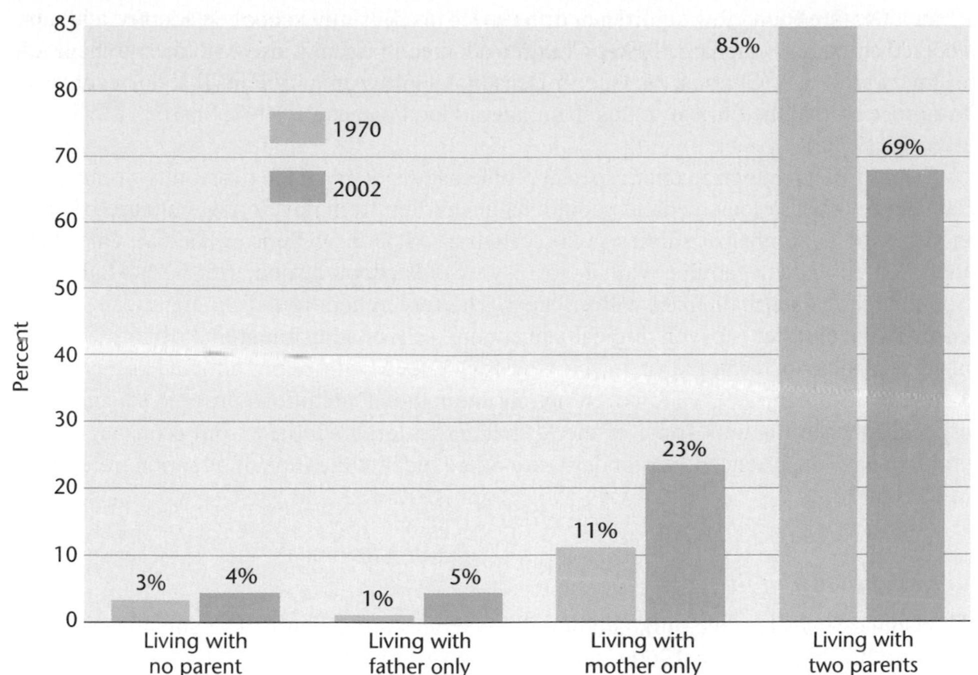

Figure 14-1

Living arrangements of children younger than 18, 1970–2002. Most children under 18 in the United States live with two parents, but this proportion dropped during the past quarter-century. Many of these two-parent families are stepfamilies.

Note: Percentages do not add up to 100 percent because fractional amounts have been dropped.

Source: Data from U.S. Department of Commerce, 1996; Lugaila, 1998, Table A; Fields, 2003.

18—2.5 percent—were adopted, at least 42,000 of them less than 1 year old; and 3.7 percent of households with children contained at least one adopted child (Kreider, 2003). An estimated 60 percent of legal adoptions are by stepparents or relatives, usually grandparents (Goodman, Emery, & Haugaard, 1998; Haugaard, 1998; Kreider, 2003).

Adoptions usually take place through public or private agencies. Agency adoptions are supposed to be confidential, with no contact between the birth mother and the adoptive parents, and the identity of the birth mother is kept secret. However, in recent years independent adoptions, made by agreement between birth parents and adoptive parents, have become more common than in the past (Brodzinsky, 1997; Goodman et al., 1998). Often these are *open adoptions,* in which the parties share information or have direct contact. Studies suggest that the presumed risks of open adoption, such as fear that a birth mother who knows her child's whereabouts will try to reclaim the child, are overstated (Grotevant, McRoy, Elde, & Fravel, 1994). In a survey of 1,059 California adoptive families, whether an adoption was open bore no relation to the children's adjustment or to the parents' satisfaction with the adoption, both of which were very high level (Berry, Dylla, Barth, & Needell, 1998).

With advances in contraception and the legalization of abortion, the proportion of babies of never-married white women placed for adoption dropped from 19.3 percent in the early 1970s to only 1.7 percent in the early 1990s (Chandra, Abma, Maza, & Bachrach, 1999). Black women have consistently been far less likely to put up their babies for adoption (Brodzinsky, 1997). Thus, increasingly children available for adoption are beyond infancy or of foreign birth or have special needs. Adoptions of foreign-born children by U.S. families nearly quadrupled between 1978 and 2001, from 5,315 to an estimated 20,000 (Bosch et al., 2003), and 13 percent of adopted children in 2000 were foreign born. Because of the cultural preference for boys in Asian countries, more girls are available for adoption there. About 17 percent of adoptions are transracial, most often involving white parents adopting an Asian or Latin American child (Kreider, 2003). Rules governing interracial adoption vary from state to state; some states give priority to same-race adoption, whereas others require that race *not* be a factor in approval of an adoption.

What's your view

- If you were infertile, do you think you would try to adopt?
- If so, would you want the adoption to be open? Why or why not?

Adopting a child carries special challenges: integrating the adopted child into the family, explaining the adoption to the child, helping the child develop a healthy sense of self, and perhaps eventually helping the child find and contact the biological parents. A review of the literature found few significant differences in adjustment between adopted and nonadopted children (Haugaard, 1998). Children adopted in infancy are least likely to have adjustment problems (Sharma, McGue, & Benson, 1996b). Any problems that do occur seem to surface around the time of sexual maturation (Goodman et al., 1998; Sharma, McGue, & Benson, 1996a).

Does foreign adoption entail special problems? Aside from the possibility of malnourishment or other serious medical conditions in children from developing countries (Bosch et al., 2003), a number of studies say no (Sharma, McGue, & Benson, 1996a). One study looked at 100 Israeli families with 7- to 13-year-olds adopted soon after birth—half from South America and half from within Israel. The researchers found no significant differences in the children's psychological adjustment, school adjustment and performance, or observed behavior at home or in the way they coped with being adopted (Levy-Shiff, Zoran, & Shulman, 1997). However, not all international adoptions proceed so smoothly, especially when (as with some of the Romanian children adopted from orphanages) the children have experienced substandard care or are older at the time of adoption (refer back to Chapter 6).

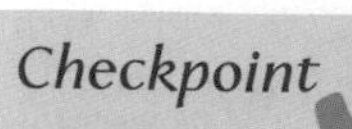

Checkpoint

Can you . . .

✔ Discuss trends in adoption and the adjustment of adopted children?

When Parents Divorce

The United States has one of the highest divorce rates in the world. The annual number of divorces has tripled since 1960 (Harvey & Pauwels, 1999), but the divorce rate has remained stable since 2001 (Munson & Sutton, 2004). One-third of first marriages dissolve within 10 years (Bramlett & Mosher, 2001), and more than 1 million children are involved in divorces each year (Harvey & Pauwels, 1999).

Influences on a child's adjustment to divorce include the child's age or maturity, gender, temperament, and psychological and social adjustment before the divorce. The way parents handle such issues as custody and visitation arrangements, finances, reorganization of household duties, household relocation, contact with the noncustodial parent, remarriage, and the child's relationship with a stepparent also make a difference. Children do better when the custodial parent creates a stable, structured, nurturing environment and does not expect the children to take on more responsibility than they are ready for (Hetherington et al., 1989).

Younger children are more anxious about divorce, have less realistic perceptions of what caused it, and are more likely to blame themselves; but they may adapt more quickly than older children, who better understand what is going on. School-age children are sensitive to parental pressures and loyalty conflicts; like younger children, they may fear abandonment and rejection. Boys generally find it harder to adjust than girls do. However, this difference may depend largely on how involved the father remains (Bray, 1991; Hetherington, Stanley-Hagan, & Anderson, 1989; Hetherington et al., 1998; Hines, 1997; Masten, Best, & Garmezy, 1990; Parke & Buriel, 1998).

In most divorce cases the mother gets custody, though paternal custody is a growing trend (Garasky & Meyer, 1996; Meyer & Garasky, 1993; U.S. Bureau of Census, 1998). The more recent the separation, the closer the father lives to his children, and the higher his socioeconomic status, the more involved he is likely to be (Amato & Keith, 1991; Parke & Buriel, 1998). According to an analysis of 63 studies, children living with divorced mothers do better when the father pays child support, which may

Although paternal custody is still relatively rare, it is a growing trend. Whether or not a father has custody, as this man does, his son is likely to adjust better if his father remains involved in his life.

The Everyday World

Box 14-1 *Should Parents Stay Together for the Sake of the Children?*

A generation ago, when divorce was far less common than it is today, it was widely believed that parents in troubled marriages should stay together for the sake of the children. More recent research suggests that marital strife harms children more than divorce does—that children are better adjusted if they grow up in a harmonious single-parent household than in a two-parent home marked by discord and discontent (Hetherington et al., 1998; Hetherington & Stanley-Hagan, 1999). However, that finding may need some qualification.

Clearly, watching parents fight can be hard on children; they may see parental rows as threatening their own security and that of the family (Davies & Cummings, 1998). Furthermore, constantly quarreling parents may fail to respond to children's needs. Children do not get used to marital conflict; the more they are exposed to it, the more sensitive they become. Young boys growing up in an atmosphere of parental anger and discord tend to become aggressive; girls to become withdrawn and anxious (E. M. Cummings, 1994). Violent clashes, conflicts about a child to which the child is directly exposed, and those in which a child feels caught in the middle are the most damaging (Hetherington & Stanley-Hagan, 1999).

However, the effects on children may depend on the *amount* of conflict in a marriage. A 15-year longitudinal study that followed a nationwide sample of 2,033 married people (Amato & Booth, 1997) suggests that in only about 30 percent of divorces involving children is there so much discord that the children are better off if the marriage ends. About 70 percent of cases, according to this research, involve low-conflict marriages, in which children would benefit "if parents remained together until children are grown" (p. 238).

Furthermore, in as many as 1 in 5 divorced families, parental conflict continues or escalates. Two years after a divorce, children suffer more from dissension in a divorced family than do children in a nondivorced family. Thus, if conflict is going to *continue,* children may be better off in an acrimonious two-parent household than if the parents divorce. On the other hand, if conflict *lessens* after a divorce, the children may be better off than they were before. Unfortunately, the amount of post-divorce wrangling is not always possible to anticipate (Hetherington & Stanley-Hagan, 1999).

In evaluating the effects of divorce, then, we need to look at particular circumstances. Sometimes divorce may improve a child's situation by reducing the amount of conflict within the family and sometimes not. Children's personal characteristics make a difference; intelligent, socially competent children without serious behavior problems, who have a sense of control over their own lives, can cope better with both parental conflict and divorce (Hetherington & Stanley-Hagan, 1999). And, although the immediate effects of a marital breakup may be traumatic, in the long run some children may benefit from having learned new coping skills that make them more competent and independent (B. L. Barber & Eccles, 1992).

What's your view?

- Would you advise parents who want a divorce to stay married until their children have grown up? Why or why not?
- What factors might you consider in giving your advice?

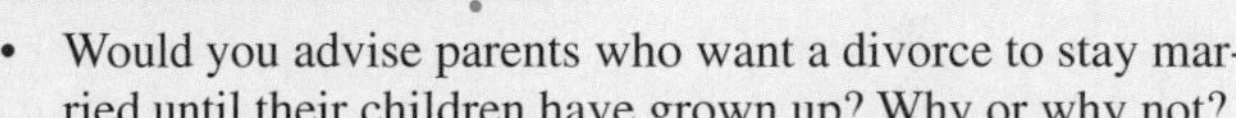

Check it out!

For more information on this topic, go to **http://divorcesource.com**. This is the Divorce Source site, a legal resource for divorce, offering information on a wide range of relevant issues. The site includes a section on children and divorce.

be a barometer of the tie between father and child and also of cooperation between the ex-spouses. Frequency of contact with the father is not as important as the quality of the father-child relationship. Children who are close to their nonresident fathers and whose fathers are authoritative parents tend to do better in school and are less likely to have behavior problems (Amato & Gilbreth, 1999). Children also perform better academically if their nonresident fathers are involved in their schools (National Center for Education Statistics [NCES], 1998) and if their custodial mothers use effective parenting practices and provide skill-building activities at home (DeGarmo, Forgatch, & Martinez, 1999).

Emotional or behavioral problems may stem from parental conflict, both before and after divorce, as well as from the separation itself (Amato, Kurdek, Demo, & Allen, 1993; E. M. Cummings, 1994; Parke & Buriel, 1998; see Box 14-1). If parents can control their anger, cooperate in parenting, and avoid exposing the children to quarreling, the children are less likely to have problems (Bray & Hetherington, 1993; Hetherington et al., 1989). Parent education programs that teach separated or divorced couples how to prevent or deal with conflict, keep lines of communication open, develop an effective co-parenting relationship, and help children adjust to divorce have been introduced in many courts, with measurable success (Amato & Gilbreth, 1999; Shifflet & Cummings, 1999). One program—a series of structured group sessions either for mothers alone or for mothers and their 9- to 12-year-old children—dramatically reduced the children's likelihood six years later of showing mental health problems, such as aggression, substance use, and sexual promiscuity, as compared with a control group who merely received books on adjusting to divorce (Wolchik et al., 2002).

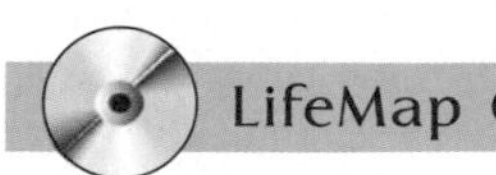

To hear some expert advice for divorcing parents, watch the video on "What Parents Can Do to Foster a Child's Smooth Adjustment to Divorce" in Chapter 14 of your CD.

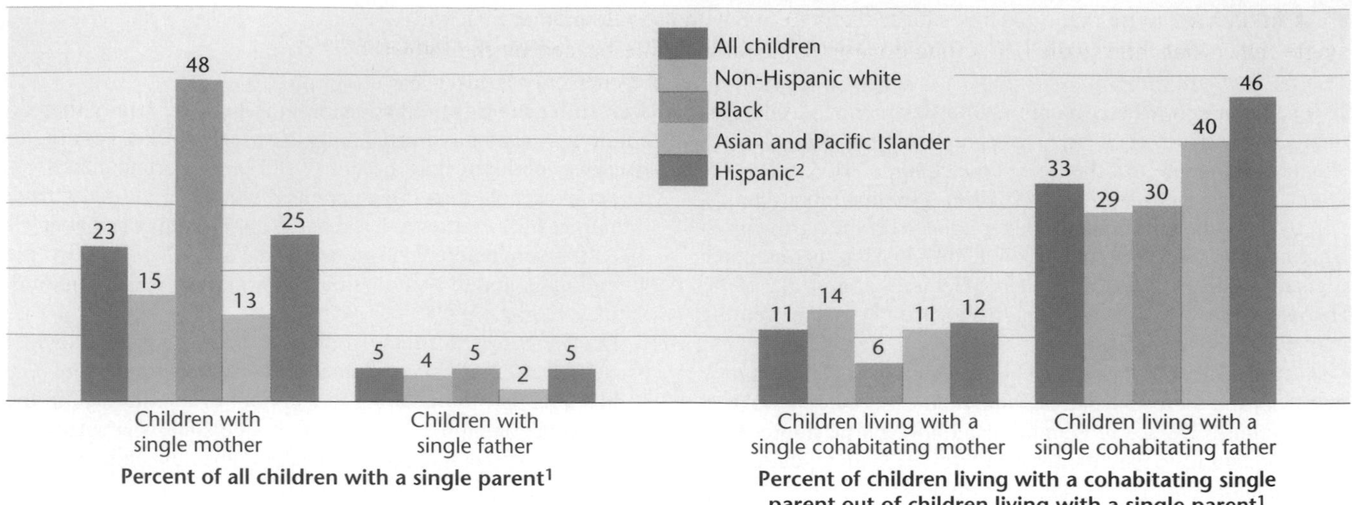

[1]The parent is the householder or partner in an unmarried-partner household. *Single* means the parent has no spouse in the household.
[2]People of Hispanic origin may be of any race.

Figure 14-2

Children living with single parents or single cohabiting parents, March 2002.

Source: Fields, 2003.

Joint custody, custody shared by both parents, can be advantageous in some cases, since both parents can continue to be closely involved with the child. When parents have joint *legal* custody, they share the right and responsibility to make decisions regarding the child's welfare. When parents have joint *physical* custody (which is less common), the child is supposed to live part-time with each of them. The main determinant of the success of joint custody is the amount of conflict between the parents (Parke & Buriel, 1998). An analysis of 33 studies of 814 children in joint custody and 1,846 children in sole custody found that children in either legal or physical joint custody were better adjusted and had higher self-esteem and better family relationships than children in sole custody, and their families experienced less conflict. In fact, the joint custody children were as well-adjusted as children in nondivorced families (Bauserman, 2002). It is likely, though, that couples who choose joint custody are those that have less conflict.

Most children of divorce eventually adjust reasonably well (Chase-Lansdale, Cherlin, & Kiernan, 1995). Still, they are more than twice as likely as children in nondivorced families to drop out of high school (McLanahan & Sandefur, 1994). They also are more likely to marry young and to form unstable, unsatisfying relationships (Ross & Mirowsky, 1999), which themselves end in divorce (Amato, 1999, 2000)—though this pattern is less prevalent than it was 30 years ago (Wolfinger, 1999). Having experienced their parents' divorce as children, some young adults are afraid of making commitments that might end in disappointment and are intent on protecting their independence (Glenn & Marquardt, 2001; Wallerstein & Corbin, 1999). Yet many overcome their fears and form solid, loving relationships (Wallerstein & Lewis, 1998). Much depends on how young people resolve and interpret the experience of parental divorce. Some, who saw a high degree of conflict between their parents, are able to learn from that negative example and to form highly intimate relationships themselves (Shulman, Scharf, Lumer, & Maurer, 2001).

Living in a One-Parent Family

One-parent families result from divorce or separation, unwed parenthood, or death. The number of single-parent families in the United States has more than doubled since 1970 (Fields & Casper, 2001) with rising rates of divorce and of parenthood outside of marriage. Today more than 1 child in 4 (28 percent) live with only one parent (Fields, 2003; refer back to Figure 14-1). Many of these "single-parent" households are actually cohabiting households that include the mother's or (more typically) the father's unwed partner (Fields, 2003; see Figure 14-2).

Children are more than four times more likely to live with a single mother than with a single father, but more than 1 in 7 single-parent U.S. families are headed by the father (Fields, 2003; refer back to Figures 14-1 and 14-2). The number of father-only families has more than quadrupled since 1974, apparently due largely to the increase in paternal custody after divorce (Garasky & Meyer, 1996; U.S. Bureau of the Census, 1998).

Some studies have found that children in one-parent families tend to do less well socially and educationally than children in two-parent families, in part because one-parent families are more likely to be poor (Seltzer, 2000). Children in one-parent families are more on their own. They tend to have more household responsibility, more conflict with siblings, less family cohesion, and less support, control, or discipline from fathers, if it is the father who is absent from the household (Amato, 1987; Coley, 1998; Walker & Hennig, 1997). However, poor outcomes are far from inevitable. Not only the father's involvement, but also the child's age and level of development, the parents' financial circumstances, whether there are frequent moves, and other aspects of the family situation affect how children turn out (Seltzer, 2000). In a longitudinal study of 1,500 white, black, and Hispanic families with 6- and 7-year-old children, the mother's educational and ability level and, to a lesser extent, family income and the quality of the home environment accounted for any negative effects of single parenting on academic performance and behavior. The same remained true when the children reached adolescence (Ricciuti, 1999, 2004; see Chapter 17). Because single mothers often lack the resources needed for good parenting, potential risks to children in these families might be reduced or eliminated through increased access to economic, social, educational, and parenting support.

Living in a Stepfamily

In 2000, 4.4 million stepchildren lived in family households, representing 5.1 percent of the children under 18 in those households. However, only 88 percent of stepchildren live with married couples (Kreider, 2003). Stepfamilies often start out as cohabiting families, when a single parent brings a new partner into the house (Seltzer, 2000).

The stepfamily is different from the "natural" family. It has a larger cast, which may include the relatives of up to four adults (the remarried pair plus one or two former spouses); and it has many stressors. A child's loyalties to an absent or dead parent may interfere with forming ties to a stepparent. Adjustment is harder when there are many children, including those from both partners' previous marriages, or when a new child is born (Hetherington et al., 1989). For these reasons, among others, remarriages are more likely to fail than first marriages, especially during the first five years (Parke & Buriel, 1998).

Findings on the impact of remarriage on children are mixed (Parke & Buriel, 1998). Some studies have found that boys—who often have more trouble than girls in adjusting to divorce and single-parent living, usually with the mother—benefit from a stepfather. A girl, on the other hand, may find the new man in the house a threat to her independence and to her close relationship with her mother and may be less likely to accept him (Bray & Hetherington, 1993; Hetherington, 1987; Hetherington et al., 1989; Hetherington et al., 1998; Hines, 1997). In a longitudinal study of a nationally representative sample of U.S. adults, mothers who remarried or formed new cohabiting relationships used less harsh discipline than mothers who remained single, and their children reported better relationships with them. On the other hand, supervision was greatest in stable single-mother families (Thomson, Mosley, Hanson, & McLanahan, 2001).

Living with Gay or Lesbian Parents

An estimated 1 to 9 million U.S. children have at least one gay or lesbian parent. Some gays and lesbians are raising children born of previous heterosexual relationships. Others conceive by artificial means, use surrogate mothers, or adopt children (Perrin and Committee on Psychosocial Aspects of Child and Family Health, 2002).

A considerable body of research has examined the development of children of gays and lesbians, including physical and emotional health, intelligence, adjustment, sense of self, moral judgment, and social and sexual functioning, and has indicated no concerns

This baby has two mothers—and both obviously dote on the child. Contrary to popular stereotypes, children living with homosexual parents are no more likely than other children to have social or psychological problems or to turn out to be homosexual themselves.

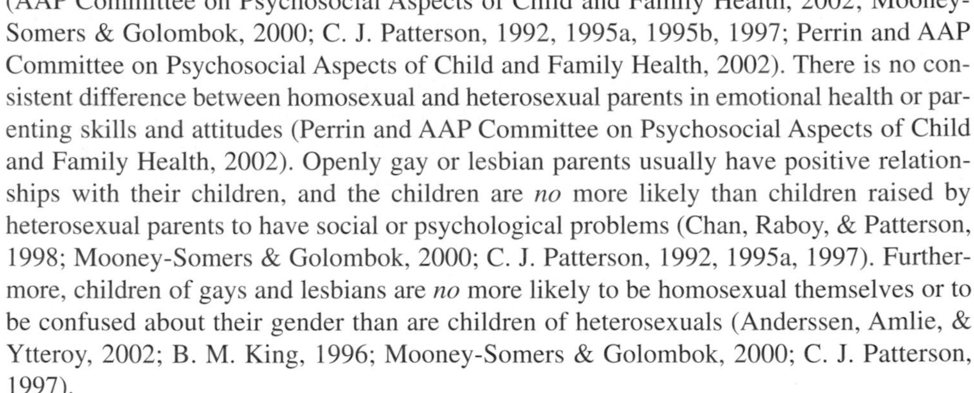

(AAP Committee on Psychosocial Aspects of Child and Family Health, 2002; Mooney-Somers & Golombok, 2000; C. J. Patterson, 1992, 1995a, 1995b, 1997; Perrin and AAP Committee on Psychosocial Aspects of Child and Family Health, 2002). There is no consistent difference between homosexual and heterosexual parents in emotional health or parenting skills and attitudes (Perrin and AAP Committee on Psychosocial Aspects of Child and Family Health, 2002). Openly gay or lesbian parents usually have positive relationships with their children, and the children are *no* more likely than children raised by heterosexual parents to have social or psychological problems (Chan, Raboy, & Patterson, 1998; Mooney-Somers & Golombok, 2000; C. J. Patterson, 1992, 1995a, 1997). Furthermore, children of gays and lesbians are *no* more likely to be homosexual themselves or to be confused about their gender than are children of heterosexuals (Anderssen, Amlie, & Ytteroy, 2002; B. M. King, 1996; Mooney-Somers & Golombok, 2000; C. J. Patterson, 1997).

Such findings have social policy implications for legal decisions on custody and visitation disputes, foster care, and adoptions. The American Academy of Pediatrics supports legislative and legal efforts to permit a partner in a same-sex couple to adopt the other partner's child, so that the child may enjoy the benefits of two parents (AAP Committee on Psychosocial Aspects of Child and Family Health, 2002).

Checkpoint

Can you . . .

- ✔ Assess the impact of parental divorce on children?
- ✔ Tell three ways in which a one-parent family can be formed, and discuss how living in such a household can affect children's well-being?
- ✔ Identify some special issues and challenges of a stepfamily?
- ✔ Summarize findings on outcomes of child raising by gay and lesbian parents?

Guidepost 6

How do siblings influence and get along with one another?

Sibling Relationships

In remote rural areas or villages of Asia, Africa, Oceania, and Central and South America, it is common to see older girls caring for three or four younger siblings: feeding, comforting, and toilet training them; disciplining them; assigning chores; and generally keeping an eye on them. In such a community, older siblings have an important, culturally defined role. Parents train children early to teach younger sisters and brothers how to gather firewood, carry water, tend animals, and grow food. Younger siblings absorb intangible values, such as respecting elders and placing the welfare of the group above that of the individual (Cicirelli, 1994). Often this culturally important teaching arises spontaneously as older siblings care for the younger (Maynard, 2002). In industrialized societies such as the United States, parents generally try not to "burden" older children with the regular care of siblings (Weisner, 1993). When older siblings do teach younger ones, this usually happens informally and not as an established part of the social system (Cicirelli, 1994).

The number of siblings in a family and their spacing, birth order, and gender often determine roles and relationships. The larger number of siblings in nonindustrialized societies helps the family carry on its work and provide for aging members. In industrialized societies, siblings tend to be fewer and farther apart in age, enabling parents to focus more resources and attention on each child (Cicirelli, 1994).

Two longitudinal studies in England and in Pennsylvania, based on naturalistic observation of siblings and mothers and interviews with the mothers, found that changes in sibling relationships were most likely to occur when one sibling was between ages 7 and 9. Both mothers and children often attributed these changes to outside friendships, which led to jealousy and competitiveness or loss of interest in and intimacy with the sibling. Sometimes the younger sibling's growing assertiveness played a part (Dunn, 1996).

These Inuit boys in a northern Canadian fishing camp enjoy caring for a baby brother. Children in nonindustrialized societies tend to have regular responsibility for siblings.

Sibling relations are a laboratory for conflict resolution. Siblings are motivated to make up after quarrels, since they know they will see each other every day. They learn that expressing anger does not end a relationship. Children are more apt to squabble with same-sex siblings; two brothers quarrel more than any other combination (Cicirelli, 1976, 1995).

Siblings influence each other's gender development. In a 3-year longitudinal study of 198 siblings (median ages 10 and 8), secondborns tended to become more like their older siblings in gender-related attitudes, personality, and leisure activities. Firstborns were more influenced by parents and less by younger siblings (McHale, Updegraff, Helms-Erikson, & Crouter, 2001).

Siblings influence each other, not only *directly,* through their own interactions, but also *indirectly* through their impact on each other's relationship with the parents. Behavior patterns established with parents tend to "spill over" into behavior with siblings. An older child's positive relationship with the mother or father can mitigate the effects of that child's "difficult" temperament on sibling interactions (Brody, Stoneman, & Gauger, 1996).

Checkpoint

Can you . . .

- ✔ Compare the roles and responsibilities of siblings in industrialized and nonindustrialized countries?
- ✔ Discuss how siblings affect each other's development?

Companion Animals

Guidepost 7

What part do pets play in children's development?

When the older daughter of one of the authors of this book brought home a collection of poetry her fifth-grade class had "published," more of the compositions dealt with pets than with sisters and brothers. The children wrote about bathing and training a dog, about the way a fish moves, about having to release a baby frog into a pond, about going to a store in winter to buy food for a hungry cat, and about the anger a pet dog showed after having been left with the veterinarian while the family went away for a weekend.

Animal companions play an important and often overlooked role in children's development. The majority of children in Western industrialized nations live with such nonhuman companions. Families with school-age children are most likely to have pets, and many families have more than one. In studies in California, the midwestern United States, and Hesse, Germany, 70 to 90 percent of families with children in this age group owned or recently had owned pets (Melson, 1998).

On the basis of Erikson's theory of personality development, one researcher (Melson, 1998) suggested that companion animals may contribute to children's sense of basic trust and help them meet the challenges of autonomy and industry. Even very young children form trustful attachments to animals and turn to them for emotional support. Having a pet may teach an older child about empathy, responsibility, and caring for others. When 22 seven- and 8-year-olds in a small English town were asked to list the people and animals most important to them, 17 of the 18 children who had pets ranked them among their 10 most important relationships. When asked to whom they would turn in various hypothetical situations (such as being ill, scared, or embarrassed; after having a bad day; or when having a problem or special secret), children often chose pets (McNicholas & Collis, 2001).

Checkpoint

Can you . . .

- ✔ Discuss ways in which pets are important to children's development?

Guidepost 8

How do relationships with peers change in middle childhood, and what influences popularity and choice of friends?

The Child in the Peer Group

In middle childhood the peer group comes into its own. Groups form naturally among children who live near one another or go to school together; thus, peer groups often consist of children of the same racial or ethnic origin (Pellegrini, Kato, Blatchford, & Baines, 2002) and similar socioeconomic status. Children who play together are usually close in age and of the same sex (Hartup, 1992). Children of the same sex have common interests; girls are generally more mature than boys, and girls and boys play and talk to one another differently. Same-sex groups help children learn gender-appropriate behaviors and incorporate gender roles into their self-concept (Hibbard & Buhrmester, 1998).

How does the peer group influence children? What determines their acceptance by peers and their ability to make friends?

Positive and Negative Effects of Peer Relations

Children benefit from doing things with peers. They develop skills needed for sociability and intimacy, they enhance relationships, and they gain a sense of belonging. They are motivated to achieve, and they attain a sense of identity. They learn leadership and communication skills, cooperation, roles, and rules (Pellegrini et al., 2002; Zarbatany, Hartmann, & Rankin, 1990).

As children begin to move away from parental influence, the peer group opens new perspectives and frees them to make independent judgments. Testing values they previously accepted unquestioningly against those of their peers helps them decide which to keep and which to discard. In comparing themselves with others their age, children can gauge their abilities more realistically and gain a clearer sense of self-efficacy (Bandura, 1994; refer back to Chapter 11). The peer group helps children learn how to get along in society—how to adjust their needs and desires to those of others, when to yield, and when to stand firm. The peer group offers emotional security. It is reassuring for children to find out that they are not alone in harboring thoughts that might offend an adult.

prejudice Unfavorable attitude toward members of certain groups outside one's own, especially racial or ethnic groups.

On the negative side, peer groups can become cliques, intent on exclusion as well as inclusion. They may reinforce **prejudice:** unfavorable attitudes toward "outsiders," especially members of certain racial or ethnic groups. A study in Montreal, Canada, where tensions exist between French-speaking and English-speaking citizens, found signs of prejudice among 254 English-speaking children in kindergarten through sixth grade (Powlishta, Serbin, Doyle, & White, 1994). The researchers asked boys and girls whether each of two cartoon children—one English speaking and the other French speaking—would be likely to be, for example, *helpful, smart, mean,* and *naughty* and which of the two pictured children they would like to play with. A similar procedure was followed using male and female figures (with regard to such gender stereotypes as *ambitious* and *gentle*) and figures of overweight and normal-weight children. Children tended to show biases toward children like themselves, but these biases, except for a preference for children of the same sex, diminished with age and cognitive development. Girls were more biased with regard to gender and boys with respect to ethnicity (Powlishta, Serbin, Doyle, & White, 1994). Children with flexible beliefs about people's ability to change are less likely to hold such stereotyped ideas (Karafantis & Levy, 2004).

What's your view

- How can parents and schools reduce racial, religious, and ethnic prejudice?

Checkpoint

Can you . . .

✔ Tell some ways in which members of a peer group tend to be alike?

✔ Identify positive and negative effects of the peer group?

The peer group also can foster antisocial tendencies. Preadolescent children are especially susceptible to pressure to conform. To be part of a peer group, a child is expected to accept its values and behavioral norms, and even though these may be socially undesirable, children may not have the strength to resist. It is usually in the company of peers that some children shoplift and begin to use drugs (Hartup, 1992). Of course, some degree of conformity to group standards is healthy. It is unhealthy when it becomes destructive or prompts people to act against their own better judgment.

Popularity

Popularity becomes more important in middle childhood. Schoolchildren whose peers like them are likely to be well adjusted as adolescents. Those who have trouble getting along with peers are more likely to develop psychological problems, drop out of school, or become delinquent (Hartup, 1992; Kupersmidt & Coie, 1990; Morison & Masten, 1991; Newcomb, Bukowski, & Pattee, 1993; Parker & Asher, 1987).

Popularity can be measured in two ways. Researchers measure *sociometric popularity* by asking children which peers they like most and least. *Perceived popularity* is measured by asking children which children are best liked by their peers. *Sociometrically* popular children typically have good cognitive abilities, are high achievers, are good at solving social problems, help other children, and are assertive without being disruptive or aggressive. They are kind, trustworthy, cooperative, loyal, and self-disclosing and provide emotional support. Their superior social skills make others enjoy being with them (Cillessen & Mayeux, 2004; LaFontana & Cillessen, 2002; Masten & Coatsworth, 1998; Newcomb et al., 1993). On the other hand, as we will discuss in a subsequent section, some children with *perceived* popularity may be dominant, arrogant, and aggressive (Cillessen & Mayeux, 2004; LaFontana & Cillessen, 2002).

Children can be *un*popular for many reasons. Although some unpopular children are aggressive, others are hyperactive, inattentive, or withdrawn (Dodge, Coie, Pettit, & Price, 1990; Masten & Coatsworth, 1998; Newcomb et al., 1993; A. W. Pope, Bierman, & Mumma, 1991). Still others act silly and immature or anxious and uncertain. Unpopular children are often insensitive to other children's feelings and do not adapt well to new situations (Bierman, Smoot, & Aumiller, 1993). Some show undue interest in being with groups of the other sex (Sroufe, Bennett, Englund, Urban, & Shulman, 1993). Some unpopular children *expect* not to be liked, and this becomes a self-fulfilling prophecy (Rabiner & Coie, 1989).

It is often in the family that children acquire behaviors that affect popularity (Masten & Coatsworth, 1998). Authoritative parents tend to have more popular children than authoritarian parents (Dekovic & Janssens, 1992). Children of authoritarian parents who punish and threaten are likely to threaten or act mean with other children; they are less popular than children whose authoritative parents reason with them and try to help them understand how another person might feel (C. H. Hart, Ladd, & Burleson, 1990).

In both western and Chinese cultures, high achievers tend to be popular and socially skilled; and, conversely, well-adjusted, well-liked children tend to do well in school (X. Chen, Rubin, & Li, 1997). One cultural difference is that shy, sensitive children are more likely to be popular in China—at least in middle childhood (see Box 14-2).

Checkpoint

Can you . . .

- ✔ Describe characteristics of popular and unpopular children, and tell how they may vary?
- ✔ Identify family and cultural influences on popularity?

Friendship

Children may spend much of their free time in groups, but only as individuals do they form friendships. Popularity is the peer group's opinion of a child, but friendship is a two-way street.

Children look for friends who are like them in age, sex, ethnicity, and interests. A friend is someone a child feels affection for, is comfortable with, likes to do things with, and can share feelings and secrets with. Friends know each other well, trust each other, feel a sense of commitment to one another, and treat each other as equals. The strongest friendships involve equal commitment and mutual give-and-take. Even unpopular children can make friends; but they have fewer friends than popular children and tend to find friends among younger children, other unpopular children, or children in a different class or a different school (George & Hartmann, 1996; Hartup, 1992, 1996a, 1996b; Newcomb & Bagwell, 1995).

With their friends, children learn to communicate and cooperate. They learn about themselves and others. They help each other weather stressful transitions, such as starting at a new school or adjusting to parents' divorce. The inevitable quarrels help children learn to resolve conflicts (Furman, 1982; Hartup, 1992, 1996a, 1996b; Hartup & Stevens, 1999; Newcomb & Bagwell, 1995).

Friendship seems to help children feel good about themselves, though it's also likely that children who feel good about themselves have an easier time making friends. Peer rejection and friendlessness in middle childhood may have long-term effects. In one longitudinal study, fifth graders who had no friends were more likely than their classmates to have low self-esteem in young adulthood and even to show symptoms of depression (Bagwell, Newcomb, & Bukowski, 1998).

Around the World

Box 14-2 *Popularity: A Cross-Cultural View*

How does culture affect popularity? Would a child who is popular in one culture be equally popular in another? Researchers compared 480 second and fourth graders in Shanghai, China, with 296 children the same ages in Ontario, Canada (X. Chen, Rubin, & Sun, 1992). Although the two samples were quite different—for example, none of the Canadian children came from peasant families, but many of the Chinese children did—both samples were representative of school-age children in the two countries.

The researchers assessed the children's popularity by two kinds of peer perceptions. The children filled out a sociometric rating telling which three classmates they most and least liked to be with and which three classmates were their best friends. The results showed that certain traits are valued similarly in both cultures. A sociable, cooperative child is likely to be popular in both China and Canada, and an aggressive child is likely to be rejected in both countries. However, one important difference emerged: shy, sensitive children are well liked in China but not in Canada. This is not surprising. Chinese children are encouraged to be cautious, to restrain themselves, and to inhibit their urges; thus, a quiet, shy youngster is considered well behaved. In a western culture, by contrast, such a child is likely to be seen as socially immature, fearful, and lacking in self-confidence.

A follow-up study at ages 8 and 10 (X. Chen, Rubin, & Li, 1995) again found shy, sensitive Chinese children to be popular with peers. They also were rated by teachers as socially competent, as leaders, and as academic achievers. However, by age 12, shy, sensitive Chinese children were no longer popular. They tended to be rejected by peers, just as in western cultures.

It may be, then, that shyness and sensitivity take on different social meanings in China as children enter adolescence, when peer relationships become more important and adult approval becomes less so. As in the west, a shy early adolescent may lack the assertiveness and communication skills needed to establish and maintain strong peer relationships.

This research suggests that the influence of culture may be tempered by developmental processes that are more or less universal. Even in China, with its strong tradition of obedience to authority, the influence of adult social standards may wane as children's urge to make their own independent judgments of their peers asserts itself.

During middle childhood, shy, sensitive children are better liked in China than in western cultures because they are considered well behaved. Children this age tend to accept adult standards of behavior.

What's your view?

What would you advise parents of a shy, sensitive child who complains of being rejected by other children?

Check it out!

For more information on this topic, go to **http://www.pbs.org/kcts/preciouschildren/resources/index.html**. Here you will find links about China from the PBS documentary "Precious Children." Or go to **http://www.pbs.org/inthemix/**. This is the Web site for the PBS program *In the Mix*, which offers transcripts. Search for the show called "Cliques: Behind the Labels."

Children's concepts of friendship and the ways they act with their friends change with age, reflecting cognitive and emotional growth. Preschool friends play together, but friendship among school-age children is deeper and more stable. Children cannot be or have true friends until they achieve the cognitive maturity to consider other people's views and needs as well as their own (Hartup, 1992; Hartup & Stevens, 1999; Newcomb & Bagwell, 1995). On the basis of interviews with more than 250 people between ages 3 and 45, Robert Selman (1980; Selman & Selman, 1979) traced changing conceptions of friendship through five overlapping stages (see Table 14-1). He found that most school-age children are in stage 2 (reciprocal friendship based on self-interest), but some older children, ages 9 and up, may be in stage 3 (intimate, mutually shared relationships).

Checkpoint

Can you . . .

- ✔ Distinguish between popularity and friendship?
- ✔ Compare two measures of popularity and discuss reasons for it?
- ✔ List characteristics children look for in friends?
- ✔ Tell how age and gender affect friendships?

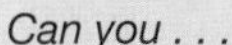

School-age children distinguish among "best friends," "good friends," and "casual friends" on the basis of intimacy and time spent together (Hartup & Stevens, 1999). Children this age typically have three to five "best" friends but usually play with only one or two at a time (Hartup, 1992; Hartup & Stevens, 1999). School-age girls care less about having many friends than about having a few close friends they can rely on. Boys have more friendships, but they tend to be less intimate and affectionate (Furman, 1982; Furman & Buhrmester, 1985; Hartup & Stevens, 1999).

Table 14-1	Selman's Stages of Friendship	
Stage	**Description**	**Example**
Stage 0: Momentary playmateship (ages 3 to 7)	On this *undifferentiated* level of friendship, children are egocentric and have trouble considering another person's point of view; they tend to think only about what they want from a relationship. Most very young children define their friends in terms of physical closeness and value them for material or physical attributes.	"She lives on my street" or "He has the Power Rangers."
Stage 1: One-way assistance (ages 4 to 9)	On this *unilateral* level, a "good friend" does what the child wants the friend to do.	"She's not my friend anymore, because she wouldn't go with me when I wanted her to" or "He's my friend because he always says yes when I want to borrow his eraser."
Stage 2: Two-way fair-weather cooperation (ages 6 to 12)	This *reciprocal* level overlaps stage 1. It involves give-and-take but still serves many separate self-interests, rather than the common interests of the two friends.	"We are friends; we do things for each other" or "A friend is someone who plays with you when you don't have anybody else to play with."
Stage 3: Intimate, mutually shared relationships (ages 9 to 15)	On this *mutual* level, children view a friendship as having a life of its own. It is an ongoing, systematic, committed relationship that incorporates more than doing things for each other. Friends become possessive and demand exclusivity.	"It takes a long time to make a close friend, so you really feel bad if you find out that your friend is trying to make other friends too."
Stage 4: Autonomous interdependence (beginning at age 12)	In this *interdependent* stage, children respect friends' needs for both dependency and autonomy.	"A good friendship is a real commitment, a risk you have to take; you have to support and trust and give, but you have to be able to let go too."

Source: Selman, 1980; Selman & Selman, 1979.

School-age friends often share confidences—and laughs–as Anna and her friend Christina are doing.

What are the most common forms of aggressive behavior in middle childhood, and what influences contribute to such behavior?

Aggression and Bullying

During the early school years, as discussed in Chapter 11, aggression generally declines and changes in form. *Hostile aggression* (aggression aimed at hurting its target) becomes more common than *instrumental aggression* (aggression aimed at achieving an objective), the hallmark of the preschool period (Coie & Dodge, 1998). *Overt* aggression (physical force or verbal threats) largely gives way to *relational,* or social, aggression. Nine-year-olds recognize such behavior as teasing and spreading rumors as "mean"; they realize that it stems from anger and is aimed at hurting others (Crick, Bigbee, & Howes, 1996; Crick et al., 2002; Galen & Underwood, 1997).

A small minority of children do not learn to control physical aggression (Coie & Dodge, 1998), and these children tend to remain physically aggressive throughout childhood. They tend to have social and psychological problems, but it is not clear whether aggression causes these problems or is a reaction to them or both (Crick & Grotpeter, 1995).

As already discussed, aggressors tend to be unpopular. In a longitudinal study of 905 children from ages 10 to 14, children who were disliked in elementary school tended to be physically aggressive in middle school, and those who were physically aggressive tended to be disliked, especially by girls, and to be seen as unpopular (Cillessen & Mayeux, 2004). However, the relationship between aggressiveness and popularity is complex. Some aggressive or antisocial boys and some relationally aggressive girls are among the most popular in the classroom (Cillessen & Mayeux, 2004; Rodkin, Farmer, Pearl, & Van Acker, 2000). In a study of "rejected" fourth graders, aggressive boys tended to gain in social status by the end of fifth grade, suggesting that behavior shunned by younger children may be seen as "cool" or glamorous by preadolescents (Sandstrom & Coie, 1999).

Highly aggressive children tend to seek out friends like themselves and egg each other on to antisocial acts (Hartup, 1989, 1992, 1996a; Hartup & Stevens, 1999; Masten & Coatsworth, 1998). Thus, school-age boys who are physically aggressive are candidates for juvenile delinquency in adolescence (Broidy et al., 2003).

Types of Aggression and Social Information Processing

What makes children act aggressively? One answer may lie in the way they process social information: what features of the social environment they pay attention to and how they interpret what they perceive (Crick & Dodge, 1994, 1996).

Instrumental (or *proactive*) aggressors view force and coercion as effective ways to get what they want. They act deliberately, not out of anger. In social learning terms, they are aggressive because they expect to be rewarded for it; and when they *are* rewarded, their belief in the effectiveness of aggression is reinforced (Crick & Dodge, 1996). By contrast, a child who is accidentally bumped in line may push back angrily, assuming that the other child bumped her on purpose. This is hostile, or *reactive,* aggression. Such children often have a *hostile attribution bias;* they see other children as trying to hurt them, and they strike out in retaliation or self-defense (Crick & Dodge, 1996; de Castro, Veerman, Koops, Bosch, & Monshouwer, 2002; Waldman, 1996).

Children who seek dominance and control may react aggressively to threats to their status, which they may attribute to hostility (de Castro et al., 2002; Erdley et al., 1997). Rejected children and those exposed to harsh parenting also tend to have a hostile bias (Coie & Dodge, 1998; Masten & Coatsworth, 1998; Weiss, Dodge, Bates, & Pettit, 1992). Since people often *do* become hostile toward someone who acts aggressively toward them, a hostile bias may become a self-fulfilling prophecy, setting in motion a cycle of aggression (de Castro et al., 2002).

Psychological differences between aggressive children and their peers become increasingly marked during middle childhood. Among a representative sample of 11,160 New York public school children who were questioned about their fantasies, their behavior, and their reactions to hypothetical situations, hostile attribution bias and aggressive fantasies became more common between ages 6 and 12, but so did more constructive responses to conflict. Although girls were less aggressive than boys at age 6, by age 11 girls were almost as likely to show hostile attribution bias and to give aggressive responses to hypothetical conflicts (Aber, Brown, & Jones, 2003).

Both instrumental and hostile aggressors need help in altering the way they process social information so that they do not interpret aggression as either justified or useful. Adults can help children curb *hostile* aggression by teaching them how to recognize when they are getting angry and how to control their anger. *Instrumental* aggression tends to stop if it is not rewarded (Crick & Dodge, 1996). In a New York City school study, children exposed to a conflict resolution curriculum that involved discussions and group role playing showed less hostile attribution bias, less aggression, fewer behavior problems, and more effective responses to social situations than children who did not participate in the program (Aber et al., 2003).

Does Televised Violence Lead to Aggression?

Children spend more time consuming entertainment media than on any other activity besides school and sleeping. On average, children spend about four hours a day in front of a television or computer screen—some much more than that (Anderson et al., 2003). Virtually all U.S. families with children have at least one television set, most have VCR or DVD players, more than half have access to the Internet, and 3 out of 4 subscribe to cable or satellite TV (Anderson et al., 2003). More than half (57 percent) of U.S. 8- to 16-year-olds have television sets in their bedrooms (Woodward & Gridina, 2000). About 6 out of 10 U.S. television programs contain violence, usually glamorized, glorified, or trivialized. The worst culprits are televised movies, which show violence 85 percent of the time (National Television Violence Study, 1995). Thirty-nine percent of children's programs on British television contain violence, mostly shootings or other physical assaults (Gunter & Harrison, 1997).

Experimental and longitudinal studies support a causal relationship between watching violent television or films and acting aggressively in childhood, adolescence, and adulthood (Anderson et al., 2001; Anderson et al., 2003; Coie & Dodge, 1998; Geen, 1994; Huesmann, Moise-Titus, Podolski, & Eron, 2003; Huston et al., 1992; Strasburger & Donnerstein, 1999). Media violence produces immediate aggressiveness by stimulating preexisting aggressive thinking and aggressive behavior patterns, increasing physiological arousal, and triggering imitation of observed behaviors (Anderson et al., 2003). Children are more vulnerable than adults to the influence of televised violence (Coie & Dodge, 1998). Classic social learning research suggests that children imitate filmed models even more than live ones (Bandura, Ross, & Ross, 1963). The influence is stronger if the child believes the violence on the screen is real, identifies with the violent character, finds that character attractive, and watches without parental supervision or intervention (Anderson et al., 2003; Coie & Dodge, 1998).

How does media violence lead to long-term aggressiveness? Children may absorb the values depicted on screen and come to view aggression as acceptable behavior. Children who see both heroes and villains on television getting what they want through violence are likely to conclude that violence is an effective way to resolve conflicts. They may become less sensitive to the pain it causes. They may learn to take violence for granted and may be less likely to intervene when they see it (Anderson et al., 2003; Gunter & Harrison, 1997; M. O. Johnson, 1996; National Television Violence Study, 1995, 1996; Sege & Dietz, 1994; Singer, Slovak, Frierson, & York, 1998; M. E. Smith, 1993; Strasburger & Donnerstein, 1999). Highly aggressive children are more strongly affected by media violence than are less aggressive children (Anderson et al., 2003).

The long-term influence of televised violence is greater in middle childhood than at earlier ages (Eron & Huesmann, 1986). Among 427 children whose viewing habits were studied at age 8, the best predictor of aggressiveness at age 19 was the degree of violence in the shows they had watched as children (Eron, 1980, 1982). In a follow-up study, the amount of television viewed at age 8 and the preference among boys for violent shows predicted the severity of criminal offenses at age 30 (Huesmann, 1986; Huesmann & Eron, 1984).

Media-induced aggressiveness can be reduced by cutting down on television use and by parental monitoring and guidance of the shows children watch (Anderson et al., 2003). Third and fourth graders who participated in a six-month curriculum aimed at motivating them to monitor and reduce the time they spent on television, videotapes, and video games showed significant decreases in peer-rated aggression, as compared with a control group (Robinson, Wilde, Navracruz, Haydel, & Varady, 2001).

What's your view 

- What can and should be done about children's exposure to violent television programs?

Checkpoint 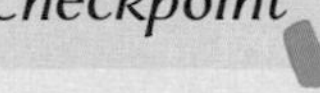

Can you . . .

✔ Tell how aggression changes during middle childhood and how social information processing and televised violence can contribute to it?

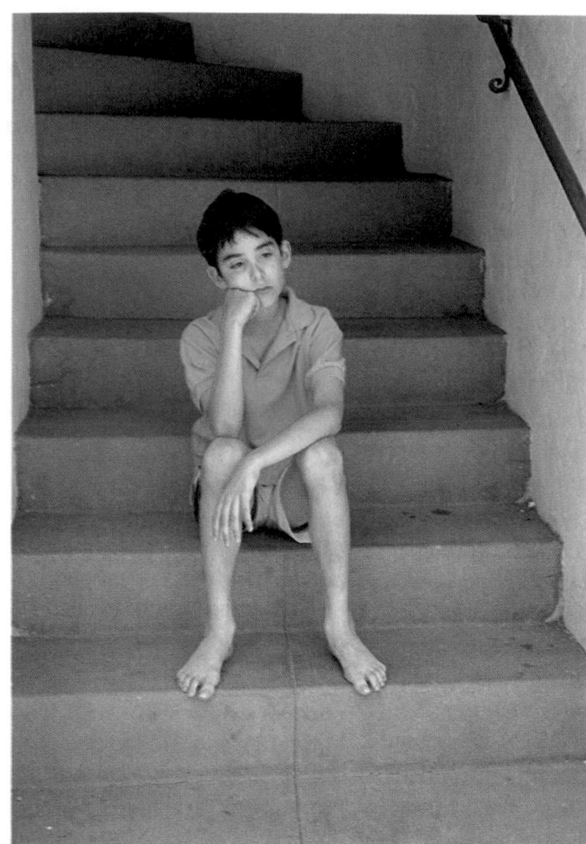

Any child may be sad or lonely at times, but sadness that lasts two weeks or more and is accompanied by such symptoms as fatigue, apathy, sleep problems, and inability to concentrate may be a sign of depression.

& Turner, 1998). Social anxiety tends to increase with age, whereas separation anxiety decreases (Costello et al., 2003).

Some children have a **generalized anxiety disorder,** not focused on any specific part of their lives. These children worry about just about everything: school grades, being on time, wars, or earthquakes. Their worry seems independent of their performance or how they are regarded by others. They tend to be perfectionists, conformists, and self-doubters. They seek approval and need constant reassurance (APA, 1994; USDHHS, 1999c). Far less common is **obsessive-compulsive disorder.** Sufferers from this disorder are obsessed by repetitive, intrusive thoughts, images, or impulses and often show compulsive behaviors, such as constant hand washing (APA, 1994; USDHHS, 1999c).

Anxiety disorders are twice as common among girls as among boys. The heightened female vulnerability to anxiety begins as early as age 6. Females also are more susceptible to depression, which is similar to anxiety and often goes hand in hand with it (Lewinsohn, Gotlib, Lewinsohn, Seeley, & Allen, 1998). Both anxiety and depression may be neurologically based or may stem from early experiences that make children feel a lack of control over what happens around them (Chorpita & Barlow, 1998).

generalized anxiety disorder Anxiety not focused on any single target.

obsessive-compulsive disorder Anxiety aroused by repetitive, intrusive thoughts, images, or impulses, often leading to compulsive ritual behaviors.

childhood depression Mood disorder characterized by such symptoms as a prolonged sense of friendlessness, inability to have fun or concentrate, fatigue, extreme activity or apathy, feelings of worthlessness, weight change, physical complaints, and thoughts of death or suicide.

Childhood Depression

"Nobody likes me" is a common complaint among school-age children, who tend to be popularity conscious; but a prolonged sense of friendlessness may be one sign of **childhood depression:** a disorder of mood that goes beyond normal, temporary sadness. At any given time, between 10 and 15 percent of children and adolescents have symptoms of depression (USDHHS, 1999c), such as inability to have fun or concentrate, fatigue, extreme activity or apathy, crying, sleep problems, feelings of worthlessness, weight change, physical complaints, or frequent thoughts about death or suicide. Any five of these symptoms, lasting at least two weeks, may point to depression (APA, 1994). If symptoms persist, the child should have psychological help. Depression may lead to attempted suicide and often signals the beginning of a recurrent problem that, if present during adolescence, is likely to persist into adulthood (Birmaher, 1998; Birmaher et al., 1996; Cicchetti & Toth, 1998; Kye & Ryan, 1995; USDHHS, 1999c; Weissman et al., 1999).

The exact causes of childhood depression are not known. Twin studies have found its heritability to be modest, though 20 to 50 percent of depressed children and adolescents have a family history of it. Depressed children tend to come from families with high levels of parental depression, anxiety, substance abuse, or antisocial behavior; and the atmosphere in such families may increase children's risk of depression (Cicchetti & Toth, 1998; USDHHS, 1999c).

Children as young as 5 or 6 can accurately report depressed moods and feelings that forecast later trouble, from academic problems to major depression and ideas of suicide (Ialongo, Edelsohn, & Kellam, 2001). Depression often emerges during the transition to middle school and may be related to stiffer academic pressures (Cicchetti & Toth, 1998). This transition seems especially stressful and depression producing in young people who do not have strong self-efficacy beliefs and who have little personal investment in academic success (Rudolph, Lambert, Clark, & Kurlakowsky, 2001). Depression becomes more prevalent during adolescence (Costello et al., 2003).

Treatment Techniques

individual psychotherapy Psychological treatment in which a therapist sees a troubled person one-on-one.

Psychological treatment for emotional disturbances can take several forms. In **individual psychotherapy,** a therapist sees a child one-on-one, to help the child gain insights into his or her personality and relationships and to interpret feelings and behavior. Such treatment may be helpful at a time of stress, such as the death of a parent or parental divorce, even when a child has not shown signs of disturbance. Child psychotherapy is usually more effective when combined with counseling for the parents.

In **family therapy,** the therapist sees the family together, observes how members interact, and points out both growth-producing and growth-inhibiting or destructive patterns of family functioning. Therapy can help parents confront their own conflicts and begin to resolve them. This is often the first step toward resolving the child's problems as well.

family therapy Psychological treatment in which a therapist sees the whole family together to analyze patterns of family functioning.

Behavior therapy, or *behavior modification* (refer back to Chapter 2), is a form of psychotherapy that uses principles of learning theory to eliminate undesirable behaviors or to develop desirable ones. A statistical analysis of many studies found that psychotherapy is generally effective with children and adolescents, but behavior therapy is more effective than nonbehavioral methods. Results are best when treatment is targeted to specific problems and desired outcomes (Weisz, Weiss, Han, Granger, & Morton, 1995).

behavior therapy Therapeutic approach using principles of learning theory to encourage desired behaviors or eliminate undesired ones; also called *behavior modification*.

When children have limited verbal and conceptual skills or have suffered emotional trauma, **art therapy** can help them describe what is troubling them without the need to put their feelings into words. The child may express deep emotions through choices of colors and subjects to depict (Kozlowska & Hanney, 1999). Observing how a family plans, carries out, and discusses an art project can reveal patterns of family interactions (Kozlowska & Hanney, 1999).

art therapy Therapeutic approach that allows a child to express troubled feelings without words, using a variety of art materials and media.

Play therapy, in which a child plays freely while a therapist occasionally comments, asks questions, or makes suggestions, has proven effective with a variety of emotional, cognitive, and social problems, especially when consultation with parents or other close family members is part of the process (Athansiou, 2001; Bratton & Ray, 2002; Leblanc & Ritchie, 2001; Ryan & Needham, 2001; Wilson & Ryan, 2001).

play therapy Therapeutic approach in which a child plays freely while a therapist observes and occasionally comments, asks questions, or makes suggestions.

The use of **drug therapy** to treat childhood emotional disorders greatly increased during the 1990s, often in combination with one or more forms of psychotherapy. However, sufficient research on its effectiveness and safety for children and adolescents is generally lacking (USDHHS, 1999c; Zito et al., 2003). Antidepressants are commonly prescribed for depression, and antipsychotics for severe psychological problems. Yet many studies have found various antidepressants no more effective than *placebos* (substances with no active ingredients) in treating depression in children and adolescents (Fisher & Fisher, 1996; Sommers-Flanagan & Sommers-Flanagan, 1996).

drug therapy Administration of drugs to treat emotional disorders.

Exceptions are the use of stimulants such as Ritalin to treat attention-deficit hyperactivity disorder and the use of *selective serotonin reuptake inhibitors (SSRIs)* to treat obsessive-compulsive, depressive, and anxiety disorders (Research Unit on Pediatric Psychopharmacology Anxiety Study Group, 2001; Rodrigues, 1999; USDHHS, 1999c). A randomly controlled trial found fluoxetine (Prozac), the most popular of the SSRIs, superior to placebos. It is safer and has more tolerable side effects than other classes of drugs (Birmaher, 1998). However, Prozac can produce sleep disturbances and behavioral changes, and its long-term effects are unknown (Rushton, Clark, & Freed, 1999). A government-sponsored study of 439 adolescents suffering from moderate to severe depression found Prozac more effective than a form of psychotherapy called *cognitive behavioral therapy,* in which patients are taught to think positively. A combination of the two therapies was most effective of all (Emslie, 2004; March, 2004).

Checkpoint

Can you . . .

- ✔ Identify causes and symptoms of disruptive behavior disorders, anxiety disorders, and childhood depression?
- ✔ Describe and evaluate five common types of therapy for emotional disorders?

Stress and Resilience

Guidepost 11

How do the stresses of modern life affect children, and what enables "resilient" children to withstand them?

Stressful events are part of childhood, and most children learn to cope with them. Stress that becomes overwhelming, however, can lead to psychological problems. Severe stressors, such as kidnapping or child abuse, may have long-term effects on physical and psychological well-being. Yet some children show remarkable resilience in surmounting such ordeals.

Stresses of Modern Life

The child psychologist David Elkind (1981, 1984, 1986, 1997) has called today's child the "hurried child." He warns that the pressures of modern life are forcing children to grow up

Summary and Key Terms

The Developing Self

Guidepost 1 How do school-age children develop a realistic self-concept, and what contributes to self-esteem?

- The self-concept becomes more realistic during middle childhood, when, according to neo-Piagetian theory, children form representational systems.
- According to Erikson, the chief source of self-esteem is children's view of their productive competence. This "virtue" develops through resolution of the crisis of industry versus inferiority. According to Susan Harter's research, however, self-esteem arises primarily from social support and self-evaluation.

representational systems (379) **industry versus inferiority (380)**

Guidepost 2 How do school-age children show emotional growth?

- School-age children have internalized shame and pride and can better understand and control negative emotions.
- Empathy and prosocial behavior increase.
- Emotional growth is affected by parents' reactions to displays of negative emotions.
- Emotional self-regulation requires effortful control.

The Child in the Family

Guidepost 13 How do parent-child relationships change in middle childhood?

- School-age children spend less time with parents and are less close to them than before; but relationships with parents continue to be important. Culture influences family relationships and roles.
- Development of coregulation may affect the way a family handles conflicts and discipline.

coregulation (382)

Guidepost 4 What are the effects of parents' work and of poverty on family atmosphere?

- The family environment has two major components: family structure and family atmosphere. Family atmosphere includes both emotional tone and economic well-being.
- The impact of mothers' employment depends on many factors concerning the child, the mother's work, and her feelings about it; whether she has a supportive partner; the family's socioeconomic status; and the kind of care the child receives.
- Homes with employed mothers tend to be more structured and more egalitarian than homes with at-home mothers. Maternal employment has a positive influence on school achievement in low-income families, but boys in middle-class families tend to do less well.
- Parents living in persistent poverty may have trouble providing effective discipline and monitoring and emotional support.

Guidepost 5 What impact does family structure have on children's development?

- Many children today grow up in nontraditional family structures. Children tend to do better in traditional two-parent families than in divorced families, single-parent families, or stepfamilies. The structure of the family, however, is less important than its effects on family atmosphere.
- Adopted children are generally well adjusted, though they face special challenges.
- Children's adjustment to divorce depends on factors concerning the child, the parents' handling of the situation, custody and visitation arrangements, financial circumstances, contact with the noncustodial parent (usually the father), and a parent's remarriage.
- The amount of conflict in a marriage and the likelihood of its continuing after divorce may influence whether children are better off if the parents stay together.
- Children living with only one parent are at heightened risk of behavioral and academic problems, in part related to socioeconomic status.
- Remarriages are more likely to fail than first marriages. Boys tend to have more trouble than girls in adjusting to divorce and single-parent living but tend to adjust better to the mother's remarriage.
- Studies have found no ill effects on children living with gay or lesbian parents.

Guidepost 6 How do siblings influence and get along with one another?

- The roles and responsibilities of siblings in nonindustrialized societies are more structured than in industrialized societies.
- Siblings learn about conflict resolution from their relationships with each other. Relationships with parents affect sibling relationships.

Guidepost 7 What part do pets play in children's development?

- Animal companions may help children achieve Erikson's tasks of trust, initiative, and industry.
- Most children regard relationships with pets as among their most important social connections.

The Child in the Peer Group

Guidepost 8 How do relationships with peers change in middle childhood, and what influences popularity and choice of friends?

- The peer group becomes more important in middle childhood. Peer groups generally consist of children who are similar in age, sex, ethnicity, and socioeconomic status and who live near one another or go to school together.

- The peer group helps children develop social skills, allows them to test and adopt values independent of parents, gives them a sense of belonging, and helps develop the self-concept. It also may encourage conformity and prejudice.
- Popularity influences self-esteem and future adjustment. Popular children tend to have good cognitive abilities and social skills. Behaviors that affect popularity may be derived from family relationships and cultural values.
- Intimacy and stability of friendships increase during middle childhood. Boys tend to have more friends, whereas girls have closer friends.

prejudice (392)

Guidepost 9 What are the most common forms of aggressive behavior in middle childhood, and what influences contribute to such behavior?

- During middle childhood, aggression typically declines. Relational aggression becomes more common than overt aggression. Also, instrumental aggression generally gives way to hostile aggression, often with a hostile bias. Highly aggressive children tend to be unpopular, but this may change as children move into adolescence.
- Aggressiveness promoted by exposure to televised violence can extend into adult life.
- Middle childhood is a prime time for bullying; patterns may be established in kindergarten. Victims tend to be weak and submissive or argumentative and provocative and to have low self-esteem.

bullying (398)

Mental Health

Guidepost 10 What are some common emotional disturbances, and how are they treated?

- Common emotional and behavioral disorders among school-age children include disruptive behavioral disorders, anxiety disorders, and childhood depression.
- Treatment techniques include individual psychotherapy, family therapy, behavior therapy, art therapy, play therapy, and drug therapy. Often therapies are used in combination.

oppositional defiant disorder (ODD) (399) **conduct disorder (CD) (399)** **school phobia (399)** **separation anxiety disorder (399)** **social phobia (399)** **generalized anxiety disorder (400)** **obsessive-compulsive disorder (400)** **childhood depression (400)** **individual psychotherapy (400)** **family therapy (401)** **behavior therapy (401)** **art therapy (401)** **play therapy (401)** **drug therapy (401)**

Guidepost 11 How do the stresses of modern life affect children, and what enables "resilient" children to withstand them?

- As a result of the pressures of modern life, many children experience stress. Children tend to worry about school, health, and personal safety.
- Resilient children are better able than others to withstand stress. Protective factors involve cognitive ability, family relationships, personality, degree of risk, and compensating experiences.

resilient children (402) **protective factors (402)**

Part 6

Adolescence: A Preview

Chapter 15
Physical Development and Health in Adolescence

- Physical growth and other changes are rapid and profound.
- Reproductive maturity occurs.
- Major health risks arise from behavioral issues, such as eating disorders and drug abuse.

Chapter 16
Cognitive Development in Adolescence

- Ability to think abstractly and use scientific reasoning develops.
- Immature thinking persists in some attitudes and behaviors.
- Education focuses on preparation for college or vocations.

Chapter 17
Psychosocial Development in Adolescence

- Search for identity, including sexual identity, becomes central.
- Relationships with parents are generally good.
- Peer group may exert a positive or negative influence.

Adolescence

In adolescence, young people's appearance changes; as a result of the hormonal events of puberty, they take on the bodies of adults. Their thinking changes, too; they are better able to think abstractly and hypothetically. And their feelings change about almost everything. All areas of development converge as adolescents confront their major task: establishing an identity, including a sexual identity, that will carry over to adulthood.

In Chapters 15, 16, and 17, we see how adolescents incorporate their drastically changed appearance, their puzzling physical yearnings, and their new cognitive abilities into their sense of self. We look at risks and problems that arise during the teenage years, as well as at characteristic strengths of adolescents.

Linkups to Look For

- Early or late physical maturation can affect emotional and social adjustment.
- Conflict between adolescents and their parents may sometimes stem from immature aspects of adolescent thinking.
- Parental involvement and parenting styles influence academic achievement.
- The ability of low-income adolescents to do well in school may depend on the availability of family and community resources.
- Physical characteristics play an important part in molding adolescents' self-concept.
- Girls who are knowledgeable about sex are most likely to postpone sexual activity.
- The intensity and intimacy of adolescent friendships is related to cognitive development.

chapter 15

Physical Development and Health in Adolescence

What I like in my adolescents is that they have not yet hardened. We all confuse hardening and strength. Strength we must achieve, but not callousness.

—Anaïs Nin, *The Diaries of Anaïs Nin*, vol. IV

Focus *Anne Frank, Diarist of the Holocaust*

Anne Frank

For her thirteenth birthday on June 12, 1942, Anne Frank's parents gave her a diary. This small, cloth-covered volume was the first of several notebooks in which Anne recorded her experiences and reflections during the next two years. Little did she dream that her jottings would become one of the most famous published accounts by victims of the Holocaust.

Anne Frank (1929–1945), her parents, Otto and Edith Frank, and her older sister, Margot, were German Jews who fled to Amsterdam after Hitler came to power in 1933, only to see the Netherlands fall to Nazi conquest seven years later. In the summer of 1942, when the Nazis began rounding up Dutch Jews for deportation to concentration camps, the family went into hiding on the upper floors of the building occupied by Otto Frank's pharmaceutical firm. Behind a door concealed by a movable cupboard, a steep stairway led to the four rooms Anne called the "Secret Annexe." For two years, they stayed in those confined quarters with the Van Daans, their 15-year-old son, Peter, and a middle-aged dentist, Albert Dussel,* who shared Anne's room. Then, on August 4, 1944, German and Dutch security police raided the Secret Annexe and sent its occupants to concentration camps, where all but Anne's father died.

Anne's writings, published by Otto Frank after the war, describe the life the fugitives led. During the day they had to be completely quiet so as not to alert people in the offices below. They saw no one except a few trusted Christian helpers who risked their lives to bring food, books, newspapers, and essential supplies. To venture outside—which would have been necessary to replace Anne's quickly outgrown clothes or to correct her worsening nearsightedness—was unthinkable.

The diary reveals the thoughts, feelings, daydreams, and mood swings of a high-spirited, introspective adolescent coming to maturity under traumatic conditions. Anne wrote of her concern about her "ugly" appearance, of her wish for "a real mother who understands me," and of her adoration for her father (Frank, 1958, pp. 36, 110). She expressed despair at the adults' constant criticism of her failings and at her parents' apparent favoritism toward

Sources of biographical information about Anne Frank are Bloom (1999), Frank (1958, 1995), Lindwer (1991), Müller (1998), and Netherlands State Institute for War Documentation (1989). Page references are to the 1958 paperback version of the diary.

*Fictional names Anne invented for use in her diary.

her sister. She wrote about her fears, her urge for independence, her hopes for a return to her old life, and her aspirations for a writing career.

As tensions rose in the Secret Annexe, Anne lost her appetite and began taking antidepressant medication. But as time went on, she became less self-pitying and more serious-minded. When she thought back to her previous carefree existence, she felt like a different person from the Anne who had "grown wise within these walls" (p. 149).

She was deeply conscious of her sexual awakening: "I think what is happening to me is so wonderful, and not only what can be seen on my body, but all that is taking place inside. . . . Each time I have a period . . . I have the feeling that . . . I have a sweet secret, and . . . I always long for the time that I shall feel that secret within me again" (pp. 115–116).

Anne originally had regarded Peter as shy and gawky—not a very promising companion; but eventually she began visiting his attic room for long, intimate talks and, finally, her first kiss. Her diary records the conflict between her stirring sexual passion and her strict moral upbringing.

One of the last diary entries is dated July 15, 1944, less than three weeks before the raid and eight months before Anne's death in the concentration camp at Bergen-Belsen: ". . . in spite of everything, I still believe that people are really good at heart. . . . I hear the ever approaching thunder, which will destroy us too, I can feel the suffering of millions and yet, if I look up into the heavens, I think that it will all come right, that this cruelty too will end, and that peace and tranquillity will return again" (p. 233).

• • •

The moving story of Anne Frank's tragically abbreviated adolescence points to the insistent role of biology and its interrelationships with inner and outer experience. Anne's "coming of age" occurred under highly unusual conditions. Yet her normal physical maturation went on, along with cognitive and psychosocial changes heightened by her stressful circumstances.

In this chapter, we examine the physical transformations of adolescence and how they affect young people's feelings. We consider the impact of early or late maturation. We discuss health issues associated with this time of life, and we examine two serious problems: depression and teenage suicide.

After you have read and studied this chapter, you should be able to answer each of the Guidepost questions that follow. Look for them again in the margins, where they point to important concepts throughout the chapter. To check your understanding of these Guideposts, review the end-of-chapter summary. Checkpoints located at periodic spots throughout the chapter will help you verify your understanding of what you have read.

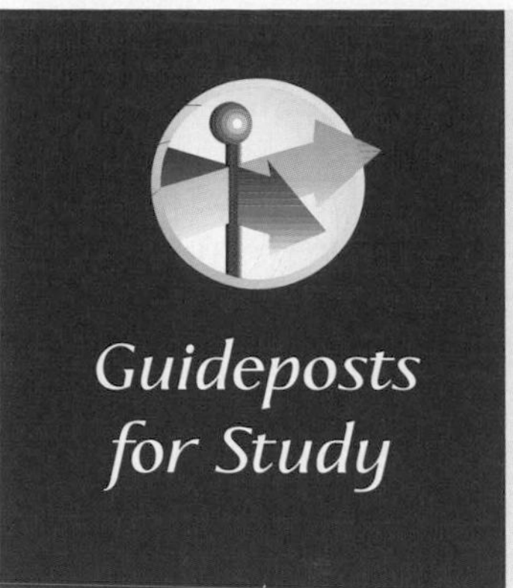

Guideposts for Study

1. What is adolescence, and when does it begin and end?
2. What opportunities and risks does adolescence entail?
3. What physical changes do adolescents experience, and how do these changes affect them psychologically?
4. What brain developments occur during adolescence, and how do they affect adolescent behavior?
5. What are some common health problems and health risks of adolescence, and how can they be prevented?

Adolescence: A Developmental Transition

Guidepost 1

What is adolescence, and when does it begin and end?

Rituals to mark a child's "coming of age" are common in many societies. Rites of passage may include religious blessings, separation from the family, severe tests of strength and endurance, marking the body in some way, or acts of magic. The ritual may be held at a certain age; for example, bar mitzvah or bat mitzvah ceremonies traditionally mark a 13-year-old Jewish boy's or girl's assumption of responsibility for following traditional religious observance. Or a ritual may be tied to a specific event, such as a girl's first menstruation, which Apache tribes celebrate with a four-day ritual of sunrise-to-sunset chanting.

In modern industrial societies the passage from childhood to adulthood is more gradual and less clear-cut. It consists of a long period known as **adolescence,** a developmental transition that entails major, interrelated physical, cognitive, and psychosocial changes. Thus, adolescence is a social construction (refer back to Chapter 1), a concept whose meaning is culturally defined.

adolescence Developmental transition between childhood and adulthood entailing major physical, cognitive, and psychosocial changes.

The Apache Indians of the southwestern United States celebrate a girl's first menstruation with a four-day ritual that includes special clothing, a symbolic blanket, and singing from sunrise to sunset.

Markers of Adolescence

puberty Process by which a person attains sexual maturity and the ability to reproduce.

Adolescence lasts about a decade, from about age 10 or 11, or even earlier, until the late teens or early 20s. Neither its beginning nor its end is plainly marked. Adolescence is generally considered to begin with **puberty,** the process that leads to sexual maturity, or fertility—the ability to reproduce.* Before the 20th century, children in western cultures entered the adult world when they matured physically or began a vocational apprenticeship. Puberty now tends to begin earlier than in the past, and entrance into a vocation tends to occur later. The complexity of modern society requires longer periods of education or vocational training before a young person can take on adult responsibilities.

Contemporary U.S. society has a variety of markers of entrance into adulthood. There are *legal* definitions: At 17, young people may enlist in the armed forces; at age 18, in most states, they may marry without their parents' permission; at 18 to 21 (depending on the state), they may enter into binding contracts. Using *sociological* definitions, people may call themselves adults when they are self-supporting or have begun a career, have married or formed a significant relationship, or have started a family. There also are *psychological* definitions. Cognitive maturity is often considered to coincide with the capacity for abstract thought. Emotional maturity may depend on discovering one's identity, becoming independent of parents, developing a system of values, and forming relationships. In the psychological sense, some people never leave adolescence, no matter what their chronological age.

Guidepost 2

What opportunities and risks does adolescence entail?

Opportunities and Risks of Adolescence

Adolescence offers opportunities for growth, not only in physical dimensions, but also in cognitive and social competence, autonomy, self-esteem, and intimacy. This period also carries great risks. Some young people have trouble handling so many changes at once and may need help in overcoming dangers along the way. Adolescence is a time of increasing divergence between the majority of young people, who are headed for a fulfilling and productive adulthood, and a sizable minority (about 1 out of 5) who will be dealing with major problems (Offer, 1987; Offer & Schonert-Reichl, 1992).

U.S. adolescents today face greater hazards to their physical and mental well-being than did their counterparts in earlier years (Petersen, 1993; Takanishi, 1993). Among these hazards are early pregnancy and childbearing (see Chapter 17) and high death rates from accidents, homicide, and suicide (NCHS, 2003). Behavior patterns that contribute to these risks, such as heavy drinking, drug abuse, sexual and gang activity, motorcycling without helmets, and use of firearms, are established early in adolescence (Petersen, 1993; Rivara & Grossman, 1996) and, as we will see, may reflect immaturity of the adolescent's brain. Across ethnic and social-class lines, use of drugs, driving while intoxicated, and sexual activity increase throughout the teenage years (see Figure 15-1).

However, a U.S. government survey shows encouraging trends. High school students are becoming less likely to engage in tobacco and marijuana use, risky sexual behavior, carrying of weapons, and riding in cars without seat belts or with drivers who have been drinking (Grunberg et al., 2002). A reduction in such risky behaviors increases the chances that young people will come through the teenage years in good physical and mental health.

Checkpoint

Can you . . .

- ✔ Compare three ways of defining entrance into adulthood?
- ✔ Identify risky behavior patterns common during adolescence?

Guidepost 3

What physical changes do adolescents experience, and how do these changes affect them psychologically?

Puberty: The End of Childhood

The biological changes of puberty, which signal the end of childhood, include rapid growth in height and weight, changes in body proportions and form, and attainment of sexual maturity. These dramatic physical changes are part of a long, complex process of maturation that begins even before birth, and their psychological ramifications continue into adulthood.

*Some people use the term *puberty* to mean the end point of sexual maturation and refer to the process as *pubescence,* but the usage here conforms to that of most psychologists today.

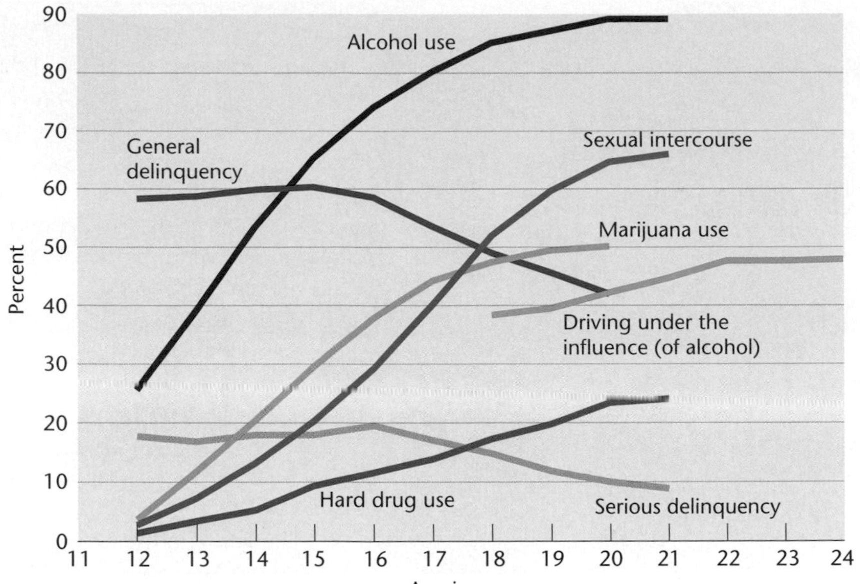

Figure 15-1
Age-specific rates for prevalence of some high-risk behaviors, averaged out over three years.
Source: Adapted from Elliott, 1993.

How Puberty Begins: Hormonal Changes

Puberty begins with a sharp increase in production of sex-related hormones and takes place in two stages: **adrenarche,** the maturing of the adrenal glands, followed a few years later by **gonadarche,** the maturing of the sex organs and the appearance of more obvious pubertal changes.

adrenarche Maturation of adrenal glands.

gonadarche Maturation of testes or ovaries.

First, sometime between ages 6 and 9 (Susman, Dorn, & Schiefelbein, 2003), the adrenal glands, located above the kidneys, secrete gradually increasing levels of androgens, principally *dehydroepiandrosterone* (DHEA). DHEA plays a part in the growth of pubic, axillary (armpit), and facial hair, as well as in faster body growth, oilier skin, and the development of body odor. By age 10, levels of DHEA are 10 times what they were between ages 1 and 4. In several studies, adolescent boys and girls—whether homosexual or heterosexual—recalled their earliest sexual attraction as having taken place at about this time (McClintock & Herdt, 1996).

The maturing of the sex organs two to four years later triggers a second burst of DHEA production, which then rises to adult levels. In this second stage, gonadarche, a girl's ovaries step up their output of estrogen, which stimulates growth of female genitals and development of breasts. In boys, the testes increase the manufacture of androgens, particularly testosterone, which stimulate growth of male genitals, muscle mass, and body hair. Boys and girls have both types of hormones, but girls have higher levels of estrogen, and boys have higher levels of androgens. In girls, testosterone influences growth of the clitoris, as well as of the bones and of pubic and axillary hair.

The signal for the increase in production of sex hormones is the secretion of a hormone called *gonadotropin-releasing hormone (GnRH)* by the hypothalamus, a structure at the base of the brain. Scientists have identified a gene, GPR54, on chromosome 19 that is essential for this development to occur (Seminara et al., 2003).

The precise time when this rush of hormonal activity begins seems to depend on reaching a critical weight level. Studies of mice and humans have found that leptin, a brain protein secreted by fatty tissue and identified as having a role in overweight (refer back to Chapter 12), is needed to trigger the onset of puberty (Chehab, Mounzih, Lu, & Lim, 1997; Clément et al., 1998; O'Rahilly, 1998; Strobel, Camoin, Ozata, & Strosberg, 1998). An accumulation of leptin in the bloodstream may stimulate the hypothalamus to send pulsating signals to the nearby pituitary gland, which in turn, may signal the sex glands to increase their secretion of hormones. Girls with a higher percentage of body fat in early childhood and those who experience unusual weight gain between ages 5 and 9 tend to show more advanced pubertal development (Davison, Susman, & Birch, 2003).

During the years from ages 11 to 13, girls are, on the average, taller, heavier, and stronger than boys, who reach their adolescent growth spurt later than girls do.

LifeMap CD

Is there a physiological basis for the idea that adolescence is a time of storm and stress? For an expert's perspective, watch the video on "Hormones and Adolescent Emotions" in Chapter 15 of your CD.

Some research attributes the heightened emotionality and moodiness of early adolescence—so apparent in Anne Frank's diary—to these hormonal developments. However, other influences, such as sex, age, temperament, and the timing of puberty, may moderate or even override hormonal ones. Hormones seem more strongly related to moods in boys than in girls and especially in early adolescents, who are still adjusting to pubertal changes (Buchanan, Eccles, & Becker, 1992).

Timing, Sequence, and Signs of Puberty and Sexual Maturity

There is about a seven-year range for the onset of puberty in boys and an eight-year range in girls. The process typically takes about four years for both sexes and begins up to three years earlier in girls than in boys. In the United States, the average age for boys' entry into puberty is 10 to 11 (Susman et al., 2003), but boys may begin to show changes any time between 9 and 16. Most girls begin to show pubertal changes at 9 or 10 years of age, but some do so as early as 6 or as late as 13 or 14.

Physical changes in both boys and girls during puberty include the development of pubic hair, deepening of the voice, the adolescent growth spurt, and muscular growth. The maturation of reproductive organs brings the beginning of menstruation in girls and the production of sperm in boys. These changes unfold in a sequence that is much more consistent than their timing (see Table 15-1), though it does vary somewhat. One girl may develop breasts and body hair at about the same rate; in another girl, body hair may reach adultlike growth a year or so before breasts develop. Similar variations occur among boys. Let's look more closely at these changes.

Primary and Secondary Sex Characteristics

primary sex characteristics Organs directly related to reproduction, which enlarge and mature during adolescence.

secondary sex characteristics Physiological signs of sexual maturation (such as breast development and growth of body hair) that do not involve the sex organs.

The **primary sex characteristics** are the organs necessary for reproduction. In the female, the sex organs are the ovaries, fallopian tubes, uterus, and vagina; in the male, they are the testes, penis, scrotum, seminal vesicles, and prostate gland. During puberty, these organs enlarge and mature. In boys, the first sign of puberty is the growth of the testes and scrotum. In girls, the growth of the primary sex characteristics is not readily apparent because these organs are internal.

The **secondary sex characteristics** (see Table 15-2) are physiological signs of sexual maturation that do not directly involve the sex organs: for example, the breasts of females and the broad shoulders of males. Other secondary sex characteristics are changes in the voice and skin texture, muscular development, and the growth of pubic, facial, axillary, and body hair.

Table 15-1 Usual Sequence of Physiological Changes in Adolescence

Female Characteristics	Age of First Appearance
Growth of breasts	6–13
Growth of pubic hair	6–14
Body growth	9.5–14.5
Menarche	10–16.5
Appearance of underarm hair	About 2 years after appearance of pubic hair
Increased output of oil- and sweat-producing glands (which may lead to acne)	About the same time as appearance of underarm hair
Male Characteristics	**Age of First Appearance**
Growth of testes, scrotal sac	9–13.5
Growth of pubic hair	12–16
Body growth	10.5–16
Growth of penis, prostate gland, seminal vesicles	11–14.5
Change in voice	About the same time as growth of penis
First ejaculation of semen	About 1 year after beginning of growth of penis
Appearance of facial and underarm hair	About 2 years after appearance of pubic hair
Increased output of oil- and sweat-producing glands (which may lead to acne)	About the same time as appearance of underarm hair

Table 15-2 Secondary Sex Characteristics

Girls	Boys
Breasts	Pubic hair
Pubic hair	Axillary (underarm) hair
Axillary (underarm) hair	Muscular development
Changes in voice	Facial hair
Changes in skin	Changes in voice
Increased width and depth of pelvis	Changes in skin
Muscular development	Broadening of shoulders

The first reliable sign of puberty in girls is the growth of the breasts. The nipples enlarge and protrude, the *areolae* (the pigmented areas surrounding the nipples) enlarge, and the breasts assume first a conical and then a rounded shape. Some adolescent boys experience temporary breast enlargement, much to their distress; this is normal and may last up to 18 months.

The voice deepens, especially in boys, partly in response to the growth of the larynx and partly in response to the production of male hormones. The skin becomes coarser and oilier. Increased activity of the sebaceous glands may give rise to pimples and blackheads. Acne is more common in boys and seems related to increased amounts of testosterone.

Pubic hair, at first straight and silky, eventually becomes coarse, dark, and curly. It appears in different patterns in males and females. Adolescent boys are usually happy to see hair on the face and chest; but girls are usually dismayed at the appearance of even a slight amount of hair on the face or around the nipples, though this is normal.

Influences on Onset of Puberty

On the basis of historical sources, developmental scientists have found a **secular trend**—a trend that spans several generations—in the onset of puberty: a drop in the age when puberty begins and when young people reach adult height and sexual maturity. The trend, which also involves increases in adult height and weight, began about 100 years ago and

secular trend Trend that can be seen only by observing several generations, such as the trend toward earlier attainment of adult height and sexual maturity that began a century ago.

has occurred in the United States, western Europe, and Japan. It still continues, at least in the United States (Anderson, Dallal, & Must, 2003). A possible explanation is a higher standard of living. Children who are healthier, better nourished, and better cared for might be expected to mature earlier and grow bigger. Thus, the average age of sexual maturity is earlier in developed countries than in developing ones. A large contributor to the secular trend in the United States during the last part of the 20th century appears to be the increase in overweight among young girls (Anderson et al., 2003).

Race/ethnicity affects the timing of puberty. African-American and Mexican-American girls generally enter puberty earlier than white girls. Black girls typically begin to show breast budding and pubic hair at age 9½, as compared with about 10 for Mexican-American girls and close to 10½ for white girls (Wu, Mendola, & Buck, 2002). However, some African-American girls experience these changes as early as age 6, and some white girls do as early as age 7 (Kaplowitz et al., 1999).

A longitudinal study suggests that the relationship with the father may be a key to pubertal timing. Girls who, as preschoolers, had close, supportive relationships with their parents—especially with an affectionate, involved father—entered puberty later than girls whose parental relationships had been cold or distant or who were raised by single mothers (Ellis, McFadyen-Ketchum, Dodge, Pettit, & Bates, 1999).

How might family relationships affect pubertal development? One suggestion is that human males, like some animals, may give off *pheromones,* odorous chemicals that attract mates. As a natural incest-prevention mechanism, sexual development may be inhibited in girls who are heavily exposed to their fathers' pheromones, as would happen in a close father-daughter relationship. On the other hand, frequent exposure to the pheromones of unrelated adult males, such as a stepfather or a single mother's boyfriend, may speed up pubertal development (Ellis & Garber, 2000). Since both a father's absence and early pubertal timing have been identified as risk factors for sexual promiscuity and teenage pregnancy, the father's early presence and active involvement may be important to girls' healthy sexual development (Ellis et al., 1999).

Another explanation is that both a father's tendency toward family abandonment and his daughter's tendency toward early puberty and precocious sexual activity may stem from a shared gene: a sex-linked variant of the androgen receptor (AR) gene, which is carried on the X chromosome of affected fathers and can be transmitted to daughters but not to sons. Among 121 men and 164 unrelated women, men with this allele tended to be aggressive, impulsive, and sexually promiscuous. Women with the same allele tended to have had early menarche and to have experienced parental divorce and father absence before age 7 (Comings, Muhleman, Johnson, & MacMurray, 2002). This hypothesis needs to be tested more directly by genetic analysis of absent fathers and their biological daughters.

The Adolescent Growth Spurt

adolescent growth spurt Sharp increase in height and weight that precedes sexual maturity.

In Anne Frank's diary, she made rueful references to her physical growth—to shoes she could no longer get into and vests "so small that they don't even reach my tummy" (Frank, 1958, p. 71). Anne obviously was in the **adolescent growth spurt**—a rapid increase in height and weight that generally begins in girls between ages 9½ and 14½ (usually at about 10) and in boys between 10½ and 16 (usually at 12 or 13). The growth spurt typically lasts about two years; soon after it ends, the young person reaches sexual maturity. Since girls' growth spurt usually occurs earlier than that of boys, girls between ages 11 and 13 are taller, heavier, and stronger than boys the same age. After their growth spurt, boys are again larger, as before. Both boys and girls reach nearly their full height by age 18.

Boys and girls grow differently, of course. A boy becomes larger overall: his shoulders wider, his legs longer relative to his trunk, and his forearms longer relative to his upper arms and his height. A girl's pelvis widens to make childbearing easier, and layers of fat accumulate under her skin, giving her a more rounded appearance.

The adolescent growth spurt affects practically all skeletal and muscular dimensions. Muscular growth peaks at age 12½ for girls and 14½ for boys. Even the eye grows faster, causing (as in Anne Frank) an increase in nearsightedness, a problem that affects about one-fourth of 12- to 17-year-olds (Gans, 1990). The lower jaw becomes longer and thicker, the jaw and nose project more, and the incisor teeth become more upright. Because each of these changes follows its own timetable, parts of the body may be out of proportion for a while. The result is the familiar teenage gawkiness Anne noticed in Peter Van Daan, which accompanies unbalanced, accelerated growth.

These dramatic physical changes have psychological ramifications. Most young teenagers are more concerned about their appearance than about any other aspect of themselves, and many do not like what they see in the mirror. Girls tend to be unhappier about their looks than boys are, reflecting the greater cultural emphasis on women's physical attributes (Rosenblum & Lewis, 1999). Girls, especially those who are advanced in pubertal development, tend to think they are too fat (Richards, Boxer, Petersen, & Albrecht, 1990; Swarr & Richards, 1996). As we will discuss in a subsequent section, this negative body image can lead to eating problems.

Signs of Sexual Maturity: Sperm Production and Menstruation

The principal sign of sexual maturity in boys is the production of sperm. The first ejaculation, or **spermarche,** occurs at an average age of 13. A boy may wake up to find a wet spot or a hardened, dried spot on the sheets–the result of a *nocturnal emission,* an involuntary ejaculation of semen (commonly referred to as a *wet dream*). Most adolescent boys have these emissions, sometimes in connection with an erotic dream.

spermarche Boy's first ejaculation.

The principal sign of sexual maturity in girls is *menstruation,* a monthly shedding of tissue from the lining of the womb—what Anne Frank called her "sweet secret." The first menstruation, called **menarche,** occurs fairly late in the sequence of female development; its normal timing can vary from ages 10 to 16½ (refer back to Table 15-1). Consistent with the secular trend mentioned previously, the average age of menarche in U.S. girls fell from greater than 14 years before 1900 to 12½ years in the 1990s. On average, a black girl first menstruates shortly after her 12th birthday and a white girl about six months later (Anderson et al., 2003).

menarche Girl's first menstruation.

A combination of genetic, physical, emotional, and environmental influences may affect the timing of menarche. The age of a girl's first menstruation tends to be similar to that of her mother. Bigger girls and those whose breasts are more developed tend to menstruate earlier. Nutrition is a factor. Strenuous exercise, as in competitive athletics, can delay menarche. Even when these factors are controlled, girls with early menarche tend to be aggressive or depressed or to have poor family relationships (Ellis & Garber, 2000; Graber, Brooks-Gunn, & Warren, 1995; Moffitt, Caspi, Belsky, & Silva, 1992; Steinberg, 1988).

Psychological Effects of Early and Late Maturation

The effects of early and late maturing vary in boys and girls. Some research over several decades has found early maturing boys to be more poised, relaxed, good-natured, popular, and less impulsive than late maturers, as well as more cognitively advanced. Other studies have found them to be more worried about being liked, more cautious, more reliant on others, and more bound by rules and routines (Graber, Lewinsohn, Seeley, & Brooks-Gunn, 1997; R. T. Gross & Duke, 1980; M. C. Jones, 1957; Tanner, 1978). Late maturers have been found to feel more inadequate, self-conscious, rejected, and dominated; to be more dependent, aggressive, insecure, or depressed; to have more conflict with parents and more trouble in school; and to have poorer social and coping skills (Graber et al., 1997; Mussen & Jones, 1957; Peskin, 1967, 1973; Siegel, 1982). Apparently there are pluses and minuses in both situations. Most boys like to mature early, and those who do so seem to gain in self-esteem (Alsaker, 1992; Clausen, 1975). However, an early maturer sometimes has trouble living up to expectations that he will act as mature as he looks.

Girls are generally happier if their timing is about the same as that of their peers. Early maturing girls tend to be less sociable, less expressive, and less poised; more introverted and shy; and more negative about menarche than later maturing girls (M. C. Jones, 1958; Livson & Peskin, 1980; Ruble & Brooks-Gunn, 1982; Stubbs, Rierdan, & Koff, 1989). Perhaps because they feel rushed into confronting the pressures of adolescence before they

What's your view 

- Did you mature early, late, or "on time"? How did the timing of your maturation affect you psychologically?

are ready, they are more vulnerable to psychological distress and remain so, at least through about age 16. They are more likely to associate with antisocial peers (Ge, Conger, & Elder, 1996). They may have a poor body image and lower self-esteem than later maturing girls (Alsaker, 1992; Graber et al., 1997; Simmons, Blyth, Van Cleave, & Bush, 1979). Early maturing girls are at increased risk of various behavioral and mental health problems, including anxiety and depression, disruptive behavior, eating disorders, early smoking and drinking, precocious sexual activity, substance abuse, and attempted suicide (Dick, Rose, Viken, & Kaprio, 2000; Graber et al., 1997). Early maturation is associated with a tendency toward risky behavior in boys as well as girls (D. P. Orr & Ingersoll, 1995).

It is hard to generalize about the psychological effects of pubertal timing because they depend on how the adolescent and other people in his or her world interpret the accompanying changes. Effects of early or late maturation are most likely to be negative when adolescents are much more or less developed than their peers; when they do not see the changes as advantageous; and when several stressful events occur at about the same time (Petersen, 1993; Simmons, Blyth, & McKinney, 1983).

Checkpoint

Can you . . .

- ✔ Tell how puberty begins and how its timing and length vary?
- ✔ Describe typical pubertal changes in boys and girls, and identify factors that affect psychological reactions to these changes?

The Adolescent Brain

Guidepost 4

What brain developments occur during adolescence, and how do they affect adolescent behavior?

Not long ago, most scientists believed that the brain is fully mature by puberty. Now brain imaging studies reveal that the adolescent brain is still a work in progress. Dramatic changes in brain structures involved in emotions, judgment, organization of behavior, and self-control take place between puberty and young adulthood and may help explain teenagers' tendency toward emotional outbursts and risky behavior (ACT for Youth, 2002).

Two major changes in the adolescent brain parallel processes that occur before birth and during infancy: the growth and pruning of gray matter. A second spurt in production of gray matter—neurons, axons, and dendrites—begins just before puberty and may be related to the surge of sex hormones at this time. The growth spurt takes place chiefly in the frontal lobes, which handle planning, reasoning, judgment, emotional regulation, and impulse control. After the growth spurt, unused connections are pruned, and those that remain are strengthened. Like the pruning that occurs early in life, this process makes the brain more efficient (ACT for Youth, 2002; NIMH, 2001).

The pattern of gray matter growth contrasts with the pattern for white matter, the nerve fibers that connect distant regions of the brain. These connections thicken and myelinate earlier in childhood, beginning with the frontal lobes and moving toward the rear of the brain. Between ages 6 and 13, striking growth takes place in connections between the temporal and parietal lobes, which deal with sensory functions, language, and spatial understanding. White matter growth then drops off precipitously at about the end of the critical period for language learning. Whereas white matter growth proceeds from front to back, gray matter growth proceeds in the opposite direction, the frontal lobes not fully maturing until young adulthood. Continuing myelination of gray matter in the frontal lobes facilitates the maturation of cognitive processing (NIMH, 2001).

Adolescents process information about emotions differently than adults do. In one line of research, researchers scanned adolescents' brain activity while they identified emotions on pictures of faces on a computer screen. Early adolescents (ages 11 to 13) tended to use the amygdala, a small, almond-shaped structure deep in the temporal lobe that is heavily involved in emotional and instinctual reactions (refer back to Figure 6-4 in Chapter 6). Older adolescents, like adults, were more likely to use the frontal lobe, which permits more accurate, reasoned judgments. This suggests a possible reason for some early adolescents' unwise choices, such as abuse of alcohol and drugs and sexual risk taking: immature brain development may permit feelings to override reason (Baird et al., 1999; Yurgelon-Todd, 2002). Underdevelopment of frontal cortical systems associated with motivation, impulsivity, and addiction may help explain adolescents' thrill and novelty seeking and also may

LifeMap CD

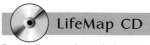

Do adolescents have their own special way of thinking? To find out, watch the video on "The Adolescent Brain" in Chapter 15 of your CD.

explain why many adolescents find it hard to focus on long-term goals (Bjork et al., 2004; Chambers, Taylor, & Potenza, 2003).

Adolescents are more vulnerable than adults to both immediate and long-term negative effects of alcohol on learning and memory (White, 2001). In one study, 15- and 16-year-old alcohol abusers showed cognitive impairments weeks after they stopped drinking, as compared with nonabusing peers (Brown et al., 2000). Addictive drugs are especially dangerous for adolescents because they stimulate parts of the brain that are changing in adolescence (Chambers et al., 2003).

Because the adolescent brain is still developing, teenagers can exert some control over that development. Adolescents who "'exercise' their brains by learning to order their thoughts, understand abstract concepts, and control their impulses are laying the neural foundations that will serve them for the rest of their lives" (ACT for Youth, 2002, p. 1). Unfortunately, the immaturity of teenage brains may keep some adolescents from heeding warnings that seem logical and persuasive to adults.

Checkpoint

Can you . . .

✔ Describe two major changes in the adolescent brain?

✔ Identify immature features of the adolescent brain, and explain how this immaturity can affect behavior?

Physical and Mental Health

What are some common health problems in adolescence, and how can they be prevented?

These years are generally healthy, as most adolescents recognize. Nine out of 10 (91.8 percent) of early and midadolescents consider themselves healthy, according to an international school-based survey of more than 120,000 eleven-, thirteen-, and fifteen-year-olds in the United States and 27 other industrialized countries under auspices of the World Health Organization (WHO) (Scheidt, Overpeck, Wyatt, & Aszmann, 2000).*

Health Problems and Health-Related Behaviors

Despite their general good health, many younger adolescents, especially girls, report frequent health problems, such as headache, stomachache, backache, nervousness, and feeling tired, lonely, or "low." Such reports are most common in the United States and Israel, where life tends to be fast paced and stressful (Scheidt et al., 2000).

Most adolescents have low rates of disability and chronic disease, and their dental health has improved. Still, about one in five 10- to 18-year-olds in the United States has at least one serious physical or mental health problem, and many more need counseling or other health services (Dougherty, 1993).

Many health problems are preventable, stemming from lifestyle or poverty. In industrialized countries, according to the WHO survey, adolescents from less affluent families tend to report poorer health and more frequent symptoms. More well-off adolescents, who are likely to be better educated, tend to have healthier diets and to be more physically active. On the other hand, socioeconomic status seems to have no effect on smoking and drinking among 15-year-olds (Mullan & Currie, 2000).

Adolescents are less likely than younger children to see a physician regularly; instead, they tend to go to school-based health centers. An estimated 18.7 percent of young people in grades 7 through 12 do not receive the medical care they need, mostly because of procrastination or fear of what a doctor will find, but in about 14 percent of cases because of inability to pay. Young people who do not receive needed care are at increased risk of physical and mental health problems, including frequent smoking and drinking (Ford, Bearman, & Moody, 1999).

Let's look at several specific health concerns: physical fitness, sleep needs, eating disorders, drug abuse, sexually transmitted diseases, depression, and causes of death in adolescence.

*The other countries were Belgium, Canada, Czech Republic, Denmark, England, Estonia, Finland, France, Germany, Greece, Greenland, Hungary, Republic of Ireland, Israel, Latvia, Lithuania, Northern Ireland, Norway, Poland, Portugal, Russian Federation, Scotland, Slovak Republic, Spain, Sweden, Switzerland, and Wales.

Physical Activity

Exercise—or lack of it—affects both physical and mental health. It improves strength and endurance, helps build healthy bones and muscles, helps control weight, reduces anxiety and stress, and increases self-confidence and well-being. Even moderate physical activity has health benefits if done regularly for at least 30 minutes almost every day. A sedentary lifestyle that carries over into adulthood may result in increased risk of obesity, heart disease, cancer, and type 2 diabetes—a growing problem among children and adolescents (Centers for Disease Control and Prevention, 2000a; Hickman et al., 2000; National Institutes of Health [NIH] Consensus Development Panel on Physical Activity and Cardiovascular Health, 1996; Troiano, 2002).

Although most young Americans exercise at least two hours a week, many become less active during adolescence. Adolescents in the United States exercise less often than in past years and less frequently than adolescents in most other industrialized countries (CDC, 2000a; Hickman, Roberts, & de Matos, 2000). Boys are more active than girls, and white students are more active than students of other racial/ethnic groups (Troiano, 2002). Three-fourths of sixth through eighth graders participate in extracurricular team sports (Kleiner, Nolin, & Chapman, 2004), but barely half (55 percent) of high school senior boys and less than one-third (30 percent) of senior girls do (Snyder & Hoffman, 2002).

Checkpoint

Can you . . .

- ✔ Summarize the status of adolescents' health and discuss prevalent health problems?
- ✔ Explain why physical activity is important in adolescence, and discuss risks and benefits of athletic activity for adolescent girls?

The decline in physical activity is greater among black girls than among white girls and may be related to higher body-mass index and greater prevalence of teenage pregnancy. Smoking is associated with lessened activity among white girls. By ages 16 and 17, 56 percent of black girls and 31 percent of white girls engage in *no* leisure-time physical activity (Kimm et al., 2002).

Many high school students are injured in sports. Some of these injuries could be avoided by grouping players by size, skill, and maturational level instead of by age; by improved equipment design; and by better supervision and enforcement of safety rules (AAP Committee on Sports Medicine and Committee on School Health, 1989; Cheng et al., 2000).

Sleep Needs

Many adolescents do not get enough sleep. They go to bed later than younger children and, on school days, get up as early or earlier. Yet adolescents need just as much sleep as before—about nine hours each night (Iglowstein, Jenni, Molinari, & Largo, 2003). "Sleeping in" on weekends does not make up for the loss. Adolescents and preadolescents who have irregular sleep schedules tend to be chronically sleep deprived and to be sleepy in the daytime (Sadeh, Raviv, & Gruber, 2000; Wolfson & Carskadon, 1998).

According to a study in Israel, this pattern is more likely to occur in families with older, less educated parents and more family stress (Sadeh, Raviv, & Gruber, 2000). In the WHO study, an average of 40 percent of adolescents (mostly boys) in 28 industrialized countries reported morning sleepiness at least once a week, and 22 percent said they are sleepy most days. Norway and Finland had the highest proportions of morning fatigue, and the United States came in third (Scheidt et al., 2000).

Sleep-deprived adolescents may have sleep problems, show symptoms of depression, and do poorly in school (Wolfson & Carskadon, 1998). In a longitudinal study of 2,259 middle school students, boys and, especially, girls got diminishing amounts of sleep between sixth and eighth grades. Sixth graders who slept less than their peers were more likely to show depressive symptoms and to have low self-esteem. These symptoms heightened with increasing loss of sleep over the three-year period (Fredriksen, Rhodes, Reddy, & Way, 2004).

Why do teenagers stay up late? In part it may be because they need to do homework, want to talk on the phone with friends or surf the Web, or wish to act "grown up." However, physiological changes also may be involved (Sadeh et al., 2000). Adolescents undergo a shift in the brain's natural sleep cycle, or *circadian timing system.* The timing of secretion of *melatonin,* a hormone detectable in saliva, is a gauge of when the brain is ready for sleep. After puberty, this secretion takes place later at night (Carskadon, Acebo,

Richardson, Tate, & Seifer, 1997). Thus, adolescents need to go to bed later and get up later than younger children; yet most secondary schools start earlier than elementary schools. Their schedules are out of sync with students' biological rhythms. These findings fit with adolescents' daily mood cycles, which also may be hormonally related. Teenagers tend to be least alert and most stressed early in the morning. Starting school later, or at least offering difficult courses later in the day, would help improve students' concentration (Crouter & Larson, 1998).

Checkpoint

Can you . . .

✔ Explain why adolescents often get too little sleep and how sleep deprivation can affect them?

Nutrition and Eating Disorders

U.S. adolescents have less healthy diets than those in most other western industrialized countries. They eat fewer fruits and vegetables and more sweets, chocolate, soft drinks, and other "junk" foods, which are high in cholesterol, fat, and calories and low in nutrients (Vereecken & Maes, 2000). Adolescents who regularly watch television consume the most junk food (Hickman et al., 2000). Deficiencies of calcium, zinc, and iron are common at this age (Lloyd et al., 1993; Bruner, Joffe, Duggan, Casella, & Brandt, 1996); iron deficiency has been linked to lower standardized math scores (Halterman, Kaczorowski, Aligne, Auinger, & Szilagyi, 2001).

Although poor nutrition is most common in economically depressed or isolated populations, it also may result from concern with body image and weight control (Vereecken & Maes, 2000). Eating disorders—both extreme overeating and extreme undereating—are most prevalent in industrialized societies, where food is abundant and attractiveness is equated with slimness (APA, 1994; Becker, Grinspoon, Klibanski, & Herzog, 1999).

Overweight

The average teenage girl needs about 2,200 calories per day; the average teenage boy needs about 2,800. Many adolescents eat more calories than they expend and thus accumulate excess body fat. Among 4,746 boys and girls in Minnesota public middle and high schools, more than 17 percent of girls and nearly 8 percent of boys reported overeating in the past year, and they were more likely than their peers to be overweight and to be trying to lose weight (Ackard, Neumark-Sztainer, Story, & Perry, 2003).

The percentage of U.S. young people who are overweight has almost doubled in the past two decades (CDC, 2000a). U.S. teens are more likely to be overweight than their age-mates in 14 other industrialized countries,* according to self-reports of height and weight from 29,242 boys and girls ages 13 and 15. Fifteen percent of all children in the 15 countries had a body mass index (BMI) at or above the 85th or 95th percentiles for age and sex. The comparable figures for U.S. teens ranged from 26 to 31 percent (Lissau et al., 2004). Similarly, a nationally representative U.S. study found nearly 31 percent of 12- to 19-year-olds overweight or at risk of overweight in 1999–2002 (Hedley et al., 2004).

Overweight teenagers tend to become overweight adults, subject to physical, social, and psychological risks (Gortmaker, Must, Perrin, Sobol, & Dietz, 1993). Overweight in adolescence can lead to life-threatening chronic conditions in adulthood, even if the excess weight is lost (Must et al., 1992).

Genetic and other factors having nothing to do with willpower or lifestyle choices seem to make some people susceptible to overweight (refer back to Chapter 12). Among these factors are faulty regulation of metabolism, inability to recognize body cues about hunger and satiation, and development of an abnormally large number of fat cells. However, some causes of overweight—too little physical activity and poor eating habits—are within a person's control. In a study of 878 California 11- to 15-year-olds, lack of exercise was the main risk factor for overweight in boys and girls (Patrick et al., 2004).

Weight-loss programs that use behavioral modification techniques to help adolescents make changes in diet and exercise have had some success. For many preadolescents and adolescents, however, dieting may be counterproductive. In a prospective three-year study of 8,203 girls and 6,769 boys ages 9 to 14, those who dieted gained more weight than those

*Austria, Czech Republic, Denmark, Flemish Belgium, Finland, France, Germany, Greece, Ireland, Israel, Lithuania, Portugal, Slovakia, and Sweden.

who did not diet (Field et al., 2003). Use of sibutramine, a weight-loss medication usually used with adults, in conjunction with behavioral modification may improve results, but more study is needed on the drug's safety and efficacy with this age group (Berkowitz, Wadden, Tershakovec, & Cronquist, 2003).

Body Image and Eating Disorders

Sometimes a determination *not* to become overweight can result in graver problems than overweight itself. As mentioned in Chapter 12, concern with body image often begins in middle childhood or earlier, intensifies in adolescence, and may lead to obsessive efforts at weight control (Davison & Birch, 2001; Schreiber et al., 1996; Vereecken & Maes, 2000). This pattern is more common among girls than among boys and is less likely to be related to actual weight problems.

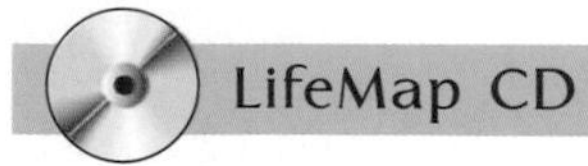

To learn what some 14-year-old girls think about social pressure to look and act a certain way, watch the "Girls and Body Image" video in Chapter 15 of your CD.

Because of girls' normal increase in body fat during puberty, many girls, especially if they are advanced in pubertal development, become unhappy about their appearance, reflecting the cultural emphasis on women's physical attributes (Richards, Boxer, Petersen, & Albrecht, 1990; Rosenblum & Lewis, 1999; Swarr & Richards, 1996). Girls' dissatisfaction with their bodies increases over the course of early to midadolescence, while boys, who are becoming more muscular, become more satisfied with their bodies (Feingold & Mazella, 1998; Rosenblum & Lewis, 1999; Swarr & Richards, 1996). By age 15, more than half the girls sampled in 16 countries were dieting or thought they should be. The United States was at the top of the list, with 47 percent of 11-year-old girls and 62 percent of 15-year-olds concerned about overweight (Vereecken & Maes, 2000). African-American girls are generally more satisfied with their bodies and less concerned about weight and dieting than white girls (Kelly, Wall, Eisenberg, Story, & Neumark-Sztainer, 2004; Wardle et al., 2004).

According to a large prospective cohort study, parental attitudes and media images play a greater part in encouraging weight concerns than do peer influences. Girls who try to look like the unrealistically thin models they see in the media tend to develop excessive concern about weight. And both girls and boys who believe that thinness is important to their parents, especially to their fathers, tend to become constant dieters (Field et al., 2001).

Excessive concern with weight control and body image may be signs of *anorexia nervosa* or *bulimia nervosa,* which involve abnormal patterns of food intake (Harvard Medical School, 2002). These chronic disorders affect an estimated 5 million Americans each year in all major ethnic groups and social classes (Becker et al., 1999), mostly adolescent girls and young women (Andersen, 1995). Anorexia and bulimia tend to run in families, suggesting a possible genetic basis. Other apparent causes are neurochemical, developmental, and social-cultural ("Anorexia nervosa—Part I," 2003; Becker et al., 1999; "Eating Disorders—Part I, Part II," 1997; Kendler et al., 1991). These disorders are especially common among girls driven to excel in ballet, competitive swimming, long-distance running, figure skating, and gymnastics ("Eating Disorders—Part II," 1997; Skolnick, 1993); girls with single or divorced parents; and girls who frequently eat alone (Martínez-González et al., 2003).

Anorexia Nervosa

anorexia nervosa Eating disorder characterized by self-starvation.

Anorexia nervosa, or self-starvation, is potentially life threatening; it may be accompanied by irregularity or cessation of menstruation and growth of soft, fuzzy body hair. Anorexics have a distorted body image; though they are constantly dieting and eat next to nothing, they think they are too fat. They often are good students, described by their parents as "model" children. They may be withdrawn or depressed and may engage in repetitive, perfectionist behavior. An estimated 0.5 percent of adolescent girls and young women and a smaller but growing percentage of boys and men in western countries are affected (AAP Committee on Adolescence, 2003; Martínez-González et al., 2003). A related disorder in nonwestern cultures involves self-starvation without an abnormal focus on weight and appearance and is rooted in religious traditions of fasting and self-mortification (Keel et al., 2003).

Anorexia has been attributed to a variety of genetic and environmental factors. A variant of a gene that may lead to decreased feeding signals has been found in anorexic patients (Vink et al., 2001). Some authorities point to a deficiency of a crucial chemical in the brain, a disturbance of the hypothalamus, or high levels of opiatelike substances in the spinal fluid ("Eating Disorders—Part I," 1997). Researchers in London, Sweden, and Germany have found reduced blood flow to certain parts of the brain in anorexics, including an area thought to control visual self-perception and appetite (Gordon, Lask, Bryantwaugh, Christie, & Timimi, 1997). Others see anorexia as a psychological disturbance related to fear of growing up or fear of sexuality or to a malfunctioning family that seems harmonious while members are actually overdependent, overly involved in each other's lives, and unable to deal with conflict ("Eating Disorders—Part I," 1997; Garner, 1993). As discussed earlier, anorexia may be in part a reaction to societal pressure to be slender.

Early warning signs include determined, secret dieting; dissatisfaction after losing weight; setting new, lower weight goals after reaching an initial desired weight; excessive exercising; and interruption of regular menstruation.

Anorexics have an unrealistic body image. Despite the evidence of their mirrors, they think they are too fat.

Bulimia Nervosa

In **bulimia nervosa,** a person regularly goes on huge eating binges within a short time, usually two hours or less, and then may try to undo the high caloric intake with self-induced vomiting, strict dieting or fasting, excessively vigorous exercise, or laxatives, enemas, or diuretics to purge the body. These episodes occur at least twice a week for at least three months (APA, 1994). People with bulimia are obsessed with their weight and shape. They become overwhelmed with shame, self-contempt, and depression over their eating habits. They have low self-esteem and a history of wide weight fluctuation, dieting, or frequent exercise (Kendler et al. 1991). Unlike self-starvation, bulimia is rare in nonwestern cultures, as it requires plenty of available food together with motivation to avoid gaining weight, a combination of conditions that exists only in the contemporary western world (Keel et al., 2003).

bulimia nervosa Eating disorder in which a person regularly eats huge quantities of food and then purges the body with laxatives, induced vomiting, fasting, or excessive exercise.

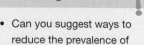

A related *binge eating disorder* involves frequent bingeing but without subsequent fasting, exercise, or vomiting. Bulimia and binge eating disorder are much more common than anorexia. About 3 percent of women and 0.3 percent of men have developed bulimia or binge eating disorder at some time in their lives, and much larger numbers have an occasional episode (Harvard Medical School, 2002). There is some overlap between anorexia and bulimia; some victims of anorexia have bulimic episodes, and some people with bulimia lose large amounts of weight ("Eating Disorders—Part I," 1997; Edwards, 1993; Kendler et al., 1991). Nevertheless, the two are separate disorders.

Bulimia seems to be related to low levels of the brain chemical serotonin ("Eating Disorders—Part I," 1997; K. A. Smith, Fairburn, & Cowen, 1999), but no causative connection has been shown. It may share genetic roots with major depression or with phobias and panic disorder (Keel et al., 2003). There also may be a psychoanalytic explanation: people with bulimia are thought to crave food to satisfy their hunger for love and attention ("Eating Disorders—Part I," 1997; Humphrey, 1986).

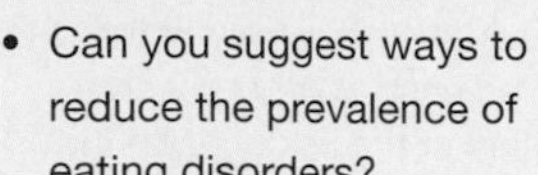

What's your view

- Can you suggest ways to reduce the prevalence of eating disorders?

Treatment and Outcomes of Anorexia and Bulimia

The immediate goal of treatment for anorexia is to get patients to eat and gain weight. They are likely to be admitted to a hospital. There they may be given 24-hour nursing, drugs to encourage eating and inhibit vomiting, and behavior therapy, which rewards eating with such privileges as being allowed to get out of bed and leave the room (Beumont et al., 1993). Bulimia, too, may be treated with behavior therapy. Patients keep daily diaries of their eating patterns and are taught ways to avoid the temptation to binge. Individual, group, or family psychotherapy can help both anorexics and bulimics, usually after initial behavior therapy has brought symptoms under control. Since these patients are at risk for depression and suicide, antidepressant drugs may be combined with psychotherapy (Becker et al., 1999; Edwards, 1993; Fluoxetine-Bulimia Collaborative Study Group, 1992; Harvard Medical School, 2002; Hudson & Pope, 1990; Kaye, Weltzin, Hsu, & Bulik, 1991).

The outlook for people with bulimia is better than for those with anorexia because bulimic patients generally want treatment ("Eating Disorders—Part II," 1997; Herzog et al., 1999; Keel & Mitchell, 1997). Recovery rates from bulimia average 50 percent after six months to five years (Harvard Medical School, 2002). People with anorexia often have long-term psychological problems even after they have stopped starving themselves (Sullivan, Bulik, Fear, & Pickering, 1998). As much as 12 years after recovery, many continue to have an unrealistic body image, to be unusually thin, and to remain preoccupied with weight and eating. Up to 25 percent of patients with anorexia progress to chronic invalidism, and 2 to 10 percent die prematurely (APA, 1994; Beumont, Russell, & Touyz, 1993; "Eating Disorders—Part I," 1997; Herzog, Keller, & Lavori, 1988).

Checkpoint

Can you . . .

- ✔ Summarize the normal nutritional needs and typical dietary deficiencies of adolescent boys and girls?
- ✔ Discuss risk factors for, effects of, treatment of, and prognoses for overweight, anorexia, and bulimia?

Use and Abuse of Drugs

Although the great majority of adolescents do not abuse drugs, a significant minority do. They turn to drugs out of curiosity or a desire for sensation, because of peer pressure, or as an escape from overwhelming problems. They thereby endanger their present and future physical and psychological health.

Substance abuse is harmful use of alcohol or other drugs. It is a poorly adaptive behavior pattern lasting more than one month, in which a person continues to use a substance after knowingly being harmed by it or uses it repeatedly in a hazardous situation, such as while driving (APA, 1994). Abuse can lead to **substance dependence** (addiction), which may be physiological, psychological, or both and is likely to continue into adulthood.

substance abuse Repeated, harmful use of a substance, usually alcohol or other drugs.

substance dependence Addiction (physical, psychological, or both) to a harmful substance.

Trends in Drug Use

Use of illicit drugs among U.S. adolescents fell 11 percent overall between 2001 and 2003 and is well below the peak during the late 1970s and early 1980s (see Figure 15-2). An upsurge during the early 1990s accompanied a decline in perception of the dangers of drug use and a softening of peer disapproval. That trend has now begun to reverse itself, including a drop in use of crack cocaine and a sharp reduction in the use of ecstasy, a hallucinatory, amphetaminelike drug popular at night-long "raves" or "trances" (L. D. Johnston,

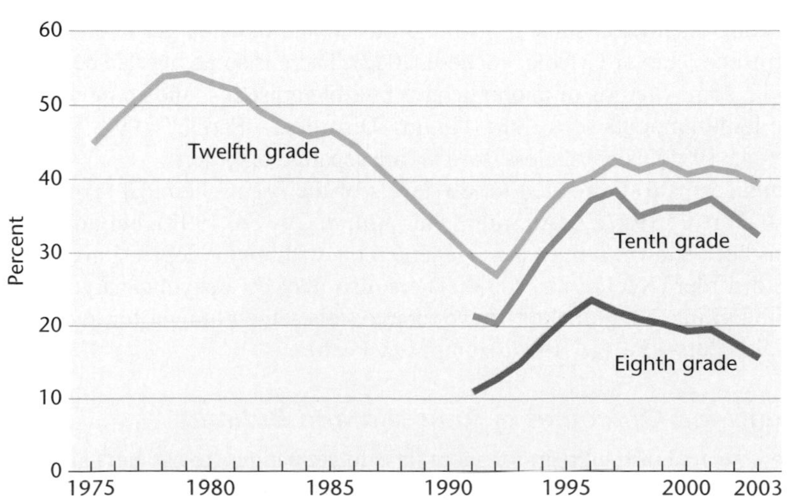

Figure 15-2
Trends in past-year use of illicit drugs by eighth, tenth, and twelfth graders. A sharp increase in marijuana use during the 1990s accounts for most of the increase in the use of illicit drugs. The rise in use of marijuana accompanied an increase in the availability of the drug and a decrease in young people's perception of the risk of harm from using it.

Source: Johnston, O'Malley, & Bachman, 2003, p. 7.

O'Malley, & Bachman, 2000, 2001, 2002a, 2002b, 2003; L. D. Johnston, O'Malley, Bachman, & Schulenberg, 2004).

These findings come from the latest in a series of annual government surveys of a nationally representative sample of 48,467 eighth, tenth, and twelfth graders in 392 schools across the United States (L. D. Johnston et al., 2004). These surveys probably underestimate adolescent drug use since they do not reach high school dropouts, who are likely to have higher rates.

One exception to the general trend is a slight rise in the use of inhalants by eighth graders in 2003. Inhalants are chemical vapors that adolescents sniff to get high, often from common household products such as glues, solvents, gasoline, butane, and aerosols. Because they are inexpensive and easy to obtain, they are most often used by younger adolescents. Sniffing can damage hearing, brain, bone marrow, liver, and kidneys and also can cause oxygen depletion, heart failure, and death. Overall, inhalant use has been on the decline, along with growing peer disapproval of its use (L. D. Johnston et al., 2003, 2004).

Risk Factors for Drug Abuse

What is the likelihood that a particular young person will abuse drugs? Risk factors include (1) "difficult" temperament; (2) poor impulse control and a tendency to seek out sensation (which may have a biochemical basis); (3) family influences (such as a genetic predisposition to alcoholism, parental use or acceptance of drugs, poor or inconsistent parenting practices, family conflict, and troubled or distant family relationships); (4) early and persistent behavior problems, particularly aggression; (5) academic failure and lack of commitment to education; (6) peer rejection; (7) associating with drug users; (8) alienation and rebelliousness; (9) favorable attitudes toward drug use; and (10) early initiation into drug use (Hawkins, Catalano, & Miller, 1992; Johnson, Hoffmann, & Gerstein, 1996; Masse & Tremblay, 1997; USDHHS, 1996b). The more risk factors that are present, the greater the chance that an adolescent or young adult will abuse drugs.

Drug use often begins when children enter middle school, where they make new friends and become more vulnerable to peer pressure. Fourth to sixth graders may start using cigarettes, beer, and inhalants and, as they get older, move on to marijuana or harder drugs (National Parents' Resource Institute for Drug Education, 1999). The earlier young people start using a drug, the more frequently they are likely to use it and the greater their tendency to abuse it.

Early smoking is a danger signal: adolescents who begin smoking by age 11 are twice as likely as other young people to engage in risky behaviors, such as riding in a car with a drinking driver; carrying knives or guns to school; using inhalants, marijuana, or cocaine; and making suicide plans. Early use of alcohol and marijuana also are associated with multiple risk behaviors (DuRant, Smith, Kreiter, & Krowchuk, 1999). Let's look more closely at alcohol, marijuana, and tobacco, the three drugs most popular with adolescents, and at influences on their use.

Alcohol, Marijuana, and Tobacco

Alcohol is a potent, mind-altering drug with major effects on physical, emotional, and social well-being; its use is a very serious problem in many countries (Gabhainn & François, 2000). Young people who begin drinking before age 15 are four times more likely to become alcohol dependent than those who do not start drinking until age 20 or later (Grant & Dawson, 1998). Alcohol use among U.S. teenagers, which had drifted upward during most of the 1990s, has begun to decline along with illicit drug use (L. D. Johnston et al., 2004).

Despite a decline in marijuana use since 1979, it is still by far the most widely used illicit drug in the United States. In 2003, 13 percent of eighth graders, 28 percent of tenth graders, and 35 percent of twelfth graders admitted to having used it in the past year (L. D. Johnston et al., 2004).

Marijuana smoke typically contains more than 400 carcinogens. Heavy use can damage the brain, heart, lungs, and immune system and cause nutritional deficiencies, respiratory infections, and other physical problems. It may lessen motivation, interfere with schoolwork and other activities, and cause family problems. Marijuana use also can impede

Marijuana is the most widely used illicit drug in the United States; about half of high school seniors say they have tried it. Aside from its own ill effects, marijuana use may lead to addiction to hard drugs.

memory and learning. It can cut down perception, alertness, attention span, judgment, and the motor skills needed to drive a vehicle and thus can contribute to traffic accidents (AAP Committee on Drugs, 1980; Farrow, Rees, & Worthington-Roberts, 1987; National Institute on Drug Abuse [NIDA], 1996; Solowij et al., 2002).

Contrary to common belief, marijuana may be addictive. Injecting rats with marijuana initially produces a "high" by increasing levels of a brain chemical called *dopamine.* As with heroin, cocaine, and other addictive drugs, the brain's ability to produce dopamine gradually diminishes with marijuana use, creating a greater craving for the drug (Tanda, Pontieri, & DiChiara, 1997). Marijuana use tends to lead to hard drug use (Lynskey et al., 2003).

Adolescent tobacco use is a less serious problem in the United States than in most other industrialized countries (Gabhainn & François, 2000). After the release of a U.S. Surgeon General's report in 1964, which linked cigarette smoking to lung cancer, heart disease, emphysema, and several other illnesses, smoking among high school seniors dropped sharply. As with other drugs, an upturn in usage during the early 1990s began to reverse itself in 1996, along with a rise in the proportion of young people who see smoking as dangerous. Still, 10 percent of eighth graders, 17 percent of tenth graders, and 24 percent of twelfth graders are current (past-month) smokers (L. D. Johnston et al., 2004).

Peer influence on smoking and drinking has been documented extensively (Center on Addiction and Substance Abuse at Columbia University [CASA], 1996; Cleveland & Wiebe, 2003). Other research points to the family. A survey of 9,225 adults found a strong relationship between smoking and several adverse childhood experiences: emotional, physical, or sexual abuse; parental separation or divorce; and growing up with a battered mother or a substance-abusing, mentally ill, or incarcerated household member (Anda et al., 1999).

Authoritative parenting can help young people internalize standards that may insulate them against negative peer influences and open them to positive ones (Collins et al., 2000; Mounts & Steinberg, 1995). Adolescents who believe their parents disapprove of smoking are less likely to smoke (Sargent & Dalton, 2001), and rational discussions with parents can counteract harmful influences and discourage or limit drinking (Austin, Pinkleton, & Fujioka, 2000; Turrisi et al., 2000).

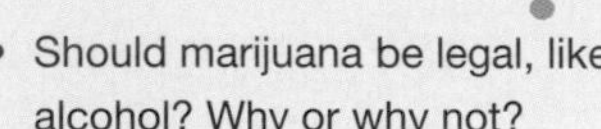

- Should marijuana be legal, like alcohol? Why or why not?
- Should there be tighter restrictions on cigarette advertising? If so, what kinds of restrictions?

Is race/ethnicity a factor? Among 6,529 California and Oregon students, African-American and Hispanic-American youths were more likely than white and Asian-American students to start smoking by age 13. However, by ages 15 and up, fewer black adolescents were regular smokers than adolescents in the other three ethnic groups. Black teens were more likely to say that their parents disapproved of smoking and, after age 13, were less likely to report having friends who smoked or approved of smoking (Ellickson, Orlando, Tucker, & Klein, 2004).

An important early influence may be the omnipresence of substance use in the media. According to one study, alcohol, tobacco, or illicit drugs are shown in 70 percent of prime-time network television dramas, 38 out of 40 top-grossing movies, and half of all music videos (Gerbner & Ozyegin, 1997). In the National Longitudinal Survey of Youth, 10- to 15-year-olds who watched at least four or five hours of television each day were 5 to 6 times more likely to start smoking within the next two years than those who watched less than two hours a day (Gidwani, Sobol, DeJong, Perrin, & Gortmaker, 2002). A random sample of major motion pictures found a decline in depiction of smoking from 10.7 incidents per hour in 1950 to 4.9 in 1980–1982, but by 2002 portrayals of smoking had reverted to 1950 levels (Glantz, Kacirk, & McCulloch, 2004). Of 50 children's animated feature films available on videotape from five major Hollywood studios, more than two-thirds show characters smoking or drinking, with no indication or warning of negative health effects (Goldstein, Sobel, & Newman, 1999). Cigarette brands popular with 10- to 15-year-olds are widely advertised in magazines aimed at young readers (King, Siegel, Celebucki, & Connolly, 1998).

Checkpoint

Can you . . .

- ✔ Summarize recent trends in drug use among adolescents?
- ✔ Discuss risk factors and influences connected with use of drugs, specifically alcohol, marijuana, and tobacco?

Sexually Transmitted Diseases (STDs)

sexually transmitted diseases (STDs) Diseases spread by sexual contact.

Sexually transmitted diseases (STDs) are diseases spread by sexual contact. Table 15-3 summarizes some common STDs: their causes, most frequent symptoms, treatment, and consequences.

Table 15-3	Common Sexually Transmitted Diseases				
Disease	**Cause**	**Symptoms: Male**	**Symptoms: Female**	**Treatment**	**Consequences If Untreated**
Chlamydia	Bacterial infection	Pain during urination, discharge from penis	Vaginal discharge, abdominal discomfort†	Tetracycline or erythromycin	Can cause pelvic inflammatory disease or eventual sterility
Trichomoniasis	Parasitic infection, sometimes passed on in moist objects such as towels and bathing suits	Often absent	Absent or may include vaginal discharge, discomfort during intercourse, odor, painful urination	Oral antibiotic	May lead to abnormal growth of cervical cells
Gonorrhea	Bacterial infection	Discharge from penis, pain during urination*	Discomfort when urinating, vaginal discharge, abnormal menses†	Penicillin or other antibiotics	Can cause pelvic inflammatory disease or eventual sterility; can also cause arthritis, dermatitis, and meningitis
HPV (genital warts)	Human papilloma virus	Painless growth that usually appear on penis but may also appear on urethra or in rectal area*	Small, painless growths on genitals and anus; may also occur inside the vagina without external symptoms*	Removal of warts; but infection often reappears	May be associated with cervical cancer; in pregnancy, warts enlarge and may obstruct birth canal
Herpes	Herpes simplex virus	Painful blisters anywhere on the genitalia, usually on the penis*	Painful blisters on the genitalia, sometimes with fever and aching muscles; women with sores on cervix may be unaware of outbreaks*	No known cure but controlled with antiviral drug acyclovir	Possible increased risk of cervical cancer
Hepatitis B	Hepatitis B virus	Skin and eyes become yellow	Same as in men	No specific treatment; no alcohol	Can cause liver damage, chronic hepatitis
Syphillis	Bacterial infection	In first stage, reddish-brown sores on the mouth or genitalia or both, which may disappear, though the bacteria remain; in the second, more infectious stage, a widespread skin rash*	Same as in men	Penicillin or other antibiotics	Paralysis, convulsions, brain damage, and sometimes death
AIDS (acquired immune deficiency syndrome)	Human immunodeficiency virus (HIV)	Extreme fatigue, fever, swollen lymph nodes, weight loss, diarrhea, night sweats, susceptibility to other diseases*	Same as in men	No known cure; protease inhibitors and other drugs appear to extend life	Death, usually due to other diseases, such as cancer

*May be asymptomatic.

†Is often asymptomatic.

About 1 in 4 new cases of STDs in the United States occurs in 15- to 19-year-olds. The chief reasons for the prevalence of STDs among teenagers are early sexual activity, which increases the likelihood of having multiple high-risk partners, failure to use condoms or to use them regularly and correctly, and, for women, the tendency to have sex with older partners (CDC, 2000c). STDs are most likely to develop undetected in adolescent girls. In a *single* unprotected sexual encounter with an infected partner, a girl runs a 1 percent risk of acquiring HIV, a 30 percent risk of acquiring genital herpes, and a 50 percent risk of acquiring gonorrhea (AGI, 1999a).

Although teenagers tend to view oral sex as less risky than intercourse, a number of STDs, especially pharyngeal gonorrhea, can be transmitted in that way (Remez, 2000). In a nationally representative sample of 15- to 17-year-olds, almost 9 out of 10 reported that sexual health issues were a personal concern, yet 1 in 3 engaged in oral sex, 4 out of 10 considered it "safer sex," and 1 out of 5 did not know that oral sex can transmit STDs (Kaiser Family Foundation, Hoff, Greene, & Davis, 2003).

The most prevalent STD, according to estimates, is human papilloma virus (HPV), which sometimes produces warts on the genitals. Also common among young people is trichomoniasis, a parasitic infection that may be passed along by moist towels and bathing suits (Weinstock, Berman, & Cates Jr., 2004).

Genital herpes simplex is a chronic, recurring, often painful, and highly contagious disease caused by a virus. This condition can be fatal to a person with a deficiency of the immune system or to the newborn infant of a mother who has an outbreak at the time of delivery. There is no cure, but the antiviral drug acyclovir can prevent active outbreaks. Both diseases have been associated, in women, with increased incidence of cervical cancer. The incidence of genital herpes has increased dramatically during the past three decades. Heptatitis B remains a prominent STD despite the availability of a preventive vaccine for more than 20 years (Weinstock et al., 2004).

The most common *curable* STDs are chlamydia and gonorrhea. These diseases, if undetected and untreated, can lead to severe health problems, including, in women, to pelvic inflammatory disease (PID), a serious abdominal infection. Forty percent of chlamydia cases are reported among 15- to 19-year-olds; more than 1 in 10 teenage girls and 1 in 5 boys are affected (CDC, 2000c).

The human immunodeficiency virus (HIV), which causes AIDS, is transmitted through bodily fluids (mainly blood and semen), usually by sharing of intravenous drug needles or by sexual contact with an infected partner. The virus attacks the body's immune system, leaving a person vulnerable to a variety of fatal diseases. Symptoms of AIDS, which include extreme fatigue, fever, swollen lymph nodes, weight loss, diarrhea, and night sweats, may not appear until six months to 10 or more years after initial infection.

Worldwide, of the 5 million new infections each year, almost 60 percent are in people younger than 15 (Summers, Kates, & Murphy, 2002). In the United States, more than 1 out of 4 persons living with HIV or AIDS were infected in their teens (Kaiser Family Foundation et al., 2003). As of now, AIDS is incurable, but increasingly the related infections that kill people are being stopped with antiviral therapy, including protease inhibitors (Palella et al., 1998; Weinstock et al., 2004). Many HIV-infected people lead active lives for years.

Because symptoms may not appear until a disease has progressed to the point of causing serious long-term complications, early detection is important. Regular, school-based screening and treatment, together with programs that promote abstention from or postponement of sexual activity, responsible decision making, and ready availability of condoms for those who are sexually active may have some effect in controlling the spread of STDs (AAP Committee on Adolescence, 1994; AGI, 1994; Cohen, Nsuami, Martin, & Farley, 1999; Rotheram-Borus & Futterman, 2000). Most young people who find out they have HIV change their sexual behavior, and half stop injecting drugs (Rotheram-Borus & Futterman, 2000). Box 15-1 lists steps young people can take to protect themselves from STDs.

Checkpoint

Can you . . .

- ✔ Identify and describe the most common sexually transmitted diseases?
- ✔ List risk factors for developing an STD during adolescence, and describe effective prevention methods?

Depression

It is not surprising that Anne Frank took an antidepressant in view of the desperate situation in which she found herself. But even in normal surroundings, the prevalence of

The Everyday World

Box 15-1 *Protecting Against Sexually Transmitted Diseases*

How can people protect themselves against sexually transmitted diseases (STDs)? Abstinence is safest, of course. For those who are sexually active, the following guidelines minimize the possibility of acquiring an STD and maximize the chances of getting good treatment if one is acquired.

- Have regular medical checkups. All sexually active persons should request tests specifically aimed at diagnosing STDs.
- Know your partner. The more discriminating you are, the less likely you are to be exposed to STDs. Partners with whom you develop a relationship are more likely than partners you do not know well to inform you of any medical problems they might have.
- Avoid having sexual intercourse with multiple partners, promiscuous persons, and drug abusers.
- Practice "safer sex": Avoid sexual activity involving exchange of bodily fluids. Use a latex condom during intercourse and oral sex (or use a dental dam for oral sex performed on a woman). Avoid anal intercourse.
- Use a contraceptive foam, cream, or jelly; it will kill many germs and help to prevent certain STDs.
- Learn the symptoms of STDs: vaginal or penile discharge; inflammation, itching, or pain in the genital or anal area; burning during urination; pain during intercourse; genital, body, or mouth sores, blisters, bumps, or rashes; pain in the lower abdomen or in the testicles; discharge from or itching of eyes; and fever or swollen glands.
- Inspect your partner for any visible symptoms.
- If you develop any symptoms yourself, get immediate medical attention.
- Just before and just after sexual contact, wash genital and rectal areas with soap and water. Males should urinate after washing.
- Do not have any sexual contact if you suspect that you or your partner is infected. Abstinence is the most reliable preventive measure.
- Avoid exposing any cut or break in the skin to anyone else's blood (including menstrual blood), body fluids, or secretions.
- Practice good hygiene routinely: frequent, thorough hand washing and daily brushing under fingernails.
- Make sure needles used for ear piercing, tattooing, acupuncture, or any kind of injection are either sterile or disposable. Never share a needle.
- If you contract any STD, notify all recent sexual partners immediately so that they can obtain treatment and avoid passing the infection back to you or on to someone else. Inform your doctor or dentist of your condition so that precautions can be taken to prevent transmission. Do not donate blood, plasma, sperm, body organs, or other body tissue.

What's your view?

- As far as you know, do adolescents seem to be taking more precautions against STDs than in the past?
- If you were trying to persuade a friend to take such precautions, on which of the guidelines listed here would you place the most emphasis?

Check it out!

For more information on this topic, go to **http://www.cdc.gov/hiv/pubs/facts.htm**. These are fact sheets from the Centers for Disease Control and Prevention about HIV/AIDS prevention. Or go to **http://www.cdc.gov/nchstp/dstd/dstdp.html**. The Centers for Disease Control and Prevention maintains this site for the National Center for HIV, STD, and TB Prevention. The URL is for the Division of Sexually Transmitted Diseases.

Source: Adapted from American Foundation for the Prevention of Venereal Disease (AFPVD), 1988; Upjohn Company, 1984.

depression increases during adolescence. About 1 percent of children and 5 percent of adolescents have depression at a given time (Brent & Birmaher, 2002). Depression in young people does not necessarily appear as sadness but as irritability, boredom, or inability to experience pleasure. It needs to be taken seriously because of the danger of suicide (Brent & Birmaher, 2002).

Adolescent girls, especially early maturing girls, and adult women are more subject to depression than males (Birmaher et al., 1996; Brent & Birmaher, 2002; Cicchetti & Toth, 1998; Ge, Conger, & Elder, 2001; Stice et al., 2001). This gender difference may be related to biological changes connected with puberty or to the way girls are socialized (Birmaher et al., 1996) and their greater vulnerability to stress in social relationships (Ge et al., 2001; USDHHS, 1999c). Besides female gender, other risk factors for depression include anxiety, fear of social contact, stressful life events, chronic illnesses such as diabetes or epilepsy, parent-child conflict, abuse or neglect, and having a parent with a history of depression (Brent & Birmaher, 2002). Body-image and eating disturbances can aggravate depressive symptoms (Stice & Bearman, 2001).

If untreated, an episode of major depression typically lasts an average of eight months, and the chance of recurrence is high. Prompt assessment is necessary to rule out medical illnesses that could cause depressivelike symptoms. Depressed adolescents who do not respond to outpatient treatment or who have substance dependence or psychosis or seem suicidal may need to be hospitalized (Brent & Birmaher, 2002). At least 1 in 5 people who experience bouts of depression in childhood or adolescence are at risk for bipolar disorder, in which depressive episodes ("low" periods) alternate with "high" periods characterized by increased energy, euphoria, grandiosity, and risk taking (Brent & Birmaher, 2002).

Treatment should begin by educating the parents and the patient about depressive illness, its symptoms, causes, and probable course. Awareness that depression is an illness can help families avoid hopelessness or blame and know what results can be expected from treatment. Often a treatment contract is drawn up, including a "no-suicide" pact—an agreement on how suicidal impulses are to be handled. A necessary precaution is to prevent the patient from having access to firearms.

SSRIs, a type of antidepressant medication (refer back to Chapter 14), are the most common treatment for adolescent depression, and their increasing use has been accompanied by a modest reduction in suicide rates (Olfson, Shaffer, Marcus, & Greenberg, 2003). Short-term cognitive behavioral therapy also can be effective. In this type of therapy, patients learn to choose pleasurable activities, improve social skills, and modify self-defeating ways of thinking that can lead to depression (Brent & Birmaher, 2002).

Death in Adolescence

Not every death in adolescence is as poignant as Anne Frank's. Still, death this early in life is always tragic and (unlike Anne's) usually accidental (Anderson & Smith, 2003)—but not entirely so. The frequency of car crashes, handgun deaths, and suicide in this age group reflects a violent culture as well as adolescents' inexperience and immaturity, which often lead to risk taking and carelessness.

Deaths from Vehicle Accidents and Firearms

Motor vehicle collisions are the leading cause of death among U.S. teenagers, accounting for 2 out of 5 deaths in adolescence. The risk of collision is greater among 16- to 19-year-olds than for any other age group and especially so among 16- and 17-year olds who have recently started to drive (McCartt, 2001; National Center for Injury Prevention and Control [NCIPC], 2004). Collisions are more likely to be fatal when teenage passengers are in the vehicle; apparently, adolescents tend to drive more recklessly in the presence of peers (Chen, Baker, Braver, & Li, 2000). In 2002, 29 percent of drivers ages 15 to 20 who died in motor crashes had been drinking alcohol, and 77 percent of those were not wearing seat belts (National Highway Traffic Safety Administration, 2003).

Most states have adopted graduated licensing systems, which allow beginning drivers to drive only with supervision at first. Only after a period of independent driving in low-risk situations can a youth qualify for an unrestricted license. More than 30 states also have restrictions on teenage night driving (McCartt, 2001). Studies in Michigan and North Carolina found significant reductions in crashes involving 16-year-olds after adoption of graduated licensing (Foss, Feaganes, & Rodgman, 2001; Shope, Molnar, Elliott, & Waller, 2001).

Firearm-related deaths of 15- to 19-year-olds (including homicide, suicide, and accidental deaths) are far more common in the United States than in other industrialized countries. They comprise about one-third of all injury deaths and more than 85 percent of all homicides in that age group. The chief reason for these grim statistics seems to be the ease of obtaining a gun in the United States (AAP Committee on Injury and Poison Prevention, 2000). Youth death rates from firearms have declined since 1993 (AAP Committee on Injury and Poison Prevention, 2000), a period during which police have been confiscating guns on the street (T. B. Cole, 1999) and fewer young people have carried them (USDHHS, 1999b).

For many adolescents, the easiest place to get a gun is at home. About one-third of U.S. homes contain firearms; and in more than one-fifth of these households, guns are loaded and unlocked (Stennies, Ikeda, Leadbetter, Houston, & Sacks, 1999). Guns in the home are 43 times more likely to kill a family member or acquaintance than to be used in self-defense (AAP Committee on Injury and Poison Prevention, 2000).

Suicide

Ready availability of guns in the home also is a major factor in teenage suicide, which caused about 12 percent of deaths among 15- to 19-year-olds in 2001—the third leading cause of death in this age group (Anderson & Smith, 2003). Although most young people who *attempt* suicide do it by taking pills or ingesting other substances, those who succeed are most likely to use firearms (Borowsky, Ireland, & Resnick, 2001). Firearms were used in 52 percent of completed suicides in 2001 (NCIPC, 2001). Restrictions on children's access to firearms may help explain the dramatic drop in gun suicides included in a 25 percent reduction in suicide rates among 10- to 19-year-olds between 1992 and 2001 (Lubell, Swahn, Crosby, & Kegler, 2004).

Adolescent boys are six times more likely than adolescent girls to take their lives. Girls are more likely to have suicidal thoughts if they feel isolated and friendless or if they know someone who has committed suicide (Bearman & Moody, 2004). Although suicide affects all ethnic groups, Native-American boys have the highest rates and African-American girls the lowest. Gay, lesbian, and bisexual youths, who have high rates of depression, also have high rates of suicide and attempted suicide (AAP Committee on Adolescence, 2000; Remafedi, French, Story, Resnick, & Blum, 1998). In a national survey of seventh to twelfth graders, almost one-fourth of the students reported that they had seriously considered suicide during the past year (AAP Committee on Adolescence, 2000). Other surveys show that as many as 12 percent of girls and 6 percent of boys actually attempt to kill themselves (Borowsky et al., 2001).

Young people who consider or attempt suicide tend to have histories of emotional illness: commonly depression, substance abuse, antisocial or aggressive behavior, or unstable personality. They tend to be either perpetrators or victims of violence and to have school problems, academic or behavioral. Often they suffered from maltreatment in childhood, leading to severe problems with relationships in adolescence. They tend to think poorly of themselves, to feel hopeless, and to have poor impulse control and low tolerance for frustration and stress. These young people are often alienated from their parents and have no one outside the family to turn to. Many come from troubled families. They also tend to have attempted suicide before or to have friends or family members who did (Borowsky et al., 2001; Deykin, Alpert, & McNamara, 1985; Garland & Zigler, 1993; Johnson et al., 2002; National Committee for Citizens in Education, 1986; NIMH, 1999; Slap, Vorters, Chaudhuri, & Centor, 1989; "Suicide—Part I," 1996; Swedo et al., 1991). Alcohol plays a part in half of all teenage suicides (AAP Committee on Adolescence, 2000).

Protective factors that reduce the risk of suicide include a sense of connectedness to family and school, emotional well-being, and academic achievement (Borowsky et al., 2001). Box 15-2 discusses ways of preventing suicide.

Checkpoint

Can you . . .

- ✔ Discuss factors affecting gender differences in adolescent depression?
- ✔ Name the three leading causes of death among adolescents, and discuss the dangers of firearm injury?
- ✔ Assess risk factors and prevention programs for teenage suicide?

Protective Factors: Health in Context

Adolescents' physical development, like that of younger children, does not occur in a vacuum. Young people live and grow in a social world. As we have discussed throughout this book, family and school environments play an important part in physical and mental health.

A study of 12,118 seventh through twelfth graders in a random sample of 134 schools across the United States (Resnick et al., 1997) took a broad overview of risk factors and protective factors affecting four major aspects of adolescent health and well-being: emotional distress and suicidal behavior; involvement in fighting, threats of violence, or use of weapons; use of cigarettes, alcohol, and marijuana; and sexual experience, including age of sexual initiation and any history of pregnancy. The students completed questionnaires and had 90-minute home interviews; during the sensitive portions of the interview, the young people listened to the questions through earphones and entered their answers on laptop computers. School administrators also filled out questionnaires.

The findings underline the linkage of physical, cognitive, emotional, and social development. Perceptions of connectedness to others, both at home and at school, positively

What's your view

- How can adolescents be helped to avoid or change risky behaviors?

The Social World

Box 15-2 *Preventing Teenage Suicide*

Many people intent on killing themselves keep their plans secret, but others send out signals well in advance. An attempted suicide is sometimes a call for help, and some people die because they are more successful than they intended to be.

Warning signs include withdrawal from relationships; talking about death, the hereafter, or suicide; giving away prized possessions; drug or alcohol abuse; personality changes, such as a rise in anger, boredom, or apathy; unusual neglect of appearance; difficulty concentrating at work or in school; staying away from work, school, or other usual activities; complaints of physical problems when nothing is organically wrong; and eating or sleeping much more or much less than usual. Friends or family may be able to help by talking to a young person about his or her suicidal thoughts to bring them out in the open; telling others who are in a position to do something—the person's parents or spouse, other family members, a close friend, a therapist, or a counselor; and showing the person that she or he has other options besides death, even though none of them may be ideal.

Access to guns is a major factor in the rise in teenage suicide.

Telephone hotlines are the most prevalent type of suicide intervention for adolescents, but their effectiveness appears to be minimal. In fact, some of these programs may do harm by exaggerating the extent of teenage suicide and painting it as a reaction to normal stresses of adolescence rather than a pathological act. Instead, programs should identify and treat young people at particular risk of suicide, including those who have already attempted it. Equally important is to attack the risk factors—for example, through programs to reduce substance abuse and strengthen families (Garland & Zigler, 1993). Programs to enhance self-esteem and build problem-solving and coping abilities can be directed toward young children and continued throughout the school years (Meehan, 1990).

What's your view?

- Have you ever experienced any of the warning signs described in this box?
- What would you do if a close friend or family member showed one or more of these signs?

Check it out!

For more information on this topic, go to **http://www.aacap.org/publications/factsfam/suicide.htm**. This is a fact sheet about teen suicide, published by the American Academy of Child & Adolescent Psychiatry. Or go to **http://www.cdc.gov/ncipc/factsheets/suifacts.htm**. The Centers for Disease Control and Prevention put together this Suicide Prevention Fact Sheet for the National Center for Injury Prevention & Control home page. It includes many good links to statistics and to prevention materials.

affected young people's health and well-being in all domains. One important factor was parents' spending time with and being available to their adolescent children. Even more important was the sense that parents and teachers are warm and caring and have high expectations for children's achievement. These findings are clear and consistent with other research: adolescents who are getting emotional support at home and are well-adjusted at school have the best chance of avoiding the health hazards of adolescence.

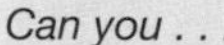

Checkpoint

Can you . . .

✔ Identify factors that tend to protect adolescents from health risks?

Refocus

- What typical pubertal changes did Anne Frank's diary describe? How did these changes affect Anne psychologically?
- What evidence did Anne show of cognitive maturation and moral development?
- In what ways might Anne's development have been similar and in what ways different had she lived under normal circumstances?

Despite the perils of adolescence, most young people emerge from these years with a mature, healthy body and a zest for life. While their bodies have been developing, their minds have continued to develop too, as we will see in Chapter 16.

Summary and Key Terms

Adolescence: A Developmental Transition

Guidepost 1 What is adolescence, and when does it begin and end?

- Adolescence is the transition from childhood to adulthood. Neither its beginning nor its end is clearly marked in western societies; it lasts about a decade, between ages 11 or 12 and the late teens or early 20s.
- Legal, sociological, and psychological definitions of entrance into adulthood vary. In some nonwestern cultures, "coming of age" is signified by special rites.

adolescence (411) **puberty (412)**

Guidepost 2 What opportunities and risks does adolescence entail?

- Adolescence is full of opportunities for physical, cognitive, and psychosocial growth but also of risks to healthy development. Risky behavior patterns, such as drinking alcohol, abusing drugs, engaging in sexual and gang activity, and using firearms, tend to be established early in adolescence. About 4 out of 5 young people experience no major problems.

Puberty: The End of Childhood

Guidepost 3 What physical changes do adolescents experience, and how do these changes affect them psychologically?

- Puberty is triggered by hormonal changes, which may affect moods and behavior. Puberty takes about four years, typically begins earlier in girls than in boys, and ends when a person can reproduce.
- During puberty, both boys and girls undergo an adolescent growth spurt. A secular trend toward earlier attainment of adult height and sexual maturity began about 100 years ago, probably because of improvements in living standards.
- Primary sex characteristics (the reproductive organs) enlarge and mature during puberty. Secondary sex characteristics appear.
- The principal signs of sexual maturity are production of sperm (for males) and menstruation (for females). Spermarche typically occurs at age 13. Menarche occurs, on average, between the ages of 12 and 13 in the United States.
- Sexual attraction seems to begin at about age 10, when the adrenal glands increase their hormonal output.
- Teenagers, especially girls, tend to be sensitive about their physical appearance. Girls who mature early tend to adjust less easily than early maturing boys.

adrenarche (413) **gonadarche (413)** **primary sex characteristics (414)** **secondary sex characteristics (414)** **secular trend (415)** **adolescent growth spurt (416)** **spermarche (417)** **menarche (417)**

The Adolescent Brain

Guidepost 4 What brain developments occur during adolescence, and how do they affect adolescent behavior?

- The adolescent brain is not yet fully mature. It undergoes a second wave of overproduction of gray matter, especially in the frontal lobes, followed by pruning of excess nerve cells. Continuing myelination of the frontal lobes facilitates the maturation of cognitive processing.
- Adolescents process information about emotions with the amygdala, whereas adults use the frontal lobe. Thus, adolescents tend to make less accurate, less reasoned judgments.
- Underdevelopment of frontal cortical systems connected with motivation, impulsivity, and addiction may help explain adolescents' tendency toward risk taking.
- Because of their developing brains, adolescents are particularly vulnerable to effects of alcohol and addictive drugs.

Physical and Mental Health

Guidepost 5 What are some common health problems in adolescence, and how can they be prevented?

- For the most part, the adolescent years are relatively healthy. Health problems often are associated with poverty or a risk-taking lifestyle. Adolescents are less likely than younger children to get regular medical care.
- Many adolescents, especially girls, do not engage in regular vigorous physical activity.
- Many adolescents do not get enough sleep because the high school schedule is out of sync with their natural body rhythms.
- Three common eating disorders in adolescence are obesity, anorexia nervosa, and bulimia nervosa. All can have serious long-term effects. Anorexia and bulimia affect mostly girls. Outcomes for bulimia tend to be better than for anorexia.
- Adolescent substance abuse and dependence have lessened in recent years; still, drug use often begins as children move into middle school.
- Marijuana, alcohol, and tobacco are the most popular drugs with adolescents. All involve serious risks. Marijuana can be a gateway to the use of hard drugs.
- Rates of sexually transmitted diseases (STDs) in the United States are highest in the world and especially high among adolescents. STDs are more likely to develop undetected in girls than in boys.
- Leading causes of death among adolescents include motor vehicle accidents, firearm use, and suicide.

anorexia nervosa (422) **bulimia nervosa (423)** **substance abuse (424)** **substance dependence (424)** **sexually transmitted diseases (STDs) (426)**

chapter 16

Cognitive Development in Adolescence

I should place [the prime of a man's life] at between fifteen and sixteen. It is then, it always seems to me, that his vitality is at its highest; he has greatest sense of the ludicrous and least sense of dignity. After that time, decay begins to set in.

—Evelyn Waugh, age 16, in a school debate, 1920

Focus *Nelson Mandela, Freedom Fighter*

Nelson Mandela

Rolihlahla, the name Nelson Mandela's father gave him at his birth in 1918, means "stirring up trouble." And that is exactly what Mandela did throughout his long and finally successful struggle to topple apartheid, South Africa's rigid system of racial separation and subjugation.

Mandela's election as his country's first black president in April 1994—only four years after his emergence from 28 years behind bars for conspiring to overthrow the white-dominated government—was the realization of a dream formed in his youth. It was a dream kindled as Mandela sat quietly listening to his tribal elders reminisce about a bygone era of self-government more than a century earlier, before the coming of white people—an era of peace, freedom, and equality.

"The land . . . belonged to the whole tribe and there was no individual ownership whatsoever," Mandela told the court that sentenced him to prison in 1962. "There were no classes, no rich or poor and no exploitation of man by man. . . . The council was so completely democratic that all members of the tribe could participate in its deliberations. Chief and subject, warrior and medicine man, all took part" (Meer, 1988, p. 12). Mandela recognized that his forebears' primitive way of life would not be viable in the modern world. But the vision of a society "in which none will be held in slavery or servitude, and in which poverty, want and insecurity shall be no more" served as a lifelong inspiration.

Mandela has royal blood: one of his ancestors ruled his Thembu tribe, and his father was chief of Mvezo, a small, isolated village in the native reservation called the Transkei where Mandela was born. Mandela seems to have inherited his "proud rebelliousness" and "stubborn sense of fairness" (Mandela, 1994, p. 6): not long after his birth, his father, a counselor to tribal kings, was deposed for refusing to honor a summons to appear before the local British magistrate. For standing on his traditional prerogatives and defying the magistrate's authority, Mandela's father paid with his lands and fortune.

Mandela's mother, his father's third of four wives, moved with her baby and his three sisters to the nearby village of Qunu, where they lived in a compound of mud huts. The family raised all their own food—cows and goats for milk and mealies (a form of corn), which his mother ground between two stones to make bread or boiled over an open fire.

The main sources of biographical information about Nelson Mandela's youth are Benson (1986), Hargrove (1989), Harwood (1987), Mandela (1994), and Meer (1988).

At 5, Mandela became a herd boy, driving sheep and cattle through the fertile grasslands. His was a simple life, governed for the most part by the time-honored rules of his tribe. His mother, who had become a Christian, had him baptized in the Methodist church; and at 7, he became the first member of his family to go to school. It was his first teacher who gave him his English name, Nelson.

When Mandela was 9, his father died, and his life changed completely. His mother sent him to live at the tribal headquarters at Mqhekezweni. The acting regent, who owed his position to Mandela's father, had offered to become his guardian and raise him as his own son.

As Mandela grew into adolescence, he observed tribal meetings, where any member could speak and the regent would listen quietly before summing up the consensus. This style of leadership deeply impressed Mandela and influenced his own demeanor as a leader in later years. He also watched his guardian preside over council meetings to which minor chiefs brought disputes to be tried. His fascination with the presentation of cases and the cross-examination of witnesses planted the seeds of an ambition to be a lawyer—an ambition he eventually fulfilled. From the visiting chiefs and headmen, he heard tales about early African warriors who had fought against Western domination. These stories stirred his interest in his people's history and laid the groundwork for his political activism.

At the age of 16, Mandela underwent circumcision, the traditional ritual by which a boy becomes recognized as a man and a participant in tribal councils. At the concluding ceremony, the main speaker, Chief Meligqili, struck a discordant note. The promise of manhood, he said, was an empty one in a land where Africans were a conquered people. "Among these young men," he said, "are chiefs who will never rule because we have no power to govern ourselves; soldiers who will never fight for we have no weapons to fight with; scholars who will never teach because we have no place for them to study. The abilities, the intelligence, the promise of these young men will be squandered in their attempt to eke out a living doing the simplest, most mindless chores for the white man. These gifts [we give them] today are naught, for we cannot give them the greatest gift of all, which is freedom and independence." Although Mandela did not appreciate it at the time, that speech sparked his political awakening.

• • •

The formative influences of Mandela's adolescent years helped shape his moral and political thinking and his life's work. The lessons he had learned about leadership and about his people's past glory stood him in good stead as he directed the resistance to an increasingly repressive regime, first in the streets and then from his island prison. Those lessons remained with him as he eventually managed to negotiate a new nonracial constitution and free elections—accomplishments for which he received the Nobel Peace Prize in 1993.

In this chapter, we examine the Piagetian stage of formal operations, which makes it possible for a young person like Nelson Mandela to visualize an ideal world. We look at adolescents' growth in information processing, including memory, knowledge, and reasoning, and in vocabulary and other linguistic skills. We note what David Elkind has identified as some immature aspects of adolescents' thought, and we examine adolescents' moral and spiritual development. Finally, we explore practical aspects of cognitive growth—issues of school and vocational choice.

After you have read and studied this chapter, you should be able to answer each of the Guidepost questions that follow. Look for them again in the margins, where they point to important concepts throughout the chapter. To check your understanding of these Guideposts, review the end-of-chapter summary. Checkpoints located at periodic spots throughout the chapter will help you verify your understanding of what you have read.

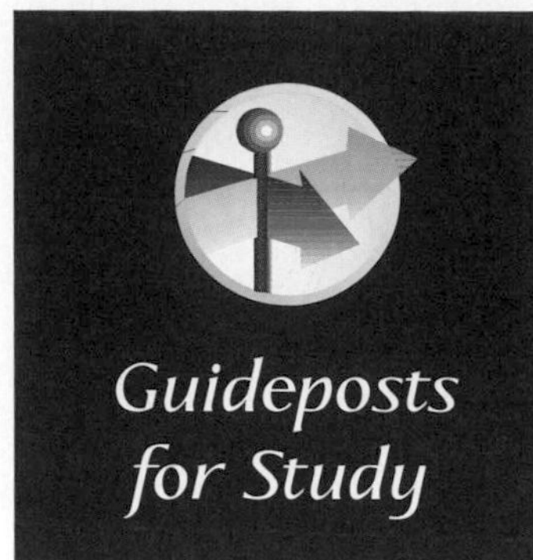

1. How do adolescents' thinking and use of language differ from younger children's?
2. On what basis do adolescents make moral judgments, and how does faith develop?
3. What influences affect adolescents' school success, and why do some students drop out?
4. What factors affect educational and vocational planning and preparation?

Aspects of Cognitive Maturation

Adolescents not only look different from younger children; they also think and talk differently. Their speed of information processing continues to increase, though not as dramatically as in middle childhood (Kail, 1991, 1997). Although their thinking may remain immature in some ways, many adolescents are capable of abstract reasoning and sophisticated moral judgments, and they can plan more realistically for the future.

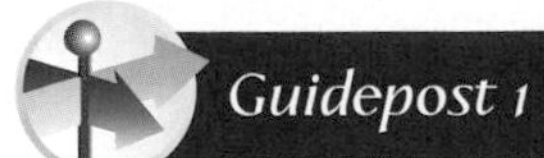

How do adolescents' thinking and use of language differ from younger children's?

Piaget's Stage of Formal Operations

According to Piaget, adolescents enter the highest level of cognitive development—**formal operations**—when they develop the capacity for abstract thought. This development, usually around age 11, gives them a new, more flexible way to manipulate information. No longer limited to the here and now, they can understand historical time and extraterrestrial space. They can use symbols for symbols (for example, letting the letter *X* stand for an unknown numeral) and thus can learn algebra and calculus. They can better appreciate metaphor and allegory and thus can find richer meanings in literature. They can think in terms of what *might be,* not just what *is.* They can imagine possibilities and can form and test hypotheses.

formal operations In Piaget's theory, final stage of cognitive development, characterized by the ability to think abstractly.

Like Nelson Mandela, people in the stage of formal operations can integrate what they have learned in the past with the challenges of the present and make plans for the future. The ability to think abstractly has emotional implications too. Earlier, a child could love a parent or hate a classmate. Now "the adolescent can love freedom or hate exploitation. . . . The possible and the ideal captivate both mind and feeling" (H. Ginsburg & Opper, 1979, p. 201).

Hypothetical-Deductive Reasoning

To appreciate the difference formal reasoning makes, let's follow the progress of a typical child in dealing with a classic Piagetian problem, the pendulum problem.* The child, Adam, is shown the pendulum, an object hanging from a string. He is then shown how he can change any of four factors: the length of the string, the weight of the object, the height from which the object is released, and the amount of force used to push the object. He is asked to figure out which factor or combination of factors determines how fast the pendulum swings. (Figure 16-1 depicts this and other Piagetian tasks for assessing the achievement of formal operations.)

When Adam first sees the pendulum, he is not yet 7 years old and is in the preoperational stage. Unable to formulate a plan for attacking the problem, he tries one thing after another in a hit-or-miss manner. First he puts a light weight on a long string and pushes it;

*This description of age-related differences in the approach to the pendulum problem is adapted from H. Ginsburg and Opper (1979).

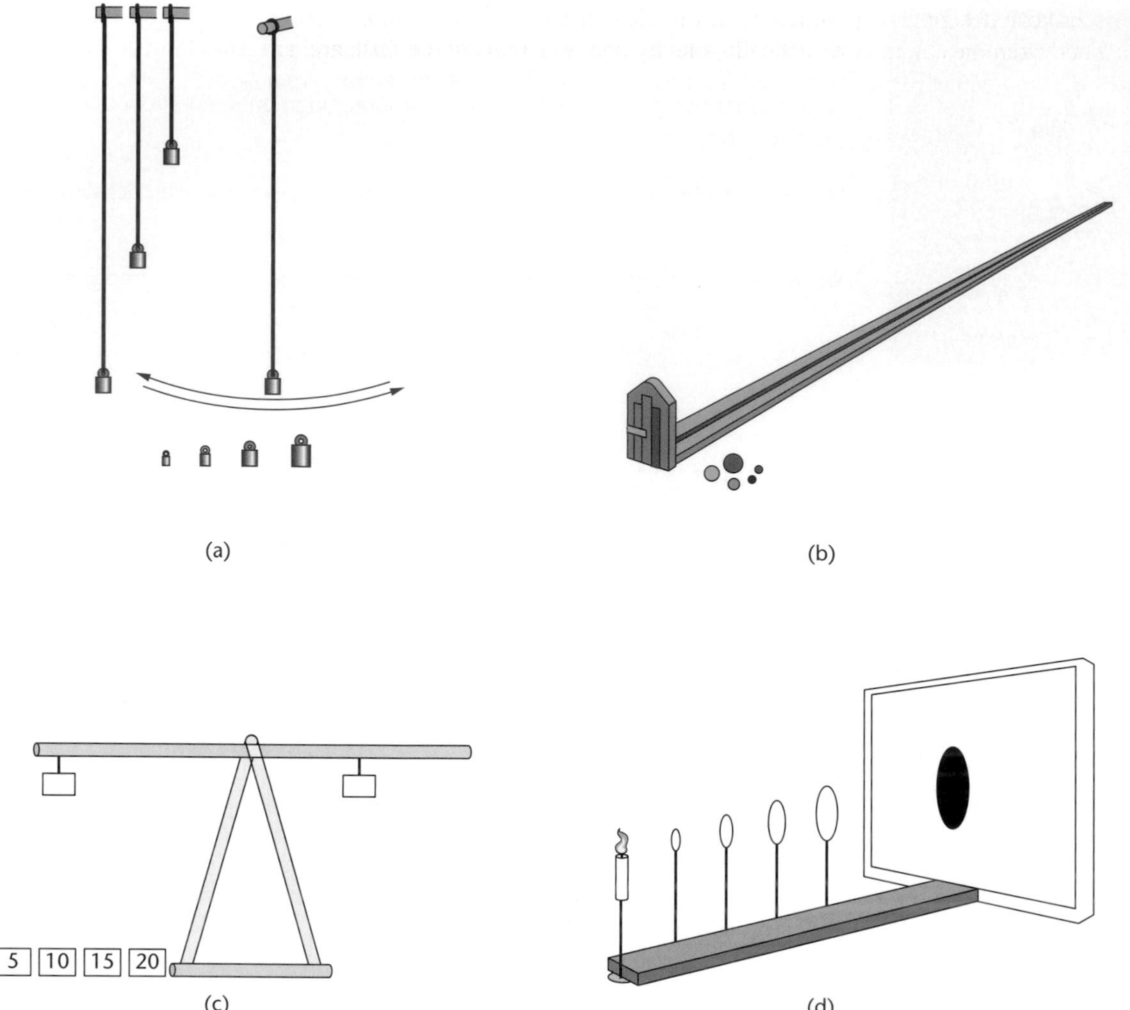

Figure 16-1

Piagetian tasks for measuring attainment of formal operations. (*a*) Pendulum. The pendulum's string can be shortened or lengthened, and weights of varying sizes can be attached to it. The student must determine what variables affect the speed of the pendulum's swing. (*b*) Motion in a horizontal plane. A spring device launches balls of varying sizes that roll in a horizontal plane. The student must predict their stopping points. (*c*) Balance beam. A balance scale comes with weights of varying sizes that can be hung at different points along the crossbar. The student must determine what factors affect whether the scale will balance. (*d*) Shadows. A board containing a row of peg holes is attached perpendicularly to the base of a screen. A light source and rings of varying diameters can be placed in the holes, at varying distances from the screen. The student must produce two shadows of the same size, using different-sized rings.

Source: Adapted from Small & Kagan, 1990, Fig. 8-12.

then he tries swinging a heavy weight on a short string; then he removes the weight entirely. Not only is his method random; he cannot understand or report what has happened.

Adam next encounters the pendulum at age 10, when he is in the stage of concrete operations. This time, he discovers that varying the length of the string and the weight of the object affects the speed of the swing. However, because he varies both factors at the same time, he cannot tell which is critical or whether both are.

Adam is confronted with the pendulum for a third time at age 15, and this time he goes at the problem systematically. He designs an experiment to test all the possible hypotheses, varying one factor at a time—first, the length of the string; next, the weight of the object; then the height from which it is released; and finally, the amount of force used—each time holding the other three factors constant. In this way, he is able to determine that only one factor, the length of the string, determines how fast the pendulum swings.

hypothetical-deductive reasoning Ability, believed by Piaget to accompany the stage of formal operations, to develop, consider, and test hypotheses.

Adam's solution to the pendulum problem shows that he has arrived at the stage of formal operations. He is now capable of **hypothetical-deductive reasoning.** He can develop a hypothesis and can design an experiment to test it. He considers all the relationships he can imagine and examines them systematically, one by one, to eliminate the false and arrive at the true. Hypothetical-deductive reasoning gives him a tool to solve problems, from fixing the family car to constructing a political theory.

What brings about the shift to formal reasoning? Piaget attributed it chiefly to a combination of brain maturation and expanding environmental opportunities. Both are essential: even if young people's neurological development has advanced enough to permit formal reasoning, they can attain it only with appropriate environmental stimulation. One way this happens is through cooperative effort. When college students (average age 18½) were given a chemistry problem and told to set up their own experiments to solve it, students randomly assigned to work in pairs solved more problems than those who worked alone. The more the partners challenged each other's reasoning, the greater were the advances in thinking (Dimant & Bearison, 1991).

As with the development of concrete operations, schooling and culture seem to play a role—as Piaget (1972) ultimately recognized. French 10- to 15-year-olds in the 1990s did better on Piagetian tests of formal operations than their counterparts two to three decades earlier, at a time when fewer French adolescents (or their parents) had secondary school educations (Flieller, 1999). When adolescents in New Guinea and Rwanda were tested on the pendulum problem, none was able to solve it. On the other hand, Chinese children in Hong Kong, who had been to British schools, did at least as well as U.S. or European children. Schoolchildren in Central Java and New South Wales also showed some formal operational abilities (Gardiner & Kosmitzki, 2005). Apparently, this kind of thinking is a learned ability that is not equally necessary or equally valued in all cultures.

What's your view 

- How can parents and teachers help adolescents improve their reasoning ability?

Evaluating Piaget's Theory

Piaget's influence on the field of developmental psychology has been compared with Shakespeare's influence on English literature and Aristotle's influence on philosophy (Beilin, 1994). His theory continues to point the way to countless avenues of investigation. In particular, Piaget's theory has had an enormous influence on education. It has given parents and teachers benchmarks for what to expect, roughly, at various ages and has helped educators design curricula appropriate to children's levels of development.

But although research has not seriously challenged the overall *sequence* of development Piaget described (Lourenco & Machado, 1996), it has questioned his assertion of definite stages of development. Adolescents *do* tend to think more abstractly than younger children, but there is debate about the precise age at which this advance emerges (Eccles, Wigfield, & Byrnes, 2003). Piaget's own writings provide many examples of children displaying aspects of scientific thinking well before adolescence. At the same time, Piaget seems to have *over*estimated some older children's abilities. Many late adolescents and adults—perhaps one-third to one-half—seem incapable of abstract thought as Piaget defined it (Gardiner & Kosmitzki, 2005; Kohlberg & Gilligan, 1971; Papalia, 1972), and those who are capable of this kind of thinking do not always use it.

Piaget, in most of his writings, paid little attention to individual differences, to variations in a child's performance of different kinds of tasks, or to social and cultural influences. In his later years, Piaget himself "came to view his earlier model of the development of children's thinking, particularly formal operations, as flawed because it failed to capture the essential *role of the situation* in influencing and constraining . . . children's thinking" (Brown, Metz, & Campione, 1996, pp. 152–153). Neo-Piagetian research suggests that children's cognitive processes are closely tied to specific content (what a child is thinking *about*) as well as to the context of a problem and the kinds of information and thought a culture considers important (Case & Okamoto, 1996).

Finally, research has found that Piaget's theory does not adequately consider such cognitive advances as gains in information-processing capacity, accumulation of knowledge and expertise in specific fields, and the role of *metacognition,* the awareness and monitoring of one's own mental processes and strategies (Flavell et al., 2002; refer back to Chapter 13).

Checkpoint 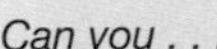

Can you . . .

✔ Explain the difference between formal operational and concrete operational thinking, as exemplified by the pendulum problem?

✔ Cite factors influencing adolescents' development of formal reasoning?

✔ Evaluate strengths and weaknesses of Piaget's theory of formal operations?

Changes in Information Processing in Adolescence

Researchers in cognitive development have identified two broad categories of measurable change in adolescent cognition: *structural change* and *functional change* (Eccles et al., 2003).* Let's look at each.

Structural Change

Structural changes in adolescence include (1) changes in information-processing capacity and (2) the increasing amount of knowledge stored in long-term memory.

The capacity of working memory, which enlarges rapidly in middle childhood, continues to increase during adolescence. In one study, 20-year-olds were better able than 14-year-olds to remember after a long delay the locations of objects that were no longer visible (Zald & Iacono, 1998). The expansion of working memory may enable older adolescents to deal with complex problems or decisions involving multiple pieces of information.

Information stored in long-term memory can be either declarative, procedural, or conceptual. **Declarative knowledge** ("knowing that . . . ") consists of all the factual knowledge a person has acquired (for example, knowing that 2 + 2 = 4 and that George Washington was the first U.S. president). **Procedural knowledge** ("knowing how to . . .") consists of all the skills a person has acquired, such as being able to multiply and divide and drive a car. **Conceptual knowledge** ("knowing why . . .") is an understanding of, for example, why the war in Iraq began or why an algebraic equation remains true if the same amount is added or subtracted from both sides.

declarative knowledge Acquired factual knowledge stored in long-term memory.

procedural knowledge Acquired skills stored in long-term memory.

conceptual knowledge Acquired interpretive understandings stored in long-term memory.

All three forms of knowledge increase steadily with age. In the United States, the National Assessment of Educational Progress (NAEP) has found that children gain in all three areas of subject-matter knowledge between fourth and eighth grades and between eighth and twelfth grades. For example, fourth graders know arithmetic facts and can solve simple word problems; twelfth graders can do algebraic manipulations and reason about geometric shapes. Similar advances occur in reading, writing, science, history, geography, and civics. Still, these gains are often modest, depending on the particular domain and on the quality of education. Even most twelfth graders do not show a deep conceptual understanding of such concepts as scarcity or civil rights, and they often exhibit misconceptions and false information.

Functional Change

Processes for obtaining, handling, and retaining information are *functional* aspects of cognition. Among these are learning, remembering, reasoning, and decision making. Mathematical, spatial, and scientific reasoning are some of the functional processes that typically improve during adolescence.

As discussed in Chapter 13, research has challenged Piaget's belief that deductive reasoning becomes possible only at the stage of formal operations. However, adolescents do gradually become more proficient in drawing conclusions, explaining their reasoning, and testing hypotheses, particularly if the premises are familiar and true. When experimental premises are contrary to common knowledge ("All elephants are small. This is an elephant. Is it small?"), fewer than half of older adolescents or adults can make the appropriate deduction.

Improvements observed in laboratory situations do not necessarily carry over to real life, where behavior depends in part on motivation and emotion regulation. Many older adolescents make poorer real-world decisions than younger adolescents do. In the game Twenty Questions, the object is to ask as few yes or no questions as necessary to discover the identity of a person, place, or thing by systematically narrowing down the categories within which the answer might fall. The efficiency with which young people can do this generally improves between middle childhood and late adolescence. However, in one study (Drumm & Jackson, 1996), high school students, especially boys, showed a greater tendency than either early adolescents or college students to jump to guessing the answer. This

*Unless otherwise referenced, the discussion in this section is indebted to Eccles et al., 2003.

pattern of guesswork may reflect a penchant for impulsive, risky behavior. As we discussed in Chapter 15, adolescents' rash judgments may be related to immature brain development, which may permit feelings to override reason.

Gender and Ethnic Differences

Girls and boys are similiar in intelligence, working memory, deductive reasoning, and decision making, but risk taking is a notable exception. Boys are more likely to drive recklessly or to take intellectual risks, such as proposing a novel idea. Girls are more likely to take health risks, such as smoking.

European-American and Asian-American students do better than African-American, Hispanic, and Native-American students on standardized achievement tests, the SAT, and the NAEP. These differences are substantially reduced when parent educational background and the student's previous course work are considered. No ethnic differences have been found in deductive reasoning, working memory, or decision making.

Checkpoint

Can you . . .

✔ Name two major kinds of changes in adolescents' cognitive development, and give examples of each?

✔ Identify gender and ethnic differences in adolescents' cognitive development?

Language Development

School-age children are quite proficient in use of language, but adolescence brings further refinements. Vocabulary continues to grow as reading matter becomes more adult. By ages 16 to 18 the average young person knows approximately 80,000 words (Owens, 1996).

With the advent of formal thought, adolescents can define and discuss such abstractions as *love, justice,* and *freedom.* They more frequently use such terms as *however, otherwise, anyway, therefore, really,* and *probably* to express logical relations between clauses or sentences. They become more conscious of words as symbols that can have multiple meanings, and they take pleasure in using irony, puns, and metaphors (Owens, 1996).

Adolescents also become more skilled in *social perspective-taking,* the ability to tailor their speech to another person's knowledge level and point of view. This ability is essential for persuasion and even for polite conversation. Conscious of their audience, adolescents speak a different language with peers than with adults (Owens, 1996; see Box 16-1). Teenage slang is part of the process of developing an independent identity separate from parents and the adult world (see Chapter 17). In creating such expressions as "That's sweet!" and "dabomb," young people use their newfound ability to play with words "to define their generation's unique take on values, tastes, and preferences" (Elkind, 1998, p. 29).

Elkind: Immature Characteristics of Adolescent Thought

We have seen how children develop from egocentric beings whose interest extends not much farther than the nipple to persons capable of solving abstract problems and imagining ideal societies. Yet in some ways adolescents' thinking seems strangely immature—and not only in risk-taking behavior. They are often rude to adults, they have trouble making up their minds what to wear each day, and they tend to act as if the whole world revolved around them.

According to the psychologist David Elkind (1998), such behavior stems from adolescents' inexperienced ventures into formal operational thought. This new way of thinking, which fundamentally transforms the way they look at themselves and their world, is as unfamiliar to them as their reshaped bodies, and they sometimes feel just as awkward in its use. As they try out their new powers, they may sometimes stumble, like an infant learning to walk.

This immaturity of thinking, Elkind suggests, manifests itself in at least six characteristic ways:

1. *Idealism and criticalness:* As adolescents envision an ideal world, they realize how far the real world, for which they hold adults responsible, falls short. They become super-conscious of hypocrisy; with their sharpened verbal reasoning, they relish magazines and entertainers that attack public figures with satire and parody. Convinced that they know better than adults how to run the world, they frequently find fault with their parents.

The Social World

Box 16-1 *"Pubilect," the Dialect of Adolescence*

"That guy's hot!"

"She's fine!"

"Chill!"

"Let's bounce!"

Adolescents' conversation is mainly about the people and events in their everyday world (Labov, 1992). They use slang (nonstandard speech) to label people ("dork" or "loser"), to pronounce positive or negative judgments ("That's cool!" or "What a beast!"), and to describe alcohol or drug-related activity ("She's wasted" or "He's blazed").

The Canadian linguist Marcel Danesi (1994) argues that adolescent speech is more than just slang (which, of course, adults use too). Instead, it constitutes a dialect of its own: *pubilect,* "the social dialect of puberty" (p. 97). Pubilect is more than an occasional colorful expression. It is the primary mode of verbal communication among teenagers, by which they differentiate themselves from adults. As they approach puberty, youngsters absorb this dialect from slightly older peers. Like any other linguistic code, pubilect serves to strengthen group identity and to shut outsiders (adults) out. Teenage vocabulary is characterized by rapid change. Although some of its terms have entered common discourse, adolescents keep inventing new ones all the time.

Analyses of recorded samples of adolescent conversation reveal several key features of pubilect. First, it is an *emotive* code. Through exaggerated tone, slow and deliberate delivery, prolonged stress, accompanying gestures, and vulgar interjections, it draws attention to feelings and attitudes ("Yeah, riiight!" "Well, duuuh!"). Such emotive utterances seem to constitute about 65 percent of adolescent speech. The use of fillers, such as the word *like,* as well as the typical pattern of narrative intonation, in which each phrase or sentence seems to end with a question mark, reflects unconscious uncertainty and serves to draw the listener into the speaker's state of mind.

A second feature of pubilect is its *connotative* function. Teenagers coin descriptive words or extend the meaning of existing words to convey their view of their world and the people in it, often in highly metaphorical ways. A person does not need a dictionary to figure out the meanings of such expressions as "space cadet" and "ditz." Such terms provide a ready lexicon for quick, automatic value judgments about others.

In the United States, there is not a single youth culture but many subcultures. Vocabulary may differ by gender, ethnicity, age, geographical region, neighborhood (city, suburban, or rural) and type of school (public or private) (Labov, 1992). Also, pubilect is *clique-coded:* it varies from one clique to another. "Druggies" and "jocks" engage in different kinds of activities, which form the main subjects of their conversation. This talk, in turn, cements bonds within the clique. Males use verbal dueling to assert power. Contenders for leadership trade insults and clever retorts in an effort to gain the upper hand in front of the group.

A study of teenage speech patterns in Naples, Italy, suggests that similar features may emerge "in any culture where teenagerhood constitutes a distinct social category" (Danesi, 1994, p. 123). Neapolitan teenagers use "mmmm" much as U.S. teenagers use "like": "Devo, mmmm, dire che, mmmm, non capisco, mmmm, . . ." ("I have, mmmm, to say that, mmmm, I don't understand, mmmm, . . ."). Exaggerated tone and rising intonation at the ends of phrases are also common. The Italian young people have terms roughly equivalent to the English "cool" (*togo*), "loser" (*grasta*), and "dork" or "nerd" (*secchione*). Other investigators report that adolescents in Milan, Bologna, and other northern Italian cities speak "the language of rock and roll." This cultural borrowing—the result of wide dissemination of English-language television channels, such as MTV—may well be creating a "symbolic universe" for teenagers around the world (Danesi, 1994, p. 123).

What's your view?

- Can you remember "pubilect" expressions from your own adolescence?
- When and why did you use such expressions?
- What was their effect on others your age? On adults?

Check it out!

For more information on this topic, go to **http://www.slanguage.com/**. This is a website called American Slanguages.

Source: Unless otherwise referenced, the source of this discussion is Danesi, 1994.

2. *Argumentativeness:* Adolescents are constantly looking for opportunities to try out and show off their reasoning abilities. They often become argumentative as they marshal facts and logic to build a case for, say, staying out later than their parents think they should.
3. *Indecisiveness:* Adolescents can keep many alternatives in mind at the same time yet may lack effective strategies for choosing among them. They may have trouble making up their minds even about such simple things as whether to go to the mall with a friend or to the computer to work on a school assignment.
4. *Apparent hypocrisy:* Young adolescents often do not recognize the difference between expressing an ideal, such as conserving energy, and making the sacrifices necessary to live up to it, such as driving less often.
5. *Self-consciousness:* Adolescents in the stage of formal operations can think about thinking—their own and other people's. However, in their preoccupation with their own mental state, adolescents often assume that everyone else is thinking about the

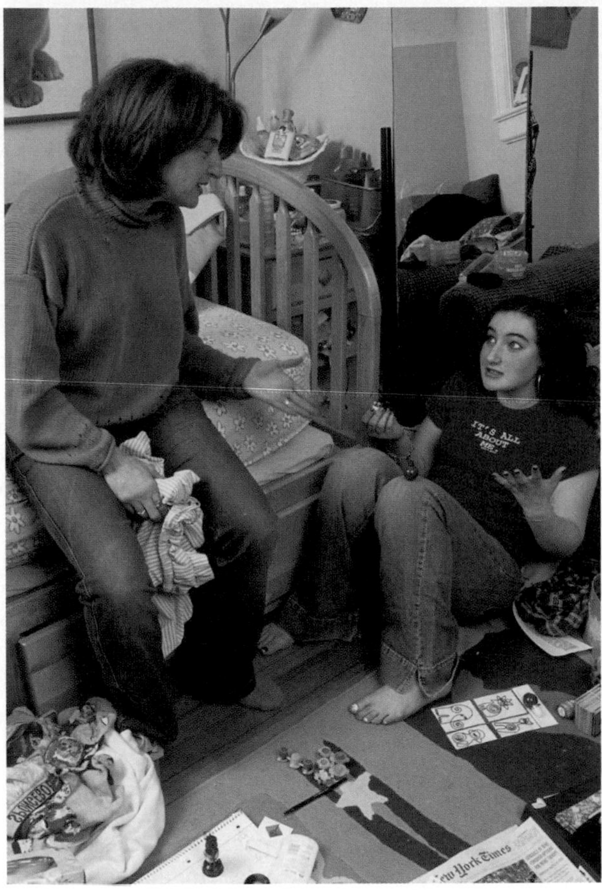

Argumentativeness—usually with parents—is a typical characteristic of adolescent thought, according to David Elkind.

same thing they are thinking about: themselves. A teenage girl may be mortified if she wears "the wrong thing" to a party, thinking that everyone else must be looking askance at her. Elkind refers to this self-consciousness as the **imaginary audience,** a conceptualized "observer" who is as concerned with a young person's thoughts and behavior as he or she is. The imaginary audience fantasy is especially strong in the early teens but persists to a lesser degree into adult life.

6. *Specialness and invulnerability:* Elkind uses the term **personal fable** to denote a belief by adolescents that they are special, that their experience is unique, and that they are not subject to the rules that govern the rest of the world ("Other people get hooked from taking drugs but not me," or, "No one has ever been as deeply in love as I am"). According to Elkind, this special form of egocentrism underlies much risky, self-destructive behavior. Like the imaginary audience, the personal fable continues in adulthood. It is the personal fable, says Elkind, that persuades people to take such everyday risks as driving a car despite statistics on highway deaths. Perhaps Elkind would say that it was in part the personal fable that led Nelson Mandela to engage in dangerous insurrectionary activities against a brutal dictatorship.

imaginary audience Elkind's term for observer who exists only in an adolescent's mind and is as concerned with the adolescent's thoughts and actions as the adolescent is.

personal fable Elkind's term for conviction that one is special, unique, and not subject to the rules that govern the rest of the world.

The concepts of the imaginary audience and the personal fable have been widely accepted, but their validity as distinct earmarks of adolescence has little independent research support. In some studies of the personal fable, adolescents were *more* likely than college students or adults to see themselves as vulnerable to certain risks, such as alcohol and other drug problems, rather than *less* likely, as the personal fable would predict (Quadrel, Fischoff, & Davis, 1993). It has been suggested that the imaginary audience and personal fable may be related to specific social experiences rather than constituting universal features of adolescents' cognitive development. Since these concepts grew out of Elkind's clinical observations, they may be more characteristic of young people who are experiencing difficulties in adjustment (Vartanian & Powlishta, 1996).

Checkpoint

Can you . . .

✔ Identify several characteristics of adolescents' language development that reflect cognitive advances?

✔ Describe Elkind's six proposed aspects of immature adolescent thought, and explain how they may grow out of the transition to formal operational thought?

On what basis do adolescents make moral judgments, and how does faith develop?

Moral and Spiritual Development

As children grow older and attain higher cognitive levels, they become capable of more complex reasoning about moral issues, and their ideas about religious questions may change as well. Let's look at Lawrence Kohlberg's influential theory of moral reasoning and then at James Fowler's theory of stages in faith development.

Kohlberg's Theory of Moral Reasoning

A woman is near death from cancer. A druggist has discovered a drug that doctors believe might save her. The druggist is charging $2,000 for a small dose—10 times what the drug costs him to make. The sick woman's husband, Heinz, borrows from everyone he knows but can scrape together only $1,000. He begs the druggist to sell him the drug for $1,000 or let him pay the rest later. The druggist refuses, saying, "I discovered the drug and I'm going to make money from it." Heinz, desperate, breaks into the man's store and steals the drug. Should Heinz have done that? Why or why not? (Kohlberg, 1969).

Heinz's problem is the most famous example of Lawrence Kohlberg's approach to studying moral development. Starting in the 1950s, Kohlberg and his colleagues posed hypothetical dilemmas like this one to 75 boys ages 10, 13, and 16 and continued to question them periodically for more than 30 years. At the heart of each dilemma was the concept of justice. By asking respondents how they arrived at their answers, Kohlberg, like Piaget, concluded that the way people look at moral issues reflects cognitive development.

Unlike socialization theory, which attributes moral behavior to internalization of societal standards, the cognitive-developmental approach holds that moral codes tend to change as people become capable of more advanced thinking. Both Piaget and Kohlberg described moral growth as progressing from externally imposed rules based on the consequences of an act to more flexible, internal judgments that take circumstances into account. This development is made possible by the shift from egocentrism to decentration—the ability to look at things from more than one point of view.

Piaget maintained that children develop concepts of fairness or justice through interaction with peers. In Kohlberg's view, *all* social relationships offer opportunities for social role-taking—taking the perspective of others—and thus stimulate moral development. Whereas peer relationships may be the most important avenue during childhood, the expanding environments of adolescence and adulthood broaden opportunities for moral growth (Gibbs, 1995).

Kohlberg's Levels and Stages

preconventional morality First level of Kohlberg's theory of moral reasoning, in which control is external and rules are obeyed in order to gain rewards or avoid punishment or out of self-interest.

conventional morality (or morality of conventional role conformity) Second level in Kohlberg's theory of moral reasoning in which standards of authority figures are internalized.

postconventional morality (or morality of autonomous moral principles) Third level in Kohlberg's theory of moral reasoning in which people follow internally held moral principles and can decide among conflicting moral standards.

On the basis of thought processes shown by responses to his dilemmas (and, later, in response to real situations), Kohlberg (1969) described three levels of moral reasoning, each divided into two stages (see Table 16-1 on pages 446–447 for detailed descriptions of each stage). Kohlberg's early stages correspond roughly to Piaget's stages of moral development in childhood, described in Chapter 13, but his most advanced stages do not occur until adulthood.

- *Level I:* ***Preconventional morality.*** People act under external controls. They obey rules to avoid punishment or reap rewards or act out of self-interest. This level, said Kohlberg, is typical of children ages 4 to 10.
- *Level II:* ***Conventional morality (or morality of conventional role conformity).*** People have internalized the standards of authority figures. They are concerned about being "good," pleasing others, and maintaining the social order. This level is typically reached after age 10; many people never move beyond it, even in adulthood.
- *Level III:* ***Postconventional morality (or morality of autonomous moral principles).*** People now recognize conflicts between moral standards and make their own judgments on the basis of principles of right, fairness, and justice. People generally do not reach this level of moral reasoning until at least early adolescence or more commonly in young adulthood, if ever.

Kohlberg later added a transitional level between Levels II and III, when people no longer feel bound by society's moral standards but have not yet developed rationally derived principles of justice. Instead, they base their moral decisions on personal feelings.

In Kohlberg's theory, it is the reasoning underlying a person's response to a moral dilemma, not the answer itself, that indicates the stage of moral development. As illustrated in Table 16-1, two people who give opposite answers may be at the same stage if their reasoning is based on similar factors.

Some adolescents and even some adults remain at Kohlberg's Level I. Like young children, they seek to avoid punishment or satisfy their own needs. Most adolescents and most adults seem to be at Level II. They conform to social conventions, support the status quo, and do the "right" thing to please others or to obey the law. For Nelson Mandela, the event that triggered his eventual emergence from this stage was his circumcision ceremony at age 16, when he listened to the shocking speech that challenged the morality of the system into which he was being initiated.

Kohlberg held that before people can develop a fully principled (Level III) morality, they must recognize the relativity of moral standards. Many young people question their earlier moral views when they enter high school or college or the world of work and encounter people whose values, culture, and ethnic background are different from their own. Still, very few people reach a level where they can choose between moral standards, as Mandela did. In fact, at one point Kohlberg questioned the validity of Stage 6, morality based on universal ethical principles, since so few people seem to attain it. Later, however, he proposed a seventh, "cosmic" stage, in which people consider the effect of their actions not only on other people but on the universe as a whole (Kohlberg, 1981; Kohlberg & Ryncarz, 1990).

Evaluating Kohlberg's Theory

Kohlberg, building on Piaget, brought about a profound shift in the way we look at moral development. Instead of viewing morality solely as the attainment of control over self-gratifying impulses, investigators now study how children and adults base moral judgments on their growing understanding of the social world.

Initial research supported Kohlberg's theory. The American boys whom Kohlberg and his colleagues followed through adulthood progressed through Kohlberg's stages in sequence, and none skipped a stage. Their moral judgments correlated positively with age, education, IQ, and socioeconomic status (Colby, Kohlberg, Gibbs, & Lieberman, 1983). However, a more recent Canadian study of children's judgments about laws and lawbreaking suggests that children can reason flexibly about such issues at an earlier age than either Piaget or Kohlberg proposed—even as early as age 6 (Helwig & Jasiobedzka, 2001).

Furthermore, research has noted the lack of a clear relationship between moral reasoning and moral behavior. People at postconventional levels of reasoning do not necessarily act more morally than those at lower levels (Colby & Damon, 1992; Kupfersmid & Wonderly, 1980). Perhaps one problem is the remoteness from young people's experience of such dilemmas as the "Heinz" situation. (Box 16-2 on page 448 describes adolescents' moral judgments on everyday issues.) On the other hand, juvenile delinquents, particularly boys, consistently show developmental delays in Kohlbergian tests of moral reasoning (Gregg, Gibbs, & Basinger, 1994).

Critics claim that a cognitive approach to moral development gives insufficient attention to the importance of emotion. Moral activity, they say, is motivated not only by abstract considerations of justice, but also by such emotions as empathy, guilt, and distress and the internalization of prosocial norms (Gibbs, 1991, 1995; Gibbs & Schnell, 1985). It has been argued that Kohlberg's stages 5 and 6 cannot fairly be called the most mature stages of moral development, since they restrict "maturity" to a select group of people who are given to philosophical reflection (J. C. Gibbs, 1995).

Some theorists today seek to synthesize the cognitive-developmental approach to moral development with the role of emotion and the insights of socialization theory (Gibbs, 1991, 1995; Gibbs & Schnell, 1985). Kohlberg himself recognized that noncognitive

When asked whether it is wrong for a teenage girl to have a baby, what would 15-year-olds say? Find out by watching the video on "Talking About Teen Pregnancy at Age 15" video in Chapter 16 of your CD.

Table 16-1 Kohlberg's Six Stages of Moral Reasoning

Levels	Stages of Reasoning	Typical Answers to Heinz's Dilemma
Level I: Preconventional morality (ages 4 to 10)	*Stage 1: Orientation toward punishment and obedience.* "What will happen to me?" Children obey rules to avoid punishment. They ignore the motives of an act and focus on its physical form (such as the size of a lie) or its consequences (for example, the amount of physical damage).	*Pro:* "He should steal the drug. It isn't really bad to take it. It isn't as if he hadn't asked to pay for it first. The drug he'd take is worth only $200; he's not really taking a $2,000 drug." *Con:* "He shouldn't steal the drug. It's a big crime. He didn't get permission; he used force and broke and entered. He did a lot of damage and stole a very expensive drug."
	Stage 2: Instrumental purpose and exchange. "You scratch my back, I'll scratch yours." Children conform to rules out of self-interest and consideration for what others can do for them. They look at an act in terms of the human needs it meets and differentiate this value from the act's physical form and consequences.	*Pro:* "It's all right to steal the drug, because his wife needs it and he wants her to live. It isn't that he wants to steal, but that's what he has to do to save her." *Con:* "He shouldn't steal it. The druggist isn't wrong or bad; he just wants to make a profit. That's what you're in business for—to make money."
Level II: Conventional morality (ages 10 to 13 or beyond)	*Stage 3: Maintaining mutual relations, approval of others, the golden rule.* "Am I a good boy or girl?" Children want to please and help others, can judge the intentions of others, and develop their own ideas of what a good person is. They evaluate an act according to the motive behind it or the person performing it, and they take circumstances into account.	*Pro:* "He should steal the drug. He is only doing something that is natural for a good husband to do. You can't blame him for doing something out of love for his wife. You'd blame him if he didn't love his wife enough to save her." *Con:* "He shouldn't steal. If his wife dies, he can't be blamed. It isn't because he's heartless or that he doesn't love her enough to do everything that he legally can. The druggist is the selfish or heartless one."

(Continued)

What's your view

- Kohlberg's method of assessing moral development by evaluating participants' reactions to moral dilemmas is widely used. Does this seem like the most appropriate method? Why or why not? Can you suggest an alternative measure?
- Can you think of a time when you or someone you know acted contrary to personal moral judgment? Why do you think this happened?

factors such as emotional development and life experience affect moral judgments. One reason the ages attached to Kohlberg's levels are so variable is that people who have achieved a high level of cognitive development do not always reach a comparably high level of moral development. A certain level of cognitive development is *necessary* but not *sufficient* for a comparable level of moral development. Thus, other processes besides cognition must be at work.

A practical problem in using Kohlberg's system is its time-consuming testing procedures. The standard dilemmas need to be presented to each person individually and then scored by trained judges. One alternative is the Defining Issues Test (DIT), which can be given quickly to a group and scored objectively (Rest, 1975). Its results correlate moderately well with scores on Kohlberg's traditional tasks.

Family Influences Neither Piaget nor Kohlberg considered parents important to children's moral development. More recent research, however, emphasizes parents' contribution in both the cognitive and the emotional realms.

In one study, parents of 63 students in grades 1, 4, 7, and 10 were asked to talk with their children about two dilemmas: a hypothetical one and an actual one that the child described (L. J. Walker & Taylor, 1991). The children and adolescents who, during the next two years, showed the greatest progress through Kohlberg's stages were those whose parents had used

Table 16-1 (continued)

Levels	Stages of Reasoning	Typical Answers to Heinz's Dilemma
	Stage 4: Social concern and conscience. "What if everybody did it?" People are concerned with doing their duty, showing respect for higher authority, and maintaining the social order. They consider an act always wrong, regardless of motive or circumstances, if it violates a rule and harms others.	*Pro:* "You should steal it. If you did nothing, you'd be letting your wife die. It's your responsibility if she dies. You have to take it with the idea of paying the druggist." *Con:* "It is a natural thing for Heinz to want to save his wife, but it's still always wrong to steal. He knows he's taking a valuable drug from the man who made it."
Level III: Postconventional morality (early adolescence or not until young adulthood or never)	*Stage 5: Morality of contract, of individual rights, and of democratically accepted law.* People think in rational terms, valuing the will of the majority and the welfare of society. They generally see these values as best supported by adherence to the law. While they recognize that there are times when human need and the law conflict, they believe it is better for society in the long run if they obey the law.	*Pro:* "The law wasn't set up for these circumstances. Taking the drug in this situation isn't really right, but it's justified." *Con:* "You can't completely blame someone for stealing, but extreme circumstances don't really justify taking the law into your own hands. You can't have people stealing whenever they are desperate. The end may be good, but the ends don't justify the means."
	Stage 6: Morality of universal ethical principles. People do what they as individuals think is right, regardless of legal restrictions or the opinions of others. They act in accordance with internalized standards, knowing that they would condemn themselves if they did not.	*Pro:* "This is a situation that forces him to choose between stealing and letting his wife die. In a situation where the choice must be made, it is morally right to steal. He has to act in terms of the principle of preserving and respecting life." *Con:* "Heinz is faced with the decision of whether to consider the other people who need the drug just as badly as his wife. Heinz ought to act not according to his feelings for his wife, but considering the value of all the lives involved."

Source: Adapted from Kohlberg, 1969; Lickona, 1976.

humor and praise, listened to them, and asked their opinions. These parents had asked clarifying questions, reworded answers, and checked to be sure the children understood the issues. They reasoned with their children at a slightly higher level than the children were currently at, much as in the method of scaffolding. The children who advanced the least were those whose parents had lectured them or challenged or contradicted their opinions.

Validity for Women and Girls On the basis of research on women, Carol Gilligan (1982) asserted that Kohlberg's theory is oriented toward values more important to men than to women. Gilligan claimed that women see morality not so much in terms of justice and fairness as of responsibility to show care and avoid harm.

Research has not supported Gilligan's claim of a male bias in Kohlberg's stages, and she has since modified her position. Moreover, in some research on gender differences in moral judgments in early adolescence, girls scored *higher* than boys (Garmon, Basinger, Gregg, & Gibbs, 1996; Skoe & Gooden, 1993). This may be because girls generally mature earlier and have more intimate social relationships (Garmon et al., 1996; Skoe & Diessner, 1994). Early adolescent girls do tend to emphasize care-related concerns more than boys do, especially when tested with open-ended questions ("How important is it to keep promises to a friend?") or self-chosen moral dilemmas related to their own experience (Garmon et al., 1996).

The Research World

Box 16-2 *How Do Psychosocial Issues Affect Adolescents' Moral Judgments?*

How many adolescents face the problem of needing a rare and expensive medicine for a mortally ill spouse? Not many do. And yet Kohlberg's theory of moral development is based on responses to dilemmas like this. Today some researchers are instead interviewing adolescents about moral issues they are likely to confront in everyday life, such as whether and how a bystander should respond to aggression, under what circumstances it might be all right to break a school rule, and whether to admit someone from a minority group to an exclusive club. The findings suggest that psychosocial issues, such as the needs for peer acceptance and personal autonomy, are important factors in adolescents' moral choices.

In one study (Tisak & Tisak, 1996), interviewers asked 111 working-class and middle-class 10-, 12-, and 14-year-olds in rural Ohio what a person their age *would* do and *should* do, and why, when witnessing a good friend or a younger sibling hit or push someone, tear a book, or break a game. The answers fell into five main categories: (1) *looking out for others' welfare* ("He [the victim] will get hurt if she [the bystander] doesn't do something to stop it"), (2) *helping the aggressor avoid punishment* ("She will get in trouble if she continues to hit"), (3) *family responsibility* ("He is supposed to make sure his brother doesn't do that"), (4) *maintaining solidarity with friends* ("She will lose her as a friend [if she intervenes]"), and (5) *importance of the consequences* ("Why should she do anything? It's not important").

Older participants were less concerned about the welfare of the victim than about maintaining solidarity with the aggressor or helping him or her avoid punishment, perhaps reflecting adolescents' growing need for peer acceptance. However, they were less inclined than younger children to expect or favor *any* intervention, perhaps because they felt that the aggressor and the victim should be able to resolve the dispute themselves. Respondents of all ages thought a bystander would be more likely to stop a sibling's aggression than a friend's and had a greater obligation to do so. Girls were more apt to expect a bystander to intervene, though boys were just as likely to think it would be wrong not to.

In another study, 120 fifth, seventh, ninth, and eleventh graders were asked about the proper scope of school rules (Smetana & Bitz, 1996). Participants agreed that three kinds of conduct should be regulated: (1) *immoral* behavior violating the rights and welfare of others, such as stealing, fighting, or failing to return textbooks; (2) *unconventional* behavior violating customary standards, such as acting up in class, swearing, coming late, or talking back to the teacher; and (3) *imprudent* behavior, such as smoking, drinking, taking drugs, and eating junk food for lunch. The young people viewed *personal* behavior, such as choice of clothing or hairstyle and eating or reading comics in class, as matters to decide for themselves.

The respondents were almost evenly split in their judgments about behavior that is customarily regulated in school but not in other contexts, such as leaving class without permission, keeping forbidden items in a school locker, and passing notes to friends in class. As compared with fifth graders, older participants were more likely to view this kind of behavior as a matter of personal discretion. Adolescents' views about the legitimate subjects of rules were important predictors of how often they broke the rules, according to their own and teachers' reports.

In a third study (Phinney & Cobb, 1996), 120 European-American (Anglo) and Hispanic-American fifth, eighth, and eleventh graders were asked how they would respond to a Hispanic or Anglo student's request to join an exclusive school club in which all the members were of the other ethnic group. In half of the cases, the hypothetical applicant was of the same ethnic group as the respondent; in the other half, of the other ethnic group.

About three-fourths of the students strongly favored accepting the applicant, mainly out of *fairness* ("Everybody should be treated the same") or *concern with individual welfare* ("So they won't hurt her feelings"). Other reasons given were *upholding social principles* ("If they choose their own people, then they're never going to get along with each other") and benefits of *cultural diversity* ("They can get to meet new people . . . learn about different cultures"). Less than 10 percent strongly favored excluding the outsider, citing the *right of club members* to select their associates ("They're the ones who started this club and . . . they should have the right . . . to choose who they want") or *cultural barriers* ("If they start speaking Spanish, she's going to feel left out"). About 12 percent of the respondents (mostly fifth and eighth graders) originally favored admission but switched when the interviewer suggested that "some people" would consider exclusion appropriate. The original reasons given by those who switched were largely pragmatic ("Let him in; otherwise it'll cause a lot of tension").

The respondents' ethnicity did not affect the decisions but did seem to influence the reasons. Anglo students tended to appeal to rights of free choice and rules ("The school says they could choose their own members") as reasons for exclusion; Hispanics appealed to cultural barriers. In line with Kohlberg's theory, older adolescents who favored inclusion were more likely than younger ones to show awareness of the impact on the social order ("If you start getting your own little groups . . . that hurts the country").

What's your view ?

What would be your answers to the three issues presented here, and why?

Check it out !

For more information on this topic, go to **http://www.usoe.k12.ut.us/curr/char_ed/default.htm**. This is the Character Education Homepage, prepared by the Center for the Advancement of Ethics and Character at Boston University. It has links to a character education reading list and many projects and reports about character education.

Early adolescent girls score have more intimate social relationships than early adolescent boys and are more concerned about caring for others. This may help explain why girls in this age group tend to score higher than boys on moral judgments.

Cross-Cultural Validity Cross-cultural studies support Kohlberg's sequence of stages—up to a point. Older people from countries other than the United States do tend to score at higher stages than younger people. However, people in nonwestern cultures rarely score above Stage 4 (Edwards, 1981; Nisan & Kohlberg, 1982; Snarey, 1985), suggesting that some aspects of Kohlberg's model may not fit the cultural values of these societies. When Kohlberg's dilemmas were tested in India, Buddhist monks from Ladakh, a Tibetan enclave, scored lower than laypeople. Apparently Kohlberg's model, while capturing the preconventional and conventional elements of Buddhist thinking, was inadequate for understanding postconventional Buddhist principles of cooperation and nonviolence (Gielen & Kelly, 1983).

Checkpoint

Can you . . .

✔ List Kohlberg's levels and stages, and discuss factors that influence how rapidly children and adolescents progress through them?

✔ Evaluate Kohlberg's theory with regard to the role of emotion and socialization, family influences, gender, and cultural validity?

Fowler's Stages of Faith

Can spiritual belief be studied from a developmental perspective? Yes, according to James Fowler (1981, 1989). Fowler defined faith as a way of seeing or knowing the world. To find out how people arrive at this way of seeing or knowing, Fowler and his students at Harvard Divinity School interviewed more than 400 people of all ages with various ethnic, educational, and socioeconomic backgrounds and various religious or secular identifications and affiliations.

Faith, according to Fowler, can be religious or nonreligious. People may have faith in a god, in science, in humanity, or in a cause to which they attach ultimate worth and that gives meaning to their lives. Faith develops, said Fowler, as do other aspects of cognition, through interaction between the maturing person and the environment. Fowler's stages correspond roughly to those described by Piaget, Kohlberg, and Erikson. New experiences—crises, problems, or revelations—that challenge or upset a person's equilibrium may prompt a leap from one stage to the next. The ages at which these transitions occur are variable, and some people never leave a particular stage; but the first three stages normally occur during childhood and adolescence.

What's your view 

- Do you agree with Fowler's definition of faith?
- From your experience and observation, can faith be nonreligious?

- *Stage 1: Primal, or intuitive-projective, faith* (ages 18–24 months to 7 years). The beginnings of faith, says Fowler, arise after toddlers become self-aware, begin to use language and symbolic thought, and have developed *basic trust:* the sense that their needs will be met by powerful others. As young children struggle to understand the forces that control their world, they form powerful, imaginative, often terrifying

attention in class and to spend less time on homework (Glasgow et al., 1997). Thus, a sense of helplessness associated with nonauthoritative parenting may become a self-fulfilling prophecy, discouraging students from trying to succeed.

Among some ethnic groups, though, parenting styles may be less important than other factors, such as peer influence, that affect motivation. In one study, Latino and African-American adolescents, even those with authoritative parents, did less well in school than European-American students, apparently because of lack of peer support for academic achievement (Steinberg, Dornbusch, & Brown, 1992). On the other hand, Asian-American students, whose parents are sometimes described as authoritarian, get high grades and score better than European-American students on math achievement tests, apparently because they like math and because both parents *and* peers prize achievement (C. Chen & Stevenson, 1995; refer back to Chapter 13). The strong school achievement of many young people from a variety of immigrant backgrounds reflects their families' and friends' strong emphasis on and support of educational success (Fuligni, 1997).

Peer influence may help explain the downward trend in academic motivation and achievement that begins for many students in early adolescence. In a longitudinal study of students entering an urban middle school after sixth grade, motivation and grades declined, on average, during the seventh-grade year. However, students whose peer group were high achievers showed less decline in achievement and enjoyment of school, while those who associated with low achievers showed greater declines (Ryan, 2001).

Checkpoint

Can you . . .

- ✔ Explain how self-efficacy beliefs can contribute to adolescents' motivation to learn?
- ✔ Assess the influences of parents and peers on academic achievement?
- ✔ Identify ethnic and gender differences in achievement and attitudes toward school?

Gender

Although adolescent boys and girls score about the same in most areas of subject-matter knowledge, girls tend to have greater confidence in their academic abilities. They earn better grades and are more likely to graduate from high school and to attend and finish college. Boys are more likely to be underachievers, to be assigned to special or remedial education, and to be expelled or drop out of school. Yet boys have a slight edge on standardized tests of math and science, probably reflecting their greater confidence and interest in these subjects and their ability to use unconventional problem solving strategies (Eccles et al., 2003).

Teachers often treat boys and girls differently. Boys tend to be disciplined more harshly than girls. On the other hand, high-achieving boys, especially European-American boys, tend to receive more favorable attention from teachers than girls do. Boys are encouraged to take honors courses, to apply to top colleges, and to aim for challenging careers (Eccles et al., 2003).

The Educational System

The modern comprehensive high school came into being in the 1920s, when adolescence was becoming recognized as a separate stage of life, and the institution has changed with the changing needs of that age group and the surrounding society. Before then, secondary education served only an elite few and was organized solely around academic disciplines. As more young people from working-class families entered high school, vocational education (then called "manual training") became an option. After the social turmoil of the 1960s, high schools found themselves serving a more diverse student body in need of greatly expanded social services. Students were given more rights, more choices, and more attention. Then, in the 1980s, a series of governmental commissions concluded that the reforms had gone too far—schools had become like cafeterias, and quality had gone by the boards (Keller, 1999).

Today educators agree that the quality of a school strongly influences student achievement. A good high school has an orderly, unoppressive atmosphere; an active, energetic principal; and teachers who take part in making decisions. Principal and teachers have high expectations for students, emphasize academics more than extracurricular activities, and closely monitor student performance (Linney & Seidman, 1989).

Students who like school do better academically. Adolescents, particularly boys, in most western industrialized countries like school less than younger children. Adolescents are more satisfied with school if they are allowed to participate in making rules and feel support from teachers and other students (Samdal & Dür, 2000).

Schools that tailor teaching to students' abilities get better results than schools that try to teach all students in the same way. Research on Sternberg's triarchic theory of intelligence (refer back to Chapter 13) found that students high in practical or creative intelligence do better when taught in a way that allows them to capitalize on those strengths and compensate for their weaknesses (Sternberg, 1997). Indeed, a combination of teaching styles may be most effective for all students. In an experiment in teaching psychology to gifted eighth graders, groups whose teachers used methods that tap creative and practical abilities as well as analysis and memory did better than groups taught by traditional memory-based or critical thinking approaches alone (Sternberg, Torff, & Grigorenko, 1998).

Innovative approaches to improving student achievement, such as charter schools (refer back to Chapter 13) and alternative schools for at-risk students, have been instituted in recent years. Some big-city school systems, such as New York's, Philadelphia's, and Chicago's, are experimenting with small schools. These schools, which may be either free-standing or located within existing school buildings, are small enough for students, teachers, and parents to form a learning community united by a common vision of good education. The curriculum may have a special focus, such as ethnic studies. Teaching is flexible, innovative, and personalized; teachers work together closely and get to know students well (Meier, 1995; Rossi, 1996). In Central Park East, a complex of four small, ethnically diverse elementary and secondary schools in New York's East Harlem, 90 percent of the students finish high school, and 9 out of 10 of those go on to college, as compared with an average citywide graduation rate of 50 percent (Meier, 1995).

The transition to college, with its higher educational standards and expectations for self-direction, can be a shock. Some educators are bridging this transition with Early College High Schools that integrate secondary education with the first two years of college-level work. These small, personalized, high-quality schools, operated in cooperation with nearby colleges, are intended primarily for low-income and minority students and first-generation English language learners, groups statistically underrepresented in higher education. By combining a nurturing atmosphere with clear, rigorous standards, these schools enable students to complete high school requirements plus the first two years of college ("The Early College High School Initiative," undated).

Dropping Out of High School

Although more U.S. youths are completing high school than ever before, 10.7 percent of U.S. 16- to 24-year-olds in 2001 were out of high school without a diploma or equivalent. This proportion has remained relatively stable since 1992 (NCES, 2003) and has decreased only modestly in the past 30 years—this during a period when high school graduation has become a minimum requirement for labor force entry (Kaufman, Alt, & Chapman, 2001).

Dropout rates are higher among boys (Kaufman et al., 2001) and in certain ethnic groups. Hispanic students are more likely to drop out than African Americans, who are more likely to drop out than non-Hispanic whites (see Figure 16-2). Hispanic immigrants

What's your view?

- How can parents, educators, and societal institutions encourage young people to finish high school?

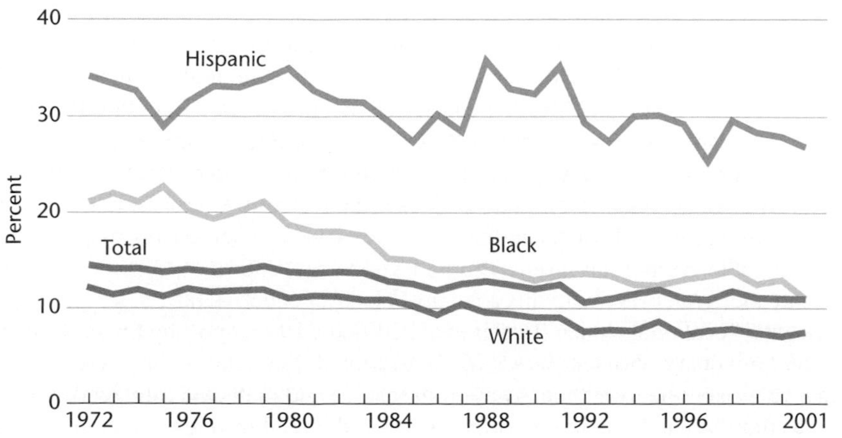

Figure 16-2

Proportion of high school dropouts among 16- to 24-year-olds by race/ethnicity: 1972–2001.

Note: Due to relatively small sample sizes, American Indians or Alaska Natives and Asians or Pacific Islanders are included in the total but not shown separately. The erratic nature of the Hispanic rates reflects, in part, the historically small sample size of Hispanics. Race categories exclude Hispanic origin.

Source: NCES, 2003.

active engagement Involvement in schooling.

have the highest dropout rates, but even Hispanics born in the United States are more likely to drop out than members of the other two groups (NCES, 2003), and low-income students are much more likely to drop out than middle- or high-income students (NCES, 2004). The higher dropout rates among minority groups living in poverty may stem in part from the poor quality of their schools as compared with those attended by more advantaged children. Among other possible reasons for the high Latino dropout rates are language difficulties, financial pressures, and a culture that puts family first, since these students often leave school to help support their families (U.S. Department of Education, 1992).

Society suffers when young people do not finish school. Dropouts are more likely to be unemployed or to have low incomes, to end up on welfare, and to become involved with drugs, crime, and delinquency. In addition, the loss of taxable income burdens the public treasury (NCES, 1999, 2001, 2003, 2004).

Perhaps the most important factor in keeping adolescents in school is **active engagement:** the extent to which the student is actively involved in schooling. On the most basic level, active engagement means coming to class on time, being prepared, listening and responding to the teacher, and obeying school rules. A second level of engagement consists of getting involved with the coursework—asking questions, taking the initiative to seek help when needed, or doing extra projects. Both levels of active engagement tend to pay off in positive school performance (Finn & Rock, 1997). Students who participate in extracurricular activities also are less likely to drop out (Mahoney, 2000; Shanahan & Flaherty, 2001). On the other hand, full-time work is a risk factor for dropping out (Shanahan & Flaherty, 2001).

Checkpoint

Can you . . .

- ✔ Give examples of educational practices that can help high school students succeed?
- ✔ Discuss trends in high school completion, and cite risk factors and protective factors?

What factors promote active engagement? Family encouragement is one. Others may be small class size and a warm, supportive school environment. Since engaged or alienated behavior patterns tend to be set early in a child's school career, dropout prevention should start early, too (Finn & Rock, 1997). Preschool experience—or the lack of it—may set the stage for high school success or failure. In a Chicago longitudinal study, young people who had been in a high-quality early childhood education program were less likely to be held back or to drop out of high school (Temple, Reynolds, & Miedel, 2000).

What factors affect educational and vocational planning and preparation?

Educational and Vocational Preparation

How do young people develop career goals? How do they decide whether to go to college and, if not, how to enter the world of work? Many factors enter in, including individual ability and personality, education, socioeconomic and ethnic background, the advice of school counselors, life experiences, and societal values. Let's look at some influences on educational and vocational aspirations. Then we'll examine provisions for young people who do not plan to go to college. We'll also discuss the pros and cons of outside work for high school students.

Influences on Students' Aspirations

Students' self-efficacy beliefs shape the occupational options they consider and the way they prepare for careers. These beliefs, as we have discussed, are often influenced by parents' beliefs and aspirations (Bandura, Barbaranelli, Caprara, & Pastorelli, 2001; Bandura et al., 1996). Parents' values with regard to academic achievement influence adolescents' values and occupational goals (Jodl, Michael, Malanchuk, Eccles, & Sameroff, 2001). This is especially apparent among children of East Asian immigrant families, who, as we have discussed, strongly value education. Although high school graduates from immigrant families in general are as likely to go on to college as peers from American-born families, the proportion of children of East Asian families who do so (96 percent) is much higher than among some other immigrant groups (Fuligni & Witkow, 2004).

Despite the greater flexibility in career goals today, gender—and gender-stereotyping—may influence vocational choice (Eccles et al., 2003). A 1992 report by the American Association of University Women (AAUW) Educational Foundation claimed that schools shortchange girls by steering them away from science and math and into gender-typed pursuits. In a study by the Foundation, even girls who did well in science and math were less likely than boys to choose careers in those fields. Some researchers suggested that young women drop out of math and science because they lack confidence in their abilities in these areas (Eccles et al., 2003). Six years later, a follow-up study (AAUW Educational Foundation, 1998a, 1998b) reported that girls were taking more science and math than before and doing better in those subjects. Male and female high school seniors are now equally likely to plan careers in math or science, though boys are much more likely to go into engineering and computer science and to get degrees in those fields (NCES, 2001), and girls are still more likely to go into nursing, social welfare professions, and teaching. European-American men and women are more likely than students of other ethnic groups to choose gender-typed occupations (Eccles et al., 2003).

The educational system itself may act as a brake on vocational aspirations. Students who can memorize and analyze tend to do well on intelligence tests and in classrooms where teaching is geared to those abilities. Thus, as predicted by the tests, these students are achievers in a system that stresses the abilities in which they happen to excel. Students whose strength is in creative or practical thinking—areas critical to success in certain fields—never get a chance to show what they can do (Sternberg, 1997). Recognition of a broader range of "intelligences" (see Chapter 9), combined with more flexible teaching and career counseling, could allow more students to get the education and enter the occupations they desire and to make the contributions of which they are capable.

Is this career counselor influenced by the student's gender in advising her about possible career choices? Even though there is little or no overall difference between boys and girls in mathematical or verbal ability, many school counselors still steer young people into gender-typed careers.

Guiding Students Not *Bound for College*

Most industrialized countries offer guidance to non-college-bound students. Germany, for example, has an apprenticeship system in which high school students go to school part-time and spend the rest of the week in paid on-the-job training supervised by an employer-mentor. About 60 percent of German high school students take advantage of this program each year, and 85 percent of those who complete it find jobs (Hopfensperger, 1996).

In the United States, vocational counseling is generally oriented toward college-bound youth. Whatever vocational training programs do exist for the approximately 38 percent of high school graduates who do *not* immediately go on to college (NCES, 2003) tend to be less comprehensive than the German model and less closely tied to the needs of businesses and industries. Most young people must get training on the job or in community college courses. Many, ignorant about the job market, do not obtain the skills they need. Others take jobs beneath their abilities. Some do not find work at all (NRC, 1993a).

In some communities, demonstration programs help in the school-to-work transition. The most successful ones offer instruction in basic skills, counseling, peer support, mentoring, apprenticeship, and job placement (NRC, 1993a). In 1994, Congress passed the School to Work Opportunities Act, which allocated $1.1 billion to help states and local governments develop vocational training programs. In 2000–2001 nearly half of public alternative schools and programs for at-risk youth offered vocational training (NCES, 2003).

What's your view 

- Would you favor an apprenticeship program like Germany's in the United States?
- How successful do you think it would be in helping young people make realistic career plans?
- What negative effects, if any, might it have?

Should High School Students Work Part-Time?

In 2002, of the 12 million U.S. adolescents ages 15 to 17, about 2.4 million were employed, 2.2 million of them part-time (Fields, 2003). Many high school students hold part-time jobs because of financial necessity. Employment while in school fits in with a basic American belief in the benefits of work. However, most high school students who work part-time have low-level, repetitive jobs in which they do *not* learn skills useful later in life. According to some research, teenagers who work are no more independent in making financial decisions and are unlikely to earn any more money as adults than those who do not hold jobs during high school. By assuming adult burdens they are not yet ready to deal with, young people may miss out on the opportunity to explore their interests and to develop close relationships. Outside work may require a student to juggle other commitments and cut down on active involvement in school (Greenberger & Steinberg, 1986). Long hours of work (more than 15 to 20 hours a week) may undermine school performance and increase the likelihood of dropping out (Larson & Verma, 1999; NCES, 1987).

Paid work can have other costs. Young people who work long hours are less likely to eat breakfast, exercise, get enough sleep, or have enough leisure time (Bachman & Schulenberg, 1993). They spend less time with their families and may feel less close to them. Some teenagers take jobs because they are uninterested in school or feel alienated from their families. Some spend their earnings on alcohol or drugs (Greenberger & Steinberg, 1986; Steinberg, Fegley, & Dornbusch, 1993).

Recent research suggests, though, that some of the alleged harmful effects of work may be overstated (Mortimer, 2003). In a four-year longitudinal study of how 1,010 randomly selected ninth graders in the St. Paul, Minnesota, public schools used their time, most of the students who worked were also heavily engaged in school and other activities (Shanahan & Flaherty, 2001). According to students' self-reports, the number of hours a student worked did not seem to reduce self-esteem, mental health, or mastery motivation. Working had no effect on homework time or grades until senior year, when students who worked more than 20 hours a week tended to do less homework than other students. Even so, their grades and achievement motivation did not suffer. And students who worked fewer than 20 hours had *higher* grades than those who did not work at all.

Research does not give a definitive answer as to whether outside work is good or bad for adolescents. For one thing, the data come entirely from self-reports, which are always subjective. Furthermore, these studies addressed only how *much* young people work and not the quality of their work experience. Other studies suggest that such factors as advancement opportunity, the chance to learn useful skills, and the kinds of responsibilities adolescents have at work help determine whether the experience is positive or negative (Call, Mortimer, & Shanahan, 1995; Finch, Shanahan, Mortimer, & Ryu, 1991; Shanahan, Finch, Mortimer, & Ryu, 1991).

Checkpoint

Can you . . .

- ✔ Discuss influences on educational and vocational planning?
- ✔ Give evidence as to the value of part-time work for high school students?

Refocus

- What signs of cognitive maturity did Nelson Mandela show as an adolescent?
- What influences played a part in his moral development? In his education? In his vocational choice?

Vocational planning is one aspect of an adolescent's search for identity. The question "What shall I do?" is very close to "Who shall I be?" People who feel they are doing something worthwhile and doing it well feel good about themselves. Those who feel that their work does not matter—or that they are not good at it—may wonder about the meaning of their lives. A prime personality issue in adolescence, which we will discuss in Chapter 17, is the effort to define the self.

Summary and Key Terms

Aspects of Cognitive Maturation

Guidepost 1 How do adolescents' thinking and use of language differ from younger children's?

- People in Piaget's stage of formal operations can engage in hypothetical-deductive reasoning. They can think in terms of possibilities, deal flexibly with problems, and test hypotheses.
- Since environmental stimulation plays an important part in attaining this stage, not all people become capable of formal operations; and those who are capable do not always use them.
- Piaget's proposed stage of formal operations does not take into account such developments as accumulation of knowledge and expertise, gains in information-processing, and the growth of metacognition. Piaget also paid little attention to individual differences, between-task variations, and the role of the situation.
- Research has found both structural and functional changes in adolescent cognition. Structural changes include increases in declarative, procedural, and conceptual knowledge and expansion of the capacity of working memory. Functional changes

include progress in deductive reasoning. However, emotional immaturity may lead older adolescents to make poorer decisions than younger ones.

- There are no gender differences in most cognitive abilities, but boys are more likely to take intellectual risks and to drive recklessly, whereas girls are more likely to take health risks.
- The superiority of European-American and Asian-American students on standardized tests seems to be attributable mainly to parental education and the student's educational experience.
- Vocabulary and other aspects of language development, especially those related to abstract thought, such as social perspective-taking, improve in adolescence. Adolescents enjoy wordplay and create their own "dialect."
- According to Elkind, immature thought patterns can result from adolescents' inexperience with formal thinking. These thought patterns include idealism and criticalness, argumentativeness, indecisiveness, apparent hypocrisy, self-consciousness, and an assumption of specialness and invulnerability. Research has cast doubt on the special prevalence of the latter two patterns during adolescence.

formal operations (437) **hypothetical-deductive reasoning (438)** **declarative knowledge (440)** **procedural knowledge (440)** **conceptual knowledge (440)** **imaginary audience (443)** **personal fable (443)**

Moral and Spiritual Development

Guidepost 2 On what basis do adolescents make moral judgments, and how does faith develop?

- According to Kohlberg, moral reasoning is based on a developing sense of justice and growing cognitive abilities. Kohlberg proposed that moral development progresses from external control to internalized societal standards to personal, principled moral codes.
- Kohlberg's theory has been criticized on several grounds, including failure to credit the roles of emotion, socialization, and parental guidance. The applicability of Kohlberg's system to women and girls and to people in nonwestern cultures has been questioned.
- According to Fowler's theory of faith development, most adolescents are in the stage of conventional faith, in which they accept established community beliefs.

preconventional morality (444) **conventional morality (or morality of conventional role conformity) (444)** **postconventional morality (or morality of autonomous moral principles) (444)**

Educational and Vocational Issues

Guidepost 3 What influences affect adolescents' school success, and why do some students drop out?

- Self-efficacy beliefs, parental practices, cultural and peer influences, gender, and quality of schooling affect educational motivation and achievement.
- Poor families whose children do well in school tend to have more social capital than poor families whose children do not do well.
- Although most Americans graduate from high school, the dropout rate is higher among poor, Hispanic, and African-American students. Active engagement in studies is an important factor in keeping adolescents in school.

active engagement (454)

Guidepost 4 What factors affect educational and vocational planning and preparation?

- Educational and vocational aspirations are influenced by several factors, including self-efficacy, parental values, and gender stereotypes.
- High school graduates who do not immediately go on to college can benefit from vocational training.
- Part-time work seems to have both positive and negative effects on educational, social, and occupational development.

chapter 17

Psychosocial Development in Adolescence

This face in the mirror
stares at me
demanding Who are you? What will you become?
And taunting, You don't even know.
Chastened, I cringe and agree
and then
because I'm still young,
I stick out my tongue.

—Eve Merriam, "Conversation with Myself," 1964

Focus *Jackie Robinson, Baseball Legend*

Jackie Robinson

On April 15, 1947, when 28-year-old Jack Roosevelt ("Jackie") Robinson (1919–1972) put on a Brooklyn Dodgers uniform and strode onto Ebbets Field, he became the first African American in the 20th century to play major league baseball. By the end of a spectacular first season in which he was named Rookie of the Year, Robinson's name had become a household word. Two years later, he was voted baseball's Most Valuable Player. During his 10 years with the Dodgers, the team won six pennants, and Robinson played in six consecutive All-Star games. After his retirement, he won first-ballot election to the Hall of Fame.

His triumph did not come easily. When the Dodgers' manager, Branch Rickey, decided to bring Robinson up from the Negro Leagues, several players petitioned to keep him off the team. But Robinson's athletic prowess and dignified demeanor in the face of racist jibes, threats, hate mail, and attempts at bodily harm won the respect of the baseball world. Within the next decade, most major league teams signed African-American players. Baseball had become "one of the first institutions in modern society to accept blacks on a relatively equal basis" (Tygiel, 1983).

Behind the Jackie Robinson legend is the story of a prodigiously talented boy growing up in a nation in which opportunities for black youth were extremely limited. His grandfather had been a slave. Jackie's father, a Georgia sharecropper, abandoned his wife and five children when the boy was 6 months old. His mother, Mallie Robinson, was a determined, deeply religious woman who imbued her children with moral strength and pride. Intent on providing them with a good education, she moved her family to Pasadena, California. But Pasadena turned out to be almost as rigidly segregated as the Deep South.

Jackie Robinson lived for sports. He idolized his older brother Mack, who won a silver medal in the 1936 Olympics. By the time Jackie was in junior high school, he was a star in his own right. He also did odd jobs after school.

Still, he had time on his hands. He joined a street gang of poor black, Mexican, and Japanese boys who seethed with "a growing resentment at being deprived of some of the advantages the white kids had" (J. Robinson, 1995, p. 6). The gang's activities—throwing rocks at cars and street lamps, smashing windows, and swiping apples from fruit stands—were serious enough to get them in trouble. But once they were taken to jail at gunpoint

Sources of biographical information about Jackie Robinson are Falkner (1995), Rampersad (1997), J. Robinson (1995), S. Robinson (1996), and Tygiel (1983, 1997).

merely for swimming in the reservoir because they were not allowed entrance to the whites-only municipal pool.

Robinson later reflected that he "might have become a full-fledged juvenile delinquent" had it not been for the influence of two men. One was an auto mechanic, Carl Anderson, who pointed out that "it didn't take guts to follow the crowd, that courage and intelligence lay in being willing to be different" (J. Robinson, 1995, pp. 6–7). The other was a young African-American minister, Karl Downs, who lured Robinson and his friends into church-sponsored athletics, listened to their worries, helped them find jobs, and got them to help build a youth center—"an alternative to hanging out on street corners" (J. Robinson, 1995, p. 8). Later, while in college, Robinson served as a volunteer Sunday school teacher at the church.

• • •

Adolescence is a time of both opportunities and risks. Teenagers are on the threshold of love, of life's work, and of participation in adult society. Yet adolescence is also a time when some young people engage in behavior that closes off their options and limits their possibilities. Today, research is increasingly focusing on how to help young people whose environments are not optimal avoid hazards that can keep them from fulfilling their potential. What saved Jackie Robinson—in addition to the influence of his indomitable, hardworking mother, his older brothers, and his adult mentors—were his talent and his passion for athletics, which ultimately enabled him to channel his drive, energy, audacity, and rebellion against racism in a positive direction.

In Chapter 16 we looked at physical and cognitive factors that contribute to an adolescent's sense of self, such as appearance and school achievement. In this chapter, we turn our attention more directly to the quest for identity. We discuss how adolescents come to terms with their sexuality. We consider how teenagers' burgeoning individuality expresses itself in relationships with parents, siblings, and peers. We examine sources of antisocial behavior and ways of reducing the risks of adolescence so as to make it a time of positive growth and expanding possibilities. Finally, we take a cross-cultural view of late adolescence and the emerging adult.

After you have read and studied this chapter, you should be able to answer each of the Guidepost questions that follow. Look for them again in the margins, where they point to important concepts throughout the chapter. To check your understanding of these Guideposts, review the end-of-chapter summary. Checkpoints located at periodic spots throughout the chapter will help you verify your understanding of what you have read.

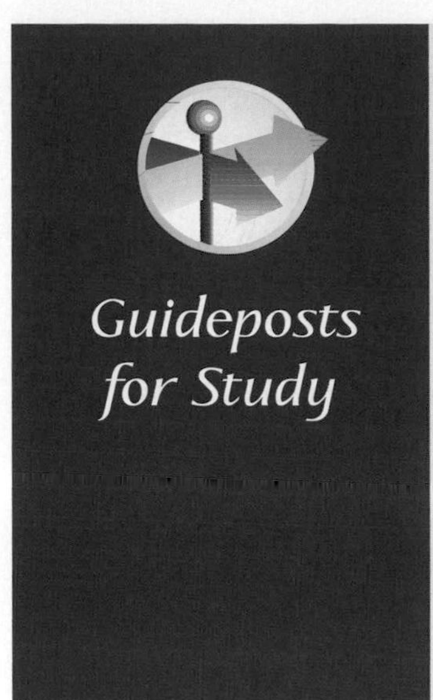

Guideposts for Study

1. How do adolescents form an identity?
2. What determines sexual orientation?
3. What sexual attitudes and practices are common among adolescents, and what leads some to engage in risky sexual behavior?
4. How common is teenage pregnancy, and what are its usual outcomes?
5. How typical is "adolescent rebellion"?
6. How do adolescents relate to parents, siblings, and peers?
7. What are the root causes of antisocial behavior and juvenile delinquency, and what can be done to reduce the risks of adolescence?
8. How do various cultures define what it means to become an adult, and what markers confer that status?

The Search for Identity

Guidepost 1

How do adolescents form an identity?

The search for identity, which Erikson defined as confidence in one's inner continuity amid change, comes into focus during the teenage years. Adolescents' cognitive development now enables them to construct a "theory of the self" (Elkind, 1998). As Erikson (1950) emphasized, a teenager's effort to make sense of the self is not "a kind of maturational malaise." It is part of a healthy, vital process that builds on the achievements of earlier stages—on trust, autonomy, initiative, and industry—and lays the groundwork for coping with the challenges of adult life.

Erikson: Identity Versus Identity Confusion

The chief task of adolescence, said Erikson (1968), is to confront the "crisis" of **identity versus identity confusion** (or *identity versus role confusion*) so as to become a unique adult with a coherent sense of self and a valued role in society. The "identity crisis" is seldom fully resolved in adolescence; issues concerning identity crop up again and again throughout adult life.

identity versus identity confusion Erikson's fifth crisis of psychosocial development, in which an adolescent seeks to develop a coherent sense of self, including the role she or he is to play in society. Also called *identity versus role confusion.*

Erikson's concept of the identity crisis was based on his own life and his research on adolescents in various societies. Growing up in Germany as the out-of-wedlock son of a Jewish woman from Denmark who had separated from her first husband, and not adopted until age 9 by her second husband, a German Jewish pediatrician, Erikson had felt confusion about his identity. He never knew his biological father; he floundered before settling on a vocation; and when he came to the United States, he needed to redefine his identity as an immigrant. All these issues found echoes in the identity crises he observed among disturbed adolescents, soldiers in combat, and members of minority groups (Erikson, 1968, 1973; L. J. Friedman, 1999).

According to Erikson, adolescents form their identity by synthesizing earlier identifications into "a new psychological structure, greater than the sum of its parts" (Kroger, 1993, p. 3)—organizing their abilities, needs, interests, and desires so they can be expressed in a social context. Identity forms as young people resolve three major issues: the choice of an *occupation,* the adoption of *values* to live by, and the development of a satisfying *sexual identity.*

During middle childhood, children acquire skills needed for success in their culture. Now, as adolescents, they need to find ways to use these skills. When young people have trouble settling on an occupational identity—or when their opportunities are artificially

Mastering the challenge of a rope course may help this adolescent boy assess his abilities, interests, and desires. According to Erikson, this process of self-assessment helps adolescents resolve the crisis of identity versus identity confusion.

limited, as they were for Jackie Robinson and his friends—they are at risk of behavior with serious negative consequences, such as criminal activity or early pregnancy.

According to Erikson, the *psychosocial moratorium,* the "time out" period that adolescence provides, allows young people to search for commitments to which they can be faithful. These youthful commitments may shape a person's life for years to come. Jackie Robinson's commitments were to develop his athletic potential and to help improve the position of African Americans in society. By remaining faithful to their commitments, as Robinson did, young people are better able to resolve the identity crisis. Adolescents who resolve that crisis satisfactorily develop the "virtue" of *fidelity:* sustained loyalty, faith, or a sense of belonging to a loved one or to friends and companions. Fidelity also can mean identification with a set of values, an ideology, a religion, a political movement, a creative pursuit, or an ethnic group (Erikson, 1982).

Fidelity is an extension of trust. In infancy, it is important for trust of others to outweigh mistrust; in adolescence, it becomes important to be trustworthy oneself. Adolescents extend their trust to mentors or loved ones. In sharing thoughts and feelings, an adolescent clarifies a tentative identity by seeing it reflected in the eyes of the beloved. However, these adolescent "intimacies" differ from mature intimacy, which involves greater commitment, sacrifice, and compromise.

Erikson saw the prime danger of this stage as identity or role confusion, which can greatly delay reaching psychological adulthood. (He himself did not resolve his own identity crisis until his mid-20s.) Some degree of identity confusion is normal. According to Erikson, it accounts for the seemingly chaotic nature of much adolescent behavior and for teenagers' painful self-consciousness. Cliquishness and intolerance of differences, both hallmarks of the adolescent social scene, are defenses against identity confusion. Adolescents also may show confusion by regressing into childishness to avoid resolving conflicts or by committing themselves impulsively to poorly thought-out courses of action.

Erikson's theory describes male identity development as the norm. According to Erikson, a man is not capable of real intimacy until after he has achieved a stable identity, whereas women define themselves through marriage and motherhood (something that may have been truer when Erikson developed his theory than it is today). Thus, said Erikson, women (unlike men) develop identity *through* intimacy, not before it. As we'll see, this male orientation of Erikson's theory has prompted criticism. Still, Erikson's concept of the identity crisis has inspired much valuable research.

Table 17-1 Identity-Status Interview

Sample Questions	Typical Answers for the Four Statuses
About occupational commitment: "How willing do you think you'd be to give up going into ______ if something better came along?"	*Identity achievement.* "Well, I might, but I doubt it. I can't see what 'something better' would be for me." *Foreclosure.* "Not very willing. It's what I've always wanted to do. The folks are happy with it and so am I." *Moratorium.* "I guess if I knew for sure, I could answer that better. It would have to be something in the general area—something related . . ." *Identity diffusion.* "Oh, sure. If something better came along, I'd change just like that."
About ideological commitment: "Have you ever had any doubts about your religious beliefs?"	*Identity achievement.* "Yes, I started wondering whether there is a God. I've pretty much resolved that now. The way it seems to me is . . ." *Foreclosure.* "No, not really; our family is pretty much in agreement on these things." *Moratorium.* "Yes, I guess I'm going through that now. I just don't see how there can be a God and still so much evil in the world. . . ." *Identity diffusion.* "Oh, I don't know. I guess so. Everyone goes through some sort of stage like that. But it really doesn't bother me much. I figure that one religion is about as good as another!"

Source: Adapted from Marcia, 1966.

Marcia: Identity Status—Crisis and Commitment

Caterina, Andrea, Nick, and Mark are all about to graduate from high school. Caterina has considered her interests and her talents and plans to become an engineer. She has narrowed her college choices to three schools that offer good programs in this field.

Andrea knows exactly what she is going to do with her life. Her mother, a union leader at a plastics factory, has arranged for Andrea to enter an apprenticeship program there. Andrea has never considered doing anything else.

Nick, on the other hand, is agonizing over his future. Should he attend a community college or join the army? He cannot decide what to do now or what he wants to do eventually.

Mark still has no idea what he wants to do, but he is not worried. He figures he can get some sort of a job and make up his mind about the future when he is ready.

These four young people are involved in identity formation. What accounts for the differences in the way they go about it, and how will these differences affect the outcome? According to research by the psychologist James E. Marcia (1966, 1980), these students are in four different **identity statuses,** states of ego (self) development.

Through 30-minute, semistructured *identity-status interviews* (see Table 17-1), Marcia distinguished these four types of identity status: *identity achievement, foreclosure, moratorium,* and *identity diffusion.* The four categories differ according to the presence or absence of **crisis** and **commitment,** the two elements Erikson saw as crucial to forming identity. Marcia defined *crisis* as a period of conscious decision making and *commitment* as a personal investment in an occupation or system of beliefs (ideology). He found relationships between identity status and such characteristics as anxiety, self-esteem, moral reasoning, and patterns of behavior. Building on Marcia's theory, other researchers have identified other personality and family variables related to identity status (see Table 17-2). Here is a more detailed sketch of young people in each identity status:

1. **Identity achievement** (*crisis leading to commitment*). Caterina has resolved her identity crisis. During the crisis period, she devoted much thought and some

identity statuses Marcia's term for states of ego development that depend on the presence or absence of crisis and commitment.

crisis Marcia's term for period of conscious decision making related to identity formation.

commitment Marcia's term for personal investment in an occupation or system of beliefs.

identity achievement Identity status, described by Marcia, that is characterized by commitment to choices made following a crisis, a period spent in exploring alternatives.

Table 17-2	Family and Personality Factors Associated with Adolescents in Four Identity Statuses*			
Factor	**Identity Achievement**	**Foreclosure**	**Moratorium**	**Identity Diffusion**
Family	Parents encourage autonomy and connection with teachers; differences are explored within a context of mutuality.	Parents are overly involved with their children; families avoid expressing differences.	Adolescents are often involved in an ambivalent struggle with parental authority.	Parents are laissez-faire in child-rearing attitudes; are rejecting or not available to children.
Personality	High levels of ego development, moral reasoning, self-certainty, self-esteem, performance under stress, and intimacy.	Highest levels of authoritarianism and stereotypical thinking, obedience to authority, dependent relationships; low level of anxiety.	Most anxious and fearful of success; high levels of ego development, moral reasoning, and self-esteem.	Mixed results, with low levels of ego development, moral reasoning, cognitive complexity, and self-certainty; poor cooperative abilities.

*These associations have emerged from a number of separate studies. Since the studies have all been correlational rather than longitudinal, it is impossible to say that any factor caused placement in any identity status.

Source: Kroger, 1993.

emotional struggle to major issues in her life. She has made choices and expresses strong commitment to them. Her parents have encouraged her to make her own decisions; they have listened to her ideas and given their opinions without pressuring her to adopt them. Caterina is thoughtful but not so introspective as to be unable to act. She has a sense of humor, functions well under stress, is capable of intimate relationships, and holds to her standards while being open to new ideas. Research in a number of cultures has found people in this category to be more mature and more socially competent than people in the other three (Marcia, 1993).

2. **Foreclosure** (*commitment without crisis*). Andrea has made commitments, not as a result of exploring possible choices, but by accepting someone else's plans for her life. She is happy and self-assured, perhaps even smug and self-satisfied, and she becomes dogmatic when her opinions are questioned. She has close family ties, is obedient, and tends to follow a powerful leader, like her mother, who accepts no disagreement.
3. **Moratorium** (*crisis with no commitment yet*). Nick is in crisis, struggling with decisions. He is lively, talkative, self-confident, and scrupulous but also anxious and fearful. He is close to his mother but resists her authority. He wants to have a girlfriend but has not yet developed a close relationship. He will probably come out of his crisis eventually with the ability to make commitments and achieve identity.
4. **Identity diffusion** (*no commitment, no crisis*). Mark has not seriously considered options and has avoided commitments. He is unsure of himself and tends to be uncooperative. His parents do not discuss his future with him; they say it's up to him. People in this category tend to be unhappy and often lonely.

foreclosure Identity status, described by Marcia, in which a person who has not spent time considering alternatives (that is, has not been in crisis) is committed to other people's plans for his or her life.

moratorium Identity status, described by Marcia, in which a person is considering alternatives (in crisis) and seems headed for commitment.

identity diffusion Identity status, described by Marcia, that is characterized by absence of commitment and lack of serious consideration of alternatives.

What's your view 

- Which of Marcia's identity statuses do you think you fit into as an adolescent?
- Has your identity status changed since then? If so, how?

These categorizations may change as young people continue to develop (Marcia, 1979). From late adolescence on, more and more people are in moratorium or achievement: seeking or finding their own identity. Still, many people, even as young adults, remain in foreclosure or diffusion (Kroger, 1993). Furthermore, although people in foreclosure seem to have made final decisions, that is often not so. When middle-aged people look back on their lives, they most commonly trace a path from foreclosure to moratorium to identity achievement (Kroger & Haslett, 1991).

Elkind: The Patchwork Self

As Erikson and Marcia observed, not everyone achieves a strong sense of identity, during or after adolescence. Why is this so?

According to Elkind (1998), there are two paths to identity. The first, and healthiest, is a process of *differentiation* and *integration:* becoming aware of the ways in which one differs from others and then integrating these distinctive parts of oneself into a unified, unique whole. This inner-directed process requires much time and reflection, and when a person has achieved identity in this way, it is almost impossible to break down. The result of this process is similar to Marcia's identity achievement.

The second, initially easier, path is that of *substitution:* replacing one childlike set of ideas and feelings about the self with another by simply adopting other people's attitudes, beliefs, and commitments as one's own. A sense of self built mainly by substitution is what Elkind calls a **patchwork self**—a self stitched together from borrowed, often conflicting, bits and pieces. Young people with patchwork selves tend to have low self-esteem. They find it hard to handle freedom, loss, or failure. They may be anxious, conforming, angry, frightened, or self-punishing. They are highly susceptible to outside influence and highly vulnerable to stress because they have no inner compass, no distinctive sense of direction to guide them. The result of this process is similar to Marcia's concept of foreclosure.

patchwork self In Elkind's terminology, sense of identity constructed by substituting other people's attitudes, beliefs, and commitments for one's own.

Elkind attributes increases in drug abuse, gun violence, risky sexual behavior, and teenage suicide to the growing number of young people who show elements of the patchwork self. Today, says Elkind, many adolescents "have a premature adulthood thrust upon them" (1998, p. 7). They lack the time or opportunity for the psychosocial moratorium Erikson described—the protected "time out" period necessary to build a stable, inner-directed self.

Authoritative parenting can help, according to Elkind. If young people see their parents acting according to firm, deeply held principles, they are more likely to develop firm, deeply held principles of their own. If parents show adolescents effective ways to deal with stress, young people will be less likely to succumb to the pressures that threaten the patchwork self.

Gender Differences in Identity Formation

Much research supports Erikson's view that, for women, identity and intimacy develop together. Rather than view this pattern as a departure from a male norm, however, some researchers see it as pointing to a weakness in Erikson's theory, which, they claim, is based on male-centered western concepts of individuality, autonomy, and competitiveness. According to Carol Gilligan (1982, 1987a, 1987b; L. M. Brown & Gilligan, 1990), the female sense of self develops not so much through achieving a separate identity as through establishing relationships. Girls and women, says Gilligan, judge themselves on their handling of their responsibilities and on their ability to care for others as well as for themselves.

Some developmental scientists question how different the male and female paths to identity really are—especially today—and suggest that individual differences may be more important than gender differences (Archer, 1993; Marcia, 1993). Indeed, Marcia (1993) argues that an ongoing tension between independence and connectedness is at the heart of all of Erikson's psychosocial stages for *both* men and women.

However, the development of self-esteem during adolescence, largely in the context of relationships with same-sex peers, seems to support Gilligan's view. Male self-esteem is linked with striving for individual achievement, whereas female self-esteem depends more on connections with others (Thorne & Michaelieu, 1996).

Some research suggests that adolescent girls have lower self-esteem than adolescent boys (Chubb, Fertman, & Ross, 1997). Highly publicized studies during the early 1990s found that girls' self-confidence and self-esteem stay fairly high until age 11 or 12 and then tend to falter (American Association of University Women [AAUW] Educational Foundation, 1992; L. M. Brown & Gilligan, 1990). However, an analysis of hundreds of studies involving nearly 150,000 respondents concluded that, although boys and men do have higher self-esteem than girls and women, especially in late adolescence, the difference is small. Contrary to the earlier finding, both males and females seemed to gain self-esteem with age (Kling, Hyde, Showers, & Buswell, 1999).

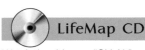

Watch the video on "Girls' Views on Self-Esteem at Age 14" in Chapter 17 of your CD to consider this important aspect of adolescent development.

A still more recent study found that children's and adolescents' perceptions of their competence in math and sports (traditionally viewed as male domains) declined from first through twelfth grades, presumably as young people gained a more realistic idea of their competitive abilities. Although girls tended to have less interest and less confidence in those areas than boys did, the gender gap with regard to perceptions of math competence steadily closed by the senior year in high school. This may reflect the increasing educational emphasis on girls' participation in math (Fredricks & Eccles, 2002; refer back to Chapter 16).

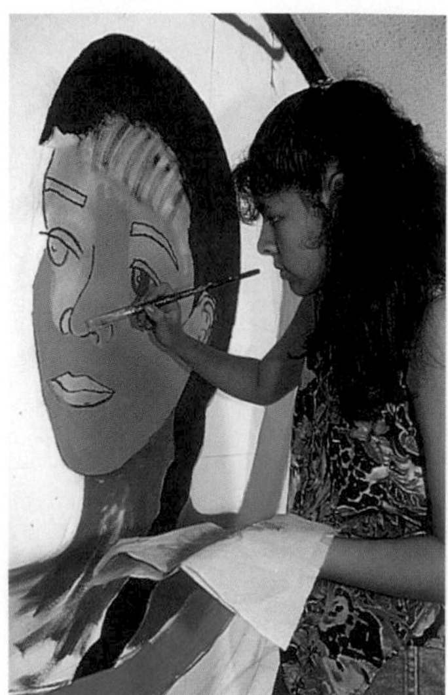

Identity development can be especially complicated for young people from minority groups. Ethnicity may play a central part in their self-concept.

Ethnic Factors in Identity Formation

How is young people's identity affected when the values of their racial or ethnic community conflict with those of the larger society—for example, when American Indians are expected to participate in a tribal ceremony on a day when they are also supposed to be in school? Or when young people face and perhaps internalize prejudice against their own ethnic group? Or when discrimination limits their occupational choices, as it did for Jackie Robinson's brother Mack, who, after his Olympic glory, came home to a succession of menial jobs? All these situations can lead to identity confusion.

Identity formation is especially complicated for young people in minority groups; in fact, for some, race or ethnicity may be central to identity formation. As Erikson (1968) pointed out, an "oppressed and exploited minority" may come to see themselves in the negative way the majority see them (p. 303). Even in a more tolerant society in which minorities have become more assertive, skin color and other physical features, language differences, and stereotyped social standing can be extremely influential in molding minority adolescents' self-concept.

Research dating back to the late 1970s and early 1980s has identified four stages of ethnic identity based on Marcia's identity statuses (Phinney, 1998):

1. *Diffuse:* Juanita has done little or no exploration of her ethnicity and does not clearly understand the issues involved.
2. *Foreclosed:* Kwame has done little or no exploration of his ethnicity but has clear feelings about it. These feelings may be positive or negative, depending on the attitudes he absorbed at home.
3. *Moratorium:* Cho-san has begun to explore her ethnicity but is confused about what it means to her.
4. *Achieved:* Diego has explored his identity and understands and accepts his ethnicity.

On the basis of interviews and questionnaires of 64 U.S.-born African-American, Asian-American, and Hispanic tenth graders in two Los Angeles high schools (Phinney, 1998), researchers assigned the respondents to three identity statuses (see Table 17-3). About half of the sample (33) were *diffuse/foreclosed.* (The researchers combined these two categories—both involving lack of exploration of ethnicity—because they could not clearly distinguish between them on the basis of the young people's responses.) The other half were either in *moratorium* (14) or had apparently *achieved* identity (13).

Members of various ethnic groups found differing issues critical. Hispanic Americans were highly conscious of prejudice against their group. Asian Americans struggled with pressures for academic achievement. African-American girls were keenly aware that they did not meet white standards of beauty, while African-American boys were more concerned about job discrimination and the negative societal image of black males. About one-fifth of the participants (some at each stage) had negative attitudes toward their own ethnic group. However, those in the achieved stage showed better overall adjustment than those in the other groups. They thought more highly of themselves, had a greater sense of mastery, and reported more positive family relationships and social and peer interactions.

Checkpoint

Can you . . .

- ✔ List the three major issues involved in identity formation, according to Erikson?
- ✔ Describe four types of identity status found by Marcia?
- ✔ Describe two paths to identity proposed by Elkind, compare them with Marcia's identity statuses, and explain the link between risky behavior and the patchwork self?
- ✔ Discuss how gender and ethnicity can affect identity formation?

Sexuality

Guidepost 2

What determines sexual orientation?

Seeing oneself as a sexual being, recognizing one's sexual orientation, coming to terms with sexual stirrings, and forming romantic or sexual attachments all are parts of achieving sexual identity. This urgent awareness of sexuality is an important aspect of identity formation, profoundly affecting self-image and relationships. Although this process is biologically driven, its expression is in part culturally defined.

Sexual Orientation

sexual orientation Gender focus of consistent sexual, romantic, and affectionate interest, either heterosexual, homosexual, or bisexual.

Although present in younger children, it is in adolescence that a person's **sexual orientation** generally becomes a pressing issue: whether that person will consistently be

Table 17-3 Representative Quotations from Each Stage of Ethnic Identity Development

Diffusion
"Why do I need to learn about who was the first black woman to do this or that? I'm just not too interested." (Black female)
Foreclosure
"I don't go looking for my culture. I just go by what my parents say and do, and what they tell me to do, the way they are." (Mexican-American male)
Moratorium
"There are a lot of non-Japanese people around and it gets pretty confusing to try and decide who I am." (Asian-American male)
Achieved
"People put me down because I'm Mexican, but I don't care anymore. I can accept myself more." (Mexican-American female)

Source: Phinney, 1998, Table 2, p. 277.

sexually, romantically, and affectionately attracted to persons of the other sex (*heterosexual*), of the same sex (*homosexual*), or of both sexes (*bisexual*).

Homosexuality is common in some cultures, such as the Melanesian Islands in the South Pacific (King, 1996) but not in the United States and other western countries. In one study of 38,000 American students in grades 7 through 12, about 88 percent described themselves as predominantly heterosexual and only 1 percent as predominantly homosexual or bisexual. About 11 percent, mostly younger students, were unsure of their sexual orientation (Remafedi, Resnick, Blum, & Harris, 1992). Social stigma may bias such self-reports, underestimating the prevalence of homosexuality and bisexuality.

Because homosexuality is less common in western societies, research has been focused primarily on efforts to explain it. Although homosexuality once was considered a mental illness, several decades of research have found no association between sexual orientation and emotional or social problems (American Psychological Association, undated; C. J. Patterson, 1992, 1995a, 1995b). These findings eventually led the psychiatric profession to stop classifying homosexuality as a mental disorder.

Other common explanations for homosexuality—all scientifically discredited—point to disturbed relationships with parents, parental encouragement of cross-gender behavior, imitation of homosexual parents, or chance learning through seduction by a homosexual. Many young people have one or more homosexual experiences as they are growing up, usually before age 15. However, isolated experiences or even homosexual attractions or fantasies do not determine sexual orientation.

Sexual orientation seems to be at least partly genetic. An identical twin of a homosexual has about a 50 percent probability of also being homosexual, while a fraternal twin has only about a 20 percent likelihood, and an adopted sibling has 10 percent or less (Gladue, 1994). In a nationally representative survey that included 794 twin pairs, the concordance rate for nonheterosexual orientation among monozygotic ("identical") twins was 31.6 percent, compared with 8.3 percent for dizygotic ("fraternal") twins (Kendler et al., 2000). Differences in neurochemical activity may play a part. A study of homosexual and heterosexual men found a link between strong sexual orientation and differences in glucose metabolism in a part of the hypothalamus—a structure critical to the expression of male sexual behavior—and other areas of the brain (Kinnunen, Moltz, Metz, & Cooper, 2003). An anatomical difference between homosexual and heterosexual men in the hypothalamus has been reported (LeVay, 1991).

Controversy remains as to whether sexual orientation is decisively shaped either before birth or at an early age. There also is dispute as to the relative contributions of biological, psychological, and social influences (Baumrind, 1995; C. J. Patterson, 1995b). These influences may well be "impossible to untangle," and their relative strength may differ among individuals (Baumrind, 1995, p. 132).

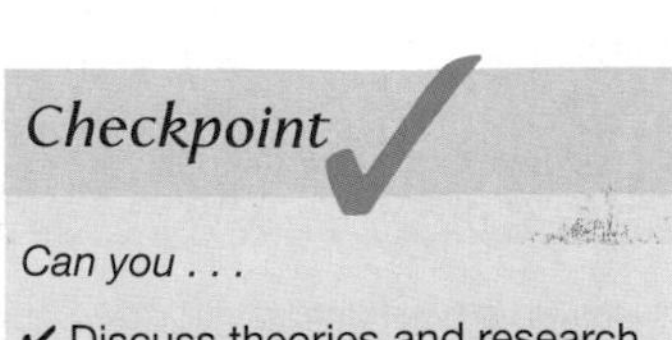

Can you . . .

✔ Discuss theories and research regarding origins of sexual orientation?

What sexual attitudes and practices are common among adolescents, and what leads some to engage in risky sexual behavior?

Sexual Attitudes and Behavior

It is difficult to do research on sexual expression. People willing to answer questions about sex tend to be sexually active and liberal in their attitudes toward sex and thus are not representative of the population. Also, there is often a discrepancy between what people say about sex and what they do, and there is no way to corroborate what people say. Problems multiply in surveying young people. For one thing, parental consent is often required, and parents who grant permission may not be typical. Methodology can make a difference: adolescent boys are more open in reporting certain types of sexual activity when surveys are self-administered by computer (C. F. Turner et al., 1998). Still, even if we cannot generalize findings to the population as a whole, within the groups that take part in surveys we can see trends that reveal changes in sexual mores.

During the 20th century the United States and other industrialized countries underwent an evolution in sexual attitudes and behavior, bringing more widespread acceptance of homosexuality and homosexual behavior, premarital sex, and other forms of sexual activity. With the advent of the Internet, casual sex with fleeting cyber-acquaintances who "hook up" through online chat rooms or singles' meeting sites has become commonplace. Cell phones, e-mail, and instant messaging make it easy for lone adolescents to arrange these hookups with disembodied strangers, insulated from adult scrutiny. All of these changes have brought increased concerns about sexual risk taking.

Homosexual Identity and Behavior

Although the "sexual evolution" has brought more acceptance of homosexuality than in the past, teenagers who openly identify as gay or lesbian or bisexual often feel isolated in a hostile environment. They may be subject to discrimination and even violence. They may be reluctant to disclose their sexual orientation, even to their parents, for fear of strong disapproval or a rupture in the family (Hillier, 2002; C. J. Patterson, 1995b). As a result, for sexual minorities the recognition and expression of sexual identity is more complex and follows a less defined timetable than for heterosexuals.

A widely proposed model for the development of gay or lesbian sexual identity goes something like this: (1) awareness of same-sex attraction (beginning at ages 8 to 11); (2) same-sex sexual behaviors (ages 12 to 15); (3) identification as gay or lesbian (ages 15 to 18); (4) disclosure to others (ages 17 to 19); and (5) development of same-sex romantic relationships (ages 18 to 20). However, this model may not accurately reflect the experience of younger gay men, many of whom feel freer than in the past to openly declare their sexual orientation; of lesbian and bisexual women, whose sexual identity development may be slower and more flexible than that of homosexual men; and of ethnic minorities, whose traditional communities and cultures may espouse strong religious beliefs or sterotypical gender roles, leading to internal and family conflict (Diamond, 1998, 2000; Dubé & Savin-Williams, 1999).

Although sexual orientation may be shaped before birth or very early in life, it is in adolescence that it becomes a pressing issue. Here, a Massachusetts high school girl who "came out" as a lesbian sits in front of a banner for a student support group.

In interviews and questionnaires, 139 young males ages 16 to 26—white, African American, Latino, and Asian American—explored what it meant to them to grow up gay or bisexual. About half felt that they had fully accepted their sexual identities, and most had become sexually and romantically involved with other men. Latino youths reported earlier awareness of same-sex attractions than the other groups, perhaps because, in a culture with rigid gender roles, boys who do not fit the male norm become aware of their "differentness" early. The first reported male-to-male sexual encounters among Asian-American youths took place about three years later than for the other young men. This pattern of delayed sexual activity, which has been found among Asian-American heterosexuals, may reflect strong cultural pressures to save sex for marriage or adulthood and then to have children who will carry on the family name (Dubé & Savin-Williams, 1999).

In Australia, where homosexuality is still strongly taboo, researchers surveyed 748 gays and lesbians, ages 14 through 21 (Hillier, 2002). Of those who had disclosed their sexuality, most had confided first in friends, who tended to be more supportive than parents. At the time of the study, only 28 percent of the respondents had "come out" to their mothers and 16 percent to their fathers. The reactions ranged from passive acceptance to "tears, screaming, and ejection of the child from the family home" (p. 84). Some parents came to terms with the situation after talking with health professionals or joining self-help groups. The children responded better when the parents were able to listen, speak honestly, and avoid black-or-white thinking.

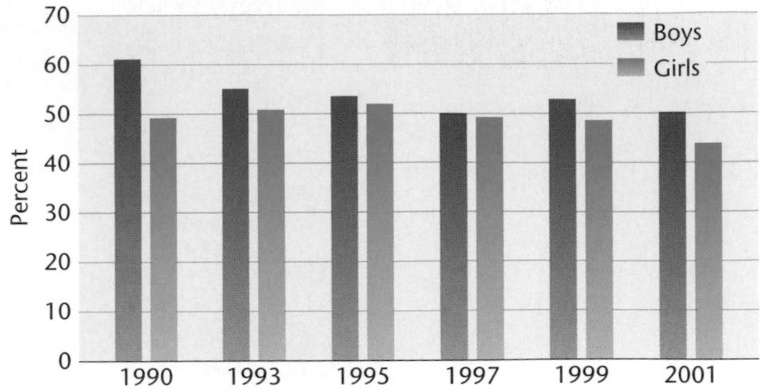

Figure 17-1

Percentage of high school students who have ever had sexual intercourse.

Source: Bernstein, 2004.

Sexual Risk Taking

Two major concerns about adolescent sexual activity are the risks of contracting sexually transmitted diseases (refer back to Chapter 15) and, for heterosexuals, of pregnancy (discussed later in this chapter). Nearly nine out of ten 15- to 17-year-olds in a nationally representative survey sponsored by the Kaiser Family Foundation said they were personally "very" or "somewhat" concerned about these risks (Kaiser Family Foundation, Hoff, Green, & Davis, 2003).

As young people became more widely aware of the risks of sexual activity, the prevalence of intercourse among high school students declined from 54.1 percent in 1991 to 45.6 percent in 2001. Although boys are more likely than girls to report having sexual intercourse (Brener et al., 2002), the difference between the genders has narrowed (see Figure 17-1). The percentage of students who have had intercourse increases with age: from 34.4 percent of ninth graders to 60.5 percent of twelfth graders (Brener et al., 2002).

Noncoital forms of genital sexual activity, such as oral and anal sex and mutual masturbation, are common and may begin in early adolescence. Many heterosexual young people do not regard these activities as "sex" but as substitutes for, or precursors of, sex. Some even define them as abstinence (Remez, 2000). In the Kaiser survey, more than one-third of 15- to 17-year-olds report having had oral sex—about 40 percent of the boys and more than 30 percent of the girls (Kaiser Family Foundation et al., 2003). Even middle school girls say they have been pressed into fellatio with the argument that "it's not really sex" (Remez, 2000). These statistics are disturbing because, contrary to what many adolescents believe, oral and anal sex involve risks of sexually transmitted disease (Remez, 2000).

Most at risk are young people who start sexual activity early, have multiple partners, do not use contraceptives regularly, and have inadequate information—or misinformation—about sex. The younger a girl is when becoming sexually active, the less likely she is to use contraception at first intercourse (Abma et al., 1997). Although the proportion of high school students reporting four or more sex partners during their lifetime decreased 24 percent between 1991 and 2001, 14.2 percent still fall in that category (Brener et al., 2002), and many of these young people do not use reliable protection (AAP Committee on Adolescence, 1999). Other risk factors are living in a socioeconomically disadvantaged community, substance use, antisocial behavior, and association with deviant peers. Parental monitoring can help reduce these risks (Baumer & South, 2001; Capaldi, Stoolmiller, Clark, & Owen, 2002).

Is it possible to predict which young people are likely to become sexual risk takers? In a multiethnic sample of 443 twelve- and thirteen-year-olds, those who were better able to regulate their emotions and behavior were less likely to engage in risky sexual behavior four years later. Self-regulation did *not* affect the age at which they began sexual activity or how often they engaged in it: but it did predict whether they would limit the number of their sexual partners and take precautions such as condom use (Raffaelli & Crockett, 2003).

Table 17-4 Some Factors Associated with Timing of First Intercourse

	Factors Associated with Early Age	Factors Associated with Later Age
Timing of puberty	Early	Late
Personality style and behavior	Risk taking, impulsive	Traditional values, religious orientation
	Depressive symptoms Antisocial or delinquent behavior	Prosocial or conventional behavior
Substance use	Use of drugs, alcohol, tobacco	Nonuse of drugs, alcohol, tobacco
Education	Fewer years of schooling	More years of schooling; valuing academic achievement
Family structure	Single-parent family	Two-parent family
Socioeconomic status	Disadvantaged	Advantaged
Race	African American	White, Latino, Asian American

Source: Dubé & Savin-Williams, 1999; B. C. Miller & Moore, 1990; Sorenstein, Pleck, & Ku, 1991.

Early Sexual Activity

Internationally, there are wide variations in timing of sexual initiation. The percentage of women who report having first intercourse by age 17 is 10 times greater in Mali (72 percent) than in Thailand (7 percent) or the Philippines (6 percent). Similar differences exist for men. Although earlier male initiation is the norm in most cultures, in Mali and Ghana more women than men become sexually active at an early age (Singh et al., 2000).

The average girl in the United States has her first sexual intercourse at 17, only one year later than the average boy (Alan Guttmacher Institute [AGI], 1999a; American Academy of Pediatrics [AAP] Committee on Adolescence, 1999; Singh, Wulf, Samara, & Cuca, 2000). Boys are more likely than girls to have their first intercourse before 13 (CDC, 2002). African Americans and Latinos tend to begin sexual activity earlier than white youth (Kaiser Family Foundation et al., 2003).

Why do some adolescents become sexually active at an early age? Various factors, including early entrance into puberty, poverty, poor school performance, lack of academic and career goals, a history of sexual abuse or parental neglect, and cultural or family patterns of early sexual experience, may play a part (AAP Committee on Adolescence, 1999; see Table 17-4). The absence of a father, especially early in life, is a strong risk factor (Ellis et al., 2003).

One of the most powerful influences is perception of peer group norms (Kinsman, Romer, Furstenberg, & Schwarz, 1998). Young people often feel under pressure to engage in activities they do not feel ready for. In the Kaiser report, nearly one-third of 15- to 17-year-olds, especially boys, said they had experienced pressure to have sex. Sixty-three percent of 15- to 17-year-olds and 53 percent of 13- and 14-year-olds agreed that "waiting to have sex is a nice idea but nobody really does" (Kaiser Family Foundation et al., 2003; see Table 17-5).

A special risk for girls is sexual violence or abuse. In some studies, 7 of 10 women whose first intercourse took place before age 13 reported that it was unwanted or not voluntary (AGI, 1999a). In a nationally representative sample of high school girls, nearly 1 in 10 reported having been victims of dating violence. These girls also tended to be involved in other forms of violence, to report extreme sadness or attempted suicide, to use illegal drugs, and to engage in risky sexual behavior (Wang, 2003).

The connection between self-esteem and early sexual activity works in opposite ways for boys as for girls. In a longitudinal study of 188 Minneapolis-area seventh graders who reported being virgins, boys with high self-esteem were 2½ times more likely than other boys to have sex by ninth grade, whereas girls with high self-esteem were three times more likely to report still being virgins (Spencer, Zimet, Aalsma, & Orr, 2002).

Table 17-5 Adolescents' Attitudes about Sexual Activity

Percent of 15- to 17-Year-Olds Who Say They "Strongly" or "Somewhat" Agree with Each of the Following

	Male	**Female**	**Sexually Active**	**Not Sexually Active**
Waiting to have sex is a nice idea but nobody really does.	66%	60%	69%	59%
There is pressure to have sex by a certain age.	59%	58%	58%	59%
Once you have had sex it is harder to say no the next time.	56%	47%	54%	50%
If you have been seeing someone for a while it is expected that you will have sex.	50%	27%	52%	31%
Oral sex is not as big of a deal as sexual intercourse.	54%	38%	52%	42%

Source: Adapted from Kaiser Family Foundation et al., 2003, Table 8, p. 12, and Table 33, p. 39.

Use of Contraceptives

According to the Kaiser report, 9 out of 10 sexually active adolescents say they use contraception at least most of the time, but only 7 out of 10 use it all of the time. Girls are more likely than boys to use protection consistently (Kaiser Family Foundation et al., 2003). A sexually active girl who does *not* use contraceptives has a 90 percent chance of becoming pregnant within a year (AGI, 1999a). Teenagers who, in their first sexual relationship, delay intercourse, discuss contraception before having sex, or use more than one method of contraception are more likely to use contraceptives consistently throughout that relationship (Manlove, Ryan, & Franzetta, 2003).

The best safeguard for sexually active teens is regular use of condoms, which gives some protection against STDs as well as against pregnancy. Condom use has increased in recent years, probably due to educational campaigns (AAP Committee on Adolescence, 2001; Abma & Sonenstein, 2001; Brener et al., 2002; see Figure 17-2). Still, only 57.9 percent of high school students report having used condoms the last time they had intercourse (Brener et al., 2002). There is *no* evidence that education about condom use and availability contributes to increased sexual activity (AAP Committee on Adolescence, 2001; Blake et al., 2003).

In the Kaiser report, 8 out of 10 adolescents said they use condoms regularly, 3 out of 10 regularly use birth control pills, 13 percent practice withdrawal, and 2 percent rely on the rhythm method. Although most young people realize that sex without condoms can be risky, 10 percent agreed that "It's not that big of a deal to have sex without a condom once in a while," and 7 percent considered condom use unnecessary "unless you have a lot of sexual partners." Many respondents showed confusion or misinformation about the efficacy of contraceptives. Twenty percent mistakenly thought condoms to be "not effective" in preventing transmission of HIV/AIDS and other STDs, while 30 percent wrongly thought birth control pills to be effective in this regard. Obstacles to condom use included the discomfort associated with talking about them and buying them; about half of the adolescents said that if a partner suggested using a condom, they would be suspicious about the partner's sexual history or would think the partner was suspicious about theirs. Only about half of these teenagers knew about the availability of contraceptive methods that can be used after unprotected sex (Kaiser Family Foundation et al., 2003).

Figure 17-2

Percentage of high school students who report using a condom the last time they had sexual intercourse, by gender and race/ethnicity.

Source: Bernstein, 2004.

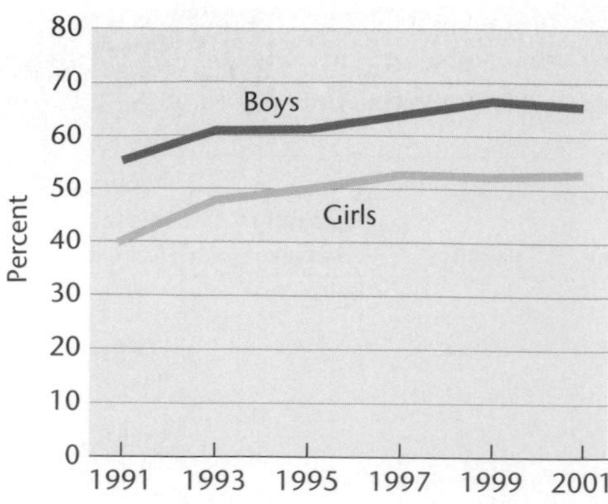

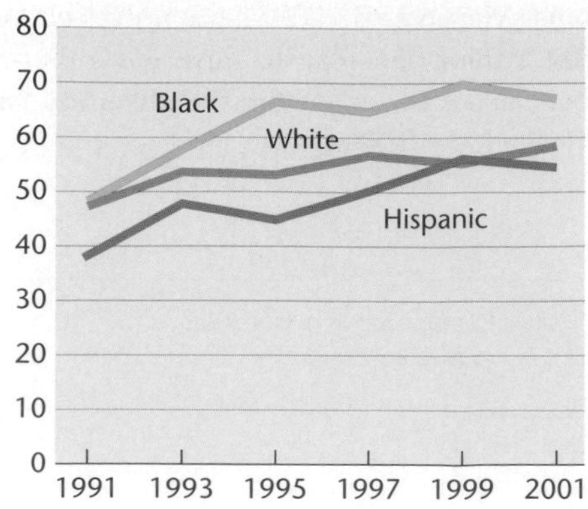

Where Do Teenagers Get Information About Sex?

Adolescents get their information about sex primarily from friends, parents, sex education in school, and the media. At least seven out of ten 15- to 17-year-olds say they have learned "some" or "a lot" from each of these four sources (Kaiser Family Foundation et al., 2003).

Adolescents whose parents have talked with them about sex from an early age, have communicated healthy attitudes, and have been available to answer questions tend to wait longer for sex (J. J. Conger, 1988; Jaslow, 1982). Adolescents who can talk about sex with older siblings as well as with parents are more likely to have positive attitudes toward safe sexual practices (Kowal & Pike, 2004).

Unfortunately, many teenagers get much of their "sex education" from the media, which present a distorted view of sexual activity, associating it with fun, excitement, competition, danger, or violence and rarely showing the risks of unprotected sex (AAP Committee on Communications, 1995; Princeton Survey Research Associates, 1996). Studies suggest a link between media influence and early sexual activity (Peterson, Moore, & Furstenberg, 1991; Strasburger & Donnerstein, 1999).

Since 1998, federally and state-funded sex education programs stressing abstinence from sex until marriage as the best or only option have become common. Many of these new programs offer a rounded approach, helping young people build healthy relationships, self-esteem, and decision-making skills and aspire to marriage and parenthood (Devaney, Johnson, Maynard, & Trenholm, 2002). Programs that encourage abstinence but also discuss HIV prevention and safer sexual practices for the sexually active have been found to delay sexual initiation and increase contraceptive use (AAP Committee on Psychosocial Aspects of Child and Family Health and Committee on Adolescence, 2001).

However, some school districts promote abstinence as the *only* option (Landry, Kaeser, & Richards, 1999), even though abstinence-only courses have *not* been shown to delay sexual activity (AAP Committee on Psychosocial Aspects of Child and Family Health and Committee on Adolescence, 2001; Satcher, 2001). Furthermore, abstinence programs do not always clearly define what abstinence means—whether it covers oral sex and other noncoital activity (Remez, 2000). After an extensive review of the research, Surgeon General David Satcher (2001) urged communities to provide thorough and medically accurate sex education.

Checkpoint

Can you . . .

- ✔ Describe trends in sexual activity among adolescents?
- ✔ Discuss homosexual identity and relationship formation?
- ✔ Identify factors that increase the risks of sexual activity?

Guidepost 4

How common is teenage pregnancy, and what are its usual outcomes?

Teenage Pregnancy and Childbearing

A dramatic drop in teenage birthrates has accompanied the steady decreases in early intercourse and in sex with multiple partners as well as increases in condom use. Birthrates for U.S. 15- to 19-year-olds fell 30 percent between 1991 and 2002 to a record low of 43 births per 1,000 women. Birth rates for unmarried teenagers, who bear about 80 percent of all babies born to adolescent mothers, have declined since 1994, especially among younger teens (Martin et al., 2003). More than half of pregnant teenagers have their babies and plan to raise them themselves. Some miscarry or abort, and a few place their infants for adoption (AAP Committee on Adolescence, 1999; Adler, Ozer, & Tschann, 2003; AGI, 1994, 1999a; Children's Defense Fund, 1998).

Although declines in teenage childbearing have occurred among all population groups, birthrates have fallen most sharply among black teenagers. Still, black and Hispanic girls are more likely to have babies than white, American-Indian, or Asian-American girls (Martin et al., 2003). And U.S. teens are more likely to become pregnant and give birth than teenagers in other western countries (see Figure 17-3 and Box 17-1).

Many of these girls are inexperienced: 50 percent had their first intercourse within the past six months (AGI, 1994; Children's Defense Fund, 1998; Ventura, Mathews, & Curtin, 1999). Many grew up without a father (Ellis et al., 2003). Some were coerced into sexual relations or sexually abused: about 1 in 5 infants born to unmarried minor girls have fathers at least five years older than the mother (AGI, 1999a). Among 9,159 women at a California primary care clinic, those who had become pregnant in adolescence were likely, as children, to have been physically, emotionally, or sexually abused and/or exposed to parental divorce or separation, domestic violence, substance abuse, or a household member who was mentally ill or engaged in criminal behavior (Hillis et al., 2004).

IT'S LIKE BEING GROUNDED FOR EIGHTEEN YEARS.
Having a baby when you're a teenager can do more than just take away your freedom, it can take away your dreams.
THE CHILDREN'S DEFENSE FUND

To teenagers, one of the most persuasive arguments against sexual risk taking is the danger that pregnancy will ruin their lives. Teenage girls respond better when the advice comes from other girls close to their own age.

Teenage pregnancies often have poor outcomes. Many of the mothers are impoverished and poorly educated, and some are drug users. Many do not eat properly, do not gain enough weight, and get inadequate prenatal care or none at all. Their babies are likely to be premature or dangerously small and are at heightened risk of neonatal death, health problems, and developmental disabilities that may continue into adolescence (AAP Committee on Adolescence, 1999; AAP Committee on Adolescence and Committee on Early Childhood, Adoption, and Dependent Care, 2001; AGI, 1999a; Children's Defense Fund, 1998).

Babies of more affluent teenage mothers may also be at risk. Among more than 134,000 white, largely middle-class girls and women, 13- to 19-year-olds were more likely than 20- to 24-year-olds to have low-birth-weight babies, even when the mothers were married and well educated and had adequate prenatal care. Prenatal care apparently cannot always overcome the biological disadvantage inherent in being born to a still-growing girl whose own body may be competing for vital nutrients with the developing fetus (Fraser et al., 1995).

Teenage unwed mothers and their families are likely to suffer financial hardship. Child support laws are spottily enforced, court-ordered payments are often inadequate, and many young fathers cannot afford them (AAP Committee on Adolescence, 1999). In the past, many teenage mothers went on public assistance, but under the 1996 federal welfare reform law such assistance is severely limited. Unmarried parents under age 18 are now eligible only if they live with their parents and go to school.

Teenage mothers are likely to drop out of school and to have repeated pregnancies. They and their partners may lack the maturity, skills, and social support to be good parents. Their children, in turn, are likely to drop out of school, to be depressed, to get in trouble with the law, and to become adolescent parents themselves (AAP Committee on Adolescence and Committee on Early Childhood, Adoption, and Dependent Care, 2001). However, these outcomes are far from inevitable. In a 20-year study of more than 400 teenage mothers in Baltimore, two-thirds of the daughters did *not* become teenage mothers themselves, and most graduated from high school (Furstenberg, Levine, & Brooks-Gunn, 1990).

Checkpoint

Can you . . .

- ✔ Summarize trends in teenage birthrates?
- ✔ Cite ways to prevent teenage pregnancy?
- ✔ Discuss risk factors, problems, and outcomes connected with teenage pregnancy?

Around the World

Box 17-1 *Preventing Teenage Pregnancy*

Although teenage pregnancy and birthrates in the United States have dropped dramatically since the early 1990s, they remain many times higher than those in other industrialized countries, where adolescents begin sexual activity at least as early (Darroch, Singh, Frost, & the Study Team, 2001). Teenage birth rates in recent years have been nearly five times higher in the United States than in Denmark, Finland, France, Germany, Italy, the Netherlands, Spain, Sweden, and Switzerland and 12 times higher than in Japan (Ventura, Mathews, & Hamilton, 2001). Twenty-two percent of American girls have had children before age 20, as compared with 15 percent of British girls, 11 percent of Canadian girls, 6 percent of French girls, and 4 percent of Swedish girls (Darroch et al., 2001).

Why are U.S. rates so high? Some observers point to the reduced stigma on unwed motherhood, media glorification of sex, the lack of a clear message that sex and parenthood are for adults, the influence of childhood sexual abuse, and failure of parents to communicate with children. Comparisons with the European experience suggest the importance of two other factors: U.S. girls are more likely to have multiple sex partners and less likely to use contraceptives (Darroch et al., 2001).

Europe's industrialized countries have provided universal, comprehensive sex education for a much longer time than the United States. Comprehensive programs encourage teenagers to delay intercourse but also encourage effective contraceptive use among sexually active adolescents. Students learn about sexuality and acquire skills for making responsible sexual decisions and communicating with partners. They learn about the risks and consequences of teenage pregnancy, about birth control methods, and about where to get medical and contraceptive help (AAP Committee on Psychosocial Aspects of Child and Family Health and Committee on Adolescence, 2001; AGI, 1994; Kirby, 1997; I. C. Stewart, 1994). Programs aimed at adolescent boys emphasize the wisdom of delaying fatherhood and the need to take responsibility when it occurs (Children's Defense Fund, 1998).

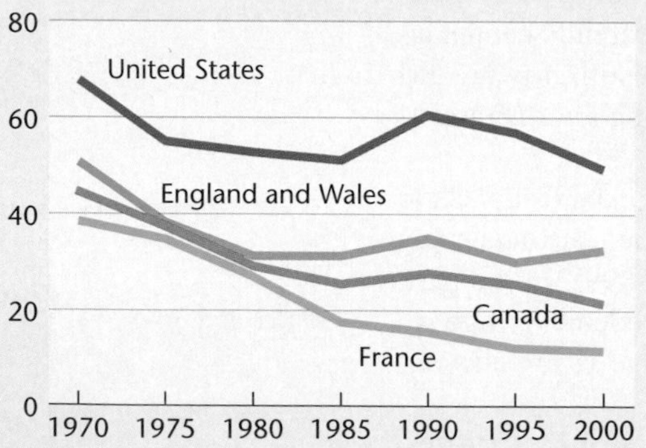

Figure 17-3

Trends in teenage birth rates per 1,000 girls ages 15 to 19 in selected western countries. The U.S. teenage birth rate has fallen since 1990, but it remains significantly higher than in England and Wales, Canada, and France.

Source: Bernstein, 2004.
© The New York Times Graphics.

In the United States the provision and content of sex education programs is a political issue. Increasingly, as mentioned in this chapter, school-based programs stress abstinence only. Critics of comprehensive sex education claim that it leads to more or earlier sexual activity, even though evidence shows otherwise (AAP Committee on Adolescence, 2001; Children's Defense Fund, 1998; Eisen & Zellman, 1987; Satcher, 2001).

An important component of pregnancy prevention in European countries is access to reproductive services, including free contraceptives. Sweden showed a fivefold reduction in the teenage birthrate following introduction of birth control education, free access to contraceptives, and free abortion on demand (Bracher & Santow, 1999).

The problem of teenage pregnancy requires a multifaceted solution. It must include programs and policies to encourage postponing or refraining from sexual activity, but it also must recognize that many young people do become sexually active and need information to prevent pregnancy and infection (AGI, 1999b). Ultimately, it requires attention to underlying factors that put teenagers and families at risk: reducing poverty, school failure, and behavioral and family problems and expanding employment, skills training, and family life education (AGI, 1994; Children's Defense Fund, 1998; Kirby, 1997). Comprehensive early intervention programs for preschoolers and elementary school students have reduced teenage pregnancy (Lonczak et al., 2002; Hawkins et al., 1999; Schweinhart, Barnes, & Weikart, 1993).

Because adolescents with high aspirations are less likely to become pregnant, programs that motivate young people to achieve and raise their self-esteem have had some success. Teen Outreach Program (TOP), which began in 1978, helps teenagers make decisions, handle emotions, and deal with peers and adults. The program also includes community service. By encouraging students to select a volunteer activity, the program helps them see themselves as autonomous and competent. Among 1,600 students in TOP and 1,600 in a control group, TOP participants had about half the risk of pregnancy or school suspension and 60 percent of the risk of failure of nonparticipants (Allen & Philliber, 2001). This is evidence that teenage pregnancy and school failure are not isolated problems but are part of a larger developmental picture.

What's your view?

- If you were designing a school-based or community-based sexuality education program, what would you include?
- Do you favor or oppose programs that provide contraceptives to teenagers?

Check it out!

For more information on this topic, go to **http://www.plannedparenthood.org/TEENISSUES/BCCHOICES/BCCHOICES.HTML**. This site, called Birth Control Choices for Teens, is located at the Planned Parenthood Web site. Or visit **http://www.teenpregnancy.org**. This is the Web site of the National Campaign to Prevent Teen Pregnancy.

Relationships with Family, Peers, and Adult Society

Guidepost 5

How typical is "adolescent rebellion"?

Age becomes a powerful bonding agent in adolescence. Adolescents spend more time with peers and less with family. However, most teenagers' fundamental values (like Jackie Robinson's) remain closer to their parents' than is generally realized (Offer & Church, 1991). Even as adolescents turn to peers for role models, companionship, and intimacy, they—much like toddlers beginning to explore a wider world—look to parents for a "secure base" from which they can try their wings. The most secure adolescents have strong, supportive relationships with parents who are attuned to the way the young people see themselves, permit and encourage their strivings for independence, and provide a safe haven in times of emotional stress (Allen et al., 2003; Laursen, 1996).

Is Adolescent Rebellion a Myth?

The teenage years have been called a time of **adolescent rebellion,** involving emotional turmoil, conflict within the family, alienation from adult society, reckless behavior, and rejection of adult values. Yet school-based research on adolescents the world over suggests that only about 1 in 5 teenagers fits this pattern (Offer & Schonert-Reichl, 1992).

adolescent rebellion Pattern of emotional turmoil, characteristic of a minority of adolescents, that may involve conflict with family, alienation from adult society, reckless behavior, and rejection of adult values.

The idea of adolescent rebellion may have been born in the first formal theory of adolescence, that of the psychologist G. Stanley Hall. Hall (1904/1916) believed that young people's efforts to adjust to their changing bodies and to the imminent demands of adulthood usher in a period of "storm and stress" that produces conflict between the generations. Sigmund Freud (1935/1953) and his daughter Anna Freud (1946) described "storm and stress" as universal and inevitable, growing out of a resurgence of early sexual drives toward the parents.

What's your view

- Can you think of values you hold that are different from those of your parents? How did you develop these values?

However, the anthropologist Margaret Mead (1928, 1935; see Chapter 2 Focus), who studied growing up in Samoa and other South Pacific islands, concluded that when a culture provides a gradual, serene transition from childhood to adulthood, "storm and stress" is not typical. Although her research in Samoa was later challenged (Freeman, 1983), this observation was eventually supported by research in 186 preindustrial societies (Schlegel & Barry, 1991).

Full-fledged rebellion now appears to be relatively uncommon even in western societies, at least among middle-class adolescents who are in school. Although adolescents may defy parental authority with some regularity, the emotions attending this transition do not normally lead to family conflict of major proportions or to a sharp break with parental or societal standards (Arnett, 1999; Offer & Church, 1991; Offer et al., 1989). Most young people feel close to and positive about their parents, share similar opinions on major issues, and value their parents' approval (J. P. Hill, 1987; Offer et al., 1989; Offer, Ostrov, Howard, & Atkinson, 1988). Furthermore, contrary to a popular belief, apparently well-adjusted adolescents are not "ticking time bombs" set to "explode" in later life. In a 34-year longitudinal study of 67 fourteen-year-old suburban boys, the vast majority adapted well to their life experiences (Offer, Offer, & Ostrov, 2004). The relatively few deeply troubled adolescents tended to come from disrupted families and, as adults, continued to have unstable family lives and to reject cultural norms. Those raised in intact two-parent homes with positive family atmosphere tended to sail through adolescence with no serious problems and, as adults, to have solid marriages and lead well-adjusted lives (Offer, Kaiz, Ostrov, & Albert, 2002).

LifeMap CD

Are the teen years really more stressful than other phases of life? For an expert's perspective on this question, watch the "Myth of Adolescence as a Time of Storm & Stress" video in Chapter 17 of your CD.

Still, adolescence can be a tough time for young people and their parents. Family conflict, depression, and risky behavior are more common than during other parts of the life span (Arnett, 1999; Petersen et al., 1993). Many adolescents feel self-conscious, embarrassed, awkward, lonely, nervous, or ignored (Larson & Richards, 1994), and most take occasional risks (Arnett, 1999). Negative emotionality and mood swings are most intense during early adolescence, perhaps due to the stress connected with puberty. By late adolescence, emotionality tends to become more stable (Larson, Moneta, Richards, & Wilson, 2002).

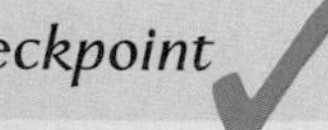

Checkpoint

Can you . . .

✔ Assess the extent of "storm and stress" during the teenage years?

Recognizing that adolescence may be a difficult time can help parents and teachers put trying behavior in perspective. But adults who assume that adolescent turmoil is normal and necessary may fail to heed the signals of the relatively few young persons who need special help.

Guidepost 6

How do adolescents relate to parents, siblings, and peers?

Changing Time Use and Changing Relationships

One way to assess changes in adolescents' relationships with the important people in their lives is to see how they spend their discretionary time. The amount of time U.S. adolescents spend with families declines dramatically between ages 10 and 18, from 35 percent to 14 percent of waking hours. This finding emerged from sequential research with 220 white middle- and working-class adolescents, who carried beepers and reported what they were doing each time the beepers sounded (Larson, Richards, Moneta, Holmbeck, & Duckett, 1996).

Disengagement is not a rejection of the family, the researchers noted, but a response to developmental needs. Early adolescents often retreat to their rooms; they seem to need time alone to step back from the demands of social relationships, regain emotional stability, and reflect on identity issues (Larson, 1997). High schoolers spend more of their free time with peers, with whom they identify and feel comfortable (Larson & Richards, 1991, 1998).

The *character* of family interactions also changes during these years. Adolescents and their parents may spend less time than before watching television together but just as much time—and, among girls, more—in one-on-one conversations. As adolescents grow older, they increasingly see themselves as taking the lead in these discussions, and their feelings about contact with parents become more positive (Larson et al., 1996).

What do 15-year-olds think about their families and peers? To find out, watch the video on "Views on Family and Peers at Age 15" in Chapter 17 of your CD.

Cultural variations in time use reflect varying cultural needs, values, and practices (Verma & Larson, 2003). Young people in tribal or peasant societies spend most of their time producing bare necessities of life and have much less time for socializing than adolescents in technologically advanced societies (Larson & Verma, 1999). In some postindustrial societies such as Korea and Japan, where the pressures of schoolwork and family obligations are strong, adolescents have relatively little free time. To relieve their stress, they spend it mainly in passive pursuits, such as watching television and "doing nothing" (Verma & Larson, 2003).

By comparison, European and U.S. adolescents have a great deal of discretionary time, most of which they spend in unstructured activities with peers (Verma & Larson, 2003). U.S. adolescents spend two to three hours a day talking and "hanging out" with peers, increasingly of the other sex (Larson & Verma, 1999; Larson & Seepersad, 2003). Weekend partying, sometimes in friends' homes without direct adult supervision, is frequent among older adolescents with access to automobiles. Parties provide emotional "highs"—fun, relief from stress, and the opportunity to experiment with unconventional behavior and to lose oneself in a group. Without appropriate parental monitoring, such activities can lead to substance use and deviant behavior (Larson & Seepersad, 2003).

African-American teenagers, who may look upon their families as havens in a hostile world, tend to maintain more intimate family relationships and less intense peer relations than white teenagers (Giordano, Cernkovich, & DeMaris, 1993). Mexican-American boys, but not girls, tend to become closer to their parents during puberty. This may reflect the unusually close-knit nature of Mexican-American families as well as the importance these families place on the traditional male role (Molina & Chassin, 1996). For Chinese-American youth from immigrant families, the need to adapt to U.S. society often conflicts with the pull of traditional family obligations (Fuligni, Yip, & Tseng, 2002).

With such cultural variations in mind, let's look more closely at relationships with parents, and then with siblings and peers.

Checkpoint

Can you . . .

✔ Identify age and cultural differences in how young people spend their time, and discuss their significance?

Adolescents and Parents

Just as adolescents feel tension between dependency on their parents and the need to break away, parents often have mixed feelings. They want their children to be independent, yet they find it hard to let go. Parents have to walk a fine line between giving adolescents enough independence and protecting them from immature lapses in judgment. These tensions often lead to family conflict, and parenting styles can influence its shape and outcome. Also, as with younger children, teenagers' relationships with their parents are affected by the parents' life situation—their work and marital and socioeconomic status.

Family Conflict

Family conflict may arise over the pace of adolescents' growth toward independence (Arnett, 1999). Most arguments concern day-to-day matters—chores, schoolwork, dress, money, curfews, dating, and friends—rather than fundamental values (Adams & Laursen, 2001; B. K. Barber, 1994). However, some of these minor issues may be proxies for more serious ones, such as substance use, safe driving, and sex. An accumulation of frequent "hassles" can add up to a stressful family atmosphere (Arnett, 1999).

Family conflict is most frequent during early adolescence but most intense in midadolescence (Laursen, Coy, & Collins, 1998). The frequency of strife in early adolescence may be related to the strains of puberty and the need to assert autonomy. The more highly charged arguments in midadolescence and, to a lesser extent, in late adolescence may reflect the emotional stress that occurs as adolescents try their wings. The reduced frequency of conflict in late adolescence may signify adjustment to the momentous changes of the teenage years and a renegotiation of the balance of power between parent and child (Fuligni & Eccles, 1993; Laursen et al., 1998; Molina & Chassin, 1996; Steinberg, 1988).

LifeMap CD

Did you have many conflicts with your parents when you were an adolescent? For an expert's perspective on this phenomenon, watch the "Adolescent-Parent Conflict" video in Chapter 17 of your CD.

The level of family discord seems to hinge primarily on adolescents' personalities and on parents' treatment of them. These factors may explain why disagreements in some families tend to blow over, whereas in other families they escalate into major confrontations. In a study of 335 two-parent rural midwestern families with teenagers, conflict declined in warm, supportive families during early to middle adolescence but worsened in a hostile, coercive, or critical family atmosphere (Rueter & Conger, 1995).

Parenting Styles

Most adolescents (like Jackie Robinson) "excel in most areas of their lives when they . . . feel that they come from a loving home with responsive parents" (Gray & Steinberg, 1999, p. 584). As we discussed in Chapter 16, although adolescents are different from younger children, authoritative parenting still seems to work best (Baumrind, 1991). Overly strict, authoritarian parenting may be especially counterproductive as children enter adolescence and want to be treated more as adults. When parents do not adjust, an adolescent may reject parental influence and seek peer support and approval at all costs (Fuligni & Eccles, 1993).

Authoritative parents insist on important rules, norms, and values but are willing to listen, explain, and negotiate (Lamborn, Mounts, Steinberg, & Dornbusch, 1991). They exercise appropriate control over a child's conduct but not over the child's sense of self (Steinberg & Darling, 1994). Parents who show disappointment in teenagers' misbehavior are more effective in motivating them to behave responsibly than parents who punish them harshly (Krevans & Gibbs, 1996).

Authoritative parenting may bolster an adolescent's self-image. A questionnaire survey of 8,700 ninth to twelfth graders in Wisconsin and California high schools concluded that "the more involvement, autonomy granting, and structure that adolescents perceive from their parents, the more positively teens evaluate their own general conduct, psychosocial development, and mental health" (Gray & Steinberg, 1999, p. 584). When adolescents thought their parents were trying to dominate their psychological experience, their emotional health suffered more than when parents tried to control their behavior. Teens whose parents were firm in enforcing behavioral rules had more self-discipline and fewer behavior problems than those with more permissive parents. Those whose parents gave them psychological autonomy tended to become self-confident and competent in both the academic and social realms. They wanted to achieve and believed they could do what they set out to do.

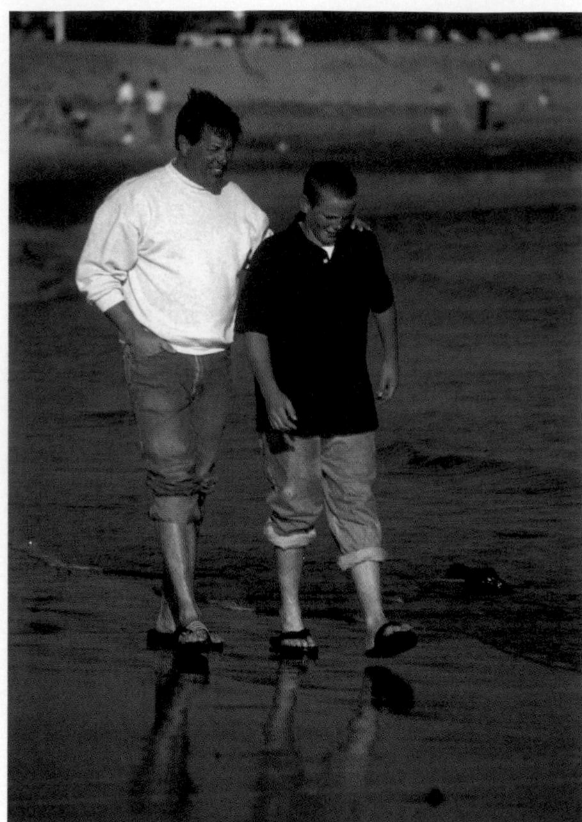

The warmth and acceptance this father shows to his son are characteristic of an authoritative parenting style. Authoritative parents set reasonable rules about, for example, what time a child must come home, but are willing to listen to and respect the child's point of view. Authoritative parenting may be especially effective as children enter adolescence and want to be treated more like adults.

Family Structure and Mothers' Employment

Many adolescents today live in families that are very different from families a few decades ago. Many households, like Jackie Robinson's, are fatherless, and many mothers, like his, work outside the home. How do these family situations affect adolescents?

A multiethnic study of 12- and 13-year-old children of single mothers—first assessed when the children were 6 and 7 years old—found no negative effects of single parenting on school performance and no greater risk of problem behavior. What mattered most, as other studies have found, were the mother's educational level and ability, family income, and the quality of the home environment (Ricciuti, 2004). In another longitudinal study, adolescent boys and girls whose parents later divorced showed more academic, psychological, and behavioral problems *before* the breakup than peers whose parents did not divorce (Sun, 2001; refer back to Box 14-1 in Chapter 14).

The impact of a mother's work outside the home may depend on whether there are two parents or only one in the household. Often a single mother like Mallie Robinson must work to stave off economic disaster; how her working affects her teenage children may hinge on how much time and energy she has left over to spend with them, how well she keeps track of their whereabouts, and what kind of role model she provides (B. L. Barber & Eccles, 1992). Without close, consistent supervision or monitoring, adolescents are more susceptible to peer pressure for risky or antisocial behavior (DiClemente et al., 2001). However, as long as working parents know where their son or daughter is and with whom, their physical absence does not significantly increase the risk of problems (Richardson, Radziszewska, Dent, & Flay, 1993).

Economic Stress

A major problem in many single-parent families is lack of money. Poverty can complicate family relationships—and also harm adolescents' development—through its impact on parents' emotional state (refer back to Chapter 14).

One study looked at single African-American mothers of seventh and eighth graders in a midwestern city that was experiencing widespread manufacturing layoffs. Unemployed mothers, especially those without outside help and support, tended to become depressed; and depressed mothers tended to perceive their maternal role negatively and punish their children harshly. Young people who saw their relationships with their mothers deteriorate tended to become depressed themselves and to have trouble in school (McLoyd, Jayaratne, Ceballo, & Borquez, 1994). A similar pattern occurred in 378 white two-parent families in an economically declining area of rural Iowa. Parental depression and marital conflict worsened financial conflicts between parents and adolescents, increasing the risk of teenage behavior problems (R. C. Conger et al., 1994).

Many adolescents in economically distressed families benefit from accumulated social capital—the support of kin and community. In 51 poor, urban African-American families in which teenagers were living with their mothers, grandmothers, or aunts, women who had strong kinship networks exercised firmer control and closer monitoring while granting appropriate autonomy, and their teenage charges were more self-reliant and had fewer behavior problems (R. D. Taylor & Roberts, 1995).

Checkpoint

Can you . . .

- ✔ Identify factors that affect conflict with parents?
- ✔ Discuss the impact on adolescents of parenting styles and of marital status, mothers' employment, and economic stress?

Adolescents and Siblings

As adolescents spend more time with peers, they have less time and less need for the emotional gratification they used to get from the sibling bond. Adolescents are less close to siblings than to either parents or friends, are less influenced by them, and become even more distant as they move through adolescence (Laursen, 1996).

Changes in sibling relationships may well precede similar changes in the relationship between adolescents and parents: more independence on the part of the younger person and less authority exerted by the older person. As children approach high school, their relationships with their siblings become progressively more equal. Older siblings exercise less power over younger ones, and younger siblings no longer need as much supervision. As relative age differences shrink, so do differences in competence and independence (Buhrmester & Furman, 1990).

Older and younger siblings tend to have different feelings about their changing relationship. As the younger sibling grows up, the older one may look on a newly assertive younger brother or sister as a pesky annoyance. Younger siblings still tend to look up to older ones—as Jackie Robinson did to his brother Mack—and try to feel more "grown up" by identifying with and emulating them (Buhrmester & Furman, 1990).

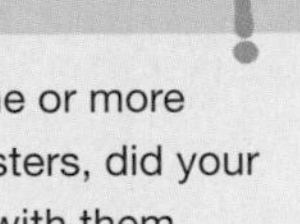

What's your view

- If you have one or more brothers or sisters, did your relationships with them change during adolescence?

Checkpoint

Can you . . .

✔ Describe typical changes in sibling relationships during adolescence?

Peers and Friends

As Jackie Robinson found, an important source of emotional support during the complex transition of adolescence is a young person's growing involvement with peers. The peer group is a source of affection, sympathy, understanding, and moral guidance; a place for experimentation; and a setting for achieving autonomy and independence from parents. It is a place to form intimate relationships that serve as "rehearsals" for adult intimacy (Buhrmester, 1996; Gecas & Seff, 1990; Laursen, 1996).

The influence of peers is strongest in early adolescence and declines during middle and late adolescence as relationships with parents are renegotiated. Attachment to peers does not forecast trouble unless the attachment is so strong that the young person is willing to give up obeying household rules, doing schoolwork, and developing his or her own talents to win peer approval and popularity (Fuligni et al., 2001).

Popularity

Sociometric studies (refer back to Chapter 14) have identified five *peer status* categories: *popular* (young people who receive many positive nominations), *rejected* (those who receive many negative nominations), *neglected* (those who receive few nominations of either kind), *controversial* (those who receive many positive and many negative nominations), and *average* (those who do not receive an unusual number of nominations of either kind). A study of 1,903 ten- to sixteen-year-olds in northern Greece used this technique along with teacher ratings and self-ratings (Hatzichristou & Hopf, 1996). The young people also were asked to name two classmates who best fit certain behavioral descriptions (for example, "quarrels often with other students," "liked by everybody and helps everybody," or "gets into trouble with the teacher"). By combining and comparing evaluations, the researchers filled out a portrait of rejected, neglected, and controversial adolescents.

The transitions from elementary to junior high school and from junior high to high school seemed to be particularly hard for the rejected and neglected groups. As in U.S. studies, the *rejected* group had the greatest adjustment problems as well as academic difficulties. Rejected boys, particularly younger ones, tended to be aggressive and antisocial; rejected girls (and older boys) were more likely to be shy, isolated, and unhappy and to have a negative self-image. The *neglected* group—which, by high school age, included more boys than girls—were less prosocial and had more learning difficulties than average, which contributed to a poor self-image.

The *controversial* group were viewed differently by teachers than by peers. Perhaps because this group tended to do well in school, teachers did not see them as having behavioral problems. Peers saw the boys as aggressive and antisocial—but also as leaders, perhaps

Adolescents show intimacy and affection for younger siblings, even though they spend less time together than before. Although differences in power and status lessen, younger siblings still look up to older ones.

because peers expect and accept aggressiveness in boys. In elementary school, peers often rated the girls in this category as snobbish and arrogant, perhaps reflecting girls' tendency to form cliques at this age. By high school, these girls were better liked than before and also were seen as leaders.

Similarly, a longitudinal study of a multiethnic group of 905 fifth through ninth graders in a northeastern U.S. city highlights the complexity and volatility of the relationship between aggressiveness and popularity as children move from middle childhood through early adolescence (Cillessen & Mayeux, 2004). Physically aggressive children became less disliked but less likely to be perceived as popular. Relationally aggressive children, especially among girls, became less well-liked but *more* likely to be seen as popular. Thus, physical aggression became less disapproved as children entered adolescence, and relational aggression was increasingly reinforced by high status among peers.

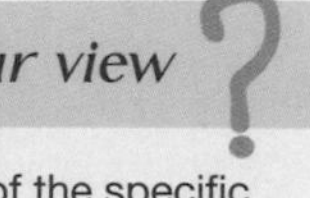

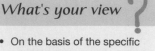

What's your view?

- On the basis of the specific characteristics of rejected and neglected children, what do you think can be done to help such children?

What might explain these developments? Adolescents may increasingly admire tough behavior as a sign of "coolness," and previously unaggressive young people may feel more free to express anger or frustration in physically aggressive ways. Also, the larger peer groups encountered in high school may allow physically aggressive—and previously unpopular—adolescents to find a social niche. Meanwhile, as physical aggression becomes more common and more accepted, it loses its power as a route to social dominance. Instead, the subtler, more manipulative methods identified as relational aggression become the key to social control (Cillessen & Mayeux, 2004).

Friendships

The intensity and importance of friendships as well as the amount of time spent with friends are probably greater in adolescence than at any other time in the life span. Friendships become more reciprocal. Early adolescents begin to rely more on friends than on parents for intimacy and support, and they share confidences more than younger friends. A stress on intimacy, loyalty, and sharing marks a transition to adultlike friendships (Berndt & Perry, 1990; Buhrmester, 1990, 1996; Hartup & Stevens, 1999; Laursen, 1996). Intimacy with same-sex friends increases during early to midadolescence, after which it typically declines as intimacy with the other sex grows (Laursen, 1996).

The increased intimacy of adolescent friendship reflects cognitive as well as emotional development. Adolescents are now better able to express their private thoughts and feelings. They can more readily consider another person's point of view, and so it is easier for them to understand a friend's thoughts and feelings. Increased intimacy reflects early adolescents' concern with getting to know themselves. Confiding in a friend helps young people explore their own feelings, define their identity, and validate their self-worth. Friendship provides a safe place to venture opinions, admit weaknesses, and get help with problems (Buhrmester, 1996). Awareness of the potential instability of friendships and of what it takes to maintain them also emerges in adolescence (Adams & Laursen, 2001; Laursen, 1996).

The capacity for intimacy is related to psychological adjustment and social competence. Friends tend to have similar academic attitudes and performance and, especially, similar levels of drug use (Hamm, 2000) and to have similar status within the peer group (Berndt & Perry, 1990). Adolescents who have close, stable, supportive friendships generally have a high opinion of themselves, do well in school, are sociable, and are unlikely to be hostile, anxious, or depressed (Berndt & Perry, 1990; Buhrmester, 1990; Hartup & Stevens, 1999). A bidirectional process seems to be at work: good friendships foster adjustment, which in turn fosters good friendships.

Sharing confidences and emotional support seem to be more vital to female friendships than to male friendships now and throughout life. Boys' friendships focus less on conversation than on shared activity, usually sports and competitive games (Blyth & Foster-Clark, 1987; Buhrmester, 1996; Bukowski & Kramer, 1986). Girls feel better after telling a friend about an upsetting experience than boys do; boys may express support by just spending time doing things together (Denton & Zarbatany, 1996). Boys tend to gain self-esteem from competition with friends, whereas girls do so from helping friends.

Romantic Relationships

In adolescence most young people experience their first romantic relationships, and the prevalence of such relationships increases with age (Furman & Buhrmester, 1992). How does the quality of romantic relationships change?

According to one research team (Furman & Wehner, 1997*), romantic development can be described on the basis of the changing roles a partner may play. Romantic partners can be attachment figures, to be sought out in times of distress; companions and friends who engage in intimacy, affection, mutual cooperation, help, care, and nurturance; and sources of sexual fulfillment. A romantic partner may fill some or all of these roles, and the relative importance of particular roles may change with age or as a relationship develops. (Although these observations are based primarily on research on heterosexual relationships, many of them may apply to gay and lesbian relationships as well.)

Before adolescence, children tend to play with others of their own sex and have little contact with the other sex. With the onset of puberty, when most children become interested in the other sex, they need to adapt to someone whose way of interacting is likely to be different from theirs. At the same time they need to deal with their budding sexual desires. Gay, lesbian, and bisexual youth may struggle with the recognition of which sex they are attracted to.

Early adolescents worry primarily about how attractive they are and how a new relationship may affect their status in the peer group. They do not generally pay attention to attachment or support needs, and their attention to sexual needs is limited to how to engage in sexual activity and which activities to engage in. During midadolescence, most young people have at least one exclusive partner, lasting for several months to about a year, and the effect of the choice of partner on peer status tends to become less important. Not until late adolescence or early adulthood, though, do romantic relationships begin to serve the full gamut of emotional needs such relationships can serve, and then only in relatively long-term relationships.

Of course, most adolescents also have other people in their social networks who can fulfill some of these needs; but, as time passes and trust develops, a romantic partner is likely to be the main person an adolescent turns to for emotional support (Furman & Buhrmester, 1992). As young people get older and more experienced in romantic relationships, their romantic interactions become more complex and their fulfillment of romantic roles more complete. Adolescents tend to view their romantic attachments as secure or insecure, depending on their experience in previous close relationships with parents and friends. On average, security tends to increase or insecurity to decrease with age.

Checkpoint ✓

Can you . . .

✔ Identify characteristics that affect adolescents' popularity?

✔ Discuss important features of adolescent friendships?

✔ Describe developmental changes in romantic relationships?

Antisocial Behavior and Juvenile Delinquency

Guidepost 7

What are the root causes of antisocial behavior and juvenile delinquency, and what can be done to reduce the risks of adolescence?

What influences young people to engage in—or refrain from—violence (see Box 17-2) or other antisocial acts? How do "problem behaviors" escalate into chronic delinquency—an outcome Jackie Robinson managed to avoid? What determines whether a juvenile delinquent will grow up to be a hardened criminal? By what processes do antisocial tendencies develop? What interventions are most effective, and why? The answers are varied, complex, multilayered, and not yet fully understood (Rutter, 2003). The interaction between environmental and genetic or biological risk factors is one of several relevant topics that need more study.

Becoming a Delinquent: How Parental, Peer, and Community Influences Interact

As Bronfenbrenner's theory would suggest, antisocial behavior seems to be influenced by multileveled, interacting factors ranging from microsystem influences, such as parenting practices and peer deviance, to macrosystem influences, such as community structure and neighborhood social support (Tolan, Gorman-Smith, & Henry, 2003). This network of interacting influences begins to be woven early in childhood.

*Unless otherwise cited, this section is indebted to Furman & Wehner, 1997.

Box 17-2 *The Youth Violence Epidemic*

On April 20, 1999, 18-year-old Eric Harris and 17-year-old Dylan Klebold entered Columbine High School in Littleton, Colorado, wearing black trench coats and carrying a rifle, a semiautomatic pistol, two sawed-off shotguns, and more than 30 homemade bombs. Laughing and taunting, they began spraying bullets at fellow students, killing 12 classmates and one teacher before fatally shooting themselves.

The massacre in Littleton was not an isolated event. Between 1994 and 1999, 253 people died in school shootings in the United States, 68 percent of them students (Anderson et al., 2001). And although the occasional youth killing may make the headlines, such crimes as forcible rape, robbery, and assault are much more prevalent (Snyder, 2000). In 1999, 4 percent of U.S. 12- through 18-year-olds reported being victims of violence at school (NCES, 2003).

Youth violence is not a peculiarly U.S. phenomenon. In a Japanese elementary school in June 2004, an 11-year-old girl stabbed her 12-year-old classmate to death after an argument over messages sent each other over the Internet—one of several such incidents in recent years ("Japan in shock at school murder," 2004). A survey by the World Health Organization found young adolescents in the United States no more likely to engage in violence than youth in four other industrialized countries: Ireland, Israel, Portugal, and Sweden. Forty percent of adolescents in all five countries had engaged in occasional fights during the previous year, about 11 percent carried weapons, and about 15 percent were injured in fights (Smith-Khuri et al., 2004).

Why do some young people engage in such destructive behavior? One answer lies in the immaturity of the adolescent brain, particularly the prefrontal cortex, which is critical to judgment and impulse suppression (refer back to Chapter 15). Another answer is ready access to guns in a culture that "romanticizes gunplay" (Weinberger, 2001, p. 2).

Youth violence is strongly related to the presence of guns and gangs at school (NCES, 2003; "Youth Violence," 2001). For many adolescents, gangs satisfy unfulfilled needs for identity, connection, and a sense of power and control. For youngsters who lack positive family relationships, a gang can become a substitute family. Gangs promote a sense of "us-versus-them." Violence against outsiders strengthens bonds of loyalty and support within the gang (Staub, 1996).

Teenage violence and antisocial behavior have roots in childhood. Children, especially boys, who are aggressive in elementary school tend to be violently antisocial in adolescence (Broidy et al., 2003). Children raised in a rejecting or coercive atmosphere or in an overly permissive or chaotic one tend to behave aggressively, and the hostility they evoke in others increases their own aggression. Their negative self-image prevents them from succeeding at school or developing other constructive interests, and they generally associate with peers who reinforce their antisocial attitudes and behavior (Staub, 1996). Boys in poor, unstable inner-city neighborhoods with high crime rates and low community involvement and neighborhood support are most likely to become involved in violence (Tolan et al., 2003), but the shootings at Columbine show that even middle-class students in a suburban school are not immune.

Adolescents are more likely to develop conduct problems, such as fighting and vandalism, if they have witnessed or have been victims of neighborhood violence or have been exposed to media violence (Pearce, Jones, Schwab-Stone, & Ruchkin, 2003; Strasburger & Donnerstein, 1999). As we discussed in Chapter 14, a steady diet of media violence can breed aggression, and adolescents are no exception to its effects (Johnson, Cohen, Smailes, Kasen, & Brook, 2002). Religiosity and parental involvement tend to buffer the negative effects of exposure to violence (Pearce et al., 2003).

Psychologists point to potential warning signs. Adolescents likely to commit violence often refuse to listen to parents and teachers; ignore the feelings and rights of others; mistreat people; rely on violence or threats to solve problems; and believe that life has treated them unfairly. They tend to do poorly in school; to cut classes or play truant; to be held back or suspended or to drop out; to be victims of bullying; to use alcohol, inhalants, and/or drugs; to engage in early sexual activity; to join gangs; and to fight, steal, or destroy property (American Psychological Association and American Academy of Pediatrics [AAP], 1996; Resnick et al., 1997; Smith-Khuri et al., 2004; "Youth Violence," 2001). Harris and Klebold showed several of these characteristics.

A report by the Surgeon General of the United States challenges some myths, or stereotypes, about youth violence ("Youth violence," 2001; see table). One of the worst is the myth that nothing can be done to prevent or treat violent behavior. School-based programs designed to prevent violent behavior by promoting social competence and emotional awareness and control have been modestly successful (Henrich, Brown, & Aber, 1999). Unfortunately, about half of the hundreds of programs being used in schools and communities fall short when rigorously evaluated. A program in Galveston, Texas, that addressed specific risk factors led to a drop in arrests for juvenile crime (Thomas, Holzer, & Wall, 2002).

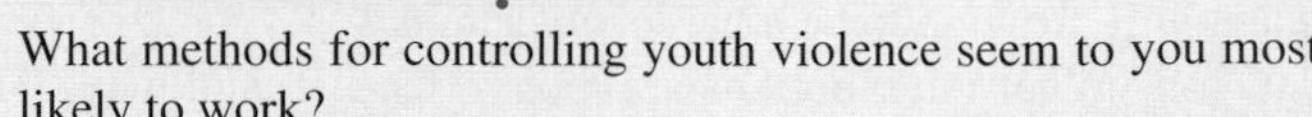

What methods for controlling youth violence seem to you most likely to work?

Check it out !

For more information on this topic, go to **http://www.search-institute.org/**. The Search Institute is an organization dedicated to "raising caring and responsible children and teenagers" by providing "developmental assets" and creating health communities.

Parents begin to shape prosocial or antisocial behavior by their responses to children's basic emotional needs (Krevans & Gibbs, 1996; Staub, 1996). Parents of children who become antisocial often failed to reinforce good behavior in early childhood and were harsh or inconsistent—or both—in punishing misbehavior (Coie & Dodge, 1998). Through the years these parents may not have been closely and positively involved in their children's lives (G. R. Patterson, DeBaryshe, & Ramsey, 1989). The children may get payoffs for antisocial behavior: when they act up, they may gain attention or get their own way. These early negative patterns pave the way for negative peer influences that promote and reinforce antisocial behavior (Collins et al., 2000; B. B. Brown, Mounts, Lamborn, & Steinberg, 1993).

These 16-year-old girls console each other at a vigil service for victims of a shooting spree by teenage gunmen at Columbine High School in Littleton, Colorado, on April 20, 1999. This and other school shootings are part of what has been called an epidemic of youth violence.

Genetic studies have found that choice of antisocial peers is affected mainly by environmental factors (Iervolino et al., 2002). Young people gravitate to others brought up like themselves who are similar in school achievement, adjustment, and prosocial or antisocial tendencies (Collins et al., 2000; B. B. Brown, Mounts, Lamborn, & Steinberg, 1993). Children with behavior problems tend to do poorly in school and do not get along with well-behaved classmates. Unpopular, low-achieving, and highly aggressive children gravitate toward each other and egg each other on to further misconduct (G. R. Patterson, Reid, & Dishion, 1992; Hartup, 1989, 1992, 1996a; Hartup & Stevens, 1999; Masten & Coatsworth, 1998; G. R. Patterson, Reid, & Dishion, 1992). As in childhood, antisocial adolescents tend to have antisocial friends, and their antisocial behavior increases when they associate with each other (Dishion, McCord, & Poulin, 1999; Hartup & Stevens, 1999; Vitaro, Tremblay, Kerr, Pagani, & Bukowski, 1997). The way antisocial teenagers talk, laugh, or smirk about rule breaking and nod knowingly among themselves constitutes a sort of "deviancy training" (Dishion et al., 1999). These "problem" children continue to elicit ineffective parenting, which predicts delinquent behavior and association with deviant peer groups or gangs (Simons, Chao, Conger, & Elder, 2001; Tolan et al., 2003).

Authoritative parenting can help young people internalize standards that may insulate them against negative peer influences and open them to positive ones (Collins et al., 2000; Mounts & Steinberg, 1995). Improved parenting during adolescence can reduce delinquency by discouraging association with deviant peers (Simons et al., 2001). As discussed, adolescents whose parents know where they are and what they are doing are less likely to engage in delinquent acts (Laird, Pettit, Bates, & Dodge, 2003) or to associate with deviant peers (Lloyd & Anthony, 2003).

Family circumstances may influence the development of antisocial behavior. Persistent economic deprivation can undermine sound parenting by depriving the family of social capital. Poor children are more likely than other children to commit antisocial acts, and those whose families are continuously poor tend to become more antisocial with time. When families rise from poverty while a child is still young, the child is no more likely to develop behavior problems than a child whose family was never poor (Macmillan, McMorris, & Kruttschnitt, 2004).

Collective efficacy—the strength of social connections within a neighborhood and the extent to which residents monitor or supervise each other's children—can make a difference (Sampson, 1997). Although collective efficacy tends to be low in poor, crime-ridden communities (Tolan et al., 2003), in some disadvantaged neighborhoods a combination of nurturant, involved parenting and collective efficacy discourages adolescents from association with deviant peers (Brody et al., 2001).

Long-Term Prospects

Many, if not most, adolescents, like Jackie Robinson and his friends, at some point engage in antisocial behavior or even in violence. The vast majority of these young people do not

Young people with antisocial tendencies tend to gravitate to others like themselves and reinforce each other's antisocial behavior.

become adult criminals but rather tame their "wild oats" (Kosterman, Graham, Hawkins, Catalano, & Herrenkohl, 2001; Moffitt, 1993).

Delinquency peaks at about age 15 and then declines as most adolescents and their families come to terms with young people's need to assert independence. However, teenagers who do not see positive alternatives are more likely to adopt a permanently antisocial lifestyle (Elliott, 1993). Those most likely to persist in violence are boys who had early antisocial influences. Least likely to persist are boys and girls who were early school achievers and girls who showed early prosocial development (Kosterman et al., 2001).

Preventing and Treating Delinquency

Because juvenile delinquency has roots early in childhood, so should preventive efforts that attack the multiple factors that can lead to delinquency. Adolescents who have taken part in certain early childhood intervention programs are less likely to get in trouble than their equally underprivileged peers (Yoshikawa, 1994; Zigler, Taussig, & Black, 1992). Effective programs are those that targeted high-risk urban children and lasted at least two years during the child's first five years of life. They influenced children directly, through high-quality day care or education, and at the same time indirectly, by offering families assistance and support geared to their needs (Berrueta-Clement et al., 1985; Berrueta-Clement, Schweinhart, Barnett, & Weikart, 1987; Schweinhart et al., 1993; Seitz, 1990; Yoshikawa, 1994; Zigler et al., 1992).

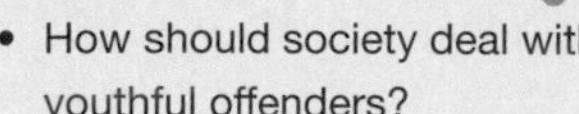

What's your view?

- How should society deal with youthful offenders?

These programs operated on Bronfenbrenner's mesosystem by affecting interactions between the home and the school or child care center. The programs also went one step further to the exosystem by creating supportive parent networks and linking parents with such community services as prenatal and postnatal care and educational and vocational counseling (Yoshikawa, 1994; Zigler et al., 1992). Through their multipronged approach, these interventions had an impact on several early risk factors for delinquency.

The Chicago Child-Parent Centers, a preschool program for disadvantaged children in the Chicago Public Schools, offers follow-up services through age 9. Participants studied at age 20 had better educational and social outcomes and fewer juvenile arrests than a comparison group who had received less extensive early interventions (Reynolds et al., 2001).

Once children reach adolescence, especially in poor, crime-ridden neighborhoods, interventions need to focus on spotting troubled adolescents and preventing gang recruitment by bolstering parenting skills and neighborhood social support (Tolan et al., 2003). Adult-monitored activities after school, on weekend evenings, and in summer, when adolescents are most likely to be idle and to get in trouble, can reduce their exposure to high-risk settings that encourage antisocial behavior. As Jackie Robinson's experience shows, getting teenagers involved in constructive activities during their free time can pay long-range dividends (Larson, 1998). Participation in extracurricular school activities tends to cut down on dropout and criminal arrest rates among high-risk boys and girls (Mahoney, 2000).

Checkpoint

Can you . . .

- ✔ Explain how parental, peer, and community influences may interact to promote antisocial behavior and delinquency?
- ✔ Give examples of programs that have been successful in preventing or stopping delinquency and other antisocial behavior?

One multifaceted intervention, Equipping Youth to Help One Another (EQUIP), uses daily, adult-guided peer support groups. Peers help teach each other how to manage anger, make moral decisions, and learn social skills (Gibbs, Potter, Barriga, & Liau, 1996; Gibbs, Potter, Goldstein, & Brendtro, 1998). Among 57 male juvenile offenders in a medium-security correctional facility, EQUIP participants improved significantly in conduct within the institution and had lower repeat offense rates during the first year after release than control groups that did not have the training (Leeman, Gibbs, & Fuller, 1993).

Fortunately, the great majority of adolescents do not get into serious trouble. Those who do show disturbed behavior can—and should—be helped. With love, guidance, and support, adolescents can avoid risks, build on their strengths, and explore their possibilities as they approach adult life.

Emerging Adulthood

Guidepost 8

How do various cultures define what it means to become an adult, and what markers confer that status?

As work becomes more complex and the need for advanced preparation more widespread, entrance into adult responsibilities often extends well beyond adolescence. Indeed, it has been suggested that the period from the late teens through the mid-20s is now, in some cultures, a distinct period of the life course that can be called *emerging adulthood.* It is a time when young people are no longer adolescents but have not yet fully become adults (Arnett, 2000). In the minds of many people today, the onset of adulthood is marked, not so much by external criteria such as driving, voting, and work, as it is by internal processes. It is more a state of mind than a discrete event.

Since the 1990s, surveys of emerging adult Americans (mostly white, urban, and middle class) have repeatedly come up with three top criteria for adulthood: "accepting responsibility for oneself, making independent decisions, and becoming financially independent"—criteria that reflect their society's values of individualism and self-sufficiency (Arnett & Galambos, 2003, p. 92). In similar studies of Israelis, Argentinians, U.S. minority groups, and Mormons, those same criteria were most widely expressed. However, emerging adults in those cultures also mentioned criteria reflecting collectivistic values. In Israel, which since its birth in 1948 has constantly been forced to defend its existence, universal military service is an important marker of adulthood (Mayseless & Scharf, 2003). Young Argentines, who have experienced severe economic crises and high unemployment in recent years, emphasize family responsibilities more than work (Facio & Micocci, 2003). Mormons cite religious rites of passage, such as being admitted to men's or women's organizations of their church (Nelson, 2003).

African Americans, Latinos, and Asian Americans are more likely than white Americans to mention criteria involving obligations to others (such as supporting one's family), recognized role transitions (such as marriage), and complying with social norms (such as avoiding illegal drug use). African Americans and Latinos who come from lower-SES families tend to believe they have reached adulthood at an earlier age than do whites and Asian Americans, probably because of greater and earlier family responsibilities (Arnett, 2003).

As research on this topic continues, it will be interesting to see what adulthood means in rural, nonwesternized cultures, which tend to hold more strongly collectivist values.

What's your view

- What criteria for adulthood do you consider most relevant?
- Do you think those criteria are influenced by the culture in which you live or grew up?

Checkpoint

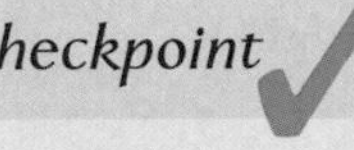

Can you . . .

✔ Explain the concept of emerging adulthood, and tell why it applies to modern westernized societies?

✔ Discuss cultural conceptions of what it means to be an adult?

Refocus

- What evidence suggests that Jackie Robinson may have gone through Erikson's stage of identity versus identity confusion?
- Which of Marcia's identity statuses did Robinson seem to fall into, both with regard to his identity in general and his ethnicity in particular?
- Did Robinson's relationships with his mother and his peers seem consistent with the findings reported in this chapter?
- Would you say that Robinson showed adolescent rebellion?
- Based on the material in this chapter, why do you think Robinson did not become a full-fledged juvenile delinquent?

The normal developmental changes in the early years of life are obvious and dramatic signs of growth. The infant lying in the crib becomes an active, exploring toddler. The young child enters and embraces the worlds of school and society. The adolescent, with a new body and new awareness, prepares to step into adulthood.

Growth and development do not screech to a stop even then. People change in important ways throughout adulthood. Human beings continue to shape their own development, as they have been doing since birth. What occurs in a child's world is significant, but it is not the whole story. We each continue to write our own story of human development for as long as we live.

Summary and Key Terms

The Search for Identity

Guidepost 1 How do adolescents form an identity?

- A central concern during adolescence is the search for identity, which has occupational, sexual, and values components. Erik Erikson described the psychosocial crisis of adolescence as the conflict of identity versus identity confusion. The "virtue" that should arise from this crisis is *fidelity.*
- James Marcia, in research based on Erikson's theory, described four identity statuses with differing combinations of crisis and commitment: identity achievement, foreclosure, moratorium, and identity diffusion.
- Researchers differ on whether girls and boys take different paths to identity formation. Although some research suggests that girls' self-esteem tends to fall at adolescence, later research does not support that finding.
- Ethnicity is an important part of identity. Minority adolescents seem to go through stages of ethnic identity development much like Marcia's identity statuses.
- According to David Elkind, healthy, stable identity development is achieved by a slow process of differentiation and integration. Today many young people instead develop a "patchwork self," highly vulnerable to stress and outside influence.

identity versus identity confusion (461) **identity statuses (463)** **crisis (463)** **commitment (463)** **identity achievement (463)** **foreclosure (464)** **moratorium (464)** **identity diffusion (464)** **patchwork self (465)**

Sexuality

Guidepost 2 What determines sexual orientation?

- Sexual orientation appears to be influenced by an interaction of biological and environmental factors and may be at least partly genetic.

sexual orientation (466)

Guidepost 3 What sexual attitudes and practices are common among adolescents, and what leads some to engage in risky sexual behavior?

- Teenage sexual activity is more prevalent and more accepted than in the past, but it involves risks of pregnancy and sexually transmitted disease. Adolescents at greatest risk are those who begin sexual activity early, have multiple partners, do not use contraceptives, and are ill-informed about sex.
- The course of homosexual identity and relationship development may vary with cohort, gender, and ethnicity.

Guidepost 4 How common is teenage pregnancy, and what are its usual outcomes?

- Teenage pregnancy and birthrates in the United States have declined. Most of these births are to unmarried mothers.
- Teenage pregnancy and childbearing often have negative outcomes. Teenage mothers and their families tend to suffer ill health and financial hardship, and the children often suffer from ineffective parenting.

Relationships with Family, Peers, and Adult Society

Guidepost 5 How typical is "adolescent rebellion"?

- Although relationships between adolescents and their parents are not always smooth, full-scale adolescent rebellion is unusual. For the majority of teens, adolescence is a fairly smooth transition. For the minority who seem more deeply troubled, it can predict a troubled adulthood.

adolescent rebellion (475)

Guidepost 6 How do adolescents relate to parents, siblings, and peers?

- Adolescents spend an increasing amount of time with peers, but relationships with parents continue to be close and influential.
- Conflict with parents tends to be most frequent during early adolescence and most intense during middle adolescence. Authoritative parenting is associated with the most positive outcomes.
- Effects of divorce, single parenting, and maternal employment on adolescents' development depend on such factors as how closely parents monitor adolescents' activity and the quality of the home environment.
- Economic stress affects relationships in both single-parent and two-parent families.
- Relationships with siblings tend to become more distant during adolescence, and the balance of power between older and younger siblings becomes more equal.
- The influence of the peer group is strongest in early adolescence. Adolescents who are rejected by peers tend to have the greatest adjustment problems.
- Friendships, especially among girls, become more intimate and supportive in adolescence.
- Romantic relationships involve several roles and develop with age and experience.

Guidepost 7 What are the root causes of antisocial behavior and juvenile delinquency, and what can be done to reduce the risks of adolescence?

- Chronic delinquency is associated with multiple interacting risk factors, including ineffective parenting, school failure, peer influence, and low socioeconomic status. Programs that attack such risk factors from an early age have had success.

Emerging Adulthood

Guidepost 8 How do various cultures define what it means to become an adult, and what markers confer that status?

- A new transitional period called *emerging adulthood* has developed in westernized cultures in recent years.
- Emerging adults in various westernized cultures hold similar views of what defines entrance into adulthood. The most widely accepted criteria are individualistic ones having to do with self-sufficiency and independence. However, some cultures also embrace collectivistic criteria, such as family responsibilities and conformity with social norms.

Glossary

A

A, not-B error Tendency for 8- to 12-month-old infants to search for a hidden object in a place where they previously found it rather than in the place where they most recently saw it being hidden.

acceleration Approach to educating the gifted that moves them through the curriculum at an unusually rapid pace.

accommodation Piaget's term for adjustments in a cognitive structure to fit new information.

acquired immune deficiency syndrome (AIDS) Viral disease that undermines effective functioning of the immune system.

active engagement Involvement in schooling.

acute medical conditions Occasional illnesses that last a short time.

adaptation Piaget's term for adjustment to new information about the environment.

adolescence Developmental transition between childhood and adulthood entailing major physical, cognitive, and psychosocial changes.

adolescent growth spurt Sharp increase in height and weight that precedes sexual maturity.

adolescent rebellion Pattern of emotional turmoil, characteristic of a minority of adolescents, that may involve conflict with family, alienation from adult society, reckless behavior, and rejection of adult values.

adrenarche Maturation of adrenal glands.

affordance In the Gibsons' ecological theory of perception, the fit between a person's physical attributes and capabilities and characteristics of the environment.

alleles Paired genes (alike or different) that affect a trait.

allocentric In Piaget's terminology, able to objectively consider relationships among objects or people.

altruism Behavior intended to help others that comes from inner concern and without expectation of external reward; may involve self-denial or self-sacrifice.

ambivalent (resistant) attachment Pattern in which an infant becomes anxious before the primary caregiver leaves, is extremely upset during his or her absence, and both seeks and resists contact on his or her return.

animism Tendency to attribute life to objects that are not alive.

anorexia nervosa Eating disorder characterized by self-starvation.

anoxia Lack of oxygen, which may cause brain damage.

Apgar scale Standard measurement of a newborn's condition; it assesses appearance, pulse, grimace, activity, and respiration.

art therapy Therapeutic approach that allows a child to express troubled feelings without words, using a variety of art materials and media.

assimilation Piaget's term for incorporation of new information into an existing cognitive structure.

asthma Chronic respiratory disease characterized by sudden attacks of coughing, wheezing, and difficulty in breathing.

attachment Reciprocal, enduring tie between infant and caregiver, each of whom contributes to the quality of the relationship.

attention-deficit/hyperactivity disorder (ADHD) Syndrome characterized by persistent inattention and distractibility, impulsivity, low tolerance for frustration, and inappropriate overactivity.

authoritarian In Baumrind's terminology, parenting style emphasizing control and obedience.

authoritative In Baumrind's terminology, parenting style blending respect for a child's individuality with an effort to instill social values.

autism Pervasive developmental disorder of the brain, characterized by lack of normal social interaction, impaired communication and imagination, and repetitive, obsessive behaviors.

autobiographical memory Memory of specific events in one's own life.

autonomy versus shame and doubt Erikson's second crisis in psychosocial development, in which children achieve a balance between self-determination and control by others.

autosomes Twenty-two pairs of chromosomes not related to sexual expression.

avoidant attachment Pattern in which an infant rarely cries when separated from the primary caregiver and avoids contact upon his or her return.

B

basic trust versus basic mistrust Erikson's first crisis in psychosocial development, in which infants develop a sense of the reliability of people and objects.

Bayley Scales of Infant Development Standardized test of infants' mental and motor development.

behavior therapy Therapeutic approach using principles of learning theory to encourage desired behaviors or eliminate undesired ones; also called *behavior modification.*

behavioral genetics Quantitative study of relative hereditary and environmental influences.

behaviorism Learning theory that emphasizes the predictable role of environment in causing observable behavior.

behaviorist approach Approach to the study of cognitive development that is concerned with basic mechanics of learning.

bilingual Fluent in two languages.

bilingual education System of teaching non-English-speaking children in their native language while they learn English and later switching to all-English instruction.

bioecological theory Bronfenbrenner's approach to understanding processes and contexts of development.

birth trauma Injury sustained at the time of birth.

body image Descriptive and evaluative beliefs about one's appearance.

brain growth spurts Periods of rapid brain growth and development.

Brazelton Neonatal Behavioral Assessment Scale (NBAS) Neurological and behavioral test to measure a neonate's responses to the environment.

bulimia nervosa Eating disorder in which a person regularly eats huge quantities of food and then purges the body with laxatives, induced vomiting, fasting, or excessive exercise.

bullying Aggression deliberately and persistently directed against a particular target, or victim, typically one who is weak, vulnerable, and defenseless.

C

canalization Limitation on variance of expression of certain inherited characteristics.

case study Study covering a single case or life.

cell death Elimination of excess brain cells to achieve more efficient functioning.

central executive In Baddeley's model, element of working memory that controls the processing of information.

central nervous system Brain and spinal cord.

centration In Piaget's theory, tendency of preoperational children to focus on one aspect of a situation and neglect others.

cephalocaudal principle Principle that development proceeds in a head-to-tail direction; that is, that upper parts of the body develop before lower parts.

cesarean delivery Delivery of a baby by surgical removal from the uterus.

child development Scientific study of processes of change and stability from conception through adolescence.

child-directed speech (CDS) Form of speech often used in talking to babies or toddlers; includes slow, simplified speech, a high-pitched tone, exaggerated vowel sounds, short words and sentences, and much repetition. Also called *parentese.*

childhood depression Mood disorder characterized by such symptoms as a prolonged sense of friendlessness, inability to have fun or concentrate, fatigue, extreme activity or apathy, feelings of worthlessness, weight change, physical complaints, and thoughts of death or suicide.

chromosomes Coils of DNA that carry genes.

chronic medical conditions Physical, developmental, behavioral, and/or emotional conditions that require special health services.

chronosystem Bronfenbrenner's term for effects of time on other developmental systems.

circular reactions Piaget's term for processes by which an infant learns to reproduce desired occurrences originally discovered by chance.

class inclusion Understanding of the relationship between a whole and its parts.

classical conditioning Learning based on association of a stimulus that does not ordinarily elicit a response with another stimulus that does elicit the response.

clone *(verb)* To make a genetic copy of an individual; (*noun*) a genetic copy of an individual.

code mixing Use of elements of two languages, sometimes in the same utterance, by young children in households where both languages are spoken.

code switching Changing one's speech to match the situation, as in people who are bilingual.

cognitive neuroscience approach Approach to the study of cognitive development that links brain processes with cognitive ones.

cognitive perspective View that thought processes are central to development.

cohort Group of people born at about the same time.

commitment Marcia's term for personal investment in an occupation or system of beliefs.

committed compliance Kochanska's term for wholehearted obedience of a parent's orders without reminders or lapses.

componential element Sternberg's term for the analytic aspect of intelligence.

conceptual knowledge Acquired interpretive understandings stored in long-term memory.

concordant Term describing tendency of twins to share the same trait or disorder.

concrete operations Third stage of Piagetian cognitive development (approximately from ages 7 to 12), during which children develop logical but not abstract thinking.

conduct disorder (CD) Repetitive, persistent pattern of aggressive, antisocial behavior violating societal norms or the rights of others.

conscience Internal standards of behavior, which usually control one's conduct and produce emotional discomfort when violated.

conservation Piaget's term for awareness that two objects that are equal according to a certain measure remain equal in the face of perceptual alteration so long as nothing has been added to or taken away from either object.

constructive play In Piaget's and Smilansky's terminology, second cognitive level of play, involving use of objects or materials to make something.

contextual element Sternberg's term for the practical aspect of intelligence.

contextual perspective View of development that sees the individual as inseparable from the social context.

control group In an experiment, group of people, similar to those in the experimental group, who do not receive the treatment under study.

conventional morality (or morality of conventional role conformity) Second level in Kohlberg's theory of moral reasoning in which standards of authority figures are internalized.

convergent thinking Thinking aimed at finding the one right answer to a problem.

coregulation Transitional stage in the control of behavior in which parents exercise general supervision and children exercise moment-to-moment self-regulation.

corporal punishment Use of physical force with the intention of causing pain but not injury so as to correct or control behavior.

correlational study Research design intended to discover whether a statistical relationship between variables exists.

crisis Marcia's term for period of conscious decision making related to identity formation.

critical period Specific time when a given event, or its absence, has the greatest impact on development.

cross-modal transfer Ability to use information gained by one sense to guide another.

cross-sectional study Study design in which people of different ages are assessed on one occasion.

cultural bias Tendency of intelligence tests to include items calling for knowledge or skills more familiar or meaningful to some cultural groups than to others.

culture A society's or group's total way of life, including customs, traditions, beliefs, values, language, and physical products—all learned behavior passed on from parents to children.

culture-fair Describing an intelligence test that deals with experiences common to various cultures, in an attempt to avoid cultural bias.

culture-free Describing an intelligence test that, if it were possible to design, would have no culturally linked content.

D

decenter In Piaget's terminology, to think simultaneously about several aspects of a situation.

declarative knowledge Acquired factual knowledge stored in long-term memory.

decoding Process of phonetic analysis by which a printed word is converted to spoken form before retrieval from long-term memory.

deductive reasoning Type of logical reasoning that moves from a general premise about a class to a conclusion about a particular member or members of the class.

deferred imitation Piaget's term for reproduction of an observed behavior after the passage of time by calling up a stored symbol of it.

Denver Developmental Screening Test Screening test given to children 1 month to 6 years old to determine whether they are developing normally.

deoxyribonucleic acid (DNA) Chemical that carries inherited instructions for the formation and function of body cells.

dependent variable In an experiment, condition that may or may not change as a result of changes in the independent variable.

depth perception Ability to perceive objects and surfaces in three dimensions.

developmental tests Psychometric tests that compare a baby's performance on a series of nonverbal tasks with standardized norms for particular ages.

differentiation Process by which neurons acquire specialized structure and function.

difficult children Children with irritable temperament, irregular biological rhythms, and intense emotional responses.

discipline Methods of molding children's character and of teaching them to exercise self-control and engage in acceptable behavior.

dishabituation Increase in responsiveness after presentation of a new stimulus.

disorganized-disoriented attachment Pattern in which an infant, after separation from the primary caregiver, shows contradictory behaviors upon his or her return.

divergent thinking Thinking that produces a variety of fresh, diverse possibilities.

dizygotic (two-egg) twins Twins conceived by the union of two different ova (or a single ovum that has split) with two different sperm cells; also called *fraternal twins.*

dominant inheritance Pattern of inheritance in which, when a child receives contradictory alleles, only the dominant one is expressed.

Down syndrome Chromosomal disorder characterized by moderate-to-severe mental retardation and by such physical signs as a downward-sloping skin fold at the inner corners of the eyes.

drug therapy Administration of drugs to treat emotional disorders.

dual representation hypothesis Proposal that children under the age of 3 have difficulty grasping spatial relationships because of the need to keep more than one mental representation in mind at the same time.

dyslexia Developmental disorder in which reading achievement is substantially lower than predicted by IQ or age.

E

early intervention Systematic process of providing services to help families meet young children's developmental needs.

easy children Children with a generally happy temperament, regular biological rhythms, and a readiness to accept new experiences.

ecological theory of perception Theory developed by Eleanor and James Gibson, which describes developing motor and perceptual abilities as interdependent parts of a functional system that guides behavior in varying contexts.

egocentric In Piaget's terminology, unable to consider any point of view other than one's own; a characteristic of young children's thought.

egocentrism Piaget's term for inability to consider another person's point of view.

elaboration Mnemonic strategy of making mental associations involving items to be remembered.

electronic fetal monitoring Mechanical monitoring of fetal heartbeat during labor and delivery.

elicited imitation Research method in which infants or toddlers are induced to imitate a specific series of actions they have seen but not necessarily done before.

embryonic stage Second stage of gestation (2 to 8 weeks), characterized by rapid growth and development of major body systems and organs.

emergent literacy Preschoolers' development of skills, knowledge, and attitudes that underlie reading and writing.

emotional maltreatment Action or inaction that may cause behavioral, cognitive, emotional, or mental disorders.

emotions Subjective reactions to experience that are associated with physiological and behavioral changes.

empathy Ability to put oneself in another person's place and feel what the other person feels.

encoding Process by which information is prepared for long-term storage and later retrieval.

English-immersion Approach to teaching English as a second language in which instruction is presented only in English.

enrichment Approach to educating the gifted that broadens and deepens knowledge and skills through extra activities, projects, field trips, or mentoring.

enuresis Repeated urination in clothing or in bed.

environment Totality of nonhereditary, or experiential, influences on development.

episodic memory Long-term memory of specific experiences or events, linked to time and place.

equilibration Piaget's term for the tendency to seek a stable balance among cognitive elements.

ethnic gloss Overgeneralization about an ethnic or cultural group that obscures differences within the group.

ethnic group Group united by ancestry, religion, language, and/or national origins, all of which contribute to a sense of shared identity.

ethnographic study In-depth study of a culture using a combination of methods including participant observation.

ethology Study of distinctive adaptive behaviors of species of animals that have evolved to increase survival of the species.

evolutionary psychology Application of Darwinian principles of natural selection and survival of the fittest to individual behavior.

evolutionary/sociobiological perspective View of development that focuses on evolutionary and biological bases of behavior.

exosystem Bronfenbrenner's term for linkages between two or more settings, one of which does not contain the child.

experiential element Sternberg's term for the insightful aspect of intelligence.

experiment Rigorously controlled, replicable procedure in which the researcher manipulates variables to assess the effect of one on the other.

experimental group In an experiment, group receiving the treatment under study.

explicit memory Intentional and conscious memory, generally of facts, names, and events.

extended family Multigenerational kinship network of parents, children, and other relatives, sometimes living together in an extended-family household.

external memory aids Mnemonic strategies using something outside the person.

F

family therapy Psychological treatment in which a therapist sees the whole family together to analyze patterns of family functioning.

fast mapping Process by which a child absorbs the meaning of a new word after hearing it once or twice in conversation.

fertilization Fusion of sperm and ovum to produce a zygote; also called *conception.*

fetal alcohol syndrome (FAS) Combination of mental, motor, and developmental abnormalities affecting the offspring of some women who drink heavily during pregnancy.

fetal stage Final stage of gestation (from 8 weeks to birth), characterized by increased detail of body parts and greatly enlarged body size.

fine motor skills Physical skills that involve the small muscles and eye-hand coordination.

fontanels Soft spots on the head of a young infant.

foreclosure Identity status, described by Marcia, in which a person who has not spent time considering alternatives (that is, has not been in crisis) is committed to other people's plans for his or her life.

formal operations In Piaget's theory, final stage of cognitive development, characterized by the ability to think abstractly.

functional play In Piaget's and Smilansky's terminology, lowest cognitive level of play, involving repetitive muscular movements.

G

gender Significance of being male or female.

gender constancy Awareness that one will always be male or female. Also called *sex-category constancy.*

gender identity Awareness, developed in early childhood, that one is male or female.

gender roles Behaviors, interests, attitudes, skills, and traits that a culture considers appropriate for males or for females.

gender-schema theory Theory, proposed by Bem, that children socialize themselves in their gender roles by developing a mentally organized network of information about what it means to be male or female in a particular culture.

gender stereotypes Preconceived generalizations about male or female role behavior.

gender-typing Socialization process by which children, at an early age, learn appropriate gender roles.

generalized anxiety disorder Anxiety not focused on any single target.

generic memory Memory that produces scripts of familiar routines to guide behavior.

genes Small segments of DNA located in definite positions on particular chromosomes.

genetic code Sequence of base pairs within DNA, which determine inherited characteristics.

genetic counseling Clinical service that advises couples of their probable risk of having children with hereditary defects.

genotype Genetic makeup of a person, containing both expressed and unexpressed characteristics.

genotype-environment correlation Tendency of certain genetic and environmental influences to reinforce each other; may be passive, reactive (evocative), or active. Also called *genotype-environment covariance.*

genotype-environment interaction Portion of phenotypic variation that results from the reactions of genetically different individuals to similar environmental conditions.

germinal stage First 2 weeks of prenatal development, characterized by rapid cell division, increasing complexity and differentiation, and implantation in the wall of the uterus.

gonadarche Maturation of testes or ovaries.

goodness of fit Appropriateness of environmental demands and constraints to a child's temperament.

gross motor skills Physical skills that involve the large muscles.

guided participation Participation of an adult in a child's activity in a manner that helps to structure the activity and to bring the child's understanding of it closer to that of the adult.

H

habituation Type of learning in which familiarity with a stimulus reduces, slows, or stops a response.

handedness Preference for using a particular hand.

haptic perception Ability to acquire information about properties of objects, such as size, weight, and texture, by handling them.

heredity Inborn influences or traits inherited from biological parents.

heritability Statistical estimate of the contribution of heredity to individual differences in a specific trait within a given population.

heterozygous Possessing differing alleles for a trait.

historical generation Group of people strongly influenced by a major historical event during their formative period.

holophrase Single word that conveys a complete thought.

Home Observation for Measurement of the Environment (HOME) Instrument to measure the influence of the home environment on children's cognitive growth.

homozygous Possessing two identical alleles for a trait.

horizontal décalage Piaget's term for inability to transfer learning about one type of conservation to other types, which causes a child to master different types of conservation tasks at different ages.

hostile aggression Aggressive behavior intended to hurt another person.

human genome Complete sequence or mapping of genes in the human body and their locations.

hypotheses Possible explanations for phenomena, used to predict the outcome of research.

hypothetical-deductive reasoning Ability, believed by Piaget to accompany the stage of formal operations, to develop, consider, and test hypotheses.

I

ideal self Self one would like to be.

identification In Freudian theory, process by which a young child adopts characteristics, beliefs, attitudes, values, and behaviors of the parent of the same sex.

identity achievement Identity status, described by Marcia, that is characterized by commitment to choices made following a crisis, a period spent in exploring alternatives.

identity diffusion Identity status, described by Marcia, that is characterized by absence of commitment and lack of serious consideration of alternatives.

identity statuses Marcia's term for states of ego development that depend on the presence or absence of crisis and commitment.

identity versus identity confusion Erikson's fifth crisis of psychosocial development, in which an adolescent seeks to develop a coherent sense of self, including the role she or he is to play in society. Also called *identity versus role confusion.*

imaginary audience Elkind's term for observer who exists only in an adolescent's mind and is as concerned with the adolescent's thoughts and actions as the adolescent is.

implicit memory Unconscious recall, generally of habits and skills; sometimes called *procedural memory.*

imprinting Instinctive form of learning in which, during a critical period in early development, a young animal forms an attachment to the first moving object it sees, usually the mother.

incomplete dominance Partial expression of a trait.

independent variable In an experiment, condition over which the experimenter has direct control.

individual differences Differences among children in characteristics, influences, or developmental outcomes.

individual psychotherapy Psychological treatment in which a therapist sees a troubled person one-on-one.

inductive reasoning Type of logical reasoning that moves from particular observations about members of a class to a general conclusion about that class.

inductive techniques Disciplinary techniques designed to induce desirable behavior by appealing to a child's sense of reason and fairness.

industry versus inferiority Erikson's fourth critical alternative of psychosocial development, in which children must learn the productive skills their culture requires or else face feelings of inferiority.

infant mortality rate Proportion of babies born alive who die within the first year.

infertility Inability to conceive after 12 to 18 months of trying.

information-processing approach Approach to the study of cognitive development by observing and analyzing the mental processes involved in perceiving and handling information.

initiative versus guilt Erikson's third stage in psychosocial development, in which children balance the urge to pursue goals with moral reservations that may prevent carrying them out.

instrumental aggression Aggressive behavior used as a means of achieving a goal.

integration Process by which neurons coordinate the activities of muscle groups.

intelligent behavior Behavior that is goal oriented and adaptive to circumstances and conditions of life.

internalization Process fundamental to socialization by which children accept societal standards of conduct as their own.

invisible imitation Imitation with parts of one's body that one cannot see.

IQ (intelligence quotient) tests Psychometric tests that seek to measure intelligence by comparing a test taker's performance with standardized norms.

irreversibility Piaget's term for a preoperational child's failure to understand that an operation can go in two or more directions.

K

Kaufman Assessment Battery for Children (K-ABC-II) Nontraditional individual intelligence test designed to provide fair assessments of minority children and children with disabilities.

L

laboratory observation Research method in which all participants are observed under the same controlled conditions.

language Communication system based on words and grammar.

language acquisition device (LAD) In Chomsky's terminology, inborn mechanism that enables children to infer linguistic rules from the language they hear.

lanugo Fuzzy prenatal body hair, which drops off within a few days after birth.

lateralization Tendency of each of the brain's hemispheres to have specialized functions.

learning disabilities (LDs) Disorders that interfere with specific aspects of learning and school achievement.

learning perspective View of development that holds that changes in behavior result from experience, or adaptation to the environment.

linguistic speech Verbal expression designed to convey meaning.

literacy Ability to read and write.

longitudinal study Study designed to assess changes in a sample over time.

long-term memory Storage of virtually unlimited capacity that holds information for very long periods.

low birth weight Weight of less than 5½ pounds (2,500 grams) at birth because of prematurity or being small-for-date.

M

macrosystem Bronfenbrenner's term for a society's overall cultural patterns.

maturation Unfolding of a natural sequence of physical and behavioral changes, including readiness to master new abilities.

mechanistic model Model that views development as a passive, predictable response to stimuli.

meconium Fetal waste matter, excreted during the first few days after birth.

menarche Girl's first menstruation.

mental retardation Significantly subnormal cognitive functioning.

mesosystem Bronfenbrenner's term for linkages between two or more microsystems.

metacognition Awareness of one's own mental processes.

metamemory Understanding of processes of memory.

microgenetic study Study design that enables researchers to directly observe change by repeated testing over a short time.

microsystem Bronfenbrenner's term for a setting in which a child interacts with others on an everyday, face-to-face basis.

mnemonic strategies Techniques to aid memory.

monozygotic (one-egg) twins Twins resulting from the division of a single zygote after fertilization; also called *identical twins.*

moratorium Identity status, described by Marcia, in which a person is considering alternatives (in crisis) and seems headed for commitment.

mother-infant bond Mother's feeling of close, caring connection with her newborn.

multifactorial transmission Combination of genetic and environmental factors to produce certain complex traits.

mutations Permanent alterations in genes or chromosomes that may produce harmful characteristics.

mutual regulation Process by which infant and caregiver communicate emotional states to each other and respond appropriately.

myelination Process of coating neural pathways with a fatty substance (myelin) that enables faster communication between cells.

N

nativism Theory that human beings have an inborn capacity for language acquisition.

natural childbirth Method of childbirth that seeks to prevent pain by eliminating the mother's fear through education about the physiology of reproduction and training in breathing and relaxation for use during delivery.

natural selection According to Darwin's theory of evolution, process by which characteristics that promote survival of a species are reproduced in successive generations, and characteristics that do not promote survival die out.

naturalistic observation Research method in which behavior is studied in natural settings without intervention or manipulation.

neglect Failure to meet a child's basic needs.

neonatal jaundice Condition, in many newborn babies, caused by immaturity of the liver and evidenced by yellowish appearance; can cause brain damage if not treated promptly.

neonatal period First four weeks of life, a time of transition from intrauterine dependency to independent existence.

neonate Newborn baby, up to 4 weeks old.

neurons Nerve cells.

niche-picking Tendency of a person, especially after early childhood, to seek out environments compatible with his or her genotype.

nonnormative Characteristic of an unusual event that has an impact on a particular person or a typical event that happens at an unusual time of life.

nonshared environmental effects Unique environment in which each child grows up, consisting of distinctive influences or influences that affect one child differently than another.

normative Characteristic of an event that is experienced in a similar way by most people in a group.

nuclear family Two-generational kinship, economic, and household unit consisting of one or two parents and their biological children, adopted children, or stepchildren.

O

obesity Overweight in relation to age, sex, height, and body type; sometimes defined as having a body mass index (weight for height) at or above the 95th percentile of growth curves for children of the same age and sex.

object permanence Piaget's term for the understanding that a person or object still exists when out of sight.

observational learning Learning through watching the behavior of others.

obsessive-compulsive disorder Anxiety aroused by repetitive, intrusive thoughts, images, or impulses, often leading to compulsive ritual behaviors.

operant conditioning Learning based on association of behavior with its consequences.

operational definition Definition stated solely in terms of the operations or procedures used to produce or measure a phenomenon.

oppositional defiant disorder (ODD) Pattern of behavior, persisting into middle childhood, marked by negativity, hostility, and defiance.

organismic model Model that views development as internally initiated by an active organism and as occurring in a sequence of qualitatively different stages.

organization (1) Mnemonic strategy of categorizing material to be remembered. (2) Piaget's term for the creation of systems of knowledge.

Otis-Lennon School Ability Test (OLSAT8) Group intelligence test for kindergarten through twelfth grade.

overt aggression Aggression that is openly directed at its target.

P

participant observation Research method in which the observer lives with the people or participates in the activity being observed.

parturition Process of uterine, cervical, and other changes, usually lasting about two weeks, preceding childbirth.

patchwork self In Elkind's terminology, sense of identity constructed by substituting other people's attitudes, beliefs, and commitments for one's own.

permissive In Baumrind's terminology, parenting style emphasizing self-expression and self-regulation.

personal fable Elkind's term for conviction that one is special, unique, and not subject to the rules that govern the rest of the world.

phenotype Observable characteristics of a person.

phonetic, or code-emphasis, approach Approach to teaching reading that emphasizes decoding of unfamiliar words.

physical abuse Action taken to endanger a child involving potential bodily injury.

Piagetian approach Approach to the study of cognitive development that describes qualitative stages in cognitive functioning.

plasticity (1) Modifiability of performance. (2) Modifiability of the brain through experience.

play therapy Therapeutic approach in which a child plays freely while a therapist observes and occasionally comments, asks questions, or makes suggestions.

polygenic inheritance Pattern of inheritance in which multiple genes affect a complex trait.

postconventional morality (or morality of autonomous moral principles) Third level in Kohlberg's theory of moral reasoning in which people follow internally held moral principles and can decide among conflicting moral standards.

postmature Referring to a fetus not yet born as of 42 weeks' gestation.

power assertion Disciplinary strategy designed to discourage undesirable behavior through physical or verbal enforcement of parental control.

pragmatics Practical knowledge needed to use language for communicative purposes.

preconventional morality First level of Kohlberg's theory of moral reasoning, in which control is external and rules are obeyed in order to gain rewards or avoid punishment or out of self-interest.

prejudice Unfavorable attitude toward members of certain groups outside one's own, especially racial or ethnic groups.

prelinguistic speech Forerunner of linguistic speech; utterance of sounds that are not words. Includes crying, cooing, babbling, and accidental and deliberate imitation of sounds without understanding their meaning.

preoperational stage In Piaget's theory, second major stage of cognitive development, in which children become more sophisticated in their use of symbolic thought but are not yet able to use logic.

prepared childbirth Method of childbirth that uses instruction, breathing exercises, and social support to induce controlled physical responses to uterine contractions and reduce fear and pain.

pretend play Play involving imaginary people or situations; also called *fantasy play, dramatic play,* or *imaginative play.*

preterm (premature) infants Infants born before completing the 37th week of gestation.

primary sex characteristics Organs directly related to reproduction, which enlarge and mature during adolescence.

private speech Talking aloud to oneself with no intent to communicate.

procedural knowledge Acquired skills stored in long-term memory.

prosocial behavior Any voluntary behavior intended to help others.

protective factors Influences that reduce the impact of early stress and tend to predict positive outcomes.

proximodistal principle Principle that development proceeds from within to without; that is, that parts of the body near the center develop before the extremities.

psychoanalytic perspective View of development as shaped by unconscious forces.

psychological aggression Verbal attack by a parent that may result in psychological harm to a child.

psychometric approach Approach to the study of cognitive development that seeks to measure the quantity of intelligence a person possesses.

psychosexual development In Freudian theory, unvarying sequence of stages of personality development during infancy, childhood, and adolescence, in which gratification shifts from the mouth to the anus and then to the genitals.

psychosocial development In Erikson's eight-stage theory, socially and culturally influenced process of development of the ego, or self.

puberty Process by which a person attains sexual maturity and the ability to reproduce.

punishment In operant conditioning, stimulus that discourages repetition of a behavior.

Q

qualitative change Change in kind, structure, or organization, such as the change from nonverbal to verbal communication.

qualitative research Research that focuses on nonnumerical data, such as subjective experiences, feelings, or beliefs.

quantitative change Change in number or amount, such as in height, weight, or size of vocabulary.

quantitative research Research that focuses on objectively measurable data.

quantitative trait loci (QTL) Interaction of multiple genes, each with effects of varying sizes, to produce a complex trait.

R

reaction range Potential variability, depending on environmental conditions, in the expression of a hereditary trait.

real self Self one actually is.

recall Ability to reproduce material from memory.

recessive inheritance Pattern of inheritance in which a child receives identical recessive alleles, resulting in expression of a nondominant trait.

recognition Ability to identify a previously encountered stimulus.

reflex behavior Automatic, involuntary, innate response to stimulation.

rehearsal Mnemonic strategy to keep an item in working memory through conscious repetition.

reinforcement In operant conditioning, stimulus that encourages repetition of a desired behavior.

relational aggression Aggression aimed at damaging or interfering with another person's relationships, reputation, or psychological well-being; also called *covert* or *indirect aggression.*

representational ability Piaget's term for capacity to store mental images or symbols of objects and events.

representational mappings In neo-Piagetian terminology, second stage in development of self-definition, in which a child makes logical connections between aspects of the self but still sees these characteristics in all-or-nothing terms.

representational systems In neo-Piagetian terminology, third stage in development of self-definition, characterized by breadth, balance, and the integration and assessment of various aspects of the self.

resilient children Children who weather adverse circumstances, function well despite challenges or threats, or bounce back from traumatic events.

retrieval Process by which information is accessed or recalled from memory storage.

risk factors Conditions that increase the likelihood of a negative developmental outcome.

rough-and tumble play Vigorous play involving wrestling, hitting, and chasing, often accompanied by laughing and screaming.

S

sample Group of participants chosen to represent the entire population under study.

scaffolding Temporary support to help a child master a task.

schemes Piaget's term for organized patterns of behavior used in particular situations.

schizophrenia Mental disorder marked by loss of contact with reality; symptoms include hallucinations and delusions.

school phobia Unrealistic fear of going to school; may be a form of *separation anxiety disorder* or *social phobia.*

scientific method System of established principles and processes of scientific inquiry.

script General remembered outline of a familiar, repeated event, used to guide behavior.

secondary sex characteristics Physiological signs of sexual maturation (such as breast development and growth of body hair) that do not involve the sex organs.

secular trend Trend that can be seen only by observing several generations, such as the trend toward earlier attainment of adult height and sexual maturity that began a century ago.

secure attachment Pattern in which an infant cries or protests when the primary caregiver leaves and actively seeks out the caregiver upon his or her return.

self-awareness Realization that one's existence and functioning are separate from those of other people and things.

self-concept Sense of self; descriptive and evaluative mental picture of one's abilities and traits.

self-conscious emotions Emotions, such as embarrassment, empathy, and envy, that depend on self-awareness.

self-definition Cluster of characteristics used to describe oneself.

self-efficacy Sense of capability to master challenges and achieve goals.

self-esteem Judgment a person makes about his or her self-worth.

self-evaluative emotions Emotions, such as pride, shame, and guilt, that depend on both self-awareness and knowledge of socially accepted standards of behavior.

self-fulfilling prophecy False expectation or prediction of behavior that tends to come true because it leads people to act as if it already were true.

self-regulation Child's independent control of behavior to conform to understood social expectations.

sensitive periods Times in development when a person is particularly open to certain kinds of experiences.

sensorimotor stage Piaget's first stage in cognitive development, during which infants learn through senses and motor activity.

sensory memory Initial, brief, temporary storage of sensory information.

separation anxiety Distress shown by an infant when a familiar caregiver leaves.

separation anxiety disorder Condition involving excessive, prolonged anxiety concerning separation from home or from people to whom a child is attached.

sequential study Study design that combines cross-sectional and longitudinal techniques.

seriation Ability to order items along a dimension.

sex chromosomes Pair of chromosomes that determines sex: XX in the normal female, XY in the normal male.

sex-linked inheritance Pattern of inheritance in which certain characteristics carried on the X chromosome inherited from the mother are transmitted differently to her male and female offspring.

sexual abuse Sexual activity involving a child and an older person.

sexual orientation Gender focus of consistent sexual, romantic, and affectionate interest, either heterosexual, homosexual, or bisexual.

sexually transmitted diseases (STDs) Diseases spread by sexual contact.

shaken baby syndrome (SBS) Form of maltreatment found mainly in children under 2 years but as old as 5, usually resulting in serious, irreversible brain trauma.

single representations In neo-Piagetian terminology, first stage in development of self-definition, in which children describe themselves in terms of individual, unconnected characteristics and in all-or-nothing terms.

situational compliance Kochanska's term for obedience of a parent's orders only in the presence of signs of ongoing parental control.

slow-to-warm-up children Children whose temperament is generally mild but who are hesitant about accepting new experiences.

small-for-date (small-for-gestational-age) infants Infants whose birth weight is less than that of 90 percent of babies of the same gestational age, as a result of slow fetal growth.

social capital Family and community resources on which a person or family can draw.

social cognition Ability to understand that other people have mental states and to gauge their feelings and intentions.

social cognitive neuroscience An emerging interdisciplinary field that draws on cognitive neuroscience, information processing, and social psychology.

social cognitive theory Albert Bandura's expansion of social learning theory; holds that children learn gender roles through socialization.

social construction Concept about the nature of reality, based on societally shared perceptions or assumptions.

social-contextual approach Approach to the study of cognitive development by focusing on environmental influences, particularly parents and other caregivers.

social interaction model Model, based on Vygotsky's sociocultural theory, which proposes that children construct autobiographical memories through conversation with adults about shared events.

social learning theory Theory that behaviors are learned by observing and imitating models. Also called *social cognitive theory.*

social phobia Extreme fear and/or avoidance of social situations.

social promotion Policy of automatically promoting children even if they do not meet academic standards.

social referencing Understanding an ambiguous situation by seeking out another person's perception of it.

social speech Speech intended to be understood by a listener.

socialization Development of habits, skills, values, and motives shared by responsible, productive members of a society.

sociocultural theory Vygotsky's theory of how contextual factors affect children's development.

socioeconomic status (SES) Combination of economic and social factors describing an individual or family, including income, education, and occupation.

spermarche Boy's first ejaculation.

spontaneous abortion Natural expulsion from the uterus of an embryo or fetus that cannot survive outside the womb; also called *miscarriage.*

Stanford-Binet Intelligence Scales Individual intelligence test used to measure memory, spatial orientation, and practical judgment.

state of arousal Infant's physiological and behavioral status at a given moment in the periodic daily cycle of wakefulness, sleep, and activity.

Sternberg Triarchic Abilities Test (STAT) Test that seeks to measure componential, experiential, and contextual intelligence.

"still-face" paradigm Research procedure used to measure mutual regulation in infants 2 to 9 months old.

storage Retention of memories for future use.

Strange Situation Laboratory technique used to study attachment.

stranger anxiety Wariness of strange people and places, shown by some infants during the second half of the first year.

stuttering Involuntary, frequent repetition or prolongation of sounds or syllables.

substance abuse Repeated, harmful use of a substance, usually alcohol or other drugs.

substance dependence Addiction (physical, psychological, or both) to a harmful substance.

sudden infant death syndrome (SIDS) Sudden and unexplained death of an apparently healthy infant.

symbolic function Piaget's term for ability to use mental representations (words, numbers, or images) to which a child has attached meaning.

syntax Rules for forming sentences in a particular language.

systems of action Increasingly complex combinations of skills that permit a wider or more precise range of movement and more control of the environment.

T

telegraphic speech Early form of sentence use consisting of only a few essential words.

temperament Characteristic disposition, or style of approaching and reacting to situations.

teratogenic Capable of causing birth defects.

theory Coherent set of logically related concepts that seeks to organize, explain, and predict data.

theory of mind Awareness and understanding of mental processes.

theory of multiple intelligences Gardner's theory that each person has several distinct forms of intelligence.

transduction In Piaget's terminology, preoperational child's tendency to mentally link particular experiences, whether or not there is logically a causal relationship.

transitive inference Understanding of the relationship between two objects by knowing the relationship of each to a third object.

triarchic theory of intelligence Sternberg's theory describing three types of intelligence: componential (analytical ability), experiential (insight and originality), and contextual (practical thinking).

two-way (dual-language) learning Approach to second-language education in which English speakers and non-English speakers learn together in their own and each other's languages.

U

ultrasound Prenatal medical procedure using high-frequency sound waves to detect the outline of a fetus and its movements so as to determine whether a pregnancy is progressing normally.

V

vernix caseosa Oily substance on a neonate's skin that protects against infection.

violation-of-expectations Research method in which dishabituation to a stimulus that conflicts with experience is taken as evidence that an infant recognizes the new stimulus as surprising.

visible imitation Imitation with parts of one's body that one can see.

visual cliff Apparatus designed to give an illusion of depth and used to assess depth perception in infants.

visual guidance The use of the eyes to guide the movement of the hands (or other parts of the body).

visual preference Tendency of infants to spend more time looking at one sight than another.

visual-recognition memory Ability to distinguish a familiar visual stimulus from an unfamiliar one when shown both at the same time.

visually-based retrieval Process of retrieving the sound of a printed word upon seeing the word as a whole.

W

Wechsler Intelligence Scale for Children (WISC-III) Individual intelligence test for schoolchildren that yields verbal and performance scores as well as a combined score.

Wechsler Preschool and Primary Scale of Intelligence, Revised (WPPSI-III) Individual intelligence test for children ages 3 to 7 that yields verbal and performance scores as well as a combined score.

whole-language approach Approach to teaching reading that emphasizes visual retrieval and use of contextual clues.

withdrawal of love Disciplinary strategy that may involve ignoring, isolating, or showing dislike for a child.

working memory Short-term storage of information being actively processed.

Z

zone of proximal development (ZPD) Vygotsky's term for the difference between what a child can do alone and what the child can do with help.

zygote One-celled organism resulting from fertilization.

Bibliography

AAP Committee on Nutrition. (2003). Prevention of pediatric overweight and obesity. *Pediatrics, 112,* 424–430.

Aaron, V., Parker, K. D., Ortega, S., & Calhoun, T. (1999). The extended family as a source of support among African Americans. *Challenge: A Journal of Research on African American Men, 10*(2), 23–36.

Abbey, A., Andrews, F. M., & Halman, J. (1992). Infertility and subjective well-being: The mediating roles of self-esteem, internal control, and interpersonal conflict. *Journal of Marriage and the Family, 54,* 408–417.

Aber, J. L., Brown, J. L., & Jones, S. M. (2003). Developmental trajectories toward violence in middle childhood: Course, demographic differences, and response to school-based intervention. *Developmental Psychology, 39,* 324–348.

Abma, J. C., & Sonenstein, F. L. (2001). Sexual activity and contraceptive practices among teenagers in the United States, 1988 and 1995. *Vital and Health Statistics,* Series 23, No. 21.

Abma, J. C., Chandra, A., Mosher, W. D., Peterson, L., & Piccinino, L. (1997). Fertility, family planning, and women's health: New data from the 1995 National Survey of Family Growth. *Vital Health Statistics, 23*(19), Washington, DC: National Center for Health Statistics.

Abramovitch, R., Corter, C., & Lando, B. (1979). Sibling interaction in the home. *Child Development, 50,* 997–1003.

Abramovitch, R., Corter, C., Pepler, D., & Stanhope, L. (1986). Sibling and peer interactions: A final follow-up and comparison. *Child Development, 57,* 217–229.

Abramovitch, R., Pepler, D., & Corter, C. (1982). Patterns of sibling interaction among preschool-age children. In M. E. Lamb (Ed.), *Sibling relationships: Their nature and significance across the lifespan.* Hillsdale, NJ: Erlbaum.

Achenbach, T. M., & Howell, C. T. (1993). Are American children's problems getting worse? A 13-year comparison. *Journal of the American Academy of Child and Adolescent Psychiatry, 32,* 1145–1154.

Ackard, D. M., Neumark-Sztainer, D., Story, M., & Perry, C. (2003). Overeating among adolescents: Prevalence and associations with weight-related characteristics and psychological health. *Pediatrics, 111,* 67–74.

Ackerman, B. P., Brown, E. D., & Izard, C. E. (2004). The relations between persistent poverty and contextual risk and children's behavior in elementary school. *Developmental Psychology, 40,* 367–377.

Ackerman, B. P., Kogos, J., Youngstrom, E., Schoff, K., & Izard, C. (1999). Family instability and the problem behaviors of children from economically disadvantaged families. *Developmental Psychology, 35*(1), 258–268.

Ackerman, M. J., Siu, B. L., Sturner, W. Q., Tester, D. J., Valdivia, C. R., Makielski, J. C., & Towbin, J. A. (2001). Postmortem molecular analysis of SCN5A defects in sudden infant death syndrome. *Journal of the American Medical Association, 286,* 2264–2269.

Acredolo, L. P. (1978). Development of spatial orientation in infancy. *Developmental Psychology, 14,* 224–234.

Acredolo, L. P. (1990). Behavioral approaches to spatial orientation in infancy. In A. Diamond (Ed.), *The development and neural bases of higher cognitive functions* (pp. 596–607). New York: New York Academy of Sciences.

Acs, G., Shulman, R., Ng, M. W., & Chussid, S. (1999). Tooth decay may slow child's growth. *Pediatric Dentistry, 21,* 109–113.

ACT for Youth Upstate Center of Excellence. (2002). *Adolescent brain development. Research facts and findings.* [A collaboration of Cornell University, University of Rochester, and the NYS Center for School Safety.] [Online]. Available: http://www.human.cornell.edu/actforyouth. Access date: March 23, 2004.

Adam, E. K., Gunnar, M. R., & Tanaka, A. (2004). Adult attachment, parent emotion, and observed parenting behavior: Mediator and moderator models. *Child Development, 75,* 110–122.

Adams, L. A., & Rickert, V. I. (1989). Reducing bedtime tantrums: Comparison between positive routines and graduated extinction. *Pediatrics, 84,* 756–761.

Adams, R., & Laursen, B. (2001). The organization and dynamics of adolescent conflict with parents and friends. *Journal of Marriage and the Family, 63,* 97–110.

Adler, N. E., Ozer, E. J., & Tschann, J. (2003). Abortion among adolescents. *American Psychologist, 58,* 211–217.

Adolph, K. E. (1997). Learning in the development of infant locomotion. *Monographs of the Society for Research in Child Development, 62*(3, Serial No. 251).

Adolph, K. E. (2000). Specificity of learning: Why infants fall over a veritable cliff. *Psychological Science, 11,* 290–295.

Adolph, K. E. & Avolio, A. M. (2000). Walking infants adapt locomotion to changing body dimensions. *Journal of Experimental Psychology: Human Perception and Performance, 26,* 1148–1166.

Adolph, K. E., & Eppler, M. A. (2002). Flexibility and specificity in infant motor skill acquisition. In J. Fagen & H. Hayne (Eds.), *Progress in infancy research* (vol. 2, pp. 121–167). Mahwah, NJ: Lawrence Erlbaum Associates.

Adolph, K. E., Vereijken, B., & Denny, M. A. (1998). Learning to crawl. *Child Development, 69,* 1299–1312.

Adolph, K. E., Vereijken, B., & Shrout, P. E. (2003). What changes in infant walking and why. *Child Development, 74,* 475–497.

Agosin, M. (1999). Pirate, conjurer, feminist. In J. Rodden (Ed.), *Conversations with Isabel Allende* (pp. 35–47). Austin: University of Texas Press.

Ahnert, L., & Lamb, M. E. (2003). Shared care: Establishing a balance between home and child care settings. *Child Development, 74,* 1044–1049.

Ainsworth, M. D. S. (1967). *Infancy in Uganda: Infant care and the growth of love.* Baltimore: Johns Hopkins University Press.

Ainsworth, M. D. S. (1969). Object relations, dependency, and attachment: A theoretical review of the infant-mother relationship. *Child Development, 40,* 969–1025.

Ainsworth, M. D. S., Blehar, M. C., Waters, E., & Wall, S. (1978). *Patterns of attachment: A psychological study of the strange situation.* Hillsdale, NJ: Erlbaum.

Akinbami, L. J., & Schoendorf, K. C. (2002). Trends in childhood asthma: Prevalence, health care utilization, and mortality. *Pediatrics, 110,* 315–322.

Alaimo, K., Olson, C. M., & Frongillo, E. A. (2001). Food insufficiency and American school-aged children's cognitive, academic, and psychosocial development. *Pediatrics, 108,* 44–53.

Alan Guttmacher Institute (AGI). (1994). *Sex & America's teenagers.* New York: Author.

Alan Guttmacher Institute (AGI). (1999a). *Facts in brief: Teen sex and pregnancy* [Online]. Available: http://www.agi_usa.org/pubs/fb_teen_sex.html#sfd. Access date: January 31, 2000.

Alan Guttmacher Institute (AGI). (1999b). Occasional report: Why is teenage pregnancy declining? The roles of abstinence, sexual activity and contraceptive use. [Online]. Available: http://www.agi_usa.org/pubs/or

_teen_preg_decline.html. Access date: January 31, 2000.

Albanese, A., & Stanhope, R. (1993). Growth and metabolic data following growth hormone treatment of children with intrauterine growth retardation. *Hormone Research, 39,* 8–12.

Alexander, K. L., Entwisle, D. R., & Dauber, S. L. (1993). First-grade classroom behavior: Its short- and long-term consequences for school performance. *Child Development, 64,* 801–814.

Alfred, Lord Tennyson (1850). "In Memoriam A. H. H., Canto 54"

Aligne, C. A., & Stoddard, J. J. (1997). Tobacco and children: An economic evaluation of the medical effects of parental smoking. *Archives of Pediatric and Adolescent Medicine, 151,* 648–653.

Allen, G. L., & Ondracek, P. J. (1995). Age-sensitive cognitive abilities related to children's acquisition of spatial knowledge. *Developmental Psychology, 31,* 934–945.

Allen, J. P., & Philliber, S. (2001). Who benefits most from a broadly targeted prevention program? Differential efficacy across populations in the Teen Outreach Program. *Journal of Community Psychology, 29,* 637–655.

Allen, J. P., McElhaney, K. B., Land, D. J., Kuperminc, G. P., Moore, C. W., O'Beirner-Kelly, H., and Kilmer, S. L. (2003). A secure base in adolescence: Markers of attachment security in the mother-adolescent relationship. *Child Development, 74,* 292–307.

Allen, K. R., Blieszner, R., & Roberto, K. A. (2000). Families in the middle and later years: A review and critique of research in the 1990s. *Journal of Marriage and the Family, 62,* 911–926.

Allende, I. (1995). *Paula* (M. S. Peden, Trans.). New York: HarperCollins.

Al-Oballi Kridli, S. (2002). Health beliefs and practices among Arab Women. *MCN, The American Journal of Maternal/Child nursing, 27,* 178–182.

Alsaker, F. D. (1992). Pubertal timing, overweight, and psychological adjustment. *Journal of Early Adolescence, 12*(4), 396–419.

Alvidrez, J., & Weinstein, R. S. (1999). Early teacher perceptions and later student academic achievement. *Journal of Educational Psychology, 91,* 731–746.

Amato, P. R. (1987). Family processes in one-parent, stepparent, and intact families: The child's point of view. *Journal of Marriage and the Family, 49,* 327–337.

Amato, P. R. (1999). Children of divorced parents as young adults. In E. M. Hetherington (Ed.), *Coping with divorce, single parenting, and marriage: A risk and resiliency perspective* (pp. 147–163). Mahwah, NJ: Erlbaum.

Amato, P. R. (2000). The consequences of divorce for adults and children. *Journal of Marriage and the Family, 62,* 1269–1287.

Amato, P. R., & Booth, A. (1997). *A generation at risk: Growing up in an era of family upheaval.* Cambridge, MA: Harvard University Press.

Amato, P. R., & Gilbreth, J. G. (1999). Nonresident fathers and children's well-being: A meta-analysis. *Journal of Marriage and the Family, 61,* 557–573.

Amato, P. R., & Keith, B. (1991). Parental divorce and adult well-being: A meta-analysis. *Journal of Marriage and the Family, 53,* 43–58.

Amato, P. R., Kurdek, L. A., Demo, D. H., & Allen, K. R. (1993). Children's adjustment to divorce: Theories, hypotheses, and empirical support. *Journal of Marriage and the Family, 55,* 23–54.

American Academy of Child and Adolescent Psychiatry (AACAP). (1997). *Children's sleep problems.* Fact sheet no. 34.

American Academy of Child and Adolescent Psychiatry (AACAP). (1997). *Children's sleep problems.* Fact sheet no. 34.

American Academy of Pediatrics (AAP). (1986). *Positive approaches to day care dilemmas: How to make it work.* Elk Grove Village, IL: Author.

American Academy of Pediatrics (AAP). (1989a, November). *The facts on breast feeding.* Fact sheet. Elk Grove Village, IL: Author.

American Academy of Pediatrics (AAP). (1989b). Follow-up on weaning formulas. *Pediatrics, 83,* 1067.

American Academy of Pediatrics (AAP). (1992, Spring). Bedtime doesn't have to be a struggle. *Healthy Kids,* pp. 4–10.

American Academy of Pediatrics (AAP). (1996, October). *Where we stand.* [Online]. Available: http://www.aap.org/advocacy/wwestand.htm.

American Academy of Pediatrics (AAP) and Canadian Paediatric Society. (2000). Prevention and management of pain and stress in the neonate. *Pediatrics, 105*(2), 454–461.

American Academy of Pediatrics (AAP) and Center to Prevent Handgun Violence. (1994). *Keep your family safe from firearm injury.* Washington, DC: Center to Prevent Handgun Violence.

American Academy of Pediatrics (AAP) Committee on Accident and Poison Prevention. (1988). Snowmobile statement. *Pediatrics, 82,* 798–799.

American Academy of Pediatrics (AAP) Committee on Adolescence. (1994). Sexually transmitted diseases. *Pediatrics, 94,* 568–572.

American Academy of Pediatrics (AAP) Committee on Adolescence. (1999). Adolescent pregnancy—Current trends and issues: 1998. *Pediatrics, 103,* 516–520.

American Academy of Pediatrics (AAP) Committee on Adolescence. (2000). Suicide and suicide attempts in adolescents. *Pediatrics, 105*(4), 871–874.

American Academy of Pediatrics (AAP) Committee on Adolescence. (2001). Condom use by adolescents. *Pediatrics, 107*(6), 1463–1469.

American Academy of Pediatrics (AAP) Committee on Adolescence. (2003). Policy statement: Identifying and treating eating disorders. *Pediatrics, 111,* 204–211.

American Academy of Pediatrics (AAP) Committee on Adolescence and Committee on Early Childhood, Adoption, and Dependent Care. (2001). Care of adolescent parents and their children. *Pediatrics, 107,* 429–434.

American Academy of Pediatrics (AAP) Committee on Bioethics. (1992, July). Ethical issues in surrogate motherhood. *AAP News,* 14–15.

American Academy of Pediatrics (AAP) Committee on Bioethics. (2001). Ethical issues with genetic testing in pediatrics. *Pediatrics, 107*(6), 1451–1455.

American Academy of Pediatrics (AAP) Committee on Child Abuse and Neglect. (2001). Shaken baby syndrome: Rotational cranial injuries—Technical report. *Pediatrics, 108,* 206–210.

American Academy of Pediatrics (AAP) Committee on Children with Disabilities. (2001). The pediatrician's role in the diagnosis and management of autistic spectrum disorder in children. *Pediatrics, 107*(5), 1221–1226.

American Academy of Pediatrics (AAP) Committee on Children with Disabilities and Committee on Drugs (1996). Medication for children with attentional disorders. *Pediatrics, 98,* 301–304.

American Academy of Pediatrics (AAP) Committee on Communications. (1995). Sexuality, contraception, and the media. *Pediatrics, 95,* 298–300.

American Academy of Pediatrics (AAP) Committee on Community Health Services. (1996). Health needs of homeless children and families. *Pediatrics, 88,* 789–791.

American Academy of Pediatrics (AAP) Committee on Drugs. (1980). Marijuana. *Pediatrics, 65,* 652–656.

American Academy of Pediatrics (AAP) Committee on Drugs. (1994). The transfer of drugs and other chemicals into human milk. *Pediatrics, 93,* 137–150.

American Academy of Pediatrics (AAP) Committee on Drugs. (2000). Use of psychoactive medication during pregnancy and possible effects on the fetus and newborn. *Pediatrics, 105,* 880–887.

American Academy of Pediatrics (AAP) Committee on Drugs and Committee on Bioethics. (1997). Considerations related to the use of recombinant human growth hormone in children. *Pediatrics, 99,* 122–128.

American Academy of Pediatrics (AAP) Committee on Environmental Health. (1997). Environmental tobacco smoke: A hazard to children. *Pediatrics, 99,* 639–642.

American Academy of Pediatrics (AAP) Committee on Environmental Health. (1998). Screening for elevated blood lead levels. *Pediatrics, 101,* 1072–1078.

American Academy of Pediatrics (AAP) Committee on Fetus and Newborn and American College of Obstetricians and Gynecologists (ACOG) Committee on Obstetric Practice. (1996). Use and abuse of the Apgar score. *Pediatrics, 98,* 141–142.

American Academy of Pediatrics (AAP) Committee on Genetics. (1996). Newborn screening fact sheet. *Pediatrics, 98,* 1–29.

American Academy of Pediatrics (AAP) Committee on Genetics. (1999). Folic acid for the prevention of neural tube defects. *Pediatrics, 104,* 325–327.

American Academy of Pediatrics (AAP) Committee on Infectious Diseases. (2000). Recommended childhood immunization schedule—United States, January-December, 2000 (pp. 105, 148).

American Academy of Pediatrics (AAP) Committee on Injury and Poison Prevention. (1995). Bicycle helmets. *Pediatrics, 95,* 609–610.

American Academy of Pediatrics (AAP) Committee on Injury and Poison Prevention. (2000). Firearm-related injuries affecting the pediatric population. *Pediatrics, 105*(4), 888–895.

American Academy of Pediatrics (AAP) Committee on Injury and Poison Prevention. (2001a). Bicycle helmets. *Pediatrics, 108*(4), 1030–1032.

American Academy of Pediatrics (AAP) Committee on Injury and Poison Prevention. (2001b). Injuries associated with infant walkers. *Pediatrics, 108*(3), 790–792.

American Academy of Pediatrics (AAP) Committee on Injury and Poison Prevention and Committee on Sports Medicine and Fitness. (1999). Policy statement: Trampolines at home, school, and recreational centers. *Pediatrics, 103,* 1053–1056.

American Academy of Pediatrics (AAP) Committee on Native American Child Health and Committee on Infectious Diseases. (1999). Immunizations for Native American children. *Pediatrics, 104,* 564–567.

American Academy of Pediatrics (AAP) Committee on Nutrition. (1992a). Statement on cholesterol. *Pediatrics, 90,* 469–473.

American Academy of Pediatrics (AAP) Committee on Nutrition. (1992b). The use of whole cow's milk in infancy. *Pediatrics, 89,* 1105–1109.

American Academy of Pediatrics (AAP) Committee on Nutrition. (2003). Prevention of pediatric overweight and obesity. *Pediatrics, 112*(2), 424–430.

American Academy of Pediatrics (AAP) Committee on Pediatric AIDS. (2000). Education of children with human immunodeficiency virus infection. *Pediatrics, 105,* 1358–1360.

American Academy of Pediatrics (AAP) Committee on Pediatric AIDS and Committee on Infectious Diseases. (1999). Issues related to human immunodeficiency virus transmission in schools, child care, medical settings, the home, and community. *Pediatrics, 104,* 318–324.

American Academy of Pediatrics Committee on Pediatric Research. (2000). Race/ethnicity, gender, socioeconomic status—Research exploring their effects on child health: A subject review. *Pediatrics, 105,* 1349–1351.

American Academy of Pediatrics (AAP) Committee on Practice and Ambulatory Medicine and Section on Ophthalmology. (1996). Eye examination and vision screening in infants, children, and young adults. *Pediatrics, 98,* 153–157.

American Academy of Pediatrics (AAP) Committee on Practice and Ambulatory Medicine and Section on Ophthalmology. (2002). Use of photoscreening for children's vision screening. *Pediatrics, 109,* 524–525.

American Academy of Pediatrics (AAP) Committee on Psychosocial Aspects of Child and Family Health. (1998). Guidance for effective discipline. *Pediatrics, 101,* 723–728.

American Academy of Pediatrics (AAP) Committee on Psychosocial Aspects of Child and Family Health. (2002). Coparent or second-parent adoption by same-sex parents. *Pediatrics, 109*(2), 339–340.

American Academy of Pediatrics (AAP) Committee on Psychosocial Aspects of Child and Family Health and Committee on Adolescence. (2001). Sexuality education for children and adolescence. *Pediatrics, 108*(2), 498–502.

American Academy of Pediatrics (AAP) Committee on Public Education (2001). Policy statement: Children, adolescents, and television. *Pediatrics, 107,* 423–426.

American Academy of Pediatrics (AAP) Committee on Sports Medicine and Fitness. (1997). Participation in boxing by children, adolescents, and young adults. *Pediatrics, 99,* 134–135.

American Academy of Pediatrics (AAP) Committee on Sports Medicine and Fitness. (December 1992). Fitness, activity, and sports participation in the preschool child (RE9265) policy statement: *Pediatrics, 90*(6).

American Academy of Pediatrics (AAP) Committee on Sports Medicine and Fitness. (1999). Human immunodeficiency virus and other blood-borne viral pathogens in the athletic setting. *Pediatrics, 104*(6), 1400–1403.

American Academy of Pediatrics (AAP) Committee on Sports Medicine and Fitness. (2000). Injuries in youth soccer: A subject review. *Pediatrics, 105*(3), 659–660.

American Academy of Pediatrics (AAP) Committee on Sports Medicine and Fitness. (2001). Risk of injury from baseball and softball in children. *Pediatrics, 107*(4), 782–784.

American Academy of Pediatrics (AAP) Committee on Sports Medicine and Committee on School Health. (1989). Organized athletics for preadolescent children. *Pediatrics, 84,* 583–584.

American Academy of Pediatrics (AAP) Committee on Substance Abuse. (2001). Tobacco's toll: Implications for the pediatrician. *Pediatrics, 107,* 794–798.

American Academy of Pediatrics (AAP) Committee on Substance Abuse and Committee on Children with Disabilities. (1993). Fetal alcohol syndrome and fetal alcohol effects. *Pediatrics, 91,* 1004–1006.

American Academy of Pediatrics (AAP) Newborn Screening Task Force (2000). Serving the family from birth to the medical home. A report from the Newborn Screening Task Force convened in Washington, DC, May 10–11, 1999. *Pediatrics, 106*(2), Part 2 of 3.

American Academy of Pediatrics (AAP) Task Force on Infant Positioning and SIDS. (1997). Does bed sharing affect the risk of SIDS? *Pediatrics, 100,* 272.

American Academy of Pediatrics (AAP) Task Force on Newborn and Infant Hearing. (1999). Newborn and infant hearing loss: Detection and intervention. *Pediatrics, 103,* 527–530.

American Academy of Pediatrics (AAP) Work Group on Breastfeeding. (1997). Breastfeeding and the use of human milk. *Pediatrics, 100,* 1035–1039.

American Association of Retired Persons (AARP) (2002). Facts about grandparents raising grandchildren. [Online]. Available: http://www.aarp.org/confacts/grandparents/ grandfacts. html. Access date: December 18, 2002.

American Association of University Women (AAUW) Educational Foundation. (1998a, October 14). *Gender gaps fact sheets.* [Online]. Available: http://www.aauw.org/home.html.

American Association of University Women (AAUW) Educational Foundation. (1998b, October 14). *Technology gender gap develops while gaps in math and science narrow, AAUW Foundation report shows.* [Online, Press Release]. Available: http://www.aauw.org/2000/ggpr.html.

American Association of University Women (AAUW) Educational

Foundation. (1992). *The AAUW report: How schools shortchange girls.* Washington, DC: Author.

American College of Obstetrics and Gynecology (ACOG). (1994). *Exercise during pregnancy and the postpartum pregnancy* (Technical Bulletin No. 189). Washington DC: Author.

American Foundation for the Prevention of Venereal Disease (AFPVD). (1988). *Sexually transmitted disease [venereal disease]: Prevention for everyone* (16th rev. ed.). New York: Author.

American Psychiatric Association (APA). (1994). *Diagnostic and statistical manual of mental disorders* (4th ed.). Washington, DC: Author.

American Psychological Association, (undated). *Answers to your questions about sexual orientation and homosexuality* [Brochure]. Washington, DC: Author.

American Psychological Association. (2002). Ethical principles of psychologists and code of conduct. *American Psychologist,* 57, 1060–1073.

American Psychological Association and American Academy of Pediatrics. (1996). *Raising children to resist violence: What you can do* [On-line, Brochure]. Available: http://www.apa.org/pubinfo/apaaap.html

American Psychological Association Commission on Violence and Youth. (1994). *Reason to Hope.* Washington, DC: Author.

American Public Health Association. (2004). Disparities in infant mortality. Fact sheet. [Online]. Available: http://www.medscape.com/viewarticle/472721.

Ames, E. W. (1997). *The development of Romanian orphanage children adopted to Canada: Final report* (National Welfare Grants Program, Human Resources Development, Canada). Burnaby, BC, Canada: Simon Fraser University, Psychology Department.

Ammenheuser, M. M., Berenson, A. B., Babiak, A. E., Singleton, C. R., & Whorton, E. B. (1998). Frequencies of hprt mutant lymphocytes in marijuana-smoking. *Mutation Research, 403,* 55–64.

Amsel, E., Goodman, G., Savoie, D., & Clark, M. (1996). The development of reasoning about causal and noncausal influences on levers. *Child Development, 67,* 1624–1646.

Anastasi, A. (1988). *Psychological testing* (6th ed.). New York: Macmillan.

Anastasi, A., & Schaefer, C. E. (1971). Note on concepts of creativity and intelligence. *Journal of Creative Behavior, 3,* 113–116.

Anastasi, A., & Urbina, S. (1997). *Psychological testing* (7th ed.). Upper Saddle River, NJ: Prentice-Hall.

Anda, R. F., Croft, J. B., Felitti, V. J., Nordenberg, D., Giles, W. H., Williamson, D. F., & Giovina, G. A. (1999). Adverse childhood experiences and smoking during adolescence and adulthood. *Journal of the American Medical Association, 282*(17), 1652–1658.

Andersen, A. E. (1995). Eating disorders in males. In K. D. Brownell & C. G. Fairburn (Eds.), *Eating disorders and obesity: A comprehensive handbook* (pp. 177–187). New York: Guilford.

Andersen, R. E., Crespo, C. J., Bartlett, S. J., Cheskin, L. J., & Pratt, M. (1998). Relationship of physical activity and television watching with body weight and level of fatness among children: Results from the Third National Health and Nutrition Examination Survey. *Journal of the American Medical Association, 279,* 938–942.

Anderson, A. H., Clark, A., & Mullin, J. (1994). Interactive communication between children: Learning how to make language work in dialog. *Journal of Child Language, 21,* 439–463.

Anderson, C. A., Berkowitz, L., Donnerstein, E., Huesmann, L. R., Johnson, J. D., Linz, D., Malamuth, N. M., & Wartella, E. (2003). The influence of media violence on youth. *Psychological Science in the Public Interest, 4,* 81–110.

Anderson, D., & Anderson, R. (1999). The cost-effectiveness of home birth. *Journal of Nurse-Midwifery, 44*(1), 30–35.

Anderson, D. R., Huston, A. C., Schmitt, K. L., Linebarger, D. L., & Wright, J. C. (2001). Early childhood television viewing and adolescent behavior. *Monographs of the Society for Research in Child Development,* Serial No. 264, *66*(1).

Anderson, M. (1992). *My Lord, what a morning.* Madison, WI: University of Wisconsin Press.

Anderson, M. (1992). Marian Anderson plans move to Portland, Oregon with her nephew, James DePriest. *Jet,* July 13, 33.

Anderson, M. (1993). Marian Anderson 1897–1993. *Time,* April 19, 24.

Anderson, M. (1993). Voice of rights struggle Marian Anderson, 96, opera pioneer succumbs. *Jet, 54,* April 26, 14–18.

Anderson, M. (1993). Song of Freedom: Marian Anderson broke barriers by touching hearts. *People Weekly,* April 26, 126.

Anderson, M., Kaufman, J., Simon, T. R., Barrios, L., Paulozzi, L., Ryan, G., Hammond, R., Modzeleski, W., Feucht, T., Potter, L., & the School-Associated Violent Deaths Study Group. (2001). School-associated violent deaths in the United States, 1994–1999. *Journal of the American Medical Association, 286*(21), 2695–2702.

Anderson, P., Doyle, L. W., and the Victorian Infant Collaborative Study Group (2003). *Journal of the American Medical Association, 289,* 3264–3272.

Anderson, P., Doyle, L. W., and the Victorian Infant Collaborative Study Group. (2003). Neurobehavioral outcomes of school-age children born extremely low birth weight or very preterm in the 1990s. *Journal of the American Medical Association, 289,* 3264–3272.

Anderson, R. N. (2002). Deaths: Leading causes for 2000. *National Vital Statistics Reports, 50*(16). Hyattsville, MD: National Center for Health Statistics.

Anderson, R. N., & Smith, B. L. (2003). Deaths: Leading causes for 2001. *National Vital Statistics Reports, 52*(9). Hyattsville, MD: National Center for Health Statistics.

Anderson, S. E., Dallal, G. E., & Must, A. (2003). Relative weight and race influence average age at menarche: Results from two nationally representative surveys of U.S. girls studied 25 years apart. *Pediatrics 2003, 111,* 844–850.

Anderson, W. F. (1998). Human gene therapy. *Nature, 392*(Suppl.), 25–30.

Anderssen, N., Amlie, C., & Ytteroy, E. A. (2002). Outcomes for children with lesbian or gay parents: A review of studies from 1978 to 2000. *Scandinavian Journal of Psychology, 43*(4), 335–351.

Angelsen, N. K., Vik, T., Jacobson, G., & Bakketeig, L. S. (2001). Breast feeding and cognitive development at age 1 and 5 years. *Archives of Disease in Childhood, 85*(3), 183–188.

Anisfeld, M. (1996). Only tongue protrusion modeling is matched by neonates. *Developmental Review, 16,* 149–161.

Ann Bancroft, 1955–. (1998). National Women's Hall of Fame. [Online]. Available: http://www.jerseycity.k12.nj.us/womenshistory/bancroft.htm. Access date: April 4, 2002.

Ann Bancroft (1955–), explorer. (1999). Women in American history by Encyclopedia Britannica. [Online]. Available: http://www.britannica.com/women/articles/Bancroft_Ann.html. Access date: April 4, 2002.

Ann Bancroft, explorer. (undated). [Online]. http://www.people/memphis.edu/~cbburr/gold/bancroft.htm. Access date: April 4, 2002.

Anorexia nervosa-Part I. (2003, February). *Harvard Mental Health Letter, 19*(8), 1–4.

Antonarakis, S. E., & Down Syndrome Collaborative Group. (1991). Parental origin of the extra chromosome in trisomy 21 as indicated by analysis of DNA polymorphisms. *New England Journal of Medicine, 324,* 872–876.

Apgar, V. (1953). A proposal for a new method of evaluation of the newborn infant. *Current Research in Anesthesia and Analgesia, 32,* 260–267.

Archer, S. L. (1993). Identity in relational contexts: A methodological proposal. In J. Kroger (Ed.), *Discussions on ego identity* (pp. 75–99). Hillsdale, NJ: Erlbaum.

Arcus, D., & Kagan, J. (1995). Temperament and craniofacial variation in the first two years. *Child Development, 66,* 1529–1540.

Arend, R., Gove, F., & Sroufe, L. A. (1979). Continuity of individual adaptation from infancy to kindergarten: A predictive study of egoresiliency and curiosity in preschoolers. *Child Development, 50,* 950–959.

Arias, E., & Smith, B. L. (2003). Deaths: Preliminary data for 2001. *National Vital Statistics Reports, 51*(5). Hyattsville, MD: National Center for Health Statistics.

Arias, E., MacDorman, M. F., Strobino, D. M., & Guyer, B. (2003). Annual summary of vital statistics—2002. *Pediatrics, 112,* 1215–1230.

Ariès, P. (1962). *Centuries of childhood.* New York: Random House.

Armistead, L., Summers, P., Forehand, R., Morse, P. S., Morse, E., & Clark, L. (1999). Understanding of HIV/AIDS among children of HIV-infected mothers: Implications for prevention, disclosure, and bereavement. *Children's Health Care, 28,* 277–295.

Arnett, J. J. (1999). Adolescent storm and stress, reconsidered. *American Psychologist, 54,* 317–326.

Arnett, J. J. (2000). Emerging adulthood: A theory of development from the late teens through the twenties. *American Psychologist, 55,* 469–480.

Arnett, J. J. (2003). Conceptions of the transition to adulthood among emerging adults in American ethnic groups. In J. J. Arnett and N. L. Galambos (Eds.), Exploring cultural conceptions of the transition to adulthood. *New Directions for Child and Adolescent Development, 100,* 63–75.

Arnett, J. J., and Galambos, N. L. (2003). Culture and conceptions of adulthood, In J. J. Arnett and N. L. Galambos (eds.). Exploring cultural conceptions of the transition to adulthood. *New Directions for Child and Adolescent Development, 100,* 91–98.

Arnold, D. S., & Whitehurst, G. J. (1994). Accelerating language development through picture book reading: A summary of dialogic reading and its effects. In D. K. Dickinson (Ed.), *Bridges to literacy: Children, families, and schools* (pp. 103–128). Oxford: Blackwell.

Ashman, S. B., & Dawson, G. (2002). Maternal depression, infant psychobiological development, and risk for depression. In S. H. Goodman, & I. H. Gotlib (Eds.), *Children of depressed parents: Mechanisms of risk and implications for treatment* (pp. 37–58). Washington, DC, American Psychological Association.

Associated Press. (2004, April 29). Mom in C-section case received probation: Woman originally charged with murder for delaying operation. [Online]. Available: http://www.msnbc.msn.com/id/4863415/. Access date: June 8, 2004.

Astington, J. W. (1993). *The child's discovery of the mind.* Cambridge, MA: Harvard University Press.

Astington, J. W., & Jenkins, J. M. (1999). A longitudinal study of the relation between language and theory-of-mind development. *Developmental Psychology, 35,* 1311–1320.

Athansiou, M. S. (2001). Using consultation with a grandmother as an adjunct to play therapy. *Family Journal—Consulting and Therapy for Couples and Families, 9,* 445–449.

Austin, E. W., Pinkleton, B. E., & Fujioka, Y. (2000). The role of interpretation processes and parental discussion in the media's effects on adolescents' use of alcohol. *Pediatrics, 105*(2), 343–349.

Autism-Part I. (2001, June). *The Harvard Mental Health Letter, 17*(12), pp. 1–4.

Autism-Part II. (2001, July). *The Harvard Mental Health Letter, 18*(1), pp. 1–4.

Aylward, G. P., Pfeiffer, S. I., Wright, A., & Verhulst, S. J. (1989). Outcome studies of low birth weight infants published in the last decade: A meta analysis. *Journal of Pediatrics, 115,* 515–520.

Azar, B. (2002, January). At the frontier of science. *Monitor on Psychology,* pp. 40–41.

Azuma, H. (1994). Two modes of cognitive socialization in Japan and the United States. In P. M. Greenfield & R. R. Cocking (Eds.), *Cross-cultural roots of minority child development* (pp. 275–284). Hillsdale, NJ: Erlbaum.

Babu, A., & Hirschhorn, K. (1992). A guide to human chromosome defects (Birth Defects: Original Article Series, 28[2]). White Plains, NY: March of Dimes Birth Defects Foundation.

Bachman, J. G., & Schulenberg, J. (1993). How part-time work intensity relates to drug use, problem behavior, time use, and satisfaction among high school seniors: Are these consequences or merely correlates? *Developmental Psychology, 29,* 220–235.

Baddeley, A. (1996). Exploring the central executive. *Quarterly Journal of Experimental Psychology: Human Experimental Psychology* (Special Issue: Working Memory), *49A,* 5–28.

Baddeley, A. (1998). Recent developments in working memory. *Current Opinion in Neurobiology, 8,* 234–238.

Baddeley, A. D. (1981). The concept of working memory: A view of its current state and probable future development. *Cognition, 10,* 17–23.

Baddeley, A. D. (1986). *Working memory.* London: Oxford University Press.

Baddeley, A. D. (1992). Working memory. *Science, 255,* 556–559.

Bagwell, C. L., Newcomb, A. F., & Bukowski, W. M. (1998). Preadolescent friendship and peer rejection as predictors of adult adjustment. *Child Development, 69,* 140–153.

Bailey, A., Le Couteur, A., Gottesman, I., & Bolton, P. (1995). Autism as a strongly genetic disorder: Evidence from a British twin study. *Psychological Medicine, 25,* 63–77.

Baillargeon, R. (1994a). How do infants learn about the physical world? *Current Directions in Psychological Science, 3,* 133–140.

Baillargeon, R. (1994b). Physical reasoning in young infants: Seeking explanations for impossible events. *British Journal of Developmental Psychology, 12,* 9–33.

Baillargeon, R. (1999). Young infants' expectations about hidden objects. *Developmental Science, 2,* 115–132.

Baillargeon, R., & DeVos, J. (1991). Object permanence in young infants: Further evidence. *Child Development, 62,* 1227–1246.

Baird, A. A., Gruber, S. A., Fein, D. A., Maas, L. C., Steingard, R. J., Renshaw, P. F., Cohen, B. M., & Yurgelon-Todd, D. A. (1999). Functional magnetic resonance imaging of facial affect recognition in children and adolescents. *Journal of the American Academy of Child and Adolescent Psychiatry, 38,* 195–199.

Baldwin, D. A., & Moses, L. J. (1996). The ontogeny of social information gathering. *Child Development, 67,* 1915–1939.

Baldwin, J. (1972). *No Name in the Street,* New York: Dial Press.

Balercia, G., Mosca, F., Mantero, F., Boscaro, M., Mancini, A., Ricciardo-Lamonica, G., & Littarru, G. (2004). Coenzyme q(10) supplementation in infertile men with idiopathic asthenozoospermia: An open, uncontrolled pilot study. *Fertility & Sterility, 81,* 93–98.

Ball, T. M., Castro-Rodriguez, J. A., Griffith, K. A., Holberg, C. J., Martinez, F. D., & Wright, A. L. (2000). Siblings, day-care attendance, and the risk of asthma and wheezing during childhood. *New England Journal of Medicine, 343,* 538–543.

Baltes, P. B., Reese, H. W., & Lipsitt, L. (1980). Life-span developmental psychology. *Annual Review of Psychology, 31,* 65–110.

Bandura, A. (1977). *Social learning theory.* Englewood Cliffs, NJ: Prentice-Hall.

Bandura, A. (1986). *Social foundations of thought and action: A social cognitive theory.* Englewood Cliffs, NJ: Prentice-Hall.

Bandura, A. (1989). Social cognitive theory. In R. Vasta (Ed.), *Annals of child development.* Greenwich, CT: JAI.

Bandura, A. (1994). Self-efficacy. In V. S. Ramachaudran (Ed.), *Encyclopedia of human behavior* (vol. 4, pp. 71–81). New York: Academic Press.

Bandura, A., & Walters, R. H. (1963). *Social learning and personality development.* New York: Holt, Rinehart, & Winston.

Bandura, A., Barbaranelli, C., Caprara, G. V., & Pastorelli, C. (1996). Multifaceted impact of self-efficacy beliefs on academic functioning. *Child Development, 67,* 1206–1222.

Bandura, A., Barbaranelli, C., Caprara, G. V., & Pastorelli, C. (2001). Self-efficacy beliefs as shapers of children's aspirations and career trajectories. *Child Development 72*(1), 187–206.

Bandura, A., Ross, D., & Ross, S. A. (1961). Transmission of aggression through imitation of aggressive models. *Journal of Abnormal and Social Psychology, 63,* 575–582.

Bandura, A., Ross, D., & Ross, S. A. (1963). Imitation of film-mediated aggressive models. *Journal of Abnormal and Social Psychology, 66,* 3–11.

Banks, E. (1989). Temperament and individuality: A study of Malay children. *American Journal of Orthopsychiatry, 59,* 390–397.

Barber, B. K. (1994). Cultural, family, and personal contexts of parent-adolescent conflict. *Journal of Marriage and the Family, 56,* 375–386.

Barber, B. L., & Eccles, J. S. (1992). Long-term influence of divorce and single parenting on adolescent, family and work-related values, behaviors, and aspirations. *Psychological Bulletin, 111*(1), 108–126.

Barker, D. J., & Lackland, D. T. (2003). Prenatal influences on stroke mortality in England and Wales. *Stroke: A Journal of Cerebral Circulation, 34,* 1598–1602.

Barkley, R. A. (1998a, February). How should attention deficit disorder be described? *Harvard Mental Health Letter,* p. 8.

Barkley, R. A. (1998b, September). Attention-deficit hyperactivity disorder. *Scientific American,* pp. 66–71.

Barkley, R. A., Murphy, K. R., & Kwasnik, D. (1996). Motor vehicle competencies and risks in teens and young adults with attention deficit hyperactivity disorder. *Pediatrics, 98,* 1089–1095.

Barlow, S. E., & Dietz, W. H. (1998). Obesity evaluation and treatment: Expert committee recommendations [Online]. *Pediatrics, 102*(3), e29. Available: http://www.pediatrics.org/cgi/content/full/102/3/e29.

Barnes, J., Sutcliffe, A., Ponjaert, I., Loft, A., Wennerholm, U., Tarlatzis, V., & Bonduelle, M. (2003, July). The European study of 1,523 ICSI/IVF versus naturally conceived 5-year-old children and their families: Family functioning and socio-emotional development. Paper presented at conference of European Society of Human Reproduction and Embryology, Madrid.

Barthel, J. (1982, May). Just a normal, naughty three-year-old. *McCall's,* pp. 78, 136–144.

Bartoshuk, L M., & Beauchamp, G. K. (1994). Chemical senses. *Annual Review of Psychology, 45,* 419–449.

Basso, O., & Baird, D. D. (2003). Infertility and preterm delivery, birth weight, and Caesarean section: A study within the Danish National Birth Cohort. *Human Reproduction, 18,* 2478–2484.

Bassuk, E. L. (1991). Homeless families. *Scientific American, 265*(6), 66–74.

Bates, E., Bretherton, I., & Snyder, L. (1988). *From first words to grammar: Individual differences and dissociable mechanisms.* New York: Cambridge University Press.

Bates, E., O'Connell, B., & Shore, C. (1987). Language and communication in infancy. In J. D. Osofsky (Ed.), *Handbook of infant development* (2d ed.). New York: Wiley.

Bateson, M. C. (1984). *With a daughter's eye: A memoir of Margaret Mead and Gregory Bateson.* New York: William Morrow & Co.

Bauer, P. J. (1996). What do infants recall of their lives? Memory for specific events by 1- to 2-year-olds. *American Psychologist, 51,* 29–41.

Bauer, P. J. (2002). Long-term recall memory: Behavioral and neuro-developmental changes in the first 2 years of life. *Current Directions in Psychological Science, 11,* 137–141.

Bauer, P. J., Wenner, J. A., Dropik, P. L., & Wewerka, S. S. (2000). Parameters of remembering and forgetting in the transition from infancy to early childhood. *Monographs of the Society for Research in Child Development,* Serial No. 263, *65*(4). Malden, MA: Blackwell Publishers.

Bauer, P. J., Wiebe, S. A., Carver, L. J., Waters, J. M., & Nelson, C. A. (2003). Developments in long-term explicit memory late in the first year of life: Behavioral and electrophysiological indices. *Psychological Science, 14,* 629–635.

Baumer, E. P., & South, S. J. (2001). Community effects on youth sexual activity. *Journal of Marriage and the Family, 63,* 540–554.

Baumrind, D. (1971). Harmonious parents and their preschool children. *Developmental Psychology, 41,* 92–102.

Baumrind, D. (1989). Rearing competent children. In W. Damon (Ed.), *Child development today and tomorrow* (pp. 349–378). San Francisco: Jossey-Bass.

Baumrind, D. (1991). Parenting styles and adolescent development. In J. Brooks-Gunn, R. Lerner, & A. C. Peterson (Eds.), *The encyclopedia of adolescence* (pp. 746–758). New York: Garland.

Baumrind, D. (1995). Commentary on sexual orientation: Research and social policy implications. *Developmental Psychology, 31,* 130–136.

Baumrind, D. (1996a). A blanket injunction against disciplinary use of spanking is not warranted by the data. *Pediatrics, 88,* 828–831.

Baumrind, D. (1996b). The discipline controversy revisited. *Family Relations, 45,* 405–414.

Baumrind, D., & Black, A. E. (1967). Socialization practices associated with dimensions of competence in preschool boys and girls. *Child Development, 38,* 291–327.

Bauserman, R. (2002). Child adjustment in joint-custody versus sole-custody arrangements: A meta-analytic review. *Journal of Family Psychology, 16,* 91–102.

Baydar, N., Greek, A., & Brooks-Gunn, J. (1997). A longitudinal study of the effects of the birth of a sibling during the first 6 years of life. *Journal of Marriage and the Family, 59,* 939–956.

Baydar, N., Hyle, P., & Brooks-Gunn, J. (1997). A longitudinal study of the effects of the birth of a sibling during preschool and early grade school years. *Journal of Marriage and the Family, 59,* 957–965.

Bayley, N. (1993). *Bayley Scales of Infant Development: II.* New York: Psychological Corporation.

Beal, C. R. (1994). *Boys and girls: The development of gender roles.* New York: McGraw-Hill.

Bearman, P. S., & Moody, J. (2004). Suicide and friendships among American adolescents. *American Journal of Public Health, 94,* 89–95.

Becker, A. E., Grinspoon, S. K., Klibanski, A., & Herzog, D. B. (1999). Eating disorders. *New England Journal of Medicine, 340,* 1092–1098.

Beckwith, L., Cohen, S. E., & Hamilton, C. E. (1999). Maternal sensitivity during infancy and subsequent life events relate to attachment representation at early adulthood. *Developmental Psychology, 35,* 693–700.

Behrman, R. E. (1992). *Nelson textbook of pediatrics* (13th ed.). Philadelphia: Saunders.

Beidel, D. C., & Turner, S. M. (1998). *Shy children, phobic adults: Nature and treatment of social phobia.* Washington, DC: American Psychological Association.

Beilin, H., (1994). Jean Piaget's enduring contribution to developmental psychology. In R. D. Parke, P. A. Ornstein, J. J. Rieser, & C. Zahn-Wexler (Eds.), *A century of developmental psychology* (pp. 257–290). Washington, DC: American Psychological Association.

Bekedam, D. J., Engelsbe1, S., Mol, B. W., Buitendijk, S. E., & van der Pal-de Bruin, K. M. (2002). Male predominance in fetal distress during labor. *American Journal of Obstetrics and Gynecology, 187,* 1605–1607.

Belizzi, M. (2002, May). *Obesity in children—What kind of future are we creating?* Presentation at the Fifty-Fifth World Health Assembly Technical Briefing, Geneva.

Bell, M. A., & Fox, N. A. (1992). The relations between frontal brain electrical activity and cognitive development during infancy. *Child Development, 63,* 1142–1163.

Bellinger, D., Leviton, A., Watermaux, C., Needleman, H., & Rabinowitz, M. (1987). Longitudinal analyses of prenatal and postnatal lead exposure and early cognitive development. *New England Journal of Medicine, 316*(17), 1037–1043.

Belsky, J. (1984). Two waves of day care research: Developmental effects and conditions of quality. In R. Ainslie (Ed.), *The child and the day care setting.* New York: Praeger.

Belsky, J. (1993). Etiology of child maltreatment: A developmental-ecological analysis. *Psychological Bulletin, 114,* 413–434.

Belsky, J., & Rovine, M. (1990). Patterns of marital change across the transition to parenthood: Pregnancy to three years postpartum. *Journal of Marriage and the Family, 52,* 5–19.

Belsky, J., Fish, M., & Isabella, R. (1991). Continuity and discontinuity in infant negative and positive emotionality: Family antecedents and attachment consequences. *Developmental Psychology, 27,* 421–431.

Belsky, J., Lang, M., & Huston, T. L. (1986). Sex typing and division of labor as determinants of marital change across the transition to parenthood. *Journal of Personality and Social Psychology, 50,* 517–522.

Bem, S. L. (1983). Gender schema theory and its implications for child development: Raising gender-aschematic children in a gender-schematic society. *Signs, 8,* 598–616.

Bem, S. L. (1985). Androgyny and gender schema theory: A conceptual and empirical integration. In T. B. Sondregger (Ed.), *Nebraska symposium on motivation, 1984: Psychology and gender.* Lincoln, NE: University of Nebraska Press.

Bem, S. L. (1993). *The lenses of gender: Transforming the debate on sexual inequality.* New Haven, CT: Yale University Press.

Benenson, J. F. (1993). Greater preference among females than males for dyadic interaction in early childhood. *Child Development, 64,* 544–555.

Benes, F. M., Turtle, M., Khan, Y., & Farol, P. (1994). Myelination of a key relay zone in the hippocampal formation occurs in the human brain during childhood, adolescence, and adulthood. *Archives of General Psychiatry, 51,* 447–484.

Benson, E. (2003). Intelligent intelligence testing. *Monitor on Psychology, 43*(2), 48–51.

Benson, J. B., & Uzgiris, I. C. (1985). Effect of self-inflicted locomotion on infant search activity. *Developmental Psychology, 21,* 923–931.

Benson, M. (1986). *Nelson Mandela: The man and the movement.* New York: Norton.

Ben-Ze'ev, A. (1997). Emotions and morality. *Journal of Value Inquiry, 31,* 195–212.

Bergeman, C. S., & Plomin, R. (1989). Genotype-environment interaction. In M. Bornstein & J. Bruner (Eds.), *Interaction in human development* (pp. 157–171). Hillsdale, NJ: Erlbaum.

Bergen, D., Reid, R., & Torelli, L. (2000). *Educating and caring for very young children: The infant-toddler curriculum.* Washington, DC: National Association for the Education of Young Children.

Berk, L. E. (1986a). Development of private speech among preschool children. *Early Child Development and Care, 24,* 113–136

Berk, L. E. (1986b). Private speech: Learning out loud. *Psychology Today, 20*(5), 34–42.

Berk, L. E. (1992). Children's private speech: An overview of theory and the status of research. In R. M. Diaz & L. E. Berk (Eds.), *Private speech: From social interaction to self-regulation* (pp. 17–53). Hillsdale, NJ: Erlbaum.

Berk, L. E., & Garvin, R. A. (1984). Development of private speech among low-income Appalachian children. *Developmental Psychology, 20,* 271–286.

Berkowitz, G. S., Skovron, M. L., Lapinski, R. H., & Berkowitz, R. L. (1990). Delayed childbearing and the outcome of pregnancy. *New England Journal of Medicine, 322,* 659–664.

Berkowitz, R. I., Wadden, T. A., Tershakovec, A. M., & Cronquist, J. L. (2003). Behavior therapy and sibutramine for the treatment of adolescent obesity: A randomized controlled trial. *Journal of the American Medical Association, 289,* 1805–1812.

Berndt, T. J., & Perry, T. B. (1990). Distinctive features and effects of early adolescent friendships. In R. Montemayor, G. R. Adams, & T. P. Gullotta (Eds.), *From childhood to adolescence: A transitional period?* (vol. 2, pp. 269–287). Newbury Park, CA: Sage.

Bernhardt, P. C. (1997). Influences of serotonin and testosterone in aggression and dominance: Convergence with social psychology. *Current Directions in Psychological Science, 6,* 44–48.

Bernstein, J. (1973). *Einstein.* New York: Viking.

Bernstein, N. (2004, March 7). Behind fall in pregnancy, a new teenage culture of restraint. *New York Times,* pp. 1, 36–37.

Bernstein, P. S. (2003). Achieving equity in women's and perinatal health. *Medscape Ob/Gyn & Women's Health, 8.* Posted 12/12/03.

Berrick, J. D. (1998). When children cannot remain home: Foster family care and kinship care. *The Future of Children, 8,* 72–87.

Berrueta-Clement, J. R., Schweinhart, L. J., Barnett, W. S., & Weikart, D. P. (1987). The effects of early educational intervention on crime and delinquency in adolescence and early adulthood. In J. D. Burchard & S. N. Burchard (Eds.), *Primary prevention of psychopathology: Vol. 10. Prevention of delinquent behavior* (pp. 220–240). Newbury Park, CA: Sage.

Berrueta-Clement, J. R., Schweinhart, L. J., Barnett, W. S., Epstein, A. S., & Weikart, D. P. (1985). *Changed lives: The effects of the Perry Preschool Program on youths through age 19.* Ypsilanti, MI: High/Scope.

Berry, M., Dylla, D. J., Barth, R. P., & Needell, B. (1998). The role of open adoption in the adjustment of adopted children and their families. *Children and Youth Services Review, 20,* 151–171.

Berry, R. J., Li, Z., Erickson, J. D., Li, S., Moore, C. A., Wang, H., Mulinare, J., Zhao, P., Wong, L.-Y. C., Gindler, J., Hong, S.-X., & Correa, A. for the China-U.S. Collaborative Project for Neural Tube Defect Prevention. (1999). Prevention of neural-tube defects with folic acid in China. *New England Journal of Medicine, 341,* 1485–1490.

Bertenthal, B. I., & Campos, J. J. (1987). New directions in the study of early experience. *Child Development, 58,* 560–567.

Bertenthal, B. I., & Clifton, R. K. (1998). Perception and action. In W. Damon (Ed.-in-Chief), D. Kuhn & R. S. Siegler (Vol. Eds.), *Handbook of child psychology, Vol. 2: Cognition perception, and language* (pp. 51–102). New York: Wiley.

Bertenthal, B. I., Campos, J. J., & Barrett, K. C. (1984). Self-produced locomotion: An organizer of emotional, cognitive, and social development in infancy. In R. N. Emde & R. J. Harmon (Eds.), *Continuities and discontinuities in development.* New York: Plenum.

Bertenthal, B. I., Campos, J. J., & Kermoian, R. (1994). An epigenetic perspective on the development of self-produced locomotion and its consequences. *Current Directions in Psychological Science, 3*(5), 140–145.

Beumont, P. J. V., Russell, J. D., & Touyz, S. W. (1993). Treatment of anorexia nervosa. *Lancet, 341,* 1635–1640.

Beversdorf, D. Q., Manning, S. E., Anderson, S. L., Nordgren, R. E., Walters, S. E., Cooley, W. C., Gaelic, S. E., & Bauman, M. L. (2001, November 10–15). *Timing of prenatal stressors and autism.* Presentation at the 31st Annual Meeting of the Society for Neuroscience, San Diego.

Bialystok, E., & Senman, L. (2004). Executive processes in appearance-reality tasks: The role of inhibition of attention and symbolic representation. *Child Development, 75,* 562–579.

Bielick, S., Chandler, K., & Broughman, S. P. (2001). *Homeschooling in the United*

States: 1999 (NCES 2001–033). Washington, DC: National Center for Education Statistics, U.S. Department of Education.

Bierman, K. L., Smoot, D. L., & Aumiller, K. (1993). Characteristics of aggressive-rejected, aggressive (nonrejected), and rejected (non-aggressive) boys. *Child Development, 64,* 139–151.

Birch, E. E., Garfield, S., Hoffman, D. R., Uauy, R. Birch, D. G. (2000). A randomized controlled trial of early dietary supply of long-chain polyunsaturated fatty acids and mental development in term infants. *Developmental Medicine & Child Neurology, 42,* 174–181.

Birmaher, B. (1998). Should we use antidepressant medications for children and adolescents with depressive disorders? *Psychopharmacology Bulletin, 34,* 35–39.

Birmaher, B., Ryan, N. D., Williamson, D. E., Brent, D. A., Kaufman, J., Dahl, R. E., Perel, J., & Nelson, B. (1996). Childhood and adolescent depression: A review of the past 10 years. *Journal of the American Academy of Child, 35,* 1427–1440.

Bishop, D. V. M., Price, T. S., Dale, P. S., & Plomin, R. (2003). Outcome of early language delay: II. Etiology of transient and persistent language difficulties. *Journal of Speech, Language, and Hearing Research, 46,* 561–575.

Bivens, J. A., & Berk, L. E. (1988, April). *A longitudinal study of the development of elementary school children's private speech.* Paper presented at the meeting of the American Educational Research Association, New Orleans, LA.

Bjork, J. M., Knutson, B., Fong, G. W., Caggiano, D. M., Bennett, S. M., & Hommer, D. W. (2004). Incentive-elicited brain activities in adolescents: Similarities and differences from young adults. *The Journal of Neuroscience, 24,* 1793–1802.

Bjorklund, D. F. (1997). The role of immaturity in human development. *Psychological Bulletin, 122,* 153–169.

Bjorklund, D. F., & Harnishfeger, K. K. (1990). The resources construct in cognitive development: Diverse sources of evidence and a theory of inefficient inhibition. *Developmental Review, 10,* 48–71.

Bjorklund, D. F., & Pellegrini, A. D. (2000). Child development and evolutionary psychology. *Child Development, 7*(6), 1687–1708.

Bjorklund, D. F., & Pellegrini, A. D. (2002). *The origins of human nature: Evolutionary developmental psychology.* Washington, DC: American Psychological Association.

Black, J. E. (1998). How a child builds its brain: Some lessons from animal studies of neural plasticity. *Preventive Medicine, 27,* 168–171.

Black, M. M., & Krishnakumar, A. (1998). Children in low-income, urban settings: Interventions to promote mental health and well-being. *American Psychologist, 53,* 636–646.

Black, M. M., Dubowitz, H., and Starr, R. H. (1999). African American fathers in low income, urban families: Development, behavior, and home environment of their three-year-old children. *Child Development, 70,* 967–978.

Black, R. E., Morris, S. S., & Bryce, J. (2003). Where and why are 10 million children dying each year? *The Lancet, 361,* 2226–2234.

Blair, C. (2002). School readiness: Integrating cognition and emotion in a neurobiological conceptualization of children's functioning at school entry. *American Psychologist, 57,* 111–127.

Blake, S. M., Ledsky, R., Goodenow, C., Sawyer, R., Lohrmann, D., & Windsor, R. (2003). Condom availability programs in Massachusetts high schools: Relationships with condom use and sexual behavior. *American Journal of Public Health, 93,* 955–962.

Blakeslee, S. (1997, April 17). Studies show talking with infants shapes basis of ability to think. *New York Times,* p. D21.

Bloom, B., & Tonthat, L. (2002). Summary health statistics for U.S. children: National Health Interview Survey, 1997. *Vital Health Statistics, 10*(203). Hyattsville, MD: National Center for Health Statistics.

Bloom, B., Cohen, R. A., Vickerie, J. L., & Wondimu, E. A. (2003). Summary health statistics for U.S. children: National Health Interview Survey, 2001. *Vital and Health Statistics, 10*(216). Hyattsville, MD: National Center for Health Statistics.

Bloom, H. (Ed.). (1999). *A scholarly look at* The Diary of Anne Frank. Philadelphia: Chelsea.

Blum, N. J., Taubman, B., & Nemeth, N. (2003). Relationship between age at initiation of toilet training and duration of training: A prospective study. *Pediatrics, 111,* 810–814.

Blyth, D. A., & Foster-Clark, F. S. (1987). Gender differences in perceived intimacy with different members of adolescents' social networks. *Sex Roles, 17,* 689–718.

Board of Education of the City of New York. (2002, May 6). Effects of the World Trade Center attack on NYC public school students. [Online]. Available: www.nycenet.edu. Access date: May 8, 2002.

Boatman, D., Freeman, J., Vining, E., Pulsifer, M., Miglioretti, D., Minahan, R., Carson, B., Brandt, J., & McKhann, G. (1999). Language recovery after left hemispherectomy in children with late onset seizures. *Annals of Neurology, 46*(4), 579–586.

Bodrova, E., & Leong, D. J. (1998). Adult influences on play: The Vygotskian approach. In D. P. Fromberg & D. Bergen (Eds.), *Play from birth to twelve and beyond: Contexts, perspectives, and meanings* (pp. 277–282). New York: Garland.

Bojczyk, K. E., & Corbetta, D. (2004). Object retrieval in the 1st year of life: Learning effects of task exposure and box transparency. *Developmental Psychology, 40,* 54–66.

Bolger, K. E., Patterson, C. J., Thompson, W. W., & Kupersmidt, J. B. (1995). Psychosocial adjustment among children experiencing persistent and intermittent family economic hardship. *Child Development, 66,* 1107–1129.

Bollinger, M. B. (2003). Involuntary smoking and asthma severity in children: Data from the Third National Health and Nutrition Examination Survey (NHANES III). *Pediatrics, 112,* 471.

Bond, C. A. (1989, September). A child prodigy from China wields a magical brush. *Smithsonian,* pp. 70–79.

Book, A. S., Starzyk, K. B., & Quinsey, V. L. (2001, November-December). The relationship between testosterone and aggression: A meta-analysis. *Aggression and Violent Behavior, 6,* 579–599.

Booth, A. E., & Waxman, S. (2002). Object names and object functions serve as cues to categories for infants. *Developmental Psychology, 38,* 948–957.

Booth, J. R., Perfetti, C. A., MacWhinney, B. (1999). Quick, automatic, and general activation of orthographic and phonological representations in young readers. *Developmental Psychology, 35*(1), 3–19.

Borman, G., Boulay, M., Kaplan, J., Rachuba, L., & Hewes, G. (1999, December 13). *Evaluating the longterm impact of multiple summer interventions on the reading skills of low-income, early-elementary students.* Preliminary report, Year 1. Baltimore, MD: Center for Social Organization of Schools, Johns Hopkins University.

Bornstein, M. H., & Sigman, M. D. (1986). Continuity in mental development from infancy. *Child Development, 57,* 251–274.

Bornstein, M. H., & Tamis-LeMonda, C. S. (1994). Antecedents of information processing skills in infants: Habituation, novelty responsiveness, and cross-modal transfer. *Infant Behavior and Development, 17,* 371–380.

Bornstein, M. H., Haynes, O. M., O'Reilly, A. W., & Painter, K. (1996). Solitary and collaborative pretense play in early childhood: Sources of individual variation in the development of representational competence. *Child Development, 67,* 2910–2929.

Bornstein, M. H., Haynes, O.M., Pascual, L., Painter, K. M., & Galperin, C. (1999). Play in two societies: Pervasiveness of process, specificity of structure. *Child Development, 70,* 317–331.

Bornstein, M. H., & Sigman, M. P. (1986). Continuity in mental development from infancy. *Child Development, 57,* 251–274.

Bornstein, M. H., Tamis-LeMonda, C. S., & Haynes, O. M. (1999). First words in the second year: Continuity, stability, and models of concurrent and predictive correspondence in vocabulary and verbal responsiveness across age and context. *Infant Behavior and Development, 22,* 65–85.

Bornstein, M., Kessen, W., & Weiskopf, S. (1976). The categories of hue in infancy. *Science, 191,* 201–202.

Borowsky, I. A., Ireland, M., & Resnick, M. D. (2001). Adolescent suicide attempts: Risks and protectors. *Pediatrics, 107*(3), 485–493.

Bosch, J., Sullivan, S., Van Dyke, D. C., Su, H., Klockau, L., Nissen, K., Blewer, K., Weber, E., & Eberly, S. S. (2003). Promoting a healthy tomorrow here for children adopted from abroad. *Contemporary Pediatrics, 20*(2), 69–86.

Bouchard, T. J. (1994). Genes, environment, and personality. *Science, 264,* 1700–1701.

Bouchard, T. J., & Loehlin, J. C. (2001). Genes, evolution, and personality. *Behavior Genetics, 31*(3), 243–273.

Boulton, M. J. (1995). Playground behaviour and peer interaction patterns of primary school boys classified as bullies, victims and not involved. *British Journal of Educational Psychology, 65,* 165–177.

Boulton, M. J., & Smith, P. K. (1994). Bully/victim problems in middle school children: Stability, self perceived competence, peer perception, and peer acceptance. *British Journal of Developmental Psychology, 12,* 315–329.

Boutin, P., Dina, C., Vasseur, F., Dubois, S. S., Corset, L., Seron, K., Bekris, L., Cabellon, J., Neve, B., Vasseur-Delannoy, V., Chikri, M., Charles, M. A., Clement, K., Lernmark, A., & Froguel, P. (2003). GAD2 on chromosome 10p12 is a candidate gene for human obesity. *Public Library of Science Biology, 1*(3), E68.

Bower, B. (1993). A child's theory of mind. *Science News, 144,* 40–42.

Bowlby, J. (1951). Maternal care and mental health. *Bulletin of the World Health Organization, 3,* 355–534.

Bowman, S. A., Gortmaker, S. L., Ebbeling, C. B., Pereira, M. A., Ludwig, D. S. (2004). Effects of fast food consumption on energy intake and diet quality among children in a national household survey. *Pediatrics, 113,* 112–118.

Boyles, S. (2002, January 27). Toxic landfills may boost birth defects. *WebMD Medical News.* [Online].

Boyum, L. A., & Parke, R. D. (1995). The role of family emotional expressiveness in the development of children's social competence. *Journal of Marriage and the Family, 57,* 593–608.

Bracher, G., & Santow, M. (1999). Explaining trends in teenage childbearing in Sweden. *Studies in Family Planning, 30,* 169–182.

Brackbill, Y., & Broman, S. H. (1979). *Obstetrical medication and development in the first year of life.* Unpublished manuscript.

Bradley, R. H. (1989). Home measurement of maternal responsiveness. In M. H. Bornstein (Ed.), *Maternal responsiveness: Characteristics and consequences* (New Directions for Child Development No. 43). San Francisco: Jossey-Bass.

Bradley, R. H., Corwyn, R. F., Burchinal, M., McAdoo, H. P., & Coll, C. G. (2001). The home environment of children in the United States: Part II: Relations with behavioral development through age thirteen. *Child Development, 72*(6), 1868–1886.

Bradley, R. H., Corwyn, R. F., McAdoo, H. P., & Coll, C. G. (2001). The home environment of children in the United States: Part I: Variation by age, ethnicity, and poverty status. *Child Development, 72*(6), 1844–1867.

Bradley, R., & Caldwell, B. (1982). The consistency of the home environment and its relation to child development. *International Journal of Behavioral Development, 5,* 445–465.

Bradley, R., Caldwell, B., & Rock, S. (1988). Home environment and school performance: A ten-year follow-up and examination of three models of environmental action. *Child Development, 59,* 852–867.

Braine, M. (1976). Children's first word combinations. *Monographs of the Society for Research in Child Development, 41*(1, Serial No. 164).

Bramlett, M. D., & Mosher, W. D. (2001). *First marriage dissolution, divorce, and remarriage: United States.* (Advance Data from Vital and Health Statistics, No. 323). Hyattsville, MD: National Center for Health Statistics.

Brass, L. M., Isaacsohn, J. L., Merikangas, K. R., & Robinette, C. D. (1992). A study of twins and stroke. *Stroke, 23*(2), 221–223.

Bratton, S. C., & Ray, D. (2002). Humanistic play therapy. In D. J. Cain (Ed.), *Humanistic psychotherapies: Handbook of research and practice* (pp. 369–402.). Washington, DC: American Psychological Association.

Braungart, J. M., Plomin, R., DeFries, J. C., & Fulker, D. W. (1992). Genetic influence on tester-rated infant temperament as assessed by Bayley's Infant Behavior Record: Nonadoptive and adoptive siblings and twins. *Developmental Psychology 28,* 40–47.

Braungart-Rieker, J., Garwood, M. M., Powers, B. P., & Notaro, P. C. (1998). Infant affect and affect regulation during the still-face paradigm with mothers and fathers: The role of infant characteristics and parental sensitivity. *Developmental Psychology, 34*(6), 1428–1437.

Braungart-Rieker, J. M., Garwood, M. M., Powers, B. P., & Wang, X. (2001). Parental sensitivity, infant affect, and affect regulation: Predictors of later attachment. *Child Development, 72,* 252–270.

Bray, J. H. (1991). Psychosocial factors affecting custodial and visitation arrangements. *Behavioral Sciences and the Law, 9,* 419–437.

Bray, J. H., & Hetherington, E. M. (1993). Families in transition: Introduction and overview. *Journal of Family Psychology, 7,* 3–8.

Brazelton, T. B. (1973). *Neonatal behavioral assessment scale.* Philadelphia: Lippincott.

Brazelton, T. B. (1984). *Neonatal behavioral assessment scale.* Philadelphia: Lippincott.

Brazelton, T. B., & Nugent, J. K. (1995). *Neonatal behavioral assessment scale* (3d ed.). Cambridge, England: Cambridge University Press.

Brehaut, J. C., Miller, A., Raina, P., McGrail, K. (February 2003). Childhood behavior disorders and injuries among children and youth: A population-based study. *Pediatrics, 111,* 262–269.

Breier, J. I., Simos, P. G., Fletcher, J. M., Castillo, E. M., Zhang, W., & Papanicolaou, A. C. (2003). Abnormal activation of temporoparietal language areas during phonetic analysis in children with dyslexia. *Neuropsychology, 17,* 610–621.

Bremner, J. G. (1989). Development of spatial awareness in infancy. In A. Slater & J. G. Bremner (Eds.), *Infant development* (pp. 123–141). London: Lawrence Erlbaum Associates.

Brener, N., Lowry, R., Kann, L., Kolbe, L., Lenhherr, J., Janssen, R., & Jaffe, H. (2002). Trends in sexual risk behaviors among high school students—United States, 1991–2001. *Morbidity and Mortality Weekly Report, 51*(38), 856–859.

Brenneman, K., Massey, C., Machado, S. F., & Gelman, R. (1996). Young children's plans differ for writing and drawing. *Cognitive Development, 11,* 397–419.

Brenner, R. A., Sismons-Morton, B. G., Bhaskar, B., Revenis, M., Das, A., & Clemens, J. D. (2003). Infant-parent bed sharing in an inner-city population. *Archives of Pediatrics and Adolescent Medicine, 57,* 33–39.

Brent, D. A., & Birmaher, B. (2002). Adolescent depression. *New England Journal of Medicine, 347,* 667–671.

Brent, R. L. (2004). Environmental causes of human congenital malformations: The pediatrician's role in dealing with these complex clinical problems caused by a multiplicity or environmental and genetic factors. *Pediatrics, 113,* 957–968.

Bretherton, I. (1990). Communication patterns, internal working models, and the intergenerational transmission of attachment relationships. *Infant Mental Health Journal, 11*(3), 237–252.

Bretherton, I. (Ed.). (1984). *Symbolic play: The development of social understanding.* Orlando, FL: Academic.

Brezina, T. (1999). Teenage violence toward parents as an adaptation to family strain: Evidence from a national survey of male adolescents. *Youth & Society, 30,* 416–444.

Brian, D. (1996). *Einstein: A life.* New York: Wiley.

Briss, P. A., Sacks, J. J., Addiss, D. G., Kresnow, M., & O'Neil, J. (1994). A nationwide study of the risk of injury associated with day care center attendance. *Pediatrics, 93,* 364–368.

Brody, G. H. (1998). Sibling relationship quality: Its causes and consequences. *Annual Review of Psychology, 49,* 1–24.

Brody, G. H., Flor, D. L., & Gibson, N. M. (1999). Linking maternal efficacy beliefs, developmental goals, parenting practices, and child competence in rural single-parent African American families. *Child Development, 70*(5), 1197–1208.

Brody, G. H., Ge., X., Conger, R., Gibbons, F. X., Murry, V. M., Gerrard, M., & Simons, R. L. (2001). The influence of neighborhood disadvantage, collective socialization, and parenting on African American children's affiliation with deviant peers. *Child Development, 72*(4), 1231–1246.

Brody, G. H., Kim, S., Murry, V. M., & Brown, A. C. (2004). Protective longitudinal paths linking child competence to behavioral problems among African American siblings. *Child Development, 75,* 455–467.

Brody, G. H., Stoneman, Z., & Flor, D. (1995). Linking family processes and academic competence among rural African American youths. *Journal of Marriage and the Family, 57,* 567–579.

Brody, G. H., Stoneman, Z., & Gauger, K. (1996). Parent-child relationships, family problem-solving behavior, and sibling relationship quality: The moderating role of sibling temperments. *Child Development, 67,* 1289–1300.

Brody, G. H., Stoneman, Z., Flor, D., McCrary, C., Hastings, L., & Conyers, O. (1994). Financial resources, parent psychological functioning, parent co-caregiving, and early adolescent competence in rural two-parent African-American families. *Child Development, 65,* 590–605.

Brody, J. E. (1995, June 28). Preventing birth defects even before pregnancy. *New York Times,* p. C10.

Brody, L. R., Zelazo, P. R., & Chaika, H. (1984). Habituation-dishabituation to speech in the neonate. *Developmental Psychology, 20,* 114–119.

Brodzinsky, D. (1997). Infertility and adoption adjustment: Considerations and clinical issues. In S. R. Leiblum (Ed.), *Infertility: Psychological issues and counseling strategies* (pp. 246–262). New York: Wiley.

Broidy, L. M., Tremblay, R. E., Brame, B., Fergusson, D., Horwood, J. L., Laird, R., Moffitt, T. E., Nagin, D. S., Bates, J. E., Dodge, K. A., Loeber, R., Lyam, D. R., Pettit, G. S., & Vitaro, F. (2003). Developmental trajectories of childhood disruptive behaviors and adolescent delinquency: A six-site cross-national study. *Developmental Psychology, 39,* 222–245.

Bronfenbrenner, U. (1986). Ecology of the family as a context for human development: Research perspectives. *Developmental Psychology, 22,* 723–742.

Bronfenbrenner, U. (1979). *The ecology of human development.* Cambridge, MA: Harvard University Press.

Bronfenbrenner, U. (1994). Ecological models of human development. In T. Husen & T. N. Postlethwaite (Eds.), *International encyclopedia of education* (2d ed., vol. 3, pp. 1643–1647). Oxford: Pergamon Press/Elsevier Science.

Bronfenbrenner, U., & Morris, P. A. (1998). The ecology of developmental processes. In W. Damon (Series Ed.) & R. Lerner (Vol. Ed.), *Handbook of child psychology: Vol. I. Theoretical models of human development* (5th ed., pp. 993–1028). New York: Wiley.

Bronfenbrenner, U., Belsky, J., & Steinberg, L. (1977). *Daycare in context. An ecological perspective on research and public policy.* Review prepared for Office of the Assistant Secretary for Planning and Evaluation, U.S. Department of Health, Education, and Welfare.

Bronner, E. (1999, January 22). Social promotion is bad; repeating a grade may be worse. *New York Times* [Online]. Available: http://search.nytimes.com/search/daily/bin/fastweb?getdocPsitePsiteP13235POPwAAAPsocial%7Epromotion.

Bronstein, P. (1988). Father-child interaction: Implications for gender role socialization. In P. Bronstein & C. P. Cowan (Eds.), *Fatherhood today: Men's changing role in the family.* New York: Wiley.

Bronstein, P., Clauson, J., Stoll, M. F., & Abrams, C. L. (1993). Parenting behavior and children's social, psychological, and academic adjustment in diverse family structures. *Family Relations, 42,* 268–276.

Brooks, P. J., Tomasello, M., Dodson, K., & Lewis, L. B. (1999). Young children's overgeneralizations with fixed transitivity verbs. *Child Development, 70,* 1325–1337.

Brooks, R., & Meltzoff, A. N. (2002). The importance of eyes: How infants interpret adult looking behavior. *Developmental Psychology, 38,* 958–966.

Brooks-Gunn, J. (2003). Do you believe in magic? What can we expect from early childhood intervention programs? *SRCD Social Policy Report, 17*(1).

Brooks-Gunn, J. Britto, P. R., & Brady, C. (1998). Struggling to make ends meet: Poverty and child development. In M. E. Lamb (Ed.), *Parenting and child development in "non-traditional" families* (pp. 279–304). Mahwah, NJ: Erlbaum.

Brooks-Gunn, J., & Duncan, G. J. (1997). The effects of poverty on children. *The Future of Children, 7,* 55–71.

Brooks-Gunn, J., & Duncan, G. J., Leventhal, T., & Aber, J. L. (1997). Lessons learned and future directions for research on the neighborhoods in which children live. In J. Brooks-Gunn, G. J. Duncan, & J. L. Aber (Eds.), *Neighborhood poverty: Context and consequences for children* (Vol. 1, pp. 279–297). New York: Russell Sage Foundation.
Brooks-Gunn, J., Britto, P. R., & Brady, C. (1998). Struggling to make ends meet: Poverty and child development. In M. E. Lamb (Ed.), *Parenting and child development in "non-traditional" families* (pp. 279–304). Mahwah, NJ: Erlbaum.
Brooks-Gunn, J., Han, W.-J., & Waldfogel, J. (2002). Maternal employment and child cognitive outcomes in the first three years of life: The NICHD study of early child care. *Child Development, 73,* 1052–1072.

Brooks-Gunn, J., Klebanov, P. K., Liaw, F., & Spiker, D. (1993). Enhancing the development of low birth weight, premature infants: Changes in cognition and behavior over the first three years. *Child Development, 64,* 736–753.

Brooks-Gunn, J., McCarton, C. M., Casey, P. H., et al. (1994). Early intervention in low-birth weight premature infants: Results through age 5 years from the Infant Health Development Program. *Journal of the American Medical Association, 272,*1257–1262.

Brosco, J. P. (1999). The early history of infant mortality rate in America: "A reflection upon the past and a prophecy of the future." *Pediatrics, 103,* 478–485.

Broude, G. J. (1995). *Growing up: A cross-cultural encyclopedia.* Santa Barbara, CA: ABC-CLIO.

Brown, A. L., Metz, K. E., & Campione, J. C. (1996). Social interaction and individual understanding in a community of learners: The influence of Piaget and Vygotsky. In A. Tryphon & J. Voneche (Eds.), *Piaget-Vygotsky: The social genesis of thought* (pp. 145–170). Hove, England: Psychology/Erlbaum (UK) Taylor & Francis.

Brown, B. (1999). Optimizing expression of the common human genome for child development. *Current Directions in Psychological Science, 8*(2), 37–41.

Brown, B. B., Mounts, N., Lamborn, S. D., & Steinberg, L. (1993). Parenting practices and peer group affiliation in adolescence. *Child Development, 64,* 467–482.

Brown, J. L. (1987). Hunger in the U.S. *Scientific American, 256*(2), 37–41.

Brown, J. R., & Dunn, J. (1996). Continuities in emotion understanding from three to six years. *Child Development, 67,* 789–802.

Brown, L. J., Kaste, L. M., Selwitz, R. H., & Furman, L. J. (1996). Dental caries and sealant usage in U.S. children, 1988–1991. *Journal of the American Dental Association, 127,* 335–343.

Brown, L. J., Wall, T. P., & Lazar, V. (1999). Trends in untreated caries in permanent teeth of children 6- to 18-years old. *Journal of the American Dental Association, 130,* 1637–1644.

Brown, L. J., Wall, T. P., & Lazar, V. (2000). Trends in untreated caries in primary teeth of children 2- to 10-years old. *Journal of the American Dental Association, 131,* 93–100.

Brown, L. M., & Gilligan, C. (1990, April). *The psychology of women and the development of girls.* Paper presented at the Laurel-Harvard Conference on the Psychology of Women and the Education of Girls, Cleveland, OH.

Brown, N. M. (1990). Age and children in the Kalahari. *Health and Human Development Research, 1,* 26–30.

Brown, S. S. (1985). Can low birth weight be prevented? *Family Planning Perspectives, 17*(3), 112–118.

Browne, A., & Finkelhor, D. (1986). Impact of child sexual abuse: A review of research. *Psychological Bulletin, 99*(1), 66–77.

Browning, E. B. (1857). *Aurora Leigh, A Poem.* London: J. Miller. (First published 1857.)

Bruck, M., & Ceci, S. J. (1997). The suggestibility of young children. *Current Directions in Psychological Science, 6,* 75–79.

Bruck, M., Ceci, S. J., & Hembrooke, H. (1998). Reliability and credibility of young children's reports: From research to policy and practice. *American Psychologist, 53,* 136–151.

Bruer, J. T. (2001). A critical and sensitive period primer. In D. B. Bailey, J. T. Bruer, F. J. Symons, & J. W. Lichtman (Eds.). *Critical thinking about critical periods: A series from the National Center for Early Development and Learning* (pp. 289–292). Baltimore, MD: Paul Brooks Publishing.

Bruner, A. B., Joffe, A., Duggan, A. K., Casella, J. F., & Brandt, J. (1996). Randomised study of cognitive effects of iron supplementation in non-anaemic iron-deficient adolescent girls. *Lancet, 348,* 992–996.

Bryant, B. K. (1987). Mental health, temperment, family, and friends: Perspectives on children's empathy and social perspective taking. In N. Eisenberg & J. Strayer (Eds.), *Empathy and its development* (pp. 245–270). Cambridge, UK; Cambridge University Press.

Buchanan, C. M., Eccles, J. S., & Becker, J. B. (1992). Are adolescents the victims of raging hormones? Evidence for activational effects of hormones on moods and behavior at adolescence. *Psychological Bulletin, 111*(1), 62–107.

Buckner, J. C., Bassuk, E. L., Weinreb, L. F., & Brooks, M. G. (1999). Homelessness and its relation to the mental health and behavior of low-income school-age children. *Developmental Psychology, 35*(1), 246–257.

Buhrmester, D. (1990). Intimacy of friendship, interpersonal competence, and adjustment during preadolescence and adolescence. *Child Development, 61,* 1101–1111.

Buhrmester, D. (1996). Need fulfillment, interpersonal competence, and the developmental contexts of early adolescent friendship. In W. M. Bukowski, A. F. Newcomb, & W. W. Hartup (Eds.), *The company they keep: Friendship in childhood and adolescence* (pp. 158–185). New York: Cambridge University Press.

Buhrmester, D., & Furman, W. (1990). Perceptions of sibling relationships during middle childhood and adolescence. *Child Development, 61,* 138–139.

Bukowski, W. M., & Kramer, T. L. (1986). Judgments of the features of friendship among early adolescent boys and girls. *Journal of Early Adolescence, 6,* 331–338.

Bulkley, K., & Fisler, J. (2002). A decade of charter schools: From theory to practice. Philadelphia: Consortium for Policy Research in Education, Graduate School of Education. University of Pennsylvania.

Bunikowski, R., Grimmer, I., Heiser, A., Metze, B., Schafer, A., & Obladen, M. (1998). Neurodevelopmental outcome after prenatal exposure to opiates. *European Journal of Pediatrics, 157,* 724–730.

Burchinal, M. R., Campbell, F. A., Bryant, D. M., Wasik, B. H., & Ramey, C. T. (1997). Early intervention and mediating processes in cognitive performance of children of low-income African American families. *Child Development, 68,* 935–954.

Burchinal, M. R., Roberts, J. E., Nabors, L. A., & Bryant, D. M. (1996). Quality of center child care and infant cognitive and language development. *Child Development, 67,* 606–620.

Bureau of Labor Statistics. (2002a). Annual social and economic supplement. *Current population survey.* Washington, DC: U.S. Department of Labor.

Bureau of Labor Statistics (2002b, March 29). Employment characteristics of families, 2000–2001 [news release] USDL 02–175. Washington, DC: U.S. Department of Labor.

Burhans, K. K., & Dweck, C. S. (1995). Helplessness in early childhood: The role of contingent worth. *Child Development, 66,* 1719–1738.

Burns, B. J., Phillips, S. D., Wagner, H. R., Barth, R. P., Kolko, D. J., Campbell, Y., & Landsverk, J. (2004). Mental health need and access to mental health services by youths involved with child welfare: A national survey. *Journal of the American Academy of Child & Adolescent Psychiatry, 43,* 960–970.

Burns, J. F. (1994, August 27). India fights abortion of female fetuses. *New York Times,* p. A5.

Bushnell, E. W., & Boudreau, J. P. (1993). Motor development and the mind: The potential role of motor abilities as a determinant of aspects of perceptual development. *Child Development, 64,* 1005–1021.

Bushnell, E. W., McKenzie, B. E., Lawrence, D. A., & Connell, S. (1995). The spatial coding strategies of 1-year-old infants in a locomotor search task. *Child Development 66,* 937–958.

Bussey, K., & Bandura, A. (1992). Self-regulatory mechanisms governing gender development. *Child Development, 63,* 1236–1250.

Bussey, K., & Bandura, A. (1999). Social cognitive theory of gender development and differentiation. *Psychological Review, 106,* 676–713

Butterworth, G., & Jarrett, N. (1991). What minds have in common in space: Spacial mechanisms serving joint visual attention in infancy. *British Journal of Developmental Psychology, 9,* 55–72.

Byrne, M., Agerbo, E., Ewald, H., Eaton, W. W., and Mortensen, P. B. (2003). Parental age and risk of schizophrenia. *Archives of General Psychiatry, 60,* 673–678.

Byrnes, J. P., & Fox, N. A. (1998). The educational relevance of research in cognitive neuroscience. *Educational Psychology Review, 10,* 297–342.

Cabrera, N. J., Tamis-LeMonda, C. S., Bradley, R. H., Hofferth, S., & Lamb, M. E. (2000). Fatherhood in the twenty-first century. *Child Development, 71,* 127–136.

Caldji, C., Diorio, J., & Meaney, M. J. (2003). Variations in maternal care alter GABA(A) receptor subunit expression in brain regions associated with fear. *Neuropsychopharmacology, 28,* 1950–1959.

Caldwell, B. M., & Bradley, R. H. (1984). *Home observation for measurement of the environment.* Unpublished manuscript, University of Arkansas at Little Rock.

Calkins, S. D., & Fox, N. A. (1992). The relations among infant temperament, security of attachment, and behavioral inhibition at twenty-four months. *Child Development, 63,* 1456–1472.

Call, K. T., Mortimer, J. T., & Shanahan, M. (1995). Helpfulness and the development of competence in adolescence. *Child Development, 66,* 129–138.

Campbell, A., Shirley, L., & Candy, J. (2004). A longitudinal study of gender-related cognition and behaviour. *Developmental Science, 7,* 1–9.

Campbell, A., Shirley, L., Heywood, C., & Crook, C. (2000). Infants' visual preference for sex-congruent babies, children, toys, and activities: A longitudinal study. *British Journal of Developmental Psychology, 18,* 479–498.

Campbell, F. A., Pungello, E. P., Miller-Johnson, S., Burchinal, M., & Ramey, C. T. (2001). The development of cognitive and academic abilities: Growth curves from an early childhood education experiment. *Developmental Psychology, 37*(2), 231–242.

Campfield, L. A., Smith, F. J., Guisez, Y., Devos, R., & Burn, P. (1995). Recombinant mouse OB protein: Evidence for a peripheral signal linking adiposity and central neural networks. *Science, 269,* 546–549.

Campos, J., Bertenthal, B., & Benson, N. (1980, April). *Self-produced locomotion and the extraction of form invariance.* Paper presented at the meeting of the International Conference on Infant Studies, New Haven, CT.

Camras, L. A., Oster, H., Campos, J., Campos, R., Vjiie, T., Miyake, K., Wang, L., & Meng, Z. (1998). Production of emotional facial expressions in European, American, Japanese, and Chinese infants. *Developmental Psychology, 34*(4), 616–628.

Canfield, R. L., Henderson, C. R., Cory-Slechta, D. A., Cox, C., Jusko, T. A., & Lanphear, B. P. (April 17, 2003). Intellectual impairment in children with blood lead concentrations below 10 μg per deciliter. *New England Journal of Medicine, 348,* 1517–1526.

Cantor, J. (1994). Confronting children's fright responses to mass media. In D. Zillman, J. Bryant, & A. C. Huston (Eds.), *Media, children, and the family: Social scientific, psychoanalytic, and clinical perspectives* (pp. 139–150). Hillsdale, NJ: Erlbaum.

Cao, A., Saba, L., Galanello, R., & Rosatelli, M. C. (1997). Molecular diagnosis and carrier screening for thalassemia. *Journal of the American Medical Association, 278,* 1273–1277.

Cao, X.-Y., Jiang, X.-M., Dou, Z.-H., Rakeman, M. A., Zhang, M.-L., O'Donnell, K., Ma, T., Amette, K., DeLong, N., & DeLong, G. R. (1994). Timing of vulnerability of the brain to iodine deficiency in endemic cretinism. *New England Journal of Medicine, 331,* 1739–1744.

Capaldi, D. M., Stoolmiller, M., Clark, S., & Owen, L. D. (2002). Heterosexual risk behaviors in at-risk young men from early adolescence to young adulthood: Prevalence, prediction, and association with STD contraction. *Developmental Psychology, 38,* 394–406.

Caplan, M., Vespo, J., Pedersen, J., & Hay, D. F. (1991). Conflict and its resolution in small groups of one- and two-year olds. *Child Development, 62,* 1513–1524.

Capute, A. J., Shapiro, B. K., & Palmer, F. B. (1987). Marking the milestones of language development. *Contemporary Pediatrics, 4*(4), 24.

Carlson, E. A. (1998). A prospective longitudinal study of attachment disorganization/disorientation. *Child Development, 69*(4), 1107–1128.

Carlson, E. A., Sroufe, L. A., & Egeland, B. (2004). The construction of experience: A longitudinal study of representation and behavior. *Child Development, 75,* 66–83.

Carlson, S. M., & Moses, L. J. (2001). Individual differences in inhibitory control and children's theory of mind. *Child Development, 72,* 1032–1053.

Carlson, S. M., Moses, L. J., & Hix, H. R. (1998). The role of inhibitory processes in young children's difficulties with deception and false belief. *Child Development, 69*(3), 672–691.

Carmichael, M. (2004, January 26). In parts of Asia, sexism is ingrained and gender selection often means murder. No girls, please. *Newsweek,* p. 50.

Carpenter, M., Akhtar, N., & Tomasello, M. (1998). Fourteen through 18-month-old infants differentially imitate intentional and accidental actions. *Infant Behavior and Development, 21,* 315–330.

Carpenter, M. W., Sady, S. P., Hoegsberg, B., Sady, M. A., Haydon, B., Cullinane, E. M., Coustan, D. R., & Thompson, P. D. (1988). Fetal heart rate response to maternal exertion. *Journal of the American Medical Association, 259*(20), 3006–3009.

Carpenter, R. G., Irgens, L. M., Blair, P. S., England, P. D., Fleming, P., Huber, J., Jorch, G., & Schreuder, P. (2004). Sudden unexplained infant death in 20 regions in Europe: Case control study. *The Lancet, 363,* 185–191.

Carraher, T. N., Schliemann, A. D., & Carraher, D. W. (1988). Mathematical concepts in everyday life. In G. B. Saxe and M. Gearhart (Eds.), Children's mathematics. *New Directions in Child Development, 41,* 71–87.

Carroll-Pankhurst, C., and Mortimer, E. A. (2001). Sudden infant death syndrome, bed sharing, parental weight, and age at death. *Pediatrics, 107*(3), 530–536.

Carskadon, M. A., Acebo, C., Richardson, G. S., Tate, B. A., & Seifer, R. (1997). Long nights protocol: Access to circadian parameters in adolescents. *Journal of Biological Rhythms, 12,* 278–289.

Casaer, P. (1993). Old and new facts about perinatal brain development. *Journal of Child Psychology and Psychiatry, 34*(1), 101–109.

Case, R. (1985). *Intellectual development: Birth to adulthood.* Orlando, FL: Academic Press.

Case, R. (1992). Neo-Piagetian theories of child development. In R. Sternberg & C. Berg (Eds.), *Intellectual development* (pp. 161–196). New York: Cambridge University Press.

Case, R., & Okamoto, Y. (1996). The role of central conceptual structures in the development of children's thought. *Monographs of the Society for Research in Child Development, 61*(1–2, serial no. 246).

Casey, B. M., McIntire, D. D., & Leveno, K. J. (2001). The continuing value of the Apgar score for the assessment of newborn infants. *New England Journal of Medicine, 344,* 467–471.

Casper, L. M. (1997). My daddy takes care of me: Fathers as care providers. *Current Population Reports* (P70–59). Washington, DC: U.S. Bureau of the Census.

Caspi, A. (2000). The child is father of the man: Personality continuity from childhood to adulthood. *Journal of Personality and Social Psychology, 78,* 158–172.

Caspi, A., & Silva, P. (1995). Temperamental qualities at age 3 predict personality traits in young adulthood: Longitudinal evidence from a birth cohort. *Child Development, 66,* 486–498.

Caspi, A., McClay, J., Moffitt, T. E., Mill, J., Martin, J., Craig, I. W., Taylor, A., & Poulton, R. (2002). Role of genotype in the cycle of violence in maltreated children. *Science, 297,* 851–854.

Cassidy, J. (1988). Child-mother attachment and the self in 6-year-olds. *Child Development, 59,* 121–134.

Cassidy, J., & Hossler, A. (1992). State and federal definitions of the gifted: An update. *Gifted Child Quarterly, 15,* 46–53.

Cassidy, K. W., Werner, R. S., Rourke, M., Zubernis, L. S., & Balaraman, G. (2003). The relationship between psychological understanding and positive social behaviors. *Social Development, 12,* 198–221.

Cavazanna-Calvo, M., Hacein-Bey, S., de Saint Basile, G., Gross, F., Yvon, E., Nusbaum, P., Selz, F., Hue, C., Certain, S., Casanova, J. L., Bousso, P., Deist, F. L., & Fischer, A. (2000). Gene therapy of human severe combined immunodeficiency (SCID)-X1 disease. *Science, 288,* 669–672.

Ceci, S. J. (1991). How much does schooling influence general intelligence and its cognitive components? A reassessment of the evidence. *Developmental Psychology, 27,* 703–722.

Ceci, S. J., & Bruck, M. (1993). Child witnesses: Translating research into policy. *Social Policy Report of the Society for Research in Child Development, 7*(3).

Ceci, S. J., & Williams, W. M. (1997). Schooling, intelligence, and income.

American Psychologist, 52(10), 1051–1058.

Celis, W. (1990). More states are laying school paddle to rest. *New York Times,* pp. A1, B12.

Center for Education Reform. (2004, August 17). Comprehensive data discounts New York Time account; reveals charter schools performing at or above traditional schools. (CER Press Release). [Online]. Available: http://edreform.com/index.cfm?fuseAction=document&documentID=1806. Access date: September 17, 2004.

Center for Weight and Health (2001). *Pediatric Overweight: A Review of the Literature: Executive summary.* Berkeley, CA: University of California at Berkeley.

Center on Addiction and Substance Abuse at Columbia University (CASA). (1996, June). *Substance abuse and the American woman.* New York: Author.

Centers for Disease Control & Prevention (CDC). (undated). Possible health effects of radiation exposure on unborn babies. Fact sheet. [Online]. Available: http://www.bt.cdc.gov/radiation/prenatal.asp. Access date: May 18, 2004.

Centers for Disease Control and Prevention (CDC). (1993). Rates of cesarean delivery—United States, 1991. *Morbidity and Mortality Weekly Report, 42,* 285–289.

Centers for Disease Control and Prevention (CDC). (1997). *Screening young children for lead poisoning: Guidance for state and local public health officials.* Atlanta, GA: U.S. Department of Health and Human Services, Public Health Service.

Centers for Disease Control and Prevention (CDC). (1999). Impact of vaccines universally recommended for children—United States, 1900–1998. *Morbidity and Mortality Weekly Report, 48,* 243–248.

Centers for Disease Control and Prevention (CDC). (2000a). *CDC's guidelines for school and community programs: Promoting lifelong physical activity.* [Online]. Available: http://www.cdc.gov/nccdphp/dash/phactaag.htm. Access date: May 26, 2000.

Centers for Disease Control and Prevention (CDC). (2000b). National, state, and urban area vaccination coverage levels among children aged 19–35 months—United States, 1999, *49*(26), 585–589.

Centers for Disease Control and Prevention (CDC). (2000c). *Tracking the hidden epidemic: Trends in STDs in the U.S., 2000.* Washington, DC: Author.

Centers for Disease Control and Prevention (CDC). (2002a). Use of assisted reproductive technology—United States, 1996 and 1998. *MMWR Weekly, 51,* 97–101.

Centers for Disease Control and Prevention (CDC). (2002b). Youth Risk Behavior Surveillance—United States, 2001. *Morbidity and Mortality Weekly Report, 51*(4). Atlanta, GA: Author.

Centers for Disease Control and Prevention (CDC). (2004). National, state, and urban area vaccination coverage among children aged 19–36 months—United States, 2003. *Morbidity and Mortality Weekly Report, 53,* 658–661.

Cernoch, J. M., & Porter, R. H. (1985). Recognition of maternal axillary odors by infants. *Child Development, 56,* 1593–1598.

Chambers, R. A., Taylor, J. R., & Potenza, M. N. (2003). *American Journal of Psychiatry, 160,* 1041–1052.

Chan, R. W., Raboy, B., & Patterson, C. J. (1998). Psychosocial adjustment among children conceived via donor insemination by lesbian and heterosexual mothers. *Child Development, 69,* 443–457.

Chandra, A., Abma, J., Maza, P., & Bachrach, C. (1999). *Adoption, adoption seeking, and relinquishment for adoption in the United States* (Advance Data from Vital and Health Statistics, No. 306). Hyattsville, MD: National Center for Health Statistics.

Chao, R. (1996). Chinese and European American mothers' beliefs about the role of parenting in children's school success. *Journal of Cross-Cultural Psychology, 27,* 403–423.

Chao, R. K. (1994). Beyond parental control and authoritarian parenting style: Understanding Chinese parenting through the cultural notion of training. *Child Development, 65,* 1111–1119.

Chao, R. K. (2001). Extending research on the consequences of parenting style for Chinese Americans and European Americans. *Child Development, 72,* 1832–1843.

Chapman, A. R., & Frankel, M. S. (2000). *Human inheritable genetic modifications: Assessing scientific, ethical, religious, and policy issues.* American Association for the Advancement of Science. [Online]. 73 pages. Available: http://www/aaas/org/spp/dspp/sfri/germline/main.htm. Access date: September 25, 2000.

Chapman, M., & Lindenberger, U. (1988). Functions, operations, and décalage in the development of transitivity. *Developmental Psychology, 24,* 542–551.

Chase-Lansdale, P. L., Cherlin, A. J., & Kiernan, K. E. (1995). The long-term effects of parental divorce on the mental health of young adults: A developmental perspective. *Child Development, 66,* 1614–1634.

Chase-Lansdale, P. L., Moffitt, R. A., Lohman, B. J., Cherlin, A. J., Coley, R. L., Pittman, L. D., Rolf, J., & Votruba-Drzal, E. (2003). Mothers' transitions from welfare to work and the well-being of preschoolers and adolescents. *Science, 299*(5612), 1548–1552.

Chehab, F. F., Mounzih, K., Lu, R., & Lim, M. E. (1997, January 3). Early onset of reproductive function in normal female mice treated with leptin. *Science, 275,* 88–90.

Chen, A., & Rogan, W. J. (2004). Breastfeeding and the risk of postneonatal death in the United States. *Pediatrics, 113,* e435–e439.

Chen, C., & Stevenson, H. W. (1995). Motivation and mathematics achievement: A comparative study of Asian-American, Caucasian-American, and East Asian high school students. *Child Development, 66,* 1215–1234.

Chen, E., Matthews, K. A., & Boyce, W. T. (2002). Socioeconomic differences in children's health: How and why do these relationships change with age? *Psychological Bulletin, 128,* 295–329.

Chen, L., Baker, S. B., Braver, E. R., & Li, G. (2000). Carrying passengers as a risk factor for crashes fatal to 16- and 17-year-old drivers. *Journal of the American Medical Association, 283*(12), 1578–1582.

Chen, W., Li, S., Cook, N. R., Rosner, B. A., Srinivasan, S. R., Boerwinkle, E., & Berenson, G. S. (2004). An autosomal genome scan for loci influencing longitudinal burden of body mass index from childhood to young adulthood in white sibships. The Bogalusa Heart Study. *International Journal of Obesity, 28,* 462–469.

Chen, X., Rubin, K. H., & Li, D. (1995). Social functioning and adjustment in Chinese children: A longitudinal study. *Developmental Psychology, 31,* 531–539.

Chen, X., Rubin, K. H., & Li, D. (1997). Relation between academic achievement and social adjustment: Evidence from Chinese children. *Developmental Psychology, 33,* 518–525.

Chen, X., Rubin, K. H., & Sun, Y. (1992). Social reputation and peer relationships in Chinese and Canadian children: A cross-cultural study. *Child Development, 63,* 1336–1343.

Cheng, T. L., Fields, C. B., Brenner, R. A., Wright, J. L., Lomax, T., Scheidt, P. C., & the District of Columbia Child/Adolescent Injury Research Network. (2000). Sports injuries; An important cause of morbidity in urban youth. *Pediatrics, 105(3).* Electronic abstracts, http://www.pediatrics.org/cgi/content/full/l05/3/e32.

Cherlin, A., & Furstenberg, F. F. (1986a). Grandparents and family crisis. *Generations, 10*(4), 26–28.

Cherlin, A., & Furstenberg, F. F. (1986b). *The new American grandparent.* New York: Basic Books.

Chervenak, F. A., Isaacson, G., & Mahoney, M. J. (1986). Advances in the diagnosis of fetal defects. *New England Journal of Medicine, 315*(5), 305–307.

Chess, S., & Thomas, A. (1982). Infant bonding: Mystique and reality. *American Journal of Orthopsychiatry, 52*(2), 213–222.

Cheung, M. C., Goldberg, J. D., & Kan, Y. W. (1996). Prenatal diagnosis of sickle cell anemia and thalassemia by analysis of fetal cells in maternal blood. *Nature Genetics, 14,* 264–268.

Childers, J. B., & Tomasello, M. (2002). Two-year-olds learn novel nouns, verbs, and conventional actions from massed or distributed exposures. *Developmental Psychology, 38,* 967–978.

Children's Defense Fund. (1998). *The state of America's children yearbook, 1998.* Washington, DC: Author.

Children's Defense Fund. (2001). *The state of America's children yearbook 2001.* Washington, DC: Author.

Children's Defense Fund. (2002a). Frequently asked questions about child poverty. Available: http://www.childrens defense.org. Access date: March 26, 2002.

Children's Defense Fund. (2002b). The state of children in America's union: A 2002 guide to "Leave No Child Behind" [Online]. Available: http://www.childrens defense.org/pdf/minigreenbook.pdf. Access date: October 10, 2002.

Children's Defense Fund. (2004). *The state of America's children 2004.* Washington, DC: Author.

Chipungu, S. S., & Bent-Goodley, T. B. (2004). Meeting the challenges of contemporary foster care. In David and Lucile Packard Foundation, Children, families, and foster care. *The Future of Children, 14*(1). Available: http://www.futureofchildren.org.

Chiriboga, C. A., Brust, J. C. M., Bateman, D., & Hauser, W. A. (1999). Dose-response effect of fetal cocaine exposure on newborn neurologic function. *Pediatrics, 103,* 79–85.

Chomitz, V. R., Cheung, L. W. Y., & Lieberman, E. (1995). The role of lifestyle in preventing low birth weight. *The Future of Children, 5*(1), 121–138.

Chomsky, C. S. (1969). *The acquisition of syntax in children from five to ten.* Cambridge, MA: MIT Press.

Chomsky, N. (1957). *Syntactic structures.* The Hague: Mouton.

Chomsky, N. (1972). *Language and mind* (2d ed.). New York: Harcourt Brace Jovanovich.

Chomsky, N. (1995). *The minimalist program.* Cambridge, MA: MIT Press.

Chorpita, B. P., & Barlow, D. H. (1998). The development of anxiety: The role of control in the early environment. *Psychological Bulletin, 124,* 3–21.

Christakis, D. A., Zimmerman, F. J., DiGiuseppe, D. L., & McCarty, C. A. (2004). Early television exposure and subsequent attentional problems in children. *Pediatrics, 113,* 708–713.

Christian, M. S., & Brent, R. L. (2001). Teratogen update: Evaluation of the reproductive and developmental risks of caffeine. *Teratology, 64*(1), 51–78.

Christie, J. F. (1991). *Psychological research on play: Connections with early literacy development.* Albany, NY: State University of New York Press.

Christie, J. F. (1998). Play as a medium for literacy development. In D. P. Fromberg & D. Bergen (Eds.), *Play from birth to 12 and beyond: Contexts, perspectives, and meanings* (pp. 50–55). New York: Garland.

Chronis, A. M., Lahey, B. B., Pelham Jr., W. E., Kipp, H. L., Baumann, B. L., & Lee, S. S. (2003). Psychopathology and substance abuse in parents of young children with attention-deficit/hyperactivity disorder. *Journal of the American Academy of Child & Adolescent Psychiatry, 42,* 1424–1432.

Chubb, N. H., Fertman, C. I., & Ross, J. L. (1997). Adolescent self-esteem and locus of control: A longitudinal study of gender and age differences. *Adolescence, 32,* 113–129.

Chugani, H. T. (1998). A critical period of brain development: Studies of cerebral glucose utilization with PET. *Preventive Medicine, 27,* 184–187.

Chugani, H. T., Behen, M. E., Muzik, O., Juhasz, C., Nagy, F., & Chugani, D. C. (2001). Local brain functional activity following early deprivation: A study of postinstitutionalized Romanian orphans. *NeuroImage 14*(6): 1290–1301.

Chun, K. M., Organista, P. B., & Marin, G. (Eds.). (2002). *Acculturation: Advances in theory, measurement & applied research.* Washington, DC: American Psychological Association.

Cibelli, J., Lanza, R. P., & West, M. D., with Carol Ezell. (2002, January). The first human cloned embryo. *Scientific American,* pp. 44–51.

Cicchetti, D., & Toth, S. L. (1998). The development of depression in children and adolescents. *American Psychologist, 53,* 221–241.

Cicero, S., Curcio, P., Papageorghiou, A., Sonek, J., & Nicolaides, K. (2001). Absence of nasal bone in fetuses with trisomy 21 at 11–14 weeks of gestation: An observational study. *Lancet, 358,* 1665–1667.

Cicirelli, V. G. (1976). Family structure and interaction: Sibling effects on socialization. In M. F. McMillan & S. Henao (Eds.), *Child psychiatry: Treatment and research.* New York: Brunner/Mazel.

Cicirelli, V. G. (1994). Sibling relationships in cross-cultural perspective. *Journal of Marriage and the Family, 56,* 7–20.

Cicirelli, V. G. (1995). *Sibling relationships across the life span.* New York: Plenum Press.

Cillessen, A. H. N., & Mayeux, L. (2004). From censure to reinforcement: Developmental changes in the association between aggression and social status. *Child Development, 75,* 147–163.

Clark, A. G., Glanowski, S., Nielsen, R., Thomas, P. D., Kejariwal, A., Todd, M. A., Tanenbaum, D. M., Civello, D., Lu, F., Murphy, B., Ferriera, S., Wang, G., Zheng, X., White, T. J., Sninsky, J. J., Adams, M. D., & Cargill, M. (2003). Inferring non-neutral evolution from human-chimp-mouse orthologous gene trios. *Science, 302,* 1960–1963.

Clarke-Stewart, K. A. (1987). Predicting child development from day care forms and features: The Chicago study. In D. A. Phillips (Ed.), *Quality in child care: What does the research tell us?* (Research Monographs of the National Association for the Education of Young Children). Washington, DC: National Association for the Education of Young Children.

Clausen, J. A. (1975). The social meaning of differential physical and sexual maturation. In S. E. Dragastin & G. H. Elder, Jr. (Eds.), *Adolescence in the life cycle.* New York: Halsted.

Clausen, J. A. (1993). *American lives.* New York: Free Press.

Clayton, E. W. (2003). Ethical, legal, and social implications of genomic medicine. *New England Journal of Medicine, 349,* 562–569.

Clayton, R., & Heard, D. (Eds.). (1994). *Elvis up close: In the words of those who knew him best.* Atlanta, GA: Turner.

Clearfield, M. W., & Mix, K. S. (1999). Number versus contour length in infants' discrimination of small visual sets. *Current Directions in Psychological Science, 10,* 408–411.

Clément, K., Vaisse, C., Lahlou, N., Cabrol, S., Pelloux, V., Cassuto, D., Gourmelen, M., Dina, C., Chambaz, J., Lacorte, J.-M., Basdevant, A., Bougnères, P., Lebouc, Y., Froguel, P., & Guy-Grand, B. (1998). A mutation in the human leptin receptor gene causes obesity and pituitary dysfunction. *Nature, 392,* 398–401.

Cleveland, H. H., & Wiebe, R. P. (2003). The moderation of adolescent-to-peer similarity in tobacco and alcohol use by school level of substance use. *Child Development, 74,* 279–291.

Clifton, R. K., Muir, D. W., Ashmead, D. H., & Clarkson, M. G. (1993). Is visually guided reaching in early infancy a myth? *Child Development, 64,* 1099–1110.

Cnattingius, S., Bergstrom, R., Lipworth, L., & Kramer, M. S. (1998). Prepregnancy weight and the risk of adverse pregnancy outcomes. *New England Journal of Medicine, 338,* 147–152.

Cnattingius, S., Bergstrom, R., Lipworth, L., & Kramer, M. S. (2000). Prepregnancy weight and the risk of adverse pregnancy outcomes. *New England Journal of Medicine, 338* 147–152.

Cobrinick, P., Hood, R., & Chused, E. (1959). Effects of maternal narcotic addiction on the newborn infant. *Pediatrics, 24,* 288–290.

Cohen, D. A., Nsuami, M., Martin, D. H., & Farley, T. A. (1999). Repeated school-based screening for sexually transmitted diseases: A feasible strategy for reaching adolescents. *Pediatrics, 104*(6), 1281–1285.

Cohen, L. B., & Amsel, L. B. (1998). Precursors to infants' perception of the causality of a simple event. *Infant Behavior and Development, 21,* 713–732.

Cohen, L. B., & Oakes, L. M. (1993). How infants perceive a simple causal event. *Developmental Psychology, 29,* 421–433.

Cohen, L. B., Rundell, L. J., Spellman, B. A., & Cashon, C. H. (1999). Infants' perception of causal chains. *Current Directions in Psychological Science, 10,* 412–418.

Cohn, J. F., & Tronick, E. Z. (1983). Three-month-old infants' reaction to simulated maternal depression. *Child Development, 54,* 185–193.

Coie, J. D., & Dodge, K. A. (1998). Aggression and antisocial behavior. In W. Damon (Series Ed.) & N. Eisenberg (Vol. Ed.), *Handbook of child psychology: Vol. 3. Social, emotional, and personality development* (5th ed., pp. 780–862). New York: Wiley.

Colby, A., & Damon, W. (1992). *Some do care: Contemporary lives of moral commitment.* New York: Free Press.

Colby, A., Kohlberg, L., Gibbs, J., & Lieberman, M. (1983). A longitudinal study of moral development. *Monographs of the Society for Research in Child Development, 48*(1–2, Serial No. 200).

Cole, M., & Cole, S. R. (1989). *The development of children.* New York: Freeman.

Cole, P. M., Barrett, K. C., & Zahn-Waxler, C. (1992). Emotion displays in two-year-olds during mishaps. *Child Development, 63,* 314–324.

Cole, P. M., Bruschi, C. J., & Tamang, B. L. (2002). Cultural differences in children's emotional reactions to difficult situations. *Child Development, 73*(3): 983–996.

Cole, T. B. (1999). Ebbing epidemic: Youth homicide rate at a 14-year low. *Journal of the American Medical Association, 281,* 25–26.

Coleman, J. S. (1988). Social capital in the creation of human capital. *American Journal of Sociology, 94*(Suppl. 95), S95–S120.

Coley, R. L. (1998). Children's socialization experiences and functioning in single-mother households: The importance of fathers and other men. *Child Development, 69,* 219–230.

Coley, R. L. (2001). (In)visible men: Emerging research on low-income, unmarried, and minority fathers. *American Psychologist, 56,* 743–753.

Collier, V. P. (1995). Acquiring a second language for school. *Directions in Language and Education, 1*(4), 1–11.

Collins, J. G., & LeClere, F. B. (1997). *Health and selected socioeconomic characteristics of the family: United Stales, 1988–90* (DHHS No. PHS 97–1523). Washington, DC: U.S. Government Printing Office.

Collins, W. A., Maccoby, E. E., Steinberg, L., Hetherington, E. M., & Bornstein, M. H. (2000). Contemporary research in parenting: The case for nature and nurture. *American Psychologist, 55,* 218–232.

Colombo, J. (1993). *Infant cognition: Predicting later intellectual functioning.* Thousand Oaks, CA: Sage.

Colombo, J. (2001). The development of visual attention in infancy. *Annual Review of Psychology, 52,* 337–367.

Colombo, J. (2002). Infant attention grows up: The emergence of a developmental cognitive neuroscience perspective. *Current Directions in Psychological Science, 11,* 196–200.

Colombo, J., & Janowsky, J. S. (1998). A cognitive neuroscience approach to individual differences in infant cognition. In J. E. Richards (Ed.), *Cognitive neuroscience of attention* (pp. 363–391). Mahwah, NJ: Erlbaum.

Colombo, J., Kannass, K. N., Shaddy, J., Kundurthi, S., Maikranz, J. M., Anderson, C. J., Bkaga, O. M., & Carlson, S. E. (2004). Maternal DHA and the development of attention in infancy and toddlerhood. *Child Development. 75,* 1254–1267.

Coltrane, S., & Adams, M. (1997). Work-family imagery and gender stereotypes: Television and the reproduction of difference. *Journal of Vocational Behavior, 50,* 323–347.

Comings, D. E., Muhleman, D., Johnson, J. P., & MacMurray, J. P. (2002). Parent-daughter transmission of the androgen receptor gene as an explanation of the effect of father absence on age of menarche. *Child Development, 73*(4), 1046–1051.

Commissioner's Office of Research and Evaluation and Head Start Bureau, Department of Health and Human Services. (2001). *Building their futures: How Early Head Start programs are enhancing the lives of infants and toddlers in low-income families. Summary report.* Washington, DC: Author.

Committee on Obstetric Practice. (2002). ACOG committee opinion: Exercise during pregnancy and the postpartum period. *International Journal of Gynaecology & Obstetrics, 77*(1), 79–81.

Conel, J. L. (1959). *The postnatal development of the human cerebral cortex.* Cambridge, MA: Harvard University Press.

Conger, J. J. (1988). Hostages to fortune: Youth, values, and the public interest. *American Psychologist,43*(4), 291–300.

Conger, R. C., Ge, X., Elder, G. H., Lorenz, F. O., & Simons, R. L. (1994). Economic stress, coercive family processes, and developmental problems of adolescents. *Child Development, 65,* 541–561.

Conger, R. D., Conger, K. J., Elder, G. H., Jr., Lorenz, F. O., Simons, R. L., & Whitbeck, L. B. (1993). Family economic stress and adjustment of early adolescent girls. *Developmental Psychology, 29,* 206–219.

Constantino, J. N. (2003). Autistic traits in the general population: A twin study. *Archives of General Psychiatry, 60,* 524–530.

Cook, E. H., Courchesne, R., Lord, C., Cox, N. J., Yan, S., Lincoln, A., Haas, R., Courchesne, E., & Leventhal, B. L. (1997). Evidence of linkage between the serotonin transporter and autistic disorder. *Molecular Psychiatry, 2,* 247–250.

Coons, S., & Guilleminault, C. (1982). Development of sleep-wake patterns and non-rapid eye movement sleep stages during the first six months of life in normal infants. *Pediatrics, 69,* 793–798.

Cooper, H. (1989, November). Synthesis of research on homework. *Educational Leadership,* 85–91.

Cooper, H., Lindsay, J. J., Nye, B., & Greathouse, S. (1998). Relationships among attitudes about homework, amount of homework assigned and completed, and student achievement. *Journal of Educational Psychology, 90,* 70–83.

Cooper, H., Valentine, J. C., Nye, B., & Lindsay, J. J. (1999). Relationships between five after-school activities and academic achievement. *Journal of Educational Psychology, 91*(2), 369–378.

Cooper, R. P., & Aslin, R. N. (1990). Preference for infant-directed speech in the first month after birth. *Child Development, 61,* 1584–1595.

Coplan, R. J., Gavinski-Molina, M., Lagacé-Séguin, D. G., & Wichman, C. (2001). When girls versus boys play alone: Nonsocial play and adjustment in kindergarten. *Developmental Psychology, 37*(4), 464–474.

Coplan, R. J., Prakash, K., O'Neil, K., & Armer, M. (2004). Do you "want" to play? Distinguishing between conflicted-shyness and social disinterest in early childhood. *Developmental Psychology, 40,* 244–258.

Corbet, A., Long, W., Schumacher, R., Gerdes, J., Cotton, R., & the American Exosurf Neonatal Study Group 1. (1995). Double-blind developmental evaluation at 1-year corrected age of 597 premature infants with birth weight from 500 to 1,350 grams enrolled in three placebo-controlled trials of prophylactic synthetic surfactant. *Journal of Pediatrics, 126,* S5–S12.

Corbin, C. (1973). *A textbook of motor development.* Dubuque, IA: Wm. C. Brown Publishers.

Correa, A., Botto, L., Liu, V., Mulinare, J., and Erickson, J.D. (2003). Do multivitamin supplements attenuate the risk for diabetes-associated birth defects? *Pediatrics, 111,* 1146–1151.

Costello, E. J., Compton, S. N., Keeler, G., & Angold, A. (2003). Relationship between poverty and psychopathology: A natural experiment. *Journal of the American Medical Association, 290,* 2023–2029.

Costello, E. J., Mustillo, S., Erkanli, A., Keeler, G., & Angold, A. (2003). Prevalence and development of psychiatric disorders in childhood and adolescence. *Archives of General Psychiatry, 60,* 837–844.

Costello, S. (1990, December). Yani's monkeys: Lessons in form and freedom. *School Arts,* pp. 10–11.

Coster, W. J., Gersten, M. S., Beeghly, M., & Cicchetti, D. (1989). Communicative functioning in maltreated toddlers. *Developmental Psychology, 25,* 1020–1029.

Courchesne, E., Carper, R., & Akshoomoff, N. (2003). Evidence of brain overgrowth in the first year of life in autism. *Journal of the American Medical Association, 290,* 337–344.

Cowan, N., Nugent, L. D., Elliott, E. M., Ponomarev, I., & Saults, J. S. (1999). The role of attention in the development of short-term memory: Age differences in the verbal span of apprehension. *Child Development, 70,* 1082–1097.

Cox, J., Daniel, N., & Boston, B. O. (1985). *Educating able learners. Programs and promising practices.* Austin, TX: University of Texas Press.

Coyle, T. R., & Bjorklund, D. F. (1997). Age differences in, and consequences of, multiple- and variable-strategy use on a multitrial sort-recall task. *Developmental Psychology, 33,* 372–380.

Crain-Thoreson, C., & Dale, P. S. (1992). Do early talkers become early readers? Linguistic precocity, preschool language, and emergent literacy. *Developmental Psychology, 28,* 421–429.

Cratty, B. J. (1986). *Perceptual and motor development in infants and children* (3rd ed.). Englewood Cliffs, NJ: Prentice-Hall.

Crick, N. R., & Dodge, K. A. (1994). A review and reformulation of social information-processing mechanisms in children's social adjustment. *Psychological Bulletin, 115,* 74–101.

Crick, N. R., & Dodge, K. A. (1996). Social information-processing mechanisms in reactive and proactive aggression. *Child Development, 67,* 993–1002.

Crick, N. R., & Grotpeter, J. K. (1995). Relational aggression, gender, and social-psychological adjustment. *Child Development, 66,* 710–722.

Crick, N. R., Bigbee, M. A., & Howes, C. (1996). Gender differences in children's normative beliefs about aggression: How do I hurt thee? Let me count the ways. *Child Development, 67,* 1003–1014.

Crick, N. R., Casas, J. F., & Nelson, D. A. (2002). Toward a more comprehensive understanding of peer maltreatment: Studies of relational victimization. *Current Directions in Psychological Science, 11*(3), 98–101.

Crijnen, A. A. M., Achenbach, T. M., & Verhulst, F. C. (1999). Problems reported by parents of children in multiple cultures: The Child Behavior Checklist syndrome constructs. *American Journal of Psychiatry, 156,* 569–574.

Crittenden, P. M. (1993). Comparison of two systems for assessing quality of attachment in the preschool years. In P. M. Crittenden (Chair). *Quality of attachment in the preschool years.* Symposium conducted at the Ninth Biennial Meeting of the International Conference on Infant Studies, Paris.

Crockenberg, S. C. (2003). Rescuing the baby from the bathwater: How gender and temperament influence how child care affects child development. *Child Development, 74,* 1034–1038.

Crockenberg, S., & Lourie, A. (1996). Parents' conflict strategies with children and children's conflict strategies with peers. *Merrill-Palmer Quarterly, 42,* 495–518.

Crouter, A. C., MacDermid, S. M., McHale, S. M., & Perry-Jenkins, M. (1990). Parental monitoring and perception of children's school performance and conduct in dual- and single-earner families. *Developmental Psychology, 26,* 649–657.

Crouter, A., & Larson, R. (Eds.). (1998). *Temporal rhythms in adolescence: Clocks, calendars, and the coordination of daily life* (New Directions in Child and Adolescent Development, No. 82). San Francisco: Jossey-Bass.

Crow, J. F. (1993). How much do we know about spontaneous human mutation rates? *Environmental and Molecular Mutagenesis, 21,* 122–129.

Crow, J. F. (1995). Spontaneous mutation as a risk factor. *Experimental and Clinical Immunogenetics, 12*(3), 121–128.

Crow, J. F. (1999). The odds of losing at genetic roulette. *Nature, 397,* 293–294.

Crowther, C. A., Hiller, J. E., Doyle, L. W., & Haslam, R. R., for the Australasian Collaborative Trial of Magnesium Sulfate (ACTOMgSO4) Collaborative Group. (2003). Effect of magnesium sulfate given for neuro protection before preterm birth: A randomized controlled trials, *Journal of the American Medical Association, 290,* 2669–2676.

Cummings, E. M. (1994). Marital conflict and children's functioning. *Social Development, 3,* 16–36.

Cummings, E. M., Iannotti, R. J., & Zahn-Waxler, C. (1989). Aggression between peers in early childhood: Individual continuity and developmental change. *Child Development, 60,* 887–895.

Cunningham, A. S., Jelliffe, D. B., & Jelliffe, E. F. P. (1991). Breastfeeding and health in the 1980s: A global epidemiological review. *Journal of Pediatrics, 118,* 659–666.

Cunningham, F. G., & Leveno, K. J. (1995). Childbearing among older women: The message is cautiously optimistic. *New England Journal of Medicine, 333,* 1002–1004.

Curtin, S. C., & Park, M. M. (1999). Trends in the attendant, place, and timing of births, and in the use of obstetric interventions: United States, 1989–97. *National Vital Statistics Reports, 47*(27). Hyattsville, MD: National Center for Health Statistics.

Curtiss, S. (1977). *Genie.* New York: Academic Press.

Cutting, A. L., & Dunn, J. (1999). Theory of mind, emotion understanding, language, and family background: Individual differences and interrelations. *Child Development, 70,* 853–865.

Cutz, E., Perrin, D. G., Hackman, R., & Czegledy-Nagy, E. N. (1996). Maternal smoking and pulmonary neuroendocrine cells in sudden infant death syndrome. *Pediatrics, 88,* 668–672.

D'Alton, M. E., & DeCherney, A. H. (1993). Prenatal diagnosis. *New England Journal of Medicine, 32*(2), 114–120.

Daiute, C., Hartup, W. W., Sholl, W., & Zajac, R. (1993, March). *Peer collaboration and written language development: A study of friends and acquaintances.* Paper presented at the meeting of the Society for Research in Child Development, New Orleans, LA.

Dale, P. S., Crain-Thoreson, C., Notari-Syverson, A., & Cole, K. (1996). Parent-child book reading as an intervention technique for young children with language delays. *Topics in Early Childhood Special Education, 16,* 213–235.

Dale, P. S., Price, T. S., Bishop, D. V. M., & Plomin, R. (2003). Outcomes of early language delay: I. Predicting persistent and transient language difficulties at 3 and 4 years. *Journal of Speech, Language, and Hearing Research, 46,* 544–560.

Dale, P. S., Simonoff, E., Bishop, D. V. M., Eley, T. C., Oliver, B., Price, T. S., Purcell, S., Stevenson, J., & Plomin, R. (1998). Genetic influence on language delay in two-year-old children. *Nature Neuroscience, 1,* 324–328.

Daley, P. (2003, July 19). "Miracle baby" speaks of life after the test tube. *The Age.* [Online]. Available:

http://www.theage.com.au/articles/2003/07/18/1058035200790.html. Access date: December 30, 2003.

Danesi, M. (1994). *Cool: The signs and meanings of adolescence.* Toronto: University of Toronto Press.

Daniel, I., Berg, C., Johnson, C. H., and Atrash, H. (2003). Magnitude of maternal morbidity during labor and delivery: United States, 1993–1997. *American Journal of Public Health, 93,* 633–634.

Daniel, M. H. (1997). Intelligence testing: Status and trends. *American Psychologist, 52,* 1038–1045.

Darling, N., & Steinberg, L. (1993). Parenting style as context: An integrative model. *Psychological Bulletin, 113,* 487–496.

Darroch, J. E., Singh, S., Frost, J. J., & the Study Team. (2001). Differences in teenage pregnancy rates among five developed countries: The roles of sexual activity and contraceptive use. *Family Planning Perspectives, 33,* 244–250, 281.

Darwin, C. (1995). *The origin of species.* New York: Gramercy. (Original work published 1859.)

David and Lucile Packard Foundation. (2004). Children, families, and foster care: Executive summary. *The Future of Children, 14*(1). Available: http://www.futureofchildren.org.

David, R. J., & Collins Jr., J. W. (1997). Differing birth weight among infants of U.S.-born blacks, African-born blacks, and U.S.-born whites. *New England Journal of Medicine, 337,* 1209–1214.

Davidson, J. I. F. (1998). Language and play: Natural partners. In D. P. Fromberg & D. Bergen (Eds.), *Play from birth to 12 and beyond: Contexts, perspectives, and meanings* (pp. 175–183). New York: Garland.

Davidson, R. J., & Fox, N. A. (1989). Frontal brain asymmetry predicts infants' response to maternal separation. *Journal of Abnormal Psychology, 948*(2), 58–64.

Davies, P. T., & Cummings, E. M. (1998). Exploring children's emotional security as a mediator of the link between marital relations and child adjustment. *Child Development, 69,* 124–139.

Davis, B. E., Moon, R. Y., Sachs, H. C., Ottolini, M. C. (1998). Effects of sleep position on infant motor development. *Pediatrics, 102,* 1135–1140.

Davis, D. L., Gottlieb, M. B., & Stampnitzky, J. R. (1998). Reduced ratio of male to female births in several industrial countries. *Journal of the American Medical Association, 279,* 1018–1023.

Davis, M., & Emory, E. (1995). Sex differences in neonatal stress reactivity. *Child Development, 66,* 14–27.

Davis-Kean, P. E., & Sandler, H. M. (2001). A meta-analysis of measures of self-esteem for young children: A framework for future measures. *Child Development, 72,* 887–906.

Davison, K. K., & Birch, L. L. (2001). Weight status, parent reaction, and self-concept in 5-year-old girls. *Pediatrics, 107,* 46–53.

Davison, K. K., Susman, E. J., & Birch, L. L. (2003). Percent body fat at age 5 predicts earlier pubertal development among girls at age 9. *Pediatrics, 111,* 815–821.

Dawson, D. A. (1991). Family structure and children's health and well-being. Data from the 1988 National Health Interview Survey on child health. *Journal of Marriage and the Family, 53,* 573–584.

Dawson, G., Frey, K., Panagiotides, H., Osterling, J., & Hessl, D. (1997). Infants of depressed mothers exhibit atypical frontal brain activity: A replication and extension of previous findings. *Journal of Child Psychology & Allied Disciplines, 38,* 179–186.

Dawson, G., Frey, K., Panagiotides, H., Yamada, E., Hessl, D. and Osterling, J. (1999). Infants of depressed mothers exhibit atypical frontal electrical brain activity during interactions with mother and with a familiar nondepressed adult. *Child Development, 70,* 1058–1066.

Dawson, G., Klinger, L. G., Panagiotides, H., Hill, D., & Spieker, S. (1992). Frontal lobe activity and affective behavior of infants of mothers with depressive symptoms. *Child Development, 63,* 725–737.

Day, S. (1993, May). Why genes have a gender. *New Scientist, 138*(1874), 34–38.

de Castro, B. O., Veerman, J. W., Koops, W., Bosch, J. D., & Monshouwer, H. J. (2002). Hostile attribution of intent and aggressive behavior: A meta-analysis. *Child Development, 73,* 916–934.

de Villiers, J. G., & de Villiers, P. A. (2000). Linguistic determination and the understanding of false beliefs. In Peter Mitchell & Kevin J. Riggs (Eds.), *Children's reasoning and the mind* (pp. 191–228). Hove, England: Psychology Press.

De Wolff, M. S., & van IJzendoorn, M. H. (1997). Sensitivity and attachment: A meta-analysis on parental antecedents of infant attachment. *Child Development, 68,* 571–591.

DeBell, M., & Chapman, C. (2003). *Computer and Internet use by children and adolescents in 2001* (NCES 2004–014). Washington, DC: National Center for Education Statistics, U.S. Department of Education.

DeCasper, A. J., & Fifer, W. P. (1980). Of human bonding: Newborns prefer their mothers' voices. *Science, 208,* 1174–1176.

DeCasper, A. J., & Spence, M. J. (1986). Prenatal maternal speech influences newborns' perceptions of speech sounds. *Infant Behavior and Development, 9,* 133–150.

DeCasper, A. J., Lecanuet, J. P., Busnel, M. C., Granier-Deferre, C., & Maugeais, R. (1994). Fetal reactions to recurrent maternal speech. *Infant Behavior and Development, 17,* 159–164.

DeGarmo, D. S., Forgatch, M. S., & Martinez, C. R. (1999). Parenting of divorced mothers as a link between social status and boys' academic outcomes: Unpacking the effects of socioeconomic status. *Child Development, 70*(5), 1231–1245.

Dekovic, M., & Janssens, J. M. A. M. (1992). Parents' child-rearing style and child's sociometric status. *Developmental Psychology, 28,* 925–932.

Del Carmen, R. D., Pedersen, F. A., Huffman, L. C., & Bryan, V. E. (1993). Dyadic distress management predicts subsequent security of attachment. *Infant Behavior and Development, 16,* 131–147.

DeLoache, J. S. (2000). Dual representation and young children's use of scale models. *Child Development, 71,* 329–338.

DeLoache, J. S., Miller, K. F., & Pierroutsakos, S. L. (1998). Reasoning and problem solving. In D. Kuhn & R. S. Siegler (Eds.), *Handbook of child psychology: Vol. 2. Cognition, perception, and language* (5th ed., pp. 801–850). New York: Wiley.

DeLoache, J. S., Miller, K. F., & Rosengren, K. S. (1997). The credible shrinking room: Very young children's performance with symbolic and nonsymbolic relations. *Psychological Science, 8,* 308–313.

DeLoache, J. S., Pierroutsakos, S. L., Uttal, D. H., Rosengren, K. S., & Gottleib, A. (1998). Grasping the nature of pictures. *Psychological Science, 9,* 205–210.

DeLoache, J. S., Uttal, D. H., & Rosengren, K. S. (2004). Scale errors offer evidence for a perception-action dissociation early in life. *Science, 304,* 1027–1029.

DeLoache, J., & Gottlieb, A. (2000). If Dr. Spock were born in Bali: Raising a world of babies. In J. DeLoache & A. Gottlieb (Eds.), *A world of babies: Imagined childcare guides for seven societies* (pp. 1–27). New York: Cambridge University Press.

Denham, S. A., Blair, K. A., DeMulder, E., Levitas, J., Sawyer, K., Auerbach-Major, S., & Queenan, P. (2003). Preschool emotional competence: Pathway to social competence? *Child Development, 74,* 238–256.

Dennis, W. (1936). A bibliography of baby biographies. *Child Development, 7,* 71–73.

Denny, F. W., & Clyde, W. A. (1983). Acute respiratory tract infections: An overview [Monograph]. *Pediatric Research, 17,* 1026–1029.

Denton, K., & Zarbatany, L. (1996). Age differences in support in conversations between friends. *Child Development, 67,* 1360–1373.

Denton, K., West, J., and Walston, J. (2003). *Reading—young children's achievement and classroom experiences: Findings from* The Condition of Education 2003. Washington, DC: National Center for Education Statistics.

Detrich, R., Phillips, R., & Durett, D. (2002). Critical issue: Dynamic debate—determining the evolving impact of charter schools. [Online]. North Central Regional Educational Laboratory. Available: http://www.ncrel.org/sdrs/areas/issues/envrnmnt/go/go800.htm.

Devaney, B., Johnson, A., Maynard, R., & Trenholm, C. (2002). *The evaluation of abstinence education programs funded under Title V, Section 510: Interim report.* Washington, DC: U.S. Department of Health and Human Services.

Devlin, B., Daniels, M., & Roeder, K. (1997). The heritability of IQ. *Nature, 388,* 468–471.

Dewey, K. G., Heinig, M. J., & Nommsen-Rivers, L. A. (1995). Differences in morbidity between breast-fed and formula-fed infants. *Journal of Pediatrics, 126,* 696–702.

Dewing, P., Shi, T., Horvath, S., & Vilain, E. (2003). Sexually dimorphic gene expression in mouse brain precedes gonadal differentiation. *Molecular Brain Research, 118,* 82–90.

Deykin, E. Y., Alpert, J. J., & McNamara, J. J. (1985). A pilot study of the effect of exposure to child abuse or neglect on adolescent suicidal behavior. *American Journal of Psychiatry, 142*(11), 1299–1303.

Diamond, A. (1991). Neuropsychological insights into the meaning of object concept development. In S. Carey & R. Gelman (Eds.), *Epigensis of mind* (pp. 67–110). Hillsdale, NJ: Erlbaum.

Diamond, A., Cruttenden, L., & Neiderman, D. (1994). AB with multiple wells: 1. Why are multiple wells sometimes easier than two wells? 2. Memory or memory inhibition? *Developmental Psychology, 30,* 192–205.

Diamond, L. M. (1998). Development of sexual orientation among adolescent and young adult women. *Developmental Psychology, 34*(5), 1085–1095.

Diamond, L. M. (2000). Sexual identity, attractions, and behavior among young sexual-minority women over a 2-year period. *Developmental Psychology, 36,* 241–250.

Diamond, M. C. (1988). *Enriching heredity.* New York: Free Press.

Diamond, M., & Sigmundson, H. K. (1997). Sex reassignment at birth: Long-term review and clinical implications. *Archives of Pediatric and Adolescent Medicine, 151,* 298–304.

Dick, D. M., Rose, R. J., Viken, R. J., & Kaprio, J. (2000). Pubertal timing and substance use: Association between and within families across late adolescence. *Developmental Psychology, 36*(2), 180–189.

DiClemente, R. J., Wingood, G. M., Crosby, R., Sionean, C., Cobb, B. K., Harrington, K., Davies, S., Hook, E. W., & Oh, M. K. (2001). Parental monitoring: Association with adolescents' risk behaviors. *Pediatrics, 107,* 1363–1368.

Dietz, W. H. (2001). Breastfeeding may help prevent childhood overweight. *Journal of the American Medical Association, 285*(19), 2506–2507.

Dimant, R. J., & Bearison, D. J. (1991). Development of formal reasoning during successive peer interactions. *Developmental Psychology, 27,* 277–284.

Ding, Y-C., Chi, H-C., Grady, D. L., Morishima, A., Kidd, J. R., Kidd, K. K., Flodman, P., Spence, M. A., Schuck, S., Swanson, J. M., Zhang, Y-P., & Moyzis, R. K. (2002). Evidence of positive selection acting at the human dopamine receptor D4 gene locus. *Proceedings of the National Academy of Science, 99,* 309–314.

Dingfelder, S. (2004). Programmed for psychopathology? Stress during pregnancy may increase children's risk for mental illness, researchers say. *Monitor on Psychology, 35*(2), 56–57.

DiPietro, J. A. (2004). The role of prenatal maternal stress in child development. *Current Directions in Psychological Science, 13*(2), 71–74.

DiPietro, J. A., Caulfield, L. E., Costigan, K. A., Merialdi, M., Nguyen, R. H. N., Zavaleta, N., & Gurewitsch, E. D. (2004). Fetal neurobehavioral development: A tale of two cities. *Developmental Psychology, 40,* 445–456.

DiPietro, J. A., Hodgson, D. M., Costigan, K. A., Hilton, S. C., & Johnson, T. R. B. (1996). Development of fetal movement-fetal heart rate coupling from 20 weeks through term. *Early Human Development, 44,* 139–151.

DiPietro, J., Hilton, S., Hawkins, M., Costigan, K., & Pressman, E. (2002). Maternal stress and affect influences fetal neurobehavioral development. *Developmental Psychology, 38,* 659–668.

Dishion, T. J., McCord, J., & Poulin, F. (1999). When intervention harms. *American Psychologist, 54,* 755–764.

Dlugosz, L., Belanger, K., Helienbrand, K., Holfard, T. R., Leaderer, B., & Bracken, M. B. (1996). Maternal caffeine consumption and spontaneous abortion: A prospective cohort study. *Epidemiology, 7,* 250–255.

Dodge, K. A., Bates, J. E., & Pettit, S. G. (1990). Mechanisms in the cycle of violence. *Science, 250,* 1678–1683.

Dodge, K. A., Coie, J. D., Pettit, G. S., & Price, J. M. (1990). Peer status and aggression in boys' groups: Developmental and contextual analysis. *Child Development, 61,* 1289–1309.

Dodge, K. A., Pettit, G. S., & Bates, J. E. (1994). Socialization mediators of the relation between socioeconomic status and child conduct problems. *Child Development, 65,* 649–665.

Dodge, K. A., Pettit, G. S., & Bates, J. E. (1997). How the experience of early physical abuse leads children to become chronically aggressive. In D. Cicchetti & S. L. Toth (Eds.), *Rochester symposium on developmental psychopathology. Vol. 8: Developmental perspectives on trauma* (pp. 263–288). Rochester, NY: University of Rochester Press.

Doherty, W. J., Kouneski, E. F., & Erickson, M. F. (1998). Responsible fathering: An overview and conceptual framework. *Journal of Marriage and the Family, 60,* 277–292.

Donovan, W. L., Leavitt, L. A., & Walsh, R. O. (1998). Conflict and depression predict maternal sensitivity to infant cries. *Infant Behavior and Development, 21,* 505–517.

Dornbusch, S. M., Ritter, P. L., Leiderman, P. H., Roberts, D. F., & Fraleigh, M. J. (1987). The relation of parenting style to adolescent school performance. *Child Development, 58,* 1244–1257.

Dorris, M. (1989). *The broken cord.* New York: Harper & Row.

Dorsey, M. J., and Schneider, L. C. (2003). Improving asthma outcomes and self-management behaviors of inner-city children. *Pediatrics, 112,* 474.

Dougherty, D. M. (1993). Adolescent health. *American Psychologist, 48*(2), 193–201.

Dougherty, T. M., & Haith, M. M. (1997). Infant expectations and reaction time as predictors of childhood speed of processing and IQ. *Developmental Psychology, 33,* 146–155.

Downey, D. B., & Condron, D. J. (2004). Playing well with others in kindergarten: The benefit of siblings at home. *Journal of Marriage and Family, 66,* 333–350.

Dozier, M., Stovall, K. C., Albus, K. E., & Bates, B. (2001). Attachment for infants in foster care: The role of caregiver state of mind. *Child Development, 72,* 1467–1477.

Dreher, M. C., Nugent, K., & Hudgins, R. (1994). Prenatal marijuana exposure and neonatal outcomes in Jamaica: An ethnographic study. *Pediatrics, 93,* 254–260.

Drumm, P., & Jackson, D. W. (1996). Developmental changes in questioning strategies during adolescence. *Journal of Adolescent Research, 11,* 285–305.

Dubé, E. M., & Savin-Williams, R. C. (1999). Sexual identity development among ethnic sexual-minority youths. *Developmental Psychology, 35*(6), 1389–1398.

Dube, S. R., Anda, R. F., Felitti, V. J., Chapman, D. P., Williamson, D. F., & Giles, W. H. (2001). Childhood abuse, household dysfunction, and the risk of attempted suicide throughout the life span: Findings from the Adverse Childhood Experiences Study. *Journal of the American Medical Association, 286*(24), 3089–3096.

Dube, S. R., Felitti, V. J., Dong, M., Chapman, D. P., Giles, W. H. & Anda, R. F. (2003 March). Childhood abuse, neglect, and household dysfunction and the risk of illicit drug use: The Adverse Childhood Experiences Study. *Pediatrics, 111*(3), 564–572.

Dubowitz, H. (1999). The families of neglected children. In M. E. Lamb (Ed.), *Parenting and child development in "nontraditional" families* (pp. 372–345). Mahwah, NJ: Erlbaum.

Duenwald, M. (2003, July 15). After 25 years, new ideas in the prenatal test tube. *New York Times.* [Online]. Available: http://www.nytimes.com/2003/07/15/health/15IVF.html?ex=1059274835&ei=1&en=21c6928d1811f348.

Duke, J., Huhman, M., & Heitzler, C. (2003). Physical activity levels among children aged 9–13 years—United States, 2002. *Morbidity and Mortality Weekly Report, 52,* 785–788.

Duncan, G. J., & Brooks-Gunn, J. (1997). Income effects across the life span: Integration and interpretation. In G. J. Duncan & J. Brooks-Gunn (Eds.), *Consequences of growing up poor* (pp. 596–610). New York: Russell Sage Foundation.

Dundy, E. (1985). *Elvis and Gladys.* New York: Dell.

Dunham, P. J., Dunham, F., & Curwin, A. (1993). Joint-attentional states and lexical acquisition at 18 months. *Developmental Psychology, 29,* 827–831.

Dunn, J. (1985). *Sisters and brothers.* Cambridge, MA: Harvard University Press.

Dunn, J. (1991). Young children's understanding of other people: Evidence from observations within the family. In D. Frye & C. Moore (Eds.), *Children's theories of mind: Mental states and social understanding.* Hillsdale, NJ: Erlbaum.

Dunn, J. (1996). Sibling relationships and perceived self-competence: Patterns of stability between childhood and early adolescence. In A. J. Sameroff & M. M. Haith (Eds.), *The five to seven year shift: The age of reason and responsibility* (pp. 253–269). Chicago: University of Chicago Press.

Dunn, J. (1999). Siblings, friends, and the development of social understanding. In W. A. Collins & B. Laursen (eds.), *The Minnesota Symposia on Child Psychology, Vol. 30. Relationships as developmental contexts* (pp. 263–279). Mahwah, NJ: Lawrence Erlbaum Associates.

Dunn, J., & Hughes, C. (2001). "I got some swords and you're dead!": Violent fantasy, antisocial behavior, friendship, and moral sensibility in young children. *Child Development, 72,* 491–505.

Dunn, J., & Kendrick, C. (1982). *Siblings: Love, envy and understanding.* Cambridge, MA: Harvard University Press.

Dunn, J., & Munn, P. (1985). Becoming a family member: Family conflict and the development of social understanding in the second year. *Child Development, 56,* 480–492.

Dunn, J., Brown, J., Slomkowski, C., Tesla, C., & Youngblade, L. (1991). Young children's understanding of other people's feelings and beliefs: Individual differences and antecedents. *Child Development, 62,* 1352–1366.

Dunne, R. G., Asher, K. N., & Rivara, F. P. (1992). Behavior and parental expectations of child pedestrians. *Pediatrics, 89,* 486–490.

Dunson, D. (2002). *Late breaking research session. Increasing infertility with increasing age: Good news and bad news for older couples.* Paper presented at 18th Annual Meeting of the European Society of Human Reproduction and Embryology, Vienna.

Dunson, D. B., Colombo, B., & Baird, D. D. (2002). Changes with age in the level and duration of fertility in the menstrual cycle. *Human Reproduction, 17,* 1399–1403.

DuPont, R. L. (1983). Phobias in children. *Journal of Pediatrics, 102,* 999–1002.

Durand, A. M. (1992). The safety of home birth: The Farm Study. *American Journal of Public Health, 82,* 450–452.

DuRant, R. H., Smith, J. A., Kreiter, S. R., & Krowchuk, D. P. (1999). The relationship between early age of onset of initial substance use and engaging in multiple health risk behaviors among young adolescents. *Archives of Pediatrics & Adolescent Medicine, 153,* 286–291.

Dwyer, T., Ponsonby, A. L., Blizzard, L., Newman, N. M., & Cochrane, J. A. (1995). The contribution of changes in the prevalence of prone sleeping position to the decline in sudden infant death syndrome in Tasmania. *Journal of the American Medical Association, 273,* 783–789.

Eating disorders—Part I. (1997, October). *The Harvard Mental Health Letter,* pp. 1–5.

Eating disorders—Part II. (1997, November). *The Harvard Mental Health Letter,* pp. 1–5.

Eaton, W. O., & Enns, L. R. (1986). Sex differences in human motor activity level. *Psychological Bulletin, 100,* 19–28.

Eccles, A. (1982). *Obstetrics and gynaecology in Tudor and Stuart England.* Kent, OH: Kent State University Press.

Eccles, J. S., Wigfield, A., & Byrnes, J. (2003). Cognitive development in adolescence. In Weiner, I. B., (Ed.), *Handbook of psychology. Vol. 6: Developmental psychology.* Vol. eds. R. M. Lerner, M. A. Easterbrooks, and J. Mistry. New York: John Wiley and Sons.

Echeland, Y., Epstein, D. J., St-Jacques, B., Shen, L., Mohler, J., McMahon, J. A., & McMahon, A. P. (1993). Sonic hedgehog, a member of a family of putative signality molecules, is implicated in the regulation of CNS polarity. *Cell, 75,* 1417–1430.

Eckenrode, J., Laird, M., & Doris, J. (1993). School performance and disciplinary problems among abused and neglected children. *Developmental Psychology, 29,* 53–62.

Eckerman, C. O., & Didow, S. M. (1996). Nonverbal imitation and toddlers' mastery of verbal means of achieving coordinated action. *Developmental Psychology, 32,* 141–152.

Eckerman, C. O., & Stein, M. R. (1982). The toddler's emerging interactive skills. In K. H. Rubin & H. S. Ross (Eds.), *Peer relationships and social skills in childhood.* New York: Springer-Verlag.

Eckerman, C. O., Davis, C. C., & Didow, S. M. (1989). Toddlers' emerging ways of achieving social coordination with a peer. *Child Development, 60,* 440–453.

Edwards, C. P. (1981). The comparative study of the development of moral judgment and reasoning. In R. Monroe, R. Monroe, & B. B. Whiting (Eds.), *Handbook of cross-cultural human development.* New York: Garland.

Edwards, C. P. (1994, April). *Cultural relativity meets best practice, or, anthropology and early education, a promising friendship.* Paper presented at the meeting of the American Educational Research Association, New Orleans.

Edwards, K. I. (1993). Obesity, anorexia, and bulimia. *Clinical Nutrition, 77,* 899–909.

Egbuono, L., & Starfield, B. (1982). Child health and social status. *Pediatrics, 69,* 550–557.

Egeland, B., & Sroufe, L. A. (1981). Attachment and early maltreatment. *Child Development, 52,* 44–52.

Egeland, B., Jacobvitz, D., & Sroufe, L. A. (1988). Breaking the cycle of abuse. *Child Development, 59,* 1080–1088.

Eiberg, H. (1995). Nocturnal enuresis is linked to a specific gene. *Scandinavian Journal of Urology and Nephrology, 173*(Supplement), 15–17.

Eiberg, H., Berendt, I., & Mohr, J. (1995). Assignment of dominant inherited nocturnal enuresis (ENUR1) to chromosome 13q. *Nature Genetics, 10,* 354–356.

Eiger, M. S., & Olds, S. W. (1999). *The complete book of breastfeeding* (3d ed.). New York: Workman.

Eimas, P. (1985). The perception of speech in early infancy. *Scientific American, 252*(1), 46–52.

Eimas, P., Siqueland, E., Jusczyk, P., & Vigorito, J. (1971). Speech perception in infants. *Science, 171,* 303–306.

Eisen, M., & Zellman, G. L. (1987). Changes in incidence of sexual intercourse of unmarrried teenagers following a community-based sex education program. *Journal of Sex Research, 23*(4), 527–544.

Eisenberg, A. R. (1996). The conflict talk of mothers and children: Patterns related to culture, SES, and gender of child. *Merrill-Palmer Quarterly, 42,* 438–452.

Eisenberg, N. (1992). *The caring child.* Cambridge, MA: Harvard University Press.

Eisenberg, N. (2000). Emotion, regulation, and moral development. *Annual Review of Psychology, 51,* 665–697.

Eisenberg, N., & Fabes, R. A. (1998). Prosocial development. In W. Damon (Series Ed.) & N. Eisenberg (Vol. Ed.), *Handbook of child psychology: Vol. 3. Social, emotional, and personality development* (5th ed., pp. 701–778). New York: Wiley.

Eisenberg, N., Fabes, R. A., & Murphy, B. C. (1996). Parents' reactions to children's negative emotions: Relations to children's social competence and comforting behavior. *Child Development, 67,* 2227–2247.

Eisenberg, N., Fabes, R. A., Guthrie, I. K., & Reiser, M. (2000). Dispositional emotionality and regulation: Their role in predicting quality of social functioning. *Journal of Personality and Social Psychology, 78,* 136–157.

Eisenberg, N., Fabes, R. A., Nyman, M., Bernzweig, J., & Pinuelas, A. (1994). The relations of emotionality and regulation to children's anger-related reactions. *Child Development, 65,* 109–128.

Eisenberg, N., Fabes, R. A., Schaller, M., & Miller, P. A. (1989). Sympathy and personal distress: Development, gender differences, and interrelations of indexes. In N. Eisenberg (Ed.), *Empathy and related emotional responses* (New Directions for Child Development No. 44). San Francisco: Jossey-Bass.

Eisenberg, N., Fabes, R. A., Shepard, S. A., Guthrie, I. K., Murphy, B. C., & Reiser, M. (1999). Parental reactions to children's negative emotions: Longitudinal relations to quality of children's social functioning. *Child Development, 70*(2), 513–534.

Eisenberg, N., Guthrie, I. K., Fabes, R. A., Reiser, M., Murphy, B. C., Holgren, R., Maszk, P., & Losoya, S. (1997). The relations of regulation and emotionality to resiliency and competent social functioning in elementary school children. *Child Development, 68,* 295–311.

Eisenberg, N., Guthrie, I. K., Murphy, B. C., Shepard, S. A., Cumberland, A., & Carlo, G. (1999). Consistency and development of prosocial dispositions: A longitudinal study. *Child Development, 70*(6), 1360–1372.

Eisenberg, N., Spinrad, T. L., Fabes, R. A., Reiser, M., Cumberland, A., Shepard, S. A., Valiente, C., Losoya, S. H., Guthrie, I. K., & Thompson, M. (2004). The relations of effortful control and impulsivity to children's resiliency and adjustment. *Child Development, 75,* 25–46.

Elder, G. H., Jr. (1974). *Children of the Great Depression: Social change in life experience.* Chicago: University of Chicago Press.

Elder, G. H., Jr. (1998). The life course and human development. In W. Damon (Series Ed.) & R. M. Lerner (Vol. Ed.), *Handbook of child psychology: Vol. 1. Theoretical models of human development* (5th ed., pp. 939–992). New York: Wiley.

Elia, J., Ambrosini, P. J., & Rapoport, J. L. (1999). Treatment of attention-deficit-hyperactivity disorder. *New England Journal of Medicine, 340,* 780–788.

Elicker, J., Englund, M., & Sroufe, L. A. (1992). Predicting peer competence and peer relationships in childhood from early parent-child relationships. In R. Parke & G. Ladd (Eds.), *Family peer relationships: Modes of linkage* (pp. 77–106). Hillsdale, NJ: Erlbaum.

Elkind, D. (1981). *The hurried child.* Reading, MA: Addison-Wesley.

Elkind, D. (1984). *All grown up and no place to go.* Reading, MA: Addison-Wesley.

Elkind, D. (1986). *The miseducation of children: Superkids at risk.* New York: Knopf.

Elkind, D. (1997). *Reinventing childhood: Raising and educating children in a changing world.* Rosemont, NJ: Modern Learning Press.

Elkind, D. (1998). Teenagers in crisis: *All grown up and no place to go.* Reading, MA: Perseus Books.

Ellickson, P. L., Orlando, M., Tucker, J. S., & Klein, D. J. (2004). From adolescence to young adulthood: Racial/ethnic disparities in smoking. *American Journal of Public Health, 94,* 293–299.

Elliott, D. S. (1993). Health enhancing and health compromising lifestyles. In S. G. Millstein, A. C. Petersen, & E. O. Nightingale (Eds.), *Promoting the health of adolescents: New directions for the twenty-first century* (pp. 119–145). New York: Oxford University Press.

Ellis, B. J., & Garber, J. (2000). Psychosocial antecedents of variation in girls' pubertal timing: Maternal depression, stepfather presence, and marital family stress. *Child Development, 71*(2), 485–501.

Ellis, B. J., Bates, J. E., Dodge, K. A., Fergusson, D. M., Horwood, L. J., Pettit, G. S., & Woodward, L. (2003). Does father-absence place daughters at special risk for early sexual activity and teenage pregnancy? *Child Development, 74,* 801–821.

Ellis, B. J., McFadyen-Ketchum, S., Dodge, K. A., Pettit, G. S., & Bates, J. E. (1999). Quality of early family relationships and individual differences in the timing of pubertal maturation in girls: A longitudinal test of an evolutionary model. *Journal of Personality and Social Psychology, 77,* 387–401.

Ellis, K. J., Abrams, S. A., & Wong, W. W. (1997). Body composition of a young, multiethnic female population. *American Journal of Clinical Nutrition, 65,* 724–731.

Eltzschig, H. K., Lieberman, E. S., and Camann, W. R. (2003). Regional anesthesia and analgesia for labor and delivery. *New England Journal of Medicine, 348,* 319–332.

Emde, R. N. (1992). Individual meaning and increasing complexity: Contributions of Sigmund Freud and René Spitz to developmental psychology. *Developmental Psychology, 28,* 347–359.

Emde, R. N., Plomin, R., Robinson, J., Corley, R., DeFries, J., Fulker, D. W., Reznick, J. S., Campos, J., Kagan, J., & Zahn-Waxler, C. (1992). Temperament, emotion, and cognition at 14 months: The MacArthur longitudinal twin study. *Child Development, 63,* 1437–1455.

Emslie, G. J. (2004). *The Treatment of Adolescents with Depression Study (TADS): Primary safety outcomes.* Presentation at the New Clinical Drug Evaluation Unit conference, Phoenix, AZ.

Engle, P. L., & Breaux, C. (1998). Fathers' involvement with children: Perspectives from developing countries. *Social Policy Report, 12*(1), 1–21.

Enloe, C. F. (1980). How alcohol affects the developing fetus. *Nutrition Today, 15*(5), 12–15.

Eogan, M. A., Geary, M. P., O'Connell, M. P., & Keane, D. P. (2003). Effect of fetal sex on labour and delivery: Retrospective review. *British Medical Journal, 326,* 137.

Erdley, C. A., Cain, K. M., Loomis, C. C., Dumas-Hines, F., & Dweck, C. S. (1997). Relations among children's social goals, implicit personality theories, and responses to social failure. *Developmental Psychology, 33,* 263–272.

Erdrich, L. (2000, March 1). Personal communication.

Erikson, E. H. (1950). *Childhood and society.* New York: Norton.

Erikson, E. H. (1950). *The life cycle completed.* New York: Norton.

Erikson, E. H. (1968). *Identity: Youth and crisis.* New York: Norton.

Erikson, E. H. (1973). The wider identity. In K. Erikson (Ed.), *In search of common ground: Conversations with Erik H. Erikson and Huey P. Newton.* New York: Norton.

Erikson, E. H. (1982). *The life cycle completed.* New York: Norton.

Erikson, E. H., Erikson, J. M., & Kivnick, H. Q. (1986). *Vital involvement in old age:*

The experience of old age in our time. New York: Norton.

Eriksson, P. S., Perfilieva, E., Björk-Eriksson, T., Alborn, A., Nordborg, C., Peterson, D. A., & Gage, F. H. (1998). Neurogenesis in the adult human hippocampus. *Nature Medicine, 4,* 1313–1317.

Eron, L. D. (1980). Prescription for reduction of aggression. *American Psychologist, 35,* 244–252.

Eron, L. D. (1982). Parent-child interaction, television violence, and aggression in children. *American Psychologist, 37,* 197–211.

Eron, L. D., & Huesmann, L. R. (1986). The role of television in the development of prosocial and antisocial behavior. In D. Olweus, J. Block, & M. Radke-Yarrow (Eds.), *The development of antisocial and prosocial behavior: Research, theories, and issues.* New York: Academic.

Etzel, R. A. (2003). How environmental exposures influence the development and exacerbation of asthma. *Pediatrics, 112*(1): 233–239.

European Collaborative Study. (1994). Natural history of vertically acquired human immunodeficiency virus-1 infection. *Pediatrics, 94,* 815–819.

Evans, G. (1976). The older the sperm . . . *Ms., 4*(7), 48–49.

Evans, G. W. (2004). The environment of childhood poverty. *American Psychologist, 59,* 77–92.

Evans, G. W., & English, K. (2002). The environment of poverty: Multiple stressor exposure, psycholophysiological stress and socioemotional adjustment. *Child Development, 73*(4), 1238–1248.

Evans, J. (1998, November). "Princesses are not into war 'n things, they always scream and run off": Exploring gender stereotypes in picture books. *Reading,* pp. 5–11.

Eyre-Walker, A., & Keightley, P. D. (1999). High genomic deleterious rates in hominids. *Nature, 397,* 344–347.

Fabes, R. A., & Eisenberg, N. (1992). Young children's coping with interpersonal anger. *Child Development, 63,* 116–128.

Fabes, R. A., & Eisenberg, N. (1996). *An examination of age and sex differences in prosocial behavior and empathy.* Unpublished data, Arizona State University.

Fabes, R. A., Eisenberg, N., Smith, M. C., & Murphy, B. C. (1996). Getting angry at peers: Associations with liking of the provocateur. *Child Development, 67,* 942–956.

Fabes, R. A., Leonard, S. A., Kupanoff, K., & Martin, C. L. (2001). Parental coping with children's negative emotions: Relations with children's emotional and social responding. *Child Development, 72,* 907–920.

Fabes, R. A., Martin, C. L., & Hanish, L. D. (2003, May). Young children's play qualities in same-, other-, and mixed-gender peer groups. *Child Development, 74*(3), 921–932.

Facio, A., & Micocci, F. (2003). Emerging adulthood in Argentina. In J. J. Arnett & N. L. Galambos (Eds.), Exploring cultural conceptions of the transition to adulthood. *New Directions for Child and Adolescent Development, 100,* 21–32.

Fagot, B. I. (1997). Attachment, parenting, and peer interactions of toddler children. *Developmental Psychology, 33,* 489–499.

Fagot, B. I., & Hagan, R. (1991). Observation of parent reaction to sex-stereotyped behaviors: Age and sex effects. *Child Development, 62,* 617–628.

Fagot, B. I., & Leinbach, M. D. (1995). Gender knowledge in egalitarian and traditional families. *Sex Roles, 32,* 513–526.

Fagot, B. I., & Leve, L. (1998). Gender identity and play. In D. P. Fromberg & D. Bergen (Eds.), *Play from birth to twelve and beyond: Contexts, perspectives, and meanings* (pp. 187–192). New York: Garland.

Faison, S. (1997, August 17). Chinese happily break the "one child" rule. *New York Times,* pp. 1, 10.

Faith, M. S., Berman, N., Heo, M., Pietrobelli, A., Gallagher, D., Epstein, L. H., Eiden, M. T., & Allison, D. B. (2001). Effects of contingent television on physical activity and television viewing in obese children. *Pediatrics, 107,* 1043–1048.

Falbo, T., & Polit, D. F. (1986). Quantitative review of the only child literature: Research evidence and theory development. *Psychological Bulletin, 100*(2), 176–189.

Falbo, T., & Poston, D. L. (1993). The academic, personality, and physical outcomes of only children in China. *Child Development, 64,* 18–35.

Falkner, D. (1995). *Great time coming: The life of Jackie Robinson, from baseball to Birmingham.* New York: Simon & Schuster.

Faltermayer, C., Horowitz, J. M., Jackson, D., Lofaro, L., Maroney, T., Morse, J., Ramirez, A., & Rubin, J. C. (1996, August 5). Where are they now? *Time,* p. 18.

Fantz, R. L. (1963). Pattern vision in newborn infants. *Science, 140,* 296–297.

Fantz, R. L. (1964). Visual experience in infants: Decreased attention to familiar patterns relative to novel ones. *Science, 146,* 668–670.

Fantz, R. L. (1965). Visual perception from birth as shown by pattern selectivity. In H. E. Whipple (Ed.), New issues in infant development. *Annals of the New York Academy of Science, 118,* 793–814.

Fantz, R. L., & Nevis, S. (1967). Pattern preferences and perceptual-cognitive development in early infancy. *Merrill-Palmer Quarterly, 13,* 77–108.

Fantz, R. L., Fagen, J., & Miranda, S. B. (1975). Early visual selectivity. In L. Cohen & P. Salapatek (Eds.), *Infant perception: From sensation to cognition: Vol. 1. Basic visual processes* (pp. 249–341). New York: Academic Press.

Farrow, J. A., Rees, J. M., & Worthington-Roberts, B. S. (1987). Health, developmental, and nutritional status of adolescent alcohol and marijuana abusers. *Pediatrics, 79,* 218–223.

Farver, J. A. M., Kim, Y. K., & Lee, Y. (1995). Cultural differences in Korean and Anglo-American preschoolers' social interaction and play behavior. *Child Development, 66,* 1088–1099.

Feingold, A., & Mazzella, R. (1998). Gender differences in body image are increasing. *Psychological Science, 9*(3), 190–195.

Feldhusen, J. F. (1992). *Talent identification and development in education (TIDE).* Sarasota, FL: Center for Creative Learning.

Feldman, R., Greenbaum, C. W., & Yirmiya, N. (1999). Mother-infant affect synchrony as an antecedent of the emergence of self-control. *Developmental Psychology, 35*(5), 223–231.

Felner, R. D., Brand, S., DuBois, D. L., Adan, A. M., Mulhall, P. F., & Evans, E. G. (1995). Socioeconomic disadvantage, proximal environmental experiences, and socioemotional and academic adjustment in early adolescence: Investigation of a mediated effect. *Child Development, 66,* 774–792.

Ferber, R. (1985). *Solve your child's sleep problems.* New York: Simon & Schuster.

Fergusson, D. M., Horwood, L. J., & Shannon, F. T. (1986). Factors related to the age of attainment of nocturnal bladder control: An 8-year longitudinal study. *Pediatrics, 78,* 884–890.

Fernald, A., & O'Neill, D. K. (1993). Peekaboo across cultures: How mothers and infants play with voices, faces, and expectations. In K. MacDonald (Ed.), *Parent-child play* (pp. 259–285). Albany, NY: State University of New York Press.

Fernald, A., Pinto, J. P., Swingley, D., Weinberg, A., & McRoberts, G. W. (1998). Rapid gains in speed of verbal processing by infants in the 2nd year. *Psychological Science, 9*(3), 228–231.

Fernald, A., Swingley, D., and Pinto, J. P. (2001). When half a word is enough: Infants can recognize spoken words using partial phonetic information. *Child Development, 72*(4), 1003–1015.

Field, A. E., Camargo, C. A., Taylor, B., Berkey, C. S., Roberts, S. B., & Colditz, G. A. (2001). Peer, parent, and media influence on the development of weight concerns and frequent dieting among preadolescent and adolescent girls and boys. *Pediatrics, 107*(1), 54–60.

Field, T. (1995). Infants of depressed mothers. *Infant Behavior and Development, 18,* 1–13.

Field, T. (1998a). Emotional care of the at-risk infant: Early interventions for infants of depressed mothers. *Pediatrics, 102,* 1305–1310.

Field, T. (1998b). Massage therapy effects. *American Psychologist, 53,* 1270–1281.

Field, T. (1998c). Maternal depression effects on infants and early intervention. *Preventive Medicine, 27,* 200–203.

Field, T., Diego, M., Hernandez-Reif, M., Schanberg, S., & Kuhn, C (2003). Depressed mothers who are "good interaction" partners versus those who are withdrawn or intrusive. *Infant Behavior & Development, 26,* 238–252.

Field, T., Fox, N. A., Pickens, J., Nawrocki, T., & Soutollo, D. (1995). Right frontal EEG activation in 3- to 6-month-old infants of depressed mothers. *Developmental Psychology, 31,* 358–363.

Field, T., Grizzle, N., Scafidi, F., Abrams, S., Richardson, S., Kuhn, C., & Schanberg, S. (1996). Massage therapy for infants of depressed mothers. *Infant Behavior and Development, 19,* 107–112.

Field, T., Hernandez-Reif, M., & Freedman, J. (2004). Stimulation programs for preterm infants. *Social Policy Report, 18*(1), 1–19.

Field, T. M. (1978). Interaction behaviors of primary versus secondary caretaker fathers. *Developmental Psychology, 14,* 183–184.

Field, T. M. (1986). Interventions for premature infants. *Journal of Pediatrics, 109*(1), 183–190.

Field, T. M. (1987). Interaction and attachment in normal and atypical infants. *Journal of Consulting and Clinical Psychology, 55*(6), 853–859.

Field, T. M., & Roopnarine, J. L. (1982). Infant-peer interaction. In T. M. Field, A. Huston, H. C. Quay, L. Troll, & G. Finley (Eds.), *Review of human development.* New York: Wiley.

Field, T. M., Sandberg, D., Garcia, R., Vega-Lahr, N., Goldstein, S., & Guy, L. (1985). Pregnancy problems, postpartum depression, and early infant-mother interactions. *Developmental Psychology, 21,* 1152–1156.

Fielden, M. R., Halgren, R. G., Fong, C. J., Staub, C., Johnson, L., Chou, K., & Zacharewski, T. R. (2002). Gestational and lactational exposure of male mice to diethylstilbestrol causes long-term effects on the testis, sperm fertilizing ability in vitro, and testicular gene expression. *Endocrinology, 143,* 3044–3059.

Fields, J. (2003). Children's living arrangements and characteristics: March 2002. *Current Population Reports* (p. 20–547). Washington, DC: U.S. Bureau of the Census.

Fields, J., & Casper, L. (2001). *America's families and living arrangements: March 2000.* (Current Population Reports, p. 20–537). Washington, DC: U.S. Census Bureau.

Fields, J. M., & Smith, K. E. (1998, April). *Poverty, family structure, and child well-being: Indicators from the SIPP* (Population Division Working Paper No. 23, U.S. Bureau of the Census). Paper presented at the Annual Meeting of the Population Association of America, Chicago, IL.

Fifer, W. P., & Moon, C. M. (1995). The effects of fetal experience with sound. In J. P. Lecanuet, W. P. Fifer, N. A. Krasnegor, & W. P. Smotherman (Eds.), *Fetal development. A psychobiological perspective* (pp. 351–366). Hillsdale, NJ: Erlbaum.

Finch, M. D., Shanahan, M. J., Mortimer, J. T., & Ryu, S. (1991). Work experience and control orientation in adolescence. *American Sociological Review, 56,* 597–611.

Finn, J. D., & Rock, D. A. (1997). Academic success among students at risk for dropout. *Journal of Applied Psychology, 82,* 221–234.

First woman to both poles—Ann Bancroft. (1997). [Online]. Available: http://www.zplace.com/rhonda/abancroft/. Access date: April 4, 2002.

Fiscella, K., Kitzman, H. J., Cole, R. E., Sidora, K. J., & Olds, D. (1998). Does child abuse predict adolescent pregnancy? *Pediatrics, 101,* 620–624.

Fischer, K. (1980). A theory of cognitive development: The control and construction of hierarchies of skills. *Psychological Review, 87,* 477–531.

Fischer, K. W., & Rose, S. P. (1994). Dynamic development of coordination of components in brain and behavior: A framework for theory and research. In G. Dawson & K. W. Fischers (Eds.), *Human behavior and the developing brain* (pp. 3–66). New York: Guilford.

Fischer, K. W., & Rose, S. P. (1995, Fall). Concurrent cycles in the dynamic development of brain and behavior. *SRCD Newsletter,* pp. 3–4, 15–16.

Fisher, C. B., Hoagwood, K., Boyce, C., Duster, T., Frank, D. A., Grisso, T., Levine, R. J., Macklin, R., Spencer, M. B., Takanishi, R., Trimble, J. E., & Zayas, L. H. (2002). Research ethics for mental health science involving ethnic minority children and youth. *American Psychologist, 57,* 1024–1040.

Fisher, R. L., & Fisher, S. (1996). Antidepressants for children: Is scientific support necessary? *Journal of Nervous Mental Disorders (United States), 184,* 99–102.

Fivush, R., & Schwarzmueller, A. (1998). Children remember childhood: Implications for childhood amnesia. *Applied Cognitive Psychology, 12,* 455–473.

Fivush, R., Hudson, J., & Nelson, K. (1983). Children's long-term memory for a novel event: An exploratory study. *Merrill-Palmer Quarterly, 30,* 303–316.

Flake, A. W., Roncarolo, M. G., Puck, J. M., Almeida-Porada, G., Evans, M. I., Johnson, M. P., Abella, E. M., Harrison, D. D., & Zanjani, E. D. (1996). Treatment of X-linked severe combined immunodeficiency by in utero transplantation of paternal bone marrow. *New England Journal of Medicine, 335,* 1806–1810.

Flavell, J. (1963). *The developmental psychology of Jean Piaget.* New York: Van Nostrand.

Flavell, J. H. (1970). Developmental studies of mediated memory. In H. W. Reese & L. P. Lipsitt (Eds.), *Advances in child development and behavior* (vol. 5, pp. 181–211). New York: Academic.

Flavell, J. H. (1992). Cognitive development: Past, present, and future. *Developmental Psychology, 28,* 998–1005.

Flavell, J. H. (1993). Young children's understanding of thinking and consciousness. *Current Directions in Psychological Science, 2,* 40–43.

Flavell, J. H., Green, F. L., & Flavell, E. R. (1986). Development of knowledge about the appearance-reality distinction. *Monographs of the Society for Research in Child Development, 51*(1, Serial No. 212).

Flavell, J. H., Green, F. L., & Flavell, E. R. (1995). Young children's knowledge about thinking. *Monographs of the Society for Research in Child Development, 60*(1, serial no. 243).

Flavell, J. H., Green, F. L., Flavell, E. R., & Grossman, J. B. (1997). The development of children's knowledge about inner speech. *Child Development, 68,* 39–47.

Flavell, J. H., Green, F. L., Flavell, E. R., & Lin, N. T. (1999). Development of children's knowledge about unconsciousness. *Child Development, 70,* 396–412.

Flavell, J. H., Miller, P. H., & Miller, S. A. (1993). *Cognitive development.* Englewood Cliffs, NJ: Prentice-Hall.

Flavell, J. H., Miller, P. H., & Miller, S. A. (2002). *Cognitive development.* Englewood Cliffs, NJ: Prentice-Hall.

Flieller, A. (1999). Comparison of the development of formal thought in adolescent cohorts aged 10 to 15 years (1967–1996 and 1972–1993). *Developmental Psychology, 35,* 1048–1058.

Flores, G., Fuentes-Afflick, E., Barbot, O., Carter-Pokras, O., Claudio, L., Lara, M., McLaurin, J. A., Pachter, L., Gomez, F. R., Mendoza, F., Valdez, R. B., Villarruel, A. M., Zambrana, R. E., Greenberg, R., & Weitzman, M. (2002). The health of Latino children: Urgent priorities, unanswered questions, and a research agenda. *Journal of the American Medical Association, 288,* 82–90.

Fluoxetine-Bulimia Collaborative Study Group. (1992). Fluoxetine in the treatment of bulimia nervosa: A multicenter placebo-controlled, double-blind trial. *Archives of General Psychiatry, 49,* 139–147.

Flynn, J. R. (1984). The mean IQ of Americans: Massive gains 1932 to 1978. *Psychological Bulletin, 95,* 29–51.

Flynn, J. R. (1987). Massive IQ gains in 14 nations: What IQ tests really measure. *Psychological Bulletin, 101,* 171–191.

Fomboone, E. (2001). Is there an epidemic of autism? *Pediatrics, 107,* 411–412.

Fomboone, E. (2003). The prevalence of autism. *Journal of the American Medical Association, 289,* 87–89.

Fontanel, B., & d'Harcourt, C. (1997). *Babies, history, art and folklore.* New York: Abrams.

Ford, C. A., Bearman, P. S., & Moody, J. (1999). Foregone health care among adolescents. *Journal of the American Medical Association, 282*(23), 2227–2234.

Ford, D. Y., & Harris III, J. J. (1996). Perceptions and attitudes of black students toward school, achievement, and other educational variables. *Child Development, 67,* 1141–1152.

Ford, R. P., Schluter, P. J., Mitchell, E. A., Taylor, B. J., Scragg, R., & Stewart, A. W. (1998). Heavy caffeine intake in pregnancy and sudden infant death syndrome (New Zealand Cot Death Study Group). *Archives of Disease in Childhood, 78*(1), 9–13.

Foss, R. D., Feaganes, J. R., & Rodgman, E. A. (2001). Initial effects of graduated driver licensing on 16-year-old driver crashes in North Carolina. *Journal of the American Medical Association, 286,* 1588–1592.

Foster, D. (1999). Isabel Allende unveiled. In J. Rodden (Ed.), *Conversations with Isabel Allende* (pp. 105–113). Austin: University of Texas Press.

Fowler, J. (1981). *Stages of faith: The psychology of human development and the quest for meaning.* New York: Harper & Row.

Fowler, J. W. (1989). Strength for the journey: Early childhood development in selfhood and faith. In D. A. Blazer, J. W. Fowler, K. J. Swick, A. S. Honig, P. J. Boone, B. M. Caldwell, R. A. Boone, & L. W. Barber (Eds.), *Faith development in early childhood* (pp. 1–63). New York: Sheed & Ward.

Fowler, M. G., Simpson, G. A., & Schoendorf, K. C. (1993). Families on the move and children's health care. *Pediatrics, 91,* 934–940.

Fox, M. K., Pac, S., Devaney, B., & Jankowski, L. (2004). Feeding Infants and Toddlers Study: What foods are infants and toddlers eating? *Journal of the American Dietetic Association, 104,* 22–30.

Fox, N. A., Henderson, H. A., Rubin, K. H., Calkins, S. D., & Schmidt, L. A. (2001). Continuity and discontinuity of behavioral inhibition and exuberance: Psychophysiological and behavioral influences across the first four years of life. *Child Development, 72,* 1–21.

Fox, N. A., Kimmerly, N. L., & Schafer, W. D. (1991). Attachment to mother/attachment to father: A meta-analysis. *Child Development, 62,* 210–225.

Fraga, C. G., Motchnik, P. A., Shigenaga, M. K., Helbock, H. J., Jacob, R. A., & Ames, B. N. (1991). Ascorbic acid protects against endogenous oxidative DNA damage in human sperm. *Proceedings of the National Academy of Sciences of the United States, 88,* 11003–11006.

Frank, A. (1958). *The diary of a young girl* (B. M. Mooyaart-Doubleday, Trans.). New York: Pocket.

Frank, A. (1995). *The diary of a young girl: The definitive edition* (O. H. Frank & M. Pressler, Eds.; S. Massotty, Trans.). New York: Doubleday.

Frank, D. A., Augustyn, M., Knight, W. G., Pell, T., & Zuckerman, B. (2001). Growth, development, and behavior in early childhood following prenatal cocaine exposure. *Journal of the American Medical Association, 285,* 1613–1625.

Frankenburg, W. K., Dodds, J. B., Fandal, A. W., Kazuk, E., & Cohrs, M. (1975). *The Denver Developmental Screening Test: Reference manual.* Denver: University of Colorado Medical Center.

Frankenburg, W. K., Dodds, J., Archer, P., Bresnick, B., Maschka. P., Edelman, N., & Shapiro, H. (1992). *Denver II training manual.* Denver: Denver Developmental Materials.

Fraser, A. M., Brockert, J. F., & Ward, R. H. (1995). Association of young maternal age with adverse reproductive outcomes. *New England Journal of Medicine, 332*(17), 1113–1117.

Frazier, J. A., & Morrison, F. J. (1998). The influence of extended-year schooling on growth of achievement and perceived competence in early elementary school. *Child Development, 69,* 495–517.

Fredricks, J. A., & Eccles, J. S. (2002). Children's competence and value beliefs from childhood through adolescence: Growth trajectories in two male-sex-typed domains. *Developmental Psychology, 38,* 519–533.

Fredriksen, K., Rhodes, J., Reddy, R., & Way, N. (2004). Sleepless in Chicago: Tracking the effects of adolescent sleep loss during the middle-school years. *Child Development, 75,* 84–95.

Freedman, D. S., Dietz, W. H., Srinivasan, S. R., & Berenson, G. S. (1999). The relation of overweight in cardiovascular risk factors among children and adolescents: The Bogalusa Heart Study. *Pediatrics, 103,* 1175–1182.

Freedman, R. (2004). *The voice that challenged a nation: Marian Anderson and the struggle for equal rights.* New York: Clarion.

Freeman, D. (1983). *Margaret Mead and Samoa: The making and unmaking of an anthropological myth.* Cambridge, MA: Harvard University Press.

French, A. P. (Ed.). (1979). *Einstein: A centenary volume.* Cambridge, MA: Harvard University Press.

Freud, A. (1946). *The ego and the mechanisms of defense.* New York: International Universities Press.

Freud, S. (1953). *A general introduction to psychoanalysis* (J. Rivière, Trans.) New York: Perma-books. (Original work published 1935.)

Freud, S. (1964a). New introductory lectures on psychoanalysis. In J. Strachey (Ed. & Trans.), *The standard edition of the complete psychological works of Sigmund Freud* (vol. 22). London: Hogarth. (Original work published 1933.)

Freud, S. (1964b). An outline of psychoanalysis. In J. Strachey (Ed. & Trans.), *The standard edition of the complete psychological works of Sigmund Freud* (vol. 23). London: Hogarth. (Original work published 1940.)

Fried, P. A., Watkinson, B., & Willan, A. (1984). Marijuana use during pregnancy and decrease length of gestation. *American Journal of Obstetrics and Gynecology, 150,* 23–27.

Friedman, J. M., & Halaas, J. L. (1998). Leptin and the regulation of body weight in mammals. *Nature, 395,* 763–770.

Friedman, L. J. (1999). *Identity's architect.* New York: Scribner.

Friend, M., & Davis, T. L. (1993). Appearance-reality distinction: Children's understanding of the physical and affective domains. *Developmental Psychology, 29,* 907–914.

Frith, U. (1989). *Autism: Explaining the enigma.* Oxford: Basil Blackwell.

Fromkin, V., Krashen, S., Curtiss, S., Rigler, D., & Rigler, M. (1974). The development of language in Genie: Acquisition beyond the "critical period." *Brain and Language, 15*(9), 28–34.

Frydman, O., & Bryant, P. (1988). Sharing and the understanding of number equivalence by young children. *Cognitive Development, 3,* 323–339.

Fuligni, A. J. (1997). The academic achievement of adolescents from immigrant families: The roles of family background, attitudes, and behavior. *Child Development, 68,* 351–363.

Fuligni, A. J., & Eccles, J. S. (1993). Perceived parent-child relationships and early adolescents' orientation toward peers. *Developmental Psychology, 29,* 622–632.

Fuligni, A. J., & Stevenson, H. W. (1995). Time use and mathematics achievement among American, Chinese, and Japanese high school students. *Child Development, 66,* 830–842.

Fuligni, A. J., & Witkow, M. (2004). The postsecondary educational progress of youth from immigrant families. *Journal of Research on Adolescence, 14,* 159–183.

Fuligni, A. J., Eccles, J. S., Barber, B. L., & Clements, P. (2001). Early adolescent peer orientation and adjustment during high school. *Developmental Psychology, 37*(1), 28–36.

Fuligni, A. J., Yip, T., & Tseng, V. (2002). The impact of family obligation on the daily activities and psychological well-being of Chinese American adolescents. *Child Development, 73*(1), 302–314.

Furman, L., Taylor, G., Minich, N., & Hack, M. (2003). The effect of maternal milk on neonatal morbidity of very low-birth-weight infants. *Archives of Pediatrics and Adolescent Medicine, 157,* 66–71.

Furman, W. (1982). Children's friendships. In T. M. Field, A. Huston, H. C. Quay, L. Troll, & G. E. Finley (Eds.), *Review of human development.* New York: Wiley.

Furman, W., & Bierman, K. L. (1983). Developmental changes in young children's conception of friendship. *Child Development, 54,* 549–556.

Furman, W., & Buhrmester, D. (1985). Children's perceptions of the personal relationships in their social networks. *Developmental Psychology, 21,* 1016–1024.

Furman, W., & Buhrmester, D. (1992). Age and sex in perceptions of networks of personal relationships. *Child Development, 63,* 103–115.

Furman, W., & Wehner, E. A. (1997). Adolescent romantic relationships: A developmental perspective. In S. Shulman & A. Collins (Eds.). Romantic relationships in adolescence: Developmental perspectives. *New Directions for Child and Adolescent Development, 78,* 21–36.

Furnival, R. A., Street, K. A., & Schunk, J. E. (1999). Trampoline injuries triple among children. *Pediatrics, 103,* e57 [Online]. Available: http://www.pediatrics.org/egi/content/full/103/5/e57. Access date: May 21, 1999.

Furrow, D. (1984). Social and private speech at two years. *Child Development, 55,* 355–362.

Furstenberg, F. F., Levine, J. A., & Brooks-Gunn, J. (1990). The children of teenage mothers: Patterns of early child bearing in two generations. *Family Planning Perspectives, 22*(2), 54–61.

Furth, H. G., & Kane, S. R. (1992). Children constructing society: A new perspective on children at play. In H. McGurk (Ed.), *Childhood social development: Contemporary perspectives* (pp. 149–173). Hillsdale, NJ: Erlbaum.

Gabbard, C. P. (1996). *Lifelong motor development* (2d ed.). Madison, WI: Brown and Benchmark.

Gabhainn, S., & François, Y. (2000). Substance use. In C. Currie, K. Hurrelmann, W. Settertobulte, R. Smith, & J. Todd (Eds.), *Health behaviour in school-aged children: A WHO cross-national study (HBSC) international report* (pp. 97–114). WHO Policy Series: Healthy Policy for Children and Adolescents, Series No. 1. Copenhagen, Denmark: World Health Organization Regional Office for Europe.

Gabriel, T. (1996, January 7). High-tech pregnancies test hope's limit. *New York Times,* pp. 1, 18–19.

Gaffney, M., Gamble, M., Costa, P., Holstrum, J., & Boyle, C. (2003). Infants tested for hearing loss—United States, 1999–2001. *Morbidity and Mortality Weekly Report, 51,* 981–984.

Gale, J. L., Thapa, P. B., Wassilak, S. G., Bobo, J. K., Mendelman, P. M., & Foy, H. M. (1994). Risk of serious acute neurological illness after immunization with diptheria-tetanus-pertussis vaccine: A population-based case-control study. *Journal of the American Medical Association, 271,* 37–41.

Galen, B. R., & Underwood, M. K. (1997). A developmental investigation of social aggression among children. *Developmental Psychology, 33,* 589–600.

Galotti, K. M., Komatsu, L. K., & Voelz, S. (1997). Children's differential performance on deductive and inductive syllogisms. *Developmental Psychology, 33,* 70–78.

Gannon, P. J., Holloway, R. L., Broadfield, D. C., & Braun, A. R. (1998). Asymmetry of chimpanzee planum temporale: Humanlike pattern of Wernicke's brain language homlog. *Science, 279,* 22–222.

Gans, J. E. (1990). *America's adolescents: How healthy are they?* Chicago: American Medical Association.

Garasky, S., & Meyer, D. R. (1996). Reconsidering the increase in father only families. *Demography, 33,* 385–393.

Garbarino, J., & Kostelny, K. (1993). Neighborhood and community influences on parenting. In T. Luster & L. Okagaki (Eds.), *Parenting: An ecological perspective* (pp. 203–226). Hillsdale, NJ: Erlbaum.

Garbarino, J., Dubrow, N., Kostelny, K., & Pardo, C. (1992). *Children in danger: Coping with the consequences of community violence.* San Francisco: Jossey-Bass.

Garbarino, J., Dubrow, N., Kostelny, K., & Pardo, C. (1998). *Children in danger: Coping with the consequences of community violence.* San Francisco: Jossey-Bass.

Garcia, M. M., Shaw, D. S., Winslow, E. B., & Yaggi, K. E. (2000). Destructive sibling conflict and the development of conduct problems in young boys. *Developmental Psychology, 36*(1), 44–53.

Gardiner, H. W. & Kosmitzki, C. (2005). *Lives across cultures: Cross-cultural human development.* Boston: Allyn & Bacon.

Gardner, H. (1993). *Frames of mind: The theory of multiple intelligences.* New York: Basic. (Original work published 1983)

Gardner, H. (1995). Reflections on multiple intelligences: Myths and messages. *Phi Delta Kappan,* pp. 200–209.

Gardner, H. (1998). Are there additional intelligences? In J. Kane (Ed.), *Education, information, and transformation: Essays on learning and thinking.* Englewood Cliffs, NJ: Prentice-Hall.

Gardner, M. (2002, Aug. 1). Meet the nanny—"Granny": Grandparents, says Census, are nation's leading child-care providers. *Christian Science Monitor.* [Online]. Available: csmonitor.com.

Garland, A. F., & Zigler, E. (1993). Adolescent suicide prevention: Current research and social policy implications. *American Psychologist, 48*(2), 169–182.

Garland, J. B. (1982, March). *Social referencing and self-produced locomotion.* Paper presented at the meeting of the International Conference on International Studies, Austin, TX.

Garmezy, N., Masten, A., & Tellegen, A. (1984). The study of stress and competence in children. A building block for developmental psychopathology. *Child Development, 55,* 97–111.

Garmon, L. C., Basinger, K. S., Gregg, V. R., & Gibbs, J. C. (1996). Gender differences in stage and expression of moral judgment. *Merrill-Palmer Quarterly, 42,* 418–437.

Garner, B. P. (1998). Play development from birth to age four. In D. P. Fromberg & D. Bergen (Eds.), *Play from birth to twelve and beyond: Contexts, perspectives, and meanings* (pp. 137–145). New York: Garland.

Garner, D. M. (1993). Pathogenesis of anorexia nervosa. *Lancet, 341,* 1631–1635.

Garner, P. W., & Power, T. G. (1996). Preschoolers' emotional control in the disappointment paradigm and its relation to temperament, emotional knowledge, and family expressiveness. *Child Development, 67,* 1406–1419.

Gartstein, M. A., & Rothbart, M. K. (2003). Studying infant temperament via the Revised Infant Behavior Questionnaire. *Infant Behavior & Development, 26,* 64–86.

Gauvain, M. (1993). The development of spatial thinking in everyday activity. *Developmental Review, 13,* 92–121.

Gazzaniga, M. S. (Ed.). (2000). *The new cognitive neurosciences* (2d ed.). Cambridge, MA: The MIT Press.

Ge, X., Conger, R. D., & Elder Jr., G. H. (1996). Coming of age too early: Pubertal influences on girls' vulnerability to psychological distress. *Child Development, 67,* 3386–3400.

Ge, X., Conger, R. D., & Elder, G. H. (2001). Pubertal transition, stressful life events, and the emergence of gender differences in adolescent depressive symptoms. *Developmental Psychology, 37*(3), 404–417.

Geary, D. C. (1993). Mathematical disabilities: Cognitive, neuropsychological, and genetic components. *Psychological Bulletin, 114,* 345–362.

Geary, D. C. (1999). Evolution and developmental sex differences. *Current Directions in Psychological Science, 8*(4), 115–120.

Gecas, V., & Seff, M. A. (1990). Families and adolescents: A review of the 1980s. *Journal of Marriage and the Family, 52,* 941–958.

Geen, R. (2004). The evolution of kinship care: Policy and practice. In David and Lucile Packard Foundation, Children, families, and foster care. *The Future of Children, 14*(1). Available: http://www.futureofchildren.org.

Geen, R. G. (1994). Television and aggression: Recent developments in research and theory. In D. Zillman, J. Bryant, & A. C. Huston (Eds.), *Media, children, and the family: Social scientific, psychoanalytic, and clinical perspectives* (pp. 151–162). Hillsdale, NJ: Erlbaum.

Gelfand, D. M., & Teti, D. M. (1995, November). How does maternal depression affect children? *The Harvard Mental Health Letter,* p. 8.

Gélis, J. (1991). *History of childbirth: Fertility, pregnancy, and birth in early modern Europe.* Boston: Northeastern University Press.

Gelman, R., & Gallistel, C. R. (1978). *The child's understanding of number.* Cambridge, MA: Harvard University Press.

Gelman, R., Spelke, E. S., & Meck, E. (1983). What preschoolers know about animate and inanimate objects. In D. R. Rogers & J. S. Sloboda (Eds.), *The acquisition of symbolic skills* (pp. 297–326). New York: Plenum.

Genbacev, O. D., Prakobphol, A., Foulk, R. A., Krtolica, A. R., Ilic, D., Singer, M. S., Yang, Z.-Q., Kiessling, L. L., Rosen, S. D., & Fisher, S. J. (2003). Trophoblash L-selectin-mediated adhesion at the maternal-fetal interface. *Science, 299,* 405–408.

Genesee, F., Nicoladis, E., & Paradis, J. (1995). Language differentiation in early bilingual development. *Journal of Child Language, 22,* 611–631.

George, C., Kaplan, N., & Main, M. (1985). *The Berkeley Adult Attachment Interview.* Unpublished protocol, Department of Psychology, University of California, Berkeley, CA.

George, T. P., & Hartmann, D. P. (1996). Friendship networks of unpopular, average, and popular children. *Child Development, 67,* 2301–2316.

Gerbner, G., & Ozyegin, N. (1997, March 20). *Alcohol, tobacco, and illicit drugs in entertainment television, commercials, news, "reality shows," movies, and music channels.* Report from the Robert Wood Johnson Foundation, Princeton, NJ.

Gertner, B. L., Rice, M. L., & Hadley, P. A. (1994). Influence of communicative competence on peer preferences in a preschool classroom. *Journal of Speech and Hearing Research, 37,* 913–923.

Gesell, A. (1929). Maturation and infant behavior patterns. *Psychological Review, 36,* 307–319.

Getzels, J. W. (1964). Creative thinking, problem-solving, and instruction. In *Yearbook of the National Society for the Study of Education* (pt. 1, pp. 240–267). Chicago: University of Chicago Press.

Getzels, J. W. (1984, March). *Problem finding in creativity in higher education.* The Fifth Rev. Charles F. Donovan, S. J., Lecture, Boston College, School of Education, Boston, MA.

Getzels, J. W., & Jackson, P. W. (1962). *Creativity and intelligence: Explorations with gifted students.* New York: Wiley.

Getzels, J. W., & Jackson, P. W. (1963). The highly intelligent and the highly creative adolescent: A summary of some research findings. In C. W. Taylor & F. Baron (Eds.), *Scientific creativity; Its recognition and development* (pp. 161–172). New York: Wiley.

Ghetti, S., & Alexander, K. W. (2004). "If it happened, I would remember it": Strategic use of event memorability in the rejection of false autobiographical events. *Child Development, 75,* 542–561.

Gibbs, J. C. (1991). Toward an integration of Kohlberg's and Hoffman's theories of moral development. In W. M. Kurtines & J. L. Gewirtz (Eds.), *Handbook of moral behavior and development: Advances in theory, research, and application* (vol. 1). Hillsdale, NJ: Erlbaum.

Gibbs, J. C. (1995). The cognitive developmental perspective. In W. M. Kurtines & J. L. Gewirtz (Eds.), *Moral development: An introduction.* Boston: Allyn & Bacon.

Gibbs, J. C., & Schnell, S. V. (1985). Moral development "versus" socialization. *American Psychologist, 40*(10), 1071–1080.

Gibbs, J. C., Potter, G. B., Barriga, A. Q., & Liau, A. K. (1996). Developing the helping skills and prosocial motivation of aggressive adolescents in peer group programs. *Aggression and Violent Behavior, 1*(3), 283–305.

Gibbs, J. C., Potter, G. C., Goldstein, A. P., & Brendtro, L. K. (1998). How EQUIP programs help youth change. *Reclaiming Children and Youth, 7*(2), 117–122.

Gibson, E. J. (1969). *Principles of perceptual learning and development.* New York: Appleton-Century-Crofts.

Gibson, E. J., & Pick, A. D. (2000). *An ecological approach to perception learning and development.* New York: Oxford University Press.

Gibson, E. J., & Walker, A. S. (1984). Development of knowledge of visual-tactual affordances of substance. *Child Development, 55,* 453–460.

Gibson, J. J. (1979). *The ecological approach to visual perception.* Boston: Houghton-Mifflin.

Gidwani, P. P., Sobol, A., DeJong, W., Perrin, J. M., & Gortmaker, S. L. (2002). Television viewing and initiation of smoking among youth. *Pediatrics, 110,* 505–508.

Gielen, U., & Kelly, D. (1983, February). *Buddhist Ladakh: Psychological portrait of a nonviolent culture.* Paper presented at the Annual Meeting of the Society for Cross-Cultural Research, Washington, DC.

Gilbert, W. M., Nesbitt, T. S., & Danielsen, B. (1999). Childbearing beyond age 40: Pregnancy outcome in 24,032 cases. *Obstetrics and Gynecology, 93,* 9–14.

Gill, B., & Schlossman, S. (1996). "A sin against childhood": Progressive education and the crusade to abolish homework, 1897–1941. *American Journal of Education, 105,* 27–66.

Gilligan, C. (1982). *In a different voice: Psychological theory and women's development.* Cambridge, MA: Harvard University Press.

Gilligan, C. (1987a). Adolescent development reconsidered. In E. E. Irwin (Ed.), *Adolescent social behavior and health.* San Francisco: Jossey-Bass.

Gilligan, C. (1987b). Moran orientation and moral development. In E. F. Kittay & D. T. Meyers (Eds.), *Women and moral theory* (pp. 19–33). Totowa, NJ: Rowman & Littlefield.

Gillman, M. W., Rifas-Shiman, S. L, Camargo, C. A., Berkey, C. S., Frazier, A. L., Rockett, H. R. H., Field, A. E., & Colditz, G. A. (2001). Risk of overweight among adolescents who were breastfed as infants. *Journal of the American Medical Association, 285*(19), 2461–2467.

Ginsburg, G. S., & Bronstein, P. (1993). Family factors related to children's intrinsic/extrinsic motivational orientation and academic performance. *Child Development, 64,* 1461–1474.

Ginsburg, H., & Opper, S. (1979). *Piaget's theory of intellectual development* (2d ed.). Englewood Cliffs, NJ: Prentice-Hall.

Ginsburg, H. P. (1997). Mathematics learning disabilities: A view from developmental psychology. *Journal of Learning Disabilities, 30,* 20–33.

Ginsburg-Block, M. D., & Fantuzzo, J. W. (1998). An evaluation of the relative effectiveness of NCTM standards-based interventions for low-achieving urban elementary students. *Journal of Educational Psychology, 90,* 560–569.

Ginzburg, N. (1985). *The Little Virtues.* (D. Davis, Trans.). Manchester, England: Carcanet.

Giordano, P. C., Cernkovich, S. A., & DeMaris, A. (1993). The family and peer relations of black adolescents. *Journal of Marriage and the Family, 55,* 277–287.

Gitau, R., Cameron, A., Fisk, N. & Glover, V. (1998). Fetal exposure to maternal cortisol. *Lancet, 352,* 707–708.

Giusti, R. M., Iwamoto, K., & Hatch, E. E. (1995). Diethylstilbestrol revisited: A review of the long-term health effects. *Annals of Internal Medicine, 122,* 778–788.

Gjerdingen, D. (2003). The effectiveness of various postpartum depression treatments and the impact of antidepressant drugs on nursing infants. *Journal of American Board of Family Practice, 16,* 372–382.

Gladue, B. A. (1994). The biopsychology of sexual orientation. *Current Directions in Psychological Science, 3,* 150–154.

Glantz, S. A., Kacirk, K. W., & McCulloch, C. (2004). Back to the future: Smoking in movies in 2002 compared with 1950 levels. *American Journal of Public Health, 94,* 261–263.

Glasgow, K. L., Dornbusch, S. M., Troyer, L., Steinberg, L., & Ritter, P. L. (1997). Parenting styles, adolescents' attributions, and educational outcomes in nine heterogeneous high schools. *Child Development, 68,* 507–529.

Gleason, T. R., Sebanc, A. M., & Hartup, W. W. (2000). Imaginary companions of preschool children. *Developmental Psychology, 36,* 419–428.

Gleitman, L. R., Newport, E. L., & Gleitman, H. (1984). The current status of the motherese hypothesis. *Journal of Child Language, 11,* 43–79.

Glenn, N., & Marquardt, E. (2001). *Hooking up, hanging out, and hoping for Mr. Right: College women on dating and mating today.* New York: Institute for American Values.

Goetz, P. J. (2003). The effects of bilingualism on theory of mind development. *Bilingualism: Language and Cognition, 6,* 1–15.

Goldberg, W. A., Greenberger, E., & Nagel, S. K. (1996). Employment and achievement: Mothers' work involvement in relation to children's achievement behaviors and mothers' parenting behaviors. *Child Development, 67,* 1512–1527.

Goldenberg, R. L., & Rouse, D. J. (1998). Prevention of premature labor. *New England Journal of Medicine, 339,* 313–320.

Goldenberg, R. L., & Tamura, T. (1996). Prepregnancy weight and pregnancy outcome. *Journal of the American Medical Association, 275,* 1127–1128.

Goldenberg, R. L., Tamura, T., Neggers, Y., Copper, R. L., Johnston, K. E., DuBard, M. B., & Hauth, J. C. (1995). The effect of zinc supplementation on pregnancy outcome. *Journal of the American Medical Association, 274,* 463–468.

Goldin-Meadow, S., & Mylander, C. (1998). Spontaneous sign systems created by deaf children in two cultures. *Nature, 391,* 279–281.

Goldman, A. (1981). *Elvis.* New York: McGraw-Hill.

Goldman, R. (1964). *Religious thinking from childhood to adolescence.* London: Routledge & Kegan Paul.

Goldsmith, M., Mackay, A., & Woudhuysen, J. S. (Eds.). (1980). *Einstein: The first hundred years.* Oxford: Pergamon.

Goldstein, A. O., Sobel, R. A., & Newman, G. R. (1999). Tobacco and alcohol use in G-rated children's animated films. *Journal of the American Medical Association, 281,* 1131–1136.

Goleman, D. (1995, July 1). A genetic clue to bed-wetting is located: Researchers say discovery shows the problem is not emotions! *New York Times,* p. 8.

Golinkoff, R. M., Jacquet, R. C., Hirsh-Pasek, K., & Nandakumar, R. (1996). Lexical principles may underlie the learning of verbs. *Child Development, 67,* 3101–3119.

Golomb, C., & Galasso, L. (1995). Make believe and reality: Explorations of the imaginary realm. *Developmental Psychology, 31,* 800–810.

Golombok, S., MacCallum, F., & Goodman, E. (2001). The "test-tube" generation: Parent-child relationships and the psychological well-being of in vitro fertilization children at adolescence. *Child Development, 72,* 599–608.

Golombok, S., MacCallum, F., Goodman, E., & Rutter, M. (2002). Families with children conceived by donor insemination: A follow-up at age twelve. *Child Development, 73,* 952–968.

Golombok, S., Murray, C., Jadva, V., MacCallum, F., & Lycett, E. (2004). Families created through surrogacy arrangements: Parent-child relationships in the 1st year of life. *Developmental Psychology, 40,* 400–411.

Gonzales, N. A., Cauce, A. M., & Mason, C. A. (1996). Interobserver agreement in the assessment of parental behavior and parent-adolescent conflict: African American mothers, daughters, and independent observers. *Child Development, 67,* 1483–1498.

Goodman, G. S., Emery, R. E., & Haugaard, J. J. (1998). Developmental psychology and law: Divorce, child maltreatment, foster care, and adoption. In W. Damon (Series Ed.), I. E. Sigel, & K. A. Renninger (Vol. Eds.), *Handbook of child psychology* (vol. 4, pp. 775–874). New York: Wiley.

Goodwin, J. (1994). *Akira Kurosawa and intertextual cinema.* Baltimore, MD: Johns Hopkins University Press.

Goodwyn, S. W., & Acredolo, L. P. (1998). Encouraging symbolic gestures: A new perspective on the relationship between gesture and speech. In J. M. Iverson & S. Goldin-Meadow (Eds.), *The nature and functions of gesture in children's communication* (pp. 61–73). San Francisco: Jossey-Bass.

Gopnik, A., Sobel, D. M., Schulz, L. E., & Glymour, C. (2001). Causal learning mechanisms in very young children: Two-, three-, and four-year-olds infer causal relations from patterns of variation and covariation. *Developmental Psychology, 37*(5), 620–629.

Gordon, I., Lask, B., Bryantwaugh, R., Christie, D., & Timini, S. (1997). Childhood onset anorexia nervosa: Towards identifying a biological substrate. *International Journal of Eating Disorders, 22*(2), 159–165.

Gorman, M. (1993). Help and self-help for older adults in developing countries. *Generations, 17*(4), 73–76.

Gortmaker, S. L., Hughes, M., Cervia, J., Brady, M., Johnson, G. M., Seage, G. R., Song, L. Y., Dankner, W. M., & Oleske, J. M. for the Pediatric AIDS Clinical Trial Group Protocol 219 Team. (2001). Effect of combination therapy including protease inhibitors on mortality among children and adolescents infected with HIV-1. *New England Journal of Medicine, 345*(21), 1522–1528.

Gortmaker, S. L., Must, A., Perrin, J. M., Sobol, A. M., & Dietz, W. H. (1993). Social and economic consequences of overweight in adolescence and young adulthood. *New England Journal of Medicine, 329,* 1008–1012.

Gottfried, A., E., Fleming, J. S., & Gottfried, A. W. (1998). Role of cognitively stimulating home environment in children's academic intrinsic motivation: A longitudinal study. *Child Development, 69,* 1448–1460.

Gottlieb, G. (1991). Experiential canalization of behavioral development theory. *Developmental Psychology, 27*(1), 4–13.

Goubet, N. & Clifton, R. K. (1998). Object and event representation in 6½-month-old infants. *Developmental Psychology, 34,* 63–76.

Gould, E., Reeves, A. J., Graziano, M. S. A., & Gross, C. G. (1999). Neurogenesis in the neocortex of adult primates. *Science, 286,* 548–552.

Graber, J. A., Brooks-Gunn, J., & Warren, M. P. (1995). The antecedents of menarcheal age: Heredity, family environment, and stressful life events. *Child Development, 66,* 346–359.

Graber, J. A., Lewinsohn, P. M., Seeley, J. R., & Brooks-Gunn, J. (1997). Is psychopathology associated with the timing of pubertal development? *Journal of the American Academy of Child and Adolescent Psychiatry, 36,* 1768–1776.

Grant, B. F., & Dawson, D. A. (1998). Age of onset of alcohol use and its association with DSM-IV alcohol abuse and dependence: Results from the National Longitudinal Alcohol Epidemiological Survey. *Journal of Substance Abuse, 9,* 103–110.

Grantham-McGregor, S., Powell, C., Walker, S., Chang, S., & Fletcher, P. (1994). The long-term follow-up of severely malnourished children who participated in an intervention program. *Child Development, 65,* 428–439.

Gray, M. R., & Steinberg, L. (1999). Unpacking authoritative parenting: Reassessing a multidimensional construct. *Journal of Marriage and the Family, 61,* 574–587.

Graziano, A. M., & Mooney, K. C. (1982). Behavioral treatment of "nightfears" in children: Maintenance and improvement at 2½ to 3-year follow-up. *Journal of Counseling and Clinical Psychology, 50,* 598–599.

Greenberger, E., & Steinberg, L. (1986). *When teenagers work.* New York: Basic Books.

Greene, M. F. (2002). Outcomes of very low birth weight in young adults. *New England Journal of Medicine, 346*(3), 146–148.

Greenfield, P. M., & Childs, C. P. (1978). Understanding sibling concepts: A developmental study of kin terms in Zinacanten. In P. R. Dasen, (Ed.), *Piagetian psychology* (pp. 335–358). New York: Gardner.

Greenhouse, L. (2000a, February 29). Program of drug-testing pregnant women draws review by the Supreme Court. *New York Times,* p. A12.

Greenhouse, L. (2000b, September 9). Should a fetus's well-being override a mother's rights? *New York Times,* pp. B9, B11.

Greenough, W. T., Black, J. E., & Wallace, C. S. (1987). Experience and brain development. *Child Development, 58,* 539–559.

Greenstone, M., & Chay, K. (2003). The impact of air pollution on infant mortality: Evidence from geographic variation in pollution shocks induced by a recession. *Quarterly Journal of Economics, 118,* 1121–1167.

Gregg, V., Gibbs, J. C., & Basinger, K. S. (1994). Patterns of developmental delay in moral judgment by male and female delinquents. *Merrill-Palmer Quarterly, 40,* 538–553.

Grigorinko, E. L., & Sternberg, R. J. (1998). Dynamic testing. *Psych Bulletin, 124,* 75–111.

Groce, N. E., & Zola, I. K. (1993). Multiculturalism, chronic illness, and disability. *Pediatrics, 91,* 1048–1055.

Gross, R. T., & Duke, P. (1980). The effect of early versus late physical maturation on adolescent behavior. [Special issue: I. Litt (Ed.), Symposium on adolescent medicine.] *Pediatric Clinics of North America, 27,* 71–78.

Grotevant, H. D., McRoy, R. G., Eide, C. L., & Fravel, D. L. (1994). Adoptive family system dynamics: Variations by level of openness in the adoption. *Family Process, 33*(2), 125–146.

Grubman, S., Gross, E., Lerner-Weiss, N., Hernandez, M., McSherry, G. D., Hoyt, L. G., Boland, M., & Oleske, J. M. (1995). Older children and adolescents living with perinatally acquired human immunodeficiency virus. *Pediatrics, 95,* 657–663.

Grunberg, J. A. (Ed. Dir.), Kann, L., Kinchen, S. A., Williams, B., Ross, J. G., Lowry, R., & Kolbe, L. (2002, June 28). Youth risk behavior surveillance—United States, 2001. *MMWR Surveillance Summaries, 51*(SS04), 1–64.

Grusec, J. E., & Goodnow, J. J. (1994). Impact of parental discipline methods on the child's internalization of values: A reconceptualization of current points of view. *Developmental Psychology, 30,* 4–19.

Guberman, S. R. (1996). The development of everyday mathematics in Brazilian children with limited formal education. *Child Development, 67,* 1609–1623.

Guerrero, L. (2001, April 25). Almost third of kids bullied or bullies: Health officials concerned either could lead to more aggressive behavior. *Chicago Sun-Times,* p. 28.

Guilford, J. P. (1956). Structure of intellect. *Psychological Bulletin, 53,* 267–293.

Guilford, J. P. (1959). Three faces of intellect. *American Psychologist, 14,* 469–479.

Guilford, J. P. (1960). Basic conceptual problems of the psychology of thinking. *Proceedings of the New York Academy of Sciences, 91,* 6–21.

Guilford, J. P. (1967). *The nature of human intelligence.* New York: McGraw-Hill.

Guilford, J. P. (1986). *Creative talents: Their nature, uses and development.* Buffalo, NY: Bearly.

Guise, J., Palda, V., Westhoff, C., Chan, B. K. S., Helfand, M., & Lieu, T. A. (2003). The effectiveness of primary care-based interventions to promote breastfeeding: Systematic evidence review and meta-analysis for the US Preventive Services Task Force. *Annals of Family Medicine, 1,* 70–80.

Gullone, E. (2000). The development of normal fear: A century of research. *Clinical Psychology Review, 20,* 429–451.

Gunnar, M. R., Larson, M. C., Hertsgaard, L., Harris, M. L., & Brodersen, L. (1992). The stressfulness of separation among 9-month-old infants: Effects of social context variables and infant temperament. *Child Development, 63,* 290–303.

Gunnoe, M. L., & Mariner, C. L. (1997). Toward a developmental-contextual model of the effects of parental spanking on children's aggression. *Archives of Pediatric and Adolescent Medicine, 151,* 768–775.

Gunter, B., & Harrison, J. (1997). Violence in children's programmes on British television. *Children & Society, 11,* 143–156.

Guralnick, P. (1994). *Last train to Memphis: The rise of Elvis Presley.* Boston: Little, Brown.

Guyer, B., Hoyert, D. L., Martin, J. A., Ventura, S. J., MacDorman, M. F., & Strobino, D. M. (1999). Annual summary of vital statistics—1998. *Pediatrics, 104,* 1229–1246.

Guyer, B., Strobino, D. M., Ventura, S. J., & Singh, G. K. (1995). Annual summary of vital statistics—1994. *Pediatrics, 96,* 1029–1039.

Guzell, J. R., & Vernon-Feagans, L. (2004). Parental perceived control over caregiving and its relationship to parent-infant interaction. *Child Development, 75,* 134–146.

Guzick, D. S., Carson, S. A., Coutifaris, C., Overstreet, J. W., Factor-Litvak, P., Steinkampf, M. P., Hill, J. A., Mastroianni, L., Buster, J. E., Nakajima, S. T., Vogel, D. L., & Canfield, R. E. (1999). Efficacy of superovulation and intrauterine insemination in the treatment of infertility. *New England Journal of Medicine, 340,* 177–183.

Hack, M., Flannery, D. J., Schluchter, M., Cartar, L., Borawski, E., & Klein, N. (2002). Outcomes in young adulthood for very low- birth-weight infants. *NEJM, 346*(3), 149–157.

Hack, M., Friedman, H., & Fanaroff, A. A. (1996). Outcomes of extremely low birth weight infants. *Pediatrics, 98,* 931–937.

Hack, M., Schluchter, M., Cartar, L., Rahman, M., Cuttler, L., and Borawski, E. (2003). Growth of very low birth weight infants to age 20 years. *Pediatrics, 112,* e30–e38.

Haddow, J. E., Palomaki, G. E., Allan, W. C., Williams, J. R., Knight, G. J., Gagnon, J., O'Heir, C. E., Mitchell, M. L., Hermos, R. J., Waisbren, S. E., Faix, J. D., & Klein, R. Z. (1999). Maternal thyroid deficiency during pregnancy and subsequent neuropsychological development of the child. *New England Journal of Medicine, 341,* 549–555.

Haddow, J. E., Palomaki, G. E., Knight, G. J., Williams, J., Polkkiner, A., Canick, J. A., Saller, D. N., & Bowers, G. B. (1992). Prenatal screening for Down's syndrome with use of maternal serum markers. *New England Journal of Medicine, 327,* 588–593.

Haden, C. A., & Fivush, F. (1996). Contextual variation in maternal conversational styles. *Merrill-Palmer Quarterly, 42,* 200–227.

Haden, C. A., Haine, R. A., & Fivush, R. (1997). Developing narrative structure in parent-child reminiscing across the preschool years. *Developmental Psychology, 33,* 295–307.

Haden, C. A., Ornstein, P. A., Eckerman, C. O., & Didow, S. M. (2001). Mother-child conversational interactions as events unfold: Linkages to subsequent remembering. *Child Development, 72*(4), 1016–1031.

Haight, W. L., Wang, X., Fung, H. H., Williams, K., & Mintz, J. (1999). Universal, developmental, and variable aspects of young children's play: A cross-cultural comparison of pretending at home. *Child Development, 70*(6), 1477–1488.

Haith, M. M. (1986). Sensory and perceptual processes in early infancy. *Journal of Pediatrics, 109*(1), 158–171.

Haith, M. M. (1998). Who put the cog in infant cognition? Is rich interpretation too costly? *Infant Behavior and Development, 21*(2), 167–179.

Haith, M. M., & Benson, J. B. (1998). Infant cognition. In D. Kuhn & R. S. Siegler (Eds.), *Handbook of Child Psychology: Vol. 2. Cognition, perception, and language* (5th ed., pp. 199–254). New York: Wiley.

Hala, S., & Chandler, M. (1996). The role of strategic planning in accessing false-belief understanding. *Child Development, 67,* 2948–2966.

Halaas, J. L., Gajiwala, K. S., Maffei, M., Cohen, S. L., Chait, B. T., Rabinowitz, D., Lallone, R. L., Burley, S. K., & Friedman, J. M. (1995). Weight reducing effects of the plasma protein encoded by the obese gene. *Science, 269,* 543–546.

Hale, S., Bronik, M. D., & Fry, A. F. (1997). Verbal and spatial working memory in school-age children: Developmental differences in susceptibility to interference. *Developmental Psychology, 33,* 364–371.

Hall, D. G. and Graham, S. A. (1999). Lexical form class information guides word-to-object mapping in preschoolers. *Child Development, 70,* 78–91.

Hall, G. S. (1916). *Adolescence.* New York: Appleton. (Original work published 1904)

Halpern, D. F. (1997). Sex differences in intelligence: Implications for education. *American Psychologist, 52*(10), 1091–1102.

Halterman, J. S., Aligne, A., Auinger, P., McBride, J. T., & Szilagyi, P. G. (2000). Inadequate therapy for asthma among children in the United States. *Pediatrics, 105*(1), 272–276.

Halterman, J. S., Kaczorowski, J. M., Aligne, A., Auinger, P., & Szilagyi, P. G. (2001). Iron deficiency and cognitive achievement among school-aged children and adolescents in the United States. *Pediatrics, 107*(6), 1381–1386.

Hamm, J. V. (2000). Do birds of a feather flock together? The variable bases for African American, Asian American, and European American adolescents' selection of similar friends. *Developmental Psychology, 36*(2), 209–219.

Hansen, D., Lou, H. C., & Olsen, J. (2000). Serious life events and congenital malformations: A national study with complete follow-up. *Lancet, 356,* 875–880.

Hansen, M., Kurinczuk, J. J., Bower, C., & Webb, S. (2002). The risk of major birth defects after intracytoplasmic sperm injection and in vitro fertilization. *New England Journal of Medicine, 346,* 725–730.

Hara, H. (2002). Justifications for bullying among Japanese school children. *Asian Journal of Social Psychology, 5,* 197–204.

Hardy, R., Kuh, D., Langenberg, C., & Wadsworth, M. E. (2003). Birth weight, childhood social class, and change in adult blood pressure in the 1946 British birth cohort. *Lancet, 362,* 1178–1183.

Hardy-Brown, K., & Plomin, R. (1985). Infant communicative development: Evidence from adoptive and biological families for genetic and environmental influences on rate differences. *Developmental Psychology, 21,* 378–385.

Hardy-Brown, K., Plomin, R., & DeFries, J. C. (1981). Genetic and environmental influences on rate of communicative development in the first year of life. *Developmental Psychology, 17,* 704–717.

Hardyck, C., & Petrinovich, L. F. (1977). Left-handedness. *Psychological Bulletin, 84,* 385–404.

Hargrove, J. (1989). *Nelson Mandela: South Africa's silent voice of protest.* Chicago: Children's Press.

Harley, K., and Reese, E. (1999). Origins of autobiographical memory. *Developmental Psychology, 35,* 1338–1348.

Harlow, H. F., & Harlow, M. K (1962). The effect of rearing conditions on behavior. *Bulletin of the Menninger Clinic, 26,* 213–224.

Harlow, H. F., & Zimmerman, R. R. (1959). Affectional responses in the infant monkey. *Science, 130,* 421–432.

Harnishfeger, K. K., & Bjorklund, D. F. (1993). The ontogeny of inhibition mechanisms: A renewed approach to cognitive development. In M. L. Howe & R. P. Pasnak (Eds.), *Emerging themes in cognitive development* (vol. 1, pp. 28–49). New York: Springer-Verlag.

Harnishfeger, K. K., & Pope, R. S. (1996). Intending to forget: The development of cognitive inhibition in directed forgetting. *Journal of Experimental Psychology, 62,* 292–315.

Harris, G. (1997). Development of taste perception and appetite regulation. In G. Bremner, A. Slater, & G. Butterworth (Eds.), *Infant development: Recent advances* (pp. 9–30). East Sussex, UK: Psychology Press.

Harris, G., Thomas, A., & Booth, D. A. (1990). Development of salt taste in infancy. *Developmental Psychology, 26,* 534–538.

Harris, L. H., and Paltrow, L. (2003). The status of pregnant women and fetuses in U.S. criminal law. *Journal of the American Medical Association, 289,* 1697–1699.

Harris, P. L., Brown, E., Marriott, C., Whittall, S., & Harmer, S. (1991). Monsters, ghosts, and witches: Testing the limits of the fantasy-reality distinction in young children. In G. E. Butterworth, P. L. Harris, A. M. Leslie, & H. M. Wellman (Eds.), *Perspective on the child's theory of mind.* Oxford: Oxford University Press.

Harris, P. L., Olthof, T., Meerum Terwogt, M., & Hardman, C. (1987). Children's knowledge of situations that provoke emotion. *International Journal of Behavioral Development, 10,* 319–343.

Harrison, A. O., Wilson, M. N., Pine, C. J., Chan, S. Q., & Buriel, R. (1990). Family ecologies of ethnic minority children. *Child Development, 61,* 347–362.

Harrist, A. W., & Waugh, R. M. (2002). Dyadic synchrony: Its structure and function in children's development. *Developmental Review, 22,* 555–592.

Harrist, A. W., Zain, A. F., Bates, J. E., Dodge, K. A., & Pettit, G. S. (1997). Subtypes of social withdrawal in early childhood: Sociometric status and social-cognitive differences across four years. *Child Development, 68,* 278–294.

Hart, B., & Risley, T. R. (1989). The longitudinal study of interactive systems. *Education and Treatment of Children, 12,* 347–358.

Hart, B., & Risley, T. R. (1992). American parenting of language learning children: Persisting differences in family-child interactions observed in natural home environments. *Developmental Psychology, 28,* 1096–1105.

Hart, B., & Risley, T. R. (1996, August). *Individual differences in early intellectual experience of typical American children: Beyond SES, race, and IQ.* Address at the annual convention of the American Psychological Association, Toronto, Canada.

Hart, C. H., DeWolf, M., Wozniak, P., & Burts, D. C. (1992). Maternal and paternal disciplinary styles: Relations with preschoolers' playground behavioral orientation and peer status. *Child Development, 63,* 879–892.

Hart, C. H., Ladd, G. W., & Burleson, B. R. (1990). Children's expectations of the outcome of social strategies: Relations with sociometric status and maternal disciplinary style. *Child Development, 61,* 127–137.

Hart, S. N., & Brassard, M. R. (1987). A major threat to children's mental health: Psychological maltreatment. *American Psychologist, 42*(2), 160–165.

Hart, S., Field, T., del Valle, C., & Pelaez-Nogueras, M. (1998). Depressed mothers' interactions with their one-year-old infants.

Infant Behavior and Development, 21, 519–525.

Harter, S. (1985a). Competence as a dimension of self-worth. In R. Leahy (Ed.), *The development of the self.* New York: Academic Press.

Harter, S. (1985b). *Manual for the Self-Perception Profile for Children.* Denver, CO: University of Denver.

Harter, S. (1990). Causes, correlates, and the functional role of global self-worth: A life-span perspective. In J. Kolligan & R. Sternberg (Eds.), *Competence considered: Perceptions of competence and incompetence across the life-span* (pp. 67–97). New Haven, CT: Yale University Press.

Harter, S. (1993). Developmental changes in self-understanding across the 5 to 7 shift. In A. Sameroff & M. Haith (Eds.), *Reason and responsibility: The passage through childhood.* Chicago: University of Chicago Press.

Harter, S. (1996). Developmental changes in self-understanding across the 5 to 7 shift. In A. J. Sameroff & M. M. Haith (Eds.), *The five to seven year shift: The age of reason and responsibility* (pp. 207–235). Chicago: University of Chicago Press.

Harter, S. (1998). The development of self-representations. In W. Damon (Series Ed.) & N. Eisenberg (Vol. Ed.), *Handbook of child psychology: Vol. 3. Social, emotional, and personality development* (5th ed., pp. 553–617). New York: Wiley.

Hartshorn, K., Rovee-Collier, C., Gerhardstein, P., Bhatt, R. S., Wondoloski, R. L., Klein, P., Gilch, J., Wurtzel, N., & Campos-de-Carvalho, M. (1998). The ontogeny of long-term memory over the first year-and-a-half of life. *Developmental Psychobiology, 32,* 69–89.

Hartup, W. W. (1989). Social relationships and their developmental significance. *American Psychologist, 44,* 120–126.

Hartup, W. W. (1992). Peer relations in early and middle childhood. In V. B. Van Hasselt & M. Hersen (Eds.), *Handbook of social development: A lifespan perspective* (pp. 257–281). New York: Plenum.

Hartup, W. W. (1996a). The company they keep: Friendships and their developmental significance. *Child Development, 67,* 1–13.

Hartup, W. W. (1996b). Cooperation, close relationships, and cognitive development. In W. M. Bukowski, A. F. Newcomb, & W. W. Hartup (Eds.), *The company they keep: Friendship in childhood and adolescence* (pp. 213–237). New York: Cambridge University Press.

Hartup, W. W., & Stevens, N. (1999). Friendships and adaptation across the life span. *Current Directions in Psychological Science, 8,* 76–79.

Harvard Medical School. (2002, July). Treatment of bulimia and binge eating. *Harvard Mental Health Letter, 19*(1), pp. 1–4.

Harvey, E. (1999). Short-term and long-term effects of early parental employment on children of the National Longitudinal Survey of Youth. *Developmental Psychology, 35*(2), 445–459.

Harvey, J. H., & Pauwels, B. G. (1999). Recent developments in close relationships theory. *Current Directions in Psychological Science, 8*(3), 93–95.

Harwood, R. (1987). *Mandela.* New York: New American Library.

Harwood, R. L., Schoelmerich, A., Ventura-Cook, E., Schulze, P. A., & Wilson, S. P. (1996). Culture and class influences on Anglo and Puerto Rican mothers' beliefs regarding long-term socialization goals and child behavior. *Child Development, 67,* 2446–2461.

Haskett, M. E., & Kistner, J. A. (1991). Social interaction and peer perceptions of young physically abused children. *Child Development, 62,* 979–990.

Haswell, K., Hock, E., & Wenar, C. (1981). Oppositional behavior of preschool children: Theory and prevention, *Family Relations, 30,* 440–446.

Hatcher, P. J., Hulme, C., & Ellis, A. W. (1994). Ameliorating early reading failure by integrating the teaching of reading and phonological skills: The phonological linkage hypotheses. *Child Development, 65,* 41–57.

Hatzichristou, C., & Hopf, D. (1996). A multiperspective comparison of peer sociometric status groups in childhood and adolescence. *Child Development, 67,* 1085–1102.

Hauck, F. R., Herman, S. M., Donovan, M., Iyasu, S., Moore, C. M., Donoghue, E., Kirschner, R. H., & Willinger, M. (2003). Sleep environment and the risk of sudden infant death syndrome in an urban population: The Chicago Infant Mortality Study. *Pediatrics, 111,* 1207–1214.

Haugaard, J. J. (1998). Is adoption a risk factor for the development of adjustment problems? *Clinical Psychology Review, 18,* 47–69.

Hawkins, J. D., Catalano, R. F., & Miller, J. Y. (1992). Risk and protective factors for alcohol and other drug problems in adolescence and early adulthood: Implications for substance abuse programs. *Psychological Bulletin, 112*(1), 64–105.

Hawkins, J. D., Catalano, R. F., Kosterman, R., Abbott, R., & Hill, K. G. (1999). Preventing adolesent health-risk behaviors by strengthening protection during childhood. *Archives of Pediatrics and Adolescent Medicine, 153,* 226–234.

Hay, D. (2003). Pathways to violence in the children of mothers who were depressed post partum. *Developmental Psychology, 39,* 1083–1094.

Hay, D. F., Pedersen, J., & Nash, A. (1982). Dyadic interaction in the first year of life. In K. H. Rubin & H. S. Ross (Eds.), *Peer relationships and social skills in children.* New York: Springer.

Hayes, A., & Batshaw, M. L. (1993). Down syndrome. *Pediatric Clinics of North America, 40,* 523–535.

Hayne, H., Barr, R., & Herbert, J. (2003). The effect of prior practice on memory reactivation and generalization. *Child Development, 74,* 1615–1627.

Heath, S. B. (1989). Oral and literate tradition among black Americans living in poverty. *American Psychologist, 44,* 367–373.

Hediger, M. L., Overpeck, M. D., Kuczmarski, R. J., & Ruan, W. J. (2001). Association between infant breastfeeding and overweight in young children. *Journal of the American Medical Association, 285*(19), 2453–2460.

Hedley, A. A., Ogden, C. L., Johnson, C. L., Carroll, M. D., Curtin, L. R., & Flegal, K. M. (2004). Prevalence of overweight and obesity among U.S. children, adolescents, and adults, 1999–2002. *Journal of the American Medical Association, 291,* 2847–2850.

Heilbut, A. (1993, April 26). Marian Anderson: Postscript. *New Yorker,* pp. 82–83.

Helms, J. E. (1992). Why is there no study of cultural equivalence in standardized cognitive ability testing? *American Psychologist, 47,* 1083–1101.

Helwig, C. C., & Jasiobedzka, U. (2001). The relation between law and morality: Children's reasoning about socially beneficial and unjust laws. *Child Development, 72,* 1382–1393.

Henderson, H. A., Marshall, P. J., Fox, N. A., & Rubin, K. H. (2004). Psychophysiological and behavioral evidence for varying forms and functions of nonsocial behavior in preschoolers. *Child Development, 75,* 251–263.

Henly, W. L., & Fitch, B. R. (1966). Newborn narcotic withdrawal associated with regional enteritis in pregnancy. *New York Journal of Medicine, 66,* 2565–2567.

Henrich, C. C., Brown, J. L., & Aber, J. L. (1999). Evaluating the effectiveness of school-based violence prevention: Developmental approaches. *Social Policy Report, SRCD, 13*(3).

Hernandez, D. J. (1997). Child development and the social demography of childhood. *Child Development, 68,* 149–169.

Hernandez, D. J. (2004, Summer). Demographic change and the life circumstances of immigrant families. In R. E. Behrman (Ed.), Children of immigrant families (pp. 17–48). *The Future of Children, 14*(2). [Online]. Available: http://www.futureofchildren.org. Access date: October 7, 2004.

Herrmann, D. (1999). *Helen Keller: A Life.* Chicago: University of Chicago Press.

Herrmann, H. J., & Roberts, M. W. (1987). Preventive dental care: The role of the pediatrician. *Pediatrics, 80,* 107–110.

Herrnstein, R. J., & Murray, C. (1994). *The bell curve: Intelligence and class structure in American life.* New York: Free Press.

Hertz-Pannier, L., Chiron, C., Jambaque, I., Renaux-Kieffer, V., Van de Moortele, P., Delalande, O., Fohlen, M., Brunelle, F., & Le Bihan, D. (2002). Late plasticity for language in a child's non-dominant hemisphere. A pre- and post-surgery fMRI study. *Brain, 125*(2), 361–372.

Herzog, D. B., Dorer, D. J., Keel, P. K., Selwyn, S. E., Ekeblad, E. R., Flores, A. T., Greenwood, D. N., Burwell, R. A., & Keller, M. B. (1999). Recovery and relapse in anorexia and bulimia nervosa: A 7.5-year follow-up study. *Journal of the American Academy of Child and Adolescent Psychiatry, 38,* 829–837.

Herzog, D. B., Keller, M. B., & Lavori, P. W. (1988). Outcome in anorexia nervosa and bulimia. *Journal of Nervous and Mental Disease, 176,* 131–143.

Hespos, S. J., & Spelke, E. S. (2004). Conceptual precursors to language. *Nature, 430,* 153–155.

Hetherington, E. M. (1987). Family relations six years after divorce. In K. Pasley & M. Ihinger-Tallman (Eds.), *Remarriage and parenting today: Research and theory.* New York: Guilford.

Hetherington, E. M., Bridges, M., & Insabella, G. M. (1998). What matters? What does not? Five perspectives on the association between marital transitions and children's adjustment. *American Psychologist, 53,* 167–184.

Hetherington, E. M., Stanley-Hagan, M., & Anderson, E. (1989). Marital transitions: Child's perspective. *American Psychologist, 44,* 303–312.

Hetherington, E. M., & Stanley-Hagan, M. (1999). The adjustment of children with divorced parents: A risk and resiliency perspective. *Journal of Child Psychology and Psychiatry, 40,* 129–140.

Hetzel, B. S. (1994). Iodine deficiency and fetal brain damage. *New England Journal of Medicine, 331,* 1770–1771.

Hewlett, B. S. (1987). Intimate fathers: Patterns of paternal holding among Aka pygmies. In M. E. Lamb (Ed.), *The father's role: Cross-cultural perspectives* (pp. 295–330). Hillsdale, NJ: Erlbaum.

Hewlett, B. S. (1992). Husband-wife reciprocity and the father-infant relationship among Aka pygmies. In B. S. Hewlett (Ed.), *Father-child relations: Cultural and biosocial contexts* (pp. 153–176). New York: de Gruyter.

Hewlett, B. S., Lamb, M. E., Shannon, D., Leyendecker, B., & Schölmerich, A. (1998). Culture and early infancy among central African foragers and farmers. *Developmental Psychology, 34*(4), 653–661.

Heyns, B., & Catsambis, S. (1986). Mother's employment and children's achievement: A critique. *Sociology of Education, 59,* 140–151.

Hibbard, D. R., & Buhrmester, D. (1998). The role of peers in the socialization of gender-related social interaction styles. *Sex Roles, 39,* 185–202.

Hickman, M., Roberts, C., & de Matos, M. G. (2000). Exercise and leisure time activities. In C. Currie, K. Hurrelmann, W. Settertobulte, R. Smith, & J. Todd (Eds.), *Health and health behaviour among young people: A WHO crossnational study (HBSC) international report* (pp. 73–82.). WHO Policy Series: Health Policy for Children and Adolescents, Series No. 1. Copenhagen, Denmark: World Health Organization Regional Office for Europe.

Hill, D. A., Gridley, G., Cnattingius, S., Mellemkjaer, L., Linet, M., Adami, H.-O., Olsen, J. H., Nyren, O., & Fraumeni, J. F. (2003). Mortality and cancer incidence among individuals with Down syndrome. *Archives of Internal Medicine, 163,* 705–711.

Hill, J. P. (1987). Research on adolescents and their families: Past and prospect. In E. E. Irwin (Ed.), *Adolescent social behavior and health.* San Francisco: Jossey-Bass.

Hillier, L. (2002). "It's a catch-22": Same-sex-attracted young people on coming out to parents. In S. S. Feldman & D. A. Rosenthal, (Eds.), Talking sexuality. *New Directions for Child and Adolescent Development, 97,* 75–91.

Hillis, S. D., Anda, R. F., Dubè, S. R., Felitti, V. J., Marchbanks, P. A., and Marks, J. S. (2004). The association between adverse childhood experiences and adolescent pregnancy, long-term psychosocial consequences, and fetal death. *Pediatrics, 113,* 320–327.

Hinds, T. S., West, W. L., Knight, E. M., & Harland, B. F. (1996). The effect of caffeine on pregnancy outcome variables. *Nutrition Reviews, 54,* 203–207.

Hines, A. M. (1997). Divorce-related transitions, adolescent development, and the role of the parent-child relationship: A review of the literature. *Journal of Marriage and the Family, 59,* 375–388.

Hines, M., Chiu, L., McAdams, L. A., Bentler, M. P., & Lipcamon, J. (1992). Cognition and the corpus callosum: Verbal fluency, visual-spatial ability, language lateralization related to midsagittal surface areas of the corpus callosum. *Behavioral Neuroscience, 106,* 3–14.

Hintz, R. L., Attie, K. M., Baptista, J., & Roche, A., for the Genentech Collaborative Group. (1999). Effect of growth hormone treatment on adult height of children with idiopathic short stature. *New England Journal of Medicine, 340*(7), 502–507.

Hirsch, H. V., & Spinelli, D. N. (1970). Visual experience modifies distribution of horizontally and vertically oriented receptive fields in cats. *Science, 168,* 869–871.

Ho, C. S.-H., & Fuson, K. C. (1998). Children's knowledge of teen quantities as tens and ones: Comparisons of Chinese, British, and American kindergartners. *Journal of Educational Psychology, 90,* 536–544.

Ho, W. C. (1989). *Yani: The brush of innocence.* New York: Hudson Hills.

Hobson, J. A., & Silvestri, L. (1999, February). Parasomnias. *Harvard Mental Health Letter,* pp. 3–5.

Hodges, E. V. E., Boivin, M., Vitaro, F., & Bukowski, W. M. (1999). The power of friendship: Protection against an escalating cycle of peer victimization. *Developmental Psychology, 35,* 94–101.

Hoff, E. (2003). The specificity of environmental influence: Socioeconomic status affects early vocabulary development via maternal speech. *Child Development, 74,* 1368–1378.

Hofferth, S. L. (1998). *Healthy environments, healthy children: Children in families* (Report of the 1997 Panel Study of Income Dynamics, Child Development Supplement). Ann Arbor, MI: University of Michigan Institute for Social Research.

Hofferth, S. L., & Jankuniene, Z. (2000, April 2). *Children's after-school activities.* Paper presented at biennial meeting of the Society for Research on Adolescence, Chicago, IL.

Hofferth, S. L., & Sandberg, J. (1998). *Changes in American children's time, 1981–1997* (Report of the 1997 Panel Study of Income Dynamics, Child Development Supplement). Ann Arbor, MI: University of Michigan Institute for Social Research.

Hoffman, H. J., & Hillman, L. S. (1992). Epidemiology of the sudden infant death syndrome: Maternal, neonatal, and postneonatal risk factors. *Clinics in Perinatology, 19,* 717–737.

Hoffman, M. L. (1970a). Conscience, personality, and socialization techniques. *Human Development, 13,* 90–126.

Hoffman, M. L. (1970b). Moral development. In P. H. Mussen (Ed). *Carmichael's manual of child psychology* (vol. 2, 3d ed., pp. 261–360). New York: Wiley.

Hoffman, M. L. (1977). Sex differences in empathy and related behaviors. *Psychological Bulletin, 84,* 712–722.

Hoffman, M. L. (1998). Varieties of empathy-based guilt. In J. Bybee (Ed.), *Guilt and children* (pp. 91–112). San Diego, CA: Academic.

Hoffrage, U., Weber, A., Hertwig, R., & Chase, V. M. (2003). How to keep children safe in traffic: Find the daredevils early.

Journal of Experimental Psychology: Applied, 9, 249–260.

Holden, C. (2000). Asia stays on top, U.S. in middle in new global rankings. *Science, 290,* 1866.

Holden, G. W., & Miller, P. C. (1999). Enduring and different: A meta-analysis of the similarity in parents' child rearing. *Psychological Bulletin, 125,* 223–254.

Holmes, L. D. (1987). *Quest for the real Samoa: The Mead-Freeman controversy and beyond.* South Hadley, MA: Bergin & Garvey.

Holowka, S., & Petitto, L. A. (2002). Left hemisphere cerebral specialization for babies while babbling. *Science, 297,* 1515.

Holtzman, N. A., Murphy, P. D., Watson, M. S., & Barr, P. A. (1997). Predictive genetic testing: From basic research to clinical practice. *Science, 278,* 602–605.

Honein, M. A., Paulozzi, L. J., Mathews, T. J., Erickson, J. D., & Wong, L.-Y. C. (2001). Impact of folic acid fortification of the U.S. food supply on the occurrence of neural tube defects. *Journal of the American Medical Association, 285,* 2981–2986.

Hood, B., Cole-Davies, V., & Dias, M. (2003). Looking and search measures of object knowledge in preschool children. *Developmental Psychology, 39,* 61–70.

Hopfensperger, J. (1996, April 15). Germany's fast track to a career. *Minneapolis Star-Tribune,* pp. A1, A6.

Hopkins, B., & Westra, T. (1988). Maternal handling and motor development: An intracultural study. *Genetic, Social and General Psychology Monographs, 14,* 377–420.

Hopkins, B., & Westra, T. (1990). Motor development, maternal expectations and the role of handling. *Infant Behavior and Development, 13,* 117–122.

Horbar, J. D., Wright, E. C., Onstad, L., & the Members of the National Institute of Child Health and Human Development Neonatal Research Network. (1993). Decreasing mortality associated with the introduction of surfactant therapy: An observational study of neonates weighing 601 to 1300 grams at birth. *Pediatrics, 92,* 191–196.

Horowitz, F. D. (2000). Child development and the PITS: Simple questions, complex answers, and developmental theory. *Child Development, 71*(1), 1–10.

Horwitz, B., Rumsey, J. M., & Donohue, B. C. (1998). Functional connectivity of the angular gyrus in normal reading and dyslexia. *Proceedings of the National Academy of Sciences USA, 95,* 8939–8944.

Horwood, L. J., & Fergusson, D. M. (1998). Breastfeeding and child achievement. *Pediatrics, 101*(1). [Online]. Available: http://www.pediatrics.org/cgi/content/full/101/1/e9. Access date: January 5, 1998.

Householder, J., Hatcher, R., Burns, W., & Chasnoff, I. (1982). Infants born to narcotics-addicted mothers. *Psychological Bulletin, 92,* 453–468.

Howe, M. L., & Courage, M. L. (1993). On resolving the enigma of infantile amnesia. *Psychological Bulletin, 113,* 305–326.

Howe, M. L., & Courage, M. L. (1997). The emergence and early development of autobiographical memory. *Psychological Review, 104,* 499–523.

Howes, C., & Matheson, C. C. (1992). Sequences in the development of competent play with peers: Social and social pretend play. *Developmental Psychology, 28,* 961–974.

Hubbard, F. O. A., & van IJzendoorn, M. H. (1991). Maternal unresponsiveness and infant crying across the first 9 months: A naturalistic longitudinal study. *Infant Behavior and Development, 14,* 299–312.

Hudson, J. I., & Pope, H. G. (1990). Affective spectrum disorder: Does antidepressant response identify a family of disorders with a common pathophysiology? *American Journal of Psychiatry, 147*(5), 552–564.

Hudson, V. M., & den Boer, A. M. (2004). *Bare branches: Security implications of Asia's surplus male population.* Cambridge, MA: MIT Press.

Huesmann, L. R. (1986). Psychological processes promoting the relation between exposure to media violence and aggressive behavior by the viewer. *Journal of Social Issues, 42,* 125–139.

Huesmann, L. R., & Eron, L. D. (1984). Cognitive processes and the persistence of aggressive behavior. *Aggressive Behavior, 10,* 243–251.

Huesmann, L. R., Moise-Titus, J., Podolski, C. L., & Eron, L. (2003). Longitudinal relations between children's exposure to TV violence and their aggressive and violent behavior in young adulthood: 1977–1992. *Developmental Psychology, 39,* 201–221.

Hughes, C., and Cutting, A. L. (1999). Nature, nurture, and individual differences in early understanding of mind. *Psychological Science, 10,* 429–432.

Hughes, M. (1975). *Egocentrism in preschool children.* Unpublished doctoral dissertation, Edinburgh University, Edinburgh, Scotland.

Huizink, A., Robles de Medina, P., Mulder, E., Visser, G., & Buitelaar, J. (2002). Psychological measures of prenatal stress as predictors of infant temperament. *Journal of the American Academy of Child & Adolescent Psychiatry, 41,* 1078–1085.

Huiznik, A. C., Mulder, E. J. H., & Buitelaar, J. K. (2004). Prenatal stress and risk for psychopathology: Specific effects or induction of general susceptibility? *Psychological Bulletin 130,* 80–114.

Hujoel, P. P., Bollen, A.-M., Noonan, C. J., & del Aguila, M. A. (2004). Antepartum dental radiography and infant low birth weight. *Journal of the American Medical Association, 291,* 1987–1993.

Humphrey, L. L. (1986). Structural analysis of parent-child relationships in eating disorders. *Journal of Abnormal Psychology, 95*(4), 395–402.

Humphreys, A. P., & Smith, P. K. (1984). Rough-and-tumble in preschool and playground. In P. K. Smith (Ed.), *Play in animals and humans.* Oxford: Blackwell.

Humphreys, G. W. (2002). Cognitive neuroscience. In H. Pashler, & D. Medin (Eds.), *Steven's handbook of experimental psychology* (3d. ed.), *Vol. 2: Memory and cognitive processes* (pp. 77–112). New York: John Wiley & Sons, Inc.

Hunsaker, S. L., & Callahan, C. M. (1995). Creativity and giftedness: Published instrument uses and abuses. *Gifted Child Quarterly, 39*(2), 110–114.

Hunt, C. E. (1996). Prone sleeping in healthy infants and victims of sudden infant death syndrome. *Journal of Pediatrics, 128,* 594–596.

Hunt, C. E., Lesko, S. M., Vezina, R. M., McCoy, R., Corwin, M. J., Mandell, F., Willinger, M., Hoffman, H. J., & Mitchell, A. A. (2003). Infant sleep position and associated health outcomes. *Archives of Pediatrics & Adolescent Medicine, 157,* 469–474.

Huntsinger, C. S., & Jose, P. E. (1995). Chinese American and Caucasian American family interaction patterns in spatial rotation puzzle solutions. *Merrill-Palmer Quarterly, 41,* 471–496.

Huntsinger, C. S., Jose, P. E., & Larson, S. L. (1998). Do parent practices to encourage academic competence influence the social adjustment of young European American and Chinese American children? *Developmental Psychology, 34*(4), 747–756.

Huston, A., Donnerstein, E., Fairchild, H., Feshbach, N. D., Katz, P. A., Murray, J. P., Rubenstein, E. A., Wilcox, B. L., & Zuckerman, D. (1992). *Big world, small screen: The role of television in American society.* Lincoln, NE: University of Nebraska Press.

Huston, H. C., Duncan, G. J., Granger, R., Bos, J., McLoyd, V., Mistry, R., Crosby, D., Gibson, C., Magnuson, K., Romich, J., and Ventura, A. (2001). Work-based antipoverty programs for parents can enhance the performance and social behavior of children. *Child Development, 72*(1), 318–336.

Huttenlocher, J. (1998). Language input and language growth. *Preventive Medicine, 27,* 195–199.

Huttenlocher, J., Haight, W., Bryk, A., Seltzer, M., & Lyons, T. (1991). Early vocabulary growth: Relation to language input and gender. *Developmental Psychology, 27,* 236–248.

Huttenlocher, J., Levine, S., & Vevea, J. (1998). Environmental input and cognitive growth: A study using time period comparisons. *Child Development, 69,* 1012–1029.

Huttenlocher, J., Newcombe, N., & Vasilyeva, M. (1999). Spatial scaling in young children. *Psychological Science, 10,* 393–398.

Huttenlocher, J., Vasilyeva, M., Cymerman, E., & Levine, S. (2002). Language input and child syntax. *Cognitive Psychology, 45,* 337–374.

Huxley, A. (1932). *Brave new world.* Toronto: Granada Publishing Ltd.

Hwang, J., & Rothbart, M .K. (2003). Behavior genetics studies of infant temperament: Findings vary across parent-report instruments. *Infant Behavior & Development, 26,* 112–114.

Hwang, S. J., Beaty, T. H., Panny, S. R., Street, N. A., Joseph, J. M., Gordon, S., McIntosh, I., & Francomano, C. A. (1995). Association study of transforming growth factor alpha (TGFa) TaqI polymorphism and oral clefts: Indication of gene-environment interaction in a population-based sample of infants with birth defects. *American Journal of Epidemiology, 141,* 629–636.

Ialongo, N. S., Edelsohn, G., & Kellam, S. G. (2001). A further look at the prognostic power of young children's reports of depressed mood and feelings. *Child Development, 72,* 736–747.

Iervolino, A. C., Pike, A., Manke, B., Reiss, D., Hetherington, E. M., & Plomin, R. (2002). Genetic and environmental influences in adolescent peer socialization: Evidence from two genetically sensitive designs. *Child Development, 73*(1), 162–174.

Iglowstein, I., Jenni, O. G., Molinari, L., & Largo, R. H. (2003). Sleep duration from infancy to adolescence: Reference values and generational trends. *Pediatrics, 111,* 302–307.

Impagnatiello, F., Guidotti, A. R., Pesold, C., Dwivedi, Y., Caruncho, H., Pisu, M. G., Uzonov, D. P., Smalheiser, N. R., Davis, J. M., Pandey, G. N., Pappas, G. D., Tueting, P., Sharma, R. P., & Costa, E. (1998). A decrease of reelin expression as a putative vulnerability factor in schizophrenia. *Proceedings of the National Academy of Science, 95,* 15718–15723.

Infant Health and Development Program (IHDP). (1990). Enhancing the outcomes of low-birth-weight, premature infants. *Journal of the American Medical Association, 263*(22), 3035–3042.

Infante-Rivard, C., Fernández, A., Gauthier, R., David, M., & Rivard, G. E. (1993). Fetal loss associated with caffeine intake before and after pregnancy. *Journal of the American Medical Association, 270,* 2940–2943.

Ingersoll, E. W., & Thoman, E. B. (1999). Sleep/wake states of preterm infants: Stability, developmental change, diurnal variation, and relation with care giving activity. *Child Development, 70,* 1–10.

Ingram, J. L., Stodgell, C. S., Hyman, S. L., Figlewicz, D. A., Weitkamp, L. R., & Rodier, P. M. (2000). Discovery of allelic variants of HOXA1 and HOXB1: Genetic susceptibility to autism spectrum disorders. *Teratology, 62,* 393–406.

Institute of Medicine (IOM) National Academy of Sciences. (1993, November). *Assessing genetic risks: Implications for health and social policy.* Washington, DC: National Academy of Sciences.

International Cesarean Awareness Network. (2003, March 5). Statistics: International cesarean and VBAC rates. [Online]. Available: http://www.ican-online.org/resources. statistics3.htm. Access date: January 20, 2004.

International Perinatal HIV Group. (1999). The mode of delivery and the risk of vertical transmission of human immunodeficiency virus type 1: A meta-analysis of 15 prospective cohort studies. *New England Journal of Medicine, 340,* 977–987.

Isabella, R. A. (1993). Origins of attachment: Maternal interactive behavior across the first year. *Child Development, 64,* 605–621.

Isley, S., O'Neil, R., & Parke, R. (1996). The relation of parental affect and control behaviors to children's classroom acceptance: A concurrent and predictive analysis. *Early Education and Development, 7,* 7–23.

Iverson, J. M., & Goldin-Meadow, S. (1998). Why people gesture when they speak. *Nature, 396,* 228.

Izard, C. E., Huebner, R. R., Resser, D., McGinness, G. C., & Dougherty, L. M. (1980). The young infant's ability to produce discrete emotional expressions. *Developmental Psychology, 16,* 132–140.

Izard, C. E., Porges, S. W., Simons, R. F., Haynes, O. M., & Cohen, B. (1991). Infant cardiac activity: Developmental changes and relations with attachment. *Developmental Psychology, 27,* 432–439.

Jackson, A. (1997a). The math wars: California battles it out over mathematics Education Reform (Part I). *Notices of the AMS.* [Online]. Available: http://www.ams.org/notices/199706/comm-calif.html. Access date: January 22, 1999.

Jackson, A. (1997b). The math wars: California battles it out over mathematics Education Reform (Part II). *Notices of the AMS.* [Online]. Available: http://www.ams.org/notices/199708/comm-calif2.html. Access date: January 22, 1999.

Jackson, R. S., Creemers, J. W. M., Ohagi, S., Raffin-Sanson, M. L., Sanders, L., Montague, C. T., Hutton, J. C., & O'Rahilly, S. (1997). Obesity and impaired prohormone processing associated with mutations in the human prohormone convertase 1 gene. *Nature Genetics, 16,* 303–306.

Jacobsen, T., & Hofmann, V. (1997). Children's attachment representations: Longitudinal relations to school behavior and academic competency in middle childhood and adolescence. *Developmental Psychology, 33,* 703–710.

Jacobson, J. L., & Wille, D. E. (1986). The influence of attachment pattern on developmental changes in peer interaction from the toddler to the preschool period. *Child Development, 57,* 338–347.

Jacobson, S. W., Chiodo, L. M., & Jacobson, J. L. (1999). Breast-feeding effects on intelligence quotient in 4- and 11-year-old children. *Pediatrics, 103*(5). [Online]. Available: http://www.pediatrics.org/cgi/content/full/103/s/e71.

Jagers, R. J., Bingham, K., & Hans, S. L. (1996). Socialization and social judgments among inner-city African-American kindergartners. *Child Development, 67,* 140–150.

Jain, A., Concato, J., & Leventhal, J. M. (2002). How good is the evidence linking breastfeeding and intelligence? *Pediatrics, 109,* 1044–1053.

Jain, T., Missmer, S. A., & Hornstein, M. D. (2004). Trends in embryo-transfer practice and in outcomes of the use of assisted reproductive technology in the United States. *New England Journal of Medicine, 350,* 1639–1645.

James, W. (1950). *The principles of psychology* (2 vols.). New York: Dover. (Original work published 1890.)

Jankowiak, W. (1992). Father-child relations in urban China. *Father-child relations: Cultural and bisocial contexts* (pp. 345–363). New York: de Gruyter.

Jankowski, J. J., Rose, S. A., & Feldman, J. F. (2001). Modifying the distribution of attention in infants. *Child Development, 72,* 339–351.

Janowsky, J. S., & Carper, R. (1996). Is there a neural basis for cognitive transitions in school-age children? In A. J. Sameroff & M. M. Haith (Eds.), *The five to seven year shift: The age of reason and responsibility* (pp. 33–56). Chicago: University of Chicago Press.

Janssen, I., Craig, W. M., Boyce, W. F., & Pickett, W. (2004). Associations between overweight and obesity with bullying behaviors in school-aged children. *Pediatrics, 113,* 1187–1194.

Japan in shock at school murder. (2004, June 2). BBC News. [Online]. Available: http://news.bbc.co.uk/go/pr/fr/-/1/hi/world/asia-pacific/3768983.stm. Access date: June 2, 2004.

Jarrell, R. H. (1998). Play and its influence on the development of young children's mathematical thinking. In D. P. Fromberg

& D. Bergen (Eds.), *Play from birth to twelve and beyond: Contexts, perspectives, and meanings* (pp. 56–67). New York: Garland.

Jaslow, C. K. (1982). *Teenage pregnancy* (ERIC/CAPS Fact Sheet). Ann Arbor, MI: Counseling and Personnel Services Clearing House.

Jefferson, T. (1999). Pediatricians alerted to five new vaccines. *Journal of the American Medical Association, 281,* 1973–1975.

Jeffery, H. E., Megevand, M., & Page, M. (1999). Why the prone position is a risk factor for sudden infant death syndrome. *Pediatrics, 104,* 263–269.

Jeffords, J. M., & Daschle, T. (2001). Political issues in the genome era. *Science, 291,* 1249–1251.

Jenkins, J. M., Turrell, S. L., Kogushi, Y., Lollis, S., & Ross, H. S. (2003). A longitudinal investigation of the dynamics of mental state talk in families. *Child Development, 74,* 905–920.

Jensen, A. R. (1969). How much can we boost IQ and scholastic achievement? *Harvard Educational Review, 39,* 1–123.

Jeynes, W. H., & Littell, S. W. (2000). A meta-analysis of studies examining the effect of whole language instruction on the literacy of low-SES students. *Elementary School Journal, 101*(1), 21–33.

Ji, B. T., Shu, X. O., Linet, M. S., Zheng, W., Wacholder, S., Gao, Y. T., Ying, D. M., & Jin, F. (1997). Paternal cigarette smoking and the risk of childhood cancer among offspring of nonsmoking mothers. *Journal of the National Cancer Institute, 89,* 238–244.

Jiao, S., Ji, G., & Jing, Q. (1996). Cognitive development of Chinese urban only children and children with siblings. *Child Development, 67,* 387–395.

Jimerson, S., Egeland, B., & Teo, A. (1999). A longitudinal study of achievement trajectories: Factors associated with change. *Journal of Educational Psychology, 91*(1), 116–126.

Jodl, K. M., Michael, A., Malanchuk, O., Eccles, J. S., & Sameroff, A. (2001). Parents' roles in shaping early adolescents' occupational aspirations. *Child Development 72*(4), 1247–1265.

Johnson, D. J., Jaeger, E., Randolph, S. M., Cauce, A. M., Ward, J., & National Institute of Child Health and Human Development Early Child Care Research Network (2003). Studying the effects of early child care experiences on the development of children of color in the United States: Toward a more inclusive research agenda. *Child Development, 74,* 1227–1244.

Johnson, J., Canning, J., Kaneko, T., Pru, J. K., & Tilly, J. L. (2004). Germline stem cells and follicular renewal in the postnatal mammalian ovary. *Nature, 428*(6979), 145–150.

Johnson, J. E. (1998). Play development from ages four to eight. In D. P. Fromberg & D. Bergen (Eds.), *Play from birth to twelve and beyond: Contexts, perspectives, and meanings* (pp. 145–153). New York: Garland.

Johnson, J. G., Cohen, P., Smailes, E. M., Kasen, S., & Brook, J. S. (2002). Television viewing and aggressive behavior during adolescence and adulthood. *Science, 295,* 2468–2471.

Johnson, K. (2004, March 27). Harm to fetuses becomes issue in Utah and elsewhere. *New York Times.* [Online]. Available: http://www.nytimes.com/2004/03027// national/27FETU.html?ex=1081399221&eu=1&en=ede725fc158cb2bd. Access date: March 29, 2004.

Johnson, K. E., Scott, P., & Mervis, C. B. (1997). Development of children's understanding of basic-subordinate inclusion relations. *Developmental Psychology, 33,* 745–763.

Johnson, M. H. (1998). The neural basis of cognitive development. In D. Kuhn & R. S. Siegler (Eds.), *Handbook of child psychology: Vol. 2. Cognition, perception, and language* (5th ed., pp. 1–49). New York: Wiley.

Johnson, M. H. (1999). Developmental cognitive neuroscience. In M. Bennett (Ed.), *Developmental psychology: Achievements and prospects* (pp. 147–164). Philadelphia, PA: Psychology Press/Taylor & Francis.

Johnson, M. H. (2001). Functional brain development during infancy. In G. Bremner & A. Fogel (Eds.), *Handbooks of developmental psychology: Blackwell handbook of infant development* (pp. 169–190). Malden, MA: Blackwell Publishers.

Johnson, M. O. (1996). Television violence and its effect on children. *Journal of Pediatric Nursing, 11,* 94–98.

Johnson, R. A., Hoffmann, J. P., & Gerstein, D. R. (1996). *The relationship between family structure and adolescent substance use* (DHHS Publication No. SMA 96–3086). Washington, DC: U.S. Department of Health and Human Services.

Johnson, S. L. (2000). Improving preschoolers' self-regulation of energy intake. *Pediatrics, 106,* 1429–1435.

Johnson, S. L., & Birch, L. L. (1994). Parents' and children's adiposity and eating styles. *Pediatrics, 94,* 653–661.

Johnson, S. P., Bremner, J. G., Slater, A., Mason, U., Foster, K., & Cheshire, A. (2003). Infants' perception of object trajectories. *Child Development, 74,* 94–108.

Johnston, B. D., Grossman, D. C., Connell, F. A., & Koepsell, T. D. (2000). High-risk periods for childhood injury among siblings. *Pediatrics, 105*(3), 562–568.

Johnston, J., & Ettema, J. S. (1982). *Positive images: Breaking stereotypes with children's television.* Newbury Park, CA: Sage.

Johnston, L. D., O'Malley, P. M., & Bachman, J. G. (2000). *Monitoring the Future results on adolescent drug use. Overview of key findings 1999.* USDHHS, PHS, NIDA, NIH Publication number 00–490. Bethesda, MD: National Institute on Drug Abuse.

Johnston, L. D., O'Malley, P. M., & Bachman, J. G. (2001). *Rise in ecstasy use among American teens begins to slow.* Ann Arbor, MI: University of Michigan News and Information Services {Online}. Available: www.monitoringthefuture.org.

Johnston, L. D., O'Malley, P. M., & Bachman, J. G. (2002a, December 16). *Ecstasy use among American teens drops for the first time in recent years and overall drug and alcohol use also decline in the year after 9/11.* Ann Arbor, MI: University of Michigan News and Information Services [Online]. Available: www.monitoringthefuture.org. Access date: January 16, 2003.

Johnston, L. D., O'Malley, P. M., & Bachman, J. G. (2002b). *Monitoring the Future national results on adolescent drug use: Overview of key findings, 2001.* NIH Publication No. 02–5105. Bethesda, MD: National Institute on Drug Abuse.

Johnston, L. D., O'Malley, P. M., & Bachman, J. G. (2003). *Monitoring the future: National results on adolescent drug use. Overview of key findings, 2002.* (NIH pub. No. 03–5374). Bethesda, MD: National Institute on Drug Abuse.

Johnston, L. D., O'Malley, P. M., Bachman, J. G., & Schulenberg, J. E. (2004). *Monitoring the future: National results on adolescent drug use. Overview of key findings, 2003.* (NIH Publication No. 04–5506). Bethesda, MD: National Institute on Drug Abuse.

Jones, H. W., & Toner, J. P. (1993). The infertile couple. *New England Journal of Medicine, 329,* 1710–1715.

Jones, M. C. (1957). The late careers of boys who were early- or late-maturing. *Child Development, 28,* 115–128.

Jones, M. C. (1958). The study of socialization patterns at the high school level. *Journal of Genetic Psychology, 93,* 87–111.

Jones, N. A., Field, T., Fox, N. A., Davalos, M., Lundy, B., & Hart, S. (1998). Newborns of mothers with depressive symptoms are physiologically less developed. *Infant Behavior & Development, 21*(3), 537–541.

Jones, N. A., Field, T., Fox, N. A., Lundy, B., & Davalos, M. (1997). EEG activation in one-month-old infants of depressed mothers. *Development and Psychopathology, 9,* 491–505.

Jones, R. T. (2004). Biographies: Marian Anderson (1897–1993). *Afrocentric Voices in "Classical" Music.* [Online]. Available: http://www.afrovoices.com/anderson.html. Access date: November 18, 2004.

Jones, S. S. (1996). Imitation or exploration? Young infants' matching of adults' oral gestures. *Child Development, 67,* 1952–1969.

Jonsson, P. (2001, July 2). Latest battle over the unborn: S. Carolina goes after pregnant drug users. *Chicago Sun-Times,* p. 4.

Jordan, B. (1993). *Birth in four cultures: A cross-cultural investigation of childbirth in Yucatan, Holland, Sweden, and the United States* (4th ed.). Prospect Heights, IL: Waveland Press. (Original work published 1978.)

Jusczyk, P. W. (2003). The role of speech perception capacities in early language acquisition. In M. T. Banich & M. Mack (Eds.), *Mind, brain, and language: Multidisciplinary perspectives.* Mahwah, NJ: Erlbaum.

Jusczyk, P. W., & Hohne, E. A. (1997). Infants' memory for spoken words. *Science, 277,* 1984–1986.

Jussim, L., Eccles, J., & Madon, S. (1996). Social perception, social stereotypes, and teacher expectations: Accuracy and the quest for the powerful self-fulfilling prophecy. In M. P. Zanna (Ed.), *Advances in experimental social psychology* (vol. 28, pp. 281–388). San Diego, CA: Academic.

Juul-Dam, N., Townsend, J. & Courchesne, E. (2001). Prenatal, perinatal, and neonatal factors in autism, pervasive developmental disorder—not otherwise specified, and the general population. *Pediatrics, 107*(4), p. e63.

Kaback, M., Lim-Steele, J., Dabholkar, D., Brown, D., Levy, N., & Zeiger, K., for the International TSD Data Collection Network. (1993). Tay-Sachs disease—Carrier screening, prenatal diagnosis, and the molecular era. *Journal of the American Medical Association, 270,* 2307–2315.

Kadhim, H., Kahn, A., & Sebire, G. (2003). High levels of immune protein in infant brain linked to SIDS. *American Academy of Neurology, 61,* 1256–1259.

Kagan, J. (1997). Temperament and the reactions to unfamiliarity. *Child Development, 68,* 139–143.

Kagan, J., & Snidman, N. (1991a). Infant predictors of inhibited and uninhibited behavioral profiles. *Psychological Science, 2,* 40–44.

Kagan, J., & Snidman, N. (1991b). Temperamental factors in human development. *American Psychologist, 46,* 856–862.

Kail, R. (1991). Processing time declines exponentially during childhood and adolescence. *Developmental Psychology, 27,* 259–266.

Kail, R. (1997). Processing time, imagery, and spatial memory. *Journal of Experimental Child Psychology, 64,* 67–78.

Kail, R., & Park, Y. (1994). Processing time, articulation time, and memory span. *Journal of Experimental Child Psychology, 57,* 281–291.

Kaiser Family Foundation, Hoff, T., Greene, L., & Davis, J. (2003). *National survey of adolescents and young adults: Sexual health knowledge, attitudes and experiences.* Menlo Park, CA: Henry J. Kaiser Foundation.

Kamerman, S. B. (2000). Parental leave policies: An essential ingredient in early childhood education and care policies. *Social Policy Report, 14*(2), 3–15.

Kanetsuna, T., & Smith, P. K. (2002). Pupil insight into bullying and coping with bullying: A bi-national study in Japan and England. *Journal of School Violence, 1,* 5–29.

Kaplan, H., & Dove, H. (1987). Infant development among the Ache of East Paraguay. *Developmental Psychology, 23,* 190–198.

Kaplowitz, P. B., Oberfield, S. E., & the Drug and Therapeutics and Executive Committees of the Lawson Wilkins Pediatric Endocrine Society. (1999). Reexamination of the age limit for defining when puberty is precocious in girls in the United States: Implications for evaluation and treatment. *Pediatrics, 104,* 936–941.

Karafantis, D. M., & Levy, S. R. (2004). The role of children's lay theories about the malleability of human attributes in beliefs about and volunteering for disadvantaged groups. *Child Development, 75,* 236–250.

Katzman, R. (1993). Education and prevalence of Alzheimer's disease. *Neurology, 43,* 13–20.

Kaufman, A. S., & Kaufman, N. L. (1983). *Kaufman Assessment Battery for Children: Administration and scoring manual.* Circle Pines, MN: American Guidance Service.

Kaufman, A. S., & Kaufman, N. L. (2003). *Kaufman Assessment Battery for Children* (2d ed.). Circle Pines, MN: American Guidance Service.

Kaufman, J., & Zigler, E. (1987). Do abused children become abusive parents? *American Journal of Orthopsychiatry, 57*(2), 186–192.

Kaufman, P., Alt, M. N., & Chapman, C. (2001). *Dropout rates in the United States: 2000.* Washington, DC: National Center for Education Statistics.

Kaye, W. H., Weltzin, T. E., Hsu, L. K. G., & Bulik, C. M. (1991). An open trial of fluoxetine in patients with anorexia nervosa. *Journal of Clinical Psychiatry, 52,* 464–471.

Keegan, R. T., & Gruber, H. E. (1985). Charles Darwin's unpublished "Diary of an Infant": An early phase in his psychological work. In G. Eckardt, W. G. Bringmann, & L. Sprung (Eds.), *Contributions to a history of developmental psychology: International William T. Preyer Symposium* (pp. 127–145). Berlin, Germany: Walter de Gruyter.

Keel, P. K., & Mitchell, J. E. (1997). Outcome in bulimia nervosa. *American Journal of Psychiatry, 154,* 313–321.

Keel, P. K., Dorer, D. J., Eddy, K. T., Franko, D., Charatan, D. L., & Herzog, D. B. (2003). Predictors of mortality in eating disorders. *Archives of General Psychiatry, 60*(2), 179–183.

Keen, R. (2003). Representation of objects and events: Why do infants look so smart and toddlers look so dumb? *Current Directions in Psychological Science, 12,* 79–83.

Keenan, K., & Shaw, D. (1997). Developmental and social influences on young girls' early problem behavior. *Psychological Bulletin, 121*(1), 95–113.

Keightley, P. D., & Eyre-Walker, A. (2001). High genomic deleterious rates in hominids. *Nature, 397,* 344–347.

Kelleher, K. J., Casey, P. H., Bradley, R. H., Pope, S. K., Whiteside, L., Barrett, K. W., Swanson, M. E., & Kirby, R. S. (1993). Risk factors and outcomes for failure to thrive in low birth weight preterm infants. *Pediatrics, 91,* 941–948.

Keller, B. (1999, February 24). A time and place for teenagers. *Education Week on the WEB.* [Online]. Available: http://www.edweek.org/ew/vol-18/24studen.h18. Access date: March 11, 2004.

Keller, H. (1905). *The story of my life.* New York: Grosset & Dunlap. (Original work published 1903.)

Keller, H. (1920). *The world I live in.* New York: Century. (Original work published 1908.)

Keller, H. (1929). *The Bereaved.* New York: Leslie Fulenwider, Inc.

Keller, H. (2003). *The Story of My Life: The Restored Edition* (J. Berger, Ed.). New York: Norton.

Keller, M., Gummerum, M., Wang, T., & Lindsey, S. (2004). Understanding perspectives and emotions in contract violation: Development of deontic and moral reasoning. *Child Development, 75,* 614–635.

Kelley, M. L., Smith, T. S., Green, A. P., Berndt, A. E., & Rogers, M. C. (1998). Importance of fathers' parenting to African-American toddler's social and cognitive development. *Infant Behavior & Development, 21,* 733–744.

Kellman, P. J., & Arterberry, M. E. (1998). The cradle of knowledge: Development of perception in infancy. Cambridge, MA: MIT.

Kellman, P. J., & Banks, M. S. (1998). Infant visual perception. In W. Damon (Ed.-in-Chief), D. Kuhn, & R. S. Siegler (Vol. Eds.), *Handbook of Child Psychology: Vol. 2. Cognition, perception, and language* (5th ed., pp. 103–146). New York: Wiley.

Kellogg, R. (1970). Understanding children's art. In P. Cramer (Ed.), *Readings in developmental psychology today.* Delmar, CA: CRM.

Kelly, A. M., Wall, M., Eisenberg, M., Story, M., & Neumark-Sztainer, D. (2004). High body satisfaction in adolescent girls: Association with demographic, socio-environmental, personal, and behavioral factors. *Journal of Adolescent Health, 34,* 129.

Kemp, J. S., Unger, B., Wilkins, D., Psara, R. M., Ledbetter, T. L., Graham, M. A., Case, M., and Thach, B. T. (2000). Unsafe sleep practices and an analysis of bedsharing among infants dying suddenly and unexpectedly: Results of a four-year, population-based, death-scene investigation study of sudden infant death and related syndromes. *Pediatrics, 106*(3), e41.

Kendall-Tackett, K. A., Williams, L. M., & Finkelhor, D. (1993). Impact of sexual abuse on children: A review and synthesis of recent empirical studies. *Psychological Bulletin, 113*(1). 164–180.

Kendler, K. S., MacLean, C., Neale, M., Kessler, R., Heath, A., & Eaves, L. (1991). The genetic epidemiology of bulimia nervosa. *American Journal of Psychiatry, 148,* 1627–1637.

Kendler, K. S., Thornton, L. M., Gilman, S. E., & Kessler, R. C. (2000). Sexual orientation in a U.S. national sample of twin and non-twin sibling pairs. *American Journal of Psychiatry, 157,* 1843–1847.

Kernan, M. (1993, June). The object at hand. *Smithsonian,* pp. 14–16.

Kerns, K A., Don, A., Mateer, C. A., & Streissguth, A. P. (1997). Cognitive deficits in nonretarded adults with fetal alcohol syndrome. *Journal of Learning Disabilities, 30,* 685–693.

Kestenbaum, R., & Gelman, S. A. (1995). Preschool children's identification and understanding of mixed emotions. *Cognitive Development, 10,* 443–458.

Khoury, M. J., McCabe, L. L., & McCabe, E. R. B. (2003). Population screening in the age of genomic medicine. *New England Journal of Medicine, 348,* 50–58.

Kier, C., & Lewis, C. (1998). Preschool sibling interaction in separated and married families: Are same-sex pairs or older sisters more sociable? *Journal of Child Psychology and Psychiatry, 39,* 191–201.

Kim, K. J., Conger, R. D., Elder, G. H., and Lorenz, F. O. (2003). Reciprocal influences between stressful life events and adolescent internalizing and externalizing problems. *Child Development, 74*(1), 127–143.

Kimball, M. M. (1986). Television and sex-role attitudes. In T. M. Williams (Ed.), *The impact of television: A natural experiment in three communities* (pp. 265–301). Orlando, FL: Academic Press.

Kimbrough, R. D., LeVois, M., & Webb, D. R. (1994). Management of children with slightly elevated blood lead levels. *Pediatrics, 93,* 188–191.

Kim-Cohen, J., Moffitt, T. E., Caspi, A., & Taylor, A. (2004). Genetic and environmental processes in young children's resilience and vulnerability to socioeconomic deprivation. *Child Development, 75,* 651–668.

Kimm, S. Y. S., Glynn, N. W., Kriska, A. M., Barton, B. A., Kronsberg, S. S., Daniels, S. R., Crawford, P. B., Sabry, Z. I., & Liu, K. (2002). Decline in physical activity in black girls and white girls during adolescence. *New England Journal of Medicine, 347,* 709–715.

King, B. M. (1996). *Human sexuality today* (2d ed.). Upper Saddle River, NJ: Prentice-Hall.

King, C., Siegel, M., Celebucki, C., & Connolly, G. N. (1998). Adolescent exposure to cigarette advertising in magazines. *Journal of the American Medical Association, 279,* 1–520.

King, W. J., MacKay, M., Sirnick, A., & The Canadian Shaken Baby Study Group. (2003). Shaken baby syndrome in Canada: Clinical characteristics and outcomes of hospital cases. *CMAJ* (Canadian Medical Association Journal), *168,* 155–159.

Kinney, H. C., Filiano, J. J., Sleeper, L. A., Mandell, F., Valdes-Dapena, M., & White, W. F. (1995). Decreased muscarinic receptor binding in the arcuate nucleus in sudden infant death syndrome. *Science, 269,* 1446–1450.

Kinnunen, L. H., Moltz, H., Metz, J., & Cooper, M. (2003). *Differential cerebral glucose metabolic patters in exclusively homosexual and exclusively heterosexual men produced by a selective serotonin reuptake inhibitor.* Washington, DC: Society for Neuroscience.

Kinsella, K., & Velkoff, V. A. (2001). *An aging world: 2001.* U.S. Census Bureau, Series P95/01-1. Washington, DC: U.S. Government Printing Office.

Kinsman, S., Romer, D., Furstenberg, F. F., & Schwarz, D. F. (1998). Early sexual initiation: The role of peer norms. *Pediatrics, 102,* 1185–1192.

Kirby, D. (1997). *No easy answers: Research findings on programs to reduce teen pregnancy.* Washington, DC: National Campaign to Prevent Teen Pregnancy.

Kisilevsky, B. S., Hains, S. M J., Lee, K., Xie, X., Huang, H., Ye, H. H., Zhang, K., & Wang, Z. (2003). Effects of experience on fetal voice recognition. *Psychological Science, 14,* 220–224.

Kisilevsky, B. S., Hains, S. M. J., Lee, K., Muir, D. W., Xu, F., Fu, G., Zhao, Z. Y., & Yang, R. L. (1998). The still-face effect in Chinese and Canadian 3- to 6-month-old infants. *Developmental Psychology, 34*(4), 629–639.

Kisilevsky, B. S., Muir, D. W., & Low, J. A. (1992). Maturation of human fetal responses to vibroacoustic stimulation. *Child Development, 63,* 1497–1508.

Kistner, J., Eberstein, I. W., Quadagno, D., Sly, D., Sittig, L., Foster, K., Balthazor, M., Castro, R., & Osborne, M. (1997). Children's AIDS-related knowledge and attitudes: Variations by grade, race, gender, socioeconomic status, and size of community. *AIDS Education and Prevention, 9,* 285–298.

Kivett, V. R. (1991). Centrality of the grandfather role among older rural black and white men. *Journal of Gerontology. Social Sciences, 46*(5), S250–S258.

Kivett, V. R. (1993). Racial comparisons of the grandmother role: Implications for strengthening the family support system of older black women. *Family Relations,* 42, 165–172.

Kivett, V. R. (1996). The saliency of the grandmother-granddaughter relationship: Predictors of association. *Journal of Women & Aging, 8*(3/4), 25–39.

Kjos, S. L., & Buchanan, T. A. (1999). Gestational diabetes mellitus. *New England Journal of Medicine,* 341.

Klar, A. J. S. (1996). A single locus, RGHT, specifies preference for hand utilization in humans. *Cold Spring Harbor Symposia on Quantitative Biology 61,* 59–65. Cold Spring Harbor, NY: Cold Spring Harbor Laboratory Press.

Klaus, M. H., & Kennell, J. H. (1982). *Parent-infant bonding* (2d ed.). St. Louis, MO: Mosby.

Klaus, M. H., & Kennell, J. H. (1997). The doula: An essential ingredient of childbirth rediscovered. *Acta Paediatrica, 86,* 1034–1036.

Klebanoff, M. A., Levine, R. J., DerSimonian, R., Clemens, J. D., & Wilkins, D. G. (1999). Maternal serum paraxanthine, a caffeine metabolite, and the risk of spontaneous abortion. *New England Journal of Medicine, 341,* 1639–1644.

Klebanov, P. K., Brooks-Gunn, J., & McCormick, M. C. (1994). Classroom behavior of very low birth weight elementary school children. *Pediatrics, 94,* 700–708.

Klebanov, P. K., Brooks-Gunn, J., & McCormick, M. C. (2001). Maternal coping strategies and emotional distress: Results of an early intervention program for low birth weight young children. *Developmental Psychology, 37*(5), 654–667.

Klebanov, P. K., Brooks-Gunn, J., McCarton, C., & McCormick, M. C. (1998). The contribution of neighborhood and family income to developmental test scores over the first three years of life. *Child Development, 69*(5), 1420–1436.

Kleiner, A., & Farris, E. (2002). *Internet access in U.S. public schools and classrooms: 1994–2001* (NCES 2002–018). Washington, DC: National Center for

Education Statistics, U.S. Department of Education.

Kleiner, B., Nolin, M. J., & Chapman, C. (2004). *Before- and after-school care, programs, and activities of children in kindergarten through eighth grade: 2001. Statistical analysis report* (NCES 2004–008). Washington, DC: National Center for Education Statistics.

Klesges, R. C., Klesges, L. M., Eck, L. H., & Shelton, M. L. (1995). A longitudinal analysis of accelerated weight gain in preschool children. *Pediatrics, 95,* 126–130.

Kling, K. C., Hyde, J. S., Showers, C. J., & Buswell, B. N. (1999). Gender differences in self-esteem: A metaanalysis. *Psychological Bulletin, 125,* 470–500.

Kochanek, K. D., & Smith, B. L. (2004). Deaths: Preliminary data for 2002. *National Vital Statistics Reports, 52*(13). Hyattsville, MD: National Center for Health Statistics.

Kochanek, K. D., Murphy, S. L., Anderson, R. N., & Scott, C. (2004). Deaths: Final data for 2002. *National Vital Statistics Reports, 53*(5). Hyattsville, MD: National Center for Health Statistics.

Kochanska, G. (1992). Children's interpersonal influence with mothers and peers. *Developmental Psychology, 28,* 491–499.

Kochanska, G. (1993). Toward a synthesis of parental socialization and child temperament in early development of conscience. *Child Development, 64,* 325–437.

Kochanska, G. (1995). Children's temperament, mothers' discipline, and security of attachment: Multiple pathways to emerging internalization. *Child Development, 66,* 597–615.

Kochanska, G. (1997a). Multiple pathways to conscience for children with different temperaments: From toddlerhood to age 5. *Developmental Psychology, 33,* 228–240.

Kochanska, G. (1997b). Mutually responsive orientation between mothers and their young children: Implications for early socialization. *Child Development, 68,* 94–112.

Kochanska, G. (1998). Mother-child relationship, child fearfulness, and emerging attachment: A short-term longitudinal study. *Developmental Psychology, 34,* 480–490.

Kochanska, G. (2001). Emotional development in children with different attachment histories: The first three years. *Child Development, 72,* 474–490.

Kochanska, G. (2002). Mutually responsive orientation between mothers and their young children: A context for the early development of conscience. *Current Directions in Psychological Science, 11,* 191–195.

Kochanska, G., & Aksan, N. (1995). Mother-child positive affect, the quality of child compliance to requests and prohibitions, and maternal control as correlates of early internalization. *Child Development, 66,* 236–254.

Kochanska, G., Aksan, N., Knaack, A., & Rhines, H. M. (2004). Maternal parenting and children's conscience: Early security as moderator. *Child Development, 75,* 1229–1242.

Kochanska, G., Coy, K. C., & Murray, K. T. (2001). The development of self-regulation in the first four years of life. *Child Development, 72*(4), 1091–1111.

Kochanska, G., Murray, K., & Coy, K. C. (1997). Inhibitory control as a contributor to conscience in childhood: From toddler to early school age. *Child Development, 68,* 263–277.

Kochanska, G., Tjebkes, T. L., & Forman, D. R. (1998). Children's emerging regulation of conduct: Restraint, compliance, and internalization from infancy to the second year. *Child Development, 69*(5), 1378–1389.

Kochenderfer, B. H., & Ladd, G. W. (1996). Peer victimization: Cause or consequence of school maladjustment? *Child Development, 67,* 1305–1317.

Koechlin, E., Dehaene, S., & Mehler, J. (1997). Numerical transformations in five-month-old human infants. *Mathematical Cognition, 3,* 89–104.

Koenig, H. G. (1994). *Aging and God.* New York: Haworth.

Kogan, M. D., Alexander, G. R., Kotelchuck, M., MacDorman, M. F., Buekens, P., Martin, J. A., & Papiernik, E. (2000). Trends in twin birth outcomes and prenatal care utilization in the United States, 1981–1997. *Journal of the American Medical Association, 284,* 335–341.

Kogan, M. D., Martin, J. A., Alexander, G. R., Kotelchuck, M., Ventura, S. J., & Frigoletto, F. D. (1998). The changing pattern of prenatal care utilization in the United States, 1981–1995, using different prenatal care indices. *Journal of the American Medical Association, 279,* 1623–1628.

Kohlberg, L. (1966). A cognitive-developmental analysis of children's sex-role concepts and attitudes. In E. E. Maccoby (Ed.), *The development of sex differences.* Stanford, CA: Stanford University Press.

Kohlberg, L. (1969). Stage and sequence: The cognitive-developmental approach to socialization. In D. A. Goslin (Ed.), *Handbook of socialization theory and research.* Chicago: Rand McNally.

Kohlberg, L. (1981). *Essays on moral development.* San Francisco: Harper & Row.

Kohlberg, L., & Ryncarz, R. A. (1990). Beyond justice reasoning: Moral development and consideration of a seventh stage. In C. N. Alexander & E. J. Langer (Eds.), *Higher stages of human development* (pp. 191–207). New York: Oxford University Press.

Kohlberg, L., Yaeger, J., & Hjertholm, E. (1968). Private speech: Four studies and a review of theories. *Child Development, 39,* 691–736.

Kolata, G. (1988, March 29). Fetuses treated through umbilical cords. *New York Times,* p. C3.

Kolbert, E. (1994, January 11). Canadians curbing TV violence. *New York Times,* pp. C15, C19.

Kopp, C. B. (1982). Antecedents of self-regulation. *Developmental Psychology, 18,* 199–214.

Kopp, C. B., & Kaler, S. R. (1989). Risk in infancy: Origins and implications. *American Psychologist, 44*(2), 224–230.

Kopp, C. B., & McCall, R. B. (1982). Predicting later mental performance for normal, at-risk, and handicapped infants. In P. B. Baltes & O. G. Brim (Eds.), *Life-span development and behaviors* (vol. 4). New York: Academic Press.

Koren, G., Pastuszak, A., & Ito, S. (1998). Drugs in pregnancy. *New England Journal of Medicine, 338,* 1128–1137.

Korner, A. (1996). Reliable individual differences in preterm infants' excitation management. *Child Development, 67,* 1793–1805.

Korner, A. F., Zeanah, C. H., Linden, J., Berkowitz, R. I., Kraemer, H. C., & Agras, W. S. (1985). The relationship between neonatal and later activity and temperament. *Child Development, 56,* 38–42.

Korte, D., & Scaer, R. (1984). *A good birth, a safe birth.* New York: Bantam.

Kosterman, R., Graham, J. W., Hawkins, J. D., Catalano, R. F., & Herrenkohl, T. I. (2001). Childhood risk factors for persistence of violence in the transition to adulthood: A social development perspective. *Violence & Victims. Special Issue: Developmental Perspectives on Violence and Victimization, 16*(4), 355–369.

Kottak, C. P. (1994). *Cultural anthropology.* New York: McGraw-Hill.

Kowal, A. K., & Pike, L. B. (2004). Sibling influences on adolescents' attitudes toward safe sex practices. *Family Relations, 53,* 377–384.

Kozlowska, K., & Hanney, L. (1999). Family assessment and intervention using an interactive art exercise. *Australia and New Zealand Journal of Family Therapy, 20*(2), 61–69.

Kraemer, H. C., Korner, A., Anders, T., Jacklin, C. N., & Dimiceli, S. (1985). Obstetric drugs and infant behavior: A reevaluation. *Journal of Pediatric Psychology, 10,* 345–353.

Kralovec, E., & Buell, J. (2000). *The end of homework.* Boston: Beacon.

Kramer, M. S., Chalmers, B., Hodnett, E. D., Sevkovskaya, Z., Dzikovich, I., Shapiro, S., Collet, J.-P., Vanilovich, I.,

Ducruet, T., Shishko, G., Zubovich, V., Mknuik, D., Gluchanina, E., Dombrovskiy, V., Ustinovich, N., Ovchinikova, L., & Helsing, E., for the PROBIT Study Group. (2001). Promotion of Breastfeeding Intervention Trial (PROBIT): A randomized trial in the Republic of Belarus. *Journal of the American Medical Association, 285,* 413–420.

Kramer, M. S., Platt, R., Yang, H., Joseph, K. S., Wen, S. W., Morin, L., & Usher, R. H. (1998). Secular trends in preterm birth: A hospital-based cohort study. *Journal of the American Medical Association, 280,* 1849–1854.

Krauss, S., Concordet, J. P., & Ingham, P. W. (1993). A functionally conserved homolog of the Drosophila segment polarity gene hh is expressed in tissues with polarizing activity in zebrafish embryos. *Cell, 75,* 1431–1444.

Kravetz, J. D., & Federman, D. G. (2002). Cat-associated zoonoses. *Archives of Internal Medicine, 162,* 1945–1952.

Kreider, R. M. (2003). Adopted children and stepchildren: 2000. *Census 2000 Special Reports.* Washington, D.C.: U.S. Bureau of the Census.

Kreutzer, M., Leonard, C., & Flavell, J. (1975). An interview study of children's knowledge about memory. *Monographs of the Society for Research in Child Development, 40*(1), Serial No. 159.

Krevans, J., & Gibbs, J. C. (1996). Parents' use of inductive discipline: Relations to children's empathy and prosocial behavior. *Child Development, 67,* 3263–3277.

Kristensen, P., Judge, M. E., Thim, L., Ribel, U., Christjansen, K. N., Wulff, B. S., Clausen, J. T., Jensen, P. B., Madsen, O. D., Vrang, N., Larsen, P. J., & Hastrup, S. (1998). Hypothalamic CART is a new anorectic peptide regulated by leptin. *Nature, 393,* 72–76.

Kristof, N. D. (1991, June 17). A mystery from China's census: Where have young girls gone? *New York Times,* pp. A1, A8.

Kristof, N. D. (1993, July 21). Peasants of China discover new way to weed out girls. *New York Times,* pp. A1, A6.

Kroger, J. (1993). Ego identity: An overview. In J. Kroger (Ed.), *Discussions on ego identity* (pp. 1–20). Hillsdale, NJ: Erlbaum.

Kroger, J., & Haslett, S. J. (1991). A comparison of ego identity status transition pathways and change rates across five identity domains. *International Journal of Aging and Human Development, 32,* 303–330.

Krueger, A. B. (February 2003). Economic considerations and class size. *The Economic Journal, 113,* F34-F63.

Krueger, A. B., & Whitmore, D. M. (April 2000). The effect of attending a small class in the early grades on college-test taking and middle school test results: Evidence from Project STAR. NBER Working Paper No. W7656.

Kuczmarski, R. J., Ogden, C. L., Grummer-Strawn, L. M., Flegal, K. M., Guo, S. S., Wei, R., Mei, Z., Curtin, L. R., Roche, A. F., & Johnson, C. L. (2000). CDC growth charts: United States. *Advance Data,* No. 314. Centers for Disease Control and Prevention, U.S. Department of Health and Human Services.

Kuczynski, L., & Kochanska, G. (1995). Function and content of maternal demands: Developmental significance of early demands for competent action. *Child Development, 66,* 616–628.

Kuhl, P. K., Andruski, J. E., Chistovich, I. A., Chistovich, L. A., Kozhevnikova, E. V., Ryskina, V. L., Stolyarova, E. I., Sundberg, U., & Lacerda, F. (1997). Cross-language analysis of phonetic units in language addressed to infants. *Science, 277,* 684–686.

Kuhl, P. K., Williams, K. A., Lacerda, F., Stevens, K. N., & Lindblom, B. (1992). Linguistic experience alters phonetic perception in infants by 6 months of age. *Science, 255,* 606–608.

Kuklinski, M. R., & Weinstein, R. S. (2001). Classroom and developmental differences in a path model of teacher expectancy effects. *Child Development, 72*(5), 1554–1578.

Kupersmidt, J. B., & Coie, J. D. (1990). Preadolescent peer status, aggression, and school adjustment as predictors of externalizing problems in adolescence. *Child Development, 61,* 1350–1362.

Kupfersmid, J., & Wonderly, D. (1980). Moral maturity and behavior: Failure to find a link. *Journal of Youth and Adolescence, 9*(3), 249–261.

Kurdek, L. A. (1999). The nature and predictors of the trajectory of change in marital quality for husbands and wives over the first 10 years of marriage. *Developmental Psychology, 35,* 1283–1296.

Kurjak, A., Kupesic, S., Matijevic, R., Kos, M., & Marton, U. (1999). First trimester malformation screening. *European Journal of Obstetrics, Gynecology, and Reproductive Biology (E4L), 85,* 93–96.

Kurosawa, A. (1993). *Something like an autobiography* (A. E. Bock, Trans.). New York: Vintage.

Kye, C., & Ryan, N. (1995). Pharmacologic treatment of child and adolescent depression. *Child and Adolescent Psychiatric Clinics of North America, 4,* 261–281.

Labov. T. (1992). Social and language boundaries among adolescents. *American Speech, 67,* 339–366.

Lackmann, G. M., Salzberger, U., Tollner, U., Chen, M., Carmella, S. G., & Hecht, S. S. (1999). Metabolites of a tobacco-specific carcinogen in the urine of newborns. *Journal of the National Cancer Institute, 91,* 459–465.

Ladd, G. W. (1996). Shifting ecologies during the 5- to 7-year period: Predicting children's adjustment during the transition to grade school. In A. J. Sameroff & M. M. Haith (Eds.), *The five to seven year shift: The age of reason and responsibility* (pp. 363–386). Chicago: University of Chicago Press.

Ladd, G. W., Birch, S. H., and Buhs, E. S. (1999). Children's social and scholastic lives in kindergarten: Related spheres of influence? *Child Development, 70,* 1373–1400.

Ladd, G. W., Kochenderfer, B. J., & Coleman, C. C. (1996). Friendship quality as a predictor of young children's early school adjustment. *Child Development, 67,* 1103–1118.

LaFontana, K. M., & Cillessen, A. H. N. (2002). Children's perceptions of popular and unpopular peers: A multi-method assessment. *Developmental Psychology, 38,* 635–647.

Lagercrantz, H., & Slotkin, T. A. (1986). The "stress" of being born. *Scientific American, 254*(4), 100–107.

Lai, C. S. L., Fisher, S. E., Hurst, J. A., Vargha-Khadem, F., & Monaco, A. P. (2001). A forkhead-domain gene is mutated in a severe speech and language disorder. *Nature, 413,* 519–523.

Lai, T., Liu, X., Guo, Y. L., Guo, N., Yu, M., Hsu, C., and Rogan, W. J. (2002). A cohort study of behavioral problems and intelligence in children with high prenatal polychlorinated biphenyl exposure. *Archives of General Psychiatry, 59,* 1061–1066.

Laible, D. J., & Thompson, R. A. (1998). Attachment and emotional understanding in preschool children. *Developmental Psychology, 34*(5), 1038–1045.

Laible, D. J., & Thompson, R. A. (2002). Mother-child conflict in the toddler years: Lessons in emotion, morality, and relationships. *Child Development, 73,* 1187–1203.

Laird, R. D., Pettit, G. S., Bates, J. E., & Dodge, K. A. (2003). Parents' monitoring-relevant knowledge and adolescents' delinquent behavior: Evidence of correlated developmental changes and reciprocal influences. *Child Development, 74,* 752–768.

Lalonde, C. E., & Werker, J. F. (1995). Cognitive influences on cross-language speech perception in infancy. *Infant Behavior and Development, 18,* 459–475.

Lamb, M. E. (1981). The development of father-infant relationships. In M. E. Lamb (Ed.), *The role of the father in child development* (2d ed.). New York: Wiley.

Lamb, M. E. (1983). Early mother-neonate contact and the mother-child relationship. *Journal of Child Psychology & Psychiatry & Allied Disciplines, 24,* 487–494.

Lamb, M. E. (1987). Predictive implications of individual differences in attachment.

Journal of Consulting and Clinical Psychology, 55(6), 817–824.

Lamb, M. E., Frodi, A. M., Frodi, M., & Hwang, C. P. (1982). Characteristics of maternal and paternal behavior in traditional and non-traditional Swedish families. *International Journal of Behavior Development, 5,* 131–151.

Lamb, M. E., Pleck, J., Charnov, E. L., & Levine, J. A. (1985). Paternal behavior in humans. *American Zoologist, 25,* 883–894.

Lamborn, S. D., Mounts, N. S., Steinberg, L., & Dornbusch, S. M. (1991). Patterns of competence and adjustment among adolescents from authoritative, authoritarian, indulgent, and neglectful families. *Child Development, 62,* 1049–1065.

Landesman-Dwyer, S., & Emanuel, I. (1979). Smoking during pregnancy. *Teratology, 19,* 119–126.

Landry, D. J., Kaeser, L., & Richards, C. L. (1999). Abstinence promotion and the provision of information about contraception in public school district sexuality education policies. *Family Planning Perspectives, 31,* 280–286.

Landry, S. H., Smith, K. E., Swank, P. R., & Miller Loncar, C. L. (2000). Early maternal and child influences on children's later independent cognitive and social functioning. *Child Development, 71,* 358–375.

Lane, H. (1976). *The wild boy of Aveyron.* Cambridge, MA: Harvard University Press.

Lange, G., MacKinnon, C. E., & Nida, R. E. (1989). Knowledge, strategy, and motivational contributions to preschool children's object recall. *Developmental Psychology, 25,* 772–779.

Lanphear, B. P. Aligne, C. A., Auinger, P., Weitzman, M., & Byrd, R. S. (2001). Residential exposure associated with asthma in U.S. children. *Pediatrics, 107,* 505–511.

Lansford, J. E., Dodge, K. A., Pettit, G. S., Bates, J. E., Crozier, J., & Kaplow, J. (2002). A 12-year prospective study of the long-term effects of early child physical maltreatment on psychological, behavioral, and academic problems in adolescence. *Archives of Pediatric and Adolescent Medicine, 156*(8), 824–830.

Lanting, C. I., Fidler, V., Huisman, M., Touwen, B. C. L., & Boersma, E. R. (1994). Neurological differences between 9-year-old children fed breastmilk or formula-milk as babies. *Lancet, 334,* 1319–1322.

Lapham, E. V., Kozma, C., & Weiss, J. O. (1996). Genetic discrimination: Perspectives of consumers. *Science, 274,* 621–624.

Larivée, S., Normandeau, S., & Parent, S. (2000). The French connection: Some contributions of French-language research in the post-Piagetian era. *Child Development, 71,* 823–839.

Larner, M. B., Stevenson, C. S., & Behrman, R. E. (1998). Protecting children from abuse and neglect: Analysis and recommendations. *The Future of Children, 8,* 4–22.

Larson, R. (1998). Implications for policy and practice: Getting adolescents, families, and communities in sync. In A. Crouter & R. Larson (Eds.), *Temporal rhythms in adolescence: Clocks, calendars, and the coordination of daily life* (New Directions in Child and Adolescent Development, No. 82, pp. 83–88). San Francisco: Jossey-Bass.

Larson, R., & Richards, M. (1998). Waiting for the weekend: Friday and Saturday nights as the emotional climax of the week. In A. Crouter & R. Larson (Eds.), *Temporal rhythms in adolescence: Clocks, calendars, and the coordination of daily life* (New Directions in Child and Adolescent Development, No. 82, pp. 37–51). San Francisco: Jossey-Bass.

Larson, R., & Richards, M. H. (1991). Daily companionship in late childhood and early adolescence: Changing developmental contexts. *Child Development, 62,* 284–300.

Larson, R., & Richards, M. H. (1994). *Divergent realities: The emotional lives of mothers, fathers, and adolescents.* New York: Basic Books.

Larson, R., & Seepersad, S. (2003). Adolescents' leisure time in the United States: Partying, sports, and the American experiment. In S. Verma and R. Larson (Eds.), Examining adolescent leisure time across cultures: Developmental opportunities and risks. *New Directions for Child and Adolescent Development, 99,* 53–64.

Larson, R. W. (1997). The emergence of solitude as a constructive domain of experience in early adolescence. *Child Development, 68,* 80–93.

Larson, R. W., & Verma, S. (1999). How children and adolescents spend time across the world: Work, play, and developmental opportunities. *Psychological Bulletin, 125,* 701–736.

Larson, R. W., Moneta, G., Richards, M. H., & Wilson, S. (2002). Continuity, stability, and change in daily emotional experience across adolescence. *Child Development, 73,* 1151–1165.

Larson, R. W., Richards, M. H., Moneta, G., Holmbeck, G., & Duckett, E. (1996). Changes in adolescents' daily interactions with their families from ages 10 to 18: Disengagement and transformation. *Developmental Psychology, 32,* 744–754.

Lash, J. P. (1980). *Helen and teacher: The story of Helen Keller and Anne Sullivan Macy.* New York: Delacorte.

Laucht, M., Esser, G., & Schmidt, M. H. (1994). Contrasting infant predictors of later cognitive functioning. *Journal of Child Psychology and Psychiatry, 35,* 649–652.

Laursen, B. (1996). Closeness and conflict in adolescent peer relationships: Interdependence with friends and romantic partners. In W. M. Bukowski, A. F. Newcomb, & W. W. Hartup (Eds.), *The company they keep: Friendship in childhood and adolescence* (pp. 186–210). New York: Cambridge University Press.

Laursen, B., Coy, K. C., & Collins, W. A. (1998). Reconsidering changes in parent-child conflict across adolescence: A meta-analysis. *Child Development, 69,* 817–832.

Law, K. L., Stroud, L. R., LaGasse, L. L., Niaura, R., Liu, J., and Lester, B. (2003). Smoking during pregnancy and newborn neurobehavior. *Pediatrics, 111,* 1318–1323.

Lawlor, D. A., Smith, G. D., Mitchell, R., & Ebrahim, S. (2004). Temperature at birth, coronary heart disease, and insulin resistance: Cross sectional analyses of the British women's heart and health study. *Heart, 90,* 381–388.

Lawson, C. (1993, October 4). Celebrated birth aside, teen-ager is typical now. *New York Times,* p. A18.

Leaper, C., Anderson, K. J., & Sanders, P. (1998). Moderators of gender effects on parents' talk to their children: A meta-analysis. *Developmental Psychology, 34*(1), 3–27.

Leblanc, M., & Ritchie, M. (2001). A meta-analysis of play therapy outcomes. *Counseling Psychology Quarterly, 14,* 149–163.

Lecanuet, J. P., Granier-Deferre, C., & Busnel, M-C. (1995). Human fetal auditory perception. In J. P. Lecanuet, W. P. Fifer, N. A. Krasnegor, & W. P. Smotherman (Eds.), *Fetal development: A psychobiological perspective* (pp. 239–262).Hillsdale, NJ: Erlbaum.

Lee, F. R. (2004, July 3). Engineering more sons than daughters: Will it tip the scales toward war? *New York Times,* pp. A17, A19.

Lee, J. (1998). Children, teachers, and the Internet. *Delta Kappa Gamma Bulletin, 64*(2), 5–9.

Leeman, L. W., Gibbs, J. C., & Fuller, D. (1993). Evaluation of a multi-component group treatment program for juvenile delinquents. *Aggressive Behavior, 19,* 281–292.

Legerstee, M., & Varghese, J. (2001). The role of maternal affect mirroring on social expectancies in 3-month-old infants. *Child Development, 72,* 1301–1313.

Leibel, R. L. (1997). And finally, genes for human obesity. *Nature Genetics, 16,* 218–220.

Leichtman, M. D., & Ceci, S. J. (1995). The effects of stereotypes and suggestions on preschoolers' reports. *Developmental Psychology, 31,* 568–578.

Lenneberg, E. H. (1967). *Biological functions of language.* New York: Wiley.

Lenneberg, E. H. (1969). On explaining language. *Science, 164*(3880), 635–643.
Leonard, William Ellery. (1925). *Two Lives: A Poem.* New York: B. W. Huebsch.
Lerner, J. V., & Galambos, N. L. (1985). Maternal role satisfaction, mother-child interaction, and child temperament: A process model. *Child Development, 21,* 1157–1164.
Lesch, K. P., Bengel, D., Heils, A., Sabol, S. Z., Greenberg, B. D., Petri, S., Benjamin, J., Müller, C. R., Hamer, D. H., & Murphy, D. L. (1996). Association of anxiety-related traits with a polymorphism in the serotonin transporter gene regulatory region. *Science, 274,* 1527–1531.
Leslie, A. M. (1982). The perception of causality in infants. *Perception, 11,* 173–186.
Leslie, A. M. (1984). Spatiotemporal continuity and the perception of causality in infants. *Perception, 13,* 287–305.
Lester, B. M., & Boukydis, C. F. Z. (1985). *Infant crying: Theoretical and research perspectives.* New York: Plenum.
Lester, B. M., & Dreher, M. (1989). Effects of marijuana use during pregnancy on newborn cry. *Child Development, 60,* 765–771.
LeVay, S. (1991). A difference in hypothalamic structure between heterosexual and homosexual men. *Science, 253,* 1034–1037.
Leve, L. D., & Fagot, B. I. (1997). Gender-role socialization and discipline processes in one- and two-parent families. *Sex Roles, 36,* 1–21.
Leventhal, T., & Brooks-Gunn, J. (2000). The neighborhoods they live in: The effects of neighborhood residence on child and adolescent outcomes. *Psychological Bulletin, 126*(2), 309–337.
LeVine, R. A. (1974). Parental goals: A cross-cultural view. *Teacher College Record, 76,* 226–239.
LeVine, R. A. (1989). Human parental care: Universal goals, cultural strategies, individual behavior. In R. A. LeVine, P. M. Miller, & M. M. West (Eds.), *Parental behavior in diverse societies* (pp. 3–12). San Francisco: Jossey-Bass.
Levine, R. A. (1994). *Child care and culture: Lessons from Africa.* Cambridge, England: Cambridge University Press.
LeVine, R. A., Dixon, S., LeVine, S., Richman, A. Leiderman, P. H., Keefer, C. H., & Brazelton, T. B. (1994). *Child care and culture: Lessons from Africa.* New York: Cambridge University Press.
Levine, S. C., Huttenlocher, J., Taylor, A., & Langrock, A. (1999). Early sex differences in spatial skill. *Developmental Psychology, 35*(4), 940–949.
Levitt, M. J., Guacci-Franco, N., & Levitt, J. L. (1993). Convoys of social support in childhood and early adolescence: Structure and function. *Developmental Psychology, 29,* 811–818.
Levron, J., Aviram, A., Madgar, I., Livshits, A., Raviv, G., Bider, D., Hourwitz, A., Barkai, G., Goldman, B., & Mashiach, S. (1998, October). *High rate of chromosomal aneupoloidies in testicular spermatozoa retrieved from azoospermic patients undergoing testicular sperm extraction for in vitro fertilization.* Paper presented at the 16th World Congress on Fertility and Sterility and the 54th annual meeting of the American Society for Reproductive Medicine, San Francisco, CA.
Levy, G. D., & Carter, D. B. (1989). Gender schema, gender constancy, and gender-role knowledge: The roles of cognitive factors in preschoolers' gender-role stereotype attributions. *Developmental Psychology, 25,* 444–449.
Levy-Shiff, R. (1994). Individual and contextual correlates of marital change across the transition to parenthood. *Developmental Psychology, 30,* 591–601.
Levy-Shiff, R., Goldschmidt, I., & Har-Even, D. (1991). Transition to parenthood in adoptive families. *Developmental Psychology, 27,* 131–140.
Levy-Shiff, R., Zoran, N., & Shulman, S. (1997). International and domestic adoption: Child, parents, and family adjustment. *International Journal of Behavioral Development, 20,* 109–129.
Lewin, T. (1997, April 23). Detention of pregnant women for drug use is struck down. *New York Times,* p. A-16.
Lewinsohn, P. M., Gotlib, I. H., Lewinsohn, M., Seeley, J. R., & Allen, N. B. (1998). Gender differences in anxiety disorders and anxiety symptoms in adolescence. *Journal of Abnormal Psychology, 107,* 109–117.
Lewis, M. (1995). Self-conscious emotions. *American Scientist, 83,* 68–78.
Lewis, M. (1997). The self in self-conscious emotions. In S. G. Snodgrass & R. L. Thompson (Eds.), *The self across psychology: Self-recognition, self-awareness, and the self-concept* (vol. 818). *Annals of the New York Academy of Sciences.* New York: The New York Academy of Sciences.
Lewis, M. (1998). Emotional competence and development. In D. Pushkar, W. Bukowski, A. E. Schwartzman, D. M. Stack, & D. R. White (Eds.), *Improving competence across the lifespan* (pp. 27–36). New York: Plenum.
Lewis, M., & Brooks, J. (1974). Self, other, and fear: Infants' reaction to people. In H. Lewis & L. Rosenblum (Eds.), *The origins of fear: The origins of behavior* (vol. 2). New York: Wiley.
Lewis, M., Worobey, J., Ramsay, D. S., & McCormack, M. K. (1992). Prenatal exposure to heavy metals: Effect on children cognitive skills and health status. *Pediatrics, 89,* 1010–1015.
Lewit, E., & Kerrebrock, N. (1997). Population-based growth stunting. *The Future of Children, 7*(2), 149–156.
Liaw, F., & Brooks-Gunn, J. (1993). Patterns of low-birth-weight children's cognitive development. *Developmental Psychology, 29,* 1024–1035.
Liberman, I. Y., & Liberman, A. M. (1990). Whole language vs. code emphasis: Underlying assumptions and their implications for reading instruction. *Annals of Dyslexia, 40,* 51–76.
Lickona, T. (Ed.). (1976). *Moral development and behavior.* New York: Holt.
Lie, R. T., Wilcox, A. J., & Skjaerven, R. (2001). Survival and reproduction among males with birth defects and risk of recurrence in their children. *Journal of the American Medical Association, 285,* 755–760.
Lillard, A., & Curenton, S. (1999). Do young children understand what others feel, want, and know? *Young Children, 54*(5), 52–57.
Lillard, A. S. (1998). Ethnopsychologies: Cultural variations in theory of mind. *Psychological Bulletin, 123,* 3–33.
Lillard, A. S., & Witherington, D. C. (2004). Mothers' behavior modifications during pretense and their possible signal value for toddlers. *Developmental Psychology, 40,* 95–113.
Lin, S. S., and Kelsey, J. L. (2000). Use of race and ethnicity in epidemiological research: Concepts, methodological issues, and suggestions for research. *Epidemiologic Reviews, 22*(2), 187–202.
Lin, S., Hwang, S. A., Marshall, E. G., & Marion, D. (1998). Does paternal occupational lead exposure increase the risks of low birth weight or prematurity? *American Journal of Epidemiology, 148,* 173–181.
Lindegren, M. L., Byers Jr., R. H., Thomas, P., Davis, S. F., Caldwell, B., Rogers, M., Gwinn, M., Ward, J. W., & Fleming, P. L. (1999). Trends in perinatal transmission of HIV/AIDS in the United States. *Journal of the American Medical Association, 282,* 531–538.
Lindwer, W. (1991). *The last seven months of Anne Frank* (A. Meersschaert, Trans.). New York: Pantheon.
Linney, J. A., & Seidman, E. (1989). The future of schooling. *American Psychologist, 44*(2), 336–340.
Lissau, I., Overpeck, M. D., Ruan, J., Due, P., Holstein, B. E., Hediger, M. L., & Health Behaviours in School-Aged Children Obesity Working Group. (2004). Body mass index and overweight in adolescents in 13 European countries, Israel, and the Untied States. *Archives of Pediatric and Adolescent Medicine, 158,* 27–33.
Litovitz, T. L., Klein-Schwartz, W., Caravati, E. M., Youniss, J., Crouch, B., & Lee, S. (1999). Annual report of the

American Association of Poison Control Centers Toxic Exposure Surveillance System. *American Journal of Emergency Medicine, 17,* 435–487.

Liu, J., Raine, A., Venables, P. H., Dalais, C., and Mednick, S. A. (2003). Malnutrition at age 3 years and lower cognitive ability at age 11 years. *Archives of Pediatric and Adolescent Medicine, 157,* 593–600.

Livson, N., & Peskin, H. (1980). Perspectives on adolescence from longitudinal research. In J. Adelson (Ed.), *Handbook of adolescent psychology.* New York: Wiley.

Llagas, C., & Snyder, T. D. (April 2003). *Status and trends in the Education of Hispanics.* Washington, DC: National Center for Education Statistics.

Lloyd, J. J., & Anthony, J. C. (2003). Hanging out with the wrong crowd: How much difference can parents make in an urban environment? *Journal of Urban Health, 80,* 383–399.

Lloyd, T., Andon, M. B., Rollings, N., Martel, J. K., Landis, J. R., Demers, L. M., Eggli, D. F., Kieselhorst, K., & Kulin, H. E. (1993). Calcium supplementation and bone mineral density in adolescent girls. *Journal of the American Medical Association, 270,* 841–844.

Lock, A., Young, A., Service, V., & Chandler, P. (1990). Some observations on the origin of the pointing gesture. In V. Volterra & C. J. Erting (Eds.), *From gesture to language in hearing and deaf children.* New York: Springer.

Lockwood, C. J. (2002). Predicting premature delivery—no easy task. *New England Journal of Medicine, 346,* 282–284.

Loeb, S., Fuller, B., Kagan, S. L., & Carrol, B. (2004). Child care in poor communities: Early learning effects of type, quality, and stability. *Child Development, 75,* 47–65.

Loewen, N., & Bancroft, A. (2001). *Four to the Pole: The American Women's Expedition to Antarctica, 1992–1993.* North Haven, CT: Shoestring Press.

Lonczak, H. S., Abbott, R. D., Hawkins, J. D., Kosterman, R., & Catalano, R. F. (2002). Effects of the Seattle Social Development Project on sexual behavior, pregnancy, birth, and sexually transmitted disease. *Archives of Pediatric and Adolescent Medicine, 156,* 438–447.

Longnecker, M. P., Klebanoff, M. A., Zhou, H., & Brock, J. W. (2001). Association between maternal serum concentration of the DDT metabolite DDE and preterm and small-for-gestational-age babies at birth. *Lancet, 358,* 110–114.

Lonigan, C. J., Burgess, S. R., & Anthony, J. L. (2000). Development of emergent literacy and early reading skills in preschool children: Evidence from a latent-variable longitudinal study. *Developmental Psychology, 36,* 593–613.

Lonigan, C. J., Fischel, J. E., Whitehurst, G. J., Arnold, D. S., & Valdez-Menchaca, M. C. (1992). The role of otitis media in the development of expressive language disorder. *Developmental Psychology, 28,* 430–440.

Lorenz, K. (1957). Comparative study of behavior. In C. H. Schiller (Ed.), *Instinctive behavior.* New York: International Universities Press.

Lorsbach, T. C., & Reimer, J. F. (1997). Developmental changes in the inhibition of previously relevant information. *Journal of Experimental Child Psychology, 64,* 317–342.

Louise Brown: From miracle baby to regular teen. (1994, February 7). *People Weekly,* p. 12.

Louise Brown: The world's first "test-tube baby" ushered in a revolution in fertility. (1984, March). *People Weekly,* p. 82.

Lourenco, O., & Machado, A. (1996). In defense of Piaget's theory: A reply to 10 common criticisms. *Psychological Review, 103*(1), 143–164.

Loveless, T. (2003). How well are American students learning? With special sections on homework, charter schools, and rural school achievement. *Brown Center Report on American Education, 1*(4). Washington, DC: Brookings Institution.

Lozoff, B., Klein, N. K., Nelson, E. C., McClish, D. K., Manuel, M., & Chacon, M. E. (1998). Behavior of infants with iron-deficiency anemia. *Child Development, 69,* 24–36.

Lubell, K. M., Swahn, M. H., Crosby, A. E., & Kegler, S. R. (2004). Methods of suicide among persons aged 10–19 years—United States, 1992–2001. *Morbidity and Mortality Weekly Report, 53,* 471–474.

Luecke-Aleksa, D., Anderson, D. R., Collins, P. A., & Schmitt, K. L. (1995). Gender constancy and television viewing. *Developmental Psychology, 31,* 773–780.

Lugaila, T. A. (1998). Marital status and living arrangements: March 1998 (update) *Current Population Reports* (p. 20–514). Washington, DC: U.S. Bureau of the Census.

Luke, B., Mamelle, N., Keith, L., Munoz, F., Minogue, J., Papiernik, E., Johnson, T. R., & Timothy, R. B. (1995). The association between occupational factors and preterm birth: A United States nurses' study. *American Journal of Obstetrics and Gynecology, 173,* 849–862.

Luman, E. T., McCauley, M. M., Shefer, A., & Chu, S. Y. (2003). Maternal characteristics associated with vaccination of young children. *Pediatrics, 111,* 1215–1218.

Lundy, B., Field, T., & Pickens, J. (1996). Newborns of mothers with depressive symptoms are less expressive. *Infant Behavior and Development, 19,* 419–424.

Lundy, B. L. (2003). Father- and mother-infant face-to-face interactions: Differences in mind-related comments and infant attachment? *Infant Behavior & Development, 26,* 200–212.

Lundy, B. L., Jones, N. A., Field, T., Nearing, G., Davalos, M., Pietro, P. A., Schanberg, S., & Kuhn, C. (1999). Prenatal depression effects on neonates. *Infant Behavior and Development, 22,* 119–129.

Luthar, S. S. (2003). The culture of affluence: Psychological costs of material wealth. *Child Development, 74*(6), 1581–1593.

Luthar, S. S., and Becker, B. E. (2002). Privileged but pressured? A study of affluent youth. *Child Development, 73*(5), 1593–1610.

Lydon-Rochelle, M., Holt, V. L., Easterling, T. R., & Martin, D. P. (2001). Risk of uterine rupture during labor among women with a prior cesarean delivery. *New England Journal of Medicine, 345,* 3–8.

Lyman, R. (1997, April 15). Michael Dorris dies at 52: Wrote of his son's suffering. *New York Times,* p. C24.

Lynskey, M. T., Heath, A. C., Bucholz, K. K., Slutske, W. S., Madden, P. A. F., Nelson, E. C., Statham, D. J., & Martin, N. G. (2003). Escalation of drug use in early-onset cannabis users versus co-twin controls. *Journal of the American Medical Association, 289,* 427–433.

Lyon, T. D., & Saywitz, K. J. (1999). Young maltreated children's competence to take the oath. *Applied Developmental Science, 3*(1), 16–27.

Lyons-Ruth, K., Alpern, L., & Repacholi, B. (1993). Disorganized infant attachment classification and maternal psychosocial problems as predictors of hostile-aggressive behavior in the preschool classroom. *Child Development, 64,* 572–585.

Lytton, H., & Romney, D. M. (1991). Parents' differential socialization of boys and girls: A meta-analysis. *Psychological Bulletin, 109*(2), 267–296.

Lyytinen, P., Poikkeus, A., Laakso, M., Eklund, K., & Lyytinen, H. (2001). Language development and symbolic play in children with and without familial risk for dyslexia. *Journal of Speech, Language, and Hearing Research, 44,* 873–885.

Maccoby, E. (1980). *Social development.* New York: Harcourt Brace Jovanovich.

Maccoby, E. E. (1984). Middle childhood in the context of the family. In W. A. Collins (Ed.), *Development during middle childhood.* Washington, DC: National Academy.

Maccoby, E. E. (1988). Gender as a social category. *Developmental Psychology, 24,* 755–765.

Maccoby, E. E. (1990). Gender and relationships: A developmental account. *American Psychologist, 45*(11), 513–520.

Maccoby, E. E. (1992). The role of parents in the socialization of children: An historical overview. *Developmental Psychology, 28,* 1006–1017.

Maccoby, E. E. (1994). Commentary: Gender segregation in childhood. In C. Leaper (Ed.), *Childhood gender segregation: Causes and consequences* (New Directions for Child Development No. 65, pp. 87–97). San Francisco: Jossey-Bass.

Maccoby, E. E., & Lewis, C. C. (2003). Less day care or different day care? *Child Development, 74,* 1069–1075.

Maccoby, E. E., & Martin, J. A. (1983). Socialization in the context of the family: Parent-child interaction. In P. H. Mussen (Series Ed.) & E. M. Hetherington (Vol. Ed.), *Handbook of child psychology: Vol. 4. Socialization, personality, and social development* (pp. 1–101). New York: Wiley.

Macfarlane, A. (1975). Olfaction in the development of social preferences in the human neonate. In *Parent-infant interaction* (CIBA Foundation Symposium No. 33). Amsterdam: Elsevier.

MacKinnon-Lewis, C., Starnes, R., Volling, B., & Johnson, S. (1997). Perceptions of parenting as predictors of boys' sibling and peer relations. *Developmental Psychology, 33,* 1024–1031.

Macklin, R. (2000). Ethical dilemmas in pediatric endocrinology: Growth hormone for short normal children. *Journal of Pediatric Endocrinology, 13*(6), 1349–1352.

Macmillan, C., Magder, L. S., Brouwers, P., Chase, C., Hittelman, J., Lasky, T., Malee, K., Mellins, C. A., & Velez-Borras, J. (2001). Head growth and neurodevelopment of infants born to HIV-1–infected drug-using women. *Neurology, 57,* 1402–1411.

MacMillan, H. M., Boyle, M. H., Wong, M. Y.-Y., Duku, E. K., Fleming, J. E., & Walsh, C. A. (1999). Slapping and spanking in childhood and its association with lifetime prevalence of psychiatric disorders in a general population sample. *Canadian Medical Association Journal, 161,* 805–809.

Macmillan, R., McMorris, B. J., & Kruttschnitt, C. (2004). Linked lives: Stability and change in maternal circumstances and trajectories of antisocial behavior in children. *Child Development, 75,* 205–220.

Madole, K. L., Oakes, L. M., & Cohen, L. B. (1993). Developmental changes in infants' attention to function and form-function correlations. *Cognitive Development, 8,* 189–209.

Madsen, K. M., Lauritsen, M. B., Pedersen, C. B., Thorsen, P. Plesner, A. M., Andersen, P. H., & Mortensen, P. B. (2003). Thimerosal and the occurrence of autism: Negative ecological evidence from the Danish population-based data. *Pediatrics, 112,* 604–606.

Mahoney, J. L. (2000). School extracurricular activity participation as a moderator in the development of antisocial patterns. *Child Development, 71*(2), 502–516.

Main, M. (1983). Exploration, play, and cognitive functioning related to infant-mother attachment. *Infant Behavior and Development, 6,* 167–174.

Main, M. (1995). Recent studies in attachment: Overview, with selected implications for clinical work. In S. Goldberg, R. Muir, & J. Kerr (Eds.), *Attachment theory: Social, developmental, and clinical perspectives* (pp. 407–470). Hillsdale, NJ: Analytic Press.

Main, M., & Solomon, J. (1986). Discovery of an insecure, disorganized/disoriented attachment pattern: Procedures, findings, and implications for the classification of behavior. In M. Yogman & T. B. Brazelton (Eds.), *Affective development in infancy.* Norwood, NJ: Ablex.

Main, M., Kaplan, N., & Cassidy, J. (1985). Security in infancy, childhood and adulthood: A move to the level of representation. In I. Bretherton & E.Waters (Eds.), Growing points in attachment. *Monographs of the Society for Research in Child Development, 50*(1–20), 66–104.

Makrides, M., Neumann, M., Simmer, K., Pater. J., & Gibson, R. (1995). Are long-chain polyunsaturated fatty acids essential nutrients in infancy? *Lancet, 345,* 1463–1468.

Malaspina, D., Harlap, S., Fennig, S., Heiman, D., Nahon, D., Feldman, D., & Susser, E. S. (2001). Advancing paternal age and the risk of schizophrenia. *Archives of General Psychiatry, 58,* 361–371.

Mandel, D. R., Jusczyk, P. W., & Pisoni, D. B. (1995). Infants' recognition of the sound patterns of their own names. *Psychological Science, 6*(5), 314–317.

Mandela, N. (1994). *Long walk to freedom: The autobiography of Nelson Mandela.* Boston: Little, Brown.

Mandler, J. (1998). The rise and fall of semantic memory. In M. A. Conway, S. E. Gathercole, & C. Cornoldi (Eds.), *Theories of memory* (vol. 2). East Sussex, England: Psychology Press.

Mandler, J. M. (1998). Representation. In D. Kuhn & R. S. Siegler (Eds.), *Handbook of child psychology,* Vol. 2: Cognition, perception, and language (5th ed., pp. 255–308). New York: Wiley.

Mandler, J. M., & McDonough, L. (1993). Concept formation in infancy. *Cognitive Development, 8,* 291–318.

Mandler, J. M., & McDonough, L. (1996). Drinking and driving don't mix: Inductive generalization in infancy. *Cognition, 59,* 307–335.

Mandler, J. M., & McDonough, L. (1998). Cognition across the life span: On developing a knowledge base in infancy. *Developmental Psychology, 34,* 1274–1288.

Manhardt, J., & Rescorla, L. (2002). Oral narrative skills of late talkers at ages 8 and 9. *Applied Psycholinguistics, 23,* 1–21.

Manlove, J., Ryan, S., & Franzetta, K. (2003). Patterns of contraceptive use within teenagers' first sexual relationships. *Perspectives on Sexual and Reproductive Health, 35,* 246–255.

Mannino, D. M., Homa, J. M., & Redd, S. C. (2002). Involuntary smoking and asthma severity in children: Data from the Third National Health and Nutrition Examination Survey (NHANES III). *Chest, 122, 409–415.*

March of Dimes Birth Defects Foundation. (1987). *Genetic counseling: A public health information booklet* (Rev. ed.). White Plains, NY: Author.

March of Dimes Foundation. (2002). *Toxoplasmosis.* (Fact Sheet). Wilkes-Barre, PA: Author.

March, J. S. (2004, June 1). *The Treatment of Adolescents with Depression Study (TADS): Primary efficacy outcomes.* Presentation at the New Clinical Drug Evaluation Unit conference, Phoenix, AZ.

Marcia, J. E. (1966). Development and validation of ego identity status. *Journal of Personality and Social Psychology, 3*(5), 551–558.

Marcia, J. E. (1979, June). *Identity status in late adolescence: Description and some clinical implications.* Address given at symposium on identity development, Rijksuniversitat Groningen, Netherlands.

Marcia, J. E. (1980). Identity in adolescence. In J. Adelson. (Ed.), *Handbook of adolescent psychology.* New York: Wiley.

Marcia, J. E. (1993). The relational roots of identity. In J. Kroger (Ed.), *Discussions on ego identity* (pp. 101–120). Hillsdale, NJ: Erlbaum.

Marcon, R. A. (1999). Differential impact of preschool models on development and early learning of inner-city children: A three-cohort study. *Developmental Psychology, 35*(2), 358–375.

Marcovitch, S., & Zelazo, P. D. (1999). The A-Not-B error: Results from a logistic meta-analysis. *Child Development, 70,* 1297–1313.

Marcus, G. F., Vijayan, S., Rao, S. B., & Vishton, P. M. (1999). Rule learning by seven-month-old infants. *Science, 283,* 77–80.

Margolis, L. H., Foss, R. D., & Tolbert, W. G. (2000). Alcohol and motor vehicle-related deaths of children as passengers, pedestrians, and bicyclists. *Journal of the American Medical Association, 283*(17), 2245–2248.

Markoff, J. (1992, October 12). Miscarriages tied to chip factories. *New York Times,* pp. A1, D2.

Marling, K. A. (1996). *Graceland: Going home with Elvis.* Cambridge, MA: Harvard University Press.

Marshall, T. A., Levy, S. M., Broffitt, B., Warren, J. J., Eichenberger-Gilmore, J. M., Burns, T. L., and Stumbo, P. J. (2003) Dental caries and beverage consumption in young children. *Pediatrics, 112,* e184–e191.

Martin, C. L., & Halverson, C. F. (1981). A schematic processing model of sex typing and stereotyping in children. *Child Development, 52,* 1119–1134.

Martin, C. L., & Ruble, D. (2004). Children's search for gender cues: Cognitive perspectives on gender development. *Current Directions in Psychological Science, 13,* 67–70.

Martin, C. L., Eisenbud, L., & Rose, H. (1995). Children's gender-based reasoning about toys. *Child Development, 66,* 1453–1471.

Martin, J. A., Hamilton, B. E., Sutton, P. D., Ventura, S. J., Menacker, F., & Munson, M. L. (2003). Births: Final data for 2002. *National Vital Statistics Reports, 52*(10). Hyattsville, MD: National Center for Health Statistics.

Martin, J. A., Hamilton, B. E., & Ventura, S. J. (2001). Births: Preliminary data for 2000. *National Vital Statistics Reports, 49*(5). Hyattsville, MD: National Center for Health Statistics.

Martin, J. A., Hamilton, B. E., Ventura, S. J., Menacker, F., & Park, M. M. (2002). Births: Final Data for 2000. *National Vital Statistics Reports, 50*(5). Hyattsville, MD: National Center for Health Statistics.

Martin, R., Noyes, J., Wisenbaker, J., & Huttunen, M. (2000). Prediction of early childhood negative emotionality and inhibition from maternal distress during pregnancy. *Merrill-Palmer Quarterly, 45,* 370–391.

Martínez-González, M. A., Gual, P., Lahortiga, F., Alonso, Y., de Irala-Estévez, J., & Cervera, S. (2003). Parental factors, mass media influences, and the onset of eating disorders in a prospective population based cohort. *Pediatrics, 111,* 315–320.

Marwick, C. (1997). Health care leaders from drug policy group. *Journal of the American Medical Association, 278,* 378.

Marwick, C. (1998). Physician leadership on national drug policy finds addiction treatment works. *Journal of the American Medical Association, 279,* 1149–1150.

Masataka, N. (1996). Perception of motherese in a signed language by 6-month-old deaf infants. *Developmental Psychology, 32,* 874–879.

Masataka, N. (1998). Perception of motherese in Japanese sign language by 6-month-old hearing infants. *Development Psychology, 34*(2), 241–246.

Mason, J. A., & Herrmann, K. R. (1998). Universal infant hearing screening by automated auditory brainstem response measurement. *Pediatrics, 101,* 221–228.

Masse, L. C., & Tremblay, R. E. (1997). Behavior of boys in kindergarten and the onset of substance use during adolescence. *Archives of General Psychiatry, 54,* 62–68.

Masten, A., Best, K., & Garmezy, N. (1990). Resilience and development: Contributions from the study of children who overcome adversity. *Development and Psychopathology, 2,* 425–444.

Masten, A. S. (2001). Ordinary magic: Resilience processes in development. *American Psychologist, 56,* 227–238.

Masten, A. S., & Coatsworth, J. D. (1998). The development of competence in favorable and unfavorable environments: Lessons from research on successful children. *American Psychologist, 53,* 205–220.

Mathews, T. J., & Ventura, S. J. (1997). *Birth and fertility rates by educational attainment: United States, 1994.* Monthly Vital Statistics Report, 45 (10, Suppl.), DHHS Publication No. PHS 97-1120. Hyattsville, MD: National Center for Health Statistics.

Mathews, T. J., Menacker, F., & MacDorman, M. F. (2003). Infant mortality statistics from the 2001 period linked birth/infant death data set. *National Vital Statistics Reports, 52*(2). Hyattsville, MD: National Center for Health Statistics.

Maurer, D., Stager, C. L., & Mondloch, C. J. (1999). Cross-modal transfer of shape is difficult to demonstrate in one-month-olds. *Child Development, 70,* 1047–1057.

May, K. A., & Perrin, S. P. (1985). Prelude: Pregnancy and birth. In S. M. H. Hanson & F. W. Bozett (Eds.), *Dimensions of fatherhood.* Beverly Hills, CA: Sage.

Mayer, D. P. (1998). Do new teaching standards undermine performance on old tests? *Educational Evaluation and Policy Analysis, 20,* 53–73.

Maynard, A. E. (2002). Cultural teaching: The development of teaching skills in Maya sibling interactions. *Child Development, 73,* 969–982.

Mayseless, O., & Scharf, M. (2003). What does it mean to be an adult? The Israeli experience. In J. J. Arnett & N. L. Galambos (Eds.), Exploring cultural conceptions of the transition to adulthood. *New Directions for Child and Adolescent Development, 100,* 5–20.

McCall, R. B., & Carriger, M. S. (1993). A meta-analysis of infant habituation and recognition memory performance as predictors of later IQ. *Child Development, 64,* 57–79.

McCarton, C. M., Brooks-Gunn, J., Wallace, I. F., Bauer, C. R., Bennett, F. C., Bernbaum, J. C., Broyles, S., Casey, P. H., McCormick, M. C., Scott, D. T., Tyson, J., Tonascia, J., & Meinert, C. L., for the Infant Health and Development Program Research Group. (1997). Results at age 8 years of early intervention for low-birth-weight premature infants. *Journal of the American Medical Association, 277,* 126–132.

McCarton, C. M., Wallace, I. F., Divon, M., & Vaughan, H. G. (1996). Cognitive and neurologic development of the preterm, small for gestational age infant through age 6: Comparison by birth weight and gestational age. *Pediatrics, 98,* 1167–1178.

McCartt, A. T. (2001). Graduated driver licensing systems: Reducing crashes among teenage drivers. *Journal of the American Medical Association, 286,* 1631–1632.

McCarty, M. E., Clifton, R. K., Ashmead, D. H., Lee, P., & Goubet, N. (2001). How infants use vision for grasping objects. *Child Development, 72,* 973–987.

McClearn, G. E., Johansson, B., Berg, S., Pedersen, N. L., Ahern, F., Petrill, S. A., & Plomin, R. (1997). Substantial genetic influence on cognitive abilities in twins 80 or more years old. *Science, 276,* 1560–1563.

McClintock, M. K., & Herdt, G. (1996). Rethinking puberty: The development of sexual attraction. *Current Directions in Psychological Science, 5*(6), 178–183.

McCord, J. (1996). Unintended consequences of punishment. *Pediatrics, 88,* 832–834.

McCormick, M. C., McCarton, C., Brooks-Gunn, J., Belt, P., & Gross, R. T. (1998). The infant health and development program: Interim summary. *Journal of Developmental and Behavioral Pediatrics, 19,* 359–371.

McCoy, A. R., & Reynolds, A. J. (1999). Grade retention and school performance: An extended investigation. *Journal of School Psychology, 37,* 273–298.

McGauhey, P. J., Starfield, B., Alexander, C., & Ensminget, M. E. (1991). Social environment and vulnerability of low birth weight children: A social-epidemiological perspective. *Pediatrics, 88,* 943–953.

McGee, R., Partridge, F., Williams, S., & Silva, P. A. (1991). A twelve-year follow-up of preschool hyperactive children. *Journal of the American Academy of Child and Adolescent Psychiatry, 30,* 224–232.

McGrath, M. M., Sullivan, M. C., Lester, B. M., and Oh, W. (2000). Longitudinal neurologic follow-up in neonatal intensive care unit survivors with various neonatal morbidities. *Pediatrics, 106*(6), 1397–1405.

McGreal, D., Evans, B. J., & Burrows, G. D. (1997). Gender differences in coping following loss of a child through miscarriage or stillbirth: A pilot study. *Stress Medicine, 13*(3), 159–165.

McGue, M. (1997). The democracy of the genes. *Nature, 388,* 417–418.

McGue, M., Bouchard, Jr., T. J., Iacono, W. G., & Lykken, D. T. (1993). Behavioral genetics of cognitive ability: A life-span perspective. In R. Plomin & G. E. McClearn (Eds.), *Nature, nurture and* *psychology* (pp. 59–76). Washington, DC: American Psychological Association.

McGuffin, P., Owen, M. J., & Farmer, A. E. (1995). Genetic basis of schizophrenia. *Lancet, 346,* 678–682.

McGuffin, P., Riley, B., & Plomin, R. (2001). Toward behavioral genomics. *Science, 291,* 1232, 1249.

McHale, S. M., Updegraff, K. A., Helms-Erikson, H., & Crouter, A. C. (2001). Sibling influences on gender development in middle childhood and early adolescence: A longitudinal study. *Developmental Psychology, 37,* 115–125.

McIntire, D. D., Bloom, S. L., Casey, B. M., & Leveno, K. J. (1999). Birth weight in relation to morbidity and mortality among newborn infants. *New England Journal of Medicine, 340,* 1234–1238.

McKay, N. Y. (1992). Introduction. In M. Anderson, *My Lord, what a morning* (pp. ix-xxxiii). Madison, WI: University of Wisconsin Press.

McKenna, J. J., & Mosko, S. (1993). Evolution and infant sleep: An experimental study of infant-parent co-sleeping and its implications for SIDS. *Acta Paediatrica, 389*(Suppl.), 31–36.

McKenna, J. J., Mosko, S. S., & Richard, C. A. (1997). Bedsharing promotes breastfeeding. *Pediatrics, 100,* 214–219.

McKinney, N. R., & Bennett, C. E. (1994). Issues regarding data on race and ethnicity: The Census Bureau experience. *Public Health Reports, 109,* 16–25.

McKusick, V. A. (2001). The anatomy of the human genome. *Journal of the American Medical Association, 286*(18), 2289–2295.

McLanahan, S., & Sandefur, G. (1994). *Growing up with a single parent.* Cambridge, MA: Harvard University Press.

McLeskey, J., Lancaster, M., & Grizzle, K. L. (1995). Learning disabilities and grade retention: A review of issues with recommendations for practice. *Learning Disabilities Research & Practice, 10,* 120–128.

McLoyd, V. C. (1990). The impact of economic hardship on black families and children: Psychological distress, parenting, and socioemotional development. *Child Development, 61,* 311–346.

McLoyd, V. C. (1998). Socioeconomic disadvantage and child development. *American Psychologist, 53,* 185–204.

McLoyd, V. C., Jayaratne, T. E., Ceballo, R., & Borquez, J. (1994). Unemployment and work interruption among African American single mothers: Effects on parenting and adolescent socioemotional functioning. *Child Development, 65,* 562–589.

McMahon, M. J., Luther, E. R., Bowes, W. A., & Olshan, A. F. (1996). Comparison of a trial of labor with an elective second cesarean section. *New England Journal of Medicine, 335,* 689–695.

McNeilly-Choque, M. K., Hart, C. H., Robinson, C. C., Nelson, L. J., & Olsen, S. F. (1996). Overt and relational aggression on the playground. Correspondence among different informants. *Journal of Research in Childhood Education, 11,* 47–67.

McNicholas, J., & Collis, G. M. (2001). Children's representations of pets in their social networks. *Child: Care, Health, & Development, 27,* 279–294.

McQuillan, J., Greil, A. L., White, L., & Jacob, M. C. (2003). Frustrated fertility: Infertility and psychological distress among women. *Journal of Marriage and Family, 65,* 1007–1018.

Mead, M. (1928). *Coming of age in Samoa.* New York: Morrow.

Mead, M. (1930). *Growing up in New Guinea.* New York: Blue Ribbon.

Mead, M. (1935). *Sex and temperament in three primitive societies.* New York: Morrow.

Mead, M. (1972). *Blackberry winter: My earlier years.* New York: Morrow.

Measelle, J. R., Ablow, J. C., Cowan, P. A., & Cowan, C. P. (1998). Assessing young children's view of their academic, social, and emotional lives: An evaluation of the self perception scales of the Berkeley Puppet Interview. *Child Development, 69,* 1556–1576.

Meehan, P. J. (1990). Prevention: The endpoint of suicidology. *Mayo Clinic Proceedings, 65,* 115–118.

Meeks, J. J., Weiss, J., & Jameson, J. L. (2003, May). Dax1 is required for testis formation. *Nature Genetics, 34,* 32–33.

Meer, F. (1988). *Higher than hope: The authorized biography of Nelson Mandela.* New York: Harper & Row.

Meier, D. (1995). *The power of their ideas.* Boston: Beacon.

Meier, R. (1991, January–February). Language acquisition by deaf children. *American Scientist, 79,* 60–70.

Meins, E. (1998). The effects of security of attachment and maternal attribution of meaning on children's linguistic acquisitional style. *Infant Behavior and Development, 21,* 237–252.

Meis, P. J., Klebanoff, M., Thom, E., Dombrowski, M. P., Sibai, B., Moawad, A. H., Spong, C. Y., Hauth, J. C., Miodovnik, M., Varner, M. W., Leveno, K. J., Caritis, S. N., Iams, J. D., Wapner, R. J., Conway, D., O'Sullivan, M. J., Carpenter, M., Mercer, B., Ramin, S. M., Thorp, J. M., Peaceman, A. M., Gabbe, S., & National Institute of Child Health and Human Development Maternal-Fetal Medicine Units Network. (2003). Prevention of recurrent preterm delivery by 17 alpha-hydroxyprogesterone caproate. *New England Journal of Medicine, 348,* 2379–2385.

Melson, G. F. (1998). The role of companion animals in human development. In D. D. Wilson & D. C. Turner (Eds.), *Companion animals in human health* (pp. 219–236). Thousand Oaks, CA: Sage.

Meltzoff, A. N. (1995). What infant memory tells us about infantile amnesia: Long-term recall and deferred imitation. *Journal of Experimental Child Psychology, 59,* 497–515.

Meltzoff, A. N., & Moore, M. K. (1983). Newborn infants imitate adult facial gestures. *Child Development, 54,* 702–709.

Meltzoff, A. N., & Moore, M. K. (1989). Imitation in newborn infants: Exploring the range of gestures imitated and the underlying mechanisms. *Developmental Psychology, 25,* 954–962.

Meltzoff, A. N., & Moore, M. K. (1994). Imitation, memory, and the representation of persons. *Infant Behavior and Development, 17,* 83–99.

Meltzoff, A. N., & Moore, M. K. (1998). Object representation, identity, and the paradox of early permanence: Steps toward a new framework. *Infant Behavior & Development, 21,* 201–235.

Mennella, J. A., & Beauchamp, G. K. (1996a). The early development of human flavor preferences. In E. D. Capaldi (Ed.), *Why we eat what we eat: The psychology of eating* (pp. 83–112). Washington DC: American Psychological Association.

Mennella, J. A., & Beauchamp, G. K. (1996b). The human infants' response to vanilla flavors in mother's milk and formula. *Infant Behavior and Development, 19,* 13–19.

Mennella, J. A., & Beauchamp, G. K. (2002). Flavor experiences during formula feeding are related to preferences during childhood. *Early Human Development, 68,* 71–82.

Ment, L. R., Vohr, B., Allan, W., Katz, K. H., Schneider, K. C., Westerveld, M., Duncan, C. C., & Makuch, R. W. (2003). Changes in cognitive function over time in very low-birth-weight infants. *Journal of the American Medical Association, 289,* 705–711.

Meyer, D. R., & Garasky, S. (1993). Custodial fathers: Myths, realities, and child support policy. *Journal of Marriage and the Family, 55,* 73–89.

Michelmore, P. (1962). *Einstein: Profile of the man.* London: Frederick Muller, Ltd.

Michelson, D., Faries, D., Wernicke, J., Kelsey, D., Kendrick, K., Sallee, F. R., Spencer, T., & the Atomoxetine ADHD Study Group from the Lilly Research Laboratories and Indiana University School of Medicine, University of Cincinnati, and Massachusetts General Hospital. (2001). Atomoxetine in the treatment of children and adolescents with attention deficit/hyperactivity disorder: A randomized, placebo-controlled, dose response study. *Pediatrics, 108,* e83.

Miedzian, M. (1991). *Boys will be boys: Breaking the link between masculinity and violence.* New York: Doubleday.

Milberger, S., Biederman, J., Faraone, S. V., Chen, L., & Jones, J. (1996). Is maternal smoking during pregnancy a risk factor for attention hyperactivity disorder in children? *American Journal of Psychiatry, 153,* 1138–1142.

Miller, B. C., & Moore, K. A. (1990). Adolescent sexual behavior, pregnancy, and parenting: Research through the 1980s. *Journal of Marriage and the Family, 52,* 1025–1044.

Miller, K. F., Smith, C. M., Zhu, J., & Zhang, H. (1995). Preschool origins of cross-national differences in mathematical competence: The role of number-naming systems. *Psychological Science, 6,* 56–60.

Miller, M. W., Astley, S. J., & Clarren, S. K. (1999). Number of axons in the corpus callosum of the mature macaca nemestrina: Increases caused by prenatal exposure to ethanol. *Journal of Comparative Neurology, 412,* 123–131.

Miller, V., Onotera, R. T., & Deinard, A. S. (1984). Denver Developmental Screening Test: Cultural variations in Southeast Asian children. *Journal of Pediatrics, 104*(3), 481–482.

Miller-Kovach, K. (2003). Childhood and adolescent obesity: A review of the scientific literature. Weight Watchers International: Unpublished ms.

Mills, D. L., Cofley-Corina, S. A., & Neville, H. J. (1997). Language comprehension and cerebral specialization from 13 to 20 months. *Developmental Neuropsychology, 13,* 397–445.

Mills, J. L., & England, L. (2001). Food fortification to prevent neural tube defects: Is it working? *Journal of the American Medical Association, 285,* 3022–3033.

Mills, J. L., Holmes, L. B., Aarons, J. H., Simpson, J. L., Brown, Z. A., Jovanovic-Peterson, L. G., Conley, M. R., Graubard, B. I., Knopp, R. H., & Metzger, B. E. (1993). Moderate caffeine use and the risk of spontaneous abortion and intrauterine growth retardation. *Journal of the American Medical Association, 269,* 593–597.

Milunsky, A. (1992). *Heredity and your family's health.* Baltimore: Johns Hopkins University Press.

Minnesota explorer Ann Bancroft (2002). Minnesota Public Radio. [Online]. http://news.mpr.org/programs/midmorning/. Access date: February 20, 2002.

Miotti, P. G., Taha, T. E. T., Kumwenda, N. I., Broadhead, R., Mtimavalye, L. A. R., van der Hoeven, L., Chiphangwi, J. D., Liomba, G., & Biggar, R. J. (1999). HIV transmission through breastfeeding: A study in Malawi. *Journal of the American Medical Association, 282,* 744–749.

Miserandino, M. (1996). Children who do well in school: Individual differences in perceived competence and autonomy in above-average children. *Journal of Educational Psychology, 88*(2), 203–214.

Misra, D. P., & Guyer, B. (1998). Benefits and limitations of prenatal care: From counting visits to measuring content. *Journal of the American Medical Association, 279,* 1661–1662.

Mistry, R. S., Vandewater, E. A., Huston, A. C., & McLoyd, V. (2002). Economic well-being and children's social adjustment: The role of family process in an ethnically diverse low income sample. *Child Development, 73,* 935–951.

Mittendorf, R. (1995). Teratogen update: Carcinogenesis and teratogenesis associated with exposure to diethylstilbestrol (DES) in utero. *Teratology, 51,* 435–445.

Mix, K. S., Huttenlocher, J., & Levine, S. C. (2002). Multiple cues for quantification in infancy: Is number one of them? *Psychological Bulletin, 128,* 278–294.

Mix, K. S., Levine, S. C., & Huttenlocher, J. (1999). Early fraction calculation ability. *Developmental Psychology, 35,* 164–174.

Miyake, K., Chen, S., & Campos, J. (1985). Infants' temperament, mothers' mode of interaction and attachment in Japan: An interim report. In I. Bretherton & E. Waters (Eds.), Growing points of attachment theory and research. *Monographs of the Society for Research in Child Development, 50*(1–2, Serial No. 109), 276–297.

Mlot, C. (1998). Probing the biology of emotion. *Science, 280,* 1005–1007.

Moffitt, T. E. (1993). Adolescent-limited and life-course persistent antisocial behavior: A developmental taxonomy. *Psychological Review, 100,* 674–701.

Moffitt, T. E., Caspi, A., Belsky, J., & Silva, P. A. (1992). Childhood experience and the onset of menarche: A test of a sociobiological model. *Child Development, 63,* 47–58.

Molina, B. S. G., & Chassin, L. (1996). The parent-adolescent relationship at puberty: Hispanic ethnicity and parent alcoholism as moderators. *Developmental Psychology, 32,* 675–686.

Molina, B. S. G., & Pelham Jr., W. E. (2003). Childhood predictors of adolescent substance use in a longitudinal study of children with ADHD. *Journal of Abnormal Psychology, 112,* 497–507.

Mondschein, E. R., Adolph, K. E., & Tamis-Lemonda, C. S. (2000). Gender bias in mothers' expectations about infant crawling. *Journal of Experimental Child Psychology. Special Issue on Gender, 77,* 304–316.

Money, J., & Ehrhardt, A. A. (1972). *Man and woman/Boy and girl.* Baltimore, MD: Johns Hopkins University Press.

Montague, C. T., Farooqi, I. S., Whitehead, J. P., Soos, M. A., Rau, H., Wareham, N. J., Sewter, C. P., Digby, J. E., Mohammed, S. N., Hurst, J. A., Cheetham, C. H., Earley, A. R., Barnett, A. H., Prins, J. B., & O'Rahilly, S. (1997). Congenital leptin deficiency is associated with severe early onset obesity in humans. *Nature, 387,* 903–908.

Montague, D. P. F., & Walker-Andrews, A. S. (2001). Peekaboo: A new look at infants' perception of emotion expressions. *Developmental Psychology, 37,* 826–838.

Montgomery, L. E., Kiely, J. L., & Pappas, G. (1996). The effects of poverty, race, and family structure on U.S. children's health: Data from the NHIS, 1978 through 1980 and 1989 through 1991. *American Journal of Public Health, 86,* 1401–1405.

Moon, C., & Fifer, W. P. (1990, April). *Newborns prefer a prenatal version of mother's voice.* Paper presented at the biannual meeting of the International Society of Infant Studies, Montreal, Canada.

Moon, C., Cooper, R. P., & Fifer, W. P. (1993). Two-day-olds prefer their native language. *Infant Behavior and Development, 16,* 495–500.

Moon, R. Y., Patel, K. M., & Shaefer, S. J. McD. (2000). Sudden infant death syndrome in child care settings. *Pediatrics, 106,* 295–300.

Mooney-Somers, J., & Golombok, S. (2000). Children of lesbian mothers: From the 1970s to the new millennium. *Sexual & Relationship Therapy 15*(2), 121–126.

Moore, S. E., Cole, T. J., Poskitt, E. M. E., Sonko, B. J., Whitehead, R. G., McGregor, I. A., & Prentice, A. M. (1997). Season of birth predicts mortality in rural Gambia. *Nature, 388,* 434.

Morelli, G. A., Rogoff, B., Oppenheim, D., & Goldsmith, D. (1992). Cultural variation in infants' sleeping arrangements: Questions of independence. *Developmental Psychology, 28,* 604–613.

Morgan, B., Maybery, M., & Durkin, K. (2003). Weak central coherence, poor joint attention, and low verbal ability: Independent deficits in early autism. *Developmental Psychology, 39,* 646–656.

Morison, P., & Masten, A. S. (1991). Peer reputation in middle childhood as a predictor of adaptation in adolescence: A seven-year follow-up. *Child Development, 62,* 991–1007.

Morison, S. J., & Ellwood, A.-L. (2000). Resiliency in the aftermath of deprivation: A second look at the development of Romanian orphanage children. *Merrill-Palmer Quarterly, 46,* 717–737.

Morison, S. J., Ames, E. W., & Chisholm, K. (1995). The development of children adopted from Romanian orphanages. *Merrill-Palmer Quarterly Journal of Developmental Psychology, 41,* 411–430.

Morissette, P., Ricard, M., & Decarie, T. G. (1995). Joint visual attention and pointing in infancy: A longitudinal study of comprehension. *British Journal of Development Psychology, 13,* 163–175.

Morris, R., & Kratochwill, T. (1983). *Treating children's fears and phobias: A behavioral approach.* Elmsford, NY: Pergamon.

Morris, R. D., Stuebing, K. K., Fletcher, J. M., Shaywitz, S. E., Lyon, G. R., Shankweiler, D. P., Katz, L., Francis, D. J., & Shaywitz, B. A. (1998). Subtypes of reading disability: Variability around a phonological core. *Journal of Educational Psychology, 90,* 347–373.

Morse, J. M., & Field, P. A. (1995). *Qualitative research methods for health professionals.* Thousand Oaks, CA: Sage.

Mortensen, E. L., Michaelson, K. F., Sanders, S. A., & Reinisch, J. M. (2002). The association between duration of breastfeeding and adult intelligence. *Journal of the American Medical Association, 287,* 2365–2371.

Mortensen, P. B., Pedersen, C. B., Westergaard, T., Wohlfahrt, J., Ewald, H., Mors, O., Andersen, P. K., & Melbye, M. (1999). Effects of family history and place and season of birth on the risk of schizophrenia. *New England Journal of Medicine, 340,* 603–608.

Mortimer, J. (2003). *Working and growing up in America.* Cambridge, MA: Harvard University Press.

Moses, L. J., Baldwin, D. A., Rosicky, J. G., & Tidball, G. (2001). Evidence for referential understanding in the emotions domain at twelve and eighteen months. *Child Development, 72,* 718–735.

Mosier, C. E., & Rogoff, B. (2003). Privileged treatment of toddlers: Cultural aspects of individual choice and responsibility. *Developmental Psychology, 39,* 1047–1060.

Moss, E., & St-Laurent, D. (2001). Attachment at school age and academic performance. *Developmental Psychology, 37,* 863–874.

Moss, M. H. (2003). Trends in childhood asthma: Prevalence, health care utilization, and mortality. *Pediatrics, 112,* 479.

Mounts, N. S., & Steinberg, L. (1995). An ecological analysis of peer influence on adolescent grade point average and drug use. *Developmental Psychology, 31,* 915–922.

MTA Cooperative Group. (1999). A 14-month randomized clinical trial of treatment strategies for attention deficit/hyperactivity disorder. *Archives of General Psychiatry, 56,* 1073–1986.

MTA Cooperative Group. (2004a). National Institute of Mental Health multimodal treatment study of ADHD follow-up: Changes in effectiveness and growth after the end of treatment. *Pediatrics, 113,* 762–769.

MTA Cooperative Group. (2004b). National Institute of Mental Health multimodal treatment study of ADHD follow-up: 24-month outcomes of treatment strategies for attention-deficit/hyperactivity disorder. *Pediatrics, 113,* 754–769.

Mullan, D., & Currie, C. (2000). Socioeconomic equalities in adolescent health. In C. Currie, K. Hurrelmann, W. Settertobulte, R. Smith, & J. Todd (Eds.), *Health and health behaviour among young people: A WHO crossnational study (HBSC) international report* (pp. 65–72). WHO Policy Series: Healthy Policy for Children and Adolescents, Series No. 1. Copenhagen, Denmark: World Health Organization Regional Office for Europe.

Müller, M. (1998). *Anne Frank: The biography.* New York: Holt.

Mumme, D. L., & Fernald, A. (2003). The infant as onlooker: Learning from emotional reactions observed in a television scenario. *Child Development, 74,* 221–237.

Munakata, Y. (2001). Task-dependency in infant behavior: Toward an understanding of the processes underlying cognitive development. In F. Lacerda, C. von Hofsten, & M. Heimann (Eds.), *Emerging cognitive abilities in early infancy.* Hillsdale, NJ: Erlbaum.

Munakata, Y., McClelland, J. L., Johnson, M. J., & Siegler, R. S. (1997). Rethinking infant knowledge: Toward an adaptive process account of successes and failures in object permanence tasks. *Psychological Review, 104,* 686–714.

Muñoz, K. A., Krebs-Smith, S. M., Ballard-Barbash, R., & Cleveland, L. E. (1997). Food intakes of U.S. children and adolescents compared with recommendations. *Pediatrics, 100,* 323–329.

Munson, M. L., & Sutton, P. D. (2004). Births, marriages, divorces, and deaths: Provisional data for November 2003. *National Vital Statistics Reports, 52*(20). Hyattsville, MD: National Center for Health Statistics.

Muntner, P., He, J., Cutler, J. A., Wildman, R. P., & Whelton, P. K. (2004, May 5). Trends in blood pressure among children and adolescents. *Journal of the American Medical Association, 291,* 2107–2113.

Murachver, T., Pipe, M., Gordon, R., Owens, J. L., & Fivush, R. (1996). Do, show, and tell: Children's event memories acquired through direct experience, observation, and stories. *Child Development, 67,* 3029–3044.

Murchison, C., & Langer, S. (1927). Tiedemann's observations on the development of the mental facilities of children. *Journal of Genetic Psychology, 34,* 204–230.

Muris, P., Merckelbach, H., & Collaris, R. (1997). Common childhood fears and their origins. *Behaviour Research and Therapy, 35,* 929–937.

Murphy, C. M., & Bootzin, R. R. (1973). Active and passive participation in the contact desensitization of snake fear in children. *Behavior Therapy, 4,* 203–211.

Murray, A. D., Dolby, R. M., Nation, R. L., & Thomas, D. B. (1981). Effects of epidural anesthesia on newborns and their mothers. *Child Development, 52,* 71–82.

Murray, B. (1998, June). Dipping math scores heat up debate over math teaching: Psychologists differ over the merits of teaching children "whole math." *APA Monitor, 29*(6), 34–35.

Murray, J. A., & Terry, D. J. (1999). Parental reactions to infant death: The effects of resources and coping strategies. *Journal of Social & Clinical Psychology, 18,* 341–369.

Mussen, P. H., & Jones, M. C. (1957). Self-conceptions, motivations, and interpersonal attitudes of late- and early-maturing boys. *Child Development, 28,* 243–256.

Must, A., Jacques, P. F., Dallal, G. E., Bajema, C. J., & Dietz, W. H. (1992). Long-term morbidity and mortality of overweight adolescents: A follow-up of the Harvard Growth Study of 1922 to 1935. *New England Journal of Medicine, 327*(19), 1350–1355.

Mustillo, S., Worthman, C., Erkanli, A., Keeler, G., Angold, A., & Costello, E. J. (2003). Obesity and psychiatric disorder: Developmental trajectories. *Pediatrics, 111,* 851–859.

Myers, J. E., & Perrin, N. (1993). Grandparents affected by parental divorce: A population at risk? *Journal of Counseling and Development, 72,* 62–66.

Naeye, R. L., & Peters, E. C. (1984). Mental development of children whose mothers smoked during pregnancy. *Obstetrics and Gynecology, 64,* 601.

Nafstad, P., Hagen, J. A., Oie, L., Magnus, P., & Jaakkola, J. J. K. (1999). Day care and respiratory health. *Pediatrics, 103,* 753–758.

Nagaoka, J., & Roderick, M. (April 2004). Ending social promotion: The effects of retention. Chicago: Consortium on Chicago School Research.

Naito, M., & Miura, H. (2001). Japanese childrens' numerical competencies: Age- and school-related influences on the development of number concepts and addition skills. *Developmental Psychology, 37,* 217–230.

Nansel, T. R., Overpeck, M., Pilla, R. S., Ruan, W. J., Simons-Morton, B., & Scheidt, P. (2001). Bullying behaviors among U.S. youth: Prevalence and association with psychosocial adjustment. *Journal of the American Medical Association, 285,* 2094–2100.

Nash, J. M. (1997, February 3). Fertile minds. *Time,* pp. 49–56.

Nash, O. (1957). *You Can't Get There From Here.* New York: Little Brown & Company.

Nathanielsz, P. W. (1995). The role of basic science in preventing low birth weight. *The Future of Our Children, 5*(1), 57–70.

National Center for Education Statistics (NCES). (1987). *Who drops out of high* school? From high school and beyond. Washington, DC: U.S. Department of Education, Office of Educational Research and Improvement.

National Center for Education Statistics (NCES). (1998, June). *Nonresident fathers can make a difference in children's school performance.* (Issue Brief, NCES 98–117).

National Center for Education Statistics (NCES). (1999). *The condition of education, 1999* (Publication No. 1999–022). Washington, DC: U.S. Government Printing Office.

National Center for Education Statistics (NCES). (2001). *The condition of education 2001* (Publication No. 2001–072). Washington, DC: U.S. Government Printing Office.

National Center for Education Statistics (NCES). (2003). *The condition of education, 2003* (Publication No. 2003–067). Washington, DC: Author.

National Center for Education Statistics (NCES). (2004). *The condition of education 2004* (NCES 2004–077). Washington, DC: U.S. Government Printing Office.

National Center for Education Statistics (NCES). (2004a). National assessment of educational progress: The nation's report card. Mathematics highlights 2003 (NCES 2004–451). Washington, DC: U.S. Department of Education.

National Center for Education Statistics (NCES). (2004b). National Assessment of Educational Progress: The nation's report card. Reading highlights 2003 (NCES 2004–452). Washington, DC: U.S. Department of Education.

National Center for Education Statistics (NCES). (2004c). *The condition of education, 2004* (Publication No. 2004–077). Washington, DC: Author.

National Center for Health Statistics (NCHS). (1994). Advance report of final natality statistics, 1992. *Monthly Vital Statistics Report, 43*(5, Suppl.). Hyattsville, MD: U.S. Public Health Service.

National Center for Health Statistics (NCHS). (1998). *Health, United States, 1998 with socioeconomic status and health chartbook.* Hyattsville, MD: Author.

National Center for Health Statistics (NCHS). (2001). *Health, United States, 2001 with urban and rural health chartbook.* Hyattsville, MD: U.S. Government Printing Office.

National Center for Health Statistics (NCHS). (2003). *Health, United States, 2003.* Hyattsville, MD: Author.

National Center for Injury Prevention and Control (NCIPC) (2001). *2001 United States suicide: Ages 15–19, all races, both sexes* (Web-based injury statistics query and reporting system) [Online]. Available: http://www.cdc.gov/ncipc. Access date: May 7, 2004.

National Center for Injury Prevention and Control (NCIPC) (2004). *Fact sheet: Teen drivers* [Online]. Available: http://www.cdc.gov/ncipc. Access date: May 7, 2004.

National Center for Learning Disabilities (2004a). *Dyslexia: Learning disabilities in reading.* Fact sheet. [Online]. Available: http://www.ld.org/LDInfoZone/InfoZone_FactSheet_Dyslexia.cfm. Access date: May 30, 2004.

National Center for Learning Disabilities (2004b). *LD at a glance.* Fact sheet. [Online]. Available: http://www.ld.org/LDInfoZone/InfoZone_FactSheet_LD.cfm. Access date: May 30, 2004.

National Center on Shaken Baby Syndrome. (2000). SBS questions. [Online]. Available: http://www.dontshake.com/sbsquestions.html.

National Child Abuse and Neglect Data System (NCANDS). (2001). *Child maltreatment 1999.* [Online]. Available: http://www.calib.com/nccanch/pubs.factsheets/canstats.cfm. Access date: April 8, 2002.

National Coalition for the Homeless. (2002, September). *How many people experience homelessness?* NCH Fact Sheet 2. Washington, DC: Author.

National Coalition for the Homeless. (2004, May). *Who is homeless?* NCH Fact Sheet 3. Washington, DC: Author.

National Commission for the Protection of Human Subjects of Biomedical and Behavioral Research. (1978). *Report.* Washington, DC: Author.

National Committee for Citizens in Education (NCCE). (1986, Winter Holiday). Don't be afraid to start a suicide prevention program in your school. *Network for Public Schools,* pp. 1, 4.

National Council of Teachers of Mathematics. (2000). *Principles and standards for school mathematics.* Reston, VA: National Council of Teachers of Mathematics.

National Enuresis Society. (1995). *Enuresis.* [Fact sheet].

National Highway Traffic Safety Administration. (2003). *Traffic safety facts 2002: Young drivers.* Washington, DC: Author.

National Institute of Child Health and Development (NICHD). (1997; updated 1/12/00). *Sudden Infant Death Syndrome.* Fact sheet. [Online]. Available: http://www.nichd.nih.gov/sids/sids_fact.htm. Access date: January 30, 2001.

National Institute of Child Health and Human Development (NICHD) Early Child Care Research Network & Duncan, G. J. (2003). Modeling the impacts of child care quality on children's preschool cognitive development. *Child Development, 74,* 1454–1475.

National Institute of Child Health and Human Development Early Child Care Research Network. (2004). Are child developmental outcomes related to before- and after-school care arrangements? Results from the NICHD Study of Early Child Care. *Child Development, 75,* 280–295.

National Institute of Mental Health (2001). *Teenage brain: A work in progress.* Available: http://www.nimh.gov/publicat/teenbrain.cfm. Access date: March 11, 2004.

National Institute of Mental Health (NIMH). (1999). *Suicide facts* [On-line]. Washington, DC: Author. Available: http://www.nimh.nih.gov/research/suifact.htm.

National Institute of Neurological Disorders and Stroke. (1999, November 10). *Autism* [Fact sheet]. NIH Publication No. 96-1877. Bethesda, MD: National Institutes of Health.

National Institute on Drug Abuse (NIDA). (1996). *Monitoring the future.* Washington, DC: National Institutes of Health.

National Institutes of Health (NIH). (1993). Early identification of hearing impairment in infants and young children. *NIH Consensus Statement, 11*(1), 1–24.

National Institutes of Health (NIH). (1998). Diagnosis and treatment of attention deficit hyperactivity disorder (ADHD). *NIH Consensus Statement, 16*(2), 1–37.

National Institutes of Health (NIH) Consensus Development Panel on Physical Activity and Cardiovascular Health. (1996). Physical activity and cardiovascular health. *Journal of the American Medical Association, 276,* 241–246.

National Institutes of Health Consensus Development Panel. (2001). National Institutes of Health Consensus Development conference statement: Phenylketonuria screening and management. October 16–18, 2000. *Pediatrics, 108*(4), 972–982.

National Parents' Resource Institute for Drug Education. (1999, September 8). *PRIDE surveys, 1998–99 national summary: Grades 6–12.* Bowling Green, KY: Author.

National Reading Panel (2000). *Report of the National Reading Panel: Teaching children to read: An evidence-based assessment of the scientific research literature on reading and its implications for reading instruction: Reports of the subgroups.* Washington, DC: National Institute of Child Health and Human Development.

National Research Council (NRC). (1993a). *Losing generations: Adolescents in high-risk settings.* Washington, DC: National Academy Press.

National Research Council (NRC). (1993b). *Understanding child abuse and neglect.* Washington, DC: National Academy Press.

National Sleep Foundation. (2004). *Sleep in America.* Washington, DC: Author.

National Television Violence Study. (1995). *Scientific papers: 1994–1995.* Studio City, CA: Mediascope.

National Television Violence Study. (1996). Key findings and recommendations. *Young Children, 51*(3), 54–55.

Nduati, R., John, G., Mbori-Ngacha, D., Richardson, B., Overbaugh, J., Mwatha, A., Ndinya-Achola, J., Bwayo, J., Onyango, F. E., Hughes, J., & Kreiss, J. (2000). Effect of breastfeeding and formula feeding on transmission of HIV-i. A randomized clinical trial. *Journal of the American Medical Association, 283*(9). 1167–1174.

Needleman, H. L., & Gatsonis, C. A. (1990). Low-level lead exposure and the IQ of children: A meta-analysis of modern studies. *Journal of the American Medical Association, 263,* 673–678.

Needleman, H. L., Riess, J. A., Tobin, M. J., Biesecker, G. E., & Greenhouse, J. B. (1996). Bone lead levels and delinquent behavior. *Journal of the American Medical Association, 275,* 363–369.

Nef, S. Verma-Kurvari, S., Merenmies, J., Vassallt, J.-D., Efstratiadis, A., Accili, D., & Parada, L. F. (2003). Testis determination requires insulin receptor family function in mice. *Nature, 426,* 291–295.

Neisser, U., Boodoo, G., Bouchard Jr., T. J., Boykin, A. W., Brody, N., Ceci, S. J., Halpern, D. F., Loehlin, J. C., Perloff, R., Sternberg, R. J., & Urbina, S. (1996). Intelligence: Knowns and unknowns. *American Psychologist, 51*(2), 77–101.

Neitzel, C., & Stright, A. D. (2003). Relations between parents' scaffolding and children's academic self-regulation: Establishing a foundation of self-regulatory competence. *Journal of Family Psychology, 17,* 147–159.

Nelson, C. A. (1995). The ontogeny of human memory: A cognitive neuroscience perspective. *Developmental Psychology, 31,* 723–738.

Nelson, C. A., & Monk, C. S. (2001). The use of event-related potentials in the study of cognitive development. In C. A. Nelson & M. Luciana (Eds.), *Handbook of developmental cognitive neuroscience* (pp. 125–136). Cambridge, MA: MIT Press.

Nelson, C. A., Monk, C. S., Lin, J., Carver, L. J., Thomas, K. M., & Truwit, C. L. (2000). Functional neuroanatomy of spatial working memory in children. *Developmental Psychology, 36,* 109–116.

Nelson, F. H., Rosenberg, B., & Van Meter, N. (2004). *Charter school achievement on the 2003 National Assessment of Educational Progress.* Washington, DC: American Federation of Teachers, AFL-CIO.

Nelson, K. (1992). Emergence of autobiographical memory at age 4. *Human Development, 35,* 172–177.

Nelson, K. (1993a). Events, narrative, memory: What develops? In C. Nelson (Ed.), *Memory and affect in development: The Minnesota Symposia on Child Psychology* (vol. 26, pp. 1–24). Hillsdale, NJ: Erlbaum.

Nelson, K. (1993b). The psychological and social origins of autobiographical memory. *Psychological Science, 47,* 7–14.

Nelson, K. B., Dambrosia, J. M., Ting, T. Y., & Grether, J. K. (1996). Uncertain value of electronic fetal monitoring in predicting cerebral palsy. *New England Journal of Medicine, 334,* 613–618.

Nelson, L. J. (2003). Rites of passage in emerging adulthood: Perspectives of young Mormons. In J. J. Arnett and N. L. Galambos (Eds.), Exploring cultural conceptions of the transition to adulthood. *New Directions for Child and Adolescent Development, 100,* 33–49.

Nelson, L. J., & Marshall, M. F. (1998). *Ethical and legal analyses of three coercive policies aimed at substance abuse by pregnant women.* Report published by the Robert Wood Johnson Substance Abuse Policy Research Foundation.

Neppl, T. K., & Murray, A. D. (1997). Social dominance and play patterns among preschoolers: Gender comparisons. *Sex Roles, 36,* 381–393.

Netherlands State Institute for War Documentation. (1989). *The diary of Anne Frank: The critical edition* (D. Barnouw & G. van der Stroom, Eds.; A. J. Pomerans & B. M. Mooyaart-Doubleday, Trans.). New York: Doubleday.

Neugebauer, R., Hoek, H. W., & Susser, E. (1999). Prenatal exposure to wartime famine and development of antisocial personality disorder in early adulthood. *Journal of the American Medical Association, 282,* 455–462.

Neville, H. J., & Bavelier, D. (1998). Neural organization and plasticity of language. *Current Opinion in Neurobiology, 8*(2), 254–258.

Newacheck, P. W., & Halfon, N. (2000). Prevalence, impact, and trends in childhood disability due to asthma. *Archives of Pediatrics and Adolescent Medicine, 154,* 287–293.

Newacheck, P. W., Stoddard, J. J., & McManus, M. (1993). Ethnocultural variations in the prevalence and impact of childhood chronic conditions. *Pediatrics, 91,* 1031–1047.

Newacheck, P. W., Strickland, B., Shonkoff, J. P., Perrin, J. M., McPherson, M., McManus, M., Lauver, C., Fox, H., & Arango, P. (1998). An epidemiologic profile of children with special health care needs. *Pediatrics, 102,* 117–123.

Newcomb, A. F., & Bagwell, C. L. (1995). Children's friendship relations: A meta-analytic review. *Psychological Bulletin, 117*(2), 306–347.

Newcomb, A. F., Bukowski, W. M., & Pattee, L. (1993). Children's peer relations: A meta-analytic review of popular, rejected, neglected, controversial, and average sociometric status. *Psychological Bulletin, 113,* 99–128.

Newman, A. J., Bavelier, D., Corina, D., Jezzard, P., & Neville, H. J. (2002). A critical period for right hemisphere recruitment in American Sign Language processing. *Nature Neuroscience, 5*(1), 76–80.

Newman, D. L., Caspi, A., Moffitt, T. E., & Silva, P. A. (1997). Antecedents of adult interpersonal functioning: Effects of individual differences in age 3 temperament. *Developmental Psychology, 33,* 206–217.

Newman, J. (1995). How breast milk protects newborns. *Scientific American, 273,* 76–79.

Newport, E., & Meier, R. (1985). The acquisition of American Sign Language. In D. Slobin (Ed.), *The crosslinguistic study of language acquisition* (vol. 1, pp. 881–938). Hillsdale, NJ: Erlbaum.

Newport, E. L. (1991). Contrasting conceptions of the critical period for language. In S. Carey & R. Gelman (Eds.), *The epigenesis of mind: Essays on biology and cognition.* Hillsdale, NJ: Erlbaum.

Newport, E. L., Bavelier, D., & Neville, H. J. (2001). Critical thinking about critical periods: Perspectives on a critical period for language acquisition. In E. Dupoux, Emmanuel (Ed.), *Language, brain, and cognitive development: Essays in honor of Jacques Mehler* (pp. 481–502). Cambridge, MA: The MIT Press.

Newson, J., Newson, E., & Mahalski, P. A. (1982). Persistent infant comfort habits and their sequelae at 11 and 16 years. *Journal of Child Psychology and Psychiatry, 23,* 421–436.

NICHD Early Child Care Research Network. (1996). Characteristics of infant child care: Factors contributing to positive caregiving. *Early Childhood Research Quarterly, 11,* 269–306.

NICHD Early Child Care Research Network. (1997a). The effects of infant child care on infant-mother attachment security: Results of the NICHD study of early child care. *Child Development. 68,* 860–879.

NICHD Early Child Care Research Network. (1997b). Familial factors associated with the characteristics of nonmaternal care for infants. *Journal of Marriage and the Family, 59,* 389–408.

NICHD Early Child Care Research Network. (1998a). Early child care and self-control, compliance and problem behavior at 24 and 36 months. *Child Development, 69,* 1145–1170.

NICHD Early Child Care Research Network. (1998b). Relations between family predictors and child outcomes: Are they weaker for children in child care? *Developmental Psychology, 34,* 1119–1127.

NICHD Early Child Care Research Network. (1998c, November). *When child-care classrooms meet recommended guidelines for quality.* Paper presented at the meeting of the National Association for the Education of Young People.

NICHD Early Child Care Research Network. (1999a). Child outcomes when child care center classes meet recommended standards for quality. *American Journal of Public Health, 89,* 1072–1077.

NICHD Early Child Care Research Network. (1999b). Chronicity of maternal depressive symptoms, maternal sensitivity, and child functioning at 36 months. *Developmental Psychology, 35,* 1297–1310.

NICHD Early Child Care Research Network. (2000). The relation of child care to cognitive and language development. *Child Development, 71,* 960–980.

NICHD Early Child Care Research Network. (2001a). Child care and children's peer interaction at 24 and 36 months: The NICHD Study of Early Child Care. *Child Development, 72,* 1478–1500.

NICHD Early Child Care Research Network. (2001b). Child-care and family predictors of preschool attachment and stability from infancy. *Developmental Psychology, 37,* 847–862.

NICHD Early Child Care Research Network. (2002). Child-care structure "process" outcome: Direct and indirect effects of child-care quality on young children's development. *Psychological Science, 13,* 199–206.

NICHD Early Child Care Research Network. (2003). Does amount of time spent in child care predict socioemotional adjustment during the transition to kindergarten? *Child Development, 74,* 976–1005.

NICHD Early Child Care Research Network (2004). Are child developmental outcomes related to before- and after-school care arrangement? Results from the NICHD Study of Early Child Care. *Child Development 75,* 280–295.

Nielsen, K., McSherry, G., Petru, A., Frederick, T., Wara, D., Bryson, Y., Martin, N., Hutto, C., Ammann, A. J., Grubman, S., Oleske, J., & Scott, G. B. (1997). A descriptive survey of pediatric human immunodeficiency virus-infected, long-term survivors [Online]. *Pediatrics, 99.* Available: http://www.pediatrics.org/cgi/content/full/99/4/e4.

Nielsen, M., Dissanayake, C., & Kashima, Y. (2003). A longitudinal investigation of self-other discrimination and the emergence of mirror self-recognitoin. *Infant Behavior & Development, 26,* 213–226.

Nin, A. (1971). *The Diaries of Anaïs Nin* (vol. IV). New York: Harcourt.

Nisan, M., & Kohlberg, L. (1982). Universality and variation in moral judgment: A longitudinal and cross sectional study in Turkey. *Child Development, 53,* 865–876.

Nishimura, H., Hashikawa, K., Doi, K., Iwaki, T., Watanabe, Y., Kusuoka, H., Nishimura, T., & Kubo, T. (1999). Sign language "heard" in the auditory cortex. *Nature, 397,* 116.

Niskar, A. S., Kieszak, S. M., Holmes, A., Esteban, E., Rubin, C., & Brody D. J. (1998). Prevalence of hearing loss among children 6 to 19 years of age: The Third National Health and Nutrition Examination Survey. *Journal of the American Medical Association, 279,* 1071–1075.

Nix, R. L., Pinderhughes, E. E., Dodge, K. A., Bates, J. E., Pettit, G. S., & McFadyen-Ketchum, S. A. (1999). The relation between mothers' hostile attribution tendencies and children's externalizing behavior problems: The mediating role of mothers' harsh discipline practices. *Child Development, 70*(4), 896–909.

Nobre, A. C., & Plunkett, K. (1997). The neural system of language: Structure and development. *Current Opinion in Neurobiology, 7,* 262–268.

Noirot, E., & Algeria, J. (1983). Neonate orientation towards human voice differs with type of feeding. *Behavioral Processes, 8,* 65–71.

Noone, K. (2000). Ann Bancroft, polar explorer. *MyPrimeTime.* [Online]. Available: http://www.myprimetime.com/misc/bae_abpro/index.shtml. Access date: April 4, 2002.

Norwitz, E. R., Schust, D. J., and Fisher, S. J. (2001). Implantation and the survival of early pregnancy. *New England Journal of Medicine, 345*(19), 1400–1408.

Notzon, F. C. (1990). International differences in the use of obstetric interventions. *Journal of the American Medical Association, 263*(24), 3286–3291.

Nourot, P. M. (1998). Sociodramatic play: Pretending together. In D. P. Fromberg & D. Bergen (Eds.), *Play from birth to twelve and beyond: Contexts, perspectives, and meanings* (pp. 378–391). New York: Garland.

Nozyce, M., Hittelman, J., Muenz, L., Durako, S. J., Fischer, M. L., & Willoughby, A. (1994). Effect of perinatally acquired human immunodeficiency virus infection on neurodevelopment in children during the first two years of life. *Pediatrics, 94,* 883–891.

Nugent, J. K., Lester, B. M., Greene, S. M., Wieczorek-Deering, D., & O'Mahony, P. (1996). The effects of maternal alcohol consumption and cigarette smoking during pregnancy on acoustic cry analysis. *Child Development, 67,* 1806–1815.

Nugent, T. (1999, September). At risk: 4 million students with asthma: Quick access to rescue inhalers critical for schoolchildren. *AAP News,* pp. 1, 10.

Nurnberger, J. I., Foroud, T., Flury, L., Su, J., Meyer, E. T., Hu, K., Crowe, R., Edenberg, H., Goate, A., Bierut, L., Reich, T., Schuckit, M., & Reich, W. (2001). Evidence for a locus on chromosome 1 that influences vulnerability to alcoholism and affective disorder. *American Journal of Psychiatry, 158,* 718–724.

O'Connor, T., Heron, J., Golding, J., Beveridge, M., & Glover, V. (2002). Maternal antenatal anxiety and children's behavioural/emotional problems at 4 years. *British Journal of Psychiatry, 180,* 502–508.

O'Rahilly, S. (1998). Life without leptin. *Nature, 392,* 330–331.

O'Sullivan, J. T., Howe, M. L., & Marche, T. A. (1996). Children's beliefs about long-term retention. *Child Development, 67,* 2989–3009.

Oakes, L. M. (1994). Development of infants' use of continuity cues in their perception of causality. *Developmental Psychology, 30,* 869–879.

Oakes, L. M., Coppage, D. J., & Dingel, A. (1997). By land or by sea: The role of perceptual similarity in infants' categorization of animals. *Developmental Psychology, 33,* 396–407.

Oakes, L. M., & Madole, K. L. (2000). The future of infant categorization research: A process-oriented approach. *Child Development, 71,* 119–126.

Ochsner, K. N., & Lieberman, M. D. (2001). The emergence of social cognitive neuroscience. *American Psychologist, 56,* 717–734.

Offer, D. (1987). In defense of adolescents. *Journal of the American Medical Association, 257,* 3407–3408.

Offer, D., & Church, R. B. (1991). Generation gap. In R. M. Lerner, A. C. Petersen, & J. Brooks-Gunn (Eds.), *Encyclopedia of adolescence* (pp. 397–399). New York: Garland.

Offer, D., & Schonert-Reichl, K. A. (1992). Debunking the myths of adolescence: Findings from recent research. *Journal of the American Academy of Child and Adolescent Psychiatry, 31,* 1003–1014.

Offer, D., Kaiz, M., Ostrov, E., & Albert, D. B. (2002). Continuity in family constellation. *Adolescent and Family Health, 3,* 3–8.

Offer, D., Offer, M. K., & Ostrov, E. (2004). *Regular guys: 34 years beyond adolescence.* Dordrecht, Netherlands: Kluwer Academic.

Offer, D., Ostrov, E., & Howard, K. I. (1989). Adolescence: What is normal? *American Journal of Diseases of Children, 143,* 731–736.

Offer, D., Ostrov, E., Howard, K. I., & Atkinson, R. (1988). *The teenage world: Adolescents' self-image in ten countries.* New York: Plenum.

Offit, P. A., Quarles, J., Gerber, M. A., Hackett, C. J., Marcuse, E. K., Kollman, T. R., Gellin, B. G., & Landry, S. (2002). Addressing parents' concerns: Do multiple vaccines overwhelm or weaken the infant's immune system? *Pediatrics, 109,* 124–129.

Ogden, C. L., Flegal, K. M., Carroll, M. D., & Johnson, C. L. (2002). Prevalence and trends in overweight among U.S. children and adolescents, 1999–2000. *Journal of the American Medical Association, 288,* 1728–1732.

Ogden, C. L., Troiano, R. P., Briefel, R. R., Kuczmarski, R. J., Flegal, K. M., & Johnson, C. L. (1997). Prevalence of overweight among preschool children in the United States, 1971 through 1994 [Online]. *Pediatrics, 99.* Available: http://www.pediatrics.org/cgi/content/full/99/4/el.

Ojito, M. (2003, July 28). A writer's heartbeats answer two calls. *New York Times,* p. E1.

Olds, D. L., Eckenrode, J., Henderson Jr., C. R., Kitzman, H., Powers, J., Cole, R., Sidora, K., Morris, P., Pettitt, L. M., & Luckey, D. (1997). Long-term effects of home visitation on maternal life course and child abuse and neglect: Fifteen-year follow-up of a randomized trial. *Journal of the American Medical Association, 278,* 637–643.

Olds, D. L., Henderson, C. R., & Tatelbaum, R. (1994a). Intellectual impairment in children of women who smoke cigarettes during pregnancy. *Pediatrics, 93,* 221–227.

Olds, D. L., Henderson, C. R., & Tatelbaum, R. (1994b). Prevention of intellectual impairment in children of women who smoke cigarettes during pregnancy. *Pediatrics, 93,* 228–233.

Olds, D. L., Henderson, C. R., Klitzman, H. J., Eckenrode, J. J., Cole, R. E., & Tatelbaum, R. C. (1999). Prenatal and infancy home visitation by nurses: Recent findings. *The Future of Children, 9,* 44–65.

Olds, S. W. (1989). *The working parents' survival guide.* Rocklin, CA: Prima.

Olds, S. W. (2002). *A balcony in Nepal: Glimpses of a Himalayan village.* Lincoln, NE: ASJA Books, an imprint of iUniverse.

Olfson, M., Shaffer, D., Marcus, S. C., & Greenberg, T. (2003). Relationship between antidepressant medication treatment and suicide in adolescents. *Archives of General Psychiatry, 60,* 978–982.

Ollendick, T. H., Yang, B., King, N. J., Dong, Q., & Akande, A. (1996). Fears in American, Australian, Chinese, and Nigerian children and adolescents: A crosscultural study. *Journal of Child Psychology and Psychiatry, 37,* 213–220.

Olthof, T., Schouten, A., Kuiper, H., Stegge, H., & Jennekens-Schinkel, A. (2000). Shame and guilt in children: Differential situational antecedents and experiential correlates. *British Journal of Developmental Psychology, 18,* 51–64.

Olweus, D. (1995). Bullying or peer abuse at school: Facts and intervention. *Current Directions in Psychological Science, 4,* 196–200.

Orr, D. P., & Ingersoll, G. M. (1995). The contribution of level of cognitive complexity and pubertal timing behavioral risk in young adolescents. *Pediatrics, 95*(4), 528–533.

Oshima-Takane, Y., Goodz, E., & Derevensky, J. L. (1996). Birth order effects on early language development: Do secondborn children learn from overheard speech? *Child Development, 67,* 621–634.

Ostrea, E. M., & Chavez, C. J. (1979). Perinatal problems (excluding neonatal withdrawal) in maternal drug addiction: A study of 830 cases. *Journal of Pediatrics, 94*(2), 292–295.

Owen, C. G., Whincup, P. H., Odoki, K., Gilg, J. A., & Cook, D. G. (2002). Infant feeding and blood cholesterol: A study in adolescents and a systematic review. *Pediatrics, 110,* 597–608.

Owens, J., Maxim, R., McGuinn, M., Nobile, C., Msall, M., & Alario, A. (1999). Television viewing habits and sleep disturbances in school children. *Pediatrics, 104*(3), e27.

Owens, R. E. (1996). *Language development* (4th ed.). Boston: Allyn & Bacon.

Ozick, C. (2003, June 16 & 23). What Helen Keller saw: The making of a writer. *New Yorker,* pp. 188–196.

Padden, C. A. (1996). Early bilingual lives of deaf children. In I. Parasnis (Ed.), *Cultural and language diversity and the deaf experience* (pp. 99–116). New York: Cambridge University Press.

Padilla, A. M., Lindholm, K. J., Chen, A., Duran, R., Hakuta, K., Lambert, W., & Tucker, G. R. (1991). The English-only movement: Myths, reality, and implications for psychology. *American Psychologist, 46*(2), 120–130.

Palella, F. J., Delaney, K. M., Moorman, A. C., Loveless, M. O., Fuhrer, J., Satten, G. A., Aschman, D. J., Holmberg, S. D., & the HIV Outpatient Study investigators. (1998). Declining morbidity and mortality among patients with advanced human immunodeficiency virus infection. *New England Journal of Medicine, 358,* 853–860.

Palkovitz, R. (1985). Fathers' birth attendance, early contact, and extended contact with their newborns: A critical review. *Child Development, 56,* 392–406.

Pally, R. (1997). How brain development is shaped by genetic and environmental factors. *International Journal of Psycho-Analysis, 78,* 587–593.

Panigrahy, A., Filiano, J., Sleeper, L. A., Mandell, F., Valdes-Dapena, M., Krous, H. F., Rava, L. A., Foley, E., White, W. F., & Kinney, H. C. (2000). Decreased serotonergic receptor binding in rhombic lip-derived regions of the medulla oblongata in the sudden infant death syndrome. *Journal of Neuropathology and Experimental Neurology, 59,* 377–384.

Papalia, D. (1972). The status of several conservation abilities across the lifespan. *Human Development, 15,* 229–243.

Park, S., Belsky, J., Putnam, S., & Crnic, K. (1997). Infant emotionality, parenting, and 3-year inhibition: Exploring stability and lawful discontinuity in a male sample. *Developmental Psychology, 33,* 218–227.

Parke, R. D. (2004). The Society for Research in Child Development at 70: Progress and promise. *Child Development, 75,* 1–24.

Parke, R. D., & Buriel, R. (1998). Socialization in the family: Ethnic and ecological perspectives. In W. Damon (Series Ed.) & N. Eisenberg (Vol. Ed.), *Handbook of child psychology: Vol. 3. Social, emotional, and personality development* (5th ed., pp. 463–552). New York: Wiley.

Parke, R. D., Grossman, K., & Tinsley, R. (1981). Father-mother-infant interaction in the newborn period: A German-American comparison. In T. M. Field, A. M. Sostek, P. Viete, & P. H. Leideman (Eds.), *Culture and early interaction.* Hillsdale, NJ: Erlbaum.

Parke, R. D., Ornstein, P. A., Rieser, J. J., & Zahn-Waxler, C. (1994). The past as prologue: An overview of a century of developmental psychology. In R. D. Parke, P. A. Ornstein, J. J. Rieser, & C. Zahn-Waxler (Eds.), *A century of developmental psychology* (pp. 1–70). Washington, DC: American Psychological Association.

Parker, J. G., & Asher, S. R. (1987). Peer relations and later personal adjustment: Are low-accepted children at risk? *Psychological Bulletin, 102,* 357–389.

Parker, L., Pearce, M. S., Dickinson, H. O., Aitkin, M., & Craft, A. W. (1999). Stillbirths among offspring of male radiation workers at Sellafield Nuclear Reprocessing Plant. *Lancet, 354,* 1407–1414.

Parmelee, A. H. (1986). Children's illnesses: Their beneficial effects on behavioral development. *Child Development, 57,* 1–10.

Parmelee, A. H., Wenner, W. H., & Schulz, H. R. (1964). Infant sleep patterns: From birth to 16 weeks of age. *Journal of Pediatrics, 65,* 576.

Parrish, K. M., Bolt, V. L., Easterling, T. R., Connell, F. A., & LeGerfo, J. P.

(1994). Effect of changes in maternal age, parity, and birth weight distribution on primary cesarean delivery rates. *Journal of the American Medical Association, 271,* 443–447.

Parten, M. B. (1932). Social play among preschool children. *Journal of Abnormal and Social Psychology, 27,* 243–269.

Patenaude, A. F., Guttmacher, A. E., & Collins, F. S. (2002). Genetic testing and psychology: New roles, new responsibilities. *American Psychologist, 57,* 271–282.

Patrick, K., Norman, G. J., Calfas, K. J., Sallis, J. F., Zabinski, M. F., Rupp, J., & Cella, J. (2004). Diet, physical activity, and sedentary behaviors as risk factors for overweight in adolescence. *Archives of Pediatric Adolescent Medicine, 158,* 385–390.

Patterson, C. J. (1992). Children of lesbian and gay parents. *Child Development, 63,* 1025–1042.

Patterson, C. J. (1995a). Lesbian mothers, gay fathers, and their children. In A. R. D'Augelli & C. J. Patterson (Eds.), *Lesbian, gay, and bisexual identities over the lifespan: Psychological perspectives* (pp. 293–320). New York: Oxford University Press.

Patterson, C. J. (1995b). Sexual orientation and human development: An overview. *Developmental Psychology, 31,* 3–11.

Patterson, C. J. (1997). Children of gay and lesbian parents. In T. H. Ollendick & R. J. Prinz (Eds.), *Advances in clinical child psychology* (vol. 19, pp. 235–282). New York: Plenum.

Patterson, G. R. (1995). Coercion—A basis for early age of onset for arrest. In J. McCord (Ed.), *Coercion and punishment in long-term perspective* (pp. 81–105). New York: Cambridge University Press.

Patterson, G. R., DeBaryshe, B. D., & Ramsey, E. (1989). A developmental perspective on antisocial behavior. *American Psychologist, 44*(2), 329–335.

Patterson, G. R., Reid, J. B., & Dishion, T. J. (1992). *Antisocial boys.* Eugene, OR: Castalia.

Pauen, S. (2002). Evidence for knowledge-based category discrimination in infancy. *Child Development, 73,* 1016–1033.

Pearce, M. J., Jones, S. M., Schwab-Stone, M. E., & Ruchkin, V. (2003). The protective effects of religiousness and parent involvement on the development of conduct problems among youth exposed to violence. *Child Development, 74,* 1682–1696.

Peirce, C. S. (1931). In C. Hartshorne, P. Weiss, and A. Burks (Eds.), *The collected papers of Charles Sanders Peirce.* Cambridge, MA: Harvard University Press.

Peisner-Feinberg, E. S., Burchinal, M. R., Clifford, R. M., Culkin, M. L., Howes, C., Kagan, S. L., & Yazejian, N. (2001). The relation of preschool child-care quality to children's cognitive and social developmental trajectories through second grade. *Child Development, 72,* 1534–1553.

Pellegrini, A. D. (1998). Rough-and-tumble play from childhood through adolescence. In D. P. Fromberg & D. Bergen (Eds.), *Play from birth to twelve and beyond: Contexts, perspectives, and meanings* (pp. 401–408). New York: Garland.

Pellegrini, A. D., & Long, J. D. (2002). A longitudinal study of bullying, dominance, and victimization during the transition from primary school through secondary school. *British Journal of Developmental Psychology, 20,* 259–280.

Pellegrini, A. D., & Smith, P. K. (1998). Physical activity play: The nature and function of a neglected aspect of play. *Child Development, 69,* 577–598.

Pellegrini, A. D., Kato, K., Blatchford, P., & Baines E. (2002). A short-term longitudinal study of children's playground games across the first year of school: Implications for social competence and adjustment to school. *American Educational Research Journal, 39,* 991–1015.

Pelletier, A. R., Quinlan, K. P., Sacks, J. J., Van Gilder, T. J., Gilchrist, J., & Ahluwalia, H. K. (2000). Injury prevention practices as depicted in G-rated and PG-rated movies, *Archives of Pediatrics and Adolescent Medicine, 154,* 283–286.

Pelleymounter, N. A., Cullen, M. J., Baker, M. B., Hecht, R., Winters, D., Boone, T., & Collins, F. (1995). Effects of the obese gene product on body regulation in ob/ob mice. *Science, 269,* 540–543.

Pellicano, E., & Rhodes, G. (2003). Holistic processing of faces in preschool children and adults. *Psychological Science, 14,* 618–622.

Pennington, B. F., Moon, J., Edgin, J., Stedron, J., & Nadel, L. (2003). The neuropsychology of Down Syndrome: Evidence for hippocampal dysfunction. *Child Development, 74,* 75–93.

Pepper, S. C. (1961). *World hypotheses.* Berkeley: University of California Press.

Perera, F. P., Rauh, V., Whyatt, R. M., Tsai, W.-Y., Bernert, J. T., Tu, Y.-H., Andrews, H., Ramirez, J., Qu, L., & Tang, D. (2004). Molecular evidence of an interaction between prenatal environmental exposures and birth outcomes in a multiethnic population. *Environmental Health Perspectives, 112,* 626–630.

Perera, F. P., Tang, D., Tu, Y.-H., Cruz, L. A., Borjas, M., Bernert, T., & Whyatt, R. M. (2004). Biomarkers in maternal and newborn blood indicate heightened fetal susceptibility to procarcinogenic DNA damage. *Environmental Health Perspectives, 112,* 1133–1136.

Perera, V. (1995). Surviving affliction. [Online.] Available: http://www.metroactive.com/papers/metro/12.14.95/allende-9550.html. Access date: April 1, 2002.

Perex, L. (1994). The households of children and immigrants in south Florida: An exploratory study of extended family arrangements. *International Migration Review, 28*(4), 736–747.

Perner, J., Sprung, M., Zauner, P., & Haider, H. (2003). *Want that* is understood well before *say that, think that,* and false belief: A test of de Villier's linguistic determinism on German-speaking children. *Child Development, 74,* 179–188.

Perozynski, L., & Kramer, L. (1999). Parental beliefs about managing sibling conflict. *Developmental Psychology, 35,* 489–499.

Perrin, E. C., and the Committee on Psychosocial Aspects of Child and Family Health. (2002). Technical report: Coparent or second-parent adoption by same-sex parents. *Pediatrics, 109*(2), 341–344.

Pérusse, L., Chagnon, Y. C., Weisnagel, J., & Bouchard, C. (1999). The human obesity gene map: The 1998 update. *Obesity Research, 7,* 111–129.

Peskin, H. (1967). Pubertal onset and ego functioning. *Journal of Abnormal Psychology, 72,* 1–15.

Peskin, H. (1973). Influence of the developmental schedule of puberty on learning and ego functioning. *Journal of Youth and Adolescence, 2,* 273–290.

Pesonen, A., Räikkönen, K., Keltikangas-Järvinen, L., Strandberg, T., & Järvenpäa, A. (2003). Parental perception of infant temperament: Does parents' joint attachment matter? *Infant Behavior & Development, 26,* 167–182.

Pesonen, A., Räikkönen, K., Keskivaara, P., Keltikangas-Järvinen, L. (2003). Difficult temperment in childhood and adulthood: Continuity from maternal perceptions to self-ratings over 17 years. *Personality and Individual Differences, 34,* 19–31.

Peters, V., Liu, K.-L., Dominguez, K., Frederick, T., Melville, S., Hsu, H.-W., Ortiz, I., Rakusan, T., Gill, B., & Thomas, P. (2003). Missed opportunities for perinatal HIV prevention among HIV-exposed infants born 1996–2000, Pediatric Spectrum of HIV Disease Cohort. *Pediatrics, 111,* 1186–1191.

Petersen, A. C. (1993). Presidential address: Creating adolescents: The role of context and process in developmental transitions. *Journal of Research on Adolescents, 3*(1), 1–18.

Petersen, A. C., Compas, B. E., Brooks-Gunn, J., Stemmler, M., Ey, S., & Grant, K. E. (1993). Depression in adolescence. *American Psychologist, 48*(2), 155–168.

Peterson, C., & McCabe, A. (1994). A social interactionist account of developing decontextualized narrative skill. *Developmental Psychology, 30,* 937–948.

Peterson, J. T. (1993). Generalized extended family exchange: A case from the

Philippines. *Journal of Marriage and the Family, 55*(3), 570–584.

Peterson, J. L., Moore, K. A., & Furstenberg Jr., F. F. (1991). Television viewing and early initiation of sexual intercourse: Is there a link? *Journal of Homosexuality, 21,* 93–118.

Peth-Pierce, R. (1998). *The NICHD study of early child care* [Online]. Available: http://www.nih.gov/nichd/html/news/early-child/Early_Child_Care.htm.

Petitto, L. A., & Kovelman, I. (2003). The bilingual paradox: How signing-speaking bilingual children help us to resolve it and teach us about the brain's mechanisms underlying all language acquisition. *Learning Languages, 8,* 5–18.

Petitto, L. A., & Marentette, P. F. (1991). Babbling in the manual mode: Evidence for the ontogeny of language. *Science, 251,* 1493–1495.

Petitto, L. A., Holowka, S., Sergio, L., & Ostry, D. (2001). Language rhythms in babies' hand movements. *Nature, 413,* 35–36.

Petitto, L. A., Katerelos, M., Levy, B., Gauna, K., Tetrault, K., & Ferraro, V. (2001). Bilingual signed and spoken language acquisition from birth: Implications for mechanisms underlying bilingual language acquisition. *Journal of Child Language, 28,* 1–44.

Pettit, G. S., Bates, J. E., & Dodge, K. A. (1997). Supportive parenting, ecological context, and children's adjustment: A seven-year longitudinal study. *Child Development, 68,* 908–923.

Pharaoh, P. D. P., Antoniou, A., Bobrow, M., Zimmern, R. L., Easton, D. F., & Ponder, B. A. J. (2002). Polygenic susceptibility to breast cancer and implications for prevention. *Nature Genetics, 31,* 33–36.

Phelps, J. A., Davis, J. O., & Schartz, K. M. (1997). Nature, nurture, and twin research strategies. *Current Directions in Psychological Science, 6*(5), 117–121.

Philipp, B. L., Merewood, A., Miller, L. W., Chawla, N., Murphy-Smith, M. M., Gomes, J. S., Cimo, S., & Cook, J. T. (2001). Baby-friendly hospital initiative improves breastfeeding initiation rates in a U. S. hospital setting. *Pediatrics, 108*(3), 677–681.

Phillips, D. F. (1998). Reproductive medicine experts till an increasingly fertile field. *Journal of the American Medical Association, 280,* 1893–1895.

Phinney, J. S. (1998). Stages of ethnic identity development in minority group adolescents. In R. E. Muuss & H. D. Porton (Eds.), *Adolescent behavior and society: A book of readings* (pp. 271–280). Boston: McGraw-Hill.

Phinney, J. S., & Cobb, N. J. (1996). Reasoning about intergroup relations among Hispanic and Euro-American adolescents. *Journal of Adolescent Research, 11,* 306–324.

Piaget, J. (1932). *The moral judgment of the child.* New York: Harcourt Brace.

Piaget, J. (1951). *Play, dreams, and imitation* (C. Gattegno & F. M. Hodgson, Trans.). New York: Norton.

Piaget, J. (1952). *The origins of intelligence in children.* New York: International Universities Press. (Original work published 1936.)

Piaget, J. (1954). *The construction of reality in the child.* New York: Basic.

Piaget, J. (1962). *The language and thought of the child* (M. Gabain, Trans.). Cleveland, OH: Meridian. (Original work published 1923).

Piaget, J. (1964). *Six psychological studies.* New York: Vintage.

Piaget, J. (1969). *The child's conception of time* (A. J. Pomerans, Trans.). London: Routledge & Kegan Paul.

Piaget, J. (1971). *The construction of reality in the child.* New York: Ballantine. (Original work published 1954, Basic Books).

Piaget, J. (1972). Intellectual evolution from adolescence to adulthood. *Human Development, 15,* 1–12.

Piaget, J., & Inhelder, B. (1967). *The child's conception of space.* New York: Norton.

Piaget, J., & Inhelder, B. (1969). *The psychology of the child.* New York: Basic Books.

Pickering, L. K., Granoff, D. M., Erickson, J. R., Mason, M. L., Cordle, C. T., Schaller, J. P., Winship, T. R., Paule, C. L., & Hilty, M. D. (1998). Modulation of the immune system by human milk and infant formula containing nucleotides. *Pediatrics, 101,* 242–249.

Pickett, W., Streight, S., Simpson, K., & Brison, R. J. (2003). Injuries experienced by infant children: A population-based epidemiological analysis. *Pediatrics, 111,* e365–e370.

Pierce, K. M., Hamm, J. V., & Vandell, D. L. (1999). Experiences in afterschool programs and children's adjustment in first-grade classrooms. *Child Development, 70*(3), 756–767.

Pillow, B. H., & Henrichon, A. J. (1996). There's more to the picture than meets the eye: Young children's difficulty understanding biased interpretation. *Child Development, 67,* 803–819.

Piña, J. A. (1999). The "uncontrollable" rebel. In J. Rodden (Ed.), *Conversations with Isabel Allende* (pp. 167–200). Austin: University of Texas Press.

Pinborg, A., Loft, A., Schmidt, L., & Andersen, A. N. (2003). Morbidity in a Danish national cohort of 472 IVF/ICSI twins and 634 IVF/ICSI singletons: Health-related and social implications for the children and their families. *Human Reproduction, 18,* 1234–1243.

Pines, M. (1981). The civilizing of Genie. *Psychology Today, 15*(9), 28–34.

Pirkle, J. L., Brody, D. J., Gunter, E. W., Kramer, R. A., Raschal, D. C., Flegal, K. M., & Matte, T. D. (1994). The decline in blood levels in the United States. *Journal of the American Medical Association, 272,* 284–291.

Pirkle, J. L., Flegal, K. M., Bernert, J. T., Brody, D. J., Etzel, R. A., & Maurer, K. R. (1996). Exposure of the U.S. population to environmental tobacco smoke: The Third National Health and Nutrition Examination Survey, 1988–1991. *Journal of the American Medical Association, 275,* 1233–1240.

Pleck, J. H. (1997). Paternal involvement: Levels, sources, and consequences. In M. E. Lamb et al. (Eds.), *The role of the father in child development* (3d ed., pp. 66–103). New York: Wiley.

Plomin, R. (1989). Environment and genes: Determinants of behavior. *American Psychologist, 44*(2), 105–111.

Plomin, R. (1990). The role of inheritance in behavior. *Science, 248,* 183–188.

Plomin, R. (1995). Molecular genetics and psychology. *Current Directions in Psychological Science, 4*(4), 114–117.

Plomin, R. (1996). Nature and nurture. In M. R. Merrens & G. G. Brannigan (Eds.), *The developmental psychologist: Research adventures across the life span* (pp. 3–19). New York: McGraw-Hill.

Plomin, R. (2001). Genetic factors contributing to learning and language delays and disabilities. *Child & Adolescent Psychiatric Clinics of North America, 10*(2), 259–277.

Plomin, R., & Crabbe, J. (2000). DNA. *Psychological Bulletin, 126*(6), 806–828.

Plomin, R., & Daniels, D. (1987). Why are children in the same family so different from one another? *Behavioral and Brain Sciences, 10,* 1–16.

Plomin, R., & DeFries, J. C. (1999). The genetics of cognitive abilities and disabilities. In S. J. Ceci & W. M. Williams (Eds.), *The nature nurture debate: The essential readings* (pp. 178–195). Malden, MA: Blackwell.

Plomin, R., & Rutter, M. (1998). Child development, molecular genetics, and what to do with genes once they are found. *Child Development, 69*(4), 1223–1242.

Plomin, R., Owen, M. J., & McGuffin, P. (1994). The genetic bases of behavior. *Science, 264,* 1733–1739.

Plotkin, S. A., Katz, M., & Cordero, J. F. (1999). The eradication of rubella. *Journal of the American Medical Association, 281,* 561–562.

Plumert, J., & Nichols-Whitehead, P. (1996). Parental scaffolding of young children's spatial communication. *Developmental Psychology, 32,* 523–532.

Plumert, J. M. (1995). Relations between children's overestimation of their physical abilities and accident proneness. *Developmental Psychology, 31,* 866–876.

Plumert, J. M., Pick Jr., H. L., Marks, R. A., Kintsch, A. S., & Wegesin, D. (1994). Locating objects and communicating about locations: Organizational differences in children's searching and direction-giving. *Developmental Psychology, 30,* 443–453.

Polit, D. F., & Falbo, T. (1987). Only children and personality development: A quantitative review. *Journal of Marriage and the Family, 49,* 309–325.

Pollock, L. A. (1983). *Forgotten children.* Cambridge, England: Cambridge University Press.

Pomerantz, E. M., & Saxon, J. L. (2001). Conceptions of ability as stable and self-evaluative processes: A longitudinal examination. *Child Development, 72,* 152–173.

Pong, S. L. (1997). Family structure, school context, and eighth-grade math and reading achievement. *Journal of Marriage and the Family, 59,* 734–746.

Pope, A. W., Bierman, K. L., & Mumma, G. H. (1991). Aggression, hyperactivity, and inattention-immaturity: Behavior dimensions associated with peer rejection in elementary school boys. *Developmental Psychology, 27,* 663–671.

Portwood, S. G., & Repucci, N. D. (1996). Adults' impact on the suggestibility of preschoolers' recollections. *Journal of Applied Developmental Psychology, 17,* 175–198.

Posada, G., Gao, Y., Wu, F., Posada, R., Tascon, M., Schoelmerich, A., Sagi, A., Kondo-Ikemura, K., Haaland, W., & Synnevaag, B. (1995). The secure-base phenomenon across cultures: Children's behavior, mothers' preferences, and experts' concepts. In E. Waters, B. E. Vaughn, G. Posada, & K. Kondo-Ikemura (Eds.), Care-giving, cultural, and cognitive perspectives on secure-base behavior and working models: New growing points of attachment theory and research (pp. 27–48). *Monographs of the Society for Research in Child Development,* 60(2–3, Serial No. 244).

Posner, J. K., & Vandell, D. L. (1999). After-school activities and the development of low-income urban children: A longitudinal study. *Developmental Psychology, 35*(3), 868–879.

Posner, M. L., & DiGirolamo, G. J. (2000). Cognitive neuroscience: Origins and promise. *Psychological Bulletin, 126*(6), 873–889.

Post, S. G. 1994 . Ethical commentary: Genetic testing for Alzheimer's disease. *Alzheimer Disease and Associated Disorders, 8,* 66–67.

Povinelli, D. J., & Giambrone, S. (2001). Reasoning about beliefs: A human specialization? *Child Development, 72,* 691–695.

Povinelli, D. J., Landau, K. R., & Perilloux, H. K. (1996). Self-recognition in young children using delayed versus live feedback: Evidence of a developmental asynchrony. *Child Development, 67,* 1540–1554.

Powell, M. B., & Thomson, D. M. (1996). Children's memory of an occurrence of a repeated event: Effects of age, repetition, and retention interval across three question types. *Child Development, 67,* 1988–2004.

Power, T. G., & Chapieski, M. L. (1986). Childrearing and impulse control in toddlers: A naturalistic investigation. *Developmental Psychology, 22,* 271–275.

Powlishta, K. K., Serbin, L. A., Doyle, A. B., & White, D. R. (1994). Gender, ethnic, and body type biases: The generality of prejudice in childhood. *Developmental Psychology, 30,* 526–536.

Prechtl, H. F. R., & Beintema, D. J. (1964). The neurological examination of the full-term newborn infant. *Clinics in Developmental Medicine* (No. 12). London: Heinemann.

Price, J. M. (1996). Friendships of maltreated children and adolescents: Contexts for expressing and modifying relationship history. In W. M. Bukowski, A. F. Newcomb, & W. W. Hartup (Eds.), *The company they keep: Friendship in childhood and adolescence* (pp. 262–285). New York: Cambridge University Press.

Price-Williams, D. R., Gordon, W., & Ramirez III, M. (1969). Skills and conservation: A study of potterymaking children. *Developmental Psychology, 1,* 769.

Princeton Survey Research Associates. (1996). *The 1996 Kaiser Family Foundation Survey on Teens and Sex: What they say teens today need to know, and who they listen to.* Menlo Park, CA: Kaiser Family Foundation.

Princiotta, D., Bielick, S., & Chapman, C. (2004). *1.1 million homeschooled students in the United States in 2003* (NCES 2004–115). Washington, DC: National Center for Education Statistics.

Proctor, B. D., & Dalaker, J. (2003). *Poverty in the United States: 2002* (Current Population Reports, Series P60–222). Washington, DC: U.S. Government Printing Office.

ProEnglish (2002). *The status of bilingual education.* Fact sheet. [Online]. Available: http://www.proenglish.org/issues/education/bestatus.html. Access date: May 30, 2004.

Purcell, J. H. (1995). Gifted education at a crossroads: The program status study. *Gifted Child Quarterly, 39*(2), 57–65.

Putallaz, M., & Bierman, K. L. (Eds.). (2004). *Aggression, antisocial behavior, and violence among girls: A developmental perspective.* New York: Guilford.

Quadrel, M. J., Fischoff, B., & Davis, W. (1993). Adolescent (in) vulnerability. *American Psychologist, 48,* 102–116.

Quasha, S. (1980). *Albert Einstein: An intimate portrait.* Larchmont, NY: Forest.

Quinlan, K. P., Brewer, R. D., Sleet, D. A., & Dellinger, A. M. (2000). Characteristics of child passenger deaths and injuries involving drinking drivers. *Journal of the American Medical Association, 283,* 2249–2252.

Quinn, P. C., Eimas, P. D., & Rosenkrantz, S. L. (1993). Evidence for representations of perceptually similar natural categories by 3-month-old and 4-month-old infants. *Perception, 22,* 463–475.

Quintero, R. A., Abuhamad, A., Hobbins, J. C., & Mahoney, M. J. (1993). Transabdominal thin-gauge embryofetoscopy: A technique for early prenatal diagnosis and its use in the diagnosis of a case of Meckel-Gruber syndrome. *American Journal of Obstetrics and Gynecology, 168,* 1552–1557.

Rabiner, D., & Coie, J. (1989). Effect of expectancy induction on rejected peers' acceptance by unfamiliar peers. *Developmental Psychology, 25,* 450–457.

Rader, N., Bausano, M., & Richards, J. E. (1980). In the nature of the visual-cliff avoidance response in human infants. *Child Development, 51,* 61–68.

Raffaelli, M., & Crockett, L. J. (2003). Sexual risk-taking in adolescence: The role of self-regulation and attraction to risk. *Developmental Psychology, 39,* 1036–1046.

Rafferty, Y., & Shinn, M. (1991). Impact of homelessness on children. *American Psychologist, 46*(11), 1170–1179.

Raine, A., Mellingen, K., Liu, J., Venables, P., & Mednick, S. (2003). Effects of environmental enrichment at ages 3–5 years in schizotypal personality and antisocial behavior at ages 17 and 23 years. *American Journal of Psychiatry, 160,* 1627–1635.

Ram, A., & Ross, H. S. (2001). Problem solving, contention, and struggle: How siblings resolve a conflict of interests. *Child Development, 72,* 1710–1722.

Ramey, C. T., & Campbell, F. A. (1991). Poverty, early childhood education, and academic competence. In A. Huston (Ed.), *Children reared in poverty* (pp. 190–221). Cambridge, England: Cambridge University Press.

Ramey, C. T., & Ramey, S. L. (1996). Early intervention: Optimizing development for children with disabilities and risk conditions. In M. Wolraich (Ed.), *Disorders of development and learning: A practical guide to assessment and management* (2d ed., pp. 141–158). Philadelphia: Mosby.

Ramey, C. T., & Ramey, S. L. (1998a). Early intervention and early experience. *American Psychologist, 53,* 109–120.

Ramey, C. T., & Ramey, S. L. (1998b). Prevention of intellectual disabilities: Early interventions to improve cognitive development. *Preventive Medicine, 21,* 224–232.

Ramey, C. T., Campbell, F. A., Burchinal, M., Skinner, M. L., Gardner, D. M., & Ramey, S. L. (2000). Persistent effects of early childhood education on high-risk children and their mothers. *Applied Developmental Science, 4*(1), 2–14.

Ramey, S. L. (1999). Head Start and preschool education: Toward continued improvement. *American Psychologist, 54,* 344–346.

Ramey, S. L., & Ramey, C. T. (1992). Early educational intervention with disadvantaged children—To what effect? *Applied and Preventive Psychology, 1,* 131–140.

Ramirez, J. M. (2003). Hormones and aggression in childhood and adolescence. *Aggression and Violent Behavior, 8,* 621–644.

Ramoz, N., Reichert, J. G., Smith, C. J., Silverman, J. M., Bespalova, I. N., Davis, K. L., & Buxbaum, J. D. (2004). Linkage and association of the mitochondrial aspartate/glutamate carrier SLC25A12 gene with autism. *American Journal of Psychiatry, 161,* 662–669.

Rampersad, A. (1997). *Jackie Robinson: A biography.* New York: Knopf.

Ramsey, P. G., & Lasquade, C. (1996). Preschool children's entry attempts. *Journal of Applied Developmental Psychology, 17,* 135–150.

Rao, R., & Georgieff, M. K. (2000). Early nutrition and brain development. *The effects of early adversity on neurobehavioral development. The Minnesota Symposia on Child Psychology* (vol. 31, pp. 1–30). Mahwah, NJ: Lawrence Erlbaum Associates.

Rapin, I. (1997). Autism. *New England Journal of Medicine, 337,* 97–104.

Rappaport, L. (1993). The treatment of nocturnal enuresis—Where are we now? *Pediatrics, 92,* 465–466.

Rask-Nissilä, L., Jokinen, E., Terho, P., Tammi, A., Lapinleimu, H., Ronnemaa, T., Viikari, J., Seppanen, R., Korhonen, T., Tuominen, J., Valimaki, I., & Simell, O. (2000). Neurological development of 5-year-old children receiving a low-saturated fat, low cholesterol diet since infancy. *Journal of the American Medical Association, 284*(8), 993–1000.

Rathbun, A., West, J., & Germino-Hausken, E. (2004). From kindergarten through third grade: Children's beginning school experiences (NCES 2004–007). Washington, DC: National Center for Education Statistics.

Ratner, H. H., & Foley, M. A. (1997, April). *Children's collaborative learning: Reconstructions of the other in the self.* Paper presented at the meeting of the Society for Research in Child Development, Washington, DC.

Rauh, V. A., Whyatt, R. M., Garfinkel, R., Andrews, H., Hoepner, L., Reyes, A., Diaz, D., Camann, D., & Perera, F. P. (2004). Developmental effects of exposure to environmental tobacco smoke and material hardship among inner-city children. *Neurotoxicology and Teratology, 26,* 373–385.

Raver, C. C. (2002). Emotions matter: Making the case for the role of young children's emotional development for early school readiness. *Social Policy Report, 16*(3).

Read, J. S., & Committee on Pediatric AIDS. (2003). Human milk, breastfeeding, and transmission of human immunodeficiency virus type 1 in the United States. *Pediatrics, 112,* 1196–1205.

Reaney, P. (2003, July 2). Test tube babies develop like normal kids—Study. Reuters.

Redding, R. E., Harmon, R. J., & Morgan, G. A. (1990). Maternal depression and infants' mastery behaviors. *Infant Behavior and Development, 113,* 391–396.

Reese, E. (1995). Predicting children's literacy from mother-child conversations. *Cognitive Development, 10,* 381–405.

Reese, E., & Cox, A. (1999). Quality of adult book reading affects children's emergent literacy. *Developmental Psychology, 35,* 20–28.

Reese, E., & Fivush, R. (1993). Parental styles of talking about the past. *Developmental Psychology, 29,* 596–606.

Reese, E., Haden, C., & Fivush, R. (1993). Mother-child conversations about the past: Relationships of style and memory over time. *Cognitive Development, 8,* 403–430.

Reid, J. R., Patterson, G. R., & Loeber, R. (1982). The abused child: Victim, instigator, or innocent bystander? In D. J. Berstein (Ed.), *Response structure and organization.* Lincoln, NE: University of Nebraska Press.

Reijo, R., Alagappan, R. K., Patrizio, P., & Page, D. C. (1996). Severe oligozoospermia resulting from deletions of azoospermia factor gene on Y chromosome. *Lancet, 347,* 1290–1293.

Reilly, J. J., Jackson, D. M., Montgomery, C., Kelly, L. A., Slater, C., Grant, S., & Paton, J. Y. (2004). Total energy expenditure and physical activity in young Scottish children: Mixed longitudinal study. *Lancet, 363,* 211–212.

Reiner, W. (2000, May 12). Cloacal exstrophy: A happenstance model for androgen imprinting. Presentation at the meeting of the Pediatric Endocrine Society, Boston, MA.

Reiner, W. G., and Gearhart, J. P. (2004). Discordant sexual identity in some genetic males with cloacal exstrophy assigned to female sex at birth. *New England Journal of Medicine, 350*(4), 333–341.

Reiss, A. L., Abrams, M. T., Singer, H. S., Ross, J. L., & Denckla, M. B. (1996). Brain development, gender and IQ in children: A volumetric imaging study. *Brain, 119,* 1763–1774.

Remafedi, G., French, S., Story, M., Resnick, M. D., & Blum, R. (1998). The relationship between suicide risk and sexual orientation: Results of a population-based study. *American Journal of Public Health, 88,* 57–60.

Remafedi, G., Resnick, M. Blum, R., & Harris, L. (1992). Demography of sexual orientation in adolescents. *Pediatrics, 89,* 714–721.

Remez, L. (2000). Oral sex among adolescents: Is it sex or is it abstinence? *Family Planning Perspectives, 32,* 298–304.

Rescorla, L. (1991). Early academics: Introduction to the debate. In L. Rescorla, M. C. Hyson, & K. Hirsh-Pasek (Eds.), *Academic instruction in early childhood: Challenge or pressure?* (New Directions for Child Development No. 53, pp. 5–11). San Francisco: Jossey-Bass.

Research Unit on Pediatric Psychopharmacology Anxiety Study Group. (2001). Fluvoxamine for the treatment of anxiety disorder in children and adolescents. *New England Journal of Medicine, 344,* 1279–1285.

Resnick, L. B. (1989). Developing mathematical knowledge. *American Psychologist, 44,* 162–169.

Resnick, M. D., Bearman, P. S., Blum, R. W., Bauman, K. E., Harris, K. M., Jones, J., Tabor, J., Beuhring, T., Sieving, R. E., Shew, M., Ireland, M., Bearinger, L. H., & Udry, J. R. (1997). Protecting adolescents from harm: Findings from the National Longitudinal Study on Adolescent Health. *Journal of the American Medical Association, 278,* 823–832.

Rest, J. R. (1975). Longitudinal study of the Defining Issues Test of moral judgment: A strategy for analyzing developmental change. *Developmental Psychology, 11,* 738–748.

Restak, R. (1984). *The brain.* New York: Bantam.

Reuters. (2004a). Canada first country to ban sale of baby walkers.

Reuters. (2004b). Senate passes Unborn Victims Bill. *New York Times.* [Online]. Available: http://www.nytimes.com/reuters/politics/politics-congress-unborn.html?ex=1081399302&ei=1&en=636394338d275008. Access date: March 29, 2004.

Reynolds, A. J. (1994). Effects of a preschool plus follow-up intervention for children at risk. *Developmental Psychology, 30,* 787–804.

Reynolds, A. J., and Temple, J. A. (1998). Extended early childhood intervention and school achievement: Age thirteen findings from the Chicago Longitudinal Study. *Child Development, 69,* 231–246.

Reynolds, A. J., Temple, J. A., Robertson, D. L., & Mann, E. A. (2001). Long-term effects of an early childhood intervention on educational achievement and juvenile arrest. *Journal of the American Medical Association, 285,* 2339–2346.

Reznick, J. S., Chawarska, K., & Betts, S. (2000). The development of visual expectations in the first year. *Child Development, 71,* 1191–1204.

Rheingold, H. L. (1985). Development as the acquisition of familiarity. *Annual Review of Psychology, 36,* 1–17.

Ricciuti, H. N. (1999). Single parenthood and school readiness in white, black, and Hispanic 6- and 7-year-olds. *Journal of Family Psychology, 13,* 450–465.

Ricciuti, H. N. (2004). Single parenthood, achievement, and problem behavior in white, black, and Hispanic children. *Journal of Educational Research, 97,* 196–206.

Rice, C., Koinis, D., Sullivan, K., Tager-Flusberg, H., & Winner, E. (1997). When 3-year-olds pass the appearance-reality test. *Developmental Psychology, 33,* 54–61.

Rice, M., Oetting, J. B., Marquis, J., Bode, J., & Pae, S. (1994). Frequency of input effects on SLI children's word comprehension. *Journal of Speech and Hearing Research, 37,* 106–122.

Rice, M. L. (1982). Child language: What children know and how. In T. M. Field, A. Huston, H. C. Quay, L. Troll, & G. E. Finley (Eds.), *Review of human development research.* New York: Wiley.

Rice, M. L. (1989). Children's language acquisition. *American Psychologist, 44*(2), 149–156.

Rice, M. L., Hadley, P. A., & Alexander, A. L. (1993). Social biases toward children with speech and language impairments: A correlative causal model of language limitations. *Applied Psycholinguistics, 14,* 445–471.

Rice, M. L., Huston, A. C., Truglio, R., & Wright, J. (1990). Words from "Sesame Street": Learning vocabulary while viewing. *Developmental Psychology, 26,* 421–428.

Rice, M. R., Alvanos, L., & Kenney, B. (2000). Snowmobile injuries and deaths in children: A review of national injury data and state legislation. *Pediatrics, 105*(3), 615–619.

Richards, M. H., Boxer, A. M., Petersen, A. C., & Albrecht, R. (1990). Relation of weight to body image in pubertal girls and boys from two communities. *Developmental Psychology, 26,* 313–321.

Richards, T. L., Dager, S. R., Corina, D., Serafini, S., Heide, A. C., Steury, K., Strauss, W., Hayes, C. E., Abbott, R. D., Craft, S., Shaw, D., Posse, S., & Berninger, V. W. (1999). Dyslexic children have abnormal brain lactate response to reading-related language tasks. *American Journal of Neuroradiology, 20,* 1393–1398.

Richardson, J. (1995). *Achieving gender equality in families: The role of males.* Innocenti Global Seminar, Summary Report. Florence, Italy: UNICEF International Child Development Centre, Spedale degli Innocenti.

Richardson, J. L., Radziszewska, B., Dent, C. W., & Flay, B. R. (1993). Relationship between after-school care of adolescents and substance use, risk taking, depressed mood, and academic achievement. *Pediatrics, 92,* 32–38.

Richie, D. (1984). *The films of Akira Kurosawa.* Berkeley, CA: University of California Press.

Riddle, R. D., Johnson, R. L., Laufer, E., & Tabin, C. (1993). Sonic hedgehog mediates the polarizing activity of the ZPA. *Cell, 75,* 1401–1416.

Rideout, V. J., Vandewater, E. A., & Wartella, E. A. (2003). *Zero to six: Electronic media in the lives of infants, toddlers and preschoolers.* A Kaiser Family Foundation Report.

Rifkin, J. (1998, May 5). Creating the "perfect" human. *Chicago Sun-Times,* p. 29.

Rios-Ellis, B., Bellamy, L., & Shoji, J. (2000). An examination of specific types of *ijime* within Japanese schools. *School Psychology International, 21,* 227–241.

Ripple, C. H., Gilliam, W. S., Chanana, N., and Zigler, E. (1999). Will fifty cooks spoil the broth? The debate over entrusting Head Start to the states. *American Psychologist, 54,* 327–343.

Ristow, M., Muller-Wieland, D., Pfeiffer, A., Krone, W., & Kahn, R. (1998). Obesity associated with a mutation in genetic regulator of adiposity differentiation. *New England Journal of Medicine,* 339, 953–959.

Ritchie, L., Crawford, P., Woodward-Lopez, G., Ivey, S., Masch, M., & Ikeda, J. (2001). *Prevention of childhood overweight: What should be done?* Berkeley, CA: Center for Weight and Health, U.C. Berkeley.

Rivara, F. P. (1999). Pediatric injury control in 1999: Where do we go from here? *Pediatrics, 103*(4), 883–888.

Rivara, F. P., & Grossman, D. C. (1996). Prevention of traumatic deaths to children in the United States: How far have we come and where do we need to go? *Pediatrics, 97,* 791–798.

Rivara, F. P., Bergman, A. B., & Drake, C. (1989). Parental attitudes and practices toward children as pedestrians. *Pediatrics, 84*(6), 1017–1021.

Rivera, J. A., Sotres-Alvarez, D., Habicht, J.-P., Shamah, T., & Villalpando, S. (2004). Impact of the Mexican Program for Education, Health and Nutrition (Progresa) on rates of growth and anemia in infants and young children. *Journal of the American Medical Association, 291,* 2563–2570.

Rivera, S. M., Wakeley, A., & Langer, J. (1999). The drawbridge phenomenon: Representational reasoning or perceptual preference? *Developmental Psychology, 35*(2), 427–435.

Rizzo, T. A., Metzger, B. E., Dooley, S. L., & Cho, N. H. (1997). Early malnutrition and child neurobehavioral development: Insights from the study of children of diabetic mothers. *Child Development, 68,* 26–38.

Roberts, G. C., Block, J. H., & Block, J. (1984). Continuity and change in parents' child-rearing practices. *Child Development, 55,* 586–597.

Robin, D. J., Berthier, N. E., & Clifton, R. K. (1996). Infants' predictive reaching for moving objects in the dark. *Developmental Psychology, 32,* 824–835.

Robinson, J. (as told to A. Duckett). (1995). *I never had it made.* Hopewell, NJ: Ecco.

Robinson, S. (1996). *Stealing home.* New York: HarperCollins.

Robinson, T. N., Wilde, M. L., Navacruz, L. C., Haydel, K. F., and Varady, A. (2001). Effects of reducing children's television and video game use on aggressive behavior: A randomized controlled trial. *Archives of Pediatric and Adolescent Medicine, 155,* 17–23.

Rochat, P., & Striano, T. (2002). Who's in the mirror? Self-other discrimination in specular images by 4- and 9-month-old infants. *Child Development, 73,* 35–46.

Rochat, P., Querido, J. G., & Striano, T. (1999). Emerging sensitivity to the timing and structure of proto conversations in early infancy. *Developmental Psychology, 35,* 950–957.

Rodden, J. (Ed.). (1999). *Conversations with Isabel Allende.* Austin: University of Texas Press.

Roderick, M., Engel, M., & Nagaoka, J. (2003). *Ending social promotion: Results from Summer Bridge.* Chicago: Consortium on Chicago School Research.

Rodier, P. M. (2000, February). The early origins of autism. *Scientific American,* pp. 56–63.

Rodkin, P. C., Farmer, T. W., Pearl, R., & Van Acker, R. (2000). Heterogeneity of popular boys: Antisocial and prosocial configurations. *Developmental Psychology, 36*(1), 14–24.

Rodrigues, D. (1999, April 26). Ensuring safe and effective psychotropic medications for children [News release]. Washington, DC: National Institute of Mental Health.

Rogan, W. J, Dietrich, K. N., Ware, J. H., Dockery, D. W., Salganik, M., Radcliffe, J., Jones, R. L., Ragan, N. B., Chisolm Jr., J. J., Rhoads, G. G., for the Treatment of Lead-Exposed Children Trial Group. (2001). The effect of chelation therapy with succimer on neuropsychological development in children exposed to lead. *New England Journal of Medicine, 344,* 1421–1426.

Rogler, L. H. (2002). Historical generations and psychology: The case of the Great

Depression and World War II. *American Psychologist, 57*(12), 1013–1023.

Rogoff, B. (1990). *Apprenticeship in thinking: Cognitive development in social context.* New York: Oxford University Press.

Rogoff, B. (1998). Cognition as a collaborative process. In W. Damon (Ed.), D. Kuhn, & R. S. Siegler (Vol. Eds.), *Handbook of child psychology: Vol. 2. Cognition, perception, and language* (5th ed., pp. 679–744). New York: Wiley.

Rogoff, B., & Morelli, G. (1989). Perspectives on children's development from cultural psychology. *American Psychologist, 44,* 343–348.

Rogoff, B., Mistry, J., Göncü, A., & Mosier, C. (1993). Guided participation in cultural activity by toddlers and caregivers. *Monographs of the Society for Research in Child Development, 58* (8, Serial No. 236).

Rolls, B. J., Engell, D., & Birch, L. L. (2000). Serving portion size influences 5-year-old but not 3-year-old children's food intake. *Journal of the American Dietetic Association, 100,* 232–234.

Rome-Flanders, T., Cronk, C., & Gourde, C. (1995). Maternal scaffolding in mother-infant games and its relationship to language development: A longitudinal study. *First Language, 15,* 339–355.

Ronca, A. E., & Alberts, J. R. (1995). Maternal contributions to fetal experience and the transition from prenatal to postnatal life. In J. P. Lecanuet, W. P. Fifer, N. A. Krasnegor, & W. P. Smotherman (Eds.), *Fetal development: A psychobiological perspective* (pp. 331–350). Hillsdale, NJ: Erlbaum.

Roopnarine, J. L., Hooper, F. H., Ahmeduzzaman, M., & Pollack, B. (1993). Gentle play partners: Mother-child and father-child play in New Delhi, India. In K. MacDonald (Ed.), *Parent-child play* (pp. 287–304). Albany: State University of New York Press.

Roopnarine, J. L., Talokder, E., Jain, D., Josh, P., & Srivastav, P. (1992). Personal well-being, kinship ties, and mother-infant and father-infant interactions in single-wage and dual-wage families in New Delhi, India. *Journal of Marriage and the Family, 54,* 293–301.

Roopnarine, J., & Honig, A. S. (1985, September). The unpopular child. *Young Children,* 59–64.

Rose, S. A. (1994). Relation between physical growth and information processing in infants born in India. *Child Development, 65,* 889–902.

Rose, S. A., & Feldman, J. F. (1995). Prediction of IQ and specific cognitive abilities at 11 years from infancy measures. *Developmental Psychology, 31,* 685–696.

Rose, S. A., & Feldman, J. F. (1997). Memory and speed: Their role in the relation of infant information processing to later IQ. *Child Development, 68,* 630–641.

Rose, S. A., & Feldman, J. F. (2000). The relation of very low birth weight to basic cognitive skills in infancy and childhood. In CA. Nelson (Ed.), The effects of early adversity on neurobehavioral development. *The Minnesota Symposia on Child Psychology* (vol. 31, pp. 31–59). Mahwah, NJ: Lawrence Erlbaum Associates.

Rose, S. A., Feldman, J. F., & Jankowski, J. J. (2001). Attention and recognition memory in the 1st year of life: A longitudinal study of preterm and full-term infants. *Developmental Psychology, 37,* 135–151.

Rose, S. A., Feldman, J. F., & Jankowski, J. J. (2002). Processing speed in the 1st year of life: A longitudinal study of preterm and full-term infants. *Developmental Psychology, 38,* 895–902.

Rosenblum, G. D., & Lewis, M. (1999). The relations among body image, physical attractiveness, and body mass in adolescence. *Child Development, 70,* 50–64.

Rosenblum, K. L., McDonough, S., Muzik, M., Miller, A., & Sameroff, A. (2002). Maternal representations of the infant: Associations with infant response to the still face. *Child Development, 73,* 999–1015.

Rosengren, K. S., Gelman, S. A., Kalish, C. W., & McCormick, M. (1991). As time goes by: Children's early understanding of growth in animals. *Child Development, 62,* 1302–1320.

Rosenthal, E. (1998, November 1). For one-child policy, China rethinks iron hand. *New York Times,* pp. 1, 20.

Rosenthal, E. (2003, July 20). Bias for boys leads to sale of baby girls in China. *New York Times,* sec. 1, p. 6, col. 3.

Rosenthal, R., & Jacobson, L. (1968). *Pygmalion in the classroom.* New York: Holt.

Rosenthal, R., & Vandell, D. L. (1996). Quality of care at school-aged childcare programs: Regulatable features, observed experiences, child perspectives, and parent perspectives. *Child Development, 67,* 2434–2445.

Rosenzweig, M. R. (1984). Experience, memory, and the brain. *American Psychologist, 39,* 365–376.

Rosenzweig, M. R., & Bennett, E. L., (Eds.). (1976). *Neural mechanisms of learning and memory.* Cambridge, MA: MIT Press.

Ross, C. E., & Mirowsky, J. (1999). Parental divorce, life-course disruption and adult depression. *Journal of Marriage and the Family, 61,* 1034–1045.

Ross, G., Lipper, E. G., & Auld, P. A. M. (1991). Educational status and school-related abilities of very low birth weight premature children. *Pediatrics, 8,* 1125–1134.

Ross, H. S. (1996). Negotiating principles of entitlement in sibling property disputes. *Developmental Psychology, 32,* 90–101.

Rossi, R. (1996, August 30). Small schools under microscope. *Chicago Sun-Times,* p. 24.

Rotenberg, K. J., & Eisenberg, N. (1997). Developmental differences in the understanding of and reaction to others' inhibition of emotional expression. *Developmental Psychology, 33,* 526–537.

Rothbart, M. K., & Hwang, J. (2002). Measuring infant temperament. *Infant Behavior & Development, 130,* 1–4.

Rothbart, M. K., Ahadi, S. A., & Evans, D. E. (2000). Temperament and personality: Origins and outcomes. *Journal of Personality and Social Psychology, 78,* 122–135.

Rothbart, M. K., Ahadi, S. A., Hershey, K. L., & Fisher, P. (2001). Investigations of temperament at three to seven years: The Children's Behavior Questionnaire. *Child Development, 72,* 1394–1408.

Rotheram-Borus, M. & Futterman, D. (2000). Promoting early detection of HIV among adolescents. *Archives of Pediatrics and Adolescent Medicine, 154,* 435–439.

Roush, W. (1995). Arguing over why Johnny can't read. *Science, 267,* 1896–1898.

Rovee-Collier, C. (1996). Shifting the focus from what to why. *Infant Behavior and Development, 19,* 385–400.

Rovee-Collier, C. (1999). The development of infant memory. *Current Directions in Psychological Science, 8,* 80–85.

Rovee-Collier, C., & Boller, K. (1995). Current theory and research on infant learning and memory: Application to early intervention. *Infants and Young Children, 7*(3), 1–12.

Rowland, A. S., Umbach, D. M., Stallone, L., Naftel, J., Bohlig, E. M., & Sandler, D. P. (2002). Prevalence of medication treatment for attention-deficit hyperactivity disorder among elementary school children in Johnston County, North Carolina. *American Journal of Public Health, 92,* 231–234.

Rozen, S., Skaletsky, H., Marszalek, J. D, Minx, P. J., Cordum, H. S., Waterston, R. H., Wilson, R. K., & Page, D. C. (2003). Abundant gene conversion between arms of palindromes in human and ape Y chromosomes. *Nature, 423,* 810–811, 813.

Rubin, D. H., Erickson, C. J., San Agustin, M., Cleary, S. D., Allen, J. K., & Cohen, P. (1996). Cognitive and academic functioning of homeless children compared with housed children. *Pediatrics, 97,* 289–294.

Rubin, D. H., Krasilnikoff, P. A., Leventhal, J. M., Weile, B., & Berget, A. (1986, August 23). Effect of passive smoking on birth weight. *Lancet,* pp. 415–417.

Rubin, K. (1982). Nonsocial play in preschoolers: Necessary evil? *Child Development, 53,* 651–657.

Rubin, K. H., Bukowski, W., & Parker, J. G. (1998). Peer interactions, relationships, and groups. In W. Damon (Series Ed.) & N. Eisenberg (Vol. Ed.), *Handbook of child psychology: Vol. 3. Social, emotional, and personality development* (5th ed., pp. 619–700). New York: Wiley.

Rubin, K. H., Fein, G. G., & Vandenberg, B. (1983). Play. In P. H. Mussen (Series Ed.) & E. M. Hetherington (Vol. Ed.), *Handbook of child psychology: Vol. 4. Socialization, personality, and social development* (pp. 694–774). New York: Wiley.

Ruble, D. M., & Brooks-Gunn, J. (1982). The experience of menarche. *Child Development, 53,* 1557–1566.

Ruble, D. N., & Dweck, C. S. (1995). Self-conceptions, person conceptions, and their development. In N. Eisenberg, (Ed.), *Social development: Review of personality and social psychology* (pp. 109–139). Thousand Oaks, CA: Sage.

Ruble, D. N., & Martin, C. L. (1998). Gender development. In W. Damon (Series Ed.) & N. Eisenberg (Vol. Ed.), *Handbook of child psychology: Vol. 3. Social, emotional, and personality development* (5th ed., pp. 933–1016). New York: Wiley.

Rudolph, K. D., Lambert, S. F., Clark, A. G., & Kurlakowsky, K. D. (2001). Negotiating the transition to middle school: The role of self-regulatory processes. *Child Development, 72*(3), 929–946.

Rueter, M. A., & Conger, R. D. (1995). Antecedents of parent-adolescent disagreements. *Journal of Marriage and the Family, 57,* 435–448.

Ruffman, T., Slade, L., & Crowe, E. (2002). The relation between children's and mothers' mental state language and theory-of-mind understanding. *Child Development, 73,* 734–751.

Ruiz, F., & Tanaka, K. (2001). The *ijime* phenomenon and Japan: Overarching consideration for cross-cultural studies. *Psychologia: An International Journal of Psychology in the Orient, 44,* 128–138.

Rushton, J. L., Clark, S. J., & Freed, G. L. (May 1999). *Newest depression medications widely prescribed for children.* Paper presented at the Pediatric Academic Societies Annual Meeting, San Francisco, CA.

Rutland, A. F., & Campbell, R. N. (1996). The relevance of Vygotsky's theory of the "zone of proximal development" to the assessment of children with intellectual disabilities. *Journal of Intellectual Disability Research, 40,* 151–158.

Rutter, M. (2002). Nature, nurture, and development: From evangelism through science toward policy and practice. *Child Development, 73,* 1–21.

Rutter, M. (2003). Commentary: Causal processes leading to antisocial behavior. *Developmental Psychology, 39,* 372–378.

Rutter, M., & the English and Romanian Adoptees (ERA) Study Team. (1998). Developmental catch-up, and deficit, following adoption after severe global early privation. *Journal of Child Psychology and Psychiatry, 39,* 465–476.

Rutter, M., Caspi, A., Horwood, L. J., Goodman, R., Maughan, B., Moffitt, T. E., Meltzer, H., & Carroll, J. (2004). Sex differences in developmental reading disability: New findings from 4 epidemiological studies. *JAMA, 291,* 2007–2012.

Rutter, M., O'Connor, T. G., and the English and Romanian Adoptees (ERA) Study Team. (2004). Are there biological programming effects for psychological development? Findings from a study of Romanian adoptees. *Developmental Psychology, 40,* 81–94.

Ryan, A. (2001). The peer group as a context for the development of young adolescent motivation and achievement. *Child Development, 72*(4), 1135–1150.

Ryan, A. S., Wenjun, Z., & Acosta, A. (2002). Breastfeeding continues to increase into the new millennium. *Pediatrics, 110,* 1103–1109.

Ryan, V., & Needham, C. (2001). Nondirective play therapy with children experiencing psychic trauma. *Clinical Child Psychology and Psychiatry* (special issue), *6,* 437–453.

Rymer, R. (1993). *An abused child: Flight from silence.* New York: HarperCollins.

Saarni, C., Mumme, D. L., & Campos, J. J. (1998). Emotional development: Action, communication, and understanding. In W. Damon (Series Ed.) & N. Eisenberg (Vol. Ed.), *Handbook of child psychology: Vol. 3. Social, emotional, and personality development* (5th ed., pp. 237–309). New York: Wiley.

Sabbagh, M. A., & Baldwin, D. A. (2001). Learning words from knowledgeable versus ignorant speakers: Links between preschoolers' theory of mind and semantic development. *Child Development, 72*(4), 1054–1070.

Sachs, B. P., Kobelin, C., Castro, M. A., & Frigoletto, F. (1999). The risks of lowering the cesarean-delivery rate. *New England Journal of Medicine, 340,* 54–57.

Sadeh, A., Raviv, A., & Gruber, R. (2000). Sleep patterns and sleep disruptions in school age children. *Developmental Psychology, 36*(3), 291–301.

Sagi, A., Koren-Karie, N., Gini, M., Ziv, Y., & Joels, T. (2002). Shedding further light on the effects of various types and quality of early child care on infant-mother attachment relationship: The Haifa Study of Early Child Care. *Child Development, 73,* 1166–1186.

Saigal, S., Hoult, L. A., Streiner, D. L., Stoskopf, B. L., & Rosenbaum, P. L. (2000). School difficulties at adolescence in a regional cohort of children who were extremely low birth weight. *Pediatrics, 105,* 325–331.

Saigal, S., Stoskopf, B. L., Streiner, D. L., & Burrows, E. (2001). Physical growth and current health status of infants who were of extremely low birth weight and controls at adolescence. *Pediatrics, 108*(2), 407–415.

Salihu, H. M., Shumpert, M. N., Slay, M., Kirby, R. S., & Alexander, G. R. (2003). Childbearing beyond maternal age 50 and fetal outcomes in the United States. *Obstetrics and Gynecology, 102,* 1006–1014.

Salisbury, A., Law, K., LaGasse, L. and Lester, B. (2003). Maternal-fetal attachment. *Journal of the American Medical Association, 289,* 1701.

Salzinger, S., Feldman, R. S., Hammer, M., & Rosario, M. (1993). Effects of physical abuse on children's social relations. *Child Development, 64,* 169–187.

Samdal. O., & Dür, W. (2000). The school environment and the health of adolescents. In C. Currie, K. Hurrelmann, W. Settertobulte, R. Smith, & J. Todd (Eds.), *Health and health behaviour among young people: A WHO cross-national study (HBSC) international report* (pp. 49–64). WHO Policy Series: Health Policy for Children and Adolescents, Series No. 1. Copenhagen, Denmark: World Health Organization Regional Office for Europe.

Sameroff, A. J., Seifer, R., Baldwin, A., & Baldwin, C. (1993). Stability of intelligence from preschool to adolescence: The influence of social and family risk factors. *Child Development, 64,* 80–97.

Sampson, R. J. (1997). The embeddedness of child and adolescent development: A community-level perspective on urban violence. In J. McCord (Ed.), *Violence and childhood in the inner city* (pp. 31–77). Cambridge, England: Cambridge University Press.

Sandler, D. P., Everson, R. B., Wilcox, A. J., & Browder, J. P. (1985). Cancer risk in adulthood from early life exposure to parents' smoking. *American Journal of Public Health, 75,* 487–492.

Sandnabba, H. K., & Ahlberg, C. (1999). Parents' attitudes and expectations about children's cross-gender behavior. *Sex Roles, 40,* 249–263.

Sandstrom, M. J., & Coie, J. D. (1999). A developmental perspective on peer rejection: Mechanisms of stability and change. *Child Development 70*(4), 955–966.

Santer, L. J., & Stocking, C. B. (1991). Safety practices and living conditions of low-income urban families. *Pediatrics, 88,* 111–118.

Santos, F., & Ingrassia, R. (August 18, 2002). The face of homelessness has changed: Family surge at shelters. *New York Daily News.* Available at www.nationalhomeless.org/housing/familiesarticle.html.

Santos, I. S., Victora, C. G., Huttly, S., & Carvalhal, J. B. (1998). Caffeine intake and low birthweight: A population-based case-control study. *American Journal of Epidemiology, 147,* 620–627.

Santrock, J. W., Sitterle, K. A., & Warshak, R. A. (1988). Parent-child relationships in stepfather families. In P. Bronstein & C. P. Cowan (Eds.), *Fatherhood today: Men's changing role in the family.* New York: Wiley.

Sapienza, C. (1990, October). Parental imprinting of genes. *Scientific American,* pp. 52–60.

Sapp, F., Lee, K., & Muir, D. (2000). Three-year-olds' difficulty with the appearance-reality distinction: Is it real or apparent? *Developmental Psychology, 36,* 547–560.

Sargent, J. D., & Dalton, M. (2001). Does parental disapproval of smoking prevent adolescents from becoming established smokers? *Pediatrics, 108*(6), 1256–1262.

Satcher, D. (2001). *Women and smoking: A report of the Surgeon General.* Washington, DC: Department of Health and Human Services.

Saudino, K. J. (2003a). Parent ratings of infant temperament: Lessons from twin studies. *Infant Behavior & Development, 26,* 100–107.

Saudino, K. J. (2003b). The need to consider contrast effects in parent-rated temperament *Infant Behavior & Development, 26,* 118–120.

Saunders, N. (1997, March). Pregnancy in the 21st century: Back to nature with a little assistance. *Lancet, 349,* s17–s19.

Savage, S. L., & Au, T. K. (1996). What word learners do when input contradicts the mutual exclusivity assumption. *Child Development, 67,* 3120–3134.

Saxe, G. B., Guberman, S. R., & Gearhart, M. (1987). Social processes in early number development. *Monographs of the Society for Research in Child Development, 52*(216).

Scarborough, H. S. (1990). Very early language deficits in dyslexic children. *Child Development, 61,* 1728–1743.

Scariati, P. D., Grummer-Strawn, L. M., & Fein, S. B. (1997). A longitudinal analysis of infant morbidity and the extent of breastfeeding in the United States. *Pediatrics, 99,* e5.

Scarr, S. (1992). Developmental theories for the 1990s: Development and individual differences. *Child Development, 63,* 1–19.

Scarr, S. (1997a). Behavior-genetics and socialization theories of intelligence: Truce and reconciliation. In R. J. Sternberg & E. Grigorenko (Eds.), *Intelligence, heredity, and environment* (pp. 3–41). Cambridge, England: Cambridge University Press.

Scarr, S. (1997b). Why child care has little impact on most children's development. *Current Directions in Psychological Science, 6*(5), 143–148.

Scarr, S. (1998). American child care today. *American Psychologist, 53,* 95–108.

Scarr, S., & McCartney, K. (1983). How people make their own environments: A theory of genotype-environment effects. *Child Development, 54,* 424–435.

Schanberg, S. M., & Field, T. M. (1987). Sensory deprivation illness and supplemental stimulation in the rat pup and preterm human neonate. *Child Development, 58,* 1431–1447.

Scheers, N. J., Rutherford, G. W., & Kemp, J. S. (2003). Where should infants sleep? A comparison of risk for suffocation of infants sleeping in cribs, adult beds, and other sleeping locations. *Pediatrics, 112,* 883–889.

Scheidt, P., Overpeck, M. D., Whatt, W., & Aszmann, A. (2000). In C. Currie, K. Hurrelmann, W. Settertobulte, R. Smith, & J. Todd (Eds.), *Health and health behaviour among young people: A WHO cross-national study (HBSC) international report* (pp. 24–38.). WHO Policy Series: Healthy Policy for Children and Adolescents, Series No. 1. Copenhagen, Denmark: World Health Organization Regional Office for Europe.

Schemo, D. J. (2004, August 19). Charter schools lagging behind, test scores show. *New York Times,* pp. A1, A16.

Scher, M. S., Richardson, G. A., & Day, N. L. (2000). Effects of prenatal crack/cocaine and other drug exposure on electroencephalographic sleep studies at birth and one year. *Pediatrics, 105,* 39–48.

Schieve, L. A., Meikle, S. F., Ferre, C., Peterson, H. B., Jeng, G., & Wilcox, L. S. (2002). Low and very low birth weight in infants conceived with use of assisted reproductive technology. *New England Journal of Medicine, 346,* 731–737.

Schilpp, P. A. (1970). *Albert Einstein: Philosopher-scientist* (3d ed.). La Salle, IL: Open Court. (Original work published 1949.)

Schlegel, A., & Barry, H. (1991). *Adolescence: An anthropological inquiry.* New York: Free Press.

Schmitt, B. D. (1997). Nocturnal enuresis. *Pediatrics in Review, 18,* 183–190.

Schmitz, S., Saudino, K. J., Plomin, R., Fulker, D. W., & DeFries, J. C. (1996). Genetic and environmental influences on temperament in middle childhood: Analyses of teacher and tester ratings. *Child Development, 67,* 409–422.

Schmuckler, M. A., & Fairhall, J. L. (2001). Visual-proprioceptive intermodal perception using point light displays. *Child Development, 72,* 954–962.

Schneider, B. H., Atkinson, L., & Tardif, C. (2001). Child-parent attachment and children's peer relations: A quantitative review. *Developmental Psychology, 37,* 86–100.

Schneider, M. (2002). *Do school facilities affect academic outcomes?* Washington, DC: National Clearinghouse for Educational Facilities.

Scholer, S. J., Mitchel, E. F., & Ray, W. A. (1997). Predictors of injury mortality in early childhood. *Pediatrics, 100,* 342–347.

Scholten, C. M. (1985). *Childbearing in American society: 1650–1850.* New York: New York University Press.

Schonfeld, D. J., Johnson, S. R., Perrin, E. C., O'Hare, L. L., & Cicchetti, D. V. (1993). Understanding of acquired immunodeficiency syndrome by elementary school children—A developmental survey. *Pediatrics, 92,* 389–395.

Schore, A. N. (1994). *Affect regulation and the origin of the self: The neurobiology of emotional development.* Hillsdale, NJ: Erlbaum.

Schreiber, J. B., Robins, M., Striegel-Moore, R., Obarzanek, E., Morrison, J. A., & Wright, D. J. (1996). Weight modification efforts reported by preadolescent girls. *Pediatrics, 96,* 63–70.

Schumann, J. (1997). The view from elsewhere: Why there can be no best method for teaching a second language. *The Clarion: Magazine of the European Second Language Acquisition, 3*(1), 23–24.

Schwartz, D., Chang, L., & Farver, J. M. (2001). Correlates of victimization in Chinese children's peer groups. *Developmental Psychology, 37*(4), 520–532.

Schwartz, D., Dodge, K. A., Pettit, G. S., Bates, J. E., & the Conduct Problems Prevention Research Group. (2000). Friendship as a moderating factor in the pathway between early harsh home environment and later victimization in the peer group. *Developmental Psychology, 36,* 646–662.

Schwartz, D., McFadyen-Ketchum, S. A., Dodge, K. A., Pettit, G. S., & Bates, J. E. (1998). Peer group victimization as a predictor of children's behavior problems at home and in school. *Developmental and Psychopathology, 10,* 87–99.

Schwebel, D. C., & Plumert, J. M. (1999). Longitudinal and concurrent relations among temperament, ability estimation, and injury proneness. *Child Development, 70,* 700–712.

Schweinhart, L. J., Barnes, H. V., & Weikart, D. P. (1993). *Significant benefits: The High/Scope Perry Preschool Study through age 27* (Monographs of the High/Scope Educational Research Foundation No. 10). Ypsilanti, MI: High/Scope.

Schwimmer, J. B., Burwinkle, T. M., Varni, J. W. (2003 April). Health-related quality of life of severely obese children and adolescents. *Journal of the American Medical Association, 289*(14), 1813–1819.

Scott, G., & Ni, H. (2004). Access to health care among Hispanic/Latino children: United States, 1998–2001. *Advance Data from Vital and Health Statistics,* No. 344. Hyattsville, MD: National Center for Health Statistics.

Sedlak, A. J., & Broadhurst, D. D. (1996). *Executive summary of the third national incidence study of child abuse and neglect* (NIS-3). Washington, DC: U.S. Department of Health and Human Services.

Sege, R., & Dietz, W. (1994). Television viewing and violence in children: The pediatrician as agent for change. *Pediatrics, 94,* 600–607.

Seifer, R. (2003). Twin studies, biases of parents, and biases of researchers. *Infant Behavior & Development, 26,* 115–117.

Seifer, R., Schiller, M., Sameroff, A. J., Resnick, S., & Riordan, K. (1996). Attachment, maternal sensitivity, and infant temperament during the first year of life. *Developmental Psychology, 32,* 12–25.

Seiner, S. H., & Gelfand, D. M. (1995). Effects of mother's simulated withdrawal and depressed affect on mother-toddler interactions. *Child Development, 60,* 1519–1528.

Seitz, V. (1990). Intervention programs for impoverished children: A comparison of educational and family support models. *Annals of Child Development, 7,* 73–103.

Selman, R. L. (1980). *The growth of interpersonal understanding: Developmental and clinical analyses.* New York: Academic.

Selman, R. L., & Selman, A. P. (1979, April). Children's ideas about friendship: A new theory. *Psychology Today,* pp. 71–80.

Seltzer, J. A. (2000). Families formed outside of marriage. *Journal of Marriage and the Family, 62,* 1247–1268.

Seminara, S. B., Messager, S., Chatzidaki, E. E., Thresher, R. R., Acierno Jr., J. S., Shagoury, J. K., Bo-Abbas, Y., Kuohung, W., Schwinof, K. M., Hendrick, A. G., Zahn, D., Dixon, J., Kaiser, U. B., Slaugenhaupt, S. A., Gusella, J. F., O'Rahilly, S., Carlton, M. B. L., Crowley Jr., W. F., Aparicio, S. A. J. R., & Colledge, W. H. (2003). The GPR54 gene as a regulator of puberty. *New England Journal of Medicine, 349,* 1614–1627.

Senghas, A., & Coppola, M. (2001). Children creating language: How Nicaraguan sign language acquired a spatial grammar. *Psychological Science, 12,* 323–328.

Serbin, L., Poulin-Dubois, D., Colburne, K. A., Sen, M., & Eichstedt. J. A. (2001). Gender stereotyping in infancy: Visual preferences for knowledge of gender-stereotyped toys in the second year. *International Journal of Behavioral Development, 25,* 7–15.

Serbin, L. A., Moller, L. C., Gulko, J., Powlishta, K. K., & Colburne, K. A. (1994). The emergence of gender segregation in toddler playgroups. In C. Leaper (Ed.), *Childhood gender segregation: Causes and consequences* (New Directions for Child Development No. 65, pp. 7–17). San Francisco: Jossey-Bass.

Serres, L. (2001). Morphological changes of the human hippocampal formation from midgestation to early childhood. In C. A. Nelson & M. Luciana (Eds.), *Handbook of developmental cognitive neuroscience* (pp. 45–58). Cambridge, MA: MIT Press.

Sethi, A., Mischel, W., Aber, J. L., Shoda, Y., & Rodriguez, M. L. (2000). The role of strategic attention deployment in development of self-regulation: Predicting preschoolers' delay of gratification from mother-toddler interactions. *Developmental Psychology, 36,* 767–777.

Sexton, A. (1964). Little girl, my string bean, my lovely woman. *The complete poems: Anne Sexton.* New York: Houghton Mifflin, 1981.

Shade, E. P., & Wissow, L. S. (2004). Spanking in early childhood and later behavior problems: A prospective study of infants and young toddlers. *Pediatrics, 113,* 1321–1330.

Shanahan, M. J., & Flaherty, B. P. (2001). Dynamic patterns of time use in adolescence. *Child Development, 72*(2), 385–401.

Shanahan, M. J., Finch, M. D., Mortimer, J. T., & Ryu, S. (1991). Adolescent work experience and depressive affect. *Social Psychology Quarterly, 54,* 299–317.

Shannon, J. D., Tamis-LeMonda, C. S., London, K., & Cabrera, N. (2002). Beyond rough and tumble: Low income fathers' interactions and children's cognitive development at 24 months. *Parenting: Science & Practice, 2*(2), 77–104.

Shannon, M. (2000). Ingestion of toxic substances by children. *New England Journal of Medicine, 342,* 186–191.

Sharma, A. R., McGue, M. K., & Benson, P. L. (1996a). The emotional and behavioral adjustment of United States adopted adolescents, Part I: An overview. *Children and Youth Services Review, 18,* 83–100.

Sharma, A. R., McGue, M. K., & Benson, P. L. (1996b). The emotional and behavioral adjustment of United States adopted adolescents, Part II: Age at adoption. *Children and Youth Services Review, 18,* 101–114.

Shatz, M., & Gelman, R. (1973). The development of communication skills: Modifications in the speech of young children as a function of listener. *Monographs of the Society for Research in Child Development, 38*(5, Serial No. 152).

Shaw, G. M., Velie, E. M., & Schaffer, D. (1996). Risk of neural tube defect affected pregnancies among obese women. *Journal of the American Medical Association, 275,* 1093–1096.

Shaywitz, S. (2003). *Overcoming dyslexia: A new and complete science-based program for overcoming reading problems at any level.* New York: Knopf.

Shaywitz, S. E. (1998). Current concepts: Dyslexia. *New England Journal of Medicine, 338,* 307–312.

Shaywitz, S. E., Shaywitz, B. A., Fulbright, R. K., Skudlarski, P., Mencl, W. E., Constable, R. T., Pugh, K. R., Holahan, J. M., Marchione, K. E., Fletcher, J. M., Lyon, G. R., & Gore, J. C. (2003). Neural systems for compensation and persistence: Young adult outcome of childhood reading disability. *Biological Psychiatry, 54*(1), 25–33.

Shaywitz, S. E., Shaywitz, B. A., Pugh, K. R., Fulbright, R. K., Constable, R. Y., Mencl, W. E., Shanweiler, D. P., Liberman, A. M., Skudlarski, P., Fletcher, J. M., Katz, L., Marchioine, K. E., Lacadie, C., Gratenby, C., & Gore, J. C. (1998). Functional disruption in the organization of the brain for reading in dyslexia. *Proceedings of the National Academy of Science, 95,* 2626–2641.

Shea, K. M., Little, R. E., & the ALSPAC Study Team (1997). Is there an association between preconceptual paternal X-ray exposure and birth outcome? *American Journal of Epidemiology, 145,* 546–551.

Shea, S., Basch, C. E., Stein, A. D., Contento, I. R., Irigoyen, M., & Zybert, P. (1993). Is there a relationship between dietary fat and stature or growth in children 3 to 5 years of age? *Pediatrics, 92,* 579–586.

Shifflett, K., & Cummings, M. (1999). A program for educating parents about the effects of divorce and conflict on children: An initial evaluation. *Family Relations, 48*(1), 79–89.

Shiono, P. H., & Behrman, R. E. (1995). Low birth weight: Analysis and recommendations. *The Future of Children, 5*(1), 4–18.

Shonkoff, J., & Phillips, D. (2000). Growing up in child care. In I. Shonkoff & D. Phillips (Eds.), *From neurons to neighborhoods* (pp. 297–327). Washington, DC: National Research Council/Institute of Medicine.

Shope, J. T., Molnar, L. J., Elliott, M. R., & Waller, P. F. (2001). Graduated driver licensing in Michigan: Early impact on motor vehicle crashes among 16-year-old drivers. *Journal of the American Medical Association, 286,* 1593–1598.

Shulman, S., Scharf, M., Lumer, D., & Maurer, O. (2001). Parental divorce and young adult children's romantic relationships: Resolution of the divorce experience. *American Journal of Orthopsychiatry, 71,* 473–478.

Shurkin, J. N. (1992). *Terman's kids: The groundbreaking study of how the gifted grow up.* Boston: Little, Brown.

Shwe, H. I., & Markman, E. M. (1997). Young children's appreciation of the mental impact of their communicative signals. *Developmental Psychology, 33*(4), 630–636.

Siegal, M., & Peterson, C. C. (1998). Preschoolers' understanding of lies and innocent and negligent mistakes. *Developmental Psychology, 34*(2), 332–341.

Siegel, A. C., & Burton, R. V. (1999). Effects of baby walkers on motor and mental development in human infants. *Journal of Developmental and Behavioral Pediatrics, 20,* 355–361.

Siegel, O. (1982). Personality development in adolescence. In B. B. Wolman (Ed.), *Handbook of developmental psychology.* Englewood Cliffs, NJ: Prentice-Hall.

Siegler, R. S. (1998). *Children's thinking* (3d ed.). Upper Saddle River, NJ: Prentice-Hall.

Siegler, R. S., & Booth, J. L. (2004). Development of numerical estimation in young children. *Child Development, 75,* 428–444.

Siegler, R. S., & Opfer, J. E. (2003). The development of numerical estimation: Evidence for multiple representations of numerical quantity. *Psychological Science, 14,* 237–243.

Siegler, R. S., & Richards, D. (1982). The development of intelligence. In R. Sternberg (Ed.), *Handbook of human intelligence.* London: Cambridge University Press.

Sigelman, C., Alfeld-Liro, C., Derenowski, E., Durazo, O., Woods, T., Maddock, A., & Mukai, T. (1996). Mexican-American and Anglo-American children's responsiveness to a theory-centered AIDS education program. *Child Development, 67,* 253–266.

Sigman, M., Cohen, S. E., & Beckwith, L. (1997). Why does infant attention predict adolescent intelligence? *Infant Behavior and Development, 20,* 133–140.

Signorello, L. B., Nordmark, A., Granath, F., Blot, W. J., McLaughlin, J. K., Anneren, G., Lundgren, S., Exbom, A., Rane, A., & Cnattingius, S. (2001). Caffeine metabolism and the risk of spontaneous abortion of normal karyotype fetuses. *Obstetrics & Gynecology, 98*(6), 1059–1066.

Silverman, W. K., La Greca, A. M., & Wasserstein, S. (1995). What do children worry about? Worries and their relation to anxiety. *Child Development, 66,* 671–686.

Silvern, S. B. (1998). Educational implications of play with computers. In D. P. Fromberg & D. Bergen (Eds.), *Play from birth to twelve and beyond: Contexts, perspectives, and meanings* (pp. 530–536). New York: Garland.

Simmons, R. G., Blyth, D. A., & McKinney, K. L. (1983). The social and psychological effect of puberty on white females. In J. Brooks-Gunn & A. C. Petersen (Eds.), *Girls at puberty: Biological and psychological perspectives.* New York: Plenum.

Simmons, R. G., Blyth, D. A., Van Cleave, E. F., & Bush, D. M. 1979). Entry into early adolescence: The impact of school structure, puberty, and early dating on self-esteem. *American Sociological Review, 44*(6), 948–967.

Simon, T. J., Hespos, S. J., & Rochat, P. (1995). Do infants understand simple arithmetic: A replication of Wynn (1992). *Cognitive Development, 10,* 253–269.

Simons, R. L., Chao, W., Conger, R. D., & Elder, G. H. (2001). Quality of parenting as mediator of the effect of childhood defiance on adolescent friendship choices and delinquency: A growth curve analysis. *Journal of Marriage and the Family, 63,* 63–79.

Simons, R. L., Lin, K.-H., & Gordon, L. C. (1998). Socialization in the family of origin and male dating violence: A prospective study. *Journal of Marriage and the Family, 60,* 467–478.

Simonton, D. K. (1990). Creativity and wisdom in aging. In J. E. Birren & K. W. Schaie (Eds.), *Handbook of the psychology of aging* (pp. 320–329). New York: Academic Press.

Simpson, G. A., & Fowler, M. G. (1994). Geographic mobility and children's emotional/behavioral adjustment and school functioning. *Pediatrics, 93,* 303–309.

Simpson, J. L., & Elias, S. (1993). Isolating fetal cells from maternal blood: Advances in prenatal diagnosis through molecular technology. *Journal of the American Medical Association, 270,* 2357–2361.

Singer, D. G., & Singer, J. L. (1990). *The house of make-believe: Play and the developing imagination.* Cambridge, MA: Harvard University Press.

Singer, J. L., & Singer, D. G. (1981). *Television, imagination, and aggression: A study of preschoolers.* Hillsdale, NJ: Erlbaum.

Singer, J. L., & Singer, D. G. (1998). *Barney & Friends* as entertainment and education: Evaluating the quality and effectiveness of a television series for preschool children. In J. K. Asamen & G. L. Berry (Eds.), *Research paradigms, television, and social behavior* (pp. 305–367). Thousand Oaks, CA: Sage.

Singer, L. T., Minnes, S., Short, E., Arendt, K., Farkas, K., Lewis, B., Klein, N., Russ, S., Min, M. O., & Kirchner, H. L. (2004). Cognitive outcomes of preschool children with prenatal cocaine exposure. *Journal of the American Medical Association, 291,* 2448–2456.

Singer, M. I., Slovak, K., Frierson, T., & York, P. (1998). Viewing preferences, symptoms of psychological trauma, and violent behaviors among children who watch television. *Journal of the American Academy of Child and Adolescent Psychiatry, 37*(10), 1041–1048.

Singh, K. K., Barroga, C. F., Hughes, M. D., Chen, J., Raskino, C., McKinney, R. E., & Spector, S. A. (2003, November 15). Genetic influence of CCR5, CCR2, and SDF1 variants on human immunodeficiency virus 1 (HIV-1)-related disease progression and neurological impairment, in children with symptomatic HIV-1 infection. *Journal of Infectious Disease, 188*(10), 1461–1472.

Singh, S., Wulf, D., Samara, R., & Cuca, Y. P. (2000). Gender differences in the timing of first intercourse: Data from 14 countries. *International Family Planning Perspectives, Part 1, 26,* 21–28.

Singhal, A., Cole, T. J., Fewtrell, M., & Lucas, A. (2004). Breastmilk feeding and lipoprotein profile in adolescents born preterm: Follow-up of a prospective randomised study. *Lancet, 363,* 1571–1578.

Sjostrom, K., Valentin, L., Thelin, T., & Marsal, K. (1997). Maternal anxiety in late pregnancy and fetal hemodynamics. *European Journal of Obstetrics and Gynecology, 74,* 149–155.

Skadberg, B. T., Morild, I., & Markestad, T. (1998). Abandoning prone sleeping: Effects on the risk of sudden infant death syndrome. *Journal of Pediatrics, 132,* 234–239.

Skaletsky, H., Kuroda-Kawaguchi, T., Minx, P. J., Cordum, H. S., Hillier, L., Brown, L. G., Repping, S., Pyntikova, T., Ali, J., Bicri, T., Chinwalla, A., Delehaunty, A., Delehaunty, K., Du, H., Fewell, G., Fulton, L., Fulton, R., Graves, T., Hou, S. F., Latrielle, P., Leonard, S., Mardis, E., Maupin, R., McPherson, J., Miner, T., Nash, W., Nguyen, C., Ozersky, P., Pepin, K., Rock, S., Rohlfing, T., Scott, K., Shultz, B., Strong, C., Tin-Wollam, A., Yang, S. P., Waterston, R. H., Wilson, R., K., Rozen, S., & Page, D. C. (2003). The male-specific region of the human Y chromosome is a mosaic of discrete sequence classes. *Nature, 423,* 825–837.

Skinner, B. F. (1938). *The behavior of organisms: An experimental approach.* New York: Appleton-Century.

Skinner, B. F. (1957). *Verbal behavior.* New York: Appleton-Century-Crofts.

Skinner, D. (1989). The socialization of gender identity: Observations from Nepal. In J. Valsiner (Ed.), *Child development in cultural context* (pp. 181–192). Toronto: Hogrefe & Huber.

Skinner, J. D., Carruth, B. R., Moran III, J., Houck, K., & Coletta, F. (1999). Fruit juice intake i[illegible] children's growth. *Pediatrics, 103,* 58–64.

Skjaerven, R., Wilcox, A. J., & Lie, R. T. (1999). A population-based study of survival and childbearing among female subjects with birth defects and the risk of recurrence in their children. *New England Journal of Medicine, 340,* 1057–1062.

Skoe, E. E., & Diessner, R. E. (1994). Ethic of care, justice, identity, and gender: An extension and replication. *Merrill-Palmer Quarterly, 40,* 272–289.

Skoe, E. E., & Gooden, A. (1993). Ethics of care and real-life moral dilemma content in male and female early adolescents. *Journal of Early Adolescence, 13*(2), 154–167.

Skolnick, A. A. (1993). "Female athlete triad" risk for women. *Journal of the American Medical Association, 270,* 921–923.

Skuse, D. H., James, R. S., Bishop, D. V. M., Coppin, B., Dalton, P., Aamodt-Leeper, G., Bacarese-Hamilton, M., Creswell, C., McGurk, R., & Jacobs, P. A. (1997). Evidence from Turner's syndrome of an imprinted X-linked locus affecting cognitive function. *Nature, 387,* 705–708.

Slade, A., Belsky, J., Aber, J. L., & Phelps, J. L. (1999). Mothers' representation of their relationships with their toddlers: Links to adult attachment and observed mothering. *Developmental Psychology, 35,* 611–619.

Slap, G. B., Vorters, D. F., Chaudhuri, S., & Centor, R. M. (1989). Risk factors for attempted suicide during adolescence. *Pediatrics, 84,* 762–772.

Slobin, D. (1971). Universals of grammatical development in children. In W. Levitt & G. B. Flores d' Arcais (Eds.), *Advances in psycholinguistic research.* Amsterdam: New Holland.

Slobin, D. (1973). Cognitive prerequisites for the acquisition of language. In C. Ferguson & D. Slobin (Eds.), *Studies of child language development.* New York: Holt, Rinehart, & Winston.

Slobin, D. (1983). Universal and particular in the acquisition of grammar. In E. Wanner & L. Gleitman (Eds.), *Language acquisition: The state of the art.* Cambridge, England: Cambridge University Press.

Sly, R. M. (2000). Decreases in asthma mortality in the United States. *Annal of Allergy, Asthma, and Immunology, 85,* 121–127.

Small, M. Y. (1990). *Cognitive development.* New York: Harcourt Brace.

Smetana, J. G., & Bitz, B. (1996). Adolescents' conception of teachers' authority and their relations to rule violations in school. *Child Development, 67,* 1153–1172.

Smilansky, S. (1968). *The effects of sociodramatic play on disadvantaged preschool children.* New York: Wiley.

Smith, B. A., & Blass, E. M. (1996). Taste-mediated calming in premature, preterm, and full-term human infants. *Developmental Psychology, 32,* 1084–1089.

Smith, D. J. (1997). Indigenous peoples' extended family relationships: A source for classroom structure. *McGill Journal of Education, 32*(2), 125–138.

Smith, G. A., & Shields, B. J. (1998). Trampoline-related injuries to children. *Archives of Pediatrics and Adolescent Medicine, 152,* 694–699.

Smith, G. C. S., Pell, J. P., Cameron, A. D., & Dobbie, R. (2002). Risk of perinatal death associated with labor after previous cesarean delivery in uncomplicated term pregnancies. *Journal of the American Medical Association, 287,* 2684–2690.

Smith, K. A., Fairburn, C. G., & Cowen, P. J. (1999). Symptomatic release in bulimia nervosa following acute tryptophan depletion. *Archives of General Psychiatry (72C), 56*(2), 171–176.

Smith, M. (1998, February 25). U.S. 12th-graders trail students of other nations in math, science. *Minneapolis Star-Tribune,* p. A5.

Smith, M., Apperly, I., & White, V. (2003). False belief reasoning and the acquisition of relative clause sentences. *Child Development, 74,* 1709–1719.

Smith, M. E. (1993). Television violence and behavior: A research summary [Online]. *ERIC/IT Digest* (ED366 329). Available: http://npin.org/respar/texts/media/viole397.html.

Smith, P. K., & Levan, S. (1995). Perceptions and experiences of bullying in younger pupils. *British Journal of Educational Psychology, 65,* 489–500.

Smith, R. (1999, March). The timing of birth. *Scientific American,* pp. 68–75.

Smith-Bindman, R., Chu, P., Bacchetti, P., Waters, J. J., Mutton, D., & Alberman, E. (2003). Prenatal screening for Down syndrome in England and Wales and population-based birth outcomes. *American Journal of Obstetrics and Gynecology, 189,* 980–985.

Smith-Khuri, E., Iachan, R., Scheidt, P. C., Overpeck, M. D., Gabhainn, S. N., Pickett, W., & Harel, Y. (2004). A cross-national study of violence-related behaviors in adolescents. *Archives of Pediatrics and Adolescent Medicine, 158,* 539–544.

Smotherman, W. P., & Robinson, S. R. (1995). Tracing developmental trajectories into the prenatal period. In J. P. Lecanuet, W. P. Fifer, N. A. Krasnegor, & W. P. Smotherman (Eds.), *Fetal development. A psychobiological perspective* (pp. 15–32). Hillsdale, NJ: Erlbaum.

Smotherman, W. P., & Robinson, S. R. (1996). The development of behavior before birth. *Developmental Psychology, 32,* 425–434.

Snarey, J. R. (1985). Cross-cultural universality of social-moral development: A critical review of Kohlbergian research. *Psychological Bulletin, 97,* 202–232.

Snow, C. E. (1990). The development of definitional skill. *Journal of Child Language, 17,* 697–710.

Snow, C. E. (1993). Families as social contexts for literacy development. In C. Daiute (Ed.), *The development of literacy through social interaction* (New Directions for Child Development No. 61, pp. 11–24). San Francisco: Jossey-Bass.

Snow, M. E., Jacklin, C. N., & Maccoby, E. E. (1983). Sex-of-child differences in father-child interaction at one year of age. *Child Development, 54,* 227–232.

Snyder, H. N. (2000). *Special analyses of FBI serious violent crimes data.* Pittsburgh, PA: National Center for Juvenile Justice.

Snyder, J., West, L., Stockemer, V., Gibbons, S., & Almquist-Parks, L. (1996). A social learning model of peer choice in the natural environment. *Journal of Applied Developmental Psychology, 17,* 215–237.

Snyder, T. D., & Hoffman, C. M. (2001). *Digest of Education Statistics, 2000.* Washington, DC: National Center for Education Statistics.

Snyder, T. D., & Hoffman, C. M. (2002). *The digest of education statistics: 2001.* Washington, DC: National Center for Education Statistics.

Snyder, T. D., & Hoffman, C. M. (2003). *Digest of education statistics, 2002* (Publication No. NCES 2003–060). Washington, DC: Author.

Society for Assisted Reproductive Technology and the American Society for Reproductive Medicine. (2002). Assisted reproductive technology in the United States: 1998 results generated from the American Society for Reproductive Medicine/Society for Assisted Reproductive Technology Registry. *Fertility & Sterility, 77*(1), 18–31.

Society for Assisted Reproductive Technology, The American Fertility Society. (1993). Assisted reproductive technology in the United States and Canada: 1991 results from the Society for Assisted Reproductive Technology generated from The American Fertility Society Registry. *Fertility and Sterility, 59,* 956–962.

Society for Research in Child Development. (1996). Ethical standards for research with children. In *Directory of members* (pp. 337–339). Ann Arbor, MI: Author.

Sokol, R. J., Delaney-Black, V., and Nordstrom, B. (2003). Fetal alcohol spectrum disorder, *Journal of the American Medical Association, 209,* 2996–2999.

Solowij, N., Stephens, R. S., Roffman, R. A., Babor, T., Kadden, R., Miller, M., Christiansen, K., McRee, B., & Vendetti, J., for the Marijuana Treatment Research Group. (2002). Cognitive functioning of long-term heavy cannabis users seeking treatment. *Journal of the American Medical Association, 287,* 1123–1131.

Sommers-Flanagan, J., & Sommers-Flanagan, R. (1996). Efficacy of antidepressant medication with depressed youth: What psychologists should know. *Professional Psychology: Research & Practice, 27,* 145–153.

Sondergaard, C., Henriksen, T. B., Obel, C., & Wisborg, K. (2001). Smoking during pregnancy and infantile colic. *Pediatrics, 108*(2), 342–346.

Sonenstein, F. L., Pleck, J. H., & Ku, L. C. (1991). Levels of sexual activity among adolescent males in the United States. *Family Planning Perspectives, 23*(4), 162–167.

Sood, B., Delaney-Black, V., Covington, C., Nordstrom-Klee, B., Ager, J., Templin, T., Janisse, J., Martier, S., & Sokol, R. J. (2001). Prenatal alcohol exposure and childhood behavior at age 6 to 7 years: I. Dose-response effect. *Pediatrics, 108*(8), e461–e462.

Sophian, C. (1988). Early developments in children's understanding of number: Inferences about numerosity and one-to-one correspondence. *Child Development, 59,* 1397–1414.

Sophian, C., & Wood, A. (1997). Proportional reasoning in young children: The parts and the whole of it. *Journal of Educational Psychology, 89,* 309–317.

Sophian, C., Garyantes, D., & Chang, C. (1997). When three is less than two: Early developments in children's understanding of fractional quantities. *Developmental Psychology, 33,* 731–744.

Sophian, C., Wood, A., & Vong, K. I. (1995). Making numbers count: The early development of numerical inferences. *Developmental Psychology, 31,* 263–273.

Sorce, J. F., Emde, R. N., Campos, J., & Klinnert, M. D. (1985). Maternal emotional signalling: Its effect on the visual cliff behavior of 1-year-olds. *Developmental Psychology, 21,* 195–200.

Sorensen, T., Nielsen, G., Andersen, P., & Teasdale, T. (1988). Genetic and environmental influence of premature death in adult adoptees. *New England Journal of Medicine, 318,* 727–732.

Sowell, E. R., & Peterson, B. (2003). Cortical abnormalities in children and adolescents with attention-deficit hyperactivity disorder. *Lancet, 362,* 1699–1707.

Spelke, E. (1994). Initial knowledge: Six suggestions. *Cognition, 50,* 431–445.

Spelke, E. S. (1998). Nativism, empiricism, and the origins of knowledge. *Infant Behavior and Development, 21*(2), 181–200.

Spencer, J. M., Zimet, G. D., Aalsma, M. C., & Orr, D. P. (2002). Self-esteem as a predictor of initiation of coitus in early adolescents. *Pediatrics, 109,* 581–584.

Spencer, J. P., Smith, L. B., & Thelen, E. (2001). Tests of a dynamic systems account of the A-not-B error: The influence of prior experience on the spatial memory abilities of two-year-olds. *Child Development, 72,* 1327–1346.

Spieker, S. J., Nelson, D. C., Petras, A., Jolley, S. N., & Barnard, K. E. (2003). Joint influence of child care and infant attachment security for cognitive and language outcomes of low-income toddlers. *Infant Behavior & Development, 26,* 326–344.

Spinath, F. M., Price, T. S., Dale, P. S., & Plomin, R. (2004). The genetic and environmental origins of language disability and ability. *Child Development, 75,* 445–454.

Spinrad, T. L., Eisenberg, N., Harris, E., Hanish, L., Fabes, R. A., Kupanoff, K., Ringwald, S., & Holmes, J. (2004). The relation of children's everyday nonsocial peer play behavior to their emotionality, regulation, and social functioning. *Developmental Psychology, 40,* 67–80.

Spitz, R. A. (1945). Hospitalism: An inquiry into the genesis of psychiatric conditioning in early childhood. In D. Fenschel et al. (Eds.), *Psychoanalytic studies of the child* (vol. 1, pp. 53–74). New York: International Universities Press.

Spitz, R. A. (1946). Hospitalism: A follow-up report. In D. Fenschel et al. (Eds.), *Psychoanalytic studies of the child* (vol. 1, pp. 113–117). New York: International Universities Press.

Spohr, H. L., Willms, J., & Steinhausen, H.-C. (1993). Prenatal alcohol exposure and long-term developmental consequences. *Lancet, 341,* 907–910.

Squire, L. R. (1992). Memory and the hippocampus: A synthesis of findings with rats, monkeys, and humans. *Psychological Review, 99,* 195–231.

Sroufe, L. A. (1979). Socioemotional development. In J. Osofsky (Ed.), *Handbook of infant development.* New York: Wiley.

Sroufe, L. A. (1997). *Emotional development.* Cambridge, England: Cambridge University Press.

Sroufe, L. A., Bennett, C., Englund, M., Urban, J., & Shulman, S. (1993). The significance of gender boundaries in preadolescence: Contemporary correlates and antecedents of boundary violation and maintenance. *Child Development, 64,* 455–466.

Sroufe, L. A., Carlson, E., & Shulman, S. (1993). Individuals in relationships: Development from infancy through adolescence. In D. C. Funder, R. D. Parke, C. Tomlinson-Keasey, & K. Widaman (Eds.), *Studying lives through time: Personality and development* (pp. 315–342). Washington, DC: American Psychological Association.

Stahl, S. A., McKenna, M. C., & Pagnucco, J. R. (1994). The effects of whole-language instruction: An update and a reappraisal. *Educational Psychologist, 29,* 175–185.

Standley, J. M. (1998). Strategies to improve outcomes in critical care—The effect of music and multimodal stimulation on responses of premature infants in neonatal intensive care. *Pediatric Nursing, 24,* 532–538.

Stapleton, S. (1998, May 11). Asthma rates hit epidemic numbers; experts wonder why [Online]. *American Medical News, 41*(18). Available: http://www.ama-assn.org/special/asthma/newsline/special/epidem.htm.

Starfield, B. (1991). Childhood morbidity: Comparisons, clusters, and trends. *Pediatrics, 88,* 519–526.

Starr, J. M., Deary, I. J., Lemmon, H., & Whalley, L. J. (2000). Mental ability age 11 years and health status age 77 years. *Age and Ageing, 29,* 523–528.

Staub, E. (1996). Cultural-societal roots of violence: The examples of genocidal violence and of contemporary youth violence in the United States. *American Psychologist, 51,* 117–132.

Stauder, J. E. A., Molenaar, P. C. M., & Van der Molen, M. W. (1993). Scalp topography of event-related brain potentials and cognitive transition during childhood. *Child Development, 64,* 769–788.

Steinberg, L. (1988). Reciprocal relation between parent-child distance and pubertal maturation. *Developmental Psychology, 24,* 122–128.

Steinberg, L., & Darling, N. (1994). The broader context of social influence in adolescence. In R. Silberstein & E. Todt (Eds.), *Adolescence in context.* New York: Springer.

Steinberg, L., Dornbusch, S. M., & Brown, B. B. (1992). Ethnic differences in adolescent achievement: An ecological perspective. *American Psychologist, 47,* 723–729.

Steinberg, L., Fegley, S., & Dornbusch, S. M. (1993). Negative impact of part time work on adolescent adjustment: Evidence from a longitudinal study. *Developmental Psychology, 29,* 171–180.

Steinberg, L., Lamborn, S. D., Dornbusch, S. M., & Darling, N. (1992). Impact of parenting practices on adolescent achievement: Parenting, school involvement, and encouragement to succeed. *Child Development, 47,* 723–729.

Stennies, G., Ikeda, R., Leadbetter, S., Houston, B., & Sacks, J. (1999). Firearm storage practices and children in the home, United States, 1994. *Archives of Pediatrics and Adolescent Medicine, 153,* 586–590.

Stephens, J. C., Schneider, J. A., Tanguay, D. A., Choi, J., Acharya, T., Stanley, S. E., Jiang, R., Messer, C. J., Chew, A.,

Han, J.-H., Duan, J., Carr, J. L., Lee, M. S., Koshy, B., Madan Kumar, A., Zhang, G., Newell, W. R., Windemuth, A., Xu, C., Kalbfleisch, T. S., Shaner, S. L., Arnold, K., Schulz, V., Drysdale, C. M., Nandabalan, K., Judson, R. S., Ruano, G., & Vovis, G. F. (2001). Haplotype variation and linkage disequilibrium in 313 human genes. *Science, 293,* 489–493.

Sternberg, R. J. (1985). *Beyond IQ: A triarchic theory of human intelligence.* New York: Cambridge University Press.

Sternberg, R. J. (1987, September 23). The use and misuse of intelligence testing: Misunderstanding meaning, users over-rely on scores. *Education Week,* pp. 22, 28.

Sternberg, R. J. (1993). *Sternberg Triarchic Abilities Test.* Unpublished manuscript.

Sternberg, R. J. (1997). The concept of intelligence and its role in lifelong learning and success. *American Psychologist, 52,* 1030–1037.

Sternberg, R. J., & Clinkenbeard, P. (1995). A triarchic view of identifying, teaching, and assessing gifted children. *Roeper Review, 17,* 255–260.

Sternberg, R. J., Torff, B., & Grigorenko, E. L. (1998). Teaching triarchically improves school achievement. *Journal of Educational Psychology, 90*(3), 374–384.

Stevens, J. H., & Bakeman, R. (1985). A factor analytic study of the HOME scale for infants. *Developmental Psychology, 21,* 1106–1203.

Stevenson, H. W. (1995). Mathematics achievement of American students: First in the world by the year 2000? In C. A. Nelson (Ed.), *The Minnesota Symposia on Child Psychology: Vol. 28. Basic and applied perspectives on learning, cognition, and development* (pp. 131–149). Mahwah, NJ: Erlbaum.

Stevenson, H. W., Chen, C., & Lee, S. Y. (1993). Mathematics achievement of Chinese, Japanese, and American children: Ten years later. *Science, 258*(5081), 53–58.

Stevenson, H. W., Lee, S. Y., Chen, C., Stigler, J. W., Hsu, C. C., & Kitamura, S. (1990). Contexts of achievement: A study of American, Chinese, and Japanese children. *Monographs of the Society for Research in Child Development, 55*(1–2, Serial No. 221).

Stevenson, H. W., Lee, S., Chen, C., & Lummis, M. (1990). Mathematics achievement of children in China and the United States. *Child Development, 61,* 1053–1066.

Stevenson-Hinde, J., & Shouldice, A. (1996). Fearfulness: Developmental consistency. In A. J. Sameroff & M. M. Haith (Eds.), *The five- to seven-year shift: The age of reason and responsibility* (pp. 237–252). Chicago: University of Chicago Press.

Steward, M. S., & Steward, D. S. (1996). Interviewing young children about body touch and handling. *Monographs of the Society for Research in Child Development, 61*(4–5, Serial No. 248).

Stewart, I. C. (1994, January 29). Two part message [Letter to the editor]. *New York Times,* p. A18.

Stice, E., & Bearman, K. (2001). Body image and eating disturbances prospectively predict increases in depressive symptoms in adolescent girls: A growth curve analysis. *Developmental Psychology, 37*(5), 597–607.

Stice, E., Presnell, K., & Bearman, S. K. (2001). Relation of early menarche to depression, eating disorders, substance abuse, and comorbid psychopathology among adolescent girls. *Developmental Psychology, 37,* 608–619.

Stick, S. M., Burton, P. B., Gurrin, L., Sly, P. D., & LeSouëf, P. N. (1996). Effects of maternal smoking during pregnancy and a family history of asthma on respiratory function in newborn infants. *The Lancet, 348,* 1060–1064.

Stifter, C. A., Coulehan, C. M., & Fish, M. (1993). Linking employment to attachment: The mediating effects of maternal separation anxiety and interactive behavior. *Child Development, 64,* 1451–1460.

Stipek, D. (2002). At what age should children enter kindergarten? A question for policy makers and parents. *SRCD Social Policy Report, 16*(2), 1–16.

Stipek, D., & Byler, P. (2001). Academic achievement and social behaviors associated with age of entry into kindergarten. *Journal of Applied Developmental Psychology, 22,* 175–189.

Stipek, D. J., & Ryan, R. H. (1997). Economically disadvantaged preschoolers: Ready to learn but further to go. *Developmental Psychology, 33,* 711–723.

Stipek, D. J., Gralinski, H., & Kopp, C. B. (1990). Self-concept development in the toddler years. *Developmental Psychology, 26,* 972–977.

Stoecker, J. J., Colombo, J., Frick J. E., & Allen, J. R. (1998). Long- and shortlooking infants' recognition of symmetrical and asymmetrical forms. *Journal of Experimental Child Psychology, 71,* 63–78.

Stolberg, S. G. (1997, May 16). Senate tries to define fetal viability: Murky concepts still clouding the debate over abortion laws. *New York Times,* p. A18.

Strasburger, V. C., & Donnerstein, E. (1999). Children, adolescents, and the media: Issues and solutions. *Pediatrics, 103,* 129–139.

Strassberg, Z., Dodge, K. A., Pettit, G. S., & Bates, J. E. (1994). Spanking in the home and children's subsequent aggression toward kindergarten peers. *Development and Psychopathology, 6,* 445–461.

Straus, M. A. (1994a). *Beating the devil out of them: Corporal punishment in American families.* San Francisco, CA: Jossey-Bass.

Straus, M. A. (1994b). Should the use of corporal punishment by parents be considered child abuse? In M. A. Mason & E. Gambrill (Eds.), *Debating children's lives: Current controversies on children and adolescents* (pp. 196–222). Newbury Park, CA: Sage.

Straus, M. A. (1999). The benefits of avoiding corporal punishment: New and more definitive evidence. Submitted for publication in K. C. Blaine (Ed.), *Raising America's Children.*

Straus, M. A., & Field, C. J. (2003). Psychological aggression by American parents: National data on prevalence, chronicity, and severity. *Journal of Marriage and Family, 65,* 795–808.

Straus, M. A., & Field, C. J. (November 2003). Psychological aggression by American parents: National data on prevalence, chronicity, and severity. *Journal of Marriage and Family, 65,* 795–808.

Straus, M. A., & Paschall, M. J. (1999, July). *Corporal punishment by mothers and children's cognitive development: A longitudinal study of two age cohorts.* Paper presented at the Sixth International Family Violence Research Conference, University of New Hampshire, Durham, NH.

Straus, M. A., & Stewart, J. H. (1999). Corporal punishment by American parents: National data on prevalence, chronicity, severity, and duration, in relation to child and family characteristics. *Clinical Child and Family Psychology Review, 2*(21), 55–70.

Straus, M. A., Sugarman, D. B., & Giles-Sims, J. (1997). Spanking by parents and subsequent antisocial behavior of children. *Archives of Pediatric and Adolescent Medicine, 151,* 761–767.

Strauss, M., Lessen-Firestone, J., Starr, R., & Ostrea, E. (1975). Behavior of narcotics-addicted newborns. *Child Development, 46,* 887–893.

Strauss, R. S. (2000). Adult functional outcome of those born small for gestational age: Twenty-six-year follow-up of the 1970 British Birth Cohort. *Journal of the American Medical Association, 283,* 625–632.

Streissguth, A. P., Aase, J. M., Clarren, S. K., Randels, S. P., LaDue, R. A., & Smith, D. F. (1991). Fetal alcohol syndrome in adolescents and adults. *Journal of the American Medical Association, 265,* 1961–1967.

Streissguth, A. P., Bookstein, F. L., Barr, H. M., Sampson, P. D., O'Malley, K., Young, J. K. (2004). Risk factors for adverse life outcomes in fetal alcohol syndrome and fetal alcohol effects. *Journal of Developmental & Behavioral Pediatrics, 25,* 228–238.

Streissguth, A. P., Martin, D. C., Barr, H. M., Sandman, B. M., Kirchner, G. L., & Darby, B. L. (1984). Intrauterine alcohol and nicotine exposure: Attention and reaction time in 4-year-old children. *Developmental Psychology, 20,* 533–541.

Strobel, A., Camoin, T. I. L., Ozata, M., & Strosberg, A. D. (1998). A leptin missense mutation associated with hypogonadism and morbid obesity. *Nature Genetics, 18,* 213–215.

Strömland, K., & Hellström, A. (1996). Fetal alcohol syndrome—An ophthalmological and socioeducational prospective study. *Pediatrics, 97,* 845–850.

Stuart, J. (1991). Introduction. In Z. Zhensun & A. Low, *A young painter: The life and paintings of Wang Yani—China's extraordinary young artist* (pp. 6–7). New York: Scholastic.

Stubbs, M. L., Rierdan, J., & Koff, E. (1989). Developmental differences in menstrual attitudes. *Journal of Early Adolescence, 9*(4), 480–498.

Sturges, J. W., & Sturges, L. V. (1998). In vivo systematic desensitization in a single-session treatment of an 11-year-old girl's elevator phobia. *Child & Family Behavior Therapy, 20,* 55–62.

Subar, A. F., Krebs-Smith, S. M., Cook, A., & Kahle, L. L. (1998). Dietary sources of nutrients among U.S. children, 1989–1991. *Pediatrics, 102,* 913–923.

Subramanian, G., Adams, M. D., Venter, J. C., & Broder, S. (2001). Implications of the human genome for understanding human biology and medicine. *Journal of the American Medical Association, 26*(18), 2296–2307.

Suddendorf, T. (2003). Early representational insight: 24-month-olds can use a photo to find an object in the world. *Child Development, 74,* 896–904.

Sue, S., & Okazaki, S. (1990). Asian-American educational achievements: A phenomenon in search of an explanation. *American Psychologist 45*(8), 913–920.

Sugarman, J. (1999). Ethical considerations in leaping from bench to bedside. *Science, 285,* 2071–2072.

Suicide—Part I. (1996, November). *The Harvard Mental Health Letter,* pp. 1–5.

Sullivan, P. F., Bulik, C. M., Fear, J. L., & Pickering, A. (1998). Outcome of anorexia nervosa: A case-control study. *American Journal of Psychiatry, 155,* 939–946.

Sullivan-Bolyai, J., Hull, H. F., Wilson, C., & Corey, L. (1983). Neonatal herpes simplex virus infection in King County, Washington. *Journal of the American Medical Association, 250,* 3059–3062.

Summers, T., Kates, J., & Murphy, G. (2002). *The tip of the iceberg: The global impact of HIV/AIDS on youth.* Menlo Park, CA: Henry J. Kaiser Family Foundation.

Sun, Y. (2001). Family environment and adolescents' well-being before and after parents' marital disruption. *Journal of Marriage and the Family, 63,* 697–713.

Suomi, S., & Harlow, H. (1972). Social rehabilitation of isolate-reared monkeys. *Developmental Psychology, 6,* 487–496.

Suomi, S. J. (2003). Gene-environment interactions and the neurobiology of social conflict. *Annals of the New York Academy of Sciences, 1008,* 132–139.

Surkan, P. J., Stephansson, O., Dickman, P. W., & Cnattingius, S. (2004). Previous preterm and small-for-gestational-age births and the subsequent risk of stillbirth. *New England Journal of Medicine, 350,* 777–785.

Susman, E. J., Dorn, L. D., & Schiefelbein, V. L. (2003). Puberty, sexuality, and health. In I. Weiner (Ed.) and R. M. Lerner, M. A. Easterbrooks, & J. Mistry (Vol. Eds.), *Handbook of Psychology. Vol. 6: Developmental Psychology* (295–324). Hoboken, NJ: Wiley.

Susman-Stillman, A., Kalkoske, M., Egeland, B., & Waldman, I. (1996). Infant temperament and maternal sensitivity as predictors of attachment security. *Infant Behavior and Development, 19,* 33–47.

Sutcliffe, A., Loft, A., Wennerholm, U. B., Tarlatzis, V., & Bonduelle, M. (2003, July). The European study of 1,523 ICSI/IVF versus naturally conceived 5-year-old children and their families: Physical development at five years. Paper presented at conference of European Society of Human Reproduction and Embryology, Madrid.

Suzuki, L. A., & Valencia, R. R. (1997). Race-ethnicity and measured intelligence: Educational implications. *American Psychologist, 52,* 1103–1114.

Swain, I. U., Zelazo, P. R., & Clifton, R. K. (1993). Newborn infants' memory for speech sounds retained over 24 hours. *Developmental Psychology, 29,* 312–323.

Swan, S. H. (2000). Intrauterine exposure to diethylstilbestrol: Long-term effects in humans. *APMIS, 108,* 793–804.

Swan, S. H., Kruse, R. L., Liu, F., Barr, D. B., Drobnis, E. Z., Redmon, J. B., Wang, C., Brazil, C., Overstreet, J. W., and Study for Future Families Research Group. (2003). Semen quality in relation to biomarkers of pesticide exposure. *Environmental Health Perspectives, 111,* 1478–1484.

Swanston, H. Y., Tebbutt, J. S., O'Toole, B. I., & Oates, R. K. (1997). Sexually abused children 5 years after presentation: A case-control study. *Pediatrics, 100,* 600–608.

Swarr, A. E., & Richards, M. H. (1996). Longitudinal effects of adolescent girls' pubertal development, perceptions of pubertal timing, and parental relations on eating problems. *Developmental Psychology, 32,* 636–646.

Swedo, S., Rettew, D. C., Kuppenheimer, M., Lum, D., Dolan, S., & Goldberger, E. (1991). Can adolescent suicide attemptors be distinguished from at-risk adolescents? *Pediatrics, 88*(3), 620–629.

Szaflarski, J. P., Holland, S. K., Schmithorst, V. J., & Weber-Byars, A. (2004). An fMRI study of cerebral language lateralization in 121 children and adults. Paper presented at the 56th Annual Meeting of the American Academy of Neurology, San Francisco, CA.

Szatmari, P. (1999). Heterogeneity and the genetics of autism. *Journal of Psychiatry and Neuroscience, 24,* 159–165.

Szkrybalo, J., & Ruble, D. N. (1999). "God made me a girl": Sex category constancy judgments and explanations revisited. *Developmental Psychology, 35,* 392–403.

Taddio, A., Katz, J., Ilersich, A. L., & Koren, G. (1997). Effect of neonatal circumcision on pain response during subsequent routine vaccination. *Lancet, 349,* 599–603.

Takanishi, R. (1993). The opportunities of adolescence—Research, interventions, and policy. *American Psychologist, 48,* 85–87.

Tamis-LeMonda, C. S., Bornstein, M. H., & Baumwell, L. (2001). Maternal responsiveness and children's achievement of language milestones. *Child Development, 72*(3), 748–767.

Tanda, G., Pontieri, F. E., & DiChiara, G. (1997). Cannabinoid and heroin activation of mesolimbic dopamine transmission by a common N1 opiod receptor mechanism. *Science, 276,* 2048–2050.

Tanner, J. M. (1978). *Fetus into man: Physical growth from conception to maturity.* Cambridge, MA: Harvard University Press.

Tao, K.-T. (1998). An overview of only child family mental health in China. *Psychiatry and Clinical Neurosciences, 52*(Suppl.), S206–S211.

Tarabulsy, G. M., Provost, M. A., Deslandes, J., St-Laurent, D., Moss, E., Lemelin, E., Bernier, A., & Dassylva, J. (2003). Individual differences in infant still-face response at 6 months. *Infant Behavior & Development, 26,* 421–438.

Tardiff, T., & Wellman, H. M. (2000). Acquisition of mental state language in Mandarin- and Cantonese-speaking children. *Developmental Psychology, 36,* 25–43.

Taveras, E. M., Capra, A. M., Braveman, P. A., Jensvold, N. G., Escobar, G. J., & Lieu, T. A. (2003). Clinician support and psychosocial risk factors associated with breastfeeding discontinuation. *Pediatrics, 112,* 108–115.

Taylor, H. S., Arici, A., Olive, D., & Igarashi, P. (1998). HOXA10 is expressed in response to sex steroids at the time of implantation in the human endometrium. *Journal of Clinical Investigation, 101,* 1379–1384.

Taylor, J. A., Krieger, J. W., Reay, D. T., Davis, R. L., Harruff, R., & Chenek, L. K. (1996). Prone sleep position and the sudden infant death syndrome in King's County, Washington: A case-control study. *Journal of Pediatrics, 128,* 626–630.

Taylor, M. (1997). The role of creative control and culture in children's fantasy/reality judgments. *Child Development, 68,* 1015–1017.

Taylor, M. G. (1996). The development of children's beliefs about social and biological aspects of gender differences. *Child Development, 67,* 1555–1571.

Taylor, M., & Carlson, S. M. (1997). The relation between individual differences in fantasy and theory of mind. *Child Development, 68,* 436–455.

Taylor, M., Cartwright, B. S., & Carlson, S. M. (1993). A developmental investigation of children's imaginary companions. *Developmental Psychology, 28,* 276–285.

Taylor, R. D., & Roberts, D. (1995). Kinship support in maternal and adolescent well-being in economically disadvantaged African-American families. *Child Development, 66,* 1585–1597.

Teachman, J. D., Tedrow, L. M., & Crowder, K. D. (2000). The changing demography of America's families. *Journal of Marriage and Family, 62,* 1234–1246.

Teller, D. Y., & Bornstein, M. H. (1987). Infant color vision and color perception. In P. Salapatek & L. B. Cohen (Eds.), *Handbook of infant perception: Vol. 1. From sensation to perception* (pp. 185–236). Orlando, FL: Academic Press.

Temple, J. A., Reynolds, A. J., & Miedel, W. T. (2000). Can early intervention prevent high school dropout? Evidence from the Chicago Child-Parent Centers. *Urban Education, 35*(1), 31–57.

Terman, L. M., & Oden, M. H. (1959). *Genetic studies of genius: Vol. 5. The gifted group at mid-life.* Stanford, CA: Stanford University Press.

Termine, N. T., & Izard, C. E. (1988). Infants' responses to their mothers' expressions of joy and sadness. *Developmental Psychology, 24,* 223–229.

Tesman, J. R., & Hills, A. (1994). Developmental effects of lead exposure in children. *Social Policy Report of the Society for Research in Child Development, 8*(3), 1–16.

Test-tube baby: It's a girl. (1978, August 7). *Time,* p. 68.

Teti, D. M., & Ablard, K. E. (1989). Security of attachment and infant-sibling relationships: A laboratory study. *Child Development, 60,* 1519–1528.

Teti, D. M., Gelfand, D. M., Messinger, D. S., & Isabella, R. (1995). Maternal depression and the quality of early attachment: An examination of infants, preschoolers, and their mothers. *Developmental Psychology, 31,* 364–376.

Teti, D. M., Sakin, J. W., Kucera, E., Corns, K. M., & Eiden, R. D. (1996). And baby makes four: Predictors of attachment security among preschoolage firstborns during the transition to siblinghood. *Child Development, 67,* 579–596.

Thacker, S. B., Addiss, D. G., Goodman, R. A., Holloway, B. R., & Spencer, H. C. (1992). Infectious diseases and injuries in child day care: Opportunities for healthier children. *Journal of the American Medical Association, 268,* 1720–1726.

Thal, D., Tobias, S., & Morrison, D. (1991). Language and gesture in late talkers: A one-year follow-up. *Journal of Speech and Hearing Research, 34,* 604–612.

Thapar, A., Fowler, T., Rice, F., Scourfield, J., van den Bree, M., Thomas, H., Harold, G., & Hay, D. (2003). Maternal smoking during pregnancy and attention deficit hyperactivity disorder symptoms in offspring. *American Journal of Psychiatry, 160,* 1985–1989.

Tharp, R. G. (1989). Psychocultural variables and constants: Effects on teaching and learning in schools. *American Psychologist, 44,* 349–359.

The Breastfeeding and HIV International Transmission Study Group. (2004). Late postnatal transmission of HIV-1 in breast-fed children: An individual patient data meta-analysis. *Journal of Infectious Diseases, 189,* 2154–2166.

The Early College High School Initiative. (undated). [Online]. Available: http://www.earlycolleges.org. Access date: March 31, 2004.

The Project CHOICES Intervention Research Group. (2003). Reducing the risk of alcohol-exposed pregnancies: A study of motivational intervention in community settings. *Pediatrics 111,* 1131–1135.

Thelen, E. (1994). Three-month-old infants can learn task-specific patterns of interlimb coordination. *Psychological Science, 5,* 280–285.

Thelen, E. (1995). Motor development: A new synthesis. *American Psychologist, 50*(2), 79–95.

Thelen, E., & Fisher, D. M. (1982). Newborn stepping: An explanation for a "disappearing" reflex. *Developmental Psychology, 18,* 760–775.

Thelen, E., & Fisher, D. M. (1983). The organization of spontaneous leg movements in newborn infants. *Journal of Motor Behavior, 15,* 353–377.

Thomas, A., & Chess, S. (1977). *Temperament and development.* New York: Brunner/Mazel.

Thomas, A., & Chess, S. (1984). Genesis and evolution of behavioral disorders: From infancy to early adult life. *American Journal of Orthopsychiatry, 141*(1), 1–9.

Thomas, A., Chess, S., & Birch, H. G. (1968). *Temperament and behavior disorders in children.* New York: New York University Press.

Thomas, C. R., Holzer, C. E., & Wall, J. (2002). The Island Youth Programs: Community interventions for reducing youth violence and delinquency. In L. T. Flaherty, Ed.), *Adolescent psychiatry: Developmental and clinical studies, Vol. 26. Annals of the American Society for Adolescent Psychiatry* (pp. 125–143). Hillsdale, NJ: Analytic Press.

Thomas, R. M. (1996). *Comparing theories of child development* (4th ed.). Pacific Grove, CA: Brooks-Cole.

Thomas, W. P., & Collier, V. P. (1997). *School effectiveness for language minority students.* Washington, DC: National Clearinghouse for Bilingual Education.

Thomas, W. P., & Collier, V. P. (1998). Two languages are better than one. *Educational Leadership, 55*(4), 23–28.

Thompson, R. A. (1990). Vulnerability in research: A developmental perspective on research risk. *Child Development, 61,* 1–16.

Thompson, R. A. (1991). Emotional regulation and emotional development. *Educational Psychology Review, 3,* 269–307.

Thompson, R. A. (1998). Early sociopersonality development. In W. Damon (Series Ed.) & N. Eisenberg (Vol. Ed.), *Handbook of child psychology: Vol. 3. Social, emotional, and personality development* (4th ed., pp. 25–104). New York: Wiley.

Thompson, S. L. (2001). The social skills of previously institutionalized children adopted from Romania. *Dissertation Abstracts International: Section B: The Sciences & Engineering, 61*(7-B), 3906.

Thomson, E., Mosley, J., Hanson, T. L., & McLanahan, S. S. (2001). Remarriage, cohabitation, and changes in mothering behavior. *Journal of Marriage and Family, 63,* 370–380.

Thorne, A., & Michaelieu, Q. (1996). Situating adolescent gender and self-esteem with personal memories. *Child Development, 67,* 1374–1390.

Thum, M. Y., Gafar, A., Wren, M., Faris, R., Ogunyeni, B., Korea, L., Scott, L., & Abdalla, H. I. (2003). Does egg-sharing compromise the chance of donors or recipients achieving a live birth? *Human Reproduction, 18,* 2363–2367.

Tiedemann, D. (1897). *Beobachtungen über die entwickelung der seelenfähigkeiten bei kindern* (*Record of an infant's life*). Altenburg, Germany: Oscar Bonde. (Original work published 1787.)

Timiras, P. S. (1972). *Developmental psychology and aging.* New York: Macmillan.

Tincoff, R., & Jusczyk, P. W. (1999). Some beginnings of word comprehension in 6-month-olds. *Psychological Science, 10,* 172–177.

Tisak, M. S., & Tisak, J. (1996). My sibling's but not my friend's keeper: Reasoning about responses to aggressive acts. *Journal of Early Adolescence, 16,* 324–329.

Tisdale, S. (1988). The mother. *Hippocrates, 2*(3) 64–72.

Tolan, P. H., Gorman-Smith, D., & Henry, D. B. (2003). The developmental ecology of urban males' youth violence. *Developmental Psychology, 39,* 274–291.

Tomashek, K. M., Hsia, J., & Iyasu, S. (2003). Trends in postneonatal mortality attributable to injury, United States, 1988–1998. *Pediatrics, 111,* 1215–1218.

Torrance, E. P. (1966). *The Torrance Tests of Creative Thinking: Technical norms manual* (Research ed.). Princeton, NJ: Personnel Press.

Torrance, E. P. (1974). *The Torrance Tests of Creative Thinking: Technical norms manual.* Bensonville, IL: Scholastic Testing Service.

Torrance, E. P., & Ball, O. E. (1984). *Torrance Tests of Creative Thinking: Streamlined (revised) manual, Figural A and B.* Bensonville, IL: Scholastic Testing Service.

Townsend, N. W. (1997). Men, migration, and households in Botswana: An exploration of connections over time and space. *Journal of Southern African Studies, Vol. 23,* 405–420.

Tramontana, M. G., Hooper, S. R., & Selzer, S. C. (1988). Research on the preschool prediction of later academic achievement: A review. *Developmental Review, 8,* 89–146.

Trautner, H. M., Ruble, D. N., Cyphers, L., Kirsten, B., Behrendt, R., & Hartmann, P. (2003). *Rigidity and flexibility of gender stereotypes in childhood: Developmental or differential?* Manuscript submitted for publication.

Treffers, P. E., Hanselaar, A. G., Helmerhorst, T. J., Koster, M. E., & van Leeuwen, F. E. (2001). [Consequences of diethylstilbestrol during pregnancy; 50 years later still a significant problem.] *Ned Tijdschr Geneeskd, 145,* 675–680.

Trimble, J. E., & Dickson, R. (in press). Ethnic gloss. In C. B. Fisher & R. M. Lerner (Eds.), *Applied developmental science: An encyclopedia of research, policies, and programs.* Thousand Oaks, CA: Sage.

Troiano, R. P. (2002). Physical inactivity among young people. *New England Journal of Medicine, 347,* 706–707.

Tronick, E. (1972). Stimulus control and the growth of the infant's visual field. *Perception and Psychophysics, 11,* 373–375.

Tronick, E. Z. (1980). On the primacy of social skills. In D. B. Sawin, L. O. Walker, & J. H. Penticuff (Eds.), *The exceptional infant: Psychosocial risk in infant environment transactions.* New York: Brunner/Mazel.

Tronick, E. Z. (1989). Emotions and emotional communication in infants. *American Psychologist, 44*(2), 112–119.

Tronick, E. Z., Morelli, G. A, & Ivey, P. (1992). The Efe forager infant and toddler's pattern of social relationships: Multiple and simultaneous. *Developmental Psychology, 28,* 568–577.

Troseth, G. L. (2003). TV Guide: 2–year-old children learn to use video as a source of information. *Developmental Psychology, 39,* 140–150.

Troseth, G. L., & DeLoache, J. S. (1998). The medium can obscure the message: Young children's understanding of video. *Child Development, 69,* 950–965.

Trottier, G., Srivastava, L., & Walker, C. (1999). Etiology of infantile autism: A review of recent advances in genetic and neurobiological research. *Journal of Psychiatry and Neuroscience, 24,* 103–115.

True, M. M., Pisani, L., & Oumar, F. (2001). Infant-mother attachment among the Dogon of Mali. *Child Development, 72,* 1451–1466.

Truffaut, François (1969). *L'enfant sauvage (The Wild Child).*

Turati, C., Simion, F., Milani, I., & Umilta, C. (2002). Newborns' preference for faces: What is crucial? *Developmental Psychology, 38,* 875–882.

Turkheimer, E., Haley, A., Waldron, J., D'Onofrio, B., & Gottesman, I. I. (2003). Socioeconomic status modifies heritability of IQ in young children. *Psychological Science, 14,* 623–628.

Turner, C. F., Ku, L., Rogers, S. M., Lindberg, L. D., Pleck, J. H., & Sonenstein, F. L. (1998). Adolescent sexual behavior, drug use, and violence: Increased reporting with computer survey technology. *Science, 280,* 867–873.

Turner, P. J., & Gervai, J. (1995). A multidimensional study of gender typing in preschool children and their parents: Personality, attitudes, preferences, behavior, and cultural differences. *Developmental Psychology, 31,* 759–772.

Turrisi, R., Wiersman, K. A., & Hughes, K. K. (2000). Binge-drinking-related consequences in college students: Role of drinking beliefs and mother-teen communication. *Psychology of Addictive Behaviors, 14*(4), 342–345.

Tuulio-Henriksson, A., Haukka, J., Partonen, T., Varilo, T., Paunio, T., Ekelund, J., Cannon, T. D., Meyer, J. M., & Lonnqvist, J. (2002). Heritability and number of quantitative trait loci of neurocognitive functions in families with schizophrenia. *American Journal of Medical Genetics, 114*(5), 483–490.

Twenge, J. M. (2000). The age of anxiety? Birth cohort change in anxiety and neuroticism, 1952–1993. *Journal of Personality and Social Psychology, 79,* 1007–1021.

Tygiel, J. (1983). *Baseball's great experiment: Jackie Robinson and his legacy.* New York: Oxford University Press.

Tygiel, J. (Ed.). (1997). *The Jackie Robinson reader.* New York: Dutton.

U.S. Bureau of the Census. (1998). *Household and family characteristics: March 1998 (Update)* (Current Population Reports, P20–514). Washington, DC: U.S. Government Printing Office.

U.S. Census Bureau. (1930). *Population in the United States: Population characteristics. January, 1930.* Washington, DC: U.S. Government Printing Office.

U.S. Census Bureau. (2003). *Population in the United States: Population characteristics. June, 2002.* Washington, DC: U.S. Government Printing Office.

U.S. Census Bureau. (2003). Table 010. Infant mortality rates and deaths, and life expectancy at birth, by sex. International Data Base. Available: http://www.census.gov/cgi-bin/ipc.agggen.

U.S. Conference of Mayors. (2003). *A status report on hunger and homelessness in America's cities: 2003.* Washington, DC: Author.

U.S. Department of Agriculture. (1999). *Household food security in the United States 1995–1998.* Washington, DC: Author.

U.S. Department of Commerce. (1996). *Statistical abstract of the United States, 1996.* Washington, DC: U.S. Government Printing Office.

U.S. Department of Commerce, Bureau of the Census. *Current Population Survey,* October 1972–2001.

U.S. Department of Education. (1992). *Dropout rates in the U.S., 1991* (Publication No. 92–129). Washington, DC: U.S. Government Printing Office.

U.S. Department of Health and Human Services (USDHHS). (1996a). *Health, United States, 1995* (DHHS Publication No. PHS 96–1232). Washington, DC: U.S. Government Printing Office.

U.S. Department of Health and Human Services (USDHHS). (1996b). *HHS releases study of relationship between family structure and adolescent substance abuse.* [Press release, online]. Available: http://www.hhs.gov.

U.S. Department of Health and Human Services (USDHHS). (1999a). *Blending perspectives and building common ground: A report to Congress on substance abuse and child protection.* Washington, DC: U.S. Government Printing Office.

U.S. Department of Health and Human Services (USDHHS). (1999c). *Mental health: A report of the surgeon general.* Rockville, MD: U.S. Department of HHS, Substance Abuse and Mental Health Services Administration, NIH, NIMH.

U.S. Department of Health and Human Services (USDHHS). (2000a). *HHS Blueprint for Action on Breastfeeding.* Washington, DC: Author.

U.S. Department of Health and Human Services (USDHHS). (2000b, December 6). *Statistics on child care help.* HHS press release [Online]. Available: http://www.hhs.gov/search/press.html. Access date: December 6, 2000.

U.S. Department of Health and Human Services (USDHHS). (2003a). State-funded pre-kindergarten: What the evidence shows. http://aspe.hhs.gov/hsp/state-funded-k/index.htm

U.S. Department of Health and Human Services (USDHHS). (2003b). Strengthening Head Start: What the evidence shows. http://aspe.hhs.gov/hsp/StrengthenHeadStart03/index.htm

U.S. Department of Health and Human Services (USDHHS). (2004). [Online]. Child maltreatment 2002. Accessed: http://www.acf.hhs.gov/programs/cb/publications/cm02/index.htm.

U.S. Environmental Protection Agency. (1994). *Setting the record straight: Secondhand smoke is a preventable health risk* (EPA Publication No. 402-F-94-005). Washington, DC: U.S. Government Printing Office.

Uller, C., Carey, S., Huntley-Fenner, G., & Klatt, L. (1999). What representations might underlie infant numerical knowledge? *Cognitive Development, 14,* 1–36.

Umberger, F. G., & Van Reenen, J. S. (1995). Thumb sucking management: A review. *International Journal of Orofacial Myology, 21,* 41–47.

UNESCO (2003). *Education for all.* Press release No. 2003–91.

UNICEF Press Centre. (2002). Five leading global health organizations announce a new initiative to save children from measles deaths in Africa as part of a global effort to reduce child mortality. (Press release). [Online]. Available: http://www.unicef.org/newsline/02prmeasles1printer.htm. Access date: January 12, 2004.

UNICEF. (2002). Official summary of *The State of the World's Children 2002.* [Online]. Available: http://www.unicef.org/pubsgen/sowc02summary/index.html. Access date: September 19, 2002.

UNICEF. (2003). *Social monitor 2003.* Florence, Italy: Innocenti Social Monitor, UNICEF Innocenti Research Centre.

Upjohn Company. (1984). *Writer's guide to sex and health.* Kalamazoo, MI: Author.

Urban Institute (2000). *A new look at homelessness in America.* Washington, DC: Author.

Vainio, S., Heikkiia, M., Kispert, A., Chin, N., & McMahon, A. P. (1999). Female development in mammals is regulated by Wnt-4 signaling. *Nature, 397,* 405–409.

Valeski, T. N., & Stipek, D. J. (2001). Young children's feelings about school. *Child Development, 72*(4), 1198–1213.

Van den Boom, D. C. (1989). Neonatal irritability and the development of attachment. In G. A. Kohnstamm, J. E. Bates, & M. K. Rothbart (Eds.), *Temperament in childhood* (pp. 299–318). Chichester, England: Wiley.

Van den Boom, D. C. (1994). The influence of temperament and mothering on attachment and exploration: An experimental manipulation of sensitive responsiveness among lower-class mothers with irritable infants. *Child Development, 65,* 1457–1477.

Van Dyck, J. (1995). *Manufacturing babies and public consent: Debating the new reproductive technologies.* New York: New York University Press.

van IJzendoorn, M. H. (1995). Adult attachment representations, parental responsiveness, and infant attachment: A meta-analysis on the predictive validity of the Adult Attachment Interview. *Psychological Bulletin, 117*(3), 387–403.

van IJzendoorn, M. H., & Kroonenberg, P. M. (1988). Cross-cultural patterns of attachment: A meta-analysis of the Strange Situation. *Child Development, 59,* 147–156.

van IJzendoorn, M. H., & Sagi, A. (1997). Cross-cultural patterns of attachment: Universal and contextual dimensions. In J. Cassidy & P. R. Shaver (Eds.), *Handbook on attachment theory and research.* New York: Guilford Press.

van IJzendoorn, M. H., & Sagi, A. (1999). Cross-cultural patterns of attachment: Universal and contextual dimensions. In J. Cassidy & P. R. Shaver (Eds.), *Handbook of attachment: Theory, research, and clinical applications* (pp. 713–734). New York: Guilford.

van IJzendoorn, M. H., Dijkstra, J., & Bus, A. (1995). Attachment, intelligence, and language: A meta-analysis. *Social Development, 4,* 115–128.

van IJzendoorn, M. H., Schuengel, C., & Bakermans-Kranenburg, M. J. (1999). Disorganized attachment in early childhood: Meta-analysis of precursors, concomitants, and sequelae. *Development and Psychopathology, 11,* 225–250.

van Noord-Zaadstra, B. M., Looman, C.W., Alsbach, H., Habbema, J. D., te Velde, E. R., & Karbaat, J. (1991). Delayed childbearing: Effect of age on fecundity and outcome of pregnancy. *British Medical Journal, 302,* 1361–1365.

Vance, M. L., & Mauras, N. (1999). Growth hormone therapy in adults and children. *New England Journal of Medicine, 341*(16), 1206–1216.

Vandell, D. L. (2000). Parents, peer groups, and other socializing influences. *Developmental Psychology, 36,* 699–710.

Vandell, D. L., & Bailey, M. D. (1992). Conflicts between siblings. In C. U. Shantz & W. W. Hartup (Eds.), *Conflict in child and adolescent development* (pp. 242–269). New York: Cambridge University Press.

Vandell, D. L., & Ramanan, J. (1992). Effects of early and recent maternal employment on children from low income families. *Child Development, 63,* 938–949.

Vargha-Khadem, F., Gadian, D. G., Watkins, K. E., Connelly, A., Van Paesschen, W., & Mishkin, M. (1997). Differential effects of early hippocampal pathology on episodic and semantic memory. *Science, 277,* 376–380.

Vartanian, L. R., & Powlishta, K. K. (1996). A longitudinal examination of the social-cognitive foundations of adolescent egocentrism. *Journal of Early Adolescence, 16,* 157–178.

Vaswani, M., & Kapur, S. (2001). Genetic basis of schizophrenia: Trinucleotide repeats: An update. *Progress in Neuro-Psychopharmacology & Biological Psychiatry, 25*(6), 1187–1201.

Vaughn, B. E., Stevenson-Hinde, J., Waters, E., Kotsaftis, A., Lefever, G. B., Shouldice, A., Trudel, M., & Belsky, J. (1992). Attachment security and temperament in infancy and early childhood: Some conceptual clarifications. *Developmental Psychology, 28,* 463–473.

Vecchiotti, S. (2003). Kindergarten: An overlooked educational policy priority. *SRCD Social Policy Report, 17*(2), 1–19.

Ventura, S. J., Hamilton, B. E., Matbews, T. J., and Cbandra, A. (2003). Trends and variations in smoking during pregnancy and low birth weight: Evidence from the birth certificate 1990–2000. *Pediatrics, 111,* 1176–1180.

Ventura, S. J., Martin, J. A., Curtin, S. C., & Mathews, T. J. (1999). Births: Final data for 1997. *National Vital Statistics Reports, 47*(18). Hyattsville, MD: National Center for Health Statistics.

Ventura, S. J., Martin, J. A., Curtin, S. C., Menacker, F., & Hamilton, B. E. (2001). Births: Final data for 1999. *National Vital Statistics Reports, 49*(1). Hyattsville, MD: National Center for Health Statistics.

Ventura, S. J., Mathews, T. J., & Curtin, S. C. (1999). Declines in teenage birth rates 1991–1998: Update of national and state trends. *National Vital Statistics Reports, 47*(6). Hyattsville, MD: National Center for Health Statistics.

Ventura, S. J., Mathews, T. J., & Hamilton, B. E. (2001). Births to teenagers in the United States, 1940–2000. *National Vital Statistics Reports, 49*(10). Hyattsville, MD: National Center for Health Statistics.

Vereecken, C., & Maes, L. (2000). Eating habits, dental care and dieting. In C. Currie, K. Hurrelmann, W. Settertobulte, R. Smith, & J. Todd (Eds.). *Health and health behaviour among young people: a WHO crossnational Study (HBSC) international report* (pp. 83–96). WHO Policy Series: Healthy Policy for Children and Adolescents, Series No. 1. Copenhagen, Denmark: World Health Organization Regional Office for Europe.

Verlinsky, Y., Rechitsky, S., Verlinsky, O., Masciangelo, C., Lederer, K., and Kuliev, A. (2002). Preimplantation diagnosis for early-onset Alzheimer disease caused by V717L mutation. *Journal of the American Medical Association, 287,* 1018–1021.

Verma, S., & Larson, R. (2003). Editors' notes. In S. Verma and R. Larson (Eds.),

Examining adolescent leisure time across cultures: Developmental opportunities and risks. *New Directions for Child and Adolescent Development, 99,* 1–7.

Verschueren, K., Buyck, P., & Marcoen, A. (2001). Self representations and socioemotional competence in young children: A 3-year longitudinal study. *Developmental Psychology, 37,* 126–134.

Verschueren, K., & Marcoen, A. (1999). Representation of self and socioemotional competence in kindergartners: Differential and combined effects of attachment to mother and to father. *Child Development, 70,* 183–201.

Verschueren, K., Marcoen, A., & Schoefs, V. (1996). The internal working model of the self, attachment, and competence in five-year-olds. *Child Development, 67,* 2493–2511.

Vgontzas, A. N., & Kales, A. (1999). Sleep and its disorders. *Annual Review of Medicine, 50,* 387–400.

Viding, E., Price, T. S., Spinath, F. M., Bishop, D. V. M., Dale, P. S., & Plomin, R. (2003). Genetic and environmental mediation of the relationship between language and nonverbal impairment in 4-year-old twins. *Journal of Speech, Language, and Hearing Research, 46,* 1271–1282.

Vink, T., Hinney, A., van Elburg, A. A., van Goozen, S. H. M., Sandkuijl, L. A., Sinke, R. J., Herpertz-Dahlmann, B.-M., Hebebrand, J., Remschmidt, H., van Engeland, H., & Adan, R. A. H. (2001). Association between an agouti-related protein gene polymorphism and anorexia nervosa. *Molecular Psychiatry, 6,* 325–328.

Vitaro, F., Tremblay, R. E., Kerr, M., Pagani, L., & Bukowski, W. M. (1997). Disruptiveness, friends' characteristics, and delinquency in early adolescence: A test of two competing models of development. *Child Development, 68,* 676–689.

von Kries, R., Koletzko, B., Sauerwald, T, von Mutius, E., Barnert, T., Grunert, V., & von Voss, H. (1999). Breastfeeding and obesity: Cross-sectional study. *British Medical Journal, 319,* 147–150.

Vondra, J. I., & Barnett, D. (1999). A typical attachment in infancy and early childhood among children at developmental risk. *Monographs of the Society for Research in Child Development, Serial No. 258, 64*(3).

Vosniadou, S. (1987). Children and metaphors. *Child Development, 58,* 870–885.

Votruba-Drzal, E., Coley, R. L., & Chase-Lansdale, P. L. (2004). Child care and low-income children's development: Direct and moderated effects. *Child Development, 75,* 296–312.

Vrijheld, M., Dolk, H., Armstrong, B., Abramsky, L., Bianchi, F., Fazarinc, I., Garne, E., Ide, R., Nelen, V., Robert, E., Scott, J. E. S., Stone, D., & Tenconi, R. (2002). Chromosomal congenital anomalies and residence near hazardous waste landfill sites. *Lancet, 359,* 320–322.

Vuchinich, S., Angelelli, J., & Gatherum, A. (1996). Context and development in family problem solving with preadolescent children. *Child Development, 67,* 1276–1288.

Vuori, L., Christiansen, N., Clement, J., Mora, J., Wagner, M., & Herrera, M. (1979). Nutritional supplementation and the outcome of pregnancy: 2. Visual habitation at 15 days. *Journal of Clinical Nutrition, 32,* 463–469.

Vygotsky, L. S. (1956). *Selected psychological investigations.* Moscow: Izdstel'sto Akademii Pedagogicheskikh Nauk USSR.

Vygotsky, L. S. (1962). *Thought and language.* Cambridge, MA: MIT Press. (Original work published 1934.)

Vygotsky, L. S. (1978). *Mind in society: The development of higher psychological processes.* Cambridge, MA: Harvard University Press.

Wade, N. (2001, October 4). Researchers say gene is linked to language. *New York Times,* p. Al.

Wade, N. (2003, June 19). Y chromosome depends on itself to survive. *The New York Times.* [Online]. Available: http://www.nytimes.com/2003/06/19/science/19GENE.html?ex=1057028641&ei=1&e=59b0008310be24b8. Access date: June 19, 2003.

Wagner, C. L., Katikaneni, L. D., Cox, T. H., & Ryan, R. M. (1998). The impact of prenatal drug exposure on the neonate. *Obstetrics and Gynecology Clinics of North America, 25,* 169–194.

Wahlbeck, K., Forsen, T., Osmond, C., Barker, D. J. P., & Erikkson, J. G. (2001). Association of schizophrenia with low maternal body mass index, small size at birth, and thinness during childhood. *Archives of General Psychiatry, 58,* 48–55.

Waisbren, S. E., Albers, S., Amato, S., Ampola, M., Brewster, T. G., Demmer, L., Eaton, R. B., Greenstein, R., Korson, M., Larson, C., Marsden, D., Msall, M., Naylor, E. W., Pueschel, S., Seashore, M., Shih, V. E., and Levy, H. L. (2003). Effect of expanded newborn screening for biochemical disorders on child outcomes and parental stress. *Journal of the American Medical Association, 290,* 2564–2572.

Wakefield, M., Reid, Y., Roberts, L., Mullins, R., & Gillies, P. (1998). Smoking and smoking cessation among men whose partners are pregnant: A qualitative study. *Social Science and Medicine, 47,* 657–664.

Wakeley, A., Rivera, S., & Langer, J. (2000a). Can young infants add and subtract? *Child Development, 71,* 1525–1534.

Wakschlag, L. S., Lahey, B. B., Loeber, R., Green, S. M., Gordon, R. A., & Leventhal, B. L. (1997). Maternal smoking during pregnancy and the risk of conduct disorder in boys. *Archives in General Psychiatry, 54,* 670–676.

Wald, N. J. (2004). Folic acid and the prevention of neural-tube defects. *New England Journal of Medicine, 350,* 101–103.

Waldman, I. D. (1996). Aggressive boys' hostile perceptual and response biases: The role of attention and impulsivity. *Child Development, 67,* 1015–1033.

Walk, R. D., & Gibson, E. J. (1961). A comparative and analytical study of visual depth perception. *Psychology Monographs, 75*(15).

Walker, D., Greenwood, C., Hart, B., & Carta, J. (1994). Prediction of school outcomes based on early language production and socioeconomic factors. *Child Development, 65,* 606–621.

Walker, L. J., & Hennig, K. H. (1997). Parent/child relationships in single-parent families. *Canadian Journal of Behavioural Science, 29,* 63–75.

Walker, L. J., & Taylor, J. H. (1991). Family interactions and the development of moral reasoning. *Child Development, 62,* 264–283.

Wallerstein, J., & Corbin, S. B. (1999). The child and the vicissitudes of divorce. In R. M. Galatzer-Levy & L. Kraus (Eds.), *The scientific basis of child custody decisions* (pp. 73–95). New York: Wiley.

Wallerstein, J. S., & Lewis, J. (1998). The long-term impact of divorce on children: A first report from a 25-year study. *Family and Conciliation Courts Review, 36,* 363–383.

Walston, J. T., & West, J. (2004). *Full-day and half-day kindergarten in the United States: Findings from the Early Childhood Longitudinal Study, Kindergarten Class of 1998–99* (NCES 2004–078). Washington, DC: National Center for Education Statistics.

Wang, D. E. (2003). Risk profiles of adolescent girls who were victims of dating violence. *Adolescence, 38,* 1–14.

Wang, Q. (2004). The emergence of cultural self-constructs: Autobiographical memory and self-description in European American and Chinese children. *Developmental Psychology, 40,* 3–15.

Wardle, J., Robb, K. A., Johnson, F., Griffith, J., Brunner, E., Power, C., & Tovée, M. (2004). Socioeconomic variation in attitudes to eating and weight in female adolescents. *Health Psychology, 23,* 275–282.

Wasik, B. H., Ramey, C. T., Bryant, D. M., & Sparling, J. J. (1990). A longitudinal study of two early intervention strategies: Project CARE. *Child Development, 61,* 1682–1696.

Watamura, S. E., Donzella, B., Alwin, J., & Gunnar, M. R. (2003). Morning-to-afternoon increases in cortisol concentrations for infants and toddlers at child care: Age differences and behavioral correlates. *Child Development, 74,* 1006–1020.

Waters, E., & Deane, K. E. (1985). Defining and assessing individual differences in attachment relationships: Q-methodology and the organization of behavior in infancy and early childhood. *Monographs of the Society for Research in Child Development, 50,* 41–65.

Waters, E., Wippman, J., & Sroufe, L. A. (1979). Attachment, positive affect, and competence in the peer group: Two studies in construct validation. *Child Development, 50,* 821–829.

Waters, K. A., Gonzalez, A., Jean, C., Morielli, A., & Brouillette, R. T. (1996). Face-straight-down and face-near-straight-down positions in healthy prone-sleeping infants. *Journal of Pediatrics, 128,* 616–625.

Watkins, M., Rasmussen, S. A., Honein, M. A., Botto, L. D., and Moore, C. A. (2003). Maternal obesity and risk for birth defects. *Pediatrics, 111,* 1152–1158.

Watson, A. C., Nixon, C. L., Wilson, A., & Capage, L. (1999). Social interaction skills and theory of mind in young children. *Developmental Psychology, 35*(2), 386–391.

Watson, J. B., & Rayner, R. (1920). Conditioned emotional reactions. *Journal of Experimental Psychology, 3,* 1–14.

Weese-Mayer, D. E., Berry-Kravis, E. M., Maher, B. S., Silvestri, J. M., Curran, M. E., & Marazita, M. L. (2003). Sudden infant death syndrome: Association with a promoter polymorphism of the serotonin transporter gene. *American Journal of Medical Genetics, 117A,* 268–274.

Wegman, M. E. (1992). Annual summary of vital statistics—1991. *Pediatrics, 90,* 835–845.

Wegman, M. E. (1994). Annual summary of vital statistics—1993. *Pediatrics, 94* 792–803.

Wegman, M. E. (1999). Foreign aid, international organizations, and the world's children. *Pediatrics, 103*(3), 646–654.

Weinberg, M. K., & Tronick, E. Z. (1996). Infant affective reactions to the resumption of maternal interaction after stillface. *Child Development, 67,* 905–914.

Weinberg, M. K., Tronick, E. Z., Cohn, J. F., & Olson, K. L. (1999). Gender differences in emotional expressivity and self-regulation during early infancy. *Developmental Psychology, 35*(1), 175–188.

Weinberg, R. A. (1989). Intelligence and IQ: Landmark issues and great debates. *American Psychologist, 44*(2), 98–104.

Weinberger, B., Anwar, M., Hegyi, T., Hiatt, M., Koons, A., & Paneth, N. (2000). Antecedents and neonatal consequences of low Apgar scores in preterm newborns. *Archives of Pediatric and Adolescent Medicine, 154,* 294–300.

Weinberger, D. R. (2001, March 10). A brain too young for good judgment. *New York Times.* [Online]. Available: http://www.nytimes.com/2001/03/10/opinion/10WEIN.html?ex_985250309&ei_1&en_995bc03f7a8c7207.

Weinreb, L., Wehler, C., Perloff, J., Scott, R., Hosmer, D., Sagor, L., and Gundersen, C. (2002). Hunger: Its impact on children's health and mental health. *Pediatrics, 110,* 816.

Weinstock, H., Berman, S., & Cates Jr., W. (2004). Sexually transmitted diseases among American youth: Incidence and prevalence estimates, 2000. *Perspectives on Sexual and Reproductive Health, 36,* 6–10.

Weisner, T. S. (1993). Ethnographic and ecocultural perspectives on sibling relationships. In Z. Stoneman & P. W. Berman (Eds.), *The effects of mental retardation, visibility, and illness on sibling relationships* (pp. 51–83). Baltimore, MD: Brooks.

Weiss, B., Dodge, K. A., Bates, J. E, & Pettit, G. S. (1992). Some consequences of early harsh discipline: Child aggression and a maladaptive social information processing style. *Child Development, 63,* 1321–1335.

Weissman, M. M., Warner, V., Wickramaratne, P. J., & Kandel, D. B. (1999). Maternal smoking during pregnancy and psychopathology in offspring followed to adulthood. *Journal of the American Academy of Child and Adolescent Psychiatry, 38,* 892–899.

Weisz, J. R., Weiss, B., Han, S. S., Granger, D. A., & Morton, T. (1995). Effects of psychotherapy with children and adolescents revisited: A meta-analysis of treatment outcome studies. *Psychological Bulletin, 117*(3), 450–468.

Weitzman, M., Gortmaker, S., & Sobol, A. (1992). Maternal smoking and behavior problems of children. *Pediatrics, 90,* 342–349.

Welch-Ross, M. K. (1997). Mother-child participation in conversation about the past: Relationships to preschoolers' theory of mind. *Developmental Psychology, 33*(4), 618–629.

Welch-Ross, M. K., & Schmidt, C. R. (1996). Gender-schema development and children's story memory: Evidence for a developmental model. *Child Development, 67,* 820–835.

Wellman, H. M., & Cross, D. (2001). Theory of mind and conceptual change. *Child Development, 72,* 702–707.

Wellman, H. M., & Gelman, S. A. (1998). Knowledge acquisition in foundational domains. In W. Damon (Series Ed.), D. Kuhn, & R. S. Siegler (Vol. Eds.), *Handbook of child psychology: Vol. 2. Cognition, perception, and language* (5th ed., pp. 523–573). New York: Wiley.

Wellman, H. M., & Liu, D. (2004). Scaling theory-of-mind tasks. *Child Development, 75,* 523–541.

Wellman, H. M., & Woolley, J. D. (1990). From simple desires to ordinary beliefs: The early development of everyday psychology. *Cognition, 35,* 245–275.

Wellman, H. M., Cross, D., & Bartsch, K. (1986). Infant search and object permanence: A meta-analysis of the A-not-B error. *Monographs of the Society for Research in Child Development, 51*(3, Serial No. 214).

Wellman, H. M., Cross, D., & Watson, J. (2001). Meta-analysis of theory-of-mind development: The truth about false belief. *Child Development, 72,* 655–684.

Wells, G. (1985). Preschool literacy-related activities and success in school. In D. R. Olson, N. Torrence, & A. Hilyard (Eds.), *Literacy, language, and learning* (pp. 229–255). New York: Cambridge University Press.

Wender, P. H. (1995). *Attention-deficit hyperactivity disorder in adults.* New York: Oxford University Press.

Wennerholm, U. B., & Bergh, C. (2000). Obstetric outcome and follow-up of children born after in-vitro fertilization (IVF). *Human Fertility, 3*(1), 52–64.

Wentworth, N., Benson, J. B., & Haith, M. M. (2000). The development of infants' reaches for stationary and moving targets. *Child Development, 71,* 576–601.

Wenzel, D. (1990). *Ann Bancroft: On top of the world.* Minneapolis, MN: Dillon.

Werker, J. F. (1989). Becoming a native listener. *American Scientist, 77,* 54–59.

Werker, J. F., Pegg, J. E., & McLeod, P. J. (1994). A cross-language investigation of infant preference for infant-directed communication. *Infant Behavior and Development, 17,* 323–333.

Werler, M. M., Louik, C., Shapiro, S., & Mitchell, A. A. (1996). Prepregnant weight in relation to risk of neural tube defects. *Journal of the American Medical Association, 275,* 1089–1092.

Werner, E. E. (1985). Stress and protective factors in children's lives. In A. R. Nichol (Ed.), *Longitudinal studies in child psychology and psychiatry.* New York: Wiley.

Werner, E. E. (1987, July 15). *Vulnerability and resiliency: A longitudinal study of Asian Americans from birth to age 30.* Invited address at the Ninth Biennial Meeting of the International Society for the Study of Behavioral Development, Tokyo, Japan.

Werner, E. E. (1989). Children of the garden island. *Scientific American, 260*(4), 106–111.

Werner, E. E. (1993). Risk and resilience in individuals with learning disabilities: Lessons learned from the Kauai longitudinal study. *Learning Disabilities Research and Practice, 8,* 28–34.

Werner, E. E. (1995). Resilience in development. *Current Directions in Psychological Science, 4*(3), 81–85.

Werner, E., & Smith, R. S. (2001). *Journeys from childhood to midlife.* Ithaca, NY: Cornell University Press.

Werner, E., Bierman, L., French, F. E., Simonian, K., Conner, A., Smith, R., & Campbell, M. (1968). Reproductive and environmental casualties: A report on the 10-year follow-up of the children of the Kauai pregnancy study. *Pediatrics, 42,* 112–127.

West, J., Denton, K., & Reaney, M. L. (2001). *America's kindergartners: Findings from the Early Childhood Longitudinal Study, Kindergarten class of 1998–99, Fall 1998.* Washington, DC: National Center for Education Statistics.

Westen, D. (1998). The scientific legacy of Sigmund Freud: Toward a psychodynamically informed psychological science. *Psychological Bulletin, 124,* 333–371.

Whalen, C. K., Jamner, L. D., Henker, B., Delfino, R. J., & Lozano, J. M. (2002). The ADHD spectrum and everyday life: Experience sampling of adolescent moods, activities, smoking, and drinking. *Child Development, 73,* 209–228.

Whalley, L. J., & Deary, I. J. (2001). Longitudinal cohort study of childhood IQ and survival up to age 76. *British Medical Journal, 322,* 819.

Whalley, L. J., Starr, J. M., Athawes, R., Hunter, D., Pattie, A., & Deary, I. J. (2000). Childhood mental ability and dementia. *Neurology, 55,* 1455–1459.

Whitaker, R. C., Wright, J. A., Pepe, M. S., Seidel, K. D., & Dietz, W. H. (1997). Predicting obesity in young adulthood from childhood and parental obesity. *New England Journal of Medicine, 337,* 869–873.

White, A. (2001). Alcohol and adolescent brain development. [Online]. Available: http://www.duke.edu/~amwhite/alc_adik_pf.html.

White, B. L. (1971, October). *Fundamental early environmental influences on the development of competence.* Paper presented at the Third Western Symposium on Learning: Cognitive Learning, Western Washington State College, Bellingham, WA.

White, B. L., Kaban, B., & Attanucci, J. (1979). *The origins of human competence.* Lexington, MA: Heath.

Whitehurst, G. J., & Lonigan, C. J. (1998). Child development and emergent literacy. *Child Development, 69,* 848–872.

Whitehurst, G. J., Falco, F. L., Lonigan, C. J., Fischel, J. E., DeBaryshe, B. D., Valdez-Menchaca, M. D., & Caulfield, M. (1988). Accelerating language development through picture book reading. *Developmental Psychology, 24,* 552–559.

Whitehurst, G. J., Zevenbergen, A. A., Crone, D. A., Schultz, M. D., Velting, O. N., and Fischel, J. E. (1999). Outcomes of an emergent literacy intervention from Head Start through second grade. *Journal of Educational Psychology, 91,* 261–272.

Whitrow, G. J. (1967). *Einstein: The man and his achievement.* New York: Dover.

Whyatt, R. M., Rauh, V., Barr, D. B., Camann, D. E., Andrews, H. F., Garfinkel, R., Hoepner, L. A., Diaz, D., Dietrich, J., Reyes, A. Tang, D., Kinney, P. L., & Perera, F. P. (in press). Prenatal insecticide exposures, birth weight and length among an urban minority cohort.

Widom, C. S. (1989). The cycle of violence. *Science, 244,* 160–166.

Wiggins, S., Whyte, P., Higgins, M., Adams, S., et al. (1992). The psychological consequences of predictive testing for Huntington's disease. *New England Journal of Medicine, 327,* 1401–1405.

Wilcox, A. J., Baird, D. B., & Weinberg, C. R. (1999). Time of implantation of the conceptus and loss of pregnancy. *New England Journal of Medicine, 340,* 1796–1799.

Wilcox, A. J., Baird, D. D., Weinberg, C. R., Hornsby, P. P., & Herbst, A. L. (1995). Fertility in men exposed prenatally to diethylstilbestrol. *New England Journal of Medicine, 332,* 1411–1416.

Wilcox, A. J., Weinberg, C. R., & Baird, D. D. (1995). Timing of sexual intercourse in relation to ovulation: Effects on the probability of conception, survival of the pregnancy, and sex of the baby. *New England Journal of Medicine, 333,* 1563–1565.

Williams, E. R., & Caliendo, M. A. (1984). *Nutrition: Principles, issues, and applications.* New York: McGraw-Hill.

Williams, G. J. (2001). The clinical significance of visual-verbal processing in evaluating children with potential learning-related visual problems. *Journal of Optometric Vision Development, 32*(2), 107–110.

Willinger, M., Hoffman, H. T., & Hartford, R. B. (1994). Infant sleep position and risk for sudden infant death syndrome: Report of meeting held January 13 and 14, 1994. *Pediatrics, 93,* 814–819.

Wilson, E. O. (1975). *Sociobiology: The new synthesis.* Cambridge, MA: Belknap Press of Harvard University Press.

Wilson, G., McCreary, R., Kean, J., & Baxter, J. (1979). The development of preschool children of heroin-addicted mothers: A controlled study. *Pediatrics, 63,* 135–141.

Wilson, K., & Ryan, V. (2001). Helping parents by working with their children in individual child therapy. *Child and Family Social Work* (special issue), *6,* 209–217.

Winerip, M. (1999, January 3). Homework bound. *New York Times:* Education Life, pp. 28–31.

Winkleby, M. A., Robinson, T. N., Sundquist, J., & Kraemer, H. C. (1999). Ethnic variation in cardiovascular disease risk factors among children and young adults: Findings from the Third National Health and Nutrition Examination Survey, 1988–1994. *Journal of the American Medical Association, 281,* 1006–1013.

Winner, E. (1997). Exceptionally high intelligence and schooling. *American Psychologist, 52*(10), 1070–1081.

Wittrock, M. C. (1980). Learning and the brain. In M. C. Wittrock (Ed.), *The brain and psychology.* New York: Academic Press.

Wolchik, S. A., Sandler, I. N., Millsap, R. E., Plummer, B. A., Greene, S. M., Anderson, E. R., et al. (2002). Six year follow-up of a randomized, controlled trial of preventive interventions for children of divorce. *Journal of the American Medical Association, 288,* 1874–1881.

Wolfe, D. A. (1985). Child-abusive parents: An empirical review and analysis. *Psychological Bulletin, 97*(3), 462–482.

Wolfe, D. A., Edwards, B., Manion, I., & Koverola, C. (1988). Early intervention for parents at risk of child abuse and neglect: A preliminary investigation. *Journal of Consulting and Clinical Psychology, 56,* 40–47.

Wolff, P. H. (1963). Observations on the early development of smiling. In B. M. Foss (Ed.), *Determinants of infant behavior* (vol. 2). London: Methuen.

Wolff, P. H. (1966). The causes, controls, and organizations of behavior in the newborn. *Psychological Issues, 5*(1, Whole No. 17), 1–105.

Wolff, P. H. (1969). The natural history of crying and other vocalizations in early infancy. In B. M. Foss (Ed.), *Determinants of infant behavior* (vol. 4). London: Methuen.

Wolfinger, N. H. (1999, August 10). *Coupling and uncoupling: Changing marriage patterns and the intergenerational transmission of divorce.* Paper presented at the annual meeting of the American Sociological Association, Chicago, IL.

Wolfson, A. R., & Carskadon, M. A. (1998). Sleep schedules and daytime functioning in adolescents. *Child Development, 69,* 875–887.

Women in History. (2004). *Marian Anderson biography.* Lakewood, OH: Lakewood Public Library. [Online]. Available: http://www.lkwdpl.org/wihohio/ande-mar.htm. Access date: November 18, 2004.

Wood, D. (1980). Teaching the young child: Some relationships between social interaction, language, and thought. In D. Olson (Ed.), *The social foundations of language and thought.* New York: Norton.

Wood, D., Bruner, J., & Ross, G. (1976). The role of tutoring in problem solving.

Journal of Child Psychiatry and Psychology, 17, 89–100.

Woodward, A. L., Markman, E. M., & Fitzsimmons, C. M. (1994). Rapid word learning in 13- and 18-month olds. *Development Psychology, 30,* 553–566.

Woodward, E. H., & Gridina, N. (2000). *Media in the home 2000: The fifth annual survey of parents and children.* Washington, DC: The Annenberg Public Policy Center of the University of Pennsylvania. Survey Series Number 7.

Woodward, S. A., McManis, M. H., Kagan, J., Deldin, P., Snidman, N., Lewis, M., & Kahn, V. (2001). Infant temperament and the brainstem auditory evoked response in later childhood. *Developmental Psychology, 37,* 533–538.

Wooley, J. D., Phelps, K. E., Davis, D. L., and Mandell, D. J. (1999). Where theories of mind meet magic: The development of children's beliefs about wishing. *Child Development, 70,* 571–587.

Woolley, J. D. (1997). Thinking about fantasy: Are children fundamentally different thinkers and believers from adults? *Child Development, 68*(6), 991–1011.

Woolley, J. D. (2000). The development of beliefs about direct mental-physical causality in imagination, magic, and religion. In K. S. Rosengren, C. N. Johnson, & P. L. Harris (Eds.), *Imagining the impossible: Magical, scientific, and religious thinking in children* (pp. 99–129). New York: Cambridge University Press.

Woolley, J. D., & Boerger, E. A. (2002). Development of beliefs about the origins and controllability of dreams. *Developmental Psychology, 38*(1), 24–41.

Woolley, J. D., & Bruell, M. J. (1996). Young children's awareness of the origins of their mental representations. *Developmental Psychology, 32,* 335–346.

World Health Organization. (2003). The world health report—shaping the future. [Online]. Available: http://www.who.int/wrh/2003/chapter1en/index2.html. Access Date: February 14, 2004.

Wright, A. L., Holberg, C. J., Taussig, L. M., & Martinez, F. D. (1995). Relationship of infant feeding to recurrent wheezing at age 6 years. *Archives of Pediatric Adolescent Medicine, 149,* 758–763.

Wright, J. C., Huston, A. C., Murphy, K. C., St. Peters, M., Pinon, M., Scantlin, R., & Kotler, J. (2001). The relations of early television viewing to school readiness and vocabulary of children from low-income families: The Early Window Project. *Child Development, 72*(5), 1347–1366.

Wright, J. T., Waterson, E. J., Barrison, I. G., Toplis, P. J., Lewis, I. G., Gordon, M. G., MacRae, K. D., Morris, N. F., & Murray Lyon, I. M. (1983, March 26). Alcohol consumption, pregnancy, and low birth weight. *Lancet,* pp. 663–665.

Wright, V. C., Schieve, L. A., Reynolds, M. A., & Jeng, G. (2003). Assisted Reproductive Technology Surveillance—United States, 2000. Division of Reproductive Health, National Center for Chronic Disease Prevention and Health Promotion. [Online]. Available: http://www.cdc.gov/reprod.

Wu, T., Mendola, P., & Buck, G. M. (2002). Ethnic differences in the presence of secondary sex characteristics and menarche among U.S. girls: The Third National Health and Nutrition Survey, 1988–1994. *Pediatrics, 11,* 752–757.

WuDunn, S. (1997, January 14). Korean women still feel demands to bear a son. *New York Times* (International Ed.), p. A3.

Wulczyn, F. (2004). Family reunification. In David and Lucile Packard Foundation, Children, families, and foster care. *The Future of Children, 14*(1). Available: http://www.futureofchildren.org.

Wynn, K. (1990). Children's understanding of counting. *Cognition, 36,* 155–193.

Wynn, K. (1992). Evidence against empiricist accounts of the origins of numerical knowledge. *Mind and Language, 7,* 315–332.

Wynn, K. (1996). Infants' individuation and enumeration of actions. *Psychological Science, 7,* 164–169.

Wynn, K. (2000). Findings of addition and subtraction in infants are robust and consistent: Reply to Wakeley, Rivera, and Langer. *Child Development, 71,* 1535–1536.

Yamada, H. (2004). Japanese mothers' views of young children's areas of personal discretion. *Child Development, 75,* 164–179.

Yamazaki, J. N. & Schull, W. J. (1990). Perinatal loss and neurological abnormalities among children of the atomic bomb. *Journal of the American Medical Association, 264,* 605–609.

Yang, B., Ollendick, T. H., Dong, Q., Xia, Y., & Lin, L. (1995). Only children and children with siblings in the People's Republic of China: Levels of fear, anxiety, and depression. *Child Development,* 66, 1301–1311.

Yazigi, R. A., Odem, R. R., & Polakoski, K. L. (1991). Demonstration of specific binding of cocaine to human spermatozoa. *Journal of the American Medical Association, 266,* 1956–1959.

Yeargin-Allsopp, M., Rice, C., Karapurkar, T., Doernberg, N., Boyle, C., & Murphy, C. (2003). Prevalence of autism in a U.S. metropolitan area. *Journal of the American Medical Association, 289,* 49–55.

Yoshikawa, H. (1994). Prevention as cumulative protection: Effects of early family support and education on chronic delinquency and its risks. *Psychological Bulletin, 115*(1), 28–54.

Youngblade, L. M., & Belsky, J. (1992). Parent-child antecedents of 5-year-olds' close friendships: A longitudinal analysis. *Developmental Psychology, 28,* 700–713.

Younger, B. (1990). Infants' detection of correlations among feature categories. *Child Development, 61,* 614–620.

Youth violence: A report of the Surgeon General. (2001, January). [Online]. Available: http://www.surgeongeneral.gov/library/youthviolence/default.htm.

Yu, S. M., Huang, Z. J., & Singh, G. K. (2004). Health status and health services utilization among U.S. Chinese, Asian Indian, Filipino, and Other Asian/Pacific Islander children. *Pediatrics, 113*(1), 101–107.

Yurgelon-Todd, D. (2002). Inside the Teen Brain. [Online]. Available: http://www.pbs.org/wgbh/pages/frontline/shows/teenbrain/interviews/todd.html.

Zahn-Waxler, C., Friedman, R. J., Cole, P. M., Mizuta, I., & Hiruma, N. (1996). Japanese and U.S. preschool children's responses to conflict and distress. *Child Development, 67,* 2462–2477.

Zahn-Waxler, C., Radke-Yarrow, M., Wagner, E., & Chapman, M. (1992). Development of concern for others. *Developmental Psychology, 28,* 126–136.

Zald, D. H., & Iacono, W. G. (1998). The development of spatial working memory abilities. *Developmental Neuropsychology, 14,* 563–578.

Zametkin, A. J. (1995). Attention-deficit disorder: Born to be hyperactive. *Journal of the American Medical Association, 273*(23), 1871–1874.

Zametkin, A. J., & Ernst, M. (1999). Problems in the management of attention-deficit-hyperactivity disorder. *New England Journal of Medicine, 340,* 40–46.

Zarbatany, L., Hartmann, D. P., & Rankin, D. B. (1990). The psychological functions of preadolescent peer activities. *Child Development, 61,* 1067–1080.

Zeedyk, M. S., Wallace, L., & Spry, L. (2002). Stop, look, listen, and think? What young children really do when crossing the road. *Accident Analysis and Prevention, 34*(1), 43–50.

Zelazo, P. D., M¸ller, U., Frye, D., & Marcovitch, S. (2003). The development of executive function in early childhood. *Monographs of the Society for Research in Child Development, 68*(3, Serial No. 274).

Zelazo, P. D., Reznick, J. S., & Spinazzola, J. (1998). Representational flexibility and response control in a multistep, multilocation search task. *Developmental Psychology, 34,* 203–214.

Zelazo, P. R., Kearsley, R. B., & Stack, D. M. (1995). Mental representations for visual sequences: Increased speed of central processing from 22 to 32 months. *Intelligence, 20,* 41–63.

Zhang, J., Meikle, S., Grainger, D. A., & Trumble, A. (2002). Multifetal pregnancy in older women and perinatal outcomes. *Fertility and Sterility, 78,* 562–568.

Zhang, Y., Proenca, R., **Maffei, M., Barone, M., Leopold, L., & Friedman, J. M. (1994).** Positional cloning of the mouse obese gene in its human homologue. *Nature, 372,* 425–431.

Zhao, Y. (2002, May 29). Cultural divide over parental discipline. *New York Times.* [Online]. Available: http://www.nytimes.com/2002/05/29/nyregion/29DISC.html?ex=1023674535&ei=1&en=5eeaee8e940eee1a.

Zhensun, Z., & Low A. (1991). *A young painter: The life and paintings of Wang Yani—China's extraordinary young artist.* New York: Scholastic.

Zhou, Q., Eisenberg, N., Wang, Y., & Reiser, M. (2004). Chinese children's effortful control and dispositional anger/frustration: Relations to parenting styles and children's social functioning. *Developmental Psychology, 40,* 352–366.

Zhu, B.-P., Rolfs, R. T., Nangle, B. E., & Horan, J. M. (1999). Effect of the interval between pregnancies on perinatal outcomes. *New England Journal of Medicine, 340,* 589–594.

Zigler, E. (1998). School should begin at age 3 years for American children. *Journal of Developmental and Behavioral Pediatrics, 19,* 37–38.

Zigler, E., & Styfco, S. J. (1993). Using research and theory to justify and inform Head Start expansion. *Social Policy Report of the Society for Research in Child Development, 7*(2).

Zigler, E., & Styfco, S. J. (1994). Head Start: Criticisms in a constructive context. *American Psychologist, 49*(2), 127–132.

Zigler, E., & Styfco, S. J. (2001). Extended childhood intervention prepares children for school and beyond. *Journal of the American Medical Association, 285,* 2378.

Zigler, E., Taussig, C., & Black, K. (1992). Early childhood intervention: A promising preventative for juvenile delinquency. *American Psychologist, 47,* 997–1006.

Zigler, E. F. (1987). Formal schooling for four-year-olds? *North American Psychologist, 42*(3), 254–260.

Zimmerman, B. J., Bandura, A., & Martinez-Pons, M. (1992). Self-motivation for academic attainment: The role of self-efficacy beliefs and personal goal setting. *American Educational Research Journal, 29,* 663–676.

Zimmerman, N., King, N. E., Laporte, J., Yang, M., Mishra, A., Pope, S. M., Muntel, E. E., Witte, D. P., Pegg, A. A., Foster, P. S., Hamid, Q., & Rothenberg, M. E. (2003). Dissection of experimental asthma with DNA microarray analysis identifies arginase in asthma pathinogenesis. *Journal of Clinical Investigation, 111,* 1863–1874.

Zimrin, H. (1986). A profile of survival. *Child Abuse and Neglect, 10,* 339–349.

Zito, J. M., Safer, D. J., dosReis, S., Gardner, J. F., Magder, L., Soeken, K., Boles, M., Lynch, F., & Riddle, M. A. (2003). Psychotropic practice patterns for youth: A 10-year perspective. *Archives of Pediatrics and Adolescent Medicine 57*(1), 17–25.

Zuckerman, B. S., & Beardslee, W. R. (1987). Maternal depression: A concern for pediatricians. *Pediatrics, 79,* 110–117.

Acknowledgments

Textual Credits

Chapter 1

Opening quote: Heraclitus, fragment (sixth century B.C.) In *The Collected Wisdom of Heraclitus,* transl. by Brooks Haxton. New York: Viking Press, 2001.

Chapter 2

Opening quote: Charles Sanders Peirce, *Collected Papers,* vol. 5, edited by Charles Hartshorne and Paul Weiss. Cambridge: Harvard University Press, 1934.

Table 2-3: Papalia, D., S. W. Olds, and R. D. Feldman (2001) From *Human Development,* Eighth Edition. Copyright © 2001. Reprinted with the permission of The McGraw-Hill Companies.

Table 2-4: Papalia, D., S. W. Olds, and R. D. Feldman (2001) From *Human Development,* Eighth Edition. Copyright © 2001. Reprinted with the permission of The McGraw-Hill Companies.

Figure 2-2: Cole, M, and S. R. Cole (1989) From *The Development of Children* by Michael Cole and Shelia R. Cole. © 1989 by Michael Cole and Shelia R. Cole. Used with permission of Worth Publishers.

Figure 2-3: Papalia, D., S. W. Olds, and R. D. Feldman (1997) From *Human Development,* Seventh Edition. Copyright © 1997. Reprinted with the permission of The McGraw-Hill Companies.

Figure 2-4: Papalia, D., S. W. Olds, and R. D. Feldman (2001) From *Human Development,* Eighth Edition. Copyright © 2001. Reprinted with the permission of The McGraw-Hill Companies.

Chapter 3

Opening quote: William Ellery Leonard, *Two Lives: A Poem.* New York: W. B. Huebsch, 1925.

Table 3-2: Milunsky, A. (1992) Adapted from Choices, *Not Chances* by Aubrey Milunsky, M.D. Copyright © 1977, 1989 by Aubrey Milunsky, M.D. By permission of Little, Brown, and Company, Inc.

Figure 3-1: Papalia, D., S. W. Olds, and R. D. Feldman (2001) From *Human Development,* Eighth Edition. Copyright © 2001. Reprinted with the permission of The McGraw-Hill Companies.

Figure 3-2: Ritter, J. (1999, November 23) From "Scientists close in on DNA code," *Chicago Sun-Times,* p. 7. Reprinted with special permission from the Chicago Sun-Times, Inc. © 2004.

Figure 3-3: Papalia, D., S. W. Olds, and R. D. Feldman (2001) From *Human Development,* Eighth Edition. Copyright © 2001. Reprinted with the permission of The McGraw-Hill Companies.

Figure 3-6: Babu, A. and K. Hirschhorn (1992) From *A Guide to Human Chromosome Defects,* Third Edition [*Birth Defects: Original Article Series,* Volume 28, Number 2].

Chapter 4

Opening quote: Anne Sexton, "Little Girl, My String Bean, My Lovely Woman" (1966). *The Complete Poems of Anne Sexton.* Boston: Houghton-Mifflin, 1981.

Ch. 4 opener, p. 85: Sexton, A. (1966) Excerpt from "My Little Girl, My String Bean, My Lovely Woman," *Live or Die.* Copyright © 1966 by Anne Sexton, renewed 1994 by Linda G. Sexton. Reprinted with the permission of Houghton Mifflin Company and SLL/Sterling Lord Literistic, Inc. All rights reserved.

Figure 4-2: Brody, J. E. (1995) From "Preventing birth defects even before pregnancy," *The New York Times,* June 28, 1995, p. C10. Copyright © 1995 by The New York Times Company. Reprinted with permission.

Chapter 5

Opening quote: James Baldwin, "No Name in the Street" (1972). *James Baldwin: Collected Essays.* New York: Library of America, 1998.

Box 5-1 Around the World, p. 113: Olds, S. W. (2002) Excerpts from *A Balcony in Nepal: Glimpses of a Himalayan Village.* New York: ASJA Press. Reprinted with permission of S. W. Olds.

Figure 5-1: Lagercrantz, H., and T. A. Slotkin (1986) Adapted from "The 'stress' of being born," *Scientific American, 254*(4), 1986, 100–107. Reprinted with the permission of Patricia J. Wynne.

Table 5-1: Timiras, P. S. (1972) From *Developmental Physiology and Aging* by P. S. Timiras, Macmillan Publishing Co. Reprinted by permission of the author.

Table 5-2: Apgar, V. (1953) Adapted from "A proposal for a new method of evaluation of the newborn infant," *Current Research in Anesthesia & Analgesia, 32,* 1953, 260–267. Reprinted with the permission of Lippincott Williams & Wilkins.

Table 5-3: Prechtl, H. F. R., and D. J. Beintema (1964) Adapted from "The neurological examination of the full-term newborn infant," *Clinics in Developmental Medicine,* No. 12. Reprinted with permission. Wolff, P. H. (1966) Adapted from "The causes, controls, and organizations of behavior in the newborn," *Developmental Psychologies of Jean Piaget (Psych Issues #5)* copyright 1973 IUP. Reprinted with permission.

Chapter 6

Opening quote: Elizabeth Barrett Browning, *Aurora Leigh,* Book VI (1857).

Figure 6-3: Casaer, P. (1993) From "Old and new facts about perinatal brain development," *Journal of Child Psychology & Psychiatry,* Vol. 34, 1993. Reprinted with permission of Blackwell Publishing Ltd. Restak, R. (1984) From "Illustration," *The Brain.* Copyright © 1984 by Educational Broadcasting Corporation and Richard M. Restak, M.D. Reprinted by permission of SLL/Sterling Lord Literistic, Inc. and Bantam Books, a division of Random House, Inc.

Figure 6-4: Lach, J. (1997) From "Cultivating the mind," *Newsweek,* Special Issue, Spring/Summer 1997, p. 39. Copyright © 1997 by Newsweek, Inc. All rights reserved. Reprinted with permission.

Figure 6-5: Conel, J. L. (1939–1967) Reprinted by permission of the publisher from *The Postnatal Development of the Human Cerebral Cortex, Vols. I-VIII* by Jesse LeRoy Conel, Cambridge, Mass.: Harvard University Press, Copyright © 1939, 1974 by the President and Follows of Harvard College.

Figure 6-6: Nash, J. M. (1997) From "Fertile Lands," *Time,* February 3, 1997, pp. 49–56. Copyright © 1997 by Time, Inc. Reprinted by permission.

Figure 6-7: Wegman, M. E. (1996) From "Infant mortality: Some international comparisons," *Pediatrics,* Vol. 98, pp. 1020–1027. Copyright 1996. Reprinted with permission.

Table 6-1: "Early human reflexes." Adapted from C. P. Gabbard (1996) From *Lifelong Motor Development,* Second Edition. Madison, WI: Brown and Benchmark. Used with the permission of the author.

Table 6-2: Frankenburg et al., (1992) Adapted from *The Denver Developmental Screening Test: Reference Manual.* Copyright © 1992. Reprinted with permission.

Chapter 7

Opening quote: Alfred, Lord Tennyson, *In Memoriam,* Canto 54 (1850).

Table 7-1: Bayley, N. (1993) From *Bayley Scales of Infant Development,* Second edition. Copyright © 1993 by The Psychological Corporation. Reproduced by permission. All rights reserved. *Bayley Scales of Infant Development* is a registered trademark of The Psychological Corporation.

Table 7-4: Papalia, D., S. W. Olds, and R. D. Feldman (2001) From *Human Development,*

Eighth Edition, Copyright © 2001. Reprinted with the permission of The McGraw-Hill Companies.

Figure 7-2: Rovee-Collier-Collier, C., and K. Boller (1995) From "Current theory and research on infant learning and memory: Application to early intervention," *Infants and young Children,* 7(3), 1–12. Reprinted with the permission of Lippincott Williams & Wilkins.

Figure 7-4: Baillargeon, R., and J. DeVos. (1991) From "Object permanence in young infants: Further evidence," *Child Development,* Vol. 62, 1991, pp. 1227–1246. Copyright © by the Society for Research in Child Development, Inc.

Figure 7-5: Hood, B., V. Cole-Davies, and M. Dias (2003) From "Looking and search measures of object knowledge in preschool children," *Developmental Psychology, 39,* pp. 61–70. Copyright © 2003 by the American Psychological Association. Reprinted with permission.

Figure 7-6: Papalia, D., S. W. Olds, and R. D. Feldman (2003) From *Human Development,* Ninth Edition. Copyright © 2003. Reprinted with the permission of The McGraw-Hill Companies.

Figure 7-7: Petitto, L. A., and P. F. Marentette (1991) From "Babbling in the manual mode: Evidence for the ontogeny of language," *Science, 251,* 1991, pp. 1493–1495. Copyright © 1991 by the American Association for the Advancement of Science. Reprinted with permission.

Box Figure 7-2: Rideout, V. J., E. A. Vandewater, and E. A. Wartella (2003) From "Zero to Six: Electronic Media in the Lives of Infants, Toddlers, and Preschoolers." (#3378). The Henry J. Kaiser Family Foundation, Fall 2003. This information was reprinted with permission of the Henry J. Kaiser Family Foundation.

Chapter 8

Opening quote: John Hartford, "Life Prayer" (1971). Copyright, Flying Fish Records.

Chapter 8 opener, p. 199: Hartford, J. (1971) Excerpt from *Life Prayer.* Words and music by John Hartford. Copyright © 1968 (renewed 1996) by Ensign Music Corporation. International copyright secured. All rights reserved.

Table 8-1: Sroufe, L. A. (1979) Adapted from "Socioemotional development." In J. Osofsky (ed.), *Handbook of Infant Development.* Copyright © 1979 by John Wiley & Sons. Adapted with permission of John Wiley & Sons, Inc.

Table 8-2: Thomas, A., and S. Chess. Adapted from "Genesis and evolution of behavioral disorders: From infancy to early adult life." *American Journal of Psychiatry, 141* (1), 1984, pp. 1–9. Copyright © 1984 by the American Psychiatric Association; http://ajp.psychiatryonline.org. Reprinted by permission.

Table 8-3: Thompson, R. A. (1998) Based on "Early sociopersonality development." In N. Eisenberg (ed.), *Handbook of Child Psychology, Volume 3,* pp. 37–39. Copyright © 1998 by John Wiley & Sons. Reprinted with permission of John Wiley & Sons, Inc.

Figure 8-1: Lewis, M. (1997) Adapted from "The self in self-conscious emotions." In S. G. Snodgrass and R. L. Thompson (eds.), "The self across psychology: Self-recognition, self-awareness, and the self-concept," *Annals of the New York Academy of Sciences,* Vol. 818. Reprinted with the permission of the New York Academy of Sciences, U.S.A. and Professor Michael Lewis.

Chapter 9

Opening quote: Michel de Montaigne, *Essays* (transl. by Charles Cotton).

Table 9-2: Corbin, C. B. (1973) From *A Textbook of Motor Development.* Copyright © 1973. Reprinted with the permission of The McGraw-Hill Companies.

Table 9-4: Kendall-Tackett, K. A., L. M. Williams, and D. Finkelhor (1993) Adapted from "Impact of sexual abuse on children: A review and synthesis of recent empirical studies," *Psychological Bulletin, 113,* 1993, pp. 164–180. Copyright © 1993 by the American Psychological Association. Adapted with permission.

Figure 9-1: Ferber, R. (1985) From *Solve Your Child's Sleep Problems.* Copyright © 1985 by Richard Ferber, M.D. Reprinted with the permission of Simon & Schuster, Inc.

Figure 9-2: Kellogg, R. (1970) From *Analyzing Children's Art.* Copyright © 1969, 1970 by Rhoda Kellogg. Reprinted by permission of The McGraw-Hill Companies, Inc.

Figure 9-3: From "The World Health Report—Shaping the future." http://www.who.int/whr/2003/chapter1/en/index2.html, accessed February 14, 2004. Used with the permission of the World Health Organization.

Figure 9-4: Wegman, M. E. (1999) Adapted from "Foreign aid, international organizations, and the world's children," *Pediatrics, 103,* 646–654. Reprinted with the permission of the American Academy of Pediatrics.

Chapter 10

Opening quote: Eugène Ionesco, *Fragments of a Journal,* transl. by Jean Steward. New York: Grove Press, Inc., 1968.

Table 10-4: Wellman, H., and D. Liu (2004) Adapted from "Scaling of theory-of-mind tasks," *Child Development,* Vol. 75, issue 2, 531. Reprinted with the permission of the Society for Research in Child Development.

Chapter 11

Opening quote: Carl Sandburg, *The People, Yes.* New York: Harcourt, Brace, 1936.

Table 11-3: Morris, R. J., and T. R. Kratochwill (1983) Adapted from "Childhood fears" in *Treating Children's Fears and Phobias: A Behavioral Approach,* p. 2. Published by Allyn and Bacon, Boston, MA. Copyright © 1983 by Pearson Education. Reprinted by permission of the publisher. Stevenson-Hinde, J., and Shouldice, A. (1996) "Fearfulness: Developmental consistency." In A. J. Sameroff & M. M. Haith (Eds.), *The five to seven year shift: The age of reason and responsibility* (pp. 237–252.) Reprinted with the permission of the University of Chicago Press.

Chapter 12

Opening quote: Ogden Nash, *You Can't Get There from Here.* Boston: Little, Brown, and Co., 1957.

Chapter 12 opener, p. 327: Nash, O. (1984) Excerpt from "The absentees," *Verses from 1929 On.* Copyright © 1942 by Ogden Nash, Renewed. Reprinted by permission of Curtis Brown, Ltd.

Chapter 13

Opening quote: Natalia Ginzburg, *The Little Virtues,* transl. by Dick Davis. New York: Little, Brown, and Co., 1985.

Table 13-3: Gardner, H. (1993, 1998) "Eight intelligences, according to Gardner." Based on *Frames of Mind: The Theory of Multiple Intelligences.* New York: Basic. Also based upon Gardner, H. (1998) "Are there additional intelligences?" In J. Kane (Ed.), *Education, Information, and Transformation: Essays on Learning and Thinking.* Englewood Cliffs, NJ: Prentice-Hall. Used with the permission of H. Gardner.

Figure 13-1: National Center for Education Statistics (NCES) (2003) The Coalition of Education, 2003, p. 21.

Chapter 14

Opening quote: Karen Crawford, age 9.

Table 14-1: Selman, R. L. (1980) From *The Growth of Interpersonal Understanding: Developmental and Clinical Analysis.* Reprinted with the permission of Elsevier. Selman, R. L., and A. P. Selman (1979) From "Children's ideas about friendship: A new theory," *Psychology Today,* April 1979, pp. 71–80. Copyright © 1979 by Sussex Publishers, Inc. Reprinted with the permission of *Psychology Today* magazine.

Table 14-2: Masten, A. S., and J. D. Coatsworth (1998) "Characteristics of resilient children and adolescents." From The development of competence in favorable and unfavorable environments: Lessons from research on successful children. *American Psychologist, 53,* 205–220. Copyright © 1998 by the American Psychological Association. Reprinted with permission.

Chapter 15

Opening quote: Anaïs Nin, *The Diaries of Anaïs Nin,* vol. IV. New York: Harcourt Brace Jovanovich, 1971.

Figure 15-1: Elliott, D. S., and B. J. Morse (1993) Adapted from "Delinquency and drug use as risk factors in teenage sexual activity," *Youth and Society, 21,* 1989, pp. 21–60. Reprinted with the permission of Sage Publications, Inc.

Chapter 16

Opening quote: Evelyn Waugh, age 16, in a school debate (1920). *The Diaries of Evelyn Waugh,* edited by Michael Davie. Boston: Little, Brown, and Co., 1976.

Table 16-1: Kohlberg, L. (1969) Adapted from "Stage and Sequence: The cognitive-developmental approach to socialization," in *Handbook of Socialization Theory and Research,* by David A. Goslin. Reprinted with the permission of David A. Goslin. Lickona, T.W. (1976) From *Moral Development and Behavior.* Reprinted with the permission of Thomas E. Lickona.

Figure 16-1: Small, M. Y., and J. Kagan (1990) From *Cognitive Development,* 1st edition by Small. © 1990. Reprinted with permission of Wadsworth, a division of Thomson Learning.

Figure 16-2: National Center for Education Statistics (NCES) (2003) The Coalition of Education, 2003, p. 42.

Chapter 17

Opening quote: Eve Merrian, "Conversation with Myself" (1964). In *Halloween abc.* Old Tappan, NJ: Simon and Schuster, 1987.

Chapter 17 opener, p. 459: Merriam, E. (1964) "Conversation with Myself," *A Sky Full of Poems.* Copyright © 1964, 1970, 1973 by Eve Merriam. All rights reserved. Used by permission of Marian Reiner.

Table 17-1: Marcia, J. E. (1966) Adapted from "Development and validation of ego identity status," *Journal of Personality and Social Psychology, 3*(5), 1966, pp. 551–558. Copyright © 1966 by the American Psychological Association. Adapted with permission.

Table 17-2: Kroger, J. (1993) From "Ego Identity: An overview," in *Discussion of Ego Identity,* edited by J. Kroger. Reprinted with permission.

Table 17-3: Phinney, J. S. (1989) "Stages of ethnic identity development in minority group adolescents," in *Journal of Early Adolescence,* 9, 34–39. Copyright © 1989 by Sage Publications. Reprinted by permission of Sage Publications, Inc.

Table 17-5: Adapted from *National Survey of Adolescents and Young Adults: Sexual Health Knowledge, Attitudes and Experiences,* (#3218), Table 6, p. 12 and Table 33, p. 39. The Henry J. Kaiser Family Foundation, 2003. This information was reprinted with the permission of the Henry J. Kaiser Family Foundation.

Figures 17-1, 17-2, 17-3: Bernstein, *New York Times,* March 17, 2004, p. 36. Copyright © 2004 The New York Times Co. Reprinted with permission.

Photo Credits

Visual Walk-Through

xxiii (top): © Visual Horizons/Getty Images; **xxiii (center):** © Jon Feingersh/Corbis Images; xxix Library of Congress; xxx

Part Openers

p. 2: (top) © Visual Horizons/Getty Images; **(bottom)** © Jon Feingersh/Corbis Images; **p. 54: (top)** © Antonio Mo/Getty Images; **(center)** © Franken/Photo Researchers; **(bottom)** © Bob Daemmrich/Stock Boston/ PictureQuest; **p. 128: (top)** © Michael Newman/PhotoEdit; **(center)** Laura Dwight/ Corbis Images; **(bottom)** © David P. Hall/ Masterfile; **p. 236: (top)** © Ariel Skelley/ Corbis Images; **(center)** © Laura Dwight; **(bottom)** © Roy Morsch/Corbis Images; **p. 324: (top)** © Rolf Bruderer/Corbis Images; **(center)** © David Young-Wolff/PhotoEdit; **(bottom)** © Tom McCarthy/Corbis Images; **p. 406: (top)** © Lori Adamski Peek/Getty Images; **(center)** © David Young-Wolff/ PhotoEdit; **(bottom)** © Pixland/Index Stock Imagery.

Chapter 1

Opener: © Visual Horizons/Getty Images; **p. 5:** © Contemporary portrait of Victor of Aveyron from DE L'EDUCATION D'UN HOMME. Reproduced by permission of The British Library; **p. 11:** © Musées Royaux d'Art et d'Histoire – Brussels; **p. 15:** © Syracuse Newspapers/The Image Works; **p. 17** Library of Congress.

Chapter 2

Opener: © Jon Feingersh/Corbis Images; **p. 23:** © Bettmann/Corbis Images; **p. 27:** © National Library of Medicine; **p. 29:** © Bettmann/ Corbis Images; **p. 32:** © Joe McNally; **p. 33:** © Yves De Braine/Black Star; **p. 38:** A.R. Luria/Dr. Michael Cole, Laboratory of Human Cognition, University of California, San Diego; **p. 47:** © James Wilson/Woodfin Camp.

Chapter 3

Opener: 56: © Antonio Mo/Getty Images; **p. 57:** © Lester Sloan/Woodfin Camp; **p. 61:** © Margaret Miller/Photo Researchers; **p. 66:** © David Young-Wolff/PhotoEdit; **p. 71:** © Ellen Senisi/The Image Works; **p. 75:** © T.K. Wanstal/The Image Works.

Chapter 4

Opener: © Franken/Photo Researchers; **p. 85:** No Credit requested.; **p. 88:** (1 mo., 7 wks.) © Petit Format/Nestle/Science Source/Photo Researchers; (3 mo.) © Lennart Nilsson/ Albert Bonniers Forlag AB, A CHILD IS BORN, Dell Publishing Company; (4 mo.) © J.S. Allen/Daily Telegraph/International Stock; (5 mo.) © James Stevenson/Photo Researchers; **p. 89:** (6 mo.): © Lennart Nilsson/Albert Bonniers Forlag AB, A CHILD IS BORN, Dell Publishing Company; (7 mo., 8 mo.) © Petit Format/Nestle/Science Source/Photo Researchers; (9 mo.) © Ronn Maratea/International Stock; **p. 92:** © PhotoDisc/Getty Images; **p. 96:** © David Young-Wolff/PhotoEdit.

Chapter 5

Opener: © Bob Daemmrich/Stock Boston/ PictureQuest; **p. 107:** © Bettmann/Corbis Images; **p. 113:** © Erol Gurian/Corbis Images; **p. 119:** © PhotoDisc/Getty Images; **p. 120:** © Nina Leen/Time Life Pictures/Getty Images; **p. 122:** © John Cole/Photo Researchers; **p. 125:** © Mike Teruya/Free Spirit Photography.

Chapter 6

Opener: © Michael Newman/PhotoEdit; **p. 131:** © Library of Congress, Prints and Photographs Division [LC-USZ62-112517]; **p. 135:** © Richard Lord/The Image Works; **p. 143: (top left):** © Mimi Forsyth; **(top center):** © Lew Merrim/Photo Researchers; **(top right):** © Laura Dwight; **(bottom left):** © Mimi Forsyth; **(bottom center):** © Elizabeth Crews; **(bottom right):** © Elizabeth Crews; **p. 145: (both)** Courtesy, Children's Hospital of Michigan; **p. 149:** © Ruth Duskin Feldman; **p. 152:** © Innervisions.

Chapter 7

Opener: © Laura Dwight/Corbis Images; **p. 161:** Neg. No. 326799 Courtesy Department Library Services/American Museum of Natural History; **p. 165:** Courtesy, Carolyn Rovee-Collier ; **p. 172:** © Laura Dwight; **p. 173:** © Brand X Pictures/Getty Images; **p. 176:** © Enrico Ferorelli; **p. 179:** © James Kilkelly; **p. 180:** © Felicia Martinez/PhotoEdit; **p. 195:** © Michael Newman/PhotoEdit.

Chapter 8

Opener: © David P. Hall/Masterfile; **p. 199:** © Ken Heyman/Woodfin Camp; **p. 203: (left)** © Bob Daemmrich/Stock Boston; **(right)** © Amy Etra/PhotoEdit; **p. 209:** © Ruth Duskin Feldman; **p. 211:** Harlow Primate Laboratory, University of Wisconsin; **p. 213:** © Cameramann/The Image Works; **p. 214:** © Jonathan Finlay; **p. 217:** © David Young-Wolff/PhotoEdit; **p. 224:** © Robert Brenner/

PhotoEdit; **p. 230:** © Syracuse Newspapers/ Dick Blume/The Image Works.

Chapter 9

Opener: © Ariel Skelley/Corbis Images; **p. 239:** © Cynthia Johnson/Getty Images; **p. 241:** © Michael Newman/PhotoEdit; **p. 247:** © Laura Dwight/PhotoEdit; **p. 253:** © Tony Freeman /PhotoEdit; **p. 254:** © Tony Freeman/PhotoEdit.

Chapter 10

Opener: © Laura Dwight; **p. 263:** © Bettmann/ Corbis Images; **p. 267:** © Laura Dwight; **p. 271:** © Sheila Sheridan; **p. 281:** © Erika Stone/Photo Researchers; **p. 283:** © PhotoDisc/Getty Images; **p. 288:** © Paul Conklin/PhotoEdit.

Chapter 11

Opener: © Roy Morsch/Corbis Images; **p. 293:** © AP/Wide World Photos; **p. 303:** © Erika Stone/Photo Researchers; **p. 308(left):** © Ellen Senisi/The Image Works; **p. 308 (right):** © Ellen Senisi; **p. 316:** © Albert Bandura; **p. 319:** © Owen Franken/Stock Boston.

Chapter 12

Opener: © Rolf Bruderer/Corbis Images; **p. 327:** © AP/Wide World Photos; **p. 331:** © Mary Kate Denny/PhotoEdit; **p. 332:** © Michael Siluk/The Image Works; **p. 338:** © Lawrence Migdale/Stock Boston; **p. 340:** © Martin Rogers/Stock Boston.

Chapter 13

Opener: © David Young-Wolff/PhotoEdit; **p. 343:** © Rene Burri/Magnum Photos; **p. 347:** © Laura Dwight; **p. 349:** © Bob Daemmrich/Stock Boston/PictureQuest; **p. 352:** © Laura Dwight/PhotoEdit; **p. 357:** © Ellen Senisi; **p. 361:** © Michael J. Doolittle/ The Image Works; **p. 365:** © David Young-Wolff/PhotoEdit; **p. 369:** © Richard S. Orton; **p. 371:** © Ken Kerbs.

Chapter 14

Opener: © Tom McCarthy/Corbis Images; **p. 377:** © Bettmann/Corbis Images; **p. 380:** © Michael Justice/The Image Works; **p. 382:** © Bernager/Explorer/Photo Researchers; **p. 383, 386:** © PhotoDisc/Getty Images; **p. 390:** © Laura Dwight; **p. 391:** © Momatiuk/Eastcott/Woodfin Camp & Associates; **p. 394:** © Dallas & John Heaton/Stock Boston; **p. 395:** © Erika Stone; **p. 400:** © Bill Aron/PhotoEdit.

Chapter 15

Opener: © Lori Adamski Peek/Getty Images; **p. 409:** © Culver Pictures; **p. 411:** © Bill Gillette/Stock Boston; **p. 414:** © Elena Rooraid/PhotoEdit; **p. 423:** © The Grand Island Independent, Barrett Stinson/ AP/Wide World Photos; **p. 426:** © PhotoDisc/Getty Images; **p. 432:** © Roy Morsch/Corbis Images.

Chapter 16

Opener: © David Young-Wolff/PhotoEdit; **p. 435:** © Bettmann/Corbis Images; **p. 443, 449:** © Laura Dwight; **p. 451:** © Erika Stone; **p. 455:** © Dana White/PhotoEdit.

Chapter 17

Opener: © Pixland/Index Stock Imagery; **p. 459:** © AP/Wide World Photos; **p. 462:** © Michael Pole/Corbis Images; **p. 466:** © Bob Daemmrich/The Image Works; **p. 468:** © Paula Lerner/Index Stock Imagery; **p. 473:** © The Children's Defense Fund; **p. 478:** © Myrleen Ferguson Cate/PhotoEdit; **p. 479:** © David Grossman/The Image Works; **p. 483:** © Laura Rauch/AP/Wide World Photos; **p. 484:** © Richard Hutchings/ PhotoEdit.

Name Index

Subject Index

NOTES

NOTES

NOTES

NOTES

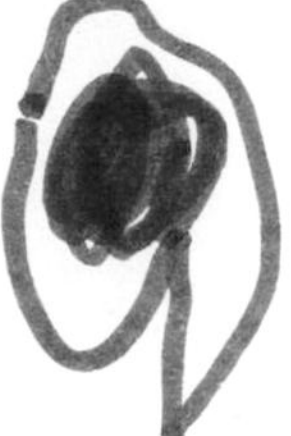

LANDMARK TABLE	Developmental Landmarks: A Holistic View							
Age	**Physical Developments**	**Neurological Developments**	**Cognitive Developments**	**Language Developments**	**Emotional Developments**	**Social Developments**	**Self/Gender/ Identity Developments**	**Moral Developments**
4 years	Child dresses self with help. Child can copy a circle and draw designs, cut with scissors, and write recognizable letters.	Myelination of pathways related to hearing is complete.	Child can classify by two criteria. Child shows intuitive understanding of fractional quantities.	Child uses longer sentences, more complex grammar. Private speech increases.	Little explicit awareness of pride or shame.	Sibling conflicts over property are common. Pretend play has sociodramatic themes.	Self-definition is concrete, focused on external traits and skills. Thinking about the self is all-or-none; real self is thought to be the same as ideal self.	Guilt and concern about wrongdoing peaks. Moral reasoning is rigid. "Problem behavior" declines among girls.
5–6 years	Child can descend stairway unaided, alternating feet. Child can hop, jump, and change directions. Child dresses self without help. Child can draw a person and copy figures (pictorial stage). Primary teeth begin to fall out, replaced by permanent teeth.	Brain is almost adult size, but not fully developed. Cortical regions connected with language are maturing.	Theory of mind matures: child can distinguish between appearance or fantasy and reality. Memory span extends to two digits. Development of metamemory enables use of memory strategies. Automatization, encoding, generalization, and strategy construction begin to become more efficient. Child can count in head.	Speech is almost adultlike. Spoken vocabulary is about 2,600 words. Child understands about 20,000 words. Child appreciates pragmatic aspects of language. Child begins to decode written words. Child can retell plot of a movie, book, or TV show.	Negativism declines. Child recognizes pride and shame in others, but not in self.	Patterns of bullying and victimization may be established.	Sense of competence is developing. Self-concept links various aspects of the self, mostly in positive terms. Gender constancy is achieved.	Moral reasoning is becoming less inflexible.
7–8 years	Balance and control of body improve. Speed and throwing ability improve.		Stage of concrete operations begins. Child shows better understanding of cause and effect, seriation, transitive inference, class inclusion, inductive reasoning, and conservation. Processing of more than one task at a time becomes easier. Children play formal games with rules. Child can solve complex story problems using addition.	Pragmatic skills improve.	Child is aware of own pride or shame.	Rough-and-tumble play is common in boys, as a way to jockey for dominance.	Self-concept is more balanced and realistic. Sense of self-worth becomes explicit.	Moral reasoning is increasingly flexible. Child believes punishment should take intent into account. Empathic and prosocial behavior increase. Aggression, especially hostile type, declines.